*Visit Our Web Site*
**www.HR-Education-Gateway.com**

# HUMAN RESOURCE MANAGEMENT

# HUMAN RESOURCE MANAGEMENT

*Eighth Edition*

GEORGE T. MILKOVICH

JOHN W. BOUDREAU

both of
Cornell University

with the assistance of Carolyn Milkovich

**IRWIN**

Chicago • Bogotá • Boston • Buenos Aires • Caracas
London • Madrid • Mexico City • Sydney • Toronto

**Irwin Book Team**

Publisher: *Rob Zwettler*
Executive editor: *Craig S. Beytien*
Developmental editor: *Jennifer R. Boxell*
Marketing manager: *Michael Campbell*
Project supervisor: *Lynne Basler*
Production supervisor: *Laurie Sander*
Designer: *Bethany Joy Stubbe*
Director, Prepress Purchasing: *Kimberly Meriwether David.*
Compositor: *Quebecor Printing/Dubuque*
Typeface: *10.5/12 Times Roman*
Printer: *Quebecor Printing/Dubuque*

**Library of Congress Cataloging-in-Publication Data**

Milkovich, George T.
Human resource management/George T. Milkovich, John W. Boudreau.
—8th ed.
p. cm.
Includes index.
ISBN 0-256-19354-1
1. Personnel management. I. Boudreau, John W. II. Title.
HF5549.M4736 1997
658.3—dc20 96–17944

*Printed in the United States of America*
2 3 4 5 6 7 8 9 0 QD 3 2 1 0 9 8 7

# PREFACE

Record sales, successful globalizing ventures in China, Korea, the Czech Republic and other countries, and a one-day stock market price increase that raised the value of AT&T by $10 billion. Sounds like a great year? It was also the year that saw the company's CEO vilified in the press for laying off 40,000 employees, above and beyond the 60,000 already laid off due to restructuring over the previous three years.

AT&T's experience shows that *decisions about managing people make a difference.* Your decisions will affect not only your own success but also your employees' behaviors and sense of fair treatment. And they affect society, too. As a manager, you will face intense pressures to achieve success through the people you lead.

We believe that what sets most successful organizations apart is how they manage human resources. The ability to achieve and sustain competitive advantage lies within the workforce. Ask executives what keeps them up at night. Without exception, they will tell you that decisions about human resources are the most difficult ones they face. How to select and develop future leaders? How to redesign the organization to better satisfy customers? How to reward good performance? How to lead a globally diverse workforce? How to control labor costs while still treating people fairly? The specific challenges depend on the pressures organizations face. But the greatest challenges involve managing human resources.

Faced with the pressures of global competition, social change, and accelerating technological advances, managers are urged to take action. Advice is plentiful and solutions appear simple. However, you will discover in this textbook that solutions are not so simple, nor are they unchanging. What works in one set of circumstances may not apply in another setting or with other employees. Thus, the search for "the answer" lies not in a book or magazine article, but in an analysis of the conditions and people involved. This book will help you understand what to consider in such an analysis so that you can make effective decisions. The potential returns from decisions about employees can match or surpass the returns from decisions on other organization resources. Rather than keeping you up at night, perhaps reading this book will even help you sleep!

## ABOUT THIS BOOK

This book is largely based on the four phases of the diagnostic approach to managing human resources. As the model in Chapter 1 illustrates, these phases include: (1) assess the conditions, both external and internal to the organization, that managers face; (2) plan and set human resources objectives for the organization that are based on these conditions; (3) choose the appropriate human resources actions that will achieve these desired objectives; and (4) evaluate the results. The major sections in the book examine these phases and discuss the human resource issues involved.

The heart of the book examines how to make effective decisions about human resources. It achieves this by analyzing the prevailing pressures and issues facing managers; discussing the concepts, theories, and research related to these issues; and describing the actions taken by leading organizations to achieve their objectives. Examples of the issues covered include: the effects of work-family pressures (Chapter 15); work force diversity (Chapter 2); global worldwide trends, such as the European Unions social charters and Asian expectations and cultural norms (integrated throughout the book); the use of high-performance work teams and new approaches to employee relations (Chapter 15); the explosion in the use of information and computers as decision aids (Chapter 16); college student recruiting (Chapter 6); workforce reductions and downsizing (Chapter 8); managing careers (Chapter 9); aligning business strategies and human resource decisions (Chapter 4); and more.

Many practices that now enjoy current popularity have potentially negative consequences. Too often attention is focused on improving the bottom line, while the potential downside for employees and their dependents is ignored. Examples include the use of contract workers, variable pay, and shifting health costs to employees; all of these actions increase the uncertainty and risk people face. These issues are discussed throughout the book.

Changes underway in the workplace are not cosmetic. We are in the midst of nothing less than a fundamental change in the employment relationship. And changes in this edition of the book are not cosmetic either. We examined every issue, reviewed the new research, searched for the emerging practices to insure the continued relevance of each chapter. Throughout every chapter you'll discover that significant developments in three areas; global impact on HR decisions, valuing and costing HR decisions, and using information systems and computers to aid decisions.

*Our objective is to help you prepare to make effective decisions about human resources and to share our belief that these decisions are crucial.* To achieve this objective, this book undertakes three basic tasks.

The first is to *examine the current theory and research* related to managing human resources and the workplace. We draw upon theory and research from organization behavior, psychology, economics, sociology, and the law. The emphasis is on relevance. This discussion is supported by extensive up-to-date references, which offer the opportunity to dig into topics beyond what is provided in the text discussion.

The *next task* is to examine the *rapidly changing state of practice* among employers. Here we draw upon practices actually used by a wide variety of employers; examples from public and private, large and small, as well as domestic and international firms, are included. We've drawn on our work across North America, Korea, Singapore, Japan, Europe, South America, Russia, Hong Kong, Australia, and China. These practices illustrate new initiatives, as well as established approaches, to human resource management.

To help you stay abreast of changes, we are introducing a new feature with this edition: a Web site for instructors who are using the book. The site offers assistance on (1) use of other relevant HRM interest sites; (2) suggestions for using internet material in the classroom; (3) "live" cases on up-to-the-minute issues; and (4) information on recent newspaper and magazine articles and legal developments that are relevant to the class. The address for this web site is <http://www.interlakes.com/mil/milld.html>. We think you will find the features there an intriguing addition to your coursework.

Finally, this book offers an opportunity *for you to develop your own decision-making skills through action-learning exercises based on actual events.* One option is

"Your Turn," included in each chapter. "Your Turn" presents a short real-life human resource problem. You make your decision and compare it to the actions actually taken by managers in the real organization. Completing these exercises will help you better understand the concepts and issues discussed in the book and help as you develop skills readily transferable to future jobs.

In the end we hope to change the way you think about managing people and how you manage your own career. We hope you will discover that human resource management is vital and challenging.

**George T. Milkovich**
**John W. Boudreau**

# ACKNOWLEDGMENTS

We relied on the contributions of many people in the preparation of this book. We owe a special debt to our students who continue to challenge and motivate us.

We appreciate the contributions of the many managers who shared their ideas and practices with us. While we can't recognize all of them here, a few who went beyond the call include:

| | |
|---|---|
| John Bronson | *PepsiCo* |
| Mishele Cheng | *Sun Microsystems* |
| Andrew Doyle | *Toshiba* |
| Stan Durda | *3M* |
| Alejandro Fernandez | *Petroleos de Venequela, S.A.* |
| Yuichi Funada | *Toshiba* |
| Rooney Mereness | *NCR Corporation* |
| Ray Olsen | *TRW* |
| Robert Rusek | *Lucent Technologies* |
| D. K. Kim | *Sunkyong* |
| Jeff McHenry | *Microsoft* |
| Toshio Sasaki | *Toshiba* |
| Gabriela Snobrova | *TRW* |
| Jay Stright | *Chevron Corporation* |
| Reese Smith | *Levi Strauss International* |
| M. J. Stone | *Chevron Corporation* |
| Fumie Urashima | *Johnson & Johnson Japan* |

Several academic colleagues were also very helpful in the preparation of this edition:.

| | |
|---|---|
| Robert Atkin | *University of Pittsburgh* |
| Melissa Barringer | *University of Massachusetts* |
| Stuart Basefsky | *Cornell University* |
| Matthew Bloom | *Notre Dame* |
| Dale Feinauer | *University of Wisconsin-Oshkosh* |
| Constance Finlay | *Cornell University* |
| Robert Gatewood | *University of Georgia* |

| | |
|---|---|
| John Hannon | *Purdue University* |
| Sookon Kim | *Kyung Hee University* |
| Kenneth A. Kovach | *George Mason University* |
| Dan Koys | *DePaul University* |
| Linda A. Krefting | *Texas Tech University* |
| Linda Lowry | *Cornell University* |
| Richard Lutz | *University of Akron* |
| Marick Masters | *University of Pittsburgh* |
| Ed Montemeyer | *Michigan State* |
| Michael Moore | *Michigan State* |
| Steve Motowidlo | *Pennsylvania State University* |
| Jerry Newman | *SUNY Buffalo* |
| Janez Prasnikar | *University of Ljubljana* |
| Jaehoon Rhee | *Yeungnam University* |
| Yoko Sano | *Keio University* |
| Mark Singer | *James Madison University* |
| Yvonne Stedham | *University of Nevada-Reno* |
| Anne S. Tsui | *Hong Kong University of Science and Technology* |
| Nada Zupan | *University of Ljubljana* |

**G. T. M**
**J. W. B**

# BRIEF CONTENTS

# CONTENTS

# A Diagnostic Approach to Human Resource Management

POSCO, the world's second largest producer of steel, extends its Pohang plant far into the sea that separates Korea and Japan. Employees and visitors to this immense modern facility pass beneath a huge sign that spans six lanes of traffic and proclaims, in Korean and English, the company's philosophy (Exhibit 1.1): "Resources are Limited: Creativity is Unlimited." To POSCO, people—Pohang's human resources—are the key to achieving competitive advantage. You don't have to go to Pohang, Korea, to learn what managers around the globe are discovering. Ask the leaders of any organization or read what executives of global companies like General Electric, Toshiba, or BMW proclaim in their speeches and operating plans. Uniformly, they assert that people are their critical resource. They believe that effective management of human resources is the key to unleashing creativity and achieving competitive advantage.

## WHY HUMAN RESOURCES ARE CRUCIAL

Although plant, equipment, and financial assets are resources required by organizations, the people—the human resources—are particularly important. Human resources (HR) provide the creative spark in any organization. People design and produce the goods and services, control quality, market the products, allocate financial resources, and set overall strategies and objectives for the organization. Without effective people, it is simply impossible for an organization to achieve its objectives. From Pohang to Petaluma, managers' decisions shape the relationship between an organization and its employees.

> *Human resource management (HRM)* is a series of integrated decisions that form the employment relationship; their quality directly contributes to the ability of the organization and the employees to achieve their objectives.

Because they directly affect people's lives as well as employers' ability to compete, HR decisions are among the most difficult yet crucial decisions that managers must make. And they are not made in isolation; the political, cultural, and economic forces in societies are interwoven with these decisions.

### Integrated Decisions . . .

Note that our definition of HRM requires that decisions be integrated, that is, blended into a whole. Decisions on different aspects of HR must be consistent with other HR decisions as shown in Exhibit 1.2. For example, a company trying to create a productive work team must *select* employees who can work well with others, *train* for communication and team building skills as well as job skills, *pay* for group output rather than individual performance, and *support* employees so that they may perform to the best of their abilities. Without all of these decisions, the team can fail. All of these decisions support the team and the organization success.

In addition to being integrated with other HR actions, decisions must also be internally consistent. For example, if incentive and overtime pay boost wages of assembly-line workers above that of their team leaders, an employer would be

**EXHIBIT 1.1** What the Korean Competition Thinks

資源은 有限 創意는 無限

Resources are Limited: Creativity is Unlimited

Source: Chinese character rendition supplied by Byoun-hoon Lee

**EXHIBIT 1.2** The Whole Picture

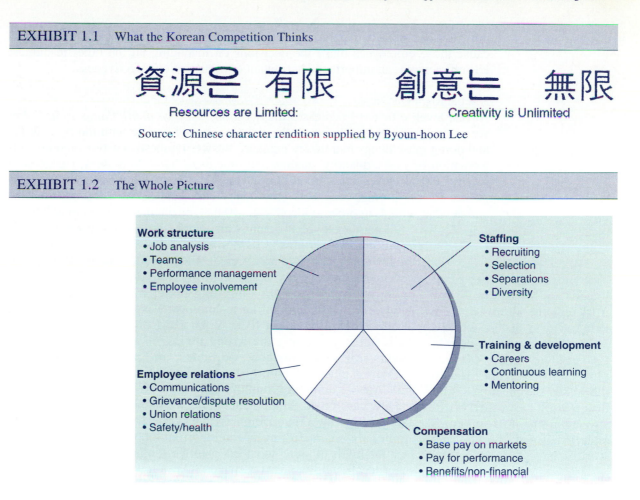

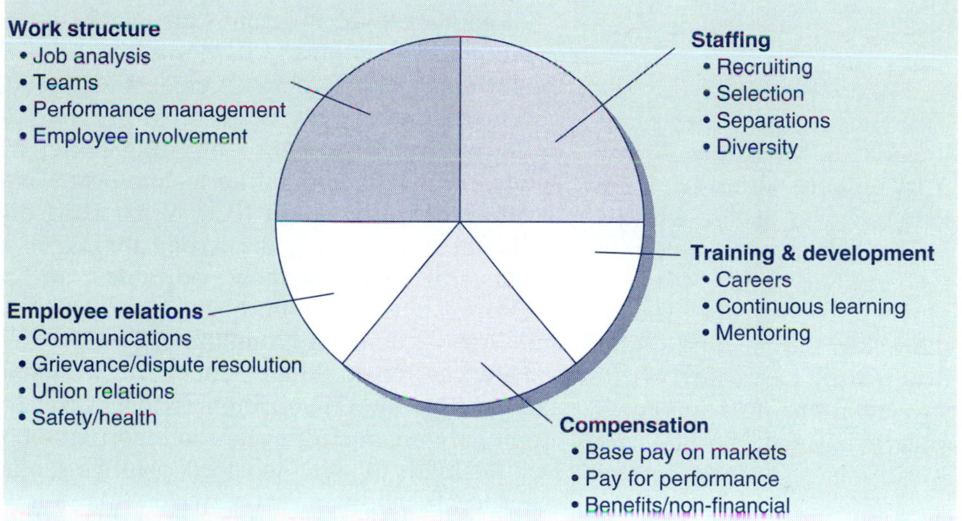


hard-pressed to find any assemblers willing to take on the extra responsibility (and lower pay) of the leadership roles. No single program stands on its own. Integrated HR programs are more likely to achieve overall organization objectives.

## . . . That Influence Effectiveness

How would we recognize an effective enterprise when we see one? Characteristics of effective organizations may include profitability, return on investment, market share, growth, adaptability and innovation, and perhaps the ultimate objective: survival. An organization is effective if it offers consumers the services and products desired in a timely manner at reasonable price and quality. Effectiveness stems from both efficiency and equity.[1]

### Efficiency

Products and services are created by combining resources and offering added value to customers. If we think of all the organization's resources—raw materials, data, technology, capital, and human resources—as inputs and the products and services that result as outputs, organizations seek to maximize outputs while minimizing inputs. HR decisions help an organization manage its employees efficiently. And because those employees make the decisions on managing all the other resources, HR efficiency is an important determinant of organization effectiveness.

### Ask the Right Questions

At one level, efficiency addresses the question, "*Are we doing things right?*" Are we controlling labor costs, hiring the right number of people with the right skills, and doing these things in a timely manner? Answering these questions requires information on costs, quantity, quality, and timeliness. How long does it take us to hire a new computer software engineer? How much do we pay for moving expenses for the average engineer? How many engineers do we need to interview and at what schools in order to identify the 10 that the engineering group will hire?

At another level, efficiency also addresses the question, "*Are we doing the right things?*" IBM's missteps in the early 1990s show the difficulties of staying efficient. Each new computer IBM introduced was undeniably better than previous models. So IBM was doing many things right—building better mainframes. Unfortunately, the whole computing technology was moving faster and in different directions than IBM. What IBM did, it did wonderfully well. But it was doing the wrong things. Its competitors and customers shifted to networks, portables, and palmtops. Applied to HRM, we must ask both questions: "Are we doing things right?" and "Are we doing the right things?"[2]

How can we do things better? Are we taking actions that do *not* add value to the organization or that waste our resources? For example, are we recruiting at engineering schools whose graduates lack the kinds of skills we need? Are we sending out recruiters who seem to alienate women engineers? Are we giving new engineers the wrong cues about performance expectations in our orientation program? Sometimes managers get so tied up in the efficient administration of procedures that they forget to ask if those procedures are adding value to the organization. Efficiency can be increased by redesigning a form to make it easier to understand or by computerizing the form; efficiency can also be increased by eliminating the need for the form in the first place.

#### WHAT DO YOU THINK?

The Bethlehem Steel plant located in Tonawanda, New York, on the shore of Lake Erie, used to be the world's largest producer of steel. At its peak, over 20,000 employees worked here. But in the 1980s the plant was shut down and eventually destroyed after it had become a safety hazard. Today, the world's largest steel producers are located in Asia. What HRM practices do you think caused the United States to lose its competitive advantage in large-scale steel production?

### Equity

Equity is the perceived fairness of both the procedures used to make HR decisions and the actual decisions.[3] In the classroom, a fair exam is not necessarily one in which all students receive the same grade. Rather, a fair exam adequately covers the material in the course and gives all students an equal chance to demonstrate their understanding of the material. Some professors adopt additional procedures to permit students to appeal a grade if they feel either the exam or the grading is unfair. Similarly, an effective organization may look at whether the amount paid to various employees is fair in comparison to what the employee does and fair in comparison to what other employees are paid. They may ask employees to serve on committees to design or review pay procedures, or they may survey employees' opinions on various HR issues. An effective organization treats its employees fairly and with respect. It strives to create conditions for all employees to contribute and to achieve success. Equity is an important aspect of effectiveness.

### Integrating Efficiency and Equity

Efficiency and equity are interrelated. For example, many organizations believe that fostering employees' sense of fair treatment by means of grievance systems, speak-up or open-door policies, dispute resolution, and employee assistance programs enable them to operate more efficiently. They reason that if employees sense they are being treated fairly, they will be more willing to accept retraining or relocation or to offer productivity improvement suggestions. For these companies, efficiency and equity are both enhanced by the same decisions.

On the other hand, efficiency and equity may sometimes conflict. For example, layoffs that retain younger employees with up-to-date skills or who are more likely to accept change may seem unfair to senior employees who believe their loyalty and years of service to the organization are being undervalued. Although all managers face questions of efficiency and equity, some of the most vivid, important, and exciting issues fall squarely within HR management. Balancing equity and efficiency is a constant challenge because both are required for an effective organization.

### Valuing Human Resources as Assets

Human resources don't come cheap. For some organizations, such as General Foods and Texaco, wages, benefits, and training make up 20 to 30 percent of total operating expenses. For organizations in labor-intensive industries, such as H&R Block, Merrill Lynch, or your local school system, labor expenses may total more than 70 percent of operating expenses.

Most important decisions in an organization are made by examining costs and benefits. When the board of regents of your college considers building a new dormitory, they want to see projected enrollment figures and cash flow statements to see whether the plan makes sense. Information on costs and benefits makes the decision process more systematic and rational, and it should make it more effective. But such rational decision making is not applied as often to HR decisions, mainly because of the difficulties of isolating the payoffs of HR programs from other initiatives and because fads and beliefs often outrun evidence.

## SEPARATING HRM COSTS AND PAYOFFS FROM OTHER INITIATIVES

To understand the difficulties of disentangling the payoffs of HRM from other organization actions, look at a recent reengineering at Pepsi-Cola. Pepsi realized that it was not getting a proper return on its $5 billion dollar purchase of its bottling franchisees. Even though the company was continuing to deliver a profit, a closer look at feedback from customers, employees, and financial analysis revealed that the company was facing a disaster. *Customers*—the grocers who sold the Pepsi beverages—complained that they couldn't understand the company's pricing, Pepsi people did not return phone calls, and customers never knew who to call on which issue because they may have had contact with up to 21 different Pepsi employees. Pepsi was not user friendly.[4] *Employees* complained that they did not believe higher-level management was dealing honestly with them, nor did there seem to be much connection between the work they were doing and what the customers or the organization needed. In the *marketplace,* cola beverages were hit by the growing popularity of alternate

EXHIBIT 1.3 More than Just Fizz?

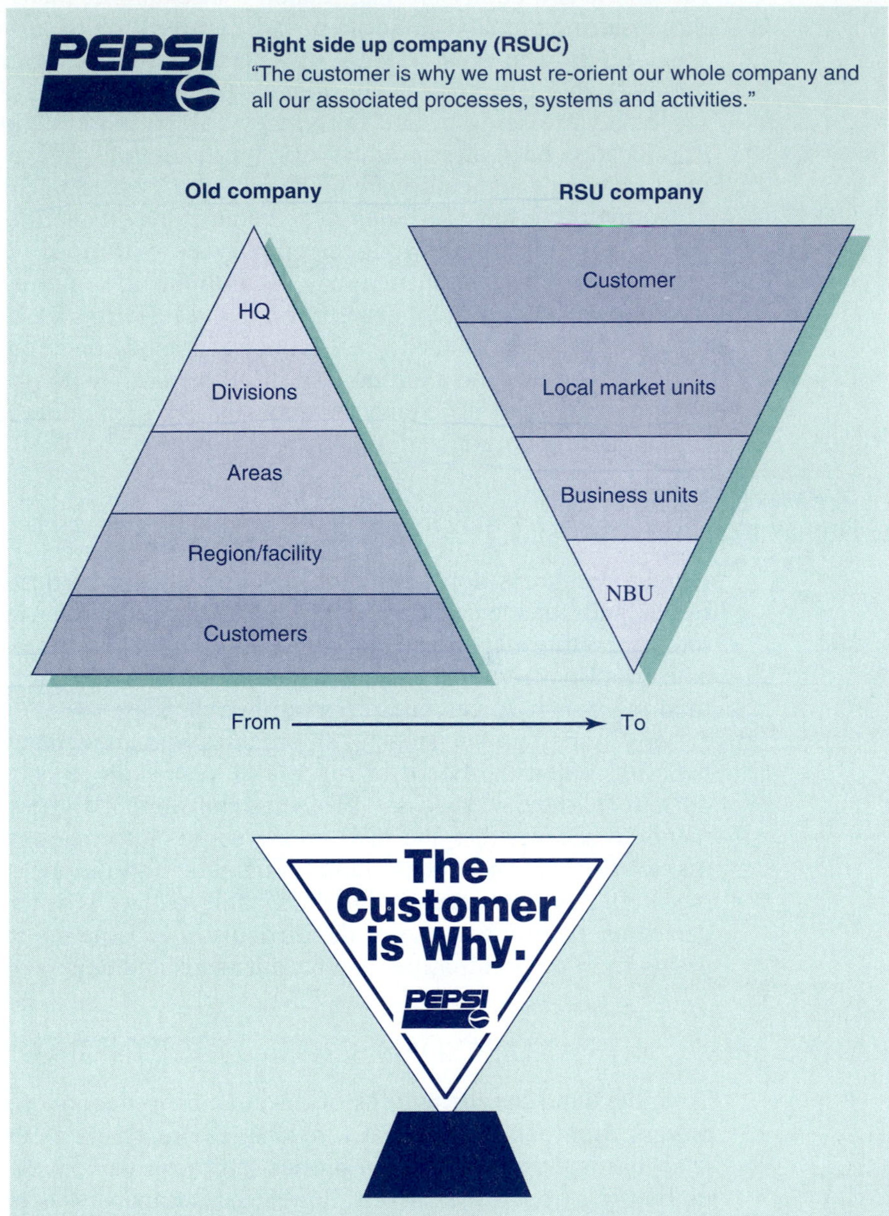


beverages (e.g., canned teas, fruit-based drinks) as well as a growing acceptance of generic colas. Customers, employees, and investors were all unhappy. Clearly, changes were needed.

Pepsi reoriented itself by putting employees closest to the customer at the top of the organization (Exhibit 1.3). The rest of the organization was dedicated to removing obstacles and providing resources so that customers' needs could be met. The company hammered home the message that "the customer is why we must re-orient our whole company and all our associated processes, systems, and activities."

EXHIBIT 1.4 Pepsi Commnicates Its Objectives and Strategies to the Troops

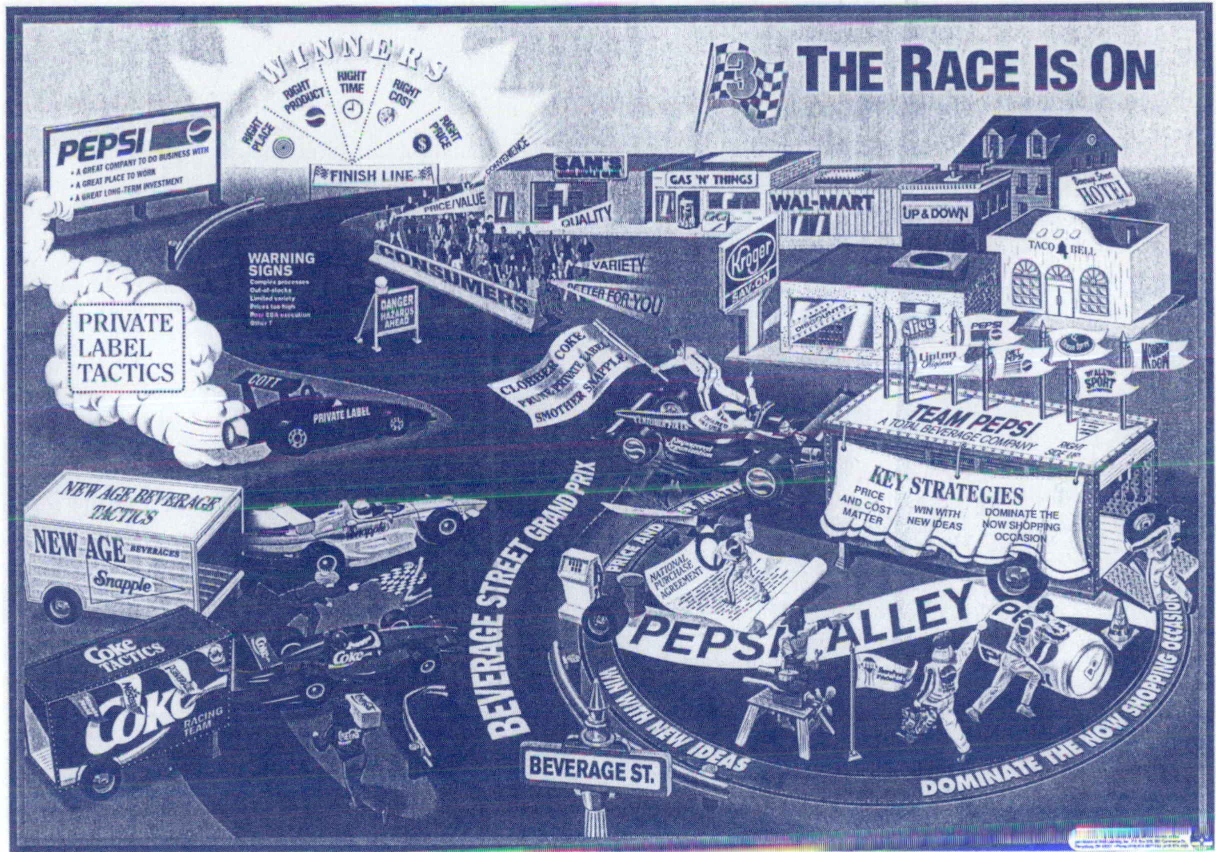


Because Pepsi is people-intensive, the vast majority of its changes were HRM-related initiatives: redesigning work processes and the jobs to focus on customers more efficiently; refocusing training to put far greater emphasis on what customers need and on how to deliver it; redesigning the compensation system to reward consistent, reliable job performance instead of seniority and "heroic" behavior that cannot be sustained over the long run; and tying pay more closely to the company's success. Pepsi recognized the importance of communicating—communicating why these changes were necessary and what the changes meant for every single employee. Exhibit 1.4 is one of a series of "learning maps" developed to help Pepsi's employees better understand their market. The maps (this one is number three in the series) are used like a board game to get employees actively involved and to make them aware of Pepsi's challenges and strategies. After a morning going through the maps by playing the game, employees know which Pepsi product has the greatest profit margin (e.g., two-liter Diet Pepsi versus a twelve-pack of regular Pepsi versus Ocean Spray fruit drink) and can see how their jobs fit into the entire process, whether they are truck drivers, bottlers, or HRM generalists.

**EXHIBIT 1.5** Business Class Fails to Discover Formula for the Pepsi-Challenged

James Smith has taken the Pepsi Challenge—and he's conceded defeat.

Every semester, Mr. Smith, a professor of finance at the Kenan-Flagler Business School at the University of North Carolina at Chapel Hill, gives his students a mathematical exercise to project corporate earnings.

The directions are simple: Select any company, take its earnings for the past 10 years, plug in some forecasts for overall economic growth, raw-material prices, etc., and predict earnings for the next four quarters.

There's only one strict rule—don't pick PepsiCo Inc.

Turns out, Pepsi is the only company among all those tested since 1988 that defies the forecasting method. Prof. Smith says that while projections for other companies almost always match up with earnings, the Pepsi predictions are way out of whack.

"You're better off flipping a coin," he says. "It's an enigma."

Not that students haven't tried. A few years ago a young woman tried to unravel the Pepsi mystery, only to wind up in Mr. Smith's office in tears. Two years ago, a national marketing manager for Pepsi who happened to be in Mr. Smith's class gave it another crack. The professor warned him, but the manager was insistent.

"He said he could get all the necessary numbers from the company, everything he needed," says Mr. Smith.

He, too, quit in frustration.

PepsiCo says it's not sure why Prof. Smith's model breaks down. A Pepsi spokesman says the company uses similar "regression analysis" to forecast earnings all the time.

"We'd have to find out more about what he's doing," says the spokesman.

Mr. Smith guesses the problem may be related to PepsiCo's unpredictable and complex structure, which includes beverage, snack-food and restaurant units. Pizza Hut may go into an earnings slump—while Mountain Dew suddenly takes off or Doritos gets into a pricing war.

Then again, Prof. Smith says, his students tackle far more complex companies, such as DuPont and Union Carbide.

"Pepsi's a fine company," he says. "But as far as modeling goes, it's a nightmare."

How does Coca-Cola Co. fare?

Says Mr. Smith: "It's a cinch."

Source: Robert Frank, *The Wall Street Journal,* November 21, 1995, p. B1.

Pepsi reports that these efforts have paid off: Profits have grown by 18 percent while demand has grown by only 4 percent. Is it fair to say that all of the increase is a result of HRM activities? No. Is it fair to say that a good deal of the increase is a result of HRM activities? Perhaps. At least it appears Pepsi's success is due to something beyond the standard economic and financial factors that most analysts use. Is it worth Pepsi's time to assign costs as well as profits to HRM compared with other initiatives? Perhaps. Those managers with short-term perspectives assert that such a task may give academics (e.g. the authors) intellectual satisfaction, but it is not consistent with the national initiatives that drive Pepsi these days. Managers more concerned with strategy recognize that assessing the constantly changing conditions facing Pepsi or diagnosing which HRM actions pay off relative to Pepsi's competitors is difficult (Exhibit 1.5), yet crucial.

## Payoffs as Expenses Avoided

Sometimes the benefits of HR actions will be estimated as costs averted. For example, Pepsi initiated "customer first" training for its truck drivers in order to avoid costly confusion and dissatisfaction among customers. A public employer,

EXPLORING THE WEB

In today's electronically-linked world, it's no surprise the HRM professionals can ask and answer questions without ever leaving their computers. HRNET is an electronic bulletin board where any member can pose a question, give an answer, or voice an opinion. Over 3,000 HR managers, professors and consultants subscribe to HRNET, which distributes every member's messages to all members, all over the world. You can catch up on these discussions in the HRNET archives. Reading the HRNET archives is as easy as sending and receiving e-mail, and it will give you a first-hand idea about the key issues facing HR professionals. Your instructor has more information to help you use HRNET in your class.

the City of Phoenix, estimates cost savings from its alcoholism assistance program at over $2 million a year.[5] The city reaches this figure by calculating the economic value of a performance decrease in specific jobs due to alcohol impairment.

### Expense of Doing Nothing

At times, HR adds value from the negative effects of doing nothing: customers not delighted, new products not developed, new marketing strategies not devised. The expense to Pepsi of not diagnosing and changing its HR actions may have been continued loss of market share and revenue growth. South Korea's Samsung Group looks at the expense of doing nothing to justify its management development program, which sends employees to live overseas for a year to become more familiar with international tastes. Samsung believes that the program will pay back its costs of over $80,000 per person per year by enabling its managers to make better judgments about international customers. Samsung has operations in 55 countries. Without understanding its customers and their cultures, Samsung managers risk squandering their company's other resources—financial assets, plants, and equipment—by leading the company's human resources in directions that do not add value.

### HR Activities Pay Off

Do HR actions—integrated, internally consistent bundles of human resource practices—contribute to organization efficiency and equity? People believe they do, and recent research offers some support that they do. For example, recent studies of U.S. manufacturing reported that production lines with integrated, innovative HRM practices have productivity levels 7 percent higher than traditional or inconsistent approaches.[6]

But it is not always clear why or how these HRM practices work. Much of this book, in addition to describing HR practices, looks into beliefs and evidence about the payoffs of HR decisions. We believe that successful managers make decisions based on careful diagnosis of the organization and the environment in which it must compete. The roles of HR managers become crucial because they involve the organization's most important resource: people. Let us turn next to the HR manager's role.

## THE HR MANAGER

Managing people is a central concern of every single manager in every single organization. The manager responsible for the assembly of personal computers, for example, must coordinate electronic components (the raw materials), production schedules, and financial budgets. Human resources are critical for this coordination. Managers of finance, marketing, distribution, operations, R&D, purchasing, and design are all managers of human resources. Even the team

EXHIBIT 1.6 Changing HR Role

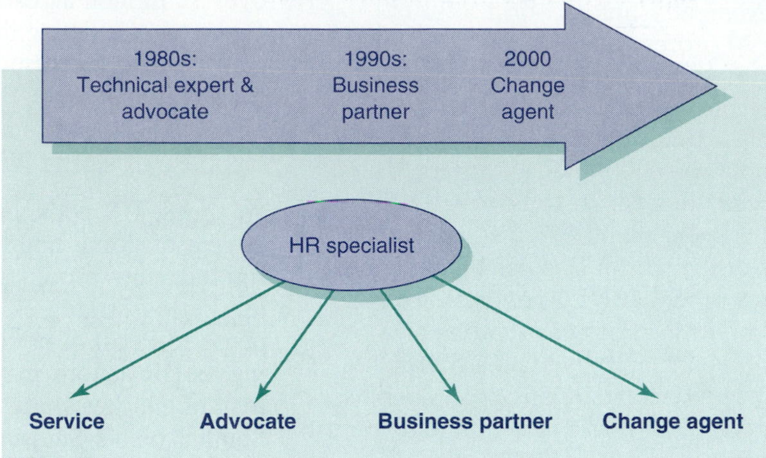


leader of a five-person software development team or the shift manager of a MacDonalds or a 7–11 convenience store is an HR manager. HR specialists may offer advice and expertise, but others actually manage the day-to-day employment relationships with people. They are responsible for the effective use of the human resources. Theirs is the ultimate responsibility for the training, performance, creativity, and satisfaction of employees whom they lead.

In a very real sense, operations managers and employees are customers or clients of the HR specialist. Providing *service* to operating managers is but one of the primary roles of the HR manager, as shown in Exhibit 1.6. Other roles include *advocate, business partner,* and *change agent.*

## Service

The service role for HRM focuses on the efficient performance of a wide variety of routine and unique tasks; for example, administering tests used for promotions or preparing government reports on hiring and diversity, or ensuring that people actually get the correct bonus once it has been determined. We know of a star software engineer who was awarded a $2,500 bonus for getting a product debugged for a key customer under tight deadlines. But when our friend opened the envelope, he discovered that the check in the envelope was for $250. Effective HR services matter. (Company name omitted to protect the guilty.)

Other services may be less routine, such as designing new pay plans to focus employees on improving product quality and delighting customers. These activities require greater expertise than issuing a new check, but the point is still to offer services that support operating managers and employees.

HR specialists bring their specialized knowledge; for example, how to design effective training programs, how to redesign work roles and organizations to fit changes in technology, how to decide where quality improvement programs may be beneficial, or how to ensure that hiring, promotion, and layoff decisions are free of discrimination. The HR specialists employ their expertise in the service of operating managers and employees. The service role is the most visible HR role in most organizations. Whether employees and managers see HR as a help or a hindrance depends on the service provided. Hence, how efficiently the service role is performed can affect profitability.

## Advocate

Fairness is important. Decisions about who to hire, promote, and train; how much to pay; how to link pay to performance; and how to assist dissatisfied employees must be made with the objective of fairness in mind. Advocating fair treatment and justice for employees is another role for the HR professional.[7] A sense of inequity among employees affects their work attitudes and behaviors. Absenteeism, low motivation, lack of concern for the quality of products or services, suggestions for improvements withheld, lack of commitment, and even sabotage may result. Examples abound from the U.S. postal workers, who have terrorized their coworkers with such frequency that "going postal" has become a catch phrase for venting uncontrolled anger, to less dramatic but more frequent reports of employees filing grievances, EEO complaints, and lawsuits accusing their employers of unfair treatment. These attitudes and behaviors affect costs, productivity, profits, and eventually the market value of the firm's stock.

### Ethics and Fiduciary Responsibility

Some argue that HR's advocacy for fairness extends beyond employees to shareholders outside the organization. For example, the food processor and trader Archer-Daniels-Midland saw its reputation severely damaged by accusations of payoffs and price fixing.[8] ADM's initial response to the charges was to accuse the informer of embezzling funds through the use of a phony compensation plan. If either charge is true, then stockholders as well as consumers have been damaged. It is not clear whether HRM people at ADM were aware of any irregularities, but as advocates of fair behavior, *all* HRM managers have a responsibility to call out lapses in behavior and to help establish a culture in the organization that tolerates no such lapses.

> EXPLORING THE WEB
>
> A discussion group whose focus is law and ethics in business can be joined by sending e-mail to
> **<listserv@moose.uvm.edu>**
> In the text (not the subject) of your message:
> SUBSCRIBE LETHICS

Sometimes ethical violations are less clear-cut. For example, government rules on pension plans focus on encouraging pensions for all employees. Yet the rules are very complex and confusing, making it difficult to comply. An organization can inadvertently run afoul of the law. People seem to vary in their sensitivity to violations. Yet HR managers are uniquely positioned—and, we argue, are responsible—for ensuring that all employee behaviors will reflect well on the company even if they find themselves grilled by Leslie Stahl on *60 Minutes*. Or satirized in a Dilbert cartoon.

Some argue that in a properly managed organization, the advocate role of HR is unnecessary and out of date.[9] The analogy is to the quality control function in manufacturing. Instead of placing all the responsibility for sorting good

WHAT DO YOU THINK?

The eye care company Bausch and Lomb fired a number of people in the early 1990s after it uncovered serious ethical lapses. As part of a concerted effort to restore the company's reputation, Deborah Smith was hired away from Xerox to become the new vice president of HR. What is it about the HR manager's position in a company that permits that person to be leader on issues of ethics?

from bad products on a specific department, make quality everyone's responsibility. Redesign jobs and train people properly to prevent the production of defective products in the first place. Similarly, if operating managers are managing their human resources effectively, the resulting training, promotion, and pay decisions will cause no ill will, and no employee advocate is required.

Experience, however, suggests otherwise. Operating managers have different orientations or objectives and face competing pressures. For example, a discount store manager may wish to pay the minimum wage necessary to attract sufficient clerks to staff the store at minimum levels of competence. On paper, the plan looks great because it holds down costs. But over time, resentful workers may take out their frustrations on customers, and inferior service may drive away formerly loyal customers. Profits may plummet, but by then the shortsighted store manager has moved on to a new location, spreading similar actions like a virus in the organization. In contrast, HR managers recommend decisions that recognize both the payoffs and the costs of those decisions. Ideally, HR specialists and other managers complement each other rather than compete. It is up to the manager of the HRM function, an HR professional, to weigh the full range of HRM activities, so that both employees and the organization are treated ethically and fairly. We believe such behavior also makes financial sense.

## Business Partner/Change Agent

The HR practitioner is also a business partner and change agent. The *business partner* role requires HR people to have hands-on knowledge of the business as well as the HR operations. The senior vice president of human resources at Novell, Inc., claims that "being a business partner means understanding the business direction of the company, including what the product is, what it's capable of doing, who the typical customers are, and how the company is positioned competitively in the marketplace."[10] In a survey of 314 leading organizations, a "savvy business perspective" was listed as the most important competency for anyone working in HRM.[11] General Electric may have carried the business partner notion the furthest. GE takes its HR managers on some sales calls. Apart from the sale of the power system, GE offers assistance to the customer's HR department.

The business partner asks the questions that help identify desired outcomes and identifies how the work force must change, as Samsung and Pepsi HR people continue to do. *Change agents* help make the changes. A change agent possesses skills such as leadership, dispute resolution, and interpersonal relations. As organizations prepare for the 21st century, change is constant. Indeed, some believe that today's reorganizations are only temporary; another one will be along soon as companies continue to adapt, amoebalike, to rapidly changing business and political environments. Consequently, the change agent role of HRM will receive greater emphasis in the future, according to Exhibit 1.6.

However, caution is required. HRM is becoming riddled with fads, resulting in change for the sake of change. Change needs to add value to the organization. Thus, the change agent and business partner are fused into a single role.

Thus, the consensus is that HR will continue to become more strategic, business oriented, customer focused, value driven, and broad in perspective. The next generation of HR practitioners will play multiple roles: client-centered service, advocate, business partner, and change agent. Sound interesting? The final chapter of this book contains additional information on becoming an accredited HR practitioner.

## A DIAGNOSTIC APPROACH

The model in Exhibit 1.7 illustrates the diagnostic approach developed in this book. This model provides a framework for thinking about HR decisions and what factors affect these decisions—the consequences as well as the causes. The diagnostic model provides a framework for the issues addressed in this book. It includes four phases: (1) assess human resource conditions, (2) set objectives based on the assessment, (3) choose a course of action from alternatives generated to achieve the objectives, and (4) evaluate the results. Evaluating the results provides feedback on the success of the actions. HR actions lead to new HR conditions. Actions can be continued or revised, depending on these new conditions. Thus, the model includes continuous learning, flexibility, and feedback. While the model breaks the HRM process into discrete phases, in reality the process is ongoing and the actions are interrelated. As with all human behavior, every action potentially affects every other action.

This diagnostic approach is used in many situations. Suppose a sharp chest pain sends you to your school's health service. The experts (we are eternal optimists) there will take your temperature, listen to your heart and lungs, record your general health history, ask for more information on your pain, and review any information already in your file. While the health professional's overall objective is to maintain the health of the entire student population, the more specific and immediate objective is to stop your pain. Based on that *objective* and their *assessment* of conditions, alternative *treatments* (actions) will be considered: admit you to a cardiac care unit, tape your cracked rib, or tell you to stop eating four jelly doughnuts before you go jogging. If problems persist, conditions will be reassessed and revised treatment considered. This process of

1. Assessing the situation
2. Planning and setting objectives
3. Choosing among alternatives
4. Evaluating results

continues throughout your relationship with the health service personnel.

### An HR Example

Apply the same diagnostic process to Paine Webber.[12] The brokerage house realized that the acquisition of its scandal-scarred competitor, Kidder Peabody, wasn't paying off (assess conditions). Paine Webber decided it needed to change its strategy. It jettisoned part of its bond operations and

EXHIBIT 1.7 The Diagnostic Model

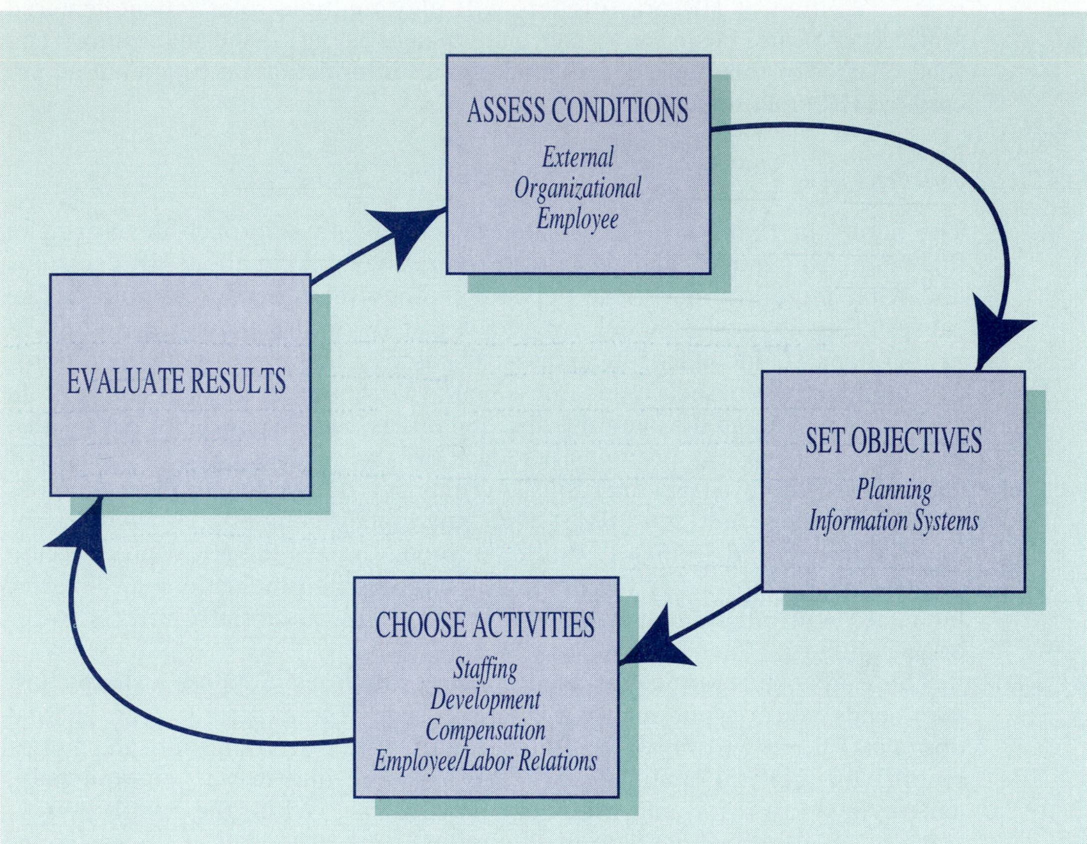


outsourced other operations by forming alliances with fund managers in other firms (work and organization design). It sharply curtailed its international initiatives by closing some of its Asian offices and moving its president of international operations to a new position, executive vice president of reengineering. Other executives were given new assignments in line with the new strategy (career development). While the company is evaluating its new strategy to see if it is paying off, it has taken immediate steps to control its labor costs by laying off 250 people (staffing; downsizing) and slashing bonuses by as much as $80 million for poorly performing traders (compensation). Paine Webber's chairman vows to focus the company more clearly on its strengths and continues to assess conditions and make whatever changes are consistent with that objective.

Rarely can a company's disappointing financial results be traced directly to human resource management issues. But as the Paine Webber example shows, it is the people who choose a strategy and carry it out. It is people who determine whether or not a firm is profitable. Managing people through an integrated bundle of HR practices thus becomes a crucial part of managing the total resources of any organization.

## ASSESS CONDITIONS

Our model of the diagnostic approach begins with assessing conditions. Conditions of particular interest to HR management fall into three broad categories: external conditions, organization conditions, and employee conditions.

### External Conditions

HRM actions are seriously influenced by conditions outside the organization. These external conditions are many and varied, but several key ones stand out. Perhaps the most important are the increasing competitive pressures, both local and global, and the dramatic changes in technology. Another crucial condition is the ever-changing laws and regulations that reflect public policy. During the 1990s in the United States, labor laws passed in the 1940s are being debated and amended, civil rights legislation of the 1960s and 1970s is being updated and extended to include the disabled, the elderly, and others, and changing pension and benefit laws also affect HR decisions. One estimate is that over half of the business decisions in the United States are shaped by federal, state, and local regulations.[13] Globally, public policy tends to have an even greater impact on HR decisions in other countries than it does in the United States. These laws, part of the social contract, require examining every single HR policy and action to ensure compliance. In these ways, external conditions influence and place constraints on the HR decisions facing managers.

### Organization Conditions

Several organization conditions directly affect HR decision making: the organization's strategy and objectives, financial situation, technology, and culture are examples. Obviously, the strategies, technologies, finances, culture, and organization structures at Iowa Beef Processors, Microsoft, and the Metropolitan Museum of Art differ from those at your local 7-11. The nature of these unique conditions influences the HR decisions managers make.

Even a single company, such as General Electric or Toshiba, may in reality be made up of many organizations based on their differing strategies and objectives, finances, technologies, and cultures, and differing external conditions among different business units. The Korean conglomerate Sunkyong has business units operating throughout the world. They range from construction to hotels to finance to oil refining. Each unit competes in different product and service markets, uses differing technologies, and faces unique financial conditions. The employment relationship within each of these units is tailored to fit the unique organization conditions at the unit.

### Employee Conditions

Employees differ in their experiences, abilities, needs, attitudes, and motivation. Information on how individuals differ is highly relevant to HRM decisions. Information about individual employees is critical for almost every HR decision. Managers must take these differences into account in setting objectives and choosing human resource activities. For example, a person failing to perform because he or she lacks a skill requires a very different HR approach than that required for a person whose family obligations cause so much stress that performance is impaired.

## PLAN AND SET OBJECTIVES

Knowing where we are is the first step. Deciding where we want to be—our objectives—is the second. Planning synthesizes information and identifies the gaps between the two.

Just as the roles of HR experts and organizations have changed, objectives also change. Two decades ago, the primary objectives of HRM dealt with employee morale and job satisfaction. Today, HRM focuses on adding value by enhancing financial performance, customer satisfaction, and employee satisfaction. An effective organization today is defined by its financial and market performance. Employee satisfaction is defined through surveys of attitudes toward HR policies and feelings of fair treatment. Customer satisfaction is variously measured in on-time deliveries, quality, and surveys of customers.

HR planning activities focus on setting objectives. HR planning involves diagnosing how an organization should move from its current HR conditions to its desired HR conditions—that is, how to close the gaps in efficiency and equity.

## HRM ACTIVITIES

HRM activities are programs designed in response to HR objectives and managed to achieve those objectives. Our diagnostic approach identifies four broad categories of activities: staffing, development, compensation, and employee/union relations. The nature of each of these activities changes over time and differs among companies, depending on their external and organization conditions as well as their objectives.

### Staffing: From Individuals to Teams

Staffing determines the composition of an organization's human resources. How many people should we employ? Which skills, abilities, and experiences should they possess? When and how should people be transferred, recruited, or laid off? How do we select the correct individuals in each case?

Traditional approaches rested on the notion of tasks grouped into jobs and individuals matched to appropriate jobs. Matching between individuals and jobs formed the basis for selection, training, compensation—almost all personnel decisions. This model still pervades much of HRM.

Currently, flexible concepts of roles are emerging to replace the original job/individual model. Instead of a fixed job defined by rigid organizational specifications, roles or work assignments are defined by the skills of the employees. In addition, teamwork and cooperation among employees rather than competition to come out ahead of co-workers is being emphasized. The team rather than the individual has emerged as the basic building block in the design of organizations.

### Development: From Training to Continuous Learning

Employee development and training activities are among the most common and costly HR activities. These activities teach new skills, refine existing skills, and affect employee attitudes. For example, newly hired employees typically undergo an orientation session soon after joining the organization. Orientation makes new employees feel part of the group. Development activities are a powerful means to enhance the efficiency and equity of the organization, especially when they are integrated with other HR activities.

Increasingly, training expenditures are regarded as strategic investments similar to those in new plants and equipment. Continuous training is vital to achieving competitiveness. While Americans on average enjoy high levels of educational attainment, about 700,000 students are dropping out of high schools each year and another 700,000 are graduating with only eighth-grade skills.[14] At the same time, the skill requirements of many employers both in the United States and around the world appear to be escalating. For example, manufacturing workers may be assigned to a team requiring continuous learning and flexibility; each team member is expected to learn every job. Quality checking, statistical process control, resetting machines, scheduling, and other tasks that were formerly the domain of supervisors are now common fare for all employees. Employee development assures that the learning necessary to perform the job takes place.

## Compensation: From Wages to Total Labor Costs and Rewarding Performance

Positioning the organization's pay relative to its competitors' pay, ensuring equitable pay differences among employees, and deciding whether pay increases should be based on individual, team, or organization performance measures are all compensation issues.

Employees are a substantial part of the operating costs of an organization. These costs are a function of the number of employees, their wages and benefits, plus costs for training, hiring, and so on. Historically, managers controlled wage levels and the number of employees. Increasingly, the focus has shifted to understanding the effects of wages and employment security on total labor costs and strengthening the links between pay and performance.

## Employee/Union Relations: From Labor Relations to Governance

Employee relations activities promote harmonious relationships among managers and employees. The relationship with unions, including collective bargaining and contract administration, is the most visible aspect of employee relations. For some managers, employee relations means reducing hostilities, or at least reducing dissatisfaction to a tolerable murmur. Others aim higher: They seek to design and manage HR activities to ensure fair and equitable treatment of all employees. Employment security provisions, grievance procedures, provisions for child care and drug counseling may all be part of employee relations activities.

From the 1940s to the 1980s, the relationship between management and unions was generally adversarial. But with the decline in their numbers and influence, joining a union is no longer the primary way employees participate in shaping their workplace. Workplace governance today includes participative management, worker councils, peer dispute resolution procedures, and quality-of-work-life programs. Managers, unions, and employees are all becoming more aware of alternatives to collective bargaining.

These, then, are the four major human resource activities listed in the diagnostic approach: staffing, developing, compensating, and employee/union relations. How these activities are designed and managed depends on the previous two phases of the model: the human resource conditions the organization faces and the objectives it has established. Decisions on these activities make up the organization's human resource strategy. Results of these activities are evaluated as part of the process of monitoring conditions.

## EVALUATING RESULTS

Evaluation determines the effects of human resource activities. Did its activities help the organization achieve its human resource objectives? For example, efficiency might be evaluated by comparing the labor costs after a staffing or training program with the labor costs before the program. Performance and absenteeism before and after a new pay system may be compared. Equity may be evaluated by comparing the number of minorities and females hired as a result of a more aggressive recruiting approach to affirmative action objectives.

HR activities change the organization's environment and lead to new conditions. This leads us back to the first phase of the diagnostic model: assess conditions. The components of the diagnostic model are thus interrelated, and their influence can be multidimensional.

## THE EMPLOYMENT RELATIONSHIP: AN IMPLICIT CONTRACT

Until the mid-1980s, many Americans thought about work in terms of regular, full-time jobs. Graduates from high schools and colleges tended to work for a single employer in stable, relatively secure, and predictable careers. They received relatively stable, predictable earnings and benefits protection in exchange for work performance. For most workers, many of the terms and conditions of these employment exchanges were left unstated, forming implicit contracts, the deal.

An *implicit employment contract* is an unwritten understanding between employers and employees over the reciprocal obligations and returns; employees contribute toward achieving the goals of the employer in exchange for returns given by the employer and valued by the employee.

To understand the notion of an implicit contract, think about the understanding between you and the class instructor. Each of you has obligations and responsibilities. Yours include actively learning the material, not dozing off in class (at least not obtrusively), doing the projects, and so on. The instructor teaches up-to-date material; presents competent, relevant instruction; offers the opportunity to learn; and so on. Each party receives returns from this exchange. Yours include credits to graduate, maybe an interesting class, and useful material. Your instructor's returns include pay and benefits funded in part by your tuition, and the pleasure of teaching intellectually engaging students. Note that some of this exchange is explicit; it is written out as in a formal agreement (e.g., credits received for the class; grading criteria). However, much of it is implicit or unspecified (e.g., how up-to-date the material will be; your participation in classroom discussions). This is how it is in the employment relationship, too: Some obligations and returns are explicit, but much might be left unstated, implicit. Thus, the expectations of the individual and the organization can be both explicit and implicit. Explicit contracts include those negotiated by unions, sports figures, and actors. But even formal, explicit contracts rely on implicit understandings to make them work.[15]

## The "New Deal": Myth or Fact?

Expectations and beliefs about the employment relationship vary widely, domestically among people working for different companies and globally among workers and employers in different cultures.[16] Traditionally, many Japanese and German companies guaranteed their employees lifetime employment in exchange for continuous improvement in productivity, learning, and peaceful relations (e.g., no strikes, take whatever job the company assigns). In the United States, the deals were more varied. Hewlett Packard and 3M offered deals similar to those of their Japanese and German competitors. GE and Microsoft offered an opportunity to contribute and perform, but not a career. Instead, job security was based on an employee's learning and contributions.

Many people think the deal is changing (Exhibit 1.8). IBM downsizes over 60,000 people, AT&T over 40,000. Even Nissan and Toyota have shifted from *lifetime* to *long-term* employment policies as old expectations no longer seem to hold.

The traditional deal is characterized by secure employment with one employer, high employee loyalty and commitment to that employer, the hiring of permanent workers and paying them based on competitive market rates, the jobs they perform, and their experience. Today's scenario is that job security is much more uncertain. Employees are urged to become loyal to themselves and committed only to their own careers and not the company.[17]

However, like so many "trends," systematic evidence about the changing deal is hard to come by. One survey of U.S. employers reports that employees are as committed as they were five years ago, job security is about the same, and the use of contract workers has remained the same or lessened in the past five years.[18] So whatever trends you read about, in this text as well as in the popular business press, you can be sure it does not apply universally.

> **WHAT DO YOU THINK?**
>
> Back to the Future: If, like Michael J. Fox, you had a chance to go back in time 20 years, how would your expectations about the workplace differ from today? Would there be differences in job security expectations? In pay expectations? Do you think a typical employer's expectations would be different? If so, how?

## A Major HR Challenge: Managing a Breached Contract

There are signs that implicit understandings based on tradition and trust are diminishing throughout the United States and the world. Changes in the employment relationship are inseparable from the continuous restructuring endemic to American society and the economy. Throughout this book we will be discussing a number of these changes. Many of the current changes in the employment relationship are designed to better fit the particular circumstances or the strategy of the employer. Yet there is some question whether the impact on employees is being considered. Increasingly, employees seem to be aligned with other factors of production.

The ramifications of the changing employment contract, for employees and their dependents, and perhaps for society, too, have been virtually ignored. Perhaps HR managers need to help individuals mitigate the increased risks and costs they must bear. Additional HR innovations are going to be required. We will return to this issue later in the book.

EXHIBIT 1.8 Let's Make a Deal

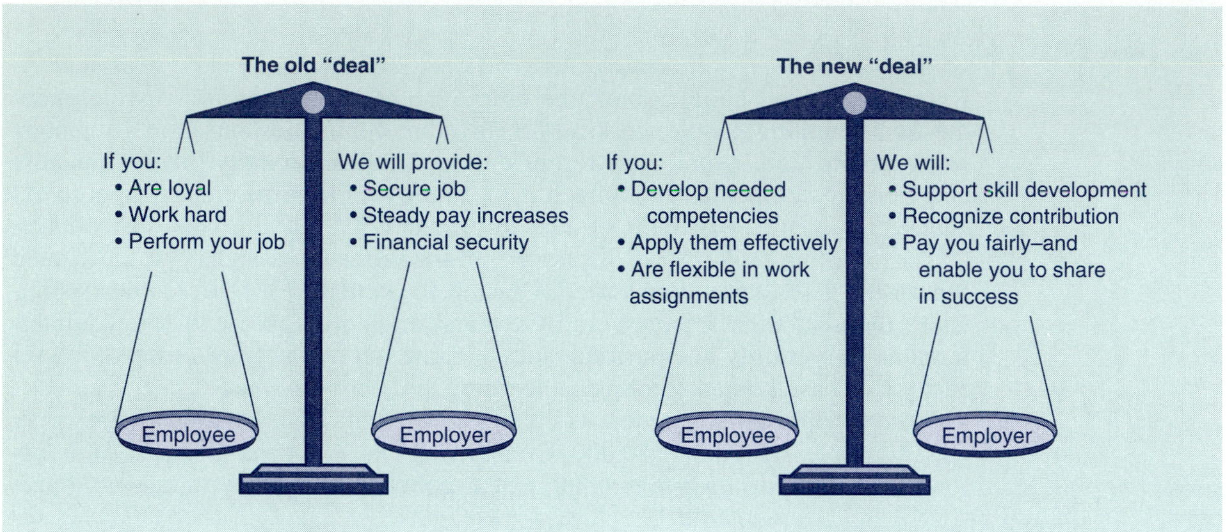


## COMBINE THE DIAGNOSTIC APPROACH WITH THEORETICAL AND TECHNICAL KNOWLEDGE

We have described the diagnostic approach for considering information on which HR decisions are based. Much of the rest of the book discusses the theoretical and technical knowledge necessary to make those decisions.

The organization of this book parallels this diagnostic approach. Part One describes external, organizational, and employee conditions relevant to human resource decisions. Then, it describes the planning process in which objectives are specified. The book then goes into detail about human resource activities. As you progress through the book, the model provides a framework for combining the decision-making process with the technical and theoretical knowledge that makes up human resource management.

## SUMMARY

Human resource management is a fascinating and important subject. The fascination lies in the fact that it involves people at work. It is important because human resources are the organization. People make the decisions; set the objectives; and design, assemble, and sell the products. The basic premise underlying this book is that decisions about how people are managed make a difference.

The diagnostic model offers a framework combining theoretical and technical knowledge with the diagnostic approach. In the diagnostic approach, external conditions, organization conditions, and employee conditions all affect human resource decisions and the organization's ability to achieve its objectives. Objectives include organizational efficiency and equity. These objectives are standards for evaluating the results of decisions.

We should emphasize that the diagnostic approach is not static. Changing conditions dictate ongoing assessment and flexible decision making. Nor do the relationships always proceed in one direction. Human resource activities can affect external conditions (such as changing the labor market by attracting more candidates), and organization conditions (such as identifying strategic directions best suited to the skills and motivations of employees), as well as employees. Managing such a dynamic process is what makes HRM so important and challenging.

## QUESTIONS

1. What are some HRM issues that have been in the news in the past two months?
2. How has the role of the HR manager changed over time?
3. Discuss the interests of various groups inside and outside the organization in HRM. In what circumstances might these interests conflict? Whose interests should prevail?
4. Describe HRM as presented in this chapter. What is it and why should it matter?
5. Apply the diagnostic approach to a personnel issue with which you are familiar.
6. Do you believe the implicit employment relationship—the deal—is changing? Give illustrations to support your view.

## NOTES AND REFERENCES


1. J. W. Walker and T. P. Bechet, "Defining Effectiveness and Efficiency Measures in the Context of Human Resource Strategy," in *Bottom Line Results from Strategic Human Resource Planning,* ed. R. J. Niehaus and K. F. Price (New York: Plenum Press, 1991).
2. Philip H. Mirvis, "Is Human Resources Out of It?" *Across The Board,* Sept. 1993, pp. 50–51.
3. R. Folger and Jerald Greenberg, "Procedural Justice: An Interpretive Analysis of Personnel Systems," in *Human Resources Management,* vol. 3, ed. K. M. Rowland and G. R. Ferris (Greenwich, CT: JAI Press, 1985), pp. 141–83.
4. John Bronson, "Turning Vision into Business Performance," Presentation at HR Executive Development Program, Cornell University, Ithaca, New York, Nov. 1995.
5. Janice Beyer and Harrison Trice, "The Best/Worst Technique for Measuring Work Performance in Organizational Research," *Organizational Behavior and Statistics,* May 1984, pp. 1-21.
6. Casey Ichniowski, Kathryn Shaw, and Giovanna Prennushi, *The Effects of Human Resources Management Practices on Productivity* (Cambridge, MA: National Bureau of Economic Research working paper No. 5333, 1996).
7. James Walker, "The Future Human Resource Function Today," Presentation at Center for Advanced Human Resource Studies, Ithaca, New York, Nov. 5, 1992.

8. Charlene Marmer Solomon, "Put Your Ethics to a Global Test," *Personnel Journal,* Jan. 1996, pp. 66–74.
9. Reuben Larson, "Zero-Defect-Based Human Asset Management," *On Center,* Fall 1992, pp. 1–2.
10. Donna Blancero and Lee Dyer, "Assessing Human Resource Competencies," Working paper, Cornell University, Ithaca, New York, 1992.
11. Louis S. Csoka, *Rethinking Human Resources* (New York: The Conference Board, 1995).
12. Anita Raghavan, "Paine Webber Plans to Slash Annual Pay," *The Wall Street Journal,* Nov. 6, 1995, pp. C1, C16.
13. Robert Reich, *Work of Nations: Preparing Ourselves for 21st-Century Capitalism* (New York: Alfred A. Knopf, 1991).
14. Laurie J. Bassi, "Upgrading the U.S. Workplace: Do Reorganization, Education Help?" *Monthly Labor Review,* May 1995, pp. 37–47.
15. Denise Rousseau and Martin Greller, "HR Practices: Administrative Contract Makers," *Human Resource Management,* Fall 1994, pp. 385–401.
16. M. Afzalur and Albert A. Blum, ed. *Global Perspectives on Organizational Conflict* (Westport, CT: Praeger, 1994); Vlado Pucik, Noel Tichy, and Carole K. Barnett, eds., *Globalizing Management* (New York: John Wiley, 1992).
17. William Bridges, "The End of the Job," *Fortune,* Sept. 19, 1994, pp. 62–68.
18. *The New Employment Relationship: Has Anything Really Changed?* (Minneapolis: Ceridian Corporation, 1995).

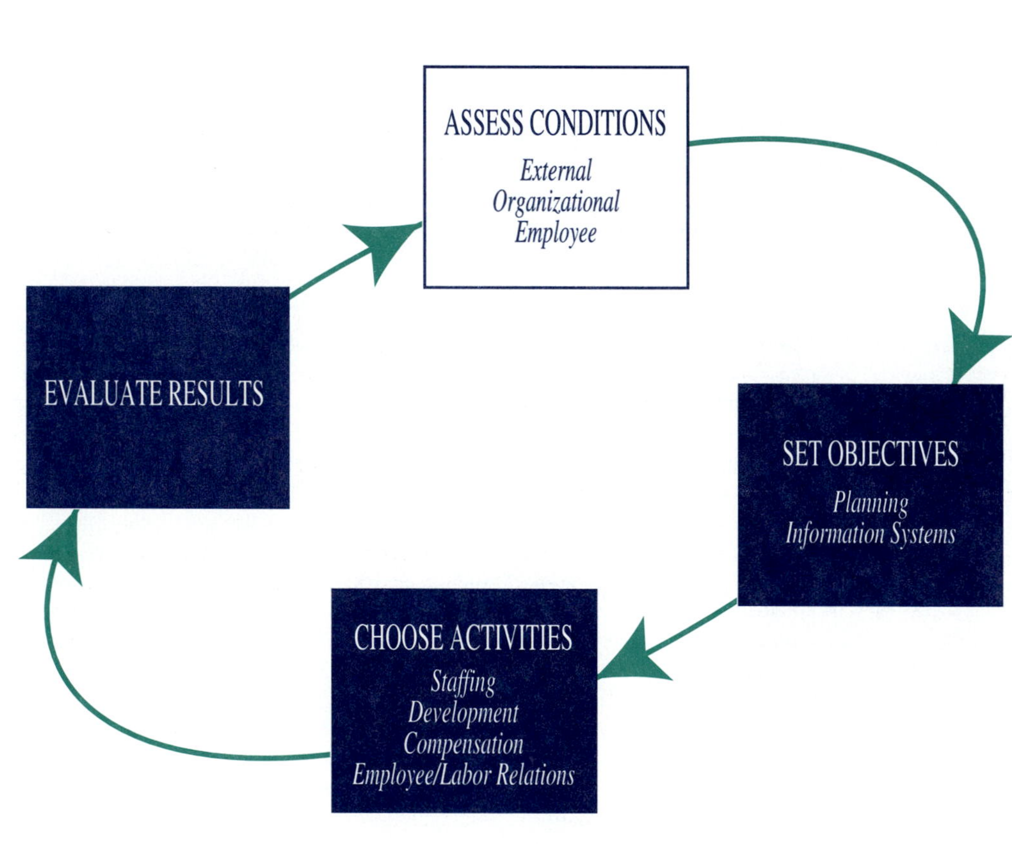
ASSESS CONDITIONS
External
Organizational
Employee
SET OBJECTIVES
Planning
Information Systems
CHOOSE ACTIVITIES
Staffing
Development
Compensation
Employee/Labor Relations
EVALUATE RESULTS

# ASSESS CONDITIONS, PLAN AND SET OBJECTIVES

Part One analyzes the relevant factors that influence human resource management (HRM). The diagnostic model on the previous page groups these factors into three categories: external, organizational, and employee conditions. This grouping provides a framework for Part One.

Chapter Two covers external conditions: sociodemographic, economic, and international conditions and their implications for HRM. Government influence through law, regulation, and policy is covered throughout the book. However, its general influence is touched here.

As the result of external conditions, the workforce today is vastly changed. Employees in the United States are far more diverse in their backgrounds and expectations; increasingly, they find themselves in a global, more competitive marketplace. For example, the skill, wages, and productivity of workers in the Czech Republic and Poland influence HR decisions in Germany and in the United States. Managing this diversity is included in Chapter Two.

Chapter Three assesses organization conditions and describes how to link organization objectives with HR activities. Chapter Three also discusses the nature of work in the organization—how tasks, behaviors, responsibilities, and outcomes are assigned to different jobs, and how jobs relate to each other.

Chapter Four considers the behavior of the individual employee. Because assessing performance is crucial to the success of the organization, HR managers are heavily involved. Other work outcomes, such as absenteeism and turnover, are also discussed, as is assessing employee attitudes, because attitudes are believed to affect performance.

Chapter Five shows how HR managers synthesize the conditions, identify gaps between actual and desired conditions, and set objectives to guide and integrate HR activities.

# External Conditions

Remember the old children's game of rock crushes scissors, scissors cut paper, and paper covers rock? Rock, scissors, and paper interact with each other in the same way that economic forces, organizations, and employees interact. External forces such as laws, demographics, and economic conditions sustain and restrain organizations and employees, who in turn influence and shape the laws and the economic conditions. Economic factors force changes in a country's laws; laws affect economic factors. Thus, the forces are inevitably intertwined.

## INTERTWINED FORCES BUILD THE EMPLOYMENT RELATIONSHIP

In Chapter One, we discussed the notion that the employment relationship involves an *exchange* between employees and employers. Employees exert effort and many contribute ideas on the employer's behalf. In return, the employer gives pay in the form of wages, benefits, and services. Other returns beyond pay may also be part of this exchange: opportunity for training, congenial colleagues, social status, a feeling of belonging, and a sense of accomplishment. If employees and employers form beliefs about their mutual obligations and returns, a psychological contract may exist based on these expectations.

## GOVERNMENT AS A THIRD PARTY IN THE EMPLOYMENT RELATIONSHIP

While employees and employers incur mutual obligations in the workforce, they are not the only parties to the exchange. Through policy and regulation, the government becomes a third party. Consequently, government actions affect HRM actions. In much of the world, government plays a far more dominant role in the workplace than the U.S. government. For example, the Pohang steel mill discussed in Chapter One was built with the encouragement and financial support of the South Korean government trying to rebuild an economy devastated by foreign occupation and civil war.[1]

Setting policy for the overall economy is just one of the ways that governments influence HR practices in their country. Governments also regulate the day-to-day workplace operations by specifying permissible conditions; for example, hours of work, rates of pay, licensing and safety requirements. In addition, the government itself is an important customer as well as employer. In the United States, 2.6 percent of the workforce is employed by the federal government and another 3.9 percent by state and local governments. U.S. federal government spending for everything from robes for the Supreme Court to submarines for the Pentagon consumes 22 percent of the gross national product.[2]

## REGULATIONS REFLECT SOCIETY

Regulations reflect the values and customs of a society. Different societies hold differing beliefs about the role of government in the workplace. Consequently, the degree of regulations and the impact of policy vary among countries.

To see how regulations reflect a society, look at the workplace regulations in Exhibit 2.1. The pattern shows how the United States has changed as a result of the

## EXHIBIT 2.1 Employment Legislation

| Year | Law or Ruling | Major Provisions |
|---|---|---|
| 1926 | Railway Labor Act | First major legislation to give any employees the right to join unions.<br>Encourages use of arbitration and mediation. |
| 1932 | Norris-LaGuardia Act | Declared union membership to be the legal right of all employees. |
| 1935 | National Labor Relations Act (Wagner Act) | Requires employers to bargain over wages, hours, and conditions of work, if a majority of employees desire such union representation.<br>Establishes the National Labor Relations Board (NLRB) to conduct representation elections and investigate charges of unfair labor practices. |
| 1938 | Fair Labor Standards Act | Establishes minimum wage, overtime pay; child labor prohibited. |
| 1947 | Labor-Management Relations Act (Taft-Hartley Act) | Employers cannot assist or establish labor organizations.<br>When a majority of employees desires a specific union, that union represents all employees in the bargaining unit, whether or not they are union members.<br>Establishes the Federal Mediation and Conciliation Service (FMCS) which offers assistance in contract settlement. |
| 1959 | Landrum-Griffin Act | Resulted from charges of labor racketeering in 40s and 50s.<br>Gives members the right to vote on union officers and dues increases, freedom of speech in union matters, and right to sue the union. |
| 1963 | Equal Pay Act | Outlaws sex differences in pay for substantially equal work. |
| 1964 | Title VII of the Civil Rights Act | Prohibits discrimination based on race, color, religion, sex, or national origin. |
| 1965 | Executive Orders 11246 and 11375 | Requires affirmative action by federal contractors to correct results of past discrimination. |
| 1967 | Age Discrimination in Employment Act | Prohibits discrimination against employees age 40 and over. |
| 1974 | Rehabilitation Act of 1973; Executive Order No. 11914 | Prohibits discrimination based on physical or mental handicap (affirmative action required). |
| 1974 | Vietnam-era Veterans Readjustment Act | Prohibits discrimination against disabled veterans and Vietnam-era veterans (affirmative action required). |
| 1990 | Americans with Disabilities Act | Prohibits discrimination against disabled persons qualified to perform the essential elements of a job. |
| 1991 | Civil Rights Act | Makes filing a lawsuit easier and more attractive. |
| 1993 | Family and Medical Leave Act | Requires employers to provide up to 12 weeks unpaid leave for family and medical emergencies. |

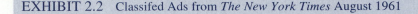

EXHIBIT 2.2 Classifed Ads from *The New York Times* August 1961

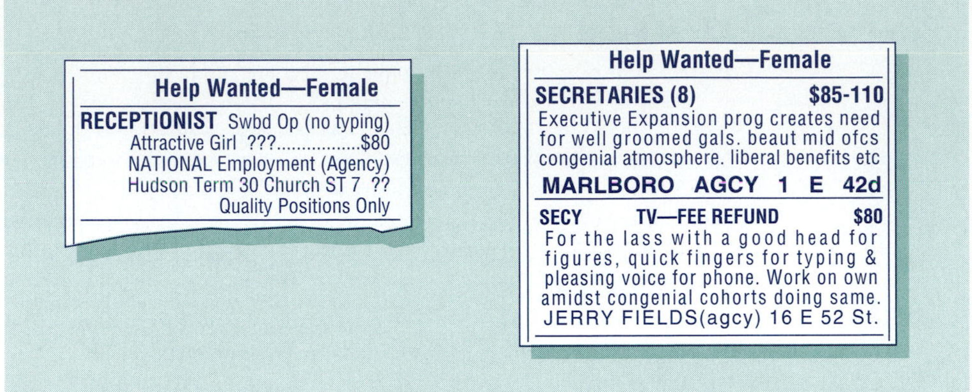
Help Wanted—Female
RECEPTIONIST Swbd Op (no typing)
Attractive Girl ???................$80
NATIONAL Employment (Agency)
Hudson Term 30 Church ST 7 ??
Quality Positions Only

Help Wanted—Female
SECRETARIES (8) $85-110
Executive Expansion prog creates need for well groomed gals. beaut mid ofcs congenial atmosphere. liberal benefits etc
MARLBORO AGCY 1 E 42d
SECY TV—FEE REFUND $80
For the lass with a good head for figures, quick fingers for typing & pleasing voice for phone. Work on own amidst congenial cohorts doing same.
JERRY FIELDS(agcy) 16 E 52 St.

civil rights movement in the 1960s.[3] Prior to the 1960s, laws dealt with wages and hours of work and union-management relations. Since then, the focus has switched to the employment rights of individuals or classes of individuals. The trend reflects an expanding notion of what is fair in the employment relationship, and to whom. For example, the newspaper help-wanted advertisements in Exhibit 2.2 reflect perfectly acceptable employment practices in the 1960s. Maybe your mother wouldn't have answered an ad for a "well-groomed gal" or a "lass with a pleasing voice," but your grandmother most likely answered similar ads or stayed home. The unremarkableness of such ads then and their unacceptability today give only a hint of the magnitude of the change in U.S. social values and resulting civil rights legislation.

### Shaping Legislation

While some employment laws limit actions of employees, most of them restrain employers. Moreover, record keeping and reporting requirements can be expensive. For these reasons, most employers as well as unions, consumer groups, and community groups try to shape legislation by lobbying legislators. Employers also influence the interpretation of legislation by defending their practices in the courts. Because this is a costly procedure, not many employers voluntarily seek it. Nevertheless, organizations and employees do shape the laws so that regulations reflect their values. As the laws change, the employment relationship changes; as economic factors change, the employment relationship changes.

## WORLDWIDE CHANGES IN THE EMPLOYMENT RELATIONSHIP

Change in the employment relationship is not limited to the United States. It is happening globally. For example, Nissan and Toyota, two of Japan's leading employers, have modified their *lifetime employment security* to *long-term security* within a group of companies, not necessarily the parent company. Many Japanese employers are relying less on seniority and more on performance in their pay and promotion systems.[4] Similarly, European companies are searching for ways to control the rate of labor cost increases. And talk about jolting change—in Russia, the former East Germany, or any number of Central and

Eastern European countries, managers in post-Communist economies are trying to revive enterprises whose policies were dictated by central government authorities and whose objectives had little to do with making profits or increasing market share.[5] In Slovenia, wage laws are so complex that in order to comply with them, one company requires 16 people working full-time to calculate wages for 200 truck drivers. After all this paperwork, the monthly pay difference between the highest and lowest-paid driver is less than $100. Good approach if the objective is to boost national employment levels; bad approach if the objective is to encourage the company to be competitive.

Thus, understanding how to manage employees in another country requires an understanding of that country's employment relationships: the role played by government, employees, and employers. However, a note of caution is in order. National and regional generalizations often can be misleading. To stereotype a country is as erroneous as stereotyping individuals. To claim that all organizations in Germany, Japan, or the United States operate similarly ignores variations and differences. Considerable variety exists among company practices within any country. Yet they all take place within the context of social, legal, and economic conditions interacting within each nation or region. Taken as a whole, they form distinct social and employment relationships. Understanding these relationships is useful for managing employees not only in the United States but around the world.[6]

## GLOBAL COMPARISONS

Picture the world as a village of 1,001 people. Of your 1,000 neighbors, 564 are Asians, 210 are Europeans, 86 are Africans, 80 are South Americans, and only 60 are North Americans. Yet, few of us realize how tightly interwoven our economies have become. One in every five United States citizens depends on international trade for employment; one of every three acres of United States farmland produces food for export. It is almost impossible to pick up any product and trace its history, its manufacture, or its raw materials, without finding a foreign connection.

However, we are not all alike. A survey of 1,200 experts from 12 countries asked about HRM goals and practices that would help achieve competitive advantage. Some of the results are shown in Exhibit 2.3. They show variations in priorities among countries. In the United States, 87 percent of the experts agreed that "rewarding employees for customer service" was the top priority. In Germany and France, "identifying high-potential employees early" was listed highest. Japanese participants rated "communicating business directions, problems, and plans" the highest.

Three related factors can help us distinguish differences in employment relationships among countries: (1) managerial autonomy based on culture and laws, (2) patterns of ownership within financial markets, and (3) structures for union and employee involvement.

### Managerial Autonomy

Managerial autonomy refers to the amount of discretion in making decisions. U.S. organizations have relatively greater freedom (i.e., it is less costly) to change employee practices than European organizations. For example, 3M, based in Saint Paul, Minnesota, is encouraging its units to consider the use of

EXHIBIT 2.3 Highest Rated Human Resource Goals by Country

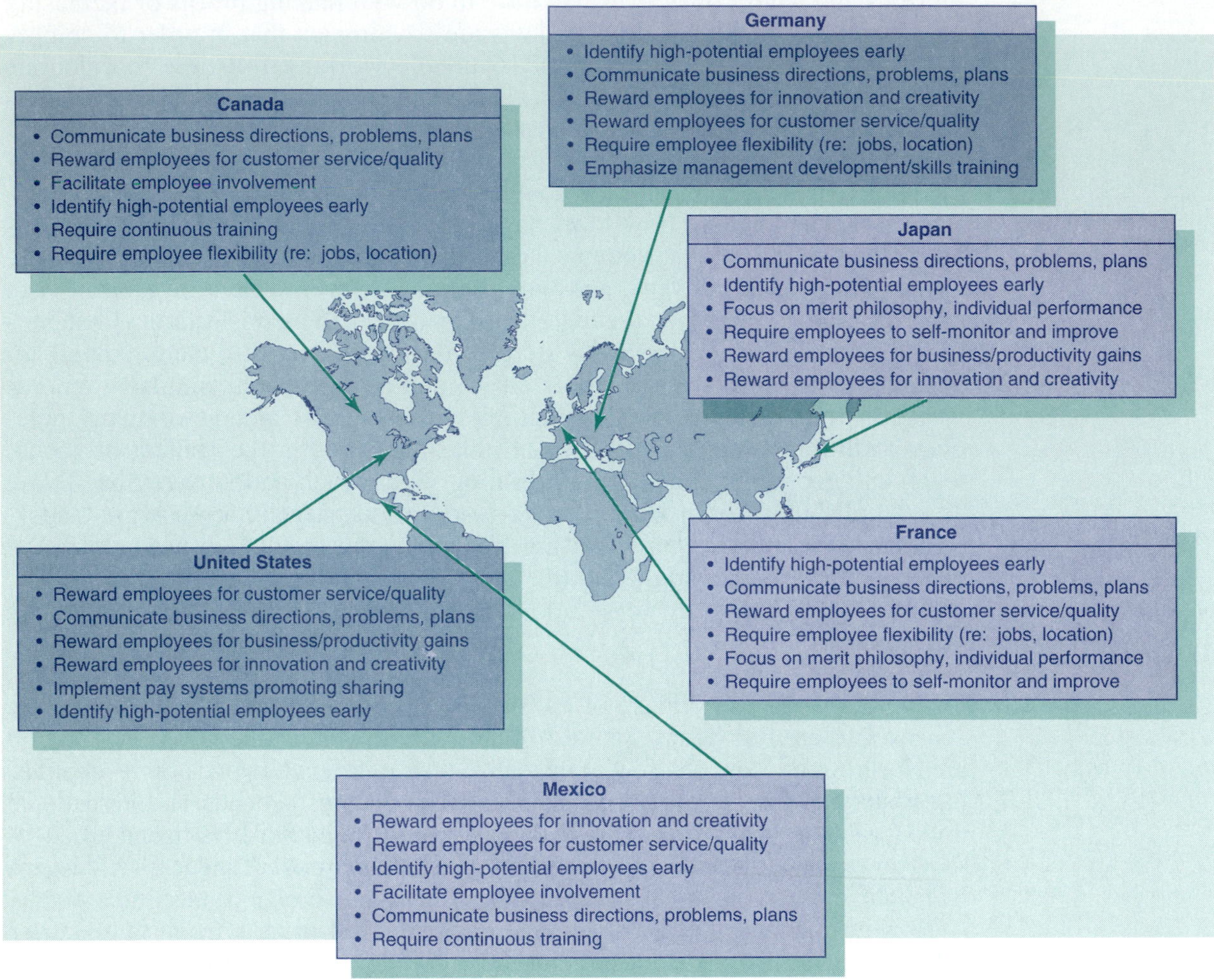
Germany
• Identify high-potential employees early
• Communicate business directions, problems, plans
• Reward employees for innovation and creativity
• Reward employees for customer service/quality
• Require employee flexibility (re: jobs, location)
• Emphasize management development/skills training
Canada
• Communicate business directions, problems, plans
• Reward employees for customer service/quality
• Facilitate employee involvement
• Identify high-potential employees early
• Require continuous training
• Require employee flexibility (re: jobs, location)
Japan
• Communicate business directions, problems, plans
• Identify high-potential employees early
• Focus on merit philosophy, individual performance
• Require employees to self-monitor and improve
• Reward employees for business/productivity gains
• Reward employees for innovation and creativity
France
• Identify high-potential employees early
• Communicate business directions, problems, plans
• Reward employees for customer service/quality
• Require employee flexibility (re: jobs, location)
• Focus on merit philosophy, individual performance
• Require employees to self-monitor and improve
United States
• Reward employees for customer service/quality
• Communicate business directions, problems, plans
• Reward employees for business/productivity gains
• Reward employees for innovation and creativity
• Implement pay systems promoting sharing
• Identify high-potential employees early
Mexico
• Reward employees for innovation and creativity
• Reward employees for customer service/quality
• Identify high-potential employees early
• Facilitate employee involvement
• Communicate business directions, problems, plans
• Require continuous training

Based on data from IBM/TPF&C Study, 1992.

performance-based pay to sustain growth. In the United States, a variety of gainsharing and bonus plans are being tried. At 3M Singapore, they've been there, done that: performance-based bonuses are old hat.

## Brussels Pouts

But at 3M Europe headquartered in Brussels, the proposed plans are running into legal problems. To control inflation and promote egalitarian values, Belgium has passed a law forbidding all new forms of pay beyond that set by nationally negotiated labor agreements. Generally, companies operating in European Union (EU) countries must comply with HR decisions made at the national level through agreements negotiated by industrywide or nationwide employers and union associations. Additionally, European governments dictate what companies must spend on training and who is to receive the training.

Overall, organizations have the greatest autonomy in the United States, have less autonomy in Japan, and appear to be the most constrained in Europe, particularly Germany.[7] But already we have an exception: The United States has by far the most detailed discrimination legislation, in part because it has the most diverse population of the leading industrialized nations.

## Ownership and Financial Markets

Ownership and financial markets also affect the employment relationship and social contract. Patterns of ownership of organizations differ greatly. In the United States, a large segment of the population participates in corporate ownership through investment in the stock market. Access to capital is far less concentrated than in most of the rest of the world. In contrast, six conglomerates control a significant portion of the South Korean economy, and the six are closely linked with specific families (e.g., Hyundai, Samsung). In Germany, most major companies are closely allied and owned largely by a small number of influential banks and the Bundesbank, the country's national bank.[8] These patterns of ownership make certain HR practices almost nonsensical. For example, the majority of U.S. firms give stock options to at least some top managers in order to link managers' financial well-being to the company's financial well-being, but such arrangements make little sense for German, South Korean, or Japanese firms where ownership is more concentrated. The Japanese, South Korean, and European governments also take a greater interventionist role in their countries' economies.

## Union and Employee Involvement

Trade unions and employee involvement clearly differ among nations. These differences influence HRM. Europe is highly unionized; 85 percent of Sweden's workforce belong to unions, about 40 percent in the United Kingdom, and about 12 percent in France. In addition, laws in France, Belgium, and Germany require the establishment of worker councils. The exact rules vary among European nations, but compared with the United States, worker councils and unions significantly affect HRM.[9]

The European Union is committed to maintaining the role of the *social partners,* as it calls employers and trade unions. The EU is trying to provide common labor standards across its member countries in order to avoid "social dumping," or relocating plants from countries with high labor standards and high associated costs to countries where standards and costs are lower. At present, hourly labor costs vary substantially among the EU countries, although sometimes the low labor costs are accompanied by low productivity, as shown in Exhibit 2.4. 1991 hourly labor costs, adjusted for purchasing power, range from 6 Ecus (the EU currency) in Portugal to 19.56 Ecus in Germany, and social protection benefits range from 1,617 Ecus in Portugal to 5,797 Ecus in Luxembourg. However, each nation's history of labor law, cultural values, and political ideologies complicate attempts to develop systemwide regulations.[10]

While compliance with the laws of any country may be expensive and time consuming, there is considerable security in knowing what the laws are and that they will be enforced. One of the major hindrances to economic development in the former Soviet Union and some less-developed countries is the lack

EXHIBIT 2.4 Disunity in the European Union

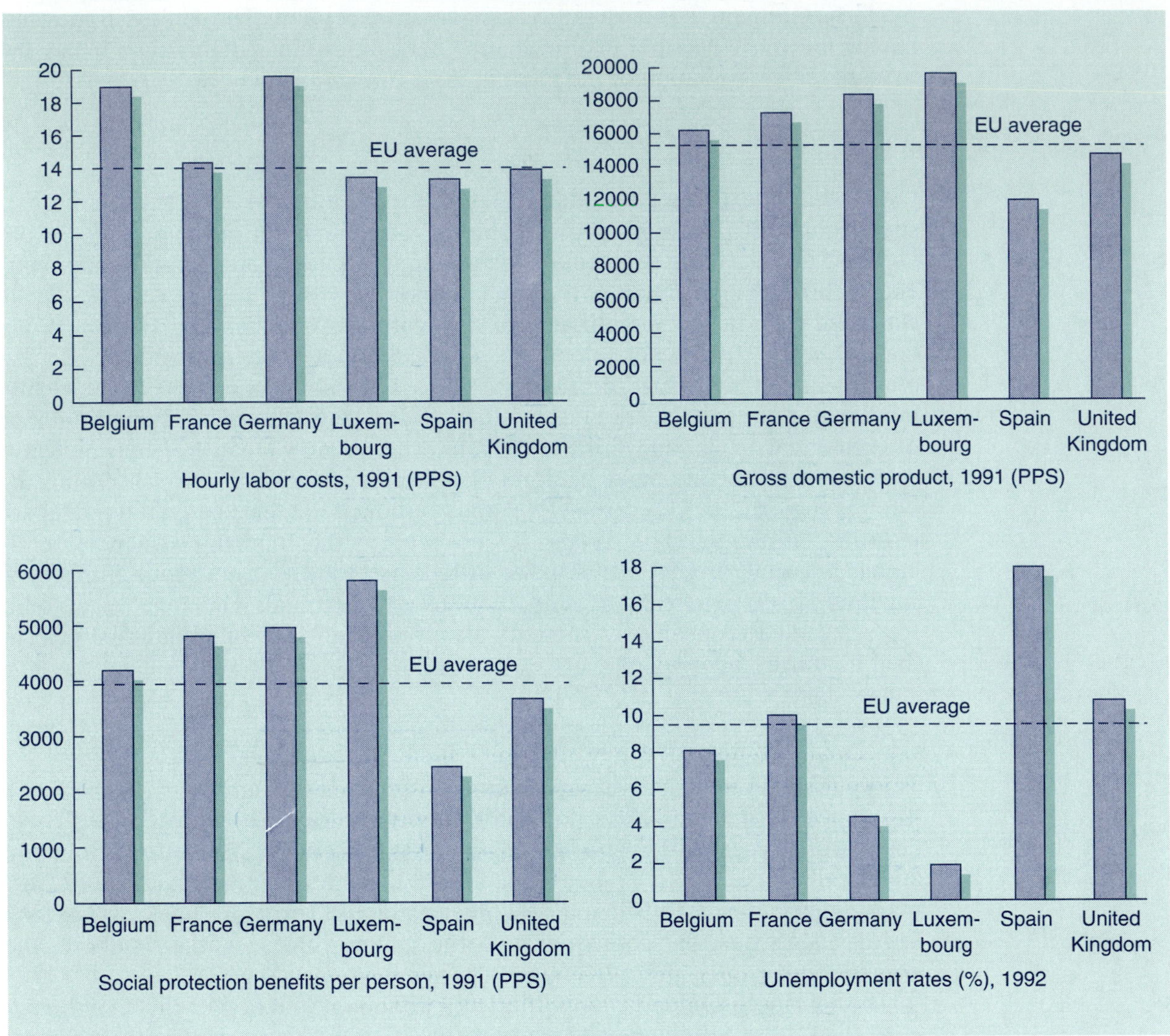


of predictability in the laws. Laws that change without advance notice or are not enforced for the protection of citizens and business interests make investment in those areas risky.

## AN INCREASINGLY DIVERSE EMPLOYEE POPULATION

In an industrialized country, the workplace becomes a vital component of the society's economic and social well-being. Tensions in society are reflected in the workplace. In no other forum do racial and ethnic groups interact so frequently; in no other forum do the sexes compete as well as cooperate. It is not surprising that governments around the world take a strong interest in trying to ensure fair treatment in the workplace.

Because an organization's employees are a subset of the population, demographic changes in a country's population will be reflected in an organization's employees and consequently in HRM practice. A number of demographic trends are changing the face of the labor supply both in the United States and around the world.

## Employee Trends: Immigration

The United States has been called a nation of immigrants. Today about 30 percent of the net population growth in the United States is a result of immigration. In Canada, the figure is 44 percent.[11] Over the last decade the United States has received the largest number of immigrants in its history, close to 10 million people. The countries from which the immigrants arrive also have changed. In the 1950s, two-thirds of the legal immigrants came from Europe or Canada. Today's immigrants come from far more diverse regions: Latin America, Asia, and Eastern Europe. This change means that many new immigrants come from cultures very different from the mainstream U.S. culture, and consequently have greater difficulty assimilating. At the same time, values in the United States have changed. The nation is divided on the extent to which we expect immigrants to *assimilate* or *adapt*—accepting some aspects of mainstream U.S. culture while rejecting others.[12] Indeed, some even question whether there is a mainstream U.S. culture.

What differences does this make for HRM? Many employers view the new immigrants as valuable links to foreign markets. Their familiarity with the language and culture can give their employers an edge in establishing a presence overseas. Foreign-born engineering talent has helped the U.S. computer industry remain competitive. On the other hand, integrating immigrants into the workplace is a major HRM challenge. Cultural misunderstandings among employees and with customers inevitably increase as interactions occur among people who do not understand or value other people's ways of doing things. More practically, if training programs or operating instructions are in English, and many employees are considerably more fluent in a language other than English, efficiency may suffer. If customers have difficulty understanding English (or foreign accents), then customer satisfaction and sales may suffer. The challenge is to turn this diversity into an asset.

## Employee Trends: The African-American Experience

One social analyst suggests that considering African-Americans as a group whose migration began in 1915 and ended in about 1965 provides fresh insight into the black experience in the United States.[13] If one starts with the black migration from the states of the Confederacy into the Northeast, the Middle West, and the Far West—and not their forced move from Africa—then their experience parallels that of the Irish, Poles, and Italians who emigrated from Europe: First generation laborer, second generation cop or civil servant, third generation anything you want to be. A distinguishing feature of the African-American experience, however, is that it applies to only about 70 percent of the group. Unfortunately, the other 30 percent is in danger of being locked into transgenerational poverty, dependence on welfare, lack of work skills, and alienation from society as a whole. This lack of economic success presents a substantial challenge to

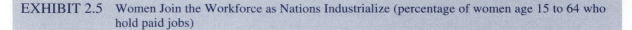

EXHIBIT 2.5 Women Join the Workforce as Nations Industrialize (percentage of women age 15 to 64 who hold paid jobs)

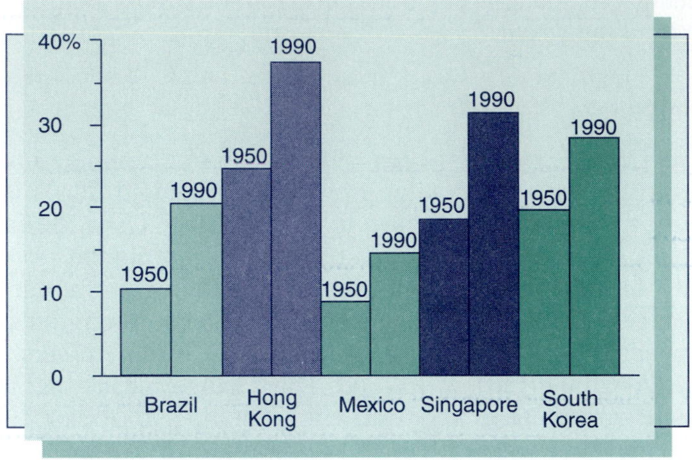


Source: International Labor Organization. *Economically Active Population Estimates and Projections, 1950–2025.* Table 2.

U.S. society as well as employers. Many companies have training programs designed to bring young and disadvantaged people into the workplace. But the restructuring of the U.S. economy—decreasing numbers of jobs that require lower skills yet pay well—and the overall decline in the level of reading and computing skills taught in public schools have made it a difficult task.

## Employee Trends: Women in the Workforce

The most significant change in the look of the U.S. labor force in the past 50 years is the dramatic increase in women's participation rates (Exhibit 2.5). The labor force participation rate is the percentage of people who are eligible to work—over 15 years of age and not in a prison, hospital, or other institution—who are actually working, looking for work, or in the military. The rising trend in women's employment is occurring internationally, although the rate of increase has slowed in the United States. The career preparations and expectations of women are also becoming more like those of men. Women are training for a wider variety of occupations and expecting to continue to work until their 60s. However, women continue to be more likely than men to interrupt their work careers for child rearing and home care.[14]

Some countries, most notably those formerly Communist countries in transition to free-market economies, have higher female participation rates than the United States. Under communism, everyone was expected to hold a job, and child care services were readily available. With the change in government, women have frequently borne a disproportionate share of the pain of transition, as both jobs and government-funded child care services have been cut.

Other countries are struggling with how to capitalize on their underused human capital. Companies in South Korea, for example, face shortages of skilled workers, whereas Japan faces a labor surplus at present. It seems likely that Korean society will act more quickly to devise ways to utilize this human capital and make women, including those with children, more welcome in the workplace.

The increased diversity in the labor force affects all HR decisions. It has increased interest in how to make access to a wide variety of jobs open and fair to more people, how to support people in organizations who may feel isolated because of their race or ethnicity, and how to provide more flexibility to make the organization attractive to employees with a wider range of expectations, needs, and perspectives. Because valuing diversity cuts across so many HR areas, we revisit this issue throughout the book.

## AN EXPANDING NOTION OF FAIRNESS

The demographic trends in the United States toward greater ethnic and racial diversity in the workforce are both a result of legislation (concerning immigration and civil rights) and a cause of further legislation. As we become aware of the unfairness of failing to consider individuals as potential technicians, assembly line workers, sales representatives, managers, or CEOs because of some characteristic unrelated to job performance, we are willing to write new laws to expand protection. Discrimination based on *age* or failure to provide accommodations for employees with *disabilities* is already illegal. Other laws address *family* needs. Some states and local government units are already considering laws outlawing discrimination based on sexual preference, too. To understand what behaviors are permitted, disallowed, and encouraged, we take a closer look at discrimination legislation.

## DEFINING DISCRIMINATION

Exhibit 2.1 gives a brief description of some of the U.S. laws and executive orders that prohibit discrimination. Groups protected by legislation include women, African-Americans, Hispanics, Native Americans, Pacific Islanders, people age 40 and over, people with handicaps, and veterans. The most important one is Title VII of the Civil Rights Act, which has had a profound impact on American society, employers, and employees. The act prohibits discrimination but does not define it. This was left to the courts.

### Title VII of the Civil Rights Act

Title VII prohibits discrimination on the basis of sex, race, color, religion, or national origin in any employment condition, including hiring, firing, promotion, transfer, compensation, and admission to training programs. Since 1964, the courts have ruled that several different behaviors by employers and unions are unlawful under Title VII. These fall into two categories: unequal treatment and unequal impact. Exhibit 2.6 contrasts the two behaviors.

#### Unequal Treatment

An HRM practice is unlawful if it supplies different or unequal standards to different employees; for example, asking applicants with disabilities how they intend to get to work if that question is not asked of all applicants.

EXHIBIT 2.6 Discriminatory Behavior

| Disparate Treatment | Disparate Impact |
|---|---|
| ✦ Different standards for different individuals or groups. | ✦ Same standards having differing consequences. |
| ✦ Impact is on individual claimants, *not* classwide. | ✦ Impact is classwide on all similarly situated employees. |
| ✦ Intent to discriminate may be inferred. | ✦ Discriminatory intent is not present. |
| ✦ Group statistics are not useful. | ✦ General statistical impact of specific practice may show discrimination. |
| ✦ Individual actions scrutinized. | ✦ Business practices, not individual actions, examined. |

However, simply prohibiting unequal treatment does not ensure that the results for all groups are equal. Even though many common job requirements are applied to all groups equally, they may have differential impact on certain groups. For example, an employer may require an applicant to have a high school diploma to run a copying machine. If Hispanics have a higher high school dropout rate than whites, Hispanics would be less able to meet such a requirement. But is the requirement related to the job? Many people think not. Permitting such requirements that have no relationship to the job in question violates a more stringent definition of discrimination: unequal impact.

### Unequal Impact

Personnel practices that have a differential effect on certain groups are illegal, unless the differences can be justified as:

1. Necessary to the safe and efficient operation of the business.
2. Work related.

The major case that established the disparate impact standard is *Griggs* v. *Duke Power Co.* in which the U.S. Supreme Court struck down requirements that screened out a greater proportion of blacks than whites.[15] The requirements in question were that applicants be high school graduates and score above a certain level on a general intelligence test. Even though the standards were applied equally—both whites and blacks had to pass them—the practices were prohibited because (1) they had the consequence of excluding blacks in greater numbers than whites, and (2) they were not related to the jobs in question. Whether or not the employer intended to discriminate is irrelevant.

## Exceptions to Title VII

Court interpretations allow several exceptions to Title VII. Among these are:

- Work-related requirements, such as the ability to lift a certain amount, if lifting is a normal part of the job's duties.[16]
- Bona fide occupational qualifications, such as possessing an engineering degree to design a bridge.[17]

- Seniority system exceptions, if the seniority system was not created to discriminate.[18]
- Preferential-treatment systems that set aside a portion of opportunities for members of groups who have been victims of discrimination.

*Equal employment* activities seek to prevent discrimination in the workplace and take remedial action to offset discrimination.

*Affirmative action* ensures that current decisions and practices enhance the employment, upgrading, and retention of minorities and women.

Initially, no one was quite sure how the Civil Rights Act would be enforced or how it would affect HRM practices. The law seemed to direct managers to provide *equal opportunities* by removing the barriers preventing women and minorities from taking advantage of job opportunities.

But by the 1970s, the emphasis shifted to *affirmative action* policies requiring a more active approach: seeking out minorities and women and helping prepare them for job opportunities.

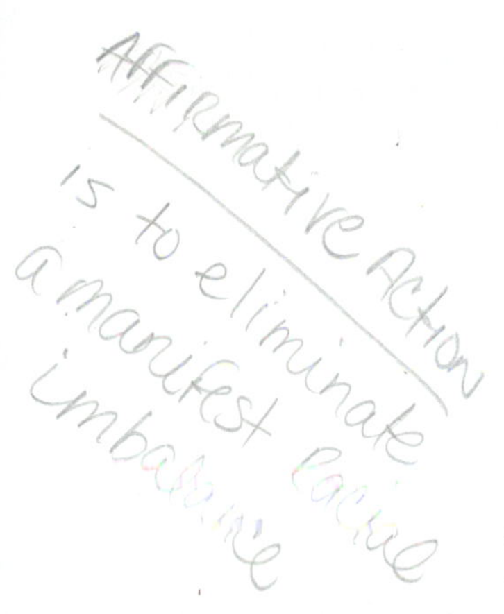


### Affirmative Action

Affirmative action goes beyond refraining from practices that discriminate. It includes positive steps to seek out, encourage, and prepare minorities and women to take advantage of job opportunities. The objective is to distribute the economic opportunities in society among a wider group and to help ensure that employers gain competitive advantage from the talents and energy of all members of the labor force. Executive orders 11246 and 11375 (Exhibit 2.1) require affirmative action by those companies who receive government contracts. In practice this translates into almost all major employers in the United States.

Preferential treatment is a continuing source of controversy. Its purpose is to overcome a long history of discrimination by setting aside a share of opportunities specifically for members of protected groups, even if the individual who receives preferential treatment has not personally experienced discrimination.

The U.S. Supreme Court has consistently ruled that employers can voluntarily give *temporary* preference to qualified members of underrepresented protected groups. In the first such case, *Weber* v. *Kaiser Aluminum and Chemicals,* an employer and union had collectively bargained access to an in-plant training program that was required to attain higher-paying jobs. Kaiser maintained separate lists of black or white workers eligible to receive the training. Fifty percent of the openings in the training program were reserved for African-Americans. The result was that qualified blacks experienced shorter waits for training than qualified whites. The court ruled such a plan was legal, noting that

> the plan does not necessarily trammel the interests of the white employees. The plan does not require the discharge of white workers and their replacement with new black hires. . . . Nor does the plan create an absolute bar to the advancement of white employees; half of those trained in the program will be white. Moreover, the plan is a temporary measure; it is not intended to maintain racial balance, but simply to *eliminate a manifest racial imbalance.*[19]

Thus, Title II permits unequal impact of personnel decisions if the practice (1) is legitimately job related, or (2) is defensible as a bona fide occupational qualification, or (3) is the result of a seniority system, or (4) is a preferential treatment system designed to overcome past discrimination.

### Preferences and Quotas: The Public Debate

Preferences become controversial when they get translated through practice into numerical quotas, when they benefit people who have never been victims of discrimination, and when they cease to be temporary. While affirmative action has always been controversial, the country has begun to debate its use with renewed vigor. Many feel it has outlived its usefulness and casts doubt on the credentials of all women and minority group members. Others say it is still needed, but the focus must change. The country's most disadvantaged citizens have not been in a position to benefit from preferential programs. Instead, the benefits have gone to women and middle-class blacks. Instead of race or gender, the criterion for affirmative action ought to be socioeconomic class. As the debate continues, employers have evolved from focusing on eliminating discrimination to trying to use their already diverse workforce as a strategic advantage.[20]

## EVALUATING COMPLIANCE

Title VII requires that organizations categorize their employees according to race and gender and report this information to the Equal Employment Opportunity Commission (EEOC) in the federal government's Department of Labor. An excerpt from a required report is shown in Exhibit 2.7. This report is the basis for further analysis to determine if employment patterns show evidence of discrimination.

Equal employment opportunity analysis has four steps:

1. *Analyze the workforce* to determine representation (percentage) of minorities and women in each job group in the organization.
2. *Analyze availability* in the relevant labor force to determine the proportion of minorities and women qualified and interested in the job opportunities.
3. *Establish goals* by comparing the present work force to availability. Goals are the percentage of job opportunities to be shared with women and minorities to increase their representation in targeted jobs.
4. *Choose programs* specifying how the goals are to be achieved and a proposed timetable for achievement.

### Availability Analysis

Availability analysis determines the number of people in the relevant labor force who are members of various protected groups and who are *qualified* and *interested* in specific job opportunities. Availability is the standard against which actual hiring and promotion rates are compared for evidence of discrimination. The availability of specific skills in each race and gender category is presumed to reflect approximately what the race and gender composition of the employer's workforce would be were it not for discrimination.

Determining availability involves considerable judgment, as you can see in Exhibit 2.8 on page 42. Hence, the results are open to controversy. Let us use the job of arc welding at the Boeing Company in Seattle, Washington, as an example. The first category in the exhibit is the entire U.S. population. But not

## EXHIBIT 2.7 Part of an EEO Form

**Section D- EMPLOYMENT DATA**

Employment at this establishment—Report all permanent, temporary, or part-time employees including apprentices and on-the-job trainees unless specifically excluded as set forth in the instructions. Enter the appropriate figures on all lines and in all columns. Blank spaces will be considered as zeros.

| JOB CATEGORIES | NUMBER OF EMPLOYEES | | | | | | | | | | |
|---|---|---|---|---|---|---|---|---|---|---|---|
| | | MALE | | | | | FEMALE | | | | |
| | OVERALL TOTAL (SUM OF COL. B THRU K) A | WHITE NOT OF HISPANIC ORIGIN B | BLACK NOT OF HISPANIC ORIGIN C | HISPANIC D | ASIAN OR PACIFIC ISLANDER E | AMERICAN INDIAN OR ALASKAN NATIVE F | WHITE NOT OF HISPANIC ORIGIN G | BLACK NOT OF HISPANIC ORIGIN H | HISPANIC I | ASIAN OR PACIFIC ISLANDER J | AMERICAN INDIAN OR ALASKAN NATIVE K |
| Officials and Managers | 700 | 572 | 10 | 1 | 3 | | 105 | 7 | | 2 | |
| Professionals | 261 | 198 | 6 | 2 | 1 | | 51 | 2 | | 1 | |
| Technicians | 71 | 40 | | 1 | | | 30 | | | | |
| Sales Workers | 40 | 35 | 3 | | | | 2 | | | | |
| Office and Clerical | 544 | 30 | 1 | | | | 502 | 10 | | 1 | |
| Craft Workers (Skilled) | 5 | 5 | | | | | | | | | |
| Operatives (Semi-Skilled) | 4 | 3 | | | | | 1 | | | | |
| Laborers (Unskilled) | 2 | | | | | | 2 | | | | |
| Service Workers | 19 | 9 | 2 | | | | 8 | | | | |
| TOTAL | 1646 | 892 | 22 | 4 | 4 | | 701 | 19 | | 4 | |
| Total employment reported in previous EEO-1 report | 1696 | 904 | 31 | 4 | 3 | | 732 | 16 | | 5 | 1 |

(The trainees below should also be included in the figure for the appropriate occupational categories above)

| Formal On-the-job trainees | A | B | C | D | E | F | G | H | I | J | K |
|---|---|---|---|---|---|---|---|---|---|---|---|
| White collar | 27 | 17 | 3 | | | | 7 | | | | |
| Production | | | | | | | | | | | |

1. Note: On consolidated report, skip questions 2-5 and Section E.
2. How was information as to race or ethnic group in Section D obtained?
   1 ☐ Visual Survey 3 ☐ Other-Specify
   2 ☒ Employment Record
3. Dates of payroll period used- 2/28/97
4. Pay period of last report submitted for this establishment
   2/28/97
5. Does this establishment employ apprentices?
   This year? 1 ☐ Yes 2 ☒ No
   Last year? 1 ☐ Yes 2 ☒ No

everyone in the entire population is qualified to be an arc welder in the aircraft industry, nor is everyone in the second category, civilian labor force (defined as those people who are either working or looking for work and not in the military). So we narrow the relevant availability to those people in the civilian labor force who are qualified or can become qualified within a reasonable amount of time. But this group may not be available or interested—some may already be employed, others may not wish to relocate or commute. The next step may be to narrow availability to applicants and to consider the percentage of minorities and women who actually apply for jobs as arc welders at Boeing.

Each time we move to a narrower category in the exhibit, the numbers become more specific. But how much narrowing of the definition of availabilities is reasonable? For example, do we assume that only those who actually apply for the welder's job and can demonstrate that they can weld should be included in an availability estimate? Limiting our estimate to welders actively seeking employment may not reflect the actual subpopulation of minority and women

EXHIBIT 2.8 Population ≠ Availability

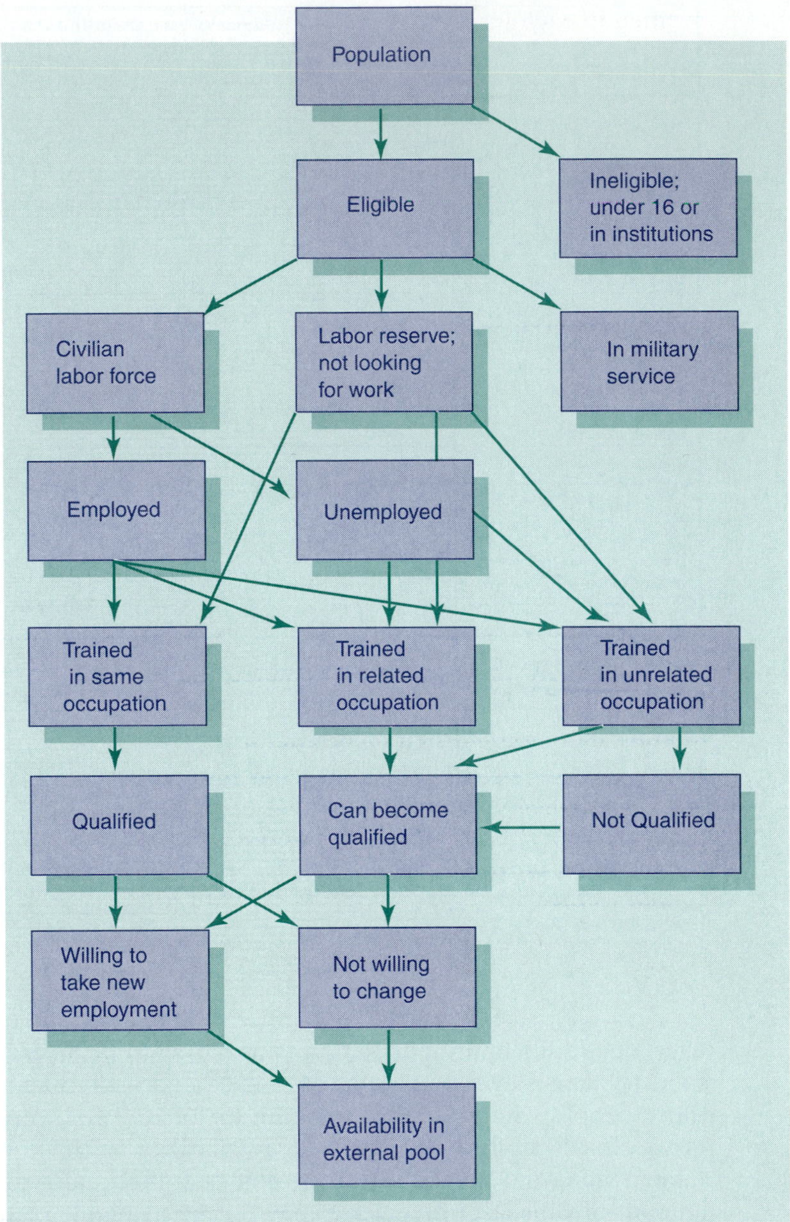


welders. Some people may not be aware of the job opportunity or may be discouraged from applying because of past discrimination. Estimating their numbers and whether to include them is an additional complication. Clearly, there is no best approach to estimating availabilities. All availability statistics have limitations. Recognizing the limitations allows an employer to make a best estimate that is useful and workable.

## Establish Goals

Comparing the employment, hiring, and/or promotion rates of minorities and women in each job to their relevant availability may produce three outcomes:

1. *Underutilization*—the employment, hiring, and/or promotion rate is below the relevant availability.
2. *Parity*—the employment, hiring, and/or promotion rate is approximately equal to the relevant authority.
3. *Overutilization*—the employment, hiring, and/or promotion rate is above the relevant availability.

Statistical guidelines are used by courts and regulatory agencies to decide if an underutilization is unlikely to be due to chance and so constitutes evidence of adverse impact.

## Programming to Achieve Goals: Affirmative Action

By diagnosing the causes of lower percentages of members of protected groups in the company's workforce, managers learn which practices must be changed. For example, the underrepresentation of women may be attributed to a host of factors including the employer's reputation or the firm's unsafe location. Flexible work schedules, child care programs, or escorted transportation home are possible options to overcome the problem. Without knowing the cause, however, managers may attempt to change the representation by lowering the requirements for some groups or by granting transfers to women while refusing to grant them to qualified men. This would not only increase the risk of reverse discrimination charges from men but may also contribute to morale problems and foster resentment against women in the company.

Often, the changes benefit all employees as well as the employer. At AT&T, for example, affirmative action efforts included the redesign of certain craft jobs so that women could perform them more readily. AT&T changed the design of an extension ladder that was hard for women to handle and a safety harness used by workers when they climb telephone poles. Also, a particularly grueling training program was redesigned to spread out the hard physical labor over a longer time—to the benefit of men as well as women. Similar redesign efforts are now under consideration for opening up jobs to employees with disabilities.

## Ensure Compliance

Many companies help ensure that EEO goals are met by making them a basis for evaluating managers' performance. For example, all Corning Glass managers are given goals for each job category in their Corning facility. These goals are based on availability and utilization information determined from published data and internal personnel records. Where underutilization is a problem, managers are asked to set goals and timetables to eliminate the underutilization. Progress toward these goals is monitored quarterly. Some companies look at the pattern of performance evaluations that each manager gives subordinates. If the patterns appear to be biased, the managers are asked to document the reasons for the ratings and to review them for possible unconscious stereotyping (i.e., assuming certain things about a person based on gender, race, culture, or age instead of the individual's behavior).

## WE'RE NOT WHAT WE USED TO BE

When Title VII was originally passed 30 years ago, minority workers comprised only 11 percent of the workforce, compared with 23 percent today. Today's minorities also represent a greater variety of ethnicities and cultures. Asian-Americans have increased from 1 million to 8.5 million, and Hispanics from 3.5 million to 23 million. In 1964, women made up 34 percent of the workforce. Today they account for 46 percent of the workforce, including 42 percent of all managers and professionals. Yet problems persist.[21]

### Unequal Occupations, Unequal Incomes

American women have made progress toward economic equality, but they are still more restricted in their occupations than males. Exhibit 2.9 shows the discrepancies in a number of categories. Well over a quarter of all women in the labor force work in administrative and clerical jobs; only 6 percent of working men hold such jobs. Twenty percent of all men in the workforce are operatives (e.g., skilled machinists or assemblers) while only 8 percent of women hold such jobs. The differences are important because they relate to pay: Clerical work is typically at the bottom of the pay scale; pay for operatives is much higher.

While women enjoy only qualified success, the experience of African-Americans is dismal. In 1970, the median income of African-American families was 60 percent that of white families. It has changed little since then. Over the past 20 years, unemployment among African-Americans has risen higher in each successive recession and fallen less with each recovery.[22] On measure after measure, African-Americans as a group continue to trail their white counterparts. As the figures in Exhibit 2.10 show, only 19 percent of African-Americans hold managerial/professional/technical positions, which typically require a college degree, even though this category includes 30 percent of all jobs. Hispanics hold even fewer of these high-paying jobs—only 15 percent.

As Exhibit 2.10 shows, despite significant educational progress by African-Americans in the 1980s, the gap between their wages and those of whites at the same educational levels has widened. High school dropout rates of blacks and whites of both sexes declined in the 1980s, but they fell far more sharply among blacks, almost eliminating the gap between black and white males. Unfortunately, such progress hasn't produced commensurate economic gains. After narrowing the gap in hourly wages during the 1970s, for example, African-Americans generally lost ground relative to whites in the 1980s, particularly college-educated black men. Education does not pay off for black males to the extent it does for others.

**Waiting to Exhale?** African-American women do better financially than African-American men. The pay gap between black and white women is only 10 percent, whereas the gap between black and white men is 30 percent, a gap that has grown since the 1970s. Sixty percent of all MBA degrees earned by African-Americans are earned by women.

> **WHAT DO YOU THINK?**
>
> The Hooters restaurant chain originally tried to sell itself as a family restaurant. But when the EEOC charged it with sex discrimination in hiring, Hooters then claimed that requiring its waitresses (females only) to wear short shorts and tight t-shirts was part of the "adult experience" that was being sold. Hooters generated so much publicity that they were able to change the focus from whether or not they discriminated to whether pursuing them was worth the EEOC's time and money. EEOC quietly dropped the investigation several months later. Do you think Hooters' hiring practices are discriminatory? Do you think EEOC did the right thing?

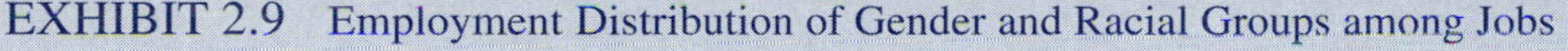

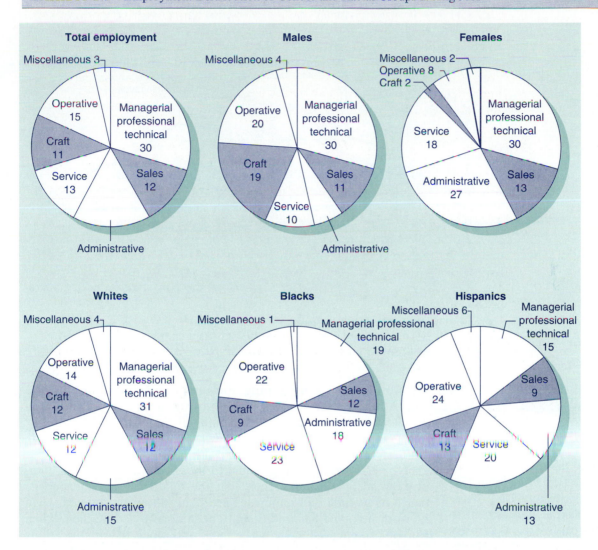

EXHIBIT 2.9 Employment Distribution of Gender and Racial Groups among Jobs



Source: U.S. Department of Labor, Bureau of Labor Statistics, *Employment and Earnings* 39, No. 1, Washington, D.C.: U.S. Government Printing Office, 1996.

Among recent university graduates, black women earn 15 cents an hour more than black men, and three cents more than white women. Yet black women often feel isolated in organizations. Many believe that neither the women's movement nor the African-American civil rights movement addresses their concerns.

Obviously, the discontent and unequal attainment stem from deeper causes than unfair HRM practices. Even though some people believe that reverse discrimination against white males has become the norm, evidence does not support this belief. Instead, discrimination still exists, though it is often subtle. Patterns of decisions appear to reveal unconscious assumptions.

EXHIBIT 2.10 A Puzzling Decline in U.S. Black Progress

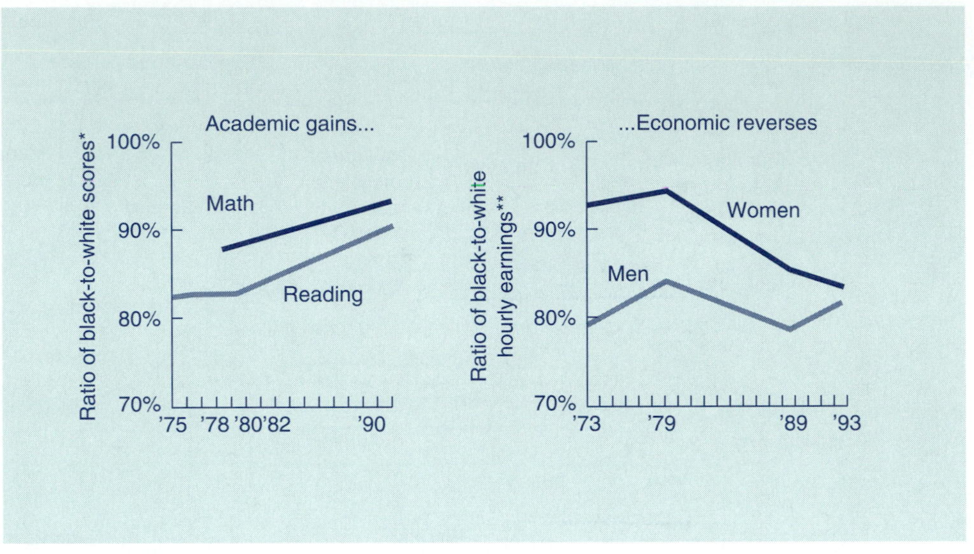


Source: Jared Bernstein, Economic Policy Institute

> **WHAT DO YOU THINK?**
>
> Several months later, Mitsubishi tried the same publicity tactic that had worked for Hooters after Mitsubishi was charged with tolerating widespread sexual harassment in its automobile assembly plant. Mitsubishi bused employees to EEOC offices for a high-publicity demonstration saying they disputed the charges. Employees' participation in the rally was voluntary, but they were paid for their time. The move was judged a public relations disaster. What do you think accounted for the difference in public response?

Unfortunately, stereotyping and unconscious assumptions die hard. A recent review of research on hiring decisions found that in 29 out of 34 studies, whites were judged more qualified than minorities who had identical qualifications.[23] Research also suggests that despite comparable performance, women and minorities do not receive performance ratings equal to those of white men.[24] A common thread in this research is that the qualifications and performance of women and minorities are likely to be discounted when the work involved has traditionally been done by white men, when it involves supervision by white men, and when the qualifications for the work are relatively general or subjectively defined. These characteristics—traditionally the domain of white men, supervised by white men, and subjectively defined qualifications—describe many managerial positions, especially those at higher levels. Thus, it is not surprising that few women and even fewer minorities hold top management jobs in U.S. companies.

## The Glass Ceiling

Lack of access to the very top positions has given rise to the term *glass ceiling*—invisible yet unbreachable barriers that prevent women and minorities from moving into the highest executive jobs in organizations. Minorities and women are consistently underrepresented at the highest levels of the corporation. For example, 97 percent of the senior managers of Fortune 1000 industrial and Fortune 500 companies are white,

**EXHIBIT 2.11** Smashing!

**If you feel your career has stalled . . .**

✦ **Find common ground**

Making people comfortable with you is the first step toward earning their trust. Promotions at the highest levels go to those who are trusted for sound judgment. You have to be trusted to be "part of the team." Learn to make casual conversation about topics of interest to others.

✦ **Learn to read your boss**

Anticipating how others will react helps you present information in a way that they will pay attention to. Your boss will look good, and so will you.

✦ **Brush up on your presentation skills**

If you come across as weak or indecisive, you won't be perceived as someone able to lead a group. Remember that everything is part of the presentation, including the way you dress and the way you sound.

✦ **Pick your projects**

Make them challenging; be sure they are strategically important, will give you high visibility with the right people, and will allow you to demonstrate your decision-making skills.

✦ **Try to find an internal sponsor**

A high-level executive who takes an interest in your career can protect you and give you valuable feedback on how you are being perceived in the company.

Source: Adapted from Hal Lancaster, "Managing Your Career," *The Wall Street Journal,* Nov. 6, 1995, p. B1.

and 95 to 97 percent are men. Only 0.4 percent of managers are of Hispanic descent, although that group makes up 8 percent of the nation's workforce. Americans of Asian and Pacific Island heritage earn less than whites in comparable positions and receive fewer promotions, despite more formal education than other groups.[25]

Potential barriers include executive recruiting practices that bypass women and minority candidates, a lack of mentoring, and few assignments to high visibility jobs, projects, or training programs. Exhibit 2.11 provides some recommendations for all employees who feel their careers are stalling rather than shattering.

Does one good metaphor deserve another? And another? The glass ceiling has given rise to *glass walls*—invisible barriers that keep people out of certain organization functions that traditionally lead to the top jobs in the organization—and *sticky floors*—invisible barriers that trap people in low-paying, dead-end jobs.[26] The point of all these metaphors is to force organizations to look at the assumptions and attitudes underlying HR decisions. The issue no longer is barriers to employment. Instead, the issue is the cultural and organizational obstacles that prevent full recognition and utilization of the diverse talent inside the organization.

### EXPLORING THE WEB

Many government reports are available on the web. The Industrial and Labor Relations Library at Cornell University serves as host for Department of Labor reports. The library can be reached at

**<http://www.ilr.cornell.edu>**

From there, go the Martin P. Catherwood Library and the Electronic Bookshelf.

## VALUING DIVERSITY

An organization that values diversity creates an environment that respects and supports employees with nontraditional backgrounds, so that they can contribute to their fullest potential. Promoting a diverse and inclusive workforce gives the organization a broader and richer base of experience. Diversity can provide a much richer environment, a variety of viewpoints, and greater productivity. Creativity and innovation can result from combining different perspectives.

It can even make a firm's share price move on Wall Street.[27] But valuing diversity requires considerable sensitivity and effort from managers. The challenge is to bring this diversity to a constructive focus that leads to greater creativity rather than creating chaos.

### Pressures for Diversity Programs

The impetus for organizations to support workplace diversity programs comes from different sources. Some companies achieve diversity through successful affirmative action. Other companies may grow so quickly or be located in areas with such a diverse population that achieving diversity takes little additional effort. For example, over half of California's population is nonwhite. Fast-growing California companies such as Hewlett-Packard may have an easier time acquiring a diverse workforce than competitors located in the more homogenous Middle West. Other companies are driven by the diversity of their customers; a diverse workforce helps them understand, accommodate, and serve customer needs. Avon, for example, believes that the diversity in its sales force helps it sell to customers of diverse backgrounds. And Avon's emphasis on diversity in the United States led the company to broaden its range of products and to consider nontraditional ways to market them outside the country.

Diverse perspectives among work group team members may lead to consideration of a greater number of alternatives. Every single alternative may be evaluated on broader criteria, so that the approach finally selected is strengthened and has a greater likelihood of succeeding. If a diverse group of employees contributes to the team, then better, more innovative work may result. The underlying belief is that the organization's diversity will become a competitive advantage.

### The Role of HRM

There can be negatives to diversity programs as well. The lack of a shared framework may result in poor communication and even conflict among employees. Motivations may become suspect. Turnover and a lack of coherent action may result. Hence, HRM can help by minimizing intergroup conflicts, offering training to help improve employees' skill in conflict resolution, and directing all groups toward organization goals.

How does a company show that it values diversity? HRM systems play a role, and flexibility seems to be a key. Hewlett-Packard incorporates flexibility and choice as one of its operating precepts. It advocates setting objectives in broad terms with a great deal of individual employee discretion over how they are achieved. IBM groups a number of diversity programs under the heading "respect for the individual." The company considers equal opportunity, corporate citizenship, and work/life programs part of its overall efforts to demonstrate this respect.[28]

EXHIBIT 2.12 Diversity Initiatives

| Policy | Programs |
|---|---|
| **Building a Culture That Values Diversity** | Discussion groups to promote tolerance and understanding<br>Diversity training for supervisors<br>Efforts to change corporate culture to value differences<br>Team building for diverse groups that must work together<br>Diversity task force to recommend policy changes where needed<br>Holding managers accountable for increasing diversity in the managerial ranks<br>Awareness training to reduce prejudice |
| **Educational Initiatives** | Incentives for younger workers to complete their education<br>Basic education classes (reading, math)<br>Classes in English for non–English-speaking employees |
| **Career Support** | Minority internships<br>Networking among minority groups<br>Programs to steer women and minorities into pivotal jobs—key positions critical to rapid advancement<br>Special goals to diversify middle and upper management |
| **Accommodating Special Needs** | Scheduled days off to accommodate religious preferences<br>Policies to hire retirees for temporary assignments<br>Day care arrangements or benefits<br>Work-at-home arrangements<br>Job redesign to accommodate disabled employees<br>Translation of written materials (manuals, newsletters) into several languages |

Source: Benson Rosen and Kay Lovelace, "Piecing Together the Diversity Puzzle," *HR Magazine,* June 1991.

Flexible benefits and flexible hours can improve a company's attractiveness to all employees. Flexible days off allow employees to celebrate Cinco de Mayo instead of Columbus Day. Rosh Hashanah or Sukkot can be observed with full support from colleagues rather than resentment over absences. To that end, the J. P. Morgan Bank has issued a *World Holiday and Time Guide* cataloging holidays. The guide lists national holidays on 285 days a year. One of our students observed that he could get 285 days off a year if he could get a large enough travel budget. Cool, huh?

A survey of 400 Society of Human Resource Management members reported that diversity brings both strengths and challenges for HR professionals.[29] Getting employers to realize the business necessity of understanding differences rather than denying them is a challenge. If a company makes this first step, perhaps a more tolerant corporate culture emerges. Managers also mentioned better business decisions, greater responsiveness to diverse groups of customers, and more loyal employees as the positive outgrowths of diversity management efforts. Exhibit 2.12 lists the variety of programs managers say their companies are doing. However, managers also said their companies need to do more work to move beyond tolerance to thoughtful appreciation.

Just Do It. Turning diversity into an asset is not that easy. Survey participants also reported that greater diversity has created some problems. Communication problems were the most frequently cited negative consequence. Increased training costs and an increase in friction among subgroups were also reported. Managers said they must now dedicate more time to dealing with special interests and advocacy groups. Rather than decreasing bias, some managers reported that diversity management efforts resulted in increased charges of bias. A minority of survey participants even reported that morale is poor, productivity is down, and bigotry is increasing despite their company's efforts.

Managing diversity means continuously evaluating all aspects of the workplace. Both attitudes and perceptions of employees and their career experiences reveal how well the employer is doing. For example, do minority group members have access to mentors who can guide their careers? Are they exposed to higher levels of management? The HR information system can identify areas where change is needed. For example, the system can tell if the organization is losing women engineers faster than men engineers, if African-American managers get bonuses equivalent to other managers, if Hispanics who break work rules receive more severe punishments than whites, if African-Americans receive fewer favorable resolutions of their sexual harassment charges than whites (EEOC data say they do).[30] The information system can uncover sources of potential bias in HR systems that may inadvertently be putting some members at a disadvantage. But it cannot act on this information. It's up to the organization's managers and employees to do so.

Some organizations use minority advisory groups as additional sources of information. These groups frequently have direct access to the most senior executives of the company. U.S. West has a 33-member Pluralism Council that advises senior management on plans for improving the company's response to increased workforce diversity. At Equitable Life Assurance, committees of women, African-Americans, and Hispanics (called business resource groups) meet with the CEO to discuss important group issues. However, nothing in HRM is that simple. The legal basis for such groups is open to question. If these groups discuss the terms and conditions of work with management, they may be considered a union. If they are a union, then companies violate labor legislation by funding them and encouraging their formation. This issue is discussed again in Chapters Fourteen and Fifteen.

## Managers and Leaders

Managers are often a company's first line of action. If a firm wishes to respect all employees, managers must provide the leadership. Managers create the culture of an organization by their daily behavior; managers help implement changes. But many managers complain that they have been given the responsibility but not the training in the interpersonal skills that may help avoid and/or resolve conflicts among employees. Such conflicts have been cited as one of the biggest headaches in managing a diverse workforce and making a multicultural organization work.

Incrementally defining the ever more specific behaviors and skills required of supervisors and managers in a multicultural organization can shape behavior. Requiring managers to demonstrate skill working with diverse employees also provides an unequivocal message that the firm is committed to a new way of doing business. Naturally, employees must be given ample opportunity and support to learn the new behaviors.

## Training

Training is a key activity in the success of a multicultural organization. Employees may need to learn new interactive skills to participate constructively in organizational activities with a more diverse group of employees. The question arises whether training should focus on behaviors or attitudes. Workplace behaviors are subject to organization control: An employee can be fired for harassing another employee. Attitudes are more controversial. Can you be fired for harboring racist or sexist attitudes if they are not made explicit? The difficulty is that subconscious prejudice can taint judgment and affect behavior. Is training to revise attitudes an unwarranted intrusion in individual privacy?

### What Works?

The sensitivity of diversity training led researchers to look at the factors that influenced the use of diversity training and its perceived success.[31] They concluded that top management support, high strategic priority of valuing diversity relative to other objectives, the presence of a diversity manager, and existence of a large number of other diversity-supportive policies increased the likelihood that training would be offered and be viewed as a success. The study also recommended mandatory attendance for all managers, long-term evaluation, and linking diversity behavior to managerial pay.

### Tell It like It Is.

Xerox has found that being very open with all employees about the specific features of a diversity initiative as well as the reasons for it was helpful in diffusing backlash by whites. Xerox provided its managers with survey results about the effectiveness of their managerial style. The feedback served as a developmental tool to help managers fine-tune their behavior. Showing each manager the results obtained by other managers (who were not identified) also allowed each manager to compare peer behavior. Corning Glass Works countered white male resistance to change by providing data showing that the promotion rate of their group was indeed much higher than that of other groups. Such a strategy provides managers with a knowledge base for identifying needed changes. Feedback may also help win workforce commitment required to implement changes.

Mentoring programs that seek to bring minorities and women into the informal networks in an organization, special career development programs that target minorities, and focus groups to examine attitudes and differences and their effects on work behaviors are among the many other techniques advocated to foster a multicultural organization. These suggestions build on affirmative action programs and extend throughout the range of human resource activities.

Although all of these programs cost money, some research indicates that cost savings can result from managing diversity.[32] For example, women and minorities typically have higher turnover rates than white males. The reasons for the turnover may vary from lack of promotion opportunities to family/work conflicts to job dissatisfaction. If the specific reasons are known, diversity initiatives may be able to address them. If turnover for all groups can be reduced to the level for white males, costs can be reduced. Ortho Pharmaceuticals has calculated savings from their diversity initiatives at more than $500,000, mainly from lower turnover among women and ethnic minorities.

The accounting firm of Deloitte & Touche calculated the costs of the heavy turnover it was experiencing among women accountants. Because of its aggressive recruiting, approximately half the accountants it hires each year are women. But many of the women weren't staying long enough to become partners, a process that typically takes nearly a decade. A task force interviewed women at all levels of the company, even women who had left the firm. The company discovered that women saw only limited advancement opportunity in their work environment, and they felt excluded from both informal mentoring and networking systems. While the company believed such exclusion was subconscious rather than deliberate, they also realized that the situation was not going to correct itself. So they developed plans for company-sponsored networking and formal career planning for women. As a result, retention of women at all levels has risen, and for the first time in the firm's history, turnover rates for senior managers—the last position before partner—are lower for women than for men. Deloitte's national director of HR says that the company's reputation as a woman-friendly firm helps in recruiting, too. The costs for retooling the work environment have been offset by reduced turnover and recruiting costs.[33]

## OTHER COUNTRIES, OTHER PERSPECTIVES

American citizens on overseas assignments at the behest of U.S. companies are covered by all federal discrimination legislation. However, they are also subject to the laws of the host country, which may be inconsistent with U.S. legislation. In the United States, the notion of fairness is at its heart a moral issue, expressed in the U.S. Constitution and subject to an ever-expanding definition of what is fair and to whom. Today, many employees expand the concept beyond moral good to competitive advantage: A diverse workforce is a worthy objective in itself, without reference to legal requirements.

### Diversity Is Not a Universal Goal

The three most diverse countries in the world are the United States, Canada, and Bosnia. The majority of countries have laws restricting immigration and citizenship to people of the same ethnic group. Such countries do not value a diverse workforce. Many Asian employers, for example, believe that competitive advantage lies in a homogeneous workforce with identical cultures and values. While Japanese women's rights to equal employment have been protected by law since 1986, the expectation is that women will leave their jobs once they marry. Japanese law does not prod companies to hire more women or prevent them from forcing out employees in their 50s. Japanese corporations were shocked when a woman won a sexual harassment lawsuit in 1992. Few, if any, Japanese companies have internal procedures for formally dealing with discrimination and harassment. Yet a Labor Ministry poll indicated that 43 percent of all women in management positions complain of sexual harassment.[34]

In the Middle East, discriminatory legislation is still common. For example, Saudi Arabian women are not allowed to drive cars. Iranian women are required to cover their heads in public. And even though they may not have the force of law, discriminatory practices are still common in Eastern Europe and Latin America.

**EXHIBIT 2.13** Gender Balancing at Samsung

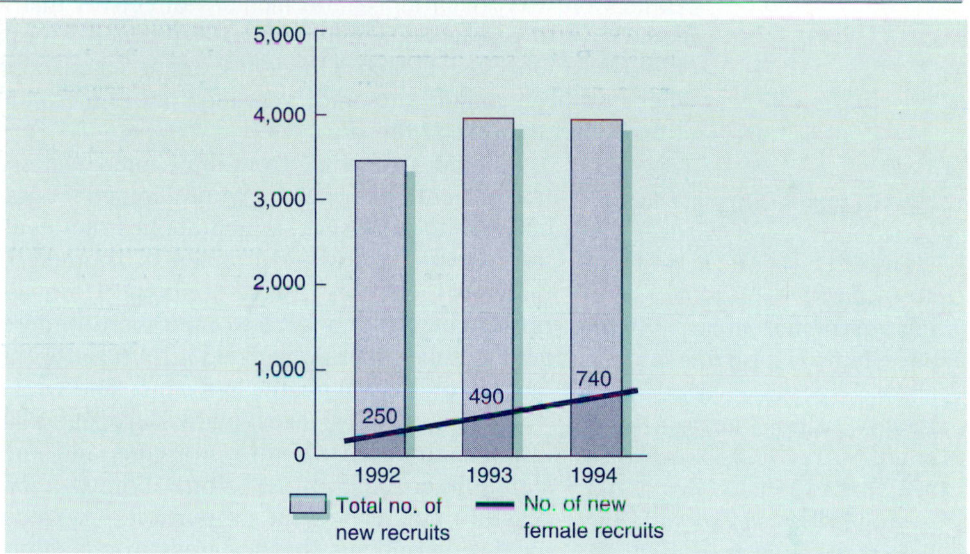


In 1993, South Korea's Samsung Group announced a new human resource policy that would "focus on quality rather than quantity" and counter South Korea's reputation for mass production of cheap goods. Working hours were reduced and examinations for hiring were opened to women on an equal basis with men, something unprecedented in the country's history. Ninety percent of the company's women section heads and assistant managers have been hired after 1993. The number of new women recruits has also risen (Exhibit 2.13). While the new policy has met some resistance internally and from outside suppliers and analysts, Samsung's "customer satisfaction index" and its employee satisfaction index rose by over 5 percent since the change. Additionally, a survey of recent college seniors found the overwhelming majority chose Samsung as their first choice for employment, citing reasons directly related to the new HR policies.[35]

Malaysia, too, has made a concerted effort to move beyond permitting its population to be viewed solely as a cheap source of labor. The Malaysian labor force is well trained and includes a high percentage of women in decision-making positions.[36]

## The European Approach

The European Union (EU) has taken a different approach than the United States to ensure fair treatment for employees. In the United States, the civil rights movement of the 1960s began with the recognition of the widespread discrimination against African-Americans in all aspects of life, including the workplace. The movement expanded to include women and other minorities, and affirmative action programs were developed that gave preferences on the basis of being a member of a protected group. Europe, on the other hand, has focused its legislation on women. While many European countries have significant ethnic minorities (e.g., Slovaks in the Czech Republic, Hungarians in Slovakia, Arabs in France), ethnicity is an extremely sensitive topic and is rarely an illegal grounds for discrimination. EU social legislation includes directives that require equal treatment on the basis of gender, equal pay, and prorated benefits for part-time and temporary employees. Only the United Kingdom extends equal opportunity to race. In no other European country are employers required to monitor the racial composition of their workforces, and few do.

Another difference from the United States is that European countries generally bar the use of preference programs. In 1995, the European Court of Justice, which applies the legal directives adopted by the EU, struck down a program in Bremen, Germany, that required municipal agencies to give preference to qualified women over men in job categories where women were underrepresented. The court held that the program violated a 1976 European Community directive that requires equal treatment for men and women in employment.[37]

> **WHAT DO YOU THINK?**
>
> Conflicts frequently arise around cultural values. Giving substantial money gifts in exchange for business contracts is perfectly acceptable in more than one non-U.S. country. Yet U.S. companies are forbidden by law from paying bribes. How can HRM help manage such conflicts?

Instead of preferences, many European countries emphasize government-financed training programs and encourages employers to step up recruiting efforts to hire more women. They have been successful in increasing the proportion of women hired by national and local governments, but progress in changing employment patterns in the private sector has been much slower. As in the United States, occupational segregation remains pervasive. European women are badly underrepresented outside traditional female jobs such as cashier, nurse, and teacher. Underrepresentation is particularly acute in the upper ranks of big corporations. The leading British retailer, Marks & Spencer, has no women among its top executives, even though 85 percent of its employees are women. London's Metropolitan Police force is 97.3 percent white, although minorities constitute approximately 20 percent of the London population. Little effort has been directed at increasing minority opportunities.

In Sweden, where the labor force of 4.4 million is almost equally split between men and women, a government report showed few women in stereotypically male jobs. Most Swedish working women are in the public sector or in traditionally female jobs such as teaching, nursing, and secretarial work despite the fact that Swedish labor unions have given women's issues a high priority in contract negotiations. Women's earnings range between 50 and 90 percent of men's throughout Europe.[38]

Hiring and firing on the basis of age still persists in Europe; want ads in the United Kingdom routinely specify that only applicants under 40 are considered.

Europeans have also avoided the use of harsh financial penalties for proven discrimination. In Germany, a 1980 antidiscrimination law provided so little financial compensation for victims of discrimination that it became known as the "stamp law"—the biggest awards available to women barely covered the cost of mailing the necessary documents. In 1985 the legislation was changed to allow compensation of up to one month's pay. Recently the limit was tripled. Oh, good.

The European approach of being less aggressive produces slower results, but its supporters believe that in the long run, it will result in more productive and harmonious workplace relationships than in the confrontational United States.

## Canada

In addition to sharing a 3,000+-mile border, the United States and Canada share many other characteristics. Canada, too, has an ethnically and culturally diverse population that is provided legal protection in employment decisions. Section 15 of the Canadian Charter of Rights and Freedoms is national legislation that prohibits discrimination.[39]

Each of the 10 provinces and two territories has its own laws. All prohibit discrimination on the basis of race, color, marital status, and sex. Except for the Yukon, every jurisdiction also includes age and disability status as prohibited grounds. In each province or territory, the human rights code or act is administered by a human rights commission or council. Thus, the courts play a smaller role in Canada than in the United States.

## DIFFERENTIAL IMPACT AND RESPONSES TO UNCERTAINTY

The difficulties of predicting external pressures for an entire society, much less their impact on a specific organization, cannot be overestimated. It is one thing to understand that the labor force in the United States is on average becoming more diverse or more susceptible to global competition. But the key question for managing HR is, So what difference will that trend make to a particular organization? For example, declining birth rates in many developed countries has meant that the average age of the population is increasing. Because of the relationship among age, length of employment, and wages, an aging workforce at General Motors and Ford Motor Company not only is more expensive, it also means fewer career opportunities for younger employees. But the Toyota Motor Corporation and Honda Motor Corporation facilities in the United States are not affected. Even though they employ the same skills as GM and Ford, they haven't been operating as long, and so have fewer employees with expensive seniority. GM and Ford are generous users of enhanced retirement programs whose objective is to increase turnover among older employees. In contrast, a rapid-growth organization such as Days Inn of America may hire some of those newly retired workers to obtain reliable employees. Thus, while an aging workforce affects all organizations, repercussions of that trend are very different among organizations.

As a result of the variability and uncertainty facing firms, some managers think it is sufficient simply to realize that the environment is changing and will continue to change. Rather than designing elaborate procedures to forecast specific changes, they urge creation of a flexible workforce and an adaptable organization structure that permits the organization and employees to adapt when necessary to whatever significant environmental changes occur.

Managers have three possible ways to approach external uncertainties: (1) reduce uncertainty by implementing scanning, forecasting, and planning mechanisms; (2) establish HR policies that create flexibility to adapt whenever necessary to whatever happens; (3) help shape external conditions. Most organizations pursue all three approaches simultaneously.

## SUMMARY

External conditions set the stage for the management of human resources. They influence the decisions organizations make; the decisions in turn influence these conditions. Because all conditions do not affect all organizations the same, responses vary. Thus, while we can say that external factors affect HRM and that these factors vary over time, consequences of these variations and the specifics of their impact on HRM are far more variable.

Although the nature of the external conditions can be discussed in general terms, it is sometimes difficult to discuss specifics for several reasons: First, the external conditions are interrelated and constantly changing. Second, organizations differ and they are constantly changing, so the same external condition may have very different implications for different organizations. External conditions may be viewed as an opportunity to improve human resource effectiveness. For instance, some managers use periods of recession to restructure their organizations and remove poor performers. Other organizations look to the HR managers to buffer the organization from external conditions. So the role of HR managers also seems to vary across organizations.

The main external factors discussed in this chapter are government laws, demographics, and diversity. In Chapter One, we discussed the employment relationship between an employee and employer. In Chapter Two we introduced a third party to that relationship: government. Through regulations and public policy, governments play a significant role in the way human resources are managed. This is true not only in the United States, but around the world. The actions of governments both reflect and influence a nation's culture and society.

As the majority of cultures around the world become increasingly interconnected through economic competition and trade, U.S. employers are finding that their increasingly diverse workforces can become a source of competitive advantage in marketing to global customers. However, such efforts are by no means universal. Metropolitan areas have had the largest growth in minority and immigrant populations. Companies operating in these areas are acutely, sometimes painfully, aware of the need to promote harmonious relations in the workplace. Companies that operate in areas of the country with stable, relatively homogeneous populations may be less aware of what their colleagues elsewhere face.

The same holds true on the global scale. Countries that have not yet expanded their definitions of rights may have very different standards of appropriate workplace actions.

Whatever the country, the program, equal opportunity, affirmative action, and diversity programs cannot succeed if managers do not support them. It is the managers who hire, promote, assign work, and terminate employees; managers can spell the difference between success and failure in meeting the company's EEO and affirmative action goals. Yet the topic remains emotion-laden and is subject to distortion on all sides, which can endanger the success of a company's efforts.

## QUESTIONS

1. Contrast the role of government in the workplaces of Western Europe and Asia with the situation in the United States. What aspects of the relationships do you feel the United States should emulate? What aspects do you feel the United States should export?
2. Russia and many other countries emerging from years of centrally planned economies are trying to rebuild their legal and employment systems. Which of the factors discussed in this chapter should be their highest priority?
3. There is considerable controversy over whether immigration is good or bad for the economy. What do you think, and why? What difference does it make for HR?

4. What skills do you think an international manager should possess?
5. How might an employer demonstrate its commitment to valuing diversity?
6. Why would an HR manager be concerned with "availability," and what makes availability difficult to quantify?

## YOUR TURN
### Levi Strauss

Levi Strauss & Company uses contractors around the world to produce its popular Levi's jeans. In 1992, Levi Strauss established operating guidelines that detail everything from environmental requirements to health and safety issues. To implement the guidelines, Levi Strauss audited its contractors and discovered that two contractors in Bangladesh were using workers in the factories who appeared to be underage. International standards have set a reasonable working age at 14. When the company brought it to the attention of the factory owners, the owners asked Levi Strauss what it wanted the factory to do; there were no birth certificates, so there was no way to know exactly how old these children were. Even if the children were younger than 14, they likely were significant contributors to family income. If the factory fired them, they probably would be forced into other ways of making a living that would be more inhumane than working in a factory, such as prostitution or begging.

Question What should Levi Strauss recommend to the subcontractor?

## NOTES AND REFERENCES

1. Soo Kon Kim, "Vietnam: Combining Human Resource and Economic Renovation Policies to Become the Next South Korea," paper presented at Center for Advanced Human Resource Sudies Sponsor Meeting, Ho Chi Minh City, Vietnam, November 6–8, 1996; Michael Byungnam Lee, "Business Strategy, Participative Human Resource Management and Organizational Performance: The Case of South Korea," working paper, Georgia State University, Oct. 1994; Byong-moo Yang, "Trends, Problems and Directions for Improvement for Korean Industrial Relations" (paper prepared for forum on Labor-Management Cooperation, Tokyo, Japan, Oct. 1994).
2. Gross national product is a measure of the prices of all goods produced in a country.
3. P. A. Katz and D. A. Taylor *Eliminating Racism: Profiles in Controversy* (New York: Plenum, 1988).
4. Yoko Sano, "Changes and Continued Stability in Japanese HRM Systems: Choice in the Share Economy," *International Journal of Human Resource Management,* Feb. 1993, pp. 11–27; Motohiro Morishima, "The Japanese Human Resource Management System: A Learning Bureaucracy," in *Human Resource Management in the Pacific Rim: Institutions, Practices and Values,* J. Devereaux Jennings and Larry Moore, eds. (New York: Walter deGruyter, in press).
5. "Pay Setting Headache in Eastern Europe," *IDS European Report* 389, May 1994, p. 21–22; Lowell Turner, "From 'Old Red Socks' to Modern

Human Resource Managers?" working paper 94-28, Cornell University Center for Advanced Human Resource Studies, 1994; Jacob C. Manakkalathil and Piotr Chelminski, "The Central European Three: Opportunities and Challenges," *SAM Advanced Management Journal,* Summer 1993, pp. 28–34; Matthew C. Bloom, George T. Milkovich, and Nada Zupan, "Contrasting Slovenian and U.S. Employment Relationships: The Links Between Social and Psychological Contracts," paper presented at 50th Anniversary of the Faculty of Economics International Conference, Ljubljana, Slovenia, September 18, 1996; Anuska Ferligoj, Janez Prasnikar, and Vesna Jordan, "Competitive Strategies and Human Resource Management in SMEs" (Working Paper, University of Ljubljana, 1994).

6. Sanford M. Jacoby, ed. *The Workers of Nations* (New York: Oxford University Press, 1995).
7. David Soskice, "Wage Determination: The Changing Role of Institutions in Advanced Industrialized Countries," *Oxford Review of Economic Policy* 6, no. 4, pp. 36–61; and David Soskice, "The German Wage Bargaining System," *IRRA 46th Annual Proceedings,* Paula Voos, ed., Boston, Oct. 1994, pp. 349–58.
8. "The German Industrial Relations System: Lessons for the United States?" *National Planning Association* 15, no. 3, Dec. 1993 (entire issue).
9. Barbara A. Lee, "The Effect of the European Community's Social Dimension on Human Resource Management in U.S. Multinationals: Perspectives from the United Kingdom and France," *Human Resource Management Review,* 4, no. 4, 1994, pp. 333–61; Neil Millward, Mark Steens, David Smart, W. R. Hawes, *Workplace Industrial Relations in Transition* (Brookfield, VT: Darmouth Publishing, 1992); Christopher L. Erickson and Sarosh Kuruvilla, "Labor Costs and the Social Dumping Debate in the European Union," *Industrial and Labor Relations Review,* Oct. 1994, pp. 28–47.
10. John T. Addison and W. Stanley Siebert, "Recent Developments in Social Policy in the New European Union," *Industrial and Labor Relations Review,* Oct. 1994, pp. 5–27.
11. Gordon Betcherman, Kathryn McMullen, Norm Leckie, and Christina Caron, eds. *The Canadian Workplace in Transition* (Kingston, Ont.: IRC Press, 1994); Vlado Pucik, Noel Tichy, and Carole K. Barnett, eds. *Globalizing Management* (New York, John Wiley, 1992).
12. Mary C. Gentile, ed. *Differences That Work* (Boston: Harvard University Press, 1994).
13. Joseph F. Coates, *Strategic Workplace Issues as We Approach Millennium 3* (Washington, DC: Coates and Jarratt, 1992).
14. T. C. Blum, D. L. Fields, and G. S. Goodman, "Organization-Level Determinants of Women in Management," *Academy of Management Journal* 37, 1994, pp. 241–68.
15. *Griggs* v. *Duke Power Co.,* 401 U.S. 424 (1971).
16. *Uniform Guidelines on Employee Selection Procedures,* 29 Code of Federal Regulations, Part 1607; *Federal Register* 43, no. 166 (1978), pp. 38295–309.
17. *Diaz* v. *Pan American World Airways, Inc.,* 5th Cir., 422 F.2d 385 (1971).

18. *Firefighters Local 1784* v. *Stotts,* 104 U.S. 2576(1984).

19. *Weber* v. *Kaiser Aluminum and Chemical Corp.,* 415 F. Sup. 761, 12 CCH *Employment Practice Decisions* 91 11, 115, S.D. La (1976).

20. J. F. Dovidio, S. L. Gaertner, and A. J. Murrell, "Why People Resist Affirmative Action" (paper presented at the annual meeting of the American Psychological Association, Los Angeles, 1994); Larry Reynolds, "As Affirmative Action Debate Heats Up, Public Support is Split," *HR Focus,* June 1995, pp. 1, 8.

21. Javed Ashraf, "Is Gender Pay Discrimination on the Wane? Evidence from Panel Data, 1968, 1989" *Industrial and Labor Relations Review* 49, 3, April 1996; Barbara R. Bergmann, *In Defense of Affirmative Action* (New York: Basic Books, 1996); Terry Eastland, *Ending Affirmative Action: The Case for Colorblind Justice* (New York: Basic Books, 1996); Clint Bolick, *The Affirmative Action Fraud: Can We Restore the American Civil Rights Vision?* (Washington: Cato Institute, 1996).

22. Augustin Kwasi Fosu, "Occupational Mobility of Black Women, 1958–1981: The Impact of Post-1964 Antidiscrimination Measures," *Industrial and Labor Relations Review,* Jan. 1992, pp. 281–94; "Minority Females Outpace Minority Males as Professionals," *Issues in HR* May/June 1994, pp. 3–4.

23. U.S. Department of Labor, *A Report on the Glass Ceiling Initiative* (Washington, D.C.: U.S. Government Printing Office, 1991); Mary Mattis, *Women in Corporate Management: The Results of a Catalyst Survey* (New York: Catalyst, 1990).

24. T. Cox, Jr. and S. M. Nkomo, "Invisible Men and Women: A Status Report on Race as a Variable in Organization Behavior Research," *Journal of Organizational Behavior* 11, 1990, pp. 419–31; G. N. Powell, "One More Time: Do Female and Male Managers Differ?" *Academy of Management Executive* 4, 1990, pp. 68–75; S. J. Spurr, "Sex Discrimination in the Legal Profession: A Study of Promotion," *Industrial and Labor Relations Review* 43, no. 4 (1990), pp. 406–17; and J. H. Greenhaus, S. Parasuraman, and W. M. Wormely, "Effects of Race on Organizational Experiences, Job Performance Evaluations, and Career Outcomes," *Academy of Management Journal* 33, 1990, pp. 64–86.

25. "The Glass Ceiling Commission Finds Workplace Still Segregated by Race and Gender," *Work in America,* June 1995, pp. 5–6; Gary N. Powell and D. Anthony Butterfield, "Investigating the 'Glass Ceiling' Phenomenon: An Empirical Study of Actual Promotions to Top Management," *Academy of Management Journal* 37, 1994, no. 1, pp. 68–86; Alison M. Konrad and Frank Linnehan, "Formalized HRM Structures: Coordinating Equal Employment Opportunity or Concealing Organizational Practices?" *Academy of Management Journal* 38, 1995, no. 3, pp. 787–820.

26. Catherine White Berheide, *The Sticky Floor: A Report on Women in Government,* Center for Women in Government, State University of New York at Albany, 1992.

27. Peter Wright, "Competitiveness Through Management of Diversity: Effects on Stock Price Valuation," *Academy of Management Journal,* Mar. 1995, pp. 37–65.

28. Ann M. Morrison, *The New Leaders: Guidelines on Leadership Diversity in America* (San Francisco: Jossey-Bass, 1992); Taylor H. Cox, Jr., "The Effects of Diversity and its Management on Organizational Performance," *The Diversity Factor,* Spring 1994, pp. 16–22; Taylor Cox and Carol Smolinski, *Managing Diversity and Glass Ceiling Initiatives as National Economic Imperatives* (Washington DC: Department of Labor, 1994); Susan E. Jackson and Associates, *Diversity in the Workplace: Human Resources Initiatives* (New York: Guilford Press, 1992); D. M. Atwater and R. J. Niehaus, "Diversity Implications from an Occupation Human Resource Forecast for the Year 2000," *Human Resource Planning* 16, no. 4, pp. 29–50; Michael L. Wheeler, *Diversity: Business Rational and Strategies* (New York: Conference Board, 1994).

29. Benson Rosen and Kay Lovelace, "Piecing Together the Diversity Puzzle," *HR Magazine,* June 1991.

30. Terr D. Egan and Charles A. O'Reilly III, "Being Different: Relational Demography and Organizational Attachment," *Administrative Science Quarterly* 37, 1992, pp. 549–79.

31. Sara Rynes and Benson Rosen, "A Field Survey of Factors Affecting the Adoption and Perceived Success of Diversity Training," *Personnel Psychology* 48, no. 2, Summer 1995, pp. 247–70.

32. Taylor H. Cox, Jr. and Stacy Blake, "Managing Cultural Diversity: Implications for Organizational Competitiveness," *Academy of Management Executives* 5, no. 3, 1991, pp. 45–56.

33. "Firm's Diversity Efforts Even the Playing Field," *Personnel Journal,* Jan. 1996, p. 56.

34. Takao Kato, "Chief Executive Compensation and Corporate Groups in Japan: New Evidence from Micro Data," *International Journal of Industrial Organization,* Laura Mazur, "Europay," *Across the Board,* Jan. 1995, pp. 40–43.

35. "New Asian Values," *Business Asia,* Mar. 13, 1995, pp. 3–4.

36. Sarosh Kuruvilla, "Linkages Between Industrialization Strategies and Industrial Relations/Human Resource Policies: Singapore, Malaysia, the Philippines, and India," *Industrial and Labor Relations Review* 49, 4, July 1996.

37. Richard W. Stevenson, "Job Discrimination in Europe: Affirmative Laissez Faire," *New York Times,* Nov. 26, 1995, p. 10.

38. Ibid.

39. Michael P. Kidd and Michael Shannon, "The Gender Wage Gap: A Comparison of Australia and Canada," *Industrial and Labor Relations Review* 49, 4, July 1996.

# Organization Conditions

"The End of the Job," trumpets the cover story of *Fortune,* a leading business magazine. The story informs us that, "Jobs as a way of organizing work . . . is a social artifact that has outlived its usefulness." If organizations expect to be successful, they need to "get rid of jobs" and "redesign to get the best out of the de-jobbed worker." If we no longer can expect to hold jobs, then can we at least hold a position? Unfortunately, no. Positions may be "too fixed." Roles? Nope. Too unitary, single-purposed. Skills and competencies then? Guess again; they will become obsolete. Like a fortune teller, *Fortune* tells us that the postjob workers will likely be self-employed contract workers hired to work on projects or teams.[1] People will work on 6 to 10 projects, possibly for different employers at one time. Some even foresee virtual employers and virtual employees.[2] A skeptic's response to this is, "OK, how about virtual performance and virtual pay to go along with the virtual organization?"

Before dismissing *Fortune*'s rhetoric as so much hype, recognize its underlying premise. We are in the midst of a revolution in the way work is organized and getting done. The old concept of work is crumbling. No longer are jobs stable; they are fluid in adapting to changing demands. Organizations are reengineering, restructuring, and removing layers of management. Change in the way work is organized is a fact of contemporary life, and the process is ongoing.

In the past, General Motors actually organized jobs into such narrow tasks as installer—front seats; installer—rear sets; installer—garnish moldings; installer—door panels. A front-seat installer would not install rear seats. Today such narrow job definitions have given way to increased employee flexibility.

Work is increasingly being designed to include an external customer focus.[3] As a result, customers and even suppliers are often included on project teams. For example, in the face of stiff competition from Airbus, Boeing solicited customers and suppliers to serve on design and engineering teams for its new commercial aircraft.[4] Cheaper maintenance, wider aisles, higher ceilings, simpler manufacturing, and adaptable seating arrangements resulted.

Much of this change in the way work is organized is a result of new technologies and cataclysmic competition that allows no margin for complacency. The *nature of the organization* and *how the work is organized* affect the types of HR actions that make sense for the organization.

## NATURE OF THE ORGANIZATION

You will not be very surprised to hear that HR practices differ between Intel and Indiana Energy. The two organizations are of different size, in different industries, and in different geographic locations. All of these differences help account for the variance in HR practice. You may be surprised to learn that HR practices differ even among organizations in the same industry, such as Intel, a global company headquartered in the U.S., and its German competitor Siemens, or Indiana Energy and Idaho Power. The most important organization factors that shape HR decisions are *financial conditions* and *technology.* The unprecedented competition on a global scale has created the need for new *business strategies* to meet market challenges and new *organization designs* to capitalize on the new technologies.

## Financial Conditions

> **WHAT DO YOU THINK?**
>
> The topic of corporate responsibility generates a lot of publicity. Robert Reich talks about creating a "corporate hall of shame" to pillory bad guys. Others say that it just is not true that businesses that are socially responsible can't also be fiscally responsible. Penalizing corporations for laying off employees, requiring "community impact studies" similar to environmental impact studies, and sharing company profits with all employees are some suggestions for eliciting corporate responsibility. To whom is an organization responsible? How should that responsibility be met? What role does HRM have in this issue?

If an organization does not generate enough cash flow over time, it cannot pay employees, fund training or retraining programs, or offer laid-off employees assistance in finding new work. However, cash flow is not an organization's only financial concern. Often an organization's market strategy postpones profits in order to increase market share. Start-up companies may take years to become profitable. Investors dreaming of future Microsofts, Netscapes, and Intels provide the necessary operating capital. From a very different perspective, the U.S. Secretary of Labor suggests that organizations ought to forgo profits for what he believes is the greater good of society; that is, avoid layoffs and pay better wages.[5]

So, while organizations' financial conditions vary for different reasons, there is little doubt that these financial conditions profoundly influence the HR decisions managers make. HR actions are often taken to improve financial conditions; downsizing and layoffs certainly affect expenses. But as we note throughout this book, HR actions such as improving training, hiring the right people, and paying them appropriately also have a significant impact on financial conditions.

In most organizations, HR decisions account for a large percentage of expenses. Most organizations are taking steps to tie these decisions more closely to the organization's financial conditions.[6] HRM decisions must be aligned with affordability and value added in mind.

## Technology and Productivity

Technology can be defined as the processes and techniques used to generate goods and services. Many dirty, dangerous, and boring jobs endured by previous generations have been eliminated through technology. However, there are trade-offs between technological applications and human resources. Perhaps these trade-offs are most obvious in developing economies such as the Philippines, Thailand, and Korea, where large pools of relatively unskilled workers are paid relatively low wages. For example, wages in the Philippines and Thailand are only 14 percent of wages in the United States, but the labor costs per unit produced are actually greater than in the United States. Low wages in developing countries often go hand in hand with lower productivity.[7] Technology, supported by sound HR actions such as training and hiring the right people, can significantly improve productivity.

**McJobs? Not.** The jobs created by applications of new technology generally require more skill than the jobs they replace, particularly analytical skill. Organizations have been scrambling to train a workforce comfortable with the new demands and greater complexity of the work.[8] Typically, fewer employees with higher skill levels and a greater number of skills are required; rather than being assigned to specific jobs, employees are usually part of a work team to which tasks are assigned. For example, Corning Glass makes ceramic components for automotive catalytic converters in both Blacksburg, Virginia, and Erwin, New York. The Blacksburg plant, which had been closed in 1984, reopened in 1988 with technology that permits small production runs and that can switch relatively easily from one component model to another. Employees in teams rotate among the tasks required by each production run. There are only two job classifications: operations associate and maintenance engineer. In contrast, the Erwin plant, which uses an older technology to produce a similar product, has 49 job classifications. The flexibility of the Blacksburg plant has allowed Corning to capture new business that the firm would previously have conceded to competitors.

Taking advantage of flexible technology frequently requires organizing employees into work teams rather than assigning specific tasks to individual employees. Because the use of teams, with or without flexible technology, is enjoying such widespread popularity, we return to the issue of designing and managing teams later in this chapter.

## Business Strategy

An organization's strategy integrates decisions and directs them toward specific goals. Strategic questions occur at various levels in the organization.

### Corporate-Level Strategy

The most fundamental strategy question is at the corporate level: *What business(es) should we be in?* During the 1980s, the answer for many organizations was to be in as many as possible. Steel companies bought oil companies and hotels, and oil companies bought department stores, office equipment manufacturers, and movie studios. While the financial logic was to acquire product lines whose product cycles complemented one another, many organizations did not have the expertise to run their new businesses. The 1990s saw a new wave of realignments, as organizations refocused on basic products and markets. However, highly successful exceptions do exist. General Electric competes in a wide variety of businesses, including entertainment (NBC), financial services (GE Capital), locomotives (GE Locomotives), appliances, chemicals and plastics, aircraft leasing and so on. PepsiCo's decision to own bottling plants rather than franchise them was a corporate-level strategic decision. (Arch rival Coca-Cola franchises its bottlers.) PepsiCo's original decision to invest in Taco Bell and Pizza Hut may have been motivated by a desire to sell more Pepsi—part of the cola wars. Today Taco Bell and Pizza Hut are major business units at PepsiCo.

### Unit-Level Strategy

Strategic decisions at the level of the business unit focus on how to compete in the unit's specific markets. PepsiCo's soft drink unit must decide where to locate its bottling plants, their capacity, and whether there is a market for a colorless cola. In contrast, managers in another PepsiCo business, Pizza Hut, need to figure out how to compete against Domino's (free delivery versus stuffed-crust pizza) as well as Olive Garden and TGI Friday's.

### Functional-Level Strategy

Functional decisions involve particular components of the organization, such as marketing, finance, and of course human resource management. At this level, managers formulate a strategy to help their function contribute to the achievement of corporate and unit objectives. So, for example, the appropriate inventory valuation and other accounting conventions are determined by corporate and unit needs. At the functional level, those decisions are translated into practice—activity-based accounting, or better inventory control systems. For HRM, a strategic approach translates into three tasks:

1. Assure that HR issues are considered in formulating business strategies: In what businesses should we compete?
2. Establish HR goals and plans—an HR strategy—to support the business strategy: How will HR decisions help us compete?
3. Work with managers to ensure implementation of the HR plan: How do we translate policies into day-to-day actions?[9]

Managers are increasingly focusing on aligning their HR decisions with other actions to help their organizations achieve and sustain competitive advantage.

A number of typologies have been proposed to relate HR decisions to a specific business strategy. Miles and Snow classified organizations as:

*Defenders:* organizations operating in a few stable product markets.

*Prospectors:* organizations that continually search for new products and market opportunities and regularly take risks.

*Analyzers:* organizations that operate in many product markets, some relatively stable, others changing.

They then proposed HR activities that would complement each of these business strategies (see Exhibit 3.1). For example, the product market stability enjoyed by Defenders allows them the time to do formal and extensive planning, and to develop people internally to meet anticipated staffing needs. In contrast, Prospectors must be more adaptable, and so are more likely to recruit people with the skills they need from outside the organization. The uncertainties that Prospectors face make formal HR planning less useful. Rather, it is sufficient to have people who are flexible enough to respond to challenges as they arise. Analyzers may resemble Defenders or Prospectors, depending on the conditions of a specific product market.

A number of other approaches also categorize strategies. The key premise is that HR decisions that fit the organization (and external conditions) are likely to be more effective.

## Organization Design

Organization design may be one of the most interesting challenges in business today. Arrangements that splendidly suited the 1960s don't necessarily serve today. New forms appear better able to capitalize on the potential of new technology as well as new demands and expectations from customers and employees.[11]

These new forms have profound implications for employment relationships. Reduced hierarchies and broadened work roles are examples of these effects. Corporate staffs and centrally controlled bureaucracies are reduced,

EXHIBIT 3.1 Organization Conditions and Human Resource Management Activities

| | **Defender** | **Prospector** | **Analyzer** |
|---|---|---|---|
| **Organizational Characteristics** | | | |
| Typical company | Lincoln Electric | Hewlett-Packard | Texas Instruments, Motorola |
| Product-market strategy | Limited, stable product line; predictable markets | Broad, changing product line; changing markets | Stable and changing product line; predictable and changing markets |
| Research and development | Limited mostly to product improvement | Extensive; emphasis on "first-to-market" | Focused; emphasis on "second-to-market" |
| Production | High volume/low cost; emphasis on efficiency and process engineering | Customized; prototypical emphasis on effectiveness and product design | High volume/low cost; emphasis on process engineering |
| Marketing | Limited mostly to sales | Focused heavily on market research | Extensive marketing campaigns |
| **Human Resource Management Activities** | | | |
| Basic role | Maintenance | Entrepreneurial | Coordination |
| Human resource planning | Formal; extensive | Informal; limited | Formal; extensive |
| Recruitment, selection, and placement | Make | Buy | Make and buy |
| Training and development | Skill building | Skill identification and application | Skill-building and application |
| Compensation | Internal pay relationships; internal equity | External pay relationships; external competitiveness | Internal consistency and external competitiveness, a blend |
| Performance appraisal | Process-oriented; focus on training needs; individual/group performance | Results-oriented; focus on staffing needs, division/corporate performance | Mostly process-oriented, training and staffing needs, individual/group/division performance |

entire layers of administrators and managers are removed from the hierarchy, and bureaucratic rules are reduced and modified. Exhibit 3.2 contrasts the most popular organization designs.

The traditional organization design has been likened to a group of ladders tied together at the top. The rungs on the ladders represent different levels of work, with each ladder representing related work. A technical ladder might include low-skilled technicians, degreed chemists and engineers, and various project managers, arrayed at various rungs in a hierarchy. Similarly, entry-level word processors, bookkeepers, and accountants make up an administrative ladder.

This traditional organization design grew out of Frederick W. Taylor's late 19th-century work on *scientific management.*[12] Prior to Taylor, workers directed and controlled production. They exercised autonomy over their labor and that of their helpers.

## EXHIBIT 3.2 HR Decisions Fit Organization Design

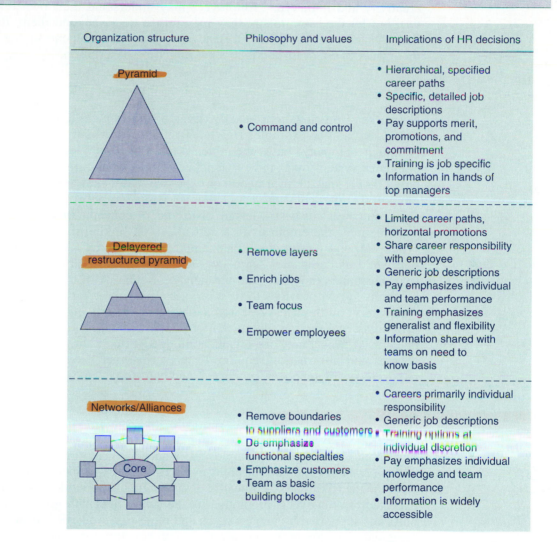

| Organization structure | Philosophy and values | Implications of HR decisions |
|---|---|---|
| Pyramid | • Command and control | • Hierarchical, specified career paths<br>• Specific, detailed job descriptions<br>• Pay supports merit, promotions, and commitment<br>• Training is job specific<br>• Information in hands of top managers |
| Delayered restructured pyramid | • Remove layers<br>• Enrich jobs<br>• Team focus<br>• Empower employees | • Limited career paths, horizontal promotions<br>• Share career responsibility with employee<br>• Generic job descriptions<br>• Pay emphasizes individual and team performance<br>• Training emphasizes generalist and flexibility<br>• Information shared with teams on need to know basis |
| Networks/Alliances<br>Core | • Remove boundaries to suppliers and customers<br>• De-emphasize functional specialties<br>• Emphasize customers<br>• Team as basic building blocks | • Careers primarily individual responsibility<br>• Generic job descriptions<br>• Training options at individual discretion<br>• Pay emphasizes individual knowledge and team performance<br>• Information is widely accessible |

Taylor calculated standards and specified methods for each job and delineated how all the jobs fit together in the organization. By reducing each job to its essential tasks, then specifying precisely how each task shall be done and how long it should take, Taylor transferred control of the workplace from the collective workers to supervisors. Supervisors also took over the functions of planning the work and training the workers, tasks formerly done by the workers.

What evolved from the Taylor approach is the traditional hierarchical organization structure, now derisively referred to as command and control. Yet the system has many advantages. Employees can see how their work fits in with the rest of the organization. Career paths are supported through promotion to a higher rung on the ladder. By making clear who reports to whom and who is responsible for what, the hierarchy coordinates work and directs employees' efforts to the objectives of the organization.

Critics claim that the precise delineation of work into so many levels stifles creativity and initiative.[13] Employees may understand their own responsibilities, but by the same token, they may refuse to go beyond them, to do more than the minimum required. Instead, they wait for someone higher up to tell them what to do, or respond, "It's not in my job description!"

## Networks

Networks of organizations usually develop based on expertise or talent in each organization. For example, Hewlett-Packard, Microsoft, and ICL (a British computer company) have assembled a team of employees to jointly develop computer system management standards. Individuals on the team are chosen based on the special information or expertise that makes them valuable contributors to this particular project. These networks are put together based on what each company does best—design, distribute, or conceptualize.

Sometimes the emphasis in a network is on linking the needs of suppliers, producers, and consumers. For example, Astra-Merck (A-M), a joint venture between drug companies Astra and Merck, proclaims that it does not sell drugs to its customers (hospitals and physicians). Rather, A-M offers "pharmaceutical solutions." A-M provides to its customers not only a variety of drugs but also information on the latest research and studies, experts on various illnesses and symptoms, and service centers that physicians can access by telephone or computer. A-M uses a network organization design that is based on the flow of resources and information required to meet customer needs. Specifications and requirements of suppliers, producers, and consumers are tightly integrated.

## HR Decisions That Fit Organization Design

Organization design goes beyond structure or architecture to reflect the management philosophy regarding employees. Under a conventional pyramid structure with a *command and control* philosophy, HR actions include clear, well-laid-out career paths (Exhibit 3.2). Specific descriptions of the work make clear what is expected of employees; promotion up the career ladder to greater job responsibilities is supported by greater status and more pay. And HR information is concentrated at the top of the organization, with key decision makers.

In contrast, a *delayered* design emphasizes empowered individuals organized into teams. Employees are encouraged to enlarge their jobs, to become more generalists, and hence, more flexible. The training and pay actions support such horizontal promotions. Both team and individual performance are recognized.

*Networks* shift the philosophy even more to participative management and recreate the organization boundaries. Now the HR decisions emphasize individual and team responsibility for careers and employment security. Team or group performance is the focus. Clearly, the design of organizations affects the HR decisions. Not surprisingly, HR departments are being redesigned, too, as Chapter Sixteen reveals.

Managers' roles shift under these different organizational designs, too, from directing and implementing in the pyramid organization to collaborating and assisting within networks. The diagnostic model specifies assessing organizations so that HR decisions can be aligned with organization conditions, including design.

## NATURE OF THE WORK

Work and the way it is organized is critical in HRM. The skills and experience required to perform a job influence the kind of education and training people seek. To a large extent, the job influences the pay that employees receive and thus their economic well-being. Many people find status and personal fulfillment at work. And the way we organize work into jobs affects the organization's ability to serve its customers, as the Astra-Merck example shows.

An organization's basic decisions about which technology to employ, what business strategy to adopt, and which organization design to use directly affect the nature of work. Allegheny Ludlum, for example, sells specialty steel that it produces from raw steel made from iron ore. Allegheny has many options. It can buy partially finished steel and finish it to customer specifications, or it can buy iron ore to smelt in its own furnace. Many factors go into Allegheny's decision on which strategy to pursue, but whatever decision it makes determines the nature of the work done at Allegheny. All organizations face similar issues. The strategies and objectives chosen by managers affect the work to be performed and how that work is organized into jobs.

### Designing Work

The design of a job is often the key to whether a job alienates or energizes the jobholder. How much freedom of action or authority do jobholders enjoy? Do they feel committed to the products they make or the services they render? Is there anything about the job that hinders employee productivity? These issues can all be influenced by job design.

Exhibit 3.3 outlines advantages and disadvantages of the major job design approaches. Taylor's scientific management was one of the first approaches to systematically design jobs. The assembly line epitomized his method and its emphasis on efficient production. Taylor's approach took into account the nature of the technology—standardization of products as well as the means of production made a wide range of affordable goods available to the average worker's family—and the nature of the employees—many were immigrants who spoke little or no English and were illiterate in their native language; consequently, jobs had to be relatively straightforward, requiring only simple training.

> *Job design* integrates work content, qualifications, and rewards for each job in a way that meets the needs of employees and the organization.

Although Taylor's principles were a systematic effort at job design, many managers distorted them. They focused on the close supervision and set standards that contained little flexibility. Rigidly enforced standards with little regard for employees' physical needs and safety—much less their psychological needs—led to boredom, dissatisfaction, alienation, and frustration.

### Human Relations

The human relations movement was in large part a reaction against the dehumanizing aspects of scientific management carried to an extreme.[14] The movement grew out of studies done in the 1920s, now referred to as the *Hawthorne studies.* The original goal of the studies at Western Electric Company's Hawthorne plant

EXHIBIT 3.3 Job Design Philosophies/Approaches

| | Techniques | Advantages | Disadvantages |
|---|---|---|---|
| **Scientific management philosophy** | Work simplification | Creates safe, simple, reliable jobs. Minimizes the mental demands on employees | Boring, demeaning. |
| | Job enlargement | Reduces waiting time between tasks, improves organization flexibility, reduces support staff needs. | May lose the advantages of work simplification without offsetting the disadvantages. |
| **Human relations philosophy** | Work groups | Recognizes importance of social needs of employees. | Less technical guidance. |
| **Work characteristics approach** | Job enrichment | Creates jobs that engage the employee, satisfaction, and production. | Costly. Accident/error potential increases. May require additional employees. Control still rests with managers. |
| **High-performance work system** | Teams | Empowers employees by giving them more control of their work. | Requires compatible organization design, careful structuring of teams. Relationships among teams must be managed. Some work may still be boring. Time devoted to nonproduction issues. |

was to test how variations in working conditions (lighting, ventilation, temperature) affected productivity. The striking conclusions were that these variations were less important than the social interaction among co-workers.[15]

Researchers discovered that workers spontaneously organized the work environment, established standards, and enforced sanctions among themselves. Therefore, management's job was to design supportive work groups that would increase worker motivation and productivity and direct efforts toward the goals of the organization.

Quality circles and other worker participation programs are contemporary applications of human relations ideas. The focus is on the sociology of groups and how individual needs can be met by these groups. However, the approach gives little guidance on how to design jobs.

## Work Characteristics Models

Work characteristics models focus on the psychological interaction between the employee and the job and identify the best way to design jobs that are intrinsically motivating.[16] Generally, they advocate *job enrichment* to give employees more responsibility, autonomy, and control in their jobs. The work characteristics model identifies five job aspects that can potentially motivate workers:

1. *Skill variety.* The degree to which the job requires a variety of different activities in carrying out the work and uses a number of an individual's skills and talents.
2. *Task identity.* The degree to which the job requires completion of a whole and identifiable piece of work—that is, doing a job from the beginning to end with a visible outcome.
3. *Task significance.* The degree to which the job has a substantial impact on the lives or work of other people.
4. *Autonomy.* The degree to which the job provides substantial freedom, independence, and discretion to the individual in scheduling the work and in determining the procedures to be used in carrying it out.
5. *Feedback.* The degree to which carrying out the work activities required by the job results in the individual's obtaining direct and clear information about the effectiveness of his or her performance.

The first three job characteristics influence whether an individual believes the work is important. Autonomy influences whether an individual feels personally responsible for good or poor performance. And feedback provides the individual with knowledge of the results of the work. The assumption is that proper arrangement of these characteristics can ensure job designs that are intrinsically rewarding. While the model has spawned a great deal of academic research, it is difficult for managers to apply because it relies on psychological states that may or may not exist in individuals.[17]

## High-Performance Work Systems

The sociotechnical approach to job design recognizes both the importance of the workplace sociology and the productivity gains of optimum technological arrangements. It assumes that the two subsystems are related to one another, serve as constraints on one another, and must be effectively fit to one another to achieve optimal functioning.

High-performance work design is an outcome of this sociotechnical approach.[18] Exhibit 3.4 contrasts the traditional and high-performance designs. In the high-performance design, operators no longer have jobs with certain specified tasks. Rather, each employee learns multiple skills; different tasks assigned to a team of employees are rotated among the team members. The team decides who will do which tasks when. This approach is consistent with delayered and network organization designs.

The team has the authority to arrange tasks and assign roles among themselves in any way they choose. They are charged with responsibility for an end product, and they are free, within technological and budgetary restrictions, to manage this responsibility as they see fit. Thus, the team manager's responsibility is not to design jobs that are intrinsically motivating, but to form work teams whose members possess the qualifications to accomplish the tasks, are compatible, and whose objectives correspond to those of the organization. The manager becomes a coach, an inspirer. But the manager must also ensure that the team has sufficient authority within the organization. The manager must still provide leadership.

**EXHIBIT 3.4** Traditional versus High-Performance Work Design

| Work-Design Element | Traditional | High Performance |
|---|---|---|
| People | Focus on a narrow set of tasks as an individual contributor | Coordinate with others, utilizing teamwork to conduct an integrated series of activities. |
| Decisions | Manage the process through command-and-control hierarchies | Empower teams to make decisions on the run to speed cycle times and process improvement. |
| Information | Information available only on a need-to-know basis | All information available in real time to all team members to facilitate decision making. |

Source: Marc J. Wallace Jr., and N. Fredric Crandall, "Winning in the Age of Execution: The Central Role of Work-Force Effectiveness," *ACA Journal* 1, no. 2, Winter 1992–93, pp. 30–47.

## Go with the Flow

Rather than focusing on the design of the job, there may be potential competitive advantage in looking at the entire work flow: concentrating on the goods and services that are delivered to the consumer and the most efficient way to deliver them. Work process analysis is an important part of total quality management (TQM). The objective is to analyze the flow of work from one area to another to determine the value added at each step. If no discernible value is added, costs or response time can be reduced by eliminating the step in the process.

Work flow is scrutinized from two standpoints:

1. From within the job itself, by having the job incumbent ask questions for each activity, such as: Could any changes in how the work is provided to me make my job easier or faster? How could I enhance the work I provide to others to expedite the next step in the work flow?
2. Through the entire process of the work flow, to determine whether a major activity can be accomplished more effectively and efficiently through reassignment or modification of tasks or responsibilities. Questions here include: What tasks are redundant or unnecessary? How can work flow be improved? How can the process be expedited without decreasing quality? What could be done differently to reduce costs or speed the process?

Answers to these questions may convince a company it needs to re-engineer itself.

## Reengineering

Reengineering looks at the entire work process in the organization. Several examples have already been discussed: Pepsi-Cola in Chapter One and Astra-Merck in this chapter. Even though these companies are very different, they both have applied reengineering principles that focus on meeting customer needs for quality, service, flexibility, and low costs. Reengineering contrasts with scientific management, which specified simple tasks knit together by complex processes. Under reengineering, work flow is kept as simple as possible.

### Benchmarking

Reengineering projects typically start with *benchmarking:* the identification of companies judged to be exceptional on a specific process, analysis of how exceptional companies achieve their results, and adaptation of the practices and techniques that are appropriate for the company conducting the benchmarking study. Benchmarking identifies the best practices in an industry or organization and spreads them by providing information to employees.[19] If a benchmarking study suggests a serious lag in some aspect of performance, reengineering may help.

According to Hammer and Champy, there are some recurring characteristics of reengineering:[20]

- *Several jobs are combined into one.* Combining jobs reduces the errors, delays, and miscommunication that are inevitable in handing off a product or customer to the next person involved. If a lengthy work process cannot be done by a single person, then the use of a team to perform the integrated process is the logical arrangement.
- *Employees make the decisions.* Employees are empowered to act, and technology gives them the information they need to make informed decisions.
- *Work is performed where it makes the most sense.* An example of this reengineering principle is placing the responsibility for recruiting and selecting team members with the team instead of in the personnel department at some corporate headquarters. Team members are trained in recruiting and selecting, so that they can make effective decisions consistent with the organization's policies (e.g., EEO), yet match the requirements of the team.
- *Controls are used only where they add value.* Checking, approving, and reconciling add up to overhead, which sometimes cost more than any amount saved by having the control system in place. For example, Wal-Mart has worked with many of its suppliers, including Pepsi, to reengineer its inventory management. Combining information from automated cash registers at each Wal-Mart store with usage patterns from retailers all over the country, Pepsi assumes responsibility for shipping Wal-Mart the amount of product it needs. Too much product ties up storage space; too little loses sales and disappoints customers.

  By giving up control of its inventory management and relinquishing this function to favored and trustworthy suppliers, both Pepsi and Wal-Mart reap advantages. Wal-Mart eliminates the costs of monitoring and maintaining its inventory, and its soft-drink stock is managed more effectively because Pepsi can do a better job of it than Wal-Mart. Space is freed up in Wal-Mart's distribution center along with money to finance that space and inventoried merchandise.

  Pepsi adds value to the cola is supplies Wal-Mart by performing the inventory management process. What does Pepsi get? As a preferred supplier, Pepsi gets prime display space and full cooperation on special promotions.

> With the improved information on product demand, Pepsi can run its bottling and transportation operations more efficiently. Instead of large lots, soda moves to Wal-Mart in smaller but more frequent shipments. Consumers potentially benefit from lower prices and fresher soda (Pepsi recently began adding freshness dating to its products). Billing is handled by Pepsi without the need for Wal-Mart to generate a purchase order ahead of time. This saves countless hours of paperwork, especially for products whose price fluctuates as much as soda does.

Just as scientific management fit the nature of the organizations and employees of an earlier day, process reengineering may be in tune with today's organizations (leaner staffing, with a host of technologies that enable educated employees to assume greater responsibility). Everything changes in a reengineered organization—work done by employees, roles of managers—consequently, the HR systems to support this organization must also change. Training, selecting, and rewarding employees able to adapt to the new requirements raise unique issues that are discussed in the upcoming chapters.

## Is This Change Really Necessary?

Many organizational transformations are driven by a quest for competitive advantage: getting close to the customer, innovative solutions, faster response time, and greater productivity. But are there any reasons why these objectives can't be met without adjusting organization structure? For example, Leighton Contractors, an Australian construction company, was seeking the best way to restructure to become more productive. More than 1,200 employees responded to a questionnaire eliciting reactions to such issues as teamwork, quality, training, management, and multiskilling. These responses provided Leighton with guidelines on how to proceed. The company discovered that all it needed was better basic employee relations.[21] Employees wanted (1) additional on-the-job skill training so that they could do their jobs better; (2) more information about the work site or project to which they were assigned, so that they could figure out how their work fit in and whether there were ways to do a better job; (3) more positive feedback when they had done their jobs well; and (4) their project managers to listen to them when they raised an issue or suggested a change. All employees, regardless of position, said they wanted to take more responsibility for their actions and wanted to feel part of a small and elite team. Hardly revolutionary techniques—yet probably extremely cost effective.

## Teams: A Fundamental Building Block

A lot of the newer technologies, newer organization designs, and newer processes discussed so far assume that employees work in teams; teams have been called a fundamental building block in today's organizations.[22]

A *team* is a distinguishable set of two or more individuals who interact independently and adaptively to achieve specified, shared, and valued objectives.

Teams come in a multitude of arrangements. They may be temporary, semiautonomous, or self-managed. They may be cross-functional and include managers. They may be organized for a specific purpose (e.g., to develop a new marketing plan), then

EXHIBIT 3.5 Range of Participation Through Teams

| Team Type | Typical Type | Degree of Authority |
|---|---|---|
| 1. Supervisor and volunteers discuss work problems once a week. | Quality circle | Contribution to solving work area problems; advice and involvement |
| 2. Cross-functional team meets weekly to work on multiarea problems or accomplish a project. | Cross-functional team | Responsibility for resolving cross-functional problems or planning cross-functional projects |
| 3. Employees within an area function as a team full-time, with supervision. | Semiautonomous | Responsibility for results and for procedures used |
| 4. Employees within an area function as full-time team, without supervision. | Self-directed work team | Accountability for results and for procedures used |
| 5. Employees replace old organization . structure. Need for support minimized as team's authority is expanded. | Process team | Completes an entire work process that delivers goods/services to external or internal customer |

disband when the plan is agreed upon by higher levels of authority. Or they may consist of employees with similar skills, such as those who assemble coffeepots for West Bend Company. The tasks of such a team remain the same, even though membership may change as people join and leave the organization.

Exhibit 3.5 categorizes some of this variety in types of teams. Teams may vary on how they interact with the rest of the organization, the nature of their task, the interdependence of team members, their size, permanency, how much authority they possess, and a host of other characteristics.[23]

Teams offer the potential to increase communication and autonomy and free employee creativity. They are continuing to proliferate in U.S. organizations. A survey of 230 companies revealed that approximately one-third of employees participate on teams; expectations are that the percentage will continue to increase.[24]

### What the Research Says

Bell South has introduced the use of teams to accomplish the task of installing, maintaining, and repairing network communication systems. Teams are given the authority for work assignments and quality control.[25]

The employees in the self-managed teams say they appreciate the greater autonomy ("no supervisor spying on you"), greater co-operation and informal training provided by teammates, and greater recognition that comes with the autonomous teams. Sixty-two percent of team members say they routinely help one another with problem solving compared with only 35 percent of traditionally organized workers, and 40 percent say that relations between co-workers have improved since the introduction of teams. However, they also acknowledge friction between self-managed teams and other workers as well as among members within the team. Over 75 percent of employees who are currently not in the autonomous

> **EXPLORING THE WEB**
>
> The ability to profit from rapidly changing global markets is the goal of the agile organization. Agility Forum, a non-profit corporation, sponsors a web site containing case studies, research projects, and illustrations of agility. Their address is **<http://www.absu.amef.lehigh.edu>**

teams said they would volunteer for teams if given the opportunity. In contrast, less than 10 percent who are now in teams said they would like to return to traditional supervision.

The Bell South researchers conclude that both workers and firms gain from self-managed teams. However, the nature of the work and technology can limit the effects of teams.[26]

Another study looked at the evolution of a team over time. At Jamestown, New York, the Cummins Engine Company uses autonomous work teams to manufacture and test diesel engines. The plant was designed to allow for work teams that would have greater responsibility and authority than traditional manufacturing facilities allowed. The original expectation was that as teams matured, they would exercise ever-greater autonomy. But that has not been the case. While employees can be given great latitude, strong leadership and direction from team leaders is still required after 10 years of team experience. Additionally, teams have typically looked to leaders to enforce discipline and to handle performance difficulties.[27]

### Making the Transition

Frederick W. Taylor identified this problem back in 1911: Workers are reluctant to tell colleagues their performance is inadequate. Taylor's solution was to assign that responsibility to management.

Advocates of high-performance work systems say that the solution is to allow sufficient time to make the transition from traditional to self-managing teams and reward the change along the way. They see a three-step transition:

1. *Multiskilling.* Every employee learns additional operational activities. The team then consists of individuals who rotate among different activities and cover for each other.
2. *A self-sustaining team.* Team members add indirect support such as preventive maintenance to their repertoire. They now operate more efficiently because they do not have to wait for outside intervention.
3. *A self-managing team.* Based on their direct monitoring of customer needs, employees decide what products to produce each day. They also do some of their own HR: They schedule their work time, including vacations, make selection decisions, and appraise individual performance. Do they set their own wages or fire themselves? Not yet.

Others point out that leaders and managers are even more important with teams; however, the skills required are different.[28] It's interesting that Taylor began with workers who were already managing their own production schedules, training workers, and enforcing discipline. The hook is that the production norms they were imposing were their own, not management's. Now managers are trying to get workers to manage production schedules, train other workers, and enforce discipline again. Who can say this time will be any different? Could it be that the more things change, the more they remain the same?

## Building Blocks or Stumbling Blocks?

With so much variety in teams, it is hard to argue that one set of HR practices works better for managing teams than another. For example, whose performance should be evaluated, that of the teams or the individual team members?

Whose responsibility is it if one team member is *free riding* (not working as hard as teammates)? Who decides on team membership, the team or a manager? You probably are familiar with many of these issues from group projects in school. Clearly, the use of teams on any long-term basis dictates the need for training that focuses on how to work with others, communicate effectively, and resolve disputes as a member of a team.[29]

Moving from focusing on the individual working in the organization to the team requires more than designing the right team. Shifting to a team-based organization demands considerable change and new skills from employees. It is not always effective to try to influence the performance of the team by focusing on the performance of the individual. Appraising the performance of individuals and paying them on the basis of that performance certainly affects what they do. However, what may be missing are the links among individual performance, team performance, and organization performance. Not only must performance among individuals, teams, and organizations fit together, but an individual's personal needs must be met at the same time that team and organization performance requirements are being met.[30] These issues in selection, training, performance management, and compensation for teams will be taken up in later chapters.

## Yosh!

Sometimes support for the use of teams takes on a messianic fervor, despite mixed research evidence. An underlying assumption of much of the writing is that employee involvement in autonomous or semiautonomous work teams "is part of a transformation to an 'industrial democracy' [where workers control the workplace] that is ethically superior because it results in stable, more satisfying jobs for employees and higher productivity for the firm." However, others don't see it that way. One writer spent six months working on the automobile assembly line of an Subaru-Isuzu plant in Indiana.[31] This plant uses workforce participation schemes, centers production on work teams, and emphasizes worker input into production improvements and quality control. She reports that she enjoyed the bright, clean, orderly work setting, a company culture that "encourages supervisors to talk to you instead of yelling at you," and an environment structured to celebrate the worker's role in production; however, tension still existed. In the traditional assembly plant based on scientific management:

> Workers are free to hate their work openly. Their attitudes are their own. The bargain they strike with the company is simple and straightforward: Make quota, and you get your pay. [This approach] did not interfere with the shop worker's personal autonomy . . . their essential freedom remained intact.

The auto worker wonders whether work teams enforce too much social control over members. For example, the day begins at 6:25 A.M. with a daily exercise routine, followed by a five-minute team meeting, followed by a team-member huddle similar to that of a sports team before a game. Each person in the huddle extends an arm into the center of the circle, hands clenched into fists. One team member is asked to deliver an inspirational message. After the

### WHAT DO YOU THINK?

At the 1996 graduation at Skidmore College, retired CBS broadcaster Charles Kuralt told graduates, "Great things are not accomplished by teams, no matter what you have heard. They are accomplished by individuals who take untraveled roads." How can HRM help an organization be sensitive to the needs of individuals who are part of teams?

message, everyone brings the other arm into the circle, with everyone's hands meeting in the center. While doing this, members shout "Yosh!" and then break up and go to work. Every team in the plant performs this same ritual at the same time. While many people find such behavior a simple expression of group cohesiveness and good will, others find such behaviors embarrassing and ultimately demeaning—"a system of social control driven by pressures for conformity to company goals."[32]

### (Dis)comfort with Conformity

A Japanese manager told us a story that further illustrates cultural differences in willingness to conform. A management team from one of Detroit's big three auto manufacturers visited a Japanese auto plant to determine why U.S. production lagged Japan's. The Detroit management team had adopted every single one of the Japanese production process innovations. They had redesigned their organization, reengineered the work to use just-in-time inventory, quality circles, empowered work teams—everything, right down to the red rope that hung within easy reach of all the U.S. assembly line workers. This red rope could be pulled at any time to halt production if a worker needed to correct a defect or merely got behind in the work. Despite these efforts, U.S. total labor costs continued to be much higher than Japan's. What was the difference? Ah, the Japanese managers confided, the answer lies in the red rope that your American workers are so fond of: no Japanese employee would *dare* to pull it!

## NATURE OF THE JOB

A member of HR Net, the largest internet discussion group related to a wide variety of HR issues, writes:

> The world of work has been undergoing profound changes; *prefigured* work (designed in advance by one person for another to do, ordinarily under stable, standardized circumstances) has all but disappeared, displacing those who used to do it. The work of many if not most people now requires of them that they figure out what to do in a given situation instead of simply invoking a canned routine. They must solve problems, make decisions, plan courses of action, marshal support and, in general, design their own work methods, techniques, and tools. We are very nearly back where we were in the late 1800s when Taylor set out to make a science of the study of work. The work back then was almost all manual and it, too, was mostly *configured* (designed on the fly by the person doing it in response to conditions faced at the time) instead of prefigured. Workers chose their own tools, worked at their own pace, and adhered to their own standards. As a result, management had no idea whatsoever what constituted a good day's work. Neither, really, did the workers. What Taylor and others did was create standardized methods and tools; they prefigured the work and, in so doing, drove costs and prices down, and wages and the standard of living up. The same fate awaits the current crop of configured work—and the people who do it. What does all this mean for job descriptions, recruiting, selection, and the HR profession in general? Nothing less than a complete reengineering of the profession, I think.

Job analysis has not been immune to this transformation turmoil. HR Net provoked one of its largest number of responses to a recent query, "What good is job analysis?" Some commentators felt the organization would have no basis for making defensible decisions without it. Others called it a bureaucratic boondoggle. Here's what all the fuss is about.

## Job Analysis

Historically, job analysis has been considered the cornerstone of personnel administration. Potential uses have been suggested to support every major personnel function. Often the type of job analysis data needed varies by function.[33] For example, training requires information on *qualifications* and job *content* so programs can be tailored to the actual qualifications required to perform the jobs. Hiring and promotion standards can be based on this same information. Job analysis information allows interviewers to assess the match between job candidates and the job, and it can help candidates decide if they are really interested in a job vacancy. In performance evaluation, both employees and supervisors look to the required *behaviors* and *results* expected in a job. Job analysis also helps document the work-relatedness of HR decisions, which is important to ensure nondiscrimination.

*Job analysis* is a systematic process of collecting data and making judgments about the nature of a specific job.

## Collecting the Data

Qualifications, job content, behaviors necessary to perform a job, and results of the job are some of the characteristics an analyst would look at to write an accurate description of each job. Three basic categories of job information commonly collected for analysis are task data, behavioral data, and knowledge data. Job analysis methodologies vary on which of these characteristics they emphasize.

### Task Data: Emphasis on Content

Task data are subparts of a job, with emphasis on the purpose of each task. An excerpt from a job analysis questionnaire that collects task data is shown in Exhibit 3.6. While the aspect of work being assessed is communication, the questionnaire describes the elemental units of communication; for example, read technical publications and consult with co-workers. The objective of the task—for example, read technical publications to keep current on industry and consult with co-workers to exchange ideas and techniques—is also emphasized. Task data reveal the actual work performed and why it is performed. This excerpt from the Position Description Questionnaire also measures time spent doing a task. Other possible measures are degree of importance of the task and prior experience required to be able to do it.

### Behavioral Data: Emphasis on Behaviors

Behavioral data use verbs describing the behaviors that occur on the job. Exhibit 3.7 shows such behavioral observations. This time, communication is described as advising, negotiating, persuading, and so on. This exhibit is from the Position Analysis Questionnaire (PAQ), which describes behavior using seven factors: information input, mental processes, work output, relationships with other persons, job context, other job characteristics, and general dimensions. The communications behavior in Exhibit 3.7 is part of the "Relationships with Other Persons" factor.

### Abilities Data: Emphasis on Qualifications

Abilities data assess the underlying knowledge or skill a worker must possess for satisfactory job performance. Abilities may be (1) psychomotor, (2) physical, or (3) cognitive. Exhibit 3.8 shows a scale used by AT&T to assess comprehension.

EXHIBIT 3.6 Job Analysis Questionnaire Using Task Data (excerpt)

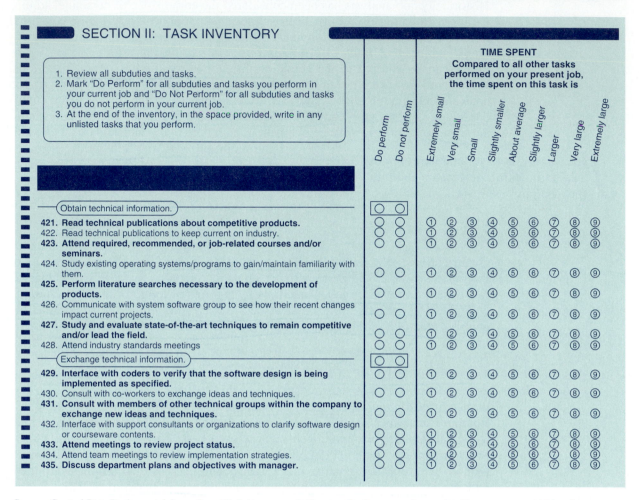

## SECTION II: TASK INVENTORY

1. Review all subduties and tasks.
2. Mark "Do Perform" for all subduties and tasks you perform in your current job and "Do Not Perform" for all subduties and tasks you do not perform in your current job.
3. At the end of the inventory, in the space provided, write in any unlisted tasks that you perform.

**TIME SPENT**
**Compared to all other tasks performed on your present job, the time spent on this task is**

| Task | Do perform | Do not perform | Extremely small | Very small | Small | Slightly smaller | About average | Slightly larger | Larger | Very large | Extremely large |
|---|---|---|---|---|---|---|---|---|---|---|---|
| Obtain technical information. | ○ | ○ | | | | | | | | | |
| **421. Read technical publications about competitive products.** | ○ | ○ | ① | ② | ③ | ④ | ⑤ | ⑥ | ⑦ | ⑧ | ⑨ |
| 422. Read technical publications to keep current on industry. | ○ | ○ | ① | ② | ③ | ④ | ⑤ | ⑥ | ⑦ | ⑧ | ⑨ |
| **423. Attend required, recommended, or job-related courses and/or seminars.** | ○ | ○ | ① | ② | ③ | ④ | ⑤ | ⑥ | ⑦ | ⑧ | ⑨ |
| 424. Study existing operating systems/programs to gain/maintain familiarity with them. | ○ | ○ | ① | ② | ③ | ④ | ⑤ | ⑥ | ⑦ | ⑧ | ⑨ |
| **425. Perform literature searches necessary to the development of products.** | ○ | ○ | ① | ② | ③ | ④ | ⑤ | ⑥ | ⑦ | ⑧ | ⑨ |
| 426. Communicate with system software group to see how their recent changes impact current projects. | ○ | ○ | ① | ② | ③ | ④ | ⑤ | ⑥ | ⑦ | ⑧ | ⑨ |
| **427. Study and evaluate state-of-the-art techniques to remain competitive and/or lead the field.** | ○ | ○ | ① | ② | ③ | ④ | ⑤ | ⑥ | ⑦ | ⑧ | ⑨ |
| 428. Attend industry standards meetings | ○ | ○ | ① | ② | ③ | ④ | ⑤ | ⑥ | ⑦ | ⑧ | ⑨ |
| Exchange technical information. | ○ | ○ | | | | | | | | | |
| **429. Interface with coders to verify that the software design is being implemented as specified.** | ○ | ○ | ① | ② | ③ | ④ | ⑤ | ⑥ | ⑦ | ⑧ | ⑨ |
| 430. Consult with co-workers to exchange ideas and techniques. | ○ | ○ | ① | ② | ③ | ④ | ⑤ | ⑥ | ⑦ | ⑧ | ⑨ |
| **431. Consult with members of other technical groups within the company to exchange new ideas and techniques.** | ○ | ○ | ① | ② | ③ | ④ | ⑤ | ⑥ | ⑦ | ⑧ | ⑨ |
| 432. Interface with support consultants or organizations to clarify software design or courseware contents. | ○ | ○ | ① | ② | ③ | ④ | ⑤ | ⑥ | ⑦ | ⑧ | ⑨ |
| **433. Attend meetings to review project status.** | ○ | ○ | ① | ② | ③ | ④ | ⑤ | ⑥ | ⑦ | ⑧ | ⑨ |
| 434. Attend team meetings to review implementation strategies. | ○ | ○ | ① | ② | ③ | ④ | ⑤ | ⑥ | ⑦ | ⑧ | ⑨ |
| **435. Discuss department plans and objectives with manager.** | ○ | ○ | ① | ② | ③ | ④ | ⑤ | ⑥ | ⑦ | ⑧ | ⑨ |



Comprehension and another factor, expression (not shown), correspond most closely to the communication aspect of work examined in Exhibits 3.6 and 3.7. Notice that this assessment can be done with or without reference to specific tasks or behaviors in a job.

As jobs become more intellectually demanding, determining the knowledge required to perform tasks may be an increasingly useful way to analyze jobs. Workers can have different kinds of knowledge about their jobs. For example, one worker may know how a machine works and how to fix it. Another may know only what the machine is supposed to do. A professor may be able to specify what a computer program should enable students to do to be an effective teaching tool without knowing the first thing about programming. An emphasis on knowledge, rather than specified tasks or behaviors, would also better accommodate jobs that continue to change as technology develops.

EXHIBIT 3.7 Job Analysis Questionnaire Using Behavioral Data (excerpt)

**Section 4 Relationships with Other Persons.**

This section deals with different aspects of interaction between people involved in various kinds of work.

*Code Importance to This Job (1)*
N Does not apply
1 Very minor
2 Low
3 Average
4 High
5 Extreme

**4.1 Communications**

Rate the following in terms of how *important* the activity is to the completion of the job. Some jobs may involve several or all of the items in this section.

**4.1.1 Oral (communicating by speaking)**

99 ___ Advising (dealing with individuals in order to counsel and/or guide them with regard to problems that may be resolved by legal, financial, scientific, technical, clinical, spiritual, and/or other professional principles).

100 ___ Negotiating (dealing with others in order to reach an agreement or solution; e.g., labor bargaining, diplomatic relations).

101 ___ Persuading (dealing with others in order to influence them toward some action or point of view; e.g., selling, political campaigning).

102 ___ Instructing (the teaching of knowledge or skills, in either an informal or a formal manner, to others; e.g., a public school teacher, a machinist teaching an apprentice).

103 ___ Interviewing (conducting interviews directed toward some specific objective; e.g., interviewing job applicants, census taking).

104 ___ Routine information exchange: job related (the giving and/or receiving of *job-related* information of a routine nature; e.g., ticket agent, taxicab dispatcher, receptionist).

105 ___ Nonroutine information exchange (the giving and/or receiving of *job-related* information of a nonroutine or unusual nature; e.g., professional committee meetings, engineers discussing new product design).

106 ___ Public speaking (making speeches or formal presentations before relatively large audiences; e.g., political addresses, radio/TV broadcasting, delivering a sermon).

**4.1.2 Written (communicating by written/printed material)**

107 ___ Writing (e.g., writing or dictating letters, reports, etc.; writing copy for ads, newspaper articles, etc).

**4.1.3 Other Communications**

108 ___ Signaling (communicating by some type of signal; e.g., hand signals, semaphore, whistles, horns, bells, lights).

109 ___ Code communications (telegraph, cryptography, etc.).

Source: PAQ Services, Inc., Logan, UT. Copyright © 1969 by Purdue Research Foundation, West Lafayette, IN 47906.

## Conventional Methods of Collecting Data

Most commonly an analyst collects job data by using a questionnaire to interview job incumbents and supervisors. The questionnaire and interviews are structured to achieve a uniform response format. The approach requires considerable involvement of employees and supervisors, which increases their understanding of

EXHIBIT 3.8 Job Analysis Questionnaire Using Ability Data (excerpt)

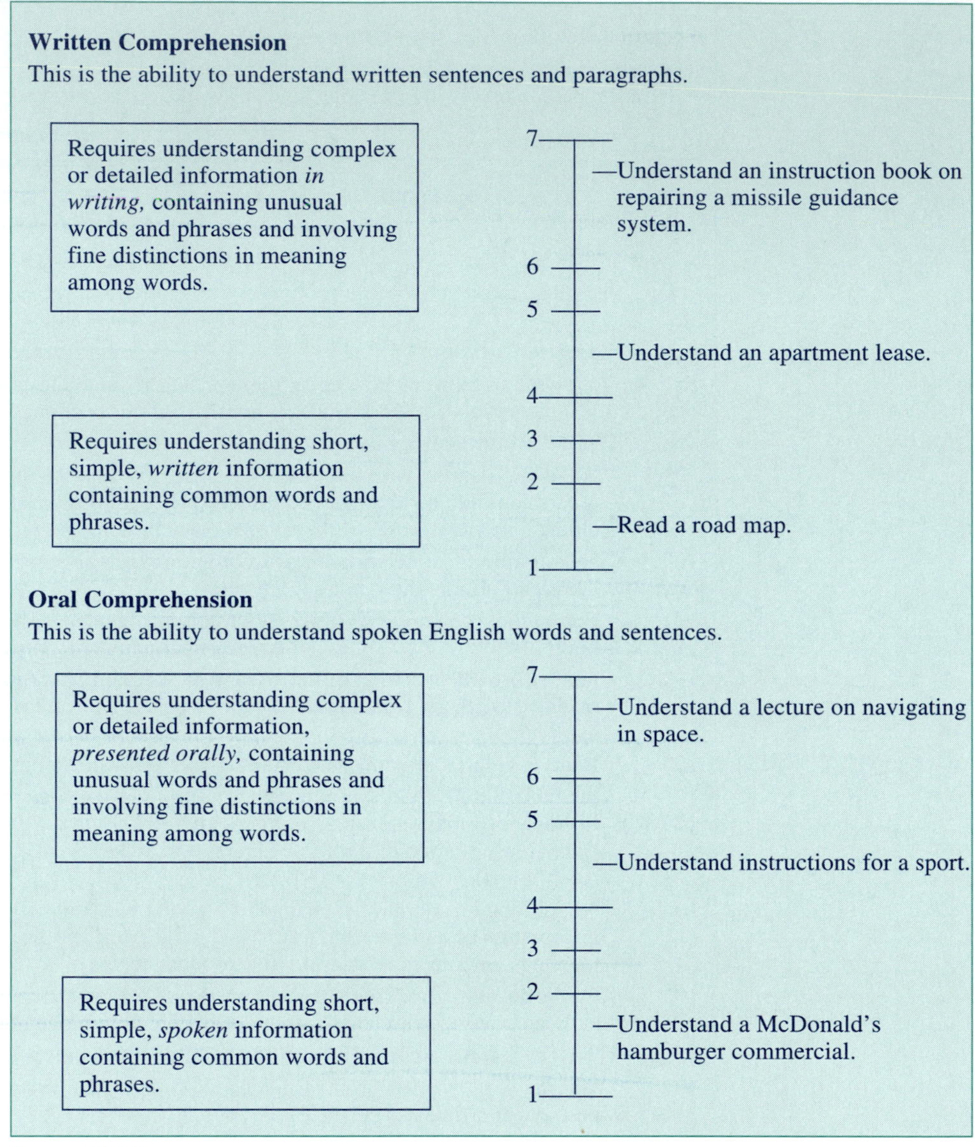


Source: AT&T.

the process, provides an opportunity to clarify their work relationships and expectations, and increases the likelihood that they will accept the results. Usually, an analyst translates the data collected to a summary job description sheet. Often, both incumbents and supervisors are given an opportunity to modify and approve the job description; this helps ensure its acceptance. In some cases the preparation of these description sheets is left to the supervisors and incumbents, and the analyst role becomes one of trainer/facilitator. The appendix provides a step-by-step procedure for collecting data and a questionnaire. Exhibit 3.9 is a job description written from information developed with conventional job analysis.

**EXHIBIT 3.9** Midway Hospital Nursing Department Job Description

**Identification**

**Job Title** Date: July 1997

Registered Nurse

**Job Summary**

Accountable for the complete spectrum of patient care from admission through transfer or discharge through the nursing process of assessment, planning, implementation, and evaluation. Each RN has primary authority to fulfill responsibility for the nursing process on the assigned shift and for projecting future needs of the patient/family. Directs and guides patient teaching and activities of ancillary personnel while maintaining standard of professional nursing.

**Definition**

**Relationships**

Reports to: Head Nurse or Charge Nurse.

Supervises: Responsible for the care delivered by L.P.N.s, nursing assistants, orderlies, and transcribers.

Works with: Ancillary Care Departments.

External relationships: Physicians, patients, patients' families.

**Qualifications**

Education: Graduate of an accredited school of nursing.

Work experience: Critical care requires one year of recent medical/surgical experience (special care nursing preferred), medical/surgical experience (new graduates may be considered for noncharge positions).

License or registration requirements: Current RN license or permit in the State of Minnesota.

Physical requirements:
A. Ability to bend, reach, or assist to transfer up to 50 pounds.
B. Ability to stand and/or walk 80 percent of eight-hour shift.
C. Visual and hearing acuity to perform job related functions.

**Description**

**Responsibilities**

1. Assess physical, emotional, and psycho-social dimensions of patients.

   Standard: Provides a written assessment of patient within one hour of admission and at least once a shift. Communicates this assessment to other patient care providers in accordance with hospital policies.

2. Formulates a written plan of care for patients from admission through discharge.

   Standard: Develops short- and long-term goals within 24 hours of admission. Reviews and updates care plans each shift based on ongoing assessment.

3. Implements plan of care.

   Standard: Demonstrates skill in performing common nursing procedures in accordance with but not limited to the established written RN skills inventory specific to assigned area. Completes patient care activities in an organized and timely fashion, reassessing priorities appropriately.

(Additional responsibilities omitted from exhibit.)

Conventional methods place considerable reliance upon analysts' abilities to understand the work performed and to translate it into a job description. One writer describes the process:

> We all know the classic procedures. One [worker] watched and noted the actions of another . . . at work on [the] job. The actions of both are biased, and the resulting information varied with the wind, especially the political wind.[34]

Techniques to quantify and computerize job data have been developed. For example, structured questionnaires that list the tasks/behaviors/abilities relevant for the jobs being analyzed have been developed and computerized. Exhibits 3.6, 3.7, and 3.8 are excerpts from such approaches. Job incumbents indicate whether each item applies to their particular job and how important it is in the overall job. Results can be easily compiled and similarities and differences among jobs can be compared.

## Job Descriptions

Because job analysis serves as the starting point for so many other HR activities, the data collected must be in a form that is accessible to all users. That form is the job description. Typical job descriptions contain three sections that identify, define, and describe the job.

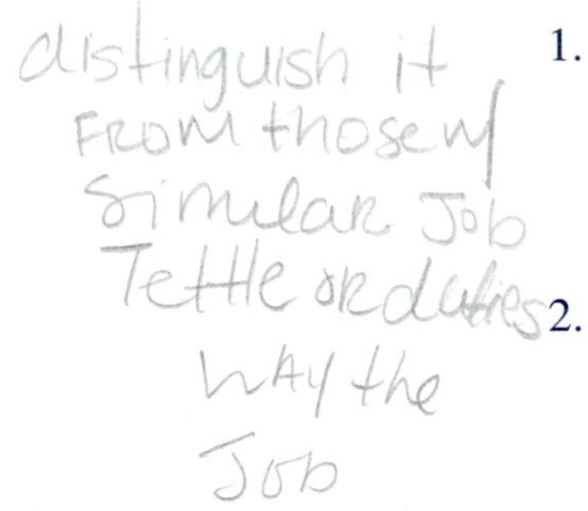

1. *Identification.* The first section may contain the job title, number of incumbents, where it is located (department, work site) and job number, if any is used. Its purpose is to clearly identify the job and to distinguish it from those with similar job titles or duties. The date of the analysis is also important. The job description in Exhibit 3.10 should indicate why.
2. *Definition.* The second section reflects the purpose of the job: why the job exists, and how it fits in with other jobs and with the organization and its overall objectives. What constitutes satisfactory performance of this job may also be included. It ought to provide an accurate word picture of the job. The word picture of the nurse position in Exhibit 3.10, making the 5 cents per day raise contingent on a debt-free employer, reflects a century of change.

   For managerial jobs, statistics on the size of the budget under the control of this job, the number (and job titles) of people supervised, and reporting relationships with other managers at both higher and lower organization levels are frequently included in the job definition.
3. *Description.* The third section is an elaboration of items in the definition, or summary section. It indicates the major duties of this job, the specific work performed, how closely supervised it is, and what controls limit the actions of the jobholder. In addition to describing the tasks performed, the training and experience required to perform them may also be included here, or in a separate section called Job Specifications.

## Generic Descriptions: Flexibility versus Fences

In practice, the amount of information collected for job analysis varies considerably. Most employers use more general descriptions, arguing that all the detailed data on tasks and behaviors are not necessary. Further, if job analysis is

**EXHIBIT 3.10** Partial Description of Job of Nurse, Cleveland Lutheran Hospital, 1887

In addition to caring for your 50 patients each nurse will follow these regulations:

1. Daily sweep and mop the floors of your ward, dust the patient's furniture and window sills.
2. Maintain an even temperature in your ward by bringing in a scuttle of coal for the day's business.
3. Light is important to observe the patient's condition. Therefore, each day, fill kerosene lamps, clean chimneys, and trim wicks. Wash the windows once a week.
4. The nurse's notes are important in aiding the physician's work. Make your pens carefully, you may whittle nibs to your individual taste.
5. Each nurse on day duty will report every day at 7 A.M. and leave at 8 P.M. except on the Sabbath on which day you will be off from 12:00 noon to 2:00 P.M.
6. Graduate nurses in good standing with the director of nurses will be given an evening off each week for courting purposes, or two evenings a week if you go regularly to church.
7. Each nurse should lay aside from each pay day a goodly sum of her earnings for her benefits during her declining years, so that she will not become a burden. For example, if you earn $30 a month you should set aside $15.
8. Any nurse who smokes, uses liquor in any form, gets her hair done at a beauty shop, or frequents dance halls will give the director good reason to suspect her worth, intentions, and integrity.
9. The nurse who performs her labors and serves her patients and doctors faithfully and without fault for a period of five years will be given an increase by the hospital administration of five cents a day, provided there are no hospital debts that are outstanding.

required, then people and resources are required to undertake it. Consequently, the cost of doing business increases. The benefits received may not justify the time and expense to collect data.

(NUMMI)

Many firms are reducing the number of separate job classifications used. New United Motors Manufacturing, Inc. (NUMMI), a joint venture between General Motors and Toyota, went from 120 separate jobs to four levels of technicians needed to perform all the tasks necessary to assemble automobiles.[35] The result is broad, generic descriptions that cover a large number of related tasks. Two employees working in the same broadly defined jobs may be doing entirely different sets of related tasks. But for pay purposes, they are doing work of equal value. Employees working in very broadly defined jobs can easily be switched to other tasks that fall within the broad range of the same job, without the bureaucratic burden of making job transfer requests and wage adjustments. Thus, employees can more easily be matched to changes in the work flow.

So where does this leave us? What data should be collected and what level of analysis should be used? There are no clear-cut answers. It depends on the situation and the resources available. The more specific and detailed the data, the more likely it is to capture differences in the work and adequately describe the work content. Whether such detailed information is worth the expense involved depends on the circumstances in the organization. Clearly, detailed data may justify pay differences to a skeptical judge presiding over a pay discrimination suit. Yet, more broadly defined jobs with generic titles and descriptions offer increased flexibility in work assignments. But equal pay for substantially different work may eventually lead to employee dissatisfaction. Herein lies one of the challenges to job analysis.

## Is Job Analysis Useful?

The usefulness of job analysis information can be judged by a number of different standards.

### Reliability

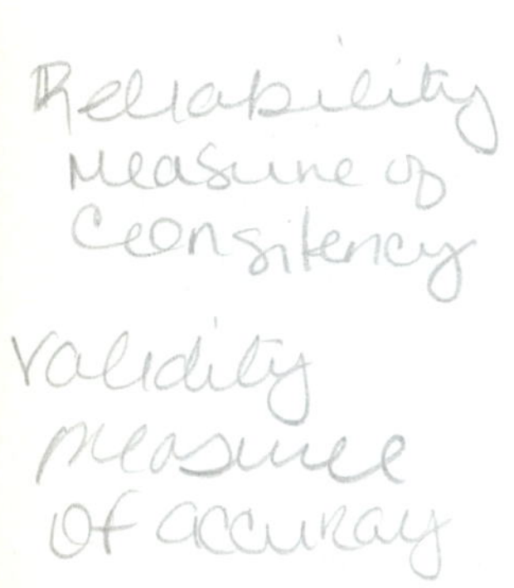

Reliability is a measure of the *consistency* of the results obtained, either from two different analyses of the same job, or from one analyst looking at a single job on two different occasions.

### Validity

Validity is a measure of the *accuracy* of the results obtained. It is quite possible for two analysts to agree completely and for both to be wrong as a result of incomplete information, biased interpretation, and the like. There is almost no way of showing statistically the extent to which a job analysis result is accurate or valid, particularly as one moves to more complex jobs. The most common method of ensuring accuracy is to collect data from multiple job holders or supervisors, or both. Requiring job holders and supervisors to sign off on results may help ensure their validity.

### Purpose of the analysis

If there is a need for uniform job data at many locations, does the method provide it? Can the method provide documentable evidence of the work-relatedness of the pay structure? Does it adequately assess the subtle difference among jobs unique to our organization? Are both the typist and the vice president of marketing convinced that it fairly describes their jobs? These challenges to job analysis provide criteria to judge a method's usefulness. However, some analysts get so taken with their statistics and computers that they ignore the role than human judgment continues to play in job analysis. As one expert cautions:

> I wish to emphasize the central role played in all these procedures by human judgment. I know of no methodology, statistical technique, or objective measurement that can negate the importance of, nor supplement, rational judgment as an important element in the process of deriving behavior and task information about jobs and of using that information to develop or justify human resources programs.[36]

Quantitative and more systematic approaches to job analysis do not remove the judgment; they only permit us to become more systematic in the way we make it.

## Yes, But Is It *Really* Useful?

Doing job analysis and writing job descriptions can help in hiring the right person; overreliance on formal descriptions can lead to rigidity and turf issues (e.g., "It's not in my job description" or "You had no authority to make that decision"). Solution: Focus on broad sets of tasks and end results. However, focusing too broadly may not provide a clear enough organizational road map nor tie employee behavior to organization objectives. Nor will it provide legal justification for hiring, promoting, training, and pay decisions.

### ADA Requirement

While no U.S. law requires job analysis, if it is done, it must be well thought-out. Additionally, the Americans with Disabilities Act (ADA) requires that essential *elements of a job* be specified in the job description. These are the elements that cannot be reassigned to other workers. If applicants can perform these essential elements, they are assumed to be able to perform the job. Once essential elements are identified, the employer must consider *reasonable accommodations* that enable an otherwise qualified handicapped person to perform them. Essential elements and reasonable accommodations have to be determined on a case-by-case basis, including legal cases. For those jobs with little discretion, it's relatively easy to list essential tasks, but fewer and fewer such jobs exist. Nevertheless, a thorough job analysis is the beginning point for compliance.[37]

In the HR Net discussion noted earlier, another participant defends job analysis and job descriptions:

> Many of the problems that have been attributed to job descriptions can be traced straight back to the mistakes made by the HR officer who assigned the job title in question to the given collection of positions. Often, the positions that share a job title (and description) are far too heterogeneous in what they do, or in what they produce, to be lumped together. But the HR manager who wrote the description or who grouped the too-diverse positions together is the culprit, not the job analysis/description process!
>
> Likewise, nobody could seriously make the argument that jobs are static entities that must remain constant across time. It is obvious that work changes over time, and that the responsibilities and desired outcomes for a given position or job may change quite rapidly in some situations. However, it is totally incorrect to use this fact as justification for the conclusion that we should just give up on trying to do job analysis right.
>
> In job descriptions . . . you get what you pay for. The main reason why so many job descriptions are worthless is because most are prepared in a haphazard way. They're vague, often written by someone with little understanding of the job, and highly questionable in terms of the validity of any personnel specifications. . . . . However, bad as most job descriptions are, it's quite fallacious to conclude that this somehow proves they can't be done correctly!

## Focus on the Person, Not the Job: Competencies

Much of the job analysis angst stems from the difficulty of aiming at a moving target. As we discussed in the introduction to this chapter, many jobs are changing so rapidly that, even with computer assistance and user-friendly description software, HR people can't keep up with the changes. In the kind of work that prevails in many organizations, the fundamental issue is separating the job from the person. Instead of trying to cope with constantly changing jobs, some organizations are focusing on the individual employee, the person who possesses the skills and competencies required to perform the work. Organizations are replacing the notion of "jobs" with considering what "roles" and "competencies" will be required for the 21st century.

Competencies are typically used for managerial, professional, and/or technical work where what is to be accomplished is not easily specified in advance.[38]

While work on competencies is still evolving and does not yet enjoy uniform definitions, it is safe to say that competencies are less specific than a description of a skill or a task. Consider, for example, the competency "product development" described in part in Exhibit 3.11. It is one of eight marketing competencies used by a major toy company. Each of the competencies has four phases of mastery: baseline expectations, competent/proficient, advanced/coach, and expert/mentor. A single individual would not be expected to reach the expert level in all competencies. Rather, a number of "roles" in the marketing function might exist that would emphasize different marketing competencies.

Because competencies are acquired over time, they can be tied to career development. The use of competencies reinforce a strategy of continuous learning and improvement. An organization that uses competencies would hire a person based on what mastery that person could already demonstrate as well as the perceived potential to develop higher levels of mastery on a number of competencies. Chapter Four examines assessing the individual employee in greater detail.

## SUMMARY

Organizations adopt different approaches to human resources: Some promote from within, while others hire experienced people; some seek cooperative relations with unions, while others aggressively avoid them. Some offer employment security and retraining, others do not; and some base pay on group performance and profit sharing, while others use individual performance schemes. These differences are not simply the result of varying external conditions. Even though pressures in the external environment affect human resource decisions, organization factors also play a significant role. To better understand differences in human resource decisions, we need to assess differences in organizations, as well as external conditions.

With a diagnostic approach, managers assess the conditions of the organizations before they make human resource decisions. We analyzed a few important conditions in this chapter, including financial, strategic, and design issues. The financial conditions underlie all the others. If an organization is not making money, it has little flexibility in its HR decisions. Strategy focuses on issues such as which business should we be in, and how should we compete. For HR, these issues translate into aligning HR decisions with other organization actions and the business strategy.

Partly as a result of financial changes (global competition) and new technologies, many organizations are being redesigned to capitalize on these new conditions. Delayered and network organizations have been popular responses. A major change is the tremendous growth in the use of teams to assume responsibility for an entire work process. The hope is that the team will be able to use new technologies and will possess the authority and skill to respond faster and better to the market. However, the use of teams raises additional HR issues of how to select, train, and pay members in order to capture the team advantage while minimizing problems that may arise.

While teams are a popular way to organize work, team members still require guidance on what constitutes their tasks and responsibility. Job analysis is the process of collecting and assessing data on tasks and responsibilities. Job analysis assesses the content of jobs. Its results provide input for a variety of

EXHIBIT 3.11 Product Development—Marketing Competency

Manages the product development process, by:

- ✦ Analyzing and evaluating marketplace to identify niches/opportunities
- ✦ Evaluating products/concepts
- ✦ Developing marketing strategies
- ✦ Coordinating and evaluating research/testing
- ✦ Generating product recommendations and obtaining management support
- ✦ Driving product schedules/activities

**Phase I: Baseline Expectations**

- ✦ Analyzes market/competitive data (e.g., TRST, NPD) and provides top-line trend analysis, with supervision
- ✦ Evaluates products/concepts (see Toy Viability competency)
- ✦ Contributes to product brainstorming sessions
- ✦ Oversees market research activities and ensures timely completion
- ✦ Obtains Account Management input to the product development effort
- ✦ Develops and implements marketing strategy, with supervision: product, positioning, pricing/financial, promotion, packaging, merchandising, and advertising
- ✦ Facilitates cost reductions to achieve price/profit goals; ensures execution of cost meeting next steps
- ✦ Ensures adherence to product schedules
- ✦ Coordinates licensor approval of product concept/models

**Phase II: Competent/Proficient**

- ✦ Monitors and analyzes market/competitive data (e.g., TRST, NPD) with minimal supervision, and provides recommendations for product development opportunities
- ✦ Makes substantial contributions in product brainstorming sessions
- ✦ Analyzes market research results and makes appropriate product recommendations
- ✦ Partners with Account Management group to obtain their buy-in to the product development effort
- ✦ Develops and implements marketing strategy, with minimal supervision
- ✦ Drives cost reductions to achieve price/profit goals
- ✦ Drives product schedules and resolves product scheduling issues (late delivery, late debug)
- ✦ Negotiates with licensors to obtain product approval

**Phase III: Advanced/Coach**

- ✦ Independently monitors and analyzes market/competitive data (e.g, TRST, NPD), provides recommendations for product development opportunities, and coaches others to do so
- ✦ Leads and facilitates formal product brainstorming sessions
- ✦ Coaches others in analyzing market research results and making product recommendations
- ✦ Develops innovative marketing plans (e.g., new channels of distribution, niche markets)
- ✦ Independently develops and implements marketing strategy, and coaches others to do so
- ✦ Identifies/evaluates cost reduction opportunities, and coaches others to do so
- ✦ Identifies and implements product schedule improvement tactics
- ✦ Coaches others to manage product schedules
- ✦ Coaches others in managing licensor relationships
- ✦ Shares product ideas/strategies with other teams/categories

**Phase IV: Expert/Mentor**

- ✦ Reviews/approves recommendations for product development opportunities
- ✦ Provides short- and long-term vision and goals for developing the corporate product portfolio across categories or brands
- ✦ Reviews/approves marketing strategy, and proactively adjusts strategy in response to internal/external changes
- ✦ Approves cost reduction recommendations
- ✦ Anticipates critical issues that may impact product schedules and develops alternate plans
- ✦ Ensures on-strategy delivery of product

human resource activities including job design. Although job analysis is a basic assessment process, not all organizations do it. Job analysis can be tedious, time consuming, and expensive. Recent advances in computerizing the process may eliminate some of these drawbacks but not all of them. Computerization raises the possibility of collecting a great deal of job information for a variety of purposes. Unfortunately, the amount of data may outrun its usefulness. Informed human judgment can never be omitted from the work assessment process.

The basic premise of this chapter is that the nature of work plays a critical role in the management of human resources. Job analysis and job design are important tools in the process of matching the nature of the individual with the nature of the work. This matching process helps achieve employee and organizational objectives.

## QUESTIONS

1. Give some examples of how financial conditions affect HRM, and how HRM can affect financial conditions.
2. This chapter described pyramid, delayered, and network organizations. Describe each and tell where each may be most appropriate. What problems is each trying to correct? What new problems may arise? What do they all have in common?
3. What are some HR issues in designing and managing teams?
4. How can an organization try to ensure that the social influences in work groups are directed toward positive organization objectives?
5. Contrast the perspectives of scientific management and human relations.
6. Give some concrete examples of the kind of job information necessary for the paying of people. Do the same for a training program.
7. What is the critical advantage of quantitative job analysis? Why is this important?
8. Describe the interaction between external pressures, organization-level factors, and work-level factors.

## YOUR TURN
### Astra-Merck

Traditionally, a drug company's approach to marketing and selling has mainly focused on the physician as an independent customer, with the size of the sales force based on the number of physicians, the number of calls per day, and the number of working days per year. If Astra-Merck were to use this approach, it would require 2,500 customer representatives to service accounts and 24 specialty sales people. But A–M's analysis of external conditions indicated that the influence of physicians is on the decline. Although an important customer group, their ability to specify products is being undermined by other segments such as managed care that control access to products for their members. A–M's marketing and sales organizations for the rest of the century need to reflect the new customer base. How might A–M reconfigure its sales force to adjust to the new environment?

# APPENDIX
# Job Analysis Procedures

## OVERVIEW

A combination of on-site observations, interviews, and preinterview preparation and study is used to develop the necessary job information. An illustrative schedule of on-site job study activities is shown in Exhibit 3.12.

The schedule illustrates one way of sequencing the interviews and job visits. The schedule may be modified to accommodate the complexity of the job being studied, the job analyst's familiarity with the job, and unforeseen operating exigencies.

### EXHIBIT 3.12 General Procedures

| Step | Things to Remember or Do |
|---|---|
| 1. Develop preliminary job information | *a.* Review existing documents to develop an initial big picture familiarity with the job: its main mission, its major duties or functions, work-flow patterns. |
| | *b.* Prepare a preliminary list of duties to serve as a framework for conducting the interviewees. |
| | *c.* Make a note of major items that are unclear, or ambiguous, or that need to be clarified during the data-gathering process. |
| 2. Conduct interviews | *a.* It is recommended that the first interview be conducted with someone who can provide an overview of the job and how the major duties fit together—a supervisor or experienced employee. |
| | *b.* The interviewers are considered subject matter experts by virtue of the fact that they perform the job (in the case of job incumbents) or are responsible for getting the job done (in the case of first-level supervisors). |
| | *c.* The job incumbent to be interviewed should represent the *typical* employee who is knowledgeable about the job (*not* the trainee who is just learning the ropes *nor* the outstanding member of the work unit). |
| | *d.* Whenever feasible, the interviewees should be selected with a view toward obtaining an appropriate race/sex mix. |
| 3. Consolidate job information | *a.* The consolidation phase of the job study involves piecing together the data obtained from several sources into one coherent and comprehensive job description. supervisor, jobholders, on-site tours, and written materials about the job. |
| | *b.* A subject matter expert should be accessible as a resource person to the job analyst during the consolidation phase. |
| | *c.* Check your initial preliminary list of duties and questions. All must be answered or confirmed. |
| 4. Verify job description | *a.* The verification phase involves bringing all the interviewees together for the purpose of determining if the consolidated job description is accurate and complete. |
| | *b.* The verification process is conducted in a group setting. Typed or legibly written copies of the job description (narrative description of the work setting *and* list of task statements) are distributed to the first-level supervisor and the job incumbent interviewees. |
| | *c.* Line by line, the job analyst goes through the entire job description and makes notes of any omissions, ambiguities, or needed clarifications. |

## DATA SOURCES

Sources of information for developing the job description include:

- ✦ Existing documents, such as job briefs, previously developed task lists, and training manuals.
- ✦ On-site observations of work operations.
- ✦ Interviews with first-level supervisors and job incumbents.

Job Analysis Report

Date 2-23-97

Job Analyst C. Davis

1. Job Title Executive Secretary
2. Department General Headquarters
3. No. incumbents 2 Interviewed 2
4. Relation to other jobs:

   Promotion: From Secretary - D To Executive Secretary

   Transfer: From Administrative Assistant To Executive Secretary

   Supervision received From President and/or Chairman of the Board. Works under minimal supervision.

   Supervision given Regularly to other clerical personnel.
5. Summary of Job:

   Personal Secretary to President and/or Chairman of the Board.
   Exercises discretion in handling confidential and specialized information, screening telephone calls and letters, arranging meetings and travel schedules, and handling inquiries during superior's absence.
6. Equipment used: Typewriter, computer, and telephone.

   Working conditions:

   Hazards (list): N/A

   Work space and quarters: Office environment

   Noise exposure: None

   Lighting: Good

   Temperature: Regulated office environment

   Miscellaneous: —

   Job training:

   A. Required experience: (include other jobs)

   Four years of secretarial experience or the equivalent.

   B. Outside educational courses:

   | | Time in semester/quarters |
   |---|---|
   | Vocational courses: Typing, office procedures | 2 semesters |
   | High school courses: Graduate | 6–8 semesters |
   | College courses: | None |
   | Continuing education required: | None |

   C. In-house training courses:

   | | Time in months |
   |---|---|
   | Courses: Basic and Advanced Word Processing, Spreadsheet | 1/2 month |

*Task Statement Worksheet*

*Task Statement:* Opens and organizes mail addressed to superior. Responds directly to routine queries.

1. Equipment used —
2. Knowledge required Must be well versed on superior's responsibilities, how superior's job fits into overall organization.
3. Skills required —
4. Abilities required Discretion. Organization skills.
5. Time spent and frequency of task performance (hourly, daily, monthly) Time varies by assignment. Daily frequency.
6. Level of difficulty/consequence of error Not difficult, some effect of error.

*Task Statement:* Establishes, maintains, and revises correspondence.

1. Equipment used Typewriter, word processor.
2. Knowledge required Understanding of organization and responsibilities of superior.
3. Skills required Typing and word processing, filing.
4. Abilities required Ability to organize and categorize information.
5. Time spent and frequency of task performance (hourly, daily, monthly) One hour spent daily.
6. Level of difficulty/consequence of error — Relatively easy, but moderate to serious consequences if information mishandled.

## NOTES AND REFERENCES


1. William Bridges, "The End of the Job," Fortune, Sept. 19, 1994, pp. 62–68.
2. Marc J. Wallace, Jr. and N. Fredric Crandall, "Winning in the Age of Execution: the Central Role of Work-Force Effectiveness," *ACA Journal Winter* 1992–93, pp. 30–47; Robert J. Greene, "Chaos Systems, A Human Resource Management Paradigm for the 1990s?" *ACA Journal,* Winter 1992–93, pp. 60–67.
3. Peter Drucker, *Post-Capitalist Society* (New York: HarperCollins, 1993).
4. Peter Leblanc, "Pay for Work: Reviving an Old Idea for the New Customer Focus," *Compensation and Benefits Review,* July-Aug. 1994, pp. 5–10.
5. Robert Reich, *The Work of Nations* (New York: Alfred A. Knopf, 1991). The role of the corporation in society is addressed in John M. Hood, *The Heroic Enterprise: Business and the Common Good* (New York: Free Press, 1996).
6. George Milkovich, Barry Gerhart, and John Hannon, "Use of Incentive Pay in R&D Firms," working paper, Cornell University, Center for Advanced Study of Human Resource Management, Ithaca, NY, Jan. 1990; Jerry Newman, "Selecting Incentive Plans to Complement Organization Strategy," in *Current Trends in Compensation Research and Practice,* ed. L. Gomez-Mejia and D. Balkin (Englewood Cliffs, NJ: Prentice Hall, 1987), pp. 14–24.
7. Mary Greiner, Christopher Kask, and Christopher Sparks, "Comparative Manufacturing Productivity and Unit Labor Costs," *Monthly Labor Review,* Feb. 1995, pp. 26–41.
8. Laurie J. Bassi, "Upgrading the U.S. Workplace: Do Reorganization, Education Help?" *Monthly Labor Review,* May 1995, pp. 37–47.
9. Patrick M. Wright and Gary C. McMahan, "Theoretical Perspectives for Strategic Human Resource Management," *Journal of Management* 18, no. 2 (1992), pp. 295–320; Lee Dyer and Gerald Holder, "A Strategic Perspective of Human Resource Management," in *Human Resource Management: Evolving Roles and Responsibilities,* ed. Lee Dyer and Gerald Holder (Washington, DC: Bureau of National Affairs, 1988), pp. 1.125–1.186.
10. R. E. Miles and C. C. Snow, *Organizational Strategy, Structure, and Processes* (New York: McGraw-Hill, 1978); C. C. Snow and R. E. Miles, "Organizational Strategy, Design, and Human Resource Management" (Paper presented at National Academy of Management meetings, Dallas, 1983).
11. Susan E. Jackson, Randall S. Shuler, and J. Carlos Rivero, "Organizational Characteristics as Predictors of Personnel Practices," *Personnel Psychology* 42, 1989, pp. 727–86.
12. Susan Parks, "Improving Workplace Performance: Historical and Theoretical Contexts," *Monthly Labor Review,* May 1995, pp. 18–28; Lucy Taksa, "Scientific Management: Technique or Cultural Ideology?" *Journal of Industrial Relations,* Sept. 1992, pp. 365–95.

13. Guillermo J. Grenier, *Inhuman Relations: Quality Circles and Anti-Unionism in American Industry* (Philadelphia: Temple University Press, 1988).

14. M. Blumberg and D. Gerwin, "Coping with Advanced Manufacturing Technology," *Journal of Occupational Behavior* 5, 1984, pp. 113–30; T. Cummings and M. Blumberg, "Advanced Manufacturing Technology and Work Design," in *The Human Side of Advanced Manufacturing Technology,* ed. T. D. Wall, C. W. Clegg, and N. J. Kemp (Chichester, West Sussex: John Wiley, 1987), pp. 37–60.

15. E. Mayo, *The Human Problems of an Industrial Civilization* (New York: Macmillan, 1933).

16. J. R. Hackman and G. R. Oldham, *Work Redesign* (Reading, MA: Addison-Wesley, 1979).

17. Michael A. Campion and Michael J. Stevens, "Neglected Questions in Job Design: How People Design Jobs, Task-Job Predictability, and Influence of Training," *Journal of Business and Psychology,* Winter 1991, pp. 169–90; John Kelly, "Does Job Re-Design Theory Explain Job Re-Design Outcomes?" *Human Relations* 45, no. 8 (1992), pp. 753–74.

18. Marc J. Wallace, Jr., and N. Fredric Crandall, "Winning in the Age of Execution: The Central Role of Work-Force Effectiveness," *ACA Journal 1,* no. 2 (Winter 1992–93), pp. 30–47.

19. Ellen F. Glanz and Lee K. Dailey, "Benchmarking," *Human Resource Management,* 31, nos. 1 and 2 (Spring/Summer 1992), pp. 9–20.

20. Michael Hammer and James Champy, *Reengineering the Corporation* (New York: Harper Business, 1993).

21. "Friends and Industrial Relations," *Australian Business Monthly,* June 1992, pp. 58–59.

22. Eric Sundstrom, Kenneth P. DeMeuse, and David Futrell, "Work Teams: Applications and Effectiveness," *American Psychologist* 45, no. 2, (Feb. 1990), pp. 120–33; Daniel R. Ilgen, Debra A. Major, John R. Hollenbeck, and Douglas J. Sego, "Team Research in the 1990s," in *Leadership and Organizational Effectiveness,* ed. M. M. Chemers and R. Aymon (New York: Academic Press, 1992).

23. Jeffrey Kling, "High Performance Work Systems and Firm Performance," *Monthly Labor Review,* May 1995, pp. 29–36.

24. *Team-Based Pay* (Washington, DC: Hay Group, 1995).

25. Eileen Appelbaum and Rosemary Batt, *The New American Workplace* (Ithaca, NY: ILR Press, 1994).

26. Paul S. Adler, "Workers and Flexible Manufacturing Systems: Three Installations Compared," *Journal of Organizational Behavior* 12, 1991, pp. 447–60.

27. Edgar H. Schein, "Corporate Teams and Totems," *Across the Board,* May 1989, pp. 12–17; Michael E. Gaffney, "The Dark Side of World-Class Manufacturing," *HR Magazine,* Dec. 1991, pp. 40–43; Robert H. Guest, "Team Management under Stress," *Across the Board,* May 1989, pp. 30–35; Paul Chance, "Redefining the Supervisor's Role," *Across the*

*Board,* May 1989, pp. 36–37; Paul Chance, "Great Experiments in Team Chemistry," *Across the Board,* May 1989, pp. 18–25.

28. Jeanne M. Wilson, Jill George, Richard S. Wellins, with William C. Byham, *Leadership Trapeze: Strategies for Leadership in Team-Based Organizations* (San Francisco: Jossey-Bass, 1994); Richard A. Guzzo, Eduardo Salas, and Associates, *Team Effectiveness and Decision Making in Organizations* (San Francisco: Jossey Bass, 1995).
29. Christopher Meyer, "How the Right Measures Help Teams Excel," *Harvard Business Review,* May–June 1994, pp. 95–103.
30. Allan M. Mohrman, Jr., Susan Albert Mohrman, and Edward E. Lawler III, The *Performance Management Teams,* Publication T91-2, 187 (Los Angeles: Center for Effective Organizations, Jan. 1991).
31. Laurie Graham, *On the Line at Subaru-Isuzu* (Ithaca, NY: ILR Press, 1995).
32. Ibid. p. 134.
33. Valerie C. Williams and Thomas J. Hackett, *Documenting Job Content* (Scottsdale, AZ: American Compensation Association, 1993); U.S. Department of Labor, Manpower Administration, *Handbook for Analyzing Jobs* (Washington, DC: U.S. Government Printing Office, 1972); S. A. Fine and W. W. Wiley, *An Introduction to Fundamental Job Analysis,* monograph no. 4 (Kalamazoo, MI: W. E. Upjohn Institute for Employment Research, 1971).
34. E. M. Ramras, "Discussion," *Proceedings of Division of Military Psychology Symposium: Collecting, Analyzing, and Reporting Information Describing Jobs and Occupations* (77th Annual Convention of the American Psychological Association, Lackland Air Force Base, Texas, Sept. 1969), pp. 75–76.
35. Paul S. Adler, "Time-and-Motion Regained," *Harvard Business Review,* Jan.–Feb. 1993, pp. 97–108.
36. M. D. Dunnette, L. M. Hough, and R. L. Rosse, "Task and Job Taxonomies as a Basis for Identifying Labor Supply Sources and Evaluating Employment Qualifications," in *Affirmative Action Planning,* ed. George T. Milkovich and Lee Dyer (New York: Human Resource Planning Society, 1979), pp. 37–51.
37. Susan Meisinger, "Emerging Issues for the Human Resources Manager Under ADA," (presentation at ADA Act: A Forum on the Progress of Implementation, Washington, DC, January, 1994).
38. Kathryn M. Cofsky, "Critical Keys to Competency-Based Pay," *Compensation and Benefits Review,* Nov.–Dec. 1993, pp. 46–52; Lyle Spencer and Signe Spencer, *Competence at Work* (New York: John Wiley 1993).

# Employee Characteristics

Microsoft has become virtually synonymous with personal computing. Your PC probably has Microsoft software. But what about Microsoft's people? Imagine that Bill Gates asked you, "What do I need to know about the employees at Microsoft to be sure that we are achieving our goal of having the best workforce in the world?" What employee characteristics would you recommend that he measure?

You might recommend measuring employee performance. Microsoft employees are legendary for their "maniacal work ethic," reinforced by a number of legends:[1]

- Lapping in the parking lot. Employees park closest to the building in order of who arrives first. I "lap" you if my car is closer to the building when you arrive *and* when you return the next day.
- Sleeping under desks. Typical offices have couches or overstuffed chairs, but the really tough folks, such as Bill Gates, take a nap under their desks and go right back to work.
- "Red-Eye" Travelers. Scott Oki launched 20 international subsidiaries by flying over 250,000 miles per year for six years.

Are these examples of superior performance? Would you assess performance by comparing people to standards like these, to each other (perhaps using ranking), or by comparing their achievements to goals? What should be measured—effort, behaviors, accomplishments, knowledge, leadership, dependability, or something else? One common Microsoft belief is that "the best way to solve a problem is to give it to the smartest person you can find, tell them to focus on nothing else until the problem is solved, and hold them personally accountable for results." This sounds good, but if the problem is not completely under the person's control, perhaps effort or behaviors should also be measured. Who should appraise performance—the supervisor, the employees' peers, the employees themselves, or some combination? Would you monitor employees' "private" behaviors such as smoking, drug use, romance in the office, or E-mail? Finally, how would you communicate with employees about their performance?

What about employee attitudes and opinions? These can offer important clues to employees' likelihood of leaving and their willingness to "go the extra mile." How would you measure attitudes and opinions? At Microsoft, they ask employees if they agree with the following statement: "I am fully committed to my work, and often do more than I have to do. My job is important to me and I am willing to give a lot for it." Across six major divisions, the lowest proportion of employees agreeing with this was 81 percent. Would you rely on this question, send out surveys with other questions, or interview employees? How could you ensure that employee opinions were honest?

## EMPLOYEE CHARACTERISTICS

Previous chapters showed how managers gather information about the organization's external environment, its structure, and its work characteristics. This information helps them make better HR decisions. In this chapter, we consider information about the people inside the organization. A huge variety of individual characteristics could be measured, and sometimes the list seems overwhelming. For instance, consider the effect of a Japanese shoe manufacturer's invention. This machine determines the dimensions of a person's foot by using laser beams and then sends those measurements to a computerized production line that cuts, sews, and glues the leather pieces together to make a custom-fitted shoe. When we told human resource managers about this, they said, "I hope my organization doesn't find out, or we'll have to add foot size to the employee files." Sometimes, it's tempting to measure everything, but that's costly and often wasteful. So, what should we measure and how?

Prior chapters have already introduced some employee characteristics, such as demographics and competencies. Later chapters will discuss employee attributes relevant to HR activities, such as ability in staffing or motivation in compensation. Here, we focus on two employee attributes that span many activities: performance and attitudes.

### Performance

Performance reflects the organization's success, so it is perhaps the most obvious employee characteristic to measure. Employee performance is fundamental to other HR activities, such as who to hire, promote, lay off, and reward. Thus, this chapter describes performance measurement in some detail. Closely related to performance is employee absence. Even very good performers provide little value if they don't come to work regularly. So, this chapter also discusses how to measure absence and what causes it.

### Attitudes and Opinions

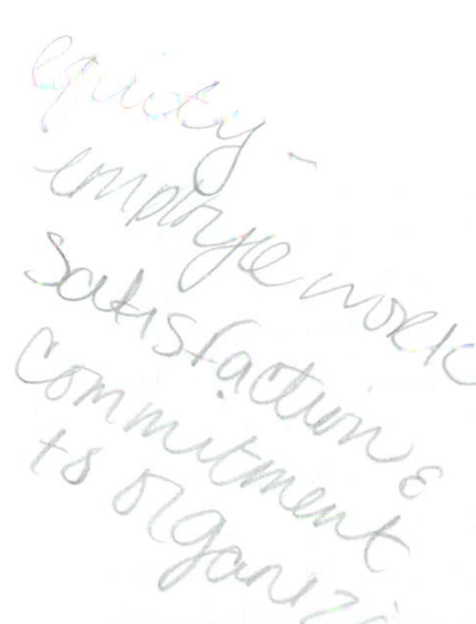

Employee performance reflects mainly the *efficiency* objectives of the organization, but *equity* objectives are also key to the diagnostic approach. A key measure of equity is employee work satisfaction and commitment to the organization. Low employee morale may signal future behavior problems, so tracking employee attitudes is also related to efficiency.

Employee performance, attendance, attitudes, and opinions are only a few of the employee characteristics that support HR decisions. While focusing on specific HR activities, later chapters describe the characteristics most relevant to each activity. Skills and abilities are relevant to recruiting and hiring. Motivation is relevant to pay. Characteristics indicating family obligations (such as aging parents or small children) are relevant to labor and employee relations.

Next, we explore how organizations know if employees are getting the job done.

## PERFORMANCE

Performance assessment tries to give employees the feedback (information about their performance) they need to improve, without diminishing their

**EXHIBIT 4.1** Six Key Questions in Performance Assessment

**Why** assess performance?
**What** performance to assess?
**How** to assess performance?
**Who** should assess performance?
**When** to assess performance?
**How to communicate** performance assessments?

*Performance assessment,* or *performance appraisal,* is the process that measures employee performance. *Employee performance* is the degree to which employees accomplish work requirements.

independence and motivation to do a good job. Designing and implementing performance assessment systems requires answering five key questions, as shown in Exhibit 4.1.

## Why Measure Performance, a "Deadly Disease"?

Must an organization measure employee performance? Many suggest that performance measurement does little good and may cause great harm. W. Edwards Deming, an expert on quality whose teachings have shaped organizations in Japan and worldwide, calls performance appraisal one of the seven deadly diseases afflicting American management practice. He views performance ratings as "a lottery, with individual ratings emanating from random factors outside individual control; therefore, performance appraisal is an affliction that should be 'purged from the earth.'"[2] Managers in one study perceived no consequences or any practical value in conducting formal performance appraisals.[3] Companies such as Ceridian Corporation and Wisconsin Power & Light dropped routine reviews for everyone except the "bad apples."[4] Also, performance assessment has costs to develop the system, to have managers and employees carry it out, and to process the results. Developing and implementing a performance assessment system can cost hundreds of thousands of dollars. Clearly, performance assessment should not be undertaken without understanding its added value.

Yet, differences in individual performance can have a huge impact. A recent study calculated the percentage performance difference between high performers and average performers in different jobs. For routine blue-collar work, high performers performed 15 percent better than average; for routine clerical work, 17 percent; for crafts, 25 percent; for clerical decision makers, 28 percent; for professionals, 46 percent; for noninsurance sales, 42 percent; and for insurance sales, 97 percent.[5] This means that the best-performing insurance salespeople sell almost twice as much as the average performers. When the tanker *Exxon Valdez* ran aground on March 24, 1989, causing the largest oil spill in Alaska, the difference between good and poor tanker captain performance became all too apparent.

### Value Added: Integrating HR Activities

Performance information can serve four general purposes: (1) providing feedback about strengths and weaknesses: (2) distinguishing between individuals to

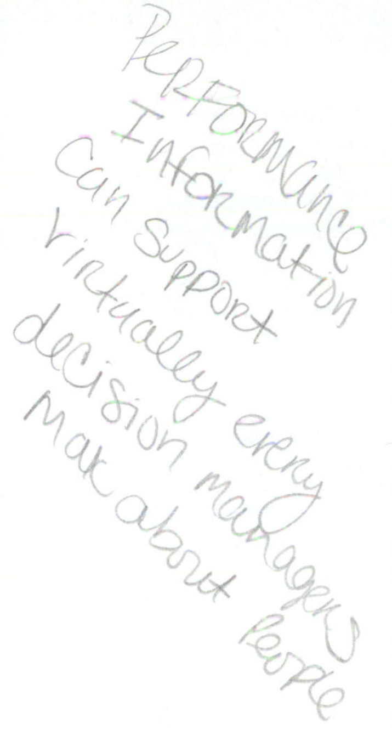

allocate rewards; (3) evaluating and maintaining the human resource systems of the organization; and (4) creating a paper trail to document the reason for certain actions, such as dismissing an employee.[6] Thus, performance information can support virtually every decision managers make about people.

Perhaps appraisals are so disparaged precisely because they are constructed to serve so many purposes. Even when the explicit purpose of appraisals is the same, managers perceive the purpose differently, and they may change their appraisals to fit the purpose—for example, giving more lenient appraisals if the purpose is to inform employees about their performance. However, when performance information is matched to the situation, it can help to integrate HR activities, so that they support each other. Performance, like other HR activity, must be tailored to achieve the right goals.[8]

Performance appraisal, like all measurements, should also be flexible. As perpetual change becomes the rule, the standards and methods used must also change. As you read this chapter, keep in mind that organizations constantly combine and recombine methods, and constantly work to fit appraisal information to organization goals.

### Potential Conflict

Unfortunately, the goals of performance measurement often conflict. You have probably experienced this. Suppose you and a classmate agree to share lecture notes when one of you misses class, but your classmate's notes are incomplete. How do you provide feedback on this performance? You want your classmate to see the problem and to improve but not to become alienated. This is the dilemma—how to provide positive feedback that accurately fits the performance.

Exhibit 4.2 shows how this conflict affects organizations. [9] Conflict within an organization reflects tension between the organization's policy to give the highest rewards to the most deserving employees (paying for high performance, promoting the most qualified, separating the clearly unacceptable performers) and the organization's desire to help employees improve by providing honest feedback. Linking rewards to performance requires comparing employees to each other (or to a standard) and focusing on the past. Helping employees improve requires considering each employee independently and focusing on the future.

### Coach or Judge? The Question of Leadership

Should today's managers be leaders? "We need to function more as coaches and less as dictators," says one senior executive.[10] The Center for Creative Leadership identifies 22 attributes of leaders, such as being daring, dynamic, considerate, empowering, entertaining, friendly, thrifty, optimistic and trusting. However, it's difficult to score highly on all of these, especially when discussing poor performance. How do you entertain and seem friendly when being "thrifty" requires telling someone they will not receive a salary increase due to poor performance? How important is leadership? In his letter to shareholders of General Electric, CEO Jack Welch declared that "GE cannot afford management styles that suppress and intimidate" subordinates. Leaders were assessed as high or low on their business results, but also on how well they exhibited these values. High on both values and results is good performance, an "easy decision." Low on both is poor performance,

> **WHAT DO YOU THINK?**
>
> Suppose you held stock shares in GE Corporation, and you were told that managers may be fired by Jack Welch because they don't exhibit certain values, even if they reach their profit and sales goals. Do you think such a policy is good for GE shareholders? Why or why not?

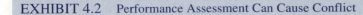

EXHIBIT 4.2 Performance Assessment Can Cause Conflict

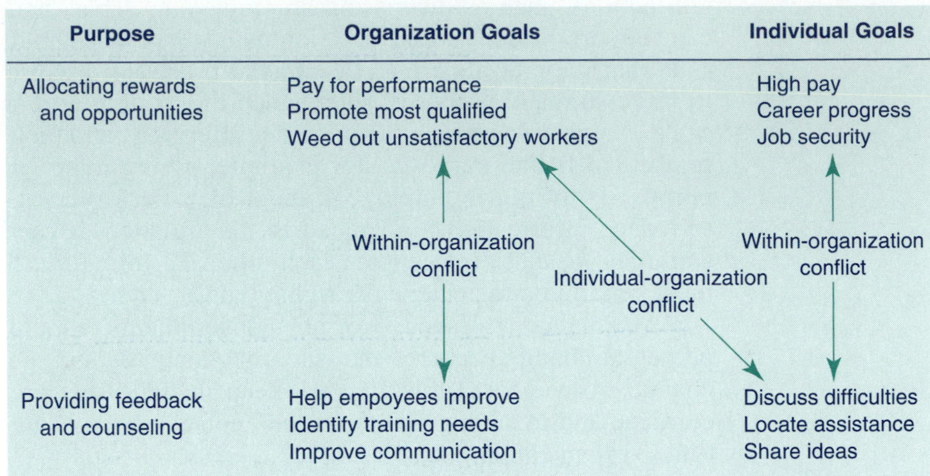


an "easy decision." Miss your results but share the values, and you get a second chance. If you make your results, but do so by force or intimidation, you may be ousted.[11]

### Honesty versus a Good Impression

Exhibit 4.2 shows that within-individual conflict affects the person being evaluated. People want to obtain rewards that come with favorable appraisals, so they may use impression management, either by promoting themselves to appear more competent or by ingratiation to make the appraiser like them more. Impression management, especially ingratiation, does raise performance evaluations.[12] However, if employees need help with problems, they must honestly share their difficulties. Painting too rosy a picture may prevent getting needed assistance, but sharing too many problems may give the impression that they can't do their jobs.

### Accuracy versus Inflation

The final conflict shown in Exhibit 4.2 exists between the individual and the organization, because the individual's goals of obtaining high rewards conflict with both of the organization's goals. Accurate information is needed to allocate rewards and provide feedback, but employees may share only the most positive information out of fear they won't be rewarded. This is especially true for poor performers and may explain why poor performance appraisals are rare and difficult. If you have ever had to tell team members they failed to pull their weight, you know how unpleasant giving a poor appraisal can be.

Despite the cost and conflict, current practice supported by research suggests that managers believe the value of performance assessment outweighs its costs. The next step is deciding what performance to measure.

## What Performance to Measure

A manager in Melbourne, Australia, tells of a new clerk in a hardware store who was confronted by a customer carrying a tire. The customer said, "This tire is defective. Look at how the tread is separating from the body. I paid $50 for this tire, and I want my money back." The clerk had been told by her supervisor to be customer-friendly, and to make every effort to satisfy the customer. So, the clerk cheerfully gave the customer a refund in exchange for the obviously defective tire. Only later did the clerk realize that the store did not sell tires.

Is this an example of very good or very bad performance? What is performance anyway? If a salesperson sells lots of merchandise, shouldn't that be enough? Not necessarily. Organizations also value long-term customer satisfaction, helping other employees, and paying attention to customers before and after the sale. In the film *Miracle on 34th Street,* Kris Kringle was applauded for sending Macy's customers to other stores if Macy's didn't have exactly what the customer wanted. PepsiCo truck driver Buck Robuck ignored the computer-generated map supplied by PepsiCo, bypassing the map's interstates for back roads and side streets that save time. Was this insubordination? PepsiCo president Roger King praises this as an example of the "ownership mentality" critical to business success.[13]

Many things could be measured to determine performance, as shown in Exhibit 4.3. On the left are individual characteristics. Although not often directly observed, these combine with tasks and organization factors to produce behaviors that can be observed. Appropriate behaviors lead to results reflecting the combined efforts of many individuals. Multiple performance measures are needed. Behaviors reflect a person's attempts to perform; individual characteristics signal the causes of the behaviors. Results ensure a link between individual behaviors and broader goals.

### Citizenship or Counterproductivity?

Performance reflects more than simply carrying out work tasks. A broad spectrum of behaviors determines the value of people to organizations. On the positive side, such extra behaviors have been called organization citizenship.

*Organization citizenship* reflects helpful and cooperative behaviors that go beyond the specific tasks of the job, including (1) helping others, (2) sharing and creating new ideas, (3) being dependable and reliable, (4) defending and promoting the organization's goals.[14]

Sometimes, citizenship may be controversial, as in the case of whistle-blowers who support the organizational value of honesty by revealing unethical or dangerous practices at work. Employees with higher work satisfaction (discussed later) may engage in more citizenship behaviors.[15]

On the other hand, counterproductive behaviors include a wide variety of harmful actions, such as theft, injuries, or violence. Employee theft costs U.S. organizations billions of dollars each year, and injuries cause over 90 lost work days per year, per 100 full-time workers. Like citizenship, theft is related to employees' satisfaction and perceptions of fairness. Organizations also monitor smoking, drug use, telephone conversations, and even excess wiggling by computer operators.[16]

A Bureau of National Affairs study of how white-collar performance was measured found that 93 percent of firms used quality of work, 90 percent used quantity of work, 87 percent used initiative, 87 percent used cooperation, 86

EXHIBIT 4.3 Examples of Performance Criteria

| Skills/Abilities/Needs/Traits | Behaviors | Results |
|---|---|---|
| Job knowledge | Perform tasks | Sales |
| Strength | Obey instructions | Production levels |
| Eye-hand coordination | Report problems | Production quality |
| Licenses | Maintain equipment | Wastage/scrap |
| Business knowledge | Maintain records | Accidents |
| Desire to achieve | Follow rules | Equipment repairs |
| Social needs | Attend regularly | Customers served |
| Dependability | Submit suggestions | Customer satisfaction |
| Loyalty | Smoking abstinence | |
| Honesty | Drug abstinence | |
| Creativity | | |
| Leadership | | |

How can an HR manager help an organization celebrate "mistakes" that indicate pursuit of organization goals, but at the same time correct mistakes made due to ignorance or wrong decisions? How would you help a supervisor see the difference?

percent used dependability, 85 percent used job knowledge, 79 percent used attendance, and 67 percent used need for supervision.[17]

Of course, sometimes, it's hard to tell if an activity is good or bad for the organization. Scientific studies have suggested that listening to stereo headsets and filing formal grievances about work may associate with higher performance. At Motorola they celebrate mistakes "in pursuit of business goals" as learning opportunities for an empowered work force.[18] Thus, there is no single best measure of performance, but there are guidelines. Performance ratings should be goal related, observable, understandable, and controllable.

### Will the Measure Contribute to Achieving Goals and Good Decisions?

The overriding goal is to improve decisions. For allocating rewards, the most valuable performance measures might reflect results. For assigning employees to training or developing their careers, individual characteristics such as knowledge may be best. To weed out the least valuable employees, identifying counterproductive behaviors or results may be useful. Many managers believe that future decisions will reflect increasingly rapid change. Rather than focusing on jobs, organizations "identify, cultivate, and exploit the core competencies that make growth possible."[19] Although Honda, for example, makes many products, its core competencies are designing and building engines regardless of how jobs are designed to do that. The key decisions for managers and employees involve how best to identify and nurture these core competencies. Here, performance assessment might focus either on the skills, abilities, needs, or traits thought to reflect those competencies or on behaviors that use those competencies. The key to supporting decisions is to ask, Who uses the appraisal information and what do they do with it?

> A *core competency* is a basic capability essential for the organization to compete and grow.

### Can the Performance Be Observed?

Performance assessment supports important decisions such as promotions, layoffs, and rewards. As you saw in Chapter Two, the United States and other countries have employment laws that protect certain groups from discrimination, so performance information often becomes a key piece of evidence. For this and other reasons, good performance criteria are observable and objective.

Even flying like an eagle can be observable. PepsiCo wants managers who "act like owners, run lean, and get big results." CEO D.W. Calloway says, "We take eagles and teach them to fly in formation," so the performance assessment process for managers includes an annual performance review between a superior and each subordinate manager, focusing on "what the manager actually did this year to make a big difference in the business, not whether he's a nice guy or wears the right color socks. Did he make his sales target? Did he develop a successful new taco chip or soda commercial?" PepsiCo combines these outcome-oriented appraisals with subordinate evaluations of their bosses, in confidential reports. The emphasis is on outcomes and behaviors, not just traits.[20]

### Are Measures Understandable?

Obviously, raters need to understand what they are looking for, but so should the person being rated. For example, meeting the production quota seems to be a very understandable performance measure. Yet, a popular cartoon in the former Soviet Union showed two people standing in front of one huge nail. One person says, "I know it's useless, but we attained our quota of producing 100 kilograms of nails this month." Understanding the meaning of good performance is even more difficult when it includes providing good customer service, achieving high quality, or displaying creativity. Not all performance measures must be based on simple behaviors, but when both raters and those being rated mutually understand what is required, they are more likely to aim for common goals. A study of financial analysts found that the more employees felt they understood the appraisal system the more likely they were to agree with their supervisor's ratings.[21]

### Can the Performer Control Performance?

It makes sense to measure performance factors that the employee can control. For example, using a customer satisfaction survey as the sole performance indicator for airline maintenance engineers probably doesn't make sense. Such surveys might be appropriate for the flight attendant who directly contacts virtually every airline passenger. Raters and those being rated may disagree about how much performance can really be controlled. For example, college students working as supervisors believed that poor performance was more likely to be caused by subordinates' motivation or ability while students working as subordinates believed that poor performance was more likely to be caused by tools and equipment, task preparation, personal constraints, and scheduling.[22] If subordinates and managers disagree about how much the performer can control performance, the rating system may fail to motivate much improvement.

## How to Measure Performance

How something is measured may be as important as what is measured. Suppose grade point averages (GPA) determine which students are on the dean's list.

GPA could be measured by ranking all students and awarding dean's list positions to the top 10 percent. If 100 students compete, only the top ten get on the list, even if the 11th-highest student's GPA is very close to the 10th. Or, we could compare every student's GPA to a fixed standard, such as 3.8 on a 4.0 scale. The 3.8 GPA cutoff might be chosen because it usually separates the top 10 percent, but the dean's list award would go to everyone who achieves 3.8 or better. Some years, this may be the top 9 percent; in other years, the top 12 percent. Both methods measure GPA, so would it make any difference? Students say it does. Ranking sends the message that students are competing with each other. Competition can get so fierce that books with key exam material mysteriously disappear from the library just before an exam, only to return afterward. The second approach, rating, allows potentially all students to be on the dean's list if they achieve the GPA standard. Rating sends the message that students don't have to beat other students to excel and may even foster cooperation among them.

Similarly, after an organization decides what performance to measure, it decides how to observe and record the information. In Exhibit 4.4 we list performance assessment approaches as comparisons to agreed objectives, to job standards, and between individuals. This exhibit also contains the most common methods for each comparison. Organizations often combine performance assessment techniques. Next, we describe the most widely used performance assessment techniques and discuss their advantages and disadvantages.

### Comparing to Objectives: MBO

Management by objectives (MBO) is like writing a contract. The person being rated and the rater set objectives to achieve by a certain date. The objectives should be measurable and observable. Performance is assessed by jointly reviewing how well the objectives are achieved. A salesperson might set a quarterly goal of 100 sales calls, selling 1,000 units of a certain product, and completing 4 sales courses. At the end of the quarter, that person and the performance appraiser might find that the salesperson made 110 calls, sold 900 units, and completed 3 courses, and the reasons for the deviations would be discussed. Some companies encourage supervisors and employees to set goals that are SMART:

**S**pecific results are obtained.

**M**easurable in quantity, quality, and impact.

**A**ttainable, challenging yet within view.

**R**elevant to the work unit, organization, career, and so forth.

**T**ime-specific, with deadlines to expect a result.

Research shows that MBO increases productivity for both individuals and groups, especially when the goals are specific, challenging, and accepted.[23] Exhibit 4.5 shows the guidelines used by General Electric Corporation for setting "stretch goals." It's also important to keep culture in mind, as AT&T learned when it required production plants in the Czech Republic to prominently display banners reading, among other things, "Work for the Team, not for the Individual." Though successful in the United States, such

> **WHAT DO YOU THINK?**
>
> Admonishing and appraising workers based on teamwork may disturb workers in cultures where "teamwork" was often a code word for following the party line, and for a reward system based on loyalty to a political party, not work performance. If you wanted to encourage teamwork in such a culture, how would you gain the trust of workers?

**EXHIBIT 4.4** Performance Assessment Comparisons

| Comparison to Agreed Objectives | Comparison to Job Standards | Comparison between Individuals |
|---|---|---|
| Management by objectives (MBO) | Physical observation | Ranking |
| | Checklists | Forced distribution |
| | Rating scales | |
| | Critical incidents | |
| | Behaviorally anchored rating scale (BARS) | |
| | Essays/diaries | |

**EXHIBIT 4.5** Guidelines for Setting "Stretch Goals" at General Electric Corporation

- By definition, stretch goals are very difficult to meet. Don't punish people for not hitting them.
- Don't set goals that stretch your employees crazily.
- Understand that stretch targets can unexpectedly affect other parts of the organization.
- Don't give tough stretch goals to those people already pushing themselves to the limit.
- Share the wealth generated by reaching stretch goals.

Source: Strat Sherman, "Stretch Goals: The Dark Side of Asking for Miracles," *Fortune,* Nov. 13, 1995, p. 231, 

banners disturbed Czech workers because they were similar to the propaganda under the old Soviet-style manufacturing systems.

MBO is attractive in fast-changing situations because it does not rely on a fixed set of behaviors or results. Computer software can help make change even quicker by guiding managers to establish unit goals, assigning these goals to individuals and teams, tracking progress (e.g., green is on schedule, yellow is behind, red is critical), reminding managers when to track performance, and suggesting rewards such as sports tickets or dinner for two.[24] Of course the flexibility of MBO may also be its greatest flaw because performance standards can change so much that they eventually bear little resemblance to the original purpose. Like all human resource processes, MBO must be monitored to achieve its goals.

### Comparing Performance to Established Standards

These methods examine the work and set standards describing desirable or undesirable performance. The characteristics of the person being rated are compared to these standards.

### Physical Observation

Watching people work might seem rather old-fashioned, suited mostly for assessing performance of manual laborers or athletes, but physical observation is indeed used for some of the world's most high-technology jobs. As many recent movies have shown, computer users can be monitored by recording keystrokes, reading their electronic mail, and even installing devices in their chairs to detect wiggling. (So far, we haven't seen a "student wiggling" method for assessing professors' classroom performance.) The World Wide Web has made "superfluous surfing" (visiting sites for games, sports, or seamier fare) cause for "disciplinary action or termination" at companies such as Pepsi-Cola and Lockheed. Employees at Olivetti Research Laboratories wear badges that constantly report their locations. Just like Star Trek, managers can call up information on employees' locations at any time.[25]

One of the most controversial physical observations is the lie detector, or polygraph. These tests were severely restricted in 1988 by the Employee Polygraph Protection Act (EPPA).[26] An equally controversial physical performance measure is testing for drug or other substance abuse. A survey of 1,200 U.S. companies revealed that drug testing increased tenfold between 1987 and 1993, driven in large part by government mandates. Ninety-one percent used urinalysis, while 13 percent used blood tests. The average cost per person was $41 in 1991. Apparently, this form of appraisal has an effect because the percentage testing positive dropped from 4.2 percent to 2.7 percent in just one year. Companies that prefer not to use physical drug tests use video games to test for drug impairment. Research suggests that substance abusers report more withdrawal behaviors (daydreaming, absence, low effort, theft) and antagonistic behaviors (filing complaints, arguing, disobeying instructions, gossiping). The legality and value of substance abuse tests continues to be debated.[27]

### Checklists

A checklist is a set of behaviors, adjectives, or descriptive statements. A rater who believes the statement describes a person's performance checks the item; if it does not, the rater leaves it blank. Each statement is scored to reflect its positive or negative impact on job performance. The performance rating is the sum of the scores for the items checked.

### Rating Scales

One of the oldest and most widely used assessment techniques is the rating scale, sometimes a *graphic rating scale* when it appears as a graph or line or series of boxes along which performance levels are marked. A graphic rating scale in Exhibit 4.6 shows some of the criteria discussed earlier. The evaluator marks the box that best describes the evaluated person's performance on each criterion. If desired, each level could be assigned a number, perhaps ranging from 5 for outstanding to 1 for unsatisfactory. When each criterion is assigned a weight according to its importance, every person's evaluation can be expressed as the sum of the importance weights times the level of each criterion achieved. *Summated scales* use more sophisticated statistical methods for assigning such weights to each item.[28] Mixed standard scales give the rater several statements, and ask how typical they are of the person's performance. Exhibit 4.7 shows such a scale for professors.

**EXHIBIT 4.6** Typical Graphical Rating Scale

Name ________________ Dept. ________________ Date ___________

| | Outstanding | Good | Satisfactory | Fair | Unsatisfactory |
|---|---|---|---|---|---|
| Knowledge of job<br>Clear understanding of the facts or factors pertinent to the job<br>Comments: | ☐ | ☐ | ☐ | ☐ | ☐ |
| Personal qualities<br>Personality, appearance, sociability, leadership, integrity<br>Comments: | ☐ | ☐ | ☐ | ☐ | ☐ |
| Cooperation<br>Ability and willingness to work with associates, supervisors, and subordinates toward common goals<br>Comments: | ☐ | ☐ | ☐ | ☐ | ☐ |

**EXHIBIT 4.7** Mixed Standard Scale for Rating Professor Performance

For each item, indicate whether the professor's performance is better than, equal to, or worse than the description:

1. Professor's response repeats a point in the lecture.
2. Professor stands behind the podium.
3. Professor misses words when reading from notes.
4. Professor insults or verbally attacks a questioner.
5. Professor uses concrete examples to clarify answers.
6. Professor varies pitch and tone of voice to emphasize points.

Note: Items 1, 4, and 5 relate to "Responding to Questions," and Items 2, 3, and 6 relate to "Speaking Style."

Source: Kevin R. Murphy and Jeannette N. Cleveland, *Understanding Performance Appraisal* (Thousand Oaks, CA: Sage, 1995), p. 437.

### Critical Incidents

*Critical incidents* are statements describing very effective and every ineffective behaviors critical to performance.[29] Critical incidents can be included in almost any performance assessment technique, such as behaviorally anchored rating scales.

### Behaviorally Anchored Rating Scales (BARS)

The BARS approach starts with a rating scale as described earlier and adds critical incidents that provide anchors for different points on the scale.[30] These

**EXHIBIT 4.8** Behaviorally Anchored Rating Scale (BARS) for a Residence Hall Adviser

**Performance Dimension**

Concern for individual dorm residents: attempts to get to know individual dorm residents and responds to their individual needs with genuine interest. This resident adviser could be expected to:

**Rating Scale**

| **Good (1)** | **(2)** | **(3)** | **(4)** | **(5) Poor** |
|---|---|---|---|---|
| Recognize when a floor member appears depressed and ask if person has problem he or she wants to discuss. | Offer floor members tips on how to study for a course he or she has already taken. | See person and recognize him/her as a floor member and say "Hi." | Be friendly with a floor member; get into discussion on problems, but fail to follow up on the problem later on with student. | Criticize a floor member for not being able to solve his or her own problems. |

anchors make the scale more job-specific and, hopefully, less subjective and less error prone. The example in Exhibit 4.8 shows a BARS for a residence hall adviser. The steps in developing a BARS are:

1. Supervisors identify performance dimensions or categories of activities that make up the job.
2. Supervisors write a set of critical incidents for each dimension.
3. An independent group of supervisors sorts the incidents into dimensions and rates each incident on a good-to-bad performance scale.
4. Incidents consistently placed in one dimension are kept and scales are constructed for each dimension, anchored with incidents showing good and bad performance.

Researchers have developed variations on BARS, including behavioral observation scales (BOS) that assess the frequency of behavior, and behavior discrimination scales (BDS) that compare the actual frequency of behavior to the opportunity and the expected frequency of the behavior.[31] These variations offer some advantages, but no evidence shows the general superiority of BARS or its variations over more easily developed appraisal techniques.[32]

### Essays/Diaries

Evaluators can write essays describing strong and weak aspects of the employee's behavior over time. Essays can be completely open-ended; however, evaluators usually follow guidelines indicating topics and purposes. Essays can be constructed from diaries in which evaluators have recorded and observed critical incidents during the assessment period. Essays can also be used with rating scales or BARS to document and elaborate on the ratings.

### Comparison between Individuals

Did you ever tell someone you wanted to break up because you had met someone more interesting or have you ever heard this from someone else? Such comparisons are unpleasant and most people avoid them. Likewise, in organizations it is often easier to compare one person's performance to a goal or standard than to another's performance. Yet, some decisions require comparisons. Just as most of can't date two people on the same night, organizations can neither promote everyone nor give everyone maximum pay increases. Such decisions require dividing a fixed set of opportunities among employees, so individuals must be compared to each other. Comparisons often reflect only a subjective general impression, but they can reflect more objective data, using the techniques mentioned earlier. Next, we discuss several comparison methods.

### Ranking

Ordering performers from highest to lowest is simple, fast, easy to understand, and inexpensive, but it becomes complicated for large numbers of employees. Alternation ranking and paired comparisons simplify the process. With *alternation ranking,* the ranker first determines who is the highest performer, then who is the lowest performer, then who is the second-highest, the second-lowest, and so on. *Paired-comparison ranking* compares every possible pair of employees, deciding which of the pair is better. After judging all possible pairs, the person with the most better-of-the-pair choices is ranked highest, and so on. In 1994, AT&T eliminated ratings completely for 37,000 U.S. managers because the fostered rivalry and discouraged teamwork. Some complain, however, that the stars don't stand out as well and that feedback is less effective, using the simple narrative descriptions.[33]

### What's the Best Way? . . . It All Depends

It would be simple if there were one best way to measure performance but the most effective way depends on the situation. There is no right answer. The three-dimensional box in Exhibit 4.9 illustrates this. From right to left, the work gets less routine; from bottom to top, the employees require more independence; and from front to back the environment gets more unstable. The lower-left-front corner represents very routine, stable situations with low employee independence, where techniques that compare to behaviors and standards, such as rating scales, are appropriate. In the middle of the box, with moderate routinization, stability, and independence, it is appropriate to focus on achieving objectives (MBO), allowing employees latitude in how they do it. The upper-right-back corner shows very unstable and nonroutine situations, with a high degree of employee independence: this calls for very unstructured comparisons, perhaps using diaries or essays.[34] Your tests and examinations reflect similar choices. Very stable, routine material might be tested with multiple-choice questions or mathematical problems. Moderately stable, changeable material might be tested with short-answer questions that give students some leeway in the language they use. Finally, less structured topics such as ethics, values, and opinions might best be tested using essays or papers, and imposing little structure on students. In organizations, a mix of different methods may be used to get a more complete picture.

EXHIBIT 4.9 How Characteristics of the Work, the Employees, and the Environment Affect Performance Assessment Methods

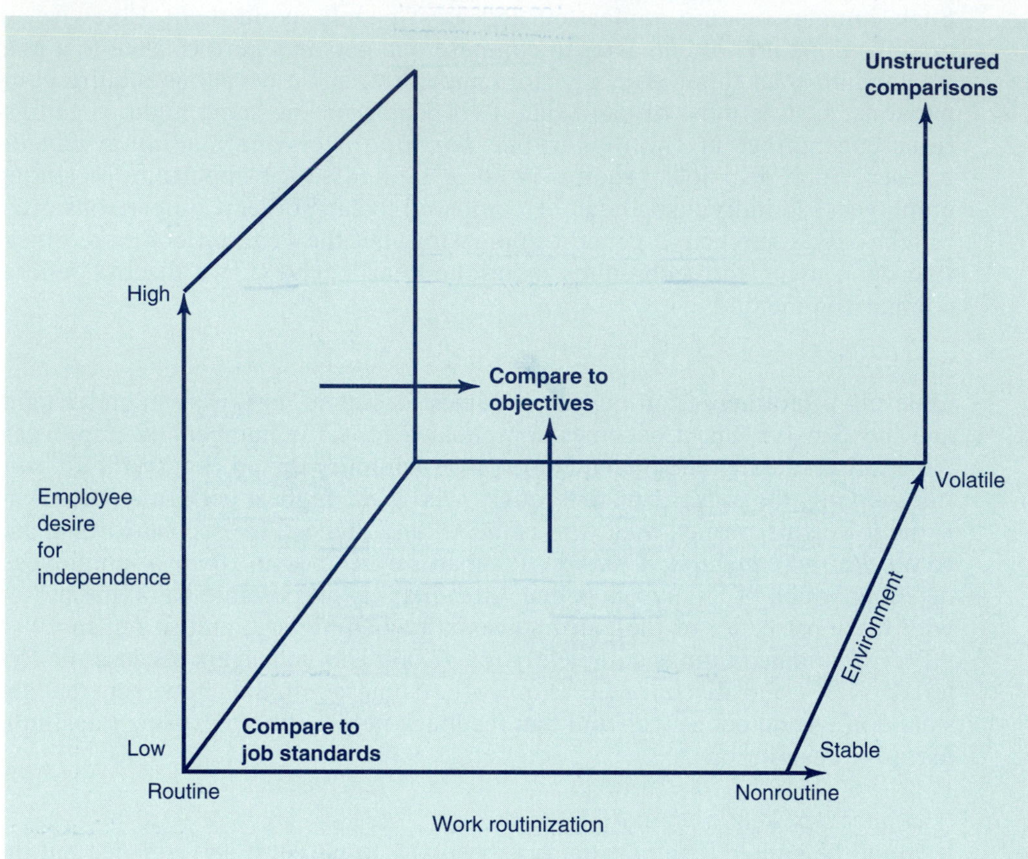


## Who Should Judge Performance?

What if you could decide your own grade in this course? Many students would leap at the chance to give themselves *A*s regardless of their learning or test performance. On further reflection, however, some students realize that an *A* means little if everyone gets one. Others realize that they would honestly assign themselves a lower grade than the instructor would. Still others simply wouldn't want to deal with the decision. We could ask the same question about having the entire class vote on each person's grade, or having everyone take a standardized test administered by an independent testing agency. Along with the usual approach, where your instructor assigns grades, all of these methods have advantages and disadvantages.

### 360-Degree Appraisal: Breakthrough or Going in Circles?

"360 Feedback Can Change Your Life" proclaims *Fortune* magazine:

> Everyone from the office screwup to your boss, including your crackerjack assistant and your rival across the hall, will fill out lengthy, anonymous questionnaires about

EXHIBIT 4.10 360-Degree Performance Feedback

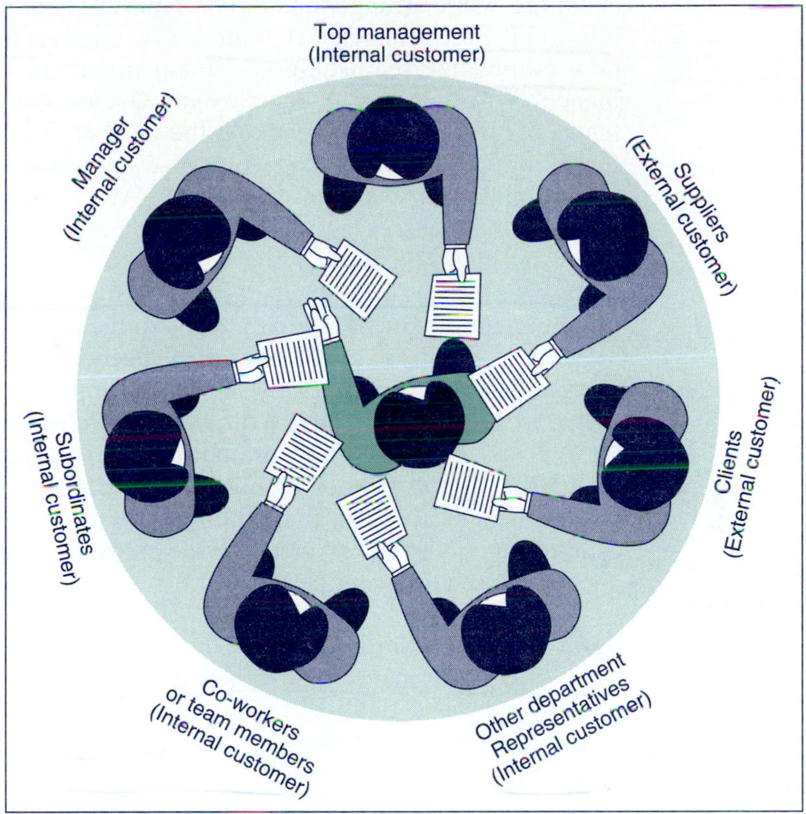


Source: John F. Millman, Robert A. Zawacki, Carol Norman, Lynda Powell, and Jay Kirksey, "Companies Evaluate Employees from All Perspectives," *Personnel Journal*, November, 1994, p. 100.

> you. You'll complete one, too. A week or two later you'll get the results, all crunched and graphed by a computer. Ideally, all this will be explained by someone from your human resources department or the company that handled the questionnaires, a person who can break bad news gently.[35]

Exhibit 4.10 shows the person being assessed ("ratee" in current parlance) in the middle of many different possible assessors. Each assessor can be perceived as a "customer," in the sense that they all need something from the ratee. Having peers or subordinates judge performance can produce insights. There is evidence that managers who receive subordinate feedback may improve over time, that leaders adjust their own self-ratings in line with follower ratings, and that managers from cultures that value uncertainty avoidance were perceived as more controlling and less likely to delegate. The 360-degree appraisal holds promise, but the evidence is still sketchy. Most performance systems still rely solely on the supervisor or higher-level manager.[36] The trick is striking a balance between gathering every bit of available information and keeping the process manageable. No matter who is involved in appraising performance, they should have three characteristics: (1) opportunity to observe performance, (2) ability to translate observations into useful assessments, and (3) motivation to provide useful assessments.

### Being in the Right Place and Time: Opportunity to Observe Performance

Although organizations typically rely on supervisor to observe performance, changing work arrangements give supervisors less opportunity to see all the important performance behaviors. You read earlier that many organizations now emphasize teams. Should team members assess each other's performance? W. L. Gore & Associates and Quaker Oats Company have used work teams for more than 20 years. At the Quaker Oats pet food plant, peer review makes up 100 percent of performance appraisal, with teams making all promotion and compensation decisions.[37] At Chrysler Corporation, subordinates evaluate their bosses on teamwork, communication, quality, leadership, planning, and development of the workforce. The boss summarizes the anonymous reports and then meets with subordinates to discuss how to improve.[38] In China, employment is guaranteed, so the Xian Department Store needed an alternative to dismissal as a way to motivate clerks who performed poorly. They created an award for the 40 worst employees and found shoppers eager to report instances of clerks throwing merchandise, being rude, and leaving their posts.[39] Though less dramatic, many employers make employees accountable to a customer or client, whether it is an actual purchaser, a coworker who depends on that employee's performance, a team, or a supervisor. Subordinates and peers can provide more information than supervisors because they see different behaviors.[40]

### Ready and Able: Ability to Make Useful Assessments

Observing performance is just the first step. Assessors must understand the purposes of appraisal, and gather and report the information in a useful way. Psychologists list three phases of the appraisal process: (1) paying attention and observing, (2) storing information in memory, and (3) recalling and making an evaluation. Attention and observation depend on the "set" or framework of the observer, which is affected by stereotypes, knowledge of the job or rating scale, and the purpose of the rating. Storage and memory appears to be less objective than once believed; people using general impressions ("he's a good worker") to guide what they observe and remember. Recalling and evaluating are affected by the age, sex, attractiveness or similarity between ratees and raters. More intelligent raters may be more accurate, long delays decrease recall and accuracy, and ratings made for pay purposes may be less accurate than those made solely for research or for providing feedback. Psychologists have focused mostly on rating scales and rater thought processes, but ratings may also be affected by organizational pressures on raters and the degree of trust between raters and ratees, where we have much less information.[41] Appraisal training (discussed later) may also improve ability, but it's difficult to train some appraisers, such as customers. Can a computer appraise performance? Not yet, but it can help. Personal computer "review writers" offer advice, store notes, provide suggested descriptions of performance (even inserting the ratee's first name to personalize it), check for "inappropriate" words, and provide a box warning that if you give a low rating, you should include supporting details in case of a legal challenge.[42]

> **EXPLORING THE WEB**
>
> On the web, you can view a description of performance review software at
> **http://www.austin-hayne.com/ea3BMfct.htm**

### Politics and Social Influence: Motivation to Provide Useful Assessments

Rater motivation may often be more important that the design of the appraisal system itself. Has your instructor ever asked you to tell him or her how you "really" feel the class is going? Was your first thought to give the most accurate and complete information that you could? More likely, you thought about what would happen to you. If you want to avoid unpleasant confrontations and increase the chance that you will receive a good grade, it may be best to avoid saying anything very negative—and this is exactly what researchers have found. The more accountable you are for your ratings and the more your rewards depend on what your boss thinks, the more incentive to inflate your appraisal. There's even an economic theory to explain it. Bosses may wonder why they don't get much feedback when they say, "I don't want yes-men around me. Tell me what you think, even if it costs you your job!"[43] This affects not only appraisals of bosses by subordinates, but also works in the other direction. Seventy-six percent of U.S. managers admitted they softened their ratings to avoid discouraging someone, to avoid conflicts, to encourage subordinates when pay raises were low, or to protect someone facing personal difficulties such as divorce. It also appears that this pattern may get worse at higher organization levels.[44] Exhibit 4.11 summarizes some of the effects of political appraisals. The reality of appraisal is social. Relationships matter, and appraiser motivation reflects not just the stated purposes of the process, but its effect on those relationships.[45] The key is to create a system where the purposes of the appraisers, appraisees, and the organization are aligned as much as possible.

**WHAT DO YOU THINK?**

Performance appraisals are often raised or lowered for quite understandable reasons, even though this lowers their accuracy. If you were advising a manager or employee, how would you help them understand the value of being accurate in their appraisal? How would you create a situation to reduce the pressure to "adjust" appraisals for expediency?

### Errors in Performance Assessment

Errors and biases in performance ratings have been widely studied. Extreme errors that lead to wrong decisions can reduce the value of an appraisal system. The most frequently studied errors are halo, leniency, severity, and central tendency. *Halo* error is when a general impression causes similar ratings on different dimensions, such as rating someone high on job knowledge because they have good social skills.[46] (When this kind of error lowers ratings, some call it *horns* error.) *Leniency* error is giving overly favorable ratings to an entire group. Author Garrison Keillor tells of Lake Woebegone, where "all the women are strong, all the men are good looking, and all the children are above average." *Severity* error is the opposite. One study found that subordinates gave harsher ratings to managers who they thought were pushing them harder than their peers.[47] *Central tendency* error is incorrectly giving all ratings near the middle of the scale (e.g., when an instructor gives grades only between B– and B+), despite large differences in student performance. Age, attractiveness, race, and similarity to the person being appraised also affect ratings. However, despite all the attention given to rating "errors," they may often reflect the actual situation. Reality isn't always free of central tendency.[48]

### Can Ability and Motivation Be Improved? Training and Rewarding Appraisers

Most large U.S. organizations train their performance appraisers. Rater training might involve *error training*, which helps raters become aware of the errors

**EXHIBIT 4.11** Politics in Executive Appraisals: Five Main Themes

1. The higher one rises in the organization, the more political the appraisal process becomes.
2. Because of the dynamic, ambiguous nature of managerial work, appraisals are susceptible to political manipulation.
3. Performance is not necessarily the bottom line in the executive appraisal process; ratings are affected by:
   - The boss's agenda.
   - The "reputation" factor.
   - The organization's current political climate.
4. Senior executives have extraordinary latitude in evaluating subordinate executives' performance; this can lead to pitfalls:
   - Superiors fail to set meaningful performance goals and standards.
   - No communication about the desired style and means of accomplishing goals.
   - The "good, but not good enough" syndrome, as an attempt to foster continuous improvement.
5. Appraisals used as a "political tool" to control people and resources.

Source: Dennis A. Gioia and Clinton O. Longenecker, "The Politics of Executive Appraisal," *Organizational Dynamics* 22, Winter 1994, p. 50. Reprinted by permission of the publisher, from Organization Dynamics, Winter 1994. American Management Association, New York. 

discussed above; *performance dimension training,* which helps raters become aware of different performance dimensions, so they avoid making only one global rating; *frame-of-reference training,* which not only defines dimensions, but also provides critical incidents, practice and feedback on how closely the rater's use of the dimensions and standards fits with expert raters; and *behavioral observation training,* which strives to improve the way behaviors are observed, not how they are evaluated. One research review found that error training did reduce errors, but an emphasis on "one best rating distribution" reduced accuracy. A combination of training approaches was most effective.[49] Considering the importance of the performance feedback, it may make sense to train ratees how best to use performance information.

## Timing Is Everything: When to Assess Performance

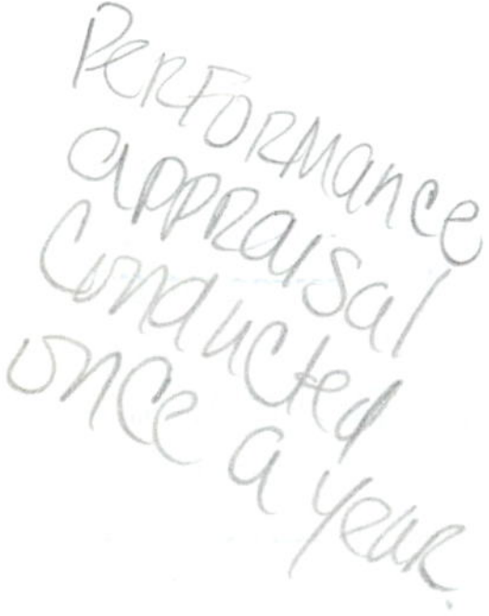

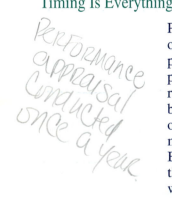

Performance appraisals are usually conducted once a year, often all at once, or on the anniversary of the date the employee was hired. More frequent appraisals may improve accuracy by reducing memory lapses and linking appraisals to key events. Students usually prefer feedback throughout the course, rather than one final grade. But too frequent appraisals are time-consuming and bothersome, especially if there's nothing new to discuss. Performance changes over time, according to research on baseball pitchers, batters, and sewing-machine operators; high performers can become low performers and vice versa. Baseball players also bat better the year before they sign new contracts (when their performance can affect their pay) than in the year after.[50] Experienced workers seem to perform better. Also, those who do best when they strive for maximum performance may not be the best at typical performance, and vice versa.[51] Perhaps the best timing is at the end of important tasks or projects, or when key results are supposed to have been completed.

EXHIBIT 4.12 Tactics Used to Influence Others

| Tactic | Definition |
| --- | --- |
| Rational persuasion | Using logical arguments and factual evidence to persuade a person that a proposal is likely to attain objectives. |
| Inspirational appeal | Making a request that arouses enthusiasm by appealing to the person's values, ideas, and aspirations or by increasing the person's self-confidence. |
| Consultation | Seeking the person's participation in planning a strategy, activity, or change, or offering to modify a proposal to deal with that person's concerns and suggestions. |
| Ingratiation | Trying to get the person in a good mood or to think favorably of the influencer before asking to do something. |
| Exchange | Offering an exchange of favors, indicating willingness to reciprocate at a later time, or promising to share the benefits if the person helps. |
| Personal appeal | Appealing to feelings of loyalty and friendship before asking for something. |
| Coalition | Seeking the aid of others to persuade the person to do something, or using the support of others as a reason for the person to agree and go along. |
| Legitimating | Claiming the authority or right to make a request because it is consistent with organization policies, rules, practices, or traditions. |
| Pressure | Using demands, threats, or persistent reminders to get a person to do something. |

Source: Adapted from Gary Yukl and J. Bruce Tracey, "Consequences of Influence Tactics Used with Subordinates, Peers, and the Boss," *Journal of Applied Psychology* 77, 1992, p. 526.

## It's All in How You Say It: How to Communicate Performance Assessment

Suppose you've been getting *B*s on your class projects, and after lots of hard work you get an *A*. You are delighted until you notice the instructor's comments: "Congratulations, you *finally* got a decent grade." Even the best-designed performance measurement system can be ruined by poor communication. Communicating results based on specific and challenging goals can improve performance.[52] Those being appraised react more favorably to the process and are more motivated to improve when they believe they have participated in the process, when the message is positive, and when the source of the assessment is viewed as expert, reliable, and attractive.[53]

Performance appraisal strives to influence people. The appraiser influences the employee to try to improve. The person being appraised influences the appraiser to give good ratings. Several influence tactics are listed in Exhibit 4.12. Which tactics do you use? Are they effective? A recent study showed that managers use different tactics with different groups and purposes. To get subordinates committed to a task, inspirational appeal and consultation had positive effects, while pressure had a negative effect. To get peers to commit, inspirational appeal, consultation, rational persuasion, and exchange had positive effects, but coalition and legitimating had negative effects. To get superiors to commit, rational persuasion and inspirational appeal had positive effect. Yet, all three group's ratings of the manager's effectiveness were influenced by rational persuasion.[54] To appear competent, be rational. To get commitment, inspire.

### Firing Up Underperformers

When someone isn't performing up to standard, there is usually a progressive set of steps to try to correct the problem. Later chapters will discuss discipline procedures and the termination process. The performance discussion is often the first opportunity to deal with such problems. There is no one best method, but a diagnostic approach can help. Identify whether the problem is with the individual, the job, the organization, or some other factor. Then, focus on changing the *behaviors* that are causing the problem. If someone says, "My boss is too stubborn," ask, "What does your boss do that seems stubborn to you?" If someone says, "I just can't do it," ask, "What would happen if you tried?" If someone says, "That other group just doesn't understand us," ask, "What has the other group done to make you think that?"[55]

Sometimes underperformance is due to destructive feedback, which tears down relationships and reduces motivation. Exhibit 4.13 shows how organizations might reduce the tendency to give destructive feedback. Notice that there are two main targets: the feedback givers' *self-control,* to help them become more aware and responsible for their behaviors; and the feedback givers' *self-esteem,* to help them feel better about themselves and their role in the feedback process. Paired with each of these targets are two general strategies: Change the "outcomes," so the results of supportive feedback are more desirable; or change the "contingencies," so there is a clearer link between supportive feedback and valuable outcomes. Finally, notice that the strategy differs depending on the type of relationship—the rows of Exhibit 4.13. "Control-dominated" relationships include supervisor, teacher, or leader, and the goal is to instruct or evaluate. "Reward-dominated" relationships include customer, supplier, or competitor, and the goal is to impress or meet expectations. "Affiliation-dominated" relationships include friends, partners, and co-workers, and the goal is to advise, persuade, and build trust. The next time you find yourself or others engaging in destructive feedback, you might try one of these strategies.

## How to Evaluate Whether Performance Assessment Works

Which techniques work best? Exhibit 4.14 shows how different techniques compare on several dimensions. Managers in the largest U.S. organizations listed the most important performance assessment goals as (1) employees being rated accept the system, (2) employees have a sense of being treated fairly, and (3) employees believe the results are fair.[56] We don't have enough evidence to say which techniques are regarded as fairest. A study of college recruiting teams in a large corporation found that leaders' reactions to subordinate ratings were not affected by any agreement of the leaders' self-ratings with the team ratings. Leaders who saw ratings from their own team members instead of average ratings across all teams, however, had higher intentions to discuss the ratings with the team, and found the process more useful and satisfying[57] In an investigative division of a government agency, subordinates appraising their managers felt the system was more useful if they believed they had sufficient

EXHIBIT 4.13 How Organizations Can Reduce Destructive Feedback

| Focus on the Source's Self-Control | | Focus on the Source's Self-Esteem | |
|---|---|---|---|
| **Change Outcomes and Outcome Values** | **Change Feedback Outcome Contingencies** | **Change Outcomes and Outcome Values** | **Change Feedback Outcome Contingencies** |
| **Control-Dominated Relationships** | | | |
| Demonstrate that leadership is enhanced by giving constructive feedback | Emphasize source's accountability for the outcome | Reward source for effective leadership; model leadership; demonstrate reward power | Chance to role-play and receive feedback on leadership skills |
| **Reward-Dominated Relationships** | | | |
| Enhance rewards to source from constructive feedback and from recipient's success (rather than failure) | Source pre-commits to a goal, tracking mechanism, and reward; model benefits of constructive feedback; demonstrate behavior outcome contingencies | Link successful behaviors to valued extrinsic rewards; recognize achievements publicly; set goals for giving feedback | Attribute successes to source; ensure a close link between desired behavior and positive outcomes |
| **Affiliation-Domination Relationships** | | | |
| Make giving feedback a required part of group process; give feedback in group forum; model empathy and respect for recipient's feelings | Clarify likely outcomes delay—how long it can take before the recipient reacts positively to constructive feedback | Demonstrate the value of being empathetic and respectful of others' feelings; learn constructive responses to visceral reactions to stress (e.g., count to 10) | Reward team outcomes and cooperative behavior |

Source: Manual London, "Giving Feedback: Source-Centered Antecedents and Consequences and Destructive Feedback," *Human Resource Management Review* 5, 1995, p. 179.

ability to rate performance, and that the manager would use the ratings to improve. The raters' motivations, the trust between raters and those being rated, and whether performance is limited by special circumstances also affect acceptability.[58]

## Does Performance Assessment Affect the Bottom Line?

Research linking performance assessment to organizational results is rare, but the research we have suggests it makes a big difference. One study estimated that introducing performance feedback for 500 managers might produce returns of $5.3 million per year.[59] At a more modest level, think about workers in a frozen-yogurt or ice-cream store. It's easy for them to make mistakes, especially by filling cups or cones too full. College-age counter workers in a Florida frozen-yogurt shop were given performance information (a scale on the

EXHIBIT 4.14 Evaluations of Performance Assessment Techniques

| Technique | Providing Feedback and Counseling | Allocating Rewards and Opportunities | Minimizing Costs | Avoiding Rating Errors |
|---|---|---|---|---|
| Management by objectives (MBO) | *Excellent:* Specific problems, deficiencies, and plans are identified | *Poor:* Nonstandard objectives across employees and units make comparisons difficult. | *Poor:* Expensive to develop. Time consuming to use. | *Good:* Tied to observations, reflects job content, low errors. |
| Checklist | *Average:* General problems identified, but little specific guidance for improvement. | *Good-Average:* Comparative scores available, and dimensions can be weighted. | *Average:* Expensive development, but inexpensive to use. | *Good:* Techniques available to increase job-relatedness and reduce errors. |
| Graphic rating scale | *Average:* Identifies problem areas, and some information on behaviors/outcomes needing improvement. | *Average:* Comparative scores available but not easily documented and defended. | *Good:* Inexpensive to develop and use. | *Average:* Substantial opportunity for errors, though they can be linked to specific dimensions. |
| Behaviorally anchored rating scales (BARS) | *Good:* Identifies specific behaviors leading to problems. | *Good:* Scores available, documented, and behavior-based. | *Average:* Expensive development, but inexpensive to use. | *Good:* Based on job behaviors, can reduce errors. |
| Essay | *Unknown:* Depends on essay topics chosen by evaluators. | *Poor:* No overall score available, not comparable across employees. | *Average:* Inexpensive development, but expensive to use. | *Unknown:* Good observation can reduce errors, but lack of structure poses a danger. |
| Comparing individuals (ranking, forced distribution) | *Poor:* Based on general factors, with few specifics. | *Poor-Average:* Overall score available, but difficult to defend. | *Good:* Inexpensive to develop and to use. | *Average:* Usually consistent, but subject to halo error and artificiality. |

Evidence suggests that firms with good performance management do better financially than those without such performance management. What are some possible connections between performance management, productivity, customer satisfaction, and ultimately, financial returns?

counter to weigh the yogurt servings), and the store doubled yearly profits by reducing waste.[60] Imagine the value of effective performance appraisal where employees handle materials even more valuable than frozen yogurt!

For example, one study compared 205 publicly traded companies with "performance management" to 232 such companies without "performance management." Performance management was indicated by setting explicit expectations, coaching and feedback, feedback, and performance-based rewards. Exhibit 4.15 shows a comparison between the two sets of companies on key financial and productivity measures. While encouraging, such results don't necessarily mean that performance management caused the returns. It could be the other way around. Still, the associations are suggestive.

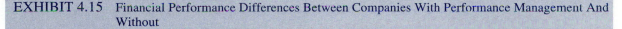

EXHIBIT 4.15 Financial Performance Differences Between Companies With Performance Management And Without

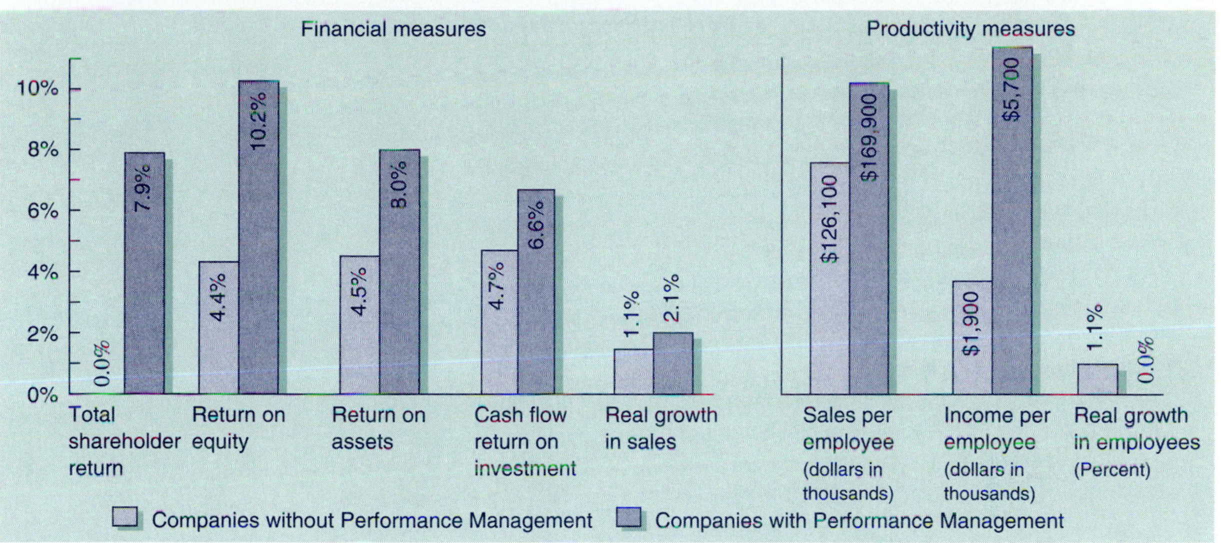


Source: Danielle MCDonald and Abbie Smith, "Performance Management and Business Results", *Compensation and Benefits Review,* January–February, 1995, p. 61. Reprinted by permission of the publisher, from Compensation and Benefits Review, January–February, 1995. American Management Association, New York. 

## Two Sides to Every Story: Handling Disagreements

Chapter Sixteen on employee relations discusses discipline and conflict in the workplace. Most organizations have methods to resolve disagreements about performance ratings. Sixty-four percent of large U.S. companies have at least an informal system, while 25 percent have a formal process. Only 10 percent have no appeals process at all.[61] A useful dispute resolution process provides ample opportunity for all parties to express their views, involve parties with many different views (such as employees, managers, and union representatives), and clearly states the duties and possible outcomes at each stage of the process. Some research suggests that the performance assessment process is based more on perceptions of "due process" or fairness, than the quest for "truth." There may not be a single objective performance level. Rather, the important thing may be the fairness of the system, and whether people feel that the process treated them properly. Exhibit 4.16 shows the features of a due-process appraisal system that was implemented in a government agency. Compared with employees and managers working in a system without these features, the employees in the due-process system reported the system was more fair, accurate, and satisfying. Managers reported decreased work problems, greater satisfaction with the appraisal system, greater job satisfaction, and less tendency to distort their appraisal ratings.

## Complying with the Law and Equal Employment Opportunity

No law requires employers to assess performance or compels them to conduct assessments in a particular way. As you saw in Chapter Two, however, when

EXHIBIT 4.16 Improving Due Process in Appraisal Systems

| Content of Due Process Appraisal System* | | |
|---|---|---|
| **System feature** | **Employees** | **Managers** |
| Adequate notice | | |
| Training to develop standards | X | X |
| Training to communicate/clarify standards | X | X |
| Expectation setting meeting | X | X |
| Training to negotiate standards | X | X |
| Training to give feedback | O | X |
| Training to participate in midstudy feedback session | X | X |
| Midstudy feedback session | X | X |
| Fair hearing | | |
| Training to encourage two-way communication in final review | O | X |
| Training on how to use form | X | X |
| Training to conduct self-appraisal | X | O |
| Conduct self-appraisal | X | O |
| Judgment based on evidence | | |
| Training to sample representative performance | O | X |
| Training to keep performance diary | X | X |
| Training to solicit performance information from employees | O | X |
| Training to make supervisor aware of accomplishments | X | O |
| Appraisal form fitted to job | X | X |
| Manual on appraisal process | X | X |

*X = present, O = absent.

Source: M. Susan Taylor; Kay B. Tracy; Monika K. Renard; J. Kline Harrison; and Stephen J. Carroll, "Due Process in Performance Appraisal: A Quasi-Experiment in Procedural Justice," *Administrative Science Quarterly* 40, 1995, p. 509.

decisions such as pay, promotion, hiring, and layoff adversely affect protected-group members, an employer may defend the decisions as being based on merit, rather than the protected characteristics of the individual. The courts examine whether merit is defined in a biased way. John Chamberlain, a 23-year employee and manufacturing manager at Bissell, was denied a wage increase because of performance problems, and his poor performance and attitude were discussed with him. Later, he was fired. He successfully sued Bissel for more than $61,000, in part because no one stated that he was in danger of being fired during the performance interview.[62] Several reviews of court cases suggest the following guidelines:

1. Base performance appraisals on job analysis.
2. Provide raters with written performance standards based on job analysis.
3. Train raters to use the rating instrument properly.
4. Provide a formal appeal mechanism and review of ratings by upper-level personnel.
5. Document evaluations and instances of poor performance.
6. Provide counseling and guidance to assist poor performers to improve.[63]

### EXHIBIT 4.17 Intel's Performance Assessment System

Intel Inc., a microprocessor company in Santa Clara, California, has a comprehensive appraisal system. Sandra Price, a manager of strategic planning and projects, describes it:

"In addition to getting a formal, annual review written to their file, managers meet to rank workers against peers performing similar jobs. A good ranking group is 10 to 30 people, and each individual is ranked on his or her contribution to the department, the division, and organization. A 'ranking manager' runs the meetings where this takes place, keeps people on track, maintains objectivity, and drives the output—a ranked list.

"Before managers go into the meeting, they fill out a short evaluation form to make their approaches similar. It captures what happened during the year—the individual's accomplishments.

"As part of the ranking process, workers go through a rating that measures how they did against the requirements of their job. After surveys found that a five-level rating system equated too closely to an A, B, C, D, E system, in which C isn't as positive, we changed it to three simple ratings—outstanding, successful, or improvement required.

"We also evaluate performance trends—how an individual is trending against his or her peers. Are individuals moving faster? Taking new responsibility? Equal to peers? About as expected? Slower? This trend evaluation is a new element, designed to give people as early a notice as possible when their performance starts to slow down.

"Intel also conducts 'focals'—a point in time when we evaluate an employee's individual performance, contribution to the group, development needs for future growth and appropriate compensation.

"We use past performance to project the future, and ask the employee to decide with the manager the areas he or she needs to improve in or wants to concentrate on over the next year. Improvement relates to defined objectives—we're an MBO company. Do employees have the skills and knowledge that enable them to meet objectives and grow as they desire? The worker and the manager agree to the skills that are required, and together devise a plan that will use both formal and informal learning systems to help the worker succeed.

"We leave it up to the manager to determine how often they meet and discuss progress, and we place the responsibility for improvement on the employee. They own that."

Price, an attorney, believes the comprehensiveness of Intel's evaluation process is one reason why the company has "for its size, been relatively untouched by litigation related to wrongful termination."

Source: Katherine G. Hauck, "Failing Evaluations." Reprinted with permission of *Human Resource Executive,* Sept. 1992, p. 52. For subscription information, call (215) 789–0860.

### Putting It All Together: The Role of the Human Resource Manager

Organizations rely on human resource managers to help them make the choices described in this chapter and to design a complete performance appraisal system. There is no one best way as our discussion has shown. Every performance assessment situation is different, and organizations must decide how much time and effort are worth the payoff. Human resource professionals usually assist with the design, administration, and evaluation of appraisal systems. See Exhibit 4.17 for the appraisal process at Intel, one of the world's most innovative and successful makers of microprocessors for personal computers. Notice how this system integrates the decisions we have discussed in this chapter.

## MORE THAN JUST PERFORMANCE: EMPLOYEE WITHDRAWAL

Performance is important, but a person has to show up and stay at work for performance to have real value. Even the best-performing employees are not valuable if they miss work frequently or leave soon after they are hired, so organizations assess *withdrawal behaviors. Work withdrawal* takes place when employees stay in the organization, but they minimize their work time by being absent, shirking their duties, and socializing with others. *Job withdrawal* occurs when employees leave the job or organization. The most visible withdrawal behaviors are absenteeism and separations. Today's absent employees are more likely to leave in the future, though the relationship is weaker when jobs are scarce.[64]

## Absenteeism

Absenteeism is often punished by discipline and dismissal because it is such an observable and obviously detrimental behavior. The formula for absence used by the Bureau of National Affairs (BNA) is:

$$\frac{\text{Worker days lost through job absence during the month}}{\text{Average number of employees} \times \text{Number of work days in month}}$$

This formula reflects both the number of absent employees and the duration of their absence. BNA does not include absences for jury duty, scheduled disciplinary time off, long-term disabilities (after the first four days), or excused absences scheduled in advance. Absence is higher in larger and nonprofit organizations.[65] However, some decisions require measuring absenteeism differently. To capture the total cost of absence, organizations might include all missed work days, regardless of the reason. Or, to capture intentionally poor attendance, they might include only absence the employee can control.[66]

*Absenteeism* is the frequency and/or duration of work time lost when employees do not come to work. *Attendance,* the opposite of absenteeism, is how often an employee is available for work.

Psychologists have long studied the causes and consequences of absence; they have found that it is affected by the employee's ability and motivation to attend and by on-the-job and off-the-job factors.[67] Study the diagnostic model of employee attendance in Exhibit 4.18. Note that perceived ability to attend can be reduced by attendance barriers such as illness and accidents, family responsibilities, and transportation problems. Attendance motivation is affected by organizational practices (such as attendance penalties or rewards); absence culture (whether absence is considered acceptable or unacceptable); and employee attitudes, values, and goals. Absence frequency and duration are related to work satisfaction, although the relationship is not extremely strong. The greater the proportion of females, the stronger the relationship between absence and satisfaction.[68] Notice how information on several employee characteristics is needed to effectively manage HR outcomes.

Absence-control programs must address the broad causes of absenteeism. Organizations influence absence motivation by disciplining absent employees, verifying excuses, communicating absence rules, and rewarding good attendance records. Dealing with other absence causes, such as family responsibilities, is much more difficult, but very important. Indeed, such tactics can backfire, as employees prohibited from one form of absence may gravitate to another. [69] This may explain why surveyed employers felt that the best control mechanism was a "paid-leave bank," where employees have a bank of paid days to use for any purpose. Once the bank is used up, the employee loses pay for every absent day. If all the days are not used, the employee receives the equivalent of the unused days' pay at the end of the year. The Commerce Clearing House estimated the 1995 cost of absenteeism to have increased to $668

EXHIBIT 4.18 A Diagnostic Model of Employee Attendance

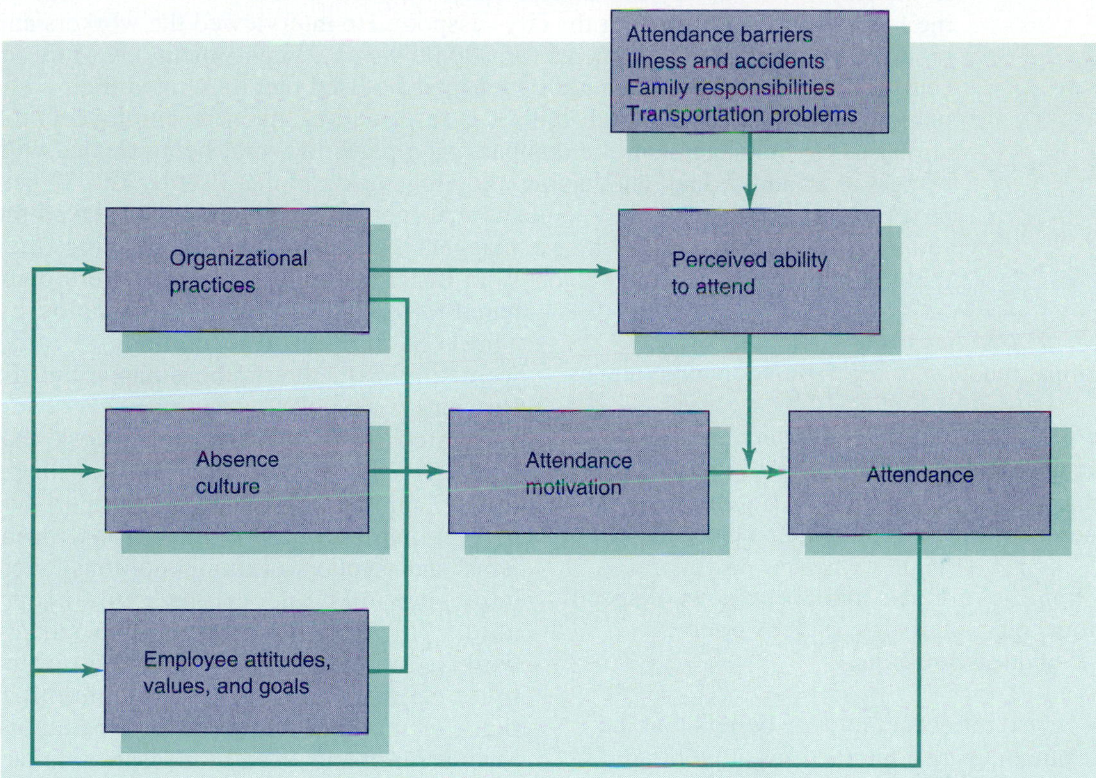


per employee per year, up 14 percent since 1992, and the increase is greatest for small employers.[70] Reducing absence can add up to big cost savings. Moreover, absence and lateness may signal other withdrawal behaviors such as lateness and future separation from the job.[71]

## Separations and Turnover

An absent employee is less valuable than one who attends regularly; an employee who leaves after a short time is less valuable than one who stays. Thus, organizations carefully track how many employees are leaving, whether the organization or the individual made the decision to separate, and how long employees stay. Chapter Five on human resource planning shows how understanding separations helps organizations plan for future human resource needs. Chapter Eight discuses how to manage employee separations, including layoffs and retirements.

Being absent and deciding to quit or retire are related to how employees feel about their jobs and the organization. So, employee attitudes and opinions provide an early warning signal about future behaviors.

## EMPLOYEE ATTITUDES AND OPINIONS

In the early 17th century in Modena, Italy, Ramazzini noted looks of dismay on the faces of men cleaning out the city cesspool. He interviewed the workers and reported on their work sentiments (or, should we say "scent-iments).[72] More recently, a survey of 750,000 middle managers showed that they rated their companies less favorably on such things as information given to employees, the ability of top management, the company as a place to work, being treated with respect as an individual, and having a top management that listens. Yet, 83 percent of top mangers said they believed that morale had improved or stayed the same.[73] U.S., Russian, and Chinese mangers were asked to rank the things they thought their subordinates wanted from their jobs, and the results were compared to the actual rankings of employees. The U.S. and Chinese managers' ranks were similar to their subordinates, but the Russians were not. Russian managers overestimated the importance of "work that keeps you interested" and "feeling in on things," and underestimated the importance of "sympathetic help with personal problems" and "good working conditions." Perhaps such misconceptions explain why about 75 percent of companies survey workers' attitudes and opinions, motivated by concerns about morale, communications, or increasing absence or separations. Such assessments usually measure satisfaction, commitment, and/or opinions.[74]

*Job satisfaction* is a pleasurable or positive emotional reaction to a person's job experiences.[75]

*Organizational commitment* is a strong belief in the organization's goals and values, a willingness to exert considerable effort on behalf of the organization, and a strong desire to remain a member of the organization.[76]

*Employee opinions* are personal evaluations of specific organizational characteristics, such as policies, procedures, and relationships.

*Perceived justice* reflects employee beliefs that the procedure, outcomes and interactions at work are fair.

The question in Exhibit 4.19 appears frequently in research measuring job satisfaction, though we've seldom actually seen people with these expressions on their faces.

Many organizations assess employee attitudes and opinions as indicators of an attractive and equitable workplace. Others track attitudes and opinions to provide an early warning of productivity-related behaviors. An avalanche of studies provides little evidence that making employees satisfied necessarily improves their performance, but satisfaction does affect individual citizenship behaviors, such as cooperation, helping co-workers, attendance, turnover, and complying with rules.[77] Evidence from U.S. schools suggests that schools with higher average satisfaction among teachers and/or students also have higher student academic achievement, standardized test scores, retention rates, attendance, and teacher tenure; though this does not provide that satisfaction caused the higher school performance.[78]

People seem to have certain predispositions to be happy or sad; and happy people tend to be more satisfied with work and life.[79] In *Winnie the Pooh* by E. E. Milne, Tigger is the ever-upbeat tiger, and Eyore is the constantly morose donkey. Some evidence suggests that people's work attitudes are affected by whether they are predisposed to be an Eyore or a Tigger. With students, we find that it all depends on whether the class meets before 9:00 a.m. (lots of Eyores), or after 10:00 a.m. (lots of Tiggers). It may be easier to alter dispositions and attitudes than we think. One study found that giving people cookies and soft

EXHIBIT 4.19 The Faces Scale for Measuring Job Satisfaction

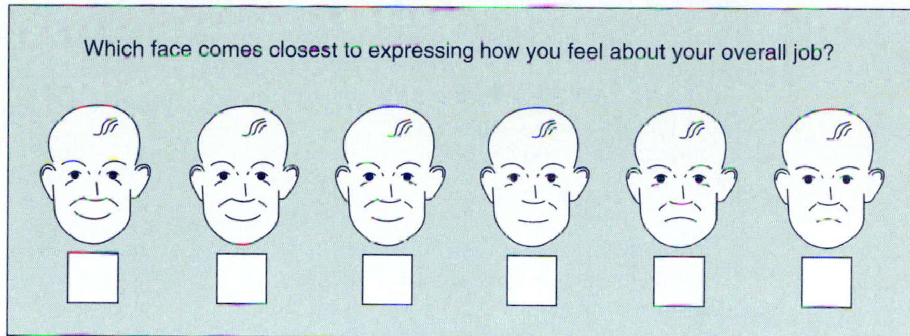
Which face comes closest to expressing how you feel about your overall job?

drinks, and a wind-up toy significantly increased their attitudes.[80] Perhaps companies should give cookies when they survey employees, or professors when they collect student course evaluations.

Attitudes also vary across nations and cultures. Exhibit 4.20 shows the results of a Louis Harris poll of 3,707 office workers in 15 countries; it found significant differences between the United States, the European Community, and Japan. With Japan's world-renowned commitment to lifetime employment, it is interesting that Japanese workers feel the least safe from layoffs.[81]

Assessing employee attitudes and opinions can be useful; for example, Motorola learned its workers craved recognition, and Ashland Oil learned employees find the grapevine the best source of information. At General Electric, the *work out* program regularly brings diverse groups of employees together to work out new ways to do business, based on employee opinions. However, organizations should not undertake attitude surveys lightly. If asked for opinions, their employees probably expect feedback about what the firms discovered and expect them to do something about the problems. As Corning Glass believes, attitude surveys can become "big traps if used to provide all the answers."

## SUMMARY

Organizations can measure many employee characteristics, from performance to absence to attitudes. HR managers provide guidance to determine what and how to measure. Such information can aid in achieving employee and organization goals. Also, the measurement and communication process has important effects. When you think about all the information we have discussed in the first four chapters, it's clear that information overload is a real occupational hazard for HR managers. Managers must have a way to choose what information to use and how to use it. Chapter Five, Planning, Objectives, and Evaluation, shows how the diagnostic model provides this framework. But first, see how well you do at solving a real performance appraisal problem at Ford Motor Company, in the Your Turn at the end of this chapter.

**EXHIBIT 4.20** International Differences in Work Attitudes and Opinions

| Percent of Those Who | United States | European Community | Japan |
|---|---|---|---|
| Are very satisfied with their work | 43% | 28% | 17% |
| Are proud of their company's products and services | 65 | 37 | 35 |
| Say the pay is good | 44 | 26 | 15 |
| Believe management is honest and ethical | 40 | 26 | 16 |
| Feel they can contribute significantly to the company | 60 | 33 | 27 |
| Believe doing a good job greatly helps them achieve their life goals | 53 | 65 | 31 |
| Think management is sensitive to family needs | 35 | 19 | 21 |
| Try to do it right the first time | 67 | 40 | 33 |
| Work too many hours | 21 | 31 | 33 |
| Feel safe from layoffs | 56 | 56 | 50 |

Source: "Office Woes East and West," *Fortune,* Nov. 4, 1991, p. 14. Source of data: Louis Harris and Associates.

## QUESTIONS

1. What are some goals of performance assessment? What decisions can performance assessment affect within an organization?
2. What are the positive and negative aspects of performance appraisal from both the organization's and the employee's point of view? When does performance appraisal put the organization's goals at odds with the employee's? What can be done to reduce this conflict?
3. How could different jobs require different assessment criteria? How could the use of different criteria in performance assessment alter decisions about pay, promotion, and hiring procedures? What problems could be caused by using different criteria on different jobs?
4. What is 360-degree appraisal? Why are leading companies embracing it so strongly? Are there any dangers to such an approach?
5. Discuss the differences between MBO, checklist, and graphic rating scales as techniques of performance appraisal. Would they be equally useful in assessing different jobs, positions, or levels within the same organization? Why or why not?
6. What types of measurement error an affect performance assessments? How can errors be minimized? What factors should be considered before spending resources to alleviate rating errors?
7. Imagine that your instructor chooses to assess your personnel management class's performance at midterm. List the criteria you would use.

Would you try to maximize your classmates' development with accurate feedback, allocate grades equitably, or both? What techniques would you adopt to accomplish your goals? How would you evaluate your system to see if it was successful?

8. Summarize reasons why absenteeism can be costly to an organization. Using the absenteeism model in Exhibit 4.18, briefly summarize what might cause members of your study group to be absent more frequently from your scheduled meetings. What would you do about it, and how does this fit with this chapter's discussion of absenteeism?
9. If employees are doing their jobs, why would an organization want to measure their attitudes/opinions? How can such information affect decisions that really have an impact on the organization? Considering the uses and effects of attitude/opinion surveys, what are the advantages and disadvantages of the common practice of measuring student opinions about a class at the end of the class?
10. In the Microsoft example at the beginning of the chapter, would sleeping under a desk be a measure of attitudes, performance, citizenship, or something else? Would you suggest that Microsoft monitor such behavior?

## YOUR TURN
### Appraising Quality Performance at Ford Motor Company

"Quality is Job 1," the familiar slogan of Ford Motor Company, goes beyond the typical focus on instituting employee involvement teams, reducing manufacturing defects, analyzing production processes with statistical process control, and ensuring high-quality materials from suppliers. As early as 1985, William Scherkenbach, Ford's executive in charge of implementing quality companywide, recognized the critical importance of the performance appraisal system in any quality enhancement effort.

Scherkenback stated, "In my opinion, the performance appraisal system is the biggest inhibitor to continuing improvement in any organization."[82] There are at least five major reasons why:

1. *It destroys teamwork* because each business function and each individual employee is evaluated on meeting performance goals that focus on a particular area. For example, manufacturing employees get rewarded for reducing product failures, which may take more time, but buyers get rewarded for negotiating many contracts, which is harder if the time costs of production go up.

2. *It fosters mediocrity* because appraisals focus on setting and meeting objectives. The person being appraised has an incentive to set the objective as low as reasonably possible, so that he or she can be sure to meet it. Employees implement their ideas for improvement slowly, so that they can use them to meet objectives over several years, rather than exceed the first objective and risk not meeting later objectives.

3. *It increases the variability of people's performance* because most appraisal systems have too many performance categories, and appraisers are forced to make impossibly fine distinctions, such as outstanding, superior, above average, below average, needs improvement, and poor. Forced distribution systems also require placing a certain proportion of employees in every category, which may force appraisers to make finer distinctions than necessary. These unrealistically fine distinctions cause employees to constantly try to change their behavior to get into the next-highest category, even if their current performance is generally satisfactory. The system becomes chaotic because a large proportion of employees are changing behaviors that really don't need changing.

4. *It confounds the contribution of people with the contribution of other resources* because performance standards such as sales, productivity, scrap levels, and so on depend on both the employees' behaviors and other factors such as material quality, equipment reliability, and advertising, Employees may get credit for good performance that they did not cause and may get blamed for poor performance caused by other factors.

5. *It focuses on the short term* because performance goals often reflect an arbitrarily limited period, and the behaviors that can improve performance in the short run, such as using low-quality but inexpensive materials, can often damage long-run quality.

Imagine that as an HR professional working for Ford Motor Company you are to respond to Scherkenbach's comments and recommend areas for improving the performance appraisal system. The following questions may be helpful as a guide to your thinking:

1. What goals should be emphasized in the appraisal system? Which of Scherkenbach's five problems are caused by the conflict between appraisal goals.
2. What are the most important performance criteria in an environment emphasizing quality improvement? What would be the best measures of these criteria?
3. How could the appraisal rating scale be improved to alleviate existing problems?
4. Who should be involved in observing and communicating appraisal results?
5. What changes in other HR activities may be required to make your new appraisal system work?

Your instructor has additional information about Ford's performance appraisal system, and some of the improvements that Ford is attempting to make.

## NOTES AND REFERENCES

1. The information in this section comes from D. Douglas McKenna and Jeffrey J. McHenry, "Microsoft Maniacal Work Ethic" (paper presented at the 10th Annual Meeting of the Society for Industrial and Organizational Psychology, May 1995).
2. Kenneth P. Carson, Robert L. Cardy, and Gregory H. Dobbins, "Performance Appraisal as Effective Management or Deadly Management Disease," *Group and Organization Studies* 16, no. 2 (June 1991), pp. 143–59; W. Edwards Deming. *Out of the Crisis* (Cambridge, MA: MIT Institute for Advanced Engineering Study, 1986).
3. N. K. Napier and Gary P. Lantham, "Outcome Expectancies of People Who Conduct Performance Appraisals," *Personnel Psychology* 39, 1986, pp. 827–37.
4. Joann S. Lublin, "It's Shape-Up Time for Performance Reviews," *The Wall Street Journal,* Oct. 3, 1994, p. B1.
5. John E. Hunter, Frank L. Schmidt, and Michael K. Judiesch, "Individual Differences in Output Variability as a Function of Job Complexity," *Journal of Applied Psychology* 75, 1990, pp. 28–42.
6. Kevin R. Murphy and Jeannette N. Cleveland, *Understanding Performance Appraisal* (Thousand Oaks, CA: Sage Publications, 1995), p. 94.
7. Cheri Ostroff, "Rater Perceptions, Satisfaction and Performance Ratings", *Journal of Occupational and Organizational Psychology* 66, 1993, pp. 345–56.
8. Murphy and Cleveland, *Performance Appraisal.*
9. Allan M. Mohrman, Jr., Susan M. Resnick-West, and Edward E. Lawler III, *Designing Performance Appraisal Systems* (San Francisco: Jossey-Bass, 1989), chap. 1; Scott M. Brooks and Robert J. Vance, "Ubiquitous

Conflict in Performance Appraisal Processes" (paper presented at the Seventh Annual Conference of the Society for Industrial and Organizational Psychology, Montreal, Quebec, May 1992).

10. Walter Kiechel III, "The Boss as Coach," *Fortune,* Nov. 4, 1991, p. 201.
11. Manuel London and Richard W. Beatty, "360-Degree Feedback as a Competitive Advantage," *Human Resource Management* 32, Summer–Fall, 1993, p. 357.
12. Gerald R. Ferris, Timothy A. Judge, Kendrith M. Rowland, and Dale E. Fitzgibbons, "Subordinate Influence and the Performance Evaluation Process: Test of a Model," *Organizational Behavior and Human Decision Processes* 58, 1994, pp. 101–35; Sandy J. Wayne and Robert C. Liden, "Effects of Impression Management on Performance Ratings: A Longitudinal Study," *Academy of Management Review* 338, 1995, pp. 232–60.
13. Dawn Anfuso, "Pepsico Shares Power and Wealth with Workers," *Personnel Journal,* June 1995, pp. 42–49.
14. Robert H. Moorman and Gerald L. Blakely, "Individualism-Collectivism as an Individual Difference Predictor of Organizational Citizenship Behavior," *Journal of Organizational Behavior* 16, 1995, pp. 127–42; Stephan J. Motowidlo and James R. Van Scotter, "Evidence That Task Performance Should Be Distinguished from Contextual Performance," *Journal of Applied Psychology* 79, 1994, pp. 475–80.
15. Dennis W. Organ and Katherine Ryan, "A Meta-Analytic Review of Attitudinal and Dispositional Predictors of Organizational Citizenship Behaviors," *Personnel Psychology* 48, 1995, pp. 775–802.
16. Ira Michael Shepard and Robert Duston, *Thieves at Work* (Washington DC: Bureau of National Affairs, 1988); Mark D. Fefer, "Taking Control of Your Workers' Comp Costs," *Fortune,* Oct. 3, 1994, p. 131; Jeffrey Rothfeder, Michele Galen, and Lisa Driscoll, "Is Your Boss Spying on You?" *Business Week,* Jan. 15, 1990, pp. 74–75; Gerald Greenberg, "Stealing in the Name of Justice," *Organizational Behavior and Human Decision Processes* 54, 1993, pp. 81–103.
17. Bureau of National Affairs, "Performance Appraisal Programs," *Personnel Policies Forum, Survey No. 135,* Feb. 1983.
18. Greg R. Oldham et al., "Listen While You Work? Quasi-Experimental Relations Between Personal Stereo-Headset Use and Employee Work Responses," *Journal of Applied Psychology,* 1995, pp. 547–64; Morris M. Kleiner, Gerald Niclesburg and Adam Pilarski, "Monitoring Grievances, and Plant Performance," *Industrial Relations,* 34, 1995, pp. 169–89; "Celebrate Misteaks?" *The Wall Street Journal,* Aug. 2, 1994, p. A1.
19. C. K. Prahalad and Gary Hamel, "The Core Competencies of the Corporation," *Harvard Business Review,* May–June 1990, pp. 79–91.
20. Brian Dumaine, "Those Highflying PepsiCo Managers," *Fortune,* Apr. 10, 1989, pp. 78–84.
21. James R. Williams and Paul E. Levy, "The Effects of Perceived System Knowledge on the Agreement between Self-Ratings and Supervisor Ratings," *Personnel Psychology* 45, 1992, pp. 835–47.

22. Carson et al., "Performance Appraisal as Effective Management"; *HR Reporter,* "Instant Feedback Assists Hoffman-LaRoche," May 1992, pp. 4–5.

23. Robert Rodgers and John E. Hunter, "The Discard of Study Evidence by Literature Reviewers," *Journal of Applied Behavioral Science* 30, 1994, pp. 329–45; Howard J. Klein and Paul W. Mulvey, "Two Investigations of the Relationships among Group Goals, Goal Commitment, Cohesion, and Performance," *Organizational Behavior and Human Decision Processes* 61, 1995, pp. 44–53.

24. Walter S. Mossberg, "Personal Technology: PC Program Lets Machines Help Bosses Manage People," *The Wall Street Journal,* Dec. 24, 1992, p. 7.

25. Laurie Flynn, "Finding On-Line Distractions, Employers Strive to Keep Workers in Line," *The New York Times,* Nov. 6, 1996, p. D5; Peter Coy, "Big Brother Pinned to Your Chest," *Business Week,* Aug. 17, 1992, p. 38.

26. Bureau of National Affairs, "Ban on Lie Detector Tests to Go into Effect Dec. 27," *Daily Labor Report,* no. 246, Dec. 22, 1988; James G. Frierson, "Labor Relations: New Polygraph Test Limits," *Personnel Journal,* Dec. 1988, pp. 40–45; David E. Nagle, "The Polygraph Shield," *Personnel Administrator,* Feb. 1989, pp. 34–39.

27. Eric Rolfe Greenberg, "Test-Positive Rates Drop as More Companies Screen Employees," *HR Focus,* June 1992, p. 7; Cory R. Fine, "Video Tests Are the New Frontier in Drug Detection," *Personnel Journal,* June 1992, pp. 149–61; Wayne E. K. Lehman and D. Dwayne Simpson, "Employee Substance Use and On-the-Job Behaviors," *Journal of Applied Psychology* 77, no. 3 (1992), pp. 309–21; Peter A. Susser, "Electronic Monitoring in the Private Sector: How Closely Should Employers Supervise Their Workers?" *Employee Relations Law Journal* 13, Spring 1988, pp. 575–98.

28. H. John Bernardin and Richard W. Beatty, *Performance Appraisal: Assessing Human Behavior at Work* (Boston: Kent Publishing, 1984), pp. 68–71.

29. Patricia Smith, "Behaviors, Results, and Organizational Effectiveness," in *Handbook of Industrial and Organizational Psychology,* ed. M. Dunnette (Skokie, IL: Rand McNally, 1976).

30. George Rosinger, Louis B. Myers, Girard W. Levy, Michael Loar, Susan Morrhman, and John R. Stock, "Development of a Behaviorally Based Performance Appraisal System," *Personnel Psychology,* Spring 1982, pp. 75–88; Richard W. Beatty, Craig Schneier, and James Beatty, "An Empirical Investigation of Perceptions of Ratee Behavior Frequency and Ratee Behavior Change Using Behavioral Expectation Studies (BES)," *Personnel Psychology* 30, 1977, pp. 647–58; Kevin R. Murphy, C. Martin, and M. Garcia, "Do Behavioral Observation Scales Measure Observation?" *Journal of Applied Psychology* 67, 1982, pp. 652–67; Jeffrey S. Kane and H. John Bernardin, "Behavioral Observation Scales and the Evaluation of Performance Appraisal Effectiveness," *Journal of Applied Psychology* 35, 1982, pp. 635–41.

31. Jeffrey S. Kane, "Performance Distribution Assessment: A New Breed of Appraisal Methodology," in Bernardin and Beatty, *Performance Appraisal;* H. John Bernardin, "Behavioral Expectation Scales versus Summated Scales: A Fairer Comparison," *Journal of Applied Psychology* 62, 1977, pp. 422–27; Gary P. Latham, Charles Fay, and Lise M. Saari, "BOS, BES, and Baloney: Raising Kane with Bernardin," *Personnel Psychology,* Winter 1980, pp. 815–22.

32. P. O. Kingstrom and A. R. Bass, "A Critical Analysis of Studies Comparing Behaviorally Anchored Rating Scales (BARS) and Other Rating Formats," *Personnel Psychology* 34, 1981, pp. 263–89; H. John Bernardin and Pat Cain Smith, "A Clarification of Some Issues Regarding the Development and Use of Behaviorally Anchored Rating Scales," *Journal of Applied Psychology* 66, 1981, pp. 458–63; Kevin R. Murphy and Joseph I. Constans, "Behavioral Anchors as a Source of Bias in Rating," *Journal of Applied Psychology* 73, no. 4 (1988), pp. 573–77.

33. Lublin, "It's Shape-Up Time for Performance Reviews."

34. Mohrman et al., *Designing Performance Appraisal Systems.*

35. Brian O'Reilly, "360 Feedback Can Change Your Life," *Fortune,* Oct. 17, 1993, pp. 93–98.

36. James W. Smither et al., "An Examination of the Effects of an Upward Feedback Program over Time," *Personnel Psychology* 48, 1995, pp. 1–47; Leanne Atwater, Paul Roush and Allison Fischthal, "The Influence of Upward Feedback on Self- and Follower Ratings of Leadership," *Personnel Psychology* 48, 1995, pp. 48–58; Lynn R. Offerman and Peta S. Hellman, "Culture's Consequences for Leadership Behavior: National Values in Action" (paper presented at the 10th Annual Meeting of the Society for Industrial and Organizational Psychology, Orlando, Florida, Apr. 1995); Mary Kay Carson, "Subordinate Feedback May Foster Better Management," *APA Monitor,* July 1995, pp. 30–31; see the special issue of *Human Resource Management,* "360-Degree Feedback," Summer–Fall, 1993; Robert D. Bretz and George T. Milkovich, "Performance Appraisal in Large Organizations," working paper 89–17, Center for Advanced Human Resource Studies, Ithaca, NY.

37. Brad Lee Thompson, "An Early Review of Peer Review," *Training,* July 1991, pp. 42–46.

38. Joyce E. Santora, "Rating the Boss at Chrysler," *Personnel Journal,* May 1992, pp. 38–45.

39. Adi Ignatius, "Now, If Ms. Wong Insults a Customer, She Gets an Award," *The Wall Street Journal,* Jan. 24, 1989, p. A1.

40. Angelo S. DeNisi and K. J. Williams, "Cognitive Approaches to Performance Appraisal," in *Research in Personnel and Human Resources Management* 6, ed. Kendrith M. Rowland and Gerald R. Ferris (Greenwich, CT: JAI Press, 1988), pp. 109–55.

41. Daniel R. Ilgen, Janet L. Barnes-Farrell, and David B. McKellin, "Performance Appraisal Process Research in the 1980's: What Has It Contributed to Appraisals in Use?" *Organizational Behavior and Human Decision Processes* 54, 1993, pp. 321–368.

42. Edward C. Baig, "So You Hate Rating Your Workers?," *Business Week,* Aug. 22, 194, p. 14.

43. David Antonioni, "The Effects of Feedback Accountability on Upward Appraisal Ratings," *Personnel Psychology* 47, 1994, pp. 349–56; Candice Prendergast and Robert H. Topel, *Favoritism in Organizations* (Cambridge, MA: National Bureau of Economic Research, 1993); Mortimer R. Feinberg, "How to Get 'No' for an Answer," *The Wall Street Journal,* Dec. 30, 1991, p. A8.

44. Clinton O. Longenecker and Dennis A. Gioia, "The Executive Appraisal Paradox," *Academy of Management Executive,* 6, 1992, pp. 18–28; Clinton O. Longenecker and Dennis A. Gioia, "The Politics of Executive Appraisal," *Organizational Dynamics* 22, Winter 1994, pp. 47–58.

45. Timothy A. Judge and Gerald R. Ferris, "Social Context of Performance Evaluation Decisions," *Academy of Management Journal* 36, 1993, pp. 80–105; J. Michael Crant and Thomas S. Bateman, "Assignment of Credit and Blame for Performance Outcomes," *Academy of Management Journal* 36, 1993, pp. 7–27; Michael M. Harris, "Rater Motivation in the Performance Appraisal Context: A Theoretical Framework," *Journal of Management* 20, 1994, pp. 737–56.

46. W. H. Cooper, "Ubiquitous Halo," *Psychological Bulletin* 90, 1981, pp. 218–44; Charles L. Hulin, "Some Reflections on General Performance Dimensions and Halo Rating Error," *Journal of Applied Psychology* 67, no. 2 (1982), pp. 165–70; Bernardin and Beatty, "Performance Appraisal"; David J. Woehr, David V. Day, Winfred Arthur, Jr., and Arthur G. Bedein, "The Systematic Distortion Hypothesis: A confirmatory Test of Two Models" (paper presented at the Seventh Annual Conference of the Society for Industrial and Organizational Psychology, Montreal, Quebec, May 1992); different definitions of halo and a summary of research is provided by William K. Balzer and Lorne M. Sulsky, "Halo and Performance Appraisal Research: A Critical Examination," *Journal of Applied Psychology* 77, no. 6 (1992), pp. 975–85.

47. Carolyn O. Lehr and Jeffrey D. Facteau, "Individual and Contextual Factors Related to Subordinate Appraisal System Effectiveness" (paper presented at the Seventh Annual conference of the Society for Industrial and Organizational Psychology, Montreal, Quebec, May 1991).

48. Bretz and Milkovich "Performance Appraisal in Large Organizations," pp. 10–11; Scott H. Oppler, John P. Campbell, Elaine D. PUlakos, and Walter C. Borman, "Three Approaches to the Investigation of Subgroup Bias in Performance Measurement: Review, Results and Conclusion," *Journal of Applied Psychology* [Monograph] 77, 1992, pp. 201–17; Illgen, Barnes-Farell and McKellin.

49. David J. Woehr and Allen I. Huffcutt, "Rater Training for Performance Appraisal: A Quantitative Review," *Journal of Occupational and Organizational Psychology* 57, 1994, pp. 189–205.

50. David A. Hofmann, Rich Jacobs, and Steve J. Gerras, "Mapping Individual Performance Over Time," *Journal of Applied Psychology* 77, 1992, pp. 185–95; Diana L. Deadrick and Robert M. Madigan, "Dynamic Criteria Revisited: A Longitudinal Study of Performance Stability and

Predictive Validity," *Personnel Psychology* 43, 1990, pp. 717–44; "Work Week," *The Wall Street Journal,* Apr. 19, 1994, p. A1.

51. Linda Argote, Chester A. Inseko, Nancy Yovetich, and Anna A. Romero, "Group Learning Curves: The Effects of Turnover and Task Complexity on Group Performance," *Journal of Applied Social Psychology* 25, 1995, pp. 512–29; Miguel A. Quinones, J. Kevin Ford, and Mark S. Teachout, "The Relationship Between Work Experience and Job Performance: A Conceptual and Meta-Analytic Review," *Personnel Psychology* 48, 1995, pp. 887–910; Paul R. Sackett, Sheldon Zedeck, and Larry Fogli, "Relations between Measures of Typical and Maximum Job Performance," *Journal of Applied Psychology* 78, no. 3 (1988), pp. 842–86.
52. Anthony J. Mento, Robert P. Steele, and Ronald J. Karren, "A Meta-Analysis of Goal Setting and Feedback," *Organizational Behavior and Human Decision Processes* 39, 1987, pp. 52–83.
53. MaryBeth DeGregorio and Cynthia D. Fisher, "Providing Performance Feedback: Reactions to Alternate Methods," *Journal of Management* 14, no. 4 (1988), pp. 605–16; Donald D. Fedor, Robert W. Eber, and M. Ronald Buckley, "The Contributory Effects of Supervisor Intentions on Subordinate Feedback Responses," *Organizational Behavior and Human Decision Processes* 44, 1989, pp. 396–414.
54. Gary Yukl and J. Bruce Tracey, "Consequences of Influence Tactics Used with Subordinates, Peers, and the Boss," *Journal of Applied Psychology* 77, 1992, pp. 525–35.
55. Marilyn J. Darling, "Coaching People through Difficult Times," *HR Magazine* 39, Nov. 1994, pp. 70–72.
56. Bretz and Milkovich, "Performance Appraisal in Large Organizations," p. 29.
57. James W. Smither, Arthur J. Wohlers, and Manuel London, "Effects of Leader Agreement and Type of Feedback on Reactions to Upward Feedback" (paper presented at the Seventh Annual Conference of the Society for Industrial and Organizational Psychology, Montreal, Quebec, May 1992).
58. Lehr and Facteau, "Individual and Contextual Factors Related to Subordinate Appraisal System Effectiveness"; Jerry W. Hedge and Mark S. Teachout, "Understanding Rater Attitudes toward Performance Ratings" (papers presented at the Annual Meeting of the Society for Industrial and Organizational Psychology, Montreal, Quebec, May 1992).
59. Frank J. Landy, James L. Farr, and Rick R. Jacobs, "Utility Concepts in Performance Measurement," *Organizational Behavior and Human Performance* 30, 1982, pp. 15–40.
60. Beth C. Florin-Thuma and John W. Boudreau, "Performance Feedback Utility Effects on Managerial Decision Processes," *Personnel Psychology* 40, 1988, pp. 693–713.
61. Jerry Greenberg, "Using Explanations to Manage Impressions of Performance Appraisal Fairness" in Jerry Greenberg and R. Bies (Chairs). *Communicating Fairness in Organizations* (symposium presented at the Annual Meeting of the Academy of Management, Anaheim, California, Aug. 1988); Jerry Greenberg, "Determinants of Perceived Fairness of

Performance Evaluation," *Journal of Applied Psychology* 71, 1986, pp. 340–42; Bretz and Milkovich, "Performance Appraisal in Large Organizations," p. 28.

62. David C. Martin, "Performance Appraisal 2: Improving the Rater's Effectiveness," *Personnel,* Aug. 1986, pp. 28–33.
63. Gerald V. Barrett and Mary C. Kernan, "Performance Appraisal and Terminations: A Review of Court Decisions since *Brito vs. Zia,* with Implications for Personnel Practices," *Personnel Psychology* 40, 1987, pp. 489–503; see also, Hubert S. Field and William H. Holley, "The Relationship of Performance Appraisal Cases," *Academy of Management Journal* 25, no. 2 (1982), pp. 392–406; David C. Martin and Kathryn M. Bartol, "The Legal Ramifications of Performance Appraisal: An Update," *Employee Relations Law Journal* 17, Autumn 1991, pp. 257–86.
64. Charles L. Hulin, "Adaptation, Persistence, and Commitment in Organizations," in *Handbook of Industrial and Organizational Psychology,* 2nd ed., ed. Marvin D. Dunnette and Leatta M. Hough (Palo Alto, CA: Consulting and Organizational Withdrawal: An Evaluation of a Causal Model," *Journal of Vocational Behavior* 39, 1991, pp. 110–28; Atul Mitra, G. Douglas Jenkins, Jr., and Nina Gupta, "A Meta-Analytic Review of the Relationship between Absence and Turnover," *Journal of Applied Psychology* 77, no. 6 (1992) pp. 879–89.
65. Bureau of National Affairs, *Quarterly Report on the Employment Outlook, Job Absence and Turnover* (Washington, DC: Bureau of National Affairs, 1986).
66. Susan R. Rhodes and Richard M. Steers, *Managing Employee Absenteeism* (Reading, MA: Addison-Wesley, 1990).
67. See Richard M. Steers and Susan R. Rhodes, "Major Influences on Employee Attendance: A Process Model," *Journal of Applied Psychology* 63, no. 4 (1978), pp. 390–96.
68. Rick D. Hackett, "Work Attitudes and Employee Absenteeism: A Synthesis of the Literature," *Journal of Occupational Psychology* 62, 1989, pp. 235–48.
69. Ian A. Miners, Michael L. Moore, Joseph E. Champoux, and Joseph J. Martocchio, "Time-Serical Substitution Effects of Absence Control on Employee Time-Use," *Human Relations* 48, 1995, pp. 207–26.
70. Commerce Clearing House, "Unscheduled Absence Survey" (Washington, DC: Commerce Clearing House, 1995).
71. Gary Blau, "Developing and Testing a Taxonomy of Lateness Behavior," *Journal of Applied Psychology* 79, 1994, pp. 959–70; Atul Mitra, G. Douglas Jenkins, Jr. and Nina Gupta, "A Meta-Analytic Review of the Relationship Between Absence and Turnover," *Journal of Applied Psychology* 77, 1992, pp. 879–89.
72. Walter Keichel III, "How Important Is Morale, Really?" *Fortune,* Feb. 13, 1989, pp. 121–22.
73. Anne B. Fisher, "Morale Crisis," *Fortune,* Nov. 18, 1991, pp. 69–81.
74. Colin P. Siverthorne, "Work Motivation in the United States, Russia, and the Republic of China (Taiwan): A Comparison," *Journal of Applied Social Psychology* 22, no. 20 (Oct. 1992), pp. 1631–39; *HR Focus,* Aug. 1992, p. 2.

75. Edward A. Locke, "The Nature and Causes of Job Satisfaction," in *Handbook of Industrial and Organizational Psychology,* ed. Marvin D. Dunnette (Skokie, IL: Rand McNally, 1976).

76. Richard Mowday, Lyman Porter, and Richard Steers. *Organizational Linkages: The Psychology of Commitment, Absenteeism and Turnover* (New York: Academic Press, 1982).

77. M. T. Iaffaladano and Paul M. Muchinsky, "Job Satisfaction and Job Performance: A Meta-Analysis," *Psychological Bulletin* 97, 1985, pp. 251–73; M. M. Petty, G. W. McGee, and J. W. Cavender, "A Meta-Analysis of the Relationships between Job Satisfaction and Individual Performance," *Academy of Management Review* 9, 1984, pp. 712–21; Dennis W. Organ, "A Restatement of the Satisfaction-Performance Hypothesis," *Journal of Management* 14, no. 4 (1988), PP. 547–57; Mel Schnake, "Organizational Citizenship: A Review, Proposed Model, and Research Agenda," *Human Relations* 44, 1991, pp. 735–59; C. J. Cranny, Patricia Cain Smith, and Eugene F. Stone, *Job Satisfaction* (Lexington, MA: Lexington Books, 1992).

78. Cheri Ostroff, "The Relationship between Satisfaction, Attitudes, and Performance: An Organization-Level Analysis," *Journal of Applied Psychology* 77, no. 6 (1992), pp. 963–74.

79. Timothy A. Judge, "The Dispositional Perspective in Human Resource Research," in *Research in Personnel and Human Resources Management* 10, 1992, pp. 31–72.

80. Arthur P. Brief, Ann Houston Butcher, and Loriann Roberson, "Cookies, Disposition, and Job Attitudes: The Effects of Positive Mood-Inducing Events and Negative Affectivity on Job Satisfaction in a Field Experiment," *Organizational Behavior and Human Decision Processes* 62, Apr. 1995, pp. 55–62.

81. Dean B. McFarlin, Paul D. Sweeney, and John L. Cotton, "Attitudes toward Employee Participation in Decision Making: A Comparison of European and American Managers in a U.S. Multinational," *Human Resource Management Journal* 31, no. 4, Winter 1991, pp. 363–83.

82. William W. Scherkenbach, "Performance Appraisal and Quality: Ford's New Philosophy," *Quality Process,* Apr. 1985, pp. 40–46.

# Planning and Evaluation

At First Chicago Bank, Chairman Barry Sullivan's strategy was to "put First Chicago at the top of the list of the country's great financial institutions." First Chicago faced a constantly changing regulatory environment, increasing competition from new kinds of financial institutions, and pressure to compete with large multinational banks from around the world. Health care costs for retired employees represented a multimillion dollar obligation. Trends suggested that health care costs will rise at 20 to 30 percent annually. Deficiencies in basic math and reading were projected to increase among clerical and operational employees, as well as among future applicants for such positions, making it difficult to staff critical positions. Recruiting costs for professional employees were rising rapidly.

How can human resource managers, working with managers in other areas, help achieve First Chicago's strategic goal and address the challenges facing the organization? Clearly, they must link HR decisions to business goals. Also, the HR decisions must complement one another. How people are trained should complement how they are selected and paid. Finally, the results of the activities must be compared to the goals.

Here's how the managers at First Chicago did it: First, they translated emerging trends and events into implications for human resources (see Chapter Two). Emerging trends in health care costs, retiree health insurance obligations, and the growing gap between the required and available skills of clerical and operational employees were identified. The scanning process, called the Human Resources Strategic Diagnostic, is continually updated as external organizations and employee characteristics change.

Second, they looked at the organization's conditions. They identified the need to become more cost-competitive, the significant portion of costs dedicated to employee health care, and the need for flexibility to respond to changing regulations and markets.

Third, they looked at the bank's employee conditions, including current and future skills, employee performance, and the understanding and commitment of all employees to the bank's broad strategic goals.

Fourth, the HR planners considered options to address the gaps. Could employees pay some of their health care insurance premiums? What other cost-reduction alternatives might avoid penalizing employees for cost increases beyond their control? Would raising the pay of clerical and operational employees attract people with higher skills? Would the increase in the bank's wage costs be worth it? Could other less costly methods of recruiting be used to acquire highly skilled applicants? What about training to enhance the skills of current employees?

Finally, the planners chose the activities to close the gaps. Health care costs would be managed using programs that emulate the most successful programs of competitors. A management information system would track and present health care cost information to highlight the effectiveness of specific programs. Child health care would be provided free during the first year of life for mothers who participate in a prenatal wellness program. The savings from reducing the costs of the complications arising during pregnancy, delivery, and premature birth would offset the additional child care costs.

To address skills shortages, the Bank Mobile visits area high schools to show students a working model of a bank, identify promising students, and give them opportunities for on-the-job training and experience. A corporate training facility was established to consolidate training activity and provide more than 50,000 participant days of training. Classes include English at Work and Gearing Up for Excellence through

Communication. Recruiting was shifted from agencies to direct sourcing, which involves targeting competing companies that employ the kind of people the bank needs. Finding and hiring people is quicker and agency costs are reduced. "Ask HR" is a 24-hour computerized telephone inquiry system that automatically provides answers to more than 100 questions about vacation, sick leave, job opportunities, and training. This frees up HR specialists to concentrate on the most important and complex employee questions.

Do these decisions, the chosen HR activities, work? At First Chicago they track results by comparing their activities and costs with those of competitors, by asking the opinions of scholars and other HR managers, and by looking at the bank's bottom line. For example, consolidating training saved the company $1.7 million a year by cutting out the costs of doing the same activities at many different locations. Getting retirees to pay more of their costs, using more cost-effective health care providers, and providing incentives to choose less-expensive options, saved $2 million in health care coverage per year.[1]

## PLANNING, SETTING OBJECTIVES, AND EVALUATING RESULTS

What would you have done as one of First Chicago's managers? Is there any other information about external, organizational, or employee characteristics you would gather? Which other activities would you consider to address the gaps, perhaps changing the way people are paid? Do the options complement each other, so that the total effect of the strategy is greater than the sum of its parts? How would you measure the success of these efforts—filling jobs, keeping costs down, making employees feel loyal and committed, enhancing company profits?

Every person makes plans, sets objectives, and evaluates results. Your plan includes taking this class and perhaps pursuing a career related to your studies. Your objectives may include a certain type of work, lifestyle, or family arrangement. You judge your progress according to how each step is achieved and according to how well the individual activities combine to produce larger outcomes such as a career, family, and lifestyle.

HR managers work with managers, employees, and others to plan for future contingencies, choose relevant information for making forecasts and setting goals, make decisions, and then evaluate results. After reading the earlier chapters, you can see the huge amount of information that could be used. Increasingly, computerized human resource information systems (HRIS) assist managers to gather and summarize information. Chapter Sixteen deals specifically with HR information systems. Even so, computers can't take the place of decision makers. Today, information is plentiful, but the time and resources to identify, process, and analyze it are scarce.[2] At exam time, most students face a similar dilemma. Therefore, managers must find ways to sort through thousands of pieces of information covering years of employee history and to identify the important information for setting goals, making decisions, and evaluating

*Human resource planning* gathers and uses information to support decisions about investing resources in HR activities. This information includes future objectives, trends, and gaps between desired and actual outcomes.

progress. HR planning does this, both informally and formally at all levels of the organization, virtually all the time.

You may wonder why we are discussing planning early in the book, rather than after you have learned more about the HR activities. How can you understand planning, objectives, and evaluation before you understand the activities themselves? Our decision to feature planning early reflects the fact that HR activities cannot be treated as detached segments. They must hang together as an integrated whole, called a strategy. Thus, you should understand how activities are identified and integrated before focusing on the individual activities. Also, planning links the information about external organization and employee conditions with decisions about activities, the subject of subsequent chapters.

## Planning Is Diagnostic Decision Making

Decisions are choices based on information. Every decision involves expending resources, usually to achieve some goal. You make decisions every day, such as deciding whether or not to come to class. When you attend, you spend your time and energy in class and give up whatever else you might have done. Your decision is probably directed toward a goal, such as listening to a fascinating lecture, learning intriguing facts about HR management, or perhaps getting to meet a visiting corporate executive who will be recruiting on campus later. Finally, your decision is based on information, such as the quality of past lectures, the material assigned for that day, or the rumor that the recruiter is especially interested in people with work experience similar to yours.

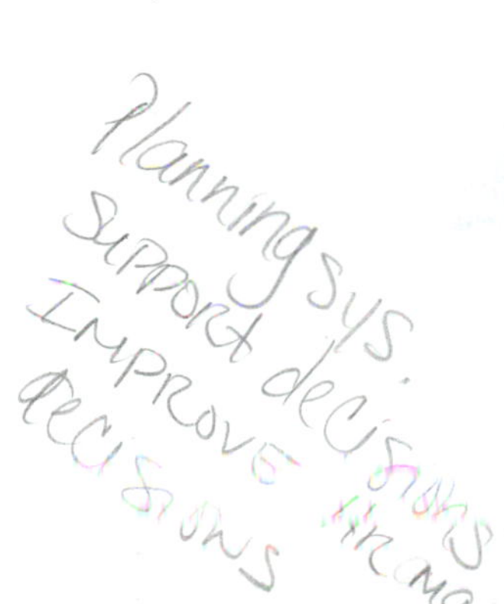

Just as you can't be sure you'll make the right decision all the time, organizations must deal with uncertainty. Information is never complete or certain, nor are people naturally good decision makers. Does this mean that planning is useless? Quite the contrary. Planning systems are needed to offset these human tendencies. Planning systems that support decisions can improve HR management and produce valuable outcomes. Adding value does not require perfect decisions, only improved ones.

## The Four Planning Questions

Exhibit 5.1 contains four key planning questions. As you can see, planning is at the heart of the diagnostic model used in this book.

### Where Are We Now?

Chapters Two through Four contain the vast array of external, organizational, and individual factors that could be used to measure the current status of HR management. We must know where we stand before we can decide where to go.

### Where Do We Want to Be?

In this step, we set goals and identify gaps between where we are now and where we want to be. The largest and most important gaps become our objectives. Setting objectives require deciding what conditions to try to change, and what to use as success measures. For example, is attending class a success if you see only the corporate recruiter? If you also talk to the recruiter? If that person takes your résumé? Or must you get invited to an interview?

EXHIBIT 5.1 The Planning Process at the Heart of the Diagnostic Approach

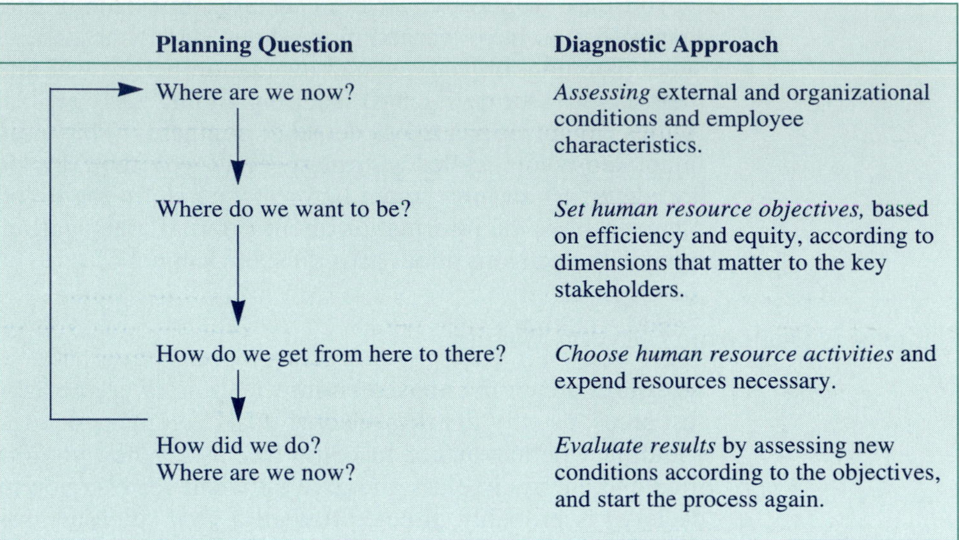

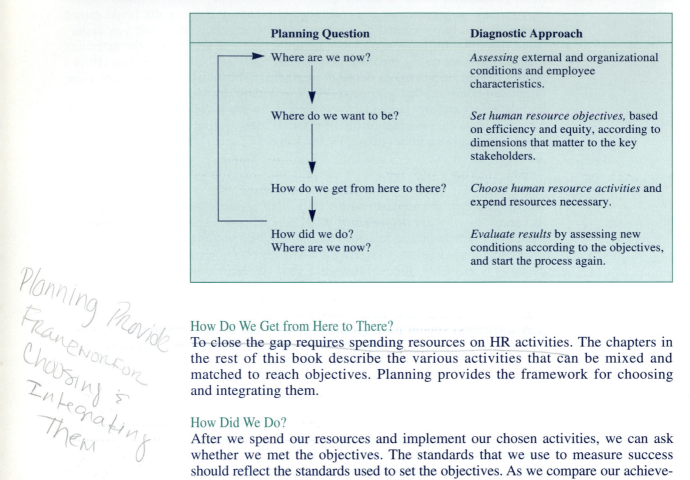

| Planning Question | Diagnostic Approach |
|---|---|
| Where are we now? | *Assessing* external and organizational conditions and employee characteristics. |
| Where do we want to be? | *Set human resource objectives,* based on efficiency and equity, according to dimensions that matter to the key stakeholders. |
| How do we get from here to there? | *Choose human resource activities* and expend resources necessary. |
| How did we do?<br>Where are we now? | *Evaluate results* by assessing new conditions according to the objectives, and start the process again. |

### How Do We Get from Here to There?

To close the gap requires spending resources on HR activities. The chapters in the rest of this book describe the various activities that can be mixed and matched to reach objectives. Planning provides the framework for choosing and integrating them.

### How Did We Do?

After we spend our resources and implement our chosen activities, we can ask whether we met the objectives. The standards that we use to measure success should reflect the standards used to set the objectives. As we compare our achievements with our objectives, we're back to assessing conditions, and we make more plans based on the new gap between where we are and where we want to be.

*Human resource decisions* are choices about how to expend resources on HR activities aimed at meeting objectives. Decisions require (1) *objectives,* which establish the gaps to be reduced; (2) *alternatives,* which are the available choices, each requiring resources and producing an anticipated set of outcomes; (3) *attributes,* which are the characteristics of the alternatives that relate to the objectives and are compared in choosing among alternatives; and (4) *evaluation standards,* which are the outcomes measured to assess success that should reflect the original objectives.

A *human resource plan* specifies the alternatives selected through HR decisions, and the attributes of the standards that are used to evaluate them.

## WHY HUMAN RESOURCE PLANNING?

Planning is time consuming, expensive, and uncertain. It seldom produces perfectly accurate predictions or guaranteed correct choices. Plans are frequently seen by employees and managers as disconnected from their concerns and useless for helping them make better decisions. Some managers describe HR plans as "where the rubber meets the sky," to illustrate how unrealistic they are. Why would organizations do human resource planning?

## Planning Links Human Resources and the Organization

A survey of general managers in large business units of Fortune 500 firms found that a majority considered human resource issues and costs in planning their business, and that the human resource "function" was rated "important" or "extremely important" by 82 percent of managers.[3] As we described in Chapter Three, organizations may choose to compete in very different ways, including innovation, cost reduction, and speed. The competitive advantage an organization achieves depends on its people. Jack Welch, CEO of General Electric, includes the following in his lessons for success: you get more productivity "by getting people involved and excited about their jobs," CEOs must have a gut belief that "people are the key to everything," and you must think constantly "about making every person more valuable [or] you don't have a chance."[4] What does this mean to managers—more training, higher pay, more careful selection, or all of the above? Planning is the process that creates the link. A good HR plan is a working document that helps employees and all managers see how human resource decisions will support the organization's goals.

## Planning Links Actions and Consequences

Without a plan, you won't know whether you're moving in the right direction. If the business strategy is to expand in international markets, some employees (e.g., key managers) should have greater language and cultural capabilities that will allow them to work with and understand customers, suppliers, and employees of different cultures. Over time, you would want to see an increasing number of managers with multiple language skills, experience in non-U.S. operations, and more managers born outside the United States progressing to positions of influence. On the other hand, a business strategy more focused on lowering production costs in the United States may call for production teams capable of identifying cost-cutting opportunities, which may mean gaining skills in creativity, communication, and an understanding of how their work relates to production costs. Without planning, the link between actions and results may be unclear. Staffing might be judged by how fast vacancies are filled, even if those vacancies are not filled with the right people. Training might focus on providing a large number of classes, even if those classes are on topics that don't build the necessary strategic abilities. Compensation might emphasize reducing payroll costs by restricting pay raises, even when this causes the best talent to leave the organization. A good HR plan shows clearly which HR actions relate to changes in people, and how those changes relate to the organization's goals.

Colgate-Palmolive Company has 35,000 employees and gets 70 percent of its revenues from outside the United States, with 500 HR people scattered around the world. Doug Reid, the vice president of human resources says, "Whether you're in Chile or Greece, Canada or Malaysia, whether you're working to implement the new career-planning system, the new succession-planning system, the competencies for finance, marketing or sales . . . you're working toward common initiatives. That's what ties people together."[5]

## Calculating the Return on Investment in Human Resources

HR activities can be evaluated using the same models as investments in new production facilities, marketing campaigns, or financial instruments. Like these investments, HR activities consume inputs, such as time, money, materials, and employee involvement. They use these inputs to create experiences for employees or to change the nature of their relationship with the organization. Compensation activities use money and management time to change the relationship between employee behaviors and their pay. Training activities use money, trainer time, and training materials to create experiences that alter trainees' skill, ability, or motivation. Staffing activities use money, tests, and managers as interviewers to improve the quality of those who are allowed to join the organization.

Exhibit 5.2 draws the analogy between evaluating an investment and evaluating HR activities. The key variables are (1) the quantity of employees or time affected by the activity, (2) the quality change produced by the activity, and (3) the costs of the activity. The bottom of the exhibit summarizes the results for a hypothetical activity to train 1,000 salespeople and give them an extra 10 percent sales bonus for four years.

### Quantity

For HR activities, the quantity of productive effort affected by an activity is not only the number of employees who go through the activity but also how long the activity affects their performance. In the example in Exhibit 5.2, we assume that the 1,000 salespeople are trained at the same time and that the effects of the training last four years. Therefore, the true quantity of productive activity affected is 4,000 person-years. When HR activities last a long time, their effects are often much more substantial than many realize. The common practice of computing costs per trainee or reporting the number of employees going through training ignores these long-run effects.

### Quality

The quality created by HR activities can be measured in many ways. The Adolph Coors Company, Johnson & Johnson, and others calculate the return on investment (ROI) for a wellness center based on reduced absence and medical costs.[6] In Exhibit 5.2 we focus on the additional sales generated by each trained employee who receives the bonus. Based on previous experience, management forecasts, or scientific studies, planners might estimate that each salesperson averages $1,000 in additional sales per year in response to the training and bonus. Another way to measure effects is to examine the dollar value of preventing unwanted employee activities such as smoking, absenteeism, theft, or separations. This approach is called behavioral costing.[7]

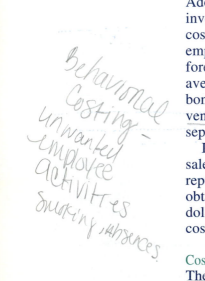

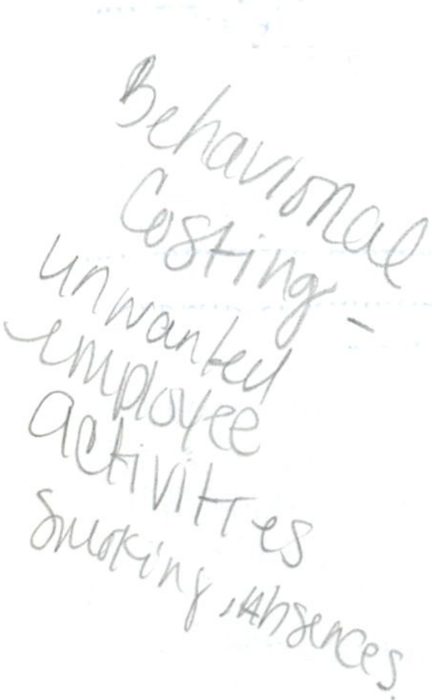

Information about quality increases might come from past productivity or sales records, management opinions, process engineering studies, or industry reports. This information is often not perfectly precise and can be difficult to obtain. However, the value of this analysis is not in precisely forecasting actual dollar values but in presenting HR activities as investments, rather than simply costs or activities.

### Cost

The costs of HR activities are the resources necessary to carry out the activity. In Exhibit 5.2 these costs include the costs of training (assumed to be $200 per person), the costs of the extra bonus (10 percent of the total additional sales), and the costs of administering and managing the training and bonus activity

EXHIBIT 5.2 Human Resource Activities as Investments

| | | | |
|---|---|---|---|
| **Formula for Calculating the Value Created by an Investment** | | | |
| Value | = [Quantity | × Quality] | – Costs |
| Profit | = Number of units produced | × Price per unit sold | – Materials + Capital + Labor |
| **Formula for Calculating the Value Created by Human Resource Activities** | | | |
| Value | = [Quantity | × Quality] | – Costs |
| Utility | = Number of employees and time periods affected | × Increased dollar value per employee and time period | – Time<br>Money<br>Materials<br>Managers' involvement |
| **Numerical Example of Applying the Cost/Benefit Formula** | | | |
| Value | = [Quantity | × Quality] | – Costs |
| | 1,000 Salespeople for 4 years | × $1,000 Additional sales per person-year | – 10% Sales bonus + $200 Training cost + $400,000 Administration |
| Utility | = [4,000 | × $1,000] | – $400,000 + $200,000 + $400,000 |
| $3,000,000 | = | $4,000,000 | – $1,000,000 |

(assumed to be $400,000 over the four-year period). Costs vary depending on the activity, as later chapters discuss. In general, wages and benefits for managers and participants represent very significant costs.

### Utility Analysis

The total utility or usefulness of the activity is calculated by multiplying the quantity by the quality and then subtracting total costs. As shown in Exhibit 5.2 this hypothetical training and compensation activity produces $4 million in additional sales over the four-year period, at a cost of $1 million, for a $3 million total utility value. This is a 300 percent return on the $1 million investment. Do not let the possibly uncertain estimates on which these figures are based bother you. Uncertainty is always a fact of life in management, and it's certainly not a reason to abandon ROI analysis for HR activities. Instead, the nature of the uncertainty can be addressed. For example, if the hurdle rate for investments is 20 percent, this program needs to generate only $200,000 in value minus costs (20 percent times the $1 million investment), which translates into $300 average sales increase per year for the 1,000 salespeople. This is far less than the estimated $4,000 sales increase. It really doesn't matter if we know exactly what the sales increase will be, only that it exceeds $300 per person per year.

While this analysis is simplified, these concepts have been applied to HR activities in virtually every area. Generally, the reported returns from HR activities range from slightly to extremely

HR managers are often called on to justify investments in HR activities by showing bottom-line effects. Suppose you were presenting the analysis show in Exhibit 5.2 to a CEO, or to a division president. What questions do you think they would ask? How would you answer them?

positive. Utility analysis can be applied to individual activities or combinations of HR activities, to identify the synergy that's possible when activities complement each other.[8]

## Planning Integrates Human Resource Activities

Planning shows how all the parts fit together. Think about a college degree. Usually, getting a degree means taking some required classes that fit together to build an integrated set of skills. A business degree is different from an engineering degree, which in turn is different from an astronomy degree. It may not always be apparent, but usually the set of classes is designed, so that each one builds on and complements the other. Understanding calculus helps a student understand both the physics of a bridge and the movement of planets.

In the same way, different human resource activities should integrate to enhance the value of human resources. Research suggests that it is hard to find relationships between any one activity and the outcomes of organizational finance. For example, organizations that base their pay on performance don't necessarily perform better than those that don't, and organizations that select people very carefully don't necessarily perform better than those that select less carefully. However, emerging studies of production systems suggests that "bundles" of HR practices are consistently associated with better organization performance. For example, combining flexible production systems with team-based work systems, pay based on team performance, and extensive training seems to associate with better performance in auto plants.[9] Unfortunately, most of this research has looked only at blue-collar workers in heavy industry, so we don't know how it applies generally. Also, while about 10 to 50 percent of organizations seem to fall into the "control" bundle (fixed jobs, little employee participation, low levels of training), and 10 to 25 percent fall into the "commitment" bundle (flexible job design, considerable employee participation, and extensive training), that leaves between 25 and 80 percent of organizations pursuing some other kind of "bundle."[10] Still, it seems logical that HR practices should reinforce each other. People benefit from multiple ways to gain skills, and they are more likely to be motivated if HR activities provide multiple reasons to be motivated. HR planning identifies these integration possibilities. Thus, planning links the conditions discussed in Chapters One to Four with the activities discussed in later chapters.

## Do Human Resources "Fit" to Strategy, or Does One Size Fit All?

Much of the evidence suggests that the "commitment bundle" of HR practices is associated with superior organizational performance in the industries and situations that have been studied. Some have gone so far as to suggest one best set of HR practices, including guaranteed employment security, employee ownership, and promotion from within. However, companies such as General Electric and Microsoft have achieved notable successes while implementing layoffs, maintaining private ownership, and establishing an employment contract that says they will seek out qualified individuals from both inside and outside the organization. Most have concluded that it makes sense to fit HR practices to business strategies in some way.[11]

## Can Human Resources Provide a Competitive Advantage?

A related question is, should organizations first establish their organizational strategy and then choose HR practices to nurture the "right" kind of human resources to support it? Or should organizations let the qualities of the human resources determine the future strategies? All organizations strive to grow and survive, and to create a purpose that is unique over time. This unique purpose that lasts over time has been called "sustainable competitive advantage."

> *Sustainable competitive advantage* occurs when an organization is implementing a value-creating strategy that is not being implemented simultaneously by any current or potential competitors, and when other organizations are incapable of duplicating the benefits of that advantage.[12]

Sustainable competitive advantage may sound like an aggressive, militaristic term, but it applies to philanthropic and public organizations as well as it does to businesses or armies. To survive and grow, any organization must acquire and use resources in unique and valuable ways or other organizations will do so over time. Consider the case of the U.S. Postal Service, which remains a basic element of U.S. society, but it no longer is the only delivery method of choice when speed is required. DHL, UPS, and Federal Express now compete for that role because they have found ways to create unique value relative to the U.S. Postal Service.

Sustainable competitive advantage derives from a "resource-based" view of organizations. Resources include *physical capital, human capital,* and *organizational capital.* Organizations influence the quality of the resources available to them, and these resources do not move easily between organizations. Companies can't fire all of their employees or sell all of their buildings to pursue every new market opportunity. Thus, organizations have a unique competitive advantage when they find ways to increase the quality of their existing resources or to use their resources more effectively than others. This advantage is sustainable when it can't be easily copied. Specifically, sustainable competitive advantage is caused by resources that:

1. Add value to the organization.
2. Are unique or rare among competitors.
3. Cannot be perfectly imitated by others.
4. Cannot be substituted by resources that others possess.[13]

Can people be managed to create sustainable competitive advantage? Yes. Indeed, it has been argued that people may be the most promising source of competitive advantage for today's organizations. Think about it for a moment: The complex relationships among people within and outside an organization can be extremely valuable, as the examples above show. Moreover, because such relationships are complex and often depend on the unique culture and history of the organization, it is very difficult to copy them. Competitors can purchase the same plants and equipment, acquire the same stocks and debt instruments, and match the pricing and distribution practices of your organization, because these are all observable. However, it is particularly difficult to peer inside an organization to decipher exactly how it creates capability and motivation among employees.[14] Employees don't show up on the financial statements, and their contributions are often very subtle. Obviously, skillful managers must find competitive advantage in all the resources they use, but people certainly rank high among those resources.

Perhaps the best HR strategy is to hire, train, and pay people, so that they create the best future strategies, no matter what the future conditions. This strategy would place less emphasis on the workforce's ability to implement today's strategy, and more emphasis on general human traits, such as creativity, intelligence, curiosity, dependability, and commitment to the organization, which will lead to superior strategies. The strategy "fits" the human resource instead of the other way around.

> **WHAT DO YOU THINK?**
>
> High-growth companies were all the rage in the mid-1990's, as initial public offerings (IPO's) of companies like Netscape and Yahoo! saw their stock prices soar. How should such companies hire people to best grow and prosper? Should they hire highly skilled technicians who have world-class talent in today's environment, such as the best internet browser programmers? Or, should they hire based on general traits such as creativity and intelligence, considering that today's technical challenges will probably change very quickly, and require new skills anyway? How can HR managers balance short- and long-run concerns? How would you measure whether the right balance is being achieved?

## HOW HUMAN RESOURCE PLANNING FITS THE BROADER PLANNING PROCESS

The jury is still out on whether there is one best set of human resource practices, and whether it's more important to get generally good people or to fit the people to the strategy. However, whether HR plans are the source of broader strategy or are derived from such strategies, it is important to understand how HR plans fit into the broader planning process.

### Planning from Mars

Sometimes examples come from Mars. No, not the planet, but the multibillion-dollar company known as M&M/Mars Company, a leader in candy, pet food, rice, and other products. An integrated set of business and human resource practices keeps the focus on constantly improving quality for customers, sharing ideas, and honestly assessing and rewarding individual and team contributions. Performance standards include time clocks for everyone (including senior executives and owners) and are linked to a pay policy that awards 10 percent punctuality bonuses. Mars' cultural signals emphasize equality and communication (no assigned parking places, everyone on the line wears hard hats and white coats) and nearby offices are arranged in concentric circles (with the top executive in the middle, surrounded by direct subordinates, etc.). Compensation and staffing reinforce each other, encouraging managers and employees to gain broad experience across many parts of the business. Mars pay scale levels are higher than 90 percent of the pay for comparable jobs, a high degree of job security is provided for good performers, and vice presidents get the same pay no matter which unit of the business they currently head. Human resource managers of today may well be the manufacturing managers of tomorrow, and vice versa.[15]

Notice how the HR decisions at Mars fit within the broader organization planning framework, and how they support organization goals. Mars wants to compete through creativity and quality, so it needs people who are willing to share ideas, who can and will learn many different roles in many different businesses, who can be creative because the company trusts them, and who feel that they are equally important to company success as top management. This translates into specific HR activities. High pay and careful selection bring in the best. Linking pay to performance and encouraging movement between businesses fosters learning and commitment to excellence. Equality of parking, clothing, and office access signals trust and communication.

EXHIBIT 5.3 How Human Resource Planning Fits the Broader Planning Process

| Level of Analysis | Goals | Type of Planning Activities | Typical Decisions |
|---|---|---|---|
| **Environment** (Chapter 2) | Financial (stock price, debt rating)<br>Government (agency ratings)<br>Union (strikes, organizing, grievances)<br>Community (attitudes, opinions) | External scanning | Should we lobby to influence laws?<br>How much should we increase diversity?<br>Should we form alliances with suppliers, customers or competitors? |
| **Organization** (Chapter 3) | Hierarchy structure<br>Norms/culture<br>Profit<br>Market share<br>Quality of product | Business planning | What business should we be in?<br>What market, process, technology, and organization design does this imply? |
| **Human resource quantity/deployment** | Quantity of employees<br>Assignment to jobs<br>Labor cost levels | Employment planning | What is future HR demand and supply?<br>What gaps should we try to reconcile? |
| **Human resource department/function** (Chapter 17) | Budget<br>Activities<br>Client opinions | HR strategic planning | How does HR management contribute to the business?<br>How many resources should we use?<br>What broad directions should we emphasize? |
| **Specific human resource management activities** | Quantity of affected employees<br>Activity costs<br>Activity results<br>Payoff/utility | HR action plans | What specific activities should we implement?<br>How extensive should each activity be? |

Exhibit 5.3 shows the five levels of analysis where HR planning takes place. At each level, the impact and role of human resource considerations is different. From the top to the bottom of the exhibit, the issues become more focused on HR activities, but decisions about the programs and HR functional configuration at the bottom of the exhibit must be clearly linked to objectives and plans at the external and organizational level at the top. As Exhibit 5.3 shows, Chapters Two and Three discussed specific issues and concerns in the environment and organization levels of analysis, so we will only touch on those here. Later in this chapter, we will discuss the main activity of HR planning—how managers decide to deploy people across the organization in response to these conditions. Each of the later chapters of the book will discuss a specific HR activity, and how it contributes to these deployments, and at the end of the book we will discuss how the HR function is organized to best deliver and support the activities and services.

## The Environment

Between 1993 and 1995, the U.S. government moved progressively closer to significant deregulation of telecommunications industries. Every company can

**EXHIBIT 5.4** How the Changing Telecommunications Environment Affects Human Resources

**Telephone Turmoil**

*Over 140,000 telephone jobs have been lost since 1993*

| Companies | Layoffs, 1993–1996 |
|---|---|
| AT&T | 63,500 |
| GTE Corp. | 17,000 |
| NYNEX | 16,800 |
| BellSouth | 11,300 |
| Pacific Bell | 10,000 |
| U.S. West | 9,000 |
| Ameritech | 6,000 |
| Bell Atlantic | 5,600 |
| MCI | 3,000 |
| Sprint | 1,600 |
| Southwestern Bell | 1,500 |
| Pacific Telesis | 500 |

Source: William J. Cook and Katia Hetter, "Hanging Up On Workers," *U.S. News & World Report,* Jan. 15, 1996, p. 50. Copyright, Jan. 15, U.S. News & World Report.

compete for long-distance and local telephone service, and businesses may soon be able to buy all their telephone, cellular, paging, and cable TV service from one provider or several. What a change in the environment from the early 1980s, when AT&T had a monopoly on telephone services. What is the implication of this turmoil for human resources? For many companies, it means laying off thousands of people, as Exhibit 5.4 shows. AT&T's stock price rose on the day it announced 40,000 layoffs, but the airwaves and news publications also were filled with interviews with CEO Robert Allen, explaining the strategy and offering quotes such as "The way I get myself mentally over the tough bridge of what happens to 40,000 people is my responsibility for 300,000 people."[16] The environment drove the decision to lay off people, but CEO Allen's decision to publicly explain the layoff also responds to the environment of AT&T stockholders, financial analysts, customers, and government legislators.

HR decisions certainly can affect progress toward external standards—to different degrees HR activities directly affect safety, equal employment opportunity (see Chapter Two), and community relations. Though HR decisions affect stock prices, debt ratings, or other financial outcomes less directly, financial analysts certainly have paid a great deal of attention to the HR decisions of AT&T.

## The Organization Level

Did you know that you can buy a book containing 301 "mission statements" from America's top companies?[17] Virtually every organization has a broad statement of goals including high quality, customer satisfaction, respect for

EXHIBIT 5.5 McDonald's 1996 Organization-Level Goals and HR Implications

**1996 Organization Goals for McDonald's USA**

- Improve customer satisfaction to 88% by year-end, 90% in 1997
- Increase employee satisfaction to 72%
- Achieve a 10-point customer satisfaction lead over Burger King, Wendy's

**Human Resource Implications for McDonald's**

- Make surprise visits to assess employee performance: Fill all orders within 90 seconds, and have no one wait more than three and one-half minutes.
- Reduce turnover rates from former very high levels.

Source: Richard Gibson, "McDonald's Approaches '96 With Goal of Making U.S. Service 'Hassle-Free,' " *The Wall Street Journal,* Dec. 26, 1995, p. A3. Reprinted by permission of The Wall Street Journal, © 1995 Dow Jones & Company, Inc. All rights reserved worldwide.

people, and so forth. These missions, and the decisions they motivate, comprise the organization level of planning, and reflect organization conditions, discussed in Chapter Three.

American Airlines decided that in addition to flying, it would sell its management services (such as its SABRE reservation system, its expertise in handling telephone calls, and its flight-yield management systems) to other airlines as well as mail-order houses and cruise lines. Amgen, a biotechnology firm, wanted to maintain "that family feeling" despite growth rates of more than 100 percent per year. U.S. industries want to close the innovation gap by producing new ideas quicker. IBM and Eastman Kodak want to restructure to achieve more competitive cost and productivity levels. Japan's organizations also are restructuring to cut costs and focus more on profits than market share.[18]

These goals reflect the second level in Exhibit 5.3, decisions about the organization. The organization usually refers to the entire firm; however, in very large or decentralized organizations, it might refer to subunits such as divisions, regions, profit centers, branches, or agencies. The key stakeholders setting organization-level standards are top managers responsible for directing and achieving organizational goals. Chapter Three described organizational characteristics and how they are assessed. The process of identifying organization-level standards and decisions to reach them is called *business planning.*

Exhibit 5.5 shows the organization-level goals of McDonald's for 1996, and the human resource implications, according to McDonald's USA President Edward H. Rensi. Notice how the organization-level goals are defined by stakeholders (top managers) within the company? Also, notice how the human resource implications link to the goals. McDonald's used human resource planning to make that link.

The right column of Exhibit 5.3 shows some of the broad business planning decisions. Can HR decisions really affect such organization-level goals? Corporate leaders seem to think so. Rich Melman, Chicago's preeminent restaurateur, created a chain of restaurants that thrive on individuality; he credits on-the-job training, rich benefits, and employee stakes in the company for their success. Economist Alan Blinder says the real secret to Japan's dynamic economy is that Japanese corporations break down the us versus them barriers impairing employee relations by narrowing pay differences between executives and ordinary workers, assigning managers to serve stints on factory floors, and pursuing growth to preserve job security and career opportunities. At drug giant Merck & Company, a key business goal is to nurture creative new drugs while internalizing tough financial standards for new product development. Judy Lewent, the chief financial officer, credits Merck's merit-based compensation, forced-distribution performance appraisal system, and low turnover for achieving this: "Competitive advantage is driven off your human resource base, the excellence of the people you recruit and retain." Frederick W. Smith at Federal Express says, "In the service sector, your product is only as good as the customer's last encounter with the employee."[19] The next time you have to deal with an uninformed or rude salesclerk at the university bookstore, perhaps you'll think, "This store should change its performance appraisal system" (in addition to other epithets).

### Quality as a Business Imperative

One of the most widely discussed organization-level objectives is *quality,* meaning value in the eyes of customers. A survey of HR managers, business leaders, consultants, and academics around the world showed a "focus on total quality/customer satisfaction" as one of the highest-ranked business imperatives for the year 2000. Thirty percent ranked its impact on HR in the future first or second, though the Japanese rated it very low, with less than 10 percent ranking its impact on HR first or second.[20] In 1987, the U.S. Congress established the Malcolm Baldrige National Quality Award to recognize and publicize successful quality achievements. This award was won in 1995 by Armstrong World Industries' Building Productions Operations unit and Corning's Telecommunications Products Division. Human resource utilization is one of the six broad categories judged by the award committee. Recent years have seen the inevitable questions about the wisdom of single-minded pursuit of quality awards, as well as questions about whether quality should reflect processes (such as a high level of quality training or suggestion systems) or outcomes (such as customer satisfaction levels or sales). Exhibit 5.6 lists some of the common pitfalls in pursuing total quality management (TQM) and indicates how HR management can help avoid them. One overriding message in this exhibit is to avoid measuring progress by the amount of *activity,* such as the number of training programs or graphs, and to focus instead on the *impact* of the programs on the organization's goals.

## Human Resource Quantity and Deployment

To further isolate the effects of HR decisions, planners typically consider the size of the workforce and how it is deployed across different work roles. This is called *employment planning*. Typical standards in employment planning might include:

- Reduce the size of our workforce by 5 percent within six months.
- Reduce employees in headquarters staff by 5,000 and redeploy at least 4,000 of them into sales/marketing within two years.
- Maintain this year's labor costs at their current level, despite inflation in overall price levels.

**EXHIBIT 5.6** How HR Can Help to Avoid the Pitfalls of Total Quality Management

| Common Pitfalls | HR Contribution |
|---|---|
| CEOs discover TQM and want it in place too fast, failing to tailor it to the organization | Tailor the approach<br>Focus the interventions<br>Move incrementally<br>Build on past successes |
| Tracking the number of training programs, instead of their results | Draw on solid organizational development techniques<br>Demonstrate resolutions of business problems |
| Focusing on implementing quality processes and rituals, but failing to make significant changes | Focus on results to be achieved<br>Integrate the process with substantial goals |
| Becoming awash with data, charts, and graphs that only add to confusion | Clarify the role of quality teams<br>Provide training on how to gather useful information and ask meaningful questions |
| Failing to change the organization culture so that new ideas can quickly flourish | Incorporate quality into the organization strategy<br>Get line management understanding<br>Monitor the progress and business impact |
| Asking for team effort, while providing only individual rewards | Revise evaluation systems to include customer and peer input<br>Develop team-based rewards<br>Time HR changes so that a critical mass of team exists |
| Enthusiasm fades after the initial euphoria | Gather feedback from employees<br>Track implementation activity<br>Monitor expansion of TQM processes and business results |

Source: Adapted from Michael S. Liebman, "Getting Results from TQM," *HR Magazine,* Sept. 1992, p. 38.

Notice how these standards focus on whether the number, costs, and qualities of employees match needs, rather than focusing on the ultimate effects of matching those needs or on the mix of programs used. Exhibit 5.3 shows that employment planning decisions focus on identifying discrepancies between the future demand and supply of employees and then making choices to reconcile the two. This planning is typical of HR management; we discuss it in detail later in this chapter.

## Human Resource Department/Function Level

External and organizational planning produces standards and decisions reflecting broad success and survival. HR management decisions can and should reflect these standards, but it is sometimes hard to tell if changes in external or organizational outcomes were achieved because of or despite a well-managed HR department/function. So, HR planners typically establish standards for how the department/function itself is managed, whether the level and mix of resources correspond to plans, and whether key stakeholders within the organization generally hold the department/function in high regard. This level of planning is called *human resource strategic planning,* and establishes the broad standards within which specific HR decisions are made.

Every year, various consultants and publications survey HR managers about their top priorities. Goals at this level include (1) introducing new technology to the workforce, (2) recruiting and retaining key people, (3) reengineering work processes, (4) becoming a business strategy player, (5) managing the outsourcing of HR functions, (6) defining internal and external HR customers, and (7) aligning HR's vision with that of top management.[21] Notice how each of these standards focuses on the combined effects of HR activities within the broad organization or external outcomes. Exhibit 5.3 indicates the kinds of decisions made at this level of planning and how such decisions translate the organization-level plan into specific choices about the HR function.

At the end of the book, we will discuss the role of the HR professional, and the specific issues facing HR departments/functions today. For now, notice how the HR function's structure and goals must complement the planning process.

## Specific Human Resource Management Activities

Perhaps the most obvious way to plan and assess HR decisions is to ask, Are our activities being carried out and producing the immediate results we want? *Human resource action plans* consider the likely effects of specific HR activities. Typical standards at this level of analysis might include:

- Extend long-term medical benefits to all employees identified as at risk for long-term disabilities before July 30.
- Implement the success sharing pay plan to recognize high performance, without increasing the compensation budget by more than $100,000, before the end of the year.
- Have every participant in literacy training pass a minimum reading competency test by the end of the year.
- Demonstrate that the benefits exceed the costs of the new team-building and worker-involvement seminar series by more than 120 percent.

Notice how these standards isolate specific HR activities, the resources they use, or the immediate outcomes they achieve.

Exhibit 5.3 shows that typical decisions in HR action planning include whether to implement particular activities, and how extensive each activity should be. Action plans translate the workforce size and deployment standards of employment planning into specific activities. Action plan standards often reflect many of the employee characteristics discussed in Chapter Four. HR action planning can provide very specific guidance for continuing, expanding, or eliminating activities. However, it must also reflect broader standards. For example, training 200 production workers in hydraulics may satisfy an action plan but provide little value if the demand for hydraulic skills is falling.

The chapters that follow will consider each of the HR activities in turn. However, it is important to keep in mind that such activities must always work together to achieve the broad goals of the organization and the proper deployment of human resources. We now turn to a detailed discussion about the third level of analysis in Exhibit 5.3, employment planning.

## EMPLOYMENT PLANNING: THE QUANTITY AND DEPLOYMENT OF HUMAN RESOURCES

*Employment planning* aims to get the right numbers and types of employees doing the right work at the right time. Exhibit 5.7 shows the employment planning process. Employment planning involves three basic phases: (1) analyzing HR demands, (2) analyzing HR supply, and (3) reconciling important discrepancies between demand and supply by maintaining or changing HR activities. Notice how this process parallels the general planning process described in Exhibit 5.1. Demand analysis asks *Where do we want to be?* Supply analysis asks *Where are we now?* and *Where will we be?* by considering both the *internal supply* (current employees), and the *external supply* (employees who join the organization from outside). The sum of internal and external supply is then compared with the projected demand. Gaps are identified and priorities are established. The most important gaps then become HR standards. In employment planning, the standards reflect the quantity and deployment of employees. Finally, the standards are *reconciled* by choosing HR activities to address the gaps, and the process starts again.

### How to Measure Human Resource Demand and Supply

What is the right number to measure the demand and supply of employees? For most people, the answer is to count "bodies" or "heads." We count the number of employees in certain categories, such as jobs, gender, race, or tenure. Thus, employment planning might focus on whether the number of people available for certain jobs or tasks equals the number that are needed. However, it might make more sense to track "capability," perhaps in the form of skills of competencies. Thus, we might track supply and demand for "leadership," "team building," or "ability to speak Malay Chinese."

> **WHAT DO YOU THINK?**
>
> Think about your own career preparation. Do you tend to set your goals in terms of a specific job, such as becoming a trial lawyer or a neurosurgeon? Or do you think of your education as building a bundle of capabilities, perhaps including knowledge of law or medicine, suited to a wide variety of possible jobs (such as a consultant to hospitals on medical legal liabilities or an author of self-help books on legal issues). An increasing number of experts are saying that you need to think of your career more in terms of what you can do than in terms of filling certain jobs. Perhaps employment planning could take a similar approach.

Considering the fast pace of change in organizations, "jobs" may not last very long. Therefore, a system based on capabilities might make more sense than one that simply tracks numbers of people. If a team needed to include both leadership and a certain technical skill, that need might be filled by one person who had both or by two persons who each had one. Such an approach might also make it easier for employees to understand how to fashion careers and learning experiences in line with future organization needs. Instead of asking, "Will there be a vacancy for me as a technician second level?" the person might ask, "Will I be eligible for more roles in the future if I get certified as a team leader?" Many organizations have adopted a capability-based approach to planning by listing the capabilities needed for various roles (such as chief financial officer or vice president of creativity) and comparing the capabilities of employees with them. This might not only identify more candidates, but also it can tell which candidates are ready and which are "close," and what to do to bring the close ones up to readiness.

For some decisions, we might measure other facets of people, such as levels of experience, diversity, or even labor costs. It all depends on what decision is being made, which links back to the organization's

EXHIBIT 5.7 Three Phases of the Employment Planning Process

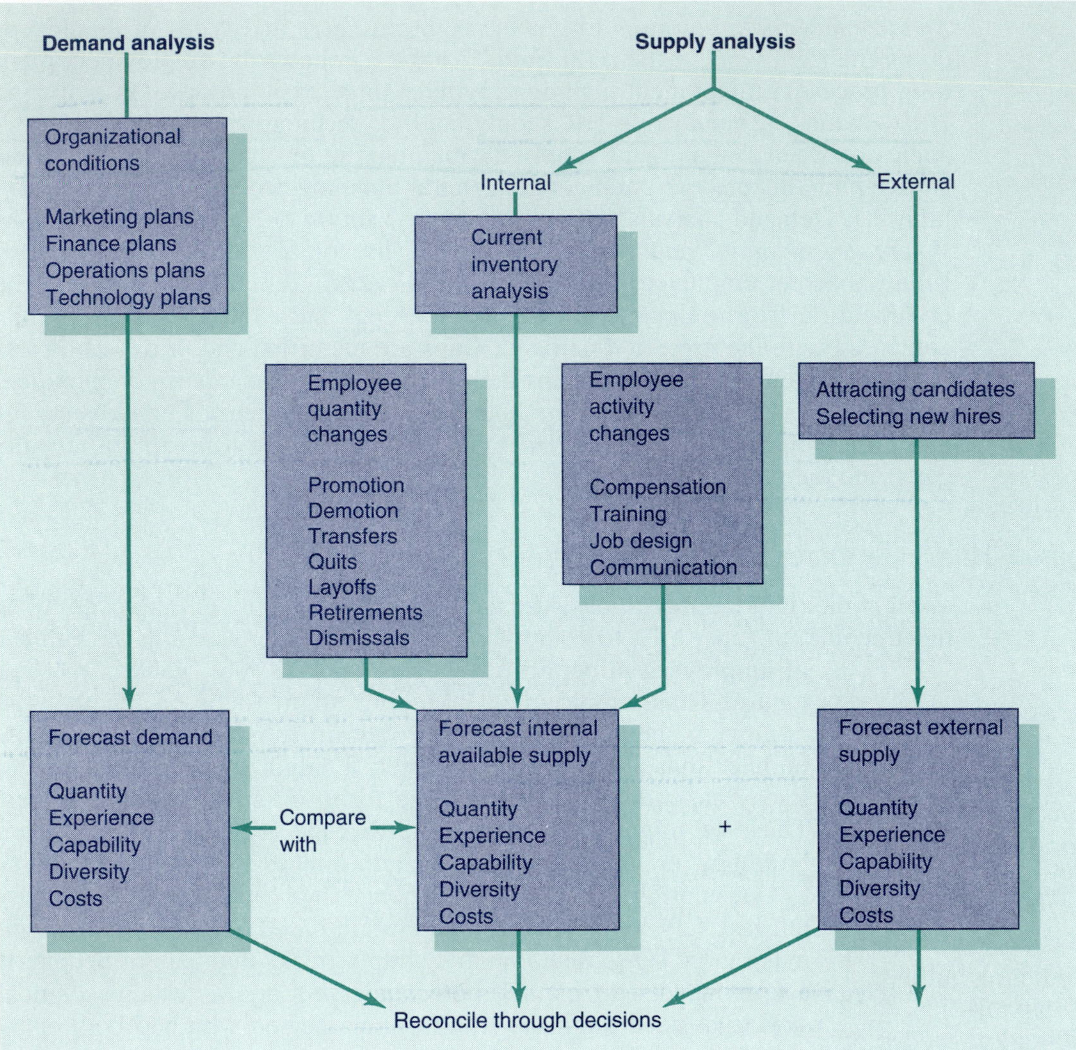


environment and business plan (see Exhibit 5.3). As you read the next sections describing analysis of demand and supply, keep in mind that while most organizations count heads, the same analysis techniques can be used with other human resource measures.

## Demand Analysis: Where Do We Want to Be?

Demand analysis describes the future human resource needs. Actual demand forecasts don't try to predict future needs down to the individual employee, competency or labor cost dollar. Instead they summarize needs into key employee groups, key competencies, or diversity targets, focusing on the most

**EXHIBIT 5.8** The Link between Business Activity and Human Resources Demand

| General Formula | | |
|---|---|---|
| **Business activity = Quantity of human resources × Productivity per employee** | | |
| **General Examples** | | |
| Sales revenues | = Number of salespeople | × Sales dollars per salesperson |
| Production levels | = Number of production hours worked | × Output per production hour |
| Operating costs | = Number of employees | × Labor cost per employee |

critical ones. At First Chicago Bank, in the beginning of this chapter, a key strategic factor was the quality of clerks and operations employees, which translated into *demands* for certain levels of basic skills.

### Linking Business Plans to Human Resource Requirements

Layoffs, costs cutting, productivity woes, downsizing, and restructuring—the headlines are full of examples of the link between business plans and human resource demand requirements. In Malaysia, managers face dilemmas such as adequately staffing a new division where demand is growing by 20 percent a year. Many American HR managers would love to have this kind of problem. Whether business is expanding or contracting, human resources should support it. How do planners translate this general idea into specific quantities, qualities, and costs of human resources?

The logic is described in Exhibit 5.8. The level of business activity that can be supported is the product of the quantity of employees and the time they work, multiplied by their average level of productivity or activity. Examples of business activity indicators are:[22]

- The 3M Company uses gross sales revenues.
- State Farm Insurance Companies use insurance policies-in-force.
- Upjohn Company uses return on investment, and still other firms use estimated production volumes or value-added (the difference between the cost of raw materials and the price of the final product).

From forecasts of business activity, some organizations estimate the number of critical-skill employees and then estimate the needed quantity of support staff (accountants, HR professionals, secretaries) based on the quantity of critical-skill employees.[23] For example, where engineering skills are critical, such as Hewlett-Packard Company or Rockwell International, planners might use a ratio of two secretaries, one-half an accountant, and one HR professional for every 10 engineers.

Business activity can also be defined as costs, in which case the goal is usually to achieve a reduced level of activity. General Motors, IBM, and Eastman Kodak are among those companies using early retirement plans to induce workers to leave, and analysts regularly estimate the effects on costs and earnings per share of stock. Another strategy is to cut costs by keeping the number of employees constant but limiting increases in wages and other costs, as USAir Group has done. Pay cuts, however, can backfire if productivity drops by more than the cost savings. "Productivity went to hell," says Frank P. Doyle, senior vice president for external affairs at General Electric, about the results of demanding that workers at the electric motors division accept an 11 percent pay cut. By increasing productivity, U.S. firms such as Birmingham Steel, Cincinnati Millacron, and Cypress Minerals found they could match the productivity/cost ratios of foreign competitors without cutting wages or employees.[24] A long-run perspective is needed; laying off or retiring employees may achieve cost reductions today but cost more later if those skills must be rebuilt when business activity picks up.

Therefore, demand analysis reveals the *desired* number and deployment of workers to support projected business activity. The next step is to determine the *actual* number and deployment of the current and projected work force.

## Internal Supply Analysis: Where Are We Now? Where Will We Be?

The Roman Catholic Church faces a crisis as older priests retire, younger priests quit, and fewer young men are recruited.[25] The loss of key competencies forces this international organization to face massive human resource supply problems. Supply analysis focuses on the organization internally and externally. As Exhibit 5.7 shows, internal supply analysis begins by asking, "Where are we now?" and examining the *current internal inventory* of employees. Then, it asks, "Where will we be?" by *forecasting internal supply,* assuming current activities are continued. This forecast accounts for movement inside the organization (promotions/demotions/transfers) and out of the organization (quits, layoffs, retirements, dismissals). The result is a summary of the current and projected work force reflecting size, experience, capability, diversity, costs, or other characteristics.[26]

Internal supply analysis is based on simple principles. First, determine how many people are in each job now. Next, for each job, estimate how many will stay where they are, how many will move to other jobs, and how many will leave their jobs and the organization. Adding up all of these movements and departures results in a projection of how many people will be in each job after all the movements are finished. The reality, however, is more complex. Will the array of jobs stay the same, will some jobs be removed or combined to create new jobs, or will new jobs be added? Will movements between jobs and out of jobs occur in the same pattern as before? Will every employee who moves to a new job be just as productive as the person who was there before? Perhaps we should abandon the idea of jobs and focus simply on competencies instead. The past is not always a good predictor of the future but it is often all we have. Therefore, internal supply forecasts are often a matter of judgment; various techniques can make internal supply analysis more systematic and grounded in experience. Some techniques, such as skill inventories and replacement charts, are based on judgments by planners or other experts, while others such as transition matrices are more statistical. Some research suggests that the judgmental techniques are more common.[27] Even so, computers are increasing the ability to use statistical models.

### Skill Inventories

A skill inventory is a list of employees showing characteristics that relate to their ability to perform different jobs.[28] These characteristics might include training classes attended, previous experience, licenses obtained, tests passed, supervisory judgments of ability, and even tests of strength or endurance. A skill inventory can help planners estimate the likelihood that given employees will move to new jobs, based on their qualifications for those jobs. Skill inventories can reflect key competencies.

Personal computers now assist both planners and individuals in tracking their skills and matching them to opportunities. For example, the "Career Architect" software package links skills to a wide variety of jobs and tracks which employees have those skills. Thus, planners can find out electronically how many people have the necessary skills for anticipated future needs, and employees can compare their skills with those needed in the jobs they want in the future. Chase Manhattan Bank uses this kind of software to plan managerial mobility around the world. The Global Mobility Information System (GMIS) links New York, São Paolo, London, and Hong Kong, allowing planners to see profiles of managerial competencies, match profiles to vacancies, and plan developmental activities when the match needs improving.[29]

You can learn more about Career Architect on the world wide web, at
**http://www.lominger.com/career.htm**

### Replacement Charts

While skill inventories list skills for individuals, replacement charts list the individuals who could move into key work roles in the organization. They list the employees available for promotion or transfer as well as each employee's current work role, level of readiness, skills/abilities, and willingness to move. Replacement charts help planners forecast movement between work roles by identifying the most ready and willing candidates. A variant of this approach that often focuses on identifying successors for top managers is called *succession planning;* we discuss it in Chapter Nine on careers.

### Transitional Matrices

While judgment-based forecasting techniques are common, organizations increasingly use statistical techniques that mathematically project past trends into the future. Such techniques may be called Markov, network flow, or renewal models, and they may use mathematical formulas such as regression or optimization. Most of them rely on the logic of the *transition probability matrix* that examines the overall pattern of movement into, between, and out of the organization.[30]

Exhibit 5.9 shows the three elements of a transition probability matrix:

1. *State definitions.* States are the divisions that segment the organization for analysis. Usually states are jobs or salary grades; they can also reflect performance levels. For EEO planning, the states might reflect race, sex, or other diversity-related factors. Some organizations, such as British Petroleum, have even replaced job descriptions with matrices reflecting skills, behaviors, and competencies. States can reflect nationalities, such as 3M's employees in Bangalore, India, or Hewlett Packard's computer

EXHIBIT 5.9 Transition Probability Matrix for Forecasting Internal Labor Supply*

| Job States† | | Destination States Time Period 2 | | | | | | | | | | | |
|---|---|---|---|---|---|---|---|---|---|---|---|---|---|
| | | **A** | **B** | **C** | **D** | **E** | **F** | **G** | **H** | **I** | **J** | **Exit** | **Total** |
| Source States Time Period I | **A Regional marketing manager** | 1.00 | | | | | | | | | | — | 1.00 |
| | **B Assistant regional marketing manager** | .15 | .80 | | | Organizational career I | | | | | | .05 | 1.00 |
| | **C Product sales manager** | | .16 | .76 | .04 | | | | | | | .04 | 1.00 |
| | **D Assistant product sales manager** | | .01 | .23 | .73 | | | | | | | .03 | 1.00 |
| | **E Plant manager** | | | | | .85 | .05 | | | | | .10 | 1.00 |
| | **F Assistant plant manager** | | | | | .25 | .65 | .05 | | | | .05 | 1.00 |
| | **G Process team liaison** | | Organizational career II | | | | .40 | .50 | .03 | | | .07 | 1.00 |
| | **H Process team leader** | | | | | | .02 | .15 | .75 | | | .08 | 1.00 |
| | **I Process operator** | | | | | | | | .20 | .50 | | .30 | 1.00 |
| | **J Truck driver** | | | | | Organizational career III | | | | | .50 | .50 | 1.00 |

*Cell entries are proportions.

plants in Guadalajara, Mexico.[31] Different job titles have been used in Exhibit 5.9 to illustrate the different "states." Jobs A through D represent sales-related jobs, with job A (regional marketing manager) being the highest job in the hierarchy, and job D (assistant product sales manager) being the lowest. Jobs E through I represent manufacturing-related jobs, with job E (plant manager) being the highest, and job I (process operator) being the lowest. Job J represents truck driver, a job outside the two groups. The right column is labeled "Exit" because it represents those who leave the organization during the analysis period.

2. *Time interval.* Movement occurs over time, so the matrix must specify a time period for analysis. The rows of the matrix (time period 1) describe the states at the beginning of the analysis; this may be some past period, the current period, or even a projected future period. The columns of the matrix (time period 2) describe the states at the end of the analyzed time period. The time period may be a day, month, year, business cycle, or whatever the planner feels is relevant to the supply forecast.
3. *Cell entries.* Each cell of the matrix is an intersection of a row and column—a state at time period 1 with a state at time period 2. Into these cells are entered the proportion of employees who were in the source state (row) at time period 1, and in the destination state (column) at time period 2. For example. cell AA has an entry of 1.00, meaning that 100 percent of the regional marketing managers at time period 1 were still in that job at time period 2. Cell BA has an entry of .15, meaning that 15 percent of the assistant regional marketing managers at time period 1 had moved up to regional marketing manager at time period 2. The cells along the diagonal (AA, BB, CC, etc.) represent the probability of remaining in the same job

over the time period of analysis. Each probability is computed by counting the number of employees who moved from the row state to the column state, and dividing that number by the original number of employees in the row state at the beginning of the analysis. Cell entries can reflect actual past movements, or they can be hypothetical what-if possibilities that we wish to achieve in the future.

### What Can the Transitional Probability Matrix Tell Us?

First, it can identify career patterns. The first four jobs in Exhibit 5.9 seem to be a marketing career path because people appear to move from assistant product sales manager (job D) through jobs B and C, to regional marketing manager (job A). Also, there is no movement between these jobs and others. Similarly, jobs E through I form a manufacturing career path because people appear to move from process operator (job I) through the ranks of jobs F, G, and H, ending up in job E, plant manager. Truck drivers (job J) don't move into either career path.

Second, transitional matrices can identify how separations affect the organization. The numbers in the exit column show the separation rate for each job. Process operators and truck drivers (states I and J) seem to have particularly high separation rates. On the other hand, no regional marketing managers (job A) left the organization during the time period of the analysis. At first this may seem like good news, but remember that the job of regional marketing manager sits atop the marketing career path (jobs A, B, C, and D). If no regional marketing managers leave, it may be difficult for employees to find career opportunities in the other marketing jobs, causing a bottleneck.

Finally, transitional matrices can reveal opportunities. Many manufacturing organizations, such as General Motors, Ford, Motorola, and Schering-Plough, have found that they can develop products faster and avoid costly mistakes by involving people from the entire production and marketing process in product design. Therefore, a design team might have someone from sales and someone from manufacturing as well as the usual design engineers. How do you build the skills to contribute to such a team? Perhaps you do it by "cross-pollinating," moving employees from manufacturing jobs to sales jobs and vice versa. Exhibit 5.9 shows this isn't happening because there are no numbers in the cells representing cross-functional movement (e.g., cells A, B, C, and D in row E), which might alert planners to the need to encourage more such movement.

### How Can the Transitional Matrix Forecast the Future Internal Supply?

A *simulation* tells what we can expect if people continue to move through and out of the organization according to past patterns. A simulation starts with the actual or assumed number of employees in each state at the beginning of the analysis (time period 1). Then the beginning number in each source state is multiplied by each probability across the row, to give the movement from that source to each destination, including exit. Finally, the forecasted number of employees staying or moving into each state is the sum down the column, including the diagonal. The total movement out of each state is the sum across the row, excluding the diagonal. For example, suppose the starting number of employees was 100 regional marketing managers (job A), 200 assistant regional marketing managers (job B), 300 product sales managers (job C), and 400 assistant product sales managers (job D). How many employees do we project to move into or stay in the job of assistant regional marketing manager (job B) by the end of the time period? The number of assistant regional marketing managers who will stay is 160 (200 × .80). The number of regional marketing managers moving down to assistant regional marketing manager (job A to job B) is zero. The number of product sales managers (job C) moving up one level to job B is 48 (300 × .16). Finally, the number of assistant product sales managers (job D) who move up two levels in one analysis period (moving from job D to job B) is four (400 × .01). Adding these numbers yields the predicted number of assistant regional sales managers at the end of one time period—212. What about those who leave the assistant regional sales manager job? Among the 40 employees who leave, we project that 30 will be promoted to job A, regional sales manager (200 × .15), and 10 will leave the organization (200 × .05).

Transitional matrices can also be used to do multiperiod analysis by simply substituting the ending numbers of employees from time period 2 as the new beginning numbers, and redoing the analysis just described. For example, the projected number of exits among the 212 assistant regional sales managers during time period 3 is 10.6 (212 × .05). Though these calculations are somewhat lengthy, today's computers can easily accomplish them.[32] It is even possible to identify the optimum movement patterns to satisfy certain goals, such as maintaining competency levels at the lowest cost.

Organizations using transitional matrices include General Motors, IBM, AT&T, Merck, and Weyerhaeuser.[33] As you've probably guessed, the actual numbers and assumptions that go into such matrices are seldom extremely precise. Such projections certainly do not forecast the future perfectly, but this is not their main purpose. Their greatest value is in providing an organized framework for describing the movement process within the organization, so that different possible future outcomes can be quickly and systematically explored. A common approach is to change one or more of the probabilities in the matrix to reflect possible human resource actions (What if we create a retirement incentive for employees in job A, and the exit rate rises to .05?).

With projected internal supplies established, the planner is part way to identifying the gaps between demand forecasts and projected supply. Now, the effects of hiring employees from outside the organization must be factored in.

WHAT DO YOU THINK?

The restructuring of AT&T in 1996 produced a new company—Lucent Technologies, which previously was the Bell Labs part of AT&T. Bell Labs was famous for inventing such things as the transistor, and still contains some of the most creative people in the world. Now, however, it must not only create, but also find ways to sell its products and services independently of AT&T. How might you use a transition matrix to present an inventory of current human resources at Lucent Technologies and to forecast the likely future internal supply?

## External Supply Analysis: Who Is Joining the Organization? Who Will Be Joining?

External supply is created by the organization's activities that attract and select job candidates. Chapters Seven and Eight discuss this process in detail. External supply analysis is similar to internal supply analysis because it forecasts the quantity, productivity, and deployment of human resources. Unlike internal supply analysis, however, external supply analysis focuses on the supply of employees projected to join the organization from outside, assuming current activities to attract and select employees are continued. Past hiring patterns suggest how many employees enter the organization in different jobs. These entering individuals can be analyzed according to their quantity, experience, abilities, race/sex, and labor costs. External scanning, discussed in Chapter Two, can provide useful information for forecasting the likely availability of different types of employees at various future time periods. Labor Department projections of future workforce skills, immigration levels, and global workforce changes can all be factored in. External supply analysis can focus on states similar to those used in transition matrix analysis. As with internal supply analysis, the numbers are seldom perfectly accurate. The value lies in providing an organized framework for considering where employees are obtained and where they enter the organization.

In Prague, Czech Republic, the large banks face explosive growth as the economies of Central Europe expand. How does this translate into external supply analysis? The human resource officer of a large Prague bank observed that the bank must consider the supply of future bank managers. The Prague School of Economics graduates 2,700 students per year. Of those, only 900 speak English, a key requirement for a bank with international clients, and of those 900, only 100 want to work in banks. Yet every year, each of 57 banks in the area are projected to need 3 new bank managers, for a total of 171! The external supply is clearly short of the projected demand.

As Exhibit 5.7 shows, the total projected supply is the sum of the supply expected from internal sources and external sources. Demand analysis has now answered the question, "Where do we want to be?" Supply analysis has answered the question, "Where are we now, and where will we be?" It's now possible to identify the gaps, establish standards, and consider how to achieve them.

### Reconciling Supply and Demand: Setting Objectives and Choosing Activities

Comparing demand and supply can produce three outcomes: (1) demand and supply closely match, (2) demand exceeds supply indicating possible shortages, or (3) supply exceeds demand indicating possible surpluses. These comparisons reflect not only the quantities of employees but also their competencies, diversity, cost levels, and perhaps other factors. The quantity of demand and supply may match, but the competencies, diversity, or labor costs may not. Some parts of the organization may be in good balance while others are out of balance. For example, although the number of layoffs in the United States increased from 1990 to 1995, the net job reductions in 1995 were only 1.1 percent, the lowest in a decade. Why? Because as companies were laying off some employees, they were hiring others with different skills. NYNEX Corporation expected to lay off more than 16,000 employees, but at the same time it was adding to sales, marketing, and technical staff to prepare for deregulation.[34] Thus, there are shortages of some skills and surpluses of others, leading to a situation where employees are added and cut at the same time.

In addition, not every gap justifies action. The stakeholders must be consulted, priorities set, and standards established that reflect the most critical gaps. Exhibit 5.10 shows how business strategy leads to projected shortages or surpluses, which leads to certain human resource goals and actions.

### Choosing Activities to Address Shortages

When the projected demand exceeds supply, an obvious solution is to hire more employees. This might involve recruiting at new sources, more aggressively pursuing job candidates, lowering entrance requirements, and expanding the use of temporary or older workers. Chapter Seven discusses these options in

### EXHIBIT 5.10 How Business Activity Goals Can Lead to Human Resource Shortages or Surpluses and Actions

**Business activity = Quantity of employees or work time × Productivity per employee or work time**

| Business Strategy | Shortage/Surplus | Human Resource Goal | HRM Example |
|---|---|---|---|
| Large increase in activity | Large shortage | Increase employee activity faster than increases in employee quantity. | Increase sales or production per employee or per hour, and add employees or person-hours. |
| Moderate increase in activity | Moderate shortage | Increase employee activity while holding employee quantity stable. | Increase sales or production per person or per hour but make no net additions to staff, replace only those who leave. |
| Moderate increases in activity | Small shortage | Hold employee activity stable while increasing employee quantity. | Maintain existing employee production or sales levels but add staff in the same proportion to the increase in business activity. |
| Large decrease in activity | Large surplus | Decrease employee activity while decreasing employee quantity. | Reduce the amount of scheduled overtime and do not replace employees who choose to leave. |
| Moderate decrease in activity followed by an increase in activity | Temporary surplus | Decrease employee activity while maintaining employee quantity, then increase employee activity. | Reduce overtime and encourage employees to take vacation time in the short run, but replace those who leave. When activity rises, add overtime and reduce vacations. |

detail. Organizations are often reluctant to add new jobs unless it's absolutely necessary. For example, before Upjohn Corporation's managers can add a new employee, they must answer the following questions:

1. What purposes does the new job serve?
2. What alternatives were considered to accomplish the same purposes?
3. If the job is filled, what are the projected five-year costs?
4. What impact will this job have on sales, earnings, improved HR utilization?[35]

A second way to deal with a shortage, as shown in Exhibit 5.10, is to expand the level of productivity per employee or time worked. Training, job design, compensation, benefits, and employee relations often expand employees' ability or motivation. Subsequent chapters discuss these activities in detail.

### Choosing Activities When Forecasts Indicate a Surplus

A surplus exists when the organization's supply of human resources exceeds its demands. Surpluses entail some of the most difficult planning choices because employees are seldom responsible for the surplus, yet they may bear the brunt of its effects. Reducing overtime or work hours, encouraging early retirement, reducing hiring so that attrition diminishes the workforce, and relying on less expensive temporary employees may be considered. As a last resort, organizations may consider layoffs. Hard times in Japan may suggest the demise of permanent employment as planners forecast long-run labor surpluses. General Motors announced a creative option, offering to let its suppliers use its idle workers and factories at reduced rates.[36] Subsequent chapters describe each of these options in detail.

### Using Surpluses to Address Shortages

Organizations could conduct employment planning on a unit-by-unit or job-by-job basis to produce an estimate of shortages and surpluses for each unit or job. A comprehensive plan that considers the entire organization can use surpluses in one area to offset shortages in others. For example, when faced with a surplus of managerial and production staff and a shortage of programmers and salespeople, IBM trained and transferred employees from managerial and production jobs into programming and sales jobs.

Employment planning can identify the shortages or surpluses and even give clues about what activities should be used to address them. Ultimately, however, decisions must be made about what resources to spend on what specific activities. Therefore, planners usually need standards geared to specific HR activities.

## OBJECTIVES AND EVALUATION STANDARDS: HOW DID WE DO?

As we have seen, the planning process integrates and analyzes a great deal of information. It is very easy for planners to get so wrapped up in the planning process that they forget the basic purpose: to improve decisions and contribute to goals. One reason for this is a common confusion between the objectives identified at the beginning of the planning process and the evaluation standards used to measure progress. Exhibit 5.1 shows that the relationship should be seamless. The same conditions that help managers understand "where are we now?" can also be tracked to see if they have changed when we ask, "How did we do?" In reality, it is common for HR planners to establish broad objectives in terms of quality, profitability, safety, and legal compliance at the beginning of the planning process, only to evaluate the results in terms of the costs of training books, the reactions of employees or managers, or the number of transactions (e.g., performance reviews completed on time or training classes offered). All are worthwhile goals but they may or may not reflect the original objectives. Thus, it is very important that the planning process specifically choose evaluation standards with a close link to the original broad objectives of the organization.

Throughout this chapter, we have shown how planning compares expected or current conditions with the desired future conditions, and then calculates the gaps. However, there are always more gaps than can be addressed, and not every gap deserves the same attention. Priorities must be established and clear measures of success must be specified. The priorities should reflect how seriously the gap affects organizational goals, and the measures of the gap and progress toward closing it should help diagnose the next round of planning. In the example of First Chicago, the need to manage retiree health insurance costs was not a critical gap until those costs began to escalate at double-digit levels. Then a key stakeholder—top management—realized the strategic importance of the gap, and closing it became a vital objective. HR planners measured the gap in meaningful terms (medical costs), forecasted its effects (bank costs at uncompetitive levels), and helped key stakeholders to understand the importance of reducing the gap (lost business or profits). The planners then tracked the effectiveness of their efforts, using meaningful success measures (e.g., did medical costs go down?).

## What Makes a Good Objective/Standard?

How hard do you look for the best bargain when you buy music CDs or tapes? Some people peruse catalogs, walk the malls, and hunt through discount stores. Others are content to go to the nearest music retailer and pay full price. Those who shop around may believe that the discounts they find outweigh the shopping time and effort (or they may just enjoy the shopping experience). Gathering information is an investment like any other resource, and the value of gathering information on a particular objective/standard is related to its usefulness. Organizations can't gather information for free, so the human resource planner must consider the value of information before gathering it.

Some information must be gathered because it is required to produce reports to government agencies. Companies that don't gather it are out of business. Safety records, financial statements, and equal employment opportunity statistics (see Chapter Two) are examples. Most information gathered by organizations is not required, especially when it relates to objectives/standards set by someone within the organization. Surprisingly, much of this internal information gathering is wasted because no one really knows what to do with it.

The value of information on an objective/standard is based on two factors:

1. How many decisions will be improved by having information?
2. How much value will each improved decision produce?

Some standards create value by correcting only a few decisions that have very important consequences. Standards regarding how executives are paid may only improve decisions about the executive pay system once every several years. However, each one of these changes can have multimillion-dollar consequences because the quality and performance of top executives affects fundamental business decisions. Some standards create value by correcting many decisions, each with modest value. Standards reflecting individual employee medical claims may detect thousands of mistakes that might have caused overpayments. Though each avoided overpayment may save less than $1,000, correcting thousands of such decisions can save an organization millions of dollars.

As previous chapters have observed, "It's hard to predict, especially the future." Fortunately, information does not have to be perfect to be valuable. Human resource management deals with people whose behaviors, feelings, and productivity are naturally uncertain. Some are tempted to forgo attempts to use information for human resource planning because "it's all based on opinions anyway." As we will see in subsequent chapters, research has revealed some very consistent patterns of human behavior at work.[37] If human behavior was so unpredictable, it would be impossible to plan in areas such as marketing and finance (who can predict tomorrow's stock prices?), yet business planning goes on. Even an imperfect prediction that improves a million-dollar decision by 50 percent can be worth half a million dollars. The key is identifying the information that can most improve decisions and then using that information with full awareness of its limitations. This has been called humble decision making.[38]

The final factor affecting the value of an objective/standard is the cost of gathering and using the information, including processing, analysis time, communication, and other factors. Even an objective/standard with high value may not be worth having if the costs of measuring it are prohibitive. For example, tracking the precise genetic susceptibility to skin rashes of every applicant for a chemical production job might be useful in screening out applicants who will file more injury claims. However, the dollar cost, privacy violations, and potential legal penalty of individual genetic screening probably vastly outweigh the benefits of such avoided claims.

Notice the importance of decisions in determining information value. If an objective/standard doesn't correct a decision, it doesn't have value. Even potentially useful standards can have little value if no one knows how to use them to make better decisions. A good objective/standard is measurable, timely, accurate, and clearly related to the decision-making process. It is also measured at a level of precision that is high enough to support decisions, but not so high that its cost exceeds its value.

## SUMMARY

Doctors must take all the information about a patient and use it to identify critical health gaps and a program of treatment. According to the diagnostic model, Human resource managers also must use information from assessments of conditions to set objectives and evaluation standards and use those standards to make decisions about investing resources in HR activities. HR planning is at the heart of the diagnostic process because planning gathers and uses the information to make decisions. Planning activities can focus on many different levels of analysis; each level contributes to improved decision making and must support the others.

While planning, objective setting, and evaluation seem essential to effective HR management, evaluation is often neither very systematic nor extensive. Reasons may include (1) fear that evaluation results will reveal problems, (2) unclear purposes of evaluation, (3) difficulty and costs of measurement, (4) lack of agreement on the level of analysis, and (5) lack of a framework for understanding evaluation.[39] These reasons argue for more careful attention and more specific goals for planning. The diagnostic model shows that planning activities are investments, with specific features that create value. Understanding the investment value of planning is the key to making it relevant and important to organizational goals.

This chapter and earlier chapters have discussed many different specific measures that can be used to support HR planning. Many of these reflect efficiency (e.g., profits, productivity levels, costs, performance ratings, and sales). Many others reflect equity (e.g., legal compliance, community relations, organizational culture, and employee attitudes). Subsequent chapters show how standards can assess effectiveness in each HR area. In a very real sense, HR management is judged according to the standards it sets.

We have discussed the planning process at the levels of assessing the environment and organization, and the quantity and deployment of human resources. The next step is to plan and choose specific human resource activities, choices that are the subject of several succeeding chapters. We will then return to the planning process and discuss how human resource departments or "functions" are constructed to support all of this activity. One of the most important results of human resource planning is to identify shortages that require bringing in new talent. See if you can solve a critical human resource planning problem facing the petroleum industry in the Your Turn at the end of the chapter.

## QUESTIONS

1. Discuss why the four questions that represent the planning process provide a never-ending series of activities.
2. What four things do human resource decisions require? How do they correspond to the four planning process questions?
3. Why would an organization spend the time and money to use HR planning?
4. Is it appropriate to judge the success of an HR activity, such as pay or training, by organizational performance standards, such as profits or stock price? Why or why not?
5. If HR information can't be used to predict with total accuracy, is it valuable to an organization to gather the information at all? Why or why not?
6. Define *sustainable competitive advantage.* Why are human resources a source of sustainable competitive advantage?
7. Discuss the use of skill inventories, replacement charts, and transitional matrices in forecasting an organization's internal supply of employees.
8. What factors determine the value of an objective or standard? Should information on every objective or standard be collected? Why or why not?
9. Which stakeholders should determine how to measure HR success? Would different stakeholders in the organization have the same opinion about the value of an HR activity? Give examples of how the same activity might produce two different opinions.
10. Discuss the HR investment concept in terms of quantity, quality, and cost.

## YOUR TURN

### Planning for the Shortage of Petroleum Engineers

In the late 1970s and early 1980s, major U.S. oil companies learned a lesson about the importance of human resources. They had weathered the OPEC oil embargoes, and oil prices were rising due to the prospects of a more robust U.S. and world economy. Most oil companies had plans for major new exploration and production (E&P) activities, such as opening new oil fields in Abu Dhabi and expanding transportation capacity. Oil companies paid meticulous attention to such things as geological forecasts, projected price levels, and transportation, but ignored HR demand and supply patterns. The petroleum and chemical industry is not very labor intensive, and these companies had always managed to staff operations adequately.

Soon their Middle East divisions began requesting the drilling engineers necessary to staff their expanded operations. Even a large drilling operation requires only a handful of these people, so Middle Eastern divisions typically requested six or nine drilling engineers from U.S. E&P divisions. Top management didn't place great importance on assuring a supply of this resource. To their surprise, the U.S. divisions often responded, "We can't spare them." Could oil property investments by some of the world's most financially secure, most technologically intensive, and largest organizations (Exxon employs over 70,000 people worldwide) really be affected by an internal request for six or nine people? Yes. If staff was unavailable, multimillion-dollar business decisions would have to be changed: Perhaps the companies would develop the fields with local engineers, or buy financial rights in fields operated by others, or offer only technical assistance.

Top management contacted their HR planners, who made it their top priority. Their first goal was to adequately staff Middle Eastern operations with six to nine drilling engineers.

Second, they compared current conditions to the goal—most companies only had 30 or so drilling engineers in their entire organization, a gap of 33 to 67 percent. Because work permits in the Middle East require five years' experience, new engineers could not be used. Engineers with children of high school age had seldom taken foreign assignments, so that eliminated those over age 45. Yet, the age distribution of existing engineers was bimodal—a large number of engineers under 30 and a large number over 30. Finally, more drilling engineers than ever were leaving because the high demand for their skills in the labor market was driving up salaries. Comparing the goal to the current workforce, there was a serious gap between demand in the Middle East and supply in the United States. The planners considered the longer-run gap: Oil demand was expected to rise into the 1990s. By then, the present engineers over age 45 would be retired and the present engineers under age 30 would be in their 40s.

Third, the planners considered options that might close these gaps. How about recruiting experienced engineers? This would require drastically raising drilling engineer pay levels, which would be costly and might foster feelings of inequity among other engineers. Moreover, in three months other companies would have raised pay as well, resulting in higher pay and no competitive advantage. How about adding career and other incentives? This would be costly and would change career progressions. How about training? Drilling engineers need very special skills that are learned through experience, so very few could be created this way.

Closing the long-run gap required creating a group of young engineers before the mid-1980s. How about recruiting from colleges? Enrollments in drilling engineer programs had dropped during the oil industry slowdown in the 1950s and 1960s. In the entire United States, only 100 such engineers graduated per year. A single firm could not be expected to hire more than 10 or 12.

Formulate an approach for identifying the gaps, possible HR activity choices, and standards for evaluating success. The following questions may guide you:

1. What is the nature of the gaps between desired and anticipated conditions? Are the gaps different in the short versus the long run? Do they mainly reflect headcount gaps, or are there gaps in other employee characteristics as well?
2. Even though you haven't read about the particular HR activities covered in later chapters, what are your general ideas about how to reduce the gaps you identified in question 1? What are the likely synergies you could attain by combining HR activities in different areas (such as tailoring a training activity to the compensation strategy)?
3. How would you measure your success? Who are the key stakeholders to be considered as you evaluate your performance? How will you combine short- and long-run standards? Do your standards link back to the gaps you identified in question 1?

Your instructor has additional information about what the oil company planners did.

## NOTES AND REFERENCES


1. Shari Caudron, "Strategic HR at First Chicago," *Personnel Journal,* Nov. 1991, pp. 50–56.
2. Peter F. Drucker, "The Coming of the New Organization," *Harvard Business Review,* Jan.–Feb. 1988, pp. 45–53; Peter F. Drucker, "Be Data Literate—Know What to Know," *The Wall Street Journal,* Dec. 1, 1992, p. A8.
3. Kathryn Martell and Stephen J. Caroll, "How Strategic *Is* HRM?" *Human Resource Management* 34, 1995, pp. 253–67.
4. "Jack Welch's Lessons for Success," *Fortune,* Jan. 25, 1993, pp. 86–93. Excerpt from Noel Tichy, *Control Your Destiny or Someone Else Will,* 1993.
5. Dawn Anfuso, "Colgate's Global HR Unites Under One Strategy," *Personnel Journal,* Oct. 1995, pp. 44–52.
6. Daniel K. Bunch, "Coors Wellness Center—Helping the Bottom Line," *Employee Benefits Journal,* Mar. 1992, pp. 14–18; John C. Erfurt, Andrea Foote, and Max A. Heirich, "The Cost-Effectiveness of Worksite Wellness Programs for Hypertension Control, Weight Loss, Smoking Cessation and Exercise," *Personnel Psychology* 45, 1992, pp. 5–27.
7. Wayne F. Cascio, *Costing Human Resources,* 2nd ed. (Boston: PWS-Kent, 1987).
8. John W. Boudreau, "Utility Analysis," chap. 1.4 in *Human Resource Management Evolving Roles and Responsibilities,* ed. Lee D. Dyer (Washington, DC: Bureau of National Affairs, 1988).
9. John Paul MacDuffie, "Human Resource Bundles and Manufacturing Performance: Organizational Logic and Flexible Production Systems in the World Auto Industry," *Industrial and Labor Relations Review* 48, 1995, pp. 197–221.
10. Lee D. Dyer and Todd Reeves, "HR Strategies and Firm Performance: What Do We Know and Where Do We Need to Go?" working paper, 94-29, 1994, Center for Advanced Human Resource Studies, presented at the

10th World Congress of the International Industrial Relations Association, Washington, DC, May 31–June 4, 1995.

11. Dyer and Reeves, "HR Strategies and Firm Performance"; Jeffrey Pfeffer, *Competitive Advantage Through People* (Boston: Harvard Business School Press, 1994).
12. J. Barney, "Firm Resources and Sustained Competitive Advantage," *Journal of Management,* 17, 1991, pp. 99–120; S. Lippman and R. Rumelt, "Uncertain Imitability: An Analysis of Interfirm Differences in Efficiency Under Competition," *Bell Journal of Economics* 13, 1982, pp. 418–38; Wright et al.
13. Barney, p. 102.
14. Wright et al.; Pfeffer; Jackson and Schuler.
15. Craig J. Cantoni, "Quality Control from Mars," *The Wall Street Journal,* Dec. 27, 1992, p. A12.
16. Allan Sloan, "For Whom the Bell Tolls," *Newsweek,* Jan. 15, 1996, pp. 44–45.
17. Jeffrey Abrahams, *The Mission Statement Book* (Berkeley, CA: Ten Speed Press, 1995).
18. "American Airlines: Managing the Future," *The Economist,* Dec. 19, 1992, pp. 68–69; Andrew Erdman, "How to Keep that Family Feeling," *Fortune,* Apr. 6, 1992, pp. 95–96; Brian Dumaine, "Closing the Innovation Gap," *Fortune,* Dec. 2, 1991, pp. 56–62; Joan E. Rigdon, "Kodak's Changes Produce Plenty of Heat, Little Light," *The Wall Street Journal,* Apr. 8, 1992, p. B4; Jacob M. Schlesinger, Clay Chandler, and John Bussey, "Era of Slower Growth Brings a Strange Sight: Japan Restructuring," *The Wall Street Journal,* Dec. 8, 1992, p. A1.
19. Lois Therrien, "Why Rich Melman Is Really Cooking," *Business Week,* Nov. 2, 1992, pp. 127–128; Alan S. Blinder, "How Japan Puts the 'Human' in Human Capital," *Business Week,* Nov. 11, 1991, p. 22; Tim W. Ferguson, "Financial Prescriptions for Mighty Merck," *The Wall Street Journal,* June 30, 1992, p. A17; Tom Belden, "High on People," *Human Resource Executive,* Sept. 1991, pp. 61–63.
20. Towers Perrin, *Priorities for Competitive Advantage: An IBM–Towers Perrin Study* (New York: Towers Perrin, 1992).
21. *HRM News,* May 22, 1995, p. 2; *HRM News,* July 10, 1995, p. 2.
22. Burton, "Manpower Planning"; Milkovich and Mahoney, "HRP and PAIR Policy"; Henry Dahl and K. S. Morgan, *Return on Investment in Human Resources* (Kalamazoo, MI: Upjohn Company, 1982).
23. Vetter, *Manpower Planning;* W. Rudelius, "Lagged Manpower Relationships in Development Projects," *IEEE Transactions on Engineering Management,* Dec. 1976, pp. 188–95.
24. Neal Templin, "GM and UAW Unveil Retirement Plan in Joint Drive to Slash Firm's Cost Woes," *The Wall Street Journal,* Dec. 15, 1992, p. A4; Brett Pulley, "USAir Group Plans Cost-Cutting Steps: Move Likely to Involve Wage Concessions," *The Wall Street Journal,* Sept. 30, 1992, p. A7; Aaron Bernstein, "GE's Hard Lesson: Pay Cuts Can Backfire," *Business Week,* Aug. 10, 1992, p. 53; Dana Milbank, "U.S. Productivity

Gains Cut Costs, Close Gap with Low-Wage Overseas Firms," *The Wall Street Journal,* Dec. 23, 1992, p. A2.

25. Gustav Niebuhr, "Mass Shortage: Catholic Church Faces Crisis as Priests Quit and Recruiting Fails," *The Wall Street Journal,* Nov. 13, 1990, p. A1.
26. Lee D. Dyer, "Human Resource Planning," in *Personnel Management,* ed. K. Rowland and Gerald Ferris (Bostn: Allyn & Bacon, 1982). pp. 52–77; D. M. Atwater, E. S. Bres III, Richard J. Niehaus, and J. A. Sheridan, "An Application of Integrated Human Resources Planning Supply-Demand Model," *Human Resource Planning* 5, no. 1 (1982), pp. 1–15; J. R. Hinrichs and Robert F. Morrison, "Human Resource Planning in Support of Research and Development," *Human Resource Planning* 3, no. 4 (1980), pp. 201–10.
27. Charles R. Greer, Dana L. Jackson, and Jack Fiorito, "Adapting Human Resource Planning in a Changing Business Environment," *Human Resource Management* 28, no. 1 (Spring 1989), pp. 105–23.
28. R. G. Murdick and F. Schuster, "Computerized Information Support for the Human Resource Function," *Human Resource Planning* 6, no. 1 (1983), pp. 25–35.
29. Hal Lancaster, "Professionals Try Novel Way to Assess and Develop Skills," *The Wall Street Journal,* Aug. 29, 1995, p. B1. "HRIS: Matching Jobs and Skills Worldwide", HRM News, July 3, 1995, p. 3.
30. Several references exist on this subject: The advanced reader is directed to R. C. Grinold and K. T. Marshall, *Manpower Planning Models* (New York: Elsevier North-Holland Publishing, 1977); D. J. Bartholomew, *Stochastic Models for Social Processes,* 2nd ed. (New York: John Wiley & Sons, 1973); and Harrison White, *Chains of Opportunity: System Models of Mobility in Organizations* (Cambridge: Harvard University Press, 1970). Students new to this topic are directed to Thomas A. Mahoney, George T. Milkovich, and Nan Weiner, "A Stock and Flow Model for Improved Human Resources Measurement," *Personnel,* May–June 1977, pp. 57–66; and Victor H. Vroom and K. R. MacCrimmon, "Towards a Stochastic Model of Management Careers," *Administrative Science Quarterly,* June 1968, pp. 26–46; K. M. Rowland and M. G. Sovereign, "Markov-Chain Analysis of Internal Manpower Supply," *Industrial Relations* 9, no. 1 (1969), pp. 88–89; T. Mahoney and G. Milkovich, "Markov Chains and Manpower Forecasts," Office of Naval Research Technical Report NR 151–323–7002, 1970; and D. J. Bartholomew and A. R. Smith, eds., *Manpower and Management Science* (London: English University Press, 1970).
31. Niehaus, "Computer-Assisted Manpower Planning"; Mahoney and Milkovich, "Markov Chains and Manpower Forecasts"; Jackson F. Gillespie, Wayne E. Leininger, and Harvey Kahalas, "A Human Resource Planning and Valuation Model," *Academy of Management Journal* Dec. 1976, pp. 650–56; E. S. Bres III, R. J. Niehaus, A. P. Schinnar, and P. Stienbuch, "Efficiency Evaluation of EEO Program Management," *Human Resource Planning* 6, no. 4 (1983), pp. 223–47; F. Krzystofiak, "Estimating EEO Liability," *Decision Sciences* 2, no. 3 (1982), pp. 10–17; J. Ledvinka and R. L. LaForge, "A Staffing Model of Affir-

mative Action Planning," *Human Resource Planning,* 1978, pp. 135–50; and G. Milkovich and F. Krzystofiak, "Simulation and Affirmative Action Planning," *Human Resource Planning* 2, no. 1 (1979), pp. 71–80. Milan Moravec and Robert Tucker, "Job Descriptions for the 21st Century," *Personnel Journal,* June 1992, pp. 37–40. Brian O'Reilly, "Your New Global Workforce," *Fortune,* Dec. 14, 1992, pp. 52–66.

32. John W. Boudreau and George T. Milkovich, "User's Corner: Employment Planning Using the PC," *Computers in HR Management* 1, no. 5 (May 1990); John W. Boudreau and George T. Milkovich, *Personnel PC* (Alexandria, VA: Society for Human Resource Management, 1989), exercise 2.
33. See note 30.
34. Catherine Arnsg, "Out One Door and In Another," *Business Week,* Jan. 22, 1996, p. 41.
35. Henry Dahl and K. S. Morgan, *Return on Investment in Human Resources* (Kalamazoo, MI.: Upjohn Company, 1982).
36. Harumi Befu and Christine Cernosia, "Demise of 'Permanent Employment' in Japan," *Human Resource Management,* Fall 1990, pp. 231–50; Neal Templin, "GM Offers Its Outside Parts Suppliers the Use of Idle Factories and Workers," *The Wall Street Journal,* July 29, 1992, p. A4.
37. Alfred L. Malabre, Jr., "Dubious Figures: Productivity Statistics for the Service Sector May Understate Gains," *The Wall Street Journal,* Aug. 12, 1992, p. A1; Frank L. Schmidt, "What Do Data Really Mean?" *American Psychologist,* Oct. 1992, pp. 1173–81.
38. Amitai Etzioni, "Humble Decision Making," *Harvard Business Review,* July–Aug. 1989, pp. 122–26.
39. Anne S. Tsui and Luis R. Gomez-Mejia, "Evaluating Human Resource Effectiveness," chap. 1.5 in *Human Resource Management Evolving Roles and Responsibilities,* ed., Lee D. Dyer (Washington, DC: Bureau of National Affairs, 1988).

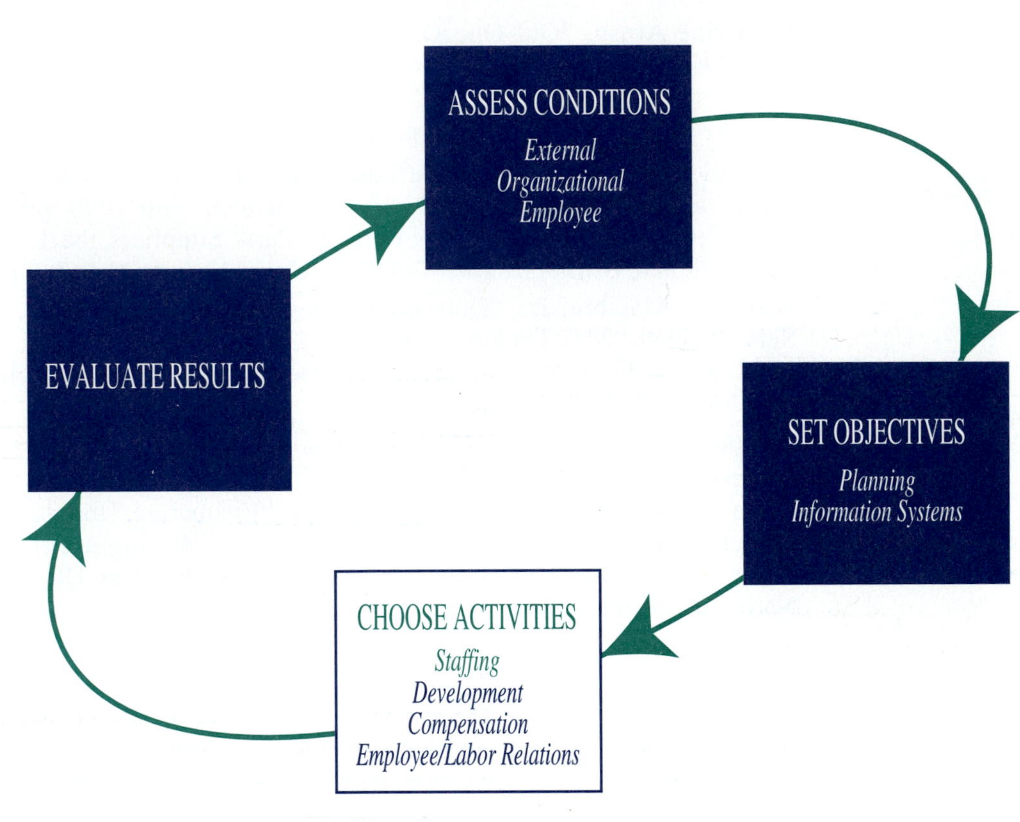
ASSESS CONDITIONS
External
Organizational
Employee
SET OBJECTIVES
Planning
Information Systems
CHOOSE ACTIVITIES
Staffing
Development
Compensation
Employee/Labor Relations
EVALUATE RESULTS

# EXTERNAL STAFFING

Employees are constantly joining, moving within, and leaving organizations. Managing this employee movement is one of the most important and influential human resource management activities. The best-designed organization's jobs, structure, and reward systems cannot function unless the right numbers and types of employees join, get assigned to the right positions, and remain with the organization.

---

*Staffing* is the process of moving employees into, through, and out of the organization, to produce the desired quantity and types of employee assignments.

*External staffing* focuses on moving employees into the organization from outside and on the pattern of employee separations from the organization.

*Internal staffing* focuses on moving employees between positions within the organization

---

The internal staffing process is discussed in Part Three, Employee Development, because it is closely linked to training and developing employee skills and abilities. In Part Two, we focus on the external staffing process of attracting, choosing, and retaining employees.

## A DIAGNOSTIC APPROACH TO EXTERNAL STAFFING

The diagnostic model shows how external staffing fits the diagnostic approach. External staffing brings human resource management into direct contact with external labor and product markets by matching the organization's requirements to them. Thus, its success is keenly affected by effective diagnosis, assessment of conditions, and objectives/standards that reflect both efficiency and equity.

### External Conditions

#### Labor markets

The number of science and engineering baccalaureates are expected to fall increasingly short of the demand for these skills throughout the 1990s and into the next century. Labor shortages have forced hospitals to cut services and to send patients to other hospitals. The American Hotel and Motel Association predicts that travel and tourism will be the country's number one employer by the year 2000, requiring "more than three quarters of a million new workers every year," according to its president. Already, businesses that traditionally relied on younger workers are facing shortages; by the year 2000, the pool of younger workers will have decreased by almost two million, or 8 percent. As Part One showed, the U.S. workforce is growing more slowly and becoming more diverse, with increasing percentages of nonwhites, immigrants, and women. In industries such as U.S. manufacturing, the headlines are filled with stories of layoffs to reduce labor surpluses, especially among white-collar workers. For these organizations, the key is to retain the best employees while selectively bringing in new ones.

These labor market trends mean that external staffing is different from before. Traditional recruitment methods, such as advertisements and employee recommendations, worked well with an abundant supply of white males; in the new labor market, they are less effective. The internet has created new sources of employees, but also more competition. Regarding employee separations and retention, downturns in the demand for a company's products can motivate early retirement incentives or even layoffs to reduce the workforce. Poor performers are less likely to voluntarily leave when unemployment is high, so some organizations must take special measures to induce them to leave.

### Governments and society

Legislation and litigation affect the external staffing process more every year. Chapter Two showed how equal employment opportunity legislation allows government agencies and the courts to review recruitment, selection, and retention practices for adverse effects on protected groups. The pool of candidates attracted by recruiting activities often defines the availability of minorities and females in the organization's labor market. As these groups comprise a greater proportion of the workforce, organizations will be expected to attract, hire, and retain more of them. The devices used to select candidates also come under government scrutiny to ensure that they are job related or do not reject a disproportionate number of minority or female candidates. Failure to consider these requirements can be costly. Burlington Northern agreed to a $40 million settlement, primarily due to its inability to demonstrate that its selection programs were job related. The increasing frequency of organizational downsizing has prompted legislators to call for expanding the role of the Equal Employment Opportunity Commission in monitoring discharge and layoff procedures for adverse effects on protected groups.

Non-EEO legislation also affects external staffing activities. For example, polygraph (lie detector) tests were severely restricted in 1988 by the Employee Polygraph Protection Act. Protection for whistle-blowers who report organizational wrongdoing, veterans' rights, drug abuse, and plant closings are just a few of the controversial issues that Congress has dealt with. Increasingly, courts and state legislatures also have profound effects on legal requirements for external staffing. Many state courts have awarded damages to fired employees who claimed that statements made during selection interviews or found in employee handbooks guaranteed them employment, pension, or severance benefits.

### Unions

Whether unionized or not, organizations must consider the effects of organized labor on staffing activities. National union lobbying is influential in shaping legislation concerning early warnings of factory closings, bans and limits on drug and lie detector tests, and changes in minimum wage legislation. More directly, unions still comprise the main applicant pool for some crafts; labor agreements stipulate specific procedures and rules regarding the timing and order of layoffs and dismissals.

## Organizational and Work Conditions

As Chapter Three showed, the organization's financial and market position directly affects external staffing activities by determining the types and quantities of employees needed. Areas of growing demand require activities focused on extensive hiring and retention, while areas of slowing demand may focus on very selective hiring (or none at all) and encouraging early retirement. Yet, simple supply and demand doesn't fully explain organizational effects. Organization reputation can help with recruiting, as Merck & Company discovered when it was named *Fortune* magazine's most admired company; it received "over 100,000 applications for jobs from New Jersey alone." Dominant management coalitions or even customers may shape external staffing policies. A study of hospitals found that when the revenues came mainly from private insurance carriers, administrators with accounting backgrounds were selected more often; when private donations provided most of the revenue, administrators were selected for their business and professional contacts. Organization values also influence external staffing policies, as those within the organization consciously or unconsciously choose applicants similar to themselves.

The nature of the work directly affects external staffing activities by establishing the qualifications needed for performance. As Chapter Three showed, teams and flexibility are in; rigid job descriptions are out. Finding and keeping people who fit these requirements means looking not only at job skills but also at traits such as leadership, communication skills, and concern for the customer. The idea is to hire for the organization, not just for the job. At Sun Microsystems, they joke that "after seven sets of interviews, we put applicants on the payroll whether they've been hired or not." The nature of the work also determines whether applicants generally find the employment relationship attractive or unattractive, which determines how easily job candidates can be found. Of course, if the work is unpleasant or difficult, employees may be more apt to leave when another opportunity comes along.

## Employee Characteristics

Applicant characteristics, such as skills, experience, and abilities, are the signals organizations use to decide who should get an employment offer. Employee characteristics such as job performance, attitudes, absenteeism, separations, and race/gender tell us if those efforts are successful. Employee demographic characteristics can also determine external staffing needs. As the baby-boomers age and retire, vacancies may emerge even with little increase in business activity. On the other hand, the immediate future will see many workers entering their most productive years (A baby-boomer turns 50 years old every few seconds in the United States), so it may be possible to support business activity with fewer workers. Finally, employee attitudes and opinions affect external staffing decisions as, for example, when the desire to increase the perceived fairness of a layoff or plant closing leads to extensive retraining or assistance for workers to find new jobs.

## Evaluating External Staffing Results

The most obvious objective/standard for external staffing is whether the organization can hire and retain employees. However, filling vacancies is not enough because the quality of the workforce also determines productivity and efficiency. External staffing activities are costly and time consuming; they should be evaluated for their return on investment just as other organization activities. Increasingly, evaluations are focusing on the effects of external staffing on profits, market share, and sales. External staffing decisions often have multimillion-dollar effects because they affect the pay, benefits, and performance of employees who may spend decades as organizational members. Perhaps the most intriguing issue is how to *combine* external staffing activities and integrate them with other HR activities to achieve objectives. It may often be more effective to focus not only on filling vacancies but also on getting the right employees to remain with the organization, so that vacancies occur less often. Spending too much on recruiting may actually be counterproductive without equal emphasis on retention. Managing separations requires changing rewards so that the most valuable employees see a clear link between their contributions and what they receive from the organization. Staffing does not occur in a vacuum.

Diversity and EEO are typically the most important equity objectives/standards for external staffing. Ensuring that candidates and employees are treated without bias toward race, gender, disability, age, and other protected characteristics is a key goal of external staffing activities. External staffing is an important factor in avoiding adverse impact (see Chapter Two), and the relative number of employees in protected groups is closely monitored when making decisions about how and where to select new employees, as well as how and where to reduce the workforce. However, external staffing activities reflect equity considerations in other ways. For example, some organizations still work hard to provide employees with some job security. This is certainly caused by the belief that such efforts contribute to efficiency; it also is often driven by a fundamental organization value—respect for the individual.

Part Two describes the external staffing process with three chapters. Chapter Six describes external recruiting, the activity that attracts the pool of employment candidates. Chapter Seven describes external selection, the activity that chooses which of the candidates receive employment offers. Chapter Eight describes retention, the activity that determines who stays and who leaves the organization.

# External Recruiting

Human resource planners in the hotel industry estimate they will add 600,000 jobs by the year 2000—an increase of 43 percent. During the same period, the labor force will increase by only 17 percent, and much of that growth will occur among people over 50, while the number of workers aged 18 to 30 continues to shrink.[1] These trends may have seemed abstract when outlined in earlier chapters, but to the service industry, they point to a serious gap between future human resource demand and supply. Hotel industry employers face a shortage of hourly employees and a tight labor market.

Even when applicants are available, their qualifications often are not suitable. For example, the vice president of Automatic Laundry Service of Newton, Massachusetts, needed a new field-service worker to repair the equipment his company sells and leases. He placed a help-wanted ad that offered a starting wage of up to $9 an hour, profit sharing, a pension plan, and full medical benefits. Three weeks later, only five people had applied. One had a severe drinking problem, three could not speak or read English, and the last one wanted $12 an hour. Three months later, the job remained unfilled.[2]

Richard A. Smith, senior vice president of administration for Days Inn of America, Inc., responded to the challenge by tapping some novel labor sources for jobs in its hotels and reservation centers. The company launched an aggressive recruitment program to hire senior workers (those over age 50). Two years later, it expanded its efforts to attract the physically challenged by establishing a hiring network with organizations such as the Shepherd Spinal Clinic in Atlanta and the Georgia Institute of Technology. Today, 30 percent of the company's staff in its Knoxville, Tennessee, and Atlanta, Georgia, reservation centers are older workers and 4 percent are physically challenged.

Perhaps the most striking decision was taken three years later, when Smith visited the Jonesboro, Georgia, shelter for the homeless. Smith says, "It was not charitable. . . . We were just trying to solve a problem."[3] More than 45 homeless people have been hired as reservation agents, and 13 are currently booking rooms and answering questions for Days Inns' customers. Even colleges need recruitment. Some small private colleges use door-to-door or telemarketing services to increase the number of student applicants, and recruiters trained to "close the sale" at prospective students' homes.[4]

How do companies decide where and how to find applicants for jobs? How do they generate the numbers of applicants necessary to fill all their vacancies? Do you think that traditional recruitment methods such as advertising, employee recommendations, and employment agencies can be sufficient in areas of labor shortages? Should job qualifications be adjusted to accommodate nontraditional applicant groups? Do applicants need a real taste of the job, including the bad parts, or should a firm hide the bad parts to get more people to take the job offer? How would a company evaluate whether it was working? For Days Inns, not only are some older employees the top telemarketing agents, but their absence rates and medical benefits costs are also lower.

## RECRUITING: THE BEGINNING OF THE STAFFING PROCESS

The preceding examples show how important it is to attract a qualified and motivated pool of individuals from which to select employees. Yet the news is filled with stories of hundreds of applicants for every job at places as diverse as a Sheraton hotel in Chicago, summer-jobs fairs in Montgomery, Maryland, and the Ashland Oil refinery at Cattlettsburg, Kentucky. This might suggest that recruiting is easy and labor shortages are not important.[5] Yet, shortages still exist. Applicants are often unqualified, as Boeing Aerospace Corporation discovered when some applicants misspelled their own street or town names on applications; one addressed the application letter to the "Blowing Air & Space Co."[6] The challenge is to recruit high-skilled applicants from a sea of unskilled job seekers. Even top-level jobs such as boards of directors or high-level executives go unfilled for a lack of good candidates. Internationally, labor shortages are particularly acute in Asia, spurring fundamental changes in social attitudes toward immigration and working women. In Japan, every new recruit got an average of 1.4 job offers and some 400,000 jobs went unfilled in 1991. By 1993, however, the ratio of jobs to applicants had dipped to less than 1.0, meaning fewer jobs than applicants.[7] Still, even companies hit by recession often recruit, if only to replace previously full-time employees with temporary workers. Few companies can survive long without hiring new blood, employees with fresh ideas. Because today's surplus can quickly become tomorrow's shortage, understanding recruiting is important.

Exhibit 6.1 shows the role of recruiting in the external staffing process. Notice how the staffing process sequentially filters individuals through a series of hurdles. As the examples at the beginning of the chapter showed, even the most accurate and effective selection and retention activities are of little use unless the recruitment process generates a sufficiently large pool of qualified applicants to select from and to replace those who leave. Some of today's applicants will be tomorrow's top executives, so recruiting has important long-run effects. Not only does recruitment affect employee qualifications, but it also affects workforce diversity. If sufficient minorities and females don't apply for jobs, there's no way to hire enough of them to meet affirmative action and diversity goals.

*Recruiting* is the process of identifying and attracting a pool of candidates, from which some will later be selected to receive employment offers.

Recruitment is not just important to the organization, however. It's a two-way communication process. Applicants desire accurate information about what it would be like to work in the organization. Organizations desire accurate information about what kind of employees applicants would make if they were hired. Both applicants and organizations send signals about the employment relationship. Applicants signal that they are attractive candidates and should receive job offers; applicants also try to get organizations to give them information to determine if they want to join. Organizations want to signal that they are good places to work; they want to get signals from applicants that give true pictures of their potential values as employees. We discuss this signaling process further in Chapter Seven.

For college students, the most important reason to understand recruitment is to survive in the job market. When a business restructures, one result is often

EXHIBIT 6.1 The Staffing Process as a Series of Filters

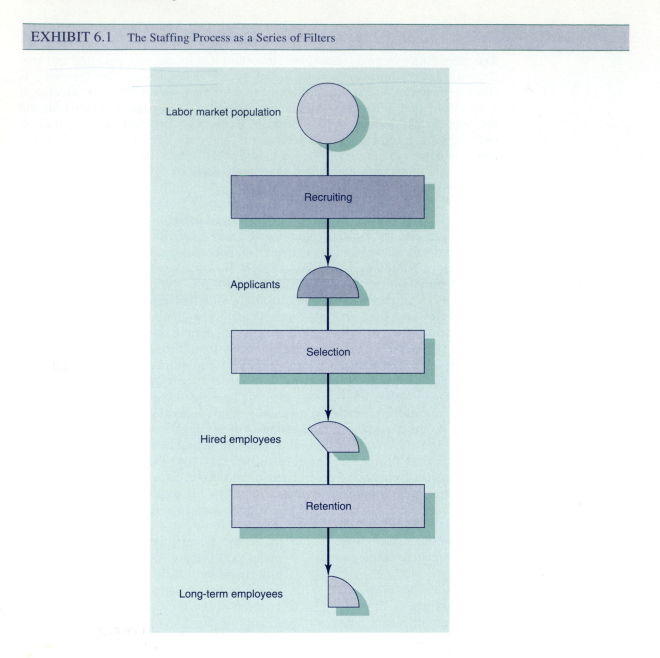

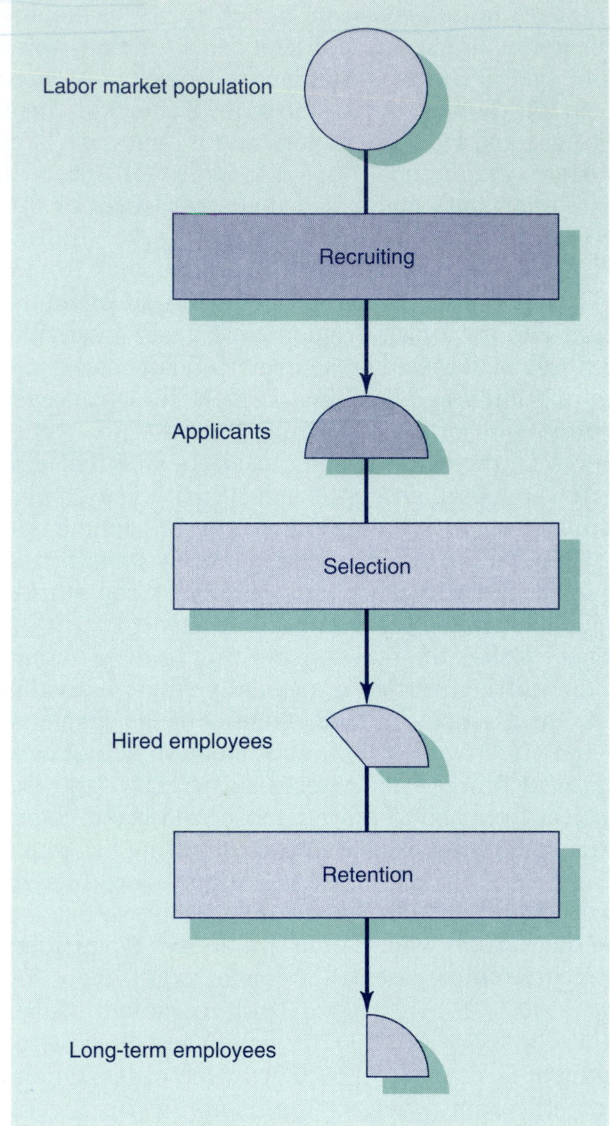


reduced college hiring. Understanding the importance of impressing recruiters, Hugo Rodriguez, an MBA student at the University of Virginia, bought a $350 plane ticket and flew 250 miles to Philadelphia to meet at a hotel cafe with the Dole Food Company recruiters visiting the Wharton School. He got a job offer.[8] While most students need not go to such lengths, understanding the recruitment process is important when you become a job candidate. Knowing how the search process works and how you can influence it are important tools no matter what kind of career you pursue. An appendix at the end of this chapter can help you in your own job search.

**EXHIBIT 6.2** The Recruitment Process

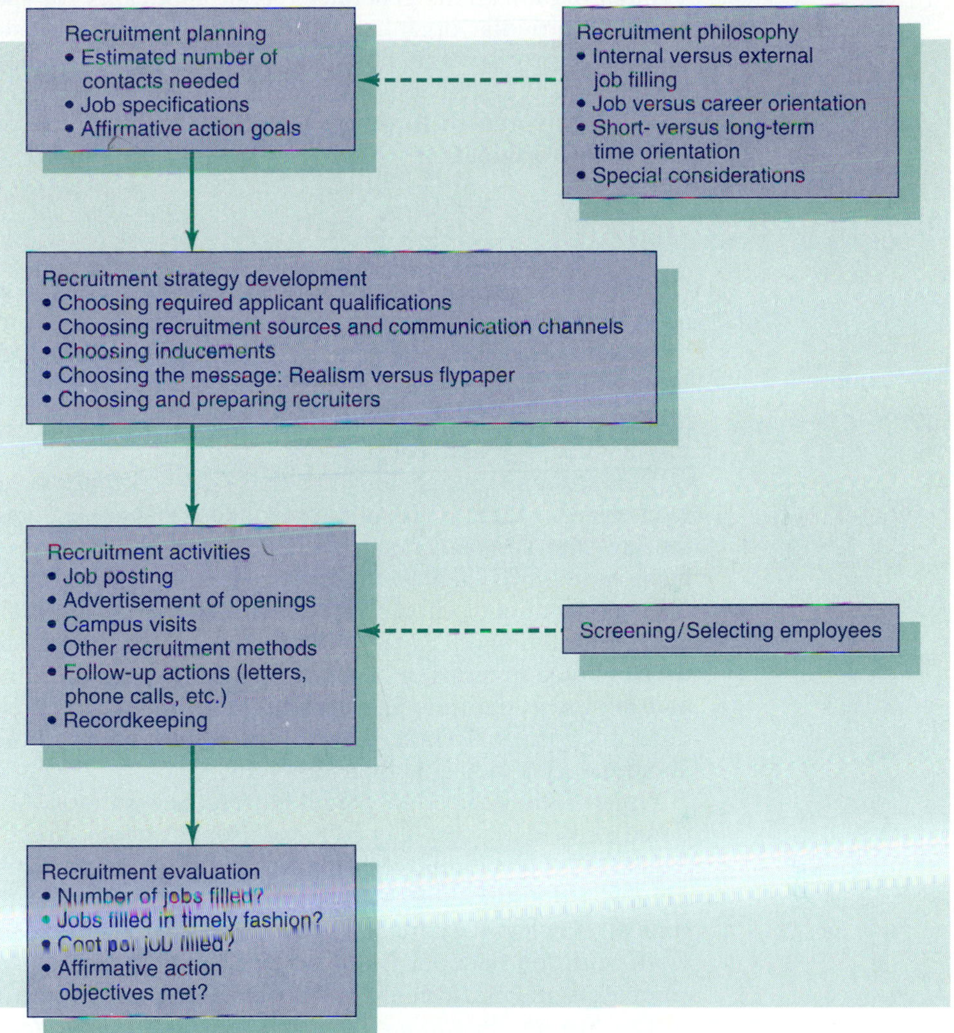


A typical recruitment process is shown in Exhibit 6.2. Notice how the process emerges from human resource planning, discussed in Chapter Five. The planning process establishes recruitment plans and the recruitment philosophy of the organization. Also, notice how recruitment activities serve as the first step in the screening and selection of applicants, which is discussed in the next chapter. In this chapter, we will focus on recruitment strategy development, recruitment activities, and recruitment evaluation. The length of the recruiting process depends on the type of position, averaging 6.8 weeks for managers/supervisors, 4.9 weeks for commissioned salespeople, 2.7 weeks for office/clerical employees, and 2.1 weeks for production/service employees.[9] These data reflect North American experiences. One study in the Netherlands found that almost all applicants arrive during the first two weeks after a position is announced, and the duration of the vacancy reflects the selection process, rather than difficulty finding applicants.[10]

## THE APPLICANT'S JOB-SEARCH PROCESS

Though organizations generally recruit applicants for specific jobs, choosing a job in a particular organization is actually the second step in most applicants' job-search processes. People begin by making occupational choices that define the general types of jobs they pursue, such as engineering, business, music, photography, and so forth. Next, these people choose organizations that offer jobs in that occupation.

### Choosing an Occupation

Occupational choice is influenced by individual as well as environmental characteristics. Psychologists have argued that people try to choose jobs that are congruent with their self-concepts; they classify jobs and people as artistic, investigative, conventional, realistic, social, or enterprising.[11] Sociologists emphasize how the family, educational system, peer group, and guidance agencies might influence and constrain occupational choice. One study of 5,000 Australian students suggested that these factors may have different effects on women from rural or urban backgrounds. When lawyers teach their sons about the law, the sons are more likely to become lawyers.[12] We presume this also happens with daughters, though that research remains to be conducted. However, occupational choice is also influenced by the realities of labor markets and the individual's capabilities and resources. Economists describe organizational choice in terms of how people seek to maximize their future income flow and minimize the time and effort it takes to obtain it. No simple formula predicts occupational choice; usually it occurs early in the lives of individuals, about the time they take their first jobs.

Organizations have only limited influence on most factors affecting occupational choice, but they can influence some factors directly. Many organizations encourage their employees to work actively with elementary and secondary schools fostering students' interest and abilities in math and science. For instance, Hewlett-Packard Company and Lockheed Missile & Space Company work with the Sequoia Union High School district on vocational programs in computers and electronics for students at high risk for dropping out of school.[13]

The *Strong Vocational Interest Blank* and the *Kuder Occupational Interest Survey* are questionnaires that measure people's interests and values, and determine their similarity to groups of people in different kinds of occupations.[14] The idea is that people tend to enter and stay in an occupation that fits their interests and values. Many college and professional placement services administer these questionnaires to help job seekers find the group that is similar to them, and help them locate an appropriate occupation. Your own career center may offer this service.

Occupational choice narrows the field of job choices. The next step is choosing what job/organization to join.

### Seeking Information about Jobs/Organizations

Before choosing a job/organization, a person should gather information about existing employment opportunities. Different people do this in different ways. Hard times have led some people to uproot their families and travel the United

States in search of work, just like the Forty-Niners of the gold rush days or the Okies of the Great Depression. Interviews with male residents of East Boston, South Boston, and Charlestown suggest that they know only about jobs that family members and peers hold, even when jobs are available from large employers who don't employ their friends or family. They also believe that luck and contacts, not education, are key factors in getting a good job. A review of 22 studies found that much job information is acquired on an informal basis. Friends and relatives are the most frequent source, with direct application (walk-ins) a close second. Managerial and clerical job seekers are more likely to use a private employment service than are blue-collar job seekers.[15] It appears that persons in less financially secure situations search more, while unemployed persons with nonwage income or receiving unemployment benefits spend fewer hours per week looking for jobs.[16] Among applicants for life insurance agent jobs, female and nonwhite applicants tended to use formal information sources, such as employment agencies, newspaper ads, and school placement offices, while white males relied on informal sources such as referrals by employees and acquaintances. One study found that some students emphasized the attractiveness of the job when choosing companies to interview with, while others emphasized the probability of receiving an offer.[17]

Does job search make a difference? It appears that those who search longer or more intensively are more satisfied with their jobs and obtain higher salary increases.[18] Males using public employment services remained unemployed longer than those using other search methods. Those who got help from friends and relatives got jobs more quickly, but took a lower wage than they were earning previously.[19] A study of undergraduate business students found that those who performed better in school expressed more confidence in their search activity; females were more confident and said they were more focused; and students with type-A tendencies reported more focused searches and greater intentions to search systematically. Yet, more focused and systematic searches did not relate to job search outcomes. School performance, environmental exploration, and confidence related positively to the number of interviews on campus. Students with greater type-A tendencies went on more company site interviews, and the number of site interviews was strongly related to the number of job offers received. Those who got more job offers were more satisfied on their jobs. High levels of environmental exploration were associated with greater job satisfaction and less search stress.[20] This suggests that while different information-seeking strategies can produce different outcomes, the results of a job search also depend on the individual's characteristics (confidence, Type-A tendencies) and environmental conditions, such as unemployment levels or work background.

Computers may make it easier to gather and consider large amounts of information about jobs. CompuServe, Prodigy, and America Online have electronic networks for job searchers. Later, we will list "web" locations for some job banks. One program constructs letters and résumés from the applicant's responses to fill-in-the-blank questions, and even reminds users to send thank-you notes and follow-up letters. In fact, one program turns ordinary language into bureaucratese, presumably to make it sound more familiar to government recruiters. We fear some of our students' term papers were prepared with this program.[21] Once an applicant has gathered job information, it must be evaluated to make a choice.

## Choosing a Job/Organization

Which strategy do you think will describe your own job search? Student approaches to job search have been classified as (1) maximizers, who had as many interviews as possible, got as many job offers as possible, and then rationally choose the best one based on self-specified criteria; (2) satisfiers, who took the first offer they got, believing that one company was about the same as any other; and (3) validators, who gathered offers until they got an acceptable one and then got one more just to see if their favorite was good, before taking the favorite offer.[22]

A *compensatory* approach to job choice involves gathering complete information on every job offered, comparing every offer to all other offers on all of the important criteria, and choosing the one with maximum overall value. Offers low on some criteria could compensate by being very high on others. People are seldom this systematic because they are bound by limits on their time, patience, or mental capacity. These limits lead to *bounded rationality.* This is the more typical search process, in which people use simplifying strategies, such as eliminating all offers that are below some standard on a couple of important factors (location, salary), and then choosing among the remaining offers, using a more complete comparison process.[23] Bounded rationality is a *noncompensatory* approach because job offers that fail to meet the initial minimum standard are eliminated and cannot compensate by being especially good on other factors.

One increasingly important issue in applicant job searches is that of the *dual career.* With more women entering the workforce, married job seekers often require jobs for both spouses. Organizations may attempt to provide both spouses with jobs in their organization or provide assistance in locating a job elsewhere for the applicant's spouse.

There is no single model of job search, nor do we know what kind of search works best under different circumstances. Most research on job search and choice has been done with graduating college students, who often have the opportunity to gather several offers before making a choice. In many other situations, such as with unemployed individuals or those who are changing jobs, there may be pressure to take the first good offer before it expires.

For organizations, understanding the applicant search process can provide guidance in designing recruitment activities. For example, an organization that can pay high starting salaries but is in a less desirable location might require a very quick response to a job offer, to reduce the chance of applicants finding better offers. It may also cause the applicant to use a noncompensatory search process that accepts minimally desirable location and emphasizes the high salary offer.

# CONFLICTING GOALS FOR APPLICANTS AND EMPLOYERS

If you have ever been through a job search, you know that the process is stressful and filled with conflicting pressures. The diagram in Exhibit 6.3 helps you to understand why the organization often faces conflicts that are just as acute. The conflicts in recruitment are similar to those discussed in Chapter Four on performance appraisal. The job candidate has an internal conflict between the goal of attracting many job offers by presenting the most attractive personal

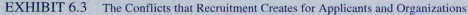

EXHIBIT 6.3 The Conflicts that Recruitment Creates for Applicants and Organizations

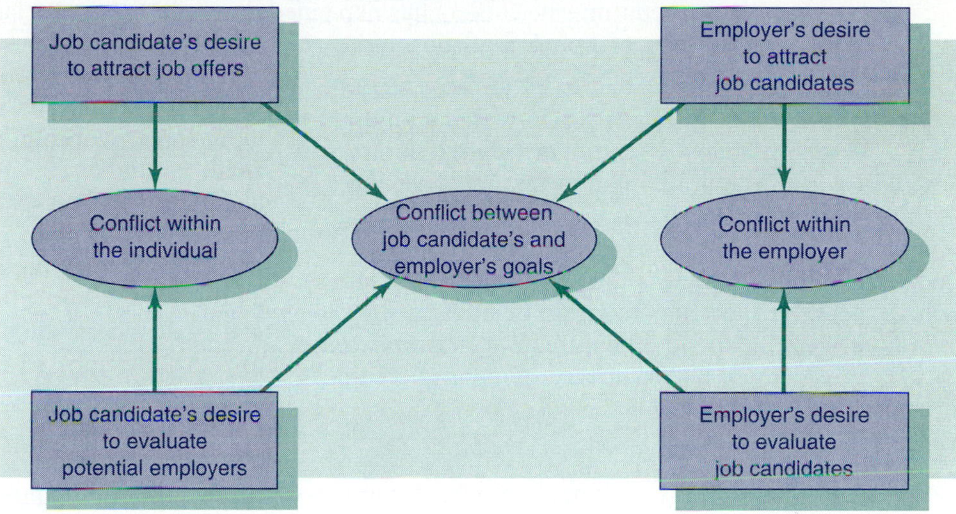


characteristics and communicating a positive reaction to the organization's messages, versus the goal of evaluating and choosing among employers by presenting the most honest picture of his or her abilities and asking tough questions about what the organization has to offer. The organization has an internal conflict between the goal of attracting a great many candidates by presenting the most attractive organizational characteristics and making candidates feel good about the process, versus the goal of evaluating job candidates by asking tough questions that weed out the qualified from the unqualified candidates.

The candidate and the organization have a conflict between them. First, the organization's efforts to appear attractive may not reveal the information the candidate needs to evaluate the employer. Second, the candidate's attempts to appear attractive may conflict with the organization's need for realistic information to evaluate the candidate's qualifications.

Therefore, organizations and candidates must try to reach an appropriate balance between realism and attractiveness.

## THE END OF PERMANENT EMPLOYMENT?

How long do you expect to stay in your present job or in the first job you take after completing your education? If you are like most people, your answer probably suggests a much shorter tenure than that of your parents or grandparents. Prior chapters have described the changing nature of employment, the more self-reliant employment contract, and the need for human resource planning to create a workforce that is extremely flexible and ready for constant change. What better way to do that than to avoid "permanent" employees altogether?

Some experts have predicted "the end of work" as we know it, as future workplaces become dominated by advanced technology and contingent workers, near workerless factories, and a labor pool consisting of highly skilled "boutique labor" brought together for specific projects and then disbanded.[25] The number of contingent workers has expanded drastically over the last several years. A Bureau of Labor Statistics survey of 60,000 American households found between 2.7 million and 6 million workers, or between 2.2 percent and 4.9 percent of the labor force, working in contingent jobs. The smaller number (2.7 million) includes wage and salary workers who have less than one year on the job and expect that job to end within a year. If you define contingent work as the first group plus self-employed persons and independent contractors who also expect their jobs to end within a year, the number is 3.4 million. The larger number (6 million) includes all of the above and anyone else who believes that his or her position will not continue, regardless of the duration of the position.[26]

*Contingent work* is any job in which an individual does not have an explicit or implicit contract for long-term employment or one in which the minimum hours worked can vary in a nonsystematic manner. It can include those working for temporary help firms, those with less than one year on the job who expect their job to end within one year, self-employed and independent contractors, and any worker who believes his or her position is temporary and not expected to continue.[24]

While the BLS surveyed employees, Exhibit 6.4 shows the results of a survey of employers, members of the Conference Board's human resource councils in the United States and Europe. Traditionally, we think of contingent workers filling clerical positions, such as bookkeeping or word processing, but Exhibit 6.4 suggests the growing use of contingent workers in production jobs and even in professional and technical areas. Though managerial jobs are less frequently filled by contingent workers, increasing layoffs and outplacement of experienced executives has created a new supply of talented managers willing and able to take temporary assignments. They may join organizations for 12 to 18 months to turn around a problem or to manage a business unit through downsizing, consolidation, or elimination. Howe Furniture Company uses temporary managers this way and is "awed by the depth of skills that are available." Caterpillar replaced 14,000 striking workers with temporary workers, including welders and technicians. Part-time employment has increased substantially in Japan and Europe as more women with children join the workforce and employment shifts to service industries.[27]

Evidence suggests that temporary agencies and employee leasing are increasingly used in the European Union, with very different regulatory environments. At one extreme, Greece, Italy, and Spain forbid the operation of temporary work agencies and temporary work contracts, although they exist illegally. Most other countries require registration of temporary agencies. Portugal has no effective regulation of any kind. One study found that French banks use temporaries as a long-term strategy to reduce the full-time workforce, while firms in Great Britain uses temps to meet short-term increases in demand.[28]

Temporary employee options include:

1. *Internal temporary pool,* where persons are on call as needed. The pool is managed internally by the company and may consist of former employees and/or external hires.
2. *Temporary agency hires,* who are persons hired through a temporary service firm and are employees of that agency, not of the firm that contracts for them.

EXHIBIT 6.4 Growing Use of Contingent Workers

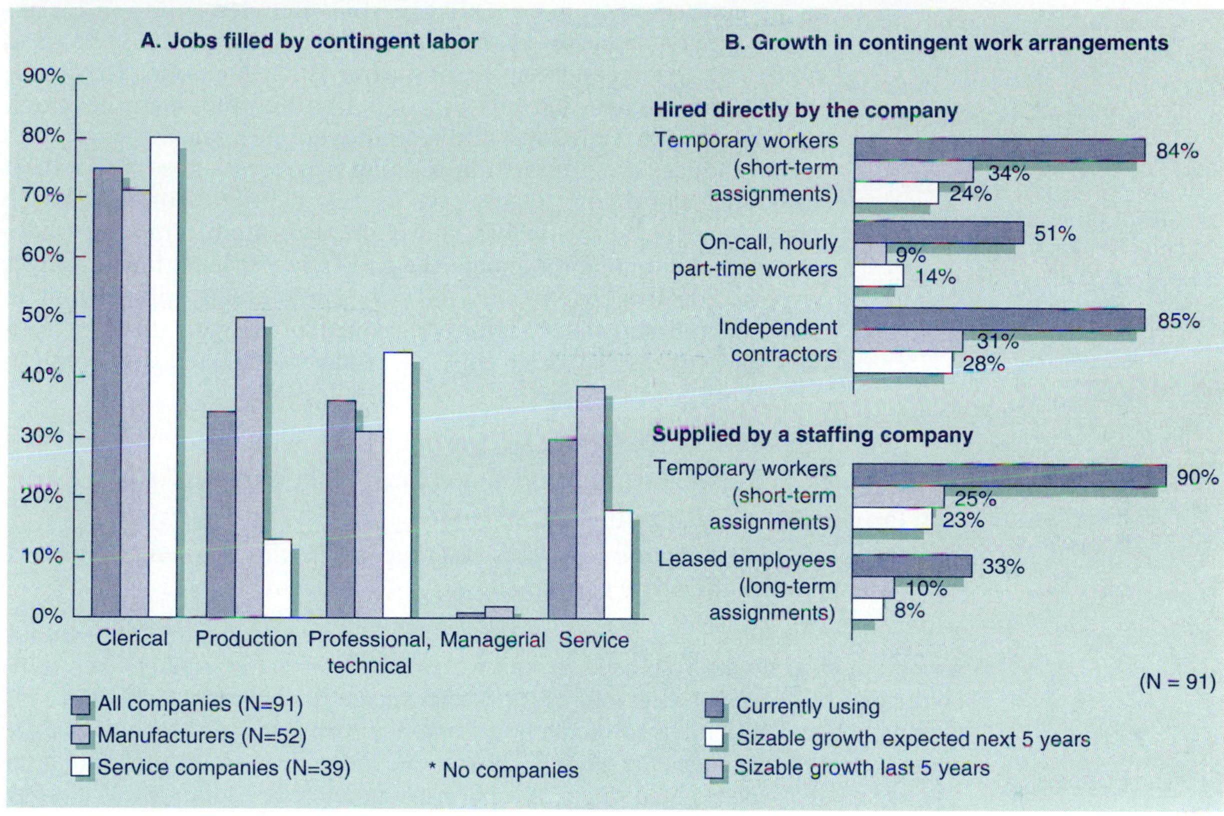


Reprinted with permission of The Conference Board.

3. *Independent contractors* who are self-employed workers hired for a finite period of time, such as freelance writers or professors acting as consultants.
4. *Short-term hires,* who are persons hired only for a specific time period (such as a busy season) or for a specific project.

How can you dismiss employees without really dismissing them? *Employee leasing* involves a long-term arrangement where an employer dismisses its existing employees, who are then hired by a leasing company and leased back to the original employer. The leasing company takes full responsibility for the employees, including payroll, benefits, taxes, and government-required paperwork, and charges the lessee a fee covering these costs and administration. Employee leasing increased after passage of the Tax Equity and Fiscal Responsibility Act (TEFRA) in 1982, as a safe harbor allowing lucrative pension plans for top executives, while avoiding the requirement to extend equal benefits to employees. Employers may also reap cost reductions, and employees may receive better benefits from the leasing firm than they would from the original company.[29]

As you read in Chapter Five, organizations face increasing challenges to meet ever-changing surpluses and shortages of human resources that often occur at the same time. Temporary workers can seem a boon to flexibility and

WHAT DO YOU THINK?

As temporary agencies and leasing companies provide a greater proportion of employees, the dilemma for managers shifts from how to choose employees, to how to choose an agency or leasing company. What criteria do you think would signify a high-quality agency? How important would be the agency's HR policies in this decision?

agility. Eighty-one percent of companies surveyed by the Conference Board said that workforce flexibility was the main reason for using contingent workers. Other reasons included filling in for absent workers—a buffer against job loss for full-time workers—and as a way to screen people for future full-time jobs. However, many argue that it disrupts the social and employment contract, and that it reduces loyalty to the employer, may cause low productivity, reduces the return from training if people leave after a short time, and can disrupt teamwork.[30] Legal subtleties often must be considered because if workers obtained through temporary-help agencies are treated too much like full-time workers, the employer may become the *employer of record,* which creates obligations to pay benefits and other rewards commensurate with those of full-time employees. To avoid this, some have suggested that employers do not:

- Offer temporary workers company business cards with their names.
- Put the names of temporary workers on their doors, cubicles, or desks.
- Provide special recognition awards to temporaries.
- Directly invite temporary workers to company parties or picnics (instead, have their agency invite them).[31]

You can see the dilemma in telling someone, "We really want you to do a good job for us, but we can't put your name up and we can't invite you to the party." Yet, some companies have success with temporaries through careful recruiting. Coors Brewing Company hires 700 temporary production workers a year, using a 10-minute video to show them how strenuous the work is, one-on-one interviews, ability and drug tests, and orientation videos about safety, alcohol use, and ethics.[32] Banc One Wisconsin Corporation solved the problem by teaming with Manpower, Inc., a temporary help company. Manpower's in-house temporary help program provides Banc One with an exclusive pool of temporary workers with better training; this has saved Banc One almost $250,000 in two years.[33] Savings come from reduced administrative costs, reduced benefit costs, and reduced hiring and separation costs.

## On the "Web": Career Help for the Contingent Worker

Exhibit 6.5 shows where to obtain more information about contingent staffing providers on the world wide web. This particular site provides information about the industry, a calendar of events, and a list of temporary help services for employers who need assistance.

Whether they are called "permanent," "temporary," or "contingent," new employees must be attracted to the organization systematically. Therefore, designing a complete recruitment strategy involves not only considering the job search strategies of applicants and determining the balance of temporary and permanent employment, but also involves choosing applicant qualifications and characteristics, communication channels and sources, inducements, messages, and recruiters. These choices interact with each other (e.g., very stringent qualifications are also frequently combined with attractive inducements) to create the recruitment strategy.

EXPLORING THE WEB

You can explore this temporary employment information site by browsing:

**http://www.natss./com/staffing/natind.htm**

EXHIBIT 6.5 Information about the Contingent Employment Industry on the Web

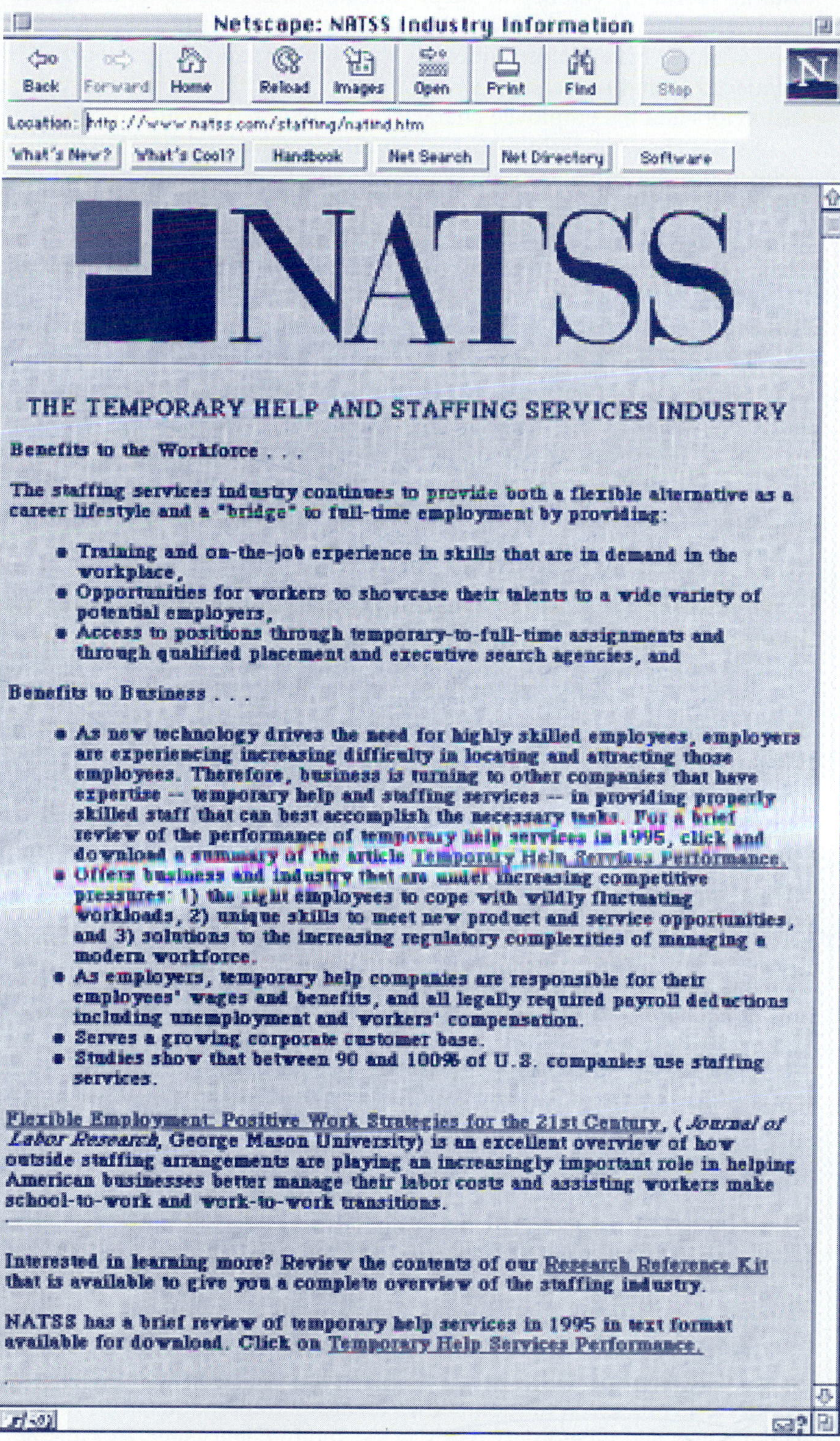

Netscape: NATSS Industry Information
Back
Forward
Home
Reload
Images
Open
Print
Find
Stop
Location: http://www.natss.com/staffing/natind.htm
What's New?
What's Cool?
Handbook
Net Search
Net Directory
Software
NATSS
THE TEMPORARY HELP AND STAFFING SERVICES INDUSTRY
Benefits to the Workforce . . .
The staffing services industry continues to provide both a flexible alternative as a career lifestyle and a "bridge" to full-time employment by providing:
• Training and on-the-job experience in skills that are in demand in the workplace,
• Opportunities for workers to showcase their talents to a wide variety of potential employers,
• Access to positions through temporary-to-full-time assignments and through qualified placement and executive search agencies, and
Benefits to Business . . .
• As new technology drives the need for highly skilled employees, employers are experiencing increasing difficulty in locating and attracting those employees. Therefore, business is turning to other companies that have expertise -- temporary help and staffing services -- in providing properly skilled staff that can best accomplish the necessary tasks. For a brief review of the performance of temporary help services in 1995, click and download a summary of the article Temporary Help Services Performance.
• Offers business and industry that are under increasing competitive pressures: 1) the right employees to cope with wildly fluctuating workloads, 2) unique skills to meet new product and service opportunities, and 3) solutions to the increasing regulatory complexities of managing a modern workforce.
• As employers, temporary help companies are responsible for their employees' wages and benefits, and all legally required payroll deductions including unemployment and workers' compensation.
• Serves a growing corporate customer base.
• Studies show that between 90 and 100% of U.S. companies use staffing services.
Flexible Employment: Positive Work Strategies for the 21st Century, (Journal of Labor Research, George Mason University) is an excellent overview of how outside staffing arrangements are playing an increasingly important role in helping American businesses better manage their labor costs and assisting workers make school-to-work and work-to-work transitions.
Interested in learning more? Review the contents of our Research Reference Kit that is available to give you a complete overview of the staffing industry.
NATSS has a brief review of temporary help services in 1995 in text format available for download. Click on Temporary Help Services Performance.

## CHOOSING APPLICANT QUALIFICATIONS: BEYOND TRADITION

Before recruiting can begin, the organization must decide on the nature of the employment vacancy and the qualifications required to fill it. Employment planning (see Chapter Five) helps to identify the number and types of workers that will be needed. Job and task analysis (see Chapter Three) helps to identify the needed job behaviors and the employee characteristics required to carry them out.

As we show in Exhibit 6.1, recruiting acts as the first filter in determining who joins the organization. We have seen that recruiting activities can affect the applicant's search process and thereby determine who applies for the job. Recruiting also filters applicants directly by choosing required applicant qualifications. An organization might try for the cream of the crop by setting stringent qualifications and spending a good deal of time and money looking for the best candidate. Or, because of a very tight labor market or the desire to reduce recruiting costs, the organization may consider lower-quality candidates, creating a larger applicant pool. Research has found that although increasing qualifications reduces the number of applicants, it can increase their quality.[34] Deciding how stringent to set the applicant requirements requires balancing the cost of searching more widely, if standards are very stringent, against the benefits of higher applicant quality. As we shall see in Chapter Seven, these trade-offs depend on how different are the applicants and how important are those differences to accomplishing goals.

*Screening,* the process of rejecting clearly unqualified candidates at the recruitment stage, is actually the first step in the selection process as discussed in Chapter Seven. We discuss screening devices such as drug tests, honesty tests, and licensing requirements there, along with other traditional methods of selection such as interviews. However, organizations are increasingly exploring ways to attract job candidates from nontraditional sources by tapping groups whose qualifications are often overlooked. These include applicants who are older, disabled, remotely located, discouraged, or lacking basic reading and writing skills.

### Tapping the Older Workforce

As Chapter Two showed, the number of people over 50 years old will increase dramatically; health and longevity allow many of these people to work long after they have retired or left their previous organizations. Long-held biases about the availability and ability of older workers often prevent organizations from tapping this valuable applicant source.[35] Yet, it can all depend on what questions a firm asks. A Louis Harris poll found that 1.9 million Americans over 50 answered yes when asked if they would prefer to work. A more careful analysis asking about specific jobs, need for money, physical ability, job search activity, and tolerance of working conditions reduced this estimate to 1.1 million.[36] Efforts such as McDonald's "McMasters," Kelly Services' "Encore," and Kentucky Fried Chicken's "the Colonel's Tradition" recognize the requirements and contributions of older workers.

Have you ever seen the Home Shopping Network (HSN) on late night cable TV (if not, we assume you were studying for a big exam)? Broadcasting 24 hours a day to seven million homes creates a tremendous need for staff to answer telephones and take orders. HSN is located in Clearwater, Florida, home to many older people, so the company set out to attract the over-55 group with flexible and part-time jobs, and by meeting managers of senior-citizen centers to give a slide show about the company and its opportunities. When this "Prime Timer" program started in 1990, it had 12 people; by 1995 it had risen to 500. In addition, those in the program, including some people 84 years old, had a 30 percent lower turnover rate than others.[37] Yet, stereotypes remain. A 1995 study of employees at a U.S. newspaper, a utility, and a state government agency found that beliefs about older workers varied by age. The older the person, the more he or she believed that older workers have fewer accidents, get fewer occupational diseases, are better and higher-quality workers, and would choose to work with older workers. The younger the person, the more he or she believed that older workers are harder to train, absent more often, grouchier, less cooperative, resistant to change, and not interested in greater responsibility or learning.[38] It appears that human resource managers may need to work hard to dispel these stereotypes, especially among younger workers.

## Creating Opportunities for the Disabled

Should minimum qualifications include physical or mental abilities? Title I of the Americans with Disabilities Act (ADA) of 1990 bars employment-related discrimination against an "individual with a disability who, with or without reasonable accommodation, can perform the essential functions of the employment position that such individual holds or desires." A person has a disability if he or she has a physical or mental impairment that substantially limits a major life activity. Unlike other laws, the ADA requires that employers make "reasonable accommodation" for disabilities, and that they avoid recruitment questions that might reveal a disability, including asking about possible necessary accommodation to do the job. In October 1995, the Equal Employment Opportunity Commission issued new guidelines giving employers more leeway in inquiring about reasonable accommodation, allowing "limited questions" about reasonable accommodation if there is an obvious disability, if the applicant volunteers that he or she needs accommodation, or if the applicant reveals that he or she has a hidden disability that will require reasonable accommodation.[39]

Technological advances and increasingly sophisticated medical treatments have opened opportunities for mentally and physically disabled persons. The Job Accommodation Network is a service of the President's Committee on Employment of People with Disabilities that provide a toll-free number advising employers on how to accommodate employees and applicants. A variety of workplace modifications can reduce barriers for those with disabilities. Thus, companies such as Holiday Inns, Domino's Pizza, and Weyerhaeuser Company have loosened applicant qualification requirements that might have excluded disabled individuals.[40]

## Removing Barriers for Discouraged Workers

Should the ability to find transportation or housing near work be a minimum qualification for employment? How can discouraged, unemployed workers be induced to apply? How can companies identify the employable unemployed? Many organizations provide transportation, relocate jobs, or provide housing. This may be especially important for attracting discouraged workers or those from inner cities who may not consider themselves eligible for jobs outside their neighborhoods. For instance, America Works is a private organization that has taken 2,000 people off welfare, saving taxpayers $20 million. The organization recruits welfare recipients, teaches them basic job skills, refers them to employers, and monitors and supports them for the first four months. Seventy percent of the employees are retained.[41]

WHAT DO YOU THINK?

Suppose you were a manager recommending that a key division of your company hire more discouraged workers, who may be homeless or shabbily dressed. How would you help a line manager understand the benefits of such a policy for achieving unit goals? What sort of preparation would be needed for those who work with the new recruits?

Century City in Los Angeles is the home of posh office buildings with high-priced lawyers, plastic surgeons, and psychiatrists. Perhaps not the first place one looks for a high school education, but the Century Plaza Hotel hosts at-risk high school students from Belmont and Fremont high schools in riot-torn South Central Los Angeles, so they can learn about hotel industry opportunities. The students spend two days at the hotel, work alongside hotel employees, and learn more about the world of work.[42] DELSTAR, which owns and operates a chain of retail specialty shops in airports and five-star resorts, reaches out through the Phoenix Urban League, Chicanos Por La Causa, and the Phoenix Indian Center to find applicants, many of whom are disadvantaged. Training includes how to budget money to pay bills and how to be on time. One of the company's top-volume sellers came to the company from a homeless shelter. She was in her mid-50s, had no teeth, and was shabbily dressed.[43] Clothes don't tell the whole story.

## Tapping Applicants with Minimum Basic Skills

Should the ability to speak and write English be a minimum qualification for applicants? Some employers have found that this requirement increasingly means shortages of qualified applicants. Fifty-seven thousand applicants took New York Telephone Company's entry-level exam, a simple test measuring basic skills in math, reading, and reasoning; 54,900 flunked. In Washington, D.C., about 90 percent of young people who apply for jobs with the Chesapeake and Potomac Telephone Company fail its entry-level employment test, set at about the ninth- or tenth-grade reading level. A survey of personnel managers found that 22 percent of job applicants were deficient in basic skills.[44] The same survey found an average of 15 percent of *current* employees were also deficient.

Companies use creative human resource activities to allow them to recruit applicants with limited basic skills, rather than face shortages. Barden, a Connecticut ball-bearing maker, responded to a demand for 125 new workers in a single year by initiating a buddy system and special courses in English. Now, the company attracts applicants representing a "veritable United Nations from such diverse countries as Cambodia, Laos, Colombia, Brazil, the Dominican Republic, Guatemala, Chile, Lebanon, Pakistan, Thailand, and Yemen" who had good educations in their home countries, but lacked sufficient English to look up operating procedures.[45] Numeracy (basic math) is apparently also a common shortcoming. Domestications, a mail-order company, includes the following helpful hint at the bottom of its 10 percent discount order form:

> Here's how to determine your 10% discount:
> 1. Add up the total for merchandise,
> 2. Multiply that figure by .10.
>
> Example: $100.00 × .10 = $10.00

EXHIBIT 6.6 Who Has the Most Qualified Workforce? Top 20 Locations

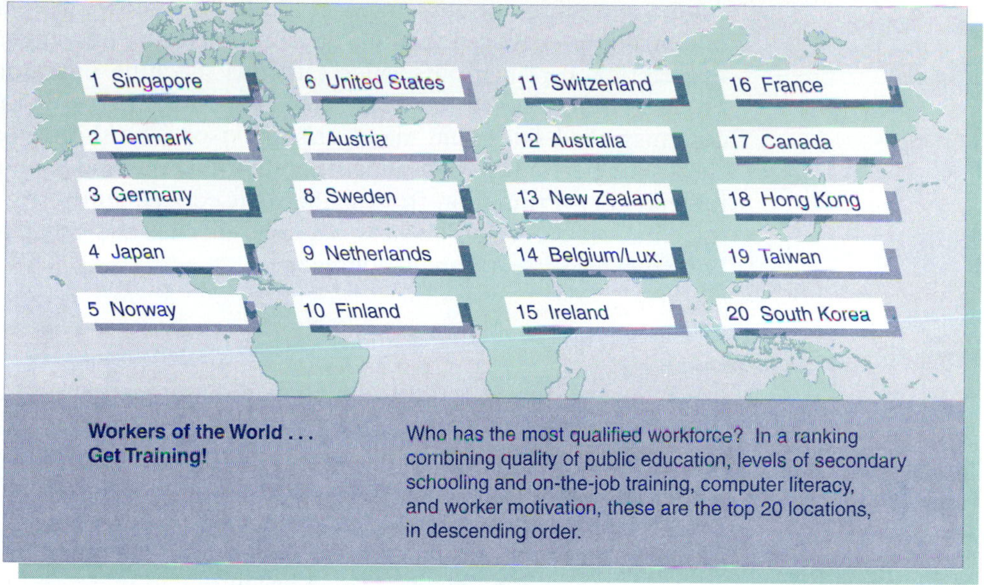
1 Singapore
2 Denmark
3 Germany
4 Japan
5 Norway
6 United States
7 Austria
8 Sweden
9 Netherlands
10 Finland
11 Switzerland
12 Australia
13 New Zealand
14 Belgium/Lux.
15 Ireland
16 France
17 Canada
18 Hong Kong
19 Taiwan
20 South Korea
Workers of the World . . .
Get Training!
Who has the most qualified workforce? In a ranking combining quality of public education, levels of secondary schooling and on-the-job training, computer literacy, and worker motivation, these are the top 20 locations, in descending order.

Source: *World Competitiveness Report* (World Economic Forum and Lausanne Institute of Management Development), in Jane A. Sasseen, Robert Neff, Shekar Hattangadi and Silvia Sansoni, "The Winds of Change Blow Everywhere," *Business Week,* Oct. 17, 1994, p. 93.

At McDonald's and other fast-food stores, pictures or short descriptions of the products have replaced numbers on the cash registers. Employees no longer need math skills to ring up customer orders or calculate how much change to give. While such tactics do allow organizations to tap less-skilled applicants, in the long run they may lead to a workforce unable to adjust to future changes. Recruitment must be integrated within the broader human resource plan.

Minimal basic skills are not only a problem in the United States. Exhibit 6.6 shows the top 20 locations in terms of the rankings of workforces. The rankings are based on the quality of public education, levels of secondary schooling and on-the-job training, computer literacy, and worker motivation. Asia and Europe are well-represented, and the United States is among the top 10. However, Mexico (not on the list) is under pressure to improve its schools to avoid losing jobs to workers in India. Even European companies are realizing that their older workforce may be less computer literate and have out-of-date skills, despite being well educated. Human resource managers considering worldwide operations must account for these differences when considering where to locate facilities and how to recruit talent.

## CHOOSING RECRUITMENT SOURCES AND COMMUNICATION CHANNELS

Whatever their qualifications, applicants must know about employment opportunities. Choosing the types of applicants to inform of vacancies and the communication channels to use determines who learns about available employment

opportunities. Recruiting channels/sources should produce a sufficient number of high-quality applicants at a reasonable cost. They are often chosen based on company tradition or past practice. Exhibit 6.7 shows the percentage of the 245 organizations surveyed that use different recruitment sources for these jobs: office/clerical, production/service (such as machine operators or retail clerks), professional/technical (such as scientists, computer programmers, or lawyers), commissioned sales, and manager/supervisor. The shorter bar in each category shows the percentage of companies rating that method as most effective for that job category. Promotion from within is used frequently; we discuss it in Chapter Nine on careers. The next sections discuss the most prevalent and well-known external recruitment sources.

## Walk-Ins

Walk-ins are simply people who come to an organization seeking employment, often responding to help-wanted notices posted at the work site. This is a very inexpensive source of recruits, especially for jobs filled primarily through the local labor market. It is used very frequently, but less often for professional/technical and manager/supervisor positions (see Exhibit 6.7). It is likely to yield the most applicants when local unemployment is high, though their quality may be mixed. An *open house* can increase walk-in applicants by inviting members of the community, college students, or others to visit the organization's site and learn about its products and technology.

Perhaps the cyberspace version of walk-ins is "E-mail-ins." Increasingly, applicants can contact companies and submit their resumes by E-mail on the Web. Indeed, the day may soon come when the best résumés are the plainest. Fancy graphics and fonts merely confuse the devices that electronically scan résumés, so some counselors recommend making résumés as plain as possible to ensure the electronic eye can read them. We'll return to "cyber-recruiting" later when we discuss advertising.

## Referrals

Did you ever recommend one of your friends as a job candidate? If so, you provided an employee referral. Exhibit 6.7 shows that this is a very common recruitment source. Referrals are particularly common for new and unfamiliar positions, which are harder to fill.[46] Even though referrals are not rated highly for their effectiveness in Exhibit 6.7, research suggests that applicants from employee referrals are less likely to leave the organization in the first year, unless the companies have low morale or substandard working conditions.[47] Perhaps the referrers prescreen the new employees or they tell the job applicants what to expect from the job; or maybe referrers exert pressure on the referred persons to stay and not make them look bad.

Referrals are also influenced by personal characteristics such as age, gender, and race; this may create difficulties in meeting diversity goals if nonwhite applicants and females are not referred for jobs held predominantly by white males (the old boy network). We all know the classic problems when a top executive hires his son-in-law for an important executive position.

Incentives can increase the quantity and quality of employee referrals. At Merck, a company admired for building talent, Chairman Roy Vagelos acts as

**EXHIBIT 6.7** Recruiting Sources Actually Used for Different Jobs (percent of companies)

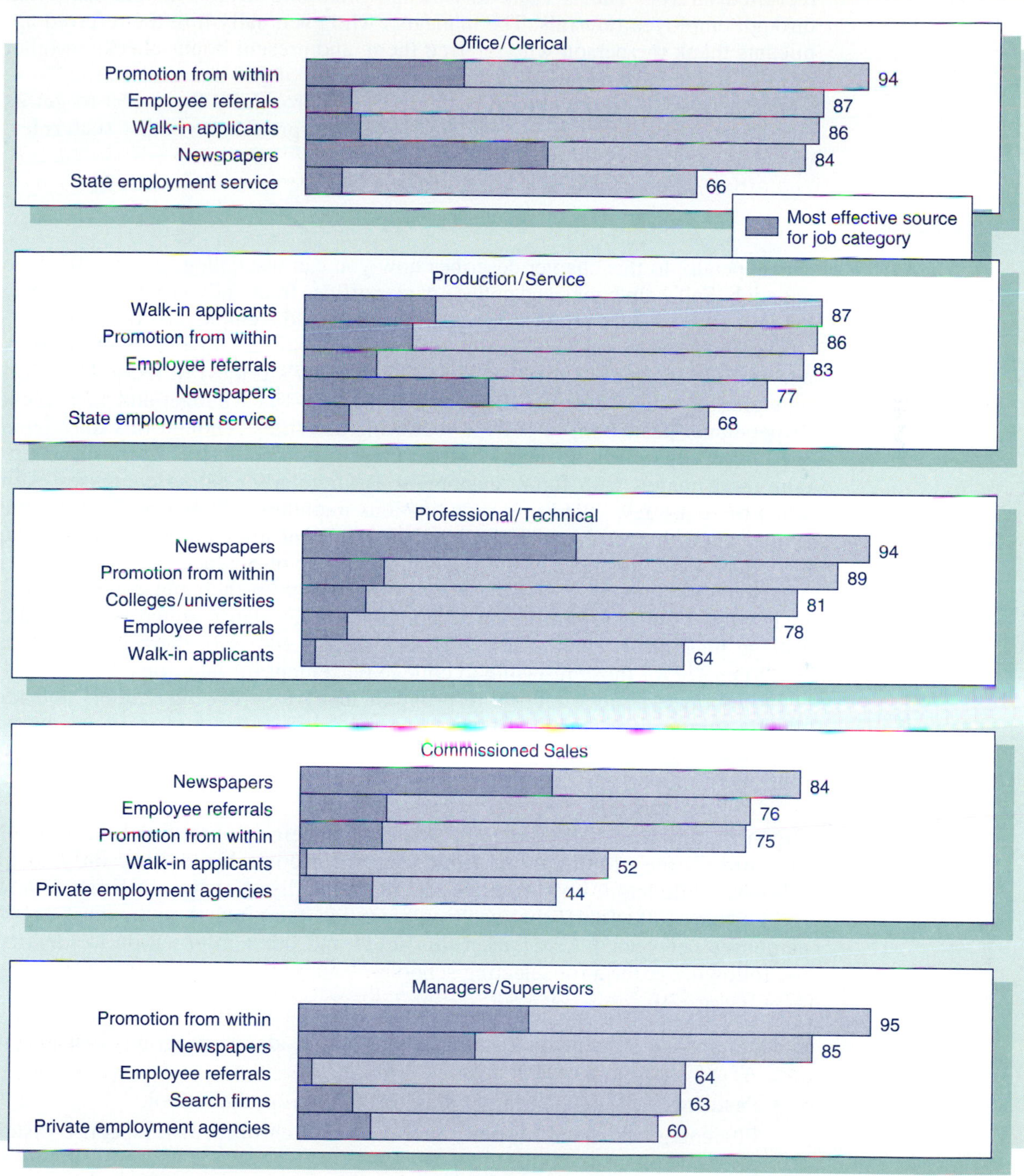


Source: Reprinted with permission from Bureau of National Affairs. *Recruiting and Selection Procedures*. Personnel Policies Forum Survey No. 146 (Washington, D.C.: Bureau of National Affairs, May 1988). p. 9. Copyright 1988 by the Bureau of National Affairs. Inc. (800-372-1033).

his own chief talent scout and often greets his managers with, "Who have you recruited lately?" Harris Bank in Chicago hires 300 to 400 people each year through employee referrals. The managers who eventually hire the referred applicants thank the person who referred them, and present bonus checks or other awards. Some have awarded the bonus in the form of 500 one-dollar bills.[48]

The ad in Exhibit 6.8 shows an interesting approach by Pizza Hut to get its customers to provide referrals. No data have been provided whether such referrals tend to eat into profits more than others.

## College Recruiting

The appendix to this chapter describes how you can use college career offices to get a job. Self-help books and college career offices frequently provide assistance; here however, college recruitment is discussed from the employer's perspective.

College recruiting is a large investment. In 1986, employers spent an average of $329,925 per year (over $500,000 at today's prices) to recruit 161 college graduates, and devoted 16 percent of the personnel budget and 17 percent of personnel headcount to college recruiting activities. Though this may seem expensive, organizations often use their presence on college campuses to maintain good images with future customers. By regularly visiting campuses even when there are few vacancies, organizations maintain valuable contacts for the future when their needs rise. Bell Labs even went after the professors at the General Physics Institute of the Russian Academy of Sciences in Moscow. Recent job shortages have prompted alumni to return to their old college placement offices for help, but this may not be wise. Evidence suggests that while college placement leads to higher wages for the first job, there is actually a wage penalty for those resorting to college placement for later jobs.[49]

Designing a college recruiting program involves choosing schools and attracting applicants for campus interviews.

## Choosing Schools

Organizations base their choice of schools on their resources and the type of position. Some organizations limit recruiting costs by visiting only local schools, while larger organizations recruit nationally. A survey of firms among the Fortune 1000 found that each organization recruited at an average of 47 campuses per year.[50] AT&T used this study and other information to identify the following criteria for selecting schools:

- Quality of academic programs in AT&T's critical skill areas.
- Number of students graduating in specific academic programs that match AT&T's needs in critical areas.
- Performance and retention of previous hires from the school.
- Percentage of racial minority and women's enrollment in specific disciplines of interest to AT&T.
- Quality of faculty in AT&T's critical skill areas.
- Previous job offer/acceptance rate.
- Student quality.
- Geographic location.[51]

EXHIBIT 6.8 Pizza Hut Advertises for Referrals for Customers

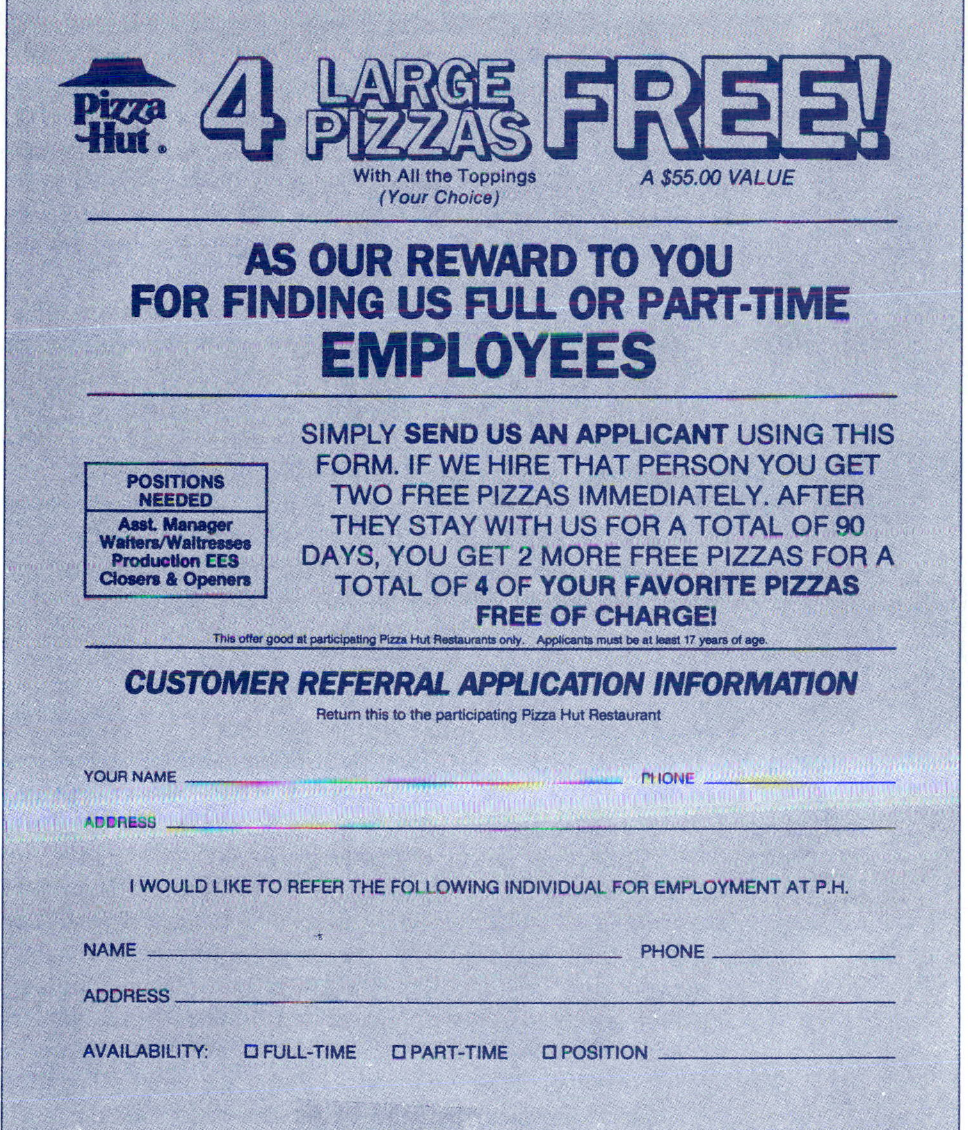


The most prestigious schools are not always the most desirable, however. PepsiCo is renowned for developing managers who understand the business. Rather than recruit hotshots from Harvard or Stanford, PepsiCo "shops around at second-tier business schools for people willing to get their hands dirty." One MBA from the University of Virginia who toils as an assistant manager in a Pizza Hut restaurant in Washington, D.C., can expect to move up in a year or two to regional manager, with 40 or so restaurants under him.[52]

WHAT DO YOU THINK?

How should an organization track and influence the quality of college degree programs? Evaluating such programs requires more than just observing how graduates fare after being hired. Many companies form partnerships with schools: Their executives speak in classes, they work with professors on projects, and they serve on college advisory boards. How would you evaluate the contribution of such partnerships to the organization? How would you choose which schools to partner with? Who should participate in the decision?

Recruiters are getting more choosy, especially about MBA degrees. Companies like GE have in-house management training that they think may be more relevant than the MBA. In response, MBA programs are racing to retool their curricula. Exhibit 6.9 shows some of the more common hot MBA topics. Perhaps you can soon get credit for an overseas junket or an Outward Bound class. Magazines such as *U.S. News & World Report, Fortune,* and *Business Week* publish ratings of MBA and other programs, but their data must be used carefully. Schools that once discouraged students with little chance for admission from applying, now encourage lots of applicants. The more applicants, the more selective the school appears. Quips one associate dean, "We'll get our acceptance rate down even if we have to pay people to apply."[53]

In fact, some MBA students complain that colleges have gotten so wrapped up in preparing students for the job search, that students don't have time to go to classes because they're so busy at wine-and-cheese parties, corporate presentations, career-club meetings, and résumé-writing seminars. One student observed, "I thought I'd have this breather period where I'd be doing class work, but everyone's walking around in interview suits." Of course, the days of person-to-person college recruiting may be numbered as more and more students contact employers by E-mail from their dorms or apartments.[54]

## Attracting Applicants

Will there be enough college graduates to fill future needs? The evidence is decidedly mixed. While college graduates' earnings have been rising relative to noncollege graduates (suggesting shortages), many college graduates are taking jobs that don't appear to require college educations (suggesting a surplus).[55] This may reflect a mismatch of skills, rather than too few graduates. Even if a surplus of college graduates exists, employers still have to attract the best applicants for their organizations.

Research shows that students are influenced by the college recruiting process. Students interpreted delays in receiving a follow-up letter and recruiter competence as symbolic of the organization's characteristics, with follow-up delays being especially discouraging for men with high GPAs and good job prospects. Students also appear to prefer organizations whose policies appear to match their personal values for such things as fairness, concern for others, and honesty.[56]

Many organizations, such as IBM, designate a small number of universities as key schools and assign high-level executives responsibility for maintaining a liaison with the schools. Each executive is expected to get to know the faculty and career professionals, and help them to understand the kind of positions and student qualifications that best fit the company. You may meet one or several human resource executives as guest speakers in your personnel management class. Executives get the opportunity to interact with students, and make students aware of employment opportunities. It's an excellent opportunity for you to express your interest in a possible future employer. Organizations can also donate equipment and money or sponsor scholarships. For

## EXHIBIT 6.9 What's Hot in the New Curriculum at B-Schools

**Case Western:** All students who want one get an executive assigned as a mentor.

**Columbia:** Spent over $1 million on initial R&D on a new curriculum that promises to integrate globalism, teamwork, ethics, and quality into all core courses.

**Georgetown:** Hearkens to Jesuit tradition in year-long required course on ethics and public policy. Inside-Beltway location inspires more-global-than-thou posture.

**NYU (Stern):** Increasing class hours by 40%, one reason it moved from Wall Street's doorstep to more spacious digs in Greenwich Village. Offers full-term foreign exchange program in lieu of the increasingly common one- to four-week study trips.

**Chicago:** Required leadership course, which in past included a weekend retreat to Wisconsin, where students watched a John Cleese film and played Desert Survival versus executives. Quality became a "recognized field of study" here in 1990.

**Denver:** Three-week MBA "boot camp" includes wilderness trip, etiquette lessons by Letitia Baldrige, "cultural sensitivity training," and work stints at soup kitchens.

**Penn (Wharton):** Experimenting with scrapping old-style semesters in favor of quickie six-week minicourses.

**Pittsburgh (Katz):** An MBA in only 11 months, unique among major U.S. schools. Saves a bundle on tuition.

**Virginia (Darden):** Twenty-student teams conduct unpaid field research for companies, often overseas. Leadership course includes management simulations and "cross-cultural exercises."

| | Global Perspective | Historical Perspective | Ethics | Foreign Language | Quality | Business Games | Leadership/ Teamwork | Overseas Junket | Consulting Projects | MBA Summer Camp | Executive Mentors | Outward Bound |
|---|---|---|---|---|---|---|---|---|---|---|---|---|
| Case Western Reserve University | • | • | | | | | • | | • | | • | |
| Columbia University | • | • | • | | • | | • | | • | | | |
| Georgetown University | • | | • | | | • | • | | • | | | |
| New York University | • | • | • | | • | | | | | | | |
| University of Chicago | • | | • | • | • | | • | | • | • | | • |
| University of Denver | • | | • | | • | • | • | • | | • | | • |
| University of Pennsylvania | • | • | • | • | • | • | • | • | • | • | | • |
| University of Pittsburgh | • | | • | • | • | | • | | • | | | |
| University of Virginia | • | | • | | • | • | • | • | • | | | • |

Circles denote required courses or strongly emphasized curricular programs or themes. Intensive foreign language courses are new options.

Source: Reprinted with permission from Alan Deutschman, "The Trouble with *MBAs,*" *Fortune,* July 29, 1991, p. 72. 

example, IBM sponsored the development of 10 personal computer human resource learning laboratories at major industrial relations centers across the United States. At some campuses, Marriott Corporation installed "Explore the World of Marriott," a computerized multimedia database with detailed descriptions of Marriott employment opportunities.[57]

*Job fairs* are employer-sponsored gatherings where students can come to speak with representatives from one or several organizations about career opportunities. *Cooperative education (co-op)* or *internship programs* hire college students in the summer to give them a taste of corporate life and to give the company a chance to evaluate the students' potential. The practice can be misused, however, when companies require applicants to work for free or to provide free consulting advice as part of the recruitment process.[58]

Companies operating internationally face unique challenges. The Japanese Labor Ministry officially prohibits college recruiting until after August 1 of the senior year. Yet students actually begin receiving thousands of recruitment mailings and telephone calls in March or April of their junior years. Motorola distinguished itself by mailing a vacuum-sealed can (like a tennis ball can), ensuring that Motorola's mailing would be separated from the thousands of cards and letters. Inside was a handkerchief printed with a story from the "Motorola Times" describing the company. The handkerchief's became a campus novelty. Candidates visit employer work sites in May of their senior year; by June and July they are receiving candy, telephone cards, books, laser disks, and videotapes. By mid-July, most students have informally decided for whom they will work. Officially, campus interviews don't begin until after August 1, but a U.S. company naively waiting until this official starting date will find the pickings very slim indeed. Japan's economic slowdown tempered this feverish activity, creating opportunities for U.S. organizations that have positions to compete for top Japanese students.[59]

## Other Educational Institutions

Starting in 1994, Los Angeles high school graduates came with warranties. Each written warranty assures companies that the graduate has the basic skills needed to enter the workforce. If the employer isn't satisfied, the school district provides remedial training at the district's expense. Sixty-eight schools in Maryland, Massachusetts, Montana, Colorado, and Illinois offer similar guarantees. Montrose County, Colorado, has had only 3 of its 600 graduates returned in four years.[60]

Organizations tap high schools, trade schools, and technical/vocational schools most frequently for office/clerical and production/service jobs. Growing labor demands for salesclerks, waiters/waitresses, nurses aides, technicians, and cashiers means that employers will come to depend even more on workers without college degrees. Former Xerox CEO David Kearns has spoken and written extensively about the need to reform U.S. high schools. The U.S. Labor Department's SCANS report (Secretary's Commission on Achieving Necessary Skills) proposed that schools fundamentally change their teaching philosophy from lectures to passive students to "applied learning" in which students use basic skills to solve everyday problems. The business community was very influential in identifying the skills and teaching methods, and sometimes helps directly when executives become mentors for students. For example, rather than learning biology by memorizing the parts of the frog, students can build ecological models that predict the birth and death of populations as well as food availability. Experts suggest that one of the best ways to encourage higher standards in high school is for employers to hire based on high-school achievement (not just getting a diploma), giving a real incentive for non-college-bound students to do well.[61]

**EXHIBIT 6.10** Intel Corporation and Chandler, Arizona Collaborate to Improve Elementary Education

**The "Vision" for the Future School**

- To create a need-fulfilling school for students, parents, teachers, community, and business partners.
- To include parents as full partners in their children's educations.
- To create a world-class instructional program with emphasis on communications, science, and mathematics.
- To create a technology-rich environment for learners.
- To create a quality/cooperative school in which people cheer for one another's learning, work together to get things done, and are committed to taking responsibility for continuous improvement.

Source: Dawn Anfuso, "Intel Educates a School District about Business," *Personnel Journal,* Apr. 1995, pp. 128–38.

Still, schools and human resource managers can do better to create the match. A survey of plant managers or site managers at 3,000 locations in the United States with more than 20 workers showed that 57 percent of managers believed that skill requirements had increased in the last three years and that 20 percent of workers were not proficient in their jobs. More troubling still was that employers ranked applicants' academic performance and reputation of their school near the bottom of the things they considered, with teacher recommendations at the bottom. Work experience, attitudes, and communication skills ranked highest. Telling high school students to do well in school may ring hollow when they find that their school performance has little to do with their job prospects.[62] Intel Corporation won *Personnel Journal's* 1995 Optima Award for Excellence for its partnership with the Chandler, Arizona, school district to create a model school in which Intel helps improve business practices and collaborates to bring problem solving, team building, and computer skills into the classroom. Exhibit 6.10 shows the "vision" for the new school. How does your elementary school system stack up? Intel also works with local two-year vocational schools and has invested $3 million in the facilities of regional colleges. Not only does this improve the pool of eventual recruits, but it makes it easier to attract families with children to Intel's plants in the area.[63]

In Japan, high schools compete for student entrants as aggressively as colleges in the United States. Businesses cultivate long-term relationships with Japanese high schools, which recommend graduates based on extensive testing that taps not only grades but also other indicators of skills and abilities. Businesses usually see only as many applicants as they have openings, and they usually hire all of them. The main screening occurs as high schools with the best business ties select the most talented students, and then as high schools match students with companies.[64]

Some have heralded vocational schools as a source of hope for filling technical job vacancies in the future. In Boston, 90 eleventh-graders participate in apprenticeships in fields such as radiology and nuclear medicine. The United

States is catching up to a long-term worldwide trend. Roughly 70 percent of German high school students study a vocation. Grade school students are placed into *gymnasium* for college prep through grade 13; *realschule* that readies 10-grade students for apprenticeships or technical training; and *hauptschule,* a lower-level school that prepares students for apprenticeships beginning after 9th or 10th grade. In Germany, about 500,000 companies every year provide on-the-job training for 1.8 million teenage apprentices, comprising 6 percent of the workforce, at a cost of roughly $10 billion.[65]

But Europe isn't the only place with apprenticeships. McDonald's "Youth Apprenticeship" will provide more than 4,000 high school students from 102 high schools in 15 states with basic business skills to begin careers in hospitality and retailing, making it the "largest corporate commitment to school-to-work programs to date," according to U.S. Secretary of Labor Robert Reich.[66]

## Public Employment Agencies

The U.S. Employment Service operates more than 2,400 employment agencies in the United States. One survey found that smaller firms used USES more often than larger ones.[68] Typically, USES places clerical, unskilled laborers, production workers, and technicians. USES offers some standardized testing and placement (see Chapter Seven). One of the largest military campaigns is Operation Transition, designed to find jobs for the 300,000 individuals discharged from the military each year. The key is the Defense Outplacement Referral System (DORS), a touch-tone service that allows employers to type in standard codes for different jobs and locations, and receive by mail or fax the résumés of interested military personnel.[69]

## Private Employment Agencies and Headhunters

Why are analogies to violent tribal customs so frequent? Psychologists sometimes resent the term *headshrinker,* and private employment agencies sometimes resent the term *headhunter.* Private agencies usually hunt for candidates with one or more specific skills, ranging from secretaries to accountants to executives. Agencies maintain an inventory of applicants and offer to fill jobs more quickly and with better screening than the employer could through its own efforts. High-level executive headhunters are constantly contacting employed executives to determine their interest in moving to new positions. One-fourth of one survey's respondents used executive search firms for higher-salary managerial positions and private agencies for entry-level and lower-salary positions.[70] A hiring organization usually pays a fee of about 30 percent of the first-year's salary for candidates from search firms, with smaller fees to other agencies. Some organizations find that the pressure to make placements can lead search firms to be too aggressive, recommending candidates that may not really fit the job. However, if revenues are any indication, the executive search business is booming. As companies outsource many human resource functions, more and more call on executive recruiters. This is especially true as multinational companies need managers who are natives of their home countries around the world. One survey found that multinational companies expect 74 percent of their managers to be host-country nationals in five years, compared with 45 percent in 1995.[71]

## Professional Associations

The American Medical Association, American Dental Association, American Management Association, Society for Women Engineers, American Psychological Association, Society for Human Resource Management, and Academy of Management are professional societies. They provide a forum for members to share ideas, make acquaintances, and improve their skills. Most also maintain placement services through which organizations can advertise position openings or attend professional conferences to meet candidates. Many professors are recruited this way by universities. Your professors may be able to describe how this process worked when they were hired.

Professional associations even exist just for recruiters. They provide a meeting place where recruiters can exchange ideas, get help with problems, and learn new developments.

> EXPLORING THE WEB
>
> On the "web," you can get a list of recruitment associations at
> **http://www.interbiznet.com/ibn/recruitassn.html**

## Cyber-Recruitment: Finding Your Dream Job on the Internet

You've already seen several examples of the Internet's growing influence on recruitment. Chapter Sixteen discusses the internet as part of the human resource professional's information management system, but here we focus on recruiting. Exhibit 6.11 shows a partial listing of the extensive recruiting and job listing services on the internet, and this in only letters *A* through *C*! Organizations can list their jobs on these services, which often allow applicants to submit their applications electronically, and forward the applications to the appropriate organization. The entire transaction may soon take place electronically, with the internet serving as the go-between. Many companies also have "home pages" on the internet, and most of them has a section available to learn more about their employment opportunities. At Cisco Systems, an "internetworking firm," almost all open positions are posted on the internet, on the firm's own home page. Net browsers can view up to 400 positions at a time.[72]

> EXPLORING THE WEB
>
> You can access this list of recruiting services at
> **http://phoenix.placement.oakland.edu/career/internet.htm**

## Advertising

Of course, not everyone is on the internet yet, so good old-fashioned advertising is still widely used, even in some unusual ways. One Nebraska man complained to Ann Landers about his six-year quest to fill six sales jobs paying $20 per hour. After Landers printed his letter, he was bombarded with letters the next week.[73] Would you ever think to look for a job by reading the restroom walls? At Chicago's Merchandise Mart, "managers live in dread of the day a prized female staffer announces, 'I'm just going to run to the ladies' room for a minute,' " because she may never return. The 26 women's restrooms at the Mart are lined with job notices placed by the home-furnishing and floor-covering wholesalers in the building. One administrative supervisor notes that it's a great prescreening tool, "because everyone using the washrooms has a knowledge of how Mart companies operate."[74] A Southern California hospital recruited nurses

EXHIBIT 6.11 Internet Job Listings and Career Assistance

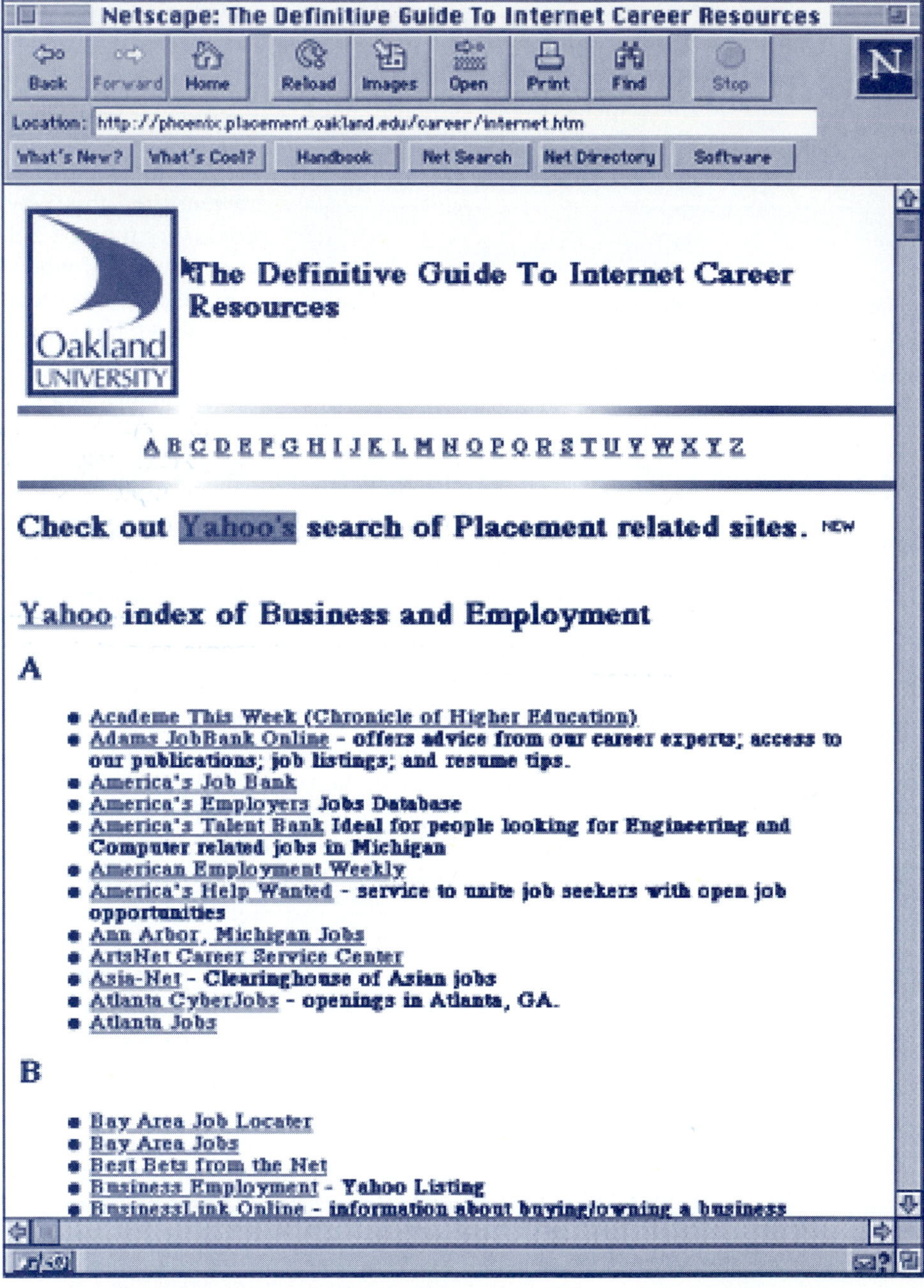

by promoting its beachside location through the mail. Each candidate received a small packet of sand and seashells inside its brochure. The outside of the mailer said, "How do you get ready for the best career move of your life? . . . Just add water."[75] This probably wouldn't work as well for New Jersey hospitals. Exxon sends candidates for its HR positions a brochure about its Human Resources Professional Development Program, an in-house series of classes in 10 modules covering such topics as Integrating HR into the Business, Advising and Consulting Skills, and Management of Change.

As we show in Exhibit 6.7, newspaper ads are one of the most frequently used communication methods for all sorts of jobs. Advertisements are also placed in trade journals or magazines, radio/television, and even mailed directly to people who fit the profiles of likely applicants. Advertisements are seen not only by those seeking employment but also by prospective applicants, customers, and the community. Thus, the message must be carefully chosen, because it presents an image of the organization, not just the recruiting process. Larger firms use national advertising and spend more on advertising than small firms. Though newspaper ads are used extensively, studies have found them to more frequently produce low-performing employees with high levels of separations.[76] Advertisements can be targeted by borrowing techniques from marketing. NEC Information Systems (NECIS) in New England used focus groups, or panels of marketing and technical applicants, to tell NECIS what they looked for in a company and in an employment advertisement. NECIS even used a tachiscope evaluation that exposed people to a slide of different ads at speeds of 1/125th, 1/30th, 1/8th, and one second to see how easily they could identify the company's name in the advertisement.[77]

## Immigrants

The Immigration Act of 1990 increased the number of immigrants allowed to enter the United States, and tripled to 140,000 the visas allotted to those with skills in high demand. Previously, immigration patterns primarily reflected the desire to reunite the families of those already in the United States. The result of this act is to create a vast new pool of skilled individuals. Gary Becker, Nobel Prize-winning economist, suggests that the value of immigration could be enhanced if immigration permits were auctioned to the highest bidder.[78] The Immigration Reform and Control Act of 1986 reflected the increasing concern about the use of illegal aliens and prohibited employers from knowingly hiring, recruiting, or referring for work aliens who have entered the country illegally or whose immigrant status does not permit their employment. Organizations who recruit immigrants may find that the stakes are high. For instance, Piedmont Quilting, a South Carolina textile firm, was fined $580,000 for employing 85 illegal aliens, including minors, and for paperwork violations involving 400 other employees. Eleven company officers and supervisors were indicted on more than 100 counts involving up to $5 million in fines and up to 653 years in jail for each if convicted. Some argue that such consequences may cause discrimination against Hispanics and other minorities as employers refuse to hire anyone who might later turn out to be an illegal immigrant.[79]

Debate continues on the effects of immigrants on the U.S. job market. The Immigration and Naturalization Service (INS) reports that the 2,400 jobs held by illegal immigrants uncovered in a recent enforcement operation earned a total of $33.6 million in annual income, some making $15 per hour. Many of those vacancies have since been filled with U.S. workers. In the high-technology area, the recruiting director for Microsoft says limiting the flow of immigrant scientists and engineers would "blow away one of the best industries the United States has going for it." It is estimated that more than 10 percent of America's scientists and engineers in 1990 were foreign-born naturalized U.S. citizens or foreign citizens. Congress continues actively to consider bills to limit immigration, fearing the loss of jobs for U.S. citizens.[80] Nonetheless, immigration remains a key recruitment source.

### Which Sources Work Best?

There is very little evidence on the effectiveness of different recruitment methods for enhancing job performance and much of the evidence is mixed.[81] However, the relationship between sources and job survival seems to be somewhat clearer. A review of 12 published studies compared inside sources, such as rehires, referrals, and in-house advertising to outside sources such as newspaper ads, employment agencies, and school placement offices. Inside sources always produced higher job survival. The worse the job survival from outside sources, the greater the improvement.[82] Therefore, it is difficult to state which sources to use for which jobs, except that inside sources should be used if job survival is the key.

## CHOOSING INDUCEMENTS

What coaxes candidates to apply for employment? Larry Drake, one of the highest-ranking African American executives at Coca-Cola Company, left for PepsiCo's Kentucky Fried Chicken unit, where he was promised a fast promotion track. His first assignment: breading onion rings and cleaning floors in an inner-city Pittsburgh restaurant. Within eight months, however, he became KFC's most senior African American executive, managing an $800 million region.[83] Despite million-dollar salaries, generous stock options, and lucrative guaranteed severance packages, troubled companies often find it hard to attract top executives. As starting salaries for MBA consulting jobs top $80,000 at some prestigious schools, many young professionals are taking salary cuts to live in small towns in rural Georgia.[84] Exhibit 6.12 shows how Comedy Central advertised for interns, including attractions such as the lack of pay and provision of water and stale bread. Obviously, it's not just the money that attracts applicants.

The main inducements for employment applicants involve the rewards, position requirements, and working conditions they gain by joining an organization. Chapter Three discussed how jobs are analyzed and designed, and how working conditions differ. Later chapters on compensation discuss how the level of pay and benefits can increase the number of applicants and their acceptance rate.[85] Opportunities for career advancement, skill training, or scholarships are frequently motivating factors and are discussed in the chapters on employee development and training. Child care costs, family needs, work values, organizational diversity, and the opportunity to "have clout" and "work on the factory floor" all affect applicants.[86] Attracting people to live in other countries can be even more complex. *The Prague Post* reports that health care is a key concern

EXHIBIT 6.12 Comedy Central's Intern Recruitment on the Web

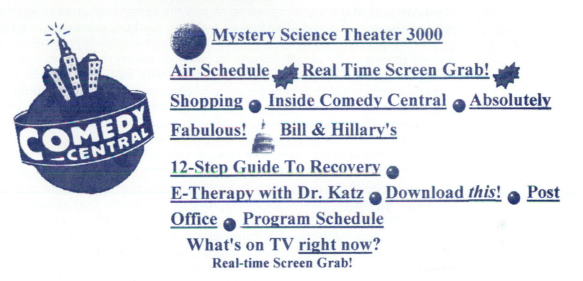

**TOTALLY FREE WEB SITE**

Air Schedule Real Time Screen Grab!

Shopping Inside Comedy Central Absolutely Fabulous! Bill & Hillary's 12-Step Guide To Recovery

E-Therapy with Dr. Katz Download *this*! Post Office Program Schedule

**What's on TV right now?**

**Real-time Screen Grab!**

**Visit Comedy Central on CompuServe. You're already in our web site, so what more could you need? You can play the big cheese and make programming suggestions, vote in the "Politically Incorrect" poll and upload your favorite jokes in Quick Laughs. "Stand-Up On-Line", a coming feature, is a closet-comic's dream where users can try out their schtick and get real-time feedback as to whether they should get an agent or keep that fancy job selling pretzels in the park. To visit Comedy Central on CompuServe, *go comedy*. If you're not already a CompuServe member, call 1-800-646-0412 for a free membership kit.**

**Comedy Central Internships: Students are needed for fall internships in the following departments:**

- **On-Line Services**
- **Program Development**
- **Production Operations**
- **Affiliate Sales**
- **Marketing**

**Comedy Central internships are hands-on positions that will enable you to develop real skills. Successful applicants will be hard working with a sense of humor and a desire to learn. Internships are unpaid and must be for college credit (water and stale bread are provided at irregular intervals). For consideration, send your cover letter and resume to Comedy Central, 1775 Broadway, New York, NY 10019, Attention: Human Resources (fax: 212-767-8581) or via e-mail to interns@comcentral.com.**

among foreigners recruited to live in Prague. Therefore, many companies are hiring Czech doctors to serve their employees. One woman started a clinic, Health Care Unlimited, to provide care for foreigners.[87]

Do the different inducements affect decisions to accept, compared with reject, job offers? In one study, people who accepted offers from a petrochemical company ranked the company, security, and the supervisor as more important, while those rejecting the offer ranked location, working conditions, and hours as more important.[88] Moreover, applicants may take certain inducements as signals of other organizational features. A study of undergraduate students found that those seeing hypothetical job descriptions with higher pay levels also believed the jobs would be more desirable in challenge, working conditions, skill requirements, and effort required.[89] Few organizations design their work, pay, and career paths solely to improve recruiting, but their importance to applicants points up the need for an integrated human resource strategy.

Certain inducements, however, are focused specifically on the recruiting process. TRW offers its employees assistance in financing new homes and actually saves money by negotiating volume discounts with real estate agents and mortgage brokers.[90] Service industries such as ski resorts, hotels, and fast-food restaurants often offer free or reduced-cost services to new hires and employees. Signing bonuses, long used by sports teams, are also becoming more common among technical/professional and managerial occupations. Inducements must be chosen carefully to avoid feelings of inequity among current employees.

## CHOOSING THE MESSAGE: REALISM VERSUS FLYPAPER

Would you rather an organization tried to recruit you using a flypaper approach that describes only the most attractive dimension of the organization, or would you prefer a more realistic treatment that includes both the positive and negative aspects? Would the organization be more successful by attracting lots of applicants with positive messages, or by having applicants obtain a more realistic idea so that if they join they already know what to expect? This is by far the most frequently studied question in recruitment. Providing realistic information is one way to ensure that new employees' expectations are met; this can increase job satisfaction, commitment, and tenure.[91]

The *realistic job preview* (RJP) is an approach that gives recruits an accurate picture of the job and the organization, including negative aspects. RJPs can be delivered through booklets, videos, conversations, advertisements, or any other means of communication. A video used by Wang Laboratories showed that workers spent a lot of time in cubicles, worked on computers, and commonly wore shorts and tank tops. Would an abundance of shorts and tank tops be classified as realism or flypaper? It probably depends on who they show in the video. Merrill Lynch & Company gives stockbroker applicants a realistic work simulation, and summer internships provide very intensive RJPs for college students.[92]

RJPs may work because (1) applicants with more accurate information self-select out of the running for jobs that don't suit them, (2) those who take the job have realistic expectations and aren't disappointed, (3) the information helps new employees cope with anticipated work problems, or (4) applicants find employers who are honest, more credible, and attractive.[93] Realistic expectations may be less important than the actual work experiences of employees.

One study found that actual work experiences were better predictors of people's opinion about whether their expectations were met, as well as their job satisfaction and intent to leave, than their expectations before being hired.[94] Key elements of an RJP include:

1. *Accuracy* of the information is the most common aspect of RJPs and the most frequently studied, although there is little research to indicate whether recipients of RJPs find them accurate.
2. *Specificity* reflects how much the information given focuses on a particular job and particular job characteristics. Many published RJPs focus on general organizational factors, such as overtime or vacation policies, providing little information about the day-to-day job environment.
3. *Breadth* refers to the number of job and organizational factors covered in an RJP. Most published RJPs appear to focus on only a limited set of factors, omitting things such as supervision, promotion opportunities, or department politics.
4. *Credibility* refers to the degree to which applicants believe the RJP information. Psychologists designing RJPs usually assume credibility, though it has seldom actually been measured.
5. *Importance* refers to whether the RJP contains information reflecting information applicants want to know about, and which they would not already know through other means. Most published RJPs appear to reflect only generally known job aspects (e.g., that bank tellers frequently work on their feet). They often do not cover hard-to-get information such as relations with supervisors, co-workers, and work groups.[95]

RJPs seem to increase employee satisfaction and reduce employee turnover (in Chapter Eight, we discuss the link between satisfaction and turnover). Exhibit 6.13 lists recommendations in five areas for improving RJP effectiveness. Your professor, for instance, was probably recruited with an RJP. Most universities bring professor candidates to the school, and schedule a series of meetings with deans, directors, and potential colleagues.

In Prague, there is a shortage of workers. Yet, Pepsi Cola Company, a division of PepsiCo, shows applicants for the job of route driver a video, depicting the realism of the job. It shows that route driving is physically demanding, sometimes tedious, and exacting. Applicants who started out thinking the job was a glamorous chance to work for a large well-known company driving through Prague in a comfortable truck soon see it's not that simple. Some choose not to pursue the job. How would you explain the value of such an RJP in an environment of severe labor shortages?

## CHOOSING AND PREPARING RECRUITERS

Virtually every recruiting process includes a meeting with one or more organization members. This group usually includes a representative from the human resource management department and may also include supervisors, co-workers, and even subordinates. Because so much about the organization and the job cannot be known in advance, applicants appear to use aspects of recruiters as signals about job attributes they cannot observe first-hand and about the likelihood of receiving an offer. One study found that 38 out of 41 graduating students said that "very good or very bad recruiters" affected their decisions to accept job offers.[96]

It's not only the first recruiter that affects applicant perceptions. One study that surveyed applicants after they had visited the site of a large firm found that the overall feeling about the site visit and the likability of the host were significantly related to the decision to

## EXHIBIT 6.13 How to Improve Realistic Job Previews' Effectiveness

**Content**

Information should be as accurate, specific, broad, credible, and important as possible.

**Sources of Information**

Multiple sources should be used, including job incumbents, the immediate supervisor, the job description, employee manuals, personnel department representatives, and exit interviews with former employees.

**Communication**

Encourage two-way conversations with job incumbents that are off the record. Use multiple methods, such as detailed job descriptions, tours of the work site, films portraying difficult job situations, and hands-on work simulations.

**Target jobs**

Don't restrict RJPs to lower-level jobs. Consider using them for professional/technical and managerial jobs, especially in the wake of restructuring or mergers.

**Timing**

If the RJP is inexpensive, give it to all applicants to maximize their chance to self-select out of jobs that don't fit them. If the RJP is expensive, prescreen applicants first and give the RJP only to clearly qualified candidates.

Source: James A. Breaugh and Robert S. Billings, "The Realistic Job Preview: Five Key Elements and Their Importance for Research and Practice," *Journal of Business and Psychology* 2, no. 4 (Summer 1988), pp. 291–305.

accept the job.[97] Studies suggest that recruiters perceived as personable and informative seem to signal desirable job characteristics and work/company environments. Recruiters perceived as competent and informative were associated with higher applicant regard for the company, while aggressive recruiters negatively affected applicants' perceived job attractiveness. When applicants perceived recruiters as more personable, they reported a higher expectancy of receiving job offers and higher intentions to accept.[98] Several studies suggest that recruiters reveal far less about the job and organization than applicants would like to know, and this has been linked to unfavorable applicant perceptions of their interview performance, lower intentions to accept job offers, and lower willingness to place follow-up phone calls after interviews.[99]

When recruiting goes wrong, it can go very wrong. The University of Chicago Law School suspended the noted Chicago law firm of Baker & McKenzie after an African American law school recruit was asked how she would react to derogatory name-calling.[100] Even the people who initially take applications or greet applicants are important. When one applicant filled out an application at the Labor Department and asked when she might hear whether she got a job, she was told "possibly never." When she asked a Labor Department employee how he got his job, he answered, "I'm lucky, my mother works downstairs."[101]

With such high stakes, you might think most employers would follow the example of Eastman Kodak, where recruiters are nominated by their managers and attend a training conference using 20-minute mock interviews, which are videotaped and reviewed. College recruiting managers reported using recruiter selection criteria such as strong interpersonal skills, enthusiasm for the company, knowledge of the company and jobs, and credibility with students and co-workers. Formal credentials, such as recruiter training or seniority, were rated as considerably less important. Although employers devote 4 to 28 weeks training sales personnel, only 48 percent of companies provide recruiter training and then only 13 hours. Recruiter success is seldom systematically tracked or rewarded.[102]

## EVALUATING RECRUITMENT

Do recruiting decisions really make any difference? What organizational goals can they affect? How do organizations measure recruiting effectiveness? The evidence suggests that recruitment is both a costly and potentially valuable activity, but that it is not evaluated very carefully.

### Efficiency

#### Costs

A recruiter at a retail electronics company estimated the costs for recruiting applicants for the 30 salesperson jobs in a new store, as shown in Exhibit 6.14. Usually, a store has one month to fill the 30 vacancies. The exhibit shows the order (top to bottom) in which the manager would use each source as more applicants were needed. A total of 297 applicants could be generated if all sources were used, at a total cost of $19,100. Recruitment cost components include (1) travel and lodging of recruiters to visit candidates, (2) training of recruiters, (3) recruiter time spent in training and traveling, (4) recruiter time spent when candidates visit the site, (5) travel costs for candidates visiting the site, (6) time employees spend processing information about applicants, and (7) relocation costs if the applicant accepts the offer. Recruiting costs vary greatly according to the level of the job and the intensiveness of the recruiting activity. Costs also differ depending on the number and type of recruiting sources used. Travel and relocation costs can be reduced by focusing on sources closer to the work site. Search firm fees can be reduced through careful shopping. Many professional journals publish buyer's guides to recruiting organizations and products that can assist managers in identifying ways to lower the costs of increased effectiveness.

The National Association of Colleges and Employers reported that the average cost per hire for entry-level college graduates in 1994 was $6,090, up from $5,672 in 1992.[103] Computers and the Internet can also be a potent way to lower costs. Many organizations now use software to "scan" résumés into a database and allow managers to search the database for specific key words that might identify qualified applicants. The Cornell Career Services office, among others, uses Resumix.

> EXPLORING THE WEB
>
> You can visit the Resumix web site at **http://www.resumix.com/.**

### Productivity and Tenure

Earlier, we discussed the evidence suggesting that employees recommended by inside sources stay longer. RJPs can also reduce employee separations. However, the evidence for the effect of recruiting on job performance or other

EXHIBIT 6.14 Recruiting Costs for Retail Salespersons

| | No. of Applicants | | Estimate Cost ($) | | Cost per Applicant ($) | |
|---|---|---|---|---|---|---|
| **Source** | **Per Source** | **Cumulative** | **Per Source** | **Cumulative** | **Per Source** | **Cumulative** |
| Walk-ins | 5 | 5 | 0 | 0 | 0 | 0 |
| Internal posting | 5 | 10 | 100 | 100 | 20 | 10 |
| Weekly newspaper ad | 50 | 60 | 2,000 | 2,100 | 40 | 35 |
| Sunday newspaper ad | 200 | 260 | 10,000 | 12,100 | 50 | 47 |
| Expand newspaper ad | 25 | 285 | 3,000 | 15,100 | 120 | 53 |
| Employee referrals | 10 | 295 | 1,500 | 16,600 | 150 | 56 |
| Job fairs | 2 | 297 | 2,500 | 19,100 | 1,250 | 64 |

Source: Reprinted with permission from Scott L. Martin and Nambury S. Raju, "Determining Cutoff Scores that Optimize Utility: A Recognition of Recruiting Costs," *Journal of Applied Psychology* 77, no. 1 (1992), p. 19.

outcomes is mixed or extremely sparse. Still, computer simulations suggest that when recruitment and selection are integrated, large dollar-valued benefits are possible. Employers are often less than optimistic about prospects of adequately filling positions. One survey found that only a third of firms believed there was a 90 percent chance or better of adequately filling a position with the first selection, half rated their chances as better than 75 percent, and one-tenth rated their chances as less than 75 percent.[104]

## Equity

In Chapter Two, we discussed that achieving a diverse workforce, meeting EEO goals, or satisfying the requirements for affirmative action often begins with recruitment. Aggressive recruitment of underrepresented minorities is one of the most acceptable and legally safe methods of enhancing diversity.[105] Also, the number of applicants who fall into the different racial and gender groups may be used to define the relevant labor market, and thus to set goals for affirmative action. This is one growing dilemma with Internet recruiting, which tends to attract applicants who are white, male, and college educated, and perhaps misses qualified people from other groups. Recruitment also affects the image of the organization in the minds of applicants who are accepted and those who are rejected. It is important to ensure that recruitment processes are perceived as fair and portray a positive image of the organization. Some evidence suggests that perceived justice and fairness may significantly affect whether employees later sue their employer.[106]

## Actual Recruiting Evaluation Practices

Evidence suggests that organizations do not carefully evaluate recruiting activities against objectives/standards. Although Fortune 1000 companies surveyed consistently indicated that objective factors such as costs, applicant quality,

## EXHIBIT 6.15 Measures to Evaluate Recruitment

**Global Criterion Measures**

Number and/or percentage of

- Jobs filled
- Jobs filled in timely fashion
- Jobs filled inexpensively (cost per hire)
- Jobs filled with above-average performers
- Jobs filled by members of underutilized groups
- Jobs filled with people who remain at least one year
- Jobs filled with people who are satisfied with their new positions

**Recruiter-Oriented Criterion Measures**

- Number of interviews conducted
- Quality of interviews as rated by interviewees
- Number and rated quality of career day presentations
- Percentage of people recommended who are hired
- Percentage of people recommended who are hired and perform well
- Number of minorities and women recruited
- Cost per interview

**Recruitment Method-Oriented Criterion Measures**

- Number of applications generated
- Number of qualified applications generated
- Number of applications generated from minorities and women
- Cost per application generated
- Time required to generate applicants
- Cost per hire
- Quality of employee hired (performance, turnover, attendance, etc.)

Source: Reprinted with permission from James A. Breaugh, *Recruitment: Science and Practice* (Boston: PWS–Kent, 1992), p. 341.

new-hire performance, and retention rates are important in evaluating recruiting strategies, less than 30 percent of responding companies actually recorded retention rates, recruiting costs by source, applicant qualifications by source, or performance differences across recruiters and sources. Filling job vacancies and following proper procedures dominate the evaluation information collected, though computerized applicant tracking systems have made it increasingly feasible to track much more information.[107]

Exhibit 6.15 contains a few examples of evaluation measures for recruitment. They reflect the activities and the results, and both efficiency and equity. Exhibit 6.16 depicts how organizations might compare recruiting results across four different colleges, reflecting both costs and efficiency. Notice that while college 4 is the most expensive and produces the highest performance rating (3.8), college 2 produces almost as high a performance level and at a much lower recruiting cost.

## EXHIBIT 6.16 Matrix for Evaluating College Recruiting

**Recruitment experience for four key colleges (based on previous two years' information)**

| | College Number | | | |
|---|---|---|---|---|
| | **1** | **2** | **3** | **4** |
| Interviews | 38 | 22 | 58 | 12 |
| Invitations | 15 | 9 | 30 | 10 |
| Site visits | 13 | 8 | 22 | 5 |
| Offers | 7 | 5 | 12 | 4 |
| Hires | 6 | 4 | 8 | 2 |
| Average performance | 2.60 | 3.10 | 2.70 | 3.80 |
| Quits in 2 years | 0 | 0 | 2 | 1 |
| Fires in 2 years | 1 | 1 | 0 | 0 |
| Cost of up to 16 interviews | $1,222 | $764 | $1,356 | $1,664 |
| Cost of 17–32 interviews | $2,525 | $1,568 | $2,769 | $3,470 |
| Cost per visit | $ 540 | $ 512 | $ 652 | $ 750 |
| Cost per hire | $ 622 | $ 320 | $ 688 | $ 810 |
| Maximum interviews per year | 24 | 12 | 32 | 20 |

It seems likely that if organizations made efforts to collect such information, they might uncover important relationships between outcomes and recruiting choices. Changes in recruiting strategies then could be better planned and implemented. Unfortunately, despite the many ways to track recruitment success, too many organizations fail to carefully track its effectiveness.

## SUMMARY

External recruiting attracts a pool of applicants from which some are chosen for employment offers. We have seen that this relatively simple-sounding activity requires a keen awareness of external and internal organizational conditions, such as increasing labor shortages and rapidly changing position requirements. Also, recruitment is a two-way process, with recruitment messages serving not only as signals to the organization regarding applicant quality but also as signals to applicants, government agencies, and communities about the organization's image and philosophy. We have described the decisions involved in recruitment: (1) choosing required applicant qualifications, (2) choosing recruitment sources and communication channels, (3) choosing inducements, (4) choosing the message, and (5) choosing and preparing recruiters. While each was treated separately, they must blend to form an integrated strategy. Choices in one area imply opportunities and constraints in others.

Attracting a large and appropriately qualified applicant pool establishes the foundation for external staffing. The next step is to choose which applicants should receive employment offers, which is the topic of Chapter Seven, External Employee Selection.

## QUESTIONS

1. How can recruiting help meet such organizational goals as EEO compliance and increasing productivity? Can it reduce the number of employees? Explain.
2. What do job applicants expect from organizations recruiting them? Does this conflict with the organizations' needs during the process?
3. Explain how understanding the various approaches to an applicant's job search could allow an organization to develop a more effective recruiting process.
4. Discuss how setting applicant qualifications can increase or decrease an applicant pool. As the traditional labor force shrinks, how can recruiters increase their effectiveness in finding workers?
5. Is a "contingent" job a good job? Will contingent work grow in the future? Explain.
6. Discuss the Internet as a recruiting source. What are some positive aspects? What are the dangers? How could it change recruiting?
7. What messages do recruiting inducements send to applicants? Can they be used to achieve organizational goals, such as EEO compliance and reducing turnover?
8. Compare the realistic and flypaper approaches to recruiting. Discuss the RJP and its effects.
9. Is the recruiter an important part of the process? What sorts of things can an individual recruiter affect?
10. Discuss the value of and criteria for evaluating recruitment.

## YOUR TURN

### Happy Meal Recruitment Advertising

Exhibit 6.17 contains an actual recruitment advertisement first included in McDonald's Happy Meals for children in September 1988. How might it be used as part of a complete recruiting strategy? Imagine that you work at a competing fast-food restaurant, and your manager asks you whether your organization should initiate a similar program. The following questions can guide you:

1. What applicant search process is McDonald's trying to appeal to? Does it involve both occupation and organizational choice? Why did McDonald's place the ad in Happy Meals in September?
2. What kinds of applicant qualifications and characteristics are likely to be generated by this kind of communication?
3. What changes in the working arrangements might need to be made if large numbers of applicants responding to this ad are hired?
4. What inducements are highlighted by the advertisement?
5. Does the advertisement adopt a flypaper or a realistic approach? What are the likely consequences of this?
6. What kinds of recruiters are respondents to this ad likely to encounter? Will these recruiters require any special selection or training?

EXHIBIT 6.17 Recruitment Advertising for Fast-Food Workers

*Dear Mom:*

*It's that time of year again. The kids have gone back to school and Christmas is just around the corner.*

*We at McDonald's would like to help you earn that extra spending money that would come in handy this season.*

*The nice thing about a job at McDonald's is that we need you when you want to work. If your kids are home, you can be also.*

*Our hours are flexible and can be changed with a short notice. Uniforms and meals are also provided.*

*Please stop in.*

7. What are the likely effects of tapping this applicant pool on both efficiency and equity?

Your instructor has additional information about this case.

## APPENDIX
## A Diagnostic Approach to Your Own Job Search

We thank Karin Ash, director of the Office of Career Services, ILR School, Cornell University, for her assistance with this appendix.

The recruiting process takes on special significance as you prepare to find a job. In tough economic times, this can be discouraging. Large companies such as AT&T and Merck receive more than 100,000 résumés a year. Being flexible, considering smaller firms, using personal contacts, and persistently keeping your name in front of prospective employers are good tips; thinking through the job-search process strategically is also helpful. This section uses the diagnostic approach to describe the steps in recruiting from a college

**EXHIBIT 6.18** Stages in the Job Search Strategy

| Assess Conditions | Prepare Your Case | Present Your Case | Consider Offers |
|---|---|---|---|
| You | Résumé | Interviews | Reply |
| Opportunities | Cover Letter | | |
| Environment | Job Sources | Site visits | Accept/reject |

student's perspective. Keep in mind, however, that most colleges have career experts who can provide additional specialized information concerning their particular job search resources.

## DECIDING ON AN OCCUPATION/VOCATION

Chances are that you've already given some thought to the general kind of occupation you'd like to enter. You may have already chosen a major area of study that will lead to jobs in a specific occupation such as chemical engineering, computer programming, marketing, or human resource management. Even within these broad occupational categories, however, many types of occupations offer very different rewards and demands. A talk with a career counselor or taking a career interest inventory may help you specify more precisely exactly what you want out of your occupation. The beginning of Chapter Nine gives an example of a career interest inventory. A widely used book that provides a good starting point is *What Color is Your Parachute?* by Richard Bolles. Assuming that you've narrowed down your occupational choice, we now discuss in detail the recruiting process for choosing a job and organization. Exhibit 6.18 lists the four major steps in a job search.

## ASSESSING CONDITIONS

The first step is to carefully consider the conditions affecting your job search. These three major areas are yourself, the available jobs, and the external environment.

### Assessing Yourself

The job you get must fit you. Therefore, the first step is to consider carefully what you need and desire from your work. For most students, the job categories they consider are largely determined by their college training. But even within fairly specialized categories, such as personnel management, there is a wide variety of job types. A good match depends on how well you know what you want. Consider the following questions:

1. How hard do I like to work?
2. Do I like to be my own boss, or would I rather work for someone else?
3. Do I like to work alone, with a few others, or with large groups?
4. Do I like to work at a steady pace or in bursts of energy?
5. Does location matter? Do I want to work near home? In warmer climates? In ski country? Am I willing to be mobile?
6. How much money do I want? Am I willing to work for less money but in a more interesting job?
7. Do I like to work in one place or many? indoors or outdoors?
8. How much variety do I want in work?

Also, consider what you want from an employer. The following questions illustrate issues to ponder:

1. Do I have a size preference?
2. Do I have a sector preference (private, not for profit, public sector)?
3. What kinds of industries interest me? (This is usually based on interests in company products or services.)
4. Have I checked to make sure that the sector or product or service has a good future and will lead to growth in opportunity?

Finally, carefully consider your own employment preparation. What do you have to offer an employer? For which jobs are your particular credentials suited? Specific areas of consideration parallel the parts of a résumé, so this process will help you prepare a résumé. At this stage it is also important to identify the job opportunities for which you are qualified.

### Assess Job Opportunities

To assess the numbers and types of jobs available to you, use as many sources of jobs and job information as you can. The right sources for you are those best tailored to your particular job desires. Some of the sources you should consider include:

**Newspapers and professional publications** Read the media ads for the type of job you want, and read the professional publications and newspapers in the area you have selected. *The Wall Street Journal* and the *New York Times* are examples of where to look. Respond to ads that sound interesting.

**College career offices** These offices, located on college campuses, often store a wealth of job search and employer information, and they usually serve as the place where recruiters offer job interviews. Many career offices today use technology to enhance opportunities. Over 300 colleges contract with Jobtrak, an internet job-posting service. Many use résumé scanning software to store résumés electronically and to allow employers to search the file for promising students who match their needs. Get to know the career office staff. Sign up for all interviews that sound interesting. Career offices also may be able to help you contact alumni of your school, which is likely to keep alumni addresses on file.

**Professional associations** Many professional associations provide job placement services. Get your name in the placement application file. Job ads appear in their publications, too.

**Private employment agencies and executive search firms** Another source of jobs is the private employment agency. Generally, you should visit them and bring a résumé. They charge a fee, often payable by the employer, but sometimes payable by you. The fee can be as much as 30 percent of the first year's salary. Executive search firms tend to recruit middle managers and up (salaries in the $50,000 range).

Some firms also offer résumé preparation, testing services, and career counseling. They often charge up to $1,500, whether or not you get a job. Though this fee is usually paid by employers, ask about any costs that you must bear.

**Personal contacts** One of the best contacts for jobs are people who work for the organization or who have worked there in the past. Develop your contacts from as many sources as you can: parents, relatives, friends, fraternity brothers, or sorority sisters. Some experts estimate that 80 percent of jobs are never advertised. Contacts get these jobs. You might consider conducting an exploration interview with someone who holds or previously held a job similar to one you are considering. Alumni from your school are often willing to participate in such interviews. Exhibit 6.19 lists several questions appropriate for such an interview.

Direct mail It is useless to mail unsolicited résumés to human resource offices without a personal approach. One way that sometimes works is to write a personalized letter to the human resource or recruiting manager of the organization explaining why you are applying to them. Find out the manager's name. Specify your preferences and advantages in the letter and tell the manager you will call in 10 days to two weeks to follow up on your letter and ask for an opportunity to meet. Sitting back and waiting for an organization to come to you is not fruitful.

### Assess Environmental Conditions

Factors in the environment affect your job-seeking behavior. If jobs are scarce, you have to start looking earlier and look harder. You may need to compromise your expectations.

## PREPARE YOUR CASE

With your job preferences established, and a firm grasp on the available job opportunities and what they offer, you are ready to begin preparing your case for employment.

### Preparing a Résumé

A résumé is the first, and sometimes the only, glimpse a prospective employer has of a job applicant. It should present a professional, organized, competent image. Thus, it should be uncluttered, balanced, grammatical, accurate, and readable. Exhibit 6.20 contains a sample résumé for a human resource management student. Most résumés include the following information:

1. Identification—name, address, and telephone number.
2. Career or job objective.
3. Educational background (including directly related course work).
4. Work experience (related to the job).
5. Activities or community involvement.
6. Interests and/or hobbies (where relevant to the job.).
7. Published papers or articles.
8. A statement indicating references.

### Preparing a Cover Letter

When you send your résumé to employers, include a cover letter. Your cover letter should make the employer want to learn more from your résumé and, perhaps, through a subsequent job interview. Keep the following guidelines in mind:

1. Each letter should be a typed original, not a photocopy.
2. Grammar, spelling, and style should be perfect. Have someone else (preferably someone skilled in editing) proofread it for you.
3. Send the letter to a *person,* not an office. If you know someone in the company, send it to them. If not, call and get the name of an executive in the area in which you want to work.

## EXHIBIT 6.19 Questions for a Job Exploration Interview

**Personal background**

1. When you were in college, what did you think your career was going to be? What was your undergraduate major field of study? What was your graduate field of study?

**Preparation**

1. Which credentials, educational degrees, or licenses are required for entry into this kind of work?
2. What kinds of prior experience are absolutely essential?
3. How did *you* prepare yourself for this work?

**Present job**

1. Describe what you do during a typical workweek.
2. Which skills or talents are most essential for effectiveness in this job?
3. What are the toughest problems with which you must deal?
4. What do you find most rewarding about the work itself, apart from external motivators, such as salary, fringe benefits, or travel?

**Prior experience**

1. Which of your past work experiences affect what you do now?
2. Have any of your job changes been for reasons of lifestyle?

**Career future**

1. If things develop as you'd like, what sort of ideal career do you see for yourself?
2. If the work you do was suddenly eliminated, which different kinds of work could you do?
3. How rapidly is your present career field growing? How would you describe or estimate future prospects in this field?

**Lifestyle**

1. What obligations outside the regular workweek does your work place on you? Do you enjoy these obligations?
2. How much flexibility do you have in dress, work hours, vacation schedules, and place of residence?

**Advice**

1. How well is my background suited to this job?
2. What additional educational preparation do you feel would be best?
3. Which kinds of experiences, paid employment or other, would you recommend?
4. If you were a college graduate and had it to do over again, what would you do differently?

**Hiring criteria**

1. If you were hiring someone to work with you today, which factors would be most important in your hiring decision and why?

Source: Adapted from *Job Search Guide* (Ithaca, NY: Cornell University, ILR, Office of Career Services, 1995).

EXHIBIT 6.20 Sample Résumé for a Human Resource Management Student

| | |
|---|---|
| **PROFESSIONAL OBJECTIVES:** | A position in human resource management utilizing my education, training, and experience while gaining exposure to a wide range of personnel functions with particular emphasis on employee relations. |
| **PERSONAL QUALIFICATIONS:** | Excellent organizational skills, well-developed leadership abilities. Strong academic and practical background.<br>Proven interpersonal skills with groups and individuals. |
| **EDUCATION:** | **Cornell University,** Ithaca, New York<br>New York State School of Industrial and Labor Relations<br>Bachelor of Science Degree, June 1, 1996<br>**Bucknell University,** Lewisburg, Pennsylvania<br>School of Arts and Sciences, September 1992–May 1993 |
| **COURSE CONCENTRATIONS:** | Organizational behavior and development<br>Labor history, law, management, and economics<br>Psychology<br>Compensation administration<br>Employee staffing and supervision<br>Human resource economics<br>Statistics<br>Collective bargaining |
| **EMPLOYMENT EXPERIENCE:** | **Resident Adviser** (August 1995–June 1996)<br>Department of Residence Life, Cornell University<br>Responsible for directly assisting 90 college freshmen adjust to university life by coordinating educational and social programming and providing personal and academic counseling.<br>**Labor Relations Intern** (May 1995–August 1996)<br>Central New York Bottle Company, a Division of Philip Morris, Inc., Auburn, New York.<br>Administered corporate quality awareness program including a 30-day participation booster campaign, researched and compiled three-year analysis of grievances, worked with employee involvement implementation, grievance resolutions, workers' compensation, disability claims, and nonexempt attendance program maintenance.<br>**Research Intern** (January 1996)<br>Buffalo-Erie County Labor Management Council, Suite 407, Convention Tower, Buffalo, New York.<br>Developed and administered several research techniques and compiled the information into a case study of labor-management participation in an abrasives company.<br>**Marketing/Public Relations Supervisor** (May 1994–August 1994)<br>Darien Lake Amusement Park, Corfu, New York.<br>Composed and supervised the administration of consumer surveys.<br>**Proposals Intern** (January 1993)<br>GTE Sylvania, Mountain View, California.<br>Organized and revamped the entire proposals department filing system.<br>**Restaurant Supervisor** (Summers 1991–1994)<br>Service Systems/Darien Lake, Corfu, New York.<br>Sole supervisor of the largest fast-food stand in an amusement park. |
| **ACTIVITIES:** | Resident adviser<br>Cornell dining employee<br>Secretary-Treasurer, college student government<br>American Society of Personnel Administrators<br>N.Y.S. School of Industrial and Labor Relations Ambassador<br>Volunteer at area nursing home; Traveling, skiing, socializing |
| **REFERENCES:** | Available on request |

Source: *Job Search Guide* (Ithaca, NY: Cornell University, ILR, Office of Career Services, 1995).

4. If someone encouraged you to apply, ask permission to use that person's name in the letter.
5. Keep the letter simple. Express interest in the position. Briefly summarize your credentials and request an interview.

Exhibit 6.21 contains a sample cover letter for a student in human resource management. It is very important to find ways to keep your name in front of company representatives. Contacts through professors or class visits are valuable.

### Interview Preparation

Initial employment interviews are usually a half-hour long, so it is very important that you be well prepared to present your case. Several steps will help you prepare:

1. *Research the employer.* This means more than reading the promotional brochure. You can check through the *New York Times Index* or recent issues of such business publications as *The Wall Street Journal* or *Business Week* for developments related to the area in which you want to work. Career offices often collect annual reports and employment manuals for companies who recruit regularly on campus.

   Use your college library CD-ROM databases such as "CD Corporate" or ABI Inform to quickly find recent financial and news stories about the company. Visit the company's home page on the World Wide Web, if they have one.
2. *Know your résumé and anticipate questions.* Have a friend or instructor read your résumé and identify obvious questions. Be prepared to emphasize your strengths and to discuss areas of weakness in a way that best represents your qualifications. Exhibit 6.22 contains 10 questions often asked by recruiters for human resource management positions.
3. *Have questions in mind for the interview.* Questions might include, "Please describe the job duties." "Why is the position open?" "Where does the job fit in the organization's hierarchy?" "What have been the best results produced by others in this job?" "What do you like most about your job and this company?"
4. *Dress neatly.* Wear clothes similar to those expected on the job.

## PRESENT YOUR CASE

The moment of truth arrives. You are about to enter the office and begin the interview. If you have prepared carefully, you will be ready to get the most out of the interview and provide the interviewer with information that best represents your qualifications.

### Interview

Though no two interviews are the same, campus interviews typically follow this sequence:

1. *Introduction.* Initiated by the interviewer, involves personal introductions, some small talk to set the applicant at ease, and perhaps a plan for the interview.
2. *Interrogation.* Also initiated by the interviewer, involves questions designed to probe the candidate's strengths and weaknesses and assess problem-solving abilities.
3. *Selling.* Initiated by the applicant, provides a chance to describe qualifications in more detail, ask questions about the job and company, and demonstrate interest and knowledge about the company.
4. *Conclusion.* Initiated by the recruiter, involves a description of the decision-making process, dates by which the candidate can expect to hear from the company (usually two or four weeks), and the end of the interview.

EXHIBIT 6.21 Sample Cover Letter

725 State Street
Ithaca, New York 14850
February 8, 1997

Mr. Samuel Staples
Personnel Manager, Federal Mogul Corporation
198 Hollywood Boulevard
Los Angeles, California 95678

Dear Mr. Staples:

I am currently a senior in the School of Industrial and Labor Relations at Cornell University and am seeking employment in the field of human resources. The Office of Career Services has informed me that your organization will be recruiting at our school this semester. I would very much like to meet with you to discuss employment opportunities at Federal Mogul. I would appreciate being included on your invitation list.

My main interest in human resources is in training and organizational development. These areas will provide me the opportunity to make a contribution in the development of an organization's human resources at both the individual and the unit levels, which I feel greatly influences operations. I plan to begin my career as a generalist or in the area of compensation to establish a solid grounding in the organization in which I am employed. Either position will provide an overall picture of an organization's human resource function as it relates to other operating functions. I believe the position at Federal Mogul would provide this opportunity.

My experience, as you can see from my résumé, is compatible with much of the industry in which your organization operates. Although limited, my knowledge of your firm will allow me to become a contributing member more rapidly. This knowledge has been acquired through several temporary part-time positions with Federal Mogul.

Once again, I am very interested in the opportunities at Federal Mogul. Thank you very much for your consideration. I look forward to hearing from you.

Cordially,

Source: *Job Search Guide* (Ithaca, NY: Cornell University, ILR, Office of Career Services, 1995).

## Handling Illegal Interview Questions

Questions about your race, gender, religion, marital status, age, or other protected group status are generally illegal as grounds for making employment decisions. Most organizations that recruit at college campuses must sign a statement asserting that they do not discriminate on the basis of these factors. Examples of such questions might be, "What is your country of citizenship?" "Do you have disabilities?" "Have you ever been arrested?" If asked a discriminatory question in an interview, you do not have to answer, but an outright refusal may be offensive to the interviewer, who may see it as an insult to his or her professionalism. You might handle the question in one of two ways: (1) Ask about the underlying concern. For example, a question about marital status or family may reflect the need to know about your ability and willingness to travel, which you can discuss; (2) Answer the question, but report the incident to the director of your career services office.

**EXHIBIT 6.22** Questions Often Asked in Interviews for Human Resource Management Jobs

1. Based on what you know about ______ company, how would you develop a training program?
2. Tell me what you know about ______ company?
3. What is your background in finance and accounting?
4. What is a 401(k) plan?
5. What is a salary structure for?
6. What would you do if you were a compensation manager and an employee wants a promotion to a higher grade, but past performance doesn't warrant a move?
7. Why do you want to work in the ______ industry? What other industries are you considering?
8. Describe your analytical abilities.
9. Human resource professionals should be a model for high standards of ethical and professional behavior. Therefore, your own values are an important issue. Relate an experience that challenged your values and how you responded.
10. Where should human resources fit in an organization? What is its role?

*Job Search Guide* (Ithaca, NY: Cornell University, ILR, Office of Career Services, 1996).

### Interview Follow-Up

Be sure to keep a record of your contacts. Immediately after leaving the interview make the following notations.

- The name of the interviewer.
- The type of opportunity for which you were considered.
- Location of work.
- Your reaction and possible interest.
- *Your next action.*

## ANSWERS TO INVITATIONS FOR VISITS

If you receive an invitation for a plant visit, acknowledge it in one of three ways:

1. Accept and set the date when you will be there.
2. Indicate your desire to accept at a later date if you need more time to consider.
3. Decline for whatever honest reason you have.

### Follow-Up to Site Visit

As soon as you return from a site visit, send a letter of thanks to the individual who issued the invitation and to any others you believe should receive a special note of appreciation.

## CONSIDERING OFFERS

With hard work and luck, your efforts will pay off with one or several employment offers. Though you may think this is the end of the process, it still requires careful handling.

### Replying to an Offer

Offers of employment may be made verbally or by letter, which is the most usual means. Again, there are innumerable ways of handling an offer. Most companies do not expect an immediate acceptance or rejection, but they do expect an acknowledgement. *Therefore, be sure to reply within three days* after receiving the offer, thanking them and stating a time when you will send definite word, provided they have not already specified a deadline date. If they have, send a letter of acknowledgement and indicate your final answer will be forthcoming by the specific date.

### Delaying a Final Answer

The occasion might arise when you need an extension of time. If so, send another letter and state quite frankly your reasons and request their indulgence. Remember always to keep in mind the employer's position as well as your own.

### Accepting an Offer

It is probably unnecessary to go into detail about how to accept an offer beyond saying that an enthusiastic note of appreciation should be sent along with an indication of when you will report for work, a point which is of course, developed by mutual agreement.

### Rejecting an Offer

Letters of rejection should be sent as soon as you realize you are definitely not interested in accepting. It is not necessary to state your exact reasons for turning down an offer, or to say where you expect to go, but it is courteous to express your sincere thanks for having been favorably considered. It is helpful for the organization to know what your true feelings are regarding them, such as preference for a different location, another product, or different initial training.

## NOTES AND REFERENCES

1. Katherine Scovel, "Room at the Inns," *Human Resource Executive,* July 1991, pp. 1–18.
2. "All Hands on Deck!" *Time,* July 18, 1988, pp. 42–43.
3. Scovel, pp. 1–18.
4. Steve Stecklow, "Peddling Schools," *The Wall Street Journal,*Sept. 5, 1995, p. A1.
5. "Labor Letter," *The Wall Street Journal,* Mar. 17, 1992. p. A1.
6. "Labor Letter," *The Wall Street Journal,* Aug. 4, 1991, p. A1.
7. Carol Hymowitz, "Board Stress Deters Prospective Directors," *The Wall Street Journal,* Dec. 22, 1992, p. B1; Robert Johnson, "Trying Harder to Find a No. 2 Executive," *The Wall Street Journal,* June 19, 1989, p. B1; Raphael Pura, "Many of Asia's Workers Are on the Move," *The Wall Street Journal,* Mar. 5, 1992, p. A11; Karen Lowry Miller, "The Mommy Track' Japanese Style," *Business Week,* Mar. 11, 1991, p. 46; Kay Itoi and Bill Powell, "Desperately Seeking Akio," *Newsweek,* Sept. 16, 1991, p. 51; Karen Lowry Miller, "Land of the Rising Jobless," *Business Week,* Jan. 11, 1993, p. 47.

8. Albert R. Karr and Robert Tomsho, "Business Graduates Scrap for Scarce Jobs," *The Wall Street Journal,* May 19, 1992, p. B1.
9. Bureau of National Affairs, *Recruiting and Selection Procedures,* Personnel Policies Forum Survey No. 146 (Washington, DC: Bureau of National Affairs, May 1988), p. 5.
10. Jan van Ours and Geert Ridder, "Vacancies and the Recruitment of New Employees," *Journal of Labor Economics* 10, no. 2 (1992). pp. 138–55.
11. J. L. Holland, *the Psychology of Vocational Choice* (New York: Blaisdell, 1966); D. Brown, "The Status of Holland's Theory of Vocational Choice," *Career Development Quarterly* 36, no. 1 (1988), pp. 13–23; J. Holland, "Current Theory of Holland's Theory of Careers: Another Perspective," *Career Development Quarterly* 36, no. 1 (1988), pp. 24–30.
12. Millicent E. Poole, Janice Langan-Fox, and Mary Omodei, "Career Orientations in Women from Rural and Urban Backgrounds," *Human Relations* 44, no. 9 (1991), pp. 983–1005; David N. Laband and Bernard F. Lentz, "Self-Recruitment in the Legal Profession," *Journal of Labor Economics* 10, no. 2 (1992), pp. 182–201.
13. Nancy J. Perry, "The New, Improved Vocational School," *Fortune,* June 19, 1989, pp. 127–38.
14. J. C. Hanson and D. P. Campbell, *Manual for the SVIB-SCII* (Stanford, CA: Stanford University Press, 1985); D. G. Zytowski, *Kuder Occupational Interest Survey for DD Manual Supplement* (Chicago: Science Research Associates, 1986).
15. Dana Milbank, "The Modern Okies," *The Wall Street Journal,* Mar. 2, 1992, p. A1; Howard Wial, "Getting a Good Job: Mobility in a Segmented Labor Market," *Industrial Relations* 30, no. 3 (Fall 1991), pp. 396–416; D. W. Stevens, "A Reexamination of What is Known about Job-Seeking Behavior in the United States" (paper presented to the Conference on Labor Market Intermediaries, sponsored by the National Commission for Manpower Policy, Nov. 16–17, 1977); C. Rosenfeld, "Job-Seeking Methods Used by American Workers," *Monthly Labor Review,* Aug. 1975, pp. 39–42.
16. L. D. Dyer, "Job Search Success of Middle-Aged Managers and Engineers," *Industrial and Labor Relations Review,* Jan. 1973, pp. 969–79; J. Barron and D. W. Gilley, "The Effect of Unemployment Insurance on the Search Process," *Industrial and Labor Relations Review,* Mar. 1979, pp. 363–66; Martin Feldstein, "The Economics of the New Unemployment," *Public Interest,* Fall 1973, pp. 3–42; Ronald G. Ehrenberg and Ronald L. Oaxaca, "Unemployment Insurance, Duration of Unemployment and Subsequent Wage Gain," *American Economic Review,* Dec. 1976, pp. 754–66; Finis Welch, "What Have We Learned from Empirical Studies of Unemployment Insurance," *Industrial and Labor Relations Review,* July 1977, pp. 451–61.
17. Jean Powell Kirnan, John A. Farley, and Kurt F. Geisinger, "The Relationship between Recruiting Source, Applicant Quality, and Hire Performance: An Analysis by Sex, Ethnicity, and Age," *Personal Psychology* 42 (1989), pp. 293–308; Sara L. Rynes and John Lawler, "A Policy-Capturing Investigation of the Role of Expectancies in Decisions to Pursue Job Alternatives," *Journal of Applied Psychology* 68, no. 4 (1983), pp. 620–31.

18. "The Higher the Pay, the Longer the Job Hunt," *The Wall Street Journal,* Dec. 15, 1989, p. B1.

19. *Empirical Analysis of the Search Behavior of Low-Income Workers* (Menlo Park, CA: Stanford Research Institute, 1975); G. L. Reid, "Job Search and the Effectiveness of Job-Finding Methods," *Industrial and Labor Relations Review,* June 1972, pp. 479–95.

20. Brian D. Steffy, Karyll N. Shaw, and Ann Wiggins Noe, "Antecedents and Consequences of Job Search Behaviors," *Journal of Vocational Behavior* 35, (1989), pp. 254–69.

21. William M. Bulkeley, "Job-Hunters Turn to Software and Databases to Get an Edge," *The Wall Street Journal,* June 16, 1992, p. B7; Diane Cole, "Letting Computers Lend a High-Tech Helping Hand," *New York Times,* Oct. 30, 1988, p. F15.

22. William Glueck, "Decision Making: Organization Choice," *Personnel Psychology,* Spring 1974, pp. 66–93; "How Recruiters Influence Job Choices on Campus," *Personnel,* Mar.–Apr. 1971, pp. 46–52.

23. J. W. Payne, "Task Complexity and Contingent Processing in Decision Making: An Information Search and Protocol Analysis," *Organizational Behavior and Human Performance* 16 (1976), pp. 366–87.

24. Daniel Roy, "Contingent Workers Cut Labor Costs While Increasing Worker Insecurity," *Daily Labor Report,* Oct. 26, 1995; Pam Ginsbach, "BLS Preparing to Launch First Survey of Contingent Workforce Next February," *Daily Labor Report,* Dec. 12, 1994.

25. "Employers Turn to Temps, Outsourcing," *BNA's Employee Relations Weekly,* 13 (Dec. 25, 1995), p. 1375.

26. "Contingent Workers: How Many Are There?" *HRM News,* Sept. 18, 1995, p. 1.

27. Vernita C. Smith, "Executives for Rent," *Human Resource Executive,* Mar. 1995, pp. 36–39; Kevin Kelly, "Picket Lines? Just Call 1-800-STRIKEBREAKER," *Business Week,* Mar. 27, 1995, p. 42; Susan N. Houseman, "Part-time Employment in Europe and Japan," *Journal of Labor Research* 16, (Summer 1995), pp. 249–62.

28. "Survey of Temporary Work Contracts," *European Industrial Relations Review,* Mar. 1989, pp. 11–16; Jacqueline O'Reilly, "Banking on Flexibility: A Comparison of the Use of Flexible Employment Strategies in the Retail Banking Sector in Britain and France," *International Journal of Human Resource Management,* May 1992, pp. 35–58.

29. George Munchus III, "Employee Leasing: Benefits and Threats," *Personnel,* July 1988, pp. 59–61; Suzanne Woolley, "Give Your Employees a Break—by Leasing Them," *Business Week,* Aug. 14, 1989, p. 135.

30. Daniel Roy, "Contingent Workers: Beware Hidden Costs," *Human Resource Management News,* Sept. 25, 1995, p. 2.

31. Shari Caudron, "Are Your Temps Doing Their Best?" *Personnel Journal,* Nov. 1995, pp. 32–38.

32. "Temporary Workers: Coors Hires Its Own," *Human Resource Management* Sept. 4, 1995, p. 2.

33. Jeffry E. Struve, "Making the Most of Temporary Workers," *Personnel Journal,* Nov. 1991, pp. 43–45.

34. Sara L. Rynes, "Recruitment, Job Choice and Post-Hire Consequences: A Call for New Research Directions," in *Handbook of Industrial and Organizational Psychology,* 2nd ed., ed. M. D. Dunnette and L. Hough (Palo Alto, CA: Consulting Psychologists Press, 1991).

35. Michael E. Borus, Herbert S. Parnes, Steven H. Sandell, and Bert Seidman, eds., *The Older Worker* (Madison, WI: Industrial Relations Research Association, 1988); Jeannette N. Cleveland, Ronald M. Festa, and Linda Montgomery, "Applicant Pool Composition and Job Perceptions: Impact on Decisions Regarding an Older Applicant," *Journal of Vocational Behavior* 32 (1988), pp. 112–25; Dane E. Herz and Philip L. Rones, "Institutional Barriers to Employment of Older Workers," *Monthly Labor Review,* Apr. 1989, pp. 14–21.

36. William McNaught, Michael C. Barth, and Peter H. Henderson, "The Human Resource Potential of Americans over 50," *Human Resource Management* 28, no. 4 (Winter 1989), pp. 455–73; Susan Dentzer, "Do the Elderly Want to Work?" *U.S. News & World Report,* May 14, 1990, pp. 48–51.

37. Charlene Marmer Soloman, "Unlock the Potential of Older Workers," *Personnel Journel,* Oct. 1995.

38. Barbara L. Hassell and Pamela L. Perrewe, "An Examination of Beliefs about Older Workers: Do Stereotypes Still Exist?" *Journal of Organizational Behavior* 16, (1995), pp. 457–468.

39. Bureau of National Affairs, "EEOC Issues Revised Guidance on the ADA," *LRR Analysis/News and Background Information,* Oct. 16, 1995, 150 LRR 193 d18.

40. Kevin R. Hopkins, Clint Bolick, and Susan L. Nestleroth, *Opportunity 2000: Creative Affirmative Action Strategies for a Changing Workforce* (Washington, DC: Employment and Standards Division of the U.S. Department of Labor, 1989); "Hiring the Handicapped Gets New Emphasis in Bid to Staff Hard-to-Fill Jobs," *The Wall Street Journal,* Oct. 3, 1989, p. A1.

41. Ibid.

42. Jennifer J. Laabs, "L.A. Hotel Gives Teens a Career Orientation," *Personnel Journal,* Nov. 1995, pp. 50–61.

43. David C. Calabria, "When Companies Give, Employees Give Back," *Personnel Journal,* Apr. 1995, pp. 75–83.

44. Eric Rolfe Greenberg, "Workplace Testing: The 1990 AMA Survey, Part 1, *Personnel,* June 1990, pp. 43–51; David Whitman, et al., "The Forgotten Half," *U.S. News and World Report,* June 26, 1989, pp. 45–53; "National Alliance of Business Chief Sees Business Problems in Growing Shortage of Qualified Workers," *BNA's Labor Relations Week* 4, no. 2 (Jan. 1990).

45. "Language Course Taps New Bank of Work Skills," *Human Resource Management News,* Dec. 30, 1989, p. 2.

46. American Management Associations, *Hiring Costs and Strategies: The AMA Report* (New York: American Management Associations, 1986).

47. J. C. Ullman, "Employee Referrals: Prime Tool for Recruiting Workers," *Personnel* 43, no. 1 (1966), pp. 30–35; D. P. Schwab, "Recruiting and

Organizational Participation," in *Personnel Management,* ed. K. Rowland and G. Ferris (Boston: Allyn & Bacon, 1982); P. J. Decker and E. T. Cornelius, "A Note on Recruiting Sources and Job Survival Rates," *Journal of Applied Psychology* 64, no. 3 (1979), pp. 463–64; M. J. Gannon, "Source of Referral and Employee Turnover," *Journal of Applied Psychology* 55, no. 1 (1971), pp. 226–28: R. E. Hill, "New Look at Employee Referrals as a Recruitment Channel," *Personnel Journal* 49, no. 1 (1970), pp. 144–48; D. F. Caldwell and W. A. Spivey, "The Relationship between Recruiting Source and Employee Success: An Analysis by Race," *Personnel Psychology* 36 (1983), pp. 67–72.

48. Andy Bargerstock and Hank Engel, "Six Ways to Boost Employee Referral Programs," *HRMagazine,* Dec. 1994, pp. 72–79.

49. Sara L. Rynes and John W. Boudreau, "College Recruiting in Large Organizations: Practice, Evaluation and Research Implications," *Personnel Psychology* 39 (1986), pp. 729–57; John J. Keller, "AT&T's Bell Labs and Corning Inc. Hire over 200 Top Scientists in Russia," *The Wall Street Journal,* May 27, 1992, p. B5; Tony Lee, "Alumni Go Back to School to Hunt for Jobs." *The Wall Street Journal,* June 11, 1991, p. B1.

50. Rynes and Boudreau, "College Recruiting in Large Organizations," p. 740.

51. Gale H. Varma and James W. Smither, "Selecting Colleges and Universities for On-Campus Recruiting," *Journal of Career Planning & Employment,* Spring 1990, pp. 34–40.

52. Brian Dumaine, "Those Highflying PepsiCo Managers," *Fortune,* Apr. 19, 1989, p. 82.

53. Alan Deutschman, "The Trouble with MBAs," *Fortune,* July 29, 1991, pp. 67–75.

54. Alex Markels, "Marketing 101: To M.B.A. Candidates, The Top Course Today Is to Land a Good Job," *The Wall Street Journal,* May 12, 1995, p. A1.

55. Daniel E. Hecker, "Reconciling Conflicting Data on Jobs for College Graduates," *Monthly Labor Review,* July 1992, pp. 3–12; John Bishop and Shani Carter, "The Worsening Shortage of College Graduates," *Educational Research and Policy Analysis,* Fall 1991, pp. 40–53; Kristina Shelley, "The Future of Jobs for College Graduates," *Monthly Labor Review,* July 1992, pp. 13–21; Robert J. Samuelson, "The Value of College," *Newsweek,* Aug. 31, 1992, p. 75.

56. Sara L. Rynes, Robert D. Bretz, Jr., and Barry Gerhart, "The Importance of Recruitment in Job Choice: A Different Way of Looking," *Personnel Psychology* 44, (1991), pp. 487–521; Timothy A. Judge and Robert D. Bretz, Jr., "Effects of Work Values on Job Choice Decisions," *Journal of Applied Psychology* 77, no. 3 (1992), pp. 261–71.

57. John W. Boudreau, "Building a PC-Based Human Resource Management Curriculum at the School of Industrial and Labor Relations, Cornell University" (paper presented at the National Industrial Relations Research Association Meeting, Dec. 1989); Albert E. Kaff, "In Depressed Job Market, Hotel Students Turn to Computerized Recruiting by Marriott," *Cornell Chronicles,* May 16, 1991, p. 1.

58. L. A. Winokur, "Job Seekers Increasingly Find They Are in Demand—As Sources of Free Expertise," *The Wall Street Journal,* Apr. 8, 1991, p. B1.
59. F. J. Logan, "Executive Recruitment, Japanese Style," *Journal of Career Planning and Employment,* Mar. 1991, pp. 66–68; Sarah O'Hagan, "Making Waves in the Japanese Labor Pool," *The Journal of ACCJ,* Dec. 1990, pp. 12–20; Ted Holden, "Suddenly, No More Jobs on a Silver Platter," *Business Week,* June 29, 1992, p. 51.
60. Susan Tifft, "Our Student-Back Guarantee," *Time,* Feb. 11, 1991; Larry Armstrong and Geoff Smith, "Productivity Assured—Or We'll Fix Them Free," *Business Week,* Nov. 25, 1991, p. 34.
61. David Whitman et al., "The Forgotten Half," *U.S. News & World Report,* June 26, 1989, pp. 45–53; Conference Board, *Corporate Mentoring in U.S. School: The Outstretched Hand* (New York: Conference Board, 1992); Tina Adler, "SCANS's Goal Is a Better U.S. Workforce," *APA Monitor,* July 1992, pp. 16–17; Aaron Bernstein, "This Is the Missing Link between Business and Schools," *Business Week,* Apr. 20, 1992, p. 42; John Bishop, "Productivity Consequences of What Is Learned in High School," *Journal of Curriculum Studies,* 1990, pp. 125–47.
62. Peter Applebome, "Employers Wary of School System," *The New York Times,* Feb. 20, 1995, p. A1.
63. Dawn Anfuso, "Intel Educates a School District About Business," *Personnel Journal,* Apr. 1995, pp. 128–38.
64. James E. Rosenbaum and Takehiko Kariya, "Market and Institutional Mechanisms for the High School to Work Transition in the U.S. and Japan" (paper presented at the Annual Meetings of the American Sociological Association, Chicago, Aug. 1987).
65. Perry, "The New, Improved Vocational School"; Thomas Toch, "Crafting the Work Force," p. 129 *U.S. News & World Report,* Aug. 19, 1991, pp. 63–64.
66. "McDonald's Starts Youth Program," *Human Resource Management,* June 12, 1995, p. 2.
67. Bureau of National Affairs, *Recruiting and Selection Procedures.*
68. American Management Associations, *Hiring Costs and Strategies.*
69. Shari Caudron, "Recruit Qualified Employees from the Military," *Personnel Journel,* May 1992, pp. 117–18.
70. American Management Associations, *Hiring Costs and Strategies.*
71. "Executive Recruitment—Don't Call Us," *The Economist,* Oct. 7, 1995, pp. 71–72.
72. Samuel Greengard, "As HR Goes Online," *Personnel Journal,* July, 1995, pp. 55–68.
73. "I Got My Job Through . . . Ann Landers?" *The Wall Street Journal,* Aug. 8, 1994, p. A1.
74. Tony Lee, "Notice: All Employees Must Wash Hands Before Applying for a Job," *The Wall Street Journal,* June 2, p. B1.
75. Jennifer J. Laabs, "Nurses Get Critical About Recruitment Ads," *Personnel Journal,* July 1991, pp. 63–68; "The Best in Recruitment Advertising," *Human Resources Executive,* Aug. 1992, pp. 43–50.

76. James A. Breaugh, "Relationships between Recruiting Sources and Employee Performance, Absenteeism, and Work Attitudes," *Academy of Management Journal* 24, (1981), pp. 142–47; James A. Breaugh and R. B. Mann, "Recruiting Source Effects: A Test of Two Alternative Explanations," *Journal of Occupational Psychology* 57 (1984), pp. 261–67; Martin J. Gannon, "Sources of Referral and Employee Turnover," *Journal of Applied Psychology* 55, (1971), pp. 226–28; P. J. Decker and Edwin T. Cornelius III, "A Note on Recruiting Sources and Job Survival Rates," *Journal of Applied Psychology* 64 (1979), pp. 463–64; Donald P. Schwab, "Recruiting and Organizational Participation," in *Personnel Management,* ed. K. M. Rowland and G. Ferris (Boston: Allyn & Bacon, 1982).

77. Albert H. McCarthy, "Research Provides Advertising Focus," *Personnel Journal,* Aug. 1989, pp. 82–87.

78. Lourdes Lee Valeriano, "Immigration Law May Help U.S. Firms, But It Also Creates Some New Headaches," *The Wall Street Journal,* Sept. 27, 1991, p. B1; Michael J. Mandel and Christopher Farrell, "The Immigrants," *Business Week,* July 13, 1992, pp. 114–22; Gary S. Becker, "An Open Door for Immigrants—The Auction," *The Wall Street Journal,* Oct. 14, 1992, p. A14.

79. "INS Proposes Record Fine over Illegal Hiring at Textile Firm," *Daily Labor Report,* Dec. 14, 1989, p. 1; Vernon M. Briggs, Jr., "Employer Sanctions and the Question of Discrimination: The GAO Study in Perspective," *International Migration Review* 24, no. 4 (Winter 1990), pp. 803–15.

80. Joe Davidson, "Nine Firms Fined for Employing Illegal Immigrants," *The Wall Street Journal,* Sept. 27, 1995, p. A5; Catherine Yang, "Give Me Your Huddled . . . High-Tech PhD's," *Business Week,* Nov. 6, 1995, pp. 161–62.

81. John Parcher Wanous, *Organizational Entry,* 2nd ed. (Reading, MA: Addison-Wesley, 1992), p. 37.

82. Wanous, *Organizational Entry,* pp. 34–37.

83. Joan E. Rigdon, "Room at the Top," *The Wall Street Journal,* Nov. 13, 1991, p. A1.

84. Joann S. Lublin, "Top Jobs at Troubled Companies Go Begging," *The Wall Street Journal,* Dec. 27, 1995, p. 13; Alex Markels, "Outlook for This Year's Top MBAs: Excellent," *The Wall Street Journal,* May 31, 1995, p. B1; Johnathan Auerbach, "Small-Town Life Lures Young Professionals," *The Wall Street Journal,* Sept. 29, 1995, p. B10.

85. Margaret L. Williams and George F. Dreher, "Compensation System Attributes and Applicant Pool Characteristics," *Academy of Management Journal* 35, no. 3 (1992), pp. 571–95: Sara L. Rynes, "Compensation Strategy in Recruiting," *Topics in Total Compensation* 1, no. 1 (1987), pp. 37–55.

86. Judge and Bretz, "Effects of Work Values," Sue Shellenbarger, "More Job Seekers Put Family Needs First," *The Wall Street Journal,* Nov. 15, 1991, p. B1; Dana Milbank, "More Business Graduates Snap Up Jobs in Rust Belt That Promise Them Clout," *The Wall Street Journal,* July 21,

1992, p. B1; Keith H. Hammonds and Monica Roman, "Itching to Get onto the Factory Floor," *Business Week,* Oct. 14, 1991, p. 64; Rachel Connelly, "The Effect of Child Care Costs on Married Women's Labor Force Participation," *Review of Economics and Statistics,* 1992; Margaret L. Williams and Talya N. Bauer, "The Effect of a `Managing Diveristy' Policy on Organizational Attractiveness" (paper presented at the Conference of the Society for Industrial and Organizational Psychology, Montreal, May 1992).

87. Rachel Sarah, "New Clinics Try to Relieve Foreigners' Anxieties," *The Prague Post,* May 10–16, 1995.
88. Daniel B. Turban, Alison R. Eyring, and James E. Campion, "Job Attributes: Preferences Compared with Reasons Given for Accepting and Rejecting Job Offers," *Journal of Occupational and Organizational Psychology* 66, (1993), pp. 71–81.
89. Alison Barber, "Pay as a Signal in Organizational Recruiting" (paper presented at the National Meeting of the Academy of Management, Washington, DC, Aug. 1989).
90. Chris W. Chen, "TRW's Housing Plan," *Personnel Journal,* Mar. 1991, pp. 83–86.
91. S. L. Rynes, "Recruitment Job Choice and Post-Hire Consequences: A Call for New Research Directions," in Marvin D. Dunnette and Leatta M. Hough, eds., *Handbook of Industrial and Organizational Psychology,* 2nd ed. (1991), pp. 399–444; S. L. Premack and John P. Wanous, "A Meta-Analysis of Realistic Job Preview Experiments," *Journal of Applied Psychology* 70 (1985), pp. 716–19; John P. Wanous, Timothy D. Poland, Stephen L. Premack, and K. Shannon Davis, "The Effects of Met Expectations on Newcomer Attitudes and Behaviors: A Review and Meta-Analysis," *Journal of Applied Psychology 77,* no. 3 (1992), pp. 288–97.
92. James A. Breaugh, *Recruitment: Science and Practice* (Boston: PWS–Kent, 1992), p. 183.
93. R. R. Reilly, B. Brown, M. Blood, and C. Malatesta, "The Effects of Realistic Previews: A Study and Discussion of the Literature," *Personnel Psychology* 34 (1981), pp. 823–34.
94. P. Gregory Irving and John P. Meyer, "On Using Direct Measures of Met Expectations: A Methodological Note," *Journal of Management* 21 (1995), pp. 1159–75.
95. James A. Breaugh and Robert S. Billings, "The Realistic Job Preview: Five Key Elements and Their Importance for Research and Practice," *Journal of Business and Psychology* 2, no. 4 (Summer 1988), pp. 291–305.
96. Rynes, Bretz, and Gerhart, "The Importance of Recruitment in Job Choice."
97. Daniel B. Turban, James E. Campion, and Alison R. Eyring, "Factors Related to Job Acceptance Decision of College Recruits," *Journal of Vocational Behavior* 47 (1995), pp. 193–213.
98. Michael M. Harris and Laurence S. Fink, "A Field Study of Applicant Reactions to Employment Opportunities: Does the Recruiter Make a

Difference?" *Personnel Psychology* 40, no. 4 (1987), pp. 765–83; Sara L. Rynes and H. E. Miller, "Recruiter and Job Influences on Candidates for Employment, "*Journal of Applied Psychology* 68 (1983), pp. 147–54; and Neil Schmitt and B. W. Coyle, "Applicant Decisions in the Employment Interview," *Journal of Applied Psychology* 61 (1976), pp. 184–92.

99. C. W. Downs, "Perceptions of the Selection Interview," *Personal Administrator,* May–June 1969, pp. 8–23; P. Herriott and C. Rothwell, "Organizational Choice and Decision Theory: Effects of Employers' Literature and Selection Interview," *Journal of Occupational Psychology* 54 (1981), pp. 17–31; M. Susan Taylor and Janet A. Sniezek, "The College of Recruitment Interview: Topical Content and Applicant Reactions," *Journal of Occupational Psychology* 57 (1984), pp. 157–68; Rynes and Miller, "Recruiter and Job Influences on Candidates for Employment"; Schmitt and Coyle, "Applicant Decisions in the Employment Interview."

100. Clare Ansberry and Alecia Swasy, "Minority Job Applicants Say Slurs Often Surface," *The Wall Street Journal,* Feb. 10, 1989, p. B1.

101. Judith Havemann, "It's Getting Harder and Harder to Find Good Help These Days," *Washington Post National Weekly Edition,* July 24–30, 1989, p. 34.

102. Steven D. Maurer, Vince Howe, and Thomas W. Lee, "Organizational Recruiting as Marketing Management: An Interdisciplinary Study of Engineering Graduates," *Personnel Psychology* 45 (1992), pp. 807–33; Rynes and Boudreau, "College Recruiting in Large Organizations."

103. Rhea Nagle, E-Mail message to HRNET, Nov. 10, 1995.

104. John W. Boudreau, "Utility Analysis," chap. 1.4 in *Human Resource Management Evolving Roles and Responsibilities,* ed. Lee D. Dyer (Washington DC: Bureau of National Affairs, 1988); American Management Associations, "Hiring Costs and Strategies,"

105. James Ledvinka and Vida Scarpello, *Federal Regulation of Personnel and Human Resource Management,* 2nd ed. (Boston: Kent Publishing, 1990).

106. Robert J. Bies and Tom Tyler, "The 'Litigation Mentality' in Organizations: A Test of Alternative Psychological Explanations," *Organization Science* 4, (Aug. 1993), pp. 352–66.

107. Rynes and Boudreau, "College Recruiting in Large Organizations"; John E. Spirig, "The ATS—Applicant Tracking System—Promises to be an Increasingly Valuable Tool for the Hiring Process in the Labor-Lean Years That Lie Ahead," *Employment Relations Today,* Summer 1990, pp. 157–60.

# External Employee Selection

External Selection
- Objectives for External Selection

Developing an External Selection Strategy

Validity: How Well Information Predicts the Future
- Validity Coefficient

Choosing Selection Techniques
- Application Forms and Résumés
- Reference and Background Checks
- Life-History Information
- Interviews
- Ability Tests
- Job Knowledge Tests, Work Samples, and Job Tryouts
- Physical/Physiological Requirements
- Personality, Honesty, and Integrity Testing

Putting the Pieces Together to Create the External Selection Process
- Single-Job Selection versus Classification
- Gathering and Scoring Predictor Information
- Combining Multiple Selection Procedures

Does It Work? Validating Selection Processes
- Criterion-Related Validation
- Content-Based Validation
- Extent of Validation
- Government Regulation of Validation

What Is the Payoff? Evaluating External Selection Activities
- Efficiency
- Equity

Your Turn: "HIO Silver" Selection at AFG Industries

How would you help your new employer choose students from your college or university? Imagine that you have completed your education program and have been hired by the organization that was your first choice. Congratulations! Now that employer has asked you to select four of your classmates to join you in the organization. The employer figures that you probably know the program and the students as well as anyone, so they think you'd do an excellent job of selecting others because you are just the type of person they had been looking for. The organization is well regarded and pays well, so many students will want the jobs. Once the employer let it be known that you would be doing the selecting for the jobs, you heard from more than 20 students who wanted you to hire them. How would you start?

You would probably begin by examining descriptions of the organization and the jobs in order to identify the important behaviors/outcomes, skills, abilities, and traits that seem necessary to accomplish them. How would you (and your employer) know if you were successful? Is it enough that the people you hire stay on the job for one year? Should you strive to select those who will get top performance ratings from their supervisors? Should you emphasize how well a person fits the values and beliefs of the organization, or should you concentrate on the skills needed for a first job? To what extent should you pick people who are a lot like you, or should you strive for diversity?

Once you've decided on your selection goals, you must decide what selection techniques and information you will gather and use. The goal is to find things you can measure before applicants are hired that will predict their behaviors and achievements after they are hired. Would you consider previous job experience? Would you call on references and, if you did, would you only call on the references listed by the applicant? Might a test of general mental abilities or specific job knowledge be appropriate? How about a personality test—do some personality types make better employees than others? Should you screen out applicants who fail a drug or honesty test? Should you impose a diversity goal? If you choose all men or all women the government may require you to demonstrate a clear performance-based reason for this preference.

Would you interview the job candidates? Who would conduct the interview—the future boss, co-workers, you? Virtually every organization interviews applicants; most job candidates expect it, and most interviewers think they are good judges of people. Yet, unless an interview is constructed and carried out in a very structured way, interviewers may not do very well at selecting good performers.

What information would you use to determine which selection techniques are likely to work? Would you be satisfied if you found that your techniques were used by other companies with good results, or would you want to test them on your particular group of candidates?

If you include several of the techniques just described, you'll be constructing a fairly involved and expensive selection process. Is it really worth all that time and effort just to find better employees? Remember, the money you spend on selection could be used to pay your first-year bonus, invest in new technology, or buy you a new car as a signing incentive. On the other hand, selection mistakes can be costly if someone you hire makes mistakes, proves to be dishonest, or leaves shortly after the company invests in his or her training. So, how would you suggest that the company evaluate whether your selection strategy works?

Your instructor may ask you to actually "select" one of the other students in the class by having the interviewee bring his or her résumé to class, and having you interview the applicant for a typical job in your field of study. How would you prepare for that assignment?

## EXTERNAL SELECTION

After external recruiting has produced an applicant pool, there are usually more applicants than job openings. A decision must be made to offer employment to some subset of the applicants while rejecting or postponing an offer to others. Exhibit 7.1 shows that the selection process acts as the filter determining whether applicants become employees.

> *External selection* gathers and uses information about externally recruited applicants to choose which of them receive employment offers. It is often preceded by *screening,* which identifies obviously unqualified applicants before gathering additional selection information.

This chapter focuses on external selection. People can join the organization at all levels, from the lowest-ranking job to chief executive officer. Deciding who to hire is a lot like deciding who should be promoted or transferred, except that promotions and transfers move people within the organization. We discuss this in Chapter Nine on internal staffing and careers. The techniques and concepts that you read about here, applied to external selection, also apply to internal selection. The big difference is that the organization usually has much more information about the people who move within it than it does about new hires. Therefore, both external selection and internal selection involve making choices based on limited information. Globalization affects external selection, as organizations such as Xerox and AT&T more frequently seek their top executives overseas.[1]

Moreover, the world of selection is changing. Increasingly, the hiring decision is made by the team of co-workers with whom the new employee will work. Team members often require training and assistance to learn how to make good selection decisions that stay within legal requirements. At Aetna, the large insurance company, the staffing process rests in the hands of managers who ultimately work with the new employee. How can you give managers the tools they need without creating a human resource "bureaucracy"? Aetna human resource managers did it with the "Staffing Toolkit," a Windows-based software package that provides assistance, instruction, and the necessary forms to follow the six steps of the staffing process:

1. Determine need
2. Source
3. Screen
4. Interview/select
5. Offer/hire
6. Orient

Thus, the role of human resource professionals changes from one of carrying out staffing activities and processes to one of developing and providing support for those who know their needs best and who will have to live with the results. In most organizations, human resource professionals play a key role in the external selection process. They often recommend and design specific selection techniques, frequently conduct the selection process, and usually help to interpret the results of selection, ensuring that the process meets organizational, employee, and legal requirements. Increasingly, however, every worker in every company is likely to play a role in the external selection process.

The "technology" of external selection, including interviews, tests, and other activities, continues to advance daily. We will discuss this technology in detail

EXHIBIT 7.1 The Staffing Process as a Series of Filters

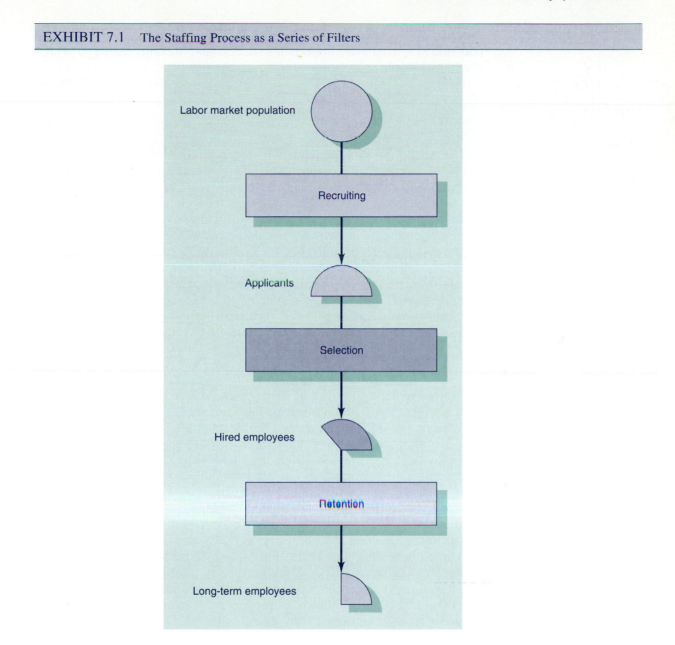

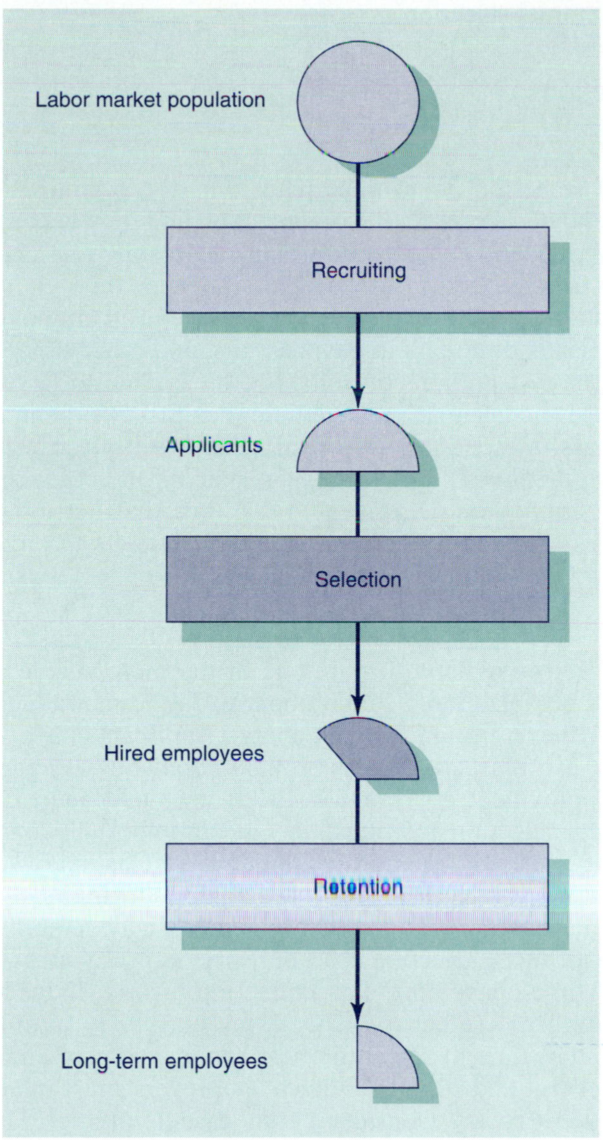


EXPLORING THE WEB

On the Internet, you can tap the experience of hundreds of professionals using and developing interviews and tests in the International Personnel Management Association Assessment Council:
**http://www.bwaldron.com/ipmaac/broch.html.**

in this chapter, but the advance of computers and the Internet brings new tools and opportunities. A recent "Buyers' Guide" includes tests for aptitudes, attitudes, drug use, honesty, leadership, personality, physical ability, safety, sales potential, office skills, and customer service, many of which can be administered and scored on personal computers.[2] Help with external staffing is just a mouse click away, and there's no shortage of experts with products to sell. This makes it even more important to understand the objectives and principles of external selection.

## Objectives for External Selection

### Efficiency

External selection determines who joins the organization. These new hires often spend decades with the organization and they become the resource the organization depends on for performance, flexibility in changing times, innovation, and candidates for further job assignments throughout their careers. It's no exaggeration to say that the decision to hire each employee costs the organization thousands of dollars in pay, benefits, and other support costs. Selection activities can cost millions of dollars when applied to large numbers of employees. However, because those employees affect organizational outcomes for many years, the one-time effort to select carefully can produce extraordinary returns on the investment. More than ever before, organizations are focusing on selecting employees who fit more than just the first job. They are looking for employees who can make long-term contributions through flexible teams, task forces, and continuous learning.[3]

### Equity

External selection activities are one of the most visible and important signals about the organization's commitment to fairness and legal compliance. Selection activities are often the first contact applicants have with the organization, and they use the activities as signals about other organizational attributes.[4] Equal employment opportunity (EEO) laws and court cases frequently focus on external selection activities; they are an important consideration in choosing and using external selection techniques. As Chapter Two described, when an organization's selection processes reject too many members of protected groups, the courts or government agencies may require that the fairness and necessity of those selection procedures be carefully assessed, often with expensive and time-consuming data collection efforts. Indeed, many organizations choose external selection procedures mainly to avoid rejecting protected groups rather than to select the best applicants from among the pool. In addition to federal and state EEO laws, employers must increasingly focus on another issue—privacy. Consider a 1989 case involving 131 Target stores in California. The national retailer required job applicants for security positions to take the Minnesota Multiphasic Personality Inventory (MMPI), which asks for true/false answers to over 700 statements such as "I am fascinated by fire," "I am strongly attracted to members of my own sex," and "I have had no difficulty starting or holding my bowel movement." Target asked these questions from 1987 to 1991, despite a class action invasion-of-privacy and employment discrimination suit, *Soroka* v. *Dayton Hudson,* filed in 1989. In 1995, the retailer settled for more than $2 million without admitting liability or wrongdoing.[5] Selection strategies can affect relations with labor unions or even prevent their formation. One study of a Japanese-owned auto parts plant in the United States suggested that the senior plant manager had been given a goal of remaining free of unions, and although none of the selection practices explicitly excluded pro-union workers, those who confidentially told the researcher they would vote for a union were more likely to withdraw their applications or quit shortly after being hired.[6]

## DEVELOPING AN EXTERNAL SELECTION STRATEGY

As the example at the beginning of this chapter illustrated, designing an external selection strategy involves making the following choices:

1. What selection criteria and evidence to use in judging selection information about applicants.
2. Which specific information-gathering techniques to use.
3. How the information will be used within the selection process.
4. How to measure the results of selection.

In later sections, we discuss different selection techniques and how to use and evaluate selection information. It is important, however, to understand the link between organization goals and external selection strategy. Ideally, external selection strategy flows directly from an analysis of the organization's goals, which translate into work roles or contributions, which suggest what applicant characteristics to look for, which in turn guides the choice of selection methods and the evaluation of their effectiveness. Exhibit 7.2 illustrates these links. It also shows how important it is to reinforce selection decisions with integrated work design, training, and rewards.

Notice that Exhibit 7.2 focuses on the overall work environment and on the notion of person-organization fit. Traditionally, external selection has been described as fitting the person to the job.[7] As Chapter Three shows, the nature of work and organizations today requires thinking in terms of long-term contributions through varied work roles and a career involving continuous learning. Organizations strive for selection that is valid not just for the job but also for the organization. One study found that when assigning undergraduate students to teams, the teams based only on ability had less communication and cohesiveness than when students chose their own teams.[8] Still, most research on selection focuses on predicting performance in a particular job.

What principles guide the selection strategy? There are many considerations, but two issues are paramount: validity and legality. Legality reflects whether the external selection strategy adheres to laws and regulations, and avoids motivating litigation. Every single step in the process is subject to legal scrutiny if it creates adverse impact, as you saw in Chapter Two. Validity refers to whether the selection strategy predicts the future. Because validity is such a central issue, we define it next, so that you will understand it when we discuss the specific selection techniques.

## VALIDITY: HOW WELL INFORMATION PREDICTS THE FUTURE

External selection decisions are predictions. Based on applicant characteristics that can be observed before hiring, organizations try to predict how applicants will behave or perform if they are hired. The only way to know for sure which applicants are the best would be to hire everyone who applies, let everyone perform on the job, and then keep only enough of the best employees to fill the

**EXHIBIT 7.2** Steps in Designing an External Selection Strategy

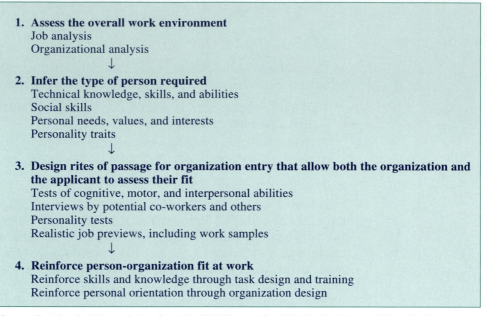

1. **Assess the overall work environment**
   Job analysis
   Organizational analysis
   ↓
2. **Infer the type of person required**
   Technical knowledge, skills, and abilities
   Social skills
   Personal needs, values, and interests
   Personality traits
   ↓
3. **Design rites of passage for organization entry that allow both the organization and the applicant to assess their fit**
   Tests of cognitive, motor, and interpersonal abilities
   Interviews by potential co-workers and others
   Personality tests
   Realistic job previews, including work samples
   ↓
4. **Reinforce person-organization fit at work**
   Reinforce skills and knowledge through task design and training
   Reinforce personal orientation through organization design

Source: Reprinted with permission from David E. Bowen, Gerald E. Ledford, Jr., and Barry R. Nathan, "Hiring for the Organization, Not the Job," *Academy of Management Executive* 15, no. 4 (1991), p. 37.

organization's needs. Unfortunately, this approach is seldom practical because of high costs, limited equipment availability, risks of damage or accidents, and the reluctance of applicants to give up other opportunities during the probationary period. Even if it were feasible for the first job, selection would still require making predictions about such things as performance in higher-level positions or the likelihood of staying with the organization.

Therefore, organizations must choose among applicants based on less direct indicators of their future behaviors. Exhibit 7.3 shows selection as a two-way signaling process, with the organization observing signals from applicants such as their performance in interviews, test scores, and knowledge of the company. These signals are interpreted for their relationship to the desired information such as applicants' knowledge, skill/ability, motivation, and other factors shown on the right side of Exhibit 7.3. The signals are called the *predictors,* and the desired information elements are called the *criteria.* Evidence regarding how well predictors actually work is called *validity* information. Note in the exhibit that the selection process acts as a signal to job applicants as well. Applicants interpret what they encounter in the selection process as they form impressions

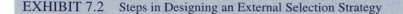

*Validity* is the degree to which predictions from selection information are supported by evidence.

*Validation* is the process of gathering information about predictor validity.

*Reliability* is the consistency with which selection information reflects an individual's characteristics. High reliability in both predictors and criteria is necessary, but not sufficient to have high validity.

**EXHIBIT 7.3** Selection as a Two-Way Signaling Process

| Applicants ◄ | | ► | Organizations |
|---|---|---|---|
| **Desired Information** | **Signals Sent ◄** | **► Signals Sent** | **Desired Information** |
| Job duties | Résumé | Advertisements | Knowledge |
| Job security | Application | Company image | Skill/ability |
| Job conditions | Background | Compensation | Motivation |
| Supervisors | References | Background checks | Loyalty |
| Co-workers | Interview | Interview | Creativity |
| Careers | Dress | Interest in candidate | Fit |
| Pay | Enthusiasm | Tests given | Performance |
| Benefits | Knowledge of the company | | Flexibility |
| Fairness | Stated job interest | | Trainability |
| | Test scores | | Promotability |
| | | | Separation probability |

about what it would be like to work in the organization. We discussed this in Chapter Six on recruitment.

For the organization, the task is to "measure" the applicants using selection information that will predict their future behaviors. To measure, the organization must distinguish among the applicants, usually by assigning a "score" to each applicant. The rating might be a test score, an interview rating, or a combination of several measures. Making a score out of an observation is often tricky. The American Management Association suggests that certain nonverbal messages "observed" in the interview may have interesting scores or interpretations. For example, is "shaking head" interpreted as "disagreeing, shocked, or disbelieving?" Should "sitting on edge of seat" be scored as "anxious, nervous, apprehensive"?[9]

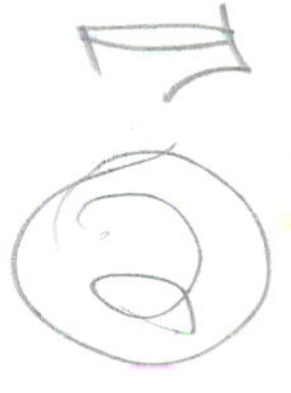

Validation simply asks, "are the differences in applicant characteristics (such as knowledge, skills, abilities, or experience) that we measure now, related to their behaviors after we hire them?" Validity information helps organizations choose predictors that can improve selection decisions and thus raise the quality of those selected. Validation is also significant legally. As Chapter Two describes when predictors seem to exclude members of legally protected groups, EEO laws and the courts consider whether the predictors are related to job performance, and thus, necessary to the business. Validity information can provide evidence that selection processes are job-related.

## Validity Coefficient

Exhibit 7.4 contains three graphs, called *scatterplots,* each one plotting the relationship between predictor scores on a selection technique (the horizontal axis) and criterion scores on a job behavior (the vertical axis). The graph is

EXHIBIT 7.4 Scatterplots and Validity Coefficients for Different Predictor-Criterion Relationships

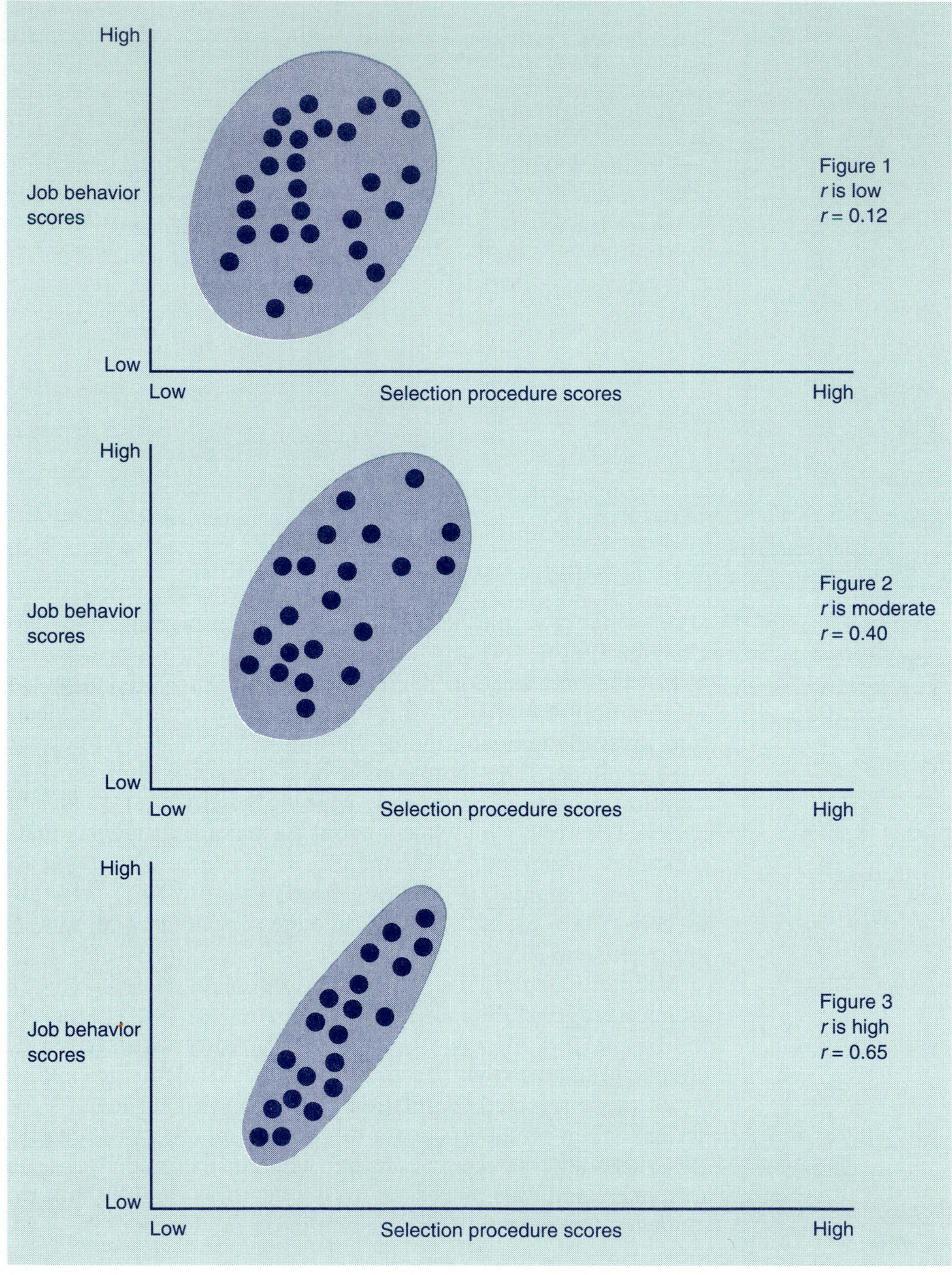

easier to understand if you imagine a particular combination of predictor and criterion. Imagine that the $X$-axis represents scores on an intelligence test and the $Y$-axis is the performance rating by a person's supervisor after one year on the job. Thus, every dot in Exhibit 7.4 represents one person's intelligence test score and one-year performance rating. This idea holds for any predictor and criterion, so you can choose your favorite if you wish. Each ellipse contains a pattern of dots for many individuals. At the top of the exhibit, those who have high intelligence scores don't necessarily seem to get high performance ratings and vice versa. At the bottom of the exhibit, the scores seem to move together more. At the top, Figure 1 shows low validity because any particular predictor score is associated with a wide range of possible criterion scores. In the middle, Figure 2 shows moderate validity because each predictor score associates with a narrower range of criterion scores. At the bottom, Figure 3 shows the highest level of validity, because the dots fall nearly on a straight line, with each predictor score associated with only a very narrow range of possible criterion scores.

The information in a scatterplot can be summarized by a single number called a *correlation coefficient.* In validation it is called a *validity coefficient.* It is represented by the symbol $r$. The values for $r$ can range from –1.0 (indicating that scores fall perfectly on a line sloping downward from left to right), to 0.0 (indicating that scores fall in a circle or have no linear relationship), to 1.0 (indicating that scores fall perfectly on a line sloping upward from left to right). In Exhibit 7.4, notice how the $r$ values of 0.12 in Figure 1. 0.40 in Figure 2, and 0.65 in Figure 3 reflect this pattern. The formula for the correlation coefficient is available in any basic statistics book. Fortunately, these calculations are now done by computer. Most basic spreadsheet programs calculate the correlation coefficient at the touch of a key.

The validity coefficient is only a calculation. You can compute it for any set of paired scores, no matter whether they are real, and no matter what their relationship. You might try calculating the correlation between the weekly hours you put into each of your classes, and the final class grades you receive. If it is positive, that may be very interesting, but does it mean that more hours and better grades will be associated next term? This is also important in selection. The validity coefficient for one group of people is less important than whether the organization will see a similar relationship with future groups of applicants. Using statistics, we can calculate the probability that a correlation from one group is large enough so that we should expect to see a relationship in other groups. If this probability is high, we say the correlation is *statistically significant.*

If study hours and grades are correlated, does that mean that the hours you put in *caused* the high grades? A validity coefficient (even a statistically significant one) does not mean that one thing causes another. Your grades and study hours may be correlated because you spend more time on classes that you like, and you get better grades because you like the class. One study found that the draft order of college basketball players into the National Basketball Association (NBA) correlated with their professional playing time and tenure with the team. Does higher draft status *cause* performance? The study found that draft order related to playing time and tenure even after taking into account on-court performance, injuries, and other factors. It appears that once NBA teams pay a lot for a player, they play them more than low-draft players with similar performance. The predictor affects how teams support the player.[10] Simply because intelligence test scores correlate with job performance ratings doesn't mean we should train employees how to do better on intelligence tests. However, it may mean we should consider intelligence when we select people.

As we discuss selection techniques in later sections, we will report the validity coefficients that have been discovered through scientific study. Keep in mind that validity coefficients closer to 1.0 mean stronger relationships and vice versa. How high must validity be to be "good"? There is no general rule. Higher validity is generally better, but even a low-validity predictor can be useful if the selection decisions are very important and if there are no alternatives. Also, keep in mind that predictor validity depends on the situation. If you are trying to select people for assignments in which they can "stretch" or "grow," then a predictor with high validity for job performance may not be useful, because it would select people who can already do the job and won't grow very much.[11]

Finally, validity is not something to be pursued at all costs. It is an indicator of a predictor's ability to help achieve goals. Sometimes validity can be improved by matching predictors to very rigid and constrained work outcomes. A typing test will be a valid predictor of how accurately a computer programmer can input characters, but it is probably not a complete selection system. A programmer also must be creative, be able to work on a team, and perhaps be able to eventually lead and influence customers, suppliers, or shareholders. Predicting future performance in a world of changing jobs and roles may require rethinking our traditional notions of validity. Keep this in mind as you learn more about the technology of external selection.

## CHOOSING SELECTION TECHNIQUES

There is probably an infinite variety of ways to measure applicant information, and new ways are being developed every day. Computerized testing and genetic screening were virtually unheard of several years ago; now many organizations use them. Still, traditional information-gathering techniques such as the application form and the interview enjoy the widest use. Despite legal scrutiny and recessionary times, U.S. employers continue to use a variety of methods to select applicants; foreign organizations often use even more.[12] In Exhibit 7.5, we summarize the techniques we discuss, as well as their validity, cost, legality, and popularity. Subsequent sections show where the information in Exhibit 7.5 came from. Clearly, selection technique popularity is not a simple matter of choosing the most valid or least-cost method. Many expensive techniques with modest validity are among the most popular, and vice versa. A better understanding of these techniques can help explain why.

### Application Forms and résumés

Shortly after his election as U.S. president in 1992, Bill Clinton's transition team received hundreds of résumés every day from job-seekers for the more than 4,000 job openings in the administration. Bob sent a new picture of himself every day. A mother sent a picture of her daughter dressed as a Clinton campaign bus. And a zookeeper said he was mauled by a hippopotamus, but is all right now. How to sort through all this? Fifty-five volunteers worked from

7:00 A.M. to midnight seven days a week feeding everything into a sophisticated computer system called Resumix that read each résumé, sorted out the duplicates, and came up with candidate lists based on the characteristics chosen by the team.[13] Electronic resume screening was unusual in 1992. Today, it's common procedure. Here's an excerpt from a discussion on HRNET:

> At Microsoft, we welcome unsolicited résumés. We receive over 100,000 per year—which is about six times the size of our workforce! A significant percent arrive over the Internet, and this is actually easier for us because we can upload them automatically into our database (the hard copy résumés we receive must be scanned before we can load them into our database). When we have a job opening, we do a key word search of our database to look for applicants who may be qualified for the job. We can then do a "manual" review of the résumés uncovered in the search to determine whether any are worth screening with interviews. We have made many hires in this manner.[14]

The first piece of information provided by most job candidates is a written summary of their personal characteristics. For blue-collar, clerical, and nommanagerial jobs, this information is typically gathered through an application form. Managers and professionals usually provide this information in the form of a résumé and cover letter, though an application form is typically part of the process for these people as well.

### Application Forms

Application forms serve as a record of the employment application and a way to keep track of the characteristics of applicants as future employment openings occur. In addition, application forms usually pose a series of questions that firms use to judge suitability for employment. Application forms almost always request an applicant's name, address, telephone, Social Security number, and citizenship or employment eligibility. They usually request information on the type of work desired and preferences about scheduling (part time, full time, evenings, etc.). Application forms also may request the names of references and prior work history.

Extensive application forms may include questions about age, race, physical characteristics, religion, gender, marital and family status, physical health, military service, arrest/conviction records, education, credit rating, medical conditions, and estimated job skills/abilities. Though Title VII of the *Civil Rights Act* does not specifically prohibit particular questions, asking questions about gender, marital status, and religion that might lead to the rejection of protected groups is risky. If too many protected-group members are rejected, the organization may be required to prove such information is job related and was not used to reject them. Many U.S. states and territories regulate preemployment inquiries, with sex, race, nationality, and age most frequently regulated. The Virgin Islands even regulate questions about political affiliation. Many organizations simply refrain from asking such questions until after people are hired.[15]

Application forms may also contain a clause requiring the applicant to undergo further testing; releasing former employers, credit sources, and references from legal liability for the information they furnish; accepting a probationary period; agreeing that the employment relationship may be terminated at any time; and stating that information provided on the form is accurate and truthful. Applicant signatures are obtained as evidence of understanding and agreement with these stipulations.[16] The questions on an application blank may be more influential than you think. One study had Canadian college students complete application blanks,

EXHIBIT 7.5 Characteristics of External Selection Techniques

| Method | Validity | Cost | Legality | Popularity |
|---|---|---|---|---|
| Application forms and résumés | Less than 0.20 for academic achievement and experience ratings. Weighted application blanks (WABs) reported as high as 0.56. | Low information acquisition cost, but higher if WAB is developed. Processing costs are moderate. | Defensible when job-related, but use of legally risky questions is common and may cause adverse impact. | Pervasive use in an unstructured way. About 11% of organizations use WABs. |
| Reference and background checks | In the range of 0.25. | Moderate, primarily costs of employee time or private investigators. | Risk of adverse impact can be reduced by avoiding risky questions, using release forms, and structuring to link to jobs. | Pervasive use of phone and mail checking. Less than 20% use outside investigators. |
| Life-history information | Biographical inventories and accomplishment records yield validity in the 0.30s or higher. Training and experience ratings show validity less than 0.20. | Moderate to high. Simple training and experience ratings involve employee time, while developing BIBs or accomplishment records can cost thousand of dollars. | General education or experience requirements can cause adverse impact, but clear links to job-related behaviors and structure can improve legality. | Very common to verify educational background. More structured and directive methods are rarely used. |
| Interview | Unstructured interview is generally very low, but with structured interview validity in the 0.60s or higher. | Relatively high. Interviewer time and travel can easily amount to thousands of dollars per candidate. Developing structured interviews involves added development and processing costs. | Subjectivity is not automatically a problem unless it produces adverse impact. Structuring and interviewer training can reduce adverse impact likelihood. | Pervasive, but only about 35% of companies use structured interviews. |

## EXHIBIT 7.5 (*concluded*)

| Method | Validity | Cost | Legality | Popularity |
|---|---|---|---|---|
| Ability tests | Generally greater than 0.40, and can range as high as 0.80. | Relatively inexpensive to administer, costing less than $100 per person. Additional modest costs involved in processing and interpreting scores. Developing a new test can cost over $100,000. | Risk of adverse impact against low-scoring minorities, but validation evidence can be used as an effective defense. | Used by about 30% of organizations, with the greatest use for office/clerical positions. |
| Job knowledge tests, work samples, and job tryouts | Validities in the 0.40s are common. | Varies widely. Standard job-knowledge tests have costs equivalent to ability tests. However, developing work samples can cost thousands of dollars, and probationary periods involve costs of paid wages and additional supervision. | Relatively little risk of adverse impact for work samples, but higher risk for job-knowledge tests. | Skill tests or work samples used by over 60% of organizations, with 31% using job knowledge tests. |
| Physical and physiological requirements | Stringently developed ability tests have shown validities in the 0.50s. Validity for most physiological tests is low or evidence sketchy. | Varies widely. Medical examinations and lab work can cost about $1,000 per employee. Drug testing and AIDS screening can cost between $500 and $1,500 per test. | Very high risk of adverse impact against females and some minority groups. Physiological testing also risks litigation over invasion of privacy. | Medical examinations and drug tests are given by about half of all organizations. Less than 10% currently use other physiological tests. |
| Personality, honesty, and graphology tests | Many early studies showed very low validity. Recent evidence suggests matching personality traits to work requirements can produce validities in the .20s, with integrity test validities as high as the .40s. | Relatively inexpensive, as standard tests and scoring systems are available from consulting and testing firms. Costs per applicant probably less than $500. | Risks of adverse impact against religious groups. Risks based on invasion of privacy. Difficult to demonstrate relationship to job behaviors. | About 17% of organizations use personality tests, mostly for salespeople. Less than 10% use other types of tests. |

some with "inappropriate questions" about age, marital status, gender, and disabilities, some with a statement that the organization was committed to "special programs designed to eliminate longstanding disadvantages in employment for women, aboriginal people, visible minorities, and disabled persons," and some with neither. Students seeing application blanks free of inappropriate questions or with the commitment to eliminate disadvantages felt more positively about pursuing the job and taking it if offered, the fairness of employee treatment, and recommending the organization to friends.[17]

An important factor in the value and legal safety of application form information is the way it is used. Checklists can be constructed to ensure that relevant information is considered, depending on the type of employment being considered for the applicant. A very elaborate form of application blank scoring is the *weighted application blank* (WAB) that scores the responses to each question, multiplies each score by a weight reflecting that question's importance in predicting performance on the job being considered, and then adds up the weighted scores to produce a total score for each applicant. About 11 percent of firms responding to a recent study indicated they used weighted application blanks. Usually weights are set either by having experts rate what factors are most important, or by examining which items seem to distinguish between high and low performers or between those who stay and those who leave. The Adolph Coors Company uses a computerized data base that allows managers to enter their own importance weights, and then have the computer list the candidates in order of their weighted scores.[18]

### Résumés

If you plan to pursue a managerial or professional job with an organization, you undoubtedly need to prepare a résumé listing your qualifications and a cover letter. The appendix to Chapter Six provides guidelines on preparing and using these tools to make your case to a prospective employer. The organization can use a cover letter and résumé similarly to an application form. Selectors scan these documents for useful selection information. Checklists and weighting schemes also can add structure and consistency to the résumé-scanning process.

As we have seen, computer technology has revolutionized the résumé-screening process. When résumés are scanned into databases, managers can easily search through thousands of them in a wink, progressively narrowing the search by using key words that reflect desired characteristics. Disney, Ford Motor Company, and the White House hire a company using artificial intelligence to analyze résumés and identify primary work experience and other factors. However, cyber-scanning may have a cost in creativity. Some experts recommend using simple black type on white paper, no folds or staples, a keyword summary at the top, and many nouns that match favorite computer-search terms. Still, it's a good idea to proofread the résumé before transmitting it. Snelling and Snelling found these résumé bloopers: "I want a position to pay my bills"; "Have Word Purpose and Locust Skills"; and "Experienced in private relations."[19]

### Validity

Grades in school, years of school, and years of experience often do not strongly relate to job performance, with validities less than 0.20. However, using a scoring scheme with weights on the most important factors can improve predictions, especially for separations. Performance predictions can be improved if the weights are developed by analyzing those factors that actually relate to job performance and weighing those most heavily.[20]

### Legality

When considering the possibilities that application form information may show different patterns for different legally protected groups, questions about arrest records, credit ratings, race, age, marital status, and so forth are risky. Applicants may later claim that by gathering such information, the organization consciously or unconsciously excluded one or more protected groups. Several surveys of U.S. and Canadian employers have found that up to 94 percent of application forms contain at least one inappropriate question, and many contain several.[21] Therefore, employers deciding what information to request on application forms should consider (1) possible adverse impact, (2) information value in identifying qualified applicants, (3) possible conflict with court decisions or EEOC guidelines, (4) possible invasion of privacy, and (5) availability of evidence that the information relates to job performance.[22]

## Reference and Background Checks

Most organizations verify information on application forms and résumés and gather additional information from references supplied by the applicant or other sources such as credit bureaus, previous employers, and educators. A survey of personnel executives in 245 U.S. organizations shows that virtually all organizations check the date of the applicant's most recent job, reason for leaving the most recent job, information about jobs prior to the most recent, salary and position in the most recent job, and legal eligibility for employment (required by the U.S. Immigration Reform and Control Act of 1986). A 1995 survey by the Society for Human Resources Management found that 92 percent of organizations spoke to the former employer, only 61 percent verify educational information, 42 percent check driving records, and 25 percent conduct credit checks.[23]

Gathering background information poses several dilemmas. On the one hand, failure to check an applicant's background can result in tragedy and significant costs. Computer Recognition Technologies, a small computer document imaging company in Skokie, Illinois, failed to check the background of the woman hired as an accounting assistant. She was on the payroll for six months, but it took only 90 days for her to forge $120,000 worth of company checks and deposit the money in a bank account opened under an alias. "We found out that she was on parole for check forgery and substance abuse when her parole officer called because she violated her parole," said Steve Gilfand, president of the company.[24] Companies can also be sued for negligent hiring should an employee commit a crime or injure someone, and a background check would have revealed such tendencies. On the other hand, employers are reluctant to offer information about former employees because they might be sued for slander if the information causes a person to lose a job. Clifford Zalay won a $25 million punitive damage settlement from John Hancock Mutual Life for slander.[25] The SHRM survey revealed that 63 percent of all human resource professionals have refused to provide information about a former employee, fearing a lawsuit. Nearly 40 percent indicated that HR professionals should refuse to provide information to

> **WHAT DO YOU THINK?**
>
> Suppose your company recently fired one of your subordinates for theft. Now, one of your former classmates, who works in another company, calls you to say the former employee has applied for a job. Would you tell your classmate about the theft?

prospective employers, even if the information is accurate and factual. Intuit Corporation, makers of Quicken software, routinely requests up to a dozen references from applicants for management positions, and then calls each one asking, "Can you describe a project in which the candidate achieved outstanding results?" and "Can you describe a situation in which the candidate's performance was disappointing." The staffing manager for Intuit says answers are usually honest and, if they are questionable, Intuit asks the candidate for additional references. APCOA, a Cleveland parking-facility operator checks applicant driving records, credit history, criminal records, education, and employment verification.[26] Of course, the computer age has come to background checking. One product allows companies to use Windows-based software and a modem to receive various reports.[27] Many employers ask employees to sign a release from liability or waive their right to see reference information. However, no such release can be an absolute protection against future suits, and many applicants might feel that these checks are an invasion of privacy.

> EXPLORING THE WEB
>
> You can see the web page for Informus, a company that provides background information such as driving records, criminal history and credit at:
> **http://www.informus.com/.**

### Validity

References recommended by applicants frequently give uniformly positive responses that make it impossible to distinguish among the candidates. However, reference checks have shown moderate validity in the vicinity of 0.25, according to many studies. If references are willing, another way to increase the comparability of information is to ask references to rate candidates on scales reflecting behaviors such as attendance, punctuality, accepting authority, and safety.[28]

### Legality

Like application blanks, reference and background checks can reduce legal vulnerability by demonstrating clear links to job-related factors and by avoiding risky questions. Having applicants sign release forms may reduce the risk of suits over invasion of privacy and slander. Even labor law affects background checks. The U.S. Supreme Court ruled in *NLRB* v. *Town & Country Electric* that the company violated the National Labor Relations Act when it refused to interview or retain 11 job applicants, even though they were union members and paid by the union to organize the company.[29]

## Life-History Information

Did you ever build a model airplane that flew? This question turned out to be a very good predictor of pilot trainee performance.[30] It's an example of one kind of life-history information going beyond the information typically contained in application forms, résumés, or background checks, and yet focusing on aspects of the candidates' previous education, experiences, and accomplishments. Past behavior is frequently a good predictor of future behavior; thus, many organizations rely on this kind of information.

### Education

Employers frequently examine the length and type of formal education reported by a job applicant and sometimes check with educators for background information. U.S. organizations emphasize college education and go to great lengths to develop relationships with university programs in areas such as engineering and management. In contrast, Japanese organizations emphasize long-term relationships with high schools that compete for students and rigorously prepare them for recommendations to the businesses having relationships with the high schools.[31]

As noted in Chapter Six, however, many of the applicants for future U.S. jobs will be those trained primarily in high schools and vocational schools. The U.S. Secretary of Labor has emphasized the importance of properly assessing and rewarding noncollege training and experience. Hundreds of American companies are supporting efforts to develop standardized tests to assess basic skills and academic achievement. The National Alliance of Business is working with the Educational Testing Service to create an employee credentialing system that would automatically track the experiences and education of people who are not college bound, such as on-the-job learning, vocational training, and so forth. By using this system, employers could easily consider the full detail of applicants' high school and subsequent performance, rather than simply checking whether they have high-school diplomas. If businesses selected and rewarded high school students based on their performance in school, they could create a very strong incentive for better student and school performance; this might motivate U.S. students to achieve math and science test scores as high as students in other countries.[32] Does education make a difference? A study of 3,000 U.S. businesses found that a 10 percent increase in the education of the workforce would produce an 8.6 percent increase in productivity, while a 10 percent increase in the capital stock would produce only a 3.4 percent increase in productivity.[33]

### Biographical Information Blanks (BIBs)

Biographical information blanks (BIBs) ask applicants questions about their backgrounds, life experiences, attitudes, and interests. Typical questions might include: "How many hours per week did you work on an outside job while you were in college?" "How carefully do you account for and budget the money you spend? "When in high school, how high were the standards you set for yourself?" In one study, these questions were related to supervisory performance.[34] Another study found that people whose past behaviors indicated a desire to make a good impression, to be helpful, and to be sociable later obtained higher ratings of their service orientation by customers in a hypothetical telemarketing experiment. Sample items included, "How many nights do you go out per week?" (sociability) and "I make a good impression on people, compared to most people."[35] This is one example where frequent dating may be good preparation for a future career! A study of thousands of U.S. Army recruits found that biodata items reflecting outdoor work or pastimes, a dependable, nondelinquent lifestyle, preference for group attachments, and diligent involvement in intellectual pastimes predicted whether new recruits would leave within their first two years of duty. Even though research suggests that such items can be faked, the danger is less with verifiable and objective items.[36]

### Training, Experience, and Accomplishments

While an application blank or résumé can list the titles of classes taken, participation in activities or clubs, and awards/honors, it is often difficult to relate these to particular job requirements. A person who worked as a fast-food manager may have simply made hamburgers or he or she may have supervised a group of 10 food preparers and servers. *Training and experience (T&E) forms* and *accomplishment records* relate experiences directly to particular job or organizational requirements.

Training and experience forms provide a list of important tasks generated through job analysis. Exhibit 7.6 shows a T&E form that might be used for the job of personnel research analyst. For each task, the T&E form asks whether the applicant has any relevant training or experience for the task. If the answer is yes, the applicant indicates the date and specific training program or job that provided the experience. Reviewing the finished form allows a manager to determine how much of the applicant's training/experience relates to specific job behaviors.

The *accomplishment record* technique was developed by a government regulatory agency to be applied to attorneys. Lawyers describe their professional achievements illustrating specific dimensions such as using knowledge. Each description has a date, a general description of the outcome of the accomplishment, a summary of exactly what the applicant did to contribute, any awards or recognition, and the name of a reference to verify the accomplishment. One study also prepared scoring keys to improve consistency for the managers who reviewed the accomplishment record summaries.[37]

### Validity

Training and experience ratings seem to produce validity levels of about 0.13, with education producing validities of about 0.10. Biographical inventories produce validities of about 0.37 across many studies. Accomplishment records have produced higher validity levels when used to predict attorneys' job success and have "face validity" because applicants believe they are appropriate and valid. Many biodata items are developed by statistically relating a large amount of biodata information to several performance measures, and then choosing the most statistically relevant. One study suggested that organizations without such data could develop biodata questions by asking experts familiar with the job.[38]

### Legality

As *Griggs* v. *Duke Power* showed, blanket application of a broad educational or training requirement, such as a high school diploma, can make companies legally vulnerable; such a requirement can produce an adverse impact and be difficult to link to job behaviors. Experience and education requirements are less vulnerable when they clearly relate to job knowledge, involve high-level or safety-related positions, and do not perpetuate past discrimination. Biographical inventories and accomplishment records have been shown to produce less adverse impact.[39]

It is also important to consider the equity issues of perceived violations of privacy with biodata. One study showed that graduate students at a state university found questions about their parents' social class, father's income, father's job, and mother's education and popularity in high school to be strongly invasive. Biodata may be threatening when it is seen as uncontrollable, not job related, or has the potential to discredit the person.[40]

#### WHAT DO YOU THINK?

Biographical information can reveal whether an applicant has past experience that directly relates to the job. However, suppose you wish to recruit among groups who haven't had the opportunity to get such experience? Can biodata still be used? What are the potential dangers of excluding people who lack such opportunity?

**EXHIBIT 7.6** Training and Experience Evaluation Form for the Job of Personnel Research Analyst

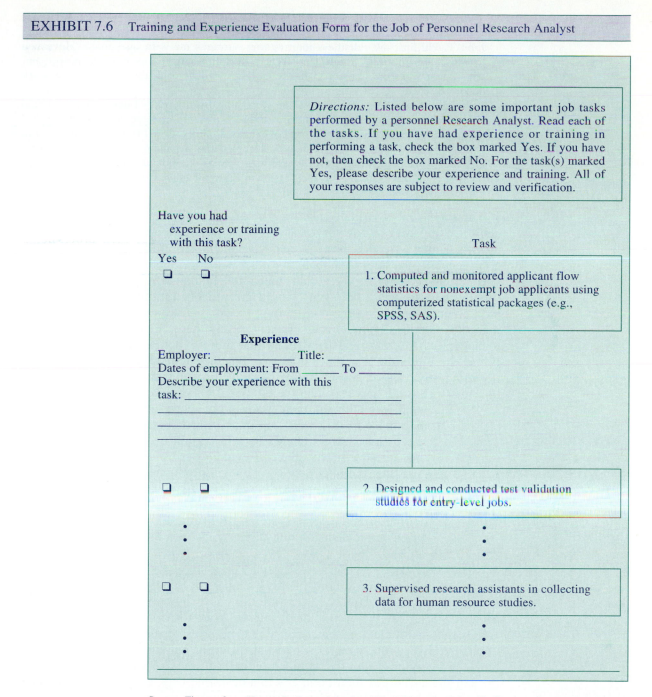

*Directions:* Listed below are some important job tasks performed by a personnel Research Analyst. Read each of the tasks. If you have had experience or training in performing a task, check the box marked Yes. If you have not, then check the box marked No. For the task(s) marked Yes, please describe your experience and training. All of your responses are subject to review and verification.

Have you had experience or training with this task?

| Yes | No | Task |
|---|---|---|
| ❑ | ❑ | 1. Computed and monitored applicant flow statistics for nonexempt job applicants using computerized statistical packages (e.g., SPSS, SAS). |

**Experience**

Employer: ____________ Title: ____________

Dates of employment: From ______ To _______

Describe your experience with this task: ______________________________

______________________________

______________________________

______________________________

| Yes | No | Task |
|---|---|---|
| ❑ | ❑ | 2. Designed and conducted test validation studies for entry-level jobs. |
| • | | • |
| • | | • |
| • | | • |
| ❑ | ❑ | 3. Supervised research assistants in collecting data for human resource studies. |
| • | | • |
| • | | • |
| • | | • |

Source: Figures from *Human Resource Selection,* Third Edition by Robert D. Gatewood and Hubert S. Field, 

## Interviews

> John T. Phillips, my relentless interrogator, barrages me with questions. "Have you led any task forces or committees? Where you didn't have any position power, but where you were the leader?" I hesitate. "How did you go about getting the work done?" Silence.
>
> Finally, I ask "Does this have to be something from work?" Luckily not, so I find myself talking, and talking. Soon, Mr. Phillips is listening to true confessions: How I tried to defuse cold-war hostilities in my extended family, how I convened a meeting to reorganize our annual holiday bash, how I lobbied cousins and commandeered an uncle into menu-planning. From this, Mr. Phillips, who is director of training and development at S. C. Johnson & Son, Inc., hopes to know whether I would fit into his company, if I were really looking for a job.[41]

The interview is virtually always part of employee selection. Fifty-six percent of companies in one survey stated that interviews are the most important aspect of their selection process, and 90 percent reported that they had more confidence in the interview than any other selection method. Yet, for decades psychologists and other researches have published studies showing that the interview has low validity.[42] Why would presumably rational managers persist with an expensive and time-consuming process that doesn't predict job performance? Undoubtedly, there is an element of faith here. A survey of hundreds of managers in different industries found that more experienced interviewers believed the interview was more effective, but they tended to reject the idea of imposing structure on the interview. A study of university admissions officer interviews showed, however, that the ratings of experienced interviewers correlated *less* with the later grade point averages (GPAs) of students than those of inexperienced interviewers, possibly because experienced interviewers tended to skip certain questions or adopt their own questions. Nonetheless, evidence from decades of study suggests that the interview can be a valid predictor, but that it must be used carefully and properly.[43] A few organizations claim that interviewer costs, inconsistency, and errors can be reduced by using computerized expert systems programmed to present questions based on the decision rules used by the best interviewers.[44]

> WHAT DO YOU THINK?
>
> Would you rather interview with a computer or a person? What would be the advantages and disadvantages for employers?

### The Interview Process

Today, interviews are still done mostly on a person-to-person basis by only one interviewer. Panels of interviewers are also used by some organizations. Exhibit 7.7 describes the employment interview as a script, proceeding through five scenes, with clear expectations about the roles of the interviewer and the applicant. Every interview is somewhat different but Exhibit 7.7 shows how both the interviewer and the applicant attempt to receive and send signals that present themselves or their company in a desirable way, and that provide clues to the match between the applicant and the organization (see Exhibit 7.3).

Exhibit 7.8 summarizes variables that research has investigated as affecting the employment interview. Although this model was proposed in 1982, it continues to form the basis for recent interview research.[45] It divides the factors affecting the interview into applicant factors, situation factors, and interviewer factors. Moreover, it shows how important it is to consider the interaction of these factors when considering the causes of interviewer behavior and the likely results of employment interviews. Some have suggested that interviewers

## EXHIBIT 7.7 The Script of a Typical Selection Interview

| Scene | Applicant Script | Interviewer Script |
|---|---|---|
| **1.** Precontact activities | Check appearance/dress.<br>Enter locale.<br>Announce arrival.<br>Review notes while waiting. | Review résumé.<br>Review interview guide.<br>Make note of questions.<br>Prepare setting. |
| **2.** Greeting and establish rapport | Shake hands.<br>Sit when asked.<br>Make good impression in small talk. | Shake hands.<br>Seat applicant.<br>Relax applicant with appropriate small talk. |
| **3.** Ask job-related questions | Provide educational history.<br>Provide details of work history.<br>Detail personal skills and abilities. | Ask about educational background.<br>Seek relevant details about work history.<br>Discuss special skills and abilities. |
| **4.** Answer applicant questions | Try to demonstrate proper motivation for the job.<br>Ask about pay and benefits.<br>Ask about opportunities for advancement. | Get to applicant's motivation to work.<br>Answer applicant questions, putting face on organization. |
| **5.** Disengagement | Ask about organization culture—work norms, and the like.<br>Wait for interviewer cue that interview is over.<br>Discuss next step.<br>Stand up and shake hands.<br>Exit. | Try to create positive impression about organization.<br>Show that interview is about to conclude.<br>Suggest what the next step will be.<br>Stand up and shake hands.<br>Show applicant out. |

Source: William L. Tullar, "The Interview as a Cognitive Performing Script," chap. 17, in *The Employment Interview,* ed. Robert W. Eder and Gerald R. Ferris (Newbury Park, CA: Sage Publications, 1989), pp. 233–46.

try to assess how well applicants would generally fit the organization and how generally qualified they are for employment; fit judgments reflect interpersonal skills, goal orientation, and physical attractiveness, but not GPA, extracurricular offices, or work experience.[46]

### Applicant Demographic Characteristics

Applicants' qualifications and experience should—and usually do—affect selection decisions. Research suggests that interviews are most valid when they avoid trying to measure everything and focus instead on interpersonal ability and good citizenship (dependability and stability). One study of corporate interviewers in a financial services organization found that interviewers rated most

EXHIBIT 7.8 Variables Affecting the Conduct and Outcomes of the Employment Interview

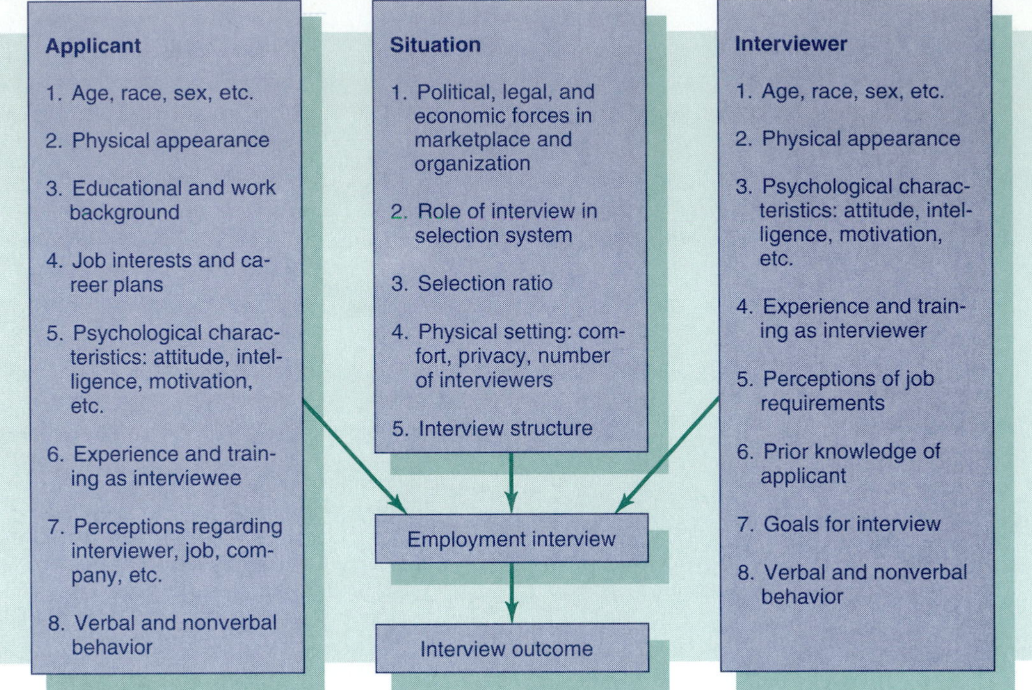


Source: Richard D. Arvey and James E. Campion, "The Employment Interview: A Summary and Review of Recent Research," *Personnel Psychology* 35, no. 3 (1982), pp. 281–322.

highly by their managers tended to emphasize applicants' interpersonal and oral communication skills. They were also more aware of their own decision processes.[47] Besides qualifications and experience, is it possible that other applicant characteristics such as sex, ethnic background, age, or disabilities also affect interview decisions?

Ann Hopkins joined Price Waterhouse in 1978; she was the only woman among 88 nominees for partnership in 1982, but was not among the 47 invited to become partners. Partners who recommended against her used such phrases as "she is a lady using foul language" and advised her to "walk more femininely, talk more femininely, dress more femininely, wear makeup, have hair styled, and wear jewelry." In *Price Waterhouse* v. *Hopkins,* the Supreme Court, in a 6–3 decision, agreed that sexual stereotyping is barred by federal antidiscrimination laws, and ordered Price Waterhouse to show that it would have reached the same employment decision even if there had been no bias.[48]

Apparently, some women students remove their wedding rings before campus interviews to avoid causing recruiters to think they might have work-family conflicts. Such *stereotypes* occur when we assume traits about a person based on that person's membership in some category, such as sex, race, or age.[49] While the *Hopkins* case involved interviews as well as other predictor information, it highlights the importance of considering whether stereotypes based on gender, race, or other applicant characteristics adversely affect interview decisions. This important question has occupied a great deal of research effort.

Early results suggested that women often received lower ratings than men. More recent research suggests that this occurs primarily when selectors are given little information about employee qualifications that correlate much more highly with hiring recommendations. The most recent evidence indicates that applicant gender has little or no effect on interview ratings.[50]

Still, the gender effect may be more complex. One study found that the evaluations by male college recruiters were not affected by applicant gender, but female recruiters found male applicants to be more similar to themselves and more qualified than female applicants.[51] Similarity of "work values" such as achievement, fairness, honesty, and helping and concern for others may also be a factor affecting the judgments of interviewers. Another study found that applicants whose independently measured values were similar to the *recruiter's personal values* were rated more employable and a better fit to the organization, but there was no such employability benefit if the applicants' idea of *organization values* was similar to the recruiter's. Perhaps being "similar to me" was more important than "similarity to my organization."[52]

Results are more mixed concerning applicant race. Some studies find that race does affect interview ratings, but not to any great degree, and that constructing mixed-race interview panels may reduce this.[53] Age also appears to affect interview decisions, but its effects are complex and depend on how accountable interviewers are for their decisions, the gender of the interviewer, and the particular dimension being evaluated.[54] There is little evidence about the effects of applicant disability on interview decisions.[55]

### Applicant Behaviors

Can applicants affect the interview decision by managing interviewer impressions?[56] Someone must think so, because every recruiting season witnesses a remarkable metamorphosis as students previously seen only in sneakers, white socks, jeans, and flannel shirts suddenly appear in new blue suits, white shirts, power ties, dress shoes, and carrying unscuffed mock-leather briefcases to their impending job interviews. Professors customarily attired in slacks, polo shirts, sweaters, and Birkenstock sandals can be found wearing suits, ties, and dress shoes in anticipation of meetings and power lunches with visiting corporate recruiters.

Evidence suggests that nonverbal behavior (smiling, leaning toward the interviewer, eye contact), wearing scent, and impression management tactics (complimenting the interviewer, self-promotion, ingratiation) can affect ratings of applicant attractiveness, and sometimes affect ratings of hiring suitability.[57] However, the effects seem to depend on the situation. Interviewer characteristics may invite different kinds of impression management. One study found that when facing older and more experienced interviewers applicants less often claimed personal credit for past outcomes and asked for explanations as a way to show interest in what the interviewer was saying. On the other hand, older and more experienced interviewers seemed to cause applicants to boast more about personal qualities and to be more demonstrative about having the specific capabilities the interviewer was looking for.[58] Yet another study found that the most aggressive applicants were more attractive to interviewers with more stereotyped views of whether a man or woman should do certain jobs. The effects can backfire if impression management is overdone, though one study found that focusing the conversation on yourself worked better than focusing the conversation on the interviewer.[59]

Exhibit 7.9 shows the results of one of the few studies to examine how much applicants *actually* use impression management in the interview. Notice the three different tactics: *entitlements, enhancements,* and *overcoming obstacles* are woven into an applicant's story. Also notice that over 30 percent of applicants used one or more of these tactics. Did it work? Statistical analysis show that site visit invitations were positively associated with claiming to fit with the organization, praising the interviewer, and nonverbal behavior. Job offers were positively associated with self-promotion and claiming to fit with the organization.

### Interviewer Behaviors and Interviewer Training

Over the years, research suggests that without training or some form of structure and guidance, interviewers may adopt potentially damaging strategies in interviews, such as the following:

1. *Overemphasis on negative information.* Often, even finding a small amount of negative information can lead to rejection of a job candidate. Some have proposed that this occurs because interviewers are seldom rewarded for selecting good candidates but are frequently penalized for hiring poor candidates. The logical reaction is to be very conservative, allowing even a hint of possible negative information to affect the decision.[61]
2. *Confirmatory biases.* If you saw information on a person's application blank that suggested a history of theft, would you tend to ask that person more questions about theft than others with no such history? Research suggests that interviewers are biased toward asking questions that confirm their initial impressions, which can be damaging if the initial impressions are false or if it leads to the interview generating little additional information.[62]
3. *Interviewer stereotypes.* As just discussed, interviewers may form incorrect impressions of applicants if they base judgments on stereotypes. This makes firms especially legally vulnerable if such stereotypes lead to rejection of protected-group members.
4. *Failure to consider job information.* Lack of relevant job information can cause interviewers to rely more on less relevant characteristics in their decisions.
5. *Different use of cues.* Interviewers may place more weight on some applicant characteristics than others or combine attributes differently.[63]
6. *Undue reliance on nonverbal cues.* As just discussed, applicant impression management may affect interview decisions, yet be unrelated to job success.
7. *Contrast effects.* Strong candidates who interview after weaker ones may appear even stronger by contrast, and vice versa for weak candidates following strong ones.
8. *Spending time discussing nonjob related issues.* This may serve other purposes, such as selling applicants on the job, but it can also reduce the ability to choose good candidates.
9. *Making snap judgments about applicants early in the interview.* Some research suggests that interviewers make their decisions quickly, though recent research calls this into some doubt.[64]

## EXHIBIT 7.9 Examples of Impression Management in Actual College Interviews

| Tactic Use | Sample Excerpt from Interview Transcripts |
|---|---|
| **Entitlements (claims of responsibility for positive events or outcomes)** | |
| Positive outcomes on jobs or class projects (36% of applicants) or in charity work (13% of applicants) | 187. *Interviewer:* OK. Is there something you've done that shows how innovative and resourceful you can be?<br>188. *Applicant:* Well, as far as my undergraduate . . . my junior year, I was on the fund-raising committee [for the crew team], and we were trying to think of a fund-raiser to do, and what we came up with . . . was a group thing that we were working with . . . so we ended up doing a row-a-thon where we had rowing machines and we were just rowing for like . . . three days straight . . . And just, that was something new that we had just done for the first time that year and we were trying to find sponsors and . . . we brought in TV exposure . . . I think we gave it to a couple radios, just letting them know this is a fund-raiser, that our—that [University] crew was trying to do. We got the faculty involved, had some of the faculty come down, and row with us . . . So that was . . . a really good fund-raiser, it turned out to be.<br>189. *Interviewer:* How much money did you raise?<br>190. *Applicant:* . . . Around $4,000, which was a pretty big size for us, because we were working on a budget of around $4,000 . . . |
| **Enhancements (claims that the value of positive events is greater than it appears)** | |
| Success in persuading others who were difficult to persuade (13% of applicants) | 110.–118. *Applicant:* And, I remember this one specific gentleman, he was so intent on getting these one skis because they were the hottest color out on the market [both laugh] . . . And there was . . . no way that the skis really were going to perform for him . . . It—it didn't make sense really for him to—to spend that much money on something that's gonna last him, not even a year really as far as ability level goes. So I felt it was my job . . . to get him into the right product. And he was very hard to convince that another ski would better suit his, his needs. So I had to go through and explain the features and the benefits of the product . . . And again go into some of the structural types of components because he wanted to know everything about the ski and why he should pay, another 70—well it was 75 or 100 or more dollars. . .<br>119. *Interviewer:* OK, good. [applicant clears throat] So basically did he end up spending more than what he wanted to?<br>120.–122. *Applicant:* Yes. And it didn't have the real flashy color . . . As it turned out, he bought that ski and at that point, he really trusted me as a salesperson . . . as a friend. And we went into the, clothing and he bought—everything that I recommended. |
| Background is stronger than it appears from resume (29% of applicants) | 123. *Interviewer:* Yeah. You could've been the largest painting contractor in town now, who knows.<br>124. *Applicant:* Could've been. Well, I was getting an awful lot of referrals . . . And it's incredible, but I kept charging more and more so that people would turn me down and they wouldn't turn me down and so I'd have to go do the job and I'd be out working till midnight, it was really, really exhausting. |
| **Overcoming Obstacles (descriptions of how barriers to progress were circumvented)** | |
| Overcoming difficulties in job or organization (29% of applicants) or in school work (13% of applicants) | 91.–97. *Applicant:* So, anyway I got, I got the [supervisor] job, and they [older co-workers] were not really happy. So, the first couple of months were really not . . . they weren't easy. I remember one specific incident . . . I was, we were loading a container . . . So, I asked this, requested this fellow to load this particular piece of heavy freight into the container in a certain way so that it would fit . . . and he refused.<br>98. *Interviewer:* He just refused?<br>99. *Applicant:* He refused. He just said, "No, I'm not going to do it that way. I think this way is better." And I said, "No, I disagree. I want you to do it this way." And, he refused again, "I'm not going to do it that way"—kind of thing, and so what do you do? Well, the way I handled it was, I just . . . said, point-blank to him, I said, "Either you do it or you go home and I'll get someone else to do it." . . . And, you know, so with that he went ahead and did it, but the antagonism did not end there. And so what I would do after that just tried to prove to him that I really knew what I was talking about . . . do a good job, so that I would earn his respect and thus his cooperation.<br>106. *Interviewer:* Were you able to do that?<br>107. *Applicant:* Oh, yeah. Yeah. At the end, you know, after, I'd say, after four or five months we were all great friends. |

Source: Cynthia K. Stevens and Amy L. Kristof, "Making the Right Impression: A Field Study of Applicant Impression Management during Job Interviews," *Journal of Applied Psychology* 80 (1995), p. 598. 

Considering the well-known potential interviewer problems, you might think that research would have focused on how to train interviewers to improve. Unfortunately, very few studies of interviewer training exist. One study trained interviewers for eight hours on general skills (such as note-taking and questioning methods) as well as avoiding rating errors (such as halo and leniency, see Chapter Four). It did not however, find an increase in agreement among interviewers. A second study found that training business students to avoid rating errors did reduce the errors. Despite mixed results, organizations continue to invest in interviewer training. Seventy-four percent of organizations responding to a survey indicated that they train their interviewers, using their own personnel professionals, outside workshops, or the company training department. Training times ranged from one-half to 60 hours, with an average of 9 hours. More recent research on training interviewers suggest that it can affect the validity of the interview, especially for unstructured interviews.[65]

While there is no single best approach to better interviewing, we provide some general steps in Exhibit 7.10 that interviewers can follow to ensure the interview is job-related and that information is carefully assessed. Different interviewers achieve different effectiveness. However, interviewer differences appear most pronounced when the interview is unstructured. When more structured interviews are used, interviewer differences are minimized, and validity seems to increase.[66]

### Structuring the Interview

If interviews suffer because different interviewers adopt various questioning strategies and focus on potentially irrelevant information, a logical remedy would be to impose a consistent structure with little interviewer opportunity to diverge from the prespecified format, and to base that interview structure on factors identified through job analysis as relevant to employment success. Many employers increasingly seem willing to accept this logic. Thirty-five percent of 245 companies responding to a survey said they use structured interviews, in which all applicants are asked identical questions. Twenty percent of firms that reported changing their interviews did so to make them more structured.[67]

Interviews can be *unstructured,* where the interviewer is completely free to cover any area; *semistructured,* where the interviewer prepared important questions in advance, but is allowed to probe those areas that seem to merit further investigation; or *structured,* where the interviewer's questions, and often their sequence, are prepared in advance, and the interviewer often fills out a form indicating applicant responses to the question. The ultimate in structured interviewing is to program a computer to ask the questions, record the responses, and analyze them mathematically. For the moment, it is still typical to involve human beings in the process.[68]

Recent research divides "structure" into two types: (1) *interview content structure,* which includes basing questions on a job analysis, asking the same questions of each candidate, placing limits on prompting and follow-up questions, using specific types of questions such as those based on behavior, using more questions, not allowing interviewers to see application forms or test scores, and not allowing candidates to ask questions until after the interview; (2) *interview evaluation structure,* which includes using rating scales for each answer, taking detailed notes, using multiple interviewers, using the same interviewer(s) for all candidates, not discussing candidates or answers between interviews, providing extensive interview training, and using statistics to

## EXHIBIT 7.10 Recommendations for Conducting Employment Interviews

**Before the interview**

Identify major interview objectives, such as:

1. Selecting.
2. Attracting.
3. Gathering information on what the applicant *can* do.
4. Gathering information on what the applicant *will* do.
5. Providing information.
6. Checking the applicant's fit with the organization.

Prepare interview content by:

1. Identifying major job responsibilities.
2. Writing hypothetical job situations to use as questions.
3. Planning and structuring the interview format consistent with its objectives.

Review each application form of résumé for information, such as:

1. Previous related work or nonwork experience.
2. Previous related training.
3. Previous related education.
4. Applicant work interests.
5. Applicant career intentions.

**During the interview**

Probe what the applicant can do through discussion and situational questions, such as:

1. Related work or nonwork experiences.
2. Related training.
3. Related education.

Probe work interests and career intentions to assess what the candidate will do.

**After the interview**

Use an applicant evaluation form to record evaluations of what the applicant:

1. Can do, based on existing skills and interests.
2. Will do, based on interests and intentions.
3. Has in the way of personal chemistry.

Record your level of interest in hiring each applicant on the *applicant evaluation form.*

James G. Goodale, "Effective Employment Interviewing," chap. 22 in *The Employment Interview,* ed. by Robert W. Eder and Gerald R. Ferris (Newbury Park, CA: Sage Publications, 1989).

combine different pieces of information rather than relying on consensus or subjectivity.[69] The most widely-studied structuring methods have to do with the kinds of interview content. Three approaches to structuring the interview are (1) the behavior description interview (BDI), (2) the situational interview (SI), and (3) the comprehensive structured interview (CSI).[70]

Behavior description interview (BDI) The BDI approach focuses on past behavior, based on the premise that the best prophet of the future is the past.[71] Interview questions are based on a job analysis of situations or decisions likely to be faced on the job. Questions are constructed based on the what-did-you-do format. For example, to assess likely attendance, interviewers might ask, "Tell me about the most recent time you had to miss work and stay at home. What was the reason? What did you actually do?" In many ways BDI is very similar to the life-history selection techniques discussed earlier, except that the interview format provides flexibility and the opportunity to probe further.

Situational interview (SI) The SI approach derives from theories about goal setting that suggest individuals' intentions are related to their future behavior. Like BDI, the SI approach derives its interview questions from job analysis that identifies important situations and decisions likely to be faced by applicants, often in the form of critical incidents (see Chapter Four). The difference is that the questions focus on intentions, not past behaviors. For example, the same attendance-related question in an SI format might be, "Your spouse and two teenage children are sick in bed with colds. There are no relatives or friends available to look in on them. Your shift starts in three hours. What would you do?"[72] By focusing on hypothetical but job-related situations and applicant intentions, the SI approach can potentially explore areas where job candidates may not have any actual previous experiences. SI approaches usually construct a scoring guide for interviewers based on input from job experts, with the best example answers receiving the highest points. Exhibit 7.11 is an SI question and scoring guide for truck driver supervisors.

Comprehensive structured interview (CSI) The CSI can contain four types of questions:

1. Situational, such as the SI approach.
2. Job knowledge, such as, "When putting a piece of machinery back together after repairing it, why would you clean all the parts first?"
3. Job simulation, such as, "Many jobs require the operation of a forklift. Please read this (90-word) forklift procedure aloud."
4. Worker requirements, such as, "Some jobs require climbing ladders to the height of a five-story building and going out on a catwalk to work. Give us your feeling about performing a task such as this."[73]

Like the SI, the CSI approach involves the construction of a scoring guide for interviewers. This can be a paper form filled out or checked by the interviewer.

### Situational Effects on the Interview

As we show in Exhibit 7.8 interviews take place within the context of forces inside and outside the organization. Exhibit 7.3 illustrates the interactive nature of selection, and this is especially apparent in the interview. Contextual factors—the complexity of the job and interview task, whether the purpose of the interview is to attract candidates to take job offers or to select among candidates, the perceived cost of making a hiring mistake, and the interviewer's accountability for interview outcomes—all affect interview processes and results.[74]

**WHAT DO YOU THINK?**

It appears that interviewer consistency and validity can be improved by imposing structure on the interview and training interviewers to follow that structure. Yet, most companies still use untrained interviewers in an unstructured format. Suppose you were asked to tell a senior line manager why she must now use a structured interview. What would you say? How would she react?

### Interview Validity

In the past, researchers lamented the low validity of the interview and cautioned employers against their tendency to use it so frequently, but recent research advances and new evidence suggests that the interview can be a valid selection technique. Research suggests that interviews can attain validities in the range of 0.25 to 0.80, with structured interviews focusing on job-relevant experience, training, or interests producing higher validity coefficients than unstructured interviews or interviews based on personality characteristics or traits.[75]

**EXHIBIT 7.11** Structured Situational Interview Question and Scoring Guide

**Interview question**

You are in charge of truck drivers in Philadelphia. Your colleague is in charge of truck drivers 800 miles away in Atlanta. Both of you report to the same person. Your salary and bonus are affected 100 percent by your costs. Your colleague is in desperate need of one of your trucks. If you say no, your costs will remain low and your group will probably win the Golden Flyer award, because they will make a significant profit for the company. Your boss is preaching costs, costs, costs as well as cooperation with one's peers. Your boss has no control over the accountants, who are the score keepers. Your boss is highly competitive and rewards winners. You are just as competitive, you are a real winner! Explain what you would do.

**Record the applicant's answer in the space below**

---

---

---

---

**Scoring guide**

(1 point) I would go for the award. I would explain the circumstances to my colleague and get his or her understanding.

(3 points) I would get my boss's advice.

(5 points) I would loan the truck to my colleague in Atlanta. I'd get recognition from my boss and my colleague that I had sacrificed my rear end for theirs. Then I'd explain the logic to my people.

Source: Adapted with permission from Gary P. Latham, "The Reliability, Validity, and Practicality of the Situational Interview," chap. 12 in *The Employment Interview,* ed. Robert W. Eder and Gerald R. Ferris (Newbury Park, CA: Sage Publications, 1989).

It appears that the interview, properly constructed and implemented, has greater value than previously believed. However, it also appears that the vast majority of interviews fail to use features that have been shown to enhance their validity.

## Improving the Legal Defensibility of the Interview

A telephone survey of 1,000 people conducted by the National Consumers League discovered that 79 percent had been asked intrusive questions during job interviews. Most said they disapproved of an employer asking about living with a nonfamily member of the opposite sex, elderly parents, religious preferences, and plans to have children.[76] Delta Air Lines faces 62 civil complaints filed by the New York City Human Rights Commission, each involving a potential penalty of $100,000. Delta applicants charge that they were asked about sexual preferences, birth control, and abortions. Such questions may not only cause animosity among applicants, but they also create legal vulnerabilities should the organization's practices be found to exclude or differentially treat protected minorities or females. A review of court cases involving interviews suggests the following guidelines to minimize legal vulnerability:

1. Develop job descriptions and use them to develop interview questions, procedures, and scoring systems.
2. Select interviewers to represent a mix of races and genders, and train them to focus on job-related topics and to avoid potentially discriminatory questions.
3. Ensure that interview questions and strategies are job relevant and are applied to all applicants.
4. Introduce review systems such as interviewer panels, committees to review interview findings and recommendations, and systems for increasing accountability.
5. Keep records of interview procedures, evaluations, and decisions in case the organization is required to reconstruct them to demonstrate job relatedness.
6. Monitor disparate impact (see Chapter Two), and take specific steps to ensure fairness if disparate impact is detected.
7. Train interviewers in proper interview techniques, and in the kinds of questions that are risky due to invasion of privacy or equal employment opportunity protection.[77]

EXPLORING THE WEB

Increasingly, managers can obtain computer programs that will help them to build interview guides based on the particular behaviors and capabilities needed in their organizations. For one example of this kind of product on the Web, including sample guides, legal advice, and even a lecture by a professor, go to:
**http://www.the-link.com/proselect/.**

## Ability Tests

Some people seem smarter, stronger, better coordinated, more skilled with people, or blessed with more "common sense." These traits are called *abilities,* or sometimes, *aptitudes.* They indicate what a person might be able to do, given an appropriate situation or the right experience or training. They do not determine performance or behavior, but they can reflect potential.

### Mental Ability: Intelligence and "Common Sense"

Will the United States someday be dominated by a "cognitive elite" of highly intelligent people, with the less cognitively gifted consigned to the lower rungs of society? Are different races or nationalities predisposed to be more or less intelligent? Is your intelligence largely determined by your genes (which means you can blame your parents the next time they berate you for low grades)? The best-selling book, *The Bell Curve,* prompted hours of televised debate and countless magazine and newspaper articles by those who felt it did (or didn't) answer yes to these questions. Scientists who study intelligence caution that *intelligence, mental ability* or *cognitive ability* has many facets and can mean many things, and that any blanket statements fail to capture the complexity of the issue. Every category of people varies widely in intelligence, environment and heritage both play a part, and success in life is determined by much more than cognitive ability.[78] Mental ability tests have been used to select and place

**EXHIBIT 7.12** Mental Ability on the Web: Questions Typical of the Wonderlic Personnel Test

Look at the row of numbers below. What number should come next?

4 2 1 1/2 1/4 ?

Assume the first 2 statements are true. Is the final one: (1) true, (2) false, (3) not certain?

The boy plays baseball. All baseball players wear hats. The boy wears a hat.

One of the numbered figures in the following drawing is most different from the others. What is the number in that figure?

1 2 3 4 5

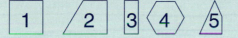

A train travels 20 feet in 1/5 second. At this same speed, how many feet will it travel in three seconds?

How many of the six pairs of items listed below are exact duplicates?

| | |
|---|---|
| 3421 | 1243 |
| 21212 | 21212 |
| 558956 | 558956 |
| 10120210 | 10120210 |
| 612986896 | 612986896 |
| 356471201 | 356571201 |

The hours of daylight and darkness in SEPTEMBER are nearest equal to the hours of daylight and darkness in

(1) June (2) March (3) May (4) November

EXPLORING THE WEB

You can visit the Wonderlic home page at **http://www.wonderlic.com/.**

people in jobs at least since 1908, when they were used to select street car operators in Paris. They became refined and widely accepted due to their success in selecting and assigning thousands of soldiers in World Wars I and II.[79] Exhibit 7.12 shows questions like those on one of the most popular such tests, the Wonderlic Personnel test. When we visited, the home page featured the role of this test in the college football draft, and even descriptions of job opportunities—we assume applicants are probably subjected to a battery of tests. One of the best known mental ability tests is the General Aptitude Test Battery (GATB), used by the U.S. Employment Service to classify applicants for job openings.[80]

Is common sense different from intelligence? A psychologist was assigned to administer intelligence tests at a school for mentally retarded boys, but when he arrived he could not test them because they had eluded the school's security system and escaped. After recapturing the boys, the psychologist gave them the test—a series of maze puzzles. The students were unable to find their way out of the mazes on the test. *Tacit intelligence* refers to knowledge that is related to action rather than facts, attaining goals rather

WHAT DO YOU THINK?

Which do you think most companies value most—"street smarts" and emotional intelligence, or "book smarts" and cognitive intelligence? What is the role of an HR manager in helping to strike a balance?

than correct answers, and it is acquired with little help from others. Tests exist for tacit knowledge in management, psychology, and other fields, and some studies suggest that these tests measure something different from general intelligence and are more closely related to success at work, although controversy among psychologists persists. Still, it's intriguing to think that "street smarts" may be measurable and different from "book smarts."[81] A special type of tacit intelligence may be *emotional intelligence,* touted in the business press as a key element in building successful teams and in achieving your career goals. Emotional intelligence has been described as (1) being aware of your feelings and using them, (2) managing your moods, (3) being optimistic and helpful, and (4) having empathy with the feelings of others.[82] This may be critical in selecting people to work with the Australian Antarctica program, where "individual privacy is mainly confined to sleeping accommodation, and people may be confined indoors for days at a time . . . Interdependence is the insurance for survival.[83]

### Teamwork Ability

Can you test people to see whether they have the ability to be good team members? Exhibit 7.13 shows 14 knowledge, skill, and ability requirements for teamwork, and an example of test items from the Teamwork-KSA Test, which contains 35 items like these, measuring the 14 areas. One study found the test related to job performance, even beyond standard aptitudes and skills.[84] We wonder if Jimmy Johnson has heard of this. You might ask classmates to take this test the next time you are forming a team for a class project.

### Physical Ability

What does it take to perform physically demanding jobs? Extended studies by psychologists have found that three components seem to capture the demands of most jobs: (1) muscular strength, (2) cardiovascular endurance, and (3) movement quality (flexibility, balance, coordination).[85] For $100,000, a company can buy the Ergos Work Simulator that allows a person to choose from a computerized database of more than 14,000 occupations. Then, the machine duplicates the physical movements required of that occupation and conducts a four-hour test for such things as range of motion, endurance, and strength. We wonder what movements it uses to simulate the one highway-construction worker who always seems to be just standing around.

Most jobs don't exact such acute physical demands that applicants' differences in physical abilities greatly affect job performance. However, for jobs that do, a good deal of research has developed job analysis methods to identify the necessary physical abilities and tests to detect them. Tests of flexibility and balance have shown validity for some jobs, and tests of static strength (especially upper-body strength) show validity for others. Explosive strength and stamina are required in fewer jobs; firefighter jobs do require prolonged cardiovascular activity, running, and jumping. One long-term research program reports validities for physical test batteries in the 0.50s and 0.60s. However, a drawback to such tests is that they are likely to produce adverse impact for females and some racial groups, particularly tests of upperbody strength.[86]

## EXHIBIT 7.13 Knowledge, Skill and Ability Requirements for Teamwork, and a Teamwork Ability Test

### Interpersonal KSAs

**Conflict Resolution KSAs**

**1.** The KSA to recognize and encourage desirable, but discourage undesirable, team conflict.
**2.** The KSA to recognize the type and source of conflict confronting the team and to implement an appropriate conflict-resolution strategy.
**3.** The KSA to employ an integrative (win-win) negotiation strategy rather than the traditional distributive (win-lose) strategy.

**Collaborative Problem Solving KSAs**

**4.** The KSA to identify situations requiring participative group problem solving and to utilize the proper degree and type of participation.
**5.** The KSA to recognize the obstacles to collaborative group problem solving and to implement appropriate corrective actions.

**Communication KSAs**

**6.** The KSA to understand communication network and to utilize decentralized networks to enhance communication where possible.
**7.** The KSA to communicate openly and supportively, that is, to send messages which are (1) behavior or event oriented, (2) congruent, (3) validating, (4) conjunctive, and (5) owned.
**8.** The KSA to listen nonevaluatively and to use active listening techniques appropriately.
**9.** The KSA to maximize consonance between nonverbal and verbal messages, and to recognize and interpret the nonverbal messages of others.
**10.** The KSA to engage in ritual greetings and small talk, and a recognition of their importance.

### Self-Management KSAs

**Goal Setting and Performance Management KSAs**

**11.** The KSA to help establish specific, challenging, and accepted team goals.
**12.** The KSA to monitor, evaluate, and provide feedback on both overall team performance and individual team member performance.

**Planning and Task Coordination KSAs**

**13.** The KSA to coordinate and synchronize activities, information, and task interdependencies between team members.
**14.** The KSA to help establish task and role expectations of individual team members, and to ensure proper balancing of workload in the team.

### Example Items from the Teamwork-KSA Test

**1.** Suppose that you find yourself in an argument with several co-workers about who should do a very disagreeable, but routine task. Which of the following would likely be the most effective way to resolve this situation?
*a.* Have your supervisor decide, because this would avoid any personal bias.
**b.* Arrange for a rotating schedule so everyone shares the chore.
*c.* Let the workers who show up earliest choose on a first-come, first-served basis.
*d.* Randomly assign a person to do the task and don't change it.

**2.** Your team wants to improve the quality and flow of the conversations among its members. Your team should:
**a.* Use comments that build upon and connect to what others have said.
*b.* Set up a specific order for everyone to speak and then follow it.
*c.* Let team members with more to say determine the direction and topic of conversation.
*d.* Do all of the above.

**3.** Suppose you are presented with the following types of goals. You are asked to pick one for your team to work on. Which would you choose?
*a.* An easy goal to ensure the team reaches it, thus creating a feeling of success.
*b.* A goal of average difficulty so the team will be somewhat challenged, but successful without too much effort.
**c.* A difficult and challenging goal that will stretch the team to perform at a high level, but attainable so that effort will not be seen as futile.
*d.* A very difficult, or even impossible, goal so that even if the team falls short, it will at least have a very high target to aim for.

*Correct answers.

Source: Michael J. Stevens and Michael A. Campion, "The Knowledge, Skill and Ability Requirements for Teamwork: Implications for Human Resource Management," *Journal of Management* 20 (1994) pp. 505, 519. JAL Press Inc, Greenwich, CT and London, England.

### Validity

One of the most important and widely accepted findings in recent psychological research is that cognitive ability tests appear to be valid predictors for a variety of different jobs. Moreover, research on validity generalization suggests that organizations can borrow validity evidence from past studies in different organizations to determine how well such tests predict in their own organizations. One theory is that such cognitive ability tests reflect a general intelligence, or "*g* factor," that translates into superior performance across a wide variety of jobs.[87] Note the validity coefficients based on many studies for several jobs and ability tests in Exhibit 7.14. The GATB has demonstrated a validity ranging from 0.2 to 0.4 in USES studies. A common cognitive ability measure is the intelligence quotient, or IQ. A high IQ does not necessarily imply goodness. Many Nazi war criminals tested after World War II proved to be quite intelligent.[88] Many students have long held a similar view of instructors who give too-difficult tests (though they are not convinced about the intelligence). Muscular strength has correlated with performance for many jobs, including law enforcement officer, firefighter, and pipeline and utility workers.[89]

### Legality and Equity

Companies using tests risk litigation because tests can produce lower scores for some minorities. The dilemma faced by the U.S. Employment Service (USES) in using the General Aptitude Test Battery (GATB) to refer applicants for job interviews is a case in point.[90] Evidence from more than 750 validity studies over many years and thousands of job applicants suggested that, on average, African American, Hispanic, and some Native American job applicants generally scored lower than white applicants on the GATB, and they also received lower average performance ratings than white applicants. The GATB had statistically significant validity for applicants from both protected and unprotected racial groups, though biased performance ratings may have caused nonwhite groups to have a slightly lower validity. If the USES referred applicants for jobs based on their raw test scores, protected minority group members would have been excluded more frequently than white applicants. A National Research Council Committee concluded that such an approach would exclude minority candidates who might have performed well more often than it would exclude nonminority candidates who might have performed well.

The committee's compromise recommendation tried to satisfy both the nation's commitment to equal employment opportunity and the USES mission to help employers and job applicants achieve the best person-job match. The committee recommended a scoring procedure called *race norming,* in which applicants' test scores are reported as the percentage of their own racial group who scored lower than they did on the test. Thus, the best employees from within each minority and nonminority group would be referred to employers, but all protected groups would be represented in the referrals.[91] The Civil Rights Act of 1991 (Section 106) now prohibits any adjustment of test scores based on protected group membership. So, if GATB scores are reported, the disparity between minority and nonminority average test scores may cause employers to exclude members of minority groups. The Labor Department considered suspending the use of GATB, but decided against it; however, many states have now suspended its use. Many employers now use only tests that do not produce different average scores for protected and unprotected groups. Debate continues

EXHIBIT 7.14 Validity Levels for Ability Tests in Various Jobs

| Job | Ability | Validity |
|---|---|---|
| First-line supervisors | General mental ability | 0.64 |
| | Mechanical ability | 0.48 |
| | Spatial ability | 0.43 |
| Mechanical repairpersons | Mechanical principles | 0.78 |
| Police officers and detectives | Quantitative ability | 0.26 |
| | Reasoning | 0.17 |
| | Spatial/mechanical ability | 0.17 |
| Computer programmers | Figure analogies | 0.46 |
| | Arithmetic reasoning | 0.57 |

Source: Robert D. Gatewood and Hubert S. Feild, *Human Resource Selection,* 3rd ed. (Fort Worth, TX: Dryden Press, 1994), p. 577.

over whether cognitive ability tests (including standardized college entrance tests) are culturally fair, and whether they artificially handicap nonwhite or non-male test takers.[92]

## Job Knowledge Tests, Work Samples, and Job Tryouts

"Name an occupation, and there's probably a test that goes with it."[93] For examples of job-knowledge test items that might be used for several occupations, see Exhibit 7.15. While riding in a taxi in Melbourne, Australia, the driver spoke with pride about the fact that his company required all drivers to score at least 120 correct out of 140 questions testing all the major landmarks, hotels, and suburbs in the Melbourne area. Perhaps there's a lesson here for major U.S. cities. *Job knowledge* items are developed through job analysis to identify the key facts or rules that job incumbents must know to do their jobs. *Work samples* are miniature replicas or simulations of actual on-the-job behaviors, such as shorthand, work processing, or blueprint reading. Assessment centers combine both and are usually used for promotion decisions, so we discuss them in Chapter Nine. Perhaps the most realistic direct test of job knowledge is to select employees for trial periods on the job, as some auto plants do for their manufacturing employees, and as some companies do through the college internship program. For instance, Connecticut General Life Insurance Company's computerized testing system presents applicants with realistic claim documents that they must process. Not only is this believed to improve selection but it also provides a realistic preview of the job (see Chapter Six) and saved the company $300,000 in training costs in the first three months.[94]

How much job knowledge is enough? Perhaps you can let supervisors set the standard. Some job knowledge tests ask applicants to rate the relative importance of work behaviors, and then compare those with the priorities reported by the supervisors with whom they would work on the job. Measures of agreement were related to job performance on several jobs.[95] If work involves

### EXHIBIT 7.15 Job Knowledge Test Items for Different Occupations

**Barber**

1. A man with a prominent nose should have a:
   a. Pyramid mustache.
   b. Large mustache.
   c. Narrow mustache.
   d. Small mustache.

**Bartender**

2. Which one of the following drinks is always shaken?
   a. California Root Beer.
   b. Screwdriver.
   c. Gibson.
   d. Sombrero.

**Building contractor**

3. What should be painted first when painting a room?
   a. Walls.
   b. Window sills.
   c. Trim and moldings.
   d. Ceilings.

**Massage therapist**

4. The best type of heat to produce relaxation prior to a massage is:
   a. Electric.
   b. Dry.
   c. Prolonged.
   d. Moist.

**Broadcaster**

5. On a telephone call-in program, you should NOT:
   a. Clarify a topic for a listener.
   b. Place a time limit on the calls, as this inhibits those persons who wish to express their opinions.
   c. Express your own opinions on the topics.

**Interior designer**

6. What one element helps to give balance to a room?
   a. A window on every wall.
   b. A fireplace.
   c. Matching wallpaper and draperies.
   d. Furniture of varied heights.

**Floral designer**

7. Which design is NOT a sympathy design?
   a. Gates ajar.
   b. Spray.
   c. Cascade bouquet.
   d. Cross.

**Travel agent**

8. To obtain the least expensive round-trip air ticket you should:
   a. Arrive at the airport two hours early.
   b. Buy two one-way tickets.
   c. Find three friends to travel with you.
   d. Book well in advance.

Answers: 1b, 2d, 3d, 4d, 5c, 6d, 7c, 8d

Source: Allen D. Bragdon, *The Book of Tests.* Copyright © 1989 by Allen D. Bragdon Publishers, Inc. Reprinted by permission of HarperCollins Publishers.

interpersonal situations, perhaps multimedia testing can help. Multimedia tests present applicants with video vignettes showing common work dilemmas, such as seeing a co-worker break a rule or steal something, and ask the applicants what they would do in that situation.[96]

#### Validity

Work samples and job tryouts carefully constructed from job analysis have demonstrated validities in the mid 0.40s. They perform best when they sample directly from the tasks that job incumbents actually do and reflect as much of the job situation as possible. Such selection devices are best suited to jobs with clearly observable and well-defined tasks.[97]

#### Legality

Work samples and job tryouts have proven relatively free from discrimination. They are also obviously job related if they contain actual job tasks. However, sometimes they tend to exclude minority groups or women, especially in jobs not historically held by these groups.[98] Therefore, work samples should be used only to assess skills and knowledge that applicants absolutely must have before starting the job. They should not reflect knowledge that is routinely learned on the job.

## Physical/Physiological Requirements

About half of all organizations give preemployment medical examinations; a similar percentage require drug tests. More specific physical/physiological testing, such as physical abilities testing, polygraph tests, genetic screening, and AIDS tests, are much rarer. Nonetheless, such measurements have stirred public and legislative attention and continue to generate controversy.[99]

### Drug Testing

The formula for a high-paying top-of-the-line job today is "six or seven interviews and a drug test" one Dartmouth College senior said in the days before graduation.[100] Many major U.S. companies, including IBM, Kodak, AT&T, Lockheed, 3M, and Westinghouse, require some or all job applicants to provide urine specimens. Large companies cite a responsibility to provide a safe, healthy, and productive environment for their workers. Drug and alcohol testing can use *bioassay* methods, which take samples of breath, blood, urine, saliva, or hair. Some of these methods may indicate only very recent drug use or exposure, making it easy to avoid detection merely by abstaining for a few days. Other tests may indicate exposure within the last several weeks, but tell little about recent use or exposure. Most companies that test refuse to hire anyone who tests positive. Smaller companies employing lower-paid service workers may not be able to afford drug tests. One government agency in a northeastern state tested 1,000 security guard applicants and 980 failed. In the south and some rural areas, employers cannot find enough drug-free workers to hire. While drug tests have been shown to relate to job behaviors such as absenteeism, the relatively low number of applicants rejected for most jobs can reduce its value. U.S. laboratory analyses incorrectly concluded that applicants were drug users more than 37 percent of the time in the past, though new standards have been issued. Drug testing may also be ruled an invasion of privacy. Recommendations include (1) testing only applicants/employees whose jobs are considered safety-specific or critical; (2) using only valid measures of drug use; (3) obtaining valid consent of the applicant or employee and then provide the examinee with the results of the tests; (4) maintaining strict confidentiality of test results; and (5) using drug tests as a small part of a comprehensive drug abuse program.[101]

### Smoking Bans

"The pay was good, the interview went well, and the job looked promising—until Art Hargreaves learned the hard way: No smokers hired." A half-pack-a-day cigarette smoker, Hargreaves was out of luck at Litho Industries, a printing company in Raleigh, North Carolina; in January 1989, Litho stopped hiring smokers—even those who agreed not to smoke at work. Though estimated at only about 6 percent, the number of companies with such no-smoking policies appears to be growing, and urine tests are often used to detect evidence of smoking.[102] Such policies are frequently designed to cut insurance and medical costs or to appease employees complaining about the effects of second-hand smoke.

### AIDS Screening

Acquired immune deficiency syndrome (AIDS) is the most prominent medical crisis of the 1990s, with thousands of confirmed AIDS cases, and over a million Americans carrying the HIV virus that causes AIDS. While the incidence of applicant or employee AIDS testing seems low among employers, blood tests may be used as part of medical examinations to support such testing. One expert concludes that AIDS testing for employment purposes is not justified because AIDS is a protected handicap, infection through routine work contacts is impossible, and presently available tests identify the antibody and not the disease.[103]

### Genetic Screening

Genetic screening involves examining an individual's genetic makeup; it has been used to identify individuals with high susceptibility to workplace toxins or those predisposed toward contracting occupational diseases. Advances in genetic research will undoubtedly expand the number of traits and characteristics that can be identified with such procedures. However, employers must proceed cautiously because the techniques are intrusive, potentially discriminatory, and it is not clear whether such characteristics are job related.

### Polygraph (Lie-Detector) Tests

Thousands of employers formerly used polygraph tests to prevent employee theft or security breaches. However, the Employee Polygraph Protection Act of 1988 prohibits polygraph test use in selection except for state, local, and federal government employees and businesses with direct involvement in secret military intelligence or nuclear power.[105] Frequently, polygraph tests were replaced by integrity tests, a form of personality test discussed next.

### Legality of Physical/Physiological Testing

Physical testing seems to be increasingly vulnerable to legal challenge. The Supreme Court ruled that employers may not bar women of childbearing age from certain jobs because of risk to their fetuses, even when medical evidence suggests exposure to the work environment can lead to fetal damage.[106] Physiological information has been cited as a potential invasion of privacy, a potential source of adverse impact against women and small-stature minorities, and a source of discrimination against disabled persons under the Americans with Disabilities Act (see Chapter Two). One dilemma concerning physiological testing is that procedures that enhance the validity of such tests, such as random testing or observing people while donating a urine specimen, also heighten feelings of invasion of privacy.

## Personality, Honesty, and Integrity Testing

"Sometimes I tease animals. Also, I feel useless at times, and I occasionally feel that I'm about to go to pieces. Once in a while I like smashing things, is that weird?" The world's most widely used personality test, the Minnesota Multiphasic Personality Inventory (MMPI), uses 567 statements like these to determine individuals' degree of paranoia, depression, mania, or anxiety. A wide variety of such tests is available through various psychological services; about 17 percent of employers use them, especially for sales occupations.[107] One writer for *The Wall Street Journal* suggested that the

> EXPLORING THE WEB
>
> You can give yourself a personality test based on the MBTI on the web at **http://sunsite.unc.edu/personality/keirsey.html.**

Meyers-Briggs Type Indicator (MBTI) "should be routinely administered to adults as they enter the workplace, to parents raising children, and to young adults thinking about getting married."[108] That's a lot of responsibility to place on a personality test!

Personality screening is used to select police officers, but it's unlikely that such tests could identify future Mark Fuhrmans or prevent Rodney King incidents.[109] Different personality tests measure different things. The MMPI contains personality scales such as hypochondriasis, depression, paranoia, and schizophrenia. Especially popular with managers is the MBTI, which looks at similar scales. Some tests measure people's preferences for intrinsically motivating work factors (task involvement, curiosity, enjoyment and interest) against extrinsically motivating work factors (competition, recognition, money).[110] Though different personality tests measure different things, there is some consensus among psychologists that a five-factor model of personality may exist.

- *Extroversion.* Sociable, agreeable, gregarious, warm, assertive, active.
- *Agreeable.* Courteous, trusting, flexible, straightforward, soft-hearted.
- *Conscientious.* Careful, thorough, hardworking, ambitious, persevering.
- *Neurotic.* Anxious, depressed, angry, embarrassed.
- *Open to experience.* Original, imaginative, daring.[111]

One study found that nuclear power industry workers "improved" their MMPI scores over time, becoming more "normal" with repeated assessment. Perhaps we'll soon see coaching services for personality. Another study found that men tended to be more assertive while women were more anxious, gregarious, trusting, and tender-minded. Do you know your own personality? Research suggests that personality ratings by supervisors, co-workers, and customers of salespeople were different from ratings by the person themselves, even predicting job performance better than the self-ratings.[112]

### Integrity and Honesty

With the prohibition of polygraph tests, there has been renewed interest in the use of written *honesty* or *integrity tests.* These tests can be specifically designed to ask applicants about their attitudes toward theft and dishonesty or to elicit admissions of theft or illegal behavior. Exhibit 7.16 shows example questions from a typical *overt honesty test.* These tests do predict behaviors such as theft. Yet, the answers seem easy to fake, so that everyone should be able to get the same high score. Scientists speculate that thieves tend to believe that "everybody does it," so they tend to fake "realistic" answers, fearing that if they appear too honest they will be caught in a lie, while more honest people tend to answer with a highly honest pattern. Another approach is to take questions from more general personality inventories and score them in ways that distinguish those who are dishonest from others. Using such *trait-based honesty tests,* integrity has been described as a combination of conscientiousness, agreeableness, and emotional stability.[113]

### Legality

Like all tests, personality and integrity tests are subject to EEO rules, which means that if they produce adverse impact against protected groups, they must be job related. Most studies show little adverse impact against women or minorities.[114]

## EXHIBIT 7.16 Example of Overt Honesty Test Items

For some, the questions asked on a typical clear-purpose integrity test, one in which the test-taker is fully aware of the test's purpose, are "no-brainers"—of *course* it's wrong to give other employees improper discounts. But others see in the questions more gray than black and white.

In *Testing Testing,* University of Kansas Professor F. Allan Hanson advises that "the most effective strategy when confronting an honesty test may be to throw honesty to the winds—to learn the kinds of considerations that go into the scoring and to answer the questions accordingly, without regard for truth."

With that in mind, ask yourself these questions, from a list of Reid Psychological Systems' sample questions, and be honest: What would you do with the $100?

- Do you believe a person who writes a check for which he or she knows there is no money in the bank should be refused a job in which honesty is important?
- Do you think a person should be fired by a company if it is found that he or she helped the employees cheat the company out of overtime once in a while?
- If you found $100 that was lost by a bank truck on the street yesterday, would you turn the money over to the bank, even though you knew for sure that there was no reward?
- Do you think it is all right for one employee to give another employee a discount even though the company does not allow it?
- Do you believe that an employee who regularly borrows small amounts of money from the place where he or she works without permission, but always pays it back, is honest?
- Do you think that the way a company is run is more responsible for employee theft than the attitudes and tendencies of employees themselves?
- On the 20th of each month, an old employee took company money to pay his mortgage installment. On the 30th of each month, payday, he paid it back. After 15 years, the man finally was seen by his boss putting the money back. No shortage was found, but the boss fired him anyway. Do you think the boss was right?
- Do you think you would ever consider buying something from somebody if you knew the item had been stolen?

Source: Mathew Budman, "The Honesty Business," *Across the Board,* Nov.–Dec. 1993, p. 36. Reprinted with permission of The Conference Board.

Another thorny legal issue is whether personality or integrity tests violate legal protection against invasion of privacy. Such legal protection may come from laws protecting federal workers, such as the Federal Privacy Act of 1974, state laws, or state constitutions that specifically define a "right to privacy." Dayton-Hudson corporation paid damages of $2 million, while admitting no wrongdoing, in a suit under California's constitutional privacy protection. Dayton-Hudson had asked test questions such as, "I believe my sins are unpardonable," "I am fascinated by fire," and "Evil spirits possess me sometimes." Users of personality tests should use professional test developers and administrators, use tests with validity evidence, keep all scores strictly confidential, combine such tests with other selection methods, and obtain written consent from the applicant before testing.[115]

### Validity

Can personality or integrity tests predict performance? Though some controversy still remains, evidence appears promising that they can, especially when personality factors match job requirements. Conscientiousness seems to predict job performance and irresponsible behaviors. Irresponsibility is also well predicted by emotional stability and openness to experience. Teamwork has been predicted by agreeableness and conscientiousness. Extroversion seems to predict success among managers and salespeople. Validities are frequently in the .20 to .30 range. One summary of many studies of integrity tests found average validities in the .30s for both counterproductive behavior and performance ratings.[116] These are respectable validities but, contrary to some recommendations, we wouldn't pick a spouse using a personality test just yet (a date, perhaps, but not a spouse).

## PUTTING THE PIECES TOGETHER TO CREATE THE EXTERNAL SELECTION PROCESS

No matter how valid the selection procedures, their effectiveness depends on how the organization uses the information. Properly constructing the process for gathering and combining predictor information often determines the success or failure of external staffing systems. Process designers make choices about selecting for one job or several, who gathers and scores the information, and how to combine multiple selection procedures.

### Single-Job Selection versus Classification

Most selection procedures are evaluated for their ability to predict performance or other behaviors on one particular job. More frequently, however, employees' careers are expected to span several jobs or to include learning many new skills and adapting to frequent work changes (see Chapter Three). Also, increasing labor shortages mean that employers often face the task of assigning virtually all applicants to some job, with the decision focusing on what job they are most qualified for. Selection decisions involving choices about placing many job candidates into one of several employment opportunities are called *classification* decisions.

The U.S. military tests thousands of applicants and assigns them to several hundred jobs based on their test scores. What priorities should be used in these assignments? Should a person who would make a superb cook but also a pretty good tank gunner be assigned to the kitchen or to the tank? How much weight should be given to the individual's stated job desires? How much should relative shortages in different assignments drive the assignment process? In principle, the system should place individuals not only by emphasizing the most important jobs, taking account of current and anticipated shortages, and giving most weight to qualifications, but also by making adjustments for job aspirations. Putting such a system in practice, however, requires massive computer programs designed to consider a large number of complex alternatives.[117] Selection techniques for such a system must be evaluated not only for their ability to predict performance in each of the jobs but also for their ability to clearly sort individuals according to their relative qualifications for several different jobs.[118] Though complex, considering candidates for several different jobs instead of only one can be beneficial. One computer simulation found that the performance of those selected can be significantly increased simply by considering applicants for a larger number of job categories.[119]

### Gathering and Scoring Predictor Information

Unless a predictor is scored in a completely mechanical way, someone must observe and record the information about applicants and translate it into some sort of report or score. Usually, the HR profession handles this task, although interviews are often shared with other managers and the hiring supervisor.[120] Microsoft, with over 15,000 employees, hires software writers "like we're a ten-person company hiring an 11th," CEO Bill Gates himself woos senior engineers and even experienced software developers are required to go through five or six hours of intense interviews.[121]

Decisions also must be made about how to score predictors, especially when adverse impact is a concern. Two general approaches involve scoring all applicants on the predictor, or set of predictors, ranking them in order of highest score, and then making selections from the top-ranked person down until you have enough to fill the vacancies. While very efficient, this approach raises some disturbing questions if the next person below the final cutoff had a predictor score very close to the last person hired. How do you feel when you get a grade of B in a class because your average was 89.5, and someone else gets an A– with an average of 89.6? One answer is to set *cutoff scores,* above which everyone is considered "qualified" on a particular predictor. Selection among those above the cutoff is based on other factors. An interesting variation on this approach is called *sliding banding,* which creates groups of scores that are so close they cannot be statistically distinguished, given the imperfections of a test. Everyone in that group is treated as having the same score. Thus, if you are "close" to the high score, you still get considered for the job.[122]

## Combining Multiple Selection Procedures

Would you hire lifeguards based solely on information from an application blank? Probably not. Most likely you would want to test applicants' knowledge of relevant regulations, have them demonstrate their strength and rescue skills in the water, and perhaps interview them. Applicants are rarely selected based on only one selection procedure. Using multiple procedures can provide more complete information and allows the election process to be adjusted in response to particular situations. The evidence cited earlier referred to single predictors, but many studies have also shown that validity is improved when multiple predictors are used, such as combining a personality test with an intelligence test.[123] However, the organization must decide how to combine multiple selection procedures to produce a single hire/reject decision for each applicant. In selecting lifeguards, for example, would everyone have to do well on the written test, the in-water demonstration, and the interview, or would a very good performance on one predictor compensate for somewhat lower performance on others? Exhibit 7.17 illustrates three methods of using multiple selection methods: compensatory, multiple hurdles, and hybrid approaches.

### Compensatory Processes

Compensatory processes allow very high performance on one selection procedure to compensate for low performance on another. Applicants are tested on all selection procedures, and the scores on individual predictors are added together before a judgment is made. This process is common in situations where there are no minimum requirements and the objective is to get an overall picture of applicant qualifications. Usually, various predictors are given different weights, depending on their relevance and importance to selected criteria. Computers can help with this weighting process.[124] Compensatory processes maximize the use of all available data. They can be expensive, however, because each applicant must complete all procedures before a decision is made.

### Multiple Hurdles

Multiple hurdles means that each predictor operates independently. Applicants must get past the first hurdles to proceed to the next; failing any hurdle leads to

EXHIBIT 7.17 Alternative Ways of Using Multiple Selection Procedures

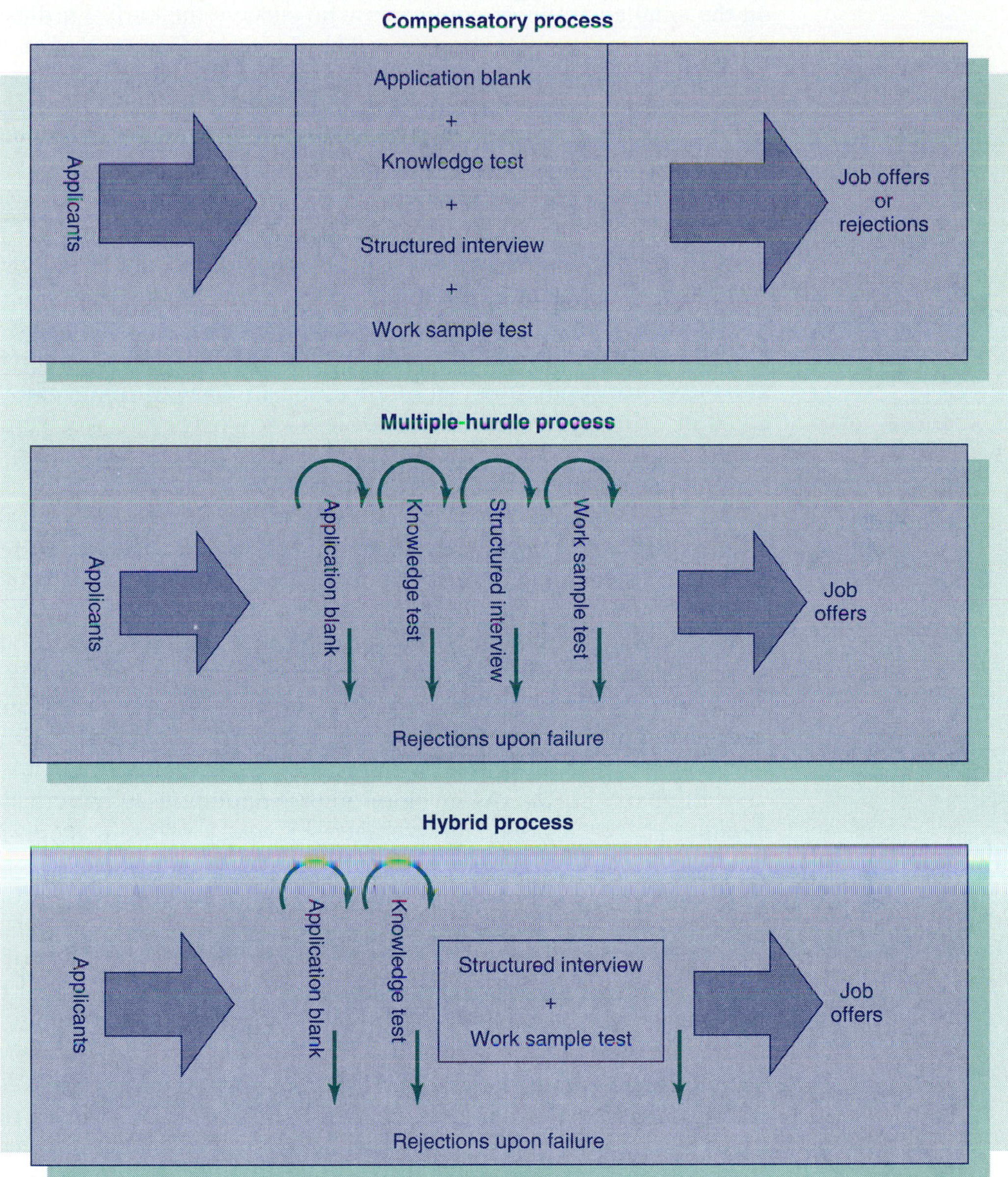


rejection. In Exhibit 7.17, applicants must be minimally qualified on the application blank to proceed to the knowledge test, and minimally qualified on the knowledge test to proceed to the structured interview. Strength on one selection measure cannot compensate for weakness on another. Multiple hurdles make sense when the work has certain minimum required characteristics: Accountants must have certain licenses, pilots must have experience in the aircraft they will fly, and lifeguards must know how to swim. Testing drug free is often a hurdle. Multiple hurdles can cut selection costs by using cheaper procedures to winnow out the applicant pool and by using more expensive procedures only on the smaller group of applicants who survive the early hurdles. Legally, such processes can be risky, however. The Supreme Court ruled in *Connecticut* v. *Teal* that every individual hurdle must either avoid rejecting protected groups or be shown to be job related (see Chapter Two).

### Hybrid Processes

A hybrid approach combines hurdles and compensatory processes. Minimum qualifications essential for the job, such as licenses, skills, or certification, are used as hurdles. Applicants who survive the hurdles are tested with other procedures whose results are combined, so that some talents can compensate for others. In selecting lifeguards, for example, ability to swim and minimum endurance levels might be hurdles. Then, a combination of predictors measuring knowledge of regulations and motivation to do well might allow highly motivated individuals to compensate for less knowledge and vice versa.

A good example of a hybrid approach is the Toyota Motor Corporation's manufacturing plant in Georgetown, Kentucky. Exhibit 7.18 shows the steps used in selecting the 3,000-member workforce. Toyota defined the target work roles as "team member, team leader, and group leader," and identified performance dimensions such as "meeting management, identifying and solving problems, initiative and oral communication," in addition to technical skills. Notice how these work role descriptions differ from the traditional job titles of assembler, painter, manager, or supervisor. As we show in Exhibit 7.18, Toyota combined multiple procedures, using some as hurdles and some as compensatory. Notice how the less-expensive selection techniques are used first, and the most expensive (such as the interview) are applied only to those who survive the early stages. More than 60,000 applicants were considered over 12 months, and each applicant averaged 15 weeks of assessment. Mazda Motors hired only about 1,300 of nearly 10,000 applicants who passed its five-step screening process. Mazda spends about 40 million dollars—roughly $13,000 per employee—to staff its U.S. plants.[125] This is a very expensive way to select! Does it pay off? Toyota managers point to turnover rates of 5 percent (the industry average is 20 percent), absenteeism of 2 percent (well below industry standards), and a sense of shared commitment to Toyota's values.[126]

Chapter Eight will show how much can be saved by reducing turnover. Let's assume that a turnover costs one and one-half times the one-year salary of an employee, and these employees earn $40,000 per year. Cutting turnover among 1,300 employees by 15 percent means 195 fewer separations per year, at a savings of $60,000 per separation, or $11.7 million dollars. The staffing system pays back in less than four years, and that's not even considering the improved performance, which we will discuss later.

## DOES IT WORK? VALIDATING SELECTION PROCESSES

You have seen that there are many valid selection technologies for managers to use. Combined, they can help managers to solve the riddle of predicting future work behavior from things that can be observed now. Validity "evidence" may be supplied by the consulting firm that is trying to sell the test, by a scientific study published in a research journal, by other organizations who have used the

**EXHIBIT 7.18** Multiple-Procedure Selection at Toyota Motor Corporation's Georgetown, Kentucky, Plant

| | |
|---|---|
| **Orientation and application blank** | Applicants completed Toyota's Kentucky application form, received a fact sheet on corporate expectations, and saw a video orientation to the selection process. Candidates were grouped in either the skilled or production track. No applicants were excluded. |
| **Technical skills assessment** | A battery of written tests including GATB, Job Fit Inventory (assesses motivation to work in a participative environment), technical skill tests. Applicants selected by top-down scoring, approximately 10 percent proceed to the next stage. |
| **Interpersonal assessment center** | Eight-hour series of four work simulations including Teamwork, Group Discussion, Problem Solving, Project T (evaluates quality of output, speed, and ideas for improvement). Top performers on the GATB and the assessment center move on to the next stage. |
| **Leadership assessment center** | Three simulations measuring decision-making and leadership skills, including in-basket requiring delegation and report writing, training and counseling, and scheduling. |
| **Technical performance assessment** | For skilled maintenance applicants only. Includes hands-on skills tests in which the written tests showed them to be most proficient. |
| **Toyota assessment interview** | Top applicants from the previous stages participate in a targeted selection interview with Toyota human resource and line managers. Ninety percent of interviewed applicants are accepted. |
| **Health assessment** | Drug and alcohol test and physical examination. Those meeting minimum health and drug-free levels are offered jobs. |

Source: Chuck Cosentino, John Allen, and Richard Wellins, "Choosing the Right People," *HR Magazine,* Mar. 1990, pp. 66–70; Gary Dessler, "Value-Based Hiring Builds Commitment," *Personnel Journal,* Nov. 1993, pp. 98–102.

For a selection device or system to be "valid," scores on the device or system must relate to future work behavior.

predictor(s), or by the organization conducting its own validation study. How do scientists, staffing consultants, or managers go about measuring validity? You may never actually participate in a validity study, but it is important to understand how validity is determined, so that you can be an informed consumer. Not all validity evidence is the same, and not all claims of validity are equally credible. Here, we will merely describe the different kinds of "validity" evidence. You can learn more about how to measure validity and conduct validation studies from books about the staffing process.[127]

*Validation methods* are the approaches used by organizations or researchers to determine whether predictors are valid. Validation makes a prediction about the predictor—this predictor will accurately forecast the applicant's future behaviors. As Exhibits 7.3 and 7.17 showed, however, the selection process involves much more than scoring applicants on predictors. Validity depends as much on how predictor information is used as it does on what predictor information is gathered. For example, a forklift license may be a valid predictor for loading dock performance, but virtually useless in predicting residence-hall advisers' performance. Thus, validity information from a study of forklift drivers is irrelevant to predicting whether a forklift license relates to residence-hall advising. Therefore, the best validation method is one that closely simulates the predictors that will actually be used, the types of applicants that will actually be selected, and the work outcomes or "criteria" that will really matter when people are placed on the job. However, this close matching is not always easy, so different validation methods have different advantages and disadvantages. Validation evidence can be gathered using *criterion-related* methods, which gather scores on predictors and criteria, or *content-based* methods, which judge similarities between the content of the predictors and criteria. To illustrate the different validation methods, consider how you decide which of your friends make reliable recommenders of movies. In a way, this involves selecting a person who will serve as your movie critic.

## Criterion-Related Validation

One way to determine whether a friend's movie recommendations fit your preferences is to have him or her make several recommendations (predictions). Then go to see those movies and judge whether you agree with the recommendations (the criterion). Criterion-related validation works the same way. It measure scores on the *predictor,* or selection device, and scores on a *criterion,* or several criteria, which are usually job behaviors such as performance, training time, absence, or career advancement. Just as you would have a predictor score and a criterion score for each movie you saw, validation studies obtain a predictor score and criterion score on each individual in the study.

### Choosing Predictors

In the movie example, the predictor seems fairly simple—movie recommendations. However, would you have your friend rate each movie on a scale (such as the number of "stars" or "turkeys"), give a simple "thumbs-up" or "thumbs-down," or rate each aspect of the film and combine those ratings into one overall score? You would want the predictor you chose to give you the right amount of information, but you also would want it to reflect how you actually use the recommendations. A very complex rating scheme is overkill if you always ask for only the bottom-line recommendation. In the same way, validation evidence should reflect predictors as they will be used by the organization. If an organization knows that its managers will tend to deviate from an interview guide when they interview candidates, a consulting firm's evidence of the guide's validity "when strictly followed" may not be very useful. Therefore, the predictors in the validation study should closely resemble the predictors that will really be used. Also, the predictors should be able to distinguish among people; if everyone gets the same predictor score it is impossible to predict anything. In the movie example, if your friend rates movies only as "really awful" or "not really awful," you may not get much variability in the ratings. In the same way, validation evidence should use predictors that give a wide range of scores on applicants.

### Choosing Criteria

At first glance, the right criterion in the movie example seems pretty obvious: Did you like the movie? However, you can think of other criteria, such as, Did the movie make you think? Did the movie leave you feeling happy or sad? Was the movie a good "date" film? Just as Eskimos have over 30 words for "snow," moviegoers have many facets to their movie tastes. You would want to judge your friend's recommendations by criteria that are most important to you. In the same way, validation evidence can reflect many different criteria. As you read in Chapters Three and Four, there are many ways to define work roles and many individual characteristics that affect organization goals. Some validation studies use absenteeism, others use training times or performance ratings by managers, and still others use "hard" data such as sales, mistakes, or customer reactions. A manager must examine carefully the criteria used in the validation study to make sure they really reflect the outcomes the organization will want to predict when the selection system is used. Validity can be very different depending on the criteria used in the study. "Typical" performance has a different relationship to predictors than "maximum" performance (when you try as hard as you can). Ability tests may predict promotional progress better than supervisory performance ratings.[128] As you have seen, today's organizations often care about employees' fit with the values, beliefs, and goals of the organization or team, in addition to their technical ability to do the job they are first hired for. No one knows exactly how to measure fit, but if that is what really matters, managers must look carefully at validity evidence that merely reflects performance in the first job, supervisory performance ratings after six months, or absence during the first year on the job.[129] Good validity evidence uses criteria that matter.

### Predictive versus Concurrent Validation

If you were validating your friend's movie recommendations against your own movie preferences, you could have your friend recommend several movies, and then go see them to test whether the recommendations matched your preferences. Or you could go to the movies with your friend, and get the recommendations at the same time that you form your own preferences. This is the difference between predictive and concurrent validation. You may get a different indication of your friend's ability, depending on which approach you take. If you go with your friend to movies that you already selected because they seemed interesting, you may never know how the friend would rate movies that didn't appear so interesting. Also, your friend's ratings after seeing the movies with you may reflect what you said or how you reacted to the movie, which isn't very helpful if you eventually want your friend to recommend movies that you haven't seen.

In the same way, validity evidence can reflect a *predictive validation* approach, which assesses the predictor on actual job applicants, places some or all of them on the job, and later measures the criteria (work behaviors) and relates criterion scores to the earlier predictor scores. Or validity evidence can reflect a *concurrent validation* approach, in which the predictor is given to employees who are already on the job. Their scores on the predictor then can be immediately related to their current job performance or other behaviors. A predictive validation study takes time while the applicants who are hired learn and perform on the job. A concurrent study can be much faster and thus much less expensive.

On the other hand, because a predictive study uses actual applicants, such evidence may more closely reflect how the selection system will perform when it is used with future applicants. Just as your friend's reviews may differ if he or she attend movies with you, employees may have learned on the job, they may have less "at stake" if they know their scores are only for a study, or their range of scores may be much smaller than those of applicants because the worst employees were already rejected or fired and the best were already promoted. From still another angle, a concurrent study may provide a much larger number of employees than a predictive study, which must rely only on the number of hired applicants, and statistical tests are more powerful with larger numbers of people. While U.S. federal guidelines favor predictive studies, evidence is mixed concerning whether predictive studies provide more useful results.[130]

### Synthetic Validation

One problem you'll have in choosing a friend to review movies for you is how many movies they should see before you analyze their reviews. Your resources may severely limit the size of your "sample" of movies, especially if you're paying for the tickets! You might have your friend rate television shows instead. Watching a television show is not the same as watching a movie—the quality and content may be different—but perhaps some of the aspects of a good reviewer could be measured by using television reviews in addition to movie reviews. In the same way, many organizations don't have a large enough number of applicants or employees to calculate meaningful validity coefficients. Consulting firms, the military, or industrial and trade associations may be able to generate larger samples, but their studies often use predictors or criteria different from those needed by the organization. One answer is *synthetic validation,* which divides up the criteria or predictors into dimensions. Across several different samples of applicants or employees, the validity of each dimension is assessed and the results are combined across dimensions.[131] For example, a teamwork ability test might be validated not only for team-based behaviors among production employees but also among clerical employees, managers, or salespeople. These jobs are very different, but a teamwork criterion can be assessed for each one, and the teamwork test scores could be correlated with only that aspect of performance across all the jobs.

### Validity Generalization

Another way to deal with the "small sample" problem in your movie reviews would be to combine evidence of the validity of your friend's movie reviews with that of three other people with similar tastes in films. If these three people had seen different movies from those you had seen, you could see how well your prospective movie reviewer predicted *their* movie preferences. If your reviewer did a pretty good job of predicting movies that all three regarded as "good," you might take that as evidence that he or she could predict your preferences. Of course, the value of this strategy depends on how similar the other people's movie tastes are to yours and how reliable their opinions are about your prospective reviewer's abilities.

These considerations also face decision makers and researchers studying selection systems. For years, scientists and managers lamented the fact that single validation studies often produced very different results, even when using very similar predictors and criteria in very similar situations. The problem is that any single validation study may have a very small sample or be plagued with a few idiosyncrasies that affect its results. However, combining many such studies, like combining the experiences of several moviegoers, can reveal general patterns of validity that weren't apparent before. This process of combining the results of many validation studies using statistical methods is called *validity generalization* or meta-analysis. Many of the validity coefficients quoted in this chapter and shown in Exhibit 7.5 were derived using validity generalization to combine results of tens or hundreds of individual studies.[132]

Human resource managers can use validity generalization to borrow validity coefficient results from other studies using similar predictors and similar criteria. This not only avoids the expense and time of conducting a situation-specific validation study but can also produce more precise information if the studies are selected carefully. Validity generalization still arouses some controversy among researchers. However, it is being used by the U.S. Employment Service. By improving the accuracy of estimates of validity coefficients, it also can help to improve the accuracy of estimates of the payoff from improved selection, as we discuss later.[133]

Within a group of similar organizations, a similar approach is to "transport" validity evidence. For example, the American Gas Association had validity data showing that a strength test predicted performance for three jobs in the gas utility industry: field service representative, crew assistant, and pipeline assistant. The validity evidence for these three jobs was transported to other jobs in the industry by using job analysis (see Chapter Three) to identify which jobs also had similar strength demands, and extrapolating the known validity results to the rest of the jobs.[134]

## Content-Based Validation

What if you can't afford to send your prospective movie reviewer to any films, the number of films you have both seen is very small, and there are no other people you can look to for evidence of the reviewer's ability? Could you still get an estimate of the validity of the prospective reviewer's opinions? Perhaps you could sit down with the reviewer and ask how he or she goes about evaluating a movie. You could listen to your reviewer's approach—the way he or she rates certain aspects of movies, places emphasis on plot, character, cinematography, and so forth—and you could compare that with your own approach to movies. If the content of your reviewer's approach seems similar to yours in evaluating movies, that would provide some evidence that the reviewer's opinions might predict yours.

As it turns out, this logic also occurred to scientists and managers searching for validity evidence.

*Content-based validation* involves choosing and constructing selection techniques so that they include the knowledge, skills, and abilities (KSAs) used on the job.[135] Unlike criterion-related validation, content-based validation computes no predictor and criterion scores or a validity coefficient. Instead, it relies on judgments comparing the job content (based on job analysis as discussed in Chapter Three) and the selection technique to determine the similarity between them.

For example, content validation for a word processing selection tool would involve listing the KSAs necessary for good word-processing performance, such as (1) ability to type at a keyboard, (2) ability to use standard business correspondence styles and formats, and (3) ability to turn on and operate a personal computer. One predictor might be a short test on the procedures for starting and operating a computer; it would have high content validity with the third skill, but low content validity for the other skills. A typing test on a typewriter would have a high content validity for the first skill, but not the other two. If the typing test involved taking a handwritten letter and producing a finished business letter in proper format, it would have content validity for the first two skills, but not for the third. Content validation is frequently used to determine how well a person must perform to be minimally competent when predictors are used as hurdles.[136]

Content validation works best when the job behaviors, KSAs, and predictor tasks are highly observable, because this minimizes the chance that judgments are highly subjective and controversial. Many organizations use content validation to construct predictors that are later validated using criterion-related methods. An interesting variation on content validation involves having selection experts predict the validity coefficient that would be produced by a particular predictor and criterion. One study found that the predictions of industrial psychologists compared favorably to the results of a typical single-organization criterion-related validation study.[137]

## Extent of Validation

Validation does not appear to be a common practice. A Bureau of National Affairs (BNA) survey of 437 organizations found that only 16 percent had validated their procedures according to the federal Uniform Guidelines on Employee Selection Procedures. Firms with more than 1,000 employees were more likely to validate than smaller firms. The most common validation criteria were formal performance evaluations, supervisory statements gathered specifically for validation, length of service, production rates, absence/tardiness, and success in training programs. Twenty-nine percent of those who validated used concurrent methods, while 18 percent used predictive methods. The other 53 percent used other methods, including some content validation, private consultants, or information from test publishers.[138] The last two sources may well base their estimates on validity generalization results. Apparently, the time and energy required to conduct organization-specific validation studies is deemed too costly an investment compared to other methods of determining whether selection procedures work, such as content validation or information from test publishers and consultants.

## Government Regulation of Validation

No law requires that organizations use valid predictors or examine predictor validity. However, validity evidence can be a defense against findings of adverse impact as discussed in Chapter Two. When such a defense is made, courts closely examine all aspects of the validation methods in considering evidence:

The *predictor,* including the adequacy of job analysis, test content, and whether the organization considered predictor alternatives less harmful to the protected group.

The *criterion,* including adequacy of job analysis, measurement quality, rating processes, and rater training.

The *validation procedure,* including sample sizes, validation strategy, and job groups used.

The *data analysis,* such as the size and statistical significance of the validity coefficient, cost-benefit evidence, setting passing scores, fair predictions for minority groups, and evidence of validity generalization.[139]

## WHAT IS THE PAYOFF? EVALUATING EXTERNAL SELECTION ACTIVITIES

We have already seen that external staffing decisions affect the productivity and qualifications of the workforce, and the legal vulnerability of the employment relationship. These two general outcomes can be measured in many different ways. We describe several alternative external selection evaluation measures in Exhibit 7.19.

### Efficiency

How can a company tell whether the money it spent on selection is really worth it? Is the money spent developing and implementing a work-sample test a good investment? As we show in Exhibit 7.19, ultimately organizations hope to improve such business results as profits, productivity, defect reductions, and cost reduction. However, selection doesn't affect these things directly—it affects them through the match between applicants chosen and work demands. Different selection processes produce different information. According to the definition of information value from Chapter Four, selection information is a good investment when it (1) improves many decisions, and/or (2) improves decisions that have very important effects, and/or (3) can be gathered at low cost.

#### Selection Cost

Selection costs vary from situation to situation; generally, they include the costs to develop the selection procedure, the costs to conduct the procedure with applicants, the costs to process the information and prepare it for the decision makers, and the costs of having decision makers evaluate the information and make a decision about who should receive employment offers. It is not possible to predict the precise costs of any selection procedure in every situation. We describe the relative cost levels of different selection devices in Exhibit 7.5. For purposes of illustration, consider the Mazda selection system described earlier, which cost $4,000 per applicant and was applied to 10,000 applicants. A total cost of $40 million. Let's see how we might calculate the payoff.

#### How Many Decisions Will Be Improved?

Obviously, the more people to be selected, the more benefit selection systems can have. However, it also depends on how many of the selection decisions would be better with the system. A selection system that improves your success by 50 percent of 200 selection decisions is just as good as one that improves your success by 10 percent of 1,000 selection decisions. Exhibit 7.20 shows how this works. Each horizontal set of graphs is related. The top set of graphs shows a situation where a selection system will do a lot of good—high improvement. The bottom set of graphs shows a situation where a selection

**EXHIBIT 7.19** Possible Measures to Evaluate External Selection Activities

| Efficiency-Related | Equity-Related |
|---|---|
| **Cost** | **Legality** |
| Cost per new hire | Adverse impact |
| **Quantity** | Number of legal challenges |
| Number hired | Adherence to legal requirements |
| Number who stay for 5 years | **Applicant perceptions** |
| Average tenure of new hires | Satisfaction with the process |
| **Quality** | Knowledge gained about the company |
| Validity of procedures | Satisfaction with the company |
| Average new-hire qualifications | |
| Proportion of new hires who succeed | |
| Performance levels of new hires | |
| Career progress of new hires | |
| **Business results** | |
| Profits | |
| Productivity | |
| Defects | |
| Production costs | |

system won't do so much good—low improvement. Each set of graphs is like the correlation coefficient graph in Exhibit 7.4, with the ellipse representing a cloud of points, each one the combination of a person's predictor score (the *X*-axis) and their criterion score (the *Y*-axis).

*Success ratio* is the measure of selection system value in Exhibit 7.20. It is simply the percentage of applicants hired who actually succeed. In the top set of graphs, the success ratio improves from 50 percent without the selection system to 75 percent with the system. In the bottom set of graphs, the success ratio improves from 70 percent without the selection system to 72 percent with it. How much improvement a selection system can make depends not only on its validity, but also on two other aspects of the situation: the "base rate" and the "selection ratio." So, if you buy a test simply because the test vendor says it is "valid," you can waste your money. Let's see why these factors affect selection system improvement.

*Base rate* is the status quo. How well would we do with our current selection system? In Exhibit 7.20, this is defined as how many applicants turn out to be satisfactory before we use the new selection system; that is, the percentage falling above the satisfactory level on the criterion. The base rate panels show that in the top situation, the status quo is only a 50 percent success while the bottom panel has a 70 percent base rate of success without the system. The applicants in the bottom panel are generally better qualified relative to the cutoff of satisfactoriness. That means there is more room to improve in the top situation, which is one factor affecting selection system value.

*Validity* is highlighted in the second set of panels in Exhibit 7.20. Having discussed the meaning of validity, you should recognize that the top situation has a highly valid predictor (the points fall near a line), and the bottom situation does not (points fall in a circle). High validity is better, all things being equal, but it's full value depends on the rest of the situation.

**EXHIBIT 7.20** How the Situation Affects the Value of Selection

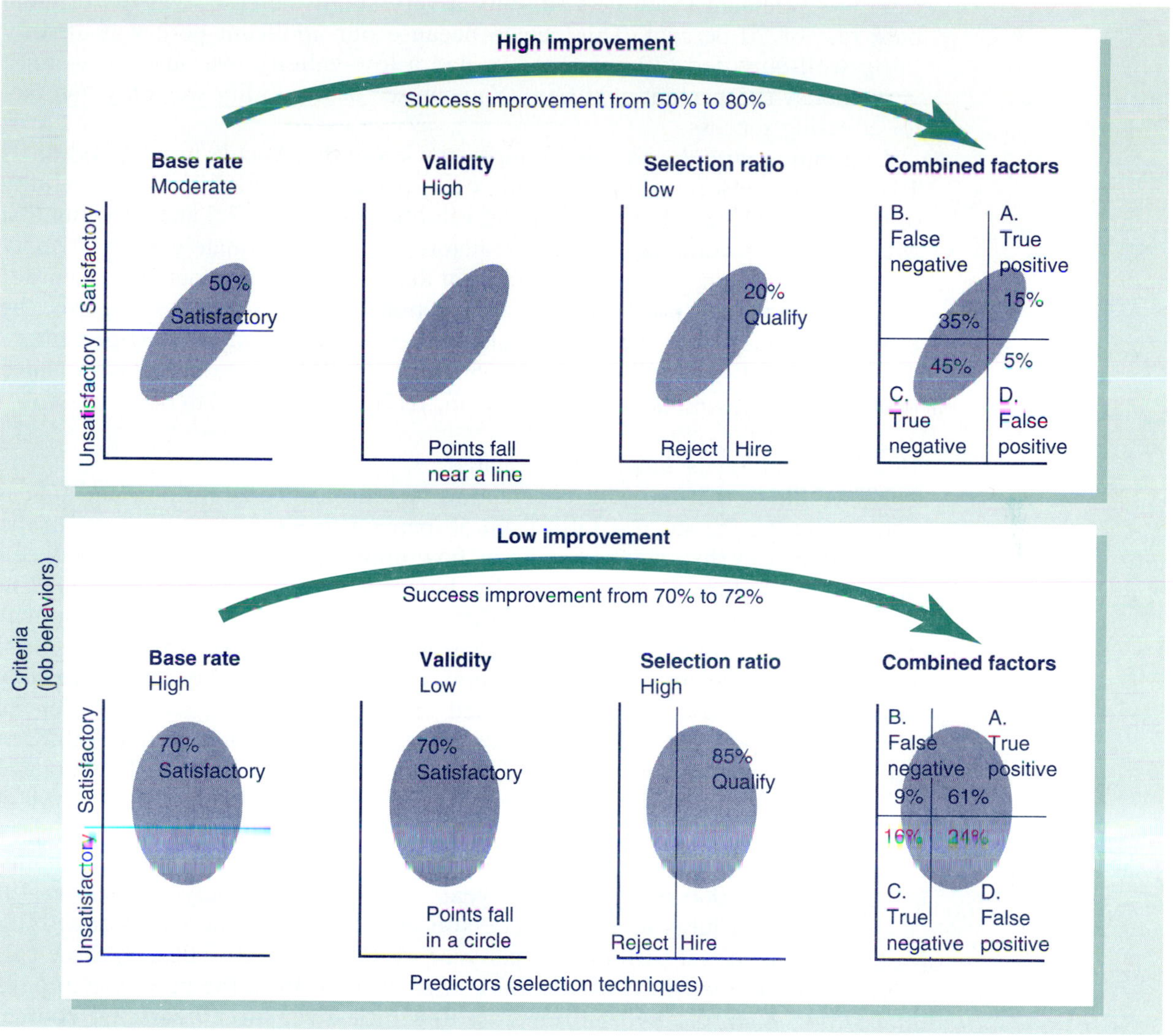


Reprinted with permission of The Conference Board.

*Selection ratio* reflects how choosy we can be. In other words, it is the percentage of applicants who "pass" our selection system and get hired. In the third pair of panels, you can see that the selection ratio is low in the high-improvement situation (20 percent qualify), but it is high in the low-improvement situation (85 percent qualify). Lower selection ratios mean more choosy systems, which generally increases the value of the selection system. However, low selection ratios also can be costly because more candidates must be considered to fill a certain number of vacancies.

The final pair of panels shows the ultimate results. In the top panel, 20 percent of the applicants are hired, of which 15 percent are successful. Therefore, the *success ratio* is 80 percent (15% ÷ 20%). Because we had a moderate base rate, a highly valid test, and a low selection ratio, the selection system improves significantly from the original base rate of 50 percent. In the bottom panel, 85 percent of the applicants are hired, of which 61 percent succeed, so the success ratio is 72 percent (61% ÷ 85%), only a very small increase over the original base rate of 70 percent. This occurs because our applicant pool was already fairly well-qualified (70 percent), we had a low-validity test, and we weren't very choosy (85 percent qualified). You can see how validity was only one factor affecting success.

Continuing with the Mazda example, we know that Mazda hired 1,300 of its 10,000 applicants, for a selection ratio of 13 percent. We don't know the validity of the Mazda system, but based on the validities in Exhibit 7.5 and knowing that Mazda's system combines several predictors, we might estimate validity at about .65. For illustration, we might assume that the base rate was about 50 percent for the Mazda applicant pool without the selection system. Using these figures, the projected success rate for the Mazda selection system would be 90 percent.[140] Thus, without the selection system, 650 of the 1,300 people hired would have been successful; with the selection system, 1,170 are projected to be successful.

### How Important Are the Improved Decisions?

Now we know that the Mazda selection system costs $40 million and that it could improve the success ratio from 50 percent to 90 percent. Is it worth the cost? To answer that, we have to know how important the difference is between success and failure or, more generally, how much is the value of variations in work performance. For some jobs, where worker decisions have huge implications or where mistakes can be disastrous (e.g., tanker or airline captains, power plant operators, or top managers), this variation is very large. For jobs where decisions are highly constrained or easily corrected, such differences may be much smaller. Estimating the difference between success and failure in terms of dollars remains more an art than a science, but reasonable estimates can be made.[141] In this case, assuming that the Mazda workers earn $40,000 per year, a typical estimate of the difference between the value of the satisfactory performers and the unsatisfactory performers would be about $25,000 per person per year. By going from only 650 successful new hires to 1,170 successful new hires, we improve productivity by about $13 million, per year, (520 × $25,000). Thus, by these calculations, the productivity improvement from the new system pays back the $40 million cost in a little over three years. Of course, these dollar figures are estimates, but so are the predictions of future interest rates, market shares, and production levels used by financial professionals, market researchers, and engineers. Just as there are techniques to refine those numbers, so there are methods to refine the numbers used here. For our purposes, the actual dollar values are less important than your understanding of how the value of a selection system depends not only on its validity, but also on the situation to which it is applied.

#### WHAT DO YOU THINK?

The dollar value of selection systems can be calculated, and often approaches millions of dollars. Yet, such estimates are never perfect. How do you think a chief financial officer would respond to evidence claiming a million-dollar payoff to improved selection?

## Equity

Selection processes are used as signals of the organization's treatment of its employees. Do you think drug testing signifies a good employer or a poor one? The acceptability of drug testing depends on whether people believe that impaired job performance poses a danger to others. One study found that applicants were less likely to apply for jobs requiring urinalysis drug tests, that using paper-and-pencil tests was no more attractive, and that applicants preferred selection without any tests at all.[142] Recent research suggests that applicants react to selection systems according to the perceived fairness of the processes and outcomes, or whether they seem to invade privacy.[143] One study found that the predictors perceived as most invasive were astrology, graphology, and polygraphs while the least invasive were interviews and work samples. Tests were perceived to be less invasive if people had firsthand experience with them.[144] Moreover, selection processes are closely monitored by regulatory agencies, especially if they tend to exclude larger numbers of minorities and women than white men. Selection systems, in combination with recruitment, greatly affect the rate at which protected group members are hired.[145] The use of clearly scorable and structured selection systems may have declined during the 1970s and 1980s because of fears that minorities and females would score lower and be more frequently rejected. It remains to be seen whether more recent civil rights legislation will have a similar effect. One reaction to such fears has been the emergence of scoring systems, such as banding (discussed earlier), that attempt to mitigate the effects of rigid top-down hiring systems by creating equivalent groups from which more affirmative selection decisions can be made. Some research has shown, however, that affirmative action success may be driven more by the applicant pool than by the selection scoring system.[146]

## SUMMARY

External selection is the final filter before offering employment. It tries to measure applicant characteristics that help forecast which applicants could be successful future employees. Within the variety of external selection techniques, many are the focus of heated debate about the balance between efficiency and equity at work. While validity is an important aspect of selection procedures, their true value is determined by the situation in which they are used. Clearly, human resource professionals, their employers, and society will continue to focus on this important human resource activity, but it's not only important to select the best. An organization needs to keep them as well as weed out the selection mistakes. That process involves managing employee separations, the topic of the next chapter. Before going on, however, see if you can construct a selection process for the organization of the future in the Your Turn at the end of this chapter.

## QUESTIONS

1. What choices must a human resource professional make when designing an external selection strategy? How can these choices affect the organization from both a legal and a long-run efficiency standpoint?
2. What is validity? What purposes does validity evidence serve? What is a validity coefficient, and what are its characteristics? When is "validity" not necessarily useful?
3. Should application forms be relied on heavily in the selection process? Discuss the positive and negative impact they may have, and what an organization can do to make them more useful.

4. What effect can stereotyping, applicant behaviors, and interviewer behavior/training have on employment interviews? What interview strategies are often found to have a damaging effect on the validity of interviews?
5. What does research suggest can be done to improve interview usefulness? How can an organization protect itself from legal repercussions?
6. Discuss the uses and drawbacks of such selection devices as emotional intelligence, physical abilities, medical examinations, drug testing, AIDS and genetic screening, and personality and honesty testing. How can an organization balance efficiency and equity in using such techniques?
7. Discuss the role of predictors and criteria in validation. What characteristics should good criteria and predictors have? How might one avoid contamination and deficiency in predictors and criteria?
8. Distinguish predictive from concurrent validation. When might a well-conducted concurrent validation study be preferable to a predictive validation study?
9. Is high validity enough to justify investing in a new selection procedure? What other situational factors affect the value of improved selection information? What difference does it make if that value is measured in terms of prediction accuracy compared with dollar-valued organizational outcomes?
10. What kind of help can the Internet offer HR professionals and managers? What might the implications be for people seeking employment?

## YOUR TURN
### "HIO Silver" Selection at AFG Industries[147]

High-involvement organizations (HIOs) are a relatively new organizational form. HIOs are designed to create very high levels of employee involvement. Power, information, skills, and rewards for performance are pushed down to the lowest levels of the organization. Self-managed teams or other structures enable employees to share decision-making power. Extensive training in technical, social, and business skills provides team members with the skills needed for effective self-management. Information systems communicate the performance data that teams need to motivate needed behaviors, such as learning and problem solving. For obvious reasons, hiring practices in HIOs typically attempt to select employees who prefer working in groups and who have high needs for personal growth and development. Thus, the hiring process is one design element of many that must fit with the overall strategy.

AFG Industries is about to start up a new float glass plant in the western United States. Management is convinced that the HIO concept will enable the new plant to achieve its goals and has decided to design the new plant and its processes to be a shining example of the HIO concept (nicknamed HIO silver). Working with the organization's strategic planners, human resource and line managers have determined that all of the HR systems must support the HIO concept. Because the plant is a new start-up, however, selecting the initial group of employees will be critical. It is your job to recommend a process for identifying the key work roles, translating them into selection activities and evaluating the results of those activities. You can use the four-step model shown in Exhibit 7.2 as a guide. The following questions may also be helpful:

1. How will you assess the work requirements of a plant that hasn't even been built? (Chapter Three may be helpful.)
2. What personal characteristics will you select for, and what specific selection techniques would you use? How would you determine if there is any evidence of their value?
3. How would you combine the selection techniques?
4. How would you reinforce the selection process with other organizational features?
5. How would you measure and communicate the effectiveness of the program you designed?

Your instructor has additional information about this case.

## NOTES AND REFERENCES

1. Michael Selz, "Hiring the Right Manager Overseas," *The Wall Street Journal,* Feb. 27, 1992, p. B2; Joann S. Lublin, "Foreign Accents Proliferate in Top Ranks as U.S. Companies Find Talent Abroad," *The Wall Street Journal,* May 21, 1992, p. B1.
2. "Buyers' Guide," *Human Resource Executive,* Nov. 1995, pp. 51–55.
3. Bureau of National Affairs, *Employee Selection Procedures,* ASPA-BNA Survey No. 45 (Washington, DC: Bureau of National Affairs, May 5, 1983); John W. Boudreau, "Utility Analysis," chap. 1.4 in *Human Resource Management Evolving Roles and Responsibilities,* ed. Lee D. Dyer (Washington, DC: Bureau of National Affairs, 1988); David E. Bowen, Gerald E. Ledford, Jr., and Barry R. Nathan, "Hiring for the Organization, Not the Job," *Academy of Management Executive* 5, no. 4 (1991), pp. 35–51; George A. Neuman, "Autonomous Work Group Selection," *Journal of Business and Psychology* 6, no. 2 (Winter 1991), pp. 283–91.
4. Sara L. Rynes, "The Employment Interview as a Recruitment Device," in *The Employment Interview,* ed. Robert W. Eder and Gerald R. Ferris (Newbury Park, CA: Sage Publications, 1989), pp. 127–42.
5. Lois Langley, "Getting Personal: Use of Psychological Tests to Screen Job Applicants Can Backfire on Employers," *Pittsburgh Post-Gazette,* Feb. 5, 1995, p. D1.
6. Gregory M. Saltzman, "Job Applicant Screening by a Japanese Transplant: A Union-Avoidance Tactic," *Industrial and Labor Relations Review* 49 (Oct. 1995), pp. 88–104.
7. Robert D. Gatewood and Hubert S. Feild, *Human Resource Selection,* 3rd ed. (Fort Worth, TX: Dryden Press, 1994).
8. Stephen M. Collarelli and Amy L. Boos, "Sociometric and Ability-Based Assignment to Work Groups: Some Implications for Personnel Selection," *Journal of Organizational Behavior* 13 (1992), pp. 187–96.
9. Diane Arthur, "The Importance Of Body Language," *HR Focus,* June 1995, pp. 22–23.
10. Barry M. Staw and Ha Hoang, "Sunk Costs in the NBA: Why Draft Order Affects Playing Time and Survival in Professional Basketball," *Administrative Science Quarterly* 40 (1995), pp. 474–94.

11. Cynthia D. McCauley, Lorrina J. Eastman, and Patricia J. Ohlott, "Linking Management Selection and Development through Stretch Assignments," *Human Resource Management* 34 (Spring 1995), pp. 93–115.
12. "Testing Report," *Human Resource Executive,* May 1991, pp. 5–7.
13. James M. Perry, "résumé-Sorting Computer Helps Clinton Team Screen Thousands Seeking Administration Jobs," *The Wall Street Journal,* Jan. 11, 1993, p. A18.
14. HRNET, Sept. 16, 1995.
15. Philip Ash, "Law and Regulation of Preemployment Inquiries," *Journal of Business and Psychology* 5, no. 3 (Spring 1991), pp. 291–308.
16. For a particularly detailed example of an application blank, see *Recruiting and Selection Procedures,* Personnel Policies Forum Survey No. 146 (Washington, DC: Bureau of National Affairs, May 1988), pp. 68–71.
17. Alan M. Saks, Joanne D. Leck, and David M. Saunders, "Effects of Application Blanks and Employment Equity on Applicant Reactions to Job Pursuit Intentions," *Journal of Organizational Behavior* 16 (1995), pp. 415–30.
18. Allen Schuh, "Application Blank and Intelligence as Predictors of Turnover," *Personnel Psychology,* Spring 1967, pp. 59–63; Allen Schuh, "The Predictability of Employee Tenure: A Review of the Literature," *Personnel Psychology,* Spring 1967, pp. 133–52; George W. England, *Development and Use of Weighted Application Blanks,* rev. ed., Bulletin 55 (Minneapolis: Industrial Relations Center, University of Minnesota, 1971); David Weiss, "Multivariate Procedures," in *Handbook of Industrial and Organizational Psychology,* ed. M. D. Dunnette (Skokie, IL: Rand McNally, 1976), pp. 344–54; Bureau of National Affairs, *Employee Selection Procedures;* Larry Stevens, "Automating the Selection Process," *Personnel Journal,* Nov. 1991, pp. 59–67.
19. "A Revolution in Resumes," *The Wall Street Journal,* May 16, 1995, p. A1; "Checkoffs: More Resume Bloopers," *The Wall Street Journal,* Aug. 8, 1995, p. A1.
20. John E. Hunter and Rhonda F. Hunter, "The Validity and Utility of Alternative Predictors of Job Performance," *Psychological Bulletin* 96 (1984), pp. 72–98. England, *Development and Use of Weighted Application Blanks;* Raymond Lee and Jerome M. Booth, "A Utility Analysis of a Weighted Application Blank Designed to Predict Turnover for Clerical Employees," *Journal of Applied Psychology* 59 (1974), pp. 516–18.
21. Stephen J. Vodanovich and Rosemary H. Lowe, "They Ought to Know Better: The Incidence and Correlates of Inappropriate Application Blank Inquiries," *Public Personnel Management* 21 (Fall 1992), pp. 363–70; J. P. Jolly and J. G. Frierson, "Playing It Safe," *Personnel Administrator* 34 (1989), pp. 44–50; D. D. Burrington, "A Review of State Government Employment Application Forms for Suspect Inquiries," *Public Personnel Management Journal* 11 (1982), pp. 55–60; D. M. Saunders, J. D. Leck and L. Marcil, "What Predicts Employer Propensity to Gather Protected Group Information from Job Applicants?" in David M. Saunders, ed., *New Approaches to Employee Management: Fairness in Employee Selection,* vol. 1 (Greenwich, CT: JAI Press, 1992, pp. 105–30.

22. Gatewood and Feild, *Human Resource Selection,* p. 421.

23. Bureau of National Affairs, *Recruiting and Selection Procedures;* Samuel Greengard, "Are You Well Armed to Screen Applicants?" *Personnel Journal,* Dec. 1995, pp. 84–95.

24. "Look before You Hire to Guard against Trouble," *Des Moines Register,* Jan. 15, 1996, p. 8.

25. "Reference Preference: Employers Button Lips," *The Wall Street Journal,* Jan. 4, 1990, p. B1.

26. Greengard, "Are You Well Armed. . ."

27. "Class of '95," *Human Resource Executive,* Dec. 1995, pp. 20–23.

28. Hunter and Hunter, "The Validity and Utility," p. 80; Kevin G. Love and Kirk O'Hara, "Predicting Job Performance of Youth Trainees under a Job Training Partnership Act Program (JTPA): Criterion Validation of a Behavior-Based Measure of Work Maturity," *Personnel Psychology* 40 (1987), pp. 323–41.

29. *National Labor Relations Board* v. *Town & Country Electric, Inc. and Ameristaff Personnel Contractors, Ltd.,* No. 94–947, 116 S. Ct. 450, 1995 U.S. Lexis 8311. Decided Nov. 28, 1995.

30. W. A. Owens, "Background Data" in *Handbook of Industrial and Organizational Psychology,* ed. Marvin D. Dunnette (Chicago, IL: Rand McNally, 1976), pp. 609–44.

31. J. E. Rosenbaum and T. Kariya, "Market and Institutional Mechanisms for the High School to Work Transition in the U.S. and Japan" (paper presented at the Annual Meeting of the American Sociological Association, Chicago, Aug. 1987).

32. David Whitman et al., "The Forgotten Half," *U.S. News and World Report,* June 26, 1989, pp. 45–53; Nancy J. Perry, "The New Improved Vocational School," *Fortune,* June 19, 1989, pp. 127–38; Cindy Skrzycki, "Test of High School Graduates' Skills Planned," *Washington Post,* Nov. 4, 1989, p. C1; "NAB Chief Sees Business Problems in Growing Shortage of Qualified Workers," *BNA Labor Relations Week* 4, no. 2 (Jan. 1990), pp. 9–14; John Bishop, "Why the Apathy in American High Schools?" *Educational Researcher* 18, no. 1 (Jan.–Feb. 1989), pp. 6–10; John Bishop and Suk Kang, "Vocational and Academic Education in High School: Complements or Substitutes?" *Economics of Education Review* 8, no. 2 (1989), pp. 133–48.

33. National Center on the Educational Quality of the Workforce, *The Other Shoe: Education's Contribution to the Productivity of Establishments* (Philadelphia: University of Pennsylvania Press, 1995).

34. Ellen H. Sides et al., "Biographical Data: A Neglected Tool for Career Counseling," *Human Resource Planning,* 1984, pp. 151–56.

35. Shawn M. Carraher, Anthony A. McBride, Jorge L. Mendoze, and M. Ronald Buckley, "Measuring Service-Orientation with Biodata and the SOI" (paper presented at the Annual Meeting of the Society for Industrial and Organizational Psychology, May 1995).

36. Fred A. Mael and Blake E. Ashforth, "Loyal from Day One: Biodata, Organizational Identification, and Turnover among Newcomers," *Personnel*

*Psychology* 48 (1995), pp. 309–33; Thomas E. Becker and Alan L. Colquitt, "Potential versus Actual Faking of a Biodata Form: An Analysis along Several Dimensions of Item Type," *Personnel Psychology* 45 (1992), pp. 389–406.

37. Leatta Hough, "Development of the Accomplishment Record Method of Selecting and Promoting Professionals," *Journal of Applied Psychology* 69, no. 1 (1984), pp. 135–46.
38. Hunter and Hunter, "Validity and Utility," p. 87; Hough, "Development of the Accomplishment Record Method," p. 138; Terry W. Mitchell, "A Priori Biodata to Predict Teamwork, Learning Rate, and Retention" (paper presented at the Seventh Annual Conference of the Society for Industrial and Organizational Psychology, Montreal, Quebec, May 1992).
39. Richard D. Arvey and Robert H. Faley, *Fairness in Selecting Employees,* 2nd ed. (Reading, MA: Addison-Wesley, 1988).
40. Dianna L. Stone, Eugene F. Stone-Romero, and Erik Eddy, "Factors That Influence the Perceived Invasiveness of Biographical Data" (paper presented at the Annual Meeting of the Society for Industrial and Organizational Psychology, May 1995).
41. Jolie Soloman, "The New Job Interview: Show Thyself," *The Wall Street Journal,* Dec. 4, 1989, p. B1.
42. Bureau of National Affairs, *Employee Selection Procedures;* Bureau of National Affairs, *Recruiting and Selection Procedures;* Milton D. Hakel, "Employment Interview," in *Personnel Management: New Perspectives,* ed. K. Rowland and G. Ferris (Boston: Allyn & Bacon, 1982); Richard D. Arvey and James E. Campion, "The Employment Interview: A Summary and Review of Recent Research," *Personnel Psychology* 35, no. 3 (1982), pp. 281–322; Eugene Mayfield, "The Selection Interview—A Re-Evaluation of Published Research," *Personnel Psychology* 17 (1964), pp. 239–60; Neal Schmitt, "Social and Situational Determinants of Interview Decisions: Implications for the Employment Interview," *Personnel Psychology* 29 (1976), pp. 79–101.
43. Robert L. Dipboye, Stacey Jackson, and Laura Galarza, "Experience and Expertise in the Employment Interview" (paper presented at the Annual Meeting of the Society for Industrial and Organizational Psychology, May 1995); Michael M. Harris, "Reconsidering the Employment Interview: A Review of Recent Literature and Suggestions for Future Research," *Personnel Psychology* 42 (1989), pp. 691–726; Michael A. McDaniel, Deborah L. Whetzel, Frank L. Schmidt and Steven D. Maurer, "The Validity of Employment Interviews: A Comprehensive Review and Meta-Analysis," *Journal of Applied Psychology* 79 (1994), pp. 599–616; Allen I. Huffcutt, Phillip L. Roth, and Michael McDaniel, "Assessment of Mental Ability in the Employment Interview: Moderating Characteristics and Implications for Incremental Validity" (unpublished manuscript, Department of Psychology, Bradley University, Peoria, IL, 1995).
44. Brooks Mitchell, "Interviewing Face-to-Interface," *Personnel,* Jan. 1990, pp. 23–24.
45. Susan M. Raza and Bruce N. Carpenter, "A Model of Hiring Decisions in Real Employment Interviews," *Journal of Applied Psychology* 72, no. 4

(1987), pp. 596–603; Gatewood and Feild, *Human Resource Selection,* chap. 11; T. H. Macan and Robert L. Dipboye, "The Relationship of Interviewers' Preinterview Impressions to Selection and Recruitment Outcomes," *Personnel Psychology* 43 (1990), pp. 745–68.

46. Sara Rynes and Barry Gerhart, "Interviewer Assessments of Applicant Fit: An Exploratory Investigation," *Personnel Psychology* 43 (1990), pp. 12–35.
47. Laura M. Graves and Ronald J. Karren, "Interviewer Decision Processes and Effectiveness: An Experimental Policy-Capturing Investigation," *Personnel Psychology* 45 (1992), pp. 313–40.
48. Stephen Wermiel, "High Court Shifts Burden to Firms in Sex-Bias Cases," *The Wall Street Journal,* May 2, 1989, p. B1; John Bales, "Sex Stereotyping Data Valid, Brief Says," *APA Monitor* 19, no. 8 (Aug. 1988), p. 23.
49. Felice N. Schwartz, "The Riddle of the Ring," *Across the Board,* Apr. 1992, pp. 32–36; Richard D. Arvey and Robert H. Faley, *Fairness in Selecting Employees* (Reading, MA: Addison-Wesley, 1988).
50. Richard D. Arvey and James E. Campion, "The Employment Interview: A Summary and Review of Recent Research," *Personnel Psychology* 35 (1982), pp. 281–322; J. S. Tosi and W. W. Einbender, "The Effects of the Type and Amount of Information in Sex Discrimination Research: A Meta-Analysis," *Academy of Management Journal* 28 (1985), pp. 712–23; Judy D. Olian, Donald P. Schwab, and Yitchak Haberfeld, "The Impact of Applicant Gender Compared to Qualifications on Hiring Recommendations: A Meta-Analysis of Experimental Studies," *Organizational Behavior and Human Decision Processes* 41 (1988), pp. 180–95; Harris, "Reconsidering the Employment Interview."
51. Laura M. Graves and Gary N. Powell, "The Effect of Sex Similarity on Recruiters' Evaluations of Actual Applicants: A Test of the Similarity-Attraction Paradigm," *Personnel Psychology* 48 (1995), pp. 85–98.
52. Cheryl L. Adkins, Craig J. Russell, and James D. Werbel, "Judgments of Fit in the Selection Process: The Role of Work Value Congruence," *Personnel Psychology* 47 (1994), pp. 605–23.
53. Thun-Rung Lin, Gregory H. Dobbins, and Jiing-Lih Farh, "A Field Study of Race and Age Similarity Effects on Interview Ratings in Conventional and Situational Interviews," *Journal of Applied Psychology* 77, no. 3 (1992), pp. 363–71; Michael A. Campion, Elliot D. Pursell, and B. K. Brown, "Structured Interviewing: Raising the Psychometric Properties of the Employment Interview," *Personnel Psychology* 41 (1988), pp. 25–42; T. McDonald and Milton D. Hakel, "Effects of Applicant Race, Sex, Suitability and Answers on Interviewer's Questioning Strategy and Ratings," *Personnel Psychology* 38 (1985), pp. 321–34.
54. Raza and Carpenter, "A Model of Hiring Decisions"; Randall A. Gordon, Richard M. Rozelle, and James C. Baxter, "The Effect of Applicant Age, Job Level, and Accountability on the Evaluation of Job Applicants," *Organizational Behavior and Human Decision Processes* 41 (1988), pp. 20–33.
55. Harris, "Reconsidering the Employment Interview."

56. Robert A. Baron, "Impression Management by Applicants during Employment Interviews: The 'Too Much of a Good Thing' Effect," chap. 15 in *The Employment Interview,* ed. Robert W. Eder and Gerald R. Ferris.
57. Neil R. Anderson, "Decision Making in the Graduate Selection Interview: An Experimental Investigation," *Human Relations* 44, no. 4 (1991), pp. 403–17; Cynthia Kay Stevens and Amy L. Kristof, "Making the Right Impression: A Field Study of Applicant Impression Management During Job Interviews," *Journal of Applied Psychology* 80 (1995), pp. 587–606.
58. John Delery and K. Michele Kacmar, "The Use of Impression Management Tactics in the Employment Interview: An Investigation of the Influence of Applicant and Interviewer Characteristics" (paper presented at the Annual Meeting of the Society for Industrial and Organizational Psychology, May 1995).
59. Cynthia Gallios, Victor J. Callan, and Jule-Anne McKenzie Palmer, "The Influence of Applicant Communication Style and Interviewer Characteristics on Hiring Decisions," *Journal of Applied Social Psychology* 22, no. 13 (1992), pp. 1041–60; Harris, "Reconsidering the Employment Interview"; Baron, "Impression Management by Applicants."
60. Schmitt, "Social and Situational Determinants of Interview Decisions"; Gatewood and Feild, *Human Resource Selection.*
61. P. M. Rowe, "Decision Processes in Personnel Selection," *Canadian Journal of Behavioural Science* 16 (1984), pp. 326–37.
62. Robert L. Dipboye, "Threats to the Incremental Validity of Interviewer Judgments," chap. 3 in *The Employment Interview,* ed. Robert W. Eder and Gerald R. Ferris.
63. Allen J. Schuh, "Interviewer Decision Styles," chap. 6, pp. 90–96; and Peter Herriott, "Attribution Theory and Interview Decisions," chap. 7, pp. 97–109, in *The Employment Interview,* ed. Robert W. Eder and Gerald R. Ferris.
64. M. R. Buckley and Robert W. Eder, "B. M. Springett and the Notion of the 'Snap Decision' in the Interview," *Journal of Management* 14 (1988), pp. 59–69.
65. Harris, "Reconsidering the Employment Interview"; Steven D. Maurer and Charles Fay, "Effect of Situational Interviews, Conventional Structured Interviews, and Training on Interview Rating Agreement: An Experimental Analysis," *Personnel Psychology* 17 (1988), pp. 329–44; Charles H. Fay and Gary P. Latham, "Effects of Training and Rating Scales on Rating Errors," *Personnel Psychology* 35 (1982), pp. 105–16; Bureau of National Affairs, *Recruiting and Selection Procedures;* Gatewood and Feild, *Human Resource Selection,* p. 536; Allen I. Huffcutt and David J. Woehr, "Further Analysis of Interview Validity: A Quantitative Evaluation of Additional Methods for Structuring the Employment Interview" (unpublished manuscript, Bradley University, Peoria, IL, 1995).
66. Elaine D. Pulakos, Neal Schmitt, David Whitney and Matthew Smith, "Individual Differences in Interviewer Ratings: The Impact of Standardization, Consensus Discussion, and Sampling Error on the Validity of a Structured Interview," *Personnel Psychology,* 49 (1996), pp. 85–102.

T. M. Gehrlein, Robert L. Dipboye and C. Shanani, "Nontraditional Validity Calculations and Differential Interviewer Experience: Implications for Selection Interviews," *Educational and Psychological Measurement* 52 (1993), pp. 457–69.

67. Bureau of National Affairs, *Recruiting and Selection Procedures.*
68. Mitchell, "Interviewing Face-to-Interface."
69. Michael A. Campion, David K. Palmer and James E. Campion, "A Review of Structure in the Selection Interview" (unpublished manuscript, Purdue University, West Lafayette, 1995).
70. Harris, "Reconsidering the Employment Interview."
71. Tom Janz, "The Patterned Behavior Description Interview: The Best Prophet of the Future Is the Past" in *The Employment Interview,* ed. Robert W. Eder and Gerald R. Ferris; Tom Janz, Lowell W. Hellervik, and D. C. Gilmore, *Behavior Description Interviewing* (Newton, MA: Allyn & Bacon, 1986).
72. Gary P. Latham, Lise M. Saari, E. D. Pursell, and Michael A. Campion, "The Situational Interview," *Journal of Applied Psychology* 69 (1984), pp. 569–73.
73. Michael A. Campion, E. D. Pursell, and B. K. Brown, "Structured Interviewing: Raising the Psychometric Properties of the Employment Interview," *Personnel Psychology* 41 (1988), pp. 25–42.
74. Sara L. Rynes, "The Interview as a Recruitment Device," chap. 9 in *The Employment Interview,* ed. Robert W. Eder and Gerald R. Ferris; Robert W. Eder, "Contextual Effects on Interview Decisions," chap. 8 in *The Employment Interview,* ed. Robert W. Eder and Gerald R. Ferris.
75. McDaniel, Whetzel, Schmidt, and Maurer, "The Validity of Employment Interviews"; Gary P. Latham and Daniel P. Skarlicki, "Criterion-Related Validity of the Situational and Patterned Behavior Description Interviews with Organizational Citizenship Behavior," *Human Performance* 8 (1995), pp. 67–80; Elaine D. Pulakos and Neal Schmitt, "Experience-Based and Situational Interview Questions: Studies of Validity," *Personnel Psychology* 48 (1995), pp. 289–308; Allen I. Huffcutt and David J. Woehr, "Further Analysis of Interview Validity . . ."; James M. Conway, Robert A. Jako, and Deborah F. Goodman, "A Meta-Analysis of Interrater and Internal Consistency Reliability of Selection Interviews," *Journal of Applied Psychology,* 1995, vol. 80, pp. 565–579. Allen I. Huffcutt and Winfred Arthur, Jr, "Hunter and Hunter (1984) Revisited: Interview Validity for Entry-Level Jobs," *Journal of Applied Psychology* 79 (Apr. 1994), pp. 184–90.
76. " 'Intrusive' Questions Are Plaguing U.S. Workers," *BNA Daily Labor Report,* no. 7, (Jan. 10, 1990), pp. 2–3.
77. James E. Campion and Richard D. Arvey, "Unfair Discrimination in the Employment Interview," chap. 4 in *The Employment Interview,* ed. Robert W. Eder and Gerald R. Ferris.
78. Richard J. Hermstein and Charles Murray, *The Bell Curve: Intelligence and Class Structure in American Life* (New York: Simon & Schuster, 1994). Tori DeAngelis, "Psychologists Question Findings of *Bell Curve,*" *APA Monitor,* Oct. 1995, p. 7; "Mainstream Science on Intelligence," *The Wall Street Journal,* Dec. 13, 1994, p. A18.

79. Gatewood and Feild, *Human Resource Selection,* p. 559.

80. D. C. Meyers, M. C. Jennings, and Edwin A. Fleishman, *Analysis of Computer Interactive Tests for Assigning Helicopter Pilots to Different Missions,* ARRO Technical Report #3075/R838 (Bethesda, MD: Advanced Research Resources Organization, 1988); Edwin A. Fleishman, "Some New Frontiers in Personnel Selection Research," *Personnel Psychology* 41 (1988), pp. 679–701.

81. Robert J. Sternberg, Richard K. Wagner, Wendy M. Williams, and Joseph A. Horvath, "Testing Common Sense," *American Psychologist* 50 (Nov. 1995), pp. 912–27.

82. Daniel Goleman, *Emotional Intelligence* (New York: Bantam Books, 1995); Sharon Nelton, "Emotions in the Workplace," *Nation's Business,* Feb. 1996, p. 25; Alan Farnham and Tim Carvell, "Managing Your Career/Special Report," *Fortune,* Jan. 15, 1996, p. 34.

83. Gordon Bain, E-mail correspondence to HRNET, May 21, 1995.

84. Michael J. Stevens and Michael A. Campion, "Staffing Teams: Development and Validation of the Teamwork-KSA Test" (paper presented at the Annual Meeting of the Society of Industrial and Organizational Psychology, May 1994); Michael J. Stevens and Michael A. Campion, "The Knowledge, Skill and Ability Requirements for Teamwork: Implications for Human Resource Management," *Journal of Management* 20 (1994), pp. 403–530.

85. Joyce Hogan, "Structure of Physical Performance in Occupational Tasks," *Journal of Applied Psychology* 76 (1991), pp. 495–507.

86. Edwin A. Fleishman, "Some New Frontiers in Personnel Selection Research," *Personnel Psychology* 41 (1988), pp. 679–701; Richard D. Arvey, Timothy E. Landon, Steven M. Nutting, and Scott E. Maxwell, "Development of Physical Ability Tests for Police Officers: A Construct Validation Approach," *Journal of Applied Psychology* [Monograph] 77, no. 6 (1992), pp. 996–1009; Joyce Hogan, "Physical Abilities," in *Handbook of Industrial-Organizational Psychology,* 2nd ed., ed. Marvin D. Dunnette and Leatta M. Hough (Palo Alto, CA: Consulting Psychologists Press, 1991), pp. 753–831.

87. Linda S. Gottredson, ed., "The *g* Factor in Employment," *Journal of Vocational Behavior* 29 (1986), pp. 293–450.

88. John A. Hartigan and Alexandra K. Wigdor, eds., *Fairness in Employment Testing,* (Washington, DC: National Academy Press, 1989); Daniel Seligman, "The Most Important Stat," *Fortune,* July 15, 1991, p. 126; Daniel Seligman, *A Question of Intelligence* (New York: Birch Lane Press, 1992).

89. Barry R. Blakley, Miguel Qui/at/nones, Marnie Swerdlin Crawford, and I. Ann Jago, "The Validity of Isometric Strength Tests," *Personnel Psychology* 47 (1994), pp. 247–74.

90. Arvey and Faley, *Fairness in Selecting Employees;* Hartigan and Wigdor, *Fairness in Employment Testing.*

91. Ramzi B. Baydoun and George A. Neuman, "The Future of the General Aptitude Test Battery (GATB) for Use in Public and Private Testing," *Journal of Business and Psychology* 7, no. 1 (Fall 1992), pp. 81–91.

92. Bureau of National Affairs, "Legal Questions about Job Aptitude Test Have Led to Its Demise in Most States," *Daily Labor Report,* Mar. 30, 1992, pp. 4–10; Niall A. Paul, "The Civil Rights Act of 1991: What Does It Really Accomplish?" *Employee Relations Law Journal* 17, no. 4 (Spring 1992), pp. 567–91; Hannah R. Rothstein and Michael A. McDaniel, "Differential Validity by Sex in Employment Settings," *Journal of Business and Psychology* 7, no. 1 (Fall 1992), pp. 45–62; Janet E. Helms, "Why Is There No Study of Cultural Equivalence in Standardized Cognitive Ability Testing?" *American Psychologist* 45, no. 9 (Sept. 1992), pp. 1083–1101; Susan Moses, "Gender Gap on Tests Examined at Meeting," *APA Monitor,* Dec. 1991, p. 38.

93. Gary Putka, "A Test for Every Task," *The Wall Street Journal,* Feb. 9, 1990, p. R19.

94. Sandy Sillup, "Applicant Screening Cuts Turnover Costs," *Personnel Journal,* May 1992, pp. 115–16.

95. Richard S. Barrett, "Employee Selection with the Performance Priority Survey," *Personnel Psychology* 48 (1995), pp. 653–62.

96. Fritz Drasgow et al., "Computerized Assessment," in *Research in Personnel and Human Resources Management* 11 (1993), pp. 163–206; Karen M. Barbera, Ann Marie Ryan, Laura Burris Desmarais, and Patricia Dyer, "Multimedia Employment Tests: Effects of Attitudes and Experiences on Validity" (paper presented at the Annual Conference of the Society for Industrial and Organizational Psychology, May 1995).

97. John E. Hunter and Rhonda Hunter, "The Validity and Utility of Alternative Predictors of Job Performance," *Psychological Bulletin* 96 (1984), pp. 72–98; Wayne F. Cascio and Neil Phillips, "Performance Testing: A Rose Among Thorns?" *Personnel Psychology* 30 (1979), pp. 187–97.

98. Cascio and Phillips, "Performance Testing"; Madeline E. Heilman, Richard F. Martell, and Michael C. Simon, "The Vagaries of Sex Bias: Conditions Regulating the Undervaluation, Equivaluation, and Overvaluation of Female Job Applicants," *Organizational Behavior and Human Decision Processes* 41 (1988), pp. 98–110.

99. Bureau of National Affairs, *Recruiting and Selection Procedures;* "Drug Testing Increases," *Human Resource Management News,* Feb. 18, 1989, p. 3; Craig Zwerling and James Ryan, "Preemployment Drug Screening, *Journal of Occupational Medicine* 34, no. 6 (June 1992), p. 595.

100. "Graduates Face Drug Tests in Joining Job Market," *The New York Times,* June 21, 1987, p. 29.

101. Andrew Kupfer, "Is Drug Testing Good or Bad?" *Fortune,* Dec. 19, 1988, pp. 133–40; *Human Resource Management News,* Jan. 13, 1990, p. 1; Zwerling and Ryan, "Preemployment Drug Testing"; Craig Zwerling, James Ryan, and E. J. Orav, "Costs and Benefits of Preemployment Drug Screening," *Journal of the American Medical Association* 267 (1992), pp. 91–93; Gatewood and Feild, *Human Resource Selection,* p. 638; Meyers, *Soroka* v. *Dayton Hudson Corp;* Deborah F. Crown and Joseph G. Rosse, "A Critical Review of the Assumptions Underlying Drug Testing," *Journal of Business and Psychology* 3, no. 1 (Fall 1988), pp. 22–41.

102. Milo Geyelin, "The Job Is Yours—Unless You Smoke," *The Wall Street Journal,* Apr. 21, 1989, p. B1.
103. Philip M. Boffey, "Spread of AIDS Is Abating, but Deaths Will Still Soar," *The New York Times,* Feb. 14, 1988, p. 36; "Few Companies Have Policies to Cover Employees with AIDS," *Resource* 6, no. 12, (Oct. 1987), pp. 6–7; Judy D. Olian, "AIDS Testing for Employment Purposes? Facts and Controversies," *Journal of Business and Psychology* 3, no. 2 (Winter 1988), pp. 135–53.
104. Judy D. Olian, "Genetic Screening for Employment Purposes," *Personnel Psychology* 37 (1984), pp. 423–38; Bureau of National Affairs, "Value of Genetic Testing Said Minimal for Gauging Workplace Risks," *BNA's Employee Relations Weekly,* Nov. 18, 1991, p. 1235.
105. James G. Frierson, "New Polygraph Test Limits," *Personnel Journal,* Dec. 1988, pp. 84–91.
106. Stephen Wermeil, "Justices Bar 'Fetal Protection' Policies," *The Wall Street Journal,* Mar. 21, 1991, p. B1.
107. Cynthia Crossen, "Bulemics Take Note: Personality Testing Is Entering the 80s," *The Wall Street Journal,* Sept. 13, 1989, p. A1; *Minnesota Multiphasic Personality Inventory-2,* (Minneapolis: University of Minnesota Press, 1989); Tina Adler, "Revision Brings Test into the 21st Century," *APA Monitor* 10, no. 11 (Nov. 1989), p. 2; Bureau of National Affairs, *Recruiting and Selection Procedures.*
108. Ernest Auerbach, "Not Your Type, but Right for the Job," *The Wall Street Journal,* Jan. 6, 1992, p. A14.
109. Wade Lambert, "Flunking Grade: Psychological Tests Designed to Weed Out Rogue Cops Get a 'D'," *The Wall Street Journal,* Sept. 11, 1995, pp. A1, A5.
110. Teresa M. Amabile, Karl G. Hill, Beth A. Hennessey, and Elizabeth M. Tighe, "The Work Preference Inventory: Assessing Intrinsic and Extrinsic Motivational Orientations," *Journal of Personality and Social Psychology* 66 (1994), pp. 960–67.
111. P. T. Costa, Jr., and R. R. McCrae, *NEO PI-R: Professional Manual* (Odessa, FL: Psychological Assessment Resources, 1992); Michael K. Mount and Murray R. Barrick, "The Big Five Personality Dimensions: Implications for Research and Practice in Human Resources Management," *Research in Personnel and Human Resources Management,* 13 (1995), pp. 153–200.
112. Patricia L. Kelley, Rick R. Jacobs, and James L. Farr, "Effects of Multiple Administrations of the MMPI for Employee Screening," *Personnel Psychology* 47 (1994), pp. 575–91; Allen Feingold, "Gender Differences in Personality: A Meta-Analysis," *Psychological Bulletin* 11 (1994), pp. 429–56; Michael K. Mount, Murray R. Barrick and J. Perkins Strauss, "Validity of Observer Ratings of the Big Five Personality Factors," *Journal of Applied Psychology* 79 (1994), pp. 272–80.
113. Daniel Seligman, "Searching for Integrity," *Fortune,* Mar. 8, 1993, p. 140; Paul R. Sackett, Laura R. Burris, and Christine Callahan, "Integrity Testing for Personnel Selection: An Update," *Personnel Psychology* 42, no. 3 (Autumn 1989), pp. 491–529; Mount and Barrick, "The Big Five Personality Dimensions," p. 276.

114. Sackett et al., "Integrity Testing for Personnel Selection."

115. Jeffrey A. Mello, "Personality Screening in Employment: Balancing Information Gathering and the Law," *Labor Law Review,* Oct. 1995, pp. 622–25.

116. Mount and Barrick, "The Big Five Personality Dimensions," p. 169. Deniz S. Ones, Chockalingam Viswesvaran, and Frank L. Schmidt, "Meta-Analysis of Integrity Test Validities: Findings and Implications for Personnel Selection and Theories of Job Performance" [Monograph] *Journal of Applied Psychology* 78 (1993), pp. 679–703; Wayne J. Camara and D. L. Schneider, "Integrity Tests: Facts and Unresolved Issues," *American Psychologist* 49 (1994), pp. 112–19; Ruth Kanfer, Phillip L. Ackerman, Todd Murtha, and Maynard Goff, "Personality and Intelligence in Industrial and Organizational Psychology," chap. 26 in Donald H. Saklofsky and Moshe Zeidner, *International Handbook of Personality and Intelligence* (New York: Plenum Press, 1995), pp. 577–602.

117. Joseph Zeidner, Cecil Johnson, Edward Schmitz, and Roy Nord, *The Economic Benefits of Predicting Job Performance,* IDA paper P-2241 (Alexandria, VA: Institute for Defense Analyses, Sept. 1989).

118. Lee J. Cronbach and Goldine C. Gleser, *Psychological Tests and Personnel Decisions,* 2nd ed. (Urbana: University of Illinois Press, 1965).

119. William E. Alley and Melody M. Darby, "Estimating the Benefits of Personnel Selection and Classification: An Extension of the Brogden Table," *Educational and Psychological Measurement* 55 (Dec. 1995), pp. 938–58.

120. Bureau of National Affairs, *Employee Selection Procedures.*

121. Alan Deutschman, "The Managing Wisdom of High Tech Superstars," *Fortune,* Oct. 17, 1994, pp. 197–205.

122. Wayne F. Cascio, James Outtz, Sheldon Zedeck, and Irwin L. Goldstein, "Statistical Implications of Six Methods of Test Score Use in Personnel Selection," *Human Performance* 8 (1995), pp. 133–64.

123. Patrick M. Wright, K. Michelle Kacmar, Gary C. McMahan, and Kevin Deleeuw, "P=f(M × A): Cognitive Ability as a Moderator of the Relationship between Personality and Job Performance," *Journal of Management* 21 (1995), pp. 1129–39; Anthony T. Dalessio and Todd A. Silverhart, "Combining Biodata Test and Interview Information: Predicting Decisions and Performance Criteria," *Personnel Psychology* 47 (1994), pp. 303–15.

124. Kenneth J. Calhoun, "Automated Objectivity for Subjective Hiring Decisions," *Computers in Personnel,* Winter 1989, pp. 5–10.

125. Norma R. Fritz, "Culture Clash," *Personnel,* Apr. 1988, pp. 6–7; William J. Hampton, "How Does Japan Inc. Pick Its American Workers?" *Business Week,* Oct. 3, 1988, pp. 84–85.

126. Gary Dessler, "Value-Based Hiring Builds Commitment," *Personnel Journal,* Nov. 1993, pp. 98–102; Saltzman, "Job Applicant Screening by a Japanese Transplant . . .", Chuck Cosentino, John Allen, and Richard Wellins, "Choosing the Right People," *HR Magazine,* March 1990, pp. 66–70.

127. Robert D. Gatewood and Hubert S. Feild, *Human Resource Selection,* 3rd ed., (Fort Worth, TX: Dryden Press, 1994), chaps. 3–5; Herbert G. Heneman III and Robert L. Heneman, *Staffing Organizations* (Middleton, WI: Mendota House, 1994).

128. Paul R. Sackett, Sheldon Zedeck, and Larry Fogli, "Relations between Measures of Typical and Maximum Job Performance," *Journal of Applied Psychology* 73, no. 3 (1988), pp. 482–86. Charles L. Hulin, Rebecca A. Henry, and S. L. Noon, "Adding a Dimension: Time as a Factor in Predictive Relationships," *Psychological Bulletin* 107 (1990), pp. 328–40; Henry Hulin, "Stability of Skilled Performance across Time: Some Generalizations and Limitations on Utilities," *Journal of Applied Psychology* 72, no. 3 (1987), pp. 457–62; Rebecca A. Henry and Charles L. Hulin, "Changing Validities: Ability-Performance Relations and Utilities," *Journal of Applied Psychology* 74, no. 2 (1989), pp. 365–67; P. L. Ackerman, "Within-Task Intercorrelations of Skilled Performance: Implications for Predicting Individual Differences?" *Journal of Applied Psychology* 74, no. 2 (1989), pp. 360–64. Herbert H. Meyer, "Predicting Supervisory Ratings versus Promotional Progress in Test Validation Studies," *Journal of Applied Psychology,* 72, no. 4 (1987), pp. 696–97.

129. Timothy A. Judge and Gerald R. Ferris, "The Elusive Criterion of Fit in Employment Interview Decisions," *Human Resource Planning* 15 (1992), pp. 47–67; Clifford E. Montgomery, "Organizational Fit Is Key to Job Success," *HR Magazine,* Jan. 1996, pp. 94–96.

130. Gerald V. Barrett, James S. Phillips, and Ralph A. Alexander, "Concurrent and Predictive Validity Designs: A Critical Reanalysis," *Journal of Applied Psychology* 66 (1981), pp. 1–6; Neal Schmitt, Richard Z. Gooding, Raymond A. Noe, and Michael Kirsch, "Meta-Analyses of Validity Studies Published between 1964–1982 and the Investigation of Study Characteristics," *Personnel Psychology* 37 (1984), pp. 407–22.

131. Robert M. Guion, "Synthetic Validity in a Small Company: A Demonstration," *Personnel Psychology* 18 (1965), pp. 49–63; John W. Hamilton and Terry L. Dickenson, "Comparison of Several Procedures for Generating J-Coefficients," *Journal of Applied Psychology* 72, no. 1 (1987), pp. 49–54.

132. See, for example, Frank L. Schmidt, I. Gast-Rosenberg, and John E. Hunter, "Validity Generalization Results for Computer Programmers," *Journal of Applied Psychology* 65 (1980), pp. 643–61; Frank L. Schmidt, John E. Hunter, and Kenneth Pearlman, "Task Differences as Moderators of Aptitude Test Validity in Selection: A Red Herring," *Journal of Applied Psychology* 66 (1981), pp. 166–85; Frank L. Schmidt, John E. Hunter, Kenneth Pearlman, and G. S. Shane, "Further Tests of Schmidt-Hunter Bayesian Validity Generalization Procedure," *Personnel Psychology* 32 (1979), pp. 257–81; N. S. Raju and Michael J. Burke, "Two New Procedures for Studying Validity Generalization," *Journal of Applied Psychology* 68 (1983), pp. 382–95; Michael J. Burke, "Validity Generalization: A Review and Critique of the Correlation Model," *Personnel Psychology* 37 (1984), pp. 93–116; Frank L. Schmidt and John E. Hunter, "A Within-Setting Empirical Test of the Situational Specificity Hypothesis in Personnel Selection," *Personnel Psychology* 37 (1984),

pp. 317–26; Frank L. Schmidt, Benjamin P. Ocasio, Joseph M. Hillery, and John E. Hunter, "Further Within-Setting Empirical Tests of the Situational Specificity Hypothesis in Personnel Selection," *Personnel Psychology* 38 (1985), pp. 509–24.

133. Ralph A. Alexander, Kenneth P. Carson, George M. Alliger, and Steven F. Cronshaw, "Empirical Distributions of Range Restricted SDx in Validity Studies," *Journal of Applied Psychology* 74, no. 2 (1989), pp. 253–58; Robert M. Madigan, K. Dow Scott, Diana L. Deadrick, and Jil A. Stoddard, "Employment Testing: The U.S. Job Service Is Spearheading a Revolution," *Personnel Administrator,* Sept. 1986, pp. 62–69.

134. Calvin C. Hoffman and Sandra C. Lamartine, "Transporting Physical Ability Test Validity via the Position Analysis Questionnaire" (paper presented at the Annual Meeting of the Society for Industrial and Organizational Psychology, May 1995).

135. American Psychological Association, Division of Industrial/Organizational Psychology, *Principles for the Validation and Use of Personnel Selection Procedures* (Washington, DC: American Psychological Association, 1979).

136. Todd J. Maurer and Ralph A. Alexander, "Methods of Improving Employment Test Critical Scores Derived by Judging Test Content: A Review and Critique," *Personnel Psychology* 45 (1992), pp. 727–62.

137. M. D. Dunnette, *Predicting Job Performance of Electrical Power Plant Operators* (Minneapolis: Personnel Decision Research Institute, 1983); Elaine D. Pulakos, Walter C. Borman and Leatta M. Hough, "Test Validation for Scientific Understanding: Two Demonstrations of an Approach to Studying Predictor-Criterion Linkages," *Personnel Psychology* 41 (1988), pp. 703–15; Frank L. Schmidt, John E. Hunter, Paul R. Croll, and Robert C. McKenzie, "Estimation of Employment Test Validities by Expert Judgment," *Journal of Applied Psychology* 68, no. 4 (1983), pp. 590–601.

138. Bureau of National Affairs, *Employee Selection Procedures.*

139. Lawrence S. Kleiman and Robert H. Faley, "The Implications of Professional and Legal Guidelines for Court Decisions Involving Criterion-Related Validity: A Review and Analysis," *Personnel Psychology* 38 (1985), pp. 803–31.

140. H. C. Taylor and J. T. Russell, "The Relationship of Validity Coefficients to the Practical Effectiveness of Tests in Selection: Discussion and Tables, *Journal of Applied Psychology* 23 (1939), pp. 565–78.

141. Boudreau, "Utility Analysis."

142. Kevin R. Murphy, George C. Thornton III, and Kristin Prue, "Influence of Job Characteristics on the Acceptability of Employee Drug Testing," *Journal of Applied Psychology* 76, no. 3 (1991), pp. 447–53; Joseph G. Rosse, Richard C. Ringer, and Janice L. Miller, "Personality and Drug Testing: An Exploration of the Perceived Fairness of Alternatives to Urinalysis" (paper presented at the National Meeting of the Academy of Management, Las Vegas, NV, Aug. 1992).

143. S. W. Gilliland, "Fairness from the Applicant's Perspective: Reactions to Employee Selection Procedures," *International Journal of Selection and*

*Assessment* 3 (1995), pp. 11–19; Richard D. Arvey and Paul R. Sackett, "Fairness in Selection: Current Developments and Perspectives," in Neal Schmitt and Walter C. Borman, eds., *Personnel Selection in Organizations* (San Francisco: Freeman, 1993), pp. 171–202.

144. David A. Kravitz, Veronica Stinson, and Tracy L. Chavez, "Evaluations of Tests Used for Making Selection and Promotion Decisions," *International Journal of Selection and Assessment,* in press.
145. Stephen Wermiel, "Workers Hurt by Affirmative Action May Sue," *The Wall Street Journal,* June 13, 1989, p. B1.
146. Kevin R. Murphy, Kevin Osten, and Brett Myors, "Modeling the Effects of Banding in Personnel Selection," *Personnel Psychology* 48 (1995), pp. 61–84.
147. This case study is based on information from David E. Bowen, Gerald E. Ledford, Jr., and Barry R. Nathan, "Hiring for the Organization, Not the Job," *Academy of Management Executive* 5, no. 4 (1991), pp. 35–50.

# Employee Separations, Workforce Reduction and Retention

The February 26, 1996, cover story of *Newsweek* paints a grim picture. It carries photos of the CEOs of Digital Equipment, Scott Paper, AT&T, IBM, Chemical/Chase Bank, GTE, Delta Airlines, McDonnell Douglas, General Motors, Sears, Philip Morris, Boeing, and NYNEX, many of whom earn millions a year. Each company is experiencing big profit increases. And each company is laying off tens of thousands of employees. Al Dunlap, former CEO of Scott Paper, reportedly pocketed $100 million after cutting 11,000 jobs in 1994, and merging the company with Kimberly-Clark. "Chain Saw Al" Dunlap was the only CEO willing to talk to *Newsweek* about the apparent paradox. His explanation is given in Exhibit 8.1. Do you agree?

Are these layoffs justified? Are such job cuts more like preventive surgery than bloodletting? Do layoffs actually increase profitability? Are employee reductions through firings, layoffs, and voluntary early-retirement incentives an effective way to cut labor costs? How do they affect those who survive the cuts? What are the costs, benefits, and alternatives? What are the causes and costs of separations that *aren't* initiated by the company? How do you retain your best performers? As an investor, an employee, or a manager, how would you decide whether layoffs, dismissals, retirements, and quits are helping or hurting an organization?

## WORKFORCE REDUCTION AND RETENTION

Downsizing, rightsizing, removing the deadwood, windows to early retirement—these phrases have become increasingly familiar as companies around the world face greater pressures to reduce their costs. This chapter discusses how organizations manage the processes by which employees leave the organization.

## A DIAGNOSTIC APPROACH TO WORKFORCE REDUCTION/RETENTION

As shown in Exhibit 8.2, the staffing process does not end when employees are hired. If an organization loses its valuable employees, improved recruitment and external selection do little good because there are too few long-term employees or their quality is insufficient. The pattern of separations from the organization affects the quantity and quality of employees as directly as the pattern of who is recruited and hired. Evidence shows that simply reducing separations can often be as counterproductive as allowing the best employees to leave. The key is to view separations as an integrated part of the staffing process, and to manage the separation process so that it complements the pattern of recruiting and selection.[2] In this way, both efficiency and equity goals can be achieved.

*Employee separations* are terminations of employment of permanent or temporary workers initiated by either the employee or the employer.[1]

## EXHIBIT 8.1 CEO Dunlap Explains Layoffs at Scott Paper Company

Albert Dunlap has become the poster boy for the folks who say that CEOs have gone too far. The 58-year-old former CEO of Scott Paper, known to detractors as "Chain Saw Al," cut 11,000 jobs in 1994. After merging the company with Kimberly-Clark, he walked away with about $100 million in salary, stock profits and other perks. Dunlap previously downsized seven other companies, including Diamond International and Lily-Tulip. When NEWSWEEK asked more than 50 CEOs of large American companies to discuss corporate restructuring, only Dunlap was willing to talk. Here's what he had to say:

When journalists and politicians spout off about corporate downsizing, it's the Al Dunlaps of the world who tend to get the blame. We're painted as villains, but we're not. We're more like doctors. We know it's painful to operate, but it's the only way to keep the patient from dying. Take the restructuring at Scott. We had to fire 35 percent of the work force. It was a difficult task. Coming from a working-class family (my father was a union steward), I know what it's like when someone in the family loses a job. But while we had to cut some jobs, we were able to give 65 percent of the work force a more secure future than they might have otherwise had. And Scott's stockholders came out $6.5 billion to the better.

So why are shareholders so important to workers? By doing a good job for them, we're encouraging them to invest, to build new plants and create new products. At the end of the day, that will mean more and better jobs down the road. And that's the point people need to remember: the only way corporate America is going to do right by its workers is to compete. And in order to compete, companies need to become efficient. That means if you have workers for whom you don't have a real job, you can't keep them on the payroll.

Let me put this in some historical perspective. In the '70s America lost its position as a leader in global business. Look at the industries we once had that barely exist: shoes, machine tools and consumer electronics. Don't blame today's executives who are having to face up to the tough decisions—blame the executives who created bloated corporations that are noncompetitive. People are always criticizing companies that bring in record profits and then announce layoffs. What they don't realize is that if an organization doesn't make record profits, it doesn't have the money to invest in new plants and new technologies.

That's not to say that I don't believe in CEOs' being accountable to their workers. I think a CEO has an obligation to communicate with workers and prepare them for the inevitable. Before the restructuring at Scott, I personally went around the world and talked to people on the shop floors. One of the things we told them was that we weren't keeping the elitist tools of corporate America at the expense of workers. Our biggest cutback was to sell the 750,000-square-foot corporate headquarters and downsize 71 percent of the corporate staff. At one plant, the workers actually applauded me. People are pretty intelligent if you tell them what's going on and explain why you're doing what you're doing.

On the other hand, the politicians don't seem to be getting the message. They pander to the public and polarize people. And they try to tell American industry how to conduct its business. The job of industry is to become competitive—not to be a social experiment. God help us if we pass legislation to make American companies less productive and compromise our global competitiveness. Then it won't be a case of a relatively small number of people losing their jobs. It will be huge numbers losing their jobs—and the death of the American free-enterprise system as we know it.

Source: Allen Sloan, "The Hit Men," *Newsweek,* Feb. 26, 1996, p. 48. From *Newsweek,* Feb. 26 © 1996, Newsweek, Inc. All rights reserved. Reprinted by permission.

## Efficiency

Employee turnover (losing and replacing employees who quit) is expensive. This is often organizations' view of separations; they see "dollars walking out the door." Later, we show just how expensive employee separations can be. IBM's U.S. workforce reductions cost $105,000 per head in 1992, and analysts estimated that cutting 75,000 more employees cost $120,000 per head, or $9 million in 1993.[3] Yet, organizations don't always want to keep every employee.

EXHIBIT 8.2 The Staffing Process as a Series of Filters

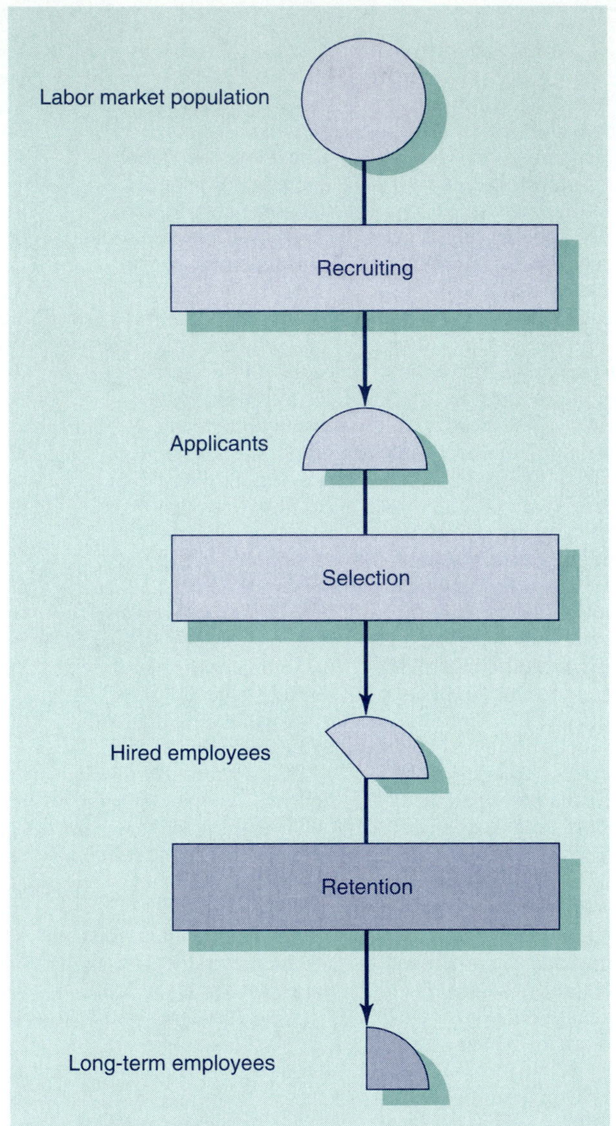

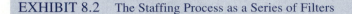

We are all too familiar with businesses that have felt compelled to dismiss or lay off employees to reduce costs. As you saw in the introduction, sometimes drastic workforce reductions reduce costs, increase profits, and raise stock prices. Clearly, if the right workers leave, an organization can be more competitive. Therefore, organizations need to look beyond simply reducing turnover in diagnosing their human resource activities. They must determine the right amount of employee separation and carefully consider when it is more efficient to allow or encourage employees to leave compared with when it is better to retain them. The key factor is not how many employees are leaving, but how valuable are the employees who are retained.

## Equity

Employee separations can have profound effects on individual self-esteem and security. Losing a job can be one of the most anguishing experiences. Is it fair to lay off employees who did nothing wrong and served loyally for many years? How much notice should employees get if they are to be laid off? What constitutes appropriate grounds for firing an employee? What if separation patterns cause an organization to lose the minorities and females that it has worked so hard to recruit and select? Government agencies and courts pay close attention to the legality and fairness of separation policies and potential discrimination based on race, gender, age, or disability (see Chapter Two). Some evidence suggests that organizations are so fearful of being sued for wrongful dismissal that they are reluctant to hire for fear they may later have to dismiss employees. Surviving employees and job applicants make judgments about an organization's attractiveness based on its approach to employee separations.[4]

## SEPARATIONS INITIATED BY EMPLOYEES OR EMPLOYERS: WHO DECIDES?

Different kinds of separations occur depending on whether the employee or the employer decides to terminate the employment relationship.

*Resignations* are separation decisions initiated by the employee. They include *quits* (employee decisions to leave the organization when retirement is not a major factor) and *retirements* (employee decisions to leave the organization that are affected by benefits and incentives associated with retirement).

*Dismissals* are separation decisions initiated by the employer. *Discharges* occur for individual-specific reasons, such as incompetence, violation of rules, dishonesty, laziness, absenteeism, insubordination, and failure to pass the probationary period. *Layoffs* occur because of an organizational need to reduce the number of employees, rather than the behavior of a particular individual.

As you can imagine, the line between the categories is frequently very faint. Employees often quit rather than face being discharged, and employers often provide early retirement incentives that include help in finding new jobs or lucrative severance pay arrangements to induce employees to retire. Both employees and employers affect the decision to terminate the employment relationship. Even more important, human resource activities affect employee decisions to separate. One study of high-technology companies in San Francisco showed that the companies' performance-based pay systems aggressively rewarded top performers, aggressively penalized very poor performers, and differentiated little among moderate performers. The result was that the very high and moderately low performers tended to stay, while the very low and moderately high performers tended to leave. The employers' decisions about how to structure the pay system directly affected employees' decisions about whether to stay or leave.[5] As Chapters Six and Seven showed, employers' decisions about how to recruit and select employees often affect the employees' propensity to leave or stay after they have been hired. Though the line may be faint, the consequences are real. One study of U.S. youth showed that wage levels went up for people who initiated their departure, and down for employer-initiated departures. Being fired reduced wages more than being laid off. Among those who said they quit for "economic reasons," men saw no significant effect on subsequent wages, but women saw their wages drop.[6]

## MEASURING THE SEPARATION RATE

Virtually every organization measures the quantity, or percentage, of separations. Many organizations try to reduce this percentage to zero or to match the rate with that of competitors. The Bureau of National Affairs reports monthly turnover rates computer with the following formula:

$$\frac{\text{Number of total separations during month}}{\text{Average number of employees during month}} \times 100$$

The separation rate per month in the United States is generally about 1 percent, implying a yearly separation rate of about 12 percent. Separation rates are higher in small companies in nonmanufacturing industries, and in the Northeast and West. In addition to measuring total separations, organizations could measure quit, retirement, discharge and layoff rates separately. Some organizations attempt to distinguish *unavoidable* separations caused by factors beyond the organization's control from *avoidable* separations affected by organizational policies. Others attempt to distinguish *dysfunctional* separations that involve losses of valued employees from *functional* separations that involve losses easily replaced or remove the least-valued employees.

Like all information, the value of measuring the separation rate depends on its usefulness in improving managerial decisions, as Chapter Five showed. The diagnostic approach emphasizes optimizing both the level and *pattern* of separations to achieve the correct balance between positive and negative separation effects. Thus, organizations must determine who uses the separation information, what decisions it is designed to affect, and what type of separation information best supports those decisions. Different organizations or organizational units probably need different separation measures. *Benchmarks,* or comparisons to industry norms, are useful for some organizations; for others, such comparisons have little significance. It depends on the relationship between separations and workforce value.

## BEYOND THE SEPARATION RATE: WORKFORCE VALUE

The idea that separations are bad or only useful in reducing labor costs pervades much of management thinking. In reality managing separations requires taking a more integrated approach. However, the basic idea is simple: The key to managing separations is to focus on who is retained rather than on who is leaving. The pattern of *retentions* determines the affect of separations on efficiency and equity goals.[7]

Exhibit 8.3 presents information about a hypothetical organization unit with 20 employees. We assume for the moment that each worker's value is represented by the amount of sales generated, though productivity is usually much more complex. The second column shows the sales figure for the most recent year. The third and fourth columns show the seniority and protected-group status of each employee. The organization contains eight protected-group members, or 40 percent.

Suppose the organization decides it must lay off 25 percent of its workforce by using either past performance or seniority. Removing the five poorest-performing employees (Oliver, Anne, Enrique, Fred, and Barney) produces a retained workforce with 15 employees averaging $30,000 in yearly sales. The

**EXHIBIT 8.3** Separation and Retention Effects on a Hypothetical Workforce

| Salesperson | Yearly Sales | Years of Seniority | Protected Group |
|---|---|---|---|
| Jeremy | $ 40,000 | 8 | No |
| Rudolfo | 40,000 | 8 | No |
| Maggie | 40,000 | 2 | Yes |
| Manuel | 40,000 | 6 | Yes |
| Herbert | 40,000 | 6 | No |
| Karl | 30,000 | 8 | No |
| Donald | 30,000 | 4 | Yes |
| Lindsey | 30,000 | 8 | Yes |
| Ralph | 30,000 | 6 | No |
| Beuford | 30,000 | 4 | No |
| Arthur | 20,000 | 8 | No |
| Dorothy | 20,000 | 2 | Yes |
| James | 20,000 | 6 | No |
| Bertram | 20,000 | 4 | No |
| Jesse | 20,000 | 4 | Yes |
| Oliver | 10,000 | 2 | No |
| Anne | 10,000 | 2 | Yes |
| Enrique | 10,000 | 2 | Yes |
| Fred | 10,000 | 6 | No |
| Barney | 10,000 | 4 | No |
| Total | $500,000 | 100 | |
| Average | $ 25,000 | 5 | |

average employee value has gone up, and there are still six protected group members left, so the representation rate is still 40 percent. In simple terms, efficiency has risen while equity has been maintained. Seniority-based layoffs would remove the five least-senior employees (Maggie, Dorothy, Oliver, Anne, and Enrique), producing a retained workforce with 15 employees averaging $27,333 in sales. The average employee value is not as high as with performance-based layoffs, and only four protected-group members (representing 26.6 percent of the workforce) would be left. Both efficiency and equity are less than with performance-based layoffs, though layoffs based on seniority may seem fairer and more objective.

Finally, suppose the organization chooses not to lay off employees, but to rely on resignations to reduce the workforce. If the best-performing salespeople have the most employment opportunities, the 5 highest performers (Jeremy, Rudolfo, Maggie, Herbert, and Manuel) may decide to quit, leaving a retained workforce of 15 people whose average sales level is only $20,000. The representation rate for protected groups would be 6 out of 15, so the representation rate is unchanged. Efficiency has fallen dramatically, though equity is the same.

The point is that evaluating employee separations is not simply a matter of counting the number of employees who leave, or adding up the savings in salary costs when the workforce is reduced. The productivity, diversity, and other characteristics of the retained employees continue to affect the organization well into the future. Evidence suggests that how employees leave an organization is interpreted by other organizations as a signal of their value. One study found that the wage level of workers laid off was no different from workers dismissed due to closing a plant. However, those displaced through layoff had longer unemployment and obtained jobs with lower starting wages.[8] Perhaps other employers assume that organizations lay off their worst employees, but that everyone must go when plants close. As you read the following sections on managing the different kinds of employee separations, keep in mind these effects, so that you can better understand the consequences of managing separations well.

## MANAGING RESIGNATIONS

It matters when people quit. When IBM acquired Lotus in 1995, part of the value it paid reflected the management and creative skills of Jim Manzi and other top Lotus managers. Yet, by early 1996, Manzi and two other top Lotus officers had left IBM, raising questions about the future value of the merger.[9] The day that Jerome York, IBM's chief financial officer, left IBM for Chrysler, the market capitalization (the value of outstanding stock) of IBM fell by $1.3 billion while that of Chrysler rose by $1.3 billion.[10] As Chapter Four showed, employees with more positive work attitudes are less likely to quit or retire; both quits and retirements are related to other forms of withdrawal behavior (absence, shirking, etc.). Here, we treat the two types of separations individually to highlight the different tools available to manage them effectively.

### Quits

The term *turnover* is often used synonymously with the term *quits.* However, turnover implies that the quit will subsequently be replaced (i.e., the organization turns over the position to a new person).[11] To avoid confusing issues of selecting replacements with issues of managing separations, we use the term *quit* to refer to the employee's leaving the organization, regardless of whether the vacancy is subsequently filled.

> WHAT DO YOU THINK?
>
> Though managers often lament the fact that human resources are "soft" and not readily measured in financial terms, the effect of Jerome York's move from IBM to Chrysler suggests markets do evaluate some people movements. What do you think the financial analysts had in mind when they bid Chrysler's value up by $1.3 billion, and IBM's down by $1.3 billion?

#### The Decision to Quit

What makes someone want to leave a job and organization? This question has fascinated industrial psychologists and others for many years.[12] Exhibit 8.4 shows a model of the employee decision to quit. Notice how the quit decision is influenced by many factors, some of which are not easily controlled by the organization, such as unemployment rates, kinship or family responsibilities, and the visibility of other organizations. However, many factors are influenced by organizations. Indeed, virtually every human resource activity influences the employee decision to quit or stay, including job design, recruitment that creates expectations, career planning and promotion opportunities, pay levels, investments in training, and the perceived justice of procedures. These factors affect the decision to quit because they affect the individual's job satisfaction,

## EXHIBIT 8.4 The Employee's Decision to Quit

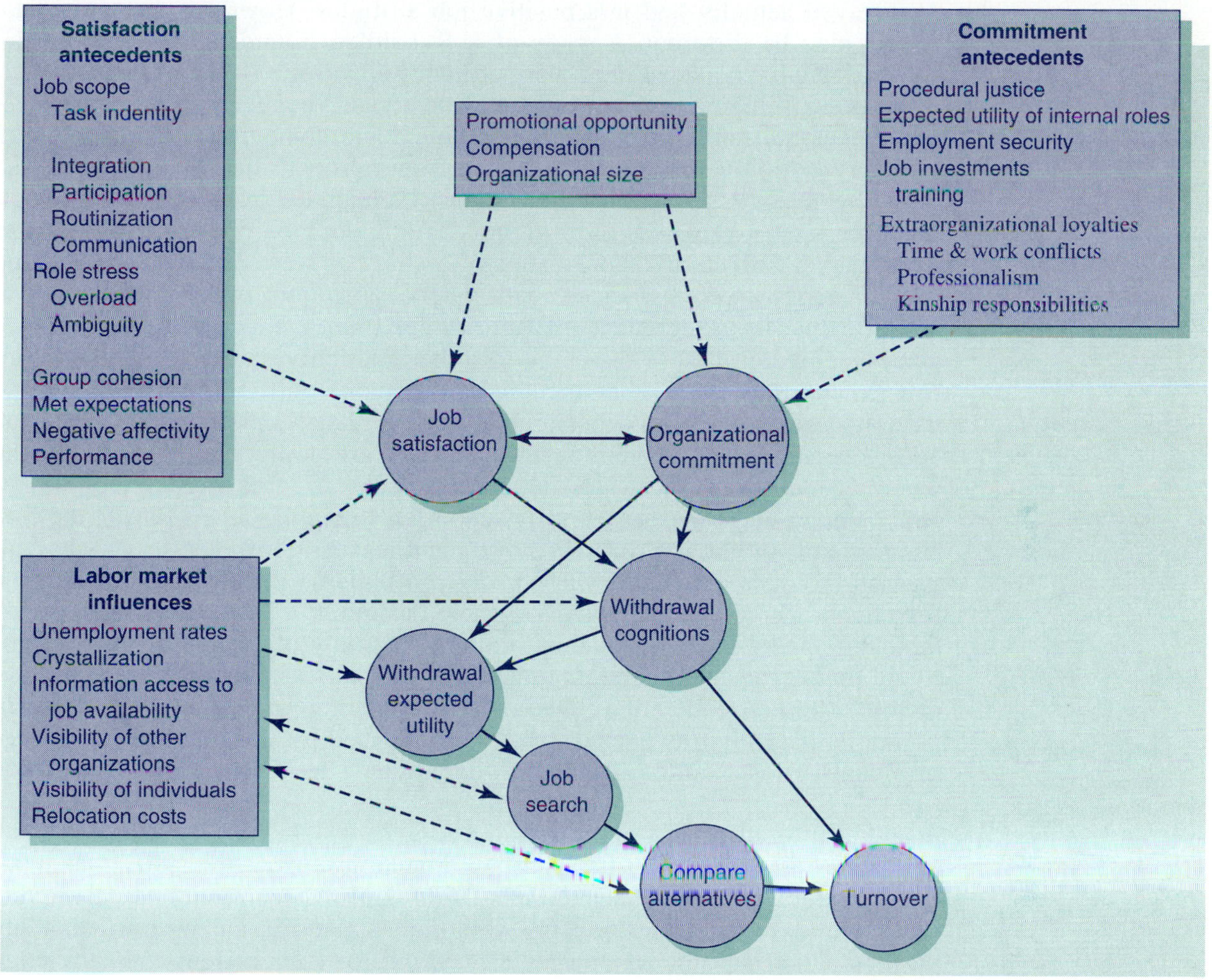

**Satisfaction antecedents**
Job scope
Task indentity
Integration
Participation
Routinization
Communication
Role stress
Overload
Ambiguity
Group cohesion
Met expectations
Negative affectivity
Performance

Promotional opportunity
Compensation
Organizational size

**Commitment antecedents**
Procedural justice
Expected utility of internal roles
Employment security
Job investments
training
Extraorganizational loyalties
Time & work conflicts
Professionalism
Kinship responsibilities

**Labor market influences**
Unemployment rates
Crystallization
Information access to job availability
Visibility of other organizations
Visibility of individuals
Relocation costs

Job satisfaction
Organizational commitment
Withdrawal cognitions
Withdrawal expected utility
Job search
Compare alternatives
Turnover

Source: Rodger W. Griffeth and Peter W. Hom, "The Employee Turnover Process," *Research in Personnel and Human Resources Management,* 1995, vol. 13, p. 255.

commitment to the organization, tendency to have "withdrawal cognitions" (thoughts of leaving), and their comparison between the value or "utility" of leaving and staying. In turn, these factors lead people to search, compare alternatives, and then perhaps to quit.

This general model has been corroborated by a great deal of research.[13] It describes the behavior of top executives, who search much more than they actually leave, and whose job satisfaction and perceived career prospects drive their decisions just as they do the rest of us. It applies to *repatriates,* managers returning from assignments overseas, who were more likely to leave if they felt there was no clear recognition or clear career paths and rewards for their overseas experience.[14] A study of Dutch workers between the ages of 18 and 26 found that attitudes also can be affected *after* leaving jobs. Those who left voluntarily had more positive job attitudes four years later in their new job, those who left involuntarily had about the same attitude level, and those who stayed actually had less positive job attitudes. However, the immediate effects may be different. A study of U.S. soldiers found that those who decided to reenlist adjusted their work attitudes upward to fit their decision.[15]

Quits are higher in times of low unemployment. Younger workers with fewer dependents quit more often, and biographical and demographic characteristics generally exhibit a strong ability to predict quit propensities. Studies have also shown fewer quits in unionized situations. Perhaps unions give employees alternative ways to express their dissatisfaction, such as grievance procedures (see Chapter Fifteen on labor relations). A study of New Zealand nurses found that separations were associated with intentions to quit, being unmarried, and being trained in a technical institute rather than a hospital.[16] Among U.S. nurses, some quit before searching for other alternatives, and their general desire to withdraw from work included thoughts of quitting and searching, so these may not always be sequential. It appears that people may leave one job before securing another either because they are compelled to abandon the workplace or because it's easier to find a new job after leaving the old one. Finally, among these nurses, job satisfaction fell to similar levels during the first eight months on the job for *both* stayers and leavers. However, leavers had increased thoughts of withdrawal, perceived a higher value of withdrawing, job search, and perceived alternatives as more desirable.[17] The relationships in Exhibit 8.4 appear to hold up across cultures; a study of Singapore accountants found that organizational commitment and job satisfaction were the main predictors of turnover intentions. Dissatisfaction with upward mobility is even important to very high-level executives, as evidenced by several IBM senior vice presidents who left after learning they did not have a shot at becoming CEO.[18]

### Implications for Reducing Quits

What does all this suggest for managing human resources? Organizations interested in reducing the number of quits might consider increasing pay, clarifying roles and job requirements, making work more satisfying, and ensuring that employees understand the advantages of working for their current company compared with moving elsewhere. Factors used to recruit and select employees, such as biographical information and realistic job previews (discussed in Chapters Six and Seven), have also predicted future quits. A study summarizing 20 experiments that used either job enrichment or realistic job previews (RJPs) to reduce separation rates found that RJPs improved separation rates by an average of 9 percent, while job enrichment improved them by an average of 17 percent.[19] Companies often try to find out why people are quitting by interviewing them before they leave. One survey found that 84 percent of companies conducted *exit interviews* with separating employees to discover their reasons for quitting.[20]

Creative approaches to reducing quits abound, especially where organizations must invest heavily in training employees and lose that investment when they leave prematurely. At Merrill Lynch, newly hired brokers receive a certificate worth $100,000 if they stay with the firm for 10 years and perform satisfactorily. KPMG Peat Marwick offers workers appreciation services such as dry cleaning pickup at the office and free weekend baby-sitting during the tax season. Continental Insurance Company sets up coaching relationships between young employees and experienced managers to help the younger employees better understand and commit to the organization.[21] Sometimes these arrangements are called "golden handcuffs" because they creative valuable incentives to tie the employee to the organization. Many companies make such effective counteroffers when key people are being recruited by search firms that one search firm mails its candidates a list of "10 reasons not to consider a counteroffer."[22] Maybe Dave Letterman had such a list when he left NBC.

### Implications for the Quality of the Retained Employees

Most organizations focus only on reducing the quantity (or rate) of employee quits, to reduce the costs incurred when employees separate. But the pattern of separations and retentions may be much more significant. A the earlier example showed, it makes a big difference whether an organization is losing high performers, who are hard to replace, or low performers. Also, workforce diversity can be significantly affected by the pattern of quits.

Though research suggests that the lower performers tend to quit, the results are mixed and some studies have found higher performers among the leavers. *Business Week* laments the brain drain among top managers at ailing U.S. companies. Earlier, we discussed research showing that rewarding extreme performance causes very good performers and moderately poor performers to stay. Among university faculty, when performance is measured by publication rate the high-performing untenured professors leave less often, but the high-performing tenured professors leave more often.[23] That may explain why untenured professors are always pounding on their word processors when students show up for office hours. Do chief executive officers go stale if they don't quit? Evidence is limited and mixed. A study of Canadian chief executive officers found that organizations with long-tenured CEOs were less likely to align strategy with the demands of the environment, and thus less likely to perform well financially, than organizations headed by shorter-tenure CEOs. However, another study of banks found that the CEOs quit less often in banks with better stock market returns.[24]

It's not clear whether merely paying more will enhance the quality of the workforce. A simulation of teacher quality showed that raising pay alone had little effect on teacher qualifications, but that raising pay for the best-qualified teachers and carefully selecting teachers based on qualifications could create significant increases in quality. Only under these conditions did the best people apply for teaching jobs and, once hired, stay on the job.[25] A study of 4,000 top managers in one company showed that over 1,000 separated during a three-year period, and that the highest performers were much more likely to leave if they didn't receive high pay increases. Cost-benefit analysis revealed that if the company had given top performers very high raises, this would indeed have increased the four-year salary costs by about $3 million a year. However, by retaining more of the high performers, the total value of the workforce would increase enough to offset this cost and produce a net return of up to $15 million over the four years.[26]

Not only the performance but also the attitudes of retained employees might be affected by quits. A study of university and city government employees in the United States found that those who stayed at their jobs felt greater personal loss and greater happiness for a departing colleague who left for reasons unrelated to the job. Stayers also felt less competitive in the labor market when a co-worker left for job-related reasons.[27]

Can employees be prohibited from going to work for competitors? Peter Bonyhard, a star engineer at IBM for five years, was working on developing disk drives when he left to take a more lucrative position at Seagate Technology. The position was—you guessed it—leader of a team developing disk drives. IBM successfully sued for an injunction to prevent Bonyhard from working on disk-drive development at Seagate, but the injunction was lifted on appeal.[28] Agreements to prevent departing employees from entering into competitive arrangements are called *restrictive covenants*. They typically prohibit revealing trade secrets and restrict a person from working in a particular "trade," for a particular time, in a specified geographic area. However, the law is vague and varies across jurisdictions. Generally, the organization must prove that such clauses protect its legitimate interests.[29]

A difficult situation arises when a "quit" is not a quit. If an employee says "I quit" and leaves, can the employer assume that the employee really quit, or is the employer required to reinstate the employee who might change his or her mind? The legal status of this question is unresolved. Decisions hinge on whether the employee clearly exhibited the intention of resigning (did the employee clean out his or her desk?), whether the person was fully capable mentally of understanding the action, whether the employee was forced into the decision by company actions, and whether the employee immediately retracted the decision. Guidelines to prevent problems include recording the actions the employee took when he or she left, getting the employee to sign a resignation document, tracking whether the employee sought alternative employment, and taking action to fill the vacancy as soon as possible.[30]

Workforce diversity goals are also affected by the organization's ability to manage the pattern of quits. Retaining qualified women remains an important goal. A study using 40 years of data on U.S. workers found that women are more likely than men to switch jobs, and that it was much harder for employers to identify women stayers than men stayers. Probability of staying was greater for those with prior experience and for whites, and less for those who left previous jobs (especially for women). However, among younger women this appears to have changed. For example, being married significantly increased the probability of leaving for women born before 1947, but not for women born between 1952 and 1954. Among younger women, the probability and pattern of leaving is similar to that for men, so it may be easier to retain women in the future.[31] Retaining older workers is another way to preserve diversity, and that brings us to retirement.

## Retirements

Retirements are similar to quits because they are initiated by employees and result from a choice process similar to the one in Exhibit 8.4. Mandatory retirement ages of 65 or 70 used to be common, making retirements similar to dismissals. However, in 1987 the Age Discrimination in Employment Act was amended to prohibit discrimination on the basis of age for anyone over age 40, to remove the previous upper limit of age 70, and to make retirement an option instead of a requirement for employees without work impairments, except in a few specific occupations such as firefighters and police officers. A study funded by the EEOC suggested that age is not a good indicator of how well a firefighter does on the job, nor are older people likely to suffer sudden death at times that would compromise public safety. The report also noted that tests exist for each of the 29 abilities needed in fire fighting and suggested it may be feasible to use tests instead of age as a determining factor.[32] Increasing the retirement age may not always benefit workers; a study of Japanese corporations found that when the mandatory retirement age was raised, the rate of salary increases went down, presumably because corporations are unwilling to pay high salaries for more years.[33]

Retirements differ from quits because they usually occur at the end of an individual's work career, though the trend is toward earlier retirement often followed by a second career, especially for managers and top executives.[34] Retirements are also different from quits because retirees collect retirement benefits. From the employer, they usually receive pension benefits and continued insurance coverage (perhaps at increased premiums); from the government they receive Social Security and Medicare benefits, usually structured to reflect an average retirement age such as 65. The increasing number of retirees (see Chapter Two) has placed Social Security and Medicare benefits among the most controversial political topics in recent elections.

While retirement decisions are affected by many of the factors shown in Exhibit 8.4, they do differ on some dimensions. Individual factors such as age, health, and family responsibilities are different for retirees than for others, as are organizational factors such as pension benefits and future promotion opportunities. Finally, instead of simply considering alternative employment relationships, retirees can consider the alternative of an employment-free lifestyle, with its unique attractions and concerns.[35]

### Managing Employee Retirements

Virtually every human resource activity has the potential to affect retirement decisions. In industries with surplus workers, retirement income and benefits are often restructured to provide *early retirement incentives.* However, labor shortages and governmental scrutiny on age discrimination have led employers to attempt to *retain older employees* with favorable HR policies.

### Early Retirement Incentives

An early retirement incentive opens the window of retirement eligibility for more employees by making retirement benefits available at a younger age and/or by adding retirement benefits so that older employees can retire more comfortably without working longer. Typical early retirement packages include (1) time added to age for pension computations (five years is typical), (2) cash-separation or severance payment, (3) extra annual payments until Social Security payments begin, and (4) continued health insurance coverage to age 65 or beyond. Such plans are usually driven by the need to cut labor costs while avoiding dismissals, or by the belief that highly paid older employees can be replaced. The United Auto Workers and General Motors proposed such an incentive to ease labor tensions in the face of competitive pressures.[36]

AT&T offered an early retirement incentive to 77,800 managers on November 15, 1995, with an expiration date of December 29, 1995. Shortly thereafter, AT&T announced 40,000 layoffs. At Boeing, more than 9,300 workers took the early retirement offer in 1995, eliminating most of the layoffs needed to meet the goal of cutting 12,000 jobs.[37] On August 12, 1991, Eastman Kodak Company announced the Resource Redeployment & Retirement (R-cubed) plan, as part of its strategy to make more effective use of company resources in its core imaging business. The plan allowed any eligible employee whose combined age and length of service totaled 75 or more years to receive a full retirement benefit. Retirees under age 62 would receive monthly payments until Social Security benefits were available at age 62. Retirees could also receive company-paid health care, dental coverage, and life insurance benefits, as well as outplacement counseling and a retraining allowance of up to $5,000. Finally, at the discretion of each unit, retirees also could receive separation payments amounting to 2 weeks of pay for each year of employment, with a minimum of 4 weeks and a maximum of 52 weeks. Some financial advisors hired by Kodak to advise employees characterized it as "the most generous plan in the U.S." The plan was expected to reduce the workforce by approximately 3,000 employees and reduce third-quarter net earnings by approximately $375 million. By late 1991, a total of 6,733 employees elected early retirement, and more than two-thirds of an after-tax restructuring charge of $495 million was reflected in the additional costs of employees taking the early retirement option. Kodak's stock price increased on the date of the original announcement and on the announcement that a larger-than-expected number of employees had taken advantage of early retirement.[38]

Consulting firms estimate that retirement acceptance rates are running at 50 percent more than expected; they speculate that some employees believe it is now or never because their companies will not be able to afford to do it again. Blue-collar workers are increasingly eligible for early retirement incentives. A 53-year-old grandmother working at General Motors' Willow Run assembly plant took early retirement, including a payment of $29,600. One reason she gave for her action was to give her 34-year-old daughter the chance to be called back after being laid off. At the same time, public outcry has made incentives for executives less lucrative, with some insurance executives being forced to renounce claims to millions of dollars in severance pay and deferred compensation.[39]

### WHAT DO YOU THINK?

Shortly after realizing the early retirement plan that induced over 6,000 people to leave Eastman Kodak, some managers noted, "There's no one over 55 left in this company. Did we go too far?" How would you evaluate the impact of these retirements on a company like Eastman Kodak?

A survey by Towers, Perrin, Forster & Crosby of 100 large employers offering retirement incentives found that retirement inducement costs averaged $50,000 per retiree, but first-year cost savings from reduced compensation and benefit obligations ranged between $61,000 and $60 million, with an average of $7.3 million. Wyatt, a benefits consulting firm, says 19 of the 50 largest U.S. companies offered early retirement to employees in 1990 or 1991. The American Management Associations's survey of 836 members found 34 percent offered early retirement in 1991.[40]

Early retirement incentives are not without their risks. Some employees are only too happy to take the money and move on. Others believe they have been coerced into retiring through sudden reductions in their performance ratings and pressure from superiors to get out before being pushed out. Before 1990, it was difficult for employers to construct such plans and still protect themselves from age discrimination suits (see Chapter Two). However, in October 1990, Congress passed the Older Workers Benefit Protection Act (OWBPA) that amended the Age Discrimination in Employment Act (ADEA) and codified what it means for a plan to be voluntary. As a stipulation for receiving additional retirement benefits, employers can require retiring employees to sign a voluntary waiver that (1) is clear and understandable, (2) specifically refers to rights or claims under the ADEA, (3) does not require waiving rights or claims arising after the date of the waiver, (4) provides extra consideration (some form of additional money or benefit) to the individual for signing the waiver, (5) advises the individual in writing to consult an attorney, (6) gives 21 days (for an individual) or 45 days (for a group plan) to consider the agreement, and (7) allows a 7-day period after signing to change one's mind.[41]

### Retaining Older Employees

The evidence suggests that companies frequently implement cost reductions by inducing older workers to retire early. However, demographic projections suggest that the workforce of the United States and many countries worldwide will soon contain a much higher proportion of older workers and that fewer qualified younger workers are entering the workforce (see Chapter Two). For many companies, this means that the appropriate strategic response is to retain the valuable older workers they have. Not only does this avoid the costs of retirement incentives and retiree benefits (see Chapter Thirteen on benefits) but also it recognizes that older workers may represent a valuable source of experience. For some organizations, age and performance are positively related. Grumman Corporation's vice president of human resources planning stated: "Between 1970 and 1977, Grumman laid off 13,000 people. The layoff was determined on the basis of performance rather than seniority. When the layoffs were completed, the average age of the workforce had increased from 37 to 45, suggesting a very positive correlation between age and performance.[42] Stanley Gault, CEO of Goodyear Tire & Rubber Company, planned to remain a "full-time Goodyear associate," even after his retirement at age 70—not surprising, considering that he began work at age 12 with the largest paper route in Worcester, Massachusetts. Experts warn of avoiding the "Dracula complex" of assuming that "old blood" must go and that "new blood" is better, because the higher pay of older workers may be offset by their higher safety or loyalty.[43]

Exhibit 8.5 contains several ideas that allow or encourage older employees to continue to contribute to organizations. Chapter Seven also discusses ways for organizations to tap into the pool of older applicants. Many of the recruitment strategies outlined in that chapter can be used to retain valuable older workers. This may prove difficult. Data on the U.S. workforce suggest that the average age of retirement has steadily declined for more than 40 years and is likely to continue at least through the 1990s.[44] Organizations wishing to retain older employees need to be very creative. On the other hand, workers who do retire early are increasingly returning to work afterward. Therefore, organizations wishing to tap this source of talent may find more willing workers even as they induce more people to retire early.

### Implications for the Quality of Retained Employees

We know very little about whether retirements tend to remove the most or least valuable employees. Pension benefits that reflect previous salary levels may provide the greatest incentive to those whose salary has risen most rapidly, probably the best performers. Substantial labor cost savings may be more than offset by the loss of key senior employees with excellent performance records. When retirement incentives are constructed as an alternative for poor performers to avoid dismissal, however they may have a more positive effect on the performance of those retained. Some have argued that managers are remiss by

**EXHIBIT 8.5** Flexible Retirement Policies That Can Lengthen the Contribution of Older Employees

Retirement counseling programs.
Increased pensions for late retirees.
Supplements to pensions to bridge Social Security.
Use older workers as mentors or consultants.
Reassign older workers to less-demanding jobs.
Redesign jobs to reduce pressure.
Arrange for working at home.
Allow flexible work schedules.
Allow cutback to half-time schedules.
Use formal performance evaluations as input to retirement planning.
Use medical evaluations as input to retirement planning.
Provide for senior exempt employees to extend their careers.

Source: Benson Rosen and Thomas Jerdee, "Retirement Policies: Evidence of the Need for Change," *Human Resource Management* 28, no. 1 (Spring 1989), pp. 87–103.

emphasizing voluntary attrition, instead of forcing out the poorest performers.[45] This naturally brings us to discuss those separations initiated by the employer rather than the employee—dismissals.

## MANAGING EMPLOYEE DISMISSALS

Losing a job has become so likely that even *U.S. News & World Report* and *Fortune* feature helpful articles describing ways to prepare for the ax (such as putting off vacations and arranging emergency home equity loans), and suggest what to do when it falls (search widely, maintain a daily routine, don't pretend you weren't fired). Business magazines even instruct you on how to negotiate a better deal after you're fired (get a lawyer, don't sign a noncompete agreement, negotiate for more money, pension, perks, and outplacement assistance).[46] Employee dismissals initiated by the employer are the most extreme action an employer can take. Thus, whether dismissals result from actions by individual employees or from the need to reduce the work force, employers may strive to avoid them. They are a fact of organizational life, however, and HR managers must manage them effectively. Dismissals also have implications for other human resource activities. For example, Chapter Thirteen on benefits describes unemployment compensation, which requires that employers pay into a fund to provide benefits to dismissed employees. Frequently, higher payments are required for employers with more dismissals.

### Discharges

"You're fired." Few of us ever hope to hear those words because they signify the organization's most extreme action—the capital punishment of an employment relationship. *Discharges* occur when the employer terminates the employment relationship because employee behaviors are believed to be seriously harmful. Chapter Fifteen on employee relations shows how organizations use progressive discipline policies that impose more stringent punishments for progressively more harmful employee behaviors. Even though these systems often culminate in the decision to fire employees, they are frequently designed to encourage and support employees in improving their performance and avoiding being dismissed. Even the wife of the president of the United States must handle discharges carefully, as public scrutiny of her role in firing White House travel employees has shown.[47]

Discharge rates appear to be higher during times of economic prosperity, perhaps because increased hiring demands lead to selection errors. Also, older and longer-tenured employees are discharged less frequently, but discharged employees have longer and more difficult job searches.[48] Still, organizations pressured to compete may increase pressure for managers to be more aggressive in getting rid of the deadwood. As noted in Chapter Four, many organizations have adopted performance systems that rank employees to identity the poor performers more clearly. The former CEO of IBM, John Akers, was reported to have admonished IBM managers to be more aggressive in weeding out poor performers. Even CEOs are finding that they, too, can be encouraged to leave if corporate performance is not improving. Robert Stempel of General Motors and John Akers of IBM are two examples. Trouble for the CEO often means that the jobs of the aides who served them are on the line as well.[49]

### Employment-at-Will?

Should an employer be allowed to discharge an employee at will, for whatever reason the employer deems appropriate? The *employment-at-will* concept in early industrial England spelled out the obligations of master and servant in law. The master could not discharge the servant unless the servant's conduct was unsatisfactory, and the servant could not quit without sufficient notice. In the United States, the Industrial Revolution modified this view by stressing people's rights to freely choose employees and employers. In 1910, the California Supreme Court stated:

> Precisely as may the employee cease labor at his whim or pleasure, and, whatever be his reason, good, bad, or indifferent, leave no one a legal right to complain; so, upon the other hand, may the employer discharge, and whatever be his reason, good, bad, or indifferent, no one has suffered a legal wrong.[50]

However, various laws and regulations limit employment-at-will. The restrictions on dismissing U.S. government employees are so stringent that they have been described as the "unemployment-at-will" doctrine because only the employee can choose to end his or her employment.[51]

### Legislation, Collective Bargaining, and Civil Service Rules Limit Employment-at-Will

The Wagner Act of 1935 made it illegal for employees to be fired because of union activity. Collective bargaining agreements frequently forbid firing union employees, except for cause. Those employed by federal, state, and local governments are typically protected from arbitrary dismissal by the civil service rules of their employers. In the 1980s, courts examined the at-will doctrine in two ways: as a violation of public policy and as a violation of implied contracts between the employer and the employee.

### Public Policy Restricts Employment-at-Will

Some dismissals *violate public policy.*[52] For example, public policy protects:

1. An employee who refuses to commit an unlawful act; the court held that an employee was protected from discharge when she refused to give false testimony in court.
2. An employee who exercises the right to perform an important public policy obligation; an employee was protected from discharge when he blew the whistle on his employer's illegal conduct.
3. An employee who exercises a statutory right or privilege; an employee was protected from discharge in retaliation for filing a workers' compensation claim as was his statutory right.

Still, a Florida court held that an employee could not sue when he was discharged for filing a workers' compensation claim, and an Alabama employer was permitted to fire an employee who refused to falsify medical records.[53] The United States currently has no national legislation; thus, no consensus exists on public policy protection. The array of individual state laws and differences across countries dictate different requirements, depending on where an organization is located.

### Employment Contracts Restrict Employment-at-Will

Employee discharges can *violate employment contracts.* Personnel policies and manuals have been construed as implied, enforceable contracts. In *Toussaint* v. *Blue Cross/Blue Shield of Michigan,* the court held that an employee's discharge was improper because the employer had discussed permanent employment during the interview and it was reinforced in the employee handbook. Therefore, simply referring to permanent employment may imply a contract, especially if the reference can be combined with statements on the application blank or oral statements during an employment interview.[54] Collective bargaining agreements frequently stipulate that decisions to discharge employees are subject to arbitration, which means an outside arbitrator can overturn a dismissal. A review of Canadian court cases suggests that employers can dismiss employees for just cause only when they can show a pattern of serious misconduct or documented evidence of poor performance. They can discharge employees only after giving them an opportunity to improve and offering clear warnings that their jobs are in jeopardy.[55] Disputes about breach of contract are not limited to lower-level employees. When Doug Morris, chairman of Warner Music was fired from Time Warner, Inc., he sued for more than $50 million based on breach-of-contract, virtually guaranteeing a protracted legal battle.[56]

### Equal Employment Opportunity Restricts Employment-at-Will

As stated in Chapter Two, U.S. civil rights legislation protects employees from dismissal based on their protected-group status, including age and physical or mental disabilities. Bernard C. Duse, an African American employee fired from IBM in 1984, charged he was fired because of his race. After eight years of court proceedings, Duse received an out-of-court settlement in which IBM admitted no liability.[57] Do these protections apply to Americans working for foreign companies? Three former Quasar executives sued Matsushita Electric Industrial, the parent company, for race and age discrimination when they and 63 other American managers—but no Japanese executives—were fired in 1986. The federal appeals judge ruled in favor of the company, noting that companies may discriminate in favor of citizenship, which is not the same as discrimination based on race. The court noted that the ruling may seem callous to Americans working for foreign companies but it serves to protect Americans working abroad for U.S. companies.[58] The 54-year-old publisher of *Field and Stream* magazine sued for age discrimination when he was fired and replaced with a younger, lower-paid executive, but the Second Circuit Court blocked the suit, saying that salary, not age, was the determining factor. Similarly, the U.S. Supreme Court ruled in 1993 against Walter Biggins, who claimed that Hazen Paper Company violated the ADEA when it fired him at age 62, after refusing his requested salary raise from $44,000 to $100,000, and after he refused to sign an agreement not to consult with competitors. The company faced damages of more than $1 million if found guilty.[59]

One area where two laws collide is sexual harassment. Companies are required by EEOC guidelines to take "immediate corrective action" against accused harassers. Yet, state law and employment contracts frequently require painstakingly gathered evidence of just cause for dismissal.[60]

### Should Neutral Arbitrators Decide Who Gets Fired?

Some companies voluntarily give firing authority to independent panels. At Federal Express, employees can appeal discharges to five-member boards; grievants choose three of the members from a company-established pool.[61] Taking this idea even further, the National Conference of Commissioners on Uniform State Laws suggests that all states pass a law stipulating that fired employees may take their cases to arbitrators. Lawsuits would no longer be permitted, and the arbitrator's decision would stand. If the employers won, the firings would stand; if the employees won, they would be reinstated or receive up to three years' pay as a severance award. Employee groups favor the proposal, especially in states where few laws protect them against unjust dismissal. Employers favor the proposal in states such as California, where workers win 70 percent of jury trials, and the average award is $300,000 to $500,000, plus an average of $75,000 in legal fees. Trial lawyers who collect the fees are not supportive. Still, this idea seems to be catching on with leading employers such as Northrup Grumman, Hughes Aircraft, Aetna Life and Casualty, Chrysler, and Eckerd Corporation. At Rockwell International, 900 senior managers were given a choice: agree to arbitrate any future dismissal or give up receiving any future stock options.[62]

Perhaps the ultimate objective arbiter would be a computer, but this might cause problems, too. For instance, a federal court case involved Transco Services' evaluation of its warehouse workers, who retrieve and load goods. The firm used a computer to estimate the time a job should take and to ensure that employees performed at least 407 minutes of work and took 73 minutes of breaks in an eight-hour workday. The least efficient workers, who fell in the lower 20 percent of employees in a given week, were subject to progressive discipline ending in dismissal. The computer found only 20 of 1,182 weekly measurements were above the 100 percent level and triggered the firing of 11 out of 52 workers, 10 of whom were age 40 or older. The company dropped the program after 48 weeks, but was sued for age discrimination by two fired workers.[63]

### Implications for Managing Employee Dismissals

The lack of a national law regarding employment-at-will limits consensus on exactly what employers may do to avoid liability for wrongful discharge. Obviously, one should avoid practices similar to those of an advertising firm, which placed notes on employees' doors that read, "You're fired. Come and see me."[64] The following recommendations are frequently mentioned.

1. Avoid any mention of permanent employment in the recruiting interviews. Telling applicants that "we may fire you at any time" may seem a bit like having a divorce lawyer at a wedding, but liability begins with the recruitment process.
2. Revise all employee handbooks to remove any implications that employment is not at will, including statements such as "this handbook is not a binding contract." This also should be done with any letters to applicants and any comments in interviews.
3. Include waivers in job applications such as this from Sears, Roebuck & Company: "My employment and compensation can be terminated, with or without cause and with or without notice at any time at the option of the company or myself."
4. Carefully document performance evaluations. Admonish appraisers to be completely truthful when evaluating subordinates, and clearly communicate to them when their performance jeopardizes their jobs.
5. Follow the disciplinary procedure carefully (see Chapter Fifteen on employee relations), and document every step. Provide a conflict-resolution procedure to allow employees to tell their side of the story—they may be right.
6. Don't offer a face-saving reason for the dismissal that's unrelated to the poor performance.[65]

### Discharges and the Quality of the Retained Employees

Employees are seldom discharged without documented evidence, and often only after an exhaustive series of reviews and appeals. If past behavior predicts future behavior, such discharges are likely to rid the organization of employees who would have been poor performers or harmful influences in the future. Evidence suggests that this is true even for CEOs younger than retirement age, who separate more frequently when reported annual earnings per share fall below financial analysts' forecasts.[66] The retained workforce is likely to be better as a result of such discharges. Thus, it is in the interest of both employer and employee to have a discharge procedure that reflects job-related behaviors and makes decisions based on evidence. A study of salespeople showed that those with lower sales, performance ratings, and job involvement were more likely to be dismissed; that mental ability and conscientiousness were associated with higher performance (and lower dismissals); and that tenure and being male were positively associated with the likelihood of being dismissed.[67]

If discharges are not handled fairly, those remaining may lose trust in the organization and consider leaving. Exhibit 8.6 shows what consultants advise to avoid problems with discharges. Notice how important it is to integrate staffing, performance assessment, and employee relations. In the future, computerized expert systems may provide managers with guides for making termination decisions, by asking managers a series of questions about the situation, ultimately recommending whether the manager should terminate the employee or not.

EXHIBIT 8.6 Guidelines for Dismissing Employees

| DOs | DON'Ts |
|---|---|
| Give as much warning as possible for mass layoffs. | Don't leave room for confusion when firing. Tell individuals in the first sentence they are terminated. |
| Sit down one-on-one with the individual, in a private office. | Don't allow time for debate during a firing session. |
| Complete a firing session within 15 minutes. | Don't make personal comments when firing someone; keep the conversation professional. |
| Provide written explanations of severance benefits. | Don't rush a fired employee off-site unless security is really an issue. |
| Provide outplacement services away from company headquarters. | Don't fire people on significant dates, like the 25th anniversary of their employment or the day their mother died. |
| Be sure the employee hears about the termination from a manager, not a colleague. | Don't fire employees when they are on vacation or have just returned. |
| Express appreciation for what the employee has contributed, if appropriate. | |

Source: Adapted from Suzanne Alexander, "Firms Get Plenty of Practice at Layoffs, But They Often Bungle the Firing Process," *The Wall Street Journal* Oct. 14, 1991, p. B1. Reprinted by permission of *The Wall Street Journal.* 

## Layoffs

> As a further restructuring, today's global challenges require the North Pole to continue to look for better, more competitive steps. Effective immediately, the following economy measures are to take place in the "Twelve Days of Christmas" subsidiary: The two turtle doves represent a redundancy that is simply not cost-effective. In addition, their romance during working hours could not be condoned. The positions are therefore eliminated. . . The six geese-a-laying constitutes a luxury that can no longer be afforded. It has long been felt that the production rate of one egg per goose per day is an example of the decline in productivity. Three geese will be let go, and an upgrading in the selection procedure by personnel will assure management that from now on every goose it gets will be a good one. . .[68] —HRNET, November 25, 1995

Humorous, perhaps, but for many Internet surfers, it must have seemed like black humor. The litany of large U.S. employers planning five-figure layoffs seemed to grow daily (see the introduction to this chapter). In the first nine months of 1995, U.S. corporations announced more than 300,000 layoffs, with over 47 percent of companies reporting workforce reductions averaging 9 percent of the workforce—and that was less than prior years! During 1991 and 1992, about 5.5 million workers permanently lost their jobs, over half losing jobs they had held more than three years. An increasing number of the jobs lost were white-collar jobs filled by older workers in the service industry.[69] No one is immune. Major universities cut core faculty. Japan, once praised for innovative ways to preserve lifetime employment for the one-fourth of the country's workforce that enjoys it, is rethinking and redesigning this commitment in light of double-digit increases in white-collar employment and the slipping of the ratio of jobs to workers below 1.0 for the first time in recent memory.[70]

One apparent bit of good news is that organizations seem to create new jobs as they lay off employees. Two-thirds of firms who laid off employees reported simultaneously hiring new employees, and 36 percent reported either no change or a net gain in total employment.[71] Still, this may be small consolation to those laid off, who might well wonder what kind of planning leads to simultaneous cuts and additions. Layoffs can be very expensive. Polaroid Corporation announced a plan to cut 1,300 jobs in 1996, resulting in a pretax charge of $195 million, taken in two consecutive quarters. Bausch & Lomb announced layoffs of 800 employees in 1996, taking a charge of $27 million, or 30 cents per share.[72] What is the logic for such actions?

### Why Companies Lay Off

As Chapter Five showed, layoffs are one of the tools organizations can use to reduce labor costs and workforce levels when forecasted labor demand is lower than the supply forecast. A 1994 survey revealed that 47 percent of American Management Association members reported workforce reductions, down from 56 percent in June 1991. Of these firms, 22 percent said a business downturn was the sole reason. When citing more than one reason for downsizing, 49 percent cited a business downturn, 42 percent cited "improved staff utilization," about 13 percent cited mergers and acquisitions, and less than 2 percent gave plant obsolescence.[73] Even low-technology can affect layoffs. In Manila, Philippines, chicken farms employed women as beak trimmers to keep chickens from scattering their feed. When food pellets were developed that didn't scatter, the beak trimmers were laid off and protested against this breach of lifetime employment. One study actually looked at financial data on company characteristics and found that the firm's "current ratio" and finished goods inventory per employee were significantly related to layoffs.[74]

The common rationale is that layoffs are necessary to financial health. Orange County laid off 1,600 workers to raise money after it suffered the largest municipal bankruptcy ever. Mexican industries announced massive layoffs in response to reduced product demand, but such layoffs could backfire and cripple the Mexican economy. Reminiscent of the Paul Bunyan story, mortgage brokers, meter readers, ticket agents, salesclerks, bank tellers, and telephone operators fear "extinction" at the hands of technology and computer networks. At Pacific Gas and Electric, hundreds of $50,000-a-year technicians are threatened by a computer program that designs new electric service and eliminates installation costs. Toyota threatens plant shutdowns and layoffs in Japan "as a last resort" because of shrinking domestic auto demand and a rising yen. While Scott Paper laid off workers when it *merged* with Kimberly-Clark, AT&T announced 40,000 layoffs because it was *breaking up* into three smaller units. The payoff estimates are astounding. Texaco estimated it would save $450 million annually after laying off 4,000 people by the end of 1996.[75]

### Do Layoffs Improve Firm Performance?

Managers and financial analysts seem to link layoffs with financial firm performance. Exhibit 8.7 shows selective statistics taken from articles in *The Wall Street Journal.* While certainly not a scientific sample, each article quoted the layoff figures and the stock price change in the same article. It's not hard to understand why top executives might get the idea that layoffs boost stock prices. In perhaps the most vivid example, Wells Fargo & Company competed with First Bank System of Minneapolis to buy First Interstate Bank in California. The financial race was dead even until Wells Fargo's top executives went

EXHIBIT 8.7 Does Stock Price Rise With Layoff Announcements?

| Date | Announcement | One-Day Percent Stock Change Price Rises |
|---|---|---|
| March 3, 1995 | Bankers Trust cuts staff 10%, 1,500 jobs | 1.80% |
| April 24, 1995 | AmSouth Bancorp cuts staff 14%, 1,000 jobs | 0.80 |
| May 8, 1995 | Republic New York Bank cuts staff 15% | 2.60 |
| May 24, 1995 | Boeing Co. cuts workforce 4%, 5,000 jobs | 0.14 |
| July 5, 1995 | Canadian Airlines cuts 394 employees | 3.00 |
| July 31, 1995 | James River Corp. cuts staff 19%, 4,000 jobs | 28.00 |
| August 23, 1995 | Kellogg Co. cuts two plants by 50%, 1,075 jobs | 0.30 |

Source: Data from *The Wall Street Journal* on the dates shown. Reprinted by permission of *The Wall Street Journal,* 

to New York City to explain to financial analysts that with their existing branches in California, they could cut 9,000 people from First Interstate's 47,000 workforce, while First Bank could cut only 6,000. The result? Wall Street liked Wells Fargo's explanation; based on stock price, Wells Fargo made the most attractive offer to First Interstate shareholders and got the prize. Other factors certainly affected the stock prices and results, but the press tells a story about how job cuts led to business success. More systematic research tells a different story. One study found that layoffs generally occurred in firms with weak earnings. Layoffs were associated with a slightly increased stock price for financially weak firms, but with a significantly lower stock price for financially healthy firms. A study of Canadian firms found that the effect of layoff announcements was to lower the stock price; larger layoffs were associated with greater price declines.[76] Another study compared firms that downsized an average of 28 percent over two years with other firms in the same industry that downsized less than 15 percent. It found that total sales in the first group were 8.8 percent higher after three years, but total sales in the second group were 25.9 percent higher. Earnings in the group with higher downsizing were up 183.4 percent after three years while they rose 422.5 percent in the comparison group; the magnitude of the cuts in the downsizing organizations was unrelated to subsequent earnings. If you invested in each group of companies, your investment in the downsizing companies would have grown by 4.7 percent after three years, but it would have grown by 34.3 percent in the comparison companies.[77] Data are very sparse, but it's certainly not obvious that downsizing helps organizations, despite vivid examples in the press.

The expense and turmoil of layoffs would suggest that companies probably go to great lengths to avoid them. Indeed, theory suggests that organizations progress through stages of decline, first recognizing the need to change, and proceeding through ever more serious crises. Companies such as Johnson & Johnson, Merck, Motorola, and Philip Morris were once cited as places where layoffs were a foreign language.[78] In Exhibit 8.8, we show the percent of companies that used different methods to minimize employee separations. You

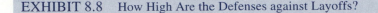

EXHIBIT 8.8 How High Are the Defenses against Layoffs?

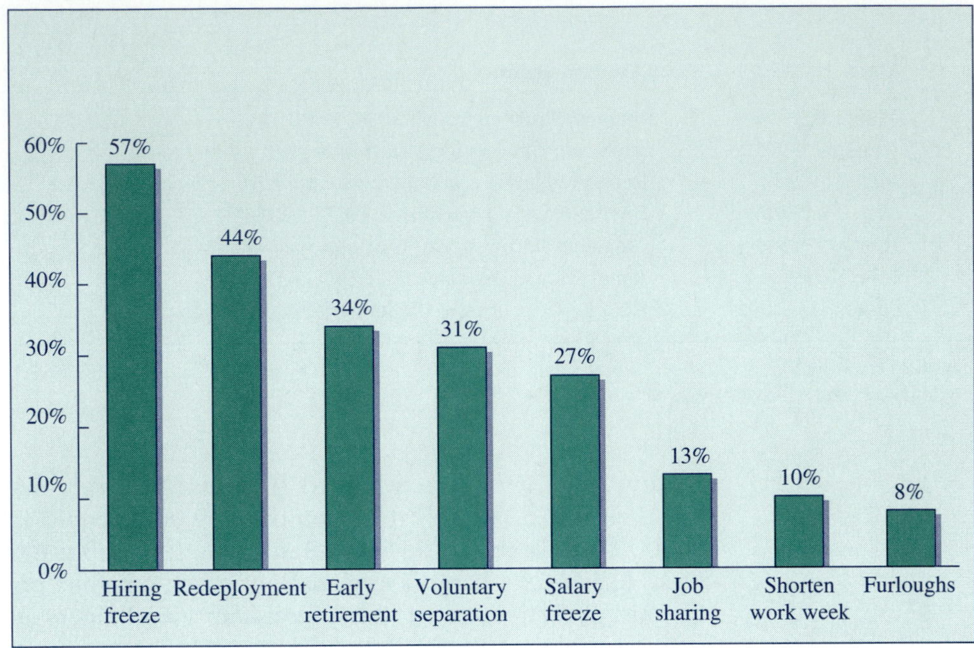


Source: American Management Association, *1994 AMA Survey on Downsizing* (New York: AMA, 1995), p. 3

might think of the bars as representing the height of the defensive wall against layoffs. Most of the walls are not very high. While 57 percent used a hiring freeze and about 44 percent used redeployment, very few took measures such as freezing pay or furloughs.

*Redeployment* means moving employees from areas of surplus to areas of shortage. For example, Canada's Ontario Hydro gave employees the option of retraining or leaving calling it "rightsizing." We discuss such internal movements in Chapter Nine. Another creative way to avoid layoffs was General Motors' offer to allow its suppliers to use its idle employees on site.[79]

The U.S. Department of Labor reviewed research findings and case studies of layoffs, and summarized the following myths about downsizing.[80] Following each of the nine myths is evidence suggesting why the myth may be false.

1. Downsizing boosts profits. Only 51 percent of downsizing companies increased profits and 20 percent saw declines.
2. Downsizing boosts productivity. While some manufacturers downsized and increased productivity, many more raised employment levels and productivity.
3. Downsizing is a last resort. The defenses against downsizing in Exhibit 8.8 suggest that firms don't often use all tools to avoid downsizing.

4. When recessions end, downsizing ends, too. Layoffs have not decreased significantly as the U.S. economy has recovered.
5. Jobs are secure at companies doing well financially. Even companies with record profits have downsized.
6. Downsizing is usually a one-time event. Of firms that downsize in one year, 66 percent do it again the next year.
7. Blue-collar workers are more likely to lose their jobs. Middle managers make up 5 percent to 8 percent of the workforce, but they have lost 18.6 percent of eliminated jobs since 1988.
8. Downsizing "cuts the fat," so there is no effect on workload, morale, or commitment. Of companies who downsized in 1994, 86 percent reported lower morale and 30 percent reported lower worker productivity.[81]
9. Victims of downsizing do not suffer any long-term income loss. Many downsized workers took jobs at lower pay levels.

### Human Resource Management Activities for Managing Layoffs

As unpleasant as workforce reductions are, they can be handled well. Most top managers say that downsizing is their toughest decision. They frequently look to their human resource managers to ensure that workforce reductions achieve both equity and efficiency goals. Exhibit 8.9 shows the guidelines recommended by the Department of Labor for "responsible restructuring. We can organize these guidelines into five specific human resource activities:

1. Planning a layoff or plant closing.
2. Communicating with and involving employees in the restructuring.
3. Giving formal notice of the layoff or plant closing.
4. Providing income maintenance and extensions of employee benefits.
5. Helping with job search or outplacement.

> **WHAT DO YOU THINK?**
>
> Can a company be too generous in helping laid-off employees? After successfully acquiring First Interstate Bank, Wells Fargo was obligated to pay very generous severance packages to 7,200 laid-off employees. The severance requirements were originally designed to be so expensive that they would protect First Interstate from takeover. Now, at least a dozen employees have threatened to sue Wells Fargo for *not* laying them off. They point to their poor performance, vacation needs, and desire for a nest egg. How would you advise top management to respond?[82]

#### Planning the restructuring

As shown in Chapter Five, it is possible to project future needs and supplies of people, and to take action to prepare people today for the challenges of tomorrow. Turbulent times make this task difficult. Sometimes no one can anticipate the significant shifts that lead to restructuring, such as the impact of technology and legislation on the U.S. telecommunications industry. Still, having no plan is worse than having an imperfect one. A plan can provide guidance to both employees and managers, and it signals the organization's commitment to anticipate and deal with future upheavals. It is also a virtual necessity for communicating and involving employees in future changes, and meeting legal requirements for advance notice. Many organizations find a "zero-base" approach helpful. At Sea-Land Service, the vice president of human resources created new job descriptions tied directly to the future vision of the company, and then oversaw a detailed examination of every single employee, top managers to janitors, rated against the job descriptions and needed capabilities,

## EXHIBIT 8.9 Guidelines for Responsible Restructuring

- Articulate a vision of what you want your organization to achieve.
- Establish a corporate culture that views people as assets to be developed instead of costs to be cut.
- Be clear about your short- and long-range objectives; for example, to cut costs (short-range) and to improve customer service and shareholder value through more effective use of assets (long-range).
- Establish an alternative menu of options for reaching the short- and long-range objectives.
- Get the people who will have to live with the changes involved in making them; provide opportunities for input at all levels.
- Communicate, communicate, communicate! Share as much information as possible about prospective changes with those who will be affected by them.
- Recognize that employees are unlikely to contribute creative, ingenious ways to cut costs if they think their own employment security will be jeopardized as a result.
- If cutting costs by cutting people is inevitable, establish a set of priorities for doing so (e.g., lay off outside contractors and temporaries first) and stick to it. Show by word and deed that full-time, value-adding employees will be the last to go.
- If employees must be let go, provide as much advance notice as possible, treat them with dignity and respect, and provide assistance (financial, counseling) to help them find new jobs.
- Consider retraining and redeploying surplus workers to promote their employment security and self-reliance and to protect your human resources investment.
- Give surviving employees a reason to stay. Explain what new opportunities will be available to them.
- View restructuring as part of a process of continual improvement—with subgoals and measurable checkpoints over time—instead of as a one-time event.

Source: U.S Department of Labor, *Guide to Responsible Restructuring,* 1995, pp. 29–30.

and matched with new jobs. The result was a clearer picture of the necessary downsizing, a coherent strategic rationale for individual decisions, and a signal that everyone's job was on the table, not only the jobs of lower-level employees.[83] AT&T took a similar approach when it laid off 40,000 employees in 1996.

### Communicating with and Involving Employees

How would you feel if your boss came to you and said, "We're going to have layoffs, and we'd like you to help." It seems paradoxical to engage people in such a traumatic process, but many theories suggest that effective coping involves taking personal control of the situation. Managers can help by getting employees to set specific goals, thus building optimism and a sense of mastery instead of powerlessness.[84] Because advance notice of layoffs is often required, the attitudes and behaviors of layoff "victims" is an important consideration. Research has shown that the attitudes of layoff victims are influenced by their perception of whether the layoff is fair, which in turn is significantly

## EXHIBIT 8.10 Ten Principles for Laying Off an Employee with Dignity

1. The employee's supervisor should conduct the termination and do so in private.
2. Keep the meeting short and to the point.
3. Offer support and compassion, but do not give hope of reversing the decision.
4. Explain why the company made the decision.
5. Don't make discriminatory statements (e.g., referring to age or gender).
6. Control your emotions, don't detain the employee, don't touch the employee, and don't yell.
7. Give the severance package in writing.
8. Encourage the employee to take positive, rather than destructive, actions.
9. Plan a graceful exit (walk with the employee to the door or bring the outplacement counselor to meet him or her).
10. Inform other employees, customers and suppliers of the decision in a nonblaming way.

Source: Joe Meissner, "How HR Can Help managers Lay Off Employees in a Dignified Way," *Personnel Journal,* Nov. 1993, p. 66.

affected by whether the bad news is delivered with adequate, open, and truthful communication. Laid-off workers who were members of quality teams and involved in their work had higher organizational commitment and favorable attitudes toward management.[85] Thus, it is important that communication and involvement include not only the layoff survivors, but also the layoff victims. The common perception that CEOs obtain great wealth as a reward for layoffs probably does little to enhance the reactions of layoff victims or survivors. Exhibit 8.10 contains a set of recommendations for laying off employees in a dignified way.

### Notice of Layoff or Plant Closing

The Worker Adjustment and Retraining Notification Act (WARN) requires employers with 100 or more workers to provide at least 60 days' notice of a plant closing or mass layoff to the affected workers or their representatives, state dislocated worker units, and the appropriate local government. Advance notice appears to reduce unemployment among displaced workers and to moderate temporary increases in area unemployment rates.[86] Managers in one survey expressed concern that advance notice causes productivity to decline, employees to jump ship, negative rumors to increase, and organizational conflict to rise. Research suggests that advance notice does not necessarily cause workers to intensify their search for new jobs and that investors react most negatively to layoff announcements caused by financial distress or negative rumors that preceded the announcements.[87] Workers can sue companies that fail to provide the required notice, and often have six months or longer in which to file their suits.[88]

### Who Goes? Order of Layoff and Bumping

Layoffs usually occur based on seniority, though job performance and transferability of skills are also frequently used. These factors may also be combined.[89] *Bumping* refers to giving more senior employees whose jobs have become obsolete the right to transfer into the jobs of less senior workers. It is frequently stipulated in collectively bargained labor contracts. Bumping maintains jobs for long-service employees, but can lead to frequent job changes or placing unqualified individuals into some jobs. Seniority-based layoffs can create legal conflicts when minority-group members have less tenure than nonminority-group members. Even a neutral seniority-based system can seriously reduce minority and women employees if they tend to have less tenure. Supreme Court decisions suggest that preferential treatment for less senior minorities may not be accepted as a way to maintain the affirmative action progress.[90]

The Older Workers Benefit Protection Act of 1990, discussed earlier with regard to retirements, applies to any worker over age 40. Therefore, the previously mentioned guidelines for extracting employee promises not to sue apply to layoffs as well as early-retirement incentives.

### Income Maintenance

Organizations often help maintain the income of laid-off employees for some period after they leave. Severance pay is a lump-sum payment upon separation; the amount of assistance is usually higher for longer-tenure employees. Hughes Aircraft Company provides 40 weeks of severance pay. One study found that it took laid-off executives an average of 25 weeks to find new jobs, and their severance pay lasted an average of 26 weeks. This may be either very good planning by the company, or evidence that the imminent loss of income is a very strong motivator to take a new job. *Supplemental unemployment benefits* augment the unemployment insurance benefits paid by states. Employees may also remain eligible for benefits such as health and life insurance, either for free or by paying the same premiums they paid before they were laid off. The Tennessee Valley Authority gives loans to laid-off employees who want to start small businesses. Thus, severance pay becomes the first step in placing the employee in a new work role.[91]

### Outplacement: Helping Employees Find a New Workplace

Organizations may provide laid-off employees with help writing résumés, training in high-demand skills, and loans or grants to pay for additional schooling. At AT&T, they measure the success of their programs by the number of safe landings, surplus employees who find suitable employment in other organizations. The U.S. Army dubs its outplacement program Operation Transition. Many programs are beneficial for the departing employees and the organization because they foster greater commitment among the survivors. However, some have suggested that organizations implement such programs because it makes firing employees easier. A growing number of states provide "one-stop" career centers, designed to put publicly available outplacement services all under one roof.[92]

Outplacement is not without its risks. In 1992, Eastman Kodak Company and Digital Equipment Company were sued for $55 million by 11 former Eastman Kodak employees, who were placed with Digital as part of a deal for Kodak to hand over management of its voice and data networks to Digital. The 11 claimed that Kodak committed age discrimination, that it pressured them to join Digital by blocking their transfer opportunities, and that Kodak and Digital misled them about their jobs at Digital. At General Motors, severance packages come with a hitch: To qualify for benefits, employees must sign waivers not to sue their former employer. Sometimes companies end up suing outplaced workers for finding jobs with competitors. When employees take recipes for key steel-protecting alloys or methods for making chardonnay or even hairstyling clients, companies may find their competitiveness threatened. Many organizations now ask employees to sign noncompete contracts agreeing not to work for competitors.[93] As in sports, free agency is hard to come by.

### Layoffs and the Quality of the Retained Employees

In the rush to cut labor costs or head count, many organizations forget that the lasting results of layoffs are their effects on the productivity, diversity, and attitudes of the survivors. The pattern of layoffs can significantly affect the value of those retained (see Exhibit 8.3). Layoffs may retain workers unaccustomed to new tasks. For example, a business executive who flew to a meeting in Taiwan soon found himself on an 18-hour flight back to his hometown of Minneapolis. The travel agency forgot to advise him he would need a visa to enter Taiwan. Why? To boost efficiency, Carlton Travel Network had cut 17 percent of its workforce, and the agent who scheduled the trip was new to the job.[94] In 1996, several of the Baby Bell regional telecommunications companies scaled back their cutback plans because of complaints and reductions in quality. After one set of cutbacks at Ameritech, the Public Service Commission of Wisconsin said it had received more complaints in one two-week period than in several years combined. Pressure and anxiety among survivors has been shown to decrease creativity and teamwork. One survivor said "the winners get to leave and the losers get to stay."[95]

Research suggests survivors react more favorably if they believe a layoff is necessary, that all other cost-cutting measures have been tried, that the layoff doesn't violate company culture, that ample notice was given, and that the process was handled with care and diligence. Two studies, one using actual managers and the other using college students in an experiment, found that survivors had less commitment to the organization if their jobs became more boring and more commitment if their jobs became more interesting. However, when layoffs were seen as fair, or if those being laid off were seen as upbeat, survivors reacted more strongly to changes in their jobs than when layoffs were seen as unfair. Even negative reactions were muted in the face of unfair layoffs, perhaps because people rationalized their decisions to stay by thinking "my job must not be so bad if I stayed with an unfair organization." It may not be wise to make survivors feel perfectly secure in their jobs. One study found productivity highest among employees who felt moderate levels of job insecurity—those with very low or very high perceived job security performed less well.[96]

Despite these findings, it appears that most layoffs have mixed effects at best. The American Management Association survey for 1995 found that among those firms that had downsized in the last five years, profits rose in 50 percent, worker productivity rose in only 34 percent, and morale declined in 86 percent. Organizations can do better to ameliorate the negative effects of

WHAT DO YOU THINK?

Telling a subordinate or colleague they've been laid off is much easier said than done. Read Exhibit 8.10 again, and imagine that you must inform someone with five years' tenure, who has worked for you for three years, that he or she is being laid off. What would you say, and how would you say it? What layoff program features would you emphasize? What assistance would you expect from the HR professionals? You may want to role-play this with a classmate.

layoffs. A study of U.S. auto manufacturers suggests that the most effective organizations had the following characteristics:[97]

1. Both top management and lower-level employees were involved in identifying redundant jobs and tasks.
2. In addition to short-term workforce reductions, long-term actions were taken to redesign the organizations to eliminate redundancies, and to foster new values focusing on continuous improvement and simplification.
3. Firms deal not only with the needs of those losing their jobs but also with the survivor guilt that is likely to afflict those who remain by showing them that new opportunities still remain.
4. After targeting downsizing surgically to those areas of greatest redundancy or waste, companies apply the same approach to outside suppliers and distributors.
5. To achieve flexibility without losing integration, firms use a clan control system relying on common values, shared vision, and collective information.
6. By setting short-term goals such as achieving cost reductions, companies can also downsize in ways that support a long-term reorganization.

## EVALUATING EMPLOYEE SEPARATIONS AND RETENTION

A typical organization might assume that quits are bad and should be reduced, and that layoffs can be evaluated solely by the reduction in labor costs. We have seen that a complete picture of the effects of employee separations requires a broader perspective. Separations are an integral part of the staffing process; many of the most important effects occur among those who are retained.

### Efficiency

Separations can be costly, especially when they involve activities such as exit interviews, outplacement assistance, counseling and severance pay, in addition to administrative and clerical support. The costs of separations can range above $100,000 per person. Turnover reduction programs are frequently justified by the cost savings they generate, often easily reaching several million dollars. In Europe, costs are even higher because many governments mandate extensive benefits for employees who are discharged or laid off. Exhibit 8.11 shows the costs for several European countries. The true pessimists may want to use these figures to decide where to seek their next jobs. In addition to costs, the lost productivity from separations can also affect efficiency. One study estimated that by extending the tenure of accountants in accounting firms, those with cultures emphasizing interpersonal values saved more than $6 million in lost productivity.[98]

### Equity

Employee separations are both a result and a cause of equity perceptions. Quits result from low employee satisfaction; the ways organizations implement and

**EXHIBIT 8.11** Costs of Dismissing One Employee in Europe

| Country | Statutory Termination Benefits (U.S. dollars) |
|---|---|
| Italy | $130,000 |
| Spain | 125,000 |
| Belgium | 94,000 |
| Portugal | 83,000 |
| Greece | 67,000 |
| Germany | 25,000 |
| United Kingdom | 19,000 |
| Ireland | 13,000 |

Costs assume a 45-year-old employee, with 20 years of service, earning $50,000.

Source: Michelle Laque Johnson, "Look Before You Leap into European Labor Market," *Investor's Business Daily,* Apr. 1, 1992, p. 4.

communicate about dismissals, retirements, and layoffs serve as an index of their commitment to fairness and equity. The employment-at-will doctrine continues to generate controversy in state courts, and federal legislation affecting separations continues to grow. Achieving equity goals is not always simple. Seniority-based separations may harm diversity goals by removing women and minority-group members who were recently hired. Before it announced 40,000 layoffs in late 1995, AT&T had already reduced its workforce by 58,000 while increasing the proportion of minority supervisors from 3 to 9 percent, and increasing the proportion of women supervisors from 2.5 to 9 percent. AT&T employed an early-retirement sweetener to induce older white men employees to leave first.[99] HR managers are constantly challenged to balance competing demands to create a fair system of separations.

## SUMMARY

The employer, the employee, or both can terminate the employment relationship. Employee separations affect efficiency and equity by affecting the retained work force. Separations are closely watched by governments, communities, and potential recruits. Managing employee separations effectively requires balancing competing demands. However, it also requires integrating separations into the staffing process. This chapter has provided a framework to help you see that recruitment, selection and separations must work together to maximize the effectiveness of the workforce. Separations determine who is retained; by understanding their link to selection and recruitment, HR managers can manage separations more effectively. Some have suggested that a hidden cost of downsizing is that it reduces available career opportunities for those who survive.[100] This shows how external staffing decisions relate to careers, the topic of our next chapter. First, however, see if you can design a strategy for a dignified plant closing at Boeing, in the Your Turn at the end of the chapter.

## QUESTIONS

1. How does the management of employee separations affect the staffing process? How does the concept of workforce value apply to the four types of employee separations/retentions?
2. Give three examples of managerial actions that might reduce the number of employee quits. Why might human resource activities fail to affect employee quit behavior?
3. Would a reduction in the number of quits necessarily be a good thing? Why or why not?
4. Under what circumstances does it benefit an organization to retain its older employees? Discuss some strategies for lengthening the contribution of older workers.
5. What is an early retirement incentive? What decisions are required for such an incentive, and how do they affect an organization?
6. Discuss why employee discharges are likely to be valid workforce reduction strategies. What is the employment-at-will issue, and how does it affect how discharges are managed? Is it likely to affect the relationship between discharges and productivity? Explain.
7. What steps can an organization take to protect itself from liability for wrongful discharge? What effect could these steps have on an organization's ability to attract and keep employees?
8. Discuss the implications of "downsizing myths" for corporations and their strategies.
9. Discuss the four human resource activities for managing layoffs in terms of their likely effect on the efficiency and equity goals of organizations. Do these goals always coincide? Give one example where they do, and one where they do not.
10. What's wrong with evaluating employee separations simply by tracking the separation rate, and by making sure it is at or below the average for your industry or geographic area?

## YOUR TURN

### Boeing Louisiana's Plant Closing[101]

Lake Charles, Louisiana, a city of 70,000 residents, was shocked by the news that Boeing Louisiana Inc. (BLI) was closing by the end of the year. The company employed more than 1,600 residents, but it hadn't received the government contract to maintain and rebuild CK 135 aircraft—the sole purpose for the Lake Charles facility. The shutdown would remove a payroll of $30 million, sharply reduce the local tax base, affect real estate values, and have an incalculable impact on local retail and restaurant businesses.

Boeing management faced difficult decisions about how to handle the plant closing. To accomplish the closing would require a close partnership between the community, the company, and the employees. Was it possible to close the plant and still preserve the local economy? How much could BLI assist the employees to accomplish safe landings, and could it afford to provide the assistance? How could BLI ensure that the plant's existing contracts to produce aircraft were completed on time and at high quality, while simultaneously preparing to close the plant?

BLI General Manager Terry Prickett was committed to "do everything we can to meet our obligations to Lake Charles and transition the employees into new jobs." At the same time, he said, "One of our main concerns is our ability to fulfill obligations and complete projects while maintaining performance standards and quality. I believe if we handle this thing in a class-act way, our employees should reciprocate."

If you were the HR manager for BLI, how would you respond to this crisis? How would you identify the key goals and objectives? What are important legal obligations? What agencies, consulting organizations, and corporate resources would you use to address the issues? What kinds of benefits and services would you put in place to accomplish the goals? How would you communicate about the program and motivate employees to participate? How would you measure your success?

Your instructor has further information about what happened to BLI.

## NOTES AND REFERENCES


1. Richard M Devens, Jr., "The Employee Turnover and Job Openings Survey," *Monthly Labor Review,* Mar. 1992, pp. 29–37.
2. John W. Boudreau. "Utility Analysis: "A New Perspective," in *Human Resource Management: Evolving Roles and Responsibilities,* ed. Lee D. Dyer (Washington, DC: Bureau of National Affairs, 1988);' John W. Boudreau and Chris J. Berger, "Decision-Theoretic Utility Analysis Applied to Employee Separations and Acquisitions," *Journal of Applied Psychology* [Monograph] 70 (1985), pp. 581–612.
3. Robert Barker and John W. Verity, "A Question of Value," *Business Week,* Jan. 18, 1993, p. 30.
4. Brian W. Bulger and Carolyn Curtis Gessner, "Sign of the Times: Implementing Reductions in Force," *Employee Relations Law Journal* 17, no. 3 (Winter 1991–1992), pp. 431–48; "Current Update," *Human Resource Management News,* Apr. 13, 1992, p. 1; Catherine Schwoerer and Benson Rosen, "Effects of Employment-at-Will Policies and Compensation Policies on Corporate Image and Job Pursuit Intentions," *Journal of Applied Psychology* 64, no. 4 (1989), pp. 653–56.
5. Todd R. Zenger, "Why Do Employers Only Reward Extreme Performance? Examining the Relationships among Performance, Pay, and Turnovers," *Administrative Science Quarterly* 37 (1992), pp. 198–219.
6. Kristen Keith and Abagail McWilliams,"The Wage Effects of Cumulative Job Mobility," *Industrial and Labor Relations Review* 49 (Oct. 1995), pp. 121–137.
7. Daniel Seligman, "Keeping Up," *Fortune,* Nov. 30, 1992, p. 80.
8. Robert Gibbons and Lawrence F. Katz, "Layoffs and Lemons," *Journal of Labor Economics* 9, no. 4 (1991), pp. 351–80.
9. Amy Cortese, "Falling Petals at Lotus," *Business Week,* Nov. 6, 1995, p. 4.
10. "Jerome York: The $1.3 Billion Man," *Fortune,* Jan. 15, 1996, p. 86.
11. John W. Boudreau and Chris J. Berger, "Toward a Model of Employee Movement Utility," in *Research in Personnel and Human Resources Management,* vol. 3, ed. Kendrith M. Rowland and Gerald R. Ferris (Greenwich: JAI Press, 1985), pp. 31–54.
12. James G. March and Herbert A. Simon, *Organizations* (New York: John Wiley & Sons, 1958); James L. Price, *The Study of Turnover* (Ames:

Iowa State University Press, 1977); William H. Mobley, "Intermediate Linkages in the Relationship between Job Satisfaction and Employee Turnover," *Journal of Applied Psychology* 62 (1977), pp. 237–40; William H. Mobley, R. W. Griffeth, H. H. Hand, and M. M. Meglino, "Review and Conceptual Analysis of the Employee Turnover Process," *Psychological Bulletin* 86 (1979), pp. 493–522.

13. Rodger W. Griffeth and Peter W. Hom, "The Employee Turnover Process," *Research in Personnel and Human Resources Management* 13 (1995), pp. 245–93.

14. Robert D. Bretz, John W. Boudreau, and Timothy J. Judge. "Job Search Behavior of Employed Managers," *Personnel Psychology* 47 (1994), pp. 275–302; Linda K. Stroh, "Predicting Turnover Among Repatriates: Can Organizations Affect Retention Rates?" *International Journal of Human Resource Management* 6 (May 1995), pp. 443–56.

15. Mandy E. G. van der Velde and Jan A. Feij, "Change of Work Perceptions and Work Outcomes as a Result of Voluntary and Involuntary Job Change," *Journal of Occupational and Organizational Psychology* 68 (1995), pp. 273–90; Arthur J. Farkas and Lois E. Tetrick, "A Three-Wave Longitudinal Analysis of the Causal Ordering of Satisfaction and Commitment on Turnover Decisions," *Journal of Applied Psychology* 74, no. 6 (1989), pp. 855–68.

16. Barry Gerhart, "The Prediction of Voluntary Turnover Using Tenure, Behavioral Intentions, Job Satisfaction, and Area Unemployment Rates," *Journal of Applied Psychology* 75 (1990), pp. 467–76; John L. Cotton and Jeffrey M. Tuttle, "Employee Turnover: A Meta-Analysis and Review with Implications for Research," *Academy of Management Review* 11, no. 1 (1986), pp. 55–70; Daniel G. Spencer "Employee Voice and Employee Retention," *Academy of Management Journal* 29, no. 3 (1986), pp. 488–502; Sik Hung Ng, Fiona Cram, and Lesley Jenkins, "A Proportional Hazards Regression Analysis of Employee Turnover among Nurses in New Zealand," *Human Relations* 44, no. 12 (1991), pp. 1313–30.

17. Peter W. Hom and Rodger W. Griffeth, "Structural Equations Modeling Test of a Turnover Theory: Cross-Sectional and Longitudinal Analyses," *Journal of Applied Psychology* 76, no. 3 (1992), pp. 350–66.

18. Samuel Aryee, Thomas Wyatt, and Ma Kheng Min, "Antecedents of Organizational Commitment and Turnover Intentions among Professional Accountants in Different Employment Settings in Singapore," *Journal of Social Psychology* 13, no. 4 (1991), pp. 545–56; Michael W. Miller, "IBM's Grabe Quits as Exodus at Top Expands," *The Wall Street Journal,* Mar. 4, 1992, p. B1.

19. Wayne F. Cascio and Glen M. McEvoy. "Strategies for Reducing Employee Turnover: A Meta-Analysis," *Journal of Applied Psychology* 70 (1985), pp. 342–53.

20. Bureau of National Affairs, *Job Absence and Turnover Control,* Personnel Policies Forum Survey No. 132 (Washington, DC: Bureau of National Affairs, 1981).

21. *Compflash,* May 1991, p. 2; Julie Amparano Lopez and Joann S. Lublin, "Bosses Seek Ways to Hold on to Workers as Recovery Encourages Job Hopping," *The Wall Street Journal,* Jan. 5, 1992, p. B1.

22. Gary McWilliams, "To Have and to Hold," *Business Week,* June 19, 1995, p. 43.

23. Boudreau and Berger, "Decision-Theoretic Utility Analysis Applied to Employee Separations and Acquisitions;" Ellen F. Jackofsky, "Turnover and Job Performance: An Integrated Process Model," *Academy of Management Journal* 9 (1984), pp. 74–83; John E. Mathieu and Joseph E. Baratta, "Turnover Type as a Moderator of the Performance-Turnover Relationship," *Human Performance* 2, no. 1 (1989), pp. 61–71; Leah Nathans Spiro, John Byrne, Bart Ziegler, and Maria Mallory, "The Flight of the Managers," *Business Week,* Feb. 22, 1993, pp. 78–81; Donald P. Schab, "Contextual Variables in Employee Performance-Turnover Relationships," *Academy of Management Journal* 34, no. 4 (1991), pp. 96–79.

24. Danny Miller, "Stale in the Saddle: CEO Tenure and the Match between Organization and Environment," *Management Science* 37, no. 1 (1991), pp. 34–52; Jason R. Barro and Robert J. Barro, "Pay, Performance and Turnover of Bank CEOs" *Journal of Labor Economics* 8, no. 4 (1990), pp. 448–81.

25. Dale Ballou and Michael Podgursky, "Recruiting Smarter Teachers," *Journal of Human Resources* 30 (1995), pp. 326–38.

26. John W. Boudreau, "Future Utility Analysis Research: Continue, but Expand the Cognitive and Strategic Focus," Center for Advanced Human Resource Studies Working Paper No. 95-35; Barry Gerhart, John W. Boudreau, and Charlie O. Trevor, "Voluntary Turnover and Job Performance: Curvilinearity and the Moderating Influences of Salary Growth, Promotions, and Labor Demand," Center for Advanced Human Resource Studies Working Paper; No. 95-33.

27. Eugene P. Sheehan, "Affective Responses to Employee Turnover," *Journal of Social Psychology* 135 (1995), pp. 63–69.

28. Michael W. Miller, "IBM Sues to Silence Former Employee." *The Wall Street Journal,* July 15, 1992, p. B1.

29. Olga Aikin, "Restraining Influences," *Personnel Management* 31, no. 6 (June 1994), pp. 65–68.

30. A. Dale Allen, Jr., "Quit and Return: Is It Resignation or Discharge?" *Labor Law Journal,* Oct. 1995, pp. 598–607.

31. Benson Rosen, Mabel Miguel, and Ellen Pierce, "Stemming the Exodus of Women Managers," *Human Resource Management* 28, no. 4 (Winter 1989), pp. 475–91; Audrey Light and Manuelita Ureta, "Panel Estimates of Male Behavior: Can Female Nonquitters Be Identified?" *Journal of Labor Economics* 10, no. 2 (1992), pp. 156–81.

32. Tina Adler, "Use Skills Tests—Not Age—to Determine Retirement?" *APA Monitor* 23, no. 2 (March 1992), pp. 4–5; B. Bower, "Mandatory Retirement: Public Safety Hazard," *Science News* 141 (Nov. 25, 1992), p. 54.

33. Robert L. Clark and Naohiro Ogawa, "The Effect of Mandatory Retirement on Earnings Profiles in Japan," *Industrial and Labor Relations Review* 45, no. 2 (Jan. 1992), pp. 258–66.

34. Amanda Bennett, "Corporate Chiefs Calling It Quits Earlier," *The Wall Street Journal,* Dec. 22, 1989, p. B1.

35. Herbert S. Parnes, "The Retirement Decision," in *The Older Worker,* ed. Michael E. Borus, Herbert S. Parnes, Steven H. Sandell, and Bert Seidman (Madison, WI: Industrial Relations Research Association, 1988), chap. 5.
36. Marc Frons, "Early Retirement: It Pays to Plan Early," *Business Week,* Feb. 27, 1989, pp. 134–35; Pamela Sherrid, "Taking an Early Out," *U.S. News & World Report,* Nov. 11, 1992, pp. 81–82; Kevin Pritchett, "Bell Atlantic Offers Early Retirement to 6,300 Workers," *The Wall Street Journal,* Aug. 5, 1991 p. A2; Ron Suskind, "Polaroid to Offer Early Retirement to Boost Growth," *The Wall Street Journal,* Nov. 18, 1992, p. A7; Neal Templin, "UAW to Unveil Pact on Slashing GM's Payroll," *The Wall Street Journal,* Dec. 14, 1992, p. A3.
37. Catherine Arnst, "For a Pink Slip, Press 2," *Business Week,* Nov. 27, 1995; Jeff Cole, "Response to Boeing Retirement Offer Eases Layoff Plans," *The Wall Street Journal,* June 19, 1995, p. A5.
38. Internal Kodak press releases and conversations with Kodak HR managers; see also Labor Letter, "Lock the Doors! Early Retirement Buy-Outs Sometimes Work Too Well," *The Wall Street Journal,* Feb. 25, 1992, p. A1.
39. *Human Resource Management News,* Dec. 1992, p. 3; Joseph B. White, "GM Tells Staff It Won't Repeat Retirement Plan Again,: *The Wall Street Journal,* Feb. 18, 1992, p. B12; Gregory A. Patterson, "More Employers Offer Early Retirement to Help Shrink Blue-collar Work Force," *The Wall Street Journal,* Aug. 30, 1991, p. B1; Joann S. Lublin, "Firms Rethink Lucrative Severance Pacts for Top Executives as Criticism Swells," *The Wall Street Journal,* Nov. 11, 1991, p. B1.
40. " 'Open-Window' Early Retirement Plans Seen Successful," *Bureau of National Affairs Daily Executive Report,* no. 48, Mar. 13, 1986; Julia Lawlor, "Buyout Game Throws Many," *USA Today,* Oct. 29, 1992, p. B1.
41. Larry I. Stein, "Through the Looking Glass: An Analysis of Window Plans," *Labor Law Journal,* Oct. 1991, pp. 665–76.
42. Conference Board, "Older Workers: Dispelling Myths," *The Conference Board's Management Briefing: Human Resources* 4, no. 9 (Sept. 1988), pp. 2–3.
43. Raju Narietti, "Retiring Gault Won't Let Go of Goodyear," *The Wall Street Journal,* Oct. 31, 1995, p. B1; "Older Workers: the 'Dracula Complex,' " *Human Resource Management News,* Feb. 13, 1995, p. 2.
44. Murray Gendell and Jacob S. Siegel, "Trends in Retirement Age by Sex, 1950–2005," *Monthly Labor Review,* July 1992, pp. 22–29; Dane E. Herz, "Work After Early Retirement: An Increasing Trend Among Men," *Monthly Labor Review,* Apr. 1995, pp. 13–20.
45. Boudreau, "Utility Analysis"; Daniel Seligman, "The Trouble with Buyouts," *Fortune,* Nov. 30, 1992, p. 124.
46. Amy Saltzman, Anne Kates Smith, and Francesca Lunzer Kritz, "Girding for a Pink Slip," *U.S. News & World Report,* Jan. 14, 1991, pp. 54–56; David Kirkpatrick, "The New Executive Unemployed," *Fortune,* Apr. 8, 1991, pp. 36–48; Marshall Loeb, "What to Do if You Get Fired," *Fortune,* Jan. 15 1996, pp. 77–78.

47. Glenn R. Simpson, "Hillary Clinton Tied to Firings in Travel Office," *The Wall Street Journal,* Jan. 15 1995, p. B4.

48. Bureau of National Affairs, *Employee Discipline and Discharge,* Personnel Policies Forum Survey No. 139 (Washington, DC: Bureau of National Affairs, 1985); Robert C. Rodgers and Jack Stieber "Employee Discharge in the 20th Century: A Review of the Literature," *Monthly Labor Review,* Sept. 1985, pp. 35–41.

49. Paul B. Carroll, "Akers to IBM Employees: Wake Up!" *The Wall Street Journal,* May 29, 1991, p. B1; Amanda Bennett and Joann S. Lublin, "Increasing Turnover at the Top Sends Many Executives' Careers into Limbo," *The Wall Street Journal,* Apr. 13, 1992, p. B1; Gabriella Stern, Paul B. Carroll, and Michel McQueen, "Fall Guys," *The Wall Street Journal,* Dec. 31, 1991, p. A1.

50. *Union Labor Hospital Association* v. *Vance Redwood Lumber Co.,* 158 Cal. 551, 112, p. 886 (1910).

51. Gary B. Brumback, "The Unemployment-at-Will Doctrine," *Labor Law Journal,* Feb. 1995, pp. 111–15.

52. *Phillips* v. *Goodyear Tire and Rubber Company,* Ca5, No. 79-2011 (1981); *Tamory* v. *Atlantic Richfield Co.,* 27 Ca.3d 167 (1980); *Murphy* v. *City of Topeka-Shawunee County Dept of Labor Services,* Kn Ct App. No. 57 (1981); *Palmateer* v. *International Harvester Company,* 85 Ill. 2d 124 (1981).

53. Clyde W. Summers, "The Need for a Statute," *ILR Report,* Fall 1982, pp. 8–12; Paul Salvatore, "Legislative Action and Private Initiative: A Practical Solution," *ILR Report,* Fall 1982, pp. 13–15.

54. *Toussaint* v. *Blue Cross/Blue Shield of Michigan,* 408 Mich. 579 (1980); Amy Dockser Marcus, "Courts Uphold Oral Pledges of Lifetime Employment," *The Wall Street Journal,* Dec. 12 1989, p. B1.

55. Terry H. Wagar and Kathy A. Jourdain, "The Determination of Reasonable Notice in Canadian Wrongful Dismissal Cases," *Labor Law Journal,* Jan. 1992, pp. 58–62.

56. Joann S. Lublin, "Companies Try to Prevent Fired Executives From Suing," *The Wall Street Journal,* June 28, 1995, p. B1.

57. "IBM Agrees to Settle Racial Bias Lawsuit by Former Executive," *The Wall Street Journal,* July 7, 1992, p. B5.

58. James P. Miller, "Japanese Firm Wins Ruling in Rights Case," *The Wall Street Journal,* Dec. 6, 1991, p. A3.

59. *Daily Labor Report,* "Court Finds No Age Bias in Firing Based on Salary," July 17, 1991; *Hazen Paper Company, et al.,* v. *Walter F. Biggins,* 1993 U.S. Lexis 2978; 61 Fair Empl. Prac. Cas. (BNA) 793.

60. Grace M. Kang, "Laws Covering Sex Harassment and Wrongful Dismissal Collide," *The Wall Street Journal,* Sept. 24, 1992, p. B1.

61. "Labor Letter," *The Wall Street Journal,* May 12, 1992, p. A1.

62. Aaron Bernstein and Zachary Schiller, "Tell It to the Arbitrator," *Business Week,* November 4, 1991, p. 109; Lublin, "Companies Try to Prevent Fired Executives from Suing."

63. Bureau of National Affairs, "Seventh Circuit Revives Age Bias Suit Challenging Computerized Evaluation," *BNA's Employee Relations Weekly,* Nov. 30, 1992, p. 1293.
64. Suzanne Alexander, "Firms Get Plenty of Practice at Layoffs, But They Often Bungle the Firing Process," *The Wall Street Journal,* Oct. 14, 1991, p. B1.
65. See, for example, Ralph H. Baxter, Jr., and Jeffrey D. Wohl, "Wrongful Termination Lawsuits: The Employers Finally Win a Few," *Employee Relations Law Journal* 10 (1985), pp. 258–75; Sami M. Abbasi, Kenneth W. Hollman, and Joe H. Murrey, Jr., "Employment at Will: An Eroding Concept in Employment Relationships," *Labor Law Journal* 38, no. 1 (Jan. 1987), pp. 261–79; Lin Grensing, "Termination—A Sensitive Issue," *Office Systems* 9, no. 8 (Aug. 1992), pp. 67–68.
66. Sheila M. Puffer and Joseph B. Weintrop, "Corporate Performance and CEO Turnover: The Role of Performance Expectations," *Administrative Science Quarterly* 36 (1991), pp. 1–19.
67. Murray R. Barrick, Michael K. Mount, and J. Perkins Strauss, "Antecedents of Involuntary Turnover Due to a Reduction in Force," *Personnel Psychology* 47 (1994) pp. 515–35.
68. HRNET, Nov. 25, 1995.
69. Bureau of Labor Statistics, "Corporate Layoffs Top 300,000 Since January, Firm Reports," *Daily Labor Reporter* no. 193 (Nov. 5, 1995), p. A–6. American Management Association, *1994 AMA Survey on Downsizing,* Summer 1994; Jennifer M. Gardner, "Worker Displacement: A Decade of Change," *Monthly Labor Review,* Apr. 1995, pp. 45–57; David S. Evans and Linda S. Leighton, "Retrospective Bias in the Displaced Worker Surveys," *Journal of Human Resources* 3 (1994), pp. 386–96.
70. Gary Putka, "Yale Committee Urges Big Cut in Core Faculty," *The Wall Street Journal,* Jan. 17, 1992, p. B1; Work in America Institute, "U.S.-Japan HR Network," *Work In America* 20 (Nov. 1995), pp. 1–3; "Salariless Man," *The Economist,* Sept. 16, 1995, p. 79; Karen Lowry Miller, "Land of the Rising Jobless," *Business Week,* Jan. 11, 1993, p. 47; Jacob M. Schlesinger and Masayoshi Kanabayashi, "Many Japanese Find Their 'Lifetime' Jobs Can Be Short-Lived," *The Wall Street Journal,* Oct. 8 1992, p. A1; Jacob M. Schlesinger, "Pioneer Electronic Forces 35 Managers to Retire, Shaking a Japanese Tradition," *The Wall Street Journal,* Jan. 11, 1993, p. A11; Masayoshi Kanabayashi, "Japanese Index Adds to Fears on Economy," *The Wall Street Journal,* Dec. 2, 1992, p. A6.
71. *1994 AMA Survey on Downsizing,* p. 1.
72. Joseph Pereira, "Polaroid to Cut Jobs, Restructure; Charge is Planned," *The Wall Street Journal,* Dec. 20, 1995, p. A5; "Bausch & Lomb Layoffs and Earnings Charge," *New York Times,* Jan. 11, 1996, p. D4.
73. *1994 AMA Survey on Downsizing,* p. 3.
74. Zahid Iqbal and Shekar Shetty, "A Multivariate Analysis of Employee Layoffs," *American Business Review* 12 (May 1994), pp. 15–21.
75. Dianne Solis and Paul B. Carroll, "Mexican Firms Are Laying Off Thousands, Imperiling Economy," *The Wall Street Journal,* Feb. 27, 1995, p.A8; "Orange County Seeks to Slash 1,600 Jobs in Recovery Plan," *The*

*Wall Street Journal,* Mar. 9 1995, p. B14; G. Pascal Zachary "Worried Workers," *The Wall Street Journal,* June 8, 1995, p. A1; Robert L. Simison and Valerie Reitman, "Toyota Says It May Have to Shut Down Plans in Japan: Layoffs Are Possibility," *The Wall Street Journal,* May 12, 1995, p. A5; John J. Keller, "AT&T Plans to Slash Workforce," *The Wall Street Journal,* Sep. 27, 1995, p. A3; Bureau of National Affairs, "Texaco Inc. Announces More Cuts," *Daily Labor Report,* Nov. 5, 1995, pp. A12–A13.

76. Allan Sloan, "Take This Job and Cut It," *Newsweek,* Feb. 5, 1996, p. 47; Zahid Iqbal and Shekar Shetty, "Layoffs, Stock Price, and Financial Condition of the Firm," *Journal of Applied Business Research* 11 (Spring 1995), pp. 67–72; Nancy Ursel and Marjorie Armstrong-Stassen, "The Impact of Layoff Announcements on Shareholders," *Industrial Relations—Quebec* 50 (Summer 1995), pp. 636–49.
77. U.S. Department of Labor, *Guide to Responsible Restructuring* (Washington, DC: Office of the American Workplace, 1995).
78. William Weitzel and Ellen Jonsson, "Decline in Organization: A Literature Integration and Extension," *Administrative Science Quarterly* 34 (1989), pp. 91–109; Jerome M. Rosow, "Cutting by the Numbers Won't Save U.S. Industry," *Work in America,* Feb. 1992, pp. 1–2.
79. Robert Harris, "Canadians Replace Layoffs with Voluntary Rightsizing," *HR Focus,* May 1991, pp. 15–16; "GM Agrees to Allow a Parts Supplier to Use Some of Its Idled Employees," *The Wall Street Journal,* Nov. 30 1992, p. B6.
80. U.S. Department of Labor, *Guide to Responsible Restructuring* pp. 7–9.
81. *1994 AMA Survey on Downsizing,* p. 4.
82. Linda Himelstein, "Take My Job, Please!" *Business Week,* July 8, 1996, p. 6.
83. Samuel Greengard, "Don't Rush Downsizing: Plan, Plan, Plan," *Personnel Journal,* Nov. 1993, pp. 64–76.
84. Marjorie Armstong-Stassen, "Coping with Transition: A Study of Layoff Survivors," *Journal of Organizational Behavior* 15 (Dec. 1994), pp. 597–621; Janina C. Latack, Angelo J. Kinicki and Gregory E. Prussia, "An Integrative Process Model of Coping with Job Loss," *Academy of Management Review* 20 (1995), pp. 311–42.
85. R. J. Bies, C. L. Martin, and Joel Brockner, "Just Laid Off But Still a Good Citizen: Only if the Process is Fair," *Employee Responsibilities and Rights Journal* (1993), pp. 227–38; Christopher L. Martin, Charles K. Parsons, and Nathan Bennett, "The Influence of Employee Involvement Program Membership during Downsizing: Attitudes Toward the Employer and the Union," *Journal of Management* 21 (1995), pp. 879–90; Marjorie Armstrong-Stassen, "Survivors' Reactions to a Workforce Reduction: a Comparison of Blue-Collar Workers and Their Supervisors," *Canadian Journal of Administrative Sciences,* 10 (Dec. 1993), pp. 334–43.
86. John T. Addison and McKinley Blackburn, "Advance Notice and Job Search: More on the Value of an Early Start," *Industrial Relations* 34 (Apr. 1995), pp. 242–63; Ronald G. Ehrenberg and George H. Jakubson,

"Advance Notification of Plant Closing: Does It Matter?" *Industrial Relations* 28, no. 1 (Winter 1989), pp. 60–71.

87. Terry H. Wagar, "The WARN Act and Perceptions of Managers Concerning the Effect of Providing Advance Notice," *Labor Law Journal,* Sept. 1992, pp. 588–92.; Paul L. Burgess and Stuart A. Low, "Preunemployment Job Search and Advance Job Loss Notice," *Journal of Labor Economics* 10, no. 3 (1992), pp. 258–87; Dan L. Worrell, Wallace N. Davidson III, and Varinder M. Sharma, "Layoff Announcements and Stockholder Wealth," *Academy of Management Journal* 34, no. 3 (1991), pp. 662–76.
88. Paul M. Barrett, "High Court Eases Limit on Workers' Suits," *The Wall Street Journal,* May 31, 1995, p. A5.
89. "Seniority versus Skills," *The Wall Street Journal,* July 7, 1992, p. A1; Joseph T. McCune, Richard W. Beatty, and Raymond V. Montagno, "Downsizing: Practices in Manufacturing Firms," *Human Resource Management* 27, no. 2 (Summer 1988), pp. 145–61.
90. *Firefighters Local Union No. 1784* v. Stotts, 467 U.S. 561 (1984); *Wygant* v. *Jackson Board of Education,* 40 FEP Cases 1321 (May 19, 1986); Bureau of National Affairs, *Affirmative Action Today* (Washington, DC: Bureau of National Affairs, 1986).
91. Sarah Lubman, "Hughes Aircraft Tries to Ease Pain of 12,000 Layoffs," *The Wall Street Journal,* July 24, 1992, p. B6; "Severance Pay Lasts as Long as Job Search," *HR Focus,* June 1992, p. 12; Charlene Marmer Soloman, "Loans Help Laid-Off Employees Find New Careers," *Personnel Journal,* Sept. 1992, pp. 77–80.
92. William J. Barkley, Jr., and Thad B. Green, "Safe Landings for Outplaced Employees at AT&T," *Personnel Journal,* June 1992, pp. 144–47; "Those Mustered Out Get Help Finding Work," *The Wall Street Journal,* Aug. 15, 1992, p. B1; Jeremy Main, "Look Who Needs Outplacement," *Fortune,* Oct. 9, 1989, pp. 85–92; Don Lee, " 'One-Stop' Centers Help Job Seekers on Career Paths," *Los Angeles Times,* Jan. 27, 1996, D1; Ellen James Martin, " 'CareerNet' is set to Go to Work," *Baltimore Sun,* Nov. 30, 1995, p. 1C.
93. "Ex-Employees Sue Kodak," *New York Times,* Mar. 23, 1992, p. D3; Lubman, "Hughes Aircraft," p. B6; Meredith K. Wadman, "More Firms Restrict Departing Workers," *The Wall Street Journal,* June 26, 1992, p. B1.
94. Lucinda Harper, "Travel Agency Learns Service Firms' Perils in Slimming Down," *The Wall Street Journal,* Mar. 20, 1992, p. A1.
95. Leslie Cauley, "Baby Bells Face a Tough Balancing Act," *The Wall Street Journal,* Jan. 14, 1996, p. A2; Teresa M. Amabile and Regina Conti, "What Downsizing Does to Creativity," *Ideas & Observations,* Center for Creative Leadership, 1995; Matt Murley, "Thanks, Goodbye," *The Wall Street Journal,* May 4, 1995, p. A1.
96. Joel Brockner, et al., "Interactive Effect of Job Content and Context on the Reactions of Layoff Survivors," *Journal of Personality and Social Psychology* 64, no. 2 (1993), pp. 187–97; Joel Brockner, Steven Grover, Thomas F. Reed, and Rocki Lee Dewitt, "Layoffs, Job Insecurity, and

Survivors' Work Effort: Evidence of an Inverted-U Relationship," *Academy of Management Journal* 35, no. 2 (1992), pp. 413–25.

97. Kim S. Cameron, Sarah J. Freeman, and Aneil K. Mishra, "Best Practices in White-Collar Downsizing: Managing Contradictions," *Academy of Management Executive* 5, no. 3 (1991), pp. 57–73.

98. John E. Sheridan, "Organizational Culture and Employee Retention," *Academy of Management Journal* 35, no. 5 (1992), pp. 1036–56.

99. Julie Amparano Lopez, "Companies Alter Layoff Policies to Keep Recently Hired Women and Minorities," *The Wall Street Journal,* Sept. 15, 1992, p. B1.

100. Boudreau and Berger, "Decision-Theoretic Utility Analysis Applied to Employee Separations and Acquisitions;" Boudreau, "Utility Analysis;" Daniel C. Feldman, "The Impact of Downsizing on Organizational Career Development Activities and Employee Career Development Opportunities," *Human Resource Management Review* 5 (1995), pp. 189–221.

101. This Your Turn is based on information from Joe A. Bowden, "The Anatomy of a Plant Closing," *Personnel Journal,* May 1992, pp. 60–72.

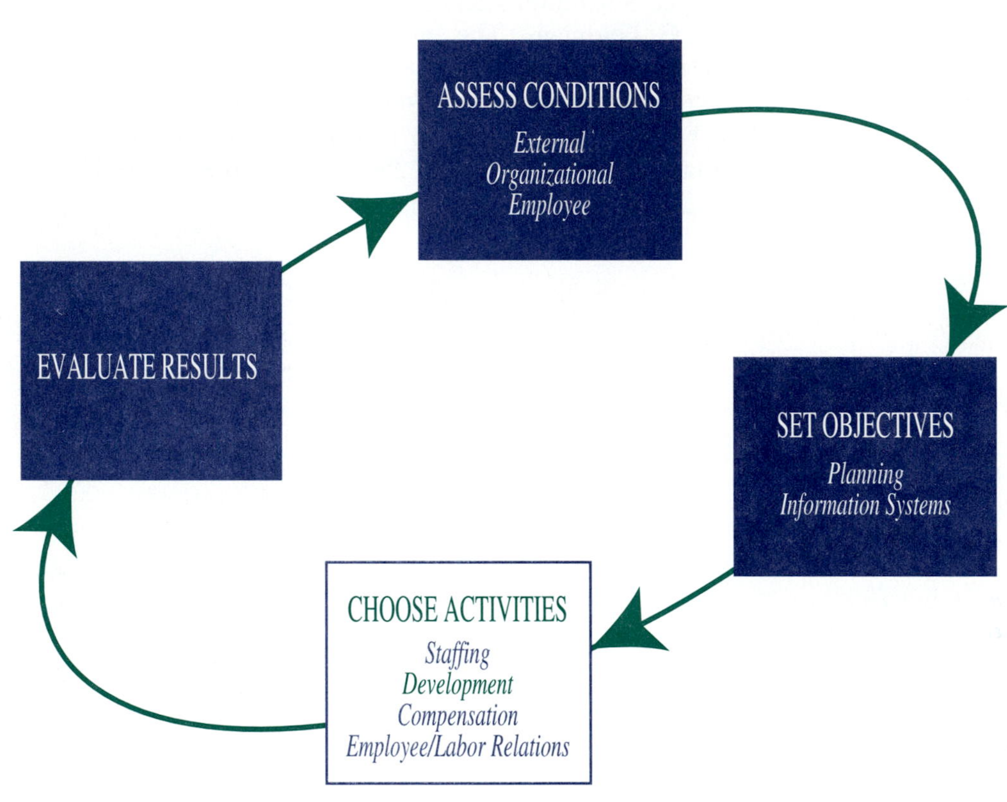
ASSESS CONDITIONS
External
Organizational
Employee
SET OBJECTIVES
Planning
Information Systems
CHOOSE ACTIVITIES
Staffing
Development
Compensation
Employee/Labor Relations
EVALUATE RESULTS

# EMPLOYEE DEVELOPMENT

According to Bill Clinton, the United States faces a national crisis because its workers are ill-prepared by the educational system for future jobs. With the drastic changes in the workforce and critical skill shortages, described earlier in Part Two on external staffing, organizations cannot expect to meet their labor force needs simply by managing external recruitment, selection, and separations. Most of the attention must be devoted to employees after they join the organization, providing them with experiences and training that will prepare them for the changing work roles of the future.

*Employee development* refers to the human resource activities designed to enhance the value of employees after they have joined the organization. It encompasses *internal staffing,* which involves moving people between jobs and work roles within the organization. It also includes *employee training and orientation,* which involves giving employees experiences designed to foster learning. These two activities go hand in hand, because they must work together if the workforce is to be properly prepared. Internal staffing bears many similarities to external staffing, but because internal staffing deals with existing employees, it also has characteristics similar to training activities. Employee training and orientation are based on principles of learning; the methods that foster adult learning in the workplace are different from the classroom education experiences most familiar to college students.

## A Diagnostic Approach to Employee Development

The accompanying exhibit shows where development fits the diagnostic approach. Because internal staffing and employee training/orientation focus on developing existing employees, they must constantly strike a balance between organizational concerns for efficiency (optimal matches between skills and demands) and equity (perceptions that activities are fair, legal, and provide adequate opportunity). They are also keenly affected by factors outside the organization as well as organization and employee characteristics.

### External Conditions

Workplace skill demands are rapidly increasing, yet workers continue to leave schools ill-prepared in even the most basic skills. The increasing number of minority and women members of the workforce present special challenges because they often require different skill-building opportunities or opportunities to acquire business knowledge than the traditional white male. Global competition means greater flexibility and continuous learning among workers to produce better products and services every year. This can only be accomplished if training and internal staffing are targeted to organizational objectives.

Legal requirements affect employee development just as they affect external staffing. The same EEO legislation that regulates external recruitment, selection, and retention policies also affects internal staffing decisions. Moreover, affirmative action does not end when people are hired. Their advancement is also a critical requirement for meeting affirmative action goals. Organizationally supplied training and career experience is often the key to giving underrepresented minorities and women the opportunity to advance. In addition, governments shape public education from public schools to vocational training to preschool programs such as

Head Start. Human resource managers have a stake in these programs because their success often depends on how well they produce trainees that fit business needs. Finally, government regulations on occupational safety often mandate training and carefully designed job experiences to assure that employees are prepared to abide by safety rules.

Collective bargaining agreements and day-to-day contract administration are frequently more concerned with internal staffing and training opportunities than with external staffing. Most union contracts award internal employment and training opportunities on the basis of seniority. Human resource managers increasingly bargain for more flexible staffing and training rules to allow the most qualified—not necessarily the most senior—employees to compete for opportunities. Unions also are key providers of training through their apprenticeship programs, especially for skilled crafts such as construction.

### Organizational Conditions

The organization's strategies and culture determine both the need and the nature of employee development. Organizations may restructure to eliminate management layers, push decision making closer to the production line or the customer, and cut costs by increasing labor productivity. These decisions must be supported by appropriate career paths, training experiences, and orientation activities if they are to succeed. It does little good to build a state-of-the-art manufacturing process if the employees do not know how to read and calculate sufficiently to operate it. Organizational values also affect employee development. In organizations choosing to compete based on employment security and employee quality, massive amounts of resources are devoted to giving employees options to move between jobs and to get the training necessary to make them successful when they do move. Many organizations have adopted the concept of *continuous learning* to describe what they expect of employees in the future. For human resource managers, this often translates into *continuous development.*

### Employee Characteristics

Employee characteristics are especially critical to internal staffing. Unlike external staffing, where new pools of applicants can be developed with different attributes, internal staffing must focus on existing employees. It is their skills, interests, abilities, and knowledge that provide the raw materials for successful internal staffing decisions. Moreover, those rejected for internal staffing opportunities remain employed by the organization. Because internal staffing decisions determine career progress, pay, and status, the reactions of employees who are chosen and those who are not affect how well objectives are achieved. The success of training activities depends on individual characteristics. Employees must be motivated and able to learn for training to succeed. Moreover, the success of training is often evaluated by examining whether such individual characteristics as knowledge, attitudes, or behavior have changed. The knowledge, skills, and abilities of individuals must match their work roles.

### Objectives/Standards for Employee Development

Subsequent chapters describe the goals and evaluation methods for employee development in detail. These activities often have effects that are not obvious at first. The goals of internal staffing may best be met by paying careful attention to the jobs that supply the promoted employees, not only the jobs that receive them. The goals of training programs may best be evaluated by calculating return on investment, even though there are no precise figures to use in the calculation. Like all human resource activities, the objectives and standards that are set for employee development must be integrated with the objectives and standards for other human resource activities.

Part III contains two chapters: Chapter Nine describes internal staffing, showing how it is related to, but distinct from, external staffing and illustrating its close relationship to employee development. Chapter Ten describes employee training, orientation, and development, showing how organizations can foster learning through both formal and informal opportunities.

# Internal Staffing and Careers

Imagine you attend a party held in a six-cornered room. An aerial view of the room is shown in Exhibit 9.1. People with similar interests have all gathered in the same corner of the room, as signified by the letters *R, I, A, S, E,* and *C.* First, decide which corner of the room you would be drawn to because that group contains the kind of people you most enjoy being with for the longest time. Write down the letter signifying that corner of the room. Second, assume that after 15 minutes, everyone in your corner leaves except you. Now, choose the corner you would move to because that group contains the kind of people you would secondmost enjoy being with for the longest time. Write down the letter signifying that corner to the right of the first letter. Finally, assume that after 15 minutes everyone in the second group leaves except you. Of the remaining corners, which one would you move to because that group contains the kind of people you would thirdmost enjoy being with for the longest time. Write down the letter signifying your third corner to the right of the second letter. You now have a three-letter combination describing people whose interests match yours.

Researchers asked people holding various jobs to do this exercise; they concluded that people drawn to certain vocational interests tend to end up in certain kinds of jobs. The letters stand for **R**ealistic, **I**nvestigative, **A**rtistic, **S**ocial, **E**nterprising, and **C**onventional. For example, **RIE** is commonly chosen by mechanical, petroleum, and mining engineers as well as mechanics and machinists. **ISA** is often chosen by physicians, psychiatrists/psychologists, and medical technologists. **AES** is often chosen by advertising executives/managers, entertainers, fashion models, and public relations persons. **SIA** is often chosen by college professors, school counselors, nurses, and social workers. **ESC** is often chosen by city managers, personnel managers, labor arbitrators, and sales clerks. **CSA** is often chosen by secretaries, library assistants, and order clerks. This career interest framework has been verified through research. There are several books and instruments available to help you pinpoint your interests and find out what kinds of occupations they match.[1]

Do you think career values differ by cultural heritage? One study compared Asian American to Caucasian American undergraduate students, and found that Asian American students were higher on the Investigative and Conventional scales, but lower on the Social scale.[2]

A more exhaustive approach is the Campbell Interest and Skill Survey (CISS), which measures likes and dislikes using names of occupations, school subjects, activities (e.g., "discussing the purpose of life," "pursuing bandits in a sheriff's posse"), types of people (e.g., "people who live dangerously"), items for you to describe yourself (e.g., "have more than share of novel ideas," "win friends easily"), and your skill and confidence in performing various activities. Using computerized scoring and databases on thousands of people, the test publishers can use the IOHCNPA scale to compare a person's answers with those of people in various professions—**I**nfluencing (leadership, public speaking), **O**rganizing (supervising, office practices), **H**elping (counseling, medicine), **C**reating (art, performing, fashion),

EXHIBIT 9.1 Occupational Interests Arranged as a Six-Cornered Room

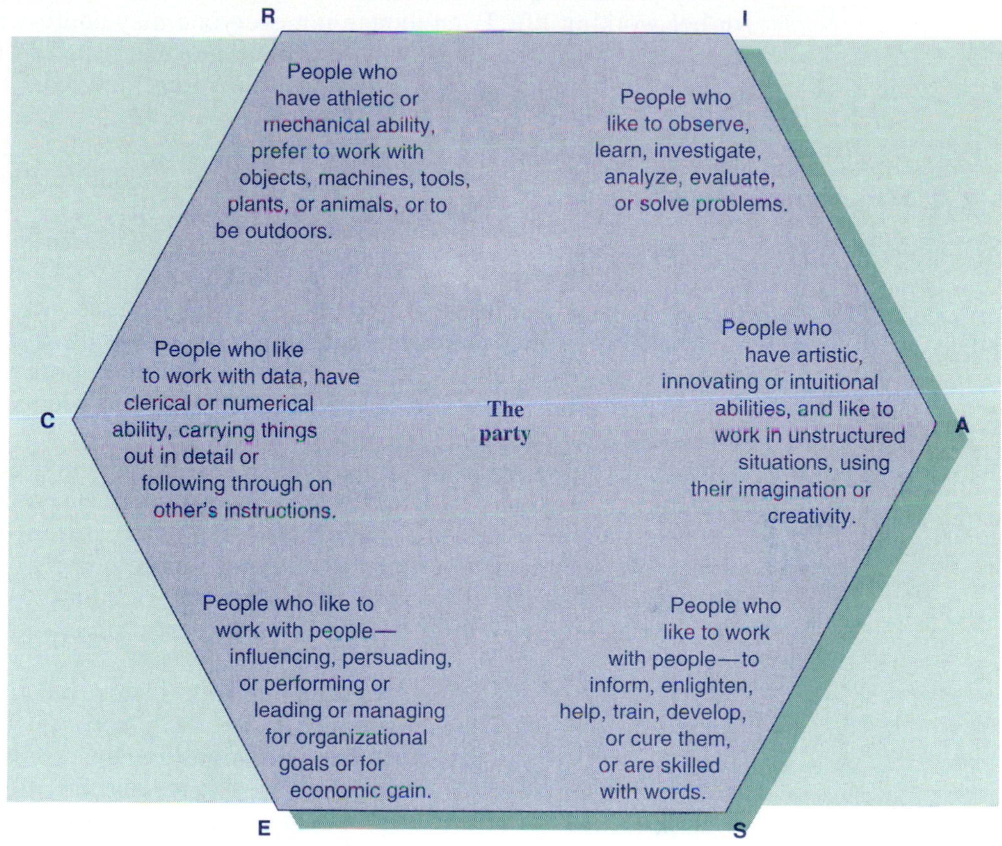


EXPLORING THE WEB

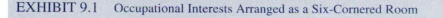

You can learn more about the Campbell Interest and Skills Survey in your college's career service office, or on the web at:
**http://www.ncs.com/cds.ciss.htm**.

A**N**alyzing (mathematics, science), **Pro**ducing (farming, animal care, woodworking), **A**dventuring (athletics, law enforcement, adventure).[3] The results report occupations where you have both high interest and high skill (pursue these), low interest and low skill (avoid these), low skill and high interest (develop these), and high skill but low interest (explore these).

Did your choices match the kind of career interests you think you'd like to pursue? Do you believe that people with these interests tend to go into these occupations? Do people change their interests throughout their careers or are they anchored to a certain kind of interest that keeps them in similar jobs or positions? Should organizations choose employees for career opportunities based on their interests or should such decisions focus simply on finding the best performer for the opportunity?

## INTERNAL STAFFING AND EMPLOYEE CAREERS

Everyone faces questions about career interests and aspirations throughout his or her working life. Even though not everyone may address them as systematically as just described, one way or another people create and follow careers.

The particular sequence of jobs, organizations, and work roles a person pursues results from conscious choices based on interests, as well as constraints and opportunities encountered throughout the person's work life. Careers include upward, lateral, and downward sequences of work experiences.

A *career* is the evolving sequence of a person's work experiences over time.[4]

As you saw in Chapter Three on organizations and work, today's companies are undergoing fundamental restructuring. For many, the traditional hierarchy is gone, replaced by flexible teams, fewer levels from bottom to top, increased individual responsibility for career development, and reduced commitments to providing lifetime employment and careers. What is a career today? It is certainly not always an orderly progression of work roles in a single area, each one providing ever more responsibility and supervisory discretion. Future careers are likely to involve work in several different organizations, to span two or three different occupations, and to rely much more heavily on the person's ability to chart a course than on an organization's traditions. Some might call this new world harsher, but for those who can adapt, it portends immense flexibility and opportunities.

We tend to think of careers affecting individuals, but they also are vitally important to organizations and are often a key activity for human resource managers. HR managers must make decisions and enact activities to retain and develop future talent. A world of greater change and flexibility presents particular challenges to HR managers responsible for ensuring a steady flow of talent. Internal staffing decisions determine how employees move between work roles within the organization. HR managers have always played a part in such decisions, but rapid change makes them even more vital today. Like the other staffing activities discussed earlier, these decisions can affect organizations for decades, so the stakes are high. Moreover, internal staffing decisions and policies determine the career progress of employees, and thus affect their status, income level, and satisfaction. This chapter examines how organizations can identify internal staffing opportunities and candidates, how individuals decide whether to accept the opportunities so that the organization can remain competitive and flexible, and the effects of such decisions on the individuals and the organization.

### Setting Objectives for Internal Staffing and Careers

Internal staffing and career choices affect which work roles are assigned to what employees. Thus, internal staffing shares many of the same effects on efficiency and equity as external recruitment, selection, and separation/retention. Whenever people move from one work role to another, the work roles they move into undertake selection and recruitment activities while the work roles they leave are affected by the separation. Again, all the principles from external staffing apply to internal staffing.

### Efficiency

Internal staffing activities incur the costs of attracting applicants for internal opportunities, assessing their characteristics and interests to determine their fitness for internal employment opportunities, moving employees from one assignment to another, and filling the vacancy created in the work role the employee leaves. All of the costs discussed in the chapters on external staffing also apply to internal staffing, but they are incurred while focusing on existing employees. Such costs are not trivial. The executive vice president of Runzheimer and Company, a national consulting firm on employee relocation, estimated that when employees were relocated in 1994, it cost an average of $50,000.[5] This doesn't even include the activities related to attracting, selecting, and replacing those who moved.

Are such costs justified? As with external selection, this depends on how well internal staffing decisions place the right people in the right work roles at the right time. Research suggests that the difference between accurate and inaccurate placements can amount to millions of dollars over time in large organizations.[6] The effects are especially obvious when you consider that every internal promotion, lateral transfer, or downward transfer creates a vacancy that also must be filled. The sequence of staffing decisions initiated by internal staffing provides immense opportunities to add value or immense opportunities to do damage if they are not considered carefully. They must be integrated with other HR activities to be truly effective. The relationships created through internal staffing are a key glue holding the organization together.[7] Moreover, careers are perhaps the most powerful tool for developing future skills, talent and values. Therefore, decisions about career systems must be closely aligned with organizational goals. As one expert put it, "every hour spent establishing top management's perceived business needs is worth 100 hours spent on program design and development.[8]

### Equity

With external staffing, those not hired usually have little impact on the organization. However, internal staffing activities deal with current employees, so rejected employees are still around and all employees watch the process carefully for clues to the fairness of the organizations's policies. Desirable career opportunities signal to employees that they are doing well, and career progressions affect employees' status and rewards. Therefore, employees regard career decisions with the same equity concerns as they have for their pay and benefits. Also, employees are usually concerned that they have some self-direction and control, that career decisions balance work and family, and that the organization provides honest and helpful information for making career decisions.[9]

Internal staffing affects progress toward equal employment opportunity (EEO) and affirmative action. These effects have been the subject of immense press coverage and even a special U.S. Labor Department study of the glass ceiling keeping women and minorities from reaching the top of organizations. Indeed, the affirmative action program in the San Francisco Fire Department has tempted some firefighters to falsely claim to belong to a minority group in hopes of getting extra consideration in promotion decisions.[10]

Finally, labor unions are keenly interested in internal staffing policies because they affect the employment security and pay levels of their members. Rules governing allowable and nonallowable internal staffing decisions are a basic issue in most collective bargaining agreements.

## INTERNAL EMPLOYEE MOVEMENT IS PART OF THE STAFFING PROCESS

Internal employee movement involves how employees are promoted, demoted, and transferred within the organization. Most organizations focus on what causes individuals to want to move from one position to another, or on how well the movers do in their new jobs. We take a broader view, recognizing that internal staffing is part of the larger staffing process, and that it must be integrated with external staffing (recruiting, selection, and separation/retention). Evidence suggests that 99 percent of organizations use internal candidate sources; many firms consider them more effective than external sources.[11] External selection is often used *only* after internal sources have been explored.

### External Staffing and Internal Staffing Create Career Systems

In Exhibit 9.2, we show how the relationship between external staffing, development/career management, and exit differs depending on the nature of the organization. The vertical dimension reflects how open the staffing system is to external candidates, with more open systems at the top and more closed systems near the bottom. The horizontal dimension reflects how much individual competition there is for internal staffing opportunities. The *Academy* (lower right, similar to a college faculty) involves a fairly closed system with entry typically only possible at entry levels early in a person's career. This system emphasizes a high degree of training and career development, based on individual merit. The *Baseball Team* (upper right, similar to sports teams) involves a very open system, with entry possible at all career levels, as well as high individual competition for internal staffing opportunities. This produces a higher degree of turnover and career paths that often span more than one organization. The *Club* (lower left, similar to a fraternity, sorority, or country club) involves low openness, with entry typically possible only at entry levels and low competition for opportunities among individuals. Career advancement is determined by standard steps at defined intervals. The *Fortress* (upper left, where those inside compete primarily with those attempting to join from the outside) has low competition among individuals for internal staffing opportunities, but high openness to external staffing at all levels. This system often characterizes industries with shortages in some areas, but surpluses in others due to rapidly changing market demands. Notice how external selection, internal development, and exit are interrelated depending on the conditions faced by the organization.

### Internal Staffing Reflects Both Internal Selection and Separation

We often overlook the fact that when organizations move people between work roles, there are consequences not only for the roles people move into but also for the roles they move out of.[12] We illustrate these relationships for two work roles in Exhibit 9.3. These work roles might be jobs or they might be assignments to teams, task forces, and so on. The vertical dotted lines represent the organization boundary. The two boxes inside the lines represent two jobs within the organization, with the source job providing employees to the receiving job. The top set of boxes shows the situation prior to the employee movements the bottom set of boxes shows the situation after the employee movements. The process begins on the right, with the receiving role experiencing

## EXHIBIT 9.2 Four Career System

| **Openness to external selection** | **Low competition** | **High competition** |
|---|---|---|
| **Highly open** | **Fortress**<br>*Entry:*<br>Passive recruitment<br>Applicant self-selection<br>*Development:*<br>Retain core talent<br>*Exit:*<br>Frequent layoffs<br>Seniority-based<br>*Examples:*<br>Airlines<br>Hotels<br>Retailing | **Baseball Team**<br>*Entry:*<br>High activity level<br>Emphasizes credentials<br>Select at all career levels<br>*Development:*<br>Informal training<br>Little career management<br>*Exit:*<br>High turnover<br>Careers cross employers<br>*Examples:*<br>Entertainment<br>Advertising<br>Law/consulting firms |
| **Low openness** | **Club**<br>*Entry:*<br>Early career<br>Emphasizes tenure<br>*Development:*<br>Builds general skills<br>Slow career paths<br>Required steps<br>Emphasizes commitment<br>*Exit:*<br>Low turnover<br>Retirement is common<br>*Examples:*<br>Utilities<br>Banks | **Academy**<br>*Entry:*<br>Strictly early career<br>Emphasizes growth potential<br>*Development:*<br>Highly emphasized activity<br>Extensive job training<br>Tracking and sponsoring high-potential employees<br>Elaborate career paths<br>*Exit:*<br>Low turnover<br>Retirement is common<br>Dismissals are common<br>*Examples:*<br>IBM<br>Kodak<br>General Motors |
| | **Low competition** ——— **High competition**<br>**Promotion Competition among Individuals** | |

Source: Adapted from Jeffrey A. Sonnefeld and Maury A. Peiperl, "Staffing Policy as a Strategic Response: A Typology of Career Systems," *Academy of Management Review* 13, no. 4 (1988), pp. 588–600.

EXHIBIT 9.3 How Internal Movement Fits the Staffing Process

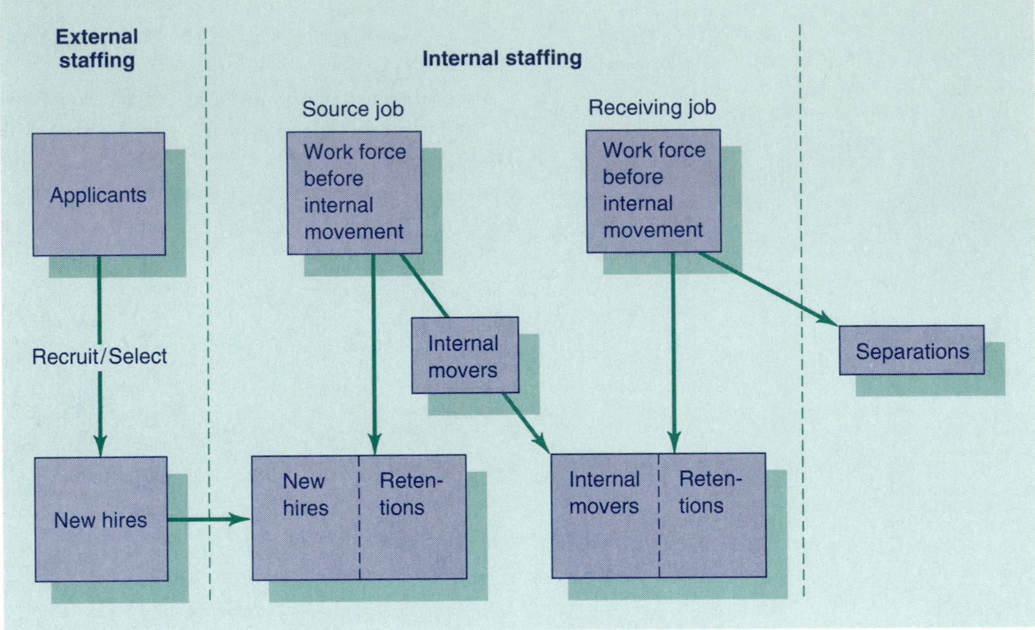


separations of employees who leave the organization. The receiving role's retained workforce is now smaller than before, so vacancies can be filled. The vacancies are filled with internal movers from the source role, so that the receiving role's workforce after the movements, is a mix of retentions and internal movers. These internal movements have the same effect on the source role as separations, so the source role workforce is smaller than before. Source role vacancies are filled through external recruitment and selection, so that the source role's workforce after the movements is a mix of retentions and new hires. These relationships obviously become more complex with more than two work roles and when more than one role is experiencing external separations. The key is that internal movement encompasses aspects of recruitment, selection, and separation/retention; thus, it uses the same models as external staffing. Research suggests decisions that affect the retention and selection process can have million-dollar consequences, depending on how it is managed.[13] Let us see how.

## Internal Staffing Affects Workforce Quality

Because internal staffing decisions serve both as rewards to employees and as strategies to enhance workforce value, they have important effects on workforce quality. In Chapter Eight we showed how different separation patterns affected the value of the workforce. In Exhibit 9.4, we have expanded the example to include a new piece of information. The last column now shows how well we expect each of the employees to perform if promoted to the job of sales manager. Ratings range from a low of 2 to a high of 10. Suppose the organization has five sales manager vacancies.

**EXHIBIT 9.4** Internal Staffing Information about a Workforce

| Salesperson | Annual Sales | Years of Seniority | Minority | Predicted Managerial Performance (points) |
|---|---|---|---|---|
| Jeremy | $40,000 | 8 | No | 10 |
| Rudolfo | 40,000 | 8 | No | 6 |
| Maggie | 40,000 | 2 | Yes | 10 |
| Manuel | 40,000 | 6 | Yes | 8 |
| Herbert | 40,000 | 6 | No | 6 |
| Karl | 30,000 | 8 | No | 8 |
| Donald | 30,000 | 4 | Yes | 10 |
| Lindsey | 30,000 | 8 | Yes | 6 |
| Ralph | 30,000 | 6 | No | 10 |
| Beuford | 30,000 | 4 | No | 6 |
| Arthur | 20,000 | 8 | No | 10 |
| Dorothy | 20,000 | 2 | Yes | 4 |
| James | 20,000 | 6 | No | 8 |
| Bertram | 20,000 | 4 | No | 4 |
| Jesse | 20,000 | 4 | Yes | 4 |
| Oliver | 10,000 | 2 | No | 8 |
| Anne | 10,000 | 2 | Yes | 4 |
| Enrique | 10,000 | 2 | Yes | 6 |
| Fred | 10,000 | 6 | No | 8 |
| Barney | 10,000 | 4 | No | 4 |
| Total | $500,000 | 100 | | |
| Average | $ 25,000 | 5 | | 7 |

One way to promote would be purely on seniority; labor unions might favor this as being objective and fair. Using seniority, Jeremy, Rudolfo, Karl, Lindsey, and Arthur would be promoted. Their average sales manager performance would be 8 out of a maximum of 10. One minority gets promoted (20 percent), the minority composition of the retained group of salespersons goes up to 47 percent (7 out of 15), and the combined sales of the retained group total $340,000. Although seniority-based promotions seem objective, high sales performers Maggie, Manuel, and Herbert may wonder whether it's worth working so hard or remaining with this organization if they have to wait up to six years to be promoted.

We might instead decide to promote the highest sales performers, to show that high performance gets rewarded. Jeremy, Rudolfo, Maggie, Manuel, and Herbert would be promoted. The average predicted sales manager performance would still be 8. The minority promotion rate is doubled to 40 percent (2 out of 5), and the minority representation rate of the retained salespeople remains what it was before (40 percent, or 6 out of 15). However, yearly sales among the retained group drops to a total of $300,000, well below the average of the group before the promotions. Lindsey and Arthur may now wonder if they will ever get promoted, after seeing less-senior employees pass them.

Finally, we might promote based simply on the employee's ability to do the sales manager job. Now, Jeremy, Maggie, Donald, Ralph, and Arthur would be promoted. The average predicted sales manager performance of this group is 10. As with performance-based promotions, the minority promotion rate is 40 percent, so the minority representation in the retained group remains 40 percent. However, this promotion pattern still removes several high-performing salespeople. It promotes two low-tenure employees (Maggie and Donald) over others with up to eight years of seniority. Finally, it promotes lower performers Donald, Ralph and Arthur over top-performing Rudolfo, Manuel, and Herbert. The high-tenure and high-performing salespeople may not find this very attractive, especially if the younger or lower performers end up as their supervisors!

WHAT DO YOU THINK?

Frequently, the best performer in a current job is not the best promotion candidate. If you had to tell a high performer they didn't get the promotion, how would you approach it? What support/assistance should HR provide?

In actual decisions, multiple work roles may compete for promising employees, and the validity of future performance predictions may vary. The best performer in a source job is not always the best candidate for the destination job. Finally, employees may or may not accept the internal movement opportunities. Clearly, internal staffing decisions and policies must constantly balance equity and efficiency goals for both the destinations and the sources of employees. This example used promotions, but the principles apply to lateral movements, movements between teams or task forces, redeployments, and downward movements.

## BALANCING EMPLOYEE AND EMPLOYER CONCERNS: CAREER MANAGEMENT AND CAREER PLANNING

Because careers affect the ongoing relationship between individuals and their organizations, both play a role in managing careers. Careers develop through the interaction of employee choices to pursue their aspirations and organization choices to provide opportunities that advance organizational goals. This dual focus is reflected in the relationship between *career development, career planning,* and *career management.*

*Career development* encompasses career management and career planning.

*Career planning* is the process through which individual employees identify and implement steps to attain career goals.

*Career management* is the process through which organizations select, assess, assign, and develop employees to provide a pool of qualified people to meet future needs.[14]

Note the different responsibilities of employees and employers in managing careers in Exhibit 9.5. The top portion illustrates how the employee, manager, and organization contribute to effective career planning, ensuring that careers match employee abilities and interests. The bottom portion illustrates how each party contributes to effective career management, ensuring that internal staffing decisions assign individuals to roles that contribute to the organization's goals.

Career development applies to all employees, although most career development activities traditionally have focused on upper-level managers. This is changing as organizations restructure to emphasize the skills and contributions of employees in nonmanagerial jobs. When attitude surveys indicated that nonexempt employees at Corning Glass felt underutilized and overlooked, Corning

## EXHIBIT 9.5 Integration between Career Planning and Career Management

**Career Planning Activities**

**Employee's responsibilities:**

- Self-assess abilities, interests, and values.
- Analyze career options.
- Decide on development objectives and needs.
- Communicate development preferences to manager.
- Map out mutually agreeable action plans with manager.
- Pursue agreed-upon action plan.

**Manager's responsibilities:**

- Act as catalyst; sensitize employee to the development planning process.
- Assess realism of employee's expressed objectives and perceived development needs.
- Counsel employee and develop a mutually agreeable plan.
- Follow up and update employee's plans as appropriate.

**Organization's responsibilities:**

- Provide career-planning model, resources, counseling, and information needed for individualized career planning.
- Provide training in career development planning to managers and employees, and career counseling to managers.
- Provide skills training programs and on-the-job development experience opportunities.

**Career Management Activities**

**Employee's responsibilities:**

- Provide accurate information to management as needed about skills, work experiences, interest, and career aspirations.

**Manager's responsibilities:**

- Validate information provided by employees.
- Provide information about vacant job positions for which the manager is responsible.
- Use all information provided by the process to (1) identify all viable candidates for a vacant position and make a selection and (2) identify career development opportunities (job openings, training programs, rotation assignments) for employees and place them accordingly.

**Organization's responsibilities:**

- Provide information system and process to accommodate management's decision-making needs.
- Organize and update all information.
- Ensure effective usage of information by (1) designing convenient methods for collecting, analyzing, interpreting, and using the information; and (2) monitoring and evaluating the effectiveness of the process.

Source: Frank J. Minor, "Computer Applications in Career Development Planning," in *Career Development in Organizations,* ed. Douglas T. Hall and Associates (San Francisco: Jossey-Bass, 1986), pp. 205–6.

implemented the Career Planning and Information System to help individuals understand and take more responsibility for their career planning. The system includes computer programs such as *Who am I?, How am I seen?* and *How can I achieve my goals?* as well as videos and informational books listing all Corning positions and their requisite skills.[15]

Do such programs induce more career planning? One study of employees in Singapore suggested that career planning was not affected by career development programs and other organizational factors, but was affected by individual factors such as the need for achievement and career commitment.[16] It seems likely that HR managers must show employees the personal value of career planning for such programs to work. Several trends illustrate the importance of individual career planning today. The partnership illustrated in Exhibit 9.5 is becoming more complex as organizations become more flexible and environments become more volatile.

## The New Employment Contract: In Business for Yourself

> *You have to accept that no matter where you work, you are not an employee; you are in a business with one employee—yourself.*
>
> *—Andrew Grove, CEO, Intel, September 1995*[17]

Chapter Three and Chapter Fifteen discuss the changing employment contract. No one owes you a job, a career, or future security. Globalization and faster change mean that you alone will be responsible for charting a successful career. Competencies and flexibility have become the currency on which careers are built while hierarchical advancement, tradition, and loyalty are less important. That means that employees must take a greater role in charting careers, amassing the knowledge and other credentials that make them attractive for future work roles, and identifying the right career experiences to gather those credentials. Where you start may be less important than where you finish, lucrative offers that don't fit your career goals may be seductive, and the best thing that can happen is often a failure or two. Indeed, the day may be coming when the whole idea of a "job" may be passé. Some researchers have suggested that promotions should be modeled more like future stock purchase "options," with candidates' value changing with the market as well as their own development, and the probability of promotion depending on many factors beyond the candidate's control.[18]

## The New Career Path: Twists and Turns, Not Straight and Narrow

In the television show *Leave it to Beaver,* Ward Cleaver went to the office every day, undoubtedly to some sort of managerial job. Cleaver's job was part of a career within a well-defined corporate hierarchy, with each successive promotion being very predictable. Promotions occurred at regular intervals in the same functional area (e.g., marketing, finance, or human resources); they involved supervising ever larger groups of people or units, and they represented rungs up a stable hierarchy. Chapter Three showed how outmoded such systems are in many of today's organizations. Pyramids are giving way to parallelograms, or simply to webs of networked alliances. Therefore, the right career move is now defined more by the capabilities it imparts than the hierarchical

WHAT DO YOU THINK?

*Fortune* magazine trumpets "famous failures" such as Sergio Zyman, who left Coca-Cola in 1986 after the disastrous introduction of New Coke, only to return in 1993 as a top marketing manager. Coca-Cola had experienced a "change in our thinking," deciding that risk taking is good.[21] What HR and career management processes could lead to such a decision? What effect do you think this had on other managers?

status it bestows. Lateral movements become more important, and work roles such as team leader, task force coordinator, and network liaison may become more critical than supervisor or manager. The new corporate ladder may be horizontal instead of upward, with rotational assignments being the plum opportunities, and it probably involves multiple employers.[19] For example, Hong Kong human resource managers have lamented the 30 percent turnover rates among their young professionals. The sheer density and growth of Hong Kong means that you can change employers simply by moving across the hall or down a causeway. With all that mobility, some Hong Kong banks track their most promising prospects and hire them back in a few years after they have obtained valuable experience. The idea of "industry communities" that agree to form multiemployer career paths has even been suggested.[20]

The career ladder may even lead downward. As you read in earlier chapters, the transition from work to school is changing, with more organizations emphasizing that careers begin even before the first job. In Japan, ranking within your graduating class significantly affects the first job, and the first job significantly affects later career opportunities. Even in the United States, it may be much harder for those who begin in lower-level jobs to work their way up than in other countries that more closely manage the school-to-work transition.[22] The concept of *the office* also is changing. For example, accounting giant Ernst & Young has only 100 Chicago offices for its 500 accountants, many of whom are on the road 60 percent of the time. Accountants who need offices call to reserve them, just like a hotel.[23] In one Singapore bank, restructuring is so common that a popular joke is, "If my boss calls, please get his or her name."

Even the changing path is up for debate because seniority still counts for big privileges among flight attendants and others, and economic studies seem to suggest that job tenure hasn't changed much in 20 years. In 1993, the proportion of workers—20 percent—who worked more than 20 years for the same employer was precisely the same percentage as in 1973. Even middle management, long the target of cost cutting, is back in vogue.[24] Exhibit 9.6 shows the results of a study of more than 1,300 top U.S. executives, indicating how much each factor is associated with their annual pay. The results suggest some traditional patterns: Older married men with spouses who stay at home, and who work longer hours and more evenings earn more; the amount of education is a significant plus; and as Cornell University professors, we were pleased to learn that an Ivy League degree pays off (no data on how many of these executives had taken our classes). There are also some surprises: Those working in smaller firms earn more, and tenure with the organization or occupation was not a significant factor in earnings.

Does the blurring of traditional career paths mean careers are less important? Quite the contrary. Career progressions that build needed capabilities and flexibility are becoming even more important to both companies and individuals. Even using a contingent workforce can enhance careers. One research study found that organizations that hired more temporary workers had slower mobility for lower-level jobs that employed the temporary workers, but faster upward mobility among the permanent group of workers in higher-level jobs. The contingent workforce created a hidden escalator for the core employees.[25]

EXHIBIT 9.6 Factors Affecting the Pay of Top U.S. Executives

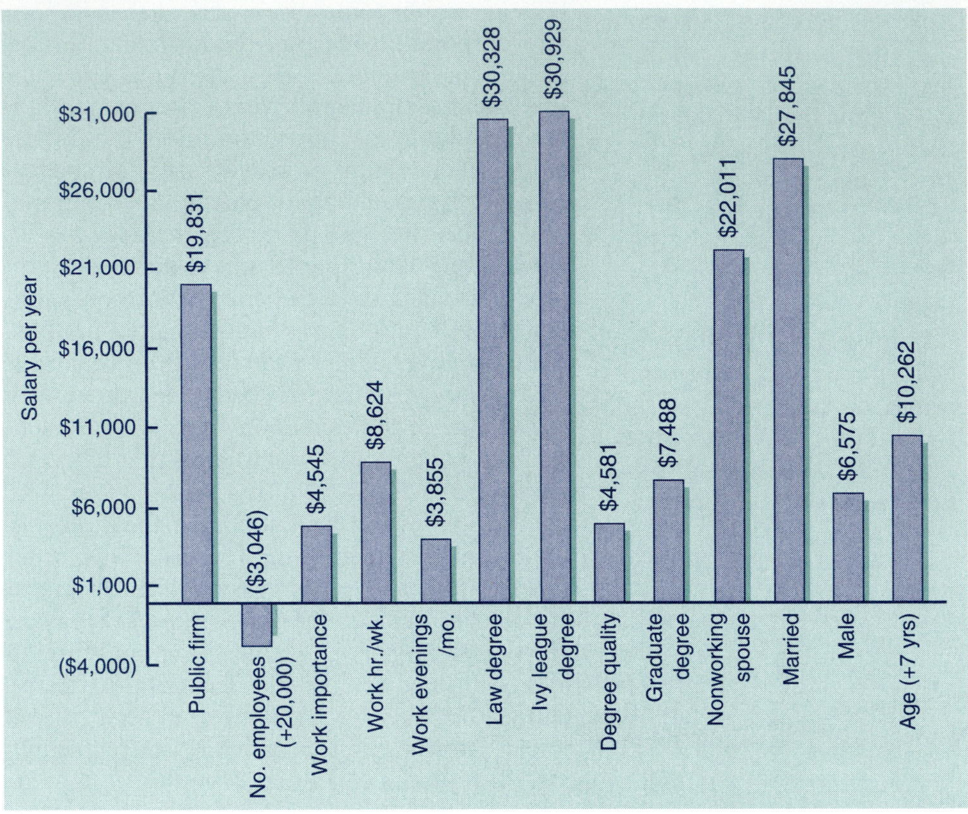


Source: Timothy A. Judge, Daniel M. Cable, John W. Boudreau, and Robert D. Bretz, "An Empirical Investigation of the Predictors of Executive Career Success," *Personnel Psychology,* 1995, vol. 48, p. 505.

Therefore, while the terrain is becoming complicated, the value of career planning and career management is increasing. For employees, this means being more vigilant in charting their own careers to match their goals, which brings us to career planning.

## CAREER PLANNING: EMPLOYEES FINDING AND PURSUING THEIR GOALS

In the opening exercise, you chose the corner of the room in which you'd like to be. That exercise illustrates the process of identifying the kinds of experiences you might find rewarding in a career. Researchers have identified two concepts to help explain the patterns of these career interests and how they may change over a person's lifetime: *career orientation* and *career stages.*

### Career Orientation: Who Do You Want to Be?

Your career aspirations and interests form patterns similar to those illustrated in Exhibit 9.1. People seem to be oriented toward certain kinds of competencies and experiences. These orientations reflect underlying motives and abilities

A *career anchor* is a self-concept based on differing work motives and abilities. This self-concept guides, stabilizes, and integrates a person's work experience.

formed before beginning work and during early work experiences. One study of adolescents found that the career interests they favored at age 13 were usually still favored 15 years later.[26] Research has suggested that these patterns reflect career anchors.

People tend to pursue work roles that remain anchored around their self-concept, although, like a ship, they may move around the anchor as well. Changing to a new anchor involves effort and some fundamental rethinking of career motives. Five career anchors have been identified.[27]

1. *Technical/functional competence.* The primary orientation of these people is the actual work they do and their wish to continue using and developing their existing skills. They avoid positions removing them from areas of established competence or pushing them into general management, preferring growth through increasing skill instead of increasing organizational level. A good example is an engineer who wishes to design semi-conductors and has no wish to supervise others.
2. *Managerial competence.* The primary orientation of these people is to develop managerial abilities of interpersonal competence, analytical competence, and emotional competence required at high levels of management. Aspirations to manage have been found to be strongly related to managerial career anchors and with specific activities such as developing career contacts, developing organizationally specific skills, and accommodating the boss's expectations.[28]

Perhaps because these studies were carried out with business school graduates, these two anchors occurred most. Even here, however, three other anchors emerged:

3. *Security.* An orientation toward working for a particular organization or in a specific geographic area.
4. *Creativity.* An orientation toward creating something that is entirely their own—whether it be a product, a company, a work of art, or a personal fortune.
5. *Autonomy/Independence.* An orientation to avoid working under the constraints of organization life, with many of these people leaving to become consultants or start their own businesses.

Understanding the career orientations of individuals makes it easier to understand which internal staffing opportunities appeal to them. It also helps individuals better evaluate potential career paths. Research suggests that individuals make decisions based on whether occupational and organizational characteristics are similar to their personal view of themselves, and that those who fit better enjoy greater eventual career success and satisfaction.[29] Of course, as any student in the job market knows, career choices are also influenced by pragmatic concerns. Research on Australian college students showed that in addition to career orientation, money, status, and gender influenced career preferences. Among Singaporean job seekers, career choices are influenced by their government's decisions regarding which industries receive subsidies and other federal support.[30] It seems likely that with the flexibility and change of future opportunities, individuals may well pursue a variety of career interests.

## Career Cycles and Stages

Traditionally, we think of careers in biological terms. A young person begins with exploration, progressing to becoming established in an organization and occupation, next enters a maintenance period of stable and productive accomplishment, and finally enters a period of decline or transition out of the work environment into retirement. However, age and tenure don't fully describe modern career paths.[31] A more modern and accurate view suggests that careers move through cycles through time, and every person may progress through these stages several times in one career. Exhibit 9.7 illustrates this cyclical pattern and the factors that determine career changes and success. Career change is triggered by a variety of opportunities or stresses; it also is determined by the person's personality and tolerance for change. The "career routine" also determines whether the person becomes aware of his or her choices. Once aware, the person goes through the stages of information (much like exploration), subidentity transition and establishment, increased adaptability and self-confidence (much like becoming established), and then the process begins again. Today, the stages are more likely to be played out across multiple work roles in multiple organizations. For example, *Business Week* suggested the new career path involves: *Starting big* by learning corporate skills in a large organization; *broadening skills* by moonlighting and developing contacts and a reputation outside the organization; *branching out* to start a new company or move to a new industry; *taking a break* to go back to school, build new credentials, or pursue a totally different kind of work; *temping,* or moving from project to project as a temporary and independent contractor with valuable skills.[32] The stages of Exhibit 9.7 may be accelerated or even repeated several times. Research suggests that people may have different levels of decidedness about their careers. *Developmentally undecided* means having little experience upon which to make a decision. *Situationally undecided* means being unsure because of a new situation, such as a merger. *Chronically undecided* means being uncertain because of general anxiety or fear. *Vigilant* means being settled on a decision after rationally weighing the alternatives and gathering information. *Hypervigilant* means rushing to make a decision without full analysis, perhaps due to anxiety.[33] Though being undecided has a negative connotation, it may be the most common and, perhaps, the most appropriate state of mind in today's volatile career environment. Research also suggests that people who switch both employers and occupations have greater increases in satisfaction and mental health than those who don't switch or only switch employers.[34]

**WHAT DO YOU THINK?**

How many organizations do you believe you will work for in the first 15 years of your career? Do your career plans reflect the cycle in Exhibit 9.7? Why should today's managers spend time helping people manage careers, if the trend is for people to spend less of their career in one organization? How can career development pay off?

### Deciding to Explore

In the information stage, a person explores activities, tries out different work roles, clarifies interests and skills, builds skills through education and training, and (in the case of young people) reduces dependence on family and school. For college students, internships with companies can help crystallize career interests. Factors such as the level and type of education, early career experiences, and even a father's occupation may relate to ultimate career choices and success.[35] Earlier, we saw the techniques for exploration, including Web-based job banks and tests of vocational and career interests and skills. In Exhibit 9.7, these processes are shown in the awareness of choice, information, and trial stages.

EXHIBIT 9.7 The Cycle of Career Changes

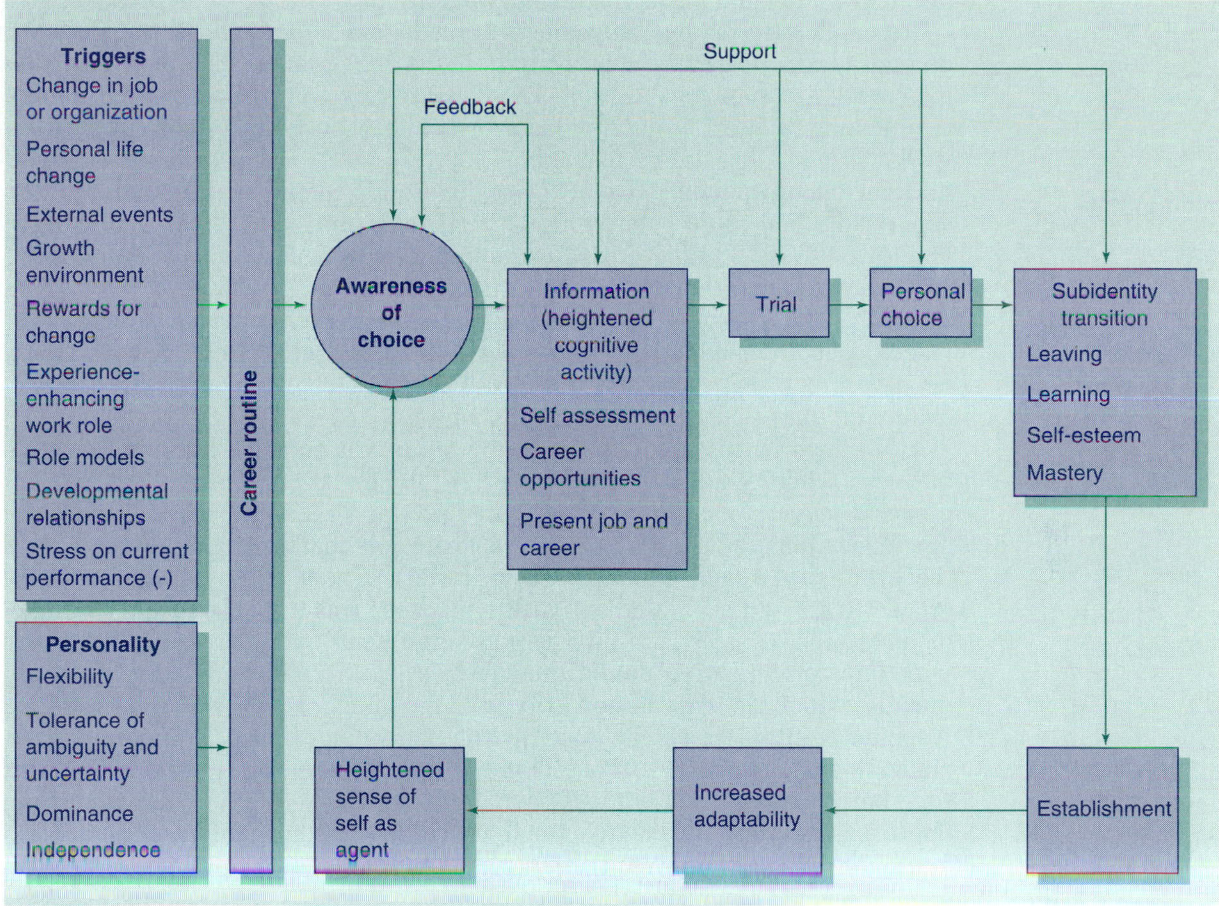


Source: Douglas T. Hall, "Unplanned Executive Transitions and the Dance of the Subidentities," *Human Resource Management,* Spring, 1995, p. 75.

## Socialization: Learning the New "Identity

Once a person has entered a new job, role, organization, or occupation, he or she embarks on a period of socialization and orientation. In Exhibit 9.7, this is called "subidentity transition" because the person is discovering his or her identity in the new situation.

Socialization occurs not only with respect to the organization, but also with respect to the work group. In both cases, the newcomer is assimilated into the new organization or group while having a reciprocal impact on its norms, culture, and perhaps structure. Most research has focused on socialization into the organization, often depicting it as a coercive process (e.g., Marine Corps boot camp) or as an administrative activity (e.g., processing the paperwork to establish membership). More

> *Socialization* involves learning to understand and make sense of a new setting, and deciding how to fit into the accepted social relationships.
>
> *Orientation* involves becoming aware of the social and organizational rules and expectations.

recent work recognizes the interactive nature of socialization and the key role that individuals play in directing their own assimilation by the kind of information they gather and the affiliations they form.[36]

Research suggests that newcomers are most concerned with learning how to do their tasks and behave appropriately in their role, rather than with aspects of their work group or organization. They tend to rely on observing others and experimenting with different approaches more than on asking supervisors or coworkers or reading policy manuals. They rely on supervisors for positive socialization outcomes. Also, those who obtained more information from supervisors had more positive organizational commitment, work adjustment, and lower stress. Among graduates joining a British oil company, early socialization worked to correct unrealistic expectations. You might expect that women entering male-dominated occupations and men entering female-dominated occupations might experience more sex-role conflict, but one study found no such effect, suggesting that those who choose such occupations have already dealt with these conflicts.[37]

How important is it to "fit" with the group you join? A study of Canadian business school graduates at 3, 9, and 14 months after joining their first employer discovered that those who entered groups where they were dissimilar in age, education, and lifestyle perceived lower job challenge and poorer fit with the group. However, dissimilarity in terms of gender was associated with greater perceived challenge and, if the manager was a man, greater likelihood of promotion. Gender dissimilarity was significantly and negatively associated with later organization commitment while later separations were most frequently associated with dissimilarity in terms of age, education, and lifestyle.[38] Apparently, fitting in can be good or bad, depending on how you define it. Socialization usually occurs through interactions with colleagues in one organization, but today's careers without boundaries mean that workers may not stay in one organization long enough for that. Therefore, the modern equivalent of guilds organized around professions or occupations have formed to offer peer support and development.[39]

What affects how well people learn new jobs? A study of 300 Navy officers suggested that these factors positively affected learning: time on the job, perceived self-efficacy, job challenge, competence of subordinates, and the job's similarity to previous jobs. Learning was less when the job was the first of a two-job tour and when the officer was married.[40] How important is being a good learner? It depends on your early career success. A study of managers in a U.S. oil company showed that cognitive ability was more strongly related to career success for those who started lower in the organization than for those who had early career success. For individuals without the advantages of early stardom, cognitive ability apparently makes a bigger difference in later success.[41]

The exploration stage is usually followed by a period of relatively permanent employment leading to the establishment stage.

### Mastery and Establishment: Making Your Mark

Once having entered a new career role, the individual proceeds to become established, to master his or her role, and to achieve a position of influence and competence. The keys to success may not hold much mystery. As Exhibit 9.6 shows, pay is associated with higher education and more devotion to work, among other factors. A study of MBA students in early careers found that those with higher cognitive ability (see Chapter Seven) and greater motivation achieved significantly higher pay and promotions. Research also shows that as tenure in the organization increases, so does the similarity between the individual's values and those expressed by other organization members.[42] Traditionally, this stage was thought to occur during a prolonged period of employment with a single stable organization. In the future, it is much more likely to occur through a series of positions in several organizations or units. At this stage, however, each new position won't represent a new exploration but a planned step along the road to establishing a position in the industry, profession, or field. For example, in the 1980s 1 Japanese manager in 100 would switch employers following an assignment in the United States. In the early 1990s, about 1 in 10 did so. These highly successful, well-educated managers were not embarking on new careers or entering exploratory positions with their new companies. Instead, they were lured by better pay and promotion prospects, greater personal freedom, and increased decision-making authority.[43] Thus, even in Japan, job-hopping is becoming a typical path toward establishment.

### Increased Adaptability: Building a Platform or Hitting the Plateau?

**Increasing influence and stature** As the establishment stage progresses, an individual becomes a more important member of the organization. The organization draws on the accumulated experience, and the person may serve as a mentor to others. This is also the time when major changes in family, financial obligations, and recognized limits may precipitate a reevaluation of career choices. Many individuals at this stage allow their current career to decline and cycle back to the exploration stage. Again, the traditional notion that maintenance is reached after progressing up the hierarchy in one organization may be outdated. Today, more organizations are looking outside, even for the top officers who exercise the greatest influence and power. The list of companies replacing loyal company men with outsiders promising to institute fundamental change includes General Motors, Digital Equipment, Tenneco, and Compaq Computers. Research suggests that poor-performing organizations are more likely to look outside for CEOs.[44]

**Plateaued careers and skill obsolescence: Getting beyond the dead end** "Plateaued," "entrenched," "obsolescent," "trapped"—these are words used to describe people who have reached a limit to their career progress, measured either by upward movement or by growth in their work skills. *Career entrenchment* consists of a high level of "career investments" that would be lost if one changed careers, high "emotional costs" that would occur if changing careers, and "limited alternatives" for alternative careers.[45] For these individuals, the rewards of career progression are limited. They are likely to be among those retained or left behind as others are promoted. Yet, they may be capable of making important contributions. Plateauing can happen when older people lose interest, or when young talented people see their upward mobility blocked by superiors who are only a few years older. One study divided 30 engineering managers with equal tenure into two groups: those actively and enthusiastically involved in the organization and those who were passive. Passive managers weren't actively dissatisfied, but had no particular enthusiasm for their jobs or the company. What accounted for the difference between the groups? The active managers reported early job assignments connected to the mainstream of the company's activities, while the passive managers did not. A second important factor was that the passive managers reported less openness and candor from the company about their career prospects. When superiors provide clear and honest feedback, employees may maintain their commitment and productivity.[46]

A study of over 2,000 Canadian managers found that the actual plateau (how long they had been in their current job) was not related to attitudes, but that *feelings* of being plateaued were related to work satisfaction. A study of senior managers found that their satisfaction tended to go down in the year before they moved, to rise significantly in the year after a move, only to fall back again if they stayed in that position—a kind of "honeymoon" and "hangover" effect.[47] How you feel about plateauing may depend on whether you think about the *content* of your work (does your job seem routine or exciting?) or the *hierarchical level* you have reached. A study of more than 1,000 U.S. managers found that perceived plateauing was reduced among those who believed they had support from top management, had training and skill development opportunities, were engaged in greater career planning and exploration, and were involved in their jobs. Interestingly, the correlation between the two perceptions (hierarchical and content plateaus) was only .17, indicating that they don't occur together.[48] You can be limited in your upward mobility and still find opportunities to grow in your work. Thus, the changing nature of organizations may help solve this problem.

As careers are defined less rigidly, more options exist to give people meaningful responsibilities. A promotion may not be possible, but movement to a key task force or team may be. This may be just the kind of mainstream experience that can rejuvenate a flagging career. One danger of career plateauing is that skills become obsolete. Again, providing a variety of ways to combat skill obsolescence can meet varied employee needs. A study of professionals in the Israeli high-technology industry found that obsolescence was perceived as a threat to their self-esteem, their social image, and their marketability. The professionals dealt with this threat differently at different career stages; younger employees used more structured methods while older employees used more informal methods.[49]

### Decline or Renewed Career Exploration?

The last part of the cycle in Exhibit 9.7 depicts the career exploration process starting again. Some characterize the period after establishment as a time of declining involvement which, as we have seen, is not confined to those reaching retirement age. Moreover, even among those over age 55, the process often begins again as they explore new opportunities. Whether it occurs at the beginning, middle, or end of a career, this is often the stage where the individual and the human resource manager must work most closely to achieve their mutual goals.

### Implications for HR Management and Career Development

Individual career aspirations and interests change with career orientation and career stage. Different kinds of opportunities and assistance are effective for people with different orientations and stages. For example, matching career counseling information with the career anchor and career stage can make it more effective in helping individuals plan their next moves. Career planning concepts can help the organization recruit, select, and retain promising candidates for internal movement opportunities. It may do little good for an organization to construct career opportunities that reflect a managerial career anchor and expect effort commensurate with the establishment career stage if the pool of internal candidates generally has a technical/functional orientation and the candidates are still in the exploration stage of their careers. It may also be important to shake up the career system occasionally to counteract the tendency to become hidebound as a larger number of people with similar skills and aspirations join organizations that they fit.

At McDonnell-Douglas Space Systems, the company gives managers and potential managers different career rotations through various jobs depending on their career stages: Rotation across units for those in the exploration stage, rotation across functions for those in the establishment stage, and rotation through upper-level corporate positions for those in the maintenance stage.[50] By reflecting individual career planning needs in its career system, McDonnell-Douglas hopes that it can improve the effectiveness of organizational career management activities designed to provide a pool of qualified people to meet future needs.

Increasingly employees bear the risk in managing their careers. Companies do not guarantee that certain actions will lead to continued employment, and more of them emphasize that it is the employees' responsibility to seek out their own best career moves. Therefore, both employee and employer must understand how the organization constructs and manages its career system. This brings us to the other side of career development—the organization's attempts to manage careers through internal recruitment, selection, and retention.

## RECRUITMENT IN CAREER MANAGEMENT

As with external staffing, internal movement candidates must be identified and attracted to apply for opportunities. Because internal staffing focuses on existing employees, the attraction/identification process is ongoing, with two-way communication throughout the individual's employment. The organization and the employee are much more active participants in building a suitable pool of applicants. Organizations can emphasize announcing employment opportunities in hopes that interested employees pursue them, or they can track or build employee characteristics and invite only the most promising candidates to apply. Combinations of these two approaches are also possible. In Exhibit 9.8, we show several approaches to internal recruitment along with their advantages and disadvantages. The techniques near the top of the chart are often quicker and cheaper, but they may miss good candidates. Techniques near the bottom are more expensive and time consuming, but they may increase the chances of attracting or creating the best candidates. The "informal staffing" method is commonly used, but it has significant pitfalls. The following sections discuss the other methods in turn.

### Job Posting

With the job posting method, the organization announces position openings through bulletin boards and company publications. These publications may resemble the help-wanted sections of newspapers and can include work

EXHIBIT 9.8 Comparison of Internal Recruitment Methods

| Approach | Advantages | Disadvantages |
|---|---|---|
| Informal staffing | Often the quickest, easiest for managers<br>Candidates are known<br>Opportunities provided first within unit | Qualified, interested employees may not be considered<br>Fosters old boy network<br>Reactive, developmental, depends on managers<br>Job requirements, individual qualifications may not be fully considered |
| Job posting | Managers consider a wide range of candidates from the overall organization<br>Better candidates may be identified<br>Supports EEO/AA objectives, promotes sense of fairness<br>Employees can participate actively, voluntarily | May be unwieldy and slow<br>Employees expect feedback<br>Credibility difficult to sustain<br>Requires job definition, use of selection criteria<br>Skills difficult to define for many positions |
| Focused internal search | Search may be wide or narrow<br>Candidates may be considered across organization<br>Individuals may provide current information<br>Can support diversity objectives | Inventories or database difficult to maintain<br>Identified candidates may not be interested or available<br>Difficult to maintain consistent practices<br>Process may be reactive, not developmental |
| Targeted development | Mobility options considered in advance of needs<br>Training or development may be provided in advance and considered in making assignments<br>Employees participate in the process | Requires time and effort from managers<br>Requires a sense of options, forecasted needs and skill requirements<br>May be unwieldy in filling positions quickly; sometimes employees assigned for development reasons are not the most qualified |
| Succession planning | Orderly succession is planned; management thinking is stimulated about future needs<br>Flexibility can be planned, talent pools identified<br>Development plans are specific and focused<br>Implementation of actions can be monitored | Process requires time and effort<br>Often does not determine actual assignment decisions<br>Can be applied only to limited numbers of positions and individuals |

Source: Reprinted with permission from James W. Walker, *Human Resource Strategy* (New York: McGraw-Hill, 1992), p. 187.

descriptions, qualifications, and locations. They can also list salary information. Copies can be placed in lounges, hallways, and other places frequented by employees. Some companies include an application form on the back that can be mailed to a coordinator. In many organizations, this process has been computerized. Employees can call up a database of available positions on their PCs or through kiosks such as those described in Chapter Sixteen. They can scan the database to find positions in specified locations or that have characteristics in which they are interested. Employees can then submit their applications, using the computer and paper application forms printed by the computer system.

Job posting systems are more prevalent for office, clerical, administrative, and technical positions. Their key advantage is that they convey a message that careers are open to all including protected groups. Job posting is often incorporated into many consent decrees to enhance affirmative action and equal employment opportunity. Such systems are most effective when it is easy for employees to determine if they are qualified for different jobs. As flexible organization structures increase, the term *job* posting should probably be modified to *position* or *work* posting, because such systems can also announce opportunities to join teams, serve on task forces, or become involved in key projects. One key to successful job posting is to handle rejected candidates carefully. As prior chapters have shown, perceived justice is important and often depends not only on the outcome of a decision but also on the process used and the interpersonal relationships encountered. This brings us to the nomination process because someone must nominate candidates once a job is posted. The nomination approaches reflect "focused internal search" in Exhibit 9.8.

## Nomination by the Employees Themselves

When positions are announced publicly, employees have the opportunity to nominate themselves. Evidence suggests that they can benefit from training in how to identify good career moves. At 3M Company, the department of career services includes a career information center, career services orientation, career growth workshop, individual counseling, supervisory development programs, and a career development library, all available to any employee during working hours. One danger with self-nomination systems is that rejected employees become even more dissatisfied than if they had never been given the choice. For example, Israeli managers who did not get their selected jobs believed they had been inequitably treated, had less commitment, and were absent more frequently.[51]

### Relocation and Dual-Career Considerations

Increasingly, employees' decisions to nominate themselves for internal staffing opportunities reflect not only their own considerations but also those of their spouses and families, a process often called *dual-career considerations.* A study of families from 10 U.S. corporations suggests that employees' willingness to relocate was a key factor in their acceptance or rejection of internal staffing opportunities. Willingness to relocate is affected by the number of children at home, the current work environment, job involvement, the attractiveness of the alternative job, general attitude toward moving, and whether the move will maintain employment or enhance a career. The wishes of a working spouse are often critical to such decisions.[52] As the proportion of working women increases, it is likely that human resource managers will need to adopt specific policies designed to accommodate the dual-career aspirations of spouses and families. Otherwise, they risk having some promising candidates eliminate themselves from the internal promotion pool. Relocation costs are also a key consideration for many companies. At GTE, worldwide relocation costs totaled nearly $60 million in 1990, including $30 million on home purchases.[53]

## Nomination by Employees' Superiors

At General Electric (GE) they call it "Session C." It consumes nearly a month of CEO Jack Welch's time each year and involves 80,000 employees filling out one-page "internal résumés" and visits by Jack Welch and other top GE managers to each operating unit to consider personally the prospects of 500 top managers. At PepsiCo, former CEO Jack Calloway shuttled promising managers through several divisions to guide their learning. The present CEO, Roger Enrico, is famous not only for his business management, but also for the private "leadership school" he runs.[54] Even when internal movement opportunities are publicly announced, and certainly when they are not, supervisors play a role in identifying and nominating employees for the opportunity. Superiors may use many types of information to decide which employees to nominate, including skills or considerations of the implications for other positions, as we discuss next. Supervisors usually significantly affect performance appraisals, which are often key considerations in internal movement. Evidence suggests that career success is positively affected by upward-influence tactics that focus on influencing supervisors, such as employees agreeing with supervisors outwardly even if they disagree privately, and employees praising supervisors' accomplishments. Some research suggests that physical attractiveness benefits men, but not women, in getting promotions. Executives seem to believe it, as many invest in hair replacement, eyelid surgery, and other cosmetic procedures. Some evidence suggests that the new careerist who tries to pursue career advancement through nonperformance-based means has more negative job attitudes but greater advancement desires and more frequent promotions.[55]

**WHAT DO YOU THINK?**

U.S. managers working for Japanese companies sometimes claim that the nomination process for high-level positions excludes non-Japanese. If you were an HR manager in such a company, how might you investigate this claim, and if true, what should be done?

## Nomination by Mentors

Frequently, the nomination process is more active with managers serving as mentors for their subordinates or protégés.

A *mentor* is a senior member of the profession or organization who provides support, coaching, feedback, acceptance, and friendship; creates opportunities for exposure; provides challenging and educational assignments; and serves as a role model and counselor.[56]

At McKinsey and Company, a large consulting firm, senior consultants work on teams with junior consultants, but it's the *junior* consultants who make presentations. The quality of those presentations depends partly on mentoring, which is considered in the appraisal of partners. The process is helped along by long trips to places like

"West Moose Lung," which tend to create personal relationships. Does Newt Gingrich support the idea of chimpanzees as mentors because he recommends the book by Frans de Waal, *Chimpanzee Politics: Power and Sex Among Apes,* in which one learns how to win power by forming coalitions and mounting psychological attacks on rivals? Marshal Loeb carries the idea one step further, suggesting the creation of your own board of advisors, including members from outside the company (so you can freely discuss your shortcomings), superiors, peers, and subordinates.[57]

When mentor relationships form naturally, research suggests that willingness to mentor is higher among better educated managers who had been mentors or protégés before and had good relationships with their supervisors. Those who felt themselves to be under a great deal of job tension perceived more barriers to being a mentor.[58] Mentor relationships usually evolve informally, but organizations can also encourage them. Hawaiian Telephone Company employees complete workbooks to help them identify their values, interests, and decision-making styles before meeting with their supervisors to discuss career possibilities. Research suggests that more mentoring is reported by those using informal job search approaches, those who are younger, those from higher socioeconomic backgrounds, and those in managerial positions.[59] Successful formal mentoring programs are characterized by top management support, careful selection of mentors and protégés, an extensive orientation program, clearly stated responsibilities for both the mentor and protégé, and established duration and frequency of contact between mentors and protégés. Good mentoring increases salaries and promotions.[60] In the future, mentors may not be limited to superiors, as team leaders and even whole teams become empowered to advise their members about future career paths.

One danger of nomination by superiors and mentors is the possibility of bias against underrepresented minorities. Factors contributing to ineffectiveness may include the lack of available mentors of the same sex or race, lack of access to information networks, perceived preferential treatment making mentors reluctant to associate with the person, stereotypes about women's or minorities' career preferences and performance, differences in socialization, and the danger of misperceptions about sexual intentions.[61] Evidence suggests that women report more barriers to obtaining mentors and that much mentoring is informal, so choosing a mentor must be done carefully. Even when mentoring is allowed to develop naturally, it can result in "ethnic drift," as a study of clerical bank employees found. New employees tended to be assigned to supervisors of the same racial group. The tendency was even more pronounced among those reassigned within the next five months. Thus, companies must be vigilant to ensure good mentoring. Some family-owned business executives hire outsiders to be mentors to their children.[62]

## Skill Inventories

Some recruitment methods go beyond simply nominating employees and focus on tracking the qualifications of employees. Then, when an internal opportunity arises, the database of qualifications can be scanned to identify qualified candidates for further consideration.

> ***S****kill inventories* are databases that contain employees' names and their characteristics relevant to internal employment opportunities.

As discussed in Chapter Sixteen on information systems, the data in a skill inventory must be tailored to the decision needs of the organization. Commonly included information includes the name, identification number, present location, birth date, employment date, current position, prior experience, training completed, skill and/or knowledge ratings, education degree and major, foreign language ability, and ratings of promotability. Increasingly, skill inventories are based on key competencies, which represent the knowledge and ability needed to help the organization compete. British Petroleum replaced its system of job descriptions with a skills matrix that tracks skills of both individuals and positions; these skills include technical expertise, leadership, business awareness, and interpersonal.[63] Skill inventories were discussed in Chapter Five on planning as tools to forecast skill imbalances. They become internal recruitment tools when a vacancy is identified and the search begins for qualified candidates.

If skill inventories are made available to all employees, an internal market for skills can combine the nomination and inventory processes. Imagine a computerized system through which any manager or team could request candidates based on the skills they need, and any employee could track which skills are sought most often. Individuals would soon realize the value in acquiring highly prized skills and increase their supply. As the organization changed, teams and managers would request different skills, providing a perpetual signal to employees about the organization's changing needs. Chase Manhattan Bank uses this kind of system to link databases in New York, São Paulo, London, and Hong Kong, which contain competency profiles on employees, competency requirements of work roles, and forecasted competency supplies throughout the organization.[64]

## Replacement and Succession Planning

In May 1995, Jack Welch, 59-year-old CEO of General Electric, was admitted to Massachusetts General Hospital for heart surgery (the very hospital where Charles Winchester III of television's *M*A*S*H* perpetually hoped to become chief of thoracic surgery). Asked to comment on a succession plan, a GE spokesperson responded, "Absolutely not. There's no need to." Could a company as well run as GE have actually forgotten to plan for a CEO replacement? Several heirs apparent had recently departed, and the remaining successors presented ticklish issues. To name one as successor risked losing all the others as they saw their upward mobility blocked.[65]

Typically, replacement planning uses charts similar to the one in Exhibit 9.9. Replacement charts can be paper-and-pencil forms, but increasingly they are created using computer software. Based on organization charts, they provide a snapshot of the top key positions in the organization and show the availability of replacements from the current workforce. Ratings of current performance, promotability, and readiness document judgments about employees' knowledge, skills, and abilities. This kind of formal record can improve decision making compared with using only informal knowledge, which may be less complete.

> *Replacement planning* requires that senior executives periodically review their top executives and those in the next-lower echelon to determine two or three backups for each senior slot. *Succession planning* goes further, attempting to anticipate changes in the requirements of future top management positions as well as the development needs, not only their fitness for the next job, of lower-level managers.

EXHIBIT 9.9 Replacement Charts

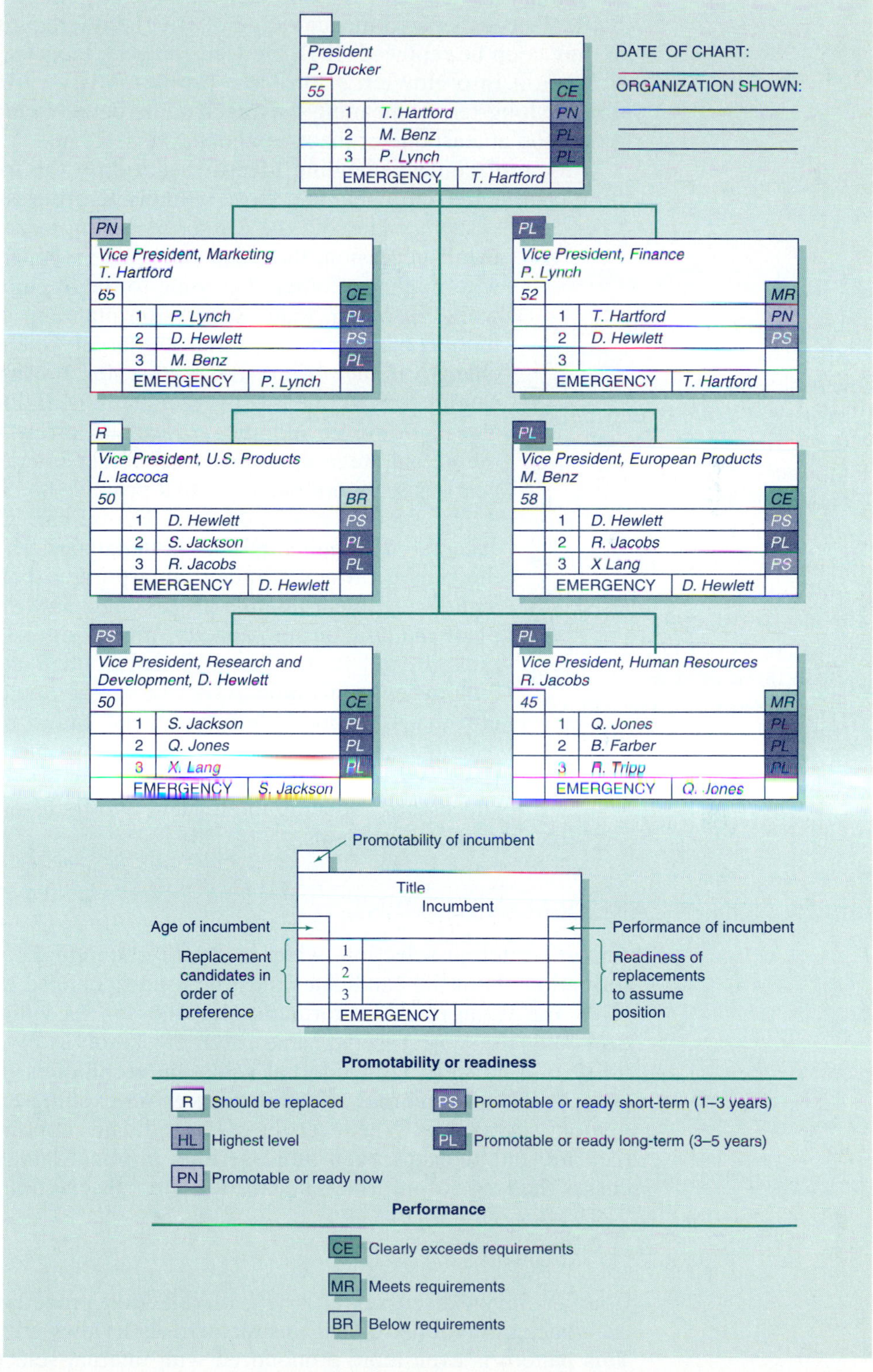

DATE OF CHART:
ORGANIZATION SHOWN:
President
P. Drucker
55
CE
1 T. Hartford PN
2 M. Benz PL
3 P. Lynch PL
EMERGENCY T. Hartford
PN
Vice President, Marketing
T. Hartford
65
CE
1 P. Lynch PL
2 D. Hewlett PS
3 M. Benz PL
EMERGENCY P. Lynch
PL
Vice President, Finance
P. Lynch
52
MR
1 T. Hartford PN
2 D. Hewlett PS
3
EMERGENCY T. Hartford
R
Vice President, U.S. Products
L. Iaccoca
50
BR
1 D. Hewlett PS
2 S. Jackson PL
3 R. Jacobs PL
EMERGENCY D. Hewlett
PL
Vice President, European Products
M. Benz
58
CE
1 D. Hewlett PS
2 R. Jacobs PL
3 X Lang PS
EMERGENCY D. Hewlett
PS
Vice President, Research and
Development, D. Hewlett
50
CE
1 S. Jackson PL
2 Q. Jones PL
3 X. Lang PL
EMERGENCY S. Jackson
PL
Vice President, Human Resources
R. Jacobs
45
MR
1 Q. Jones PL
2 B. Farber PL
3 R. Tripp PL
EMERGENCY Q. Jones
Promotability of incumbent
Title
Incumbent
Age of incumbent
Performance of incumbent
Replacement candidates in order of preference
Readiness of replacements to assume position
1
2
3
EMERGENCY
Promotability or readiness
R Should be replaced
HL Highest level
PN Promotable or ready now
PS Promotable or ready short-term (1–3 years)
PL Promotable or ready long-term (3–5 years)
Performance
CE Clearly exceeds requirements
MR Meets requirements
BR Below requirements

In Exhibit 9.9, for example, career planners might note that T. Hartford is a top candidate for both the job of vice president of finance and president, though she is 65 years old and may be considering retirement. They might also note that L. Iaccoca's performance rating of BR (below requirements) indicates that he may soon be replaced. If D. Hewlett replaces Iaccoca, all the candidates for promotion into Hewlett's job have promotability ratings of only PL (promotable long-term), meaning they need some development. It may be essential to develop at least one of these candidates very soon.

Thus, replacement planning identifies not only the top candidates but also those needing development and those unlikely to progress further. Ideally, such systems can avoid the danger of failing to prepare for top-management succession; they also can open up consideration to candidates who might not otherwise come to the attention of the old boy network. However, many succession planning systems fail to live up to this potential because they are largely subjective, fail to adjust to changes in the positions over time, fail to warn managers when one candidate is in line for several positions, fail to consider needed lateral moves or development processes, rarely include input from the individuals regarding their own career interests, and often become yearly paperwork exercises that produce no decisions.

> WHAT DO YOU THINK?
>
> The traditional succession planning system at Pfizer was similar that given in Exhibit 9.9, and Bruce Ellig, the former vice president of human resources says, "We ended up with a lot of beautiful charts of the three best candidates . . . but when we got to the time when a position would open up, typically, it would not be one of those three people who filled the position."[66] Why do you think the system failed to identify the eventual promotions? What should be done? What is HR's role?

Yet, success stories do exist. Scott Paper Company refocused its succession planning system on updated work descriptions linked to the organization's strategy, incorporated performance assessment and development into the process, and saw a 35 percent increase in plant manufacturing capacity, plus a significant decline in defect rates. Recall from Chapter 8 that Scott Paper was also laying off employees at this time. AT&T built a computerized, worldwide system that links individual managers' career planning and identifies candidates who could be developed into successors. The system allows managers to scan AT&T's worldwide workforce for qualified successors, reducing the tendency to focus on single nations or demographic groups.[67]

## SELECTION IN CAREER MANAGEMENT

As with external selection, when there are more candidates than openings, information about the candidates must be used to choose who should receive the offer; the value of this information depends on its validity. Internal selection decisions are subject to the same EEO legislation as external selection, so validity is a concern with internal selection techniques that exclude protected groups. Because internal selection focuses on existing employees, more information is available. Whenever rejected candidates continue as employees, how they are handled has even more serious implications. The next section discusses the types of information used for internal selection.

### Selection Procedures Used for Internal Staffing

Chapter Seven discusses a variety of selection procedures, noting that reference/background checks and unstructured interviews are used most frequently. This pattern is even more pronounced with internal selection. A survey of U.S.

promotion procedures for skilled employees found that about 60 percent of companies checked with previous supervisors and had unstructured interviews with candidates, about 25 percent of companies used structured interviews, and 12 percent of companies used skills tests/work samples. Other procedures such as weighted application blanks, ability tests, and personality tests were used by less than 10 percent of companies.[68] The advent of more flexible and volatile career environments has probably increased the use of informal methods because formal tests and work samples become harder to develop in volatile environments.

Companies that test candidates for supervisory roles may use personality tests such as the Myers-Briggs Type Indicator (MBTI). This test includes questions that assess a person's preference for extraversion versus introversion, sensing versus intuition, thinking versus feeling, and judging versus perceiving. The results are compiled into reports that suggest a person's strong and weak points. For example, a person expressing preferences for introversion, sensing, thinking, and judging (ISTJ) would be described as "thorough, painstaking, systematic, hardworking and careful with detail." Potential pitfalls might indicate "May neglect interpersonal niceties." Suggestions for development might include "May need to try fresh alternatives to avoid ruts."[69] Exhibit 9.10 shows excerpts from the MBTI. You can see the similarity to the Campbell Interest and Skill Survey (CISS) introduced at the beginning of the chapter. The Campbell test is used more frequently with applicants or to help individuals identify careers. The MBTI is used more often with managers and teams as a diagnostic and feedback tool.

## Assessment Centers

When selecting internal candidates, especially for supervisory/managerial jobs, it might seem logical to have them complete a work sample simulating the kinds of things that such jobs require. They might work on a typical set of letters, memos, notes, and statistical information from a manager's in-basket. They could counsel a poor-performing subordinate, meet with an angry customer, analyze an organization's financial status, and compete for funds in a business meeting. With the recent emphasis on teams, they could work with a team to accomplish a particular task. All candidates would also be interviewed. Finally, to improve accuracy and completeness, a team of assessors might observe all of these tasks and discuss and confer before giving their ratings. This kind of selection procedure is called an *assessment center.* An assessment center is not a location, but a set of selection tasks judged by a team of assessors.[70] The dimensions typically measured in an assessment center are listed in Exhibit 9.11. These dimensions are very subjective, which is why a team approach is attractive. A team is presumed to cancel out the biases of any one person. What traits relate to success in assessment centers? One study found that the cognitive ability of managers related to virtually all tasks such as in-baskets, projects, and presentations, but not to the structured interview. Personality traits such as extroversion related to a few tasks such as the interview and discussions or presentations.[71]

As we saw in Chapter Seven, assessment centers are sometimes used to select new employees for the organization; here we focus on their use as an internal selection device. Less than 10 percent of companies reported using assessment centers for promotion in one national survey, and 12 percent reported

EXHIBIT 9.10 Sample Items from the Myers-Briggs Type Indicator

**Testing Time**

**PART 1: Which answer comes closer to telling how you usually feel or act?**

*When you go somewhere for the day, would you rather*

*a.* Plan what you will do and when, or

*b.* Just go?

*Do you more often let*

*a.* Your heart rule your head, or

*b.* Your head rule your heart?

*In reading for pleasure, do you*

*a.* Enjoy odd or original ways of saying things, or

*b.* Like writers to say exactly what they mean?

*Would you rather have as a friend*

*a.* Someone who is always coming up with new ideas, or

*b.* Someone who has both feet on the ground?

*Do you*

*a.* Talk easily to almost anyone for as long as you have to, or

*b.* Find a lot to say only to certain people or under certain conditions?

**PART II: Which word in each pair appeals to you more?**

| | |
|---|---|
| Compassion | Foresight |
| Soft | Hard |
| Forgive | Tolerate |
| Who | What |
| Build | Invent |
| Foundation | Spire |
| Party | Theater |

Source: Consulting Psychologists Press Inc. quoted in Diane Goldner, "Fill in the Blank," *The Wall Street Journal,* Feb. 27, 1995, p. R5. Reprinted by permission of *The Wall Street Journal* © 1995 Dow Jones & Company, Inc. All Rights Reserved Worldwide.

using such centers for external selection, especially for managers/supervisors.[72] Yet, because many of the largest U.S. organizations have used assessment centers, they have frequently been investigated and described by academics and professionals.[73] Even though assessment centers are usually more expensive than simpler selection procedures, they have been strongly associated with later promotions, with validity coefficients of about 0.40.[74] Even expensive assessment centers can pay off when applied to many hiring decisions, as Chapter Seven shows, though it is not clear that assessment centers are actually better predictors than less expensive alternatives.[75] A study of 382 management candidates in an Israeli corporation found assessment center validity to be only about .25, but other predictors such as cognitive ability were less valid. Although the center cost $111,953 to develop and implement, utility analysis calculations suggested that the payoff over the two years of subsequent manager tenure was $326,103 after subtracting the costs.[76] At the end of Chapter Seven, we discussed the type of model used to calculate such figures. The same logic that applied to external staffing applies to internal staffing.

EXHIBIT 9.11 Typical Dimensions Measured in Assessment Centers

| Dimension | Definition |
|---|---|
| Oral communication | Effective expression in individual or group situations (includes gestures and nonverbal communications) |
| Planning and organizing | Establishing a course of action for self and/or others to accomplish a specific goal; planning proper assignments of personnel and appropriate allocation of resources |
| Delegation | Utilizing subordinates effectively; allocating decision making and other responsibilities to the appropriate subordinates |
| Control | Establishing procedures to monitor and/or regulate processes, tasks, or activities of subordinates and job activities and responsibilities; taking action to monitor the results of delegated assignments or projects |
| Decisiveness | Readiness to make decisions, render judgments, take action, or commit oneself |
| Initiative | Active attempts to influence events to achieve goals; self-starting rather than passive acceptance. Taking action to achieve goals beyond those called for; originating action |
| Tolerance for stress | Stability of performance under pressure and/or opposition |
| Adaptability | Maintaining effectiveness in varying environments, with various tasks, responsibilities, or people |
| Tenacity | Staying with a position or plan of action until the desired objective is achieved or is no longer reasonably attainable |

Source: Reprinted with permission from Robert D. Gatewood and Hubert S. Feild, *Human Resource Selection* (Hinsdale, IL: Dryden Press, 1994). p. 641.

There is also some debate about why assessment centers really work, with the following explanations frequently suggested:

1. Assessment centers are good measures of the traits needed for success.
2. Those who make future promotion decisions know who did well on the assessment center, so such centers don't add any information, they just "crown the prince or princess."
3. Assessment centers only measure the factors the organization eventually uses to make promotions, so they don't add any information beyond what would have been used anyway.
4. Being selected to participate in assessment centers, and doing well, gives managers a feeling of self-confidence that causes them to do well, so the center's value is not for selection as much as for building attitudes and motivation.
5. Assessors simply react to the candidates' past performance, not the traits measured by the center.
6. Assessment centers measure candidates' intelligence.[77]

Assessment centers may also provide valuable training for the assessors themselves, by helping them better understand the traits and characteristics expected of successful managers. Assessors may go on to be better at appraising managerial performance and/or better at their own managerial tasks.

Organizations also have a responsibility to those who participate in the centers and fail to achieve assessments justifying promotion to higher levels. Such individuals often can make valuable contributions if the opportunity to do so is not reduced because they are seen as failures. In a United Kingdom bank, successful candidates' self-assessments agreed with the assessment center, but unsuccessful candidates' assessments were negatively correlated. The worse they did, the better they thought they did. This was true on one dimension even after the candidates received feedback on their results.[78] Clearly, assessment center information must be handled carefully. The assessment center must be seen as one of many ways future potential is assessed, and there must be a commitment to providing opportunities for valued employees who may not be suitable for promotion. Indeed, some have suggested that a significant benefit of assessment centers is their capability to develop future managers by helping them identify areas needing improvement.[79]

## Past Performance, Experience, and Seniority

What factors do you expect to influence your career advancement? Do you think that promotions should be solely a reward for good performance in the current job? Should promotions hinge on gaining certain key experiences that prepare you for future jobs? Or should career advancement be tied to seniority, with those staying the longest getting preference when upper-level opportunities arise? Unions often prefer seniority, believing it is the most objective and observable factor. Yet, evidence suggests that job seniority may not predict future performance and training times as well as the similarity between past and future jobs, and performance in past jobs.[80]

Although employees potentially always develop knowledge, skills, and personal characteristics as they progress through different work roles, organizations can capitalize on this process by creating specific sequences of experiences designed to prepare employees for future work roles. Increasingly, these work roles are defined in skills or competencies rather than job titles. General Electric's power systems division had a reputation for being stodgy and bureaucratic, rigidly following the 28 numbered steps from entry-level management up to the chairman's job. People expected each new job to move them up one number. Because international experience wasn't one of the numbers, they saw foreign postings as roadblocks. The GE unit abolished the 28 steps and replaced them with six broad bands to allow lateral moves. International experience is a prerequisite to advancement. One fast-track candidate was named environmental health and safety manager. While not a traditional fast-track job, the move sends a signal that future GE manages must have experience in a variety of current issues.[81]

Research suggests that career progressions often operate as a tournament in which fast-trackers who succeed early progress to future rounds, but those without early success are less likely to be considered for future opportunities. This was true in a German mechanical engineering company.[82] It also appears to be true in Japanese companies; the diagram in Exhibit 9.12 shows the career progression of 71 college graduates who stayed in a Japanese firm for 13 years. Notice how the managers were separated into three distinct groups shown vertically, with the first, second, and third groups signifying the order in which managers received promotions. The three promotion grades and their timing

EXHIBIT 9.12 Career Mobility of 71 Japanese Executives over 13 Years

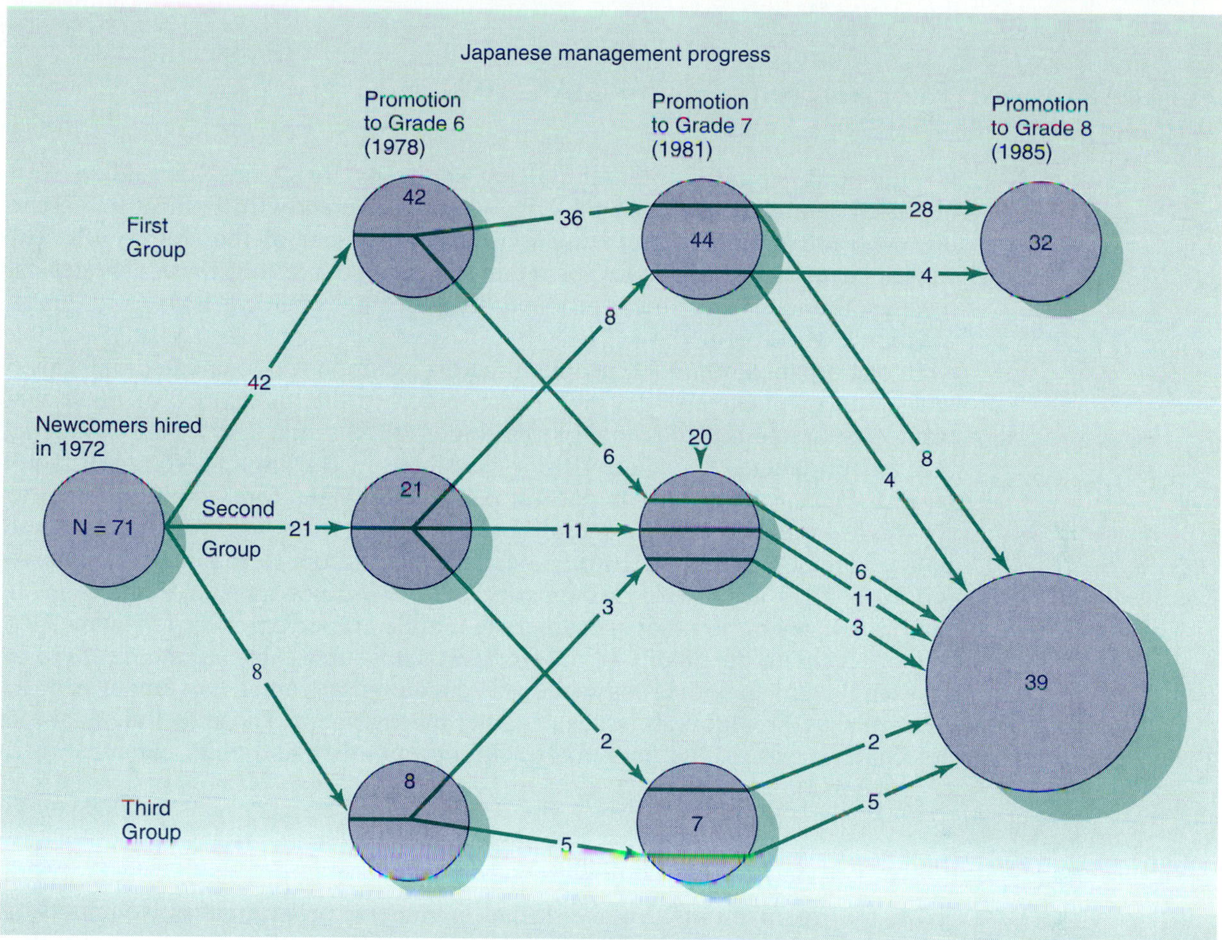


Source: Reprinted from "Japanese Management Progress: Mobility into Middle Management," by Mitsuru Wakabayashji, George Graen, Michael Graen, and Martin Graen, *Journal of Applied Psychology* 73, 1988, p. 221. Copyright 1988 by the American Psychological Association. Reprinted by permission.

appear horizontally with the second and third groups combined in the big circle under 1985. As the diagram shows, the groups are formed within the first six years, and there is very little movement between them. Twenty-eight of the 42 managers in the first group in 1978 made it to grade 8 by 1985, while only 4 of the 21 managers in the second group and none of the 8 managers in the third group progressed to this level.

Clearly, information on past experience, seniority, and recent work performance can be used in very different ways by various organizations. In this age of downsizing, companies such as Household International have found that the best candidates for new positions are those forced out of positions being eliminated to cut costs.[83] What should a good fast-track career experience emphasize? The 276 employees of a Fortune 100 company rated "receive constructive coaching and feedback, be exposed to managers who can serve as role models, gain cross-functional experience, take responsibilities, start a project and work on it until completion, and experience crises and adversity" as the six top tactics.[84]

## SEPARATION AND RETENTION IN CAREER MANAGEMENT: WHO'S LEFT WHEN THEY LEAVE?

It's tempting to judge internal staffing solely by its success in finding well-qualified candidates for new jobs. However, as we show in Exhibit 9.3, someone who moves into a receiving job must move out of the source job. This causes changes in the employees retained in the source job; these changes can have profound effects on the productivity and other characteristics of the organization's workforce.[85]

In one organization, "All people hired off a campus are evaluated in terms of what kind of managers they will make, much to the annoyance of those who wanted to create a professional sales force." IBM's managers were concerned that redeployments to reduce IBM's workforce in Burlington, Vermont, would leave the plant with only the poorest performers. Therefore, although other locations were encouraged to recruit and hire Burlington workers, the corporate policy included the 10-80-10 rule: Managers could opt to retain workers in the top 10 percent at least for six months; they could not transfer workers in the bottom 10 percent to other sites; and the middle 80 percent were fair game.[86]

Concern with the quality of the workforce in source jobs and the desire to retain employees in some jobs while still encouraging career movement is at the heart of several important issues in career management. These include dual-ladder career progressions, mommy-track opportunities, and chief executive officer succession.

### Dual-Ladder Career Paths: Keeping Technical Talent on Track

In many organizations, highly skilled engineers, programmers, scientists, or salespeople face a career dilemma. They may be excellent performers in their skill areas and have a strong desire to grow within that area (a *technical/functional* career anchor), but the organization's technical career track has an early ceiling. At first, individuals can advance quickly within their technical skill; however, they soon reach a point where further advancement requires more supervisory or managerial tasks. Not all engineers have the aspiration to manage.[87] The organization also faces a dilemma: when it forces its best people to leave their technical careers to advance, it may find itself removing top technical performers only to produce mediocre managers who really don't desire their managerial responsibility. The overall value of the workforce may actually decline due to a policy of promoting the best technical performer.

A dual-ladder or two-track career progression establishes parallel career tracks: Some pursue a managerial career, while others pursue a technical or professional career.[88] Movement up the managerial ladder leads to greater decision-making authority and responsibility. Movement up the technical ladder leads to greater independence and more resources to practice in the procession. Organizations such as IBM, AT&T, and Mobil Corporation have long used such career tracks.

Look at the example of multiple career paths for technical workers in Exhibit 9.13; it derives from surveys and interviews with 20 organizations. The

## EXHIBIT 9.13 Multiple-Ladder Career Paths for Technical Workers

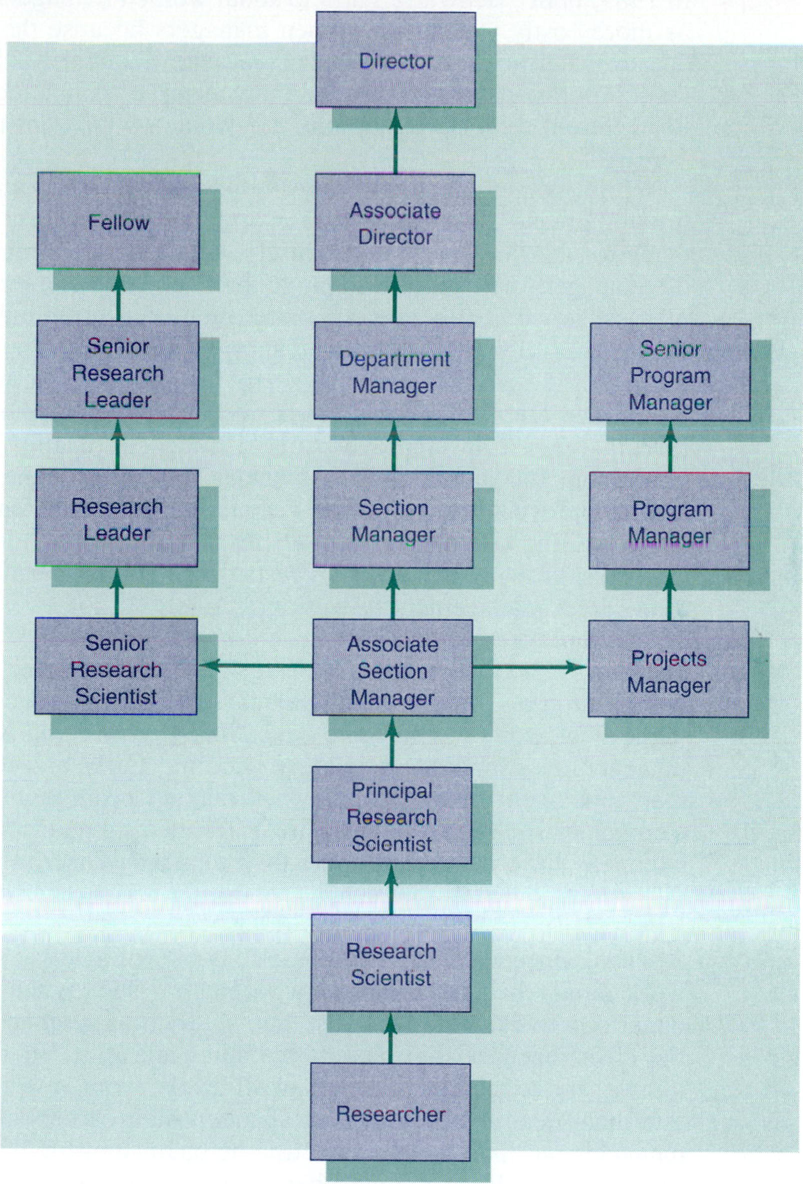


Source: Reprinted with permission from Zandy B. Leibowitz, Beverly L. Kaye, and Caela Farren, "Multiple Career Paths," *Training and Development Journal,* October 1992, p. 32. Copyright 1992, the American Society for Training and Development. All rights reserved.

middle path is the managerial track, the left track emphasizes research expertise and independence, and the right track maintains a technical connection to specific programs with some management responsibility. In a survey of 107 large corporations, Hewitt Associates found multiple career paths most frequently used for engineering, research and development, and information systems employees. Two-thirds of companies felt they achieved their desired results.[89]

## "Mommy Tracks," "Parent Tracks," and Work-Life Balance

In 1989, Felice Schwartz's article about women managers suggested that it may be more costly to employ women managers because they separate more often due to maternity and other dependent care demands. Schwartz also suggested that corporations should provide more flexible arrangements, including options for different career progressions, for women who want to combine career and family.[90]

While women are often very high performers as managers, they may feel greater pressure to refuse career opportunities unless accommodations are made for their commitment to family. An up or out mentality, whereby all middle managers are expected to prove their full-time commitment to the company, may cause women to separate more often. Yet, providing special accommodations for family responsibilities, such as allowing a period of part-time work during child-rearing years, may seem discriminatory if applied only to women. Many men are also opting for a period of reduced career activity during child-rearing years. Can employers afford the costs of allowing slower career advancement for some employees? Does stepping off the fast track necessarily mean employees can't ultimately catch up and advance to higher levels?[91]

As leading companies implement programs to accommodate work-family demands, growing evidence suggests the programs must be carefully integrated with career management to work effectively. If not, even with good intentions, many employees believe they would pay a high price if they actually took advantage of flextime or family leave. The percentage of women who return to work within one year of having a baby was only 53 percent in 1990, and it was highest for women with more education. Corning and Xerox are now training managers to administer flexible scheduling fairly and to "stress results rather than time spent in the office" when making promotions. The stakes are high. Companies such as Goodyear Tire & Rubber, Imagematrix, and Warshawsky & Company have been sued under the Pregnancy Discrimination Act of 1978 for discrimination in granting leave or for giving women who return after pregnancy leave less responsible positions.[92]

Thus, since the "Mommy-Track" books of 1989 it has become clear that work-family balance is hardly a women's issue. When the Bank of Montreal undertook to examine the myth that "cultivating women employees isn't worth the effort because they just have babies and quit," it found that women had longer service records than men at all levels, women weren't quitting at a faster rate than men, and they did not abandon their careers after childbirth.[93] "Self-management" skills—the art of finding balance in life—is becoming part of the curriculum at Wharton and other prestigious business schools. Merck's former director of human resources said, "You can't build an effective company on a foundation of broken homes and strained personal relationships."[94] Human resource managers will need increasingly to tailor career systems to meet needs for balance, or risk losing their most talented employees.

## Chief Executive Officer Succession

Vector Aeromotive makes high-performance cars from materials used in fighter jets. When its founder was fired by his board of directors, he changed the locks, posted armed guards, and holed up in his Los Angeles corporate compound.[95]

For most organizations, CEO succession is not nearly so dramatic; nonetheless, it requires careful handling. Many organizations have traditions or policies stipulating that top officers step down at a certain age, usually in their early sixties. If properly planned, this can be an advantage because it opens up room for upward mobility, provides continuity, and brings in new ideas from below. If unplanned, or if CEOs are unwilling to relinquish their positions when they should, it becomes much more difficult to manage this separation process. It is often difficult to remove a CEO who doesn't want to go because few are in a position to encourage the top corporate officer to leave. Difficulties that must be overcome include (1) the *denial of death,* or reluctance to accept the end of a successful career; (2) *loss of control,* which may hamper an executive's ability to allow successors to take over critical duties; (3) *fear of reprisal* from those not chosen as successors, which could make a CEO reluctant to decide upon a successor; and (4) *romancing the past* by inflating memories of past accomplishments, making it difficult for the successor to institute needed changes and improvements.[96] Mandatory retirement ages are generally prohibited by the Age Discrimination in Employment Act, but many organizations often promote an informal understanding among top executives that the CEO is expected to step down at a certain age, such as 65.

One study found that succession was toughest on CEOs in their 50s. Older CEOs tended to move on to advisory roles, while younger CEOs moved on to other executive positions. One solution is the "papa farm," a peaceful setting in Strausstown, Pennsylvania, where ousted executives receive counseling, comraderie with others like them, and outplacement assistance.[97]

## MANAGING GLOBAL CAREERS

People accustomed to working for American bosses may soon be in for a surprise. At General Motors, Corp., a Spaniard is the new head of worldwide purchasing, responsible for spending more than $30 billion a year. The new president of Esprit de Corp., a major U.S. Sportswear maker, was born in Switzerland. And Xerox Corp.'s newest executive vice president comes from Italy. American corporations picked foreigners for between 7 and 10 percent of their high-level assignments in 1991. Foreign executives accounted for fewer than 1 percent of such placements in 1986.[98]

The race is on to create the global corporation of the future. Success depends on how well companies can identify worldwide talent and create career systems that include international experience as a valued development opportunity. Unfortunately, many Western corporations face great difficulties managing international careers. Between 16 and 40 percent of expatriate U.S. managers do not even complete their foreign assignments because of poor performance or inability to adjust; up to 80 percent perform under par in foreign assignments. For Japanese managers working in the United States, the percent having difficulties or failing is closer to 5 percent.[99] The cost of an international relocation can easily exceed $100,000, so failure in these assignments directly affects the bottom line, not to mention the indirect effect of poor performance.

Exhibit 9.14 presents different factors that may affect the success of international assignments. The horizontal axis shows the time frame of the effects, proceeding from pre-move variables: organizational structure and strategies, past personal experience, family support, and cultural factors. Next, intervening

EXHIBIT 9.14 Factors Related to Expatriate Adjustment and Success

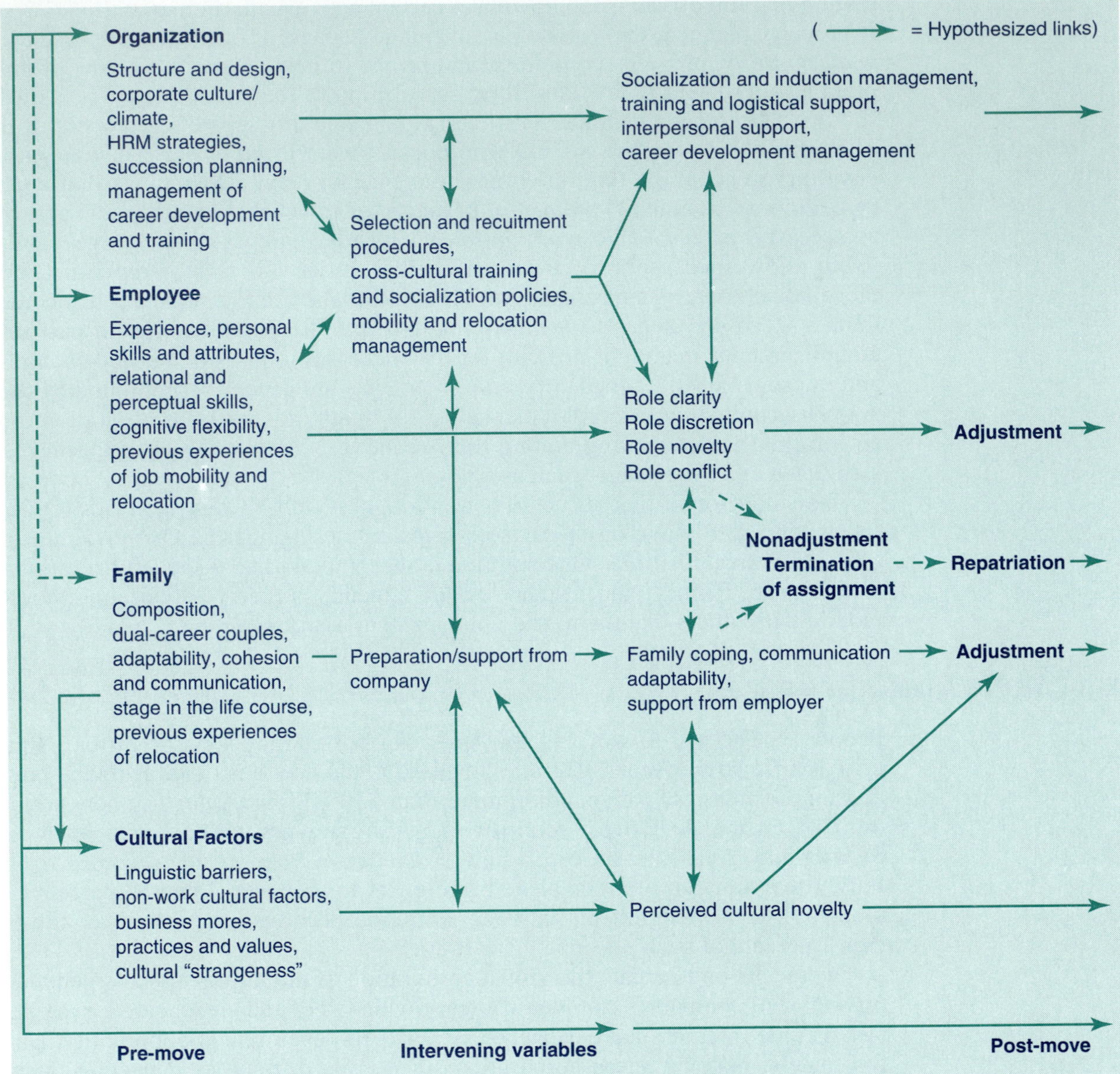

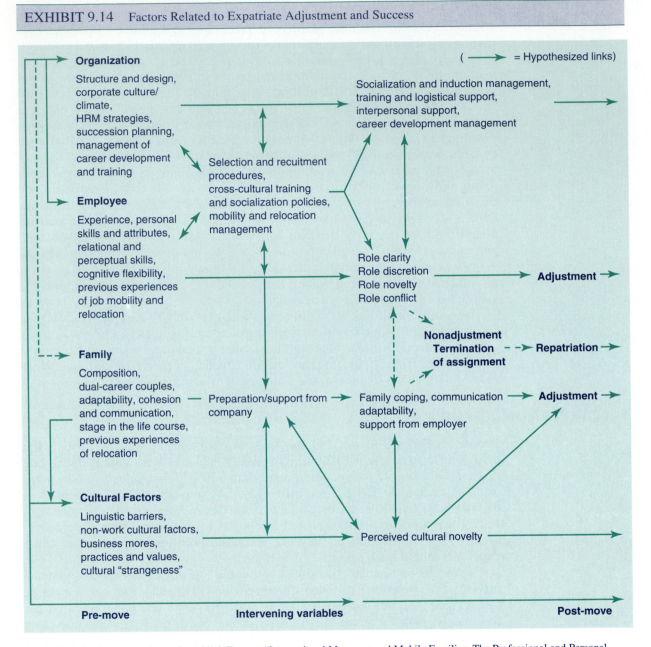

Source: Reprinted with permission from Nick Forster, "International Managers and Mobile Families: The Professional and Personal Dynamics of Trans-National Career Pathing and Job Mobility in the 1990s." *The International Journal of Human Resource Management* 3, no. 3 (December 1992), p. 618.

variables reflect the activities taken to facilitate the move. Once the move has occurred, factors such as on-site support, characteristics of the role, family coping ability, and the novelty of the culture affect adjustment. The right side of the exhibit shows the outcomes. The person may not adjust and be repatriated, or adjust and complete the assignment. One of the most important factors affecting successful international career systems is the post-move phase. If subsequent career opportunities are attractive and challenging, the best candidates are available for international assignments. If not, no amount of pre-move and intervening management compensates for the lack of good candidates. We now briefly discuss what we know about how these factors affect expatriate adjustment.

## Organizational Factors

The most important decision an organization must make in planning international careers is the purpose of international assignments.

*Control-based* strategies aim to ensure that the home-country headquarters maintains authority over company operations around the world. These strategies make sure that experienced and competent home-country nationals are assigned to oversee international units, as is typical in Japanese companies.

*Development-based* strategies emphasize the career growth and learning of those in the assignment, dictating that younger or less internationally experienced people should be given priority, and rotated across several assignments.

*Expertise-based* strategies impart particular expertise to international units, such as sending a top scientist, marketer, or engineer to different locations temporarily to help with specific issues. The movie, *The Coca-Cola Kid,* chronicles the adventures of just such an expert, assigned to raise Coca-Cola sales in Australia.

*Rapid-expansion* strategies involve sending international assignees to establish a presence or explore potential opportunities in countries where expansion is desired. One drawback of such a strategy is that there may be few links to the mainstream of career development because the target country may not develop as expected.

*Joint-venture* strategies involve sending candidates to countries where operations are jointly owned with local governments (such as India) or where local experts have knowledge key to success (such as Japan's product distribution channels.) Obviously, each strategy has very different implications for HR decisions.[100]

## Employee Characteristics: Arnold Schwarzenegger Would Be Ideal

When asked what makes expatriate managers successful, at least 20 percent of executives from 130 multinationals listed one or more of the following: flexibility and tolerance, knowledge of business, interpersonal skills, past job performance, traveled and lived abroad, eagerness to work abroad, or results-oriented management.[101] Unfortunately, little research supports or refutes these beliefs. It remains largely unknown whether certain types of people are more likely to succeed. This can lead to unfounded but self-fulfilling prophesies, such as assigning only host-country managers to overseas operations. This in turn leads to the best local-country employees feeling discriminated against and leaving, which can cause the impression that only host-country managers have the skills to manage foreign operations. A computerized expert system developed by two professors claims to "diagnose employees' readiness for any of over 100 countries" by rating personal characteristics such as adaptability, expectations, and so on. The program has been tested by companies including Avon Products and AT&T.[102]

## Family Support: Whither Thou Goest Shall I Go?

Does having a supportive (or unsupportive) family play a key role in expatriate success? The evidence is limited and mixed, though the business press frequently suggests that the adjustment of spouses and teens is critical. There is strong evidence that family and lifestyle issues are a key reason for refusing expatriate assignments, with many surveys showing that more than 50 percent of those refusing list family as a main concern. When women go overseas, they are usually single; when men do, they are usually accompanied by a spouse. Therefore, although issues of spouse adjustment and employment are more important for men today, they are likely to increase as organizations attempt to send more women overseas. FMC Corporation screens not only the expatriate manager candidates but also spouses for flexibility, patience, and adaptability.[103]

## Cultural Adaptability: Don't Sneeze into Your Handkerchief in Tokyo

There is no doubt that different cultures have different rules. Using a handkerchief is considered disgusting by many Japanese, and some cultures consider it an insult if people put their feet up on a desk, displaying the soles of their shoes to their office guests. Variations are also very wide in management cultures and practices, leadership styles, and group working practices. Familiarity or training in cultural differences is essential. One study of American expatriate managers in Japan, Korea, Taiwan, and Hong Kong showed that adjustment to interacting with host-country residents was enhanced by culture-related training and greater association with host-country residents.[104] A trial period with a short-term visit may help to acclimate expatriates.

## Human Resource Management: How Can We Help?

Senior executives agree that HR decisions play a central role in successful international career management. A Conference Board study of 130 multinational companies touching on several HR areas revealed that more than 80 percent of companies included international candidates in their forecasts and succession plans. However, more than 50 percent had no international HR information system and less than 15 percent found the system very useful. Seventy-nine percent of foreign companies routinely send hiring managers candidates from other countries while only 55 percent of U.S. companies do. Recruitment costs are usually paid by the hiring organization, which may explain their reluctance to search extensively for international candidates. Regarding selection methods, the pattern was similar to the trends discussed in Chapter Seven, with virtually everyone using interviews of the candidates, many using site visits or temporary assignments, and very few using more objective tests, biodata, or background checks. Most companies do not have formal international management development programs; 83 percent of U.S. companies and 61 percent of non-U.S. companies did not. Regarding compensation, even though companies still offer hardship differentials for particularly difficult assignments they are becoming rarer.[105]

### WHAT DO YOU THINK?

Look at the questions asked by AT&T of overseas candidates and their spouses (see Exhibit 9.15) and compare these with the factors related to expatriate adjustment (in Exhibit 9.14) to see whether AT&T is getting at all the important factors.

Companies such as Whirlpool, Unisys, and Colgate-Palmolive had batteries of assessments designed to evaluate candidates'

**EXHIBIT 9.15** Questions Posed by AT&T to Prospective Overseas Candidates and Spouses

- Would your spouse be interrupting a career to accompany you on an international assignment? If so, how do you think this will [affect] your spouse and your relationship with each other?
- Do you enjoy the challenge of making your own way in new situations?
- Securing a job upon reentry will be primarily your responsibility. How do you feel about networking and being your own advocate?
- How able are you in initiating new social contacts?
- Can you imagine living without television?
- How important is it for you to spend significant amounts of time with people of your own ethnic, racial, religious, and national background?
- As you look at your personal history, can you isolate any episodes that indicate a real interest in learning about other peoples and cultures?
- Has it been your habit to vacation in foreign countries?
- Do you enjoy sampling foreign cuisines?
- What is your tolerance for waiting for repairs?

Source: Reprinted with permission from Gilbert Fuschberg, "As Costs of Overseas Assignments Climb, Firms Select Expatriates More Carefully," *The Wall Street Journal,* Jan. 9, 1992, p. B1. Reprinted by permission of *The Wall Street Journal,* 

qualifications as well as such things as their sense of humor and the strength of their family unit. One of the key tasks for human resources is managing the flow of "inpatriates," foreign nationals entering the United States and "repatriates," expatriates reentering their home culture.[106] A survey of 338 internal assignees from a variety of countries and companies found that the most important factors for their success were (1) family situation, (2) flexibility/adaptability, (3) relational skills, (4) job knowledge, and (5) extracultural openness. Assignees in service-oriented industries gave somewhat higher ratings to job knowledge and relational skills than those from manufacturing or utility companies.[107]

## EVALUATING INTERNAL STAFFING AND CAREER DEVELOPMENT

When people are moved within the organization, all the activities of recruitment, selection, and separation/retention become involved. Frequently, such movements also increase training and compensation activities. Therefore, internal staffing has the potential to significantly affect virtually every organization goal. Managed effectively, the organization reaps long-term benefits. Managed poorly, it may be impossible to overcome the problems.

### Efficiency

Recruitment, selection, and separation processes are seldom evaluated very rigorously, and this holds for internal staffing as well. We know some things about what factors affect promotion and transfer decisions, but little about their effectiveness, though some validity evidence exists for assessment centers. The validity of building career systems around competencies remains uninvestigated.

The costs of relocation can easily exceed $40,000 and expatriate moving costs frequently top $100,000. Exhibits 9.3 and 9.4 show examples of the information firms use to analyze the effects of internal staffing. A simulation using these concepts suggested that internal staffing could have million-dollar effects on workforce value when it involves large numbers of employees staying with the organization for many years. Interestingly, it is just as important to monitor the effects of internal movements on the positions that serve as sources of candidates, as it is to monitor whether they produce good candidates in the destination positions.[108] Virtually any of the effectiveness measures discussed at the ends of the previous three chapters can be adapted to measure internal staffing effects. Clearly, organizations could benefit from ensuring that internal staffing policies are carefully implemented and effective.

## Equity

Internal staffing, like all HR activities, must consider EEO and affirmative action implications (see Chapter Two on managing diversity). Government agencies assess the adverse impact created by internal staffing practices. Also, unions are keenly interested in internal staffing practices, with labor contracts frequently stipulating in detail the appropriate factors to consider in making promotions or transfers. Finally, perceptions of promotion fairness affect general attitudes about jobs and occupations; there may be a tendency for promotions of people of the opposite sex to be viewed as unfair.[109] Perhaps the most disturbing aspect of equity in internal staffing is the possibility that women and minorities are artificially held back in their career progress by invisible, but very real barriers called "glass ceilings" or "glass walls."

## Glass Ceilings and Walls

The *glass ceiling* refers to invisible, artificial barriers that prevent qualified individuals from advancing within their organization and reaching full potential. The term originally described the point beyond which women managers and executives, particularly white women, were not promoted. Today it is evident that ceilings and walls exist throughout most workplaces for minorities and women. These barriers result from institutional and psychological practices, and limit the advancement and mobility opportunities of men and women of diverse racial and ethnic backgrounds.[111]

In 1995, 97 percent of senior managers were men, and about the same proportion were white.[110] While promotion rates of minorities and women is rising, the top ranks of organizations remain a white male bastion.

Catalyst studied 481 women who had broken through the glass ceiling and attained positions where 40 percent report directly to the CEO. Their average salaries were $248,000. The women attributed their success to "consistently exceeding performance expectations" and "developing a style with which male managers are comfortable." The women's views were compared with the views of male CEOs in a survey of Fortune 500 companies. The women were more than twice as likely to consider inhospitable work environments and male stereotyping and preconceptions of women as barriers, but both women and CEOs felt that the lack of significant general management or line experience was a key factor. Eighty-five percent of the women and 97 percent of the CEOs felt that opportunities for women had improved during the past five years, and one-third of the

**EXHIBIT 9.16** Recommendations to Shatter the Glass Ceiling

**Recommendations for Business**

- Demonstrate CEO commitment
- Include diversity in all strategic business plans and hold line managers accountable for progress
- Use affirmative action as a tool
- Select, promote and retain qualified individuals
- Prepare minorities and women for senior positions
- Educate the corporate ranks to sensitize employees about gender, racial, and ethnic challenges
- Initiate work/life and family-friendly policies
- Adopt high-performance workplace practices

**Recommendations for Government**

- Lead by example with innovative policies
- Strengthen enforcement of antidiscrimination laws
- Improve data collection to better show progress in breaking the glass ceiling
- Increase disclosure of diversity data by companies

Source: Glass Ceiling Commission, *A Solid Investment: Making Full Use of the Nation's Human Capital* (Washington DC: Glass Ceiling Commission, Nov. 1995) pp. 13–14.

> EXPLORING THE WEB
>
> You can read the entire report of the Glass Ceiling Commission at Cornell's School of Industrial and Labor Relations library on the World Wide Web at **http://www.ilr.cornell.edu/library/e-archive/glassceiling/.**

women believed that 20 percent of senior management positions will be held by women by the year 2000, compared with only 5 percent in 1996.[112] There is evidence that women face different challenges as they progress through their careers, with men's challenges reflecting task-related factors and women facing obstacles to overcome.[113] Are women better leaders than men? It depends. A study summarizing a large amount of prior research showed that across all studies, women and men were equally effective, but that women tended to be more effective in roles defined in less masculine terms or where the subordinate groups were less male dominated.[114] What to do? The 1995 report of the Glass Ceiling Commission offers the recommendation shown in Exhibit 9.16.

## SUMMARY

Changes in organizational structures, gender roles, and demographics all significantly affect internal staffing. In an age when many wonder whether the word *job* will be replaced by *competency* or *temporary work role,* and when the concept of a career may have more to do with amassing marketable capabilities than steadily moving up the hierarchy, it is no wonder that internal staffing presents some of the most important challenges for HR managers. Internal staffing is a powerful tool because it incorporates the effects of recruitment, selection, and separation into every internal movement decision. Because internal staffing does not operate in a vacuum, it must integrate with external staffing, compensation, labor relations, and other human resource functions. Perhaps the closest integration is with training activities. Training and internal movement work hand in hand to create opportunities for employees to develop new capabilities. This should become clearer as we discuss training in the next chapter. Before going on, see how well you can do in helping Corning Glass Works shatter its glass ceiling in Your Turn at the end of the chapter.

## QUESTIONS

1. How does internal staffing integrate the processes of recruitment, selection, and separation/retention? How is it different from external staffing?
2. Is it always best to promote the highest performers? Which other factors should be considered? Why must internal staffing activities be especially attuned to employee equity perceptions?
3. How is the idea of a career changing? How will this affect the employee's strategy for advancement?
4. How are internal recruiting activities similar to external recruiting? How could you judge the effectiveness of a job posting, skills inventory, or succession planning system? Could you use the same evaluation methods as used for external recruiting? Why or why not?
5. How does internal staffing affect internal employee separations/retentions? Why is this effect often overlooked? Could this effect ever offset what appears to be a valuable selection process? Or, is the effect of internal movements on the retained workforce probably not very important?
6. What is a career anchor? How important is this concept in developing an internal staffing strategy? Should career stage be used to determine which employees will be offered new opportunities? What factors are important in this decision from an organization's viewpoint?
7. How is selection for an international assignment different from selection for domestic assignments?
8. What is a "plateaued" employee? How can career systems be designed to minimize the chance that employees will face plateaus? Should such plateaus be seen as a problem? Why or why not?
9. Discuss dual-ladder career progressions and the mommy track. Why have they been introduced and are they producing the desired effects? Give examples.
10. What is a glass ceiling? What are its effects and how can the ceiling be broken?

## YOUR TURN
### Shattering the Glass Ceiling at Corning Glass Works

Corning Glass Works is known as a good employer. It has many progressive programs, including competitive benefits, child care, and flexible time schedules. So why can't the company retain its women and African American managers? Former chairman James

R. Houghton challenged his executives to figure this out and correct it, saying, "We do a good job at hiring but a lousy job at retention and promotion. And it's not good enough just to bring them through the front door." While just 1 in 14 white male professionals left the concern each year between 1980 and 1987, about 1 in 6 African American professionals departed, as did 1 in 7 women professionals. Asked in company exit interviews why they had resigned, most women and blacks cited lack of career opportunities. Corning's manufacturing activities range from space-age ceramic components, to housewares, to collector-quality glass. Most of its operations are located in or around its headquarters in Corning, New York, a rural town with so few minorities living locally that Corning attracted an African American hairdresser to town at the request of African American managers who said they were driving an hour or more to Ithaca or Rochester for a haircut.[115]

Imagine you are a top personnel executive at Corning. How will you help Corning respond to the chairman's challenge? What potential biases or cultural histories may be causing the shortage of women and minority top managers? What kind of internal staffing policies could improve the attractiveness of women and minorities for upper-level positions? How can ingrained biases and ignorance be attacked? How would you convince line managers of the need to act? Finally, how would you measure your success?

## NOTES AND REFERENCES


1. Terence J. Tracey and James Rounds, "Evaluating Holland's and Gati's Vocational-Interest Models: A Structural Meta-Analysis," *Psychological Bulletin* 113, no. 2 (1993), pp. 229–246; Howard A. Tinsley, "Special Issue on Holland's Theory," *Journal of Vocational Behavior* 40, no. 2 (Apr. 1992), pp. 109–215; John L. Holland, *The Occupations Finder* (Palo Alto, CA: Consulting Psychologists Press, 1978); John L. Holland, *Professional Manual for the Self-Directed Search* (Odessa, FL: Psychological Assessment Resources, 1990); John L. Holland, *Making Vocational Choices,* 2nd ed. (Englewood Cliffs, NJ: Prentice Hall, 1985).
2. Sahng Ern Park and Albert A. Harrison, "Career-Related Interests and Values, Perceived Control, and Acculturation of Asian-American and Caucasian-American College Students," *Journal of Applied Social Psychology* 25 (1995), 25, pp. 1184–1203.
3. Ida C. Hansen and David P. Campbell, *Manual for the SVIB-SCII,* 4th ed. (Palo Alto, CA: Stanford University Press, 1985); *The Campbell Interest and Skill Survey,* Web page, **http://www.ncs.com/cds/ciss.htm**, Feb. 1996.
4. Michael B. Arthur, Douglas T. Hall, and Barbara S. Lawrence, "Generating New Directions in Career Theory: The Case for a Transdisciplinary Approach," in *Handbook of Career Theory,* ed. Arthur, Hall, and Lawrence (New York: Cambridge University Press, 1989), chap. 1.
5. David Young, "Corporation Relocation Tab; People Movers Pay $50,000," *Chicago Tribune,* May 1, 1995, p. C3.
6. John W. Boudreau, "Utility Analysis: A New Perspective on Human Resource Management Decisions," in *ASPA Handbook of Personnel and Industrial Relations,* vol. 1, ed. Lee D. Dyer (Washington, DC: Bureau of National Affairs, 1988).
7. "Gluing the Organization Together," *HRM News,* Dec. 21, 1992, p. 2.
8. Douglas T. Hall, "Executive Careers and Learning, Aligning Selection, Strategy and Development," *Human Resource Planning* 18 (1995), pp. 14–23.

9. Douglas T. Hall and Associates, *Career Development in Organizations* (San Francisco: Jossey-Bass, 1986); "Self-Assessment Said to Be First Step in Employee Career Development Process," Bureau of National Affairs, *Employee Relations Weekly* 5, no. 18 (May 4, 1987), p. 547; Richard K. Broszeit, "'If I Had My Druthers. . .' A Career Development Program," *Personnel Journal,* Oct. 1986, pp. 84–90.

10. Joan E. Rigdon, "Room at the Top: PepsiCo's KFC Scouts for Blacks and Women for its Top Echelons," *The Wall Street Journal,* Nov. 13, 1991, p. A1; Felice Schwartz, *Breaking with Tradition—Women, Work and the New Facts of Life* (New York: Catalyst, 1992); Charles McCoy, "Some Pose as Members of Minority Groups to Promote Careers," *The Wall Street Journal,* Feb. 12, 1991, p. A1.

11. Bureau of National Affairs, *Recruiting and Selection Procedures,* Personnel Policies Forum Survey No. 146 (Washington, DC: Bureau of National Affairs, May 1988).

12. J. E. Rosenbaum, *Career Mobility in a Corporate Hierarchy* (New York: Academic Press, 1984); Shelby Stewman and Suresh L. Konda, "Careers and Organizational Labor Markets: Demographic Models of Organizational Behavior," *American Journal of Sociology* 40 (1983), pp. 298–321; Victor H. Vroom and K. R. MacCrimmon, "Toward a Stochastic Model of Managerial Careers," *Administrative Science Quarterly* 13 (1968), pp. 26–46; George T. Milkovich and John C. Anderson, "Career Planning and Development Systems," in *Personnel Management,* ed. Kendrith M. Rowland and Gerald R. Ferris (Boston: Allyn & Bacon, 1982).

13. John W. Boudreau, "Utility Analysis Applied to Internal and External Employee Movement: An Integrated Theoretical Framework," working paper, Cornell University, NYSSILR 1988; John W. Boudreau, "Utility Analysis: A New Perspective on Human Resource Management Decisions"; John W. Boudreau, "Utility Analysis for Human Resource Management Decisions," in *Handbook of Industrial and Organizational Psychology,* 2nd ed., ed., M. D. Dunnette (Palo Alto, CA: Consulting Psychologists Press, 1991).

14. Hall et al., *Career Development in Organizations.*

15. Zandy B. Leibowitz, Barbara H. Feldman, and Sherry H. Mosely, "Career Development Works Overtime at Corning, Inc.," *Personnel,* Apr. 1990, pp. 38–45.

16. Samuel Aryee and Yaw A. Debrah, "Career Planning: An Examination of Individual, Non-Work and Work Determinants," *International Journal of Human Resource Management* 3, no. 1 (May 1992), pp. 85–104.

17. Andrew S. Grove, "A High-Tech CEO Updates His Views on Managing and Careers," *Fortune,* Sept. 18, 1995, p. 229.

18. Hal Lancaster, "Life Lessons: The Adaptable Survive Corporate Chaos," *The Wall Street Journal,* Feb. 14, 1995, p. B1; William Bridges, *Job Shift,* (Reading, MA: Addison-Wesley, 1994); Stanley B. Malos and Michael A. Campion, "An Options-Based Model of Career Mobility in Professional Service Firms," *Academy of Management Review* 20 (1995), pp. 611–44.

19. Arno Penzias, "New Paths to Success," *Fortune,* June 12, 1995, pp. 90–94; Michael A. Campion, Lisa Cheraskin, and Michael J. Stevens, "Career-Related Antecedents and Outcomes of Job Rotation," *Academy of Management Journal* 37 (1994), pp. 1518–42.

20. Robert J. DeFillippi and Michael B. Arthur, "The Boundaryless Career: A Competency-Based Perspective," *Journal of Organizational Behavior* 15 (1994), pp. 307–24.

21. Patricia Sellers, "Now Bounce Back!" *Fortune,* May, 1995, pp. 49–66.

22. A. Sakamoto and D. A. Power, "Education and the Dual Labor Market for Japanese Men," *American Sociological Review* 60 (Apr. 1995), pp. 222–46; Aaron Bernstein, "Is America Becoming More of a Class Society?" *Business Week,* Feb. 26, 1996, pp. 86–91.

23. Timothy D. Schellhardt, "Mobile Work Force Checks into Office," *The Wall Street Journal,* July 22, 1992, p. B1.

24. Susan Carey, "Flight Attendants Stay Aloft for Decades, Piling Up the Privileges of Job Seniority," *The Wall Street Journal,* May 16, 1995, p. B1; G. Pascal Zachary, "Data about Job Instability May Be Shaky," *The Wall Street Journal,* Mar. 31, 1995, p. A2; "The Salaryman Rides Again," *The Economist,* Feb. 4, 1995.

25. William P. Barnett and Anne S. Miner, "Standing on the Shoulders of Others: Career Interdependence in Job Mobility," *Administrative Science Quarterly* 37 (1992), pp. 262–81.

26. David Lubinski, Camilla P. Benbow, and Jennifer Ryan, "Stability of Vocational Interests among the Intellectually Gifted from Adolescence to Adulthood: A 15-Year Longitudinal Study," *Journal of Applied Psychology* 80 (1995), pp. 196–200.

27. Edgar H. Schein, *Career Anchors: Discovering Your Real Values* (San Diego, CA: University Associates, 1985); Edgar H. Schein, "A Critical Look at Current Career Development Theory and Research," in Douglas T. Hall and Associates, *Career Development in Organizations* (San Francisco: Jossey-Bass, 1986).

28. Sara L. Rynes, Pamela S. Tolbert, and Pamela G. Strausser, "Aspirations to Manage: A Comparison of Engineering Students and Working Engineers," *Journal of Vocational Behavior* 32 (1988), pp. 239–53.

29. Robert D. Bretz, Jr., and Timothy .A Judge, "The Relationship between Person-Organization Fit and Career Success," Working Paper 92-11, Cornell University Center for Advanced Human Resource Studies, Ithaca, NY, 1992.

30. G. V. Crockett, "A Logit Model of Labour Market Influences on the Choice of Occupation," *Journal of Industrial Relations,* Sept. 1991, pp. 309–25; Samuel Aryee, "The Impact of Government Policy on Managerial and Professional Singaporean Careers," (paper presented at the National Academy of Management Meeting, Las Vegas, Aug. 1992).

31. John O. Crites, "A Comprehensive Model of Career Adjustment in Early Adulthood," *Journal of Vocational Behavior* 9 (1976), pp. 105–18; Solomon Cytrynbaum and John O. Crites, "The Utility of Adult Development Theory in Understanding Career Adjustment Process," in *Handbook of Career Theory,* ed. Michael B. Arthur, Douglas T. Hall, and Bar-

bara S. Lawrence, chap. 4; Donna K. Cooke, "Measuring Career Change," *Human Resource Management Review* 4 (1994), pp. 383–98.

32. Bruce Nussbaum, "I'm Worried About My Job," *Business Week,* Oct. 7, 1991, pp. 94–97.
33. Gerard A. Callahan and Jeffrey Greenhaus, "The Career Indecision of Managers and Professions: An Examination of Multiple Subtypes," *Journal of Vocational Behavior* 41 (1992) pp. 212–13.
34. John D. Krumboltz, "The Wisdom of Indecision," *Journal of Vocational Behavior* 41, (1992), pp. 239–44; Thomas .A Wright and Douglas G. Bonett, "The Effect of Turnover on Work Satisfaction and Mental Health: Support for a Situational Perspective," *Journal of Organizational Behavior* 13 (1992), pp. 603–15.
35. M. Susan Taylor, "Effects of College Internships on Individual Participants," *Journal of Applied Psychology* 73, no. 3 (1988), pp. 393–401; Joel E. Ross and Darab Unwalla, "Making it to the Top: A 30-Year Perspective," *Personnel,* Apr. 1988, pp. 70–78.
36. Neil Anderson and Helena D. C. Thomas, "Work Group Socialization," in M. West, ed.,*Handbook of Work Groups* (Chichester, England: Wiley, forthcoming).
37. Cheri Ostroff and Steve W. J. Kozlowski, "Organizational Socialization as a Learning Process: The Role of Information Acquisition," *Personnel Psychology* 45 (1992), pp. 849–74; Nigel Nicholson and John Arnold, "From Expectation to Experience: Graduates Entering a Large Corporation," *Journal of Organizational Behavior* 12 (1991), pp. 413–29; Christine S. Koberg and Leonard H. Chusmir, "Sex Role Conflict in Sex-Atypical Jobs: A Study of Female-Male Differences," *Journal of Organizational Behavior* 12 (1991), pp. 461–65.
38. Catherine Kirchmeyer, "Demographic Similarity to the Work Group: A Longitudinal Study of Managers at the Early Career Stage," *Journal of Organizational Behavior* 16 (1995), pp. 67–83.
39. Hal Lancaster, "As Company Programs Fade, Workers Turn to Guild-Like Groups," *The Wall Street Journal,* Jan. 16, 1996, p. B1.
40. Robert F. Morrison and Thomas M. Brantner, "What Enhances or Inhibits Learning a New Job? A Basic Career Issue," *Journal of Applied Psychology* 77, no. 6 (1992), pp. 926–40.
41. George F. Dreher and Robert D. Bretz, Jr., "Cognitive Ability and Career Attainment: Moderating Effects of Early Career Success," *Journal of Applied Psychology* 76, no. 3 (1991), pp. 392–97.
42. Charles A. O'Reilly III and Jennifer A. Chatman, "Working Smarter and Harder: A Longitudinal Study of Managerial Success," *Administrative Science Quarterly* 39 (1994), pp. 603–27; Cheri Ostroff and Teresa J. Rothausen, "Tenure's Role in Fit: An Individual and Organization Level Analysis," paper presented at the 10th Annual Meeting of the Society for Industrial and Organizational Psychology (Orlando, FL, May 1995).
43. Joann S. Lublin, "Japanese Are Doing More Job Hopping," *The Wall Street Journal,* Nov. 18, 1991, p. B1.

44. Thomas C. Hayes, "Faltering Companies Seek Outsiders," *New York Times,* Jan. 18, 1993, p. D1; Warren Boeker and Jerry Goodstein, "Performance and Successor Choice: The Moderating Effects of Governance and Ownership," *Academy of Management Journal* 36, no. 1 (1993), pp. 172–86.

45. Kerry D. Carson, Paula Phillips Carson, and Arthur G. Bedeian, "Development and Construct Validation of a Career Entrenchment Measure," *Journal of Occupational and Organizational Psychology* 68 (1995), pp. 301–20.

46. Jay W. Lorsch and Haruo Takago, "Keeping Managers off the Shelf," *Harvard Business Review,* July–Aug. 1986, pp. 60–65.

47. Michel Tremblay, Alain Roger, and Jean-Marie Toulouse, "Career Plateau and Work Attitudes: An Empirical Study of Managers," *Human Relations* 48 (1995), pp. 221–37; Anne B. Fisher, "Why the Grass is Looking Greener," *Fortune,* Oct. 2, 1995, pp. 45–46.

48. Tammy D. Allen, Joyce E. A. Russell, Mark L. Poteet, and Gregory H. Dobbins, "Learning and Development Factors Related to Perceptions of Job Content and Hierarchical Plateauing," paper presented at the 10th Annual Meeting of the Society for Industrial and Organizational Psychology, May 1995.

49. Asya Pazy, "The Threat of Professional Obsolescence: How Do Professionals at Different Career Stages Experience It and Cope with It?" *Human Resource Management* 29, no. 3 (Fall 1990), pp. 251–69.

50. "Grooming Managers through Rotation," *Human Resource Management News,* Dec. 6, 1989, p. 3.

51. John D. Krumboltz et al., "Teaching a Rational Approach to Career Decision Making: Who Benefits Most?" *Journal of Vocational Behavior* 29, no. 1 (Aug. 1986), pp. 1–6; Bureau of National Affairs, "Self-Assessment Said to Be First Step in Employee Career Development Process," *Employee Relations Weekly* 5, no. 18 (May 4, 1987), p. 54; Dan R. Dalton and Debra J. Mesch, "The Impact of Employee-Initiated Transfer on Absenteeism: A Four-Year Cohort Assessment," *Human Relations* 45, no. 3(1992), pp. 291–304; Joseph Schwarzwald, Meni Koslowsky, and Boaz Shalit, "A Field Study of Employees' Attitudes and Behaviors after Promotion Decisions," *Journal of Applied Psychology* 77, no. 4(1992), pp. 511–14.

52. Jeanne M. Brett and Anne H. Reilly, "On the Road Again: Predicting the Job Transfer Decision," *Journal of Applied Psychology* 73, no. 4 (1988), pp. 614–20; Daniel B. Turban, James E. Campion, and Alison R. Eyring, "Factors Relating to Relocation Decisions of Research and Development Employees," *Journal of Vocational Behavior* 41 (1992), pp. 183–99; William T. Bielby and Denise D. Bielby, "I Will Follow Him: Family Ties, Gender-Role Beliefs, and Reluctance to Relocate for a Better Job," *American Journal of Sociology* 97, no. 5 (Mar. 1992), pp. 1241–67; Jacqueline C. Landau, Boas Shamir, and Michael B. Arthur, "Predictors of Willingness to Relocate for Managerial and Professional Employees," *Journal of Organizational Behavior* 13 (1992), pp. 667–80.

53. Neville .C Tompkins, "GTE Managers on the Move," *Personnel Journal,* Aug. 1992, pp. 86–91.
54. Stratford Sherman and Ani Hadjian, "How Tomorrow's Leaders Are Learning Their Stuff," *Fortune,* Nov. 27, 1995, p. 90.
55. Rebecca A. Thacker and Sandy J. Wayne, "An Examination of the Relationship Between Upward Influence Tactics and Assessments of Promotability," *Journal of Management* 21 (1995), pp. 739–56; Timothy A. Judge and Robert D. Bretz, Jr., "Political Influence Behavior and Career Success," *Journal of Management* 20 (1994), pp. 43–65; Timothy D. Schellhardt, "Attractiveness Aids Men More than Women," *The Wall Street Journal,* Oct. 18, 1991, p. B2; Rodney Ho, "Men Try to Put a New Face on Careers," *The Wall Street Journal,* Aug. 28, 1991, p. B1; Daniel C. Feldman and Barton A. Weitz, "From the Invisible Hand to the Gladhand: Understanding a Careerist Orientation to Work," *Human Resource Management* 30, no. 2(Summer 1991), pp. 237–57; Deborah L. Jacobs, "Suing Japanese Employers," *Across the Board,* Oct. 1991, pp. 30–37.
56. Judy D. Olian, Stephen J. Carroll, Christina M. Giannantonio, and Dena B. Feren, "What Do protégés Look for in a Mentor? Results of Three Experimental Studies," *Journal of Vocational Behavior* 33 (1988), pp. 15–37.
57. Sherman and Hadjian, "How Tomorrow's Leaders Are Learning Their Stuff"; Elizabeth Lesly, "Manager See, Manager Do," *Business Week,* Apr. 3, 1995, pp. 90–91; Marshall Loeb, "The New Mentoring," *Fortune,* Nov. 27, 1995, p. 213.
58. Tammy D. Allen, Mark L. Poteet, Joyce E. A. Russell, and Gregory H. Dobbins, "A Field Study of Factors Related to Supervisors' Willingness to Mentor Others," *Journal of Vocational Behavior,* in press, 1996.
59. David Jacoby, "Rewards Make the Mentor," *Personnel,* Dec. 1989, pp. 10–14; Bureau of National Affairs, "Hawaiian Telephone Co. Career Program Encourages Employee Growth," *Employee Relations Weekly* 4, no. 44 (Nov. 10, 1986), p. 1406; William Whitely, Thomas W. Dougherty, and George F. Dreher, "Correlates of Career-Oriented Mentoring for Early Career Managers and Professionals," *Journal of Organizational Behavior* 13 (1992), pp. 141–54.
60. Raymond A. Noe, "Women and Mentoring: A Review and Research Agenda," *Academy of Management Review* 13, no. 1(1988), pp. 65–78; Terri A. Scandura, "Mentorship and Career Mobility: An Empirical Investigation," *Journal of Organizational Behavior* 13 (1992), pp. 169–74.
61. Noe, "Women and Mentoring."
62. Joel Lefkowitz, "Race as a Factor in Job Placement: Serendipitous Findings of 'Ethnic Drift,'" *Personnel Psychology* 47 (1994), pp. 497–513; Barbara Marsh, "Families Hire Mentors to Ease Succession," *The Wall Street Journal,* July 23, 1992, p. B1.
63. Milan Moravec and Robert Tucker, "Job Descriptions for the 21st Century," *Personnel Journal,* June 1992, pp. 37–44.
64. "HRIS: Matching Jobs and Skills Worldwide," *HRM News,* July 3, 1995, pp. 3–4.

65. William M. Carley, "CEO's Heart Surgery Is Giving GE a Case of Succession Jitters," *The Wall Street Journal,* May 24, 1995, p. A1.

66. "The Right Dose of HR," *Human Resource Executive,* Oct. 1995, pp. 1–29.

67. Robert J. Sahl, "Succession Planning Drives Plant Turnaround," *Personnel Journal,* Sept. 1992, pp. 67–70; Victoria J. Brush and Ren Nardoni, "Integrated Data Supports AT&T's Succession Planning," *Personnel Journal,* Sept. 1992, pp. 103–9.

68. Bureau of National Affairs, *Employee Selection Procedures,* ASPA-BNA Survey No. 45 (Washington, DC: Bureau of National Affairs, May 5, 1983).

69. *1991 Business Catalog* (Palo Alto, CA: Consulting Psychologists Press, 1991).

70. Paul R. Sackett and Michael M. Harris, "A Further Examination of the Constructs Underlying Assessment Center Ratings," *Journal of Business and Psychology* 3, no. 2 (Winter 1988), pp. 214–29; Robert .D Gatewood and Hubert S. Feild, *Human Resource Selection* (Hinsdale, IL: Dryden, 1994), p. 641.

71. Carol A. Vance and Paul E. Spector, "The Relation of Cognitive Ability and Personality Traits to Assessment Center Performance," paper presented at the 10th Annual Meeting of the Society for Industrial and Organizational Psychology, May 1995.

72. Bureau of National Affairs, *Employee Selection Procedures;* Bureau of National Affairs, *Recruiting and Selection Procedures.*

73. William C. Byham, "Starting an Assessment Center the Correct Way," *Personnel Administrator,* Feb. 1980, pp. 27–32; P. R. Sackett, "A Critical Look at Some Common Beliefs about Assessment Centers," *Public Personnel Management* 11, no. 1 (1982), pp. 140–47; Frederick D. Frank and James R. Preston, "The Validity of the Assessment Center Approach and Related Issues," *Personnel Administrator,* June 1982, p. 94; Milan Marovee, "A Cost-Effective Career Planning Program Requires Strategy," *Personnel Administrator,* Jan. 1982, p. 30; Anthony J. Plento, *A Review of Assessment Center Research* (U.S. Office of Personnel Management, Washington, DC, May 1980), p. 8; Stephen L. Cohen, "The Bottom Line on Assessment Center Technology: Results of a Cost-Benefit Analysis Survey," *Personnel Administrator,* Feb. 1980, p. 57; Donald H. Bush and Lyle F. Schoenfeldt, "Identifying Managerial Potential: An Alternative to Assessment Centers," *Personnel* (AMACOM), May–June 1980, p. 69; Stephen L. Cohen, G. L. Hart, and P. H. Thompson, "Assessment Centers: For Selection or Development—IBM Workshop Experience," *Organization Dynamics,* Spring 1979, p. 63; D. W. Bray and D. L. Grant, "The Assessment Center in the Measurement of Potential for Business Management," *Psychological Monographs* 80, no. 625 (1966).

74. Paul R. Sackett and George F. Dreher, "Constructs and Assessment Center Dimensions: Some Troubling Empirical Findings," *Journal of Applied Psychology* 67, no. 4 (1982), pp. 401–10; V. R. Boehm, "Assessment Centers and Management Development," in *Personnel Management,* ed.

K. Rowland and G. R. Ferris (Boston: Allyn & Bacon, 1982); Janet J. Turnage and Paul M. Muchinsky, "A Comparison of the Predictive Validity of Assessment Center Evaluations versus Traditional Measures in Forecasting Supervisory Job Performance: Interpretive Implications of Criterion Distortion for the Assessment Paradigm," *Journal of Applied Psychology* 69, no. 4 (1984), pp. 595–602; George F. Dreher and Paul R. Sackett, *Perspectives on Employee Staffing and Selection* (Homewood, IL: Richard D. Irwin, 1983); John R. Hinrichs, "An Eight-Year Follow-Up of a Management Assessment Center," *Journal of Applied Psychology* 63 (1978), pp. 596–601; Paul R. Sackett, "Assessment Centers and Content Validity: Some Neglected Issues," *Personnel Psychology* 40 (1987), pp. 13–25; Manuel London and Stephen Stumpf, "Effects of Candidate Characteristics on Management Promotion Decisions: An Experimental Study," *Personnel Psychology* 36 (1983), pp. 241–59.

75. Wayne .F Cascio and Val Silbey, "Utility of the Assessment Center as a Selection Device," *Journal of Applied Psychology* 64 (1979), pp. 107–81; John F. Hunter and Rhonda F. Hunter, "Validity and Utility of Alternative Predictors of Job Performance," *Psychological Bulletin* 96 (1984), pp. 72–98.
76. Aharon Tziner, Elchanan I. Meir, Mihal Dahan, and Assa Birati, "An Investigation of the Predictive Validity and Economic Utility of the Assessment Center for the High-Management Level," *Canadian Journal of Behavioral Science* 26 (1994), pp. 228–45.
77. Richard Klimoski and Mary Brickner, "Why Do Assessment Centers Work? The Puzzle of Assessment Center Validity," *Personnel Psychology* 40 (1987), pp. 243–60.
78. Clive Fletcher and Claire Kerslake, "The Impact of Assessment Centers and Their Outcomes on Participants' Self-Assessments," *Human Relations* 45, no. 3(1992), pp. 281–89.
79. A. S. Engelbrecht and A. H. Fischer, "The Managerial Performance Implications of a Developmental Assessment Center Process," *Human Relations* 48 (1995), pp. 387–404.
80. Michael E. Gordon and E. J. Fitzgibbons, "Empirical Test of the Validity of Seniority as a Factor in Staffing Decisions," *Journal of Applied Psychology* 67 (1982), pp. 311–19; Michael E. Gordon and W. A. Johnson, "Seniority: A Review of Its Legal and Scientific Standing," *Personnel Psychology* 35 (1974), pp. 255–80; Michael E. Gordon, John L. Cofer, and P. Michael McCullough, "Relationships among Seniority, Past Performance, Interjob Similarity, and Trainability," *Journal of Applied Psychology* 71, no. 3 (1986), pp. 518–21.
81. Amanda Bennett, "GE Redesigns Rungs of Career Ladder," *The Wall Street Journal,* Mar. 15, 1993, p. B1.
82. J. E. Rosenbaum, *Career Mobility in a Corporate Hierarchy* (Orlando, FL: Academic Press, 1984); Josef Bruderl, Andreas Diekmann, and Peter Preisendorfer, "Patterns of Intraorganizational Mobility: Tournament Models, Path Dependency, and Early Promotion Effects," *Social Science Research* 20 (1991), pp. 197–216.

83. Peggy Stuart, "New Internal Jobs Found for Displaced Employees," *Personnel Journal,* Aug. 1992, pp. 50–56.

84. Hubert S. Feild and Stanley G. Harris, "Entry-Level, Fast-Track Management Development Programs: Developmental Tactics and Perceived Effectiveness," *Human Resource Planning* 14, no. 4 (1991), pp. 261–73.

85. John W. Boudreau, "Utility Analysis: A New Perspective on Human Resource Management Decisions."

86. Rosabeth Moss Kanter, *Men and Women of the Corporation* (New York: Basic Books, 1977), p. 130; D. Quinn Mills, *The IBM Lesson* (New York: Random House, 1988).

87. Rynes, Tolbert, and Strausser, "Aspirations to Manage."

88. Joseph A. Raelin, "Two-Track Plans for One-Track Careers," *Personnel Journal,* January 1987, pp. 96–101; Conference Board, "Dual Career Paths in Sales," *Management Briefing: Human Resources* (New York: Conference Board, 1987).

89. "Dual-Career Ladders: Keeping Technical Talent on Track," *HR Focus,* Dec. 1992, p. 24.

90. Felice Schwartz, "Management Women and the New Facts of Life," *Harvard Business Review,* Jan.–Feb. 1989, pp. 65–76.

91. T. Bennett, "Fathers Make More Use of On-Site Day Care," *The Wall Street Journal,* Sept. 4, 1991; Elizabeth Erlich, "Is the Mommy Track a Blessing—Or a Betrayal?" *Business Week,* May 15, 1989, pp. 98–99; Carol Hymowitz, "Stepping off the Fast-Track," *The Wall Street Journal,* June 13, 1989, p. B1; Victor Fuchs, "Mommy Track Is Good for Both Business and Families," *The Wall Street Journal,* Mar. 13, 1989, p. A14.

92. Meredith K. Wadman, "Mothers Who Take Extended Time off Find Their Careers Pay a Heavy Price," *The Wall Street Journal,* July 16, 1992, p. B1; Aaron Bernstein, "The Mommy Backlash," *Business Week,* August 10, 1992, pp. 42–44; Walter Kiechel III, "A Guide for the Expectant Executive," *Fortune,* Sept. 9, 1991, p. 191; Sue Shellenbarger, "Averting Career Damage from Family Policies," *The Wall Street Journal,* June 24, 1992, p. B1.

93. Sue Shellenbarger, "Shedding Light on Women's Records Dispels Stereotypes," *The Wall Street Journal,* Dec. 20, 1995, p. B1.

94. Sue Shellenbarger, "Keeping your Career a Manageable Part of Your Life," *The Wall Street Journal,* Apr. 12, 1995, p. B1.

95. "Fired CEO Seizes 4 Buildings," *Ithaca Journal,* Mar. 25, 1992, p. 2A.

96. Manfred F. R. Kets De Vries, "The Dark Side of CEO Succession," *Harvard Business Review,* Jan.–Feb. 1988, pp. 56–60.

97. Andrew Ward, Jeffrey A. Sonnenfeld, and John R. Kimberley, "In Search of a Kingdom: Determinants of Subsequent Career Outcomes for Chief Executives Who Are Fired," *Human Resource Management* 34, (Spring 1995), pp. 117–39; Pamela Sebastian, "Some Senior Executives Get Sent Out to Pasture; Others Go to the Papa Farm," *The Wall Street Journal,* Oct. 4, 1995, p. B1.

98. Joann S. Lublin, "Foreign Accents Proliferate in Top Ranks as U.S. Companies Find Talent Abroad," *The Wall Street Journal,* May 21, 1992, p. B1.

99. Nick Forster, "International Managers and Mobile Families; The Professional and Personal Dynamics of Trans-National Career Pathing and Job Mobility in the 1990s," *International Journal of Human Resource Management* 3, no. 3 (Dec. 1992), pp. 605–23; J. Black and Mark Mendenhall, "Cross-Cultural Training Effectiveness: A Review and a Theoretical Framework for Future Research," *Academy of Management Review* 15, no. 1 (1990), pp. 113–36; L. Copeland and L. Griggs, *Going International* (New York: Random House, 1985); Rosalie Tung, "Selection and Training Procedures of U.S., European and Japanese Multinationals," *California Management Review* 25, no. 1 (1982), pp. 57–71.

100. David A. Weeks, *Recruiting and Selecting International Managers,* Report No. 998 (New York: Conference Board), 1992.

101. Ibid.

102. Forster, "International Managers and Mobile Families." Moshe Banai, "The Ethnocentric Staffing Policy in Multinational Corporations: A Self-Fulfilling Prophecy," *International Journal of Human Resource Management* 3, no. 3 (Dec. 1992), pp. 451–72; H. Fuschberg, "Calling on Electronics to Limit Culture Shock," *The Wall Street Journal,* May 4, 1992, p. B1.

103. "Family Support Keeps Expatriates in the Field," *The Wall Street Journal,* Aug. 19, 1992, p. B1, Karen Dawn Stuart, "Teens Play a Role in Moves Overseas," *Personnel Journal,* Mar. 1992, pp. 72–78; Robin Pascoe, "Employers Ignore Expatriate Wives at Their Own Peril," *The Wall Street Journal,* Mar. 2, 1992, p. A12; Weeks, "Recruiting and Selecting International Managers," *Relocating Managers and Professional Staff,* Report No. 139 (Sussex University, Institute for Manpower Studies, 1987); C. Cooper and P. Makin, "The Mobile Managerial Family," *Journal of Management Development* 4, no. 3 (1985), pp. 56–66; Calvin Reynolds and Rita Bennett, "The Career Couple Challenge," *Personnel Journal,* March 1992, pp. 46–48; Betty Jane Punnett, Olga Crocker, and Mary Ann Stevens, "The Challenge for Women Expatriates and Spouses: Some Empirical Evidence," *International Journal of Human Resource Management* 3, no. 3 (Dec. 1992), pp. 585–92; Sue Shellenbarger, "Spouses Must Pass Test before Global Transfers," *The Wall Street Journal,* Sept. 6, 1991, p. B1.

104. P. Smith, "Organisational Behaviour and National Cultures," *British Journal of Management* 3 (1992), pp. 39–51; J. Stewart Black and Hal B. Gregersen, "Antecedents to Cross-Cultural Adjustment for Expatriates in Pacific Rim Assignments," *Human Relations* 44, no. 3 (1991), pp. 497–515.

105. Weeks, "Recruiting and Selecting International Managers."

106. Karen E. Theurmer, "World Class," *Human Resource Executive,* Nov. 1995, pp. 27–30; John R. Engen, "Coming Home," *Training,* Mar. 1995, pp. 37–40; Charlene Marmer Solomon, "HR's Helping Hand Pulls Global Inpatriates Onboard," *Personnel Journal,* Nov. 1995, pp. 40–49.

107. Winfred Arthur, Jr., and Winston Bennett, Jr., "The International Assignee: The Relative Importance of Factors Perceived to Contribute to Success," *Personnel Psychology* 48 (1995), pp. 99–114.

108. Boudreau, "Utility Analysis Applied to Internal and External Employee Movement"; Boudreau, "Utility Analysis: A New Perspective on Human Resource Management Decisions"; John W. Boudreau, "MOVUTIL: A Spreadsheet Program for Analyzing the Utility of Internal and External Employee Movement," (working paper, Cornell University, NYSSILR, 1986); Leon E. Wynter and Jolie Solomon, "A New Push to Break the 'Glass Ceiling,'" *The Wall Street Journal,* Nov. 15, 1989, p. B1.
109. Vida Scarpello and Robert J. Vandenberg, "Generalizing the Importance of Occupational and Career Views to Job Satisfaction Attitudes," *Journal of Organizational Behavior* 13, 1992, pp. 125–40; Frank E. Saal and S. Craig Moore, "Perceptions of Promotion Fairness and Promotion Candidates' Qualifications," *Journal of Applied Psychology* 78, no. 1 (1993), pp. 105–110.
110. "Work Week," *The Wall Street Journal,* Mar. 14, 1995, p. A1.
111. Glass Ceiling Commission, *A Solid Investment: Making Full Use of the Nation's Human Capital* (Washington, DC: Glass Ceiling Commission, Nov. 1995).
112. "Catalyst Surveys Senior Women Executives and CEOs on Women's Progress in Corporate Leadership," *PR Newswire,* Feb. 27, 1996.
113. Patricia J. Ohlott, Marian N. Ruderman, and Cynthia D. McCauley, "Gender Differences in Managers' Developmental Job Experiences," *Academy of Management Journal* 37 (1994), pp. 46–67.
114. Alice H. Eagly, Steven J. Karau, and Mona G. Makhijani, "Gender and the Effectiveness of Leaders: A Meta-Analysis," *Psychological Bulletin* 117 (1995), pp. 125–145.
115. Carol Hymowitz, "One Firm's Bid to Keep Blacks, Women," *The Wall Street Journal,* Feb. 16, 1989, p. B1.

# Training

Motorola, Inc., faced a critical dilemma. In 1982, its sales had been even with Texas Instruments, Inc., the world's largest maker of semiconductors. In only five years, its semiconductor sales had slipped to fourth place, and its other electronics products were under siege from innovative foreign competitors. While other companies might have turned to massive layoffs or plant closings, Motorola's chairman, Robert W. Galvin, and his successor, George M. C. Fisher, decided to bet that their employees could provide the necessary competitive edge. In 1984, Galvin mandated that at least 1.5 percent of each manager's payroll be devoted to training. By 1992, Motorola was spending $120 million, or 3.6 percent of its payroll, on education, providing an average of 36 hours of training per employee per year. In 1993, *Fortune* magazine called Motorola the "gold standard" of corporate training.[1]

By 1995, Motorola had sales of $22.2 billion, spent $150 million to deliver a minimum of 40 hours of training to each of its 132,000 employees, and devoted 4 percent of payroll to training. Galvin's son and Motorola's current president, Christopher, has an equally strong commitment to training. By the end of the decade, every worker will get 80 to 100 hours of training per year, and the annual training budget will grow to $300 million. Employees and managers are expected to choose from 600 courses offered at Motorola University in Schaumburg, Illinois, and in 13 other locations worldwide. A sampling of the courses at Motorola University includes computer-based business games in which customers go bankrupt, CEOs get fired, and factories burn down; a 24-hour class on how to deal with hard-to-manage employees, building Tinkertoy towers to learn about customer specifications, using catapults to launch golf balls into baskets to learn quality; and a 12-hour basic math course in fractions, graphs, and algebra.[2] Clearly, Motorola executives believe that inventiveness and adaptability are critical to succeeding in a competitive and volatile global marketplace, and that training can contribute to that success.

Put yourself in the position of Motorola University president William Wiggenhorn. Getting the strongest commitment to corporate education from the company president is rare and valuable. It means you can probably design a companywide training strategy, get the resources and management support you need to implement it, and have a real impact on the organization's goals. However, it also means that you're probably going to be held accountable for showing that your strategy pays off by improving total customer satisfaction. How would you design and implement such a strategy? How would you assess the organization's training needs? Is it possible some of the problems are not training issues at all, but require interventions such as staffing or compensation? How will you establish the right motivation among employees and tailor the training to their learning abilities? What areas of training will you pursue, and how will you choose them? Should everyone get similar training in customer needs, or should training for different positions such as managers and production workers, be different? Should the training groups comprise a mix of different kinds of employees or should they have similar jobs and organizational status? What training delivery methods would you use? Should you opt for modern high-tech methodssuch as computer-based videodisks, or stick with more traditional lecture and group discussion formats? Finally, how will you later show the CEO that the $150 million spent on training paid off better than investing that money in new tools, plants, or technologies?

## TRAINING AND THE EMPLOYEE DEVELOPMENT PROCESS

Motorola's factory workers learn computer-aided design, robotics, and customized manufacturing not only from manuals and lectures but also by inventing and building plastic knickknacks. Motorola University houses computer-equipped classrooms and laboratories. Not only employees but also suppliers and customers receive training. Instructors are not full-time professors; they are experienced engineers, scientists, and managers rigorously selected and trained to rely on action learning that emphasizes having participants learn by doing. Motorola calculates that every $1 it spends on training delivers $30 in productivity gains within three years; between 1987 and 1993, the company cut costs by $3.3 billion as workers were trained to simplify processes and reduce waste. Sales per employee doubled and profits increased 47 percent.[3] Perhaps a good stock-picking strategy is to invest in companies that train the best?

Training is clearly big business. In Exhibit 10.1 we show that U.S. organizations with more than 100 employees spent a total of $52 billion in 1995, an increase of 30 percent over 1988 levels. Notice that 72 percent went to pay training staff salaries, with the rest paying for materials, outside services, conferences, and facility overhead. In France, training expenses averaged 3 percent of the total wage bill in 1990, with firms employing more than 2,000 people spending 5 percent. Japan is estimated to spend 6 percent of payroll on training. Yet, this is only the tip of the iceberg. Motorola estimates that staff time off the job is equal to formal training expenditures, so that would bring the total U.S. cost to over $100 billion. Many workers get their training through informal on-the-job activities, or through partnerships with outside universities or local schools; this also involves resource costs.[4]

- *Training* is a systematic process to foster the acquisition of skills, rules, concepts, or attitudes that result in an improved match between employee characteristics and employment requirements.
- *Development* is the long-term process of enhancing employee capabilities and motivation to make them valuable future members of the organization. Development includes not only training but also careers and other experiences.

### Training Is Not for Training's Sake

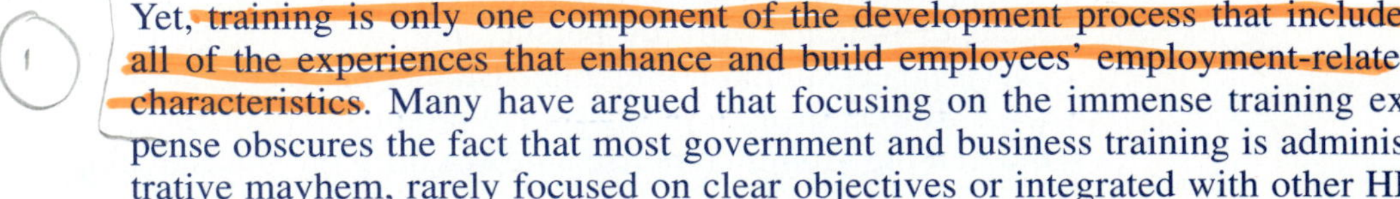
Yet, training is only one component of the development process that includes all of the experiences that enhance and build employees' employment-related characteristics. Many have argued that focusing on the immense training expense obscures the fact that most government and business training is administrative mayhem, rarely focused on clear objectives or integrated with other HR

EXHIBIT 10.1 Dollars Budgeted for Formal Training by U.S. Organizations

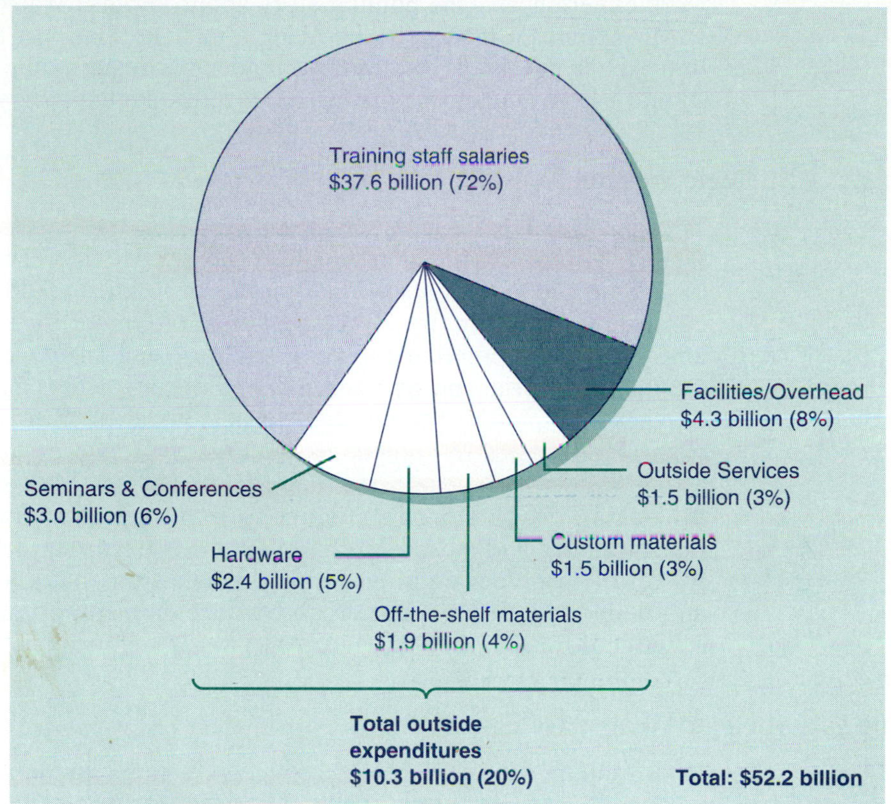


"Vital Statistics," *Training,* October 1995, p. 42. Adapted with permission from the Oct. 1995 issue of *Training Magazine.* Copyright 1995. Lakewood Publications, Minneapolis, MN. All rights reserved. Not for resale.

activities.[5] Training programs too frequently occur because a few people decide a particular program is needed, or that the latest training fad can be sold to top management. They find the money to get it started and measure success by how many people enroll. Effectiveness is seldom ever measured. The programs often remain in the company course catalog long after anyone can remember why they occurred or whether they work.

In contrast, the best companies integrate training within a systematic set of HR activities, including external and internal staffing, rewards, and job design. Federal Express spends 3 percent of its total expenses, or $225 million a year on training. It also uses a pay-for-knowledge system to reward employees for what they learn, biannual tests of job knowledge (with results tied to pay increases), and a precise service quality indicator that scores problems such as wrong delivery (5 points) and missed pick up (10 points), to correlate knowledge with results.[6] Similar examples can be found at Apple Computer, Mirage Resorts, and J. P. Morgan, where every training activity is explicitly linked to specific business-unit needs, root causes of business problems, and key business outcomes that drive the training requirement.[7] In many organizations, the focus is on learning, whether it occurs in training classes or through work experiences. One popular story about Thomas Watson, an early leader at IBM, involves a manager who made a mistake that cost the company $2 million. When the manager came to tender his resignation, Watson said, "Why should I let you resign? I just spent $2 million educating you."

## Training as a Strategic Weapon for Nations

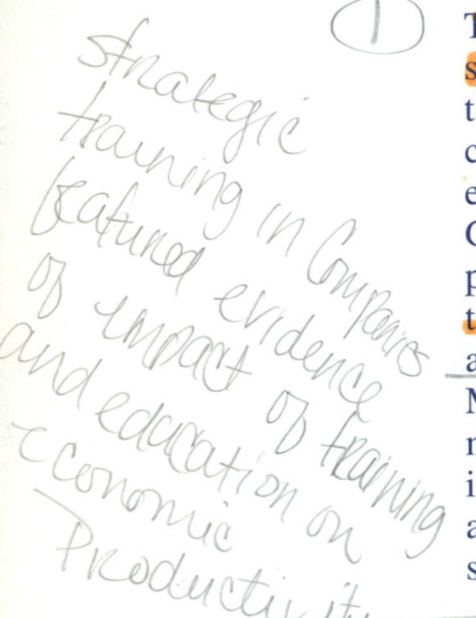

There is growing evidence and awareness that training and education are key strategic investments for national prosperity. Mexico used a World Bank loan to double the size of its adult training program to 700,000 and implement competency training, trying to stem unemployment by making workers more employable. Apprenticeship programs are rare in the United States, but in Germany, Austria, and Switzerland they occupy 5 to 6 percent of civilian employees and one-third to one-half of persons ages 15 to 18.[8] A conference on training strategies in companies featured evidence of the impact of training and education on economic productivity in Mexico, Colombia, and Malaysia.[9] South Korea's attempt to import cooperative employer-government training and master crafts universities from Germany did not necessarily result in higher employee skills, suggesting that governmental, cultural, and economic differences across countries are important in determining the success of training.[10]

## Training as a Strategic Weapon for Organizations

Does training pay off? There is growing economic evidence that investments in training are associated with long-run profitability, and that firms that reorganize work using programs such as teams and quality circles report greater productivity if those programs are associated with worker education. There is also evidence that organizations do more training for higher-level jobs and high-performance work systems.[11] More frequently, top executives consider it a key mission to be a "knowledge-creating company"; organizations such as Philips, General Electric, Royal Dutch Shell, and Daimler-Benz have invested significantly in employee education. Motorola, GE, and Disney can point to a more direct effect of training on organization goals—they sell their educational programs, or use them as a way to attract customers.[12]

In this chapter, we focus primarily on how organizations can use training as a strategic tool for attaining the goals of the organization and the employees. The link between training and goals seems obvious, but is often lost in the day-to-day struggle to implement programs and deal with crises. Training becomes an activity, not a strategy. There is a big difference between training as an activity and training for impact, as we show in Exhibit 10.2. Training for impact requires careful identification of objectives, systematic evaluation of alternatives, and strict evaluation of achievements. In short, it is a diagnostic approach.

> **WHAT DO YOU THINK?**
>
> A visit to the cafeteria at the General Electric training facility in Crotonville, New York, is as likely to find you sitting with managers from GE's suppliers or customers, as to find you sitting with GE employees. Customers pay more for GE bids on large projects, and suppliers charge GE lower prices, in part for the privilege of getting training in "Work Out" and the "Change Acceleration Process." How do you think GE's customers and suppliers justify such decisions?

**EXHIBIT 10.2** Difference between Training as an Activity and Training for Impact

| Training for Activity | Training for Impact |
|---|---|
| Characterized by | Characterized by |
| ◆ No client | ◆ Partnership with client |
| ◆ No business need | ◆ Link to business need |
| ◆ No assessment of performance effectiveness or of cause | ◆ Assessment of performance effectiveness and of cause |
| ◆ No effort to prepare the work environment to support training | ◆ Preparation of work environment to support training |
| ◆ No measurement of results | ◆ Measurement of results |

Source: Reprinted with permission from Dana Gaines Robinson and James C. Robinson, *Training for Impact* (San Francisco: Jossey-Bass, 1992), p. 28.

## ACHIEVING IMPACT: DIAGNOSTIC APPROACH TO TRAINING

Note the three stages in developing, implementing, and evaluating training activities in Exhibit 10.3. Needs assessment involves examining goals at the levels of the organization, the job/task/knowledge-skill-ability (KSA), and the person/individual. This process identifies gaps that become instructional objectives. In the training and development stage, the objectives are used to select and design the instructional program and to deliver the training. Finally, the evaluation phase involves using criteria and evaluation models to determine whether the training achieved the original objectives. The results of this evaluation become the basis for a new needs assessment, and the process continues. Each stage is important if training is to have an impact on employee and organization goals.

One training approach gives students a mnemonic reminder to help them remember things. The concepts in Exhibit 10.3 are the framework for this entire chapter, so it is important that you remember them. Students in our classes have noted that the letters in the model, **N**eeds assessment, **O**bjectives, **C**riteria, **D**esign of programs, **T**raining, and **E**valuation, can be easily remembered with the phrase, "**N**ice **O**ld **C**ats **D**on't **T**ease **E**lephants." Perhaps you can come up with an even better one.

### Assessing the Organization's Needs

Linking training to assessed needs and evaluating its effects based on those needs may seem obvious, but this doesn't always occur. For instance, an *Alaska Daily News* editorial called for stricter oversight of training programs after the Alaska Peace Officers in Christ used public funds to bring in an Arizona consultant to teach that Smurfs are agents of Satan![13] In 1991, Digital Equipment Corporation realized it had never assessed the skills or interests of its human resources staff. Central European countries attempting to transform state-owned industries into market-driven enterprises are assessing their needs with help from a host of eager international training centers.[14]

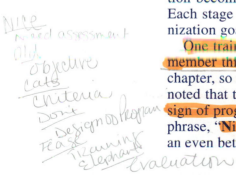

EXHIBIT 10.3 Diagnostic Model of the Training Process

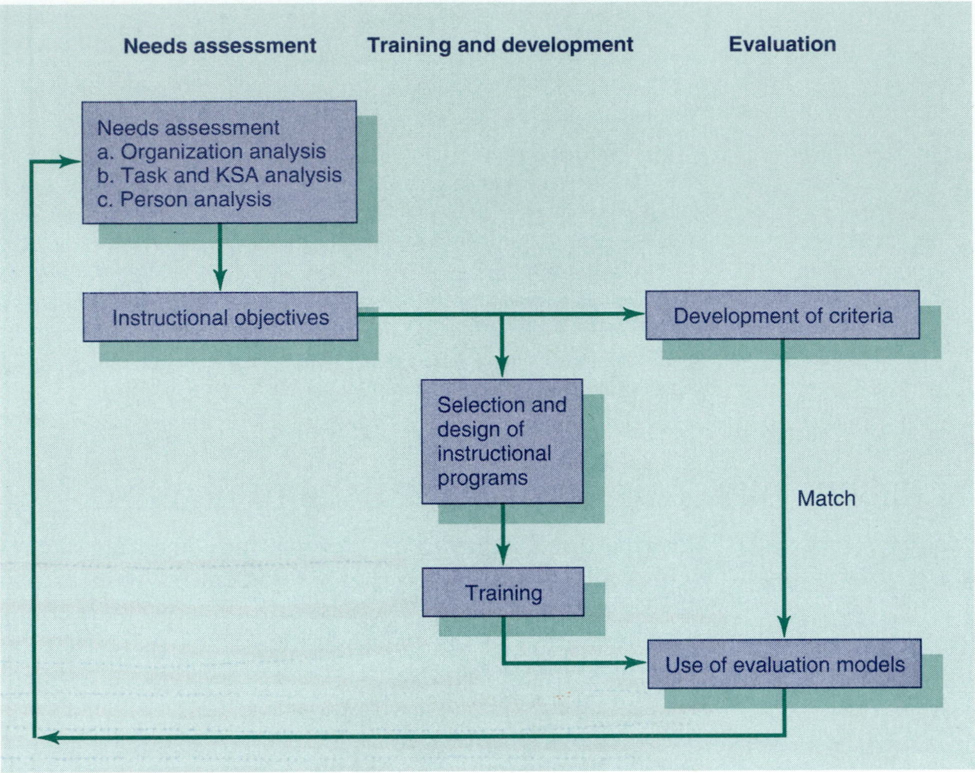


## Commitment from the Top

Many studies claim that top management commitment is a key to success for management programs, and this is probably true for training as well.[15] Such support flows from showing that training is clearly linked to organization objectives, so assessing the organization's goals is a key first step. Companies that do training well link their training directly to organizational goals. Xerox does "training to understand customer needs"; KPMG Peat Marwick touts "training for more value added, faster and more cost-effective service for clients"; and Aetna aims to "reengineer for a labor force that responds to change." Research suggests that organizations pursuing different production and marketing strategies do use training differently, and that the use of flexible production is strongly associated with greater training efforts.[16]

Analyzing organizational needs goes beyond simply identifying goals. It also must include establishing support from top management and other key decision makers, ensuring that the organization is prepared to support and nurture the new knowledge and behaviors that training will create, and identifying any legal or external constraints that might impede conducting the training or applying it. For example, at Corning's Celcor plant in Erwin, New York, managers gained agreement from unionized assembly workers to junk 21 job classifications and replace them with 1, the Celcor specialist. Then the work was restructured to give teams new authority concerning machine placement, work assignments, and production scheduling. After the changes, new barriers cropped up as interpersonal squabbles and confusion reigned. Only then was it clear that training must be restructured to focus on a defined set of competencies (see Chapters Three and Four), and to certify all workers for each type of work role.[17]

In 1990, Peter Senge argued that the "learning organization" was the wave of the future, dedicated to "systems thinking," "personal mastery", "mental models", "shared vision," and "team learning."[18] How can you diagnose whether your organization's conditions are fertile ground for learning? One proposal is the "Learning Organization Quiz" (see Exhibit 10.4), whose idea is that the organization and its leaders will significantly determine the success of training activities. Therefore, a careful diagnosis of organizational conditions and needs is essential to make training strategic.

## Job, Task, Competency, and Knowledge-Skill-Ability (KSA) Analysis

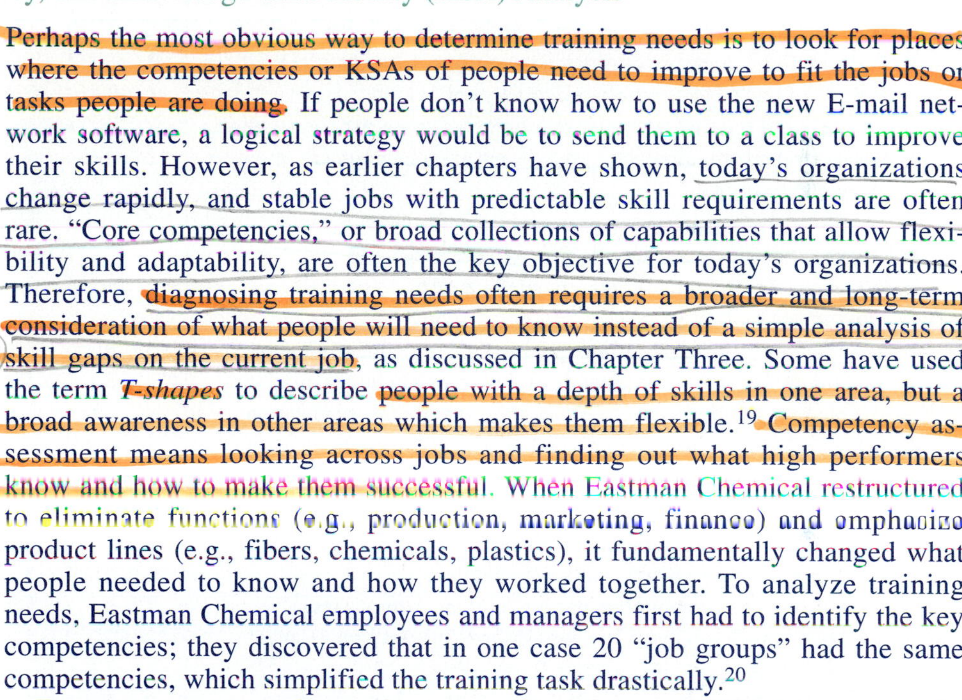

Perhaps the most obvious way to determine training needs is to look for places where the competencies or KSAs of people need to improve to fit the jobs or tasks people are doing. If people don't know how to use the new E-mail network software, a logical strategy would be to send them to a class to improve their skills. However, as earlier chapters have shown, today's organizations change rapidly, and stable jobs with predictable skill requirements are often rare. "Core competencies," or broad collections of capabilities that allow flexibility and adaptability, are often the key objective for today's organizations. Therefore, diagnosing training needs often requires a broader and long-term consideration of what people will need to know instead of a simple analysis of skill gaps on the current job, as discussed in Chapter Three. Some have used the term *T-shapes* to describe people with a depth of skills in one area, but a broad awareness in other areas which makes them flexible.[19] Competency assessment means looking across jobs and finding out what high performers know and how to make them successful. When Eastman Chemical restructured to eliminate functions (e.g., production, marketing, finance) and emphasize product lines (e.g., fibers, chemicals, plastics), it fundamentally changed what people needed to know and how they worked together. To analyze training needs, Eastman Chemical employees and managers first had to identify the key competencies; they discovered that in one case 20 "job groups" had the same competencies, which simplified the training task drastically.[20]

Does empowerment change the nature of training needs? When a guest at the Ritz-Carlton Hotel in McLean, Virginia, complained about the housekeeping and the fitness center attendant, the front-desk clerk waived a two-night bill of $405.25. Since 1992, Ritz-Carlton front-desk clerks have been allowed to take off up to $2,000 from a guest's bill at their own discretion. Without training, however, such programs can get very costly. This was the case after a bellhop at San Francisco's Fairmont Hotel mistakenly put a couple's luggage in someone else's rental car headed for Oregon. The manager told the staff to allow the couple free clothes, toiletries, and other necessities. The guests spent $3,000 on these necessities, though the suitcases were eventually returned.[21] In some industries, job-based needs assessment leads to proposed skill standards and certification requirements, especially for basic skills. Labor unions react strongly, noting that unions and workers should be involved in setting such standards. At

## EXHIBIT 10.4 The Learning Organization Quiz

Step One: Decide the organization you want to rate. It can be your entire company, department, or working group as long as the organization has an identifiable leader. Write the name of the organization below.

Organization:______________________________________________

Step Two: In the first column, rate your organization according to how true each statement *currently* is. In the second column, rate your organization according to how you *desire* your organization to become. After rating each statement, total all circled numbers in each column. On the scale at the bottom on the page, put a * by your organization's *current* score and a + by the *desired* score.

| | **Current*** | | | | | **Desired+** | | | | |
|---|---|---|---|---|---|---|---|---|---|---|
| | **Not True** | | | | **Very True** | **Not True** | | | | **Very True** |
| 1. Our leader has a clear vision. | 1 | 2 | 3 | 4 | 5 | 1 | 2 | 3 | 4 | 5 |
| 2. Our leader's vision is clearly communicated and understood by all. | 1 | 2 | 3 | 4 | 5 | 1 | 2 | 3 | 4 | 5 |
| 3. Our leader is admired by the troops. | 1 | 2 | 3 | 4 | 5 | 1 | 2 | 3 | 4 | 5 |
| 4. Our leaders walk their talk. | 1 | 2 | 3 | 4 | 5 | 1 | 2 | 3 | 4 | 5 |
| 5. We have a clear plan to transform our vision into reality. | 1 | 2 | 3 | 4 | 5 | 1 | 2 | 3 | 4 | 5 |
| 6. We effectively measure our processes, progress, and results. | 1 | 2 | 3 | 4 | 5 | 1 | 2 | 3 | 4 | 5 |
| 7. Results of our metrics are shared rapidly and widely. | 1 | 2 | 3 | 4 | 5 | 1 | 2 | 3 | 4 | 5 |
| 8. External and internal customer requirements are clearly understood. | 1 | 2 | 3 | 4 | 5 | 1 | 2 | 3 | 4 | 5 |
| 9. Our customers are involved in the design and development of our products or services. | 1 | 2 | 3 | 4 | 5 | 1 | 2 | 3 | 4 | 5 |
| 10. We routinely learn from the best practices of other companies whose capabilities are better than ours in critical areas. | 1 | 2 | 3 | 4 | 5 | 1 | 2 | 3 | 4 | 5 |
| 11. We avoid the problem of "not invented here" by using the good ideas of others. | 1 | 2 | 3 | 4 | 5 | 1 | 2 | 3 | 4 | 5 |
| 12. Other company's learnings are quickly transmitted and acted on. | 1 | 2 | 3 | 4 | 5 | 1 | 2 | 3 | 4 | 5 |
| 13. We rapidly identify a best practice in one part of our organization and share it so it can be used by another part of our organization. | 1 | 2 | 3 | 4 | 5 | 1 | 2 | 3 | 4 | 5 |
| 14. Our people readily share their good ideas with others to help our organization be more successful. | 1 | 2 | 3 | 4 | 5 | 1 | 2 | 3 | 4 | 5 |
| 15. The training we do is actively supported by the work environment. | 1 | 2 | 3 | 4 | 5 | 1 | 2 | 3 | 4 | 5 |
| 16. We often accept challenges even when not sure how to meet them. | 1 | 2 | 3 | 4 | 5 | 1 | 2 | 3 | 4 | 5 |
| 17. We are inventive in how we meet our challenges. | 1 | 2 | 3 | 4 | 5 | 1 | 2 | 3 | 4 | 5 |
| 18. We hold people accountable, but do not punish "mistakes." | 1 | 2 | 3 | 4 | 5 | 1 | 2 | 3 | 4 | 5 |
| 19. We are a "make it happen" organization. We have a bias toward action and take pride in our accomplishments. | 1 | 2 | 3 | 4 | 5 | 1 | 2 | 3 | 4 | 5 |
| 20. We find work fun. | 1 | 2 | 3 | 4 | 5 | 1 | 2 | 3 | 4 | 5 |
| Total: | | | | | | | | | | |

Source: Calhoun W. Wick and Lu Stanton Leon, "From Ideas to Action: Creating a Learning Organization," *Human Resource Management* 34 (Summer 1995), pp. 299–311.

companies such as Texas Instruments and Eastman Kodak, gaining the support of managers for workplace literacy and basic skills training requires showing how the training reflects specific jobs and tasks, based on job descriptions.[22] Even today, however, technology can reduce job-skill demands rather than raise them. Computers that can understand speech or read documents are changing the meaning of workplace literacy.

## Person Analysis

Even when organizational conditions are conducive to training effectiveness and the training addresses the right competencies or KSAs, individual differences still matter. Among 106 junior managers free to choose their training, learning was associated with using an analytic strategy, having a generally positive attitude toward training, and being younger. Managers anxious beforehand about the training found it more difficult and enjoyed it less. Among 967 state government employees, those who perceived greater organization support had greater incentives to do well. Those who felt that the training was of high quality had greater motivation going into training and felt it transferred more to their later work. *Self-efficacy,* or the perception that you can successfully perform certain tasks and behaviors, has been shown to be a strong predictor of training success and an important outcome of successful training. A study of 154 accountants found that those with *low* self-efficacy benefited more from training, in terms of their post-training self-efficacy, ability to cope, job performance and intention to quit.[23]

Person-specific factors can help identify who will benefit most from training. A study of Russians being trained to work at a Western-owned luxury hotel in Moscow found that those with greater English-language ability and general service orientation achieved higher service training performance at the end of training, but that behavior-modeling training (involving practice, games and role-plays) created the greatest training benefit for those with the *lowest* language ability and pretraining service orientation.[24] Another study of hotel/resort employees found that those high in conscientiousness (see Chapter Seven) tended to get better supervisor evaluations, and that training in self-leadership improved the performance of those originally low on conscientiousness, but not those who originally were high on this attribute.[25] Even how the training is "framed" can interact with individual factors. One study gave undergraduate psychology students a test, after which they were assigned to either "remedial" or "advanced" training. Those who expected to be placed in the training group they were assigned had higher fairness perceptions than those who were placed differently than they expected; these fairness perceptions associated with later training motivation, even though the actual training assignments were random.[26]

## Comparison and Use of Needs Assessment Methods

In Exhibit 10.5, we compare several assessment techniques in terms of the opportunity for participant involvement, the necessary involvement by management or supervisors, the time required, the cost, and whether the process produces data that can be quantified (expressed as numbers). Trainee involvement can be useful to promote motivation and a sense of responsibility for training success. Management involvement can help lay a foundation for supporting and encouraging trainees to use their new skills when they return to the job. All things being equal, methods that require less time, cost less, and produce information that can be documented as numbers would be preferable, but these factors are usually less important than trainee and management involvement. The most commonly cited reasons for training failures include a lack of managerial support, no reward for the new behaviors, and a lack of employee motivation.

EXHIBIT 10.5 Needs Assessment Methods Compared

| Technique | Potential Participant Involvement | Management Involvement | Time Required | Cost | Relevant Quantifiable Data |
|---|---|---|---|---|---|
| Advisory committees | Low | Moderate | Moderate | Low | Low |
| Assessment centers | High | Low | Low | High | High |
| Attitude (opinion) surveys | Moderate | Low | Moderate | Moderate | Low |
| Group discussions | High | Moderate | Moderate | Moderate | Moderate |
| Interviews with potential participants | High | Low | High | High | Moderate |
| Management requests | Low | High | Low | Low | Low |
| Observations of behavior (on-the-job performance) | Moderate | Low | High | High | Moderate |
| Performance appraisals | Moderate | High | Moderate | Low | High |
| Performance documents | Low | Moderate | Low | Low | Moderate |
| Critical incident method | High | Low | Moderate | Low | High |
| Questionnaire surveys and inventories (needs assessment) | High | High | Moderate | Moderate | High |
| Skills test | High | Low | High | High | High |
| Evaluations of past programs | Moderate | Low | Moderate | Low | High |

Source: John Newstrom and John Lilyquist, "Selecting Needs Analysis Methods," *Training and Development Journal,* Oct. 1979, p. 56. 

Though systematic needs analysis seems quite logical—indeed essential for making rational training program decisions—it does not occur frequently. One study found that 81 percent of companies surveyed identified training needs only by reacting to problems as they occurred.[27] The most effective needs analysis is closely linked to the activities discussed in Chapter Five on planning.

## IDENTIFYING TRAINING OBJECTIVES: WHAT'S THE TARGET?

As Chapter Five showed, objectives and evaluation standards (or criteria in Exhibit 10.3) go hand in hand. Objectives must be measurable and specific enough to serve as measures of success. Objectives also are constantly changing, as training programs are implemented and new information comes to light that can be used in the next stage of needs analysis. Therefore, objectives and criteria for training must meet the same general standards described in Chapter Five for all information: (1) they must reflect information that will improve future decisions, (2) they must improve important decisions, and (3) the cost of gathering the information must not exceed its benefit. Good objectives are measurable, specific, set a deadline, and reflect outcomes important to key

> **WHAT DO YOU THINK?**
>
> Toyota implemented a coordinated training effort to reduce costs. Suppose costs fell following the training. Would you be willing to credit training for reduced costs? Why or why not? What is the role of HR in assessing such effects?

constituents. For example, when Chrysler Corporation observed a major cost disadvantage compared with Toyota, the company developed three integrated training programs to address the goal of bringing costs down. Senior executives trained in cross-functional groups to discuss Toyota's cost-control program and to identify what they could do to create fundamental change. Middle managers focused less on external competition and more on ideas for streamlining their internal efforts and integrating their operations. Supervisors took classes to improve their analytical and productivity improvement skills. The goal was to create a significant cost reduction and to make costs comparable with those of Toyota and other competitors.[28]

## SELECTION AND DESIGN OF TRAINING PROGRAMS

The middle two boxes of Exhibit 10.3 describe the process of selecting and designing training, and then implementing it. This process involves establishing conditions conducive to learning, choosing the content of the training program, and choosing how the training will be delivered and who will deliver it.

### Establishing Supportive Conditions for Learning

For training to have any effect at all, trainees must learn something from it. When training is effectively designed and trainees are motivated, learning can occur. Notice that learning is defined broadly and includes much more than simply being able to declare facts or new knowledge. Before training ever takes place, certain preconditions must exist for learning to occur.

> *Learning* is a relatively permanent change in knowledge, skills, beliefs, attitudes, or behaviors, produced by experience.

### Trainee Ability to Learn

Individuals enter training with different experiences, different familiarity with the material, and different innate mental and physical abilities. Training designers must ensure that their training demands match the abilities of trainees. Training that is either too difficult or too easy is likely to be less effective. Even though general intelligence or other abilities can predict later performance, the abilities that contribute to performance differ depending on where trainees are in the learning process. Testing trainees prior to beginning training can help ensure a good match. Evidence suggests that work sample tests can predict trainability, though they predict short-term trainability better than long-term trainability.[29] There is ongoing debate about whether some abilities are more important at different stages of learning. It may be that initial stages of learning are enhanced by broad cognitive abilities, but that later stages may depend on such things as perceptual speed and psychomotor ability. Personality variables may also affect trainee learning.[30]

*Self-efficacy*, or people's judgments of their capability to successfully execute a course of action, has been suggested as an important determinant of the individual's ability to learn and shown to relate to the effects of training on newcomer adjustment and to their level of training anxiety. Helping people to feel confident may be a way to enhance training effects.[31]

## Trainee Motivation to Learn

Perhaps the most important motivation trainees need is the desire to change their behaviors and results on the job. Motivating job-related behaviors requires integration of training with compensation, discussed later in this book. Research suggests that supportive supervisors and the expectation that training results will be assessed later on the job contribute to higher trainee motivation. However, trainee motivation also affects learning during the training program.[32] Sometimes trainee motivation can be decreased even with the best intentions. One study found that when trainees were given a choice of attending and got their choice, training outcomes were high. On the other hand, when trainees were asked to choose but did not get their choice, their response to training was even worse than for trainees who received no choice at all.[33] We now discuss several specific factors that affect trainee motivation.

**Goal setting** Goal-setting theory says that individuals' conscious goals regulate their behavior. The trainer's job is to get the trainees to adopt or internalize the goals of the program. This would suggest using tactics such as:

- Convey the learning objectives at the outset and at various strategic points throughout the training program.
- Make goals difficult enough to be a challenge, so that trainees receive satisfaction in achieving them, but not so difficult that they are unattainable and frustrating.
- Supplement the overall goals with subgoals (periodic quizzes and work samples), to maintain feelings of accomplishment.

**Reinforcement** Reinforcement theory says that the frequency of a behavior is influenced by its consequences. Behavior can be shaped by reinforcing progressively closer approximations to the desired goal, so reinforcement should be administered as soon as possible after the desired behavior occurs. Because the same reinforcers may not be effective for all trainees, a trainer should tailor them to individual differences. Research suggests that training can be more reinforcing if described in playful terms, like a game with players who are solving puzzles, rather than as an exercise with employees of the organization solving real problems.[34]

**Expectancy theory** Expectancy theory says that individuals are motivated to choose a behavior or alternative that has the greatest chance of producing desired consequences. Therefore, trainees must believe that acquiring the knowledge, skills, or other material from the training will lead to desired outcomes, and that the training can provide that knowledge or skill. This underscores the importance of linking the needs analysis, which identified how training contributes to employee and organization goals, with the training content.

**Social learning theory** Social learning theory notes that if individuals could learn only by direct experiences and reinforcers, human development would be stifled. Humans learn by processing information and understanding links between actions and consequences. Thus, building individuals' skills by allowing them to see models of good and poor performance, and giving trainees confidence in their abilities to apply their skills, become important aspects of training.[35]

### Active Practice

Trainees learn better if they can practice their skills. After sufficient practice, the skills may become automatic, requiring very little conscious thought. If you have ever practiced a sport or music technique until you could do it in your sleep, you have experienced *automaticity,* resulting from practice. *Overlearning* refers to giving trainees opportunities to continue practicing even after they have achieved proficiency the first time. Research suggests that while designing training to include overlearning may add to its costs, extended practice does aid in retaining what is learned.[36] For example, firefighters, nurses, or combat soldiers must carry out their tasks under great stress, almost without thinking. Overlearning and automaticity are needed. That's why even experienced firefighters have fire drills and experienced Navy Seals continue to practice assembling their weapons in the dark. Practice need not be physical. A review of studies of mental practice found that practice did indeed improve performance, especially for mental tasks, but that the most significant effects occurred in the early part of practice. Longer practice had diminishing effects.[37] So, the next time you rehearse asking for a favor or a date, perhaps running through it once will be enough.

### Whole versus Part Learning

Should a training task be divided into subparts or taught as a whole operation? The difference between teaching the whole task at once and teaching it in parts (sometimes called "massed" versus "spaced" training) depends on the difficulty of the task and the degree of relationship between the subtasks. For example, you could probably learn an inventory clerk task by first learning to correctly identify the stock, and then learning the computerized system for maintaining the inventory. On the other hand, you can't learn to turn a car unless it's moving, so you have to learn both turning-speed control and steering at the same time. Generally, when a task has highly related components, the higher its complexity the better whole methods work. When a task has low relationships, the higher its complexity, the better part methods work.[38]

### Knowledge of Results and Feedback

Imagine learning to bowl with a curtain preventing you from seeing whether your ball hits any pins. Without knowing the results of your tries, it would be very difficult to improve. Errors are eliminated faster when trainees have feedback about their mistakes and successes. Such feedback can come from the task itself or from role models or trainers. It's important that feedback occur close to the actions that cause the outcomes, so that learners can associate their actions with outcomes. Perceived accuracy may vary with the source of the feedback. Also, too much feedback may be as bad as too little, when it gives trainees the impression that they are out of control or causes them to rely on the feedback rather than learning to monitor their performance. A study of helicopter pilot trainees found that both asking questions and watching others were more frequent among people who had a general desire for external information, and in situations where it was not costly to get the feedback. Surprisingly, trainees sought more feedback when performance was rated as low.[39]

### Instructional Environment and Instructors

The characteristics of the instructional environment and the instructors obviously affect the effectiveness of training. Even the best materials are less effective if trainees can't see or hear them, or if the room is uncomfortable. Modern training facilities bear little resemblance to a simple blackboard and desk. When the editorial staffs of *Training* and *Presentations* magazines sought out the top training facilities, they found that "almost universally, they include integrated systems that control both media and the room environment, often with a high degree of automation, plus projection of video, computer graphics, and other media. Most include videoconferencing as an option, and several have computer workstations or audience-response systems for each training participant."[40] Whatever the environment, it is good to keep in mind the basics. Below, we list several basic considerations in the environment and instructor preparation.

**Instructional environment** The instructional environment can be designed around nine basic events:

1. Gaining attention.
2. Informing learners of objectives.
3. Stimulating recall of prerequisites.
4. Presenting the training stimulus material.
5. Providing learning guidance, such as verbal cues, hints, and context.
6. Eliciting performance, such as asking for a problem solution.
7. Providing feedback.
8. Assessing performance.
9. Enhancing retention and transfer, such as by providing a variety of different examples or problem types.[41]

**Instructor preparation** It's also important that the instructor be prepared. Instructors should ensure that they have:

1. Publicized the program.
2. Informed everyone about the time, place, and arrangements.
3. Arranged the facilities.
4. Checked the physical requirements such as seating, food, and supplies.
5. Secured necessary equipment and ensured that it is working properly.
6. Established training objectives.
7. Studied the lesson plan to anticipate group responses and to prepare experiences, examples, and stories.
8. Developed personal enthusiasm for the topic.[42]

While these may seem obvious, you can probably recall either giving or attending a class that was disrupted because one or more of these things was overlooked.

**Accelerated learning** *Accelerated learning* is an approach to the training environment that emphasizes principles such as (1) being positive and accepting, (2) providing a natural and comfortable setting, (3) exalting the trainee, (4) reducing trainee anxiety or stresses, (5) being supportive of trainees and trainers, (6) using multiple learning approaches, (7) allowing for different learning styles, speeds, and needs instead of forcing everyone to learn in the same way, (8) making learning fun, (9) emphasizing group-based learning, and (10) presenting material that uses pictures as well as words. Such training has received enthusiastic response in some organizations; it has also provided tremendous savings in learning time and costs in organizations such as Bell Atlantic. One study suggested that such tactics improved participant reactions to the training but had no effect on participant learning. Still, it might be interesting to consider how many of these principles are followed in the classes you attend. One area of some debate is whether it is effective to tailor training approaches to the preferences or *learning styles* of trainees. Some may prefer to learn orally, others visually.[43]

## Choosing the Content of Training

In Exhibit 10.6, we show the percentage of organizations with more than 100 employees that provide training in different skills. Management skills training has been and continues to be extremely popular. Basic computer skills training has increased dramatically. Notice that 65 percent of corporations report training their customers, a trend that reflects increasing emphasis on customer satisfaction. You can now get plenty of help locating and choosing training content. One company even offers a "Training Media Toolkit," an updated CD-ROM listing many training resources on video, audio, and computers, as well as consultants and developers. In the next sections, we discuss several of the categories of training content. Keep in mind that choosing training content must be driven by the needs analysis discussed earlier. In each section, we describe the kinds of needs that the particular type of training fulfills.

### Orientation

Often the first training experience of new employees is orientation to their new employer. Orientation starts before the person joins the organization, because activities such as recruiting, realistic job previews (RJPs), selection interviews, and other recruiting and selection activities send signals to potential employees, as earlier chapters have discussed. Many organizations augment this process with training. Orientation includes relinquishing certain attitudes, values, and behaviors as the new recruit learns the organization's goals, the means for attaining those goals, basic job responsibilities, effective job behaviors, and work rules. Much of this is learned on the job from co-workers and work teams.[44] Orientation strives to help new employees learn work procedures, establish relationships with co-workers, develop realistic expectations and positive attitudes, and show newcomers how their work fits with the organization's goals.

At Walt Disney World in Orlando, Florida, fast-food and other service positions are called *roles* to stress the employees' job of entertaining the customers, called *guests*. The recruitment and hiring process is called *casting*. Orientation begins with a one-day program called Disney Traditions I, which presents the history of the organization with pride and enthusiasm. On the second day, the program is Disney Traditions II, which describes company procedures, policies, and rules. Finally, the new recruit spends several days or weeks in on-the-job training, working with an assigned buddy who exposes the new employee to learning experiences that go along with the new *role*.[45]

Orientation training is often a response to new-employee turnover (see Chapter Eight). However, its effects may be unexpected. A study of new entry-level hospital and fast-food employees gave one group warnings about negative job aspects and information on how to cope, but another group received

## EXHIBIT 10.6 Skills Taught by U.S. Corporations

| Types of Training | Percent of Companies Providing Training* |
|---|---|
| Basic computer skills | 93% |
| Management skills/development | 86 |
| Technical skills/knowledge | 85 |
| Supervisory skills | 85 |
| Communication skills | 85 |
| Customer relations/services | 82 |
| New methods/procedures | 80 |
| Executive development | 75 |
| Personal growth | 71 |
| Clerical/secretarial skills | 68 |
| Employee/labor relations | 66 |
| Customer education | 65 |
| Wellness | 58 |
| Sales | 55 |
| Remedial/basic education | 43 |

Source: "Vital Statistics: Industry Training Report," *Training,* Oct. 1995, p. 60. Adapted with permission from the Oct. 1995 issue of *Training Magazine*. 

this information in addition to training in positive self-talk and encouraging statements to bolster self-efficacy. The second group actually had *more* turnover in the first four weeks, perhaps due to increased sensitivity to negative job aspects. However, of those staying four weeks or longer, the second group had greater intentions to stay for at least a year and had greater job satisfaction.[46] Did the organizations consider the training a success? No data are provided. What would you say?

### Nonmanagement Skills Training

Which types of jobs receive the most training? Some of the most newsworthy training activities (white-water rafting, junkets to Hawaii) make it seem that senior managers or salespeople receive the most training. Indeed, the highest percentage of organizations report offering training to executives, professionals and middle managers, and only about 40 percent report offering training to production workers. However, the average number of workers trained is much higher for production workers and others. Therefore, the total hours of training delivered to production workers and customer service people is more than 100 times that for executives and 3 times that for salespeople.[47] Many technical skills are also learned on the job, outside of formally scheduled training programs. This kind of training is usually closely related to job skills, such as operating machinery, understanding work documents, or requirements for licenses or certification. Thus, the link between the training and the need is often very direct. However, this kind of training also can include instruction in "softer" areas such as team processes and quality.

### Team Processes and Quality

Though training in such skills as delegation, communication, decision making, and conflict resolution was traditionally reserved for managers, the changing nature of work means that these skills are more frequently becoming a part of work roles that are much closer to the production process. As the number of hierarchical levels decreases, more employees at lower levels are called on to lead teams, set goals for projects, and facilitate group work. The U.S. Army now trains new recruits in topics such as empowering the people in the trenches, working in teams, and adapting to change.[48] Xerox and Texas Instruments' Defense Systems and Electronics Group (DSEG) are both Malcolm Baldrige National Quality Award winners that credit training for part of their success. Xerox spent $100 million and five years training employees in the tools of quality by throwing out the pie charts and providing simple step-by-step methods emphasizing interactive skills and teamwork. DSEG empowered 700 work teams to take responsibility for meeting customer requirements at all levels, with training that included changes in work roles, decision making, holding meetings, communication, and cross-functional skills.[49]

Growing research showing how to effectively create and train teams suggests the following guidelines for team training:

- Encourage team communication that supports the desire to work as well as to encourage and support team members' input.
- Emphasize interaction and the need for members to depend on each other.
- Emphasize the team and member goals and responsibilities, and allow learning of all team members' responsibilities.
- Challenge the team to react to changes and unexpected events.
- Emphasize teamwork skills and provide examples of both acceptable and unacceptable teamwork.[50]

Team training needn't be "dry." Some organizations use movies such as *Twelve Angry Men* and *Apollo 13* to illustrate the principles. Others assign team projects, such as how to build a box capable of keeping an egg from breaking after a 10-foot drop. Listening to Miles Davis's "Freddie Freeloader" and identifying team and quality lessons from the jazz ensemble has also been recommended.[51] Chapter Seven discussed the skills needed for teamwork, and selection tests to identify them. The same skills also can serve as the basis of team-building training.

### Workplace Literacy

In the 1940s, *functional literacy* was defined as the ability to read and write at a fourth-grade level. Today, it's often considered the ability to read and write at the eighth-grade level. *Workplace literacy* refers to the basic communication and computation skills needed to successfully do the job. Some have estimated that 70 percent of on-the-job reading materials are written at the ninth-grade to college levels, yet 65 percent of the American work force reads below the ninth-grade level.[52]

As we show in Exhibit 10.6, 43 percent of companies report providing formal training in basic skills such as reading and mathematics. A Work in America Institute survey of U.S. organizations suggests why: More than 45 percent of responding companies said that inadequate literacy skills led to one or more of the following: slow production, errors, inability to promote employees, and decreased work unit productivity. Despite his inability to read, write, and solve basic math problems, Jimmy Wedmore finally stopped refusing promotions after years of working at General Motors, admitted his problems, received training, and now runs a high-technology machine.[53] The chapter on recruiting pointed out that employers frequently encounter shortages of applicants and employees with even the most basic level of skills needed to perform their jobs. When public schools fail to prepare workers, U.S. companies often become the educators of last resort.

Major unions, the National Alliance of Business, the Department of Labor, and other organizations are increasingly calling on businesses to achieve an educational partnership with public and private schools. Motorola refuses to hire people who cannot do fifth-grade math and seventh-grade reading. The company tested 3,000 applicants in Arlington Heights, Illinois, and half failed. As a result, Motorola spent $35 million—four times its investment in a new state-of-the-art plant—to teach basic reading skills to employees.[54] Frequently, organizations extend literacy training to employees' families as well. A study by Work-in-America Institute suggests the following training design principles:

- Help students understand the purpose of the education in their lives.
- Develop new knowledge on the basis of old knowledge the student has.
- Integrate basic skills into the technical or academic content area of the work.
- Set objectives based on the demands of the work role for which the course is designed.
- Use contexts, tasks, materials, and procedures from actual work settings.[55]

WHAT DO YOU THINK?

Companies spend millions to train workers how to read at above a ninth-grade level. Is this the appropriate task for businesses? Is it a failure of public education? Do you think such sums would be better spent directly in schools, rather than training people after graduation? Why or why not?

### Management Training

Management skills training is usually reserved for those who supervise other employees. It is frequently tied to managerial career development. At Whirlpool Corporation and many other large organizations, management training is linked directly to the succession planning process (see Chapter Nine), as managers are recommended for training based on the need to build their competencies for specific future career moves.[56] Digital Equipment Corporation has developed such a career-focused curriculum for HR professionals. Entry-level education includes overviews of HR functional areas, as well as discussions of consulting skills and valuing differences. At mid-level, the curriculum includes prevention skills, creating and maintaining positive business partnerships, and implementing strategic plans. At the senior level (12 years or more), the curriculum includes international business acumen, valuing difference leadership, and strategic organizational consulting. Business schools such as Harvard, Wharton, and Stanford even offer courses on how to become a member of a board of directors, costing up to $5,000 for a three-day course.[57] Increasingly, resources for management training are diverse and computerized.

EXPLORING THE WEB

Exhibit 10.7 contains a Web page offering resources for management and leader developers and trainers. You can visit this site at

**http://www.oise.on.ca/~bwillard/leadaid.htm.**

## EXHIBIT 10.7 Leadership/Management Development on the Internet

**What is available on the Internet to help *facilitators* of leadership/management development?**

**What is available on the Internet to help *leaders/managers* improve?**

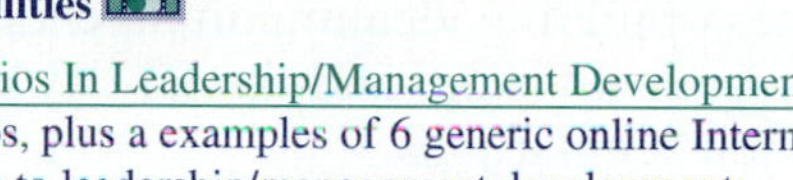

**1. The Desired Capabilities**

- Potential Scenarios In Leadership/Management Development...
  3 possible scenarios, plus a examples of 6 generic online Internet facilities that relate to leadership/management development; includes a review of current versus "future" Internet facilities in the scenarios.

**2. Internet Resources for Facilitators** 

- Good Conferences For Facilitators To Subscribe To...
  the Top 3 "Bob's Best Bets", plus severalother good ones.

- Useful Information Sources for Facilitators...
  the Top 5 "Bob's Best Bets", plus many other good ones.

- Writing Your Own Courseware...
  pointers to course-writing templates, sample quizzes, online HTML guides and resources, and books about HTML.

**3. Internet Resources for Leaders/Managers**  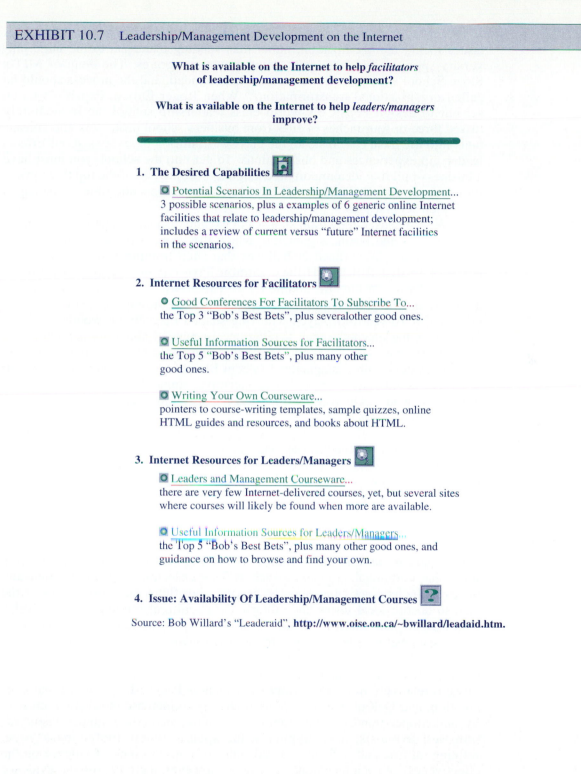

- Leaders and Management Courseware...
  there are very few Internet-delivered courses, yet, but several sites where courses will likely be found when more are available.

- Useful Information Sources for Leaders/Managers...
  the Top 5 "Bob's Best Bets", plus many other good ones, and guidance on how to browse and find your own.

**4. Issue: Availability Of Leadership/Management Courses** 

Source: Bob Willard's "Leaderaid", **http://www.oise.on.ca/~bwillard/leadaid.htm.**

Increasingly, companies customize management programs to focus on actual issues facing the organization, rather than sending managers to the large university-sponsored management development programs. The dean of MIT's Sloan School says executive education is outmoded, and the process should be called organizational transformation.[58] When Roger Enrico, PepsiCo's CEO, set out to design PepsiCo's world-class leadership school, he immediately tossed three or four inches of files from business school professors and consultants into the trash can. Instead, the class was built on interviews about Erico's leadership experiences and observations. To get into the school, you must have a business-building idea important enough to become one of the top three priorities of your division, and the 90-day class runs at the same time as managers work their regular jobs.[59]

At Weyerhaeuser, they train spouses of executives using outdoor team-building exercises and business games in which the spouses run a simulated business.[60] Perhaps Weyerhaeuser believes that such training fosters the kind of partnership that Bill and Hillary Clinton have developed. If you train the spouse, why not include the children, too? Creativity is a topic more frequently included in management training. At Texas Utilities Mining Company, an executive and a 10-year-old played with ring-shaped magnets on wooden dowels. Sometimes the magnets repel, leaving one suspended above its neighbor. The boy tells the manager, "It seems to me that you could replace a hydraulic suspension system with a magnetized system like this, and it would last forever. There are no parts to wear out." The executive, stunned, says, "That's a multibillion-dollar idea. Do you mind if I use it?" The kid shrugs, "Nah. Go ahead. I've got lots of ideas."[61]

### Training to Prepare for International Assignments

Chapter Nine showed how frequently expatriates fail in their new-country assignments and how costly such failures can be. Faced with such costs, organizations have frequently turned to training to help, though one survey showed 57 percent reported having no formal expatriate training programs.[62] Note the percentages of companies offering different types of expatriate training services in Exhibit 10.8. GE routinely sends its managers outside the United States to pursue action learning case studies. While the services in Exhibit 10.8 are somewhat traditional, companies such as Sanyo Electric in Japan and Samsung in Korea include activities such as making clay flutes and goofing off at the mall to absorb local tastes and culture. Cross-cultural training usually works, with virtually all studies showing it aids in expatriate adjustment, and most showing a positive relationship with job performance.[63]

### Is There a New Age in Consciousness-Raising?

Though relatively rare, some employers such as Pacific Bell, Sundstrand Corporation, and DeKalb Farmers' Market attempt to increase motivation, creativity, and cooperation by using programs involving meditation, guided visualization, self-hypnosis, mass-hypnosis, therapeutic touch, biofeedback yoga, walking on fire, and inducing altered states of consciousness. Evidence on the effectiveness of such techniques is sparse. However, there is growing evidence that such practices are vulnerable to lawsuits from employees who believe they violate the protection from infringement of religious beliefs.[64]

**EXHIBIT 10.8** Expatriate Training Activities Offered by Companies

| Service | Percent Using the Activity |
|---|---|
| Summary of culture, history, and background of country | 79% |
| Previsit orientation | 60 |
| Meet with former expatriates | 57 |
| Foreign language lessons | 53 |
| Career-path counseling | 7 |

Source: Joann S. Lublin, "Companies Use Cross-Cultural Training to Help Their Employees Adjust Abroad," *The Wall Street Journal,* Aug. 4, 1992, p. B1. Reprinted by permission of *The Wall Street Journal*. 

## Choosing Training Delivery Methods: On-the-Job Training

Once training content has been established, it must be delivered. The two main delivery methods are on the job and off the job. Most training takes place on the job, especially for nonmanagerial employees. On-the-job training (OJT) is often informal and seldom shows up in formal estimates of training activity. If you ever held a job, you probably received some initial OJT from your supervisor or co-workers.

A typical OJT program places the trainee into the real work situation, where an experienced worker or the supervisor demonstrates the job and the tricks of the trade. An advantage to OJT is that it virtually automatically creates the same environment, cues, and rewards in the training that the individual experiences when actually doing the job. Realism is maximized. However, the cost for this realism is frequently that the training experience is poorly designed, is not linked to any goals, and is carried out by an instructor with little training. Frequently, OJT is used merely because it does not involve direct costs, and thus it appears inexpensive. In addition to the risks of having poorly trained individuals on the job after training, OJT carries more risks during training. Novice workers can damage machinery, produce low-quality output, annoy customers, and waste valuable materials.

One advantage of OJT is that it frequently involves training supervisors, managers, and employees to be the trainers. This can not only benefit the trainees, but it adds skills to the trainers as well. When the senior-level system maintenance workers at a Monsanto Chemical plant in South Carolina couldn't spare the time to become trainers and write the training manuals, junior-level workers did it. These workers took the training and, while they were doing that, also learned to write training manuals and prepared the teaching materials for the next class. There is some evidence that Japanese firms use OJT much more than U.S. firms, perhaps because Japanese firms select employees based on academic standing instead of job proficiency.[65]

There is no reason that OJT cannot be designed according to the diagnostic model proposed here. We depict one framework for assessing OJT needs, designing the OJT program, and assuring follow-up in Exhibit 10.9. You might find the technique helpful if you are called on to train a friend or co-worker,

**EXHIBIT 10.9** Job Instruction Training (JIT) Procedure for On-the-Job Training

Here's what you *must do* to get ready to teach a job:

1. Decide what the learner must be taught to do the job efficiently, safely, economically, and intelligently.
2. Have the right tools, equipment, supplies, and material ready.
3. Have the workplace properly arranged, just as the worker will be expected to keep it.

*Then,* you should *instruct* the learner by the following *four basic* steps:

Step I—*Preparation* (of the learner)

1. Put the learner at ease.
2. Find out what is already known about the job.
3. Get the learner interested in and desirous of learning the job.

Step II—*Presentation* (of the operations and knowledge)

1. *Tell, show, illustrate,* and *question* to put over the new knowledge and operations.
2. Instruct slowly, clearly, completely, and patiently, one point at a time.
3. Check, question, and repeat.
4. Make sure the learner really knows.

Step III—*Performance tryout*

1. Test by having the learner perform the job.
2. Ask questions beginning with *why, how, when,* or *where.*
3. Observe performance, correct errors, and repeat instructions if necessary.
4. Continue until you *know* the learner knows.

Step IV—*Follow-up*

1. Check frequently to be sure instructions are being followed.
2. Taper off extra supervision and close follow-up until the learner is qualified to work with normal supervision.

*Remember*—if the learner hasn't learned, the teacher hasn't taught.

even if it's not on the job. OJT trainers also should be chosen carefully, not only for their job performance but also for their interest and motivation to instruct effectively. Unfortunately, there is little research on the effectiveness of OJT.[66]

### Apprenticeships

A high school student in Carol Stream, Illinois, learns about vacuums, but not in science class. He has to figure out why the Sears vacuum cleaner won't suck up dirt. He comes to Sears during the school day as part of a joint pilot apprenticeship program paid for by his high school but designed by Sears. In Boston, 11th-graders work in hospitals, learning how to be surgical technicians and medical secretaries.[67] Such programs offer an alternative route to high-paying employment for students not interested in college. They combine off-the-job and on-the-job training. More traditional apprenticeships have existed for decades and involve a commitment of up to 10 years learning crafts such as meat cutting, electrical work, plumbing, and tool-and-die making.

The United States has far fewer opportunities for youth than other countries, especially Germany. In the United States, there are formal apprenticeship programs for some 415 trades involving more than 300,000 registered apprentices,

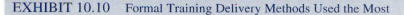

EXHIBIT 10.10 Formal Training Delivery Methods Used the Most

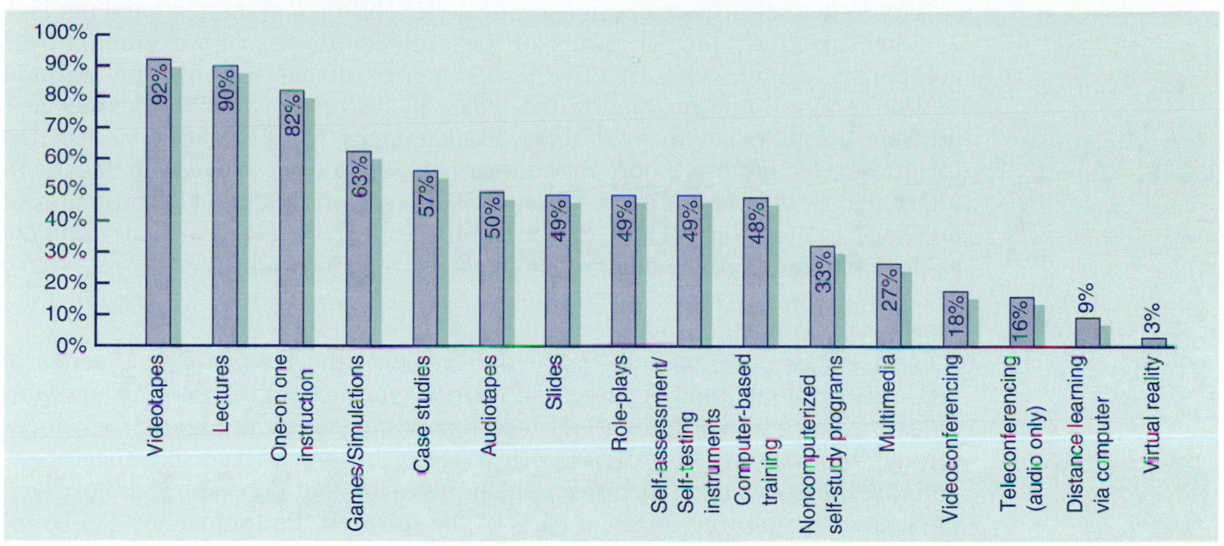


with an average age of 27. Germany, in contrast, has had an apprenticeship program in place for 700 years, and gets 70 percent of its workforce through youth apprenticeships, including banking and insurance. The total cost of apprenticeships to German industry is about 25 percent of total government spending on education. The rest of the European Union looks to Germany as a model. In the United States, barriers include parents' worries that students tracked into apprenticeships will needlessly forgo college, that unions will find apprenticeships a threat to established training programs, that businesses will fail to see a connection to profits, and that federal student aid rules will not be modified to fund apprenticeships as they now fund a college education.[68]

## Choosing Training Methods: Off-the-Job Training

Off-the-job, or formal, training gets a lot of attention, in part because its costs are more direct and obvious. Though OJT is probably much more common, research and company attention are frequently focused on managing one or more formal training programs. Note the popularity of different off-the-job techniques listed in Exhibit 10.10. Obviously, the use of videotapes has risen meteorically with the advent of the camcorder. Multimedia didn't even show up in the 1991 survey, yet it is gaining rapid acceptance. Still, lectures and one-on-one instruction continue to be highly popular.

### Lectures

Lectures are the mainstay of high schools and colleges. An instructor presents material to a group of learners. Lectures are relatively inexpensive to develop and deliver; they can impart factual knowledge quickly and efficiently. Their claimed shortcomings include the one-way nature of the communication; insensitivity to learner differences in learning style, ability, and interest; and the lack of feedback to the learner. Many of these difficulties can be overcome by a competent lecturer who effectively intersperses discussion into the learning session. One-on-one instruction that pairs an instructor with one learner at a time can also alleviate many of these disadvantages. Most scientific studies that include the lecture use it only for comparison with a more interesting new technique that is the study's focus. Comparisons with programmed instruction or televised instruction suggest that a lecture is no less likely to foster student achievement, though the other methods may cover material faster.[69]

### Programmed Instruction (PI)

Self-paced, or programmed, instruction presents the learner with a series of tasks, allows evaluation of success at intervals throughout the training, and provides feedback about correct and incorrect responses as the learner advances through the training. PI programs can proceed through a fixed sequence of experiences or they can branch from one point to another depending on how well the learner is grasping different parts of the material. PI approaches can be incorporated into books, machines, and computers; they have been used to train everything from mathematics in elementary school to air traffic control rules. The cultural assimilator, a PI for expatriate candidates, presents a series of 37 to 100 short incidents between a visitor and a host-country national. Trainees answer a question following the incident and are directed to a page in a book showing why the response is correct or incorrect. Evidence suggests that trainees learn more and perform better using this technique in combination with behavioral modeling (discussed later).[70] Many new multimedia training methods incorporate PI principles.

The advantages of PI include encouraging careful attention to learning sequences and objectives, the probability of learners progressing faster with PI than with lectures, materials that can be packaged and distributed, learners who can use the materials at their convenience and when they are ready, reinforcement that can increase motivation, and self-pacing that allows flexibility according to different abilities. Its major limitations are the expense of developing and preparing a PI course, the difficulty in teaching nonfactual material (such as interpersonal interactions), and some learner isolation and resistance. PI techniques seem to enhance training speed, but their effectiveness in promoting learning is mixed.[71]

### Breaking Barriers of Time and Space: Audio, Video, and Teleconferencing

> It's a gray Thursday afternoon and about 60 human resources types are scattered around a semidarkened movie theater in Woodbury; the scent of popcorn hangs heavy in the air. The screen lights up. A voice intones, "Welcome to another milestone in telecommunications." Live from Salt Lake City, two clean-cut guys in suits perch in an "Oprah"-style studio, rolling out Visendus Incorporated's answer to workplace training—interactive satellite sessions that beam experts simultaneously to theaters and offices across the country. Wait. What's that? It's Linda from Minneapolis, calling with a question. Linda's face flashes on the screen. She wants to know what programs Visendus will offer in the future. The folks back at the studio are glad she asked. With the help of wireless remote keypads, they poll the audience in Denver to see what kinds of programs they want.[72]

The future of training may well lie in "distance learning," using a wide variety of technologies to tie groups together electronically, or exporting expertise through audio and video technology and the World Wide Web. Recordings, films, and slides can be distributed to learners and used independently, or used in conjunction with other training methods. *America's Funniest Home Videos* provides a weekly demonstration that anyone with a camcorder can make a video and often does. While video training in organizations also can suffer from poor production standards, it is increasingly possible for organizations to produce effective training videos at relatively low cost. Although professional-quality training videos are more expensive, they can have greater appeal and impact. John Cleese, of *Monty Python* fame, has made quite a name for himself as an actor in videos, training managers to interview, provide feedback, and perform other tasks.[73] With *video teleconferencing,* learners are in remote classrooms equipped with televisions and microphones, and the instructor provides the training from a video studio, often linked to the learners via satellite. Learners can see the instructor and ask questions via audio links to the studio. Picture-phones are rapidly making this sort of conference the standard. *Audio teleconferencing* provides a similar arrangement but uses only audio connections. Often, systems originally installed to meet the communication needs of executives are appropriated by the trainers when they realize the potential cost savings.[74]

The advantage of audiovisual techniques is their ability to quickly distribute a consistent training experience to a large number of individuals, without being constrained by the time limits of instructors or the logistical requirements of getting instructors and learners in the same location. Professionally produced audiovisual techniques can also generate greater attention and involvement when well constructed.

### High-Technology Training: Computers and Multimedia

If programmed instruction and audiovisual techniques have separate advantages, why not combine them? The appeal of computer-based training is obvious to anyone who has watched a child (of any age) captivated by video games. At Federal Express, both needs assessment and training are computer-based. At least once a year, every Federal Express courier and customer service agent plugs into an interactive PC-based program that tests job knowledge, records skill levels, and helps plan future career and personal development. The program is supplemented by a curriculum on 25 laser disks that provide *interactive video,* in which trainees see and hear video vignettes chosen by the computer program based on the student's demonstrated proficiency.[75]

Computer-based training shares many of the advantages of programmed instruction, while increasing the ability to tailor training to the learner, to use dramatic audio and video to illustrate learning points, and to provide an engaging training environment. Evidence from the U.S. Defense Department suggests that learning may occur faster with computer-assisted instruction (CAI) than with instructor-led classes.[76] Though expensive to develop, such programs can quickly become cost-effective by reducing the amount of off-the-job time required by training, and by allowing trainees to receive their training without extensive travel. Federal Express has more than 1,200 interactive video training locations.

### Learning by Doing: Simulations, Business Games, Action Learning, and Behavior Modeling

Learning by doing training techniques copy the essential elements of real-world situations; they allow learners to play a role or make decisions about the situation and receive feedback about their effectiveness. *Simulations* such as flight simulators duplicate the audio, visual, and physical environment of the cockpit or other work situation. Cockpit resource training is believed to have helped the pilots of United Flight 811 successfully land their Boeing 747 after a cargo door and part of the fuselage ripped open in February 1988.[77]

*Business games* grew out of traditional war games; they allow learners to make decisions about business variables, often competing against other individuals or teams. Computers are frequently used to track and compute the results. Sometimes the notion of a game is taken literally. At Target Stores, sales clerks learn the importance of helping each other by forming a human chain and passing two hula hoops in opposite directions down the chain without dropping them or letting them touch the ground.[78]

The *case study* presents learners with a written report about a realistic situation; learners analyze the information and prepare solutions for discussion.

*Role-playing* has trainers act out simulated roles, sometimes interacting with other trainees who are also acting. To help men understand the women's point of view, U.S. West and Motorola stage mock beauty contests for men, to let male managers switch places mentally with female colleagues. When these men have been in the room where everyone except one is labeled a loser based on his body, they may gain a different understanding of a woman's perspective.[79]

> **WHAT DO YOU THINK?**
>
> At GE, classes of 40 executives were divided into six-person teams that race around the world gathering information to solve a real GE problem. Why all the effort on a training class? At the end of the class, the teams present their findings to CEO Jack Welch.[80] Why do you think Jack Welch takes his valuable time to attend such presentations?

Case studies, business games, and role-playing are frequently combined in *action learning,* where the content of the game, case, or role-play comes from actual business problems faced by the company. Frequently, the students themselves identify the problems and tackle them as part of the training process. For example, Chrysler managers studied the product-development cycle at Mitsubishi and discovered the management process at Chrysler was impeding progress.

*Behavior-modeling,* which draws on learners' ability to imitate appropriate behavior once they have seen it, is based on the theory that people can form mental models of appropriate behavior. This technique involves introducing the skills to be learned, viewing an example of successful behavior that has been related to the learning points, group discussion of the effectiveness of the behaviors, practicing the behaviors in front of others, and feedback about the effectiveness of the behaviors. Target Store trainees confront customers from hell including Bad Mouth Betty and Hysterical Harold.[81]

Advantages of these training methods include the potential for a high degree of transfer to the work situation, high participant involvement providing specific feedback, and helping learners deal with incomplete data and realistic levels of complexity. Behavior modeling has consistently been shown to affect behaviors and learning. Such techniques can be expensive to develop and must be constructed carefully to accomplish the realism necessary for high transfer to the job. For example, case-study methods are supposed to involve participants in confronting and questioning assumptions, have only minimal dependence on faculty, recognize that there is rarely one right answer, and create drama to involve learners. Yet one study of executive training found that faculty members frequently dominated the group interaction, failed to relate the case to situations on the job, and usually led the group to the preferred solution.[82]

### Universities, Colleges, Vocational Schools, and Public Schools

The National Center on the Educational Quality of the Workforce estimates that there is a 3.4 percent productivity output when a company increases the book value of its stock, but a one-year increase in average workforce schooling produces an increase in output of 8.6 percent—a compelling reason for a company to consider the value of educational institutions in the training effort.[83] Why build expensive training centers and pay instructors, when hundreds of public and private institutions are already available to offer training? This logic partly explains the explosion of executive education programs at business schools such as Michigan, Cornell, Harvard, and Wharton. *Business Week* now runs a yearly evaluation of executive education programs at business schools. Increasing competition has brought with it criticism that these programs are outmoded and too traditional. Even though U.S. companies may be sending fewer executives, foreign companies are taking up the slack. Many of the action learning techniques and the emphasis on globalization are emerging in the top programs. Many are also using teleconferencing technology to reach out to executives around the world. A study that interviewed past participants in Harvard's Advanced Management Placement program found that they reported short-term learning in areas such as measuring productivity, customer satisfaction, make-or-buy decisions, and global structures. Long-term learning included broadened perspective, knowledge of other industries, and knowledge of the political and social environment. Some spouses even reported that the executives became more self-confident and developed broader perspectives as a result of the program.[84]

An interesting twist on the university idea is to establish a "corporate university." These are large, well-funded training centers, located in idyllic settings, often with residence facilities and state-of-the-art training equipment. GE's facility in Crotonville, New York, Motorola University in Schaumberg, Illinois, and Xerox's "Document University" in Leesburg, Virginia, are examples.[85]

Partnerships with local colleges, vocational schools, and high schools are increasingly evident, as both business and government see a common benefit in improving the quality of schools and their relevance to workplace skills. Perhaps the simplest partnership is to pay students to do their homework, as one McDonald's franchise owner has done. More intensive partnerships involve customizing technical college or vocational school curricula to fit the needs of the company, as Graco Inc. did with the St. Paul technical college. Some companies adopt public schools or train school administrators; RJR Nabisco awards $2,000 grants for school improvements to parents who achieve leadership roles in the PTA or school board. Evidence does suggest that technical skills and education can add significantly to wages, and perhaps even more significantly to worker productivity.[86]

International businesses are attracted to the United States by skilled labor, as South Carolina has discovered with its network of 16 technical colleges that recruit and train employees to meet the specific needs of incoming companies.[87] Australia's government requires companies to spend 1% of payroll on training, prompting ads similar to the one from Sydney University in Australia in Exhibit 10.11.

**EXHIBIT 10.11** Is the United States Next? Advertisement for University Training in Australia



Source: Advertisement from the *Sydney Morning Herald,* June 16, 1992, p. 22.

Perhaps the ultimate outside training approach is *outdoor training,* including having trainees climb trees, swing through the air, traverse canyons hanging from ropes, and fall backward into each other's arms. It remains a subject of debate: Proponents suggest that it provides a stimulating opportunity to foster communication, trust, and awareness while critics call it a waste of time. Rigorous research is sparse, but participants often believe the training enhances their teamwork and communication.[88]

## TRANSFER FROM THE TRAINING ENVIRONMENT TO THE JOB

After all the design and implementation are finished, training is effective only if in-class results translate to job behaviors. Transfer is enhanced when the training activities, environment, and responses closely resemble the work situation, as when secretaries use the same computers and work materials in training as they use on the job. While this may seem obvious, changes in technology frequently make it tricky. For example, a pilot attempting to avoid undershooting the landing strip pulled back on the throttle and pushed the stick forward, exactly the opposite of the correct combination, causing the plane to nose into the ground. Fortunately, the pilot was able to explain afterward that he had been trained on planes in which the throttle was operated with the right hand and the stick with the left. In the crashed plane, the controls were the opposite.[89]

Perhaps, the most important element of training transfer has little to do with the training program itself. Transfer climate is the degree to which the work situation provides opportunities and rewards for using what is learned in training. This requires creating situational cues to show when to use the training, and consequences that reward trainees appropriately for using it.[90]

Exhibit 10.12 shows 24 items used to measure whether supermarket stores had a culture that encouraged continuous learning and application of skills learned in training. A study of the perception of the culture by supermarket

**EXHIBIT 10.12** Sample Questions for Measuring if the Work Environment Supports Transfer of Training

**In your store . . .**

1. Job assignments are challenges that stretch managers' knowledge to the limit.
2. Supervisors give recognition and credit to those who apply new knowledge and skills to their work.
3. Co-workers are able to provide reliable information about ways to improve job performance.
4. There is a performance appraisal system that ties financial rewards to technical competence.
5. Job assignments consistently expose managers to new technical information.
6. Supervisors match an associate's need for personal and professional development with opportunities to attend training.
7. Co-workers tell each other about new information that can be used to increase job performance.
8. There is excellent on-the-job training.
9. Job assignments are made in the manager's area of interest and are designed to promote personal development.
10. Independent and innovative thinking are encouraged by supervisors.
11. Co-workers consistently suggest new approaches to solving problems based on their own experiences.
12. Associates are provided with equipment and facilities to acquire and apply new knowledge and skills.
13. Job assignments include free time to explore new, advanced ideas and methods for improving performance.
14. Supervisors ask for ideas about how to solve technical, work-related problems.
15. Co-workers are willing to listen to new ideas.
16. There is a job rotation program to give managers diverse job assignments during the first years of employment.
17. Job assignments continually require the evaluation of alternative solutions to problems.
18. Supervisors openly express their support of continuous learning.
19. Co-workers encourage each other to use new knowledge and skills on the job.

**This corporation . . .**

20. Is highly innovative.
21. Expects continuing technical excellence and competence.
22. Has a progressive atmosphere.
23. Attempts to be better than its competitors.
24. Expects high levels of work performance.

Source: J. Bruce Tracey, Scott I. Tennenbaum and Michael J. Kavanagh, "Applying Trained Skills on the Job: The Importance of the Work Environment," *Journal of Applied Psychology* 80 (1995), p. 252. Copyright © 1995 by the American Psychological Association. Reprinted with permission.

store managers receiving basic supervisory training, using the 24 items, significantly predicted trainees' post-training behaviors even more than their knowledge at the end of the training.[91] Because the real-world job often has many obstacles to using newly-trained skills, many have advocated *relapse training,* which provides specific skills and coping responses for trainees, so that they can deal with the barriers encountered on the job.

## EVALUATING TRAINING OUTCOMES: THE PROOF IS IN THE RESULTS

Flight attendants in four major accidents between 1989 and 1992 were unable to locate or operate emergency equipment or follow proper emergency procedures. In one case, an emergency exit was opened while the plane was moving. The National Transportation Safety Board notes that airline companies often focus on reducing training costs while unions often focus on the hours of training provided. Neither of these measures really gets at the effectiveness of the training.[92]

Evaluation is a vital part of the training process, as shown in Exhibit 10.3, just as it should be a vital part of every human resource activity. It is tempting to think of evaluation as the final step in training, but that's incorrect. Evaluation must be planned when objectives are set, and must become a part of subsequent needs analysis to plan future programs. Evaluation is valuable when it improves important future decisions. However, evaluation is like brushing your teeth after every meal—everyone advocates it but few actually do it. Too often, managers do not use training evaluation as an ongoing planning tool, but only when it is needed to sell expensive training programs or repel threatened program cuts. Or they avoid evaluation, fearing that evaluations may show some programs to be ineffective and threaten established procedures. They often believe that the inability to measure all training outcomes perfectly makes it impossible to evaluate training at all. Yet, an effective and ongoing planning and evaluation system for training is essential to ensure adequate return on investment in the millions of dollars spent.[93] Next, we discuss how to create effective evaluation systems.

## Choosing Training Criteria: What Is Effectiveness?

Training effectiveness can be judged using virtually any outcome that the organization considers relevant. Evaluation on only one, or a small subset, of criteria can lead to biased conclusions. Since the late 1950s, researchers have grouped evaluation criteria into four levels:

1. Do the trainees feel good about the training? (trainee reactions)
2. Can the trainees recall and understand the concepts they were taught? (learning)
3. Do the trainees apply the concepts to their behaviors? (behavior changes)
4. Do these changed behaviors affect organizational outcomes? (results)[94]

Exhibit 10.13 shows the percentage of 982 companies surveyed, that evaluate their training programs using one of the four levels. The top percentage represents organizations that evaluate *any* program in this way while the bottom percentage represents all courses in the organization that are evaluated this way. The percentages are very high, suggesting that companies believe they are evaluating their training activities. However, careful choice of criteria and data are needed for group evaluation, for example, it is not enough merely to observe that profits went up after training if it's possible that many factors may have caused the increase.

Recently, some have added a fifth dimension:

5. Do the trainees leave with more positive feelings about the organization or their work? (attitudes)[95]

New England Telephone evaluated an executive development program using measures of training activity, interviews with executives at several points after training, performance appraisals both before and after development, and competency ratings. Economists often use increased wages to measure the effects of public training programs, though wages may not capture the true value of such programs.[96] When Tom Roney, training director for Circle K Corporation, asked for $40,000 to develop a computer-based training (CBT) and orientation

EXHIBIT 10.13 Use of Different Training Evaluation Criteria

| All Industries | |
|---|---|
| **Trainees' Reactions to the course will be measured.** | |
| Percent measuring reactions* | 84 |
| Percent of courses† | 85 |
| **Trainees will be tested to determine what they learned.** | |
| Percent testing* | 69 |
| Percent of courses† | 50 |
| **Trainees' behavior will be evaluated when they return to the job.** | |
| Percent evaluating behavior* | 60 |
| Percent of courses† | 50 |
| **Changes in business results attributable to the training will be measured.** | |
| Percent measuring business results* | 43 |
| Percent of courses† | 46 |

*Of all organizations with 100 or more employees, the percent that evaluate any of their training courses in this way.

†Average percentage of all courses in an organization's curriculum that are evaluated in this way (considering only organizations that evaluate some courses).

Based on 982 responses.

Source: "1995 Industry Report," *Training,* Oct. 1995, p. 64. Adapted with permission from the Oct. 1995 issue of *Training Magazine*. 

program for new store clerks, his managers asked him to prove that it was worth it. So, he gave the new training to 100 new clerks in Phoenix and tracked them against another 100 trained in the usual way. Roney discovered that CBT reduced training time from four days to two because it was self-paced. Store manager reports showed CBT-trained employees to be quicker on the cash register, to make fewer errors, and to be more focused on customer service than other clerks. Circle K hires about 27,000 new clerks a year. Roney calculated the cost to set up 55 CBT labs in 26 states and the benefits of saved time and salaries in cutting the training time by two days. The result? A saving of $1.6 million in the first year, *plus* the benefits of better-trained clerks.[97]

Roney approached the training evaluation carefully, choosing criteria that mattered to key decision makers (cost savings and clerk behaviors). Moreover, he adopted an *evaluation design* that gave clear information about training effects. In this case, he compared trainees with a *control group* of clerks trained the usual way. Of course, it's possible that the CBT-trained clerks were somehow different to begin with, in which case the training wouldn't really make any difference. Roney could have tested this situation by having both sets of clerks work a trial period prior to training, showing that CBT trainees not only ended up better performers but also improved more than the other clerks. Much as we know you'd like a short course in statistical design, we can't go into that here; the point is that it is important to gather training evaluation data systematically if the data are going to give useful information for decisions. Researchers have investigated innovative ways to demonstrate effects while avoiding very costly or complicated experimental designs. One recent suggestion is to measure both criteria that should and should not be changed by training, and prove that training had an effect if the first set of criteria are changed, but the second set are not.[98] The matrix shown in Exhibit 10.14 uses these four criterion levels to develop questions and general measurement approaches. Though this particular matrix was developed in the 1970s, it still provides a good general idea of how evaluation can be accomplished.

Research suggests that the different levels of criteria are related, but often in complex ways, and that they often depend on factors outside the training environment, such as trainees' prior expectations, education, knowledge, and whether they volunteered. The most appropriate criteria are those that can be gathered at a reasonable cost and that have the greatest meaning to the key decision makers.[99] Increasingly, these criteria include training costs and benefits.

WHAT DO YOU THINK?

Considering the expense of training, and the available ways to evaluate training, why don't top managers insist that training be carefully evaluated, just as investments in technology or facilities?

## Efficiency: Training Costs

The dollar amounts in Exhibit 10.1 show that training is big business. For human resource managers in organizations, the most compelling evidence is the size of their training cost budget. Cost estimates vary, because different organizations include different ingredients in their formulas. Digital Equipment Company estimated the costs of each offering at its Sales Management School for entry-level sales managers to be as high as $174,369, including $96,501 in salaries and $21,780 in travel. At the other extreme, Clorox Company estimated that it spent less than $10,000 on the first three sessions of its literacy training program.[100] In Exhibit 10.15, we list several training cost examples. Generally, training cost estimates should include all the resources necessary to implement the program, including the lost opportunity to use the resources in other useful ways.

Focusing only on costs can cause decision makers to emphasize cost reduction. This can lead to creative actions, such as those used by EDS and Lockheed Corporation requiring trainees to sign *repayment agreements* that require them to work for one or several years beyond the training or pay the training expenses. Other firms, such as Florida Power Corporation, sell company-developed training programs as products to outside organizations.[101] However, a cost focus also can cause organizations to cut training programs for short-term cost reductions that may cost much more in long-term lost productivity. To see the whole picture, we must consider training benefits.

## Efficiency: Benefits

Training can be treated as an investment and analyzed using the same investment models that apply to purchases of new equipment, investments in new plants, or underwriting new marketing programs. In fact, the Labor Department has considered encouraging a change in accounting rules that would allow companies to record training expenditures as investments, rather than costs, and to treat training as an asset.[102] Note one training consulting firm's approach to

EXHIBIT 10.14 Training Evaluation Criteria and Measurement Approaches

| What We Want to Know | What Might Be Measured | Measurement Dimensions | What to Look at (sources of data) | Alternative Data Gathering Methods |
|---|---|---|---|---|
| I. Are the trainees happy? If not, why?<br>a. Concepts not relevant.<br>b. Workshop design.<br>c. Trainees not properly positioned. | Trainee reaction during workshop. | Relevance.<br>Threat.<br>Ease of learning. | Comments between trainees.<br>Comments to instructor.<br>Questions about exercises. | Observation.<br>Interview.<br>Questionnaire. |
| | Trainee reaction after workshop. | Perceived "worth."<br>Relevance; or<br>Learning energy. | "Approach behavior" to project.<br>Questions about project concepts. | Observation.<br>Interview.<br>Questionnaire. |
| II. Do the materials teach the concepts? If not, why not?<br>a. Workshop structure.<br>b. Lessons:<br>—Presentation<br>—Examples<br>—Exercises | Trainee performance during workshop. | Understanding.<br>Application. | Learning time.<br>Performance on exercises.<br>Presentations. | Observation<br>Document review. |
| | Trainee performance at end of workshop. | Understanding.<br>Application.<br>Facility.<br>Articulation. | Action plan for project.<br>Use of tools on exercises.<br>Presentations. | Observation.<br>Document review.<br>Interview.<br>Questionnaire. |
| III. Are the concepts used? If not, why not?<br>a. Concepts:<br>—Not relevant.<br>—Too complex.<br>—Too sophisticated.<br>b. Inadequate tools.<br>c. Environment not supportive. | Performance improvement projects. | Analysis.<br>Action plan.<br>Results. | Discussions.<br>Documentation.<br>Results. | Observation.<br>Interview.<br>Document review.<br>Questionnaire (critical incident). |
| | Problem-solving technique. | Questioned asked.<br>Action proposed.<br>Action taken. | Discussions.<br>Documentation.<br>Results. | Observation.<br>Interview.<br>Document review.<br>Questionnaire (critical incident). |
| | Ongoing management approach. | Dissemination effort.<br>Language.<br>People management process. | Discussions.<br>Meetings.<br>Documentation. | Observation.<br>Interview.<br>Document review.<br>Questionnaire (critical incident). |
| IV. Does application of concepts positively affect the organization? If not, why not? | Problem solving. | Problem identification.<br>Analysis.<br>Action.<br>Results. | Discussions.<br>Documentation.<br>Results. | Interview.<br>Document review.<br>Questionnaire (critical incident). |
| | Problem prediction and prevention. | Potential problem identification.<br>Analysis.<br>Action. | Discussions.<br>Documentation.<br>Results. | Interview.<br>Document review.<br>Questionnaire (critical incident). |
| | Performance measures. Specific to a particular workshop. | Output measures.<br>Interim or diagnostic measures. | Performance data. | Document review. |


Source: K. Brethower and G. Rummler, "Evaluating Training," *Training and Development Journal,* May 1979, pp. 14–22.

**EXHIBIT 10.15** Training Cost Categories and Examples

| Equipment | Facilities |
|---|---|
| Training devices: | Classrooms |
| Computer | Laboratories |
| Video | Offices |
| Trainers | Libraries/learning centers |
| Telecommunications | Carrels |
| Laboratory equipment | |
| **Personnel** | **Materials** |
| Instructors | Workbooks |
| Managers/administrators | Texts |
| Clerks | Slides, tapes |
| Programmers | Programs |
| Analysts/designers | Tests |
| Evaluators | Paper |
| Consultants | Film |
| Artists | |

Source: Greg Kearsley, Costs, Benefits, and Productivity in Training Systems (Reading, MA: Addison-Wesley, 1982), p. 24.

calculating the return from training in Exhibit 10.16. Initially, the calculation identifies the objective, audience, and time frame to ensure the information is appropriate for the decision maker. Also, notice how the revenue with training is compared with revenue without training, to isolate the effects of the training program.

Measuring the investment value of training presents two problems: First, the outcomes of training are hard to measure in the same tangible, dollar-valued units as training costs. Second, it's often difficult to be sure how much of a change in dollar-valued outcomes should be attributed to the training program. The first problem can be addressed by focusing on dollar-valued aspects of performance, as in Exhibit 10.16 and as discussed in the chapter on performance appraisal. The second problem can be addressed with rigorous study design, as discussed earlier.

A review of 17 research studies suggested that training does generally have a positive effect on supervisors' performance ratings. We have already seen that some companies estimate very large returns from training. Motorola estimates it gets $30 in productivity gains for every $1 it spends on training. Target Stores notes that employee turnover peaked at 89 percent per year in 1989 before a new training program; turnover dropped to 59 percent by 1992.[103] Yet, all of these are merely estimates and subject to some imprecision. Fortunately, a method is available that makes perfect precision unnecessary.

## Break-Even Analysis

Precise estimates of training costs and benefits are seldom, probably never, available. This is also true for virtually any human resource management activity.

## EXHIBIT 10.16 Calculating the Return on Investment in Training

Objective: ______________________________________________

______________________________________________

Audience: ______________________________________________

Returns measured over: __________One year__________Other __________

### Part 1: Calculating the Revenue Produced by Training

#### Option A—Itemized Analysis

| | | |
|---|---|---|
| Increased sales: | _______ | Additional sales per employee |
| | × _______ | Revenue (or margin) per sale |
| | × _______ | Number of employees |
| | = _______ | Revenue produced by training |
| Higher productivity: | _______ | Percent increase in productivity |
| | × _______ | Cost per employee (salary plus benefits plus overhead) |
| | × _______ | Number of employees |
| | = _______ | Revenue produced by training |
| Reduced errors: | _______ | Average cost per error |
| | × _______ | Number of errors avoided per employee |
| | × _______ | Number of employees |
| | = _______ | Revenue produced by training |
| Client retention: | _______ | Average revenue per client |
| | × _______ | Number of clients retained |
| | = _______ | Revenue produced by training |
| Employee retention: | _______ | Average cost of a new employee (training plus lost productivity) |
| | × _______ | Number of employees retained |
| | = _______ | Revenue produced by training |
| Other: | _______ | ____________________ |
| Total revenue produced by training: | | $ ____________________ |

#### Option B—Summary Analysis

| _________ | − | _________ | = | _________ |
|---|---|---|---|---|
| Revenue After Training | | Revenue Without Training | | Revenue Produced by Training |

### Part 2: Calculating the Return

| _________ | − | _________ | = | _________ |
|---|---|---|---|---|
| Revenue Produced by Training | | Cost of Training | | Total Return on Training Investment |

Source: James Hassett, "Simplifying ROI." Reprinted with permission from the Sept. 1992 issue of *Training*, Lakewood Publications, Minneapolis, MN. 

Indeed, it is typically true for any management activity, including marketing, production, and finance. HR managers frequently lament this imprecision because it makes it impossible to do cost/benefit analysis, but such imprecision doesn't stop the finance, marketing, and production officers from using dollars to justify their programs. Perhaps human resource managers just aren't aware of systems for using imprecise information.

In Exhibit 10.17 we show how *break-even analysis,* a system commonly used in management, can be applied to evaluate a training program when the training benefits are not precisely known. This system uses the investment analogy and the concept of quality, quantity, and cost developed in Chapter Seven.

### Quantity

The number of employees and time periods affected by a human resource decision or activity is the quantity, or "leverage," of human resource activities. In Exhibit 10.17, we depict the leverage for a training program. The program is applied for five years and trains the existing 200-person workforce in the first year. After that, five trained employees leave each year. The 25 new employees who join the workforce each year are trained using the program—a gain of 20 employees. Therefore, the program produces 200 trained employees in the workforce in the first year, 220 in the second year, 240 in the third year, and so on. By training 300 people, the organization reaps 1,200 person-years of productivity effects over the five years. When human resource decisions affect the productivity of employees for many years, they can quickly amass large leverage values.

### Quality

The effects of a human resource decision on employee quality reflect two factors: First, they reflect any enhancements in employee service value to the organization, such as increased sales or better-quality production. Second, they reflect any additional service costs required to maintain and improve the enhanced employee value, such as increased inventories to support increased sales or higher productivity-based pay. The difference between enhanced employee service value and increased employee service cost is the net increase in employee value for the program. Thus, the effect of human resource activities on quality is the average increase in net employee value per employee per year. Though this concept is very difficult to measure, precision usually is not necessary.

In Exhibit 10.17, assume that the most pessimistic managers said the training program could produce an increase in net value averaging at least $1,000 per person-year, while the most optimistic managers said it could increase net value as much as $10,000 per person-year.

### Cost

The cost of a human resource activity refers to the value of the resources used in implementing that decision. These resources include the out-of-pocket expenses to develop and carry out the decision and the value of employees' time as participants, administrators, or in-house instructors. Relevant costs include those to develop and establish the activity, as well as those to keep it going.

In Exhibit 10.17, this training program requires building a state-of-the-art system of training studios capable of receiving closed-circuit audiovideo

EXHIBIT 10.17 Break-Even Analysis Applied to a Training Program

**Computing Quantity/Leverage**

| Year | Trained Employees Added to the Workforce | Trained Employees Leaving the Workforce | Net Increase in Trained Employees in the Workforce | Total Trained Employees in the Workforce |
|---|---|---|---|---|
| 1 | 200 | 0 | 200 | 200 |
| 2 | 25 | 5 | 20 | 220 |
| 3 | 25 | 5 | 20 | 240 |
| 4 | 25 | 5 | 20 | 260 |
| 5 | 25 | 5 | 20 | 280 |
| | | | | 1,200 |

Total person-years of productivity affected

**Estimating Program Quality**

Supervisors estimate the dollar value of the expected increase in employee service value from the training program, on a per person, per year basis, less the increased service costs that would have to be incurred to maintain that increased service value. The estimates of net value ranged from a low of $1,000 to a high of $10,000 per person-year.

**Computing Program Costs**

| Year | Start-up Costs | Ongoing Program Costs | Total Costs |
|---|---|---|---|
| 1 | $500,000 | $100,000 | $ 600,000 |
| 2 | 0 | 100,000 | 100,000 |
| 3 | 0 | 100,000 | 100,000 |
| 4 | 0 | 100,000 | 100,000 |
| 5 | 0 | 100,000 | 100,000 |
| Total program costs over 5 years | | | $1,000,000 |

**Computing Total Program Returns**

Total program returns = (Program quality × leverage) − Program costs

| Program Quality | Leverage | Program Costs | Total Program Returns |
|---|---|---|---|
| $ 833/person-year | 1,200 | $1,000,000 | $ 0 |
| 1,000/person-year | 1,200 | 1,000,000 | $ 200,000 |
| 10,000/person-year | 1,200 | 1,000,000 | $11,000,000 |

Adapted from John W. Boudreau, "Utility Analysis: A New View of Strategic Human Resource Management," in ASPA-BNA *Handbook of Human Resource Management,* vol. 1, chap. 4, ed. Lee D. Dyer (Washington, DC: Bureau of National Affairs, 1988).

transmissions of live training broadcasts and communicating with the instructors through a remote two-way audio system. Costs to build, maintain, and staff the studios, and to develop and carry out the training decision, would be $1 million for the five-year program, with half spent in the first year to build the studios.

## Total Program Returns

The organization depicted in Exhibit 10.17 faces the decision of whether to spend $1 million to train 300 employees over five years, a cost of $3,333 per trainee. However, this cost level is misleading. Because of the leverage factor, the training program need only produce an average increase in net employee value of $833 per trainee, per year, to cover its costs (i.e., $1 million divided by 1,200). This is the break-even value of quality improvement.[104] If it produces the conservatively estimated $1,000 average increase in net employee value per person-year, the total return will be $200,000 ($1.2 million minus the $1 million cost), for a 20 percent return on the original $1 million investment. If it produces the optimistic $10,000 average increase in net employee value per person-year, the total return of $11 million ($12 million minus the $1 million cost) is a 1,100 percent return on investment.

Rather than dwell on the imperfections of the training effectiveness measures, we can focus on the minimum level of training benefits necessary to cover the training costs. This minimum return equals $833 (i.e., $1 million divided by 1,200). If the increase in workforce value created by the training program (per person, per year) is greater than $833, the investment pays off, and vice versa. Several studies have suggested that break-even effect levels are often quite low.[105] When this is true, it may be possible that even imperfect training assessments based on only a portion of the possible training outcomes may be sufficient to justify the training investment. Such an approach is certainly superior to attempting to measure training program effects precisely to the last dollar.[106]

## Equity

Training has important effects on employee perceptions of fairness. A study of Norway's third largest private industrial enterprise suggested that training can backfire. After managers received training to change the organizational climate, their climate perceptions actually dropped, apparently because they were now sensitized to the climate problems.[107] Access to training leading to advancement can be seen as a reward for good performance or loyalty. Being forced to undergo remedial training can be seen as a punishment. Training can arouse employees' anger and even stimulate lawsuits. We have already discussed the controversy associated with new age training and employees' religious beliefs. Some employees have sued employers for endangering them by failing to adequately train them to avoid unsafe job behaviors.[108]

Training is also a key tool as part of a complete EEO or affirmative action program, often providing protected groups with the skills they need to compete with others on an equal footing. Though adverse impact analysis usually focuses on staffing decisions, training can be implicated as well when: (1) successfully completing training is a prerequisite for some jobs; (2) persons are competitively selected for training; (3) training performance is used as a selection predictor or to allocate compensation.[109] Organizations often use training directly to help foster appreciation of the value of diversity. A study of more than 700 human resource professionals found that adopting diversity training was associated with larger organizations, positive top management beliefs about diversity, high strategic priority on diversity, presence of a diversity manager, and other diversity-related policies. The success of diversity training was associated with mandatory attendance for all managers, long-term evaluation of results, rewards to managers for increasing diversity, and a broad and inclusive definition of diversity.[110]

## SUMMARY

U.S. organizations spend more than $50 billion on formal training every year. When all the time, materials, and energy devoted to on-the-job-training and educational partnerships are included, this figure is undoubtedly much higher. Training plays a vital part in preparing and upgrading the workforce when it is carefully planned and integrated with other activities such as compensation and external and internal staffing. Indeed, training and internal staffing are so closely tied that we have discussed them as two components of a single process—employee development. Many have argued that training holds the key to competitiveness and social equity by bringing previously excluded groups into the mainstream.

While the effort spent on training is astonishing, even more astonishing is how little we know about effectively managing training investments. Financial, marketing, and production managers, who are responsible for the consequences of their decisions, devote considerable effort to ensure that comparable capital and financial outlays are well managed. Imagine the reaction if a manager proposed building a multimillion dollar plant based only on the opinion of a few people, with little systematic analysis. Yet, of all the personnel activities, training seems most subject to passing fads and fashions.

Managers need to approach training decisions more systematically by using the diagnostic approach suggested here. The key is to focus on the impact of training, rather than the training activity. While research on training is improving, there are still large blank spots in our knowledge about training effects. Therefore, managers need to be flexible and creative in their use of information. If you need help, the Web is there for a start.

Perhaps the most fundamental trend affecting training is its merger with other forms of development. Increasingly, work roles, career progressions, and pay systems are being designed to support and foster continuous learning. The boundary between on-the-job and off-the-job training becomes ever more blurred as organizations use apprenticeships, classroom materials derived from real company problems, and computerized training that simulates the sights and sounds of real job situations. In short, training and learning principles will play an even larger role in future organizations, though it may become more difficult to identify training activities as distinct from other human resource activities.

> EXPLORING THE WEB
>
> You can visit the "Learning Exchange" with a training FAQ (frequently asked questions), addresses of organizations that focus on training and development, suggested books and journals, and even an on-line discussion list. Point your browser to: **http://www/tcm.com/trdev/faq/index.html.**

## QUESTIONS

1. What is training, and why do organizations regard it as a strategic investment?
2. Discuss how training is linked to other HR activities used by organizations. How can these links be used to increase the value of training?
3. Why is training sometimes considered a strategic weapon for organizations? What is training for impact?

4. What are organization-level needs, and how can training address them? How can an organization maximize training benefits?
5. What factors affect whether trainees actually learn what is being taught? What does this imply for organizational efforts to improve learning?
6. Discuss the concept of *learning* in training, and the importance of transfer between training and the job.
7. What are the most common training content areas? How do different content areas affect the type of training chosen? Pick a content area and give examples of an appropriate and an inappropriate training delivery method.
8. Compare on-the-job training and apprenticeships. What are their similarities, differences, advantages, and disadvantages?
9. How important is training likely to be in the future? What changes are facing organizations that will increase the importance of training to human resource management?
10. How can the value of training be evaluated? Is it ever possible to evaluate training when so many of its effects are hard to predict or measure precisely?

## YOUR TURN

### Training to Build the Saturn Difference[111]

All over the United States, auto dealers were saying to customers, "Thanks to you, we have sold every car in our stock. New cars will arrive soon. Order yours today!" Honda, Toyota, Nissan? No. Saturn Corporation, an American success story that credits training with the success of a revolutionary new way to sell cars.

In the early 1980s, with U.S. automakers suffering sales declines, plant closings, and an image among consumers for quality far below Japanese rivals, General Motors Corporation sought to recapture the small-car market through a new automobile company that would make a fresh start toward building customer satisfaction. Saturn Corporation, a subsidiary of GM, was formed to "aim beyond providing customer satisfaction: We must exceed customer expectations and provide an unparalleled buying and vehicle-ownership experience that results in customer enthusiasm." The new company defined five values: (1) a commitment to customer enthusiasm, (2) a commitment to excel, (3) teamwork, (4) trust and respect for the individual, and (5) continuous improvement.

Transferring these values to the manufacturing process was tough enough, but transferring them to the retail sales force was even tougher. It even required changing the company's vocabulary, with dealers becoming *retailers,* dealerships becoming *retail facilities,* and salespeople becoming *sales consultants.* This required shifting from the traditional car sales game that often pitted salespersons against customers in attempting to get the best deal, to a new philosophy exemplified by Saturn's Six Steps to Customer Enthusiasm:

1. Listen to your customer.
2. Create an environment of mutual trust.
3. Exceed customer expectations.
4. Create a win-win culture.
5. Follow up with customers to make sure their expectations are met.
6. Continually improve customers' perceptions of the quality of products and services.

How would you design a cost-effective training approach for the new breed of Saturn sales consultants? How would you assess the needs of the typical automobile sales trainee? What conditions for learning would be essential, and how would you create them through your training design? Would you use internal or external trainers? What specific training methods would you use? How would you bridge the distance between the training and the actual job? Finally, how would you measure and evaluate effectiveness to ensure continuous improvement in the training process?

## NOTES AND REFERENCES

1. Ronald Henkoff, "Companies that Train Best," *Fortune,* Mar. 22, 1993, pp. 62–75; William Wiggenhorn, "Motorola U.: When Training Becomes an Education," *Harvard Business Review,* July–Aug. 1990, pp. 71–83; Lois Therrien, "Motorola Sends Its Work Force Back to School," *Business Week,* June 6, 1988, pp. 80–81.
2. Linda Grant, "A School for Success," *U.S. News and World Report,* May 22, 1995, pp. 53–55.
3. Henkoff, "Companies that Train Best," p. 68.
4. Centre d'Etudes et de Recherches sur les Qualifications, *Statistique de la Formation Professionnelle Continue Financée par les Entreprises: Années 1989–1990;* Susan Dentzer, "How to Train Workers for the 21st Century," *U.S. News & World Report,* Sept. 21, 1992, p. 74; Thomas Amirault, "Training to Qualify for Jobs and Improve Skills, 1991," *Monthly Labor Review,* Sept. 1992, pp. 31–36.
5. "Training and the Workplace," *The Economist,* Aug. 22, 1992, p. 21.
6. Patricia A. Galagan, "Training Delivers Results to Federal Express," *Training & Development,* Dec. 1991, pp. 27–33.
7. Linda Keegan and Betsy Jacobson, "Training Goes Mod(ular) at Apple," *Training & Development,* July 1995, pp. 38–39; Dawn Anfuso, "Las Vegas Resort Bets on Training—And Wins," *Personnel Journal,* Sept. 1995, pp. 78–86; Calhoun W. Wick and Lou, Stanton Leon, "Individual Learning Nurtures J. P. Morgan," *Personnel Journal,* Nov. 1993, pp. 50–54; Patricia Galagan, "Building Capability at Pacific Bell," *Training & Development,* Feb. 1995, pp. 23–31.
8. Dianne Solis, "Mexico, Amid Growing Jobless Rate, Steps Up Programs to Train Workers," *The Wall Street Journal,* Oct. 23, 1995, p. A13; Bernard Elbaum and Nirvikar Singh, "The Economic Rationale of Apprenticeship Training: Some Lessons from British and U.S. Experience," *Industrial Relations* 34 (Oct. 1995), pp. 593–622.
9. World Bank Conference on Enterprise Training Strategies and Productivity, June 12–13, 1995.
10. Jooyean Jeong, "The Failure of Recent State Vocational Training Policies in Korea from a Comparative Perspective," *British Journal of Industrial Relations,* June 1995, pp. 237–52.
11. Lisa M. Lynch and Sandra Black, "Beyond the Incidence of Employer-Provided Training: Evidence from a National Employers Survey," Working paper, National Bureau of Economic Research, Cambridge, MA, 1995; Lisa M. Lynch, "Employer-Provided Training in the Manufacturing Sector: First Results from the United States," paper presented at the

Conference on Enterprise Training Strategies and Productivity, June 12–13, 1995; Urs E. Gattiker, "Firm and Taxpayer Returns from Training of Semiskilled Employees," *Academy of Management Journal,* 38 (1995), pp. 1152–73; Laurie J. Bassi, "Upgrading the U.S. Workplace: Do Reorganization, Education Help?" *Monthly Labor Review,* May 1995, pp. 37–47; Paul Osterman, "Skill Training and Work Organization in American Establishments," *Industrial Relations* 34 (Apr. 1995), pp. 125–46.

12. Ikujiro Nonaka, "The Knowledge-Creating Company," *Harvard Business Review* 69 (Nov.–Dec. 1995), pp. 96–104; Douglas A. Ready, "Educating the Survivors," *Journal of Business Strategy* 16 (Mar.–Apr. 1995), pp. 28–37; "Learning Organizations," *The Economist,* Oct. 28, 1995, pp. 79–80.
13. "The Eighth Annual Training Zone Awards," *Training,* Dec. 1992, p. 31.
14. Betty Bailey, "Ask What HR Can Do for Itself," *Personnel Journal,* July 1991, pp. 35–39; Robert O'Connor, "Retraining Eastern Europe," *Training,* Nov. 1992, pp. 41–45.
15. Robert Rodgers, John E. Hunter, and Deborah L. Rogers, "Influence of Top Management Commitment on Management Program Success," *Journal of Applied Psychology* 78, no. 1 (1993), pp. 151–55.
16. Linda Thornburg, "Training in a Changing World," *HR Magazine,* Aug. 1992, pp. 44–47; John Paul MacDuffie and Thomas A. Kochan, "Does the U.S. Underinvest in Human Resources? Determinants of Training in the World Auto Industry" (paper presented at the National Academy of Management Meetings, August 1991, New York); J. A. Ettlie, "What Makes a Manufacturing Firm Innovate?" *Academy of Management Executive* 4 (1990), pp. 7–20.
17. Henkoff, "Companies that Train Best," p. 73.
18. Peter Senge, *The Fifth Discipline: The Art and Practice of the Learning Organization* (New York: Doubleday, 1990).
19. "The Knowledge," *The Economist,* Nov. 11, 1995, p. 63.
20. Joseph D. Keith and Ellen Smith Payton, "The New Face of Training," *Training & Development,* Feb. 1995, pp. 49–51; Donald J. McNerney and Angela Briggins, "Competency Assessment Gains Favor Among Trainers," *HR Focus,* June 1995, p. 19.
21. James M. Hirsch, "Now Hotel Clerks Provide More than Keys," *The Wall Street Journal,* Mar. 19, 1993, p. B1.
22. "Cooperation Key to Setting Skill Standards, Certification, AFL-CIO Official Testifies,"*HRDI Advisory* 20, no. 5 (May/June 1992), p. 1; "Enough Talk: Time to Set Skill Standards," *HR Focus,* June 1992, p. 1; Linda T. Henderson and Kathy Price, "TI Locks in Supervisory Support for Basic Skills," *Work in America,* Feb. 1993, pp. 1–3; "How Kodak Helps Managers and Supervisors Play Their Part," *Work in America,* Jan. 1992, p. 1.
23. Peter Warr and David Bunce, "Trainee Characteristics and the Outcomes of Open Learning," *Personnel Psychology* 48 (1995), pp. 347–75; Jeffrey D. Facteau et al., "The Influence of General Perceptions of the Training Environment on Pretraining Motivation and Perceived Training

Transfer," *Journal of Management* 21 (1995), pp. 1–25; Alan M. Saks, "Longitudinal Field Investigation of the Moderating and Mediating Effects of Self-Efficacy on the Relationship Between Training and Newcomer Adjustment," *Journal of Applied Psychology* 80 (1995), pp. 211–25; R. A. Noe, "Trainees' Attributes: Neglected Influences on Training Effectiveness," *Academy of Management Review* 11 (1986), pp. 736–49; R. A. Noe and N. Schmitt, "The Influence of Trainee Attitudes on Training Effectiveness: Test of a Model," *Personnel Psychology* 39 (1986), pp. 497–523.

24. Michelle Najjar and John W. Boudreau, "The Effect of Behavior Modeling Training, Service Orientation and Language Skills on Service Skills and Behaviors: Extending Social Learning Theories to Collectivist Cultures" Working Paper #96-01, Center for Advanced Human Resource Studies, Ithaca, NY, 1996.

25. Greg L. Stewart, Kenneth P. Carson, and Robert L. Cardy, "The Joint Effects of Conscientiousness and Self-Leadership Training on Employee Self-Directed Behavior in a Service Setting," *Personnel Psychology,* 49 (1996), pp. 143–164.

26. Miguel A. Qui/at/nones, "Pretraining Context Effects: Training Assignment as Feedback," *Journal of Applied Psychology* 80 (1995), pp. 226–38.

27. L. A. Digman, "Determining Management Development Needs," *Human Resource Management,* Winter 1980, pp. 12–17.

28. Lloyd Baird, Jon Briscoe, Lydia Tuden, and L. M. H. Rosansky, "World Class Executive Development," *Human Resource Planning* 17 (1994), pp. 1–15.

29. Edwin A. Fleishman and Michael D. Mumford, "Abilities as Causes of Individual Differences in Skill Acquisition," *Human Performance* 2, no. 3 (1989), pp. 201–23; Beverly Geber, "The Limits of HRD," *Training,* May 1989, pp. 25–33; Ivan T. Robertson and Sylvia Downs, "Work Sample Tests of Trainability: A Meta-Analysis," *Journal of Applied Psychology* 74, no. 3 (1989), pp. 402–10.

30. Paul L. Ackerman, "Determinants of Individual Differences during Skill Acquisition: Cognitive Abilities and Information Processing," *Journal of Experimental Psychology General* 117 (1988), pp. 288–318; Scott I. Tannenbaum and Gary Yukl, "Training and Development in Work Organizations," *Annual Review of Psychology* 43 (1992), pp. 399–441; Michael D. Mumford et al., "Personality Variables and Skill Acquisition: Performance While Practicing a Complex Task," *Human Performance* 6 (1993), pp. 345–81.

31. Cynthia Lee and Phillip Bobko, "Self-Efficacy Beliefs: Comparison of Five Measures," *Journal of Applied Psychology* 79 (1994), pp. 364–69; Allan M. Saks, "Longitudinal Field Investigation of the Moderating and Mediating Effects of Self-Efficacy on the Relationship between Training and Newcomer Adjustment," *Journal of Applied Psychology* 80 (1995), pp. 211–25; Allan M. Saks, "Moderating Effects of Self-Efficacy for the Relationship between Training Method and Anxiety and Stress Reactions of Newcomers," *Journal of Organizational Behavior* 15 (1994), pp. 639–54.

32. D. J. Cohen, "What Motivates Trainees," *Training and Development Journal,* Nov. 1990, pp. 91–93; Timothy T. Baldwin and R. J. Magjuka, "Organizational Training and Signals of Importance: Effects of Per-Training Perceptions on Intentions to Transfer," *Human Resource Development* 2, no. 1 (1991), pp. 25–36; T. C. Williams, Paul W. Thayer, and S. B. Pond, "Test of a Model of Motivational Influences on Reactions to Training and Learning" (paper presented at the Sixtieth Annual Conference of the Society for Industrial and Organizational Psychology, Washington, DC, June 1991).
33. Timothy T. Baldwin, Richard J. Magjuka, and Brian T. Lohrer, "The Perils of Participation: Effects of Choice of Training on Trainee Motivation and Learning," *Personnel Psychology* 44 (1991), pp. 51–65.
34. Joseph J. Martocchio, "Microcomputer Usage as an Opportunity: The Influence of Context in Employee Training," *Personnel Psychology* 45 (1992), pp. 529–552; Jane Webster and Joseph Martocchio, "Turning Work into Play: Implications for Microcomputer Software Training," *Journal of Management* 19 (1993), pp. 127–146.
35. R. Wood and Albert Bandura, "Social Cognitive Theory of Organizational Management," *Academy of Management Review* 14 (1989), pp. 361–84.
36. James E. Driskell, Ruth P. Willis, and Carolyn Copper, "Effect of Overlearning on Retention," *Journal of Applied Psychology* 77, no. 5 (1992), pp. 615–22.
37. James E. Driskell, Carolyn Copper & Aidan Moran, "Does Mental Practice Enhance Performance?" *Journal of Applied Psychology* 79 (1994) pp. 481–492.
38. Goldstein, *Training in Organizations,* p. 109.
39. Ibid., p. 117; Donald B. Fedor, Roger B. Rensvold, and Susan M. Adams, "An Investigation of Factors Expected to Affect Feedback Seeking: A Longitudinal Field Study," *Personnel Psychology* 45 (1992), pp. 779–805.
40. "Top Training Facilities," *Training,* Apr. 1994, pp. A–O.
41. R. M. Gagne and L. J. Briggs, *Principles of Instructional Design* (New York: CBS College Publishing, 1979).
42. Goldstein, *Training in Organizations,* p. 140; J. S. Randall, "You and Effective Training," *Training and Development Journal* 32 (1978), pp. 10–19.
43. Mary Jane Gill and David Meier, "Accelerated Learning Takes Off," *Training and Development Journal,* Jan. 1989, pp. 63–65; Robert D. Bretz, Jr., and Robert E. Thompsett, "Comparing Traditional and Integrative Learning Methods in Organizational Training Programs," *Journal of Applied Psychology* 77, no. 6 (1992), pp. 941–51; Peggy Stuart, "New Directions in Training Individuals," *Personnel Journal,* Sept. 1992, pp. 86–94.
44. Jane S. Mouton and Robert R. Blake, *Synergogy: A New Strategy for Education, Training and Development* (San Francisco: Jossey-Bass, 1984).
45. Manuel London, *Managing the Training Enterprise* (San Francisco: Jossey-Bass, 1989), pp. 33–34.

46. Marie Waung, "The Effects of Self-Regulatory Coping Orientation on Newcomer Adjustment and Job Survival," *Personnel Psychology* 48 (1995), pp. 633–650.

47. "Vital Statistics: Industry Report," *Training,* Oct. 1995, p. 56.

48. Henkoff, "Companies That Train Best," p. 70.

49. Shari Caudron, "How Xerox Won the Baldrige," *Personnel Journal,* Apr. 1991, pp. 98–102; Samantha Drake, "Empowering the People," *Human Resource Executive,* Dec. 1992, pp. 32–35.

50. Goldstein, *Training in Organizations,* pp. 267–68; R. W. Swezy and Eduardo Salas, eds., *Teams: Their Training and Performance* (Norwood, NJ: Ablex, 1991).

51. Ronald E. Purwer and Alfonso Montouri, "Miles Davis in the Classroom: Using the Jazz Ensemble Metaphor for Enhancing Team Learning," *Journal of Management Education,* Feb. 1994, pp. 21–31.

52. Donald J. Ford, "Toward a More Literate Workforce," *Training and Development,* Nov. 1992, pp. 53–54; Teresa L. Smith, "Finding Solutions for Illiteracy," *HR Focus,* Feb. 1995, p. 7.

53. Krystal Miller, "At GM, the Three R's Are the Big Three," *The Wall Street Journal,* July 3, 1992, p. B1.

54. Kirkland Ropp, "A Reform Movement for Education," *Personnel Administrator,* Aug. 1989, pp. 39–41; "Employers Are the Key to Basic Skills," *Human Resource Management News,* Jan. 6, 1990, p. 4; Gary Putka, "Learning Curve: Lacking Good Results, Corporations Rethink Aid to Public Schools," *The Wall Street Journal,* June 27, 1989, p. A1; Cindy Skrzycki, "Before You Can Work You Have to Read," *Washington Post National Weekly Edition,* Oct. 2–8, 1989, p. 19; Wiggenhorn, "Motorola U."

55. Jerome M. Rosow and Robert Zager, *Training—The Competitive Edge* (San Francisco: Jossey-Bass, 1990), pp. 182–83.

56. Linda Stockman Vines, "Training the Top," *Human Resource Executive,* Aug. 1991, pp. 5–10.

57. Philip R. Theibert, "Training Agenda," *HR Magazine,* Oct. 1995, p. 66.

58. Jay Stuller, "Practical Matters," *Across the Board,* Jan.–Feb. 1993, pp. 14–19; Brian O'Reilly, "How Execs Learn Now," *Fortune,* Apr. 5, 1993, pp. 52–58.

59. Noel Tichy, Christopher DeRose, and Anne Faircloth, "Roger Enrico's Master Class," *Fortune,* Nov. 27, 1995, pp. 105–7.

60. Peter G. Beinetti, "Spouse Programs: Developing the 'Whole' Executive," *HR Focus,* May 1992, p. 24.

61. Marc Hequet, "Creativity Training Gets Creative," *Training,* Feb. 1992, pp. 41–46.

62. Joann S. Lublin, "Companies Use Cross-Cultural Training to Help Their Employees Adjust Abroad," *The Wall Street Journal,* Aug. 4, 1992, p. B1.

63. James L. Noel and Ram Charan, "GE Brings Global Thinking to Light," *Training & Development,* July 1992, pp. 29–33; Jim Impoco, "Basic Training Sanyo Style," *U.S. News & World Report,* July 13, 1992,

pp. 46–48; "Korea's Biggest Firm Teaches Junior Execs Strange Foreign Ways," *The Wall Street Journal,* Dec. 30, 1992, p. A1; J. Stewart Black and Mark Mendenhall, "Cross-Cultural Training Effectiveness: A Review and a Theoretical Framework for Future Research," *Academy of Management Review* 15, no. 1 (1990), pp. 113–36.

64. Thomas D. Brierton, "Employers' New Age Training Programs Fail to Alter the Consciousness of the EEOC," *Labor Law Journal,* July 1992, pp. 411–20.

65. Vicente F. Estrada, "Are Your Factory Workers Know-it-alls?" *Personnel Journal,* Sep. 1995, pp. 128–34; "U.S.-Japan HR Network," *Work in America,* Dec. 1995, p. 3.

66. Goldstein, *Training in Organizations,* pp. 227–29.

67. Rick Wartzman, "Apprenticeship Plans Springs Up for Students Not Headed for College," *Wall Street Journal,* May 19, 1992, p. A1.

68. Susan E. Tift, "Youth Apprenticeships: Can They Work in America?" *EQW Issues,* Oct. 1992, pp. 2–8; Philip Glouchevitch, *Juggernaut: The German Way of Business* (New York: Simon & Schuster, 1992), chap. 7.

69. Goldstein, *Training in Organizations,* p. 232.

70. J. Kline Harrison, "Individual and Combined Effects of Behavior Modeling and the Cultural Assimilator in Cross-Cultural Management Training," *Journal of Applied Psychology* 77, no. 6 (1992), pp. 952–62.

71. Goldstein, *Training in Organizations,* pp. 242–43.

72. Jill Hodges, "Not So Basic Training," *Minneapolis Star Tribune,* Dec. 24, 1995, p. D1.

73. Video Arts, 4088 Commercial Ave., Northbrook, IL.

74. David Sheridan, "Off the Road Again—Training through Teleconferencing," *Training,* Feb. 1992, pp. 63–68.

75. Henkoff, "Companies That Train Best"; Diane Filipowski, "How Federal Express Makes Your Package Its Most Important," *Personnel Journal,* Feb. 1992, pp. 40–46.

76. N. Madlin, "Computer-Based Training Comes of Age," *Personnel* 64, no. 11 (1987), pp. 64–65.

77. Judith Valente and Bridget O'Brian, "Airline Cockpits Are Not Place to Solo," *The Wall Street Journal,* Aug. 2, 1989, p. B1; Joseph Oberle, "Teamwork in the Cockpit," *Training,* Feb. 1990, pp. 34–38.

78. Henkoff, "Companies that Train Best," p. 71.

79. Laura L. Castro, "More Firms 'Gender Train' to Bridge the Chasms that Still Divide the Sexes," *The Wall Street Journal,* Jan. 2, 1992, p. B1.

80. Brian O'Reilly, "How Execs Learn Now," *Fortune,* Apr. 5, 1993, p. 54.

81. Goldstein, *Training in Organizations,* pp. 285–91; Timothy T. Baldwin, "Effects of Alternative Modeling Strategies on Outcomes of Interpersonal Skills," *Journal of Applied Psychology* 77, no. 2 (1992), pp. 147–54; Marilyn E. Gist, Catherine Schwoerer, and Benson Rosen, "Effects of Alternative Training Methods on Self-Efficacy and Performance in Computer Software Training," *Journal of Applied Psychology*

74, no. 6 (1989), pp. 884–91; Henkoff, "Companies that Train Best," p. 70.

82. Chris Argyris, "Some Limitations of the Case Method: Experiences in a Management Development Program," *Academy of Management Review* 5, no. 2 (1980), pp. 201–98.
83. "Productivity: Education's Big Payoff," *HRM News,* July 26, 1995, p. 2.
84. John A. Byrne, "Back to School," *Business Week,* Oct. 28, 1991, pp. 102–7; O'Reilly, "How Execs Learn Now"; George P. Hollenbeck, "What Did You Learn in School? Studies of a University Executive Program," *Human Resource Planning* 14, no. 4 (1991), pp. 247–60.
85. Jeanne Meister, *Corporate Quality Universities: Lessons in Building a World Class Work Force* (Alexandria VA: American Society for Training and Development, 1994).
86. "McPay for McStudying," *Training & Development,* July 1992, p. 9; Bill Kelley, "Back to Class," *Human Resource Executive,* Feb. 1993, pp. 37–38; Troy Segal et al., "Saving Our Schools," *Business Week,* Sept. 14, 1992; Joyce E. Santora, "Nabisco Tackles Tomorrow's Skills Gap," *Personnel Journal,* Sept. 1992, pp. 47–50; John Bishop, "Educational Reform and Technical Education?" (paper presented at the American Economics Association Meetings, Anaheim, CA., Jan. 6, 1993).
87. Barbara Harrison, "South Carolina Offers Glimpse of Clinton Way," *Financial Times,* Jan. 5, 1993.
88. Richard J. Wagner and Christopher C. Roland, "How Effective Is Outdoor Training?" *Training & Development,* July 1992, pp. 61–66; Jennifer J. Laabs, "Team Training Goes Outdoors," *Personnel Journal,* June 1991, pp. 56–63.
89. Goldstein, *Training in Organizations,* p. 126.
90. J. Z. Rouillier and Irwin L. Goldstein, "Determinants of the Climate for Transfer of Training" (paper presented at the Society for Industrial and Organizational Psychology, Saint Louis, MO, 1990).
91. J. Bruce Tracey, Scott I. Tennenbaum and Michael J. Kavanagh, "Applying Trained Skills on the Job: The Importance of the Work Environment," *Journal of Applied Psychology* 80 (1995), pp. 239–52.
92. Jonathan Weil, "Flight Attendants' Training Is Lax, Board Tells FAA," *The Wall Street Journal,* June 10, 1992, p. A8.
93. Cynthia A. Lombardo, "Do the Benefits of Training Justify the Costs?" *Training and Development Journal,* Dec. 1989, pp. 60–64; John W. Boudreau, "Utility Analysis," chap. 4 in *Human Resource Management: Evolving Roles and Responsibilities,* vol. 1 of the *ASPA/BNA Handbook of Personnel and Industrial Relations,* ed. Lee D. Dyer (Washington, DC: Bureau of National Affairs, 1988).
94. Donald L. Kirkpatrick, *Evaluating Training Programs—The Four Levels* (San Francisco: Barrett-Koehler, 1994).
95. Scott I. Tannenbaum and Steven B. Woods, "Determining a Strategy for Evaluating Training: Operating within Organization Constraints," *Human Resource Planning* 15, no. 2 (1991), pp. 63–81.

96. Martin Smith, "Evaluation of Executive Development: A Case Study," *Performance Improvement Quarterly* 6, no. 1 (1993), pp. 26–42; Kenneth A. Couch, "New Evidence on the Long-Term Effects of Employment Training Programs," *Journal of Labor Economics* 10, no. 4 (1992), pp. 380–88; John H. Bishop, "Toward More Valid Evaluations of Training Programs Serving the Disadvantaged," *Journal of Policy Analysis and Management* 8 (1989), pp. 209–28.

97. "Training: Eyes on the ROI," *HRM News,* Mar. 6, 1995, pp. 2–3.

98. Richard D. Arvey, Scott E. Maxwell, and Eduardo Salas, "The Relative Power of Training Evaluation Designs under Different Cost Configurations," *Journal of Applied Psychology* 77, no. 2 (1992), pp. 155–60; Robert R. Haccoun and Thierry Hamtiaux, "Optimizing Knowledge Tests for Inferring Learning Acquisition Levels in Single Group Training Evaluation Designs: The Internal Referencing Strategy," *Personnel Psychology* 47 (1994), pp. 593–604.

99. Robert D. Bretz, Jr., and Robert E. Thompsett, "Comparing Traditional and Integrative Learning Methods in Organizational Training Programs," *Journal of Applied Psychology* 77, no. 6 (1992), pp. 941–51; S. E. Maxwell, D. A. Cole, Richard A. Arvey, and Eduardo Salas, "A Comparison of Methods for Increasing Power in Randomized Between-Subjects Designs," *Psychological Bulletin,* 1991, pp. 328–37; Scott I. Tannenbaum and Gary Yukl, "Training and Development in Work Organizations," *Annual Review of Psychology* 43 (1992), pp. 399–441.

100. Rob Hartz, Richard P. Niemiec, and Herbert J. Walberg, "The Impact of Management Education," *Performance Improvement Quarterly* 6, no. 1 (1993), pp. 67–76; Stephanie Overman, "Retraining Puts Workers Back on Track," *HRM Magazine,* Aug. 1992, pp. 40–43.

101. Anthony W. Kraus, "Repayment Agreements for Employee Training Costs," *Labor Law Journal,* Jan. 1993, pp. 49–55; Diane Filipowski, "Florida Power Turns Training into Dollars," *Personnel Journal,* May 1991, pp. 47–50.

102. Beverly Geber, "A Capital Idea," *Training,* Jan. 1992, pp. 31–34; Christine D. Keen, "Moving Training from 'Cost' to 'Investment.' " *HR News,* March 1992, p. 5.

103. Michael J. Burke and Russell R. Day, "A Cumulative Study of the Effectiveness of Managerial Training," *Journal of Applied Psychology* 71 (1986), pp. 232–45; Henkoff, "Companies that Train Best."

104. John W. Boudreau, "Decision Theory Contributions to HRM Research and Practice," *Industrial Relations* 23 (1984), pp. 198–217.

105. Ibid.; John W. Boudreau, "Utility Analysis: A New View of Strategic Human Resource Management," in *ASPA-BNA Handbook of Human Resource Management,* vol. 1, ed. Lee D. Dyer (Washington, DC: Bureau of National Affairs, 1988); Beth C. Florin-Thuma and John W. Boudreau, "Effects of Performance Feedback Utility Analysis on Managerial Decision Processes," *Personnel Psychology* 40 (1987), pp. 693–713; Joe R. Rich and John W. Boudreau, "Effects of Variability and Risk on Selection Utility Analysis: An Empirical Comparison," *Personnel Psychology* 40 (1987), pp. 55–84; John W. Boudreau, "Utility Analysis in Human Re-

source Management Decisions," in *Handbook of Industrial and Organizational Psychology,* 2nd ed., M. D. Dunnette (Palo Alto, CA: Consulting Psychologist Press, 1991); John E. Mathieu and Russell L. Leonard, Jr., "Applying Utility Concepts to a Training Program in Supervisory Skills and a Time-Based Approach," *Academy of Management Journal* 30, no. 2 (1987), pp. 316–35.

106. Boudreau, "Decision Theory Contributions to HRM Research and Practice."

107. Paul Moxnes and Dag-Erik Eilertsen, "The Influence of Management Training upon Organizational Climate: An Exploratory Study," *Journal of Organizational Behavior* 12 (1991), pp. 399–411.

108. James W. Fenton, William N. Ruud, and James A. Kimbell, "Negligent Training Suits: A Recent Entry into the Corporate Employment Negligence Arena," *Labor Law Journal,* June 1991, pp. 351–56.

109. David Mank, John Oorthuys, Larry Rhodes, Dennis Sandow, and Tim Weyer, "Accommodating Workers with Disabilities," *Training & Development,* Jan. 1992, pp. 49–52; C. J. Bartlett, "Equal Employment Opportunity Issues in Training," *Human Factors* 20 (1988), pp. 179–88.

110. Sara Rynes and Benson Rosen, "A Field Survey of Factors Affecting the Adoption and Perceived Success of Diversity Training," *Personnel Psychology* 48 (1995), pp. 247–70.

111. This Your Turn is based on Dorothy Cottrell, Larry Davis, Pat Detrick, and Marty Raymond, "Sales Training and the Saturn Difference," *Training & Development,* Dec. 1992, pp. 38–43.

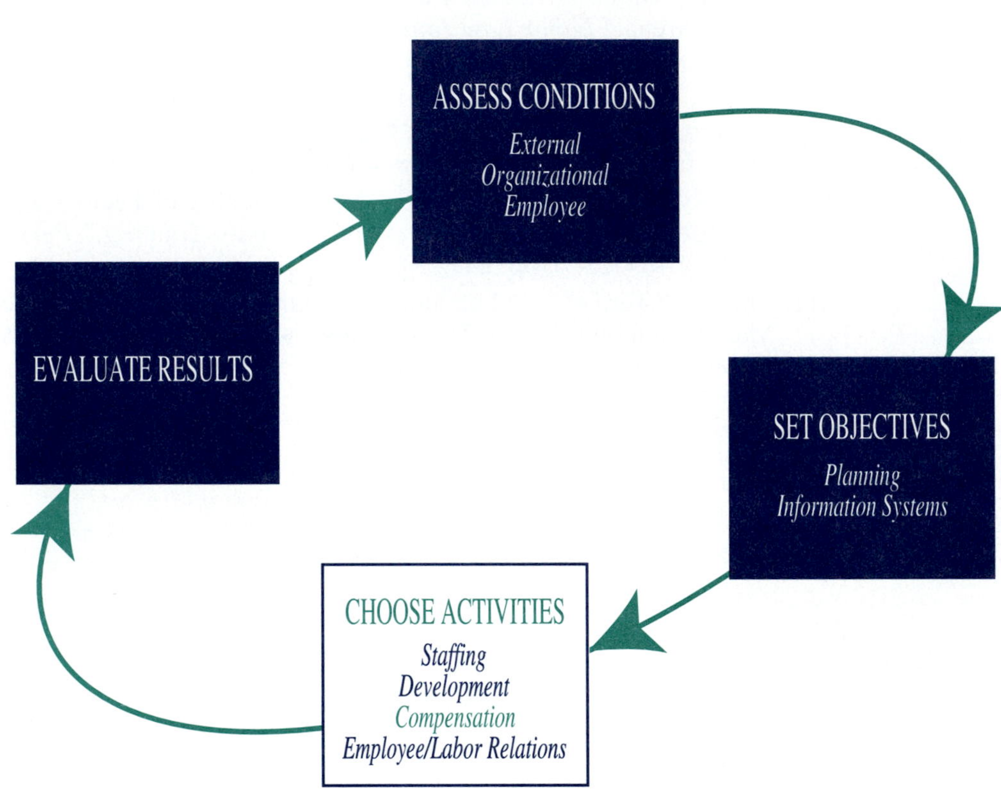
ASSESS CONDITIONS
External
Organizational
Employee
SET OBJECTIVES
Planning
Information Systems
CHOOSE ACTIVITIES
Staffing
Development
Compensation
Employee/Labor Relations
EVALUATE RESULTS

# COMPENSATION

The country's in a bind, but I'm cheerful and I'm chipper,
As I slash employee wages like a fiscal Jack the Ripper,
And I take away their health care and never mind their hollers,
And pay myself a bonus of a couple of million dollars.

Managing compensation is so fascinating that even comedians are getting into the act. Mark Russell's satire on executive pay confirms what everyone suspects: that pay, particularly one's own, is determined without apparent justice or reason.

We are in a period in which traditional approaches to pay are increasingly scrutinized. Managers face economic pressures to improve productivity, boost the quality of products and services, and control labor costs. Social pressures stem from shifting employee expectations and continued government regulations. In light of these pressures, traditional, often bureaucratic, approaches to pay are being reexamined. Different approaches—some new, some simply old goods in new wrappings—are being tried.

Because pay is one of the most important means employers have to attract, retain, and motivate employees, as well as a major cost of doing business, it requires careful management. The three chapters in Part Four explore compensation: Chapters Eleven and Twelve examine the decisions related to cash compensation; benefits decisions is the subject of Chapter Thirteen.

Before turning to these chapters, let's once again place the compensation activities into the diagnostic perspective. As shown in the diagnostic model, compensation may be influenced by external, organizational, and employee conditions. Managers need to assess each of these factors when making pay decisions.

## EXTERNAL INFLUENCES ON PAY

Pay decisions may be affected by the economic conditions facing the firm, the firm's policies and practices, its relations with unions, and the types of people employed. Important external influences include the economy and government regulations.

### Economy: Product and Labor Markets

Although some may believe that people should not be subject to forces of supply and demand, they are. During times of expanding demand for products and services, job opportunities expand and employers are more willing and able to increase pay to attract and retain employees who possess the needed skills and experience.

Increased wages translate into increased costs of production. Organizations usually pass these costs on to consumers in the form of higher prices. This is easier to do if there is strong demand for products. Even public sector employers, such as states or universities, pass on increased labor costs as tax increases or tuition hikes.

Labor market conditions affect pay, also. During periods of shortages of qualified employees, pay tends to increase. In recessions, or when surpluses of qualified employees are available, rates of pay increases are slowed; pay may even decrease.

### Government Regulations

Government policy and regulations influence pay more than any other human resource activity. State and federal laws regulate wage rates (e.g., minimum wages) and hours of work, prevent discrimination, and require certain benefits (e.g., social security, unemployment insurance). Government also competes in the labor market to hire employees. Government tax policy shapes the type of pay offered. Differences in tax policy among countries are reflected in pay differences. For example, Japanese employers do not offer stock options to their top executives in part because there is no tax advantage in doing so. Similarly, employer-provided health insurance in the United States became widespread as an attempt to get around wage and price controls. In many other countries such as the Czech Republic, France, Japan, and Canada, the national government provides health care insurance paid from general income taxes.

### Unions

Although fewer than one in five U.S. workers is a member of a labor union, it would be a mistake to conclude that the impact of unions on pay is minor. Frequently, the threat of becoming unionized encourages managers to improve wages, benefits, and other conditions of employment. In unionized organizations, the union is one of the main players in determining pay. Outside the United States, unions play a much more dominant role in wage setting, particularly in Europe and Asia.

## ORGANIZATION INFLUENCES ON PAY

The old axiom, you get what you pay for, has a flip side: You don't get what you don't pay for. This is the philosophy underlying incentive pay systems.

All pay systems have a purpose. Answer the question, For what do we want to pay? and you will begin to specify the objectives of the pay system. Some objectives are clearly identified; others are implied. Both should support the organization's strategies.

Because pay is only one of the many systems that make up an organization, its design must be partially influenced by how well it fits with the rest of the organization. A highly centralized and confidential pay system, controlled by a few people in a corporate unit, will not operate effectively in a highly decentralized, team-based open organization.

The importance of the fit of pay programs is most clear with other HRM programs. For example, some employers do not maintain significant pay differences between manufacturing workers (such as assemblers or inspectors) and their supervisors. This diminishes the incentive to acquire the training required to be a supervisor or to accept the promotion to supervisor. The situation is reversed for many engineering and research jobs, where the pay for managerial positions induces people to leave engineering and research positions. Pay coexists with other systems in the organization.

## EMPLOYEE CHARACTERISTICS

The simple fact that employees differ is too easily and too often overlooked in designing pay systems. For example, older, highly paid workers may wish to defer taxes by putting their pay into retirement funds, while younger employees may have high cash needs to buy a house, support a family, finance an education, or purchase a Miata. Dual-career couples who are overinsured medically may prefer to use more of their combined pay for child care, automobile insurance, financial counseling, or other benefits

How to motivate productive behaviors and control labor costs while satisfying employees' needs and sense of fair treatment are the objectives of the compensation system.

# The Pay System

Did you brush your teeth this morning? Now that you are older and no longer wonder how they get all that toothpaste into that tiny tube, we offer a new question to engage you while brushing. How do they decide what to pay the people who put that toothpaste there? How do they decide what to pay the driver who delivers the toothpaste from the warehouse to the retailer, the brand manager who worries about shelf space, the accountant who decides what overhead costs to allocate to the toothpaste, the engineer who is working on better ways to get the toothpaste in and out of the tube, the chemist fooling around with new flavors, the global strategist who recommends building a new plant in Tanzania, and the manager of that plant? How is pay for all these different jobs determined?

Compensation is endlessly fascinating because work and the people doing it are so fascinating. Employees may be indifferent to their company's training policy or be completely unaware of retirement benefits, but questions of pay—*my* pay, and more particularly, my pay compared with *your* pay—are of stunning importance. How organizations set pay for different jobs and different people is addressed in the next three chapters.

## MULTIPLE FORMS OF PAY

The stub of your paycheck is so wonderfully useful because it is the endpoint of a host of decisions shaped by our diagnostic model. Look at the check stub in Exhibit 11.1. Once you get over the shock of the size of the deductions for federal and state taxes (external conditions), look at the section labeled current earnings. Hillary Jones worked 87 hours in this time period, but her job is exempt from legislation requiring one and one-half times the base pay per hour when working more than 40 hours per week. Hillary is not yet eligible for profit sharing at Hewlett-Packard, nor is she part of any *incentive* plan that bases pay on production (i.e., printers delivered or revenue targets achieved).

> *Compensation* includes financial returns and tangible services and benefits employees receive as part of an employment relationship.

Move now to the deductions. Hillary's deductions are federal and state income taxes, health insurance, and Social Security. The last two, in addition to retirement and parking, are examples of *benefits* whose costs may be shared between employers and employees. Other benefits can include health programs, tuition subsidies, paid time off, and child care services. If the cost of a service or benefit is paid completely by the employer, no deduction appears on the paycheck. The paycheck shows only some of the variety of forms compensation can take. Employer contributions to Social Security, health care, vacations, sick leave, and the like are excluded.

### Total Compensation versus Total Rewards

Exhibit 11.2 lists the elements in IBM's *total compensation.* IBM does not include promotions, choice office locations, training opportunities, awards that

**EXHIBIT 11.1** Paycheck Stubs Reflect Pay System Decisions

HEWLETT PACKARD
EARNINGS STATEMENT
RETAIN FOR YOUR RECORDS

| EMPLOYEE'S NAME & ADDRESS | EMPLOYEE NO. | LOCATION | SHIFT | BLDG | ISSUE DATE |
|---|---|---|---|---|---|
| Hillary R. Jones | 123456 | 47 | 1 | | 01/06/97 |
| | CHECK | | | | |

| SOCIAL SECURITY NUMBER | MARITAL STATUS | FED EXEMPT. | FED % | FED ADD. $ | STATE EXEMPT. | SPEC. STATE | STATE ADD. $ | CK CNTRL NO |
|---|---|---|---|---|---|---|---|---|
| 474-74-7474 | M | 2 | | | 2 | | | |

(TAX INFORMATION)

| PAY PERIOD FROM | PAY PERIOD THROUGH | PAY RATE MONTHLY | PAY RATE HOURLY | PROFIT SHARING BASE EARNINGS | RETIREMENT BASE EARNINGS |
|---|---|---|---|---|---|
| 12/16/96 | 12/31/96 | 3,140.00 | | | |

DEDUCTIONS

| DESCRIPTION | CURRENT | CUMULATIVE | DESCRIPTION | CURRENT | CUMULATIVE |
|---|---|---|---|---|---|
| FEDWH | 263.00 | 263.00 | | | |
| STWH CA | 27.01 | 27.01 | | | |
| FICA | 118.08 | 118.08 | | | |

CURRENT EARNINGS

| DESCRIPTION | AMOUNT |
|---|---|
| REG 87.00HRS | 1,570.00 |
| TOTAL GROSS | 1,570.00 |

ADJUSTMENTS TO GROSS

| | |
|---|---|
| PRETX MEDINS | -26.50 |

PAID TIME OFF

| | |
|---|---|
| PTO EARNED | 31.33 |
| PTO AVAIL. | 31.33 |
| PTO TAKEN | 24.00 |

YEAR-TO-DATE INFORMATION

| GROSS EARNINGS | TAXCAP DEFERRAL | ADJ. GROSS EARNINGS | INC. NOT SUBJ. TO W/H |
|---|---|---|---|
| 1,570.00 | | 1,543.50 | |
| | PRETX MED 26.50 | | |

| | |
|---|---|
| ADJ. GROSS PAY | 1,543.50 |
| CURRENT DEDUCTIONS | 308.09 |
| NET PAY | $1,235.41 |

recognize outstanding work, or even employment security in its definition of total compensation, even though IBM knows that these elements are important. IBM's *total rewards system* does include these elements and more, such as feelings of accomplishment, self-esteem, friendship, and opportunities for personal growth. Wherever and whenever possible, these elements should be coordinated with compensation, but many of them are not under the organization's control.[1] Psychological factors and work were discussed in greater detail in Chapters Three and Four. Our compensation chapters will look at the items in the exhibit.

## MULTIPLE PAY OBJECTIVES

Pay systems can be designed to achieve a number of objectives, including:

1. Improve productivity and customer satisfaction.
2. Control costs.
3. Treat employees fairly.
4. Comply with laws.
5. Enhance individual and/or team performance.[2]

In Exhibit 11.3, we show Hewlett-Packard's and Astra-Merck's statements of objectives for their pay systems. Both companies' objectives emphasize innovative performance (productivity), competitiveness (controlling costs), and fair treatment for all employees.

## EXHIBIT 11.2 IBM's Total Compensation

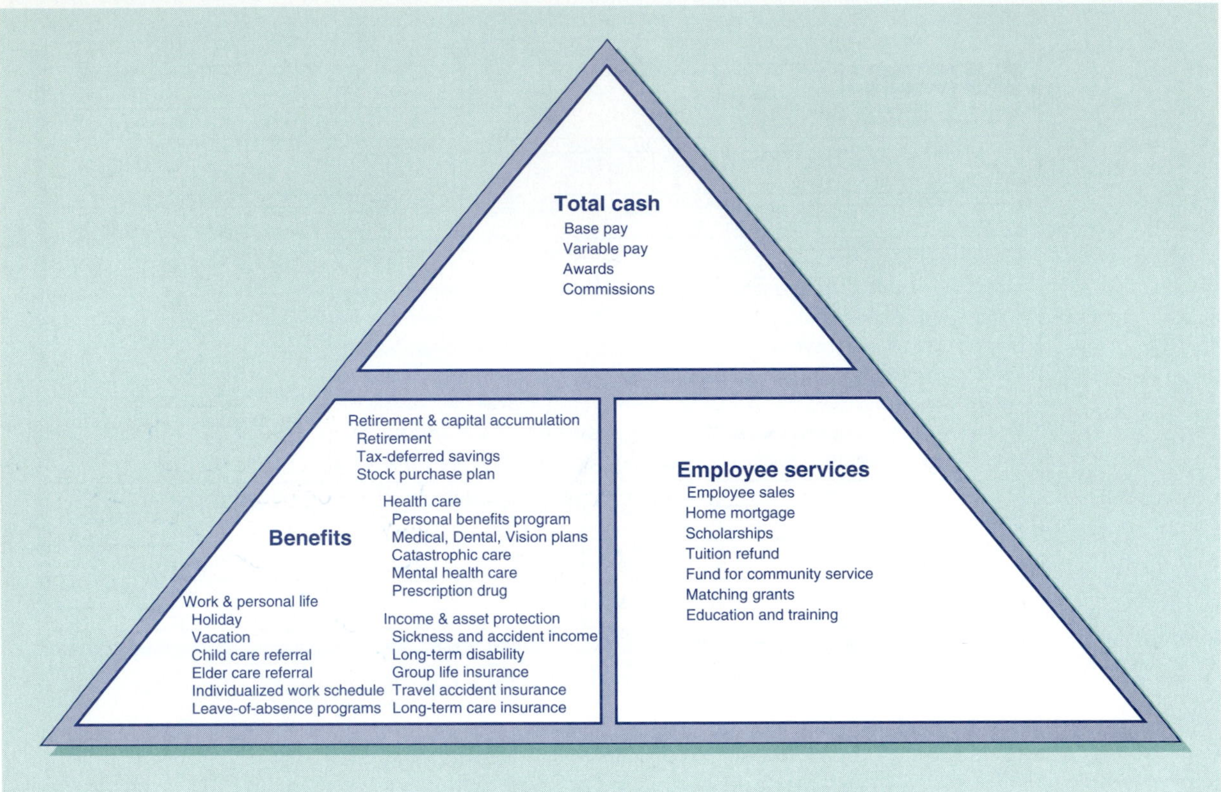


## EXHIBIT 11.3 Comparisons of Pay System Objectives

**Astra-Merck**

- Share commitment and responsibility; foster teamwork
- Balance immediate and strategic interests
- Celebrate performance
- Promote fairness
- Achieve simplicity
- Be market competitive; pay at the 75th percentile of competitors

**Hewlett-Packard**

- Help H-P continue to attract creative and enthusiastic people who contribute to its success
- Pay among the leaders
- Reflect sustained relative contribution of unit, division, and H-P
- Be open and understandable
- Ensure fair treatment
- Be innovative, competitive, and equitable

There are probably as many statements of pay objectives as there are employers. The multiple objectives are the reason for the complexity of many pay plans. Unfortunately, sometimes plans get so complex that neither employees nor managers understand how they work, much less why certain conventions persist. Instead of helping achieve objectives, these systems build fences. Instead of directing employee behavior toward organization purposes, the pay system engenders feelings of inequity among employees and hinders productivity.

Objectives serve several purposes. First, they guide the design of the pay system. Consider the employer whose objective is to reward outstanding performance. That objective determines the pay policy (e.g., pay for performance) as well as the elements of pay plans (e.g., merit and/or incentives). Another employer may emphasize a flexible, continuously learning workforce. This employer's pay system may base pay increases on increased skills or knowledge. Different objectives guide the design of different pay systems.

Objectives also serve as the standards against which the success of the pay system is evaluated. If the objective is to attract and retain a highly competent staff, yet skilled employees are leaving to take higher paying jobs at other employers, the system may not be performing effectively. If you and all of your classmates have signed up with MCI, then AT&T's pay system may need another look.

EXPLORING THE WEB

If you are thinking of moving out of town when you get your next job, check the relocation salary calculator that is part of the relocation information on the Homebuyer's Fair homepage at

**http://www.homefair.com**

Just enter your salary, current city, and potential new city to see if the salary offered will meet your needs based on cost-of-living differences.

# PAY POLICY DECISIONS

In an effective compensation system, pay policies are chosen to help achieve the objectives of the pay system. The policies form the building blocks, the foundation on which the pay system is designed. Exhibit 11.4 demonstrates the relationship between objectives, policies, and techniques. The four basic pay policies include external competitiveness, internal alignment employee contributions, and implementation.

## External Competitiveness: Comparisons among Organizations

*External competitiveness* refers to the pay relationships among organizations. The heart of the concept of external competitiveness is its relative nature: comparisons with other employers.

How much do other employers pay accountants, and how much do we wish to pay accountants in comparison to what other employers pay? Some set pay levels higher than their competition, hoping to attract the best accountants. Of course, this assumes that someone is able to identify and hire the "best" from the pool of applicants. Another employer may offer lower base pay but greater potential bonuses, better benefits, or more flexible working hours than those offered by others.

External competitiveness has a twofold effect on objectives. First, pay rates must be high enough to attract and retain employees. If employees do not see their pay as *equitable* in comparison with what other organizations pay for similar work, they are likely to leave.[3] Second, because labor costs make up a substantial percentage of an organization's total labor costs; they directly affect the price the organization must charge for goods and services.[4] Labor costs must be set at a level that permits the organization to maximize its efficiency

**EXHIBIT 11.4** Pay Objectives are Achieved through Four Pay Policies

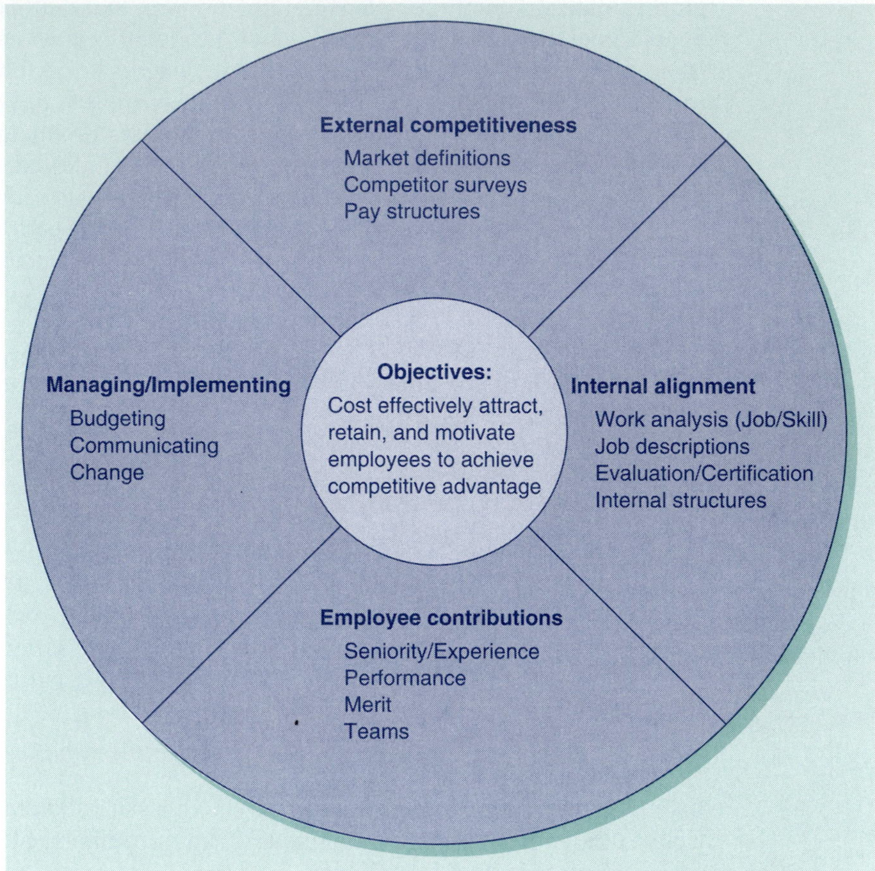


in producing goods and services. Hewlett-Packard refers to external competitiveness in its objectives when it says it wants to "Pay among the leaders." Astra-Merck's policy is to "pay at the 75th percentile of competitors."

## Internal Alignment: Comparisons within an Organization

*Internal alignment* refers to comparisons among jobs or skill levels inside a single organization.

Alignment may be based on the work content, the skills and/or competencies required to do it, or some combination. The focus is on comparisons based on relative contribution of the work to the organization's overall objectives. Internal alignment is a consideration in determining pay rates for employees in both similar jobs and dissimilar jobs. The emphasis is on the work, not the individual doing it. To understand the distinction, imagine someone with a college degree driving a taxi. No matter how well the person drives, nor how enlightening the conversation on the way to the airport, the pay for driving the taxi is the same whether the driver has a PhD or can read

nothing beyond road signs. The fare is based on the work—providing transportation—not the person doing it.

Managers have several policy options that address internal relationships. They can opt for many (or few) levels of work (e.g., a machinist I, electronics specialist I, laboratory assistant I, all with different pay, or opt for a single job titled technical assistant); managers can set larger (or smaller) differences in pay rates among the various jobs. Hewlett-Packard is addressing internal consistency when it seeks to "reflect sustained *relative contribution* of unit, division, and H-P." Astra-Merck wants to "foster teamwork."

## Employee Contributions

*Employee contributions* refers to the relative emphasis placed on the performance and/or seniority of people doing the same job or possessing the same skills: comparisons among employees.

Should all employees receive the same pay? Or should one programmer be paid differently from another if one has better performance and/or greater seniority? Should a more productive team of employees be paid more than less-productive teams? The emphasis given to performance and/or seniority directly affects employee attitudes and work behaviors, which affect all of the compensation objectives. Hewlett-Packard addresses performance with its objective of attracting "creative and enthusiastic people who contribute." Astra-Merck's objective is to "celebrate performance."

Both internal alignment and employee contributions are judged according to organization objectives. The first looks at the contribution of the work itself, without regard to the person doing it. The second looks at the performance of the people doing the work. To return to our PhD taxi driver, every person driving the taxi gets paid the same hourly rate. However, the driver also gets to keep a percentage of fares. Therefore, the incentive plan is based on performance, but the hourly rate is based on the job.

## Implementation

While it is possible to design a system that is externally competitive, that aligns jobs internally with each other and with organization objectives, and that recognizes employee contributions, the system will not achieve its objectives unless it is properly implemented. The greatest design in the world is useless without competent implementation and administration. Determining the costs of the system, judging whether it is achieving its objectives, surveying how employees feel about their pay, and communicating the system to employees are all as important as the initial design. Hewlett-Packard's objectives include a plan that is "open and understandable." Astra-Merck hopes to "achieve simplicity."

## Balancing Policy Decisions

The multiple objectives and policy options available explain a great deal of the variety in compensation systems. Does it ever make sense to emphasize one policy over another? For example, many firms match outside offers employees receive from competing employers (an external competitiveness issue). These offers may be outside the range recommended by the pay system and, therefore, inconsistent with the policy on internal alignment. Matching the outside offer means paying more than is warranted based on the job's contributions to the organization's objectives or the employee's performance. Ignoring internal alignment and employee contributions may increase dissatisfaction and vulnerability to lawsuits. If the person next to you is doing the same job but is paid more than you are, there had better be a good reason for this differential. But ignoring the outside offer may mean the loss of key employees. Balancing policies is a key part of managing compensation.

As our model of the pay system shows, pay techniques translate policy into compensation decisions. The rest of this chapter addresses the first two policies shown in the model: external competitiveness and internal alignment. The last two policies, employee contributions and implementation, are saved for Chapter Twelve.

## EXTERNAL COMPETITIVENESS

External competitiveness focuses on three key issues:

- Measuring the market (what competitors are paying).
- Setting a pay level relative to competitors that reflects external competitiveness policy.
- Implementing programs to achieve that targeted pay level.

> *Pay level* refers to the average of the array of rates paid by an employer.

Pay level may be called the average of all the averages. It may refer to the average for a job family (e.g., clerical support) or the entire company. The employer's pay level decisions translate policy on external competitiveness into practice. These decisions focus on two objectives: (1) attracting and retaining employees, and (2) controlling labor costs.

**Attract and retain employees** Although pay level is a primary determinant of external competitiveness, other factors such as benefits, career opportunities, and/or the financial stability may also influence how attractive an organization appears to potential and current employees.[5]

**Labor costs** Exhibit 11.5 shows how pay level affects labor costs. Other things being equal, the higher the pay level, the higher the labor costs. Furthermore, the higher the pay level relative to the pay level of competitors, the greater the relative costs to produce similar products or provide similar services.

### Measure the Market

Organizations find out what other employers are paying through wage surveys.[6] Exhibit 11.6 is an example of the kind of information gleaned in a wage survey. It shows the results of a survey done to determine pay for word processors in Dallas.

EXHIBIT 11.5 Calculating Labor Costs

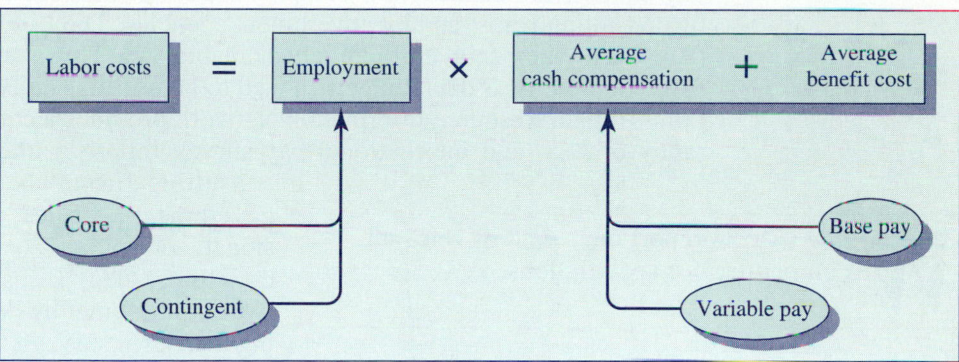


EXHIBIT 11.6 Salary Survey Results

Date: January 1

**Word Processing Operator, Lead**

**Duties**

Assumes responsibility for directing work flow through the word processing center and provides administrative support to principals to improve overall productivity. Uses word processor to type high priority and confidential work.

High school graduate or equivalent, plus three years of processing (diskette) experience required.

| Company Code | Minimum Rate | Mid Rate | Maximum Rate | Average Rate | Employee Population |
|---|---|---|---|---|---|
| D | $9.34 | $10.88 | $12.40 | $10.53 | 1 |
| Y | 8.23 | 9.69 | 11.14 | 10.53 | 1 |
| E | 8.53 | 10.07 | 11.60 | 10.17 | 3 |
| Y | 8.71 | 10.14 | 11.56 | 10.01 | 1 |
| B | 7.66 | 9.59 | 11.49 | 9.37 | 2 |
| N | 7.69 | 9.62 | 11.55 | 9.37 | 14 |
| W | 6.68 | 10.07 | 11.51 | 9.05 | 1 |
| X | 7.72 | 9.07 | 10.89 | 9.02 | 12 |
| O | 6.19 | 8.05 | 9.90 | 8.57 | 2 |
| Q | 7.22 | 8.63 | 11.46 | 8.49 | 3 |
| M | 6.38 | 7.99 | 9.59 | 8.29 | 2 |
| G | 6.14 | 7.59 | 9.05 | 8.24 | 1 |
| R | 6.94 | 8.55 | 10.14 | 8.24 | 3 |

Source: Dallas Area Electronics Survey. Survey sponsors: Recognition Equipment. Rockwell International, Collins Radio Group, and Texas Instruments, Inc.

## Conducting a Survey

Pay surveys are conducted by employers, either individually or in associations; by consulting firms; and by government agencies. The Bureau of Labor Statistics (BLS) is a major source of publicly available data. However, many private sector firms find the BLS data too generalized to be useful. The Bureau of National Affairs' Human Resource Information Network provides a computer-based bibliography of U.S. and international pay survey reports gathered from publishers, consulting firms, chambers of commerce, government agencies, and technical, professional, and trade associations. In spite of all these data, many firms still find their objectives are best met by designing and conducting their own surveys.[7]

> *Wage surveys* report rates paid by relevant competitors for specific jobs.

How are these surveys done? A personal interview develops the most accurate responses, but is also the most expensive method. Mailed questionnaires are probably the most frequently used because this method is cheapest. The jobs being surveyed by mail must be clearly defined, or the data may be suspect. Telephone inquiries can be used to follow up the mailed questionnaires or to gather additional data.

### Relevant Market

The companies involved in the survey in Exhibit 11.6—Recognition Equipment, Rockwell International, Collins Radio Group, and Texas Instruments—are all similar in size, industry, and geographic location. This grouping of companies makes up the relevant labor market for this survey. Not all employers of word processors in the Dallas area are included—only those who compete to hire the same kinds of employees within an area.

A relevant market will vary with the job being surveyed. For example, this same group of employers probably uses regional or even national market data for wages for engineers. Exhibit 11.7 shows how job qualifications interact with geography to define the relevant labor market.

### Key Jobs

A brief description of the job being surveyed helps survey users decide if the tasks and responsibilities of the internal job match the survey job. In practice, employers do not seek market data for all jobs; only selected jobs, called *key* or *benchmark* jobs, are included in the survey. Key jobs have the following characteristics:

- The work content is relatively stable over time.
- A large number of employees hold them.
- They are common across a number of different employers.
- They are free of discriminatory employment patterns.
- They are not subject to recent shortages or surpluses in the marketplace.

Examples of key jobs may include data entry clerks, word processors, design engineers, project engineers, compensation analysts, or even human resource managers.

### Survey Results

To provide a sense of the distribution of rates paid for the job by each firm, the survey collects a number of salary measures. Data are not identified by

**EXHIBIT 11.7** Relevant Labor Markets by Geographic and Employee Groups

| | Employee Groups/Occupations | | | | | |
|---|---|---|---|---|---|---|
| **Geographic Scope** | **Production** | **Office and Clerical** | **Technicians** | **Scientists and Engineers** | **Managerial Professional** | **Executive** |
| *Local:* within relatively small areas, such as cities or MSAs (Metropolitan Statistical Areas; e.g., Dallas metropolitan area) | Most likely | Most likely | Most likely | — | — | — |
| *Regional:* within a particular area of the state or county or several states (e.g., Greater Boston area) | Only if in short supply or critical | Only if in short supply or critical | Most likely | Likely | Likely | — |
| *National:* across the country | — | — | — | Most likely | Most likely | Most likely |
| *International:* across several countries | — | — | — | Only for critical skills or those in very short supply | Only for critical skills or those in very short supply | Likely |

Source: George T. Milkovich and Jerry Newman, *Compensation,* 5th ed. (Homewood, IL: Richard D. Irwin, 1996).

company name. Identifying data by companies violates confidentiality and risks violating U.S. antitrust law.[8]

Exhibit 11.6 shows that there is no single "going rate" in Dallas for word processors. Instead, the rates paid by these firms vary from $6.14 to $12.40 an hour. These variations may be attributable to differences in seniority or experience among employees; they may also reflect different pay policies among employers.

The results gained from a survey are a distribution of rates paid by competitors for similar jobs. In Exhibit 11.8, we show the distribution of average rates for the word processing operator. The distribution summarizes the data from Exhibit 11.6 and allows survey users to make comparisons between what their organizations are paying for this single job and market rates—what competitors are paying.

However, a survey rarely focuses on a single job. Instead, data are gathered for any number of different jobs, which may be related (e.g., computer programmers, computer operators, and software engineers) or may cover a broader range of work. If the purpose of the survey is to set pay rates for a number of jobs with respect to the market, a way is needed to combine data from all the surveyed jobs. A market pay line does this by summarizing the rates of the various jobs found in the market.

A market pay line In Exhibit 11.9, the distributions of rates for four key jobs have been rotated and combined in a single graph. Drawing a line that connects the frequency distributions reveals a market pay line. Such a line may be drawn

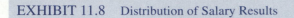

## EXHIBIT 11.8 Distribution of Salary Results

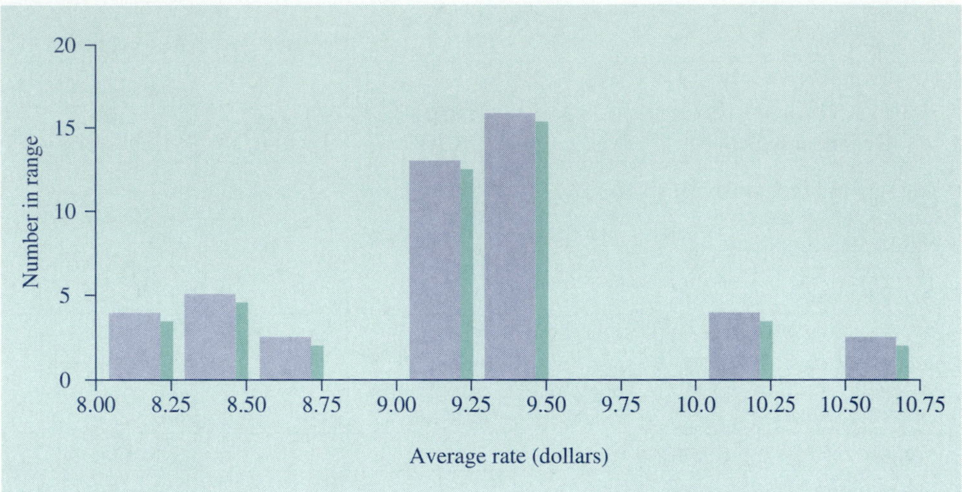


## EXHIBIT 11.9 Constructing a Market Pay Line

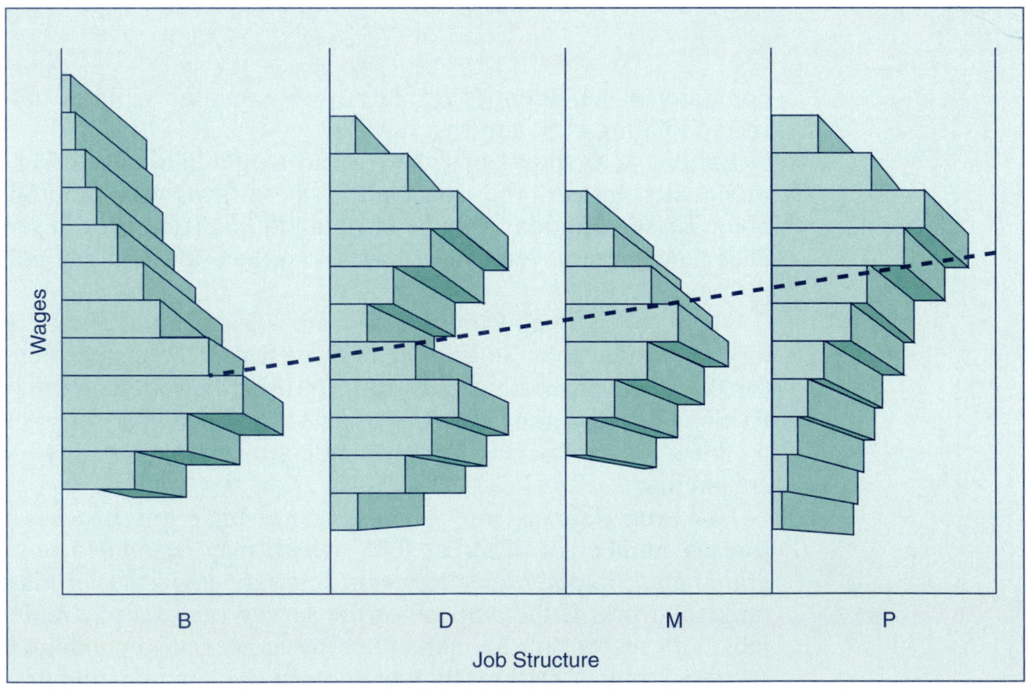

in a number of ways: (1) all the distribution midpoints can be connected, (2) a straight line may be drawn, even though the midpoints for some jobs may not fall on this line, or (3) regression analysis can be used to make a statistically more accurate line.

The market line summarizes the survey data and reveals what competitors are paying for similar positions. Whether an employer sets pay rates equal to, above, or below the market line is a function of the employer's pay level policy.[9]

## What Pay Level to Set?

Decisions about external competitiveness directly affect the organization's total expenses. Other things being equal, the higher the pay level, the higher the labor costs. Furthermore, the higher the pay relative to what competitors pay, the greater the relative costs to produce similar products. Therefore, it would seem that the obvious conclusion is to set the minimum pay as low as possible.

However, other things are rarely equal. For example, high pay may make it easier to attract and retain a qualified workforce. High-wage employers should not have to train or recruit as extensively as low-paying ones. Yet, evidence suggests that high-wage employers also expend greater efforts on recruiting. This dichotomy is explained by the greater selectivity in hiring that is made possible by the larger number of applicants attracted by the high wages.[10] If better applicants are hired, greater productivity may offset the higher labor costs per employee. So, a decision to set a high pay level can also be justified. In fact, employers often set different pay levels to meet different objectives for different groups of jobs.

There are three pure alternatives in setting a pay level—to set pay so it (1) leads competition, (2) matches competition, or (3) falls below what others are paying. Evidence suggests that the most common policy is to match what is paid by competition.[11] What difference does the pay level make? The potential effects are shown in Exhibit 11.10.

**Match competition** Matching organizations try to ensure that their wage rates are approximately equal to those of competitors. Equal wage rates place competing employers on an equal footing in their ability to attract and maintain a qualified workforce.

**Lead** Employers who offer higher pay rates than their competitors maximize their ability to attract and retain quality employees and minimize employee dissatisfaction with pay. The idea is that higher pay increases the number of applicants and permits the selection process to skim the cream of the applicants.

### WHAT DO YOU THINK?

Every year the Business Placement Office at Indiana University collects average starting salary data for its graduates. In 1996, it reported the following data, by business school major:

|  |  |
|---|---|
| Accounting: | $30,481 |
| Computer information systems | $34,149 |
| Finance | $31,131 |
| Management | $27,212 |
| Marketing | $28,905 |

How do these salaries compare to those at your school? What might account for any difference? Is the ranking by specialty the same at your school?

EXHIBIT 11.10 Probable Relationships between Pay Level Policies and Objectives

| | Compensation Objectives | | | | |
|---|---|---|---|---|---|
| **Policy** | **Ability to Attract** | **Ability to Retain** | **Contain Labor Costs** | **Reduce Pay Dissatisfaction** | **Increase Productivity** |
| Pay above market (lead) | + | + | ? | + | ? |
| Pay with market (match) | = | = | = | = | ? |
| Pay below market (lag) | − | ? | + | − | ? |

Source: George T. Milkovich and Jerry M. Newman, *Compensation,* 5th ed. (Homewood, Ill.: Richard D. Irwin, 1996).

Lag Letting pay rates fall below competitors' rates may hinder an employer's ability to attract or retain employees. However, the opportunity to work overtime, to secure promotions and avoid layoffs, or to be part of a friendly work environment may offset lower pay rates for many potential employees.

## Translating Pay Level Policy into Practice

If an organization's pay level policy is to match competition, this policy can be translated into practice by projecting market rates forward to the middle of the next budget period and then paying those rates at the start of the next budget period. For example, look back at Exhibit 11.6, the Dallas word processor survey data. The survey report told us that these were the wage rates in effect last January 1. But the organization's adjusted rates will not go into effect until next January 1, at which time the survey data will be a year old. If market rates are increasing steadily by 5 percent a year, survey data are simply adjusted upward by 5 percent to represent the rates *next* January 1 (see Exhibit 11.11).

When an organization adjusts salaries next January 1 to *match* projected rates for that date, the organization's pay matches the market only on January 1. After that, the market rates continue to rise, but unless the organization continues to increase its rates, its pay will begin to *lag* the market, rather than match it. Most organizations get around this dilemma by projecting survey rates forward an additional six months; that is, by an additional 2 percent, then matching these adjusted rates on January 1. With this technique, an organization actually leads the market for the first six months, matches the market at mid-year, then lags the market for six months.

For a *lead* pay policy, the market line may simply be redrawn higher, the rates may be multiplied by some constant, or the frequency distributions may be connected at the 75th or the 90th percentile. How closely the organization's actual pay corresponds to its specified pay policy depends on the techniques used.[12] Once pay level has been determined, we turn to the second policy in the pay model, internal alignment.

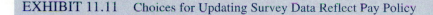

**EXHIBIT 11.11** Choices for Updating Survey Data Reflect Pay Policy

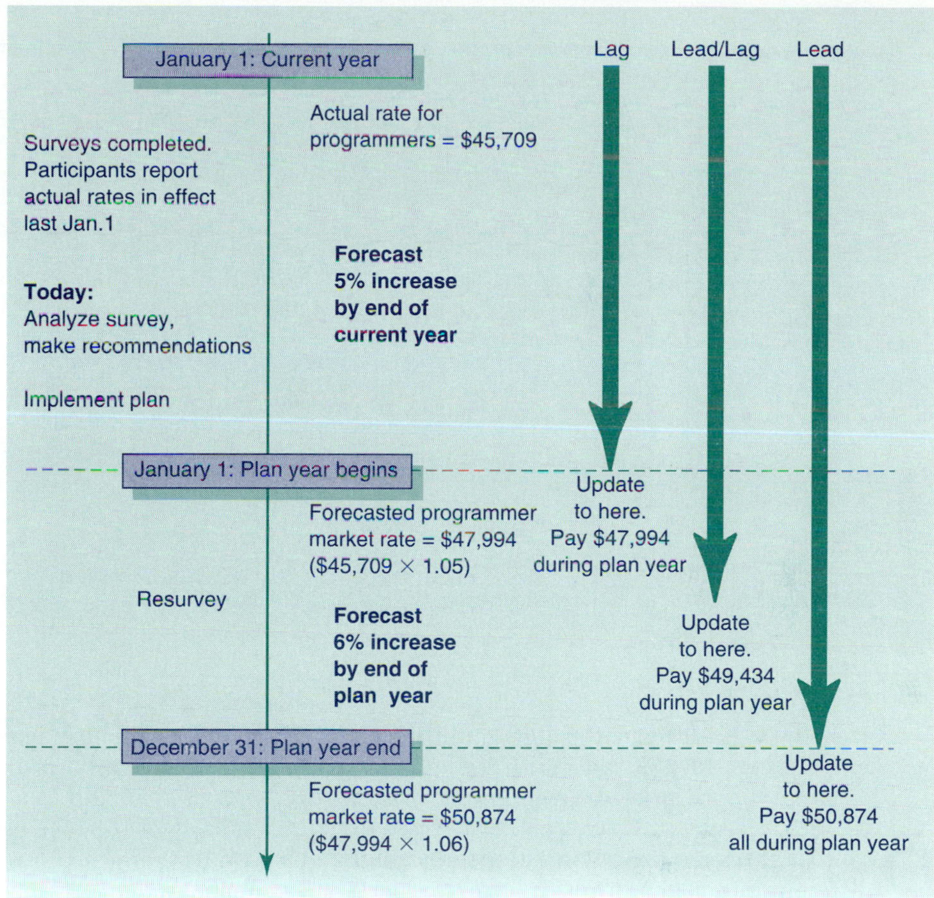


## INTERNAL ALIGNMENT

Internal alignment focuses on similarities and differences among jobs within a single organization, and the relative contribution of the jobs to organization objectives. The similarities and differences form an internal structure of work relationships. Key decisions include:

1. Whether to use egalitarian or hierarchical structures.
2. Whether to base the structure on jobs, skills, competencies, or the market.
3. How to meld the internal structure with external pay data.

In Chapter Three, we defined job analysis as the systematic process of collecting data and making judgments about the nature of jobs. The end result of job analysis is job descriptions that permit judgments about the jobs' relative complexity, difficulty, responsibility, or worth. The criteria for judgment can vary among organizations. The result of these judgments is a job structure.

Exhibit 11.12 depicts four hypothetical job structures within a single organization. Organizations commonly have multiple structures that may be

EXHIBIT 11.12 Resulting Internal Structures—Job, Skill, and Competency Based

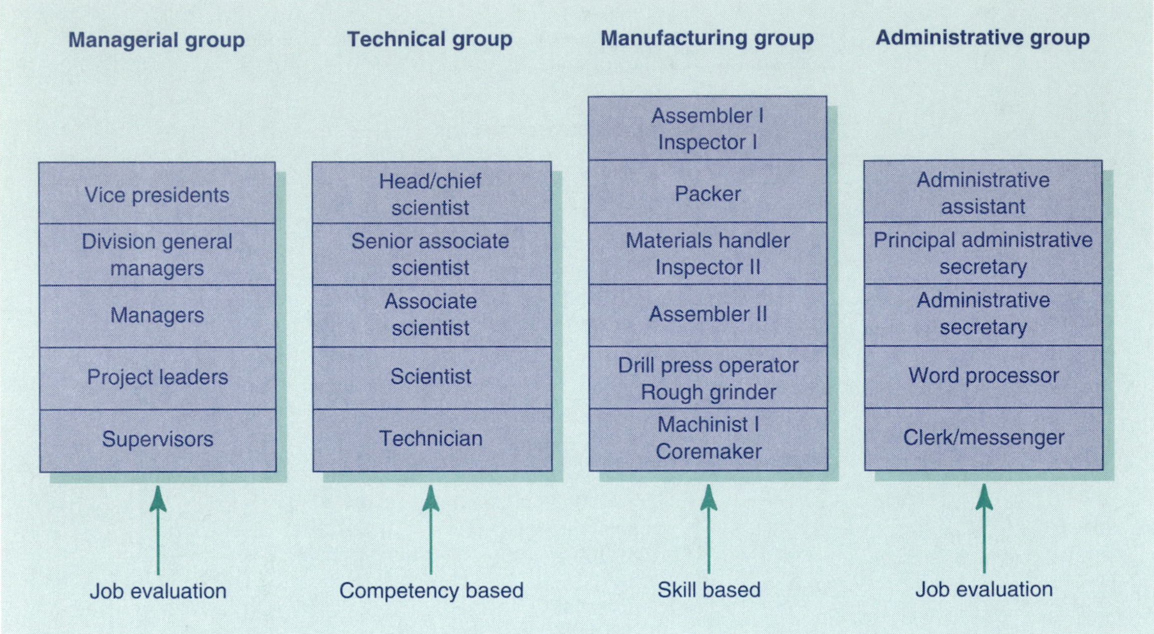


derived through multiple approaches and evaluated against multiple criteria. When pay rates are attached to the different levels in the structures, they become pay structures.

> *Pay structures* are the pay relationships among different jobs within a single organization.

One key issue is the size of the pay differentials among jobs. Pay structures are considered internally equitable if they pay more for doing jobs that (1) require greater knowledge or skill to perform, (2) are performed under less desirable conditions, and/or (3) make a greater contribution to the organization.

These pay differentials may influence employee decisions to stay or leave the organization or to invest in additional training for promotions and new assignments. Employee satisfaction or dissatisfaction can be affected if pay differences are too small or too large. Achieving an equitable pay structure is an important part of compensation.

## Egalitarian versus Hierarchical Structures

Imagine that your family has encouraged you to open an ice-cream shop to sell the delicious vanilla ice cream that you make so well along with a few other flavors. You will hire employees to churn, freeze, and pack the ice cream and deliver it to your shop where other employees will scoop it out, embellish it, and serve it to hordes of customers. Congratulations! You are now so successful that you need to hire an accountant and a financial planner, as well as plant managers and shop managers, so that you will be free to manage human resources, which is, after all, a lot more fun.

How will you structure your organization? Egalitarian structures have fewer levels and smaller pay differentials between adjacent levels and between the highest-paid (you) and lowest-paid workers. Maybe two levels will be sufficient: you, and everyone else. Hierarchical structures have more levels and greater differentials. Perhaps there is a senior management level, management level, supervisory level, and so forth.

All pay structures contain some degree of hierarchy, but some have more than others.[13] An egalitarian structure implies that minimizing differentials will improve employee satisfaction, aid team unity, and affect worker performance positively, all of which will lead to greater competitive advantage. A hierarchical structure implies that differentials are an important part of recognizing more knowledgeable employees who perform more responsible jobs. Failure to reward their greater contribution will cause them to quit, which will lessen competitive advantage. Thus, a case can be made for either egalitarian or hierarchical structures.

In the United States, the differentials between CEOs and operatives (unskilled and low-skilled manual workers) is 35 to 1, the highest among industrialized countries. In Japan, the differential is only 15 to 1. Many people believe that the U.S. differentials are excessive and reflect unfair treatment of employees.[14]

Egalitarian structures often result from reengineering efforts, where organization designers try to take out layers of management and give that authority and responsibility to lower-level employees.[15] But egalitarian structures can cause problems, too. For example, Ben and Jerry's Homemade, a purveyor of premium ice cream, maintains a spread of only seven to one between its highest-paid and lowest-paid employees. (When the company started, the spread was only five to one.) The relatively narrow range reflects company philosophy that the prosperity of its production workers and its management should be closely linked. But it also hurts the company's ability to recruit. When Ben and Jerry's could not find a qualified chief financial officer for what it was willing to pay, it decided instead to hire an accounting manager and provide backup support from a consultant two days a month. Similarly, when the company needed a new CEO to replace one of the original partners, it invited customers nationwide to write in saying why they would like to be CEO. However, the actual hiring was done with the assistance of a professional executive placement service. The CEO's salary was not within the seven-to-one ratio. While Ben and Jerry's reaped a lot of favorable publicity for its pay philosophy, neither of the original partners was eager to publicize the lucrative stock arrangements which put their own returns well beyond the seven-to-one ratio.

How egalitarian or hierarchical should pay structures be? Neither theory nor research yet provide much help in defining the ideal structure. The answer probably lies in how the work is organized. As we discussed in Chapter Three, it can be organized around teams or individual performers. The pay structure should support the underlying organization structure. Every single layer in the structure ought to add value. If it doesn't, it should be cut.

**Structures based on jobs, skills, competencies, and markets** An internal structure can be based on job content, the skills or competencies demonstrated by employees, or simply reflect the market. Job-based structures are the most common. A job-based structure uses job evaluation to compare the similarities and differences in the content and value of jobs.

## Designing a Job-Based Structure: Job Evaluation

*Job evaluation* systematically assesses jobs as a basis for deciding pay. It includes assessing job duties and responsibilities, the skills required to perform jobs, and the relative contribution of each job to the organization's objectives.

Job evaluation has been criticized as cumbersome and time consuming.[16] Why bother with it? Because it aids in establishing a pay structure based on the work performed and because it is internally equitable to employees and consistent with the goals of the organization. Hence, managers can explain differences in pay (for different work) to employees on a work-related basis. The job of manager of accounting is paid higher than the job of accountant because of the responsibilities and skills required, as well as the jobs' relative contributions to the success of the organization.

Three basic job evaluation methods are in common use: ranking, classification, and point method.

**Ranking** Ranking simply orders the job descriptions from highest to lowest based on some definition of relative value or contribution to the organization's success. Ranking is the simplest, fastest, easiest to understand, and least expensive job evaluation method. However, ranking is seldom the recommended approach. The criteria on which jobs are ranked are usually so crudely defined that the results are subjective opinions, difficult to explain or justify. Furthermore, ranking requires familiarity with every single job under study. In larger, changing organizations, this becomes a formidable task. Because its results are difficult to explain and defend, costly solutions are often required to overcome problems that the ranking method creates.

**Classification** Classification slots job descriptions into a series of classes or grades covering the range of jobs in the organization. The method is similar to labeling all the shelves of your bookcase, and then sorting books according to those labels.

Exhibit 11.13 contains some class descriptions used in manufacturing. The classification method is widely used in the public sector and for managerial and engineering/scientific jobs in the private sector. In practice, the most troublesome feature of the classification method is the need to describe each class properly. The description must be general enough to cause little difficulty in slotting jobs, yet capture sufficient detail to have meaning.

## Point Methods: The Most Common Job Evaluation Method

Point methods have three common features:

1. Compensable factors.
2. Numerically scaled factor degrees.
3. Weights reflecting the importance of each factor.

### Compensable Factors

Compensable factors are valued by the organization because they help the organization achieve its objectives. Common factors include skills, effort, responsibility, and working conditions. Typically, a committee chooses compensable factors based on what is judged to be important in the work. The appendix to

**EXHIBIT 11.13** Definitions and Benchmarks for Use with the Classification Job Evaluation Method

**CLASS IV**

**Definition of Class IV Jobs**

Ability to perform work of a skilled or specialized nature. Must have the mechanical ability to set up, repair, overhaul, and maintain machinery and mechanical equipment without being subject to further check. Must have ability to read blueprints, material specifications, and the use of basic shop mathematics or comparable experience with the company layout to offset these requirements.

Work may be specialized or of a nonmechanical nature, requiring the ability to plan and perform work where only general operations methods are available. Requires the making of decisions involving the use of considerable ingenuity, initiative, and judgment. Work under limited supervision.

**Benchmark Jobs Class IV**

Skilled machinist, packaging supervisor, skilled electrician, skilled mechanic, shipping supervisor.

**CLASS V**

**Definition of Class V Jobs**

Ability to perform work of the highest level in a trade or craft. This skill may be recognized with a license or other certification after formal apprenticeship training; or, after a considerable period of formal on-the-job training, by demonstrated competence to perform equivalent level of skill.

Other employees to be considered for classification into class V must regularly supervise others in the technical and other aspects of the work, perform other supervisory functions and may, in addition, perform work of a nonsupervisory nature.

**Benchmark Jobs Class V**

Master electrician, factory supervisor, master (chief) mechanic, maintenance planner, power plant—chief engineer.

A *compensable factor* is a work-related job attribute of value to the organization that provides a basis for comparing relative worth.

this chapter includes a point plan for manufacturing jobs. The eight compensable factors used are basic knowledge, electronic skills, mechanical skills, graphics, mathematical skills, communication, safety, and decision making.

## Choose Compensable Factors

Compensable factors flow from the work itself and the strategic direction of the business. To select factors, an organization asks itself (typically in a committee drawn from different levels in the organization), What is it about the work that adds value?

One company chose "decision making" as a compensable factor. As shown in Exhibit 11.14, it defines decision making according to three dimensions: (1) the risk and complexity (hence, the availability of guidelines to assist in making the decision), (2) the impact of the decisions, and (3) the time that must pass before the impact is evident. In effect, this firm decided that its competitive advantage

## EXHIBIT 11.14 Example of a Compensable Factor Definition: Decision Making

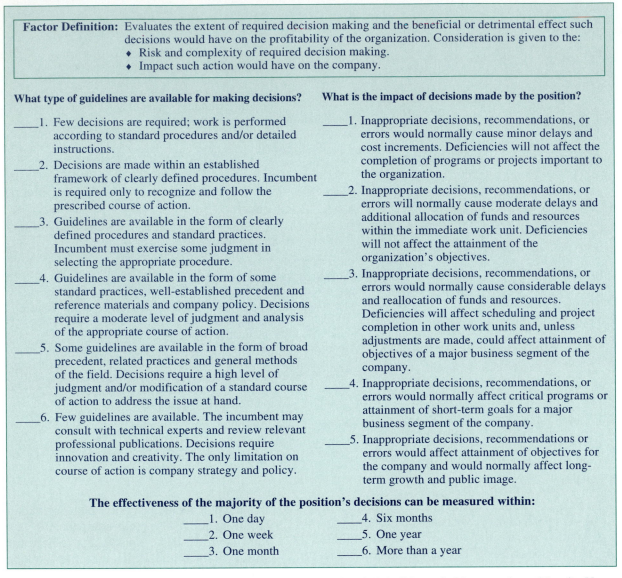

**Factor Definition:** Evaluates the extent of required decision making and the beneficial or detrimental effect such decisions would have on the profitability of the organization. Consideration is given to the:

- Risk and complexity of required decision making.
- Impact such action would have on the company.

**What type of guidelines are available for making decisions?**

____1. Few decisions are required; work is performed according to standard procedures and/or detailed instructions.

____2. Decisions are made within an established framework of clearly defined procedures. Incumbent is required only to recognize and follow the prescribed course of action.

____3. Guidelines are available in the form of clearly defined procedures and standard practices. Incumbent must exercise some judgment in selecting the appropriate procedure.

____4. Guidelines are available in the form of some standard practices, well-established precedent and reference materials and company policy. Decisions require a moderate level of judgment and analysis of the appropriate course of action.

____5. Some guidelines are available in the form of broad precedent, related practices and general methods of the field. Decisions require a high level of judgment and/or modification of a standard course of action to address the issue at hand.

____6. Few guidelines are available. The incumbent may consult with technical experts and review relevant professional publications. Decisions require innovation and creativity. The only limitation on course of action is company strategy and policy.

**What is the impact of decisions made by the position?**

____1. Inappropriate decisions, recommendations, or errors would normally cause minor delays and cost increments. Deficiencies will not affect the completion of programs or projects important to the organization.

____2. Inappropriate decisions, recommendations, or errors will normally cause moderate delays and additional allocation of funds and resources within the immediate work unit. Deficiencies will not affect the attainment of the organization's objectives.

____3. Inappropriate decisions, recommendations, or errors would normally cause considerable delays and reallocation of funds and resources. Deficiencies will affect scheduling and project completion in other work units and, unless adjustments are made, could affect attainment of objectives of a major business segment of the company.

____4. Inappropriate decisions, recommendations, or errors would normally affect critical programs or attainment of short-term goals for a major business segment of the company.

____5. Inappropriate decisions, recommendations or errors would affect attainment of objectives for the company and would normally affect long-term growth and public image.

**The effectiveness of the majority of the position's decisions can be measured within:**

____1. One day
____2. One week
____3. One month
____4. Six months
____5. One year
____6. More than a year

Source: Jill Kanin-Lovers, "The Role of Computers in Job Evaluations: A Case in Point," *Journal of Compensation and Benefits* (New York: Warren Gorham and Lamont, 1985).

depends on the decisions employees make in their work. And the relative value of those decisions depends on their risk, their complexity, and their impact on the company. Jobs that require riskier decisions with greater impact have a higher relative worth than jobs that require fewer decisions of relatively little consequence. To be useful, compensable factors should be:

1. Based on the work performed.
2. Based on the strategy and values of the organization.
3. Acceptable to those affected by the resulting pay structure.

### Numerically Scaled Factors

Scaling allows judgments of how much of a factor (degrees) is present in a job. Different degrees of each factor are defined, and examples of each degree are included. For example, in the job evaluation plan in the appendix, "Ability to read, write, and add and subtract basic mathematics" is the first degree of the basic knowledge factor. A job that required "extensive specific skills training in a specialized field" would have four degrees of basic knowledge, as defined in this plan.

### Factor Weights

The weight of a factor corresponds to the factor's importance. Suppose that a plan uses these four factors: skills, effort, responsibility, and working conditions. The compensation committee members first decide the number of points they plan to use in their plan, say 1,500, and then they allocate those points according to each factor's importance. If skills, for example, is weighted 40 percent in a 1,500-point plan, then a total of 600 points is available to be assigned to different degrees of skill. If the plan uses five degrees of skill, then each degree is worth 40 points.

A job's total point value is the sum of these numerical values. In the plan in the appendix, the factor *decision making* carries the greatest weight. Over one-quarter of the total points (180 out of 680) are allocated to this factor. Exhibit 11.15 shows how degrees and weights for four compensable factors are combined to evaluate the job of bookstore manager.

### Apply the Plan to All Jobs

Usually a point plan is initially developed using a subset of jobs, similar to the use of key jobs for determining external competitiveness. Once total points for these jobs are computed and a hierarchy established, the rest of the organization's jobs to be covered by the point plan can be similarly compared and slotted into the hierarchy.

The Hay Guide Chart-Profile Method, used by 5,000 employers worldwide, is perhaps the most widely used job evaluation plan. It uses the Hay factors—know-how, problem solving, and accountability.[17] Because the Hay method is so widely used, these factors are almost universally accepted for describing managerial work.

Several compensation consulting firms offer computer-based job evaluation plans. Their software does everything from analyze the job analysis questions and provide computer-generated job descriptions to predict the pay classes for each job. Job evaluation remains a subjective process that involves substantial judgment, even though computers may help reduce the frequent bureaucratic burden of job evaluation and help make the process more systematic.

## Skill-Based Structures

Skill-based structures pay employees based on what they have demonstrated they know, rather than on the particular *job* they are doing. Generally, skill-based plans can be grouped into two types:

1. *Knowledge-based* plans link pay to depth of knowledge related to *one* job (e.g., scientists and teachers).
2. *Multiskill-based* plans link pay to the number of *different jobs* (breadth) an employee is certified to perform (e.g., related production jobs).[18]

EXHIBIT 11.15 Job Evaluation Form

Job BOOKSTORE MANAGER

Check one: Administrative X Technical ____

| Compensable factors | Degree 1 | 2 | 3 | 4 | 5 | × Weight | = Total |
|---|---|---|---|---|---|---|---|
| **Working conditions:** | | | | | | | |
| Environment | X | | | | | 10% | 10 |
| Hazards | X | | | | | 10% | 10 |
| **Skill:** | | | | | | | |
| Education | | | X | | | 40% | 120 |
| Experience | | | X | | | 40% | 120 |
| Mental | | | | X | | 40% | 160 |
| Manual/specific | | X | | | | 40% | 80 |
| **Effort:** | | | | | | | |
| Physical | | X | | | | 30% | 60 |
| Mental | | | | X | | 30% | 120 |
| **Responsibility:** | | | | | | | |
| Effect of error | | | | X | | 20% | 80 |
| *Inventiveness/ innovation | | | X | | | 20% | 60 |
| | | | | | | | 820 |

Knowledge based: depth Basing pay structures on knowledge possessed by individual employees is not new. The pay structures for elementary or high school teachers have long been based on their knowledge as measured by education level. A typical teacher's contract specifies a series of steps, with each step corresponding to a level of education. A bachelor's degree in education is step one and the minimum required for hiring. To advance a step to higher pay requires additional education. For example, an additional nine semester hours of course work earns an increase of $275 per month in Ithaca, New York. The result can be that two teachers may receive different pay rates for doing essentially the same job—teaching English to high school juniors. The pay is based on the knowledge of the individual doing the job (measured by number of college credits) instead of job content. The presumption is that teachers with more knowledge are more effective and more valuable—able to teach seniors, too.

Multiskill based: breadth As with the teachers, employees in a multiskill system earn pay increases by acquiring new knowledge, but the knowledge is specific to a range of related jobs. For example, Borg-Warner Corporation assembles drive chains for automobile transmissions; its job hierarchy is shown in Exhibit 11.16. Previously, seven different jobs were involved in the assembly process,

EXHIBIT 11.16 Borg-Warner Automotive Assembly Classifications

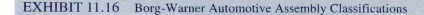

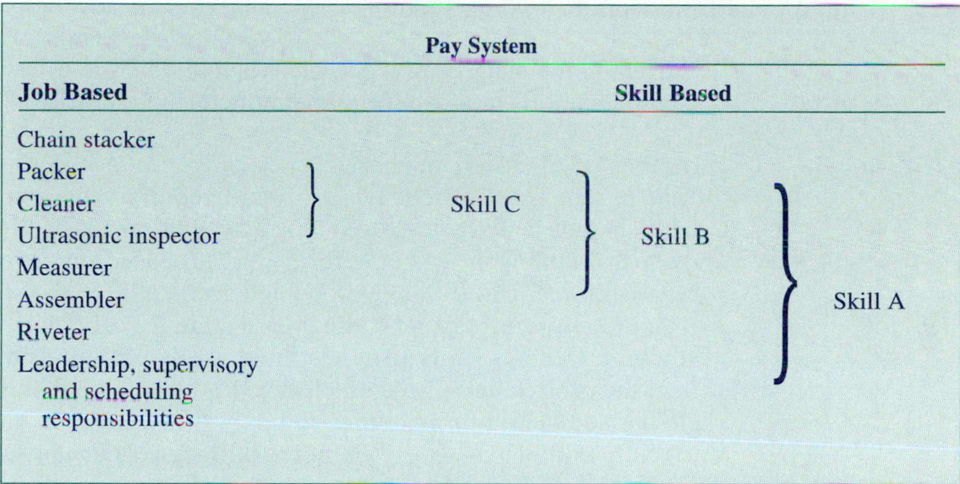


starting with stackers, and moving up through packers, assemblers, and riveters. When Borg-Warner switched to a skill-based pay system, these seven jobs were reorganized into three broad categories: Cell Operators A, B and C. Cell Operator C is an entry-level position. Once Operator Cs are able to satisfactorily demonstrate that they have mastered the jobs of stacker through measurer, they become eligible to train for the Operator B jobs. With each job mastery comes a pay raise. Operator Bs can be rotated among any of the jobs for which they have demonstrated mastery, including C-level jobs. An Operator B can do all the jobs required, including stacking, and still receive Operator B pay. Operator As also can perform all jobs; in addition, they assume responsibility for scheduling and supervising teams. The advantage to Borg-Warner is workforce flexibility and, hence, lower staffing levels.

The multiskilled system differs from the knowledge-based system of teachers because the job responsibilities of an employee in a multiskill system can change drastically over a short time. Whereas teachers increase the *depth* of their skills on the same basic job, employees in multiskill systems can perform a variety of jobs. Pay is based on the highest level of individual skill mastery. Typically, training and evaluation systems are established to ensure that individuals have adequately mastered the skills for which they are being paid and that those skills are maintained.

WHAT DO YOU THINK?

The Ithaca, New York City School District employs a second-grade teacher who possesses a PhD from Cornell University. She recently observed that in spite of her advanced degree and her twelve years of experience, she was paid only a few thousand dollars more than a new teacher with a master's degree. Her PhD is in collective bargaining. Should the school district's pay system place higher value on her PhD? Does her PhD degree increase her value to the school system? Her flexibility?

### Designing a Skill-Based Structure: Skill Analysis

Building a skill-based structure parallels the process for a job-based structure. Instead of job analysis, the process begins with skill analysis.

The basic premise is that blocks of skill required are more likely to be described, certified, and valued fairly if accurate work-related data about them are

*Skill analysis* is a systematic process of collecting information about the knowledge or skills required to perform work in an organization.

available. These are the same issues managers face in job analysis. However, skill analysis in compensation is so new that very little research exists to offer guidance. Currently, the state of practice must be culled from a few case studies describing applications in a handful of manufacturing facilities.[19]

### Determine Skill Blocks and Levels

*Skill blocks* are different types of skill required to perform the work. Just as with compensable factors used in job evaluation, skills blocks should be (1) derived from the work to be performed, (2) focused on developing a highly flexible workforce, and (3) understood and acceptable to the stakeholders involved.

*Skill levels* correspond to degrees within a particular block of skill. For example, a General Mills plan has three levels within each block. The levels reflect the proficiency of the employee. In the technical skill block, the three levels include (1) limited abilities to apply principles, (2) partially proficient, and (3) fully competent. Borg-Warner's skill-based plan in Exhibit 11.16 uses levels of each skill block, similar to degrees of a compensable factor in a job evaluation plan.

A skill-based plan for technicians at FMC Corporation is shown in Exhibit 11.17. The plan has three skill blocks: (1) foundation, which includes material on quality, safety, and a general orientation, (2) core electives, which are necessary for operations (e.g., fabrication, welding, painting, assembly inspection), and (3) optional electives, ranging from computer applications to team leadership and consensus building.

The levels within the core elective block are calibrated by points assigned to each specific skill. The technician pay structure has five rates ranging from an entry rate of $10.50 per hour to a $14.50 rate for a Technician IV. A Technician IV is able to perform all work in a cell.

The FMC approach should look familiar to any college student: required courses, required electives, and optional electives. There is a minor difference, of course—FMC employees get paid for passing these skills, whereas college students pay their schools to take courses!

### Certification Methods

How should employees certify that they possess the skill and are able to apply it? Who should be involved in the process? Practice varies widely. Some organizations use successful completion of courses as evidence of certification. Elementary and secondary school teachers get pay increases for completing additional college courses. Other organizations use peer review, on-the-job demonstrations, and tests for certification. This is similar to the traditional craft approach (i.e., apprentice, journeyman, and master). Still others require successful completion of formal courses, plus time on the job. Northern Telecom uses a preassessment meeting between supervisor and employee to discuss skill accomplishments, goals, and training needs. Subsequently, a certification committee made up of employees and supervisors examines employees to determine whether they can be certified in the skills. Honeywell's plan calls for evaluating employees during the six months after they have learned the skills. Again, supervisors and peers are used in the certification process.

EXHIBIT 11.17 Skill-Based Structure for Techician

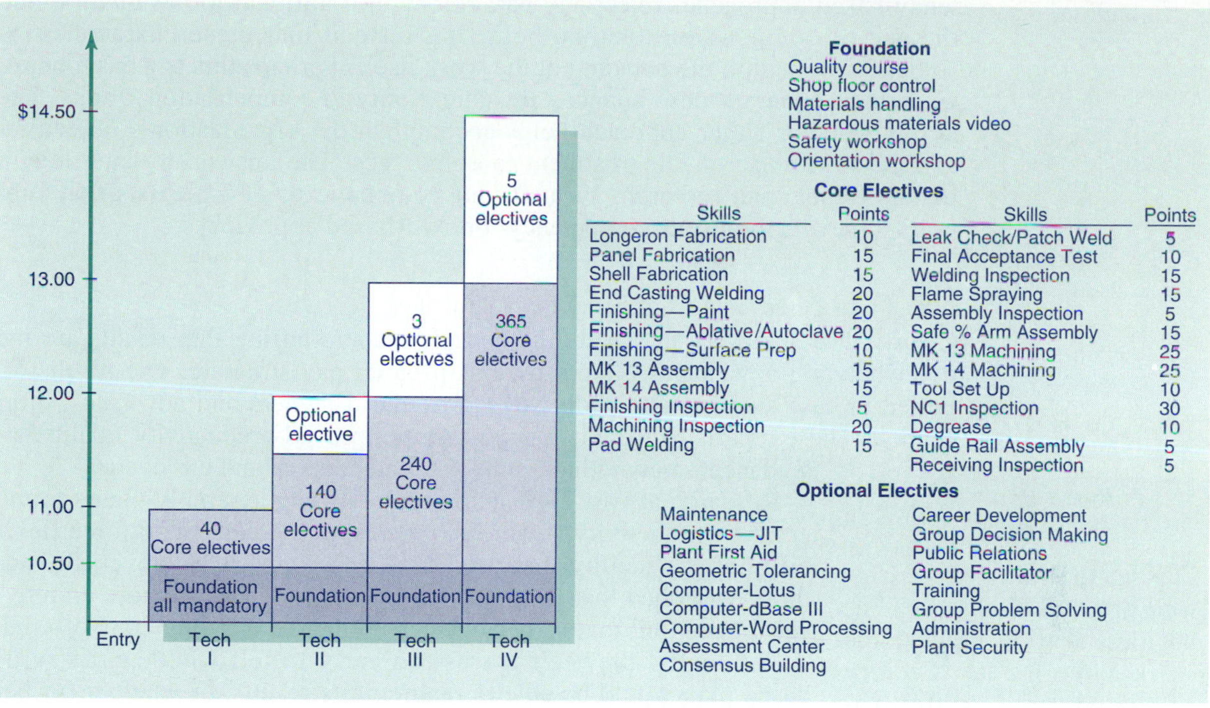


This whole approach to certification may be fraught with potential legal vulnerabilities if employees who fail to be certified challenge the process. Little attention has been devoted thus far to assessor training or validating the certification process. On the face of it, certification procedures used to determine pay increases are vulnerable to regulatory pressures, just like the employment tests used in hiring and promotion decisions. Clearly, there is a need to ensure that procedures are work related and bias free.

## Competency-Based Structures

As noted in Chapter Three, competencies address what human resource characteristics are required to achieve and sustain a competitive advantage. Competencies tend to be more general than skill blocks. At this point in development, competencies usually refer to managerial and professional work, whereas skills are used to value technical and blue-collar work. Nevertheless, like compensable factors, they are derived from the executive leadership's beliefs about the organization and its strategic intent. In essence, competencies are the basic attributes of employees that create value for the organization. One consultant calls competencies "the DNA of organizations."[20]

Determining competencies is relatively new; however, the procedures seem to parallel those used with compensable factors. However, advocates of competency-based approaches reject any parallels with traditional job evaluation and the use of compensable factors, believing instead that these characteristics somehow lie within the person, not the work itself. Perhaps this is a basic point, or perhaps some of these nuances are salient only to compensation wonks. The key is whether either approach helps accomplish the organization's objectives and offers a sense of fair treatment to employees. The answer, to date, lies in beliefs rather than research. Virtually no systematic evidence exists that supports job evaluation over competency- or skill-based approaches.

### Advantages/Disadvantages of Various Pay Structures

Clearly, the flexibility in scheduling and the leaner staffing that results are the overwhelming advantages offered by a skill-based pay structure. The results reported in case studies, admittedly written by the designers and advocates, offer support. These reports list results ranging from improved productivity, quality, attendance, safety ratings, employee satisfaction, and turnover.

Research at two TRW automobile air-bag assembly plants found greater productivity, lower labor costs, and greater workforce flexibility at the facility that used skill-based pay.[21] However, the authors cautioned that labor costs were likely to rise as more employees topped out; that is, became certified for the top pay rate offered. Additionally, they felt it was too early to tell whether the skill-based plan would be able to maintain its results, or whether further HR innovation would be required.

One of Motorola's cellular phone plants has already shifted back from a skill-based plan to a more conventional approach. A Canadian survey found that one-third of those who reported using a skill-based system were no longer using it after five years.[22] Many companies have instituted holding patterns to slow down the rate of progression through the plan. Others set starting pay slightly below competitors. But thus far, the topping-out dilemma seems insurmountable. A skill system requires that higher wage rates must be offset by a smaller workforce or greater productivity, or the organization's labor costs become a significant competitive disadvantage.

In addition, questions still remain about a skill-based system's compliance with the Equal Pay Act. If a member of a protected group is doing the same job as a white male but is being paid less for it (because of a difference in skill mastery), does this violate the equal pay/equal work standard specified in the legislation? The next chapter discusses this and other pay legislation at length.

Exhibit 11.18 contrasts the job evaluation, skill-based, and competency-based approaches to aligning the internal structure. Every approach has advantages as well as disadvantages. The main criticism of job evaluation is that it can become an expensive bureaucratic burden. The difficulty with a skill-based system is that it can become expensive if not properly managed. While competency-based structures are still new, they have not yet demonstrated usefulness in actually setting wages. However, they do focus employees on what the organization says it values.

During the mid-1980s, Motorola saw skill-based pay as an ideal way to prepare the work force for its "Factory of the Future," which required that employees have advanced skills to support the company's future needs. However, within a couple of years of implementing the plan, management started questioning if paying more money for certain skills, whether or not a new skill was used regularly, was "giving money away." Additionally, the company began moving toward greater use of teams. This created conflicts with the pay system because their skill-based pay focused on individual performance. Motorola is a very labor-intensive organization with rapidly changing jobs. With the benefit of hindsight, could anything have been done up-front that would have made skill-based pay a better fit for Motorola?

**EXHIBIT 11.18** Contrasting Approaches

| Criteria | Job Evaluation | Skill Based | Competency Based |
|---|---|---|---|
| What is valued | Compensable factors | Skill blocks | Competencies |
| Quantify the value | Factor degrees and weights | Skill levels | Competency levels |
| Mechanisms to translate into pay | Assign points that reflect criterion pay structure | Certification and market pricing | Certification and market pricing |
| Advantages | Pay based on value of work performed | Flexibility; reduced workforce; rewards continuous learning | Flexibility; rewards development |
| Disadvantages | Potential bureaucracy; inflexible | Can become expensive and/or bureaucratic; can become obsolete | Vague; hard to define or measure; can become obsolete |

## Market-Based Structures

By now, some readers may fear that job evaluation and skills analysis produce bureaucracies to rival the federal government. Why not simply set wages based on what competitors are paying in the market? Some employers do. Their internal structure reflects pay relationships in the external market. *Market pricers* match a large percentage of their jobs with market data. Opting for market pricing emphasizes external competitiveness and deemphasizes internal job relationships.

The potential problems with market pricing stem from giving up internal alignment among jobs to the vagaries of the external market and therefore to competitors' decisions. In effect, marketing pricing lets competitors determine an employer's internal pay structure.

Market pricers often use the ranking method to determine the pay for jobs unique to the firms. Often called *rank to market,* the method involves first determining the competitive rates for positions for which external market data are available and then blending the remaining (nonbenchmark) jobs into the pay hierarchy.

At Pfizer, for example, job analysis results in written job descriptions. This is immediately followed by labor market analysis and market pricing for as many jobs as possible. Exhibit 11.19 shows Pfizer's pay comparisons with comparable jobs at surveyed companies. After that, the internal job relationships are reviewed to be sure they are "reasonable in light of organization needs." The final step is pricing those jobs not included in the survey. These remaining jobs are compared with the survey positions "in terms of their total value to Pfizer." This internal evaluation seeks to ensure consistency with promotion opportunities and to properly reflect cross-functional job values (e.g., production versus clerical jobs).

**EXHIBIT 11.19** Market Pricing at Pfizer

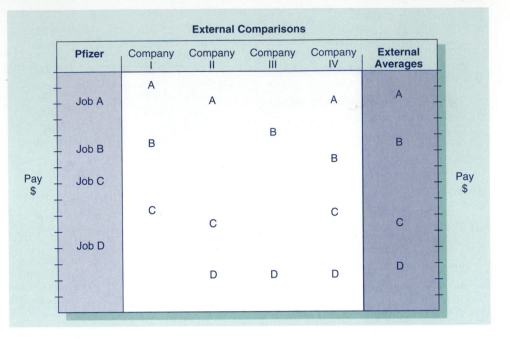

External Comparisons

Pfizer | Company I | Company II | Company III | Company IV | External Averages

Pay $

Job A
Job B
Job C
Job D

A A A A
B B B B
C C C C
D D D D

## Building Bureaucracies?

The techniques used to build internal structures have come in for a lot of criticism for building internal boundaries that hinder an organization's ability to compete. The rigid structures have become walls that prevent the communication and joint efforts required to respond to today's customers. There is some evidence that this criticism is deserved. Stories of employees who refuse to do work outside their job classes are legion. Probably the height of folly was reached by the city government of Philadelphia, where it used to take three people to change a lightbulb. (One to provide access to the fixture, another to remove the old bulb and install the new one, and a third to clean up after the operation.) In the face of a taxpayer revolt, the unions and city managers eventually redesigned work rules.

At 3M, a proposed job evaluation plan was shot down by managers who said most engineers were routinely taking on responsibilities that properly belonged at a higher level. But who would be so foolish as to tell these innovative, creative employees to throttle back? A redesigned plan addressed these issues.

While advocates of skill-based structures say they are less bureaucratic, the advantage may be temporary. As the inevitable challenges arise, additional bureaucracy to resolve them may accumulate like barnacles on a racing boat.

To put the boundaries/bureaucracies issue in the proper light, think back to the basic issue involved. We are trying to build a fair pay structure that recognizes the relative contribution of jobs toward achieving certain objectives. To achieve such a structure, some way must be devised to set pay equal for similar jobs and to ensure that differences in pay for dissimilar jobs are equitable.

Setting equitable pay differences is the real issue. With them we can encourage employees to invest in training and to seek greater responsibility, thus maintaining an experienced workforce. If differences in pay are not grounded in work and business-related factors, then we run the risk of disgruntled employees, undesired turnover, grievances, strikes, and possible lawsuits.

Properly designed and administered, skill-based, job evaluation-based, or market-based systems can provide equitable pay structures. The challenge is to be sure that we do not inhibit creative and productive employees. In the next chapter, we examine some approaches to recognize the contributions of valued employees.

## SUMMARY

Part Four began by examining why differences in pay exist. Differences in organizations, work, employees, and labor markets help account for pay differences. The premise of this chapter is that managers need to design pay systems to fit their organizations. Instead of one size fitting all situations, pay systems must be custom-tailored to be effective. They are contingent on the context—the environment, the organization, and employees. These are the factors in our diagnostic model.

Within this context, we have begun our analysis of how to design pay systems. We looked at competitively pricing work (external competitiveness) and building fair pay differences among jobs within the organization (internal alignment). External competitiveness involves setting a relative pay level against what competitors are paying. Market surveys are used to determine what others are paying. This information is used to design the pay policy line.

Internal alignment is established in the pay structure. The structure, supported through job analysis and job evaluation, or through use of a skill-based or competency-based plan, focuses on pay differentials between similar and dissimilar jobs. Market pricers de-emphasize internal alignment and price the vast majority of their jobs in the external market.

External competitiveness and internal alignment are the first two policies in our pay model. In the next chapter, we cover the last two, employee contributions and administration.

## QUESTIONS

1. Give examples where organizations may adopt different pay policies, depending on the external and organization conditions they face.
2. What is a key job?
3. What is a pay structure? How do you construct one?
4. What are the main job evaluation methods? What is the major advantage and disadvantage of each?

5. How does market pricing differ from job evaluation? How is it similar?
6. How can an organization adjust its pay system to its strategy?
7. What are the criticisms of evaluation? Do they have merit?

8. How should an organization decide who to include in a market survey?
9. How might an organization's design affect its compensation system?
10. Distinguish between skill- and competency-based pay, and what are the advantages and disadvantages of each?

## YOUR TURN
### Evaluating Jobs

Use the plan included in the appendix to evaluate these six jobs. Include a chart that gives the points for each factor, as well as total points for each job. Rank the jobs according to points so results can be compared. Your instructor will share with you the company's actual decisions.

### JOB 1: JOURNEYMAN TOOL AND DIE MAKER

#### General Purpose

Provide specific diversified tooling and assemblies to meet engineering and production requirements by performing various complex technical Tool Room functions with limited supervision.

#### General Duties

Journeyman Tool and Die Maker has a complete knowledge of all Tool Room operations and utilizes the skill and ability to perform complex layouts and complex machine tool setups for the purpose of adjusting, repairing, heat treating, and constructing various tools, dies, fixtures, gages, and the like. Must be able to work to extremely close tolerances, perform design and development without the aid of blueprints, assemble various tooling projects and electromechanical assemblies, and be able to set up and operate all Tool Room equipment with a general responsibility for work involved.

#### Job Specifications

- **Technical Know-How** Specific training and work experience equivalent to a Journeyman Trade Certificate, with the understanding of complex blueprints, assembly prints, and mathematics up to and including the fundamentals of trigonometry. Knowledge to set up, operate, adjust, and troubleshoot all Tool Room equipment and precision measuring devices is required. Understand the application of the principles of electrical circuitry, and the disassembly/assembly of machines and die equipment.
- **Training** Extensive specific skills training in the tool- and die-making field for a minimum of six (6) years, or Journeyman Certificate obtained through an apprenticeship program.
- **Decision Making/Accountability** The Journeyman Tool and Die Maker works in an environment that requires limited supervision, periodic guidance of others, and the latitude to deviate on Tool Room practices and procedures. Review of work results is usually after the fact.
- **Communication/Interpersonal Skills** Relationship usually involves discussion or recommendations, or both, on issues in regard to tooling practices. Impact is considerable and may be limited to an individual project or department or it could possibly affect the facility as a whole.

- **Safety** The Journeyman Tool and Die Maker performs work in a highly variable environment where safety principles and procedures need to be tailored to deal with unforeseen hazards to minimize high potential for serious injury, both to incumbent and others who will use equipment that is made/modified by incumbent.
- **Physical/Mental/Visual** The Journeyman Tool and Die Maker performs work with a high mental application and close visual attention required for extended time periods, with the possibility of exposure to hazardous conditions.

## JOB 2: TOOL ROOM SERVICE OPERATOR

### General Purpose

Provide perishable tooling to meet production requirements by performing specific machine tool functions under limited supervision.

### General Duties

Operate specific machines in a Tool Room environment, performing repetitive, long-term basic operations required to maintain perishable tooling. Has a complete knowledge of various setup and operational functions of machines involved, skill and ability to work and inspect to very close tolerances. Must be capable of operating other basic machines in the Tool Room.

### Job Specifications

- **Technical Know-How** Tool Room Service Operator will have specific training or work experience, or both, exceeding vocational trade school or high school. Knowledge to set up, operate, and adjust specific Tool Room equipment with basic math and blueprint reading ability at a job-related intermediate level capable of working to close tolerances.
- **Training** Tool Room Service Operator requires minimum of two (2) years specific training to perform duties effectively.
- **Decision Making/Accountability** Supervision is usually limited and review of work results is after the fact. High potential for major impact on production if work quality is not of the highest standards.
- **Communication/Interpersonal Skills** Provide or receive technical information that may require an explanation or interpretation to proceed with a specific job involved.
- **Safety** Tool Room Service Operator works in accordance with a wide range of safety procedures to minimize potential for injury.
- **Physical/Mental/Visual** Extremely close mental and visual effort required for extended periods. Work environment is moderately disagreeable, with possibility of hazardous conditions.

## JOB 3: TOOL ROOM MACHINIST

### General Purpose

Provide tooling to meet engineering and production requirements by performing general or all-purpose machine tool setups and operations under limited supervision.

### General Duties

Machinist has a general knowledge of various specific machine tool setups and operations. Inspection, print reading, setup, and machine operation is performed at an intermediate level with a general responsibility for work involved.

### Job Specifications

- **Technical Know-How** Tool Room Machinist will have specific training or work experience exceeding vocational trade school or high school. Knowledge to set up, operate, and adjust a variety of Tool Room equipment, work to close tolerances, and perform layouts, print reading, and math computations at an intermediate level.
- **Training** Tool Room Machinist requires a minimum of four (4) years specialized training in various machine operations and Tool Room functions to perform duties effectively.
- **Decision Making/Accountability** Subject to routine decision making based on established Tool Room practices and technical procedures. Progress of work is periodically checked by others.
- **Communication/Interpersonal Skills** Provide or receive technical information that may require an explanation or interpretation to proceed with specific job involved.
- **Safety** Perform work in accordance with a wide range of safety procedures to minimize potential for injury.
- **Physical/Mental/Visual** Close mental and visual effort required for extended periods. Work environment moderately disagreeable, with possibility of hazardous conditions.

## JOB 4: MASTER JOURNEYMAN TOOL AND DIE MAKER

### General Purpose

Provide specific diversified tooling and assemblies to meet engineering and production requirements by performing various complex technical Tool Room functions under limited supervision.

### General Duties

The Master Journeyman Tool and Die Maker has an extensive knowledge of all Tool Room operations and utilizes skill and ability to perform complex layouts and complex machine tool setups for the purpose of adjusting, repairing, and constructing various tools, dies, fixtures, gages, and the like. Must be able to work to extremely close tolerances, perform design and development without blueprints, assemble various tooling projects, and have knowledge of setup and operation of all Tool Room equipment. Job duties place a strong emphasis on electromechanical assemblies, new die systems, and collaboration with designers and engineers on prototype projects. Extensive communication, evaluation, and decision making are required both in-house and outside the facility, which will at times include travel. Assistance in the education and training of other Tool Room employees and input on future tooling and projects is often required. Receiving, recording, inspecting, and advising changes in tooling, along with knowledge in the fields of electricity, hydraulics, heat treat, and fabrication is also required of this position.

## Job Specifications

- **Technical Know-How** Minimum of eight (8) years extensive skill training or a Journeyman Trade Certificate with additional minimum of two (2) years extensive skills training. Knowledge in electrical, hydraulic, heat treat, tooling, and fabrication fields. Setup and operation of all Tool Room equipment and precision measuring devices. Knowledge of tooling, production, assembly, and manufacturing equipment in other departments is required. Knowledge of math up to and including trigonometry.
- **Training** This Master Journeyman Tool and Die Maker position requires eight (8) years as a minimum amount of training in the Tool Room and related skills to perform the duties effectively.
- **Decision Making/Accountability** The Master Journeyman Tool and Die Maker has the latitude to deviate on practices and technical procedures that encompass a wide range of department objectives or programs to meet an objective, often with no review of work results by others.
- **Communication/Interpersonal Skills** The Master Journeyman Tool and Die Maker position usually includes extensive communication in a broad sense and will have considerable impact in areas both within and outside the facility. Extensive communications with other departments, vendors, engineering, sales, management, and so forth are usual.
- **Safety** The Master Journeyman Tool and Die Maker performs work in a highly variable environment both within and outside the department or facility that requires tailoring safety principles and procedures to deal with unforeseen hazards to minimize high potential for serious injury both to the incumbent and others who will use the equipment produced.
- **Physical/Mental/Visual** The Master Journeyman Tool and Die Maker position requires intensive mental application and visual attention for extended time periods, with the possibility of exposure to hazardous conditions.

# JOB 5: MASTER DRAW DIE MAKER

## General Purpose

Provide specific and prototype draw die tooling to meet production and engineering requirements by performing specialized draw die maker techniques under limited supervision.

## General Duties

The Master Draw Die Maker develops and constructs drifts, laps, electrodes, draw dies, and so on pertaining to draw die tooling from sketches, prints, or verbal instructions. Operates profilers, die sizers, and EDM machines for the purpose of hand or machine lapping, sizing, polishing, and EDMing various new rough core dies and maintenance of existing draw dies and cut-off tooling. Inspects, records, and assists in ordering new draw die tooling. Investigates tooling problems in draw die area and makes recommendations for correction. Assists in the design and development of new draw die tooling in collaboration with engineering. Works to very close tolerances with a general responsibility for work involved. Assists in the education and training of other Draw Die Makers.

### Job Specifications

- **Technical Know-How** Specific skills training exceeding vocational trade school or high school plus skills applicable to wire mill tooling requirements. Set up, operate, adjust, and troubleshoot all draw die making equipment plus Tool Room equipment applicable to draw die making. Work to close tolerances, read drawings, develop layouts, grind and lap, follow instructions, and use math at a complex level. Must be totally capable of investigating, diagnosing, and correcting draw dies to satisfy close tolerances and form requirements.
- **Training** Extensive specific skills in draw die making requires up to five (5) years training in the draw die maker field plus one (1) year Tool Room training to perform duties effectively.
- **Decision Making/Accountability** These positions have a degree of independence to deviate on certain practices and procedures in draw die making with often no review of work.
- **Communication/Interpersonal Skills** Master Draw Die Maker position involves discussion and recommendations in draw die making and could possibly affect the facility as a whole. Extensive communications with other production departments, Product Engineering, and Manufacturing Engineering are common.
- **Safety** Draw die making is performed in accordance with a wide range of safety procedures to minimize potential for injury.
- **Physical/Mental/Visual** Extreme physical effort, high mental application, or extreme close visual attention, or both, required for extended periods. Work environment highly disagreeable, with possible exposure to hazardous conditions.

## JOB 6: TOOL ROOM MACHINE OPERATOR

### General Purpose

Provide basic machined parts by performing specific Tool Room functions under direct supervision.

### General Duties

The Tool Room Machine Operator is an entry-level position that performs a variety of basic machine tool setups and operations under direct supervision. Print reading, inspection, and machine operations are performed at introductory levels.

### Job Specifications

Working from verbal/written direction, the Tool Room Machine Operator will have the skill, training, and abilities of the following degree:

- **Technical Know-How** The Tool Room Machine Operator will have knowledge equivalent to a high school diploma. Understand and follow basic drawings and instruction with a basic math background.
- **Training** Introductory level with no necessary training upon arrival. Training up to and including two (2) years.
- **Decision Making/Accountability** This position is subject to routine decision making based on established practices and technical procedures. Progress of work is periodically checked by others.

- **Communication/Interpersonal Skills** Limited in nature to receiving and interpreting information on Tool Room tasks.
- **Safety** The Tool Room Machine Operator performs specific tasks with several specific safety procedures required.
- **Physical/Mental/Visual** Moderate physical/mental/visual application is required for short periods in this position.

---

# APPENDIX
## Factor Definitions and Points for a Skill-Based Job Evaluation Plan for Manufacturing Jobs

### FACTOR 1: BASIC KNOWLEDGE

**1st Degree (22 points)**
Ability to read, write, add and subtract basic mathematics, interpret and complete simple instructions.

**2nd Degree (47 points)**
Knowledge of higher mathematical calculations, such as basic decimal and fractional equations, ability to read and follow semicomplicated written instructions and to use basic measuring equipment.

**3rd Degree (72 points)**
Knowledge of a variety of manufacturing skills, specific training, work experience equivalent to trade school or high school, ability to read semicomplicated measuring equipment, graphics, technical or written reports.

**4th Degree (111 points)**
Extensive specific skills training in a specialized field; equivalent to one to two years of college or vocational (technical) training or master trade certificate.

### FACTOR 2: ELECTRICAL/ELECTRONIC SKILLS

Application of the principles of electricity, electronics, electronic logic, and integrated transmission technologies, such as lasers. This includes understanding of circuits, their component parts, and how they work together.

**1st Degree (7 points)**
Operational knowledge of electrical/electronic equipment without understanding the electrical/electronic principles on which the equipment operates.

**2nd Degree (15 points)**
Operational knowledge of electrical/electronic equipment with understanding the electrical/electronic principles on which the equipment operates.

**3rd Degree (23 points)**
Application of principles of electronic circuity and appropriate wiring procedures.

**4th Degree (37 points)**
Application of principles of miniaturized electronic circuits and digital analog transmission concepts.

## FACTOR 3: MECHANICAL SKILLS

The application of mechanical knowledge of how/why mechanical equipment works. It includes the operation, repair, or maintenance of machinery/mechanical systems.

**1st Degree (5 points)**
This includes the use of basic mechanical ability to operate/adjust single or multiple pieces of mechanical or electromechanical equipment. It includes, but is not limited to, such elements as clearing jams and setting feed speeds and/or pressure changes.

**2nd Degree (12 points)**
This includes all elements of 1st degree basic mechanical ability, with the exceptions that the incumbent is required to have the skills to perform preventive maintenance, disassemble/assemble specific components, change tools, and the like.

**3rd Degree (25 points)**
Perform servicing and procedural repair activities on mechanical systems/machinery as the primary function.

**4th Degree (31 points)**
Apply advanced principles of mechanical skills to repair, rebuild, service to a close tolerance level of fit.

**5th Degree (37 points)**
Perform sophisticated diagnostic and repair activities on complex mechanical or electromechanical machinery/systems.

## FACTOR 4: GRAPHICS

Reading, interpreting, and/or preparing graphic representations of information, such as maps, plans, drawings, blueprints, diagrams, schematics, and timing/flowcharts.

**1st Degree (5 points)**
Understand basic blueprints and/or prepare rough sketches.

**2nd Degree (12 points)**
Understand more complex blueprints and/or prepare simple graphic information.

**3rd Degree (25 points)**
Understand complex, technical graphic representations of information and/or prepare technical graphics.

**4th Degree (31 points)**
Prepare and/or interpret complex, technical graphic representations of a wide range of information.

**5th Degree (37 points)**
Develop, prepare, and/or interpret highly complex, sophisticated graphic representations.

## FACTOR 5: MATHEMATICAL SKILLS

The selection and application of mathematical methods or procedures to solve problems or to achieve desired results.

**1st Degree (8 points)**
Simple arithmetic computations involving addition, subtraction, multiplication, or division.

**2nd Degree (15 points)**
Computations involving decimals, percentages, fractions, and/or basic statistics.

**3rd Degree (23 points)**
Computations involving algebra (e.g., solving for an unknown) or geometry (e.g., areas, volumes).

**4th Degree (38 points)**
Computations involving the use of trigonometry (properties of triangles and circles including sine, cosine, and tangent functions), logarithms and exponents, and advanced statistics.

## FACTOR 6: COMMUNICATION/INTERPERSONAL SKILLS

This factor measures the scope and nature of relationships with others.

**1st Degree (28 points)**
Little or no contact with others. Relationships involve providing and/or receiving information or documents.

**2nd Degree (56 points)**
Some contact with others. Relationships often require explanation or interpretation of information.

**3rd Degree (84 points)**
Substantial contact with others. Relationships usually involve discussions with stakeholders or recommendations on issues regarding policies, programs, and so on. Impact is considerable and may be limited to individual departments/programs.

**4th Degree (140 points)**
Extensive contact with others. Relationships usually include decisions in a broad sense and will affect several areas within the manufacturing unit.

## FACTOR 7: SAFETY SKILLS

This factor measures the requirements for adherence to prescribed safety and personal security practices in the performance of required tasks. These safety and personal security practices are generally required to minimize exposure to hazard or risk in the work environment.

**1st Degree (10 points)**
Perform work in accordance with a few simple safety procedures to minimize potential for injury.

**2nd Degree (40 points)**
Perform work in accordance with several specific safety procedures to minimize potential for injury.

**3rd Degree (80 points)**
Perform work in accordance with a wide range of safety procedures to minimize some potential for injury.

**4th Degree (100 points)**
Perform work in a highly variable environment where safety principles and procedures need to be tailored to deal with unforeseen hazards to minimize high potential for serious injury.

### FACTOR 8: DECISION MAKING/SUPERVISION REQUIRED

This factor measures the degree of decision making required without being checked by others, and the degree to which immediate supervisor is required to outline the procedures to be followed and/or the results to be attained on the job.

**1st Degree (36 points)**
Limited decision making by the incumbent. Progress of work is checked by others most of the time, and/or 60–90 percent of activities are defined by other than the incumbent.

**2nd Degree (89 points)**
Routine decision making based on specific criteria. Progress of work is often checked by others, and/or 40–60 percent of activities are defined by other than the incumbent.

**3rd Degree (112 points)**
Significant decision making based on established guidelines and experience. Progress of work is checked by others some of the time, and/or 25–40 percent of activities are defined by other than the incumbent.

**4th Degree (180 points)**
Extensive decision making based on broad policies, procedures, and guidelines. Progress of work is seldom checked by others, and/or less than 25 percent of activities are defined by other than the incumbent.

## NOTES AND REFERENCES


1. V. Fuehrer, "Total Reward Strategy," *Compensation and Benefits Review,* Jan.–Feb. 1994, pp. 44–53.
2. George T. Milkovich and Jerry Newman, *Compensation,* 5th ed. (Burr Ridge, IL: Richard D. Irwin, 1996).
3. D. Kahneman, J. Knetsch, and R. Thaler, "Fairness as a Constraint on Profit Seeking: Entitlements in the Market," *American Economic Review,* Sept. 1986, pp. 730–36; Edward E. Lawler III, *Pay and Organization Development* (Reading, MA: Addison-Wesley, 1981).
4. H. J. Holzer, "Wages, Employer Costs, and Employee Performance in the Firm," *Industrial and Labor Relations Review* 43 (1990), pp. 147S–164S.
5. M. Bloom and G. Milkovich, "Money, Managers, and Metamorphosis," in *Trends in Organizational Behavior,* 3rd ed., ed. D. Rousseau and C. Cooper (New York: John Wiley, 1996).
6. Jane A. Bjorndal and Linda Ison, *Mastering Market Data* (Scottsdale, AZ: American Compensation Association, 1991).
7. Frederic W. Cook, "Compensation Surveys Are Biased," *Compensation and Benefits Review,* Sept.–Oct. 1994, pp. 19–22.
8. Michael B. Shea, "Decrees Offer Survey Guidelines," *ACA News,* June 1994, p. 15.
9. Chockalingam Viswesvaran and Murray Barrick, "Decision Making Effects on Compensation Surveys: Implications for Market Wages," working paper, University of Iowa, 1991; L. S. Hartenian and N. B. Johnson, "Establishing the Reliability and Validity of Wage Surveys," *Public Personnel Management* 20, no. 3 (1991), pp. 367–83.

10. S. L. Rynes and A. E. Barber, "Applicant Attraction Strategies: An Organizational Perspective," *Academy of Management Review* 15 (1990), pp. 286–310; Margaret L. Williams and George Dreher, "Compensation System Attributes and Applicant Pool Characteristics," *Academy of Management Journal,* Aug. 1992, pp. 510–35; Daniel Turban and Thomas W. Dougherty, "Influences of Campus Recruiting on Applicant Attraction to Firms," *Academy of Management Journal* 4, no. 35 (1992), pp. 739–65.
11. George Milkovich, "Compensation Systems in High Technology Companies," in *Human Resource Management in High Technology Firms,* ed. A. Kleingartner and C. S. Anderson (Lexington, MA: Lexington Books, 1987), pp. 103–14; Barry Gerhart and George T. Milkovich, "Organizational Differences in Managerial Compensation and Financial Performance," *Academy of Management Journal* 33 (1990), pp. 663–91; and Barry Gerhart and George Milkovich, "Employee Compensation: Research and Practice," in *Handbook of Industrial and Organizational Psychology,* 2nd ed. M. D. Dunnette and L. M. Hough (Palo Alto, CA: Consulting Psychologists Press, 1992).
12. Charles Brown, "Firms' Choice of Method of Pay," *Industrial and Labor Relations Review* 40 (1990), pp. S165–S182.
13. Elliott Jaques, "In Praise of Hierarchies," *Harvard Business Review,* Jan.–Feb. 1990, pp. 11–35.
14. Arne L. Kalleberg and James R. Lincoln, "The Structure of Earnings Inequality in the United States and Japan," *American Journal of Sociology* 94 (1994), supplement pp S121–S153; T. A. Kochan and P. Osterman, *The Mutual Gains Enterprise: Forging a Winning Partnership among Labor, Management, and Government* (Cambridge: Harvard Business School Press, 1994).
15. E. Montemayer, "Aligning Pay Systems with Market Strategies," *ACA Journal,* Winter 1994, pp. 44–53; Scott A. Snell and James W. Dean, Jr., "Strategic Compensation for Integrated Manufacturing: The Moderating Effects of Jobs and Organizational Inertia," *Academy of Management Journal,* Oct. 1994, pp. 1109–40.
16. Sandra M. Emerson, "Job Evaluation: A Barrier to Excellence?" *Compensation and Benefits Review,* Jan.–Feb. 1991, pp. 38–51.
17. For a copy of the Hay Guide Charts and a detailed description of their use, see Al Bellak, "Specific Job Evaluation Systems: The Hay Guide Chart-Profile Method," in *Handbook of Wage and Salary Administration,* ed. Milton L. Rock (New York: McGraw-Hill, 1984), pp. 15/1–16.
18. E. E. Lawler III, G. E. Ledford, Jr., and L. Chang, "Who Uses Skill-Based Pay and Why," *Compensation and Benefits Review* 2, no. 5 (1993), pp. 22–26; Graham L. O'Neill and Deirdre Lander, "Linking Employee Skills to Pay: A Framework for Skill-Based Pay Plans," *ACA Journal,* Winter 1993–1994, pp. 14–27.
19. Gerald E. Ledford, Jr., "Three Case Studies on Skill-Based Pay: An Overview," *Compensation and Benefits Review,* Mar.–Apr. 1991, pp. 11–23.

20. Sandra O'Neal, "Competencies: The DNA of the Corporation," *Perspectives in Total Compensation,* Winter 1994, pp. 6–12; see also Kathryn M. Cofsky, "Critical Keys to Competency-Based Pay," *Compensation and Benefits Review,* Nov.–Dec. 1993, pp. 46–52; and E. E. Lawler III, "From Job-Based to Competency-Based Organizations," *Journal of Organization Behavior* 15 (1994), pp. 3–15.

21. Brian Murray and Barry Gerhart, "Early Organization Outcomes from Introduction of Skill-Based Pay," Working Paper 94-26, Cornell University Center for Advanced Human Resource Studies, Ithaca, NY, 1994.

22. Gordon Betcherman and Anil Verma, "Follow-Up to the New Technology Survey" (paper presented to the Annual Meeting of the Canadian Industrial Relations Research Association, Halifax, Nova Scotia, June 1993).

# Paying Individual Employees

The most important pay question for most of us is, How much of it do we get? The topics discussed in the previous chapter—external competitiveness, internal alignment, pay levels, and structures—seem abstract in comparison. How much should one employee be paid relative to another when both hold the same job in the organization? For example, should all team leaders working at Exxon Chemical's Baytown, Texas, facilities receive the same pay? Or should those with better performance and/or seniority receive more? Should the pay increase employees receive be based on their individual performance, the performance of a team to which they belong, or the plant or corporate performance? This chapter examines various approaches to paying individual employees. It also considers a variety of issues associated with administering the entire pay system. These include gaining acceptance of the plan, pay legislation, discrimination, and special plans designed to pay special groups of employees.

## EMPLOYEE CONTRIBUTIONS

The pay model in Exhibit 11.4 shows that employee contributions is the third basic policy decision. This policy refers to pay relationships among employees performing the same work within a single organization and using pay to affect employees' work behaviors.[1] Three basic issues are:

1. *Why should employees be paid differently?* Should different employees (or teams) performing the same work or possessing the same skills be paid the same—or should managers pay them differently?
2. *How to do it?* What approaches (and techniques) do managers have available to determine differences in individual employees' pay? Should the differences be based on performance, experience, or some combination of the two?
3. *Does it really matter?* What are the payoffs of paying for experience and/or performance? Do productivity, efficiency, and employee satisfaction improve? Or, do employees perceive a lack of fairness in those decisions?

## SHOULD EMPLOYEES BE PAID DIFFERENTLY?

Many employers pay different rates to employees doing the same job. The different rates paid to the Dallas word processors (Exhibit 11.6) are an example. According to the pay model, these differences certainly reflect differences in *external competitive* policies (lead, match, lag competitors' pay) and differences in *internal alignment* policies (how valuable the job is to each organization's objectives). Their differences in pay may also reflect managers' decisions to pay for *employee contributions* (performance and/or experience). Therefore, if word processor A does better and more timely work than word processor B, A is paid more even though they are both word processors.

Employers use a wide array of techniques to determine how to pay for employee contributions. Before discussing these techniques, think about how employees would be paid if their contributions were *not* recognized with pay. Flat rates would result.

## Flat Rates

In cases where wages are established by collective bargaining, single flat rates are common. An example might be if all senior machinists receive $14.50 per hour, regardless of performance or experience. This flat rate is often set to correspond to some midpoint on a market survey for that job. Or it may simply reflect the patterns established across various union/employer negotiations.

Existence of a flat rate does not mean that performance or experience variations do not exist. It means that the parties choose not to recognize these variations with pay. There may be several reasons for ignoring performance differences. Unions may argue that performance measures are biased. Or the work may be designed in a manner that requires cooperative efforts that would be hindered by different pay rates. Skill-based pay structures, for example, result in flat rates for each skill level.[2]

Some managers pay a flat rate for a job (or skill level) and then attach a bonus or incentive to recognize performance differences. Gainsharing plans follow this logic. Under these plans, differences in team or unit performance, rather than individual differences, are recognized with pay.

## Pay Ranges

Ranges set limits on the rates a manager pays for a particular job. Exhibit 12.1 shows pay ranges constructed for the pay level and structure designed in the last chapter. Five pay ranges (I–V), one for each key job (B, D, G, M, and P), have been established.

Designing ranges is relatively simple. Although there is no best approach, two basic steps are typically involved. The logic is that the value of employees' contributions on a job can range between some minimum and some maximum.

1. *Develop grades.* In the graph in Exhibit 12.1, the horizontal axis is the structure generated through job evaluation. Jobs A through P form a hierarchial structure, with P the most valued job. The structure can now be divided into grades. A grade is a grouping of different jobs; each grade may be made up of a number of jobs. In the exhibit there are five grades (I–V): grade I has two jobs (A and B) in it, grade II has jobs C, D, E, and F, and so on. The jobs in each grade are considered substantially similar for pay purposes.

   Each grade has its own pay range. All the jobs within the grade have that same range. Jobs within a grade (e.g., jobs K, L, M, and N in grade IV) should be dissimilar from jobs in other grades (e.g., jobs G, H, I, and J in grade III). Each grade has a different pay range. Designing the grade structure that fits each organization involves trial and error until one seems to fit the best without too many problems.[3]

2. *Design midpoints, maximums, and minimums.* Exhibit 12.2 shows the pay range for grade II jobs with a maximum, midpoint, and minimum.

EXHIBIT 12.1 Establishing Ranges

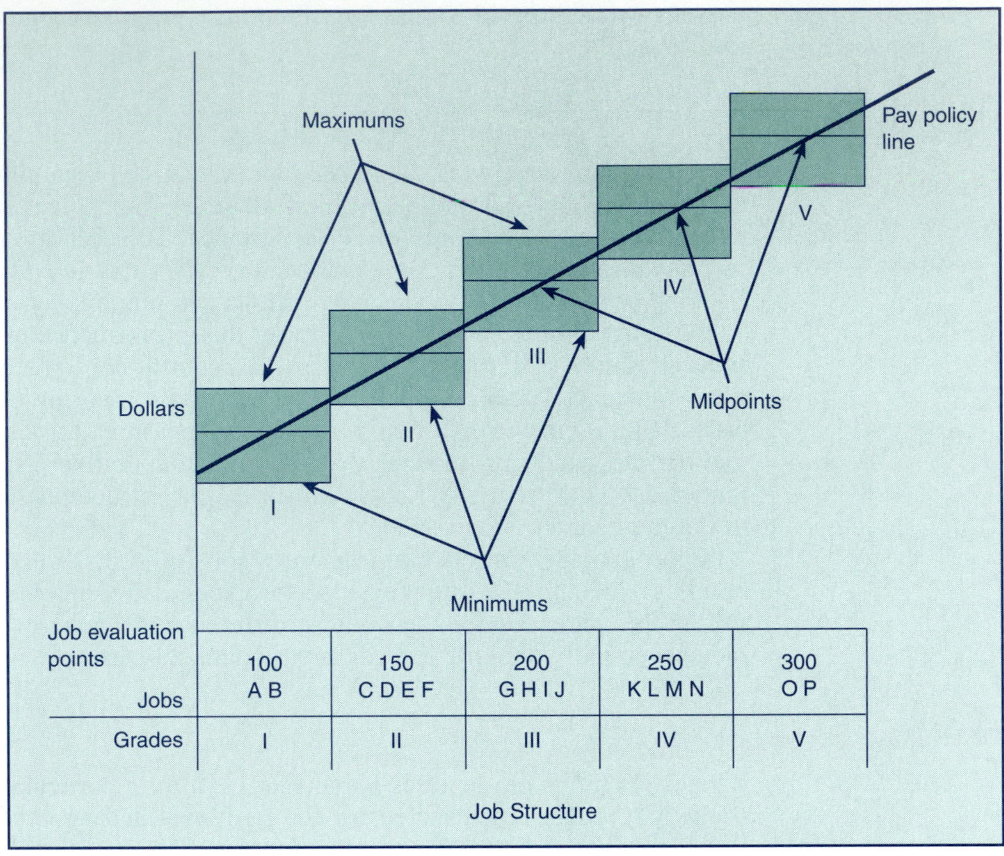


Source: George T. Milkovich and Jerry M. Newman. *Compensation.* 5th ed. (Homewood, IL: Richard D. Irwin. 1996).

Ranges give managers the freedom to pay on the basis of employee experience or performance. The pay range for any job should approximate the range of differences in performance and/or experience that managers wish to recognize. For example, the job of vice president of marketing accommodates a wide variation in performance level and experience, so the pay range for this job may be quite large. But there is less latitude in the job of word processor and consequently a narrower pay range. Ranges also act as control devices. A range maximum signals the ceiling on what the manager is willing to pay for the job; the range minimum sets the floor. So, no matter how excellent a word processor is, the value of that person's contributions to the organization has a limit (maximum).

The midpoint of each range is usually set to correspond to the employer's *pay policy line,* which represents the organization's pay level policy relative to what competition pays for similar jobs. The maximums and minimums are usually based on a combination of what other employers are doing and a judgment

EXHIBIT 12.2 Typical Pay Range

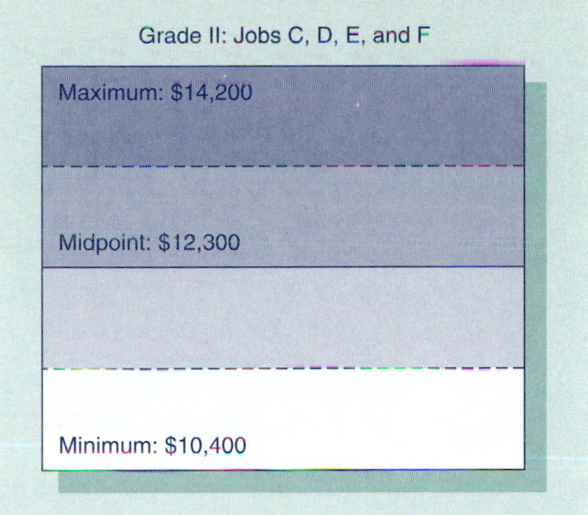


about the relative value of the contribution of that job to the organization's goals. Surveys usually provide data on both the actual maximum and minimum rates paid, as well as the established ranges. These survey data provide a starting point to design the ranges. The range spread can vary from 10 to 50 percent on either side of the midpoint with ± 20 to 30 percent of the midpoint most common.

Progression through ranges can be based on seniority or performance. *Experience-based pay increases* recognize the value of an experienced, stable workforce. However, as the workforce grows older on the job, it also grows more expensive. Therefore, without turnover or productivity increases, labor costs per unit of output increase under seniority-based systems. *Merit pay increases* link pay to employee performance. If pay is tied to productivity, unit labor costs are less likely to increase than in seniority-based systems.

## Broadbanding

Exhibit 12.3 collapses the number of salary grades within the structure into only a few broad grades (or bands) with much wider ranges. This technique, known as *broadbanding,* consolidates as many as four or five traditional grades into a single band with one minimum and one maximum. Because the band encompasses so many jobs of differing values, a range midpoint is usually not used.[4]

Supporters of broadbands say they offer two advantages over traditional grade-and-range approaches. By acting as *"fat" grades,* they provide flexibility to define job responsibilities more broadly. Thus, they support redesigned, downsized, or boundaryless organizations that have eliminated layers of managerial jobs. They are consistent with a competency- or skill-based structure. Second, they foster cross-functional growth and development in these new organizations. Employees can move laterally across functions within a band in order to gain depth of experience.

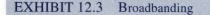

EXHIBIT 12.3 Broadbanding

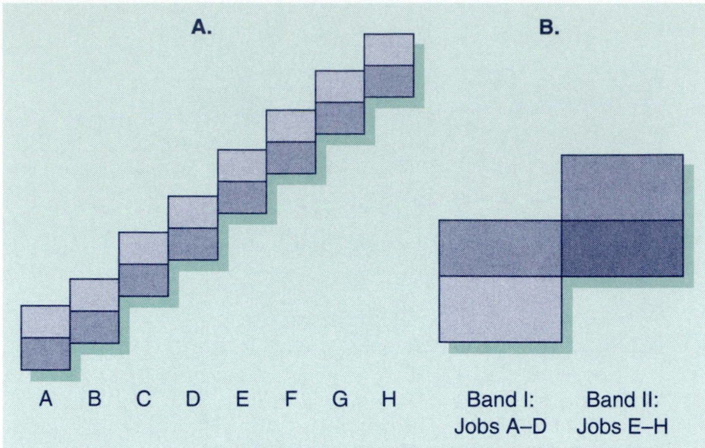


## HOW TO PAY FOR EMPLOYEE CONTRIBUTIONS

The variety among performance-based pay plans is so great that you almost need a field guide to keep track of them. In Exhibit 12.4, our field guide, we categorize the variety of available plans using the following two dimensions:

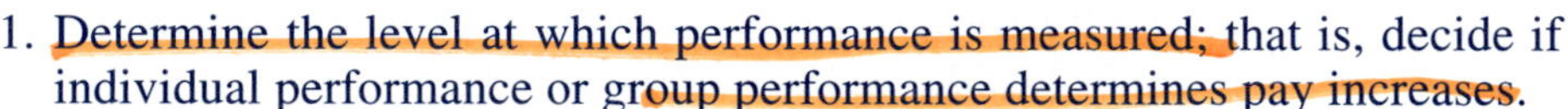

1. Determine the level at which performance is measured; that is, decide if individual performance or group performance determines pay increases.
2. Determine whether the performance payment increases base pay; for example, traditional merit pay increases add onto employees' base pay. Increases in following years are calculated using the new base, whereas awards or profit-sharing plans do not increase the employees' base pay—the increase has to be re-earned each period. Plans that do not add into base can be triggered by either individual performance as in sales commissions and piece-rate incentives, or group performance as in gainsharing and profit sharing. These plans are loosely grouped under the heading "variable pay."

The percentage of companies using each type of plan is shown in Exhibit 12.5. Merit pay is be far the most widespread, with about 93 percent of firms reporting that they use it. Groupwide pay such as gainsharing is used by about 19 percent, and profit sharing by 24 percent. These variable plans, while widely used, are still not as popular as individual bonuses (49 percent).

### Merit Pay: Individual Employees Matter

Because merit pay is based on *individual performance*, its message is that individual employees matter; employees can make a difference to the organization, and that difference is valued and recognized with pay increases.[5] Most managers believe that merit pay fits into an overall human resources system that emphasizes meritocracy as the basis in making pay and promotion decisions.

## EXHIBIT 12.4 Performance-Based Pay

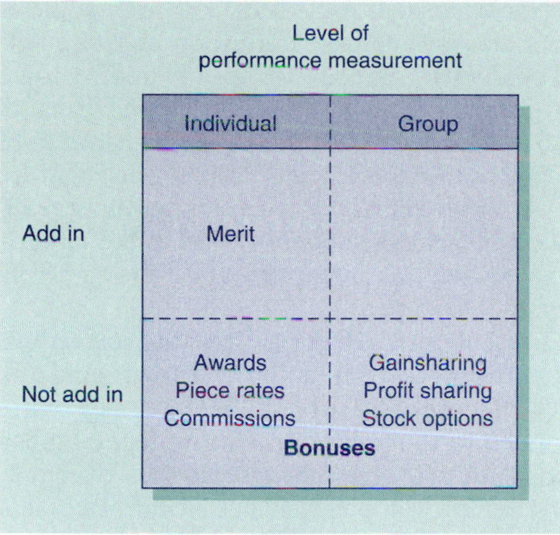


## EXHIBIT 12.5 Pay Plans

| | Percentage of Companies Using Plan | Average Size Percentage of Pay |
|---|---|---|
| Merit pay | 93% | 3.5% |
| Individual performance awards | 49% | 8.4% |
| Gainsharing/teams | 19 | 6.0 |
| Profit sharing/company-wide | 24 | 5.2 |
| Combination incentives | 24 | 8.8 |
| Special recognition awards | 51 | 3.3 |
| Stock awards/options | 17 | 9.1 |

Source: Adapted from Hewitt, 1995 survey of 2,400 U.S. companies; Conference Board 1994 Surveys; Mercer 1995 Surveys.

Merit pay combines the following three elements, the first two of which have already been discussed:

1. Individual performance evaluation (Chapter Four).
2. Pay ranges designed to reflect differences in performance and/or experience that managers wish to recognize with pay.
3. Merit increase guidelines that translate a specific performance rating and position in the pay range to a percent merit increase.

**Increase guidelines** An example of merit increase guidelines used by the Bank of America is shown in Exhibit 12.6. The pay ranges are divided into performance levels (far exceeded, exceeded, met, met some but not all objectives) and the appropriate pay increase corresponding to each performance level is calculated. Lower performance ratings are tied to lower pay increases, and higher ratings get the largest increases. In many firms, the poorest performers may receive no pay increases under a pay-for-performance guideline.

Guidelines help control costs and ensure consistent treatment across different managers. At the Bank of America, for example, employees whose performance exceeds expectations should be paid in the upper half of their job's pay range. All Bank of America managers who follow the plan treat their star performers the same way.

The bulk of research on merit pay has focused on ways to reduce the subjectiveness of performance evaluation.[6] Critical incidents, management by objectives (MBO), and behaviorally anchored rating scales are some of the approaches discussed in Chapter Four. Unfortunately, most of this research is of only marginal use to managers because it often overlooks whether any subsequent effects on employee performance occur. Two separate perspectives on performance appraisal exist. On one side are researchers honing it as a measurement device to eliminate errors. On the other side are managers who view performance appraisal as a communication, reinforcement, and motivation tool.[7] While managers are certainly concerned with the accuracy and fairness of the performance measurement, a greater concern is how employees feel at the end of the appraisal process and how these feelings affect their subsequent work behavior. There is little research that examines merit pay's direct effect on employee performance. Studies of job satisfaction and performance indicate that they may be positively affected by merit pay, but other studies equivocate. And few controlled studies examine the factors that might mediate merit pay's effects, such as the size of the merit budget or the tenure of the workforce.

## Is Merit Mismanaged? Too Much Money Has Too Little Effect

Given the widespread use of merit pay, why aren't there clear-cut research results showing substantial effects on performance? The answer may lie in the way merit pay is administered. First, most plans call for yearly performance evaluations and pay increases. This time horizon makes it hard for an employee to connect today's pay increase with behavior that occurred months ago. In addition, an annual increase results in only a small change in a weekly paycheck. Over the last few years, annual merit increases have hovered around 5 percent. Five percent on $40,000 base pay comes to $38 before taxes in a weekly paycheck; if taxes are around 30 percent, the new paycheck is only $27 higher than the old paycheck. Twenty-seven dollars is probably not a meaningful difference to most employees.

A second problem is the size of the differentials among performance levels. The difference between the pay increase for employees whose performance *exceeds* expectations and that for employees' whose performance *meets* expectations is rarely enough to change performance. Assume employees who perform at a "meets expectations" level are given a 5 percent increase and those who

**EXHIBIT 12.6** Excerpt from Bank of America's Pay-for-Performance Plan

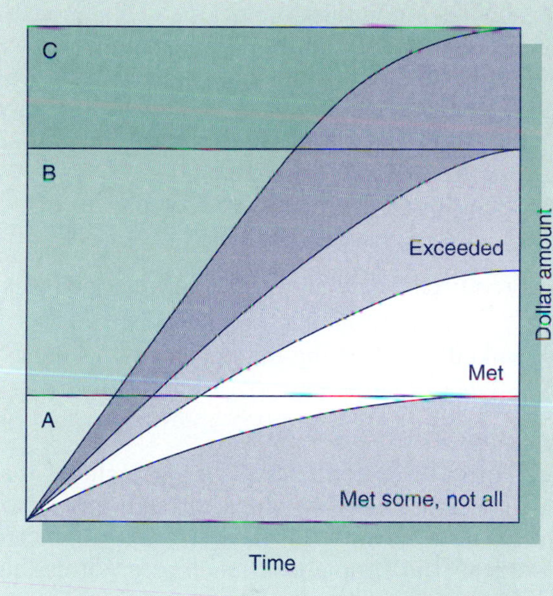


Your performance affects your pay in two ways.

First, it affects the size of the raise you receive. For example, if two employees started in the same job at the same time, at the same salary, over time the salary level of the one whose performance far exceeds will be greater than the salary level of the employee whose performance is rated as only having "met" an acceptable level of results. So, the better you do your job, the higher your salary can grow.

Second, the timing of your salary increase will be based on your performance and your position in your salary range. If two employees are in the same sector of their salary range, the better performer can expect to receive an increase sooner than the employee performing at a lower level. Thus, your performance determines how much of an increase you receive, as well as when you receive it.

perform at the "exceeds" level are given 8 percent. Those who rate 8 percent receive over $15 more after taxes per paycheck than their co-workers whose work is average. Even if employees are absolutely certain that extra effort on their part would lead to a higher performance rating (a certainty not all employees possess), the extra $15 may not be perceived to be worth the effort.

### Merit—The Compounding Effect

The weekly impact of 5 percent or even 8 percent may seem inconsequential. However, the extra $27, $38, or $53 recurs every week in every year that the employee stays. Few employees or managers seem to realize the financial impact of adding increases into a base. If a $40,000 employee receives 5 percent increases every year, after 10 years the new base salary is $62,000. The total cash paid to this employee over the 10 years is $403,116. In addition, costs for benefits tied to wages, such as pensions, Social Security taxes, and life insurance, have also increased. Unfortunately, few employees view merit increases in the context of one's entire career, as the beginning of an income stream—and equally unfortunately, so do few managers.

The example illustrates how pay for performance plans and the lack of realistic communications can dilute any motivational value that merit pay may possess. There is a growing belief that merit is mismanaged: Too much money is going to too many people with too little effect. The heart of the problem lies in the way merit is managed—as a cost control, not a performance motivation approach. If performance motivation were an objective, rather than cost control, more attention would be devoted to designing merit grids that motivate people rather than control costs.

## Individual Incentives

Individual incentive systems avoid the pitfalls of performance evaluation by using objective measures of performance, such as a commission as a percentage of the sales price of a car or piece rates on production, as a basis for calculating pay. As shown in our field guide in Exhibit 12.4, the key features are (1) performance is measured at the individual level and (2) the pay increase is *not* added to base pay. Although the size of the incentive payment is often larger than a merit increase, it does not add into base pay. There is also the risk of no payout at all.

Behavioral theories tell us three conditions are necessary for pay to affect performance:

1. The behaviors and conditions required to achieve the goal must be under the control of the individual.
2. The payment must be clearly linked to achieving the goals.
3. The payment must be big enough to justify the effort required to reach the goal.

Properly designed incentive plans can meet these conditions. Research shows that increases in productivity of up to 30 percent can be obtained through the use of properly designed incentives.[8] Unfortunately, most of this research was conducted in artificial settings where college students did simple tasks such as proofreading or sorting colored objects and earned extra points for grades. In real-world situations, the unintended negative effects of imposing individual incentives are well documented. Studies in retail sales, for example, have shown that employees won't bother doing job tasks such as restocking displays if these tasks are not the basis for payments, even though they are part of the job.[9] Some even sabotage coworkers by hiding the most salable merchandise. Sears, the retail giant, found its integrity attacked when attorneys general in California and New Jersey charged its automotive stores with consistently selling repairs that weren't needed and replacing parts that weren't broken. Sears laid the blame on its incentive pay system that not only paid mechanics based on the number of repairs done but also imposed quotas that required a certain number of repairs per month. Instead of furthering organizational financial performance, the offending pay-for-performance plan caused a scandal that decreased customer satisfaction and trust.

Numerous studies have also documented clashes between high producers and other members of a work group. Such clashes appear motivated by fear of new, higher performance standards or even job loss.[10]

Individual incentives can have a positive effect on individual performance, but few jobs today completely fulfill the conditions required by behavioral theory for individual incentives to affect performance. Most work is complex, and employees are interdependent. It is not surprising that surveys of managers report tremendous interest in group incentives to influence performance rather than individual-based plans.

## Team/Unit Based Plans: Teamwork as a Key to Improved Performance

Managers are limited in their ability to link pay to performance by their inability to measure performance. Some jobs don't have easily definable performance outcomes. How do we measure the performance of an engineer whose job involves making cars more aerodynamic? What is the increased dollar value of a car with a

EXHIBIT 12.7 Pay-for-Performance Plan Decisions

| Decision | Merit | Gainsharing | Profit Sharing |
|---|---|---|---|
| **Objectives and philosophy** | Signals meritocracy<br>Individual contributions matter<br>Support longer term commitment<br>Control costs | Signals performance philosophy<br>Team contributions matter<br>Short term<br>Control costs | Signals performance philosophy<br>Total unit membership matters<br>Short term<br>Control costs |
| **Eligibility** | All employees | Team members | Professionals and managers |
| **Cost effects** | Increases fixed costs | Variable | Variable |
| **Performance measures** | Performance appraisal ratings | Team level measures (Costs, quality, quantity) | Unit level financials (return on assets, return on capital) |
| **Threshold** | Minimum performance rating required | Minimum cost, quality, quantity required | Minimum financial return required |
| **Cap** | Merit budget | Ceiling on payouts | Ceiling on payouts |
| **Award schedule (size and timing)** | Merit grid | By performance achieved | By performance achieved |
| **Form of pay** | Cash spread over budget cycle | Cash lump | Cash lump |
| **Manage plan and changes** | Communication | Communication participation | Communication and participation |

better drag coefficient? Other jobs have a defined output, but no single individual is responsible for the entire product or service. Working on an assembly line in Detroit yields cars at the rate of one every minute or less, but the added value of any single worker is difficult to separate from the contributions of other employees. Group incentives are used when it is difficult to measure each individual employee's output, and/or when teamwork is important.[11] The performance of a team of employees or the entire plant is used to determine pay increases. Employees who manufacture pumps and electric motors for Dresser Rand, automobile components for TRW, and toothpaste and soap for Colgate-Palmolive Company receive group incentives. A recent survey of more than 200 group-based plans reported that 43 percent used financial measures (profitability, revenues, cost per unit, cost savings), 30 percent used productivity measures (output to input ratios), 36 percent quality (errors, units within tolerances), and 15 percent, customer satisfaction as a basis for group pay.[12]

Generally, it is convenient to contrast two basic types of group-based plans: *gainsharing* plans and *profit sharing*. Exhibit 12.7 contrasts merit, gainsharing, and profit sharing. Each plan faces similar design issues. However, the decisions vary. The typical gainsharing plan measures production or cost-saving performance and focuses on team or facility levels. A portion of the savings in

current production or labor costs compared with past costs is paid out to all team members. Profit-sharing plans focus on changes in profitability as the performance measure at the division or total corporate level. A portion of profits above a targeted level is distributed among all employees, generally as a percentage of base salary. Gainsharing and profit sharing are similar in many ways, but the level of performance measurement differs in ways that may influence performance. For example, gainsharing's focus on team results may make it easier for employees to see how they can influence it, but it may also result in competition among teams. Profits at the corporate level may be beyond the line of sight of most employees; that is, they have difficulty seeing how their behaviors influence corporate profits.

## Gainsharing

According to its advocates, gainsharing is more than a group incentive scheme. It is part of a total management approach or philosophy. Exhibit 12.8 lists the organizational characteristics favoring a gainsharing plan. Key characteristics include small-size operation, production and costs under employee control, a trusting participative relationship between managers and employees, and a technically competent workforce. Experience suggests that a plant manager totally committed to making the incentive plan work is also required.

### An Illustration

A Dresser Rand plant in Painted Post, New York, illustrates the key features of the gainsharing plan (see Exhibit 12.9). Employees earn a bonus by increasing productivity, improving quality, or saving shop supplies. This plan is a variation on the Scanlon Plan, an early group (plant or facility wide) gainsharing plan. Plans of this type were developed by Joseph Scanlon, a union leader in the steel industry during the 1930s.

The Dresser Rand plan includes the three key features of a Scanlon Plan. First is a *philosophy of management* that is participatory and involves pay incentives and a suggestion system. Each unit in the plant has a production committee made up of foremen and employee representatives. Employee involvement teams (EIT) provide employees the opportunity to make suggestions for improvements.

The second key feature is that a *committee of employees and managers* administer the plan, including evaluating the improvement suggestions, applying the bonus formula, redesigning the formula, and so on. The bonus committee at Dresser Rand screens the improvement suggestions made by employees and managers. If accepted, the gains (e.g., cost savings of improved production) are shared with the work group, not just the individual who suggested it.

Third, companies using the Scanlon Plan use widely varying *formulas for calculating the amount of bonuses employees receive,* usually a percentage of their pay. For example, some base the bonus on a ratio of total sales volume to total payroll expenses. This measure reflects labor cost changes (corrected for inflation). Others focus on payroll costs for each type of product. The Dresser Rand plan utilizes three measurements to calculate the bonus payout as shown in Exhibit 12.9:

1. Productivity (as measured by savings in labor costs).
2. Quality (as measured by reductions in spoilage and scrap).
3. Shop supplies (as measured by reductions in costs for tools and aprons).

EXHIBIT 12.8 Conditions Favoring Gainsharing Plans

| Organizational Characteristic | Favorable Condition |
|---|---|
| Size | Small unit, usually less than 500 employees. |
| Age | Old enough so that learning curve has flattened and standards can be set based on performance history. |
| Financial measures | Simple, with a good history. |
| Market for output | Good, can absorb additional production. |
| Product costs | Controllable by employees. |
| Organizational climate | Open, high level of trust. |
| Style of management | Participative. |
| Union status | No union, or one that is favorable to a cooperative effort. |
| Overtime history | Limited to no use of overtime in the past. |
| Seasonal nature of business | Relatively stable across time. |
| Work floor interdependence | High to moderate interdependence. |
| Capital investment plans | Little investment planned. |
| Product stability | Few product changes. |
| Comptroller/chief financial officer | Trusted, able to explain financial measures. |
| Communication policy | Open, willing to share financial results. |
| Plant manager | Trusted, committed to plan, able to articulate goals and ideals of plan. |
| Management | Technically competent, supportive of participative management style, good communications skills, able to deal with suggestions and new ideas. |
| Corporate position (if part of larger organization) | Favorable to plan. |
| Workforce | Technically knowledgeable, interested in participation and higher pay, financially knowledgeable and/or interested. |
| Plant support services | Maintenance and engineering groups competent, willing, and able to respond to increased demands. |

The plan permits gains in productivity to be enhanced by savings in scrap and shop supplies, as well as through suggestions for productivity improvements from the employee involvement teams. Thus, a bonus is determined by the following formula:

$$\text{Gainsharing bonus} = \frac{\text{Productivity}}{\text{(Labor costs)}} \pm \frac{\text{Quality}}{\text{(Scrap savings)}} \pm \frac{\text{Shop supplies}}{\text{(Cost savings)}}$$

In Exhibit 12.9, the improvement in labor costs, product quality, and shop supplies yielded $120,000. One-third of the bonus is set aside in a reserve; the remainder is divided between the employees' share (65 percent) and the firm's share (35 percent). The 65 percent employee share translates to about 5.2 percent per employee. Therefore, if the average annual salary is $30,000, the bonus the average employee takes home is $1,560.

The main objective underlying gainsharing is to use pay to tie the goals of individuals to the goals of the organization and to emphasize that improved performance involves both individual and team effort.[13] A number of case studies and surveys report impressive increases in performance connected with gainsharing. There are only a few controlled studies, however.

EXHIBIT 12.9 Dresser Rand Gainsharing Plan

| | | | |
|---|---|---|---|
| **Total All Savings Bonus Pools** | | | $ 120,000 |
| Labor | + $ 50,000 | | |
| Quality | + 40,000 | | |
| Supplies | + 30,000 | | |
| | $120,000 | | |
| Less 1/3 as current quarter reserve provision* | | 40,000 | |
| Apply to prior quarter loss | | + 0 | |
| | | 40,000 | − 40,000 |
| **Available for Distribution: 2/3** | | | 80,000 |
| Employee share of savings 65% | | | 52,000 |
| Participating payroll (total wages for all hours worked.) | | | 1,000,000 |
| Employee share—% of participating payroll | | | 5.20% |

*The reserve is established to provide some safeguard for the plan against quarters with lower than normal efficiency where the stated labor costs, spoilage, scrap and reclamation, and shop supplies goals are not met. At the end of the gainsharing year, the money remaining in the reserve account will be distributed.

The first study of the effect of gainsharing on 28 plants with complex, interdependent jobs found that significant gains in productivity occurred immediately in half the plants and continued throughout the five-year study period. Those plants where improvement did not occur were hampered by infrequent bonus payouts, poor union-management relations before and during the study period, and a lack of employee input into the plan design and production standards.[14]

A second study examined a foundry's productivity data for four years before and six years after a gainsharing plan was implemented. Productivity improved at a faster rate after the introduction of gainsharing; labor costs and grievance rates were reduced.[15]

A third study found that the way the payoffs of a gainsharing plan are distributed affects results. Payment of equal dollars to all employees regardless of base pay (i.e., everyone got $250) had no effect on productivity. Payments of equal percentages of base pay (i.e., employees got 3 percent of their base pay) had a positive effect on quality, safety, production, and revenues.[16]

Outliers: stars, loafers, and free riders There is negative evidence about gainsharing as well. The study of a gainsharing plan at AT&T found that the least productive employees improved, but the most productive employees apparently reduced their efforts.[17] Does this matter? In some cases no. If the work allows for little range in performance, lower productivity of some high performers may be offset by the overall increase in productivity. Some argue that so-called *social loafers* and *free riders*—those who take advantage of others on the team—are placed under great pressure to perform, with pressure coming from peers rather than managers. In some situations, however, the diminished performance of the stars can be devastating. Outliers may provide the creative spark that inspires, leads, and motivates. If three members of the Chicago Bulls basketball team each play 10 percent better, it is still uncertain if they can offset a 30 percent decline in Michael Jordan's performance. At this point, there is little research to help inform us about the effects of gainsharing on individuals at the extremes. Nevertheless, studies offer documentation that gainsharing can result in increases in productivity that can be sustained over a long time. However, they caution that gainsharing must be part of an overall approach to human resources that is built on solid employee relations and that emphasizes employee participation in decision making.

### Profit Sharing and Bonus Plans

Essentially, profit sharing is the payment to employees of a portion of profits that exceed some preestablished level. Many firms have adopted such plans. Union Carbide Corporation, for example, shares profits that reflect an 8 percent or better return on capital.

Profit-sharing plans vary in the timing of the payouts (e.g., quarterly, annually) and in the form the payout takes (e.g., cash or deferred payment until retirement or severance). The assumption underlying profit sharing is that employees who have profit-sharing plans identify more closely with the company and its profit goal and thus reduce waste and increase productivity.

One of the best-known profit-sharing plans is at Lincoln Electric Company in Cleveland, Ohio. Lincoln Electric is the world's leading manufacturer of welding equipment. Each of Lincoln Electric's 3,400 U.S. employees is accountable for the quality and quantity of her or his work. Employees receive performance evaluations twice a year based on quality, output, dependability, cooperation, and ideas. These ratings determine how much of the total corporation profit-sharing bonus pool each employee gets. The bonus is added to each employee's base pay, which is above average for the Cleveland area. The profit-sharing bonus can double the pay of some employees; however, total earnings of employees vary widely—from roughly $32,000 to more than $100,000 for the best performers—because the bonus size depends on individual performance.

Despite the system's success, Lincoln Electric is being forced to reexamine it. In its drive to remain globally competitive, management has acquired welding manufacturing plants in several countries, including Canada, Mexico, and Malaysia. Not only have these acquisitions dragged down corporate profits, but the newly acquired plants aren't as efficient as the Cleveland facility. Over the last several years, Lincoln Electric has borrowed over $100 million to pay bonuses to its U.S. employees even though the company lost money on its acquisitions.

Lincoln Electric is wrestling with what it should do with its profit-sharing plans when the weak profits are the result of management's decisions (poor acquisitions) or external factors (changes in currency exchange rates) and not under the control of employees. Stay tuned for further developments.

The greatest problem with profit sharing plans in general may be their failure to pay off when the targets are not achieved. Many companies end up sharing some payment, attributing the weak performance to "exceptional unanticipated events." A 3M plant in Canada launched a profit-sharing system under which all employees could put up to 6 percent of their annual salary, in effect placing up to 6 percent "at risk." In return, employees could earn up to

18 percent ($3 for $1) if the plant's financial performance exceeded goals by certain amounts. The first year, employees earned 2.5 for 1; the second year 2 for 1, and the third year the plan paid nothing, thereby causing employees to lose up to 6 percent of their pay. Employees complained, arguing that unforeseen foreign competition caused the results. 3M managers acquiesced and restored whatever money employees had put at risk. When Dupont's profit-sharing plan failed to pay off, the company not only made employees whole, Dupont dumped the whole plan.

## DOES PAYING FOR EMPLOYEE CONTRIBUTIONS PAY OFF?

### Pay for Performance Affects Equity

From the employees' perspective, pay is a major determinant of economic well-being. But pay is more than that; it can also affect social standing and psychological well-being. The reaction of employees to a variable pay plan is probably related as much to their own financial needs as the specifics of the plan.

In examining employees' acceptance of variable pay plans, three characteristics are salient: leverage, level of risk, and procedural justice.

**Leverage** is the ratio of variable pay to base pay. The leverage that is appropriate may differ among employee groups and among organizations. Executive pay, for example, is typically more leveraged than that of other employees.

**Risk** is the probability that an employee will get an increase commensurate with his or her effort. Many executive pay plans are highly leveraged but relatively risk-free. That is, the probability of payoff is very high. Different risks may be more appropriate for different employee groups.

**Procedural justice** refers to the fairness of the process by which the plan is designed and managed. The actual results—the amount each employee receives, the criteria for allocating payments—pertain to distributive justice. The distinction between procedural and *distributive justice* is important. Suppose you are given a ticket for speeding. Procedural justice refers to the process by which a decision is reached: the right to an attorney, the right to an impartial judge, and the right to receive a copy of the arresting officer's statement. Distributive justice refers to the fairness of the decision: Guilty! Researchers have found that employees' perceptions of the fairness of procedures significantly influence acceptance of the results.[18] Pay plans are most likely to be perceived as fair if (1) they are consistently applied to all employees, (2) employee participation and/or representation is included, (3) appeals procedures are available, and (4) the data used are accurate.

In a comparison of gainsharing plans that focused on rules versus results, researchers found that employees considered fairness with the rules a more important issue when the payouts were small. Where payouts were large, the opposite pattern occurred: Fairness with the amount was more important than fairness of the rules. Perhaps the rules for slicing the pie are less important if it is a big pie.[19]

WHAT DO YOU THINK?

A painting business employs 20 people whose average pay is $9 an hour. The owner decides to restructure and go into the building custodial services, where the average wage is $7 an hour. He reduces the workers' wages from $9 to $7 an hour. Do you think this action is fair? What impact will it have on results?

The current employees leave, the owner pays new employees $7 an hour. Do you think this action is fair? What impact will this have on results?

What if the current employees stay, and the owner guarantees them $8 an hour, with a profit-sharing bonus that will range from $0 to $4 an hour, depending on how the new market plan works out. Do you think this action is fair? What impact will this have on results?

## The Dark Side of Variable Pay

Many employees are not in a position to manage a risky financial portfolio of such personal importance. Employees often begin to count on their bonus pay regardless of the likelihood of receiving it.[20] Some employees' base pay is relatively low, so putting any of it at risk is unacceptable. Others undertake financial obligations consistent with their earnings *potential* rather than the realities of the company's economic situation. Because employees usually hold only one job at a time, they cannot minimize risk through diversification as they might when investing in stocks and bonds. An AFL-CIO officer points out that "banks holding mortgages and utilities that provide services do not adjust monthly bills to fit changes in worker income. Until they do, it is unlikely that workers will ask their unions to support variable pay packages."[21]

The UAW's experience with profit sharing provides ammunition for critics. Payouts to Ford employees from their profit-sharing plan totaled $1,350 per employee in 1993 and $4,000 in 1994; General Motors employees received $0 in 1993 and $550 in 1994. It would be only human for General Motors employees to feel penalized for factors beyond their control and attribute the difference in profitability to poor decision making on management's part rather than superior performance of the rank and file at Ford.

## Pay for Performance Affects Efficiency

One of the key reasons for being systematic about pay decisions is to control costs. A simple model shows the three main factors that determine labor costs:

Costs = Employment × (Cash compensation + Benefits) where

- Employment includes both number of employees and number of hours worked.
- Cash compensation includes wages and variable pay.
- Benefit costs includes health and life insurance, pensions, and the like.

Varying any of these factors varies costs. If a greater proportion of compensation can be made variable rather than fixed, costs can be better controlled. Think about the cost controls built into incentives and awards. The essence of variable pay is that it must be re-earned each period, whereas conventional merit pay increases or across-the-board increases (an equal percent for all employees) are added to the base pay. From a labor cost perspective, conventional increases affect not only the average cash compensation but also the cost of those benefits contingent on base pay (e.g., pensions). Consequently, the greater the ratio of variable pay to base pay, the more variable (flexible) are labor costs.

### It's Not How Much But How

The preponderance of research evidence reported from recent studies strongly suggests that pay for performance, designed and managed properly, does work.

One study looked at 16,000 managers in more than 200 companies over six years. It reported pay for performance plans were related to the subsequent financial success of these firms. For example, a 10 percent increase in the bonus was associated with a 1.5 percent increase in return on assets in the following year. And a 10 percent increase in the number of managers eligible for bonuses was associated with a 0.20 percent increase in return on assets.[22] Here the percent of pay that was variable was strongly related to profitability.

While advocates emphasize the link between pay and performance, in practice this link is often a challenge to achieve. Several conditions must be met, including a constructive, trusting relationship with employees; fair, understandable criteria for measuring performance; a plan for providing employees with honest feedback; simple, easily understood mechanisms for payouts (or non-payouts); and some means to handle the inevitable changes that are required. In many cases, these supports are simply not there.[23]

Remember also that these plans are only part of a total compensation system, which is part of an overall human resource management system. A pay system that is consistent with the company's strategic approach to managing human resources communicates the philosophy and values of the organization and strengthens the links between behaviors and rewards. Performance-based pay plans can benefit employers and link their financial success with that of employees, but not unless managers give serious thought to both the company's business situation and the employees' needs. Then, employees are more likely to feel they receive equitable returns for their efforts and managers are more likely to see greater success for the organization.

## PAY IMPLEMENTATION

Proper administration is the fourth block in the pay model (see Exhibit 11.4). To achieve the objectives for which it was designed, the system must be administered properly and fairly. Two key administrative issues are (1) gaining employee acceptance and (2) ensuring legal compliance.

### Gaining Acceptance

One common approach to gaining acceptance, understanding, and valuable ideas from managers and employees is by using compensation committees that include key managers, nonmanagerial employees, and/or union officials.

Research strongly suggests that attending to the fairness of the procedures, rather than results alone, is likely to foster commitment, trust, and acceptance of results. Employee participation may help achieve this fairness. Researchers observe that if people do not participate in decisions, there is little to prevent them from assuming that things would have been better, had they been in charge.[24]

A design process that includes employees can be successful in overcoming resistance to change. Employees are more likely to be committed to the system if they have some control over what happens.

#### Communication and Appeals

The literature on pay administration usually exhorts employers to communicate pay information. One reason is that according to some research, employees seem to misperceive the pay system. For example, they overestimate the pay of those with lower-level jobs and underestimate the pay of those in higher-level jobs. They think that the pay structure is more compressed than it actually is. Consequently, the pay differentials have no opportunity to motivate employees. There is even some evidence to suggest that the good will engendered by the act of being open about pay also affects employee satisfaction with pay.[25]

Despite managers' best attempts to help employees understand how their pay is set, employees sometimes feel they have been unjustly treated. They may believe their performance was unjustly evaluated, their jobs improperly evaluated, or even that the external market comparisons excluded relevant firms. Many firms design procedures to handle these disagreements. These mechanisms are discussed in Chapter Fifteen on employee relations.

## Ensuring Legal Compliance

No matter its form, pay systems must comply with legislation. If an employer is operating in several different countries, there are several different sets of legislation to comply with. In the United States, legislation affects wages and hours of work, and benefits. Antidiscrimination legislation, designed to ensure that all employees of similar ability, seniority, and qualifications receive the same pay for the same work, is discussed in Chapter Two. The effect of this legislation on pay systems in the past 25 years cannot be overestimated. Benefits legislation is discussed in Chapter Thirteen.

### Wage and Hour Regulations

The Fair Labor Standards Act of 1938 (FLSA) is the basic pay regulation act in the United States. Many countries have similar legislation. FLSA has been amended many times. It has a number of important provisions.

**Minimum wages** All employers covered by the law must pay an employee at least a minimum wage per hour. In 1938, the minimum wage was 25 cents per hour. In 1996, the minimum became $5.15. Proposals to increase it again began shortly after that.

Most economists argue that a minimum wage is harmful, because it can price workers with few skills out of the market. Others argue that a higher minimum is an antipoverty program, since people who work full time at the minimum wage earn only slightly above the federal poverty level.

While one immediately thinks of teenage employees of fast-food restaurants when we think of a minimum wage earners, only one-third of the roughly four million minimum-wage earners are teenagers. The rest are adults over 25. An additional 5.5 million workers, or nearly 5 percent of the workforce, receive wages within 50 cents of the minimum. As legislation forces pay rates at the lowest end of the scale to move up, pay rates above the minimum may also be increased in order to maintain

> **EXPLORING THE WEB**
>
> Interested in labor force data, information on government regulations, or other government information? The web site for the Bureau of Labor Statistics is
>
> **http://stats.bls.gov/blshome.html**
>
> The web site containing labor force data is
>
> **http://stats.bls.gov:80/cgi-bin/surveymost**
>
> You can link to it from the bls home page. In addition, the US House of Representative's Internet Law Library Code of Federal Regulations, at
>
> **http://www.pls.com:80-1/his/cfr.html**
>
> will keep you current on compliance.

differentials. This shift in pay structure does not affect all industries equally. For example, the lowest rates paid in the steel, chemical, oil, and pharmaceutical industries are already well above minimum; any legislative change would have little direct impact on employers in these industries. However, retailing and service firms tend to pay many clerks and sales personnel at or near minimum wage. When legislation results in substantially higher labor costs for these firms, the possibility of substituting capital for jobs (e.g., automated inventory control systems, prepacked frozen french fries) or holding down employment level increases, thus reducing the number of jobs available.

Conventional economic theory says that this job loss falls most heavily on inexperienced and unskilled workers because their value added does not equal their cost. The high rate of unemployment among teenagers supports this theory. However, a number of studies cast doubt on this belief. A decade ago, most studies concluded that 1 percent or more of all minimum wage workers lost their jobs for each 10 percent increase in the minimum wage.[26] But more recent studies put the job losses at less than 1 percent, or roughly 40,000 people, if the proposed increase to $5.15 were passed. One study goes even further; it claims no employment effects among fast-food restaurants in New Jersey when that state's minimum wage was increased from $4.25 to $5.05 in 1992.[27] (Forty-seven states also have minimum wage laws to cover employees exempt from FLSA.) However, that study relied on phone interviews rather than actual payroll records to confirm interviews. Critics have attacked the methodology and say that a closer examination finds that "the laws of economics have not been repealed": Increasing the minimum wage prices some people out of the job market.

Minimum wage discussion is tied up in the social good of people who are not faring well in the market economy.[28] Some make the case that continuing a low minimum wage permits the continuation of boring, dead-end jobs that ought to be modernized. Many employers won't bother doing the necessary upgrading and training of employees if they can get by with paying low wages. Others believe that a higher wage will make it more attractive to people to leave welfare or other government assistance and join the labor market. The topic stirs endless debate.

**Overtime pay** An employee covered by the law who works more than 40 hours per week must be paid one-and-one-half times the base wage for overtime hours.

**Child labor prohibition** The law prohibits employing persons between 16 and 18 in hazardous jobs, such as meatpacking and logging. Persons under 16 cannot be employed in jobs involving interstate commerce except for nonhazardous work for a parent or guardian. However, there are exceptions and limitations to the law.

**Exemptions** For jobs covered by the FLSA, strict record keeping of hours and pay is required so the Department of Labor, which enforces the act, can ensure compliance. However, FLSA does not cover all jobs. The list of exemptions is probably the most complex part of the act. Most organizations make distinctions in their pay systems between "nonexempts" (jobs subject to FLSA overtime and hours provisions) and "exempts." In practice, however, the changing nature of work has muddied this distinction. In general, professional, executive, and administrative jobs are exempt. Most jobs in the transportation industry are also exempt, because of the practical difficulty of tracking exact hours of work.

The Department of Labor provides strict criteria for which jobs qualify for various exemptions. For example, to meet the executive exemption, employees must:

- Primarily undertake management duties.
- Supervise two or more employees.
- Have control (or at least great influence) over hiring, firing, and promotion.
- Exercise discretionary powers.
- Devote at least 80 percent of their work hours to such activities.

### Prevailing Wage Laws

Several laws, most notably the Davis-Bacon Act of 931 and the Walsh-Healey Act of 1936, require that workers on covered projects receive at least a government-defined prevailing wage in an area. Covered projects include government-financed construction costing more than $2,000 (Davis-Bacon) and production or supply contracts for government purchases over $10,000 (Walsh-Healey). The government theoretically surveys wages in the area and then sets the prevailing rate as the minimum to be paid on the government project. In practice, it takes the union rates in an area. Therefore, a government-set prevailing rate may correspond to the actual rate of only a minority of an area's laborers.

### Wage Controls and Guidelines

Several times in the past quarter century or so, the federal government has established wage freezes and guidelines. Wage freezes are government orders that permit no wage increases; wage controls limit the size of wage increases. Wage guidelines are similar to wage controls, but they are voluntary rather than legally required restrictions.

Economists differ on the usefulness of wage and price freezes. Critics argue that the controls disrupt market forces and lead to frustration and strikes. However, during times of national emergencies, and for relatively brief periods, the controls can slow (but not indefinitely postpone) inflation. The important point is that compensation decisions must fit any governmental wage guidelines or controls.

## Comparable Worth

As you recall from Chapter Two, the Equal Pay Act and the Civil Rights Act embody the principle of "equal pay for equal work." Equal work is defined by four factors: (1) equal skills, (2) equal effort, (3) equal responsibility, and (4) equal working conditions. These are strikingly similar to the compensable factors found in most job evaluation plans.

Differences in pay for equal work are permitted if they result from (1) differences in seniority, (2) differences in quality of performance, (3) differences in quantity and quality of production (incentives), or (4) some factor other than gender or race (e.g., premiums for night hours).

### Earnings Gap

There is a continuing debate over the causes of the earnings gap between men and women and how to define and subsequently eliminate pay discrimination. The debate is not over whether all employees should be paid equally when they are doing the same jobs. This is required by the Equal Pay Act and the Civil

Rights Act. What is at issue is pay differences for *dissimilar jobs.* Should jobs that are dissimilar in content but in "some sense of comparable value" be paid the same? For example, should nurses be paid equally with plumbers or office and clerical workers equally with assemblers or carpenters?

Several basic issues underlie the controversy:

1. Is the persistent gap in earnings between men and women (the average earnings of fully employed women is approximately 70 percent of the earnings of fully employed men) due to pay discrimination, or is it due to productivity-related factors (nature of the jobs, seniority, continuity of employment) and/or the collective bargaining process?
2. Should the currently accepted standard for pay determination (equal pay for equal or substantially equal work) be replaced with another standard—equal pay for work of comparable worth or value?
3. What is comparable worth and can it be assessed?
4. What are the consequences of adopting comparable worth as the standard for pay determination? Will the earnings gap between men and women be reduced? What will be the effects of adjusting the pay structure on inflation, labor costs, or individual career decisions?

### A Definition of Comparable Worth

Comparable worth, the principal mechanism suggested to reduce the earnings gap, has been defined as "jobs that require comparable (not identical) skill, responsibility, and effort."[29] The basic approach involves equal pay for all jobs with the same total job evaluation points. Thus, internal equity would dominate external market concerns. In Washington and Minnesota, for example, jobs such as public health nurse and secretary received the same job evaluation points as carpenters and other craft jobs.[30] In order to comply with comparable worth legislation passed by these states, the rates paid to nurses and secretaries were raised to match those paid to crafts.

Consider Exhibit 12.10. The black circles are jobs held predominantly by women (i.e., greater than or equal to 70 percent women). The other circles are jobs held predominantly by men (i.e., greater than or equal to 70 percent men). The policy line (solid) for the women's jobs is below and less than the policy line for men's jobs (dotted line). A comparable worth policy would use the results of the single job evaluation plan (*x* axis) and price all jobs as if they were male-dominated jobs. Thus, all jobs with 100 job points would receive $700, all those with 200 points would receive $800, and so on.

The courts have not interpreted present laws in a manner that encompasses comparable worth. However, several other countries have adopted comparable worth as the standard for pay determination.[31] Most notable is the Canadian Pay Equity legislation. Ontario requires all employers, public and private, to adopt plans that are similar to the comparable worth approach already described.

## Special Groups

In every organization, special groups emerge. Often they are special because of the value of their contribution to the organization's success. The decisions

EXHIBIT 12.10 Job Evaluation Points and Salary

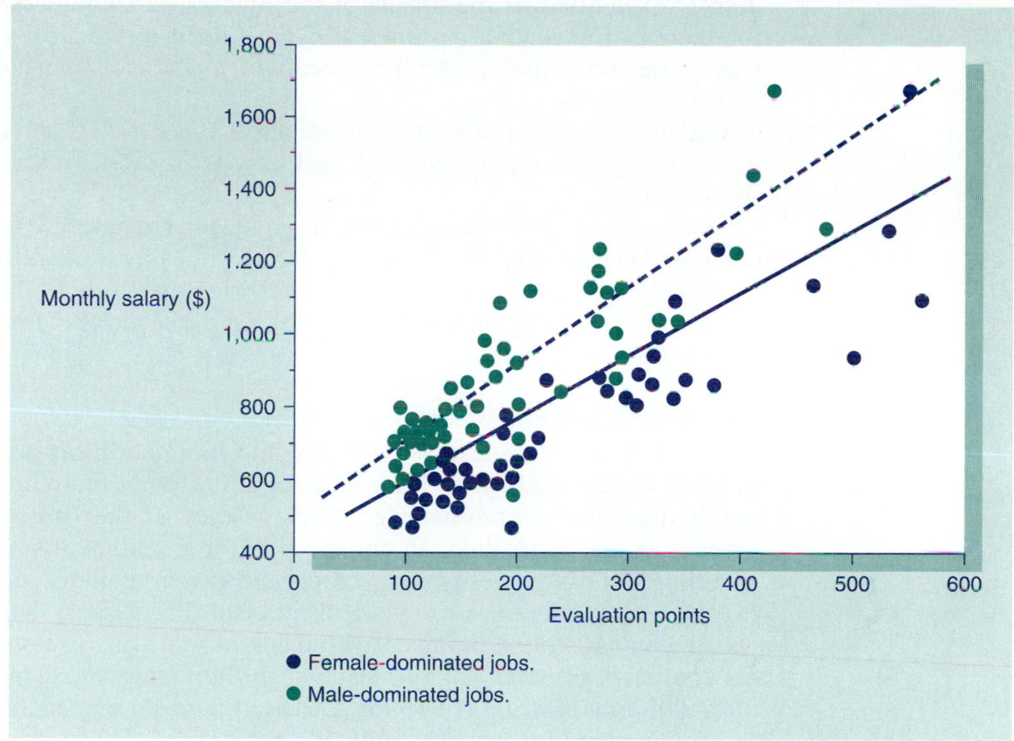


they make significantly affect the revenues and resources on which the organization depends. Examples include research and development scientists at Amgen, marketing and salespeople at General Mills, research and marketing at Merck, and so on. Or they are special because of unique market conditions (i.e., a shortage of computer system engineers) or unique circumstances (i.e., managers on international assignments). These external and organizational conditions often require the design of unique pay plans. Probably the most obvious one is executive pay. We discuss executive pay to illustrate how pay plans are tailored for these special groups. The point is that managers typically design several pay plans (e.g., executive, managerial, international, sales, clerical), not just a single plan.

### Executives: A Really Special Group

For purposes of compensation, executives are usually defined as individuals in the very highest levels of the organization (e.g., the top 2 to 5 percent). Designers of executive pay plans face some of the same issues discussed earlier. Only the answers may differ, because external compensation and internal consistency differ. An important difference in executive pay is that it is often tied to the performance of the *entire organization* rather than a team or unit.

### Executive Incentives

Executive incentive plans are based on notions from the *agency theory,* which depicts executives as the agents of the owners (stockholders).[32] According to the theory, if executive pay increases are linked to the firm's performance by way of incentive plans, then the executives make decisions consistent with the owner's interests.

Usually, two types of incentives are used: short-term cash bonuses (based on one or two years of performance), and long-term capital accumulation, such as stock options.

*Stock options* give the executive the right to purchase a fixed number of the company's shares at a fixed price (exercise price) by a fixed time in the future. The executive gains as long as the stock price increases in the future. Options are a form of profit sharing, which links the executives' financial success to that of the shareholders.

### The Critics: Greed, Sticky Downward, and Trust Gap

Public skepticism about executive pay and its relationship to the performance of firms has a long history. Fifty years ago, President Franklin D. Roosevelt inveighed against corporate executives as part of the forces of "entrenched greed." At that same time, an opinion poll reported that "over half of those responding felt executives of large corporations were paid too much." Since then, executive pay continues to evoke skepticism. Particularly befuddling to some was the pay of Robert Stempel, who made nearly $2.2 million in the same year his company, General Motors, lost $4.5 billion and announced the elimination of 74,000 jobs. During the 1990s, CEO pay rose an average 212 percent while factory workers' increased by only 53 percent.

These examples highlight one of the major criticisms underlying executive pay; namely, that executives' total pay (base, bonus, and value of their stock options) is "sticky downward"—their pay seems to suffer little or not at all if performance goes down, yet their pay increases if performance improves.[33]

Research on the relationship between executive pay and firm performance yields mixed results so far. Some report that "on average, compensation plans encourage executives to act on behalf of their shareholders." Others find that executive pay is highly related to performance only during periods when firm performance is improving.

One highly publicized structural issue is the gap between returns received by executives and those received by other employees. For example, the chief executive officer at Disney received *cash* payments of more than $10 million in one year. This is 10 times more than a ride operator in the Disney theme park earns in *an entire lifetime.* Labeled the *trust gap,* many people believe the gap between pay for executives and other employees is unfair. This gap is most obvious when large cash bonuses are paid to executives at the same time that concessions are demanded from other employees. But such comparisons are oversimplified. The effectiveness of executive pay is assumed to show up in later corporate results, in the returns to shareholders, and in more complex ways than a few financial indexes. More rigorous research on these issues is underway.

> **WHAT DO YOU THINK?**
>
> The CEO of Walt Disney Company continues to be one of the highest-paid executives in the world. However, his supporters say that the bulk of his remuneration is the direct result of the phenomenal stock market performance of the company, which shows that performance-based pay really does work. Do you think the Disney Company is helped or hurt by its approach to executive compensation?

## INTERNATIONAL PAY SYSTEMS

The internationalization of businesses, financial markets, trade agreements, and even labor markets is affecting every workplace and employment relationship. Employee compensation, so central to the workplace, is embedded in the social contracts found in each nation.

As we noted in earlier chapters, looking at human resource management as part of the employment relationship among employees, employers, and government offers a useful framework for understanding contemporary changes as well as global differences in practices. The U.S. and German pay systems illustrate the contrasts.[34] "In the United States you work hard to advance to keep a good job, to keep from falling into a shallow social safety net . . . whereas the German pay system and social benefits system is close to a guaranteed annual income".[35] A typical German employee's marginal tax rate (percent of tax on each additional dollar or mark earned) is 30 percent higher than in the United States. As a result, the return for working extra hours or working harder to receive a gainsharing bonus is smaller in Germany. But in exchange for their higher taxes, German employees receive more generous social benefits such as welfare and unemployment payments, national health care, and subsidized college and apprenticeship programs.[36]

Thus, understanding how to manage employee compensation in Germany requires an understanding of the role played by government, employees, and employers. Efforts to change employee compensation systems—for example, to make them more responsive to customers, encourage innovative and quality service, or control costs—must be managed within the context of the employment relationship in each country. However, we must add a note of caution: National and regional generalizations often mislead, often as incorrectly as personal stereotypes. To claim that all organizations in Germany or Japan or the United States operate in some similar way ignores variations and differences. Considerable variety among company practices within any country exists.

### Comparing Wages and Productivity

Japan and many Western European countries pay higher wages than the United States. Exhibit 12.11 shows that Japan's hourly compensation costs for manufacturing workers are about 125 percent of the U.S. average. Germany holds the highest compensation costs at 160 percent that of the United States.

However, interpret such direct compensation comparisons with caution. If compensation in Korea, Taiwan, and Hong Kong is so low, isn't it a no-brainer to relocate your manufacturing in these low-wage places? Not if productivity is also considered. Lower wages often go hand in hand with lower productivity. Consequently, international comparisons of productivity and labor costs per unit produced become crucial. For example, Korean unit labor costs are 86 percent of U.S. costs (compared to wages at 38 percent).[37] In the Philippines and Malaysia, unit labor costs are 112 percent those of the United States. Therefore, even though the wages in these two countries are only a small fraction of U.S. wages, it may be more cost effective to manufacture goods in the United States.

Even more important than these country-level comparisons are relative differences among companies and their direct competitors. In Chapter Eleven we discussed measuring a market wage rate. Comparisons of wages among societies as

EXHIBIT 12.11 Index of Hourly Compensation Costs for Manufacturing Workers in Selected Countries, 1990–1994

United States = 100

| Country or area | 1990 | 1991 | 1992 | 1992 | 1994 |
|---|---|---|---|---|---|
| United States | 100 | 100 | 100 | 100 | 100 |
| Canada | 106 | 110 | 105 | 98 | 92 |
| Mexico | 11 | 12 | 14 | 15 | 15 |
| Australia | 88 | 87 | 81 | 75 | 80 |
| Hong Kong | 21 | 23 | 24 | 26 | 28 |
| Israel | 57 | 56 | 56 | 53 | 53 |
| Japan | 86 | 94 | 101 | 114 | 125 |
| Korea | 25 | 30 | 32 | 33 | 37 |
| New Zealand | 56 | 54 | 49 | 48 | 52 |
| Singapore | 25 | 28 | 31 | 31 | 37 |
| Sri Lanka | 2 | 3 | 2 | 3 | - |
| Taiwan | 26 | 28 | 32 | 31 | 32 |
| Austria | 119 | 116 | 126 | 122 | 127 |
| Belgium | 129 | 127 | 138 | 128 | 134 |
| Denmark | 120 | 117 | 124 | 114 | 120 |
| Finland | 141 | 136 | 123 | 99 | 110 |
| France | 102 | 98 | 105 | 97 | 100 |
| Germany | 147 | 146 | 157 | 154 | 160 |
| Greece | 45 | 44 | 46 | 41 | - |
| Ireland | 79 | 78 | 83 | 73 | - |
| Italy | 119 | 119 | 121 | 96 | 95 |
| Luxembourg | 110 | 107 | 116 | 110 | - |
| Netherlands | 123 | 117 | 126 | 119 | 122 |
| Norway | 144 | 139 | 143 | 121 | 122 |
| Portugal | 25 | 27 | 32 | 27 | 27 |
| Spain | 76 | 78 | 83 | 69 | 67 |
| Sweden | 140 | 142 | 152 | 106 | 110 |
| Switzerland | 140 | 139 | 144 | 135 | 145 |
| United Kingdom | 85 | 88 | 89 | 76 | 80 |

Dash indicates data not available.

different as the United States and Japan, for example, can be very misleading. Even if wages appear the same, expenses for health care, living costs, and typical company-provided perquisites such as dormitories and commuting allowance complicate the picture. Comparing a specific U.S. firm and a specific Japanese firm may be even more misleading.[38] Statistics may not be publicly available or may not completely specify what is or is not included. A number of different comparisons may all be valid, but all may paint different pictures. Mexico provides an example closer to home. The Bureau of Labor Statistics comparison of hourly compensation costs in 29 countries calculates wages in Mexico at only 14 percent those of the United States. However, another source puts the "effective labor costs" in Mexico at about 36 percent.[39] The difference between the two estimates stems largely from supplemental pay required by either Mexican law or custom.[40] Another consulting firm reports that because of shortages of trained Mexican managers, these managers often get 120 to 130 percent the pay of their U.S. counterparts. The point of including these variations is to show that some data are useful only for gross comparisons and for understanding trends over time. But to design a pay system in one of these countries, current local data and an understanding of local culture and customs are required.

## Comparing Systems

The pay system model used in this and the previous chapter guides our discussion of pay systems in different countries. While our experience suggests that organizations face similar strategic issues in every country, the relative importance among them differs greatly. You will recognize the basic choices, which seem universal:

- Objectives of pay systems
- External competitiveness
- Internal alignment
- Employee contributions
- Implementation.

If the choices are universal, the decisions are not. Some of these differences are best explained by governmental laws and regulations which reflect national cultures and politics. For example, German and Japanese tax laws make stock options unattractive. Not surprisingly, the use of stock options is practically nil in both countries. Pay and benefits regulations vary widely among countries. The majority of European Union countries specify a minimum wage, maximum hours, and formal methods for employee participation through work councils.[41]

Another striking difference in regulations is that many Western and Central European countries have nationally negotiated wage agreements which set the floor for all wages of unionized employees in the country. Such national-level decision making reduces the ability of organization-level managers to attempt to tailor their pay system to fit their organization's unique business strategy.

In addition to nationally negotiated agreements, national laws in some countries regulate wages so strictly that it is difficult to manage any part of employee compensation to help achieve competitive advantage. In effect, decisions about pay are taken out of the hands of the organization and placed in the hands of regulators and nationwide associations. For example, Sweden is so constrained by laws and national agreements that all Swedish organizations have very similar pay systems. However, global competitive forces are pressuring organizations in all countries to seek to control labor costs and attempt to use performance-based pay approaches. Even the strong unions in Germany are beginning to offer employees greater flexibility in setting wages in exchange for guaranteeing employment levels and job security.[42]

## Global Snapshots

Exhibit 12.12 offers some highlighted comparisons based on the major strategic decisions in the pay model.

## EXHIBIT 12.12 Global Comparisons

| | People's Republic of China | Egypt | Germany | India | Japan |
|---|---|---|---|---|---|
| **External Competitiveness** | ◆ Lack of data and markets<br>◆ Emphasis on preferential access to scarce goods and services<br>◆ Government agencies control wages; shift to noncash and off-the-books forms | ◆ Lack salary surveys<br>◆ Government guarantees jobs with low pay to college graduates | ◆ National rates negotiated by employers and union association<br>◆ Government and Bundesbank (national bank) major players in negotiations<br>◆ Increasing interest in surveys and market data | ◆ Oversupply of highly qualified labor, forcing wages down; many highly educated workers leave the country | ◆ Comparisons within industry<br>◆ Relative labor costs and workforce productivity important factors<br>◆ Private comparisons among Japanese firms<br>◆ Consultant surveys among multinationals |
| **Internal Alignment** | ◆ Hierarchical levels<br>◆ Small differentials<br>◆ Job based and negotiated with government agencies | ◆ Relatively hierarchical<br>◆ Skill/knowledge based, especially technical<br>◆ Small differentials | ◆ Relatively hierarchical<br>◆ Primarily job based<br>◆ Modest differentials between levels | ◆ Jobs at the bottom levels determined by social class<br>◆ Higher level jobs are job based | ◆ Person based; seniority-ability factors<br>◆ Hierarchical with small differentials<br>◆ Differences compound with tenure |
| **Employee Contribution** | ◆ Growing interest in incentives based on individual and facility performance | ◆ High interest in performance based; up to 40% of pay based on company results<br>◆ High inflation and high taxes decrease impact of performance increases | ◆ Increases based on seniority, inflation, and across-the-board guarantees<br>◆ Increasing interest in performance bonuses, tip to 20% in some cases<br>◆ Performance small percentage of total pay | ◆ Low-level workers have little incentive to do better; excellence by the individual threatens the social system and is not rewarded<br>◆ Payment Bonus Act of 1965 requires profit sharing with a minimum of 8.33% | ◆ Increased interest in individual merit and group-based pay<br>◆ Traditional bonuses (twice yearly) used as variable costs<br>◆ Performance based pay small percentage of total pay<br>◆ Emerging use of performance appraisal |
| **Benefits** | ◆ Major strategic tool; company provides services such as housing, showers, medical, scarce commodities, transportation, and day care | ◆ Moderate mandatory benefits of vacation pay, medical, and retirement | ◆ National health care and national pensions<br>◆ High mandated; costly layoff severance allowance<br>◆ Discretionary; cars | ◆ Mandatory retirement and pension benefits<br>◆ Typical package includes housing, traveling, and geographic allowances | ◆ Mandated; national health care, and retirement; layoff allowances<br>◆ Discretionary; commuting, housing, family, sports facilities, vacations retreats |
| **Nature of Administration** | ◆ Centralized<br>◆ Emphasize government connections<br>◆ Focus on benefits/services | ◆ Governmental taxes and regulations limit the use of pay as a strategic tool<br>◆ Centralized with low participation<br>◆ Search for nontaxable "payments" | ◆ Government policies and regulations major factor<br>◆ Centralized<br>◆ Less use of pay as strategic source of competitive advantage | ◆ Government laws major factor; regardless of profit level or performance level, employee's pay cannot go down<br>◆ Layoffs are illegal | ◆ Increasingly using pay as strategic device<br>◆ Tax regulations major influence; retaining allowances; only base pay included in pension, medical, retirement calculations |

EXHIBIT 12.12 (concluded)

| | Korea | Mexico | Russia | Slovenia | United Kingdom |
|---|---|---|---|---|---|
| **External Competitiveness** | ♦ Mobility among companies relatively common<br>♦ Surveys of wages and labor costs<br>♦ Competitive position important for attracting and retaining workers | ♦ Competitive forces influencing pay of higher-skilled workers<br>♦ Surveys based upon work conduct<br>♦ Overall labor cost relatively low; yet, 10 to 25% premium for scarce talent | ♦ Lacks markets and data, setting pay is guessing game<br>♦ Personal negotiators based on expertise | ♦ National negotiated rates with unions, employers, and the government<br>♦ Rates paid above negotiated rate to attract needed talent | ♦ Reduced reliance on national rates negotiated by employers and union associations, more on industry specific data<br>♦ White-collar based on "London rates"<br>♦ Increasing use of surveys and competitive market data |
| **Internal Alignment** | ♦ Person based, seniority, ability, and competencies<br>♦ Hierarchical with small differentials | ♦ Relatively hierarchical levels<br>♦ Primarily job based with skill based in high tech<br>♦ Modest differentials | ♦ Hierarchical<br>♦ Appearance of job based<br>♦ Small differentials | ♦ Modest to low hierarchies<br>♦ Small differentials<br>♦ Job and skill based | ♦ Relatively hierarchical levels<br>♦ Primarily job based<br>♦ Modest differences among levels |
| **Employee Contribution** | ♦ Increasing use of performance-based pay<br>♦ Companywide bonuses at least once a year | ♦ Increases based on seniority, inflation, and across-the-board guarantees<br>♦ Growing interest in performance based<br>♦ Performance about 5% of total pay | ♦ Transition from old, out-of-date piece rates and across-the-board government mandated increases<br>♦ Facility level incentives | ♦ Increasing use of profit sharing, gain-sharing, and performance appraisals | ♦ Increase based on seniority, inflation, and across-the-board guarantees<br>♦ Growing use of performance based (75% use individual based and 50% use unit or firm based)<br>♦ Performance still small percentage of total pay |
| **Benefits** | ♦ Mandatory national health care and retirement<br>♦ Generally sparse benefits; few companies pay overtime or holidays | ♦ Moderate mandatory medical, retirement, low cash allowances<br>♦ Christmas bonus (15 days pay) and Vacation Bonus (25% of pay)<br>♦ Mandated profit sharing; 10% of pretax profits | ♦ Major strategic tool; offer scarce goods and services, medical care, improved housing, access to quality products | ♦ High mandated coverage; medical care, pensions, and vacations/-holidays | ♦ Slight trend away from company cars, though it is still a major symbol of status<br>♦ National health care and pensions<br>♦ Paid leaves (25 days) plus national holidays<br>♦ Lunch and parking allowance |
| **Nature of Administration** | ♦ Government policies and regulations not enforced stringently | ♦ Government regulations major factor<br>♦ Acquired rights; if a benefit or bonus is paid for two years, employee has a right to it<br>♦ Centralized<br>♦ Low costs and increased use of incentives as strategic aspects | ♦ High inflation and uncertainty<br>♦ Preferential access to scarce goods and service (nontaxed)<br>♦ Individual negotiations | ♦ Government policies major factor<br>♦ Increased use of performance based as a strategic tool | ♦ Government policies and regulations a major influence<br>♦ Centralized and open<br>♦ Early efforts at using pay strategically have not had impact on administration<br>♦ Increasing effort to the employee reviews |

### External Competitiveness

North America (United States and Canada) and the United Kingdom remain relatively unique in the importance placed on labor and product market competitors to set base pay. Japanese and Korean companies emphasize internal more than external factors.[43] As already noted, employers and union associations negotiate national rates of pay in several countries in Europe and Asian countries. These rates act as the going rates for entire industries. By establishing national rates for different types of work, pay is no longer a variable to be managed.

### Internal Alignment

Person-based systems are used to determine base pay in Japan and Korea and in high technology firms in Egypt and Mexico.[44] Most companies in the European Union and the United States use some form of job basis for setting base pay, though some careers (engineering and computers) are based on person factors (types of degree and years since degree). And person-based approaches (knowledge and competency) are increasingly being considered. Exhibit 12.13 shows that pay differentials vary among countries. While German manufacturing employees are the highest paid in this particular comparison, German CEOs are near the bottom.

### Employee Contributions

An increased interest in performance-based pay seems to be a global trend. The percent of total pay that is based on performance varies greatly owing to tax rates, culture, and ideology. For example, the Communist party objected to wage differences by saying they do no good and lead to inequality in society. In China, this was rationalized by a Confucian saying, "Do not worry about scarcity, only about unevenness." The United Kingdom and United States seem to place greatest emphasis on performance-based approaches.

## Expatriate Pay

When multinational organizations decide to open facilities in an international location, one of the many decisions they face is what type of personnel to hire. International subsidiaries choose among a mix of *expatriates* (i.e., someone whose citizenship is that of the employer's base country; such as a Japanese citizen working for Sony in Toronto), *third-country nationals* (TNCs; someone whose citizenship is neither that of the employer's base country nor of the location of the subsidiary, such as a German citizen working for Sony in Toronto), and *local country nationals* (LCNs; citizens of the country in which the subsidiary is located, such as a Canadian citizen working for Sony in Toronto). One obvious choice is to staff the subsidiary with individuals whose citizenship corresponds to the country of origin for the subsidiary: LCNs. Hiring LCNs has a number of advantages: (1) relocation expenses are saved, (2) concerns about adapting to the local culture are avoided, and (3) employment of LCNs satisfies nationalist demands for hiring locals. Only rarely do organizations decide that hiring LCNs is inappropriate. Only about 1 percent of the international workforces of U.S. and European multinational companies are expatriates, and about 4.2 percent are for Japanese manufacturing companies.

## EXHIBIT 12.13 Pay Through the Ranks

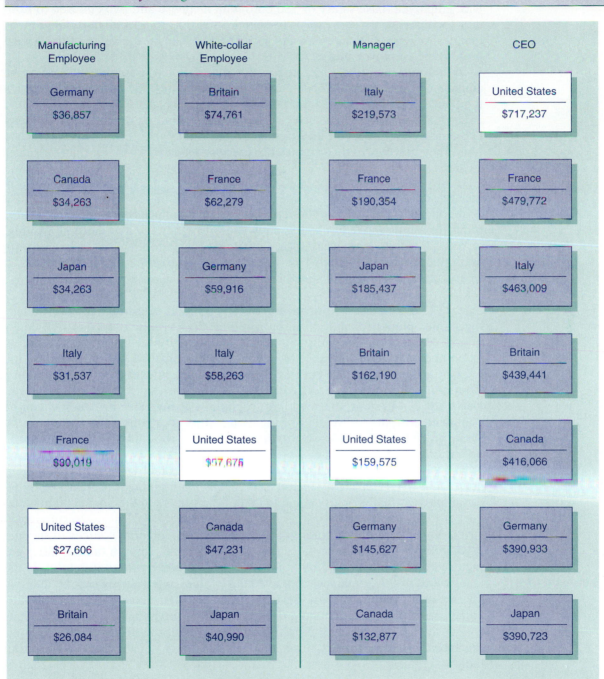

| Manufacturing Employee | White-collar Employee | Manager | CEO |
|---|---|---|---|
| Germany $36,857 | Britain $74,761 | Italy $219,573 | United States $717,237 |
| Canada $34,263 | France $62,279 | France $190,354 | France $479,772 |
| Japan $34,263 | Germany $59,916 | Japan $185,437 | Italy $463,009 |
| Italy $31,537 | Italy $58,263 | Britain $162,190 | Britain $439,441 |
| France $30,019 | United States $57,675 | United States $159,575 | Canada $416,066 |
| United States $27,606 | Canada $47,231 | Germany $145,627 | Germany $390,933 |
| Britain $26,084 | Japan $40,990 | Canada $132,877 | Japan $390,723 |

Expatriate assignments are expensive. For example, a company that sends a U.S. employee (base salary of $80,000) with a spouse and two children to London for three years can expect to spend $800,000 to $1,000,000. Obviously, that cost of expatriate assignments needs to be offset by the value of the contributions the employee makes.[45]

In addition, employee preferences for international assignments need to be considered. For many European and Asian companies, the home markets are a relatively small part of the total product market. Therefore, working in another country at some point in a career is part of understanding the market. For many U.S.employees, however, leaving the United States may mean leaving the action. They may worry that expatriate experience sidetracks rather than enhances a career.

## Elements of Expatriate Pay

A shopping list of items comprising expatriate compensation includes everything from household furnishing allowances to language and cultural training, to spousal employment assistance, to rest and relaxation leaves for longer-term assignments. Usually such lists are organized into four major components: salary, taxes, housing, and general services allowances and premiums.

**Salary** The base salary plus incentives (e.g., merit, eligibility for profit sharing, bonus plans) for the job to be filled by the expatriate needs to be determined. More often than not, this is accomplished by means of job evaluation or competency-based plans. 3M, for example, designed an international job evaluation plan which it applies globally for its international assignments. Common factors describe different 3M jobs in various regions of the world. Using the 3M system, the work of a regional HR manager in Brussels can be compared with one in Austin or Singapore. Most companies attempt to use the same procedures for valuing expatriate jobs that they use for their domestic operations.

Beyond salaries and incentives, the intent of the other components is to help keep employees financially intact. This means maintaining a standard of living for employees that is nearly equal to that of their peers in the home country.

**Taxes** Income earned in foreign countries has two potential sources of income tax liability. With few exceptions (e.g., Saudi Arabia), foreign tax liabilities are incurred on income earned by a non-citizen. The other potential liability is the taxes owed in the employees' home country. The United States has the dubious distinction of being the only developed country that taxes its citizens for income earned in another country, even though that income is taxed by the country in which it was earned. Employers handle this through *tax equalization* allowances to ensure that expatriates do not have any negative tax effects from their assignments.[46]

**Housing** Most international companies pay allowances for housing or provide company-owned housing for expatriates. Providing expatriates with appropriate housing seems to have a major impact on the success of the assignment.

**Service Allowances** A friend in Moscow cautions that when taking the famed Moscow subway, we must be sure to pay the fare at the beginning of the ride because inflation is so high that if we wait to pay at the end of the ride, the fare will be more than we can afford! Cost-of-living allowances, club memberships, transportation assistance, child care and education, spousal employment, local culture training, and personal security are some of the many items that may be included in service allowances.

### The Balance Sheet Approach

The balance sheet approach, illustrated in Exhibit 12.14, is used by most North American, European, and Japanese global firms to pay expatriates.[47] As you can tell from its name, this approach borrows from accounting, where credits and debits must balance. All of the elements just discussed—taxes, housing, service allowances—are included, plus a "reserve" to cover discretionary payments that may be negotiated on an individual basis. The premise of the balance sheet approach is that employees on overseas assignments should have the same spending power as an employee in the home country. Therefore, the home country is the standard for all payments. The approach has three objectives:

1. Ensure that mobility of expatriate talent to global assignments is as cost-effective as feasible.
2. Ensure that expatriates neither gain nor lose financially.
3. Minimize adjustments required of expatriates and their dependents.

Of these, the last two seem to receive the major emphasis. Until recently, efforts to link expatriate pay to improving performance and cost effectiveness received less attention.

Despite the inherent difficulties in comparing apples and oranges (and other goods and services), most major companies use some index of cost of living abroad provided by consulting firms, the State Department, or the United Nations. For example, Runzheimer International provides comparative cost-of-living data for different cities around the globe. A $75,000 cost-of-living for a typical family of four in Chicago would translate into about $41,000 in Warsaw, $73,000 in Rome, $151,000 in Seoul, and a whopping $210,000 in Tokyo.

### The Hamburger Standard

If comparing labor costs is difficult, comparing living costs and standards is even more complex. The Bank of Switzerland takes one approach by using a uniform basket of goods based on European consumer habits, which includes the prices for 137 items from clothing to transportation to personal care. A woman shopping for a summer dress, jacket, skirt, shoes, and tights will find Tokyo the most expensive place to shop ($2,300), whereas Nairobi ($50) and Bombay ($120) are best buys. Tokyo is equally expensive for a man. If he wants a blazer, shirt, jeans, socks and shoes, he will need to come up with $1,800 for a medium-priced outfit.[48]

If your tastes don't run to blazers and jackets, *The Economist* takes a Big Mac approach. Instead of pricing a complex basket of goods and services, the magazine uses the price of a Big Mac in different locations. The average price of a Big Mac in the United States is $2.30 (a four-city average), in China 9.00 yuan (U.S. $1.03), in Canada $2.86 (U.S. $2.06), and Russia 2,900 rubles (about U.S. $1.66).[49] No word yet on an Arch Deluxe approach.

EXHIBIT 12.14 Balance Sheet Approach

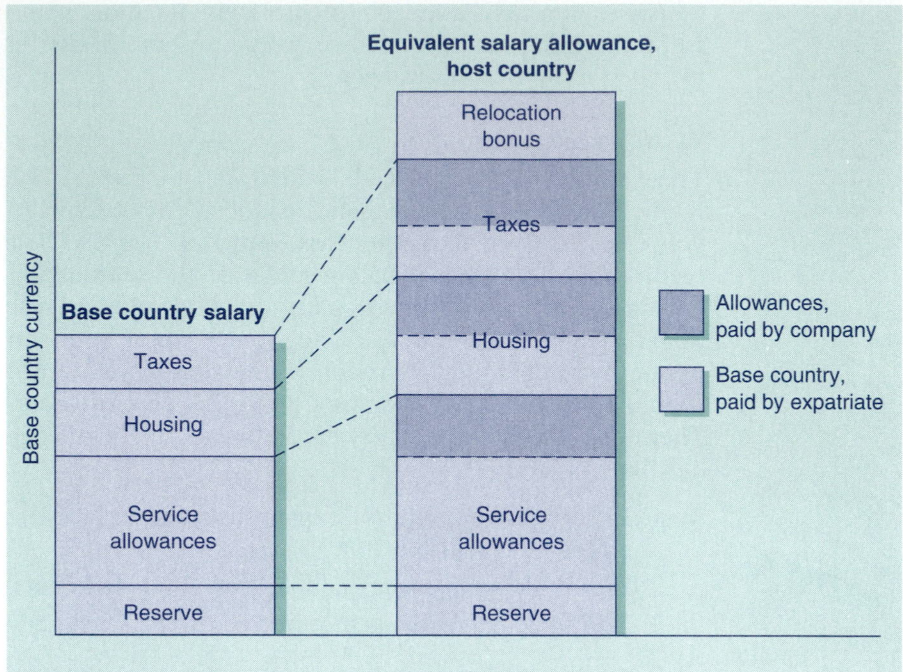


## SUMMARY

The last two chapters have examined the basic pay issues and illustrated alternative techniques designed to aid managers facing these issues. This chapter examined pay for individual employees and some common techniques for varying pay based on the contributions of the employees toward the achievement of organization objectives. Employers who choose not to vary pay with performance or seniority may opt for flat rates and across-the-board increases. Employers who wish to pay for performance have a number of options from which to choose. We categorized the options based on (1) whether the performance payment was added onto base pay, and (2) whether individual or group levels of performance triggered the payment. Merit pay is by far the most common pay for performance approach. Pay ranges and merit increase guidelines translate merit pay. Though individual incentives, like merit pay, are also based on individual performance, incentives do not increase base pay.

By far, the hottest pay for performance approach is gainsharing. Even though it is not a new technique, it is enjoying renewed popularity as employers look for new ways to enhance competitiveness by increasing productivity and controlling costs. Gainsharing plans may be based on the work results of a work team or the entire organization. Gainsharing with employees shares the gains that result from changed behaviors.

Some employee groups, including executives, are likely to be paid under a separate pay plan. As with gainsharing, the objective of executive pay is to tie the pay system to the results of performance.

In today's economy, it is shortsighted to ignore what is happening around the world. Because compensation reflects society and government as well as economic pressures, compensation practices vary considerably among countries. We use the pay model from Chapter Eleven to provide a framework for understanding pay systems around the world. The model emphasizes the concepts of external competitiveness, internal alignment, employee contributions, and implementation.

The next chapter examines a major form of compensation: benefits. Rising costs, concerns about their tax-free status, and questions about their value make benefits a timely topic.

## QUESTIONS

1. In what circumstances may an employer wish to pay individuals performing the same job different wages? In what circumstances may an employer wish to pay all individuals performing the same job the same wages?
2. What are the most common employee differences used for individualizing pay?
3. What are some of the difficulties in a merit pay system?
4. When would you use group pay incentives instead of individual pay incentives?
5. What are some of the problems with variable pay?
6. How do gainsharing and profit sharing affect motivation of different employee groups? Are the effects always positive?
7. What employee groups might need a separate pay system? Why?
8. What is comparable worth, and how does it differ from equal pay? What is legally required? What are some approaches to putting comparable worth into operation? What are some difficulties?
9. Why are international productivity comparisons important?
10. What is the main consideration in expatriate pay as it is commonly operationalized today? What are some criticisms of this approach?

## YOUR TURN
### The Class Comparison

With your classmates, prepare a list of items that you feel properly reflect living standards for your group. Get very specific so that comparisons can be made. Once the class has decided on a list, enlist the help of friends and relatives who live in different parts of your city, and in different cities, and in different states. Ask them to price the items on the list and return the information to you. If there are special circumstances that cause them to feel any of their information is wrong or distorted, ask for that information, too. Then, as a group, compare all the information and propose a class index of price comparisons. What conclusions can you make from your information?

## NOTES AND REFERENCES


1. George T. Milkovich and Jerry Newman. *Compensation,* 5th ed. (Homewood, IL: Richard D. Irwin, 1996).
2. G. Douglas Jenkins, Jr.; Gerald E. Ledford, Jr.; Nina Gupta; and D. Harold Doty, *Skill-Based Pay* (Scottsdale, AZ: American Compensation Association. 1992).
3. Luis R. Gomez-Meja, ed. *Compensation and Benefits* (Washington, DC: Bureau of National Affairs. 1989).
4. Kenan S. Abosch and Janice S. Hand, *Broadbanding Models* (Scottsdale, AZ: American Compensation Association, 1994).
5. George Milkovich and Carolyn Milkovich, "Making Pay for Performance Work," *Compensation and Benefits Review,* Sept.–Oct. 1992, pp. 53–62.
6. Robert Heneman, *Merit Pay: Linking Pay Increases to Performance Ratings* (Reading, MA: Addison-Wesley, 1992).
7. Robert Bretz, Jr., George Milkovich, and Walter Read, "The Current State of Performance Appraisal Research and Practice: Concerns, Directions, and Implications," *Journal of Management* 18, (1992), pp. 321–52.
8. A. Kohn, *Punished by Rewards* (Boston: Houghton-Mifflin, 1993).
9. Andrew Weiss, "Incentives and Worker Behavior: Some Evidence," NBER Working Paper No. 2194, March 1987.
10. Edward E. Lawler III, *Pay and Organization Development* (New York: McGraw-Hill, 1981); Edward E. Lawler III and G. Douglas Jenkins, Jr., "Strategic Reward Systems," in *Handbook of Industrial and Organizational Psychology,* 2nd ed., vol. 3 (Palo Alto, CA: Consulting Psychologists Press, 1992), pp. 1009–49.
11. Richard A. Guzzo, Eduardo Salas, and Associates, *Team Effectiveness and Decision Making in Organizations* (San Francisco: Jossey Bass, 1995); A. Blinder, ed., *Paying for Productivity* (Washington, DC: Brookings Institution, 1990).
12. Jerry McAdams and Elizabeth Hawk, "Capitalizing on Human Assets through Performance-Based Rewards," *ACA Journal* 1, no. 1 (Autumn 1992), pp. 60–73.
13. Brian Graham-Moore and Timothy Ross, *Gainsharing* (Washington, DC: Bureau of National Affairs, 1990).
14. Michael H. Schuster, "The Scanlon Plan: A Longitudinal Analysis," *Journal of Applied Behavioral Science* 20, no. 4 (1984), pp. 23–28.
15. John Wagner, Paul Rubin, and Thomas Callahan, "Incentive Payment and Non-Managerial Productivity: An Interrupted Time Series Analysis of Magnitude and Trend," *Organizational Behavior and Human Decision Processes* 42 (1988), pp. 47–72.
16. Theresa M. Welbourne and Daniel M. Cable, "Group Incentives and Pay Satisfaction: Understanding the Relationship through an Identity Theory Perspective," working paper, Cornell University Center for Advanced Human Resource Studies, Ithaca, NY, 1993.

17. Barry Gerhart and George Milkovich, "Employee Compensation," in *Handbook of Industrial and Organizational Psychology,* 2nd ed., vol. 3 (Palo Alto, CA: Consulting Psychologists Press, 1992).
18. Robert Folger and Mary Konovsky, "Effects of Procedural and Distributive Justice on Reactions to Pay Raise Decisions." *Academy of Management Journal,* March 1989, pp. 115–30; Jerald Greenberg, "Looking Fair vs. Being Fair: Managing Impressions of Organizational Justice," in *Research in Organizational Behavior,* vol. 12, ed. B. M. Staw and L. L. Cummings (Greenwich, CT: JAI Press, 1990).
19. Theresa M. Welbourne, David B. Balkin, and Luis R. Gomez-Mejia, "Gainsharing and Mutual Monitoring: A Combined Agency-Organizational Justice Interpretation," *Academy of Management Journal,* 38, no. 3 (1995), pp. 881–99.
20. George T. Milkovich and Matt Bloom, *Does Performance-Based Pay Really Work? Conclusions Based on the Scientific Research* (Ithaca, NY: Center for Advanced Human Resource Studies, 1995).
21. Ronald E. Ehrenberg, ed. *Do Compensation Policies Matter?* (Ithaca, NY: ILR Press, Cornell University, 1990).
22. Working papers from Cornell University Center for Advanced Human Resource Studies, Ithaca, NY, 1992, address the pay/performance relationship. They include John M. Abowd, "Does Performance-Based Managerial Compensation Affect Subsequent Corporate Performance?"; Barry Gerhart and George T. Milkovich, "Organizational Differences in Managerial Compensation and Financial Performance," and George T. Milkovich, Barry Gerhart, and John Hannon, "The Effects of Research and Development Intensity on Managerial Compensation in Large Organizations."
23. Lee Dyer and Gerald Holder, "A Strategic Perspective of Human Resource Management," in *Human Resource Management: Evolving Roles and Responsibilities,* ed., Lee Dyer and Gerald Holder (Washington, DC: Bureau of National Affairs, 1988) pp. 1:125–86.
24. Edward E. Lawler III, *Strategic Pay* (San Francisco: Jossey-Bass, 1990).
25. G. Douglas Jenkins, Jr., and E. E. Lawler III, "Impact of Employee Participation in Pay Plan Development," *Organization Behavior and Human Performance* 28, no. 2 (1981), pp. 111–28.
26. Finis Welch, Donald Deere, and Kevin Murphy, "Estimates of Job Loss with Increasing Minimum Wage," (paper presented at the American Economic Association, Washington, DC, Jan. 8, 1995); David Neumark and William Wascher, "Employment Effects of Minimum and Subminimum Wages: Panel Data on State Minimum Wage Laws," *Industrial and Labor Relations Review* 46, no. 1 (Oct. 1992), pp. 55–81.
27. David Card and Alan Krueger, "Minimum Wages and Employment: A Case Study of the Fast-Food Industry in New Jersey and Pennsylvania," *American Economic Review,* Sept. 1994, pp. 772–93; Lawrence F. Katz and Alan B. Krueger, "The Effect of the Minimum Wage on the Fast-Food Industry," *Industrial and Labor Relations Review* 46, no. 1 (Oct. 1992), pp. 6–21.

28. David Neumark, "Employment Effects of Minimum and Subminimum Wages: Recent Evidence" mimeo (Washington, DC: Employment Policies Institute, Feb. 1993).
29. Helen Remick, *Comparable Worth and Wage Discrimination* (Philadelphia: Temple University Press, 1984).
30. Erica Groshen, "The Structure of the Female/Male Wage Differential," *Journal of Human Resources* 26, no. 3, pp. 457–72. Doug Grider and Leslie A. Toombs, "Disproving Valuation Discrimination: A Study of Evaluator Gender Bias," *ACA Journal,* Autumn 1993, pp. 24–33.
31. Al Bellak, "Comparable Worth: A Practioner's View," in *Comparable Worth: Issue for the 80's,* vol. 1 (Washington, DC: U.S. Civil Rights Commission, 1985); Victor Fuchs, *Women's Quest for Economic Equality* (Cambridge: Harvard University Press, 1988); T. A. Mahoney, "Job Evaluation: Endangered Species or Anachronism? *Human Resource Management Review* 1 (1991), pp. 155–62.
32. Bruce Ellig, *Executive Compensation—A Total Pay Perspective* (New York: McGraw-Hill, 1982).
33. Graef Crystal, *In Search of Excess* (New York: W. W. Norton, 1991).
34. David Soskice, "Wage Determination: The Changing Role of Institutions in Advanced Industrialized Countries," *Oxford Review of Economic Policy* 6, no. 4, pp. 36–61; David Soskice, "The German Wage Bargaining System," *IRRA 46th Annual Proceedings,* ed., Paula Voss, (1994), pp. 349–58; Anuska Ferligoj, Janez Prasnikar, and Vesna Jordan, "Competitive Strategies and Human Resource Management in SMEs," working paper, University of Ljubljana, 1994.
35. "Pay Setting Headache in Eastern Europe," *IDS European Report* 389 (May 1994), pp. 21–22; Lowell Turner, "From 'Old Red Socks' to Modern Human Resource Managers?" working paper 94–28, Cornell University Center for Advanced Human Resource Studies, (Ithaca, NY, 1994); Jacob C. Manakkalathil and Piotr Chelminski, "The Central European Three: Opportunities and Challenges," *SAM Advanced Management Journal,* Summer 1993, pp. 28–34.
36. Linda Bell and Richard Freeman, *Why Do Americans and Germans Work Different Hours?* (Cambridge, MA: National Bureau of Economic Research, Oct. 1994.)
37. Michael Byungnam Lee, Vida Scarpello, and B. Wayne Rockmore, "Strategic Compensation in South Korea's Publicly Traded Firms" paper presented at the 10th World Congress of the International Industrial Relations Association, Washington, DC, June 1995; Michael Byungnam Lee, "Business Strategy, Participative Human Resource Management and Organizational Performance: The Case of South Korea," working paper, Georgia State University, Oct. 1994.
38. Yoko Sano, "Changes and Continued Stability in Japanese HRM Systems: Choice in the Share Economy," *International Journal of Human Resource Management* Feb. 1993, pp. 11–27; Motohiro Morishima, "The Japanese Human Resource Management System: A Learning Bureaucracy," in *Human Resource Management in the Pacific Rim: Institutions, Practices and Values,* ed., J. Devereaux Jennings and Larry Moore (New York: Walter deGruyter, in press).

39. Mary Grenier, Christopher Kask, and Christopher Sparks, "Comparative Manufacturing Productivity and Unit Labor Costs," *Monthly Labor Review,* Feb. 1995, pp. 26–41; Melvin M. Brodsky, "Labor Market Flexibility: A Changing International Perspective, *Monthly Labor Review,* Nov. 1994, pp. 53–60.
40. "Mexican Labor's Hidden Costs," *Fortune,* Oct. 17, 1994, p. 32.
41. Barbara A. Lee, "The Effect of the European Community's Social Dimension on Human Resource Management in U.S. Multinationals: Perspectives from the United Kingdom and France," *Human Resource Management Review* 4, no. 4 (1994), pp. 333–61; Neil Millward, Mark Steens, David Smart, and W. R. Hawes, *Workplace Industrial Relations in Transition* (Brookfield, T: Dartmouth Publishing, 1992); John T. Addison and W. Stanley Siebert, "Recent Developments in Social Policy in the New European Union," *Industrial and Labor Relations Review,* Oct. 1994, pp. 5–27; Christopher L. Erickson and Sarosh Kuruvilla, "Labor Costs and the Social Dumping Debate in the European Union," *Industrial and Labor Relations Review,* Oct. 1994, pp. 28–47.
42. "The German Industrial Relations System: Lessons for the United States?" *National Planning Association* 14, no. 3 (Dec. 1993), entire issue; also Soskice, "German Wage Bargaining System."
43. Michael Byungnam Lee, "South Korea," in Raoul C. Nacamulli, Miriam Rothman, and Dennis R. Brisco, ed., *Industrial Relations around the World* (New York: Walter DeGruyter, 1993), pp. 245–69; Korea Labor Institute, *Korea's Labor Unions* (Seoul, 1989); Michael Byungnam Lee, "Bonuses, Unions, and Labor Productivity in South Korea" *Journal of Labor Research,* in press; *Benefit Policies for Third Country Nationals, U.S. Expatriates, and Key Local Nationals* (New York: Kwasha Lipton, 1994); William Brown and Janet Walsh, "Pay Determination in Britain in the 1980s: The Anatomy of Decentralizations," *Oxford Review of Economic Policy* 7, no. 1, pp. 44–59; Tony Buxton, Paul Chapman, and Paul Temple, *Britain's Economic Performance* (London: Routledge, 1994); Byong-moo Yang, "Trends, Problems and Directions for Improvement for Korean Industrial Relations" (paper prepared for the forum on Labour-Management Cooperation, Tokyo, Japan, Oct. 1994.
44. Gordon Betcherman, Kathryn McMullen, Norm Leckie, and Christina Caron, ed., *The Canadian Workplace in Transition* (Kingston, Ont.: IRC Press, 1994); "Focus on International Benefits," *Employee Benefit Plan Review,* Nov. 1994, pp. 32–37; Gillian Flynn, "Human Resources in Mexico: What You Should Know," *Personnel Journal,* Aug. 1994, pp. 34–44; Richard D. Kantor and Michael Richerson, "The Egyptian Compensation Environment: Where Change is the Only Constant," *Benefits and Compensation International,* Mar. 1993, pp. 18–22; Arturo, J. Fisher and Douglas J. Carey, "Mexico in the Dawn of NAFTA: The Human Resources Environment," *Journal of International Compensation and Benefits,* July–August 1994, pp. 9–15.
45. *International Total Remuneration,* Certification Course T9; Cal Reynolds, "International Compensation," in *Compensation Guide,* ed., William A. Caldwell (Boston: Warren, Gorham and Lamont, 1994).

46. Monica M. Sabo, "Tax-Effective Compensation Planning for International Assignments," *International Compensation and Benefits,* Jan.–Feb. 1995, pp. 24–28; Charles J. Boyland, "A Short Guide to U.S. Expatriate Taxes," *Journal of International Compensation and Benefits,* July–Aug. 1992, pp. 45–50.

47. Carolyn Gould, "Can Companies Cut Costs by Using the Balance-Sheet Approach?" *International Compensation and Benefits,* July–August 1993, pp. 36–41; David E. Molnar, "Repatriating Executives and Keeping Their Careers on Track," *International Compensation and Benefits,* Nov.–Dec. 1994, pp. 31–35; Ken I. Kim, Hun-Joon Park, and Nori Suzuki, "Reward Allocations in the United States, Japan, and Korea: A Comparison of Individualistic and Collectivistic Cultures," *Academy of Management Journal* 33, no. 1 (1990), pp. 188–98.

48. Daniel Kalt and Manfred Gutmann, ed., *Prices and Earnings Around the Globe* (Zurich: Union Bank of Switzerland, 1994).

49. "Big Mac Currencies," *The Economist,* Apr. 9, 1994, p. 88.

# Benefits

June Betts, an Ohio speech pathologist, developed an Alzheimer's-related disease that left her unable to work at age 61. Ohio's pension plan included $350 a month disability pay plus medical benefits. But the law allowed disability retirements only through age 60. Since Betts was 61, she would have to take early retirement instead, and receive only $158 a month, with no medical benefits. Betts sued, charging that offering disability retirement to only employees age 60 or under was illegal age discrimination. The Supreme Court disagreed: Age-based benefits differences are acceptable, as long as they do not affect employment conditions outside of fringe benefits.[1] In response, Congress passed the Older Workers Benefit Protection Act outlawing age-based differences.

Years ago, Continental Can negotiated an expensive pension plan that was payable to eligible employees in the event of a plant shutdown or extended involuntary layoff. Eligibility for the plan was based on age and years of service. Once eligible, an employee would receive full normal retirement benefits well before normal retirement age. Thus, there was a significant (and apparently irresistible) economic incentive to lay off employees *before* they became eligible and to protect the jobs of those who were already eligible, so that the extra benefits would not have to be paid. Continental developed a sophisticated computer program to identify who was not yet eligible. These employees were not only targeted for dismissal, but their names were continuously tracked so they would not be inadvertently recalled to work and allowed to become eligible. When these targeted workers found out about Continental's tracking, they filed suit.

Continental argued that the decline in demand for steel cans meant that the aggrieved workers would have been laid off anyway. Structuring layoffs with costs—including pension costs—in mind was good business sense. But a federal district court judge said the firm went too far and its action was illegal. Potential benefit consequences had driven its business decisions, rather than the other way around.[2]

These two cases demonstrate some very important benefits issues: the importance of employer-provided benefits to the social welfare of employees and the importance of controlling benefits costs to employers.

This chapter addresses the basic decisions managers make in the design and administration of benefits programs. We consider the conditions affecting benefits decisions, discuss the objectives managers try to achieve with benefits, examine the alternative forms benefits have taken, and highlight what is known about their effects.

## THE GROWTH OF BENEFITS

Although the first recorded profit-sharing plan in the United States occurred at a Pennsylvania glass works in 1794, the big push for increasing benefits occurred during World War II.[3] Wartime needs created serious shortages of workers. Since increases in wages were controlled by the federal government, employers and labor unions came up with new ways to attract and retain employees. Managers

**Employee benefits** are the indirect forms of total compensation; they include paid time away from work, insurance and health protection, employee services, and retirement income.

offered inducements that were not subject to government controls. If the government would not permit managers to offer greater wages, then the mangers would offer to pay medical bills, to provide life insurance, and to subsidize cafeterias instead.

Tax policies encouraged the continued growth in benefits. Most benefits are nontaxable income to employees and are deductible expenses to employers. Today, benefits constitute a major portion of labor costs. In 1929, they amounted to only 3 percent of total payroll; by 1969, they were 31 percent; and in 1995, they topped 40 percent.[4] The average employer pays more than $14,500 a year per employee for benefits. We depict this growth in Exhibit 13.1.

Unions have been a dominant force to improve benefits.[5] In the 1960s and 1970s, a major thrust of unions' bargaining strategy was for increased levels and new forms of benefits. Group auto insurance, dental care, eyeglasses, and prepaid legal fees became common issues at the bargaining table. The success of unions at the bargaining table has a spillover effect on nonunionized employees in the same facility. One study found evidence that benefits for nonunion employees improved 15 to 50 percent when blue-collar employees in that facility belonged to unions.[6]

At General Motors, the company used to pay all health care insurance premiums for its workers and retirees, their dependents, and survivors. Those who were covered by the premiums paid nothing. The result was that, for every vehicle GM produces, health insurance premiums cost $929. GM's foreign competitors paid less than $300 per car for health insurance.[7]

Recently, unions have played a major role in employers' efforts to control health care costs. Since most benefits are a form of tax-free income to their members, unions actively opposed congressional efforts to tax benefits, particularly health insurance. And unions have actively worked with management in seeking approaches to contain rising health care costs, since many members view health care coverage as important as pay increases.

## Contributions versus Entitlements

Benefit strategies are mirrored in the specific benefit decisions managers make. Overemphasizing to illustrate the point, some organizations may foster a sense of caring and belonging as part of a family; it follows that all employees are entitled to benefits that help maintain their economic and physical well-being. Other employers pursue a strategy that is more performance driven; their compensation programs, including some benefits, are linked to the performance of the firm and individual employees. In reality, many firms use a combination of these two extremes.

Critics argue that as benefits increase, contributions, responsibility, and initiative are less and less linked to compensation and rewards.

> Workers have an expanding sense of what is due them as rights of employment. From pension, health care, and long vacations to a high standard of living, the perception by workers of what constitutes their rights is inexorably being enlarged. Concomitant with the spiraling sense of rights has been a declining sense of responsibility.[8]

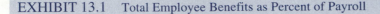

EXHIBIT 13.1 Total Employee Benefits as Percent of Payroll

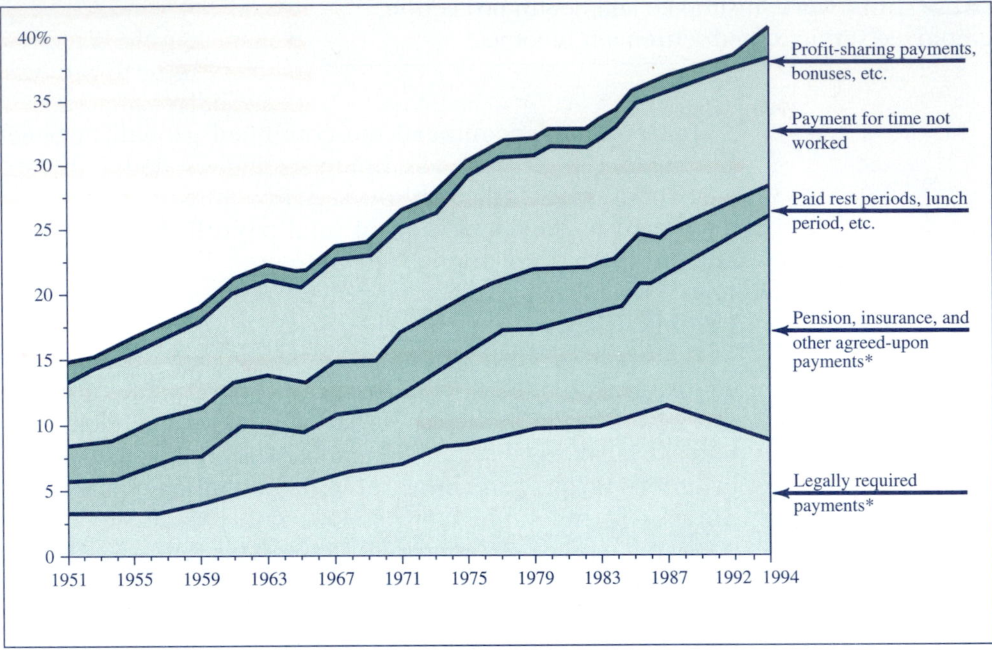


*Employers' share only.

Source: *Monthly Labor Review,* 1992, 1996.

For example,

> The largest single item in the Los Angeles City operating budget: Pensions for police and fire fighters. It accounts for about 50 percent of all property tax revenues. The pension fund has an uncapped cost-of-living adjustment and is based on the salary of the worker on the last day before retirement—thus encouraging last-minute promotions to captain shortly before "retirement" at age 38.[9]

Decision makers face a basic trade-off between entitlements and contributions. The trade-off is between the proportion of total compensation received in the form of benefits (entitlements) for simply holding a job or belonging to the organization, and the proportion allocated to increasing unit productivity, superior performance, innovation, and risk taking (contributions).

## A Benefits Gap

A countering position of the previous argument is that all members of society have certain rights, including the right to adequate health care and freedom from poverty. Is it the government's responsibility to ensure coverage to every citizen, whether through welfare programs or through mandated employer-provided programs? For those in society who are employed, employer-financed insurance and pensions provide a convenient method to ensure protection. For those not employed, employed in part-time jobs, or employed by small businesses, a benefits gap between the haves and the

EXPLORING THE WEB

*Compensation and Benefits Review* is a publication whose focus is compensation strategies and plan design. The magazine also maintains a network of compensation professionals who have agreed to exchange information on related concerns. Individual network members pose questions, which magazine editors then send out to all network members for comment. In addition, the editors invite prominent consultants to provide expert commentary. For more information on the network, e-mail to: **L_Bennet@amanet.org**

have-nots exists. One study even shows the benefits gap increasing, with changes in employer-sponsored health care having a disproportional effect on low-wage workers.[10] Many believe that society's best interests are served if parental leave, child care, and other benefits are available to all employees who require them. It then follows that a minimal level of benefits should be a required part of any compensation system. These are issues of public interest. Benefit managers should be part of that dialogue.

## SETTING BENEFIT OBJECTIVES AND STRATEGIES

Organization strategies and objectives shape the benefit decisions managers make.[11] A large, well-established employer in a growing or mature industry, for example, may offer a relatively generous benefit package. But a smaller, emerging firm may find that the high fixed costs attached to many benefits, particularly pensions, entail too great a financial risk. Instead, such firms may emphasize incentive pay or profit sharing, where costs vary with the firm's profitability, and de-emphasize benefits with fixed costs. For example, Impac, a medical software company in California, does not provide pensions for its 50 employees. Rather, all 50 belong to a profit-sharing plan, which typically pays out amounts equal to 18 percent of income. Profit sharing supports Impac's entrepreneurial strategy and young workforce better than pensions that focus on retirement instead of firm performance. In contrast, Medtronics, an older, established medical company, offers stock options, profit sharing, and pensions to different employee groups. Medtronics is better able financially to undertake the fixed costs of a pension plan. Its larger size also enables it to tune its offerings among categories of employees.

WHAT DO YOU THINK?

In earlier chapters we discussed the role of the organization in society. Now that you are more familiar with the nature of HRM, has your view changed on this issue? How can the HRM practitioner be a force for the good of society?

Many companies become aware of the need for strategic benefit plans as the result of a crisis or an environmental jolt. The skyrocketing costs for health care, which now costs five times as much as it did ten years ago, is frequently the jolt.[12] Concerns over controlling costs prompt managers to examine their entire benefits portfolio to address whether the offerings are well managed and make strategic sense. Other crises that prompt a plan include new legislation that may be inconsistent with present benefits, or corporate restructurings that require previously separate plans to merge.

Typically, benefits are designed to accomplish three objectives:

1. Competitiveness, including cost effectiveness.
2. Compliance with legal regulations.
3. Choices tailored to the individual employee, including needs and preferences.

J. C. Penney Company's benefits objectives put costs in the context of sharing (see Exhibit 13.2). The connections to productivity and specific employee behaviors are more tenuous. The reason is that benefits were intended to help protect employees' physical well-being and provide for retirement. They were not intended to be tied to an individual's performance.

EXHIBIT 13.2 Benefit Objectives

**To Our Penney Partners:**

Teamwork, sharing, and mutual support—the same kind of cooperative effort that provides outstanding value and service for our customers—are all part of our benefits philosophy. Associates in the Penney family support one another's benefits during our active careers and in retirement. The Company shares in this team effort by contributing financial support where benefits help is most needed. Part of this help is by creating new plans responsive to associate needs, such as tax-deferred savings and the Penney Stock Ownership Plan (PenSOP). The result . . . a strong, vital program that gives substantial financial security—providing the greatest amount of protection at least cost to you.

## COMPETITIVENESS

Competitive pressures impact benefit decisions in conflicting ways. On the one hand, labor costs must be controlled to price products and services competitively. At 39 percent of labor costs, approaches to reduce or manage benefits expenses have high priority.[13]

On the other hand, competition in labor markets to attract and retain productive employees creates pressure to match the benefits offered by other employers. If others include dental insurance and recreational facilities in their offer, employers who do not may be at a disadvantage.

As with cash compensation, an employer adopts a policy to position its total compensation, including benefits, in the marketplace. Traditionally, choices have been to lead, lag, or match competition. More often than not, benefits are designed to meet those offered by competitors. By offering employees choices among various benefits, some firms, such as TRW, Honeywell, and others, emphasize a unique competitive posture regarding benefits. They try to use their benefits programs to make them an employer of choice.

EXPLORING THE WEB

The following web site contains a lot of information on employee benefits:

**http://galaxy.einet/galaxy/Business and Commerce/Business Administration.html**

### Cost Comparisons

Assessing the benefits of external competitors is accomplished through market surveys providing data on the different forms of benefits offered by competitors, their coverage, eligibility, and costs.

Comparisons can be made on total benefit costs, costs per employee, or percentage of payroll. These costs can then be compared with the averages of competitors. The (dubious) assumption underlying cost analysis is that if an organization is spending the same amount on benefits as its competitors, its benefits package must be competitive.[14]

## COMPLIANCE

Benefits may be one of the most heavily regulated areas of human resource management. Three categories of regulation exist: civil rights, fiduciary responsibility, and mandatory benefits.

## Civil Rights Laws

Four laws, Title VII of the Civil Rights Act, the Age Discrimination in Employment ACT (ADEA), the Older Workers Benefit Protection Act, and the Pregnancy Discrimination Act are particularly important in benefits administration.

*Title VII* prohibits discrimination in terms and conditions of employment (including benefits) based on race, color, religion, sex, or national origin. Sex discrimination existed in two types of pension plans:

1. Plans that require women to contribute a higher premium than men to receive the same benefits as men, other things being equal.
2. Plans that require women to contribute the same amount but pay them smaller benefits than men, other things being equal.

The insurance industry justified such differences by reasoning that women as a class live longer than men; therefore, the pension cost to the employer for the average retired woman was greater than the cost for the average retired man. But the Supreme Court ruled that Title VII of the Civil Rights Act applies to *individuals,* not classes. Since not all individual women live longer than all individual men, differential payments discriminate against those women required to pay more.[15] Women must also receive the same pensions.[16] Lower benefits paid to women than to men who made the same contributions are illegal. Thus, actuarial tables used to determine the cost of employer-provided insurance must be based on the *combined* illness, accident, and death rates for men and women.

### Age Discrimination in Employment Act (ADEA) and the Older Workers Benefit Protection Act

Passed in 1967 and amended in 1978 and 1986, these laws prohibit job-related discrimination against workers age 40 and above. Mandatory retirement, formerly legal at age 70, is with a few exceptions forbidden. For people who work past age 65, however, special rules regarding pensions, life insurance, and health care may be applied:

1. *Pensions.* A pension can be frozen at whatever level employees would have received had they retired at 65.
2. *Life insurance.* Coverage cannot be eliminated after age 65. However, reduction in the amount is permitted if an employer can demonstrate that continuing benefit coverage at the pre-65 level results in higher costs.
3. *Health care.* Total health benefits cannot be reduced for those employees 65 and over. The employer may only reduce health insurance by the amount of Medicare coverage available.

### Pregnancy Discrimination Act (1973)

The Pregnancy Discrimination Act "prohibits the denial of health, disability, or sick leave benefits to pregnant women temporarily disabled by childbirth itself or by a medical condition incurred before or after childbirth if such coverage is provided for nonpregnancy-related conditions." Such coverage only applies if a valid benefits plan is already in effect. It does not require an employer to offer a medical benefits program. But if a program is offered, pregnancy must be treated the same as any other medical condition. In addition, benefits that distinguish in coverage between employees and dependents, including spouses, are legal, but benefits that distinguish between male dependents and female dependents are not.[17]

### Tax Laws

As we already stated, the tax-free status of benefits has been a major impetus for their growth. But tax law also affects benefits by ensuring that they are nondiscriminatory.[18] In this sense, nondiscriminatory means that benefits must be received by a large portion of the firm's employees to qualify for favorable tax treatment. For example, very specific financial rules regulate capital accumulation plans (e.g., pensions, stock ownership, savings plans). The purpose of these regulations is to prevent the bulk of benefits from being given only to executives.

## Fiduciary Responsibility

In the early 1970s, thousands of retirees and workers who thought their pensions were guaranteed found out they weren't. When the former employers went bankrupt during a recession, the retirees were abandoned. As a result, Congress passed legislation regulating private pensions and imposing strict financial measures on employers.

### Employee Retirement Income Security Act

The 1974 Employee Retirement Income Security Act (ERISA), the 1984 Retirement Equity Act, the 1986 Tax Reform Act, and the Retirement Protection Act of 1994 all regulate private pension plans. They do not require employers to provide pension plans, but if one is offered, it must conform to ERISA regulations.[19] Unfortunately, the complex government rules have caused many companies to drop their pensions, instead of complying with the reporting and paperwork requirements. ERISA has five main regulations.

**Eligibility** All employee earnings from age 21 on must be included. Because only 1,000 hours of work are required during a year to be eligible, many part-time employees are now covered by pensions.

**Vesting and portability** Full vesting means employees own the pension benefits if they leave the employer prior to retirement. Prior to ERISA, employees could lose all pension rights if they left (or were terminated) before retirement. Now they must be fully vested after five years of service with an employer.

Many pensions are also portable; that is, an employee changing jobs can transfer vested pension funds from one employer to another. ERISA does not mandate portability.

**Funding and fiduciary liabilities** Because financial mismanagement of pension plans was the primary impetus for the passage of ERISA, an employer offering a pension must now conform to rigorous funding guidelines. Pension fund administrators have legal and financial obligations under ERISA. Pension funds are to be managed solely for the benefit of participating employees and their beneficiaries. No favoritism or nepotism is allowed.

**Termination responsibilities** The Pension Benefit Guaranty Corporation (PBGC), a nonprofit agency, was formed under ERISA to protect employees whose employers failed to provide intended benefits. These payments come from a reserve fund created from yearly premiums paid by all employers.

### Accounting Regulations

The Financial Accounting Standards Board (FASB) requires self-insured companies to include health care obligations on their balance sheets.[20] To comply with this regulation, companies can (1) take an immediate charge-off or phase it in over 20 years, (2) reduce the liability by putting more money into the plan, perhaps from an overfunded pension plan, or (3) reduce liability by reducing coverage.

## Mandated Benefits

Employers are legally required to offer certain programs to employees. These mandated benefits include Social Security, unemployment compensation, workers' compensation, and unpaid leave to care for a newborn or sick child or family member.

### Social Security

The Social Security System, established in 1935, provides some income protection to employees who have retired, died, or are disabled. Payments are based on past earnings and years of work. Exhibit 13.3 shows the growth in Social Security tax rates. In 1995, employers paid 6.2 percent on incomes up to $61,200 and another 1.45% for Medicare. (There is no upper income limit for Medicare coverage.) These rates are about double what they were ten years earlier. Employees pay an equal amount.

The benefits one receives depend on past earnings and length of work experience.[21] Social Security provides income protection beyond pensions; these include survivor benefits for children under age 18, disability benefits, and Medicare health coverage for those beyond 65.

### Unemployment Compensation

Unemployment compensation (UC) was set up in the United States as part of the Social Security Act of 1935. It is designed to provide a subsistence payment for employees between jobs. The employer pays into the UC fund at a rate based on the average number of former employees who have drawn benefits from the fund.

To be eligible for compensation, the employee must have worked a minimum number of weeks, be without a job, and be willing to accept a suitable position offered through the state Unemployment Compensation Commission. New York is the only state that permits payments to strikers.

To fund unemployment compensation, the employer pays a payroll tax to the state and federal governments on total wages paid. Currently, the tax is 3.4 percent of the first $6,000 earned by each worker. However, if an organization had laid off very few employees, it may qualify for a lower tax rate. The state unemployment commissions receive the bulk of the funds.

Each state has its own set of interpretations and payments. Payments by employers and to employees vary because the benefits paid vary, experience ratings of employers may vary, and some states are much more efficient in administering the program than others.

### Workers' Compensation Insurance

Workers' compensation (WC) is an employer-paid insurance program designed to compensate an employee for the expenses sustained from a work-related

EXHIBIT 13.3 Tax Rates, Maximum Earnings Base, and Maximum Social Security Tax

| | Taxation Rate on Covered Earnings | | | | |
|---|---|---|---|---|---|
| Year | For Retirement Survivors and Disability Insurance (percent) | For Hospital Insurance (percent) | Total × (percent) | Maximum Earnings Base (dollars) | Maximum Social Security Tax (dollars) |
| 1978 | 5.05% | 1.00% | 6.05% × | $17,700 | $1,070.85 |
| 1980 | 5.08 | 1.05 | 6.13 × | 25,900 | 1,587.67 |
| 1983 | 5.40 | 1.30 | 6.70 × | 35,700 | 2,391.90 |
| 1986 | 5.70 | 1.45 | 7.15 × | 42,000 | 3,003.00 |
| 1993 | 6.2 | 1.45 | 7.65 × | 57,600 | 4,406.40 |
| 2000 | 6.2 | 1.45 | 7.65 × | | |

Automatic adjustments based on average earnings level.

Source: Social Security Administration Annual Statistical Supplement, 1990, 1992, 1996.

injury. An injury is compensable if it is the result of an accident that arose out of, and while in, the course of employment. Diseases that result from occupations (e.g., black lung disease in miners) are also compensable.

Payments are made in the event of disability or death. Medical expenses are also covered. Disability payments are often based on formulas that take into account the employee's earnings, number of dependents, and other factors. Detailed accident and death records are also required of employers in order to learn how to make the workplace safer.

Workers' compensation insurance laws exist in every state. Because each state offers its own program, the levels of protection and associated costs differ considerably. Because of their close ties to medical costs, WC costs are soaring. Additionally, the number and type of medical problems covered, particularly some that are not easily diagnosed or agreed upon, have resulted in a consensus that the system needs an overhaul. Because WC costs are so high (more than income taxes for many employers), many states use their lower rates as an inducement to lure businesses across state lines.

A recent study examined the effect of workers' compensation on time out of work by comparing the experience of individuals injured before and after increases in the maximum weekly benefit amount. The increases examined in Kentucky and Michigan raised the benefit amount for high-earnings individuals by approximately 50 percent, while low-earnings individuals, who were unaffected by the benefit maximum, did not experience a change in their benefit amount. Time out of work increased for those eligible for the higher benefits and remained unchanged for those whose benefits were constant.[22]

### Family Leave

The very first piece of legislation signed by President Bill Clinton was the Family Leave Bill in 1993. The bill requires employers with more than 50 employees to provide up to 12 weeks of unpaid leave for an employee to care for a newborn child or handle family medical emergencies, such as caring for an elderly parent. After the leave, employers must offer a returning employee the same job or one similar in responsibilities. The United States was one of the last developed countries to mandate this benefit. Most EU countries require longer leaves, some as long as one year.

## COVERAGE

In addition to those legally required, four kinds of benefits are typically provided to employees: employer-purchased insurance, paid time away from work, employee services, and retirement income. Exhibit 13.4 ranks the popularity of various benefits. It shows that health insurance is the benefit employees value most.

### Employer-Purchased Insurance

The expense associated with risks encountered throughout life—illness, accident, and early death, among others—can be diminished by pooling the risk through buying insurance. In addition to the tax advantage of employer-purchased insurance, employers can usually buy insurance cheaper because the rate is based on group risk, rather than individual risk. Insurance may be free to the employee (noncontributory) or the employee may pay a share of the premium (contributory). Three major forms of insurance are common: health, life, and disability-accident.

*Health insurance* is costly, but as Exhibit 13.4 shows, it is extremely popular with employees.[23] In addition to doctor and hospital bills, coverage may include prescription drugs, mental health services, and dental care. The Consolidated Omnibus Reconciliation Act (COBRA) of 1986 requires employers to continue coverage up to three years for employees who have been laid off. As a result of increasing contributory payments from employees and greater use of managed care plans, the rate of increase in health care costs has decreased dramatically. Exhibit 13.5 compares the increases in health care costs with increases in the consumer price index. In 1982, health care costs shot up 12 percent while the overall price index increased only 6 percent. In 1994, health care costs actually fell 1 percent. However, the cost of retiree health care increased 10 percent in 1995, which is likely to cause employers to reduce their retiree health care programs.

*Group life insurance* is one of the oldest and most widely available employee benefits. Yet, as Exhibit 13.4 shows, it is not particularly popular. The amount of insurance provided typically increases as salary increases.

*Long-term sickness and accident/disability insurance* protects employees who have accidents at work that leave them unable to work, temporarily or permanently. Workers' compensation pays only a very small part of these costs because it is designed primarily to take care of short-term disability problems. Employer-funded long-term disability insurance supplements benefits from workers' compensation, Social Security, and other agencies.

**Domestic Partners** Some employers have extended eligibility for insurance coverage to domestic partners of employees. A domestic partner is defined as an

## EXHIBIT 13.4 Ranking of Importance of Different Employee Benefits

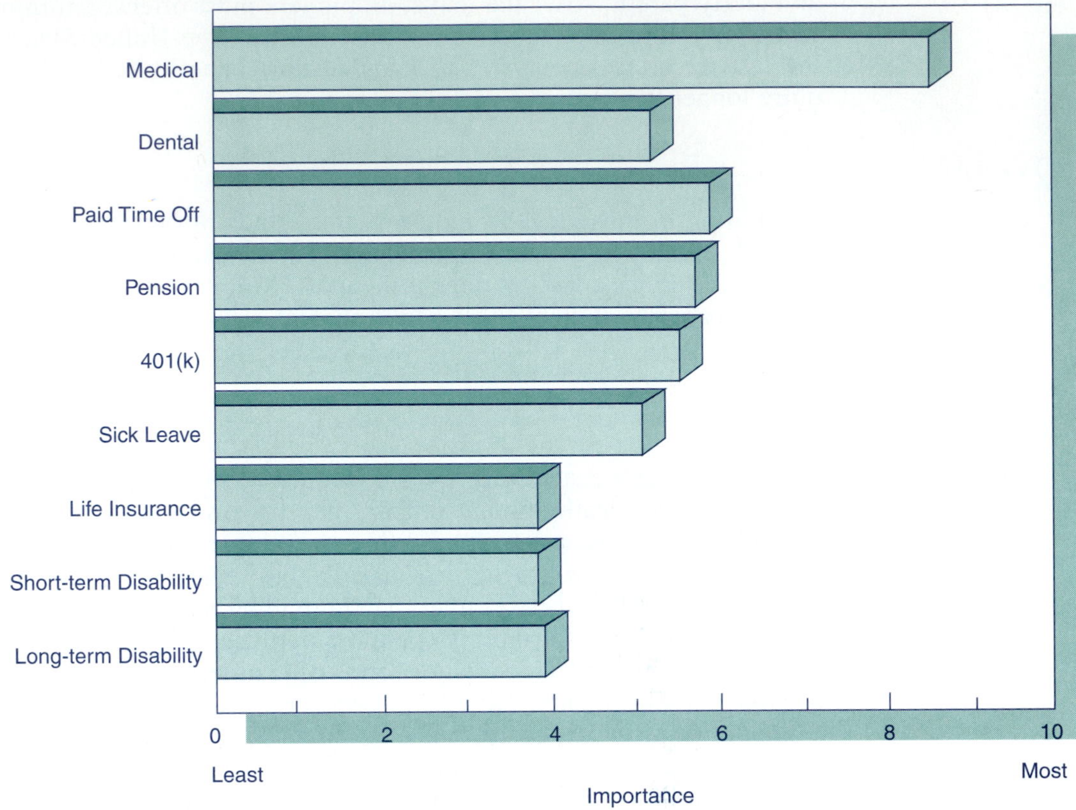


Source: Jeff Klein, "Total Remuneration Solutions: The Benefits Perspective," Presentation at Human Resources Executive Seminar, Cornell University, November 3, 1995. Data from Hewitt Associates surveys.

## EXHIBIT 13.5 Health Care Inflation

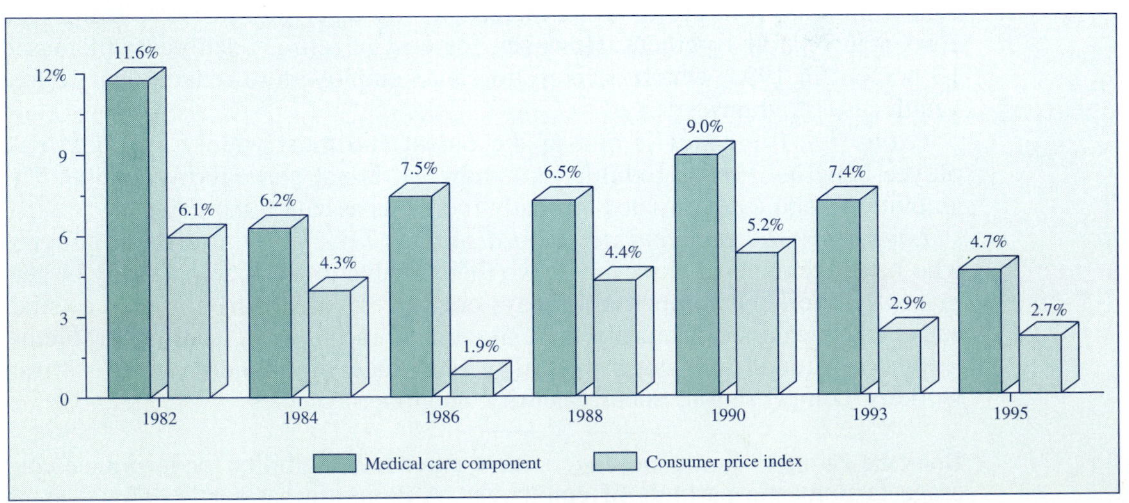


Source: *Monthly Labor Review,* U.S. Department of Labor, Bureau of Labor Statistics, May 1989, 1992, 1993.

adult with whom the employee shares a long-term relationship. A few companies require registration or some kind of legal statement testifying that the relationship is long-term. Agreements with insurance companies must be modified to accommodate this extension. The premium differential for the additional coverage is relatively small, especially when compared with the costs for retiree coverage.

## Paid Time Away from Work

Paid vacations and holidays are a relatively popular benefit. However, they did not always exist. People used to work 12 hours a day, six days a week, 52 weeks a year. Now, most employers compensate employees for rest periods, coffee breaks, and time when they are not actually at work—holidays, vacations, or sick leave. Vacations with pay usually begin after a minimum period of employment. The cost of these benefits is influenced by the employee's base salary. An executive away from the job for a week costs the company more than a missing messenger.

## Employee Services

Services is something of a catchall category of voluntary benefits. It includes all other benefits provided by employers, such as cafeterias, saunas and gyms, free parking lots, commuter vans, infirmaries, discounts on company products, financial counseling, and child care assistance.

Child care deserves a special word because the entry of record numbers of women into the labor force has dramatically increased the demand for quality child care centers. Working parents frequently list adequate child care as the most important problem they face.[24]

There are several approaches to child care assistance. One is a *flexible spending account,* which lets employees put aside pretax wages for certain expenses, including help for elderly parents and child care. This arrangement saves the employee taxes on the money put into this account. A second approach is the corporation as caregiver. Many companies have set up operations at or near the office, but these arrangements may raise concerns about liability and possible favoritism in admissions. Another alternative for many employers is to help subsidize community care providers both directly and indirectly through vouchers. A recent study of on-site care found that its strongest effect was on employee attitudes and membership (i.e., retention and recruitment) rather than performance.[25] Child care assistance is discussed again in Chapter Fifteen, Employee Relations.

In order to become more "family friendly," employers are starting to add services ranging from on-site ATM machines to delivery of flowers and dry cleaning. Do you think these services will help the organization to achieve its objectives? How might you measure any impact of such services?

## Retirement Income

Employees' retirement income comes from four sources—mandated Social Security benefits, private pensions, asset income, and earnings. Employers play a role in all of these categories.

### Asset Income

Asset income is money generated by personal savings and investments. There are a wide variety of employer-assisted savings or capital accumulations plans.

Deferred compensation plans, such as 401(k) plans (named for the section of the Internal Revenue Code that authorizes them) permit employees to postpone income taxes on a portion of salary if that salary is contributed to a qualified plan. Frequently, an employer matches an employee's contribution to a plan, typically on a 50 cents per $1 rate.

A number of compensation-deferred plans exist. Basically, all of them have the similar strategy of shifting income to postretirement years.[26]

### Employee Stock Ownership Plans

Under these plans, employers make payments to a trust, which purchases the employer's stock, for the benefit of employees. Employers get a tax deduction for the contribution, and employees accumulate equity in the organization.

Employee ownership theoretically has the potential to "improve corporate performance, create a more equitable distribution of wealth, and build a society in which enriching one group will not automatically mean taking something away from another group."[27] However, the success of employee stock ownership plans (ESOPs) in accomplishing such lofty objectives depends on the health of the organization before the transfer of ownership. A dying company is not made healthy by a change in ownership alone. Ownership may have nothing to do with problems that may exist, but it does represent another retirement income option for employees and managers to consider.

In addition to stock ownership, incentive stock options (ISOs) are frequently used for executives in companies whose stock is likely to increase in value. All of these variations on employee ownership are the result of legislation intended to accommodate a particular social goal or to curb a particular abuse. Thus, further revisions can be anticipated.

### Private Pensions

Many employers provide pension funds to retired employees, with the amount usually based on years of service and income level while employed. An astounding variety in pensions cover about two-thirds of all U.S. employees. The most generous pensions are in the public sector: the federal government offers pensions that are double the rate of those in private industry. Many government employees qualify for retirement at full pension when they are only 38 years old.

There are two basic types of pension plans. A *defined benefit* plan pays out a guaranteed amount every month for the life of the retiree, but the total costs of the plan cannot be specified in advance because they vary with the life expectancy of retirees. Consequently, many employers have switched to *defined contribution* plans, which specify the amount of money paid in, rather than the amount paid out. Knowing what the total costs will be has become more important as the workforce gets older and life expectancies increase.

## CHOICE

Employees close to retirement and with college-age children clearly have different benefit preferences than newly hired employees with working spouses and preschool children. A study of choices made by 1,500 employees of a computer manufacturer among six different health care plans found that decisions were influenced by age, income, marital status, and gender.[28] As age and salary increased, more expensive options with greater coverage were chosen more frequently.

A few studies found that higher-income employees preferred more benefits to cash, but the majority of employees preferred cash. For lower-paid employees, fewer tax advantages exist, or perhaps these employees may have more immediate needs that only cash can satisfy. But because benefits are so tied in with a country's tax policy, these generalizations may not hold true outside the United States.

The degree of employee choice varies across organizations. Most firms allow employees to specify if they wish health insurance to cover their dependents, and their insurance beneficiaries. The greatest choice in contemporary systems is found in flexible benefit plans.

### How Flexible Benefits Work

Although there are varying types of programs, the *core cafeteria plan* is the most common. Under its provisions, employees have identical minimum levels of benefits (e.g., health and life insurance, pensions). They are then given a choice among additional life insurance, more vacation time, better health insurance coverage, dependent health insurance, long-term disability, dental coverage, child care services, and so on. Employees purchase these choices by using benefit "credits" designed into the plan. Different options require different levels of credits. Primerica's flexible benefits plan is illustrated in Exhibit 13.6. Employees periodically recertify or revise their choices. In this way, changes in employee needs are recognized.

Another approach to broadening the choices available is the use of *flexible spending accounts*. Employees specify the dollar amount they want deducted from each paycheck for their flexible account. They then use this fund to pay medical or dependent care bills with pretax dollars. The disadvantage is the "use it or lose it" rule: any money left in the account at the end of the year goes to the employer.

### Advantages

The basic advantage of flexible benefits is that they are designed to meet employee preferences. If employees' benefits preferences are satisfied, they may be less likely to be absent, more reluctant to quit, have fewer accidents, and so on. However, there is little research to support these speculations.

### Disadvantages

Administering a flexible-benefits plan requires significant administrative effort. Administration includes communications, counseling employees about available choices, and sophisticated record-keeping and accounting systems. Computerized human resource information systems simplify these tasks.

An additional problem is "adverse selection." Employees may take extensive dental coverage in one year, then opt out of dental care the following year. For the next few years, they may pay for routine dental care themselves and then opt back into the dental care program when major work is needed again. This results in erratic cost patterns for the company as premiums increase according to the use or overuse of the provision.

### Flexible Benefits as a Cost-Control Strategy

Employees also can face some disadvantages under flexible plans. Many employers use their introduction as an opportunity to raise employee contributions and deductibles. However, flexible plans also may lower the costs of

EXHIBIT 13.6 Flexible Benefits at Primerica Corporation

## The Concept

The idea behind flexible benefits is very simple. It reflects our belief that each individual should have the ability to choose the benefits that are most meaningful to him or her. Under flexible benefits, you'll have a basic foundation—or core—of coverage and an allowance to use in putting together your own benefit program around that core.

**The Development of Flexible Benefits**

Think of our pre-flexible benefit program (the program we had before flexible benefits) as a circle divided into five parts—medical benefits, life insurance benefits, vacation, disability, and retirement and capital accumulation benefits. Over the past few decades, we worked hard to build a benefit program that stands among the best available in industry today. The trouble is, no one program—however rich—can ever meet everyone's needs equally well. People are too different for that.

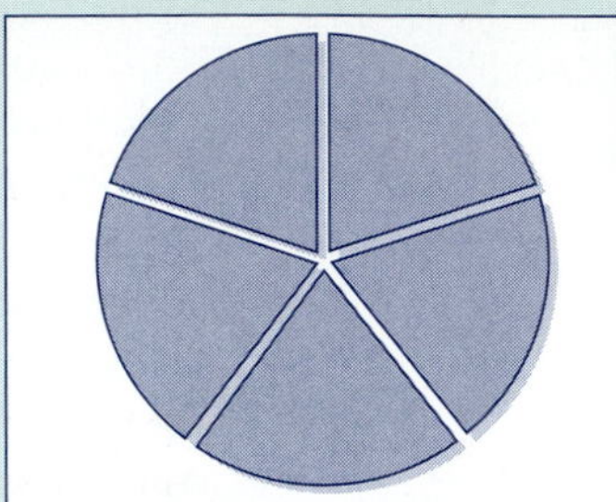

Now picture an inner circle of benefits which we'll call the core. This core area represents fundamental protection that can't be changed under the flexible benefits system. It's a basic foundation of security for all employees—security no one can opt out of.

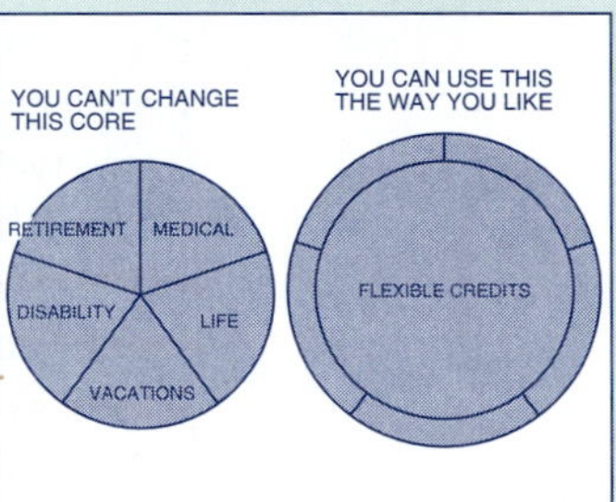

**How Flexible Credits Are Figured**

The difference between the core and your pre-flexible benefits is transformed by insurance and actuarial calculations into flexible credits which are allocated to you in dollars. You can then use those dollars for benefit options. With them, you can build your own benefit program around the core. The amount of flexible credits you are allotted will vary from year to year. That's because they depend on your particular age, pay, family status, and years of service with the company. You'll be given your flexible credit allowance on the form you use to make your benefit option decisions. This same principle holds even if you joined us without having ever been covered by the pre-flexible program. Your flexible credit allowance will be figured the same way.

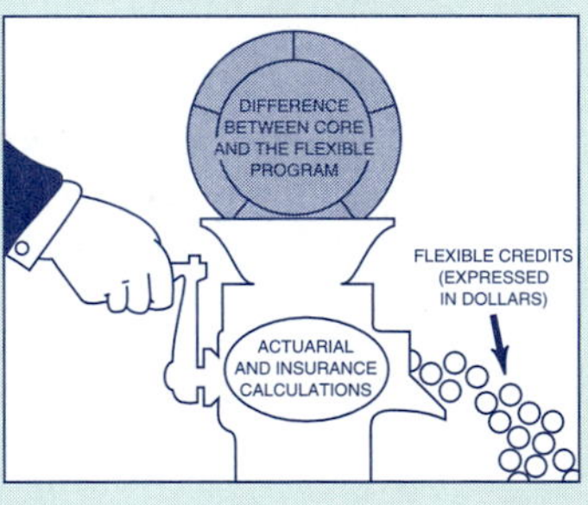


introducing new forms of benefits. By adopting a flexible approach, the company can offer, say, a dental plan at no additional expense to the company. Employees pay the cost by reducing other benefit coverages. Employees satisfy their needs while the employer does not increase the costs of providing an additional benefit.[29]

In addition, flexible benefits can be used to address unique concerns. For example, including child care services as part of a flexible-benefits package permits employees who need the service to select it.[30] At the same time, the employer avoids the appearance of favoring one group of employees—those who require child care services—over other employees. Flexible benefits permit a wider variety of benefits and a greater degree of employee choice than may otherwise be affordable.

## COMMUNICATION

Writer after writer bemoans the fact that employees do not appreciate or value their benefits, largely because they are unaware of them. But given the frequency of uncoordinated, haphazard administration, many employers seem equally unaware of them. Except for costs. Failure to understand benefits components and their value is a root cause of employee dissatisfaction with benefits.[31] Therefore, perhaps some training in effective communication should be a prerequisite for benefits administrators. ERISA requires employers to communicate with employees by sending them an annual report on their pension plan and basic information on their pensions. In its annual report, J. C. Penney emphasizes how much employees would need to save to provide this coverage on their own. Some employers even send employees copies of bills paid by the company for medical expenses on their behalf.

Communication is not a one-way process. A basic premise underlying benefits management is that employees need to be involved in choosing benefits; if some choice is available, the chances are that (1) employees will understand their benefits and (2) they will be more satisfied with benefits. But employees can only choose an appropriate mix of benefits if they are given proper information and make a careful assessment of their own needs. Lack of interest or understanding by employees can lead to inappropriate and expensive choices that do not increase satisfaction.

One study tested the use of an expert system on benefits selection. An *expert system* is a computer program that models the decision making of individuals designated as experts on a specific topic. The benefits expert system recommended benefits choices for individuals based on their specific circumstances (e.g., age, income, number and ages of any dependents, other benefits available through an employed spouse, approximate savings for retirement, and special needs). The study found that when the benefits choices recommended by the expert system differed from their current choices, employees who used the system were more likely to change their choices than employees who made their choices without the expert system. Those who used the system were also more satisfied with their benefits than employees who used a spreadsheet computer program or those who did not use a computer.[32] It appears that benefits satisfaction, as well as choices, can be managed.

Xerox made a similar discovery when it surveyed its employees on benefits. A key finding was that changes previously made to Xerox's retirement and savings plan were perceived by many employees as a takeaway. In reality, the changes had improved the value of the program by increasing the benefit guaranteed at retirement. Continuing communications efforts have resulted in significant improvement in employee understanding and appreciation of benefits, according to the Xerox benefits manager.[33]

## INTERNATIONAL VARIATIONS

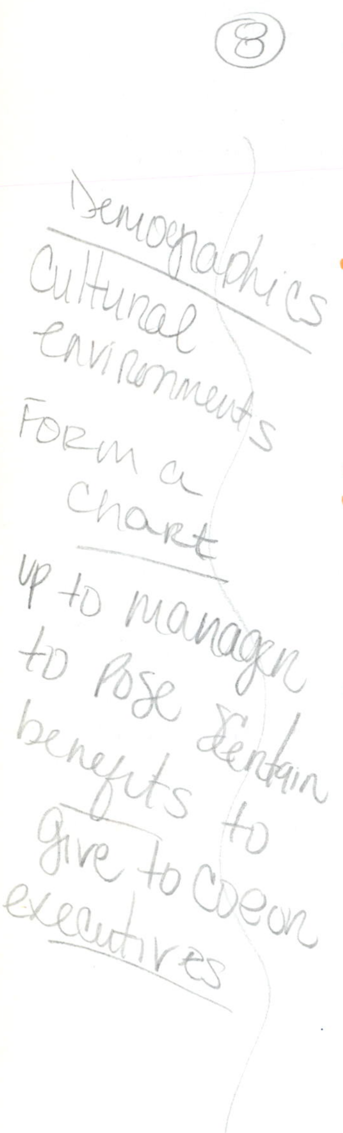

Every benefit is offered for a reason. In many countries, pressure from organized labor contributed to the growth of benefits in the 1960s and 1970s. In other countries, employer benefits supply employees with goods that are difficult for them to obtain on their own. In China, for example, access to a shower after work is a popular benefit. In Japan, most mortgages for housing are arranged through large employers. Those who are not employed by the large companies are less able to secure financing on their own. In much of Eastern Europe, German employers who are eager to secure access to a well-trained, low-wage labor force are providing housing, particularly in the large cities where existing housing stock is still controlled by the government. Variations among countries are consistent with their economic development, culture, and customs.

### Japan

Japanese benefits emphasize uniformity for everyone. For example, Japanese employees are covered by employment-based health insurance, just as in the United States, and are assured free choice of their physicians and hospitals. However, to provide equal access to all employees, health insurance is strictly regulated across the board by the Japanese government. Employees of a small company on the verge of bankruptcy are provided basically the same coverage as employees of Honda or Toyota. Thus, if a company believes that its health care costs are too high, law prohibits the company from introducing an alternative plan.

This uniformity is a common feature in pension plans, too. Consequently, Japanese companies seem to pay much less attention to benefit issues than their American counterparts. The central government has taken the key role in planning and implementing the system.[34]

Because of its low birthrates and growing life expectancy, Japan will have by the year 2020 the highest proportion of people age 65 and over among developed countries: 25 percent. At the same time, the extended family is disappearing, so the demand for long-term care and child care is growing.

It is the custom of large Japanese employers to provide extra payments to mark the life passages of their employees. However, economic and social conditions in Japan have changed a great deal since these payments were originally instituted. While such traditions may long continue after they are needed (e.g., a rice shortage no longer exists), it is less likely that payments will be extended for new situations such as elder care.

### Europe

In Eastern Europe, benefits have a relatively low priority. Employees place a higher value on cash and housing. In the European Union countries, two types of health care systems exist. Belgium, France, Germany, Luxembourg, and the Netherlands use private health insurance institutions. Denmark, Greece, Ireland, Italy, Portugal, Spain, and the United Kingdom have national health services. The EU tends to have higher levels of benefits such as parental leave and subsidized child care, in part because of higher rates of unionism than in the United States.

The European Union has tried several times to specify a benefits standard for member countries, but has been unsuccessful. In 1996 it considered, then shelved, proposals to make pensions portable within the EU. The move would have made it easier for workers to move from one country to another. But

Germany's private pension system has the opposite objective. In order to encourage loyalty to a company and discourage movement, employees are required to wait 10 years to qualify for a pension.

## OUTSOURCING

*utsourcing* is the practice of subcontracting work outside a company, often to nonunion or foreign organizations.

The outsourcing of benefits administration is not particularly new; processing pay checks and medical claims has been handled for years outside the primary employer by third parties. For example, if you call the 800 number to discuss a medical claim, the person who answers your call is likely to be an employee of a "vendor" such as Aetna Insurance or a consulting firm such as Towers Perrin or Hewitt. Benefit representatives are trained in the intricacies of your particular medical plan. Like customer representatives at L. L. Bean, they will take your information, punch up your employer's benefit plan on their screen, and handle your transaction.

### Why Outsource?

Exhibit 13.7 shows the reasons that 175 firms gave to the Conference Board. Improving quality of service and freeing time to spend on strategic issues were more important than cost containment.[35] Specialized outside vendors develop computerized technology that provides better service quicker to employees. Additionally, the vendors reduce the costs required to keep pace with the increasingly complex legal and technical aspects of benefits administration.

Rhône Poulenc, a French chemical and drug company, reports that outsourcing has saved the company $400,000 on administering its 401(k) plan, $60,000 on pensions, and $200,000 on flexible benefits on its United States operations. The company reduced its benefits staff from eight to four employees. Additionally, an employee survey found increased employee satisfaction with the quality of benefit services after the outsourcing.

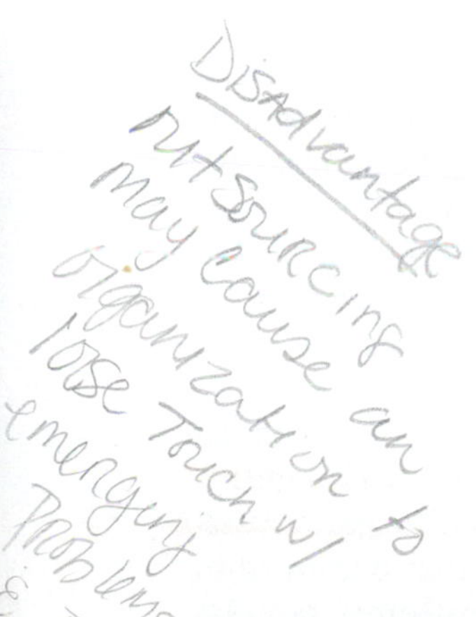


### The Downside of Outsourcing

Outsourcing is not always an effective way to manage. Many managers believe that diagnosing what benefits to offer employees is strategic policy, and should therefore be retained. Outsourcing may cause an organization to lose touch with emerging problems and issues, or to become too dependent on its vendors and suppliers.[36] Over time, an organization will lose its benefit expertise and not be able to adequately judge the quality and value of the service delivered by the vendor. Once an activity has been outsourced, it is not easy to bring it back. An emerging role for the human resource department may be to become skilled at locating and managing human resource vendors, similar to a purchasing manager.

## EVALUATING THE RESULTS OF BENEFIT DECISIONS

From a decision-making perspective, benefits are evaluated in terms of their objectives. Three objectives deserve special attention. The first is the cost-effectiveness of benefit decisions. A second is the impact of benefits on employee work behaviors, and the third is the fairness or equity with which benefits are viewed by employees.

EXHIBIT 13.7 Reason for Outsourcing

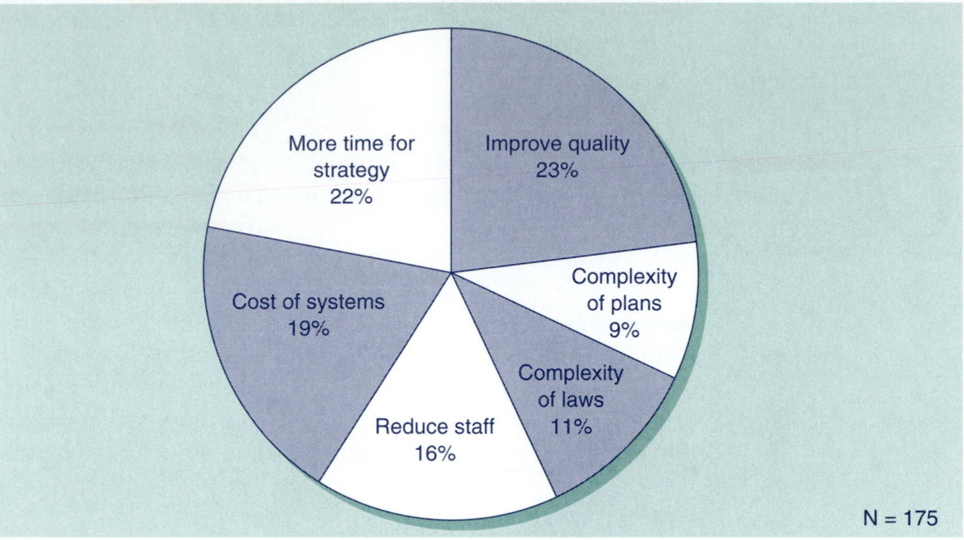


## Effects on Costs

Because health care costs have experienced the greatest growth, increasing almost three times faster than overall price increases in the economy, they have received most of the attention. Tactics for controlling costs include changing employee consumption patterns, changing financing methods, and managing competition among providers.

### Changing Consumption Patterns

Copaid benefit plans require that employees pay a share of costs. For example, employees may be required to pay a share of medical insurance premiums, and/or they may be required to pay a part of total medical expenses. By requiring employees to pay a portion of costs, employers hope to heighten cost awareness and increase selectivity in using services. While this is currently one of the most popular cost-containment strategies, it has the potential to backfire. Without effective communication, employees may see copayment and increased deductibles as cutbacks in benefit levels. Many employees are more willing to take a pay cut than reduce health care coverage.

Case management—programs to plan and coordinate cost-effective medical care—is becoming a popular approach to managing consumption. Emphasis is on exploring alternative sources of care and developing a plan to meet a patient's needs in the most cost-effective way. One study reports that one-third of yearly health insurance claims stem from 2 to 5 percent of the insured population.[37] This is the population on which managers concentrate their efforts to manage consumption. After extensive data analysis, Sony Corporation of America discovered that as much as 50 percent of its medical care costs were incurred by individuals with modifiable or lifestyle-related conditions. As a result, Sony launched a highly targeted wellness program for about 12,000 employees nationwide. Sony's plan design changes have helped Sony keep its annual medical cost increases to about 15 percent.

Requiring second opinions or preauthorization before covering certain medical expenses are other ways employers hope to motivate employees to be more selective in using medical services. Unfortunately, many of these approaches generate more ill will than cost savings.

More and more employers are negotiating rates with hospitals, doctors, laboratory services, and druggists. Sometimes these special rates are in exchange for a certain volume of business. This approach, called *preferred provider,* is growing rapidly. Employees who use preferred providers pay little or nothing. Choosing nonparticipating doctors means high deductibles and copayments.

## Effects on Employee Behaviors

The effects of benefits on behaviors, such as applicants' decision to join an employer or work hard once employed, are less well documented. Some benefits may, at best, have an indirect effect on performance. The argument in support of an indirect effect is that unhealthy, worried, or troubled employees are not likely to perform at their best, which lowers productivity. Consequently, benefits designed to assist employees to maintain their health, financial security, and personal stability (drug counseling, child care, legal assistance) help avoid these problems. ESOPs also are thought to affect productivity. Partial ownership of the company is believed to have a positive effect on employee motivation and, hence, performance. Again, these views are based more on belief than on analysis.

### Absenteeism

General Motors took a novel approach to finding out whether benefits matter. They link absenteeism and reduced benefits in their collective bargaining agreement with the UAW.[38] Employees who are absent more than 20 percent of their scheduled work time during the first six months of the contract were offered counseling. If they exceeded the 20 percent rate during the second six months of the contract, their benefits were cut equal to the individual's absence rate. Cuts occurred in paid holidays, jury duty pay, and sickness and accident benefits. GM reported an 11 percent drop in controllable absences the first year and 10 percent and 9 percent in subsequent years of the contract.

### Early Retirement

Modified benefit programs have also been used to reduce workforce size or to engineer an exit for a specific employee.[39] Health and disability insurance may be extended beyond the period of employment, or retirement provisions may be sweetened. For example, IBM added five years of age and service to employees' actual age and service for calculating retirement benefits, to induce employees to retire in 1986 during IBM's initial downsizing. IBM cut staffing levels again in subsequent years. However, later inducements have not been as generous. Organizations must be sure their retirement incentives are consistent with age discrimination laws and that acceptance is voluntary. Many companies require employees accepting early retirement programs to sign waivers indicating they will not file age discrimination charges. Nevertheless, some employees charge they are being coerced and face a possible layoff if they do not accept the retirement offer.

## Effects on Equity

An important objective of benefits decisions is to positively affect employee attitudes about the fairness and adequacy of benefits.[40] Research does show that the overall level of benefits is positively related to employees' satisfaction with their benefits—no surprise here. And there also is some support for the proposition that communication and choice increase satisfaction.

However, more research is required to provide a better understanding of employees' reactions to various coverages and types of benefits. Opinion Research Corporation found a sharp drop in the satisfaction with benefits over the past decade, a drop they attribute to a failure to restructure benefits in response to the changing demographics of the labor force.

# SUMMARY

In spite of the hefty price tab of benefits—almost 40 percent of payroll costs—it has only been in the last few years that employers have placed a high priority on managing benefits. Not only are benefits expensive, but they aren't always the benefits that employees want. Satisfaction with benefits has slipped dramatically because benefits have not kept step with changes in the demographics of the workplace.

The chapter has described the major benefits decisions: competitiveness, compliance, alternate coverage, communication, and choice. Competitiveness refers to structuring one's benefit package in relationship to one's competitors. Some of the issues are similar to those discussed in the previous chapter on external competitiveness.

Some benefits are required by law: unemployment compensation, government pensions, and workers' compensation. In addition, most employers offer additional benefits, such as compensation for time off (holidays, vacations), employer-purchased insurance (health, life, and disability), private pensions, and other services, such as prepaid legal services, health club memberships, or child care centers.

Communication to employees about their benefit coverage deserves greater attention than most organizations give. Communication tends to increase employee satisfaction with benefits, but this may occur because employees typically underestimate the value of their benefits.

One innovative approach to tuning benefits to individual preferences, as well as to control costs, is flexible benefits. Under these plans, employees are given a core group of benefits, plus credits for additional benefit coverage that they may allocate in any way they choose. The Internal Revenue Service has a number of requirements that must be met for such plans. Nevertheless, flexible benefit plans are very popular.

While the effects of benefits on costs are easily calculated, their effects on employee behaviors and equity are less easily documented. Benefits may even be dysfunctional because few of them are tied to performance. Rather, they are entitlements—given to employees as part of the conditions of employment. Benefits provide a social good, but by steadily increasing them, fewer dollars remain to reward the risk-taking behavior or performance levels that may be required for an organization to maintain its competitive edge.

## QUESTIONS

1. Why do employers provide benefits plans?
2. How and why can benefits be tailored to individual needs?
3. Why are copayment strategies not always successful?
4. What effect does communication have on the various benefits objectives?
5. What effect will demographic changes have on benefits? How can an employer capitalize on such changes?
6. What are the advantages and disadvantages of mandating benefits from the perspective of the entire society? From the perspective of the organization?
7. How can benefits be tailored to the strategic objectives of an organization?
8. How and why do benefits vary among countries?
9. Why are defined contribution pension plans becoming increasingly common?
10. What are the advantages to the employer of outsourcing? To the employee?

### YOUR TURN
### National Health Insurance

You are a member of the House of Representatives. The economy of your Michigan district is heavily dependent on the economy of the auto industry. The number one issue for many of your constituents, as well as fellow representatives, is affordable health care.

A proposal on national health insurance is on your desk. The Heritage Foundation has sent over a copy of its proposal. One of your staffers has collected information on national health insurance plans in Canada and Japan. Compare the approaches and decide which of them you would vote for. Your instructor will provide information on the various proposals.

## NOTES AND REFERENCES


1. *Public Employees Retirement System of Ohio* v. *Betts,* U.S. Sup. Ct. 88-389, June 23, 1989; 50 FEP Cases 104.
2. *McLendon* v. *The Continental Group, Inc.,* D.N.N., Civ. Act. No. 83-1340, May 10, 1989.
3. J. Cohen, "The Evolution and Growth of Social Security," in *Federal Policies and Worker Status since the Thirties,* ed. J. P. Goldberg, E. Ahern, W. Haber, and R. A. Oswald (Madison, WI: Industrial Relations Research Association, 1976).
4. Robert M. McCaffery, *Employee Benefits Programs: A Total Compensation Perspective* (Boston: PWS-Kent Publishing, 1992); U.S. Chamber of Commerce, *Employee Benefits 1996* (Washington, DC: Chamber of Commerce, 1996).
5. Richard Freeman and James Medoff, *What Do Unions Do?* (New York: Basic Books, 1984).

6. Loren Solnick, "The Effect of Blue-Collar Unions on White-Collar Wages and Fringe Benefits," *Industrial and Labor Relations Review,* Jan. 1985, pp. 236–43.
7. Bruce Shutan, "Should Unionized Firms Approach Salarieds before Rank and File?" *Employee Benefit News,* Dec. 1992, pp. 3–4.
8. James O'Toole, "The Irresponsible Society," in *Working in the 21st Century,* ed. C. Stewart Sheppard and Donald C. Carroll (New York: John Wiley, 1980), p. 156.
9. Ibid., p. 163.
10. Research by Jane Snedon Little was discussed in *Business Week* August 21, 1995, p. 20; Stephen Woodbury and Wei-jang Huang, *The Tax Treatment of Fringe Benefits* (Kalamazoo, MI: Upjohn Institute, 1991); Robert Paul and Dale Grant, "The Next Generation of Benefits Plans: What the Past Says about the Future," *ACA Journal,* Winter 1992–1993, pp. 6–17.
11. Victor S. Barocas, *Strategic Benefit Planning* (New York: Conference Board, 1992).
12. "The Rising Cost of Providing Medical Benefits," *Compflash* August 1995, p. 9.
13. Theresa Brothers, *Controlling the Costs of Employee Benefits* (New York: Conference Board, 1992).
14. J. M. Pergande, *Organization Choice: The Role of Job Characteristics,* Report No. 88–2, (Brookfield, WI: International Foundation of Employee Benefit Plans, 1988).
15. *Los Angeles Dept. of Water and Power* v. *Manhart,* 435 U.S. 702 (1978).
16. *Arizona Governing Committee* v. *Norris,* 32 Fair Empl. Prac. Cas. 233 (1983).
17. We emphasize that these civil rights laws apply only in the United States. Other countries will have their own laws concerning the treatment of employees and members of their family.
18. Alan L. Gustman, Olivia S. Mitchell, and Thomas L. Steinmeier, "The Role of Pensions in the Labor Market," Working Paper 93–07, Cornell University, Center for Advanced Human Resource Studies, Ithaca, NY, 1993.
19. Gordon Goodfellow and Sylvester Schieber, "Death and Taxes: Can We Fund for Retirement between?" (paper presented at symposium on the Future of Pensions in the United States, Pension Research Council, Philadelphia, May 1992).
20. "Honest Balance Sheets, Broken Promises," *Business Week,* Nov. 23, 1992, pp. 106–7.
21. Olivia Mitchell, *New Jobs in an Aging Economy: Costs, Benefits and Policy Challenges* (Ithaca, NY: Cornell University Press, 1993).
22. Bruce D. Meyer, W. Kip Viscusi, and David L. Durbin, "Workers' Compensation and Injury Duration: Evidence from a Natural Experiment," *American Economic Review* 85, no. 3 (June 1995), pp. 322–40.
23. Regina E. Herzlinger and Jeffrey Schwartz, "How Companies Tackle Health Care Costs: Part I," *Harvard Business Review,* July–Aug. 1985, pp. 69–81; Herzlinger, "How Companies Tackle Health Care Costs: Part II," *Harvard Business Review,* Sept.–Oct. 1985, pp. 108–20; and

Regina E. Herzlinger and David Calkins, "How Companies Tackle Health Care Costs: Part III," *Harvard Business Review,* Jan.–Feb. 1986, pp. 70–80.

24. David E. Bloom and Todd P. Steen, "Why Child Care Is Good for Business," *American Demographics,* Aug. 1988, pp. 22–27, 58–59.
25. Jean Kimmel, "The Role of Child Care Assistance in Welfare Reform," *Upjohn Institute Employment Research,* Fall 1994, pp. 1–4.
26. Michael D. Hurd, "The Joint Retirement Decision of Husbands and Wives," in *Issues in the Economics of Aging,* ed. David A. Wise (Chicago: University of Chicago Press, 1990).
27. Corey Rosen, "Growth versus Equity: The Employee Ownership Solution," *ILR Report,* Spring 1985; Poly Taplin, "ESOPs Meet the Needs of a Variety of Companies," *Employee Benefit Plan Review,* June 1983, pp. 10–14.
28. Melissa W. Barringer, George T. Milkovich, and Olivia S. Mitchell, "Employee Health Insurance Decisions in a Flexible Benefits Environment," working paper, Cornell University Center for Advanced Human Resource Studies, Ithaca, NY, 1991.
29. A. Barber, R. B. Dunham, and R. A. Formisano, "The Impact of Flexible Benefits on Employee Benefit Satisfaction," *Personnel Psychology* 46, no. 1 (1992), pp. 55–76.
30. William J. Wiatrowski, "Who Really Has Access to Employer-Provided Health Benefits?" *Monthly Labor Review,* June 1995, pp. 36–44.
31. George Dreher, Ronald Ash, and Robert Bretz, "Benefit Coverage and Employee Cost: Critical Factors in Explaining Compensation Satisfaction," *Personnel Psychology* 41 (1988), pp. 237–54.
32. George T. Milkovich, Michael Sturman, and John Hannon, "The Effect of a Flexible Benefits Expert System on Employee Decisions and Satisfaction," working paper, Cornell University Center for Advanced Human Resource Studies, Ithaca, NY, 1993.
33. "Xerox Applies Total Quality Process to Benefit Communication," *On Employee Benefits,* Apr.–May 1992, pp. 1–3.
34. Tomomi Kodama, "Observations on the Differences and Similarities in the Japanese and U.S. Benefits Systems," *Employee Benefit Notes,* Aug. 1992, pp. 1–2.
35. *HR Executive Review—Outsourcing HR Services,* Volume 1, Number 2, The Conference Board, 1994.
36. Brian Hackett, *Transforming the Benefit Function* (New York: The Conference Board, 1995).
37. "Sony Translates Data into Action with Wellness Incentives and Preventive Care," *On Health Care,* Oct. 1991, pp. 1–4.
38. George Ruben, "GM's Plan to Combat Absenteeism Successfully," *Monthly Labor Review,* Sept. 1983, pp. 36–37.
39. James C. Berkovec and Steven Stern, "Job Exit Behavior of Older Men," *Econometrica* 59, no. 1 (Jan. 1991), pp. 189–210.
40. R. D. Bretz, R. A. Ash, and G. F. Dreher, "Do People Make the Place? An Examination of the Attraction-Selection-Attrition Hypothesis," *Personnel Psychology* 42 (1989), pp. 561–81.

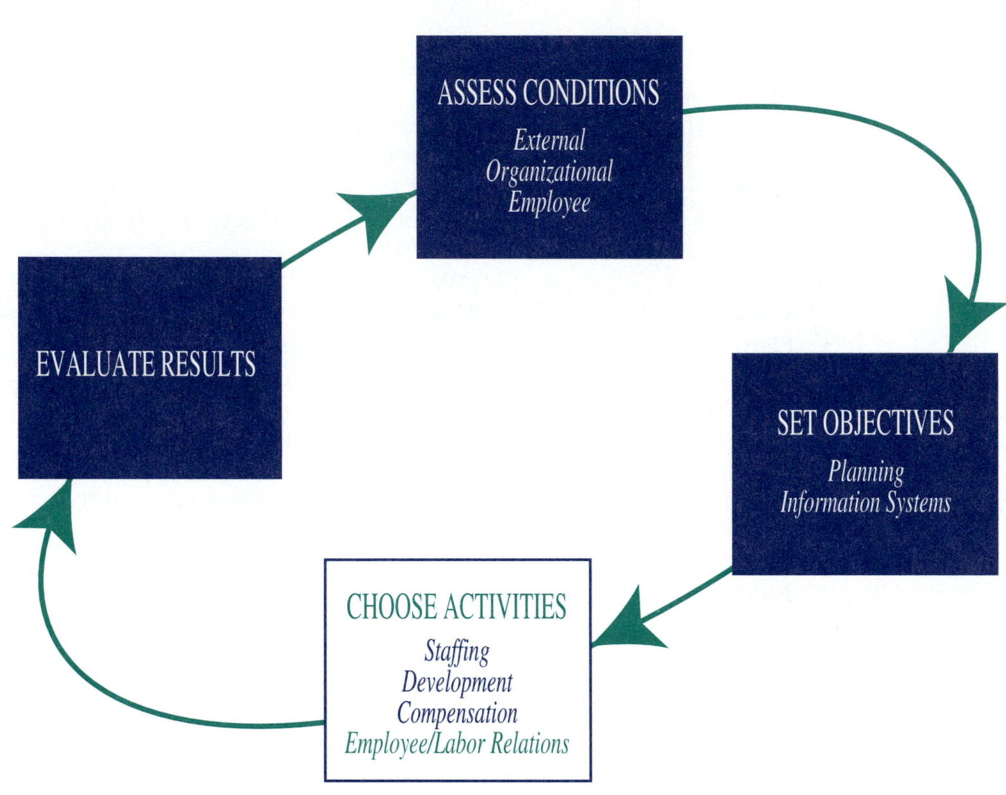

ASSESS CONDITIONS
External
Organizational
Employee
SET OBJECTIVES
Planning
Information Systems
CHOOSE ACTIVITIES
Staffing
Development
Compensation
Employee/Labor Relations
EVALUATE RESULTS

# EMPLOYEE/LABOR RELATIONS

One-to-one relationships at work, the daily human relationships, are the focus of Part Five of the book: How to ensure that managers treat employees fairly and with respect. How to help employees who come to work with personal or job-related problems (e.g., sick preschoolers, overburdening debts, or stress from marital problems or even drug abuse). And how to handle the disagreements that are inevitable in any organization.

Part Five explores the way managers and employees may relate to each other to ensure fair treatment. Employers are frequently accused, rightly or wrongly, of being insufficiently concerned about the conditions and treatment employees face at work.

Rather than tolerate unfair conditions, employees may form unions and collectively bargain improved employment conditions. In Chapter Fourteen, "Unions," we analyze the critical influences unions have on managing human resources. We examine the collective bargaining process and its impact on employers and employees as well as the current status of labor relations in the United States.

The effects of unions extend beyond their members; gains won during negotiations and the potential threat of union activity influence working conditions for all employees. Unions are part of the social and political fabric in whichever country they operate. As we have discussed in earlier chapters, the fabric varies among countries. Although there are many similarities, unions in Western and Central Europe, South America, and in Asia differ from U.S. unions in important ways that are described in this chapter.

Chapter Fifteen, "Employee Relations," explores the ways managers and employees may relate to each other to ensure fair treatment outside the collective bargaining framework. We also look at the changing nature of the implied contract that exists between employer and employee. Changes in assumptions are reflected throughout this text. Many of these changes raise disturbing issues for HR managers.

Chapter Sixteen, "The Evolving Human Resource Management and Profession," addresses how the human resource function has changed over time and where its future may lie. The fundamental question addressed in the chapter is, How can HR accomplish the goals discussed throughout the text in a way that adds value to the organization. Information systems as an important human resource tool are also discussed.

## A DIAGNOSTIC APPROACH TO EMPLOYEE/LABOR RELATIONS

The quality of employee/labor relations, as the diagnostic model shows, is affected by external conditions. Collective bargaining agreements are legal contracts subject to regulation by national laws. The whole unionizing and negotiating process is regulated, too, to provide some semblance of a balance of power among participants. Economic conditions affect these relations by limiting what options each side can afford to utilize.

## External Conditions

Economic A company that is making a profit and experiencing growth finds it easier to make a commitment to supportive employee relations policy. Child care and elder care, drug rehabilitation, and financial counseling become affordable. Fairness and trust are harder to maintain when the pie to be divided is shrinking and cutbacks are required. Product market conditions set the context for employee relations. However, some employee relations activities may receive insufficient attention when there are extreme competitive pressures. Attention to health and safety may wane in an all-out effort to get products out the door.

Perhaps more than any other human resource activity, labor relations are affected by economic conditions on a global scale. Foreign competition has had a devastating impact on union membership, employment, and wage scales in the U.S. auto and steel industries. Other industries, notably transportation and communications, have experienced the dislocations that have accompanied deregulation. Largest employers like AT&T and IBM have downsized, while new competitors like Compaq, MCI, or Gateway have enjoyed phenomenal growth.

Hard times for an employer constitute hard times for the union. Membership declines when declining demand for a firm's products or services reduces employment levels. In contrast, labor market conditions affect unions and employers inversely. If the labor market is tight, the union's power may be enhanced. If unemployment is high, management may have an advantage: It can sustain a strike and perhaps even benefit economically by replacing employees with new hires at lower pay rates.

Government The government creates the legal environment within which employee/labor relations take place. The government's attitude toward labor relations has varied over time. The courts continued to find collective activity illegal well into the 19th century. However, a number of laws passed between 1926 and 1959 have given unions a more equal footing with employers. Union supporters say greater government action is required to permit unions to regain the power they enjoyed during the 1930s and 1940s.

## Organization Conditions

The employee/labor relations atmosphere reflects the values and culture of the organization. Many employee relations programs emphasize safeguarding employees' rights. Others provide a forum for input into work and job decisions. Communication programs make employees aware of problems/objectives of the organization and make managers aware of problems/objectives of the employees.

Unions play a substantial role in shaping employee relations. For example, they can ensure the success of a quality of work life program by their support and participation. They also play an indirect role, in that many employee relations programs are motivated by a desire to maintain a union-free status for the organization. Many employers believe that they have more flexibility in the absence of a union. For example, promotions can be on the basis of merit or potential instead of strictly on the seniority that most union contracts require. People can be switched among jobs, and jobs can more easily be changed to adopt new technologies or to adjust to changing market conditions. But the discretion to promote and change people's jobs permits abuse, too. Still, many employers believe that the services a union may provide—job security, grievance procedures, good wages—can and should be provided by an enlightened management without the intervention of a union.

Therefore, assessing the conditions in which people are managed—the external, organization, and employee conditions—helps managers diagnose the situation, set objectives, and make proper human resource decisions, including those regarding unions and employee relations.

# Unions

In early August 1980, Polish authorities in Gdańsk caught Anna Walentynowicz collecting the remains of candles from graves in a local cemetery. Walentynowicz, a fiftyish forklift operator at the Lenin Shipyard, was gathering the wax to make new candles for a memorial to the victims of a 1970 shipyards protest during which at least 45 people were killed and over a thousand injured. On August 9 she was accused to stealing and was fired from her job. At 6 A.M. five days later, workers in two sections of the shipyard put down their tools and demanded her reinstatement and a 1,000-zloty pay increase. By nightfall the shipyard's 17,000 workers were on strike. Within days, the strike had spread to nearly two dozen factories in the area. On August 31, the government and the leader of the strike, a forklift electrician named Lech Walesa, signed the Gdańsk accords granting workers wage increases, more days off, better food supplies, changes in the party selection process, and—free trade unions. Walentynowicz got her job back, and the martyrs of 1970 received their memorial: the birth of the most sweeping and effective grassroots social movement the world had ever seen: Solidarity. Of the 12.5 million workers eligible to join Solidarity, nearly 10 million did, more than a fourth of all Poles. One-third of the Communist Party's three million members were also members of Solidarity. When Solidarity told them to strike and the party ordered them to work, they struck. Even in the 150,000-strong police force, Solidarity boasted 40,000 members. The actions of Solidarity members and its remarkable leader, Lech Walesa, inspired citizens everywhere in the Soviet bloc who eventually brought down the Berlin Wall and overturned the Soviet domination that had crippled not only their economies but every aspect of their lives. Heady days for a labor union.[1]

## THE UNION MOVEMENT IN THE UNITED STATES

Back in the United States, labor's headiest days often appear to be in the past. U.S. labor, too, has an honorable history of standing up to tyrants, of fighting for the rights of the powerless, and of being part of a grassroots social movement. Unions traditionally have sought to gain greater power to influence employers' decisions and to control the work life of their members. But today, unions are suffering from declining membership as the economy shifts from large-plant manufacturing to smaller, more flexible factories and a service economy peopled with workers who view unions as a hindrance rather than a help. Forty years ago, more than a third of the nation's nonagricultural workers belonged to labor unions. Today, less than 15 percent of the workforce is organized; if government employees are excluded, the figure drops to 12 percent.[2] Employers no longer quail before the thought of a strike; indeed, some even seem to be pushing for one, and begin hiring replacement workers before the picket lines are formed. Exhibit 14.1 shows this long membership decline.

EXHIBIT 14.1 Union Membership as a Percentage of the Nonagricultural Labor Force, 1930–1995

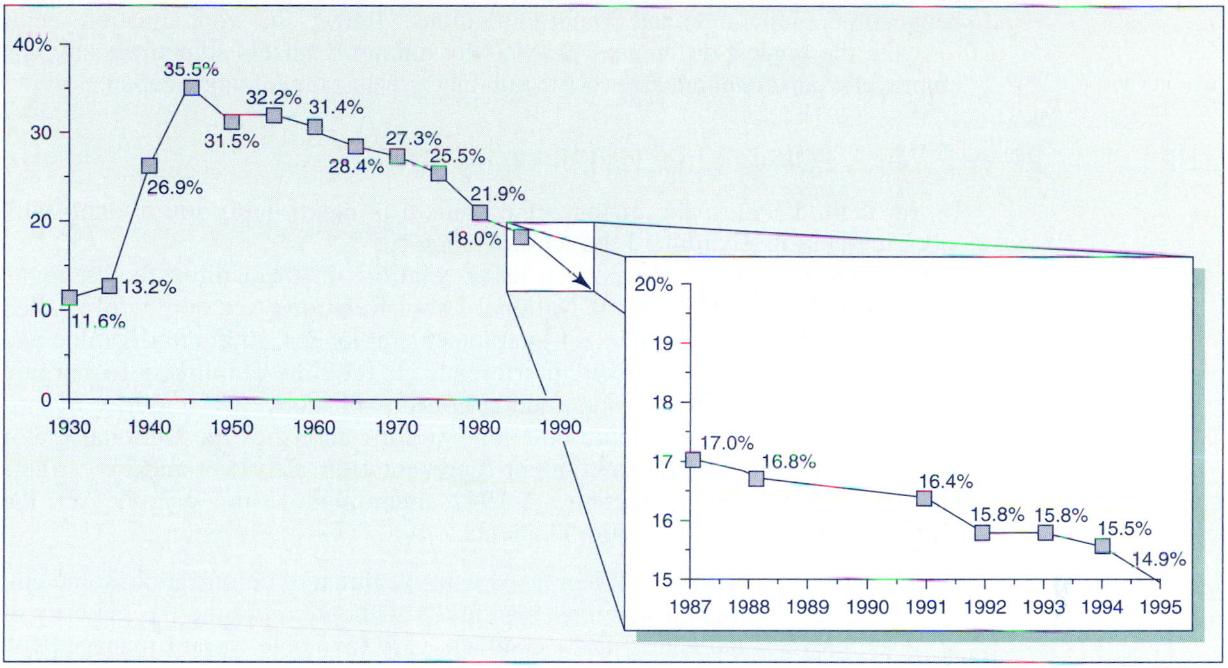

Source: *Employment & Earnings,* Jan. 1996.

*Labor relations* is a continuous relationship between a defined group of employees (represented by a union or association) and an employer.

*Collective bargaining* is the process by which union representatives for member employees negotiate employment conditions that will apply to all employees, union and nonunion.

Because it is at heart an issue of control, labor relations is frequently an emotionally charged activity. Both unions and employers are adopting new approaches to their relationship and setting new objectives. We will examine these approaches as well as the collective bargaining process—organizing, negotiating, and administration—in this chapter.

## WHY DO EMPLOYEES JOIN UNIONS?

Pragmatically, people join unions if they perceive the benefits to be greater than the costs. At the extreme, potential increases in wages must be greater than the amount of dues paid. Psychologically, however, there are more important reasons for joining. Probably the most important one has to do with frustration caused by not being listened to by others in the organization, especially in times of turmoil and retrenchment.

Dissatisfaction with bread-and-butter aspects of the job, such as wages and benefits, with supervision, or with the treatment of one group of employees compared with another can translate into a greater interest in unionism, particularly if employees feel they lack other alternatives for influence turns employees to unions.[3]

Some researchers have taken this theme a step further and analyzed why people *don't* join unions. The overall conclusion is that there are no substantial differences between people who do and do not join unions.[4] Rather, the work situation seems to make the biggest difference. That is why union organizers sometimes say that employers' personnel practices are the unions' greatest organizing weapon.

## THE LEGAL FRAMEWORK FOR COLLECTIVE BARGAINING

In the United States, the history of unionism is inextricably intertwined with labor legislation. Exhibit 14.2 traces this history.

For practical purposes, modern labor relations in the United States began with the passage in 1935 of the National Labor Relations Act, commonly called the Wagner Act. The Wagner Act guarantees employees' rights to organize and to bargain free from employer interference. It requires employers to bargain with a union over wages, hours, and conditions of work, if a majority of employers desire such union representation. And it establishes the National Labor Relations Board (NLRB) to conduct representation elections and investigate charges of unfair labor practices. A 1947 amendment to the Wagner Act, the Taft-Hartley Act, has five major elements.

1. *Sweetheart contracts.* When faced with the threat of unionization, some employers and established their own union without consulting the majority of employees and signed labor contracts very favorable toward management. These sweetheart contracts were outlawed by Taft-Hartley; employers are now forbidden from assisting or establishing labor organizations. This provision formed the basis for a 1993 ruling forbidding certain employee-management committees if management instigated the committees and if they dealt with wages, hours, or conditions of work. Because the majority of U.S. workers want a stronger voice in the workplace, but not necessarily through formal union representation, we return to this issue later in the chapter.[5]
2. *Exclusive representation.* When a majority of employees desires a specific union, that union represents all employees in the bargaining unit, whether or not they are union members. Exclusive representation is a major difference between unions in the United States and many other countries.
3. *Federal Mediation and Conciliation Service (FMCS).* The FMCS offers assistance in contract settlement and maintains a list of arbitrators to help interpret contract language and resolve disputes.
4. *Closed shop and union shop.* Taft-Hartley makes illegal the *closed shop,* which requires that employees be union members at the time of hiring. Requiring all employees in a bargaining unit to join a unit as a condition of *continued* employment is legal, if such a stipulation is agreed to by both employer and union. This is called a *union shop.* If the collectively bargained contract does not contain such a clause, it is illegal for an employer to either require or forbid employee union activity or to use union status as a promotion decision factor.
5. *Emergency powers of presidents.* If a strike threatens the public welfare, the president of the United States has power to order an 80-day cooling-off period. During this time, employees return to work and a board of inquiry tries to settle issues.

EXHIBIT 14.2 Legal Framework for Collective Bargaining

| Law or Ruling | Major Provisions | Significance |
| --- | --- | --- |
| Railway Labor Act (1926) | First major legislation to give any employees the right to join unions.<br>Encourages use of arbitration and mediation. | Applies only to railway and airline employees. |
| Norris-LaGuardia Act (1932) | Declared union membership to be the legal rights of all employees.<br>Forbids yellow dog contracts forcing employees to agree not to join a union or participate in any union activity.<br>Forbids federal judges from issuing injunctions against lawful union activities, unless there is a clear and present danger to life or property. | Applies to all private sector employees and unions. |
| Wagner Act (1935) | Guarantees employees' rights to organize and to bargain free from employers' interference.<br>Requires employers to bargain over wages, hours, and conditions of work, if a majority of employees desire such union representation.<br>Establishes the National Labor Relations Board (NLRB) to conduct representation elections and investigate charges of unfair labor practices. | Spurred growth in union membership. |
| Taft-Hartley Act or Labor-Management Relations Act (1947) | Employers cannot assist or establish labor organizations.<br>When a majority of employees desires a specific union, that union represents all employees in the bargaining unit, whether or not they are union members.<br>Established the Federal Mediation and Conciliation Service (FMCS), which offers assistance in contract settlement and maintains a list of arbitrators to help interpret contract language and resolve disputes.<br>Forbids the closed shop, requiring that employees be union members at the time of hiring. Allows the union shop, which stipulate union membership as a condition of continued employment.<br>Gives the president power to order an 80-day cooling off period if a strike threatens the public welfare. | Corrects abuses by unions, and to a lesser extent, employers. |
| Landrum-Griffin Act (1959) | Gives members the right to vote on union officers and dues increases, freedom of speech in union matters, and right to sue the union.<br>Requires union officers to report certain financial transactions.<br>Permits union job referrals (closed shops) for construction trades if the union agrees not to discriminate on the basis of membership. | Resulted from charges of labor racketeering in 1940s and 1950s. |
| "Right-to-Work" Laws | Outlaws union shop clauses. Twenty-one states, mainly in the South and Southwest, have such laws. | Outlaws compulsory unionism. |
| NLRB versus Electromation (1993) | Forbids the employer from setting up or creating employee committees or labor organizations, even for dealing with problems such as absenteeism and pay scales.<br>Ruling cited Wagner Act, which prohibits companies from setting up sham unions to undercut real ones. | Some consider the ruling a setback for cooperative efforts outside unionized workplaces. |

## LABOR RELATIONS OBJECTIVES

As we have already noted, less than 12 percent of private sector employees belong to unions. There are a number of reasons postulated for the decline of unions: an economic restructuring that shifted jobs away from heavy manufacturing, greater employer resistance, and a workforce whose expectations changed faster than unions could accommodate them. A closer look at the data reveals that most of the drop in membership occurred in the early 1980s. In the 1990s, membership has plateaued and even shown an increase in the 1993–94 time period. These signs of revival have come about because unions have begun targeting service workers on the increasingly crowded bottom tiers of the economy—people who do the dirty, dangerous, unpleasant jobs, at low wages.[6] As a result, organized labor is beginning to reclaim its traditional role of supporter of the underdog and regain public sympathy for the workers it represents. However, many people believe that a major cause of union difficulties is a change in organization objectives. More and more employers have made remaining (or becoming) nonunion part of their business strategy, and they have taken human resource actions consistent with this strategy.[7]

### Maintain a Union-Free Status

Sometimes employee relations programs are motivated in part by a desire to maintain a union-free status. Such programs have the objective of demonstrating concern and respect for employees and giving them substantial control over their work lives. The intended message is that "employees do not need a union, they are part of the organization which is as fair and equitable as possible."

A number of organization conditions appear related to whether or not a union is present. Three important ones are the location and size of the facility and the nature of the work.

#### Plant Location

In the United States, union membership is concentrated geographically. New York is the most highly unionized state, with a union membership that is double the rate nationwide. Over half the New York State union members are public sector employees, where unionism is 73 percent. Virtually all teachers and nonmanagerial municipal workers are unionized. Labor is also far stronger in the nearby states of New Jersey, Connecticut, and Pennsylvania than in the nation as a whole. Hawaii, too, is heavily unionized, as is the heavily industrialized state of Michigan. In contrast, the southern states have relatively few union members and share a strong antiunion bias. For example, union membership in South Carolina is under 4 percent, by far the lowest in the nation. Within a geographic region, small towns or the outskirts of large cities are also viewed as less favorable for unions. Employers take this information into consideration when deciding where to locate new facilities.

#### Plant Size

For a number of reasons, including technical and economic, many companies have shifted from large, centralized organizations to smaller business units with more independence from the corporate headquarters. The smaller size gives organizations greater flexibility to respond quickly to market changes. Smaller plants are also less likely to be unionized. Perhaps their size and multiple locations make it less cost effective for an outside union to mount an organizing campaign.

### Nature of the Work

Historically, some occupations have contained a high percentage of union members. Printing is one example; truck driving is another. Some nonunion employers subcontract their own printing and trucking to avoid having printers or truck drivers on their payroll. By doing so, they hope to reduce the likelihood of a union campaign. If subcontracting is not possible, some employers go to great lengths to ensure that its employees in those occupations enjoy wages, benefits, and working conditions directly comparable to those earned by union members doing the same jobs for different organizations.

Exhibit 14.3 shows current membership in some major U.S. unions. The largest is the Teamsters, which is an old union that has been extremely successful in organizing workers outside its original occupation group of truck drivers. Airline attendants, nurses, and even the actors who play Mickey Mouse and Snow White at Disneyland belong to the Teamsters.

### Anti-Union Tactics

Antiunion tactics include a variety of actions, not all of which are legal. The most extreme behavior is to fire employees who are perceived to be union activists. While such a move is clearly and absolutely illegal, it unfortunately continues to occur. The penalties for such activity are slight. If the NLRB rules that an employee was illegally fired for union activity, the employer must reinstate the worker and pay any difference between wages the worker would have earned absent the firing and wages actually earned.

The appeals process takes time; it may be several years before the union activist is back. This delay typically works to the employer's advantage and so makes many of them willing to run the risk. The payoffs of remaining nonunion are viewed as greater than the financial penalties of illegal behavior.

## Collaboration

Although labor relations disputes—strikes, violence, and allegations of illegal behavior—capture the attention of the public, the vast majority of contract negotiations and day-to-day administration is done in an atmosphere of mutual respect. If not harmonious, most relationships are at least cooperative, though some employers do not become cooperative until they have exhausted all other possibilities. "Resigned to the inevitable" may be more descriptive.

A more positive approach is collaboration, in which "management attempts to improve labor/management relations through joint union/management committees, employee involvement, and giving union leaders input into strategic business decisions."[8]

Which objective—union avoidance, maintain union-free status, or collaboration—or mix of objectives, is most common? It's a safe bet that almost all nonunionized firms in the United States prefer to remain so. They believe that a union reduces their flexibility in HR as well as capital decisions. Whether firms already unionized pursued an avoidance or a collaboration strategy (or a mix of the two) is heavily dependent on market pressures.[9] When the market worsens, as measured by industry employment levels, companies are more likely to

EXHIBIT 14.3 Service and Government Union Membership Strengthens

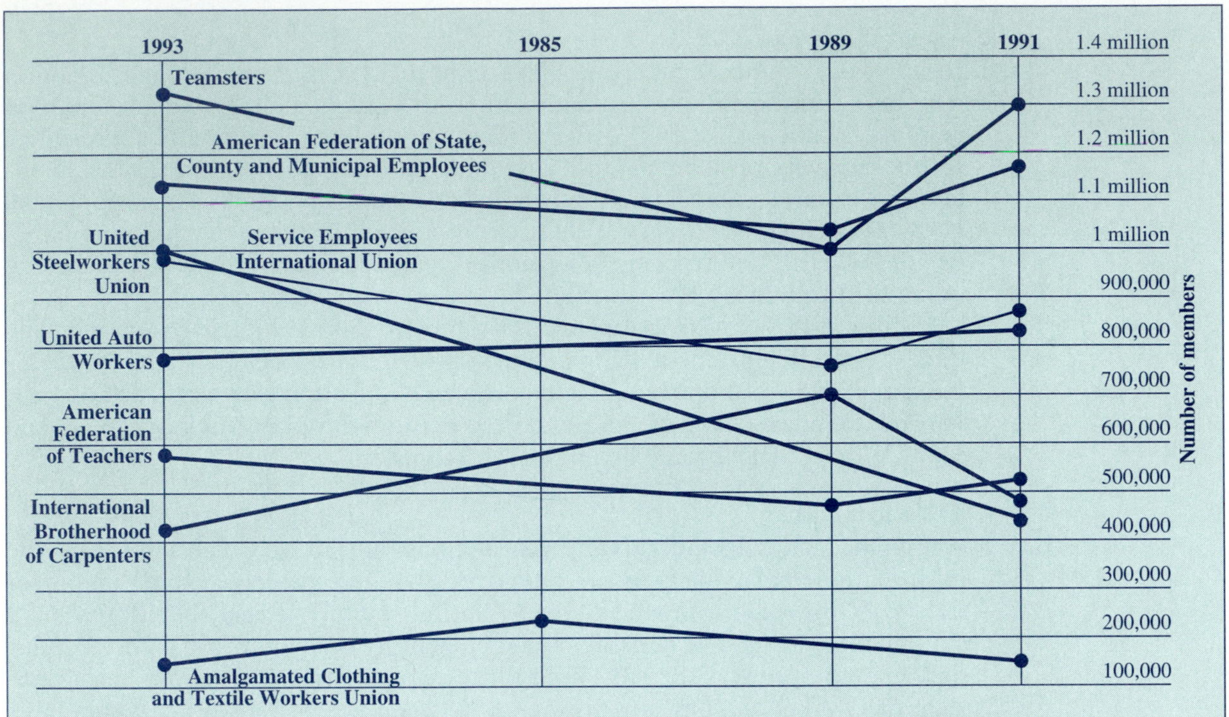

*Note: Numbers represent the membership figures the AFL-CIO uses to calculate per-capita dues of member unions.*

Note: Numbers represent the membership figures the AFL-CIO uses to calculate pre-capita dues of member unions.

choose union avoidance. The higher the proportion of plants unionized, the more likely the organization is to choose collaboration. Thus, external and organizational conditions clearly affect the choice of a labor relations strategy.

## THE ORGANIZING CAMPAIGN

The collective bargaining process includes the initial recognition of the rights and responsibilities of union and management, the negotiation of a written contract concerning wages, hours, and other conditions of employment, and the interpretation and administration of this contract over its period of coverage. When the employees are not represented by a union, either the employees themselves or a union can initiate unionization. Union organizers who are not employees may assist employees to start a campaign if there is a good chance of success. A union tries to mobilize discontent and steer employees toward union formation as a solution.

### Authorization Cards

Union organizers try to get employees to sign cards authorizing that union to represent them in collective bargaining. In the United States, 30 percent of the employees in the proposed bargaining unit must sign cards before the union can call for representation election. In most Canadian provinces, if 60 percent of the workers

> **WHAT DO YOU THINK?**
>
> How would you go about organizing such small employers as 7-11, McDonalds, or Nordstroms department store?

sign authorization cards, the union is certified without a representation election. There is no campaign on either side.

In general, the union tries to keep the initial stages of the campaign secret, so it can gather momentum before management can mount a counteroffensive. During the organizing period, unions and management pursue campaigns to affect employee attitudes toward unionization. Typically, the union stresses how it can improve the workers' compensation, benefits, and working conditions, and increase their control over decisions related to their jobs. Management mounts a countercampaign stressing how well off the employees are already and how union membership will cost them in dollars and "loss of freedom." It is illegal for either side—in mass meetings, literature, or individual meetings—to threaten employees with discharge or violence. Both sides must be truthful or the procedure can be set aside.

### Hearings

After the authorization, the NLRB holds a hearing to decide whether there is enough evidence to hold an election. The NLRB seeks to determine two things:

1. *Valid signatures.* Do the people who signed authorization cards actually work there, and do they constitute 30 percent of employees?
2. *Appropriate bargaining unit.* A bargaining unit delineates which group of employees will be involved in the representation election; for example, all employees in technician job categories at a particular plant location or all nonexempt employees at multiple locations.

Typically, a union proposes a bargaining unit. The NLRB must determine if this unit is appropriate, using two criteria: Will it ensure employees freedom of choice, and does it foster "industrial peace and stability"? It is not the NLRB's role to choose the *best* bargaining unit, only an *appropriate* unit. Employers frequently challenge the union's specification of a unit to influence which employees are eligible to vote in the election or just to delay the procedure.

### The Election

To win an election, 50 percent plus one of the people who vote in the election must vote for the union. Occasionally, there may be more than one union on the ballot. If this is the case, a runoff election is held between the two top choices; for example, either between the two unions, or between no union and the more popular union. When a union wins an election, the NLRB certifies that union's exclusive right to represent everyone in the bargaining unit. No other union may represent employees in the unit, and all employees in the unit are represented, whether or not they join the union.

Researchers have spent a great deal of effort trying to specify what factors affect the outcomes of union elections.

1. Employees are more likely to unionize if an employer is perceived to have demanded different behavior of employees than was expected, or failed to provide expected rewards.
2. An individual must believe that there is little likelihood of changing conditions except through collective bargaining.
3. Some critical mass of like-minded activists is necessary to begin the unionizing attempt.

Most union elections are very close. One study found that a shift of eight votes would have changed the outcome of the average election.[10] Therefore, it is no wonder that participation rates are high—typically 90 percent—in union elections, compared to roughly 50 percent in major political elections. Employees accurately perceive that their vote *can* make a difference.

#### Decertification

If a union has not served its members, or if employee membership has so changed that there is no longer support for the union, decertification is a possibility. The same group of employees who vote in a union can vote one out, using much the same procedure as in certification. An election, supervised by the NLRB, can be called for by either the employees in the unit involved or a labor organization acting on their behalf. Whoever requests the election must provide evidence that at least 30 percent of the employees want a decertification election. A petition signed by a majority of the bargaining unit employees is the most common evidence.

A decertification election cannot be held within 12 months of the certification election or while a labor contract is in effect.

## NEGOTIATING A CONTRACT

Once a union is recognized as the bargaining representative for a group of employees, its officials are authorized to negotiate an employment contract. This contract differs in several important ways from a typical legal contract. It is unusual because:

1. So many people are bound by it. If you buy a car, you may feel that many people are involved: the salesperson, the salesperson's supervisor, the loan processor, and the license bureau. But a union contract involves all the people who are employed in the bargaining unit. This number may run into the hundreds.
2. The contract is not strictly voluntary because neither side can walk away from it. Workers are already employed, the union cannot say "I'll go get another employer," and the employer is legally required to bargain.
3. Most contracts specify all details of a one-time event. By contrast, the collective bargaining agreement governs a day-to-day relationship, but it may be incomplete and purposely vague. If there is no meeting of the minds, a statement of general principle may be given. For example, a statement supporting worker participation plans was contained in GM-UAW contracts for years before any programs actually began.

### Preparation

Little research has been done on the preparation for negotiation mainly because the parties to the negotiation prefer secrecy. The more complex the bargaining, the further ahead preparations begin.

The beginning part of the preparation analyzes problems in contract administration and possible changes in contract language. If management or the union wishes to make changes in a contract, it must notify the other party and the FMCS in writing of its desire at least 60 days before the contract expires. This notification also should include an offer to meet with the other side to discuss the issues.

> **WHAT DO YOU THINK?**
>
> Free collective bargaining, some claim, is essential for market-based democratic societies to function efficiently and fairly. What should public policy be regarding collective bargaining and unions in emerging and transforming countries such as those in Central Europe, parts of Asia, and Latin America? What are the pros and cons of unions and free collective bargaining?

Since the signing of the last contract, both sides probably have compiled lists of issues to bring up the next time. Management has asked its supervisors how they would like the contract modified to avoid problem areas. Both sides may study patterns in grievances to identify problems.

Based on these data, both sides gather statistical information and prepare bargaining positions. For example, management seeks information on economic conditions affecting the job (e.g., wage rates, productivity) from its staff, industry data, and published sources. Management also attempts to determine the cost of each likely union demand. Computer simulation can help here.

Often there are differences within management groups over bargaining objectives. A common complaint is: "I'm having more trouble with my company than I am with the union." When these management differences are worked out before the negotiations start, the bargaining process is more effective. If an employer negotiates with more than one union (e.g., different unions representing various bargaining units within the employer), careful preparation is essential, for what is negotiated with one union is likely to be brought up by the others. Typically, a careful balance of wage, benefit, and status differentials is maintained among unions.

The union also prepares for negotiations by preparing lists of problems with the contract. It, too, gathers statistical information, studies the issues likely to be raised, and coordinates with any other unions involved. Unions may also have internal differences, usually over what the bargaining objectives are; for example, younger workers may want job security, while older workers favor better pensions. Women members may prefer obtaining schedule flexibility, men may prefer greater opportunity for overtime.[11]

## Negotiation Issues

Any labor contract can have a large number of clauses. The clauses in the agreement set out the rules of the job for the contract period. They restrict some behavior and require other behavior. Proper wording of the agreement can prevent future difficulties in interpretation. Both sides should thoroughly discuss the meaning of each clause to prevent misunderstanding, if possible.

1. *Union security.* This is usually the first bargaining issue for a union. Most unions prefer a *union shop clause:* When workers take jobs in this bargaining unit, they must join the union after a certain time period or lose the job. Requiring union membership as a condition for continued employment is legal. A *closed shop,* where union membership is a condition of hiring, is illegal. Sometimes states can further restrict what kinds of security clauses are permitted.

   If a union shop clause cannot be won, a union may settle for an *agency shop:* Even if workers do not join, they must still pay the equivalent of dues to the union.[12]

   Another option is a *maintenance of membership clause:* Workers may or may not join the union, but once they join, they must maintain (continue) their membership for the duration of the contract. Membership can only be dropped within 30 days of contract expiration. A maintenance of membership clause guarantees stability in numbers for a union.

2. *Contract administration.* The contract specifies its duration, commonly two to three years, and procedures to ensure that it is applied/enforced as intended.
3. *Employee security and seniority.* Seniority is continuous service in a work unit, plant, or organization. Most contracts stipulate that seniority should be the determining factor in promotions, layoffs, and recalls.

   Seniority rights can sometimes conflict with diversity objectives. The Supreme Court has upheld the legality of seniority systems as long as the original intent of the system was not to discriminate. Because minorities and women are more likely to have low seniority, layoffs on a seniority basis hurt them disproportionately.
4. *Management rights.* This issue usually presents an especially difficult set of problems. Management lists certain decisions as management rights, excluded from bargaining. Management tries to make these lists long, and unions try to chip away at them. In many cases, the wage concessions that unions made in the 1980s were in exchange for reduction in the items of management's sole discretion.
5. *Compensation and working conditions.* All contracts stipulate compensation and working conditions, such as direct compensation rates, benefits, and hours of work. Issues concern whether overtime should be voluntary, and the size of any cost-of-living adjustments. For example, unions may bargain about not only payments for pensions but also the details of early retirement provisions.

### Two-Tier Provisions

One wage clause that has generated a great deal of controversy is the two-tier wage structure, in which the top rate of pay for new employees is substantially lower than that for previously hired employees.

Because employees with identical job titles, duties, responsibilities, and performance receive substantially different pay rates, two-tier structures seem particularly hard to reconcile with the objective of equity. Fortunately, most such plans phase new employees into the higher rates after several years, so eventually the differential disappears. Equity issues raise serious concerns about two-tier provisions. Nevertheless, General Motors and the UAW agreed to one in 1996.

## Refusal to Bargain

In spite of the legal requirement to bargain in good faith, a lot of newly certified unions are unable to negotiate a contract. A study found that employer discrimination against union activists—mostly firings—and refusal by employers to bargain have substantial negative effects on the likelihood of obtaining a first contract.[13] Even though employers are legally required to bargain, they can delay by throwing up legal challenges. A fledgling union rarely has the resources to fight or wait out these delaying tactics. However, when bargaining units are large and cohesive, and when national union representatives participate in the process, first contracts are more likely obtained. Therefore, employers in effect don't bargain unless the union has the strength to force the issue.

### Pattern Bargaining

Another way of gaining advantage is by pattern bargaining, which is the use of a settlement in one setting as the target in another setting. Pattern bargaining was common into the 1970s, but it has declined in the 1990s.

### Formalizing the Contract

An agreement comes about when both sides believe they have produced the best contract they can. Their perceptions are influenced by the negotiations, their relative power at the time, and other factors. Power factors, such as a weak union or a strong employer, are very important in the settlement of the contract.

After the two sides have tentatively agreed, the union members must ratify the contract. Ratification is not automatic and union negotiators must keep an eye toward membership ramifications or the negotiation process will have to be repeated.

Even if the contract is accepted at one level, it may require adjustments at other levels. For example, when Ford Motor Company signs a contract with the UAW at the national level, local plants must then settle disputes on work rules and other issues at each plant. Only when these are settled is the contract negotiation process over for a while.

# IMPASSES IN COLLECTIVE BARGAINING

The description of contract negotiation above suggests a smooth flow, from presentation of demands to settlement. This flow is not always so smooth; impasses may develop that do not allow one or both sides to keep the process moving. Three things can happen when an impasse develops: mediation, a strike or lockout, or arbitration.

## Mediation

> *Mediation* is the process by which a professional, neutral third party is invited in by both parties to help remove an impasse to the contract negotiations.

All experts agree that it is better for the two parties to negotiate alone. When it appears this process has broken down, however, they can invite in a mediator, usually a government mediator, such as those provided by the FMCS. The FMCS offers services such as developing factual data if the two sides disagree, setting up joint study committees on difficult points, or trying to help the two sides find common grounds for further bilateral negotiations. Instead of waiting until an impasse, the FMCS also offers preventive mediation when the two parties anticipate serious problems prior to strike deadlines.

In general, fact-finding appears to work best when the negotiators are inexperienced and to be least effective when major differences exist between the expectations of each party to the dispute.

Mediators have no power to compel the two sides to reach an agreement. Instead, they seek to persuade employers and unions that it is in their best interest to reach an agreement without resorting to a strike.

## Strikes

If an impasse in negotiations is quite serious, a strike or lockout can take place.

A *strike* is a refusal by employees to work.

A *lockout* is a refusal by management to allow employees to work.

Strikes can be categorized by the objectives they seek. A *contract strike* occurs when management and the union cannot agree on terms of a new contract. More than 90 percent of strikes are contract strikes.

A *grievance strike* occurs when the union disagrees on how management is interpreting the contract or handling day-to-day problems, such as discipline. Strikes over grievances are prohibited in about 5 percent of contracts, but they occur fairly frequently in mining, transportation, and construction industries.

A *jurisdictional strike* takes place when two or more unions disagree on which jobs should be organized by each union. The Taft-Hartley Act gives the NLRB the power to settle jurisdictional issues.

About 1 percent of strikes are *recognition strikes.* These occur as a strategy to force an employer to accept the union. *Political strikes* take place to influence government policy and are extremely rare in the United States.

Strikes differ, too, in the percentage of employees who refuse to work. A *total strike* takes place when all unionized employees walk out; if only a percentage of the workers does so, the result may be a partial strike, semistrike, or slowdown. In a *slowdown,* all employees come to work but they do little work; the union insists on all work rules being followed to the letter, with the result that output slows down. This is also called "working to the contract." This old tactic is being used with increasing frequency as an alternative to a total strike, because many employers are simply replacing striking workers with new hires.

Public employees in the federal sector and in almost half of the states do not have the right to strike. Instead, impasses in negotiating contracts that cannot be resolved through mediation go to arbitration. However, arbitration is rarely used in negotiations in the private sector in the United States (see the discussion of arbitration in the next section).

### Anatomy of a strike

For a strike to take place, both sides must make decisions. Management must decide it can afford to "take a strike;" that is, it has built up its inventories, has sufficient financial resources, thinks it will not lose too many customers during a strike, and believes it can win. The union must believe it will win more than it loses, that the employer will not go out of business, and that management will not replace the union employees with permanent replacements. Union members must be willing to live with hardships, to receive *no* paychecks, and to give the union a strike vote. When members give the union the authority to strike, the union's bargaining hand is strengthened, and it can then time the strike to occur when it will hurt management the most.

> EXPLORING THE WEB
>
> Information on international labor unions in many countries outside the United States is available on the web. Your instructor has a list of addresses for much of this information.

During the strike, the union sets up the legally allowed number of pickets at the plants and tries to mobilize support among allies in other unions and the public. Sometimes the union will conduct a *corporate campaign* by going to the bankers, major customers, and members of the company's board to present negative information about the targeted company. The hope is that outside alliances and negative publicity can put additional pressure on the company to settle.

What does management do if there is a strike? Lockouts are rarely used. In general, it tries to encourage the workers to return to work by advertising circulars, phone calls, and so on. The longer the strike, the harder it is on the strikers. If the union has only limited strike funds and workers' savings run out, a back-to-work movement can cause this strike to collapse. In recent years, management has tended to play a defensive "wait-them-out" game and to keep operating during a strike. Nonunionized employees, such as white-collar workers and managers, may try to keep things going. If management goes on the offensive, it can hire replacements or threaten to close the plant. A strike ends when both sides negotiate an agreement they can live with, or the weaker side gives in.

### Replacement Workers

The hiring of permanent replacements has always been legal. However, prior to the strike by air traffic controllers in 1981, it was a weapon that management rarely used. The air traffic controllers are federal employees and thus forbidden by law from striking. When they did anyway, President Ronald Reagan fired them and authorized the hiring of replacements. The air traffic controllers received sympathy and support neither from the public, most of whom earned a great deal less than the strikers, nor from organized labor, who had not forgotten that the controllers had supported Reagan in the 1980 election while the rest of organized labor had strongly supported Reagan's opponent. When private sector employers saw that there were few repercussions from hiring replacements, many soon followed the government's example. Caterpillar, Cargill, Hormel and TWA are just some of the large employers who replaced legal strikers with permanent hires. Unions have not yet found effective ways to counteract these tactics, although legislation outlawing hiring replacement workers has been proposed.[14]

In 1995, President Clinton issued an executive order banning companies that hired permanent replacements during a strike from doing business with the government. As a practical measure, the order affected all major employers, because of the pervasiveness of government as a purchaser of goods and services. However, an appeals court struck down the ban, ruling that it was inconsistent with the Wagner Act, which offsets the employees' right to strike with an employer's right to hire replacements.

## CONTRACT ADMINISTRATION

The labor contract governs the day-to-day employment relationships; it is a living document. The union steward and the supervisor are the principal interpreters and enforcers of the contract. Differences in interpretation are resolved through the grievance process. The grievance process is a mechanism for employees to voice their disagreement with the way the contract is administered; hence it is a key part of administering the contract. The ability to provide a channel for grievances is a key selling point for union organizers.

A *grievance* is a formal dispute between an employee and management on the conditions of employment.

Grievances arise because of (1) differing interpretations of the contract by employees, stewards, and management; (2) a violation of a contract provision; (3) a violation of law; (4) a violation of work procedures or other precedents; or (5) perceived unfair treatment of an employee by management. The rate of grievances may increase when the contract language is unclear, employees are dissatisfied or frustrated on their jobs or they resent the supervisory style, or because the union is using grievances as a tactic against management.[15] Grievances may also be due to employees with personal problems that affect job performance (see Chapter Fifteen) or who are otherwise difficult.

The Department of Labor has found that the most frequent incidents that lead to the filing of a grievance are employee discipline, seniority decisions at promotion or layoff time, and work assignments.

The grievance process has at least three purposes and consequences. First, by settling smaller problems early, it may prevent larger problems from occurring in the future. Second, grievances identify ambiguities in the contract for negotiation at a future date. Finally, the grievance process is an effective communication channel from employees to management.

## Steps in the Grievance Process

The employee grievance process involves a systematic set of steps for handling an employee complaint. Most union contracts specify the mechanisms for processing these grievances, though the process varies with the contract.

1. *Initiation of the formal grievance.* An employee who feels mistreated or believes that some action or application of policy violates rights in the contract files a grievance with the supervisor. It can be done in writing or (at least initially) orally. The grievance can be formulated with the help and support of the union steward. If the steward believes no grievance has occurred, the process ends here. Most grievances are settled between the steward, the employee, and the supervisor.

   The supervisor must attempt to accurately determine the reason for the grievance. The effective approach is to try to solve the problem, rather than to assess blame or find excuses. A supervisor and a steward who have a good working relationship can work together to settle the problem at that level.
2. *Department head or unit manager.* If the steward, supervisor, and employee together cannot solve the grievance, it goes to the next level in the hierarchy. At this point, the grievance must be presented in writing, and both sides must document their cases.
3. *Arbitration.* If the grievance cannot be settled at this intervening step (or steps), an independent arbitrator may be called in to settle the issue.

A sexual harassment lawsuit filed by Mitsubishi union members identifies a dilemma for the traditional union grievance process when the mistreatment is at the hands of a fellow unionist rather than management. Female union members who complained about the behavior of male co-workers discovered that union stewards were reluctant to file a grievance that might jeopardize the job of a union member. If a union member would be disciplined or fired for sexual harassment, the union would be compelled to file a grievance on behalf of the accused employee, even at the expense of another union member.

## Arbitration

No other topic in labor relations has more confusing jargon and labels. Arbitration refers to a process that ends in a *decision,* not a recommendation. In the United States, arbitration is typically used to settle grievance issues arising from contract administration. Bargaining impasse arbitration is only used in the public sector, where strikes are illegal.

> *Arbitration* is the process by which two parties to a dispute agree in advance of the hearing to abide by the decision of an independent quasijudge called an *arbitrator.*

Exhibit 14.4 clarifies the different forms of arbitration. Under *voluntary arbitration,* the parties agree to submit their differences to arbitration, whereas under *compulsory arbitration* the law requires the parties' impasses to be submitted to arbitration. Compulsory arbitration in the United States is common only in the public sector, where employees may be legally forbidden to strike. Australia and some other countries specify compulsory arbitration for all labor disputes; no one has the right to strike. In these circumstances, arbitration resolves disputes arising from contract administration *and* contract negotiation.

Under *conventional arbitration,* the arbitrator is free to generate any resolution that seems appropriate. *Final-offer arbitration* requires the arbitrator to choose either the employer's or the union's last proposal. Professional baseball uses this system. Arbitrators may deal with a single issue or the total contract, and it may be done by a single individual or by a panel of arbitrators.

After hearing all the evidence, the arbitrator writes an arbitration award binding both parties. The award attempts to clarify the situation to prevent future problems from arising. More than 75 percent of grievances are settled at the first step and another 20 percent are settled at the second. Only about 1 percent go to arbitration.

Studies of the personal characteristics of those who have filed grievances revealed some differences when contrasted with those who have not. In general, those who filed grievances were younger, had more formal education, and got more wage increases. One study found gender differences in the handling of grievances: women employees are more likely to have disciplinary actions overturned than men.[16] Handling grievances is time consuming and expensive for both unions and management. Thus, the sooner and more informally grievances or just complaints or inquiries can be handled, the better.

# THE UNION ORGANIZATION

To become a union member in the United States, a person joins one of the 70,000 or so local unions. The local is a subunit of one of the national unions, most of which belong to the American Federation of Labor—Congress of Industrial Organizations (AFL-CIO). This federation represents 80 percent of unionized employees.

National union headquarters provides many services to subsidiary unions: training for regional and local union leaders, organizing help, strike funds, and

**EXHIBIT 14.4** The Terminology of Alternative Forms of Arbitration

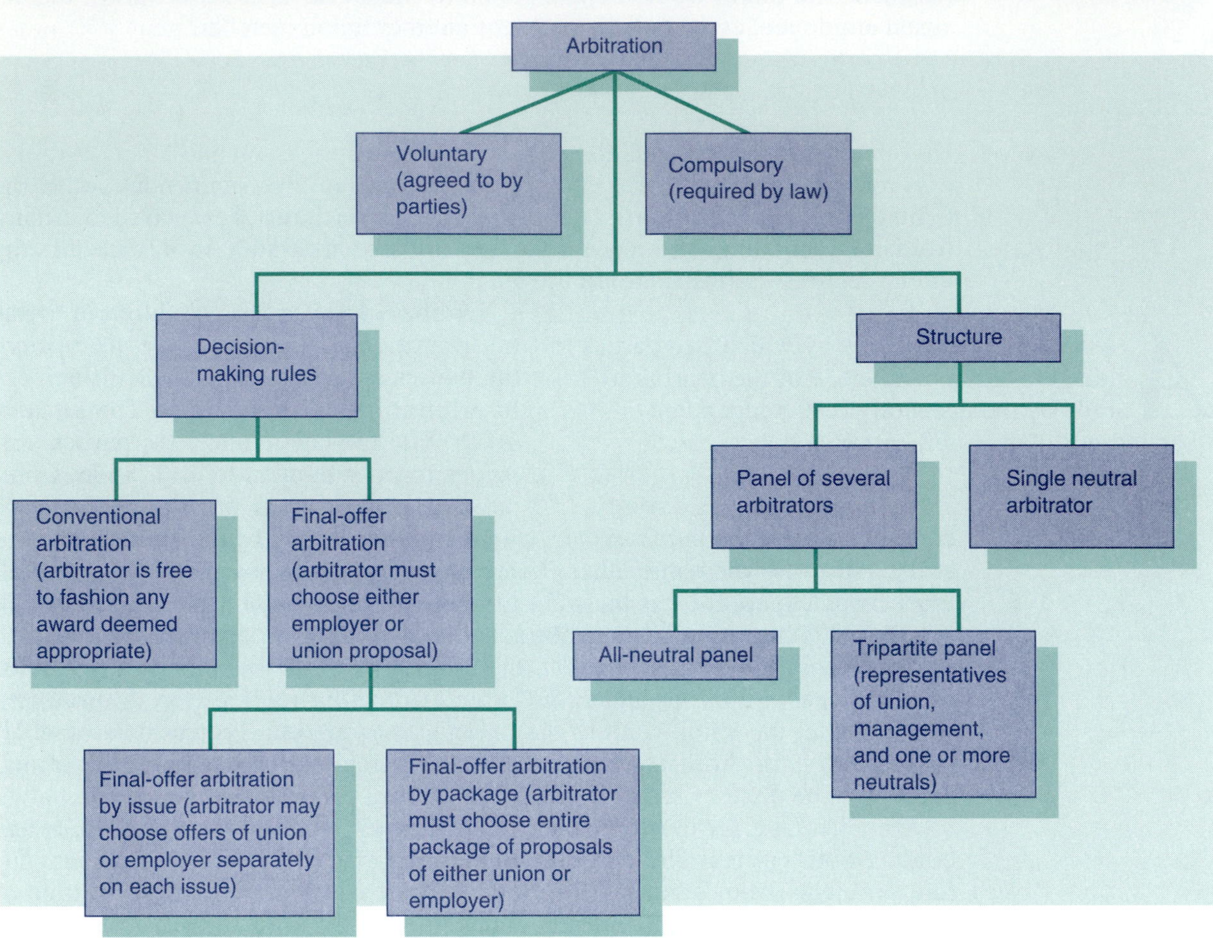


Source: Adapted from Thomas Kochan, *Collective Bargaining and Industrial Relations* (Homewood, IL: Richard D. Irwin, 1980), p. 290.

data to be used in negotiating contracts. Specialists available for consultation include lawyers, public relations specialists, and research personnel.

The keystone of the trade union movement is the local union, representing all the union members in a geographic area for a craft union (e.g., all carpenters in San Francisco) or in a plant for an industrial union (e.g., UAW members at GM's Saturn plant in Spring Hill, Tennessee). In general, the local union is a branch of the national union, and has little legal autonomy. In many unions, the local must get permission from the national union before it can strike. The national can charter or disband a local, suspend it, or put it under national trusteeship.

## Union Leaders

There is as great a variety in the size and power of the local unions as there is in the nationals. The local elects officials, such as president, secretary-treasurer, business representative, and committee representatives. If the local is large enough, the business representative and a secretary-treasurer are full-time employees. The business representative plays a crucial role in contract negotiations and grievances. The president and other officials hold full-time jobs in the trade or industry. Typically, they get some released time for union duties and are paid expenses.

### Union Steward

The steward represents the union on the job site and is charged with handling grievances and disciplinary matters. Normally, the steward is elected by members in the unit for a one-year term. The effectiveness of the local is usually judged by its effective grievance handling.

The steward functions as a gatekeeper who can encourage employees to file grievances (or even file in their behalf). Or the steward can seek to resolve problems informally, in consultation with management.

Both employees and unions can be viewed as political entities. But politics are more fundamental to unions. Union leaders, especially local union leaders, have much less power than their managerial equivalents. They are always subject to reelection, and the contracts they negotiate must be ratified by union members. Members also can keep union leaders in line by voting them out or by engaging in wildcat strikes. Typically, union members are apathetic about union affairs except in times of crisis, such as the decision to strike. Usually only 10 to 15 percent of the members attend an ordinary union meeting.

In theory, unions are democratic; their members are supposed to influence their policies and decisions. However, the typical union is run by a small percentage of members. The effective union leader realizes, however, that the demands made by the union must not put the employer out of business. Good union leaders help employers by policing the contract and keeping maverick members in line. The union leader's job should be to represent the diverse and often conflicting demands and interests of the membership.

## Union Strategies

The union movement today is in trouble. In the 1980s, many unions became victims of their successes in the 1950s and 1960s. The appalling working conditions and arbitrary employer behaviors that had gained unions public sympathy earlier in this century had vastly improved. Legally, they were no longer the underdog. They had negotiated generous agreements for their members. Good times for employers meant that generous labor settlements could be passed on to consumers in the form of higher prices. A highly structured, formalized relationship between unions and management evolved with detailed contracts enforced through grievance procedures. But the base of the unions' power—the detailed contract, the uniformity of its administration, the narrow job rules, and the emphasis on stability—were the very factors that constrained employers' ability to respond to the economic dislocation and competition of the 1980s. Formalized procedures that could only be changed through lengthy negotiation made it difficult to react fast enough to changes in external conditions. As a result, the union image changed from being a friend of the worker to one of a protector of the status quo; a hindrance to necessary change. Big unions were held in low esteem, and while money and volunteers from union ranks were still welcomed by political candidates, they did not seek to publicize the relationship. In the 1990s, however, the national union leadership is giving a higher priority, and more funding, to organizing efforts that focus on low-paying jobs such as building maintenance workers, clerical and office workers, or hospital and nursing home aides and attendants. In addition, three of the nation's largest industrial unions—the UAW, Machinists, and United Steelworkers—merged. Their goal in creating a mega-union is to span multiple industries and gain a presence in every region of the country, which they hope will translate into more leverage in negotiating companywide or industrywide contracts. Prior to the merger, the three unions often represented different plants of the same company and different companies in the same industries.

Unions are changing the way they interact with employers. Cooperative programs are becoming more common, and some unions are getting involved in employer's strategic decisions.

## Cooperative Programs

Resistance to unions dies hard. Unless they have no choice, most employers prefer to remain nonunion. If they are only partially unionized, they may try to redirect their business to favor growth in the nonunionized segments, often at the expense of unionized segments. However, successful examples of union/management cooperation also exist.

### Employee Involvement at Saturn

GM's Saturn plant in Spring Hill, Tennessee, is the most well known. The Saturn automobile has not only proven popular with customers, it also established a reputation as a pioneer in workplace changes. Even before the plant was built, GM management and UAW workers collaboratively designed the physical plant, chose all the technology to be used, produced the marketing and advertising strategy, and developed the recruitment and education programs used to select and train the workforce, drawn from the ranks of UAW membership. Members of a work team interview applicants to determine not only the applicants' skills but also their leadership qualities and adaptability to the Saturn culture. The team reaches consensus on which applicants are acceptable and extends offers to them. Union representatives also participate in hiring managerial staff. Training programs are administered jointly. Half the training is devoted to developing the human relations skills necessary to operate successfully in the democratized system.[17]

The union also participated in other strategic decisions. For example, the initial plan was to produce a small car with great emphasis on fuel economy. But after sampling customer reaction to the proposed car, the joint committee turned instead to a larger design with a more powerful engine and a sporty appearance.

While the Saturn automobile and its marketing strategy have successfully created a mystique among owners, the next challenge is to see if GM and the UAW can hold fast to principles as the nature of competitive pressures changes.

Part of the challenge stems from Saturn's success. As Saturn has hired additional "partners" to staff a second shift, it has cut back the amount of training the new hires receive. Unfortunately, the training cutback may be affecting those employees who need the training the most, since the most enthusiastic supporters among UAW membership for the new system were among the initial hires.

Among many other lessons, Saturn's experience demonstrates the enormous efforts that must constantly occur to maintain the trust necessary for the partnership to deliver benefits to labor and management equally. Saturn is currently planning to enter the Japanese market with a smaller-sized car.

## What Does the Research Tell Us?

Union-management cooperation and employee involvement has been the topic of a great deal of research. The results frequently disagree with people's beliefs. A study of the auto industry found that the use of teams had a *negative* impact on productivity. In plants where teams were utilized, the ratio of supervisors to production workers was actually higher, not lower, and on average it took seven and a half hours longer to assemble each car. On the other hand, representative union participation in decision making had a *positive* impact. In plants where the union played a greater role through joint action committees, the supervisor/worker ratio was lower, and it took almost five hours less to build a car. These results were corroborated by another study of more than 1,000 metal-working and machinery firms. Nonunion firms that had adopted employee involvement plans were on average significantly less productive than firms without such experiments. Unionized firms adopting participatory schemes had no such loss in efficiency, although unionized firms without an employee involvement plan had the highest efficiency of all. These studies conclude that the biggest predictor of productivity is the presence of a union.[18]

On the other hand, an analysis of 47 statistical studies concerned with the productivity impact of employee participation found that more than half showed improved productivity as a result of employee involvement or worker ownership; only two reported negative effects. The differing results indicate that the context of cooperation makes a difference: "Workers respond only when there exists some sense of reciprocal obligation, a sense that management actually values skilled workers, will make sacrifices to retain them, and is willing to delegate responsibility to the team. Merely changing the organization chart to show 'teams' and introducing quality circles to find ways to improve productivity processes are unlikely to make much difference."[19]

Another study raises further doubts. After examining a wide variety of employee involvement programs in Pennsylvania, researchers found management much more enthused about the programs, with unions either neutral or somewhat positive. Both union and management agree that the social and psychological impact of such programs is greater than their economic impact.[20]

Why does union involvement appear to be a necessary ingredient? Unions keep companies from reverting to old ways when difficulties hinder the progress of employee participation. Unions provide a mechanism for addressing the glitches without throwing out the whole participation process, and they allow workers to participate meaningfully without risking their jobs. Further, unions can help educate workers for better-informed participation. Where unions do not exist or employee involvement is promoted unilaterally by management, employee commitment is likely to be weak.

Employee involvement can certainly increase employees' sense of commitment to an organization, even through a layoff. One study found that participants in an employee involvement program felt they had received better information delivered in a considerate, respectful manner than had nonparticipants.[21]

On the other hand, the vice president of HR for Merck cautions against prescriptive rules governing employee involvement:

> Cooperation cannot be mandated nor can cooperative programs be tailored to fit the particular circumstances of individual workplaces by federal regulation writers. If there is a role for government here, it is to provide the soil in which the seed of cooperative relationships can sprout, and to provide the nutriments and conditions in which the plant can flourish. It is not the government's role to prescribe the size of each leaf, the points on the stem at which a branch is permitted, and the acceptable number of flowers, the failure to produce that number being sufficient grounds for ripping up the plant by its roots.[22]

## PUBLIC SECTOR UNIONS

One segment of the economy that presents a brighter picture for unionism is the public sector. While private sector unionism represents less than 12 percent of the workforce and continues to shrink, public sector unionism is over 43 percent—and growing. Two unique attributes of public employment account for the phenomenal growth.

First is the lack of managerial opposition to union organization. Because public sector employees also are voters, managers who oppose the union run the risk of losing their own jobs by being voted out of office.

Second, the interests of public sector employees and managers frequently overlap. They may be allies in lobbying for increased government spending. Managers may welcome union help in obtaining larger budgets, which translate into employment growth and consequent higher union membership.

Only a small number of states allow public employees to strike, and then it is usually only certain groups of employees. Instead, mediation is commonly used to resolve public sector disputes. Teachers are the most strike-prone public employees.[23]

## NEW LEGISLATIVE INITIATIVES

As with any HR activity, legislation, court cases, and rulings by enforcement agencies—in this case, the National Labor Relations Board—influence actions. The Wagner Act was a strong force encouraging unionism. Since then, the climate has changed. Although the Department of Labor promotes cooperative efforts to "enhance the quality of working life, while improving the productivity and competitiveness of American industry," many blame the federal government for setting the tone of adversarial relationships throughout the 1980s, beginning with their firing of the air traffic controllers and continuing with their tepid responses to antiunion behavior.

Many say existing legislation fails to take into account the changed nature of jobs and competition. What is required is new legislation to curb major abuses by:

- Making it illegal to permanently replace strikers.[24]
- Increasing the penalties for wrongfully firing union activists.
- Speeding up the organizing campaign.
- Allowing unions to represent those who vote for a union even if they are less than a majority.

### Electromation

A more fundamental issue today is the fluid nature of the workplace in contrast with the command-and-control structures that prevailed when unions were at their peak membership. As employers try to involve employees in organization decision making, they are running up against the NLRB's interpretation of labor-management committees as employer-dominated bogus unions, which the Wagner Act outlaws. The act defines a union as any organization in which employees participate for the purpose of "dealing with" the employer over "pay, wages, hours of employment, or other conditions of employment."

The issue first arose in a ruling involving Electromation Inc., a small manufacturer of electrical parts. In late 1988, after a year of heavy losses, Electromation decided to replace wage increases with length-of-service bonuses. When employees objected, the company met with selected employees and eventually established a number of committees to issue recommendations to management on certain prescribed topics: Absenteeism/infractions, no smoking policy, communication network, pay progression for premium positions, and an attendance bonus program. Participation was voluntary. Soon after, the Teamsters began an organizing drive at the company. When they lost the election, they complained to the NLRB that the committees violated the Wagner Act.

To determine whether the committees were lawful requires a two-part test: First, does the committee meet the definition of a labor organization as defined in the National Labor Relations Act? A committee is a labor organization if (1) employees participate, (2) the committee "deals with" the employer, and (3) the subject matter of the committee includes wages, rates of pay, hours of employment, or working conditions. All three requirements must be met if the organization is to be considered a labor union. Second, does the employer dominate or interfere with the committee? Because Electromation management helped form the committees and had the option of discontinuing them at will, the NLRB ruled that Electromation had unlawfully interfered with the formation of a union chosen freely by the employees.

### Employee Involvement

In response to this ruling, legislation has been proposed that would modify the law's definition of a labor organization. The Teamwork for Employers and Managers Act (TEAM) permits team-based employee involvement structures in nonunion settings. Employers support the proposed legislation because it permits increased cooperation and joint decision making. Unions, however, oppose the legislation, arguing that it ignores the inherent issue of power. Any structure such as teams or committees that are not negotiated through a union are inherently dominated by management and so cannot really "empower" employees. True empowerment comes only through a collective voice of a union. The legislation was passed in 1996 but vetoed by President Clinton.

## LABOR RELATIONS IN OTHER COUNTRIES

As we have seen, labor relations in the United States are intertwined with political and economic history. This is true for other countries as well. Each country's employment relationship must fit the unique conditions of its society and adapt over time to changes in those conditions.

Labor relations systems in the United States have been relatively slow to adapt to changes in external factors.[25] Unions (and many organizations, too) have frequently continued to follow policies and practices long after they had become obsolete. The increase in international and multinational organizations provides an opportunity for us to compare innovations in labor relations in other countries.

Union membership is declining in many nations. France, the United Kingdom, and Japan have all seen the percentages fall.[26] In Japan, coverage fell from 32 percent to 26 percent in the 1980s. But as Exhibit 14.5 shows, membership is thriving in Norway and Australia, and other countries where laws support their growth and political power. Structural differences that help account for this difference in membership levels include a high degree of centralization of unions (nationally negotiated contract structures), legally binding participation in influential worker councils, and other social legislation that strengthens the rights of employees, such as requirements of advance notice of layoffs, and lenient terms of qualification for unemployment insurance.

## Centralized Bargaining

We have seen how thousands of local U.S. unions bargain over detailed contracts that set members' wages while management determines the wages for nonunion workers subject to market constraints. But in most of the rest of the world, bargaining is much more centralized, with nationwide or at least industrywide agreements that acquire the force of law. For example, Scandinavian and Austrian unions often negotiate national wage agreements with employer associations and enter into agreements with the government and employer federations that link wages settlements to national economic policies. Australian unions argue wage cases before arbitration tribunals that issue orders covering the bulk of the workforce. French and German unions negotiate industrywide or regional agreements whose terms the ministry of labor can extend to nonunion workers. In Japan, enterprise unions bargain at the firm level while union federations determine national wage patterns.[27]

## Worker Councils

Many Western European countries require employee involvement in a firm's strategic decisions. Participation is in the form of worker councils, who must approve major decisions. The councils represent all workers, union and nonunion, on local workplace issues. Their membership is mandated in many Western European countries. The councils make diffusion of new practices relatively easy. The analogy may be to outsourcing a lot of HR decisions to vendors who can do it more efficiently or can bring a higher level of skill to the task. The councils and the individual employers negotiate the details within the parameters established by the "framework agreements" signed by the trade union confederation and the employer/industry associations.

Although Japan has no formal structure for worker participation in business decision making or in government policy making, most large Japanese firms engage union leaders in informal consultations. Union gains are made through these consultations, rather than negotiation. This approach is consistent with Japanese values of conformity to group norms. Japanese unions traditionally

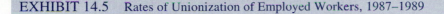

EXHIBIT 14.5 Rates of Unionization of Employed Workers, 1987–1989

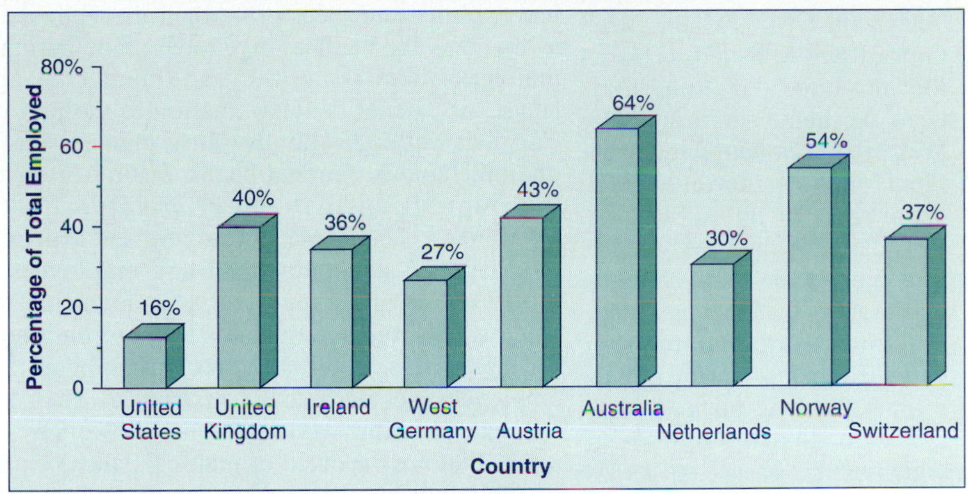


emphasize employment security over other HR practices. One study found that they are less likely to resist changes in performance evaluation and pay practices than employment security changes.[28]

## Social Legislation: Intensive versus Extensive

Government regulations play a strong role in each country's labor relations. Regulations affect discretion managers have in making decisions.

Government involvement in labor relations in the United States can be characterized as "intensive, detailed and controlling" where it is involved, but not extensive in the areas of involvement. For example, the NLRB establishes precisely which workers can or cannot be part of a bargaining unit. The intensity has become onerous enough that U.S. firms often go to great lengths to prevent unionization in the first place. But government involvement is not so extensive that management cannot retain control over strategic decisions such as investments, plant location, or business strategies. This narrowly focused involvement contrasts with the German government's intervention. The government's objective is to provide a broad framework that stabilizes the economy through interlocking webs of influence; for example, company ownership concentrated in the hands of a small number of banks, other social legislation that limits managerial options, and centralized bargaining structures that set wages for an entire industry or region. Within this framework, it is very difficult for a single German firm to adopt a unilateral strategy to manage its workforce.[29]

The same contrast between the focused legislation in the United States and the extensive legislation of Western Europe also extends to other social legislation. Most Western Europe countries specify minimum pay, maximum pay, hours during which an establishment may be open, vacation pay, and of course employee participation.[30] To maintain a "proper balance" of what goods are available and to prevent unfair competition, a shopkeeper in Italy must comply with government orders on what products can and cannot be carried in the store. In Germany generous payments for unemployment and family allowances reduce the incentive for job hunting.

WHAT DO YOU THINK?

Television hostess Kathie Lee Gifford was appalled to learn that the line of clothing that bears her name and is sold by Wal-Mart is manufactured in Guatemalan factories where children as young as 14 work long days for only a few dollars. She made many public appearances to denounce such practices. But Guatemalans defended themselves by pointing out the long lines of people who desire such jobs, which are far easier, far better paid, and performed under much better conditions than other jobs available to the unskilled labor force. Is it appropriate for union activists to try to impose U.S. labor standards on another country? Is it appropriate for U.S. consumers to benefit from the low wages paid by many non-U.S. clothing manufacturers? What would you recommend as the U.S. government policy and U.S. union policies to deal with such matters?

Most countries have a greater proportion of government-provided or mandated social welfare benefits—health care, maternity leave, child care, pensions—than the United States. Although runaway costs for medical care have made national health insurance a major political issue, the traditional U.S. approach has been to leave most benefits determination to the private sector. In contrast, Canada's public health insurance plan covers 90 percent of its population. Japan's national health insurance covers the 39 percent of the population that is not covered by employer-provided insurance.[31] Japanese employers even provide dormitories and mortgage assistance to attract new employees in areas where housing is scarce and expensive. The downside to this housing assistance is that it is not available to those employees who do not work for large firms. Those who work for subcontractors or as temporary employees get no housing assistance. They also are ineligible for the matchmaking service, family allowances, and life passage payments that are expected of major Japanese employers.

While not required by law, many large employers in many countries provide employees access to items that are scarce in a particular economy. For example, Prague employers provide housing, while Chinese employers provide hot showers. One of the Japanese allowances is a rice allowance which dates to postwar years when food was scarce. The tradition persists long after the original need. Rather than rice, the payment today is in yen.

Layoffs, discharges, and plant closings are closely regulated by the individual governments of most European countries. Agreements crossing all industries and sectors throughout the European Union may soon be possible.

All of the preceding statements necessarily oversimplify a wide diversity of practices. However, they do allow interested readers to question many patterns and traditions that might otherwise be taken for granted. Additionally, they may make us more objective when we discuss criteria for evaluating labor relations decisions.

## EVALUATING THE EFFECTS OF LABOR RELATIONS ACTIVITIES

Labor relations and collective bargaining affect both efficiency and equity either positively or negatively. Economic theory depicts unions as a constraint on the organization. In a competitive market, unions attempt to obtain monopolistic control over the supply of labor to raise wages above the market-determined rate. Moreover, as unions are likely to attempt to establish restrictive work rules to protect their members, productivity is likely to fall. Consequently, people frequently view unions as promoting inefficiency and inequality in society. Is that view accurate? Let us examine the research on the impact of unions.

### Efficiency: Union Impact on Wages

Does the presence of a union in an organization raise the level of wages for workers above what it would be if the company was not unionized? The commonly

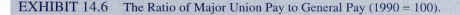

EXHIBIT 14.6 The Ratio of Major Union Pay to General Pay (1990 = 100).

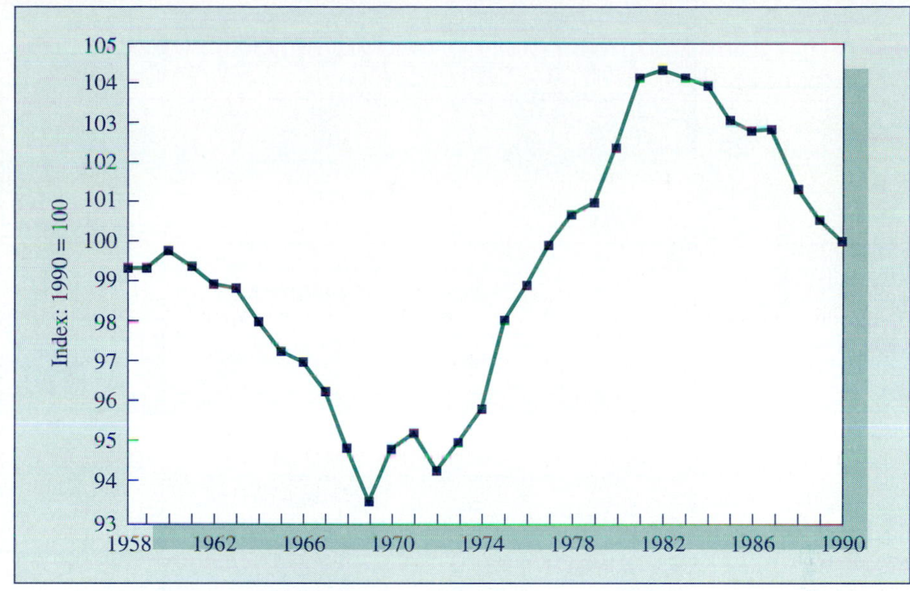


Source: U.S. Bureau of Labor Statistics.

held belief among workers is that unions do have a wage impact. More than 80 percent of the respondents to a quality of employment survey conducted by the Survey Research Center of the University of Michigan believed that unions improve the wages of workers.[32] Efforts to determine if this perception is accurate have been a focus of research for over 40 years.

Part of the reason for the continuing interest in this area is that the question of union impact on wages has not been totally resolved. Efforts to determine union impact on wages run into several measurement problems. The ideal situation would compare numerous organizations that were identical except for the presence or absence of a union. Any wage differences among these organizations could than be attributed to the unionization. Unfortunately, few such situations exist. But even if they did, one could make the case that employers pay nonunionized employees wages close to those paid to union members to reduce the attractiveness of unions to employees. This union influence on nonunion wages and benefits is called a *spillover* effect.

Nevertheless, the best evidence we have suggests that unions make a positive difference in wage levels, and the extent of the union effect varies over time.[33] During the 1932–1933 period, union presence meant much higher wages for union workers than nonunion workers. As the Great Depression receded in the late 1930s, the differential declined. An increased union premium in the 1970s may have provided an economic incentive for increased management opposition in negotiations and organizing campaigns and for a subsequent drop in membership. Exhibit 14.6 tracks this variance over time.

In the public sector, a summary of 13 studies concludes that the average wage effect is approximately +5 percent. This wage differential is smaller than typically assumed, and certainly smaller than the estimate for the private sector. The largest

EXHIBIT 14.7 Unionism and Productivity

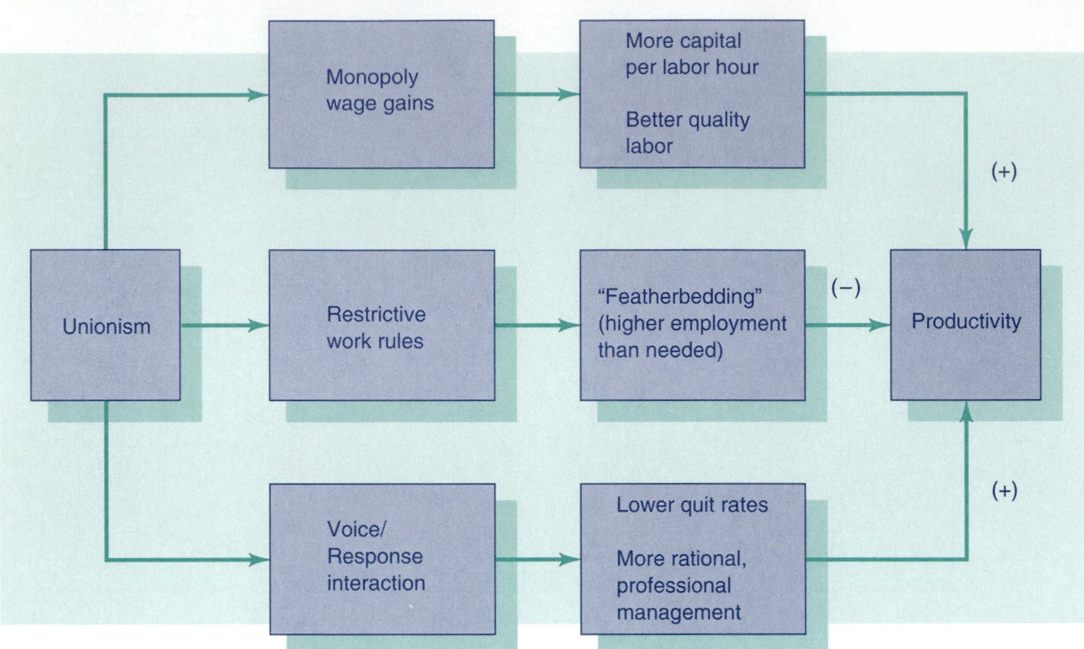


Source: Richard Freeman and James Medoff, *What Do Unions Do?* (New York: Basic Books, 1984). © 1984 by Basic Books, Inc. Reprinted by permission of the publisher.

gains for the public sector employees are reported for fire fighters, with some studies reporting as much as an 18 percent wage differential attributable to the presence of a union. At the other extreme, however, teachers (primarily affiliates of the National Education Association and the American Federation of Teachers) have not fared as well, with reported wage impact of unionization generally in the range of 1 percent to 4 percent.[34]

## Efficiency: Union Impact on Productivity

The model in Exhibit 14.7 indicates that unions can have a positive or negative effect on productivity, depending on the quality of the union-management relationship. The model suggests some specific ways that union and employer behavior can affect productivity. Based on their analysis of the research, Richard Freeman and James Medoff conclude that, "with management and unions working together to produce a bigger 'pie' as well as fighting over the size of their slice, productivity is likely to be higher under unionism. If industrial relations are poor, with management and labor ignoring common goals to battle one another, productivity is likely to be lower under unionism."[35] Incentive systems, profit-sharing plans, and merit-based are all examples of efforts to increase the link between productivity and wages. Even productivity bargaining and quality control circles show an increasing emphasis on the level of productivity in unionized and nonunionized organizations alike.

## Equity: Union Impact on Employees' Voice

In addition to its effect on members' wages, the other positive effect claimed for unionism is that it provides workers a collective voice on subjects affecting their work.[36] By providing workers with a voice in work-related decisions, unions are likely to have a number of positive effects for both employees and organizations. First, unions act as *information collectors* for organizations, obtaining a clearer picture of the preferences of all employees, rather than just new entrants to or leavers from organizations. As a result, employers are able to develop better personnel practices that reflect the needs of the existing work force. Second, unions are likely to *increase worker satisfaction by reducing inequality* among workers and guaranteeing some degree of due process in organizational decision making. Unions have a significant positive effect on employees' satisfaction with pay. However, job dissatisfaction appears to be higher among union members than nonunion members. Absenteeism rates may be higher among union members, too.[37] Because absenteeism can be interpreted as an expression of job dissatisfaction, it may be that any voice the union provides has only limited effect on job satisfaction.

## Different Countries, Different Effects

Based on his analysis of 1987–1989 data from the countries in Exhibit 14.5, Freeman concludes that

- Unions raise wages by widely different amounts across countries, with union-nonunion wage gaps being largest in the United States.
- Unions reduce the dispersion of earning among members in virtually all countries.
- Union workers generally report lower job satisfaction and more conflict with management at workplaces than nonunion workers.

After reviewing other existing studies, Freeman concludes:

- Unions raise fringe benefits in several countries besides the United States, but they are unlikely to do as much in countries where government mandates large fringe-benefit expenditures.
- Unions reduce voluntary quitting and turnover in other countries, as in the United States.
- Unions have disparate effects on the level and growth of productivity.
- Unions reduce profits in the United States and the United Kingdom—countries with decentralized bargaining—but are unlikely to have such effects in countries with centralized wage setting.

Why does unionism have similar effects on wage dispersion, exit, fringes, and satisfaction across countries, but different effects on wages, productivity, and profits? Freeman characterizes unionism's effect on dispersion, fringes, exit, and satisfaction as the "voice" of unions—the ability of employees to influence and have control of their work life. Unionism's differential effects on wages and profits reflect the centralized versus decentralized wage-setting system. Where wages are centrally negotiated, no company can achieve competitive advantage by offering an alternate wage. If everyone receives the union wage, unionism makes no difference. But in the United States and the United Kingdom, where wage setting is decentralized, various firms pay various wages, and there may be financial payoffs for opposing unions.[38]

## SUMMARY

Labor relations is a major activity in unionized organizations. It also is an activity of major interest in society as well. Cataclysmic events in the 1930s awoke the public to the wretched conditions faced by American workers. The public's identification with union goals led to a changed regulatory climate and phenomenal growth in union strength in the 1940s and 1950s. After that, unions began a long decline.

The industries that were most heavily unionized were typically the ones hit hardest by competitive pressures in the 1980s. Foreign competition, deregulation, and a changed climate of public opinion have severely weakened unions.

Perhaps changing public attitudes toward unions have enabled employers to become more aggressive in their efforts to avoid becoming unionized. Private sector employers appear more willing to engage in illegal behavior because they believe the benefits of being nonunion outweigh the penalties. However, changed union leadership and changed strategies may help unions regain public sympathy as supporters of low-skilled, low-wage workers.

The public sector offers a brighter picture. Even though most public sector unions are forbidden to strike, public sector unionism is increasing to the point where it is a major influence on the U.S. labor movement.

Internationally, there is a wide variety of forms that unionism can take. In all cases, the nature of unionism is affected by the politics, culture, and history of a country. Many European and South American unions are political movements that seek major change in their societies. This contrasts with the focus on economic gains for members in U.S. unions.

Unions can be evaluated on how well they contribute to their members' economic well-being and how well they help resolve conflict at the workplace. Unions affect both efficiency and equity, because an effective union can provide employees a voice to change organization conditions and enhance equitable treatment of unionized employees. Having a more satisfied, stable, unionized workforce can result in higher productivity for the employer. However, unions can have a negative effect on productivity if work rules hinder performance. Whether the effect on productivity is positive depends on the quality of the employer-employee relationship.

## QUESTIONS

1. Why do people join unions?
2. Contrast different methods of dispute settlement.
3. What factors have contributed to the past success of unions in the United States?
4. What factors have contributed to the recent decline in union membership in the United States?
5. How do unions differ in the public sector?

6. How do unions affect productivity?
7. How do unions affect wages?
8. What changes in legislation could be made to encourage union growth? Do you think such changes are a good idea?
9. What is "employee voice"? What are some indicators of employee voice in a non-union organization?
10. How and why do U.S. unions differ from those in other countries?

## YOUR TURN
### Caterpillar and the United Auto Workers

### From Adversaries to Cooperation to Adversaries

### HISTORY OF CATERPILLAR-UAW RELATIONS:

#### Prior to 1987: Adversarial Relationship

- The past 10 contract negotiations between Cat and the UAW included 8 strikes, the last one for 205 days.
- One observer described Cat factories as "playgrounds." Many workers came in drunk or stoned on drugs.
- Grievances and absenteeism were high, and a high percentage of grievances had to be settled through arbitration.

#### From 1987 to 1990: Cooperative Culture Emerges

- After the 205-day strike, both UAW leaders and Cat management began to search for a change. They initiated an employee involvement process in which employees helped plan everything from purchasing machinery to reorganizing the assembly line. In just three weeks at one plant, employees offered 240 ideas that generated about $5 million in savings. In another plant, over $13 million in savings were generated in 12 months.
- Cat continued to maintain the number one position in its industry but faced increasingly serious competition from Komatsu Limited, Japan.
- Cat CEO George Schaefer, who had pursued better relations with the UAW, retired, and Don Fites became the CEO. Faced with the serious threats from Komatsu Limited, Japan, Fites launched a cost-cutting drive and reorganized the company into profit centers. He also faced negotiations with the UAW for a new labor contract.
- The UAW demanded the same terms it had successfully negotiated with Deere and Company, a Cat competitor. The terms included (1) a 26 percent increase in wages and benefits over the two-year term of the contract, (2) a voice in which parts were made in-house and which were purchased from outside suppliers, and (3) a requirement that Cat remain neutral in any future UAW organizing campaigns.
- Cat management responded by offering a 17 percent increase in wages and benefits, arguing that management's responsibility to stockholders, not only employees, meant that costs must be better controlled. They indicated that cost control was particularly important because global competition was threatening jobs as well as financial returns.

### 1991: Strike

- In November 1991, the UAW launched a strike at two plants and a partial walkout at another. Negotiations continued.
- On April, 1992, Cat announced it would replace strikers who did not return to work.
- Two weeks later, the union ended the strike and employees returned to work under the management's imposed conditions (17 percent raise).

### 1994: Strike Again

- Another strike began in June 1994. Close to 14,000 UAW members hit the picket lines.
- Union said issues were staffing levels, job security, health, and safety.
- Caterpillar kept operating, in part by using replacement workers.
- Caterpillar increased dividends by 40 percent and spent $1.2 billion to buy back stock.

### 1995:

- UAW selected new leader, Stephen Yokich, who said he wanted to settle dispute. Union members were hopeful that Yokich possessed the right degree of militancy. One member said, "The era of working together and jointness has kind of lulled the union to sleep."[38]
- The UAW announced plans to merge with the Machinists and the United Steelworkers to become a 2 million member megaunion by the year 2000.
- President Clinton signed an executive order barring use of replacement workers.

### 1996:

- Executive order overturned by court.

### Current Situation

- The old "them versus us" attitudes are back.
- Grievance and arbitration rates are up.
- Management claims that costs are reduced and productivity and quality are high. They claim to have saved $80 million in wages and benefits.

### Discussion Questions

Generate a list of possible actions for both the UAW and the HR director of Caterpillar. List the objectives you would try to achieve. Then evaluate each option for the likelihood that it will achieve its objectives and any possible risks. What would you need from the other side to achieve your objectives? How could you get what you need?

## NOTES AND REFERENCES


1. Description taken from Tina Rosenberg, *The Haunted Land: Facing Europe's Ghosts After Communism* (New York: Random House, 1995).
2. Henry S. Farber and Alan Krueger, "Union Membership in the United States: The Decline Continues," Working Paper No. 306, Princeton University Industrial Relations Section, Aug. 1992.
3. Tom Kochan, Robert McKersie, and Harry Katz, *The Transformation of American Industrial Relations* (New York: Basic Books, 1986); Sanford Jacoby, ed., *Masters to Managers* (New York: Columbia University Press, 1990).
4. Gary Chaison and Dileep G. Dhavale, "The Choice between Union Membership and Free-Rider Status," *Journal of Labor Research,* Fall 1992, pp. 355–69.
5. Survey by Princeton Survey Research Associates reported in *Personnel Journal,* March 1995, p. 44.
6. Paula B. Voos, *Contemporary Collective Bargaining in the Private Sector* (Madison, WI.: Industrial Relations Research Association, 1994).
7. Terry H. Wagar and Kent F. Murrmann, "An Examination of the Relationship between Union Status and Organizational Characteristics and Constraints," *Proceedings of the Forty-Fourth Annual Meeting of the Industrial Relations Research Association,* Jan. 1992; Kay Stratton-Devine, "Unions and Strategic Human Resource Planning," *Proceedings of the Forty-Fourth Annual Meeting of the Industrial Relations Research Association,* Jan. 1992, pp. 424–31; Lloyd Buckwell, Robert A. Figler, and Stephen J. Holoviak, "The Effects of Corporate Strategic Policy on Unionization: A Case Study," *Proceedings of the Forty-Fourth Annual Meeting of the Industrial Relations Research Association,* Jan. 1992.
8. William N. Cooke, "Improving Productivity and Quality through Collaboration," *Industrial Relations,* Spring 1989, pp. 299–319.
9. William N. Cooke and David G. Meyer, "Structural and Market Predictors of Corporate Labor Relations Strategies," *Industrial and Labor Relations Review,* Jan. 1990, pp. 280–93.
10. John J. Lawler, *Unionization and Deunionization: Strategy, Tactics, and Outcomes* (Columbia: University of South Carolina Press, 1990).
11. Steven Mellor, "Gender Composition and Gender Representation in Local Unions: Relationship Between Women's Participation in Local Office and Women's Participation in Local Activities," *Journal of Applied Psychology* Vol. 8, no. 6, 1995, pp. 706–20.
12. Chaison and Dhavale, "The Choice between Union Membership and Free-Ridership."
13. William N. Cooke, "The Failure to Negotiate First Contracts: Determinants and Policy Implications," *Industrial and Labor Relations Review,* Jan. 1985, pp. 163–78.

14. Daniel J. B. Mitchell, "A Decade of Concession Bargaining," in *Labor Economics and Industrial Relations,* ed. Clark Kerr and Paul D. Staudohar (Cambridge: Harvard University Press, 1994), pp. 435–76.
15. Brian S. Klass, Herbert G. Heneman III, and Craig A. Olson, "Effects of Grievance Activity on Absenteeism," *Journal of Applied Psychology* 76, no. 6 (1991), pp. 1–7; Richard B. Peterson, "Perceptions of Grievance Procedure Effectiveness: Evidence from a Nonunion Company," *Proceedings of the Forty-Fourth Annual Meeting of the Industrial Relations Research Association,* Jan. 1992.
16. Brian Bemmels, "Gender Effects in Discharge Arbitration," *Industrial and Labor Relations Review,* Oct. 1988, pp. 63–76.
17. Beverly Geber, "Saturn's Grand Experiment," *Training,* June 1992, pp. 27–35; S. Rubinstein, *Rethinking Labor and Management: Saturn and the UAW; The Governance and Supervision of High Performance Team Based Work Systems,* PhD dissertation, MIT Sloan School of Management, forthcoming.
18. Maryellen R. Kelley and Bennett Harrison, "Unions, Technology, and Labor-Management Cooperation," in *Unions and Economic Competitiveness,* ed. Lawrence Mishel and Paula B. Voos (Armonk, NY: Sharpe, 1992).
19. David I. Levine and Laura D'Andrea Tyson, "Participation, Productivity, and the Firm's Environment," in *Paying for Productivity,* ed. Alan S. Blinder (Washington, DC: Brookings Institution, 1990); James P. Womack, Daniel T. Jones, and Daniel Roos, *The Machine that Changed the World* (New York: Rawson, 1990), p. 99.
20. Tom Juravich, Howard Harris, and Andrea Brooks, "Mutual Gains? Labor and Management Evaluate Their Employee Involvement Programs," *Journal of Labor Research,* Spring 1993, pp. 165–85.
21. Christopher L. Martin, Charles K. Parson, and Nathan Bennett, "The Influence of Employee Involvement Program Membership During Downsizing: Attitudes Toward the Employer and the Union," *Journal of Management* 21, no. 5 (1995), pp. 879–90.
22. Testimony by Steve Darien, vice president of HR for Merck and Co. at Congressional Hearings on Workplace Cooperation, Washington, D.C.: 1994.
23. Peter Feuille, "Changing Patterns in Dispute Resolution," in *Labor Economics and Industrial Relations,* ed. Clark Kerr and Paul D. Staudohar (Cambridge: Harvard University Press, 1994), pp. 475–511.
24. Thomas A. Kochan, "Principles for a Post–New Deal Employment Policy," in *Labor Economics and Industrial Relations,* ed. Clark Kerr and Paul D. Staudohar (Cambridge: Harvard University Press, 1994), pp. 646–72.
25. Thomas A Kochan and Thomas A. Barocci, *Human Resource Management and Industrial Relations* (Boston: Little, Brown, 1985), pp. 495–99.

26. Richard B. Freeman, "American Exceptionalism in the Labor Market: Union-Nonunion Differentials in the United States and Other Countries," in *Labor Economics and Industrial Relations,* ed. Clark Kerr and Paul D. Staudohar (Cambridge: Harvard University Press, 1994), pp. 272–302.
27. Ibid.
28. Motohiro Morishima, "Union Loyalty Among White-Collar Workers in Japan," *Journal of Organizational Behavior* 16 (1995), pp. 609–25.
29. Kirsten S. Wever, "Human Resource Management and Organizational Strategies in German- and U.S.-owned Companies," *International Journal of Human Resource Management,* Sept. 1995, pp. 606–25.
30. Barbara A. Lee, "The Effect of the European Community's Social Dimension on Human Resource Management in U.S. Multinationals: Perspectives from the United Kingdom and France," *Human Resource Management Review* 4, no. 4 (1994) pp. 331–61.
31. Tadashi Amaya, *Recent Trends in Human Resource Development* (Tokyo: Japan Institute of Labour, 1992); John Salmon, "The Impact of Developments in Welfare Corporatism upon Japanese Workplace Trade Unionism," *International Journal of Human Resource Management,* Sept. 1992, pp. 247–63; Yoko Sano, "Changes and Continued Stability in Japanese HRM Systems: Choice in the Share Economy," *International Journal of Human Resource Management,* Feb. 1993, pp. 11–27.
32. David Neumark and Michael L. Wachter, "Union Threat Effects and Nonunion Industry Wage Differentials," Working Paper No. 4046, National Bureau of Economic Research, April 1992.
33. Daniel J. B. Mitchell, "A Decade of Concession Bargaining," in *Labor Economics and Industrial Relations,* ed. Clark Kerr and Paul D. Staudohar (Cambridge: Harvard University Press, 1994), pp. 435–76.
34. Richard Freeman, "Contraction and Expansion: The Divergence of Private Sector and Public Sector Unionism in the United States," Working Paper 2399, National Bureau of Economic Research, Cambridge, MA., Jan. 1988; Rene Saran and John Sheldrake, *Public Sector Bargaining in the 1980s* (Brookfield, VT: Gower, 1988) Joel Cutcher-Gershenfeld, Matthew Bodah, and Terry Patterson, "Determinants and Consequences of a Mutual Gains Orientation in Public Sector Collective Bargaining," *Proceedings of the Forty-Fourth Annual Meeting of the Industrial Relations Research Association,* Jan. 1992.
35. Richard B. Freeman and James L. Medoff, *What Do Unions Do?* (New York: Basic Books, 1984); David Card, "The Effect of Unions on the Distribution of Wages: Redistribution or Relabeling?" Working Paper No. 4195, National Bureau of Economic Research, 1992.
36. Sandra E. Gleason and Karen Roberts, "The Impact of Union Membership on Perceptions of Procedural Justice of Injured Workers," *Proceedings of the Forty-Fourth Annual Meeting of the Industrial Relations Research Association,* Jan. 1992.

37. Thomas A. Kochan, *New Directions in Human Resource Management,* Industrial Relations Centre, Queen's University, Kingston, Ont., 1992.
38. Freeman, "American Exceptionalism in the Labor Market," pp. 272–302.

# Employee Relations

An "Embarrassing Incident at Work" contest was recently overwhelmed with contestants. The winner was not the traveling sales representative whose underwire bra set off the metal detector at the airport, though she came in second. Instead, the winner was the supervisor who had taken off his hard hat to help demonstrate his lecture to the new hires on the protection provided by wearing the hard hat at all times—when a pigeon flew overhead.[1]

The safety and well-being of employees is a long-standing concern of managers. A century ago, safety issues were more clearcut. The *Scientific American* for June 1896 reports that, "Sixteen thousand railroad employees were killed, and 170,000 crippled, in the seven years from 1888 to 1894. The awful record of the killed and injured seems incredible; few battles in history show so ghastly a fatality. A large percentage of these deaths were caused by the use of imperfect equipment by the railroad companies."

Today, the well-being of employees implies more than refraining from jeopardizing their lives. However, sometimes the careless or thoughtless actions of one employee or manager jeopardizes the health, safety, or comfort of another. Perhaps the checkout cashier suspects he has been singled out unfairly for special scrutiny by his supervisor, and the stress from this possible scrutiny affects his job performance. What happens if the supervisor suspects the cashier is stealing? Suppose an employee is frequently late. Is it because of difficulties with child care arrangements, or drugs? These examples illustrate a time-consuming and worrisome aspect of today's manager's job: protecting all employees, including troubled employees. Personal problems on and off the job can affect employee work behavior. Because social as well as economic relationships are involved, an employer is frequently in the best position to provide assistance to employees at such times.

*Employee relations activities* are those which seek greater organizational effectiveness by removing the barriers that inhibit full employee participation and compliance with organization policies.

Many organizations go beyond changing negative behavior or assisting troubled employees. They wish to build on strengths: to provide a work environment where employees can flourish. They also wish to tap into employee expertise on how to do jobs better. Employee relations activities are those whose objective is to create an atmosphere of trust, respect, and cooperation.

Barriers to a relationship of respect and cooperation may arise from organizational or personal factors. Whatever their source, employee relations activities seek to establish direct two-way communication to provide mutual assistance and involvement in overcoming them.

An employer's approach to employee relations permeates all other human resource activities. Job sharing, retraining programs, and career management could all be considered employee relations activities. Therefore, while the term *employee relations* can refer to specific activities, it also can describe the intangible quality of management-employee relationships, part of the philosophy of the organization, which says an organization ought to treat employees with respect and ought to be responsive to the personal and family needs of employees.

Survey after survey identifies family/work conflicts as a major problem for employees. Dual-career couples may be unable to make career-enhancing job moves. Whether managers can design alternatives for dual-career couples reflects an organization's employee relations policy. So do work schedules; can they be adjusted to mesh with family demands? Participation in management is another way organizations can respond to employee needs. These topics are all discussed in this chapter.

## THE IMPORTANCE OF EMPLOYEE RELATIONS

Employee relations has been characterized by some as hardly more than a union avoidance strategy.[2] That is too simple. While union avoidance can certainly be an objective of employee relations activities, many organizations in which the likelihood of unionization is quite low still maintain strong employee relations. Union avoidance is not the only objective; indeed, it may be only an indirect effect. More typically, the objective is to provide an atmosphere in which all employees can perform their jobs to the best of their abilities and creatively contribute to the organization.

Employee relations activities affect efficiency, in that potential reasons for performance problems are confronted and help is offered to remove them. When the problem is an individual employee's behavior, employee assistance and conflict resolution systems seek constructive solutions. If the problem is the organization's behavior, employee-management committees or other two-way communication forums can identify possible changes that remove the problem.

Equity is also affected. Much of employee relations is designed to send the message that the organization is a concerned institution that will help protect, assist, and deal fairly with all its members. How well this message comes through depends in large measure on how well employers deliver on these policies. Good intentions only go so far. Managers' decisions need to support these intentions.

The typical decisions that managers face in designing employee relations programs include:

- *Communication.* How best can we convey our philosophy to employees and solicit their opinions and suggestions on work issues?
- *Cooperation.* To what extent should decision making and control be shared?
- *Protection.* Do some aspects of the workplace threaten the well-being of employees?
- *Assistance.* How shall we respond to special needs of specific employees?
- *Discipline and conflict.* How shall we deal with it?

While most of these topics have been touched on before, in this chapter we focus more directly on their employee relations aspects.

## COMMUNICATION

An employee handbook is a necessary part of communicating an employee relations program. The handbook sets out the rules and policies within which employees and managers must operate. How the organization sets wages, allocates training and promotion opportunities, what services it provides, and what it expects from employees is discussed in the handbook. Later exhibits in this chapter provide examples from employee handbooks.

Organizations today are routinely advised to include a disclaimer that, although general policies, rules, and regulations are specified, the handbook does not form the basis of a binding employment contract. Attorneys representing discharged employees have successfully argued in courts that handbooks *can* imply a contract that forbids dismissal without just cause. However, interpretations vary among judicial districts.

Obviously, merely writing a handbook is not enough. It must be continuously updated, publicized to employees, and supervisors must be thoroughly familiar with it, since they are the ones who translate policy into action.

### Both Ways

Handbooks provide communication in only one direction. Many organizations have formats for providing communication from employees to supervisors and managers. These can range from "speak-up" and open-door policies, to work improvement suggestion systems, to "sensing" sessions, opinion surveys, or conflict resolution procedures. Unfortunately, there is evidence of a growing communications gap between employees and top management.[3] Messages that managers think they are sending aren't being received by employees. Statistics show a dramatic drop in employee confidence in top management in the 1980s and 1990s. Many employees believe they aren't being heard or that their concerns are not being factored into strategic decisions.

However, an increasing number of employers are actively listening. They systematically assess employee opinions. A survey of HR executives found that almost half had surveyed employees within the past three years.[4] However, only half were satisfied with the changes that resulted from survey information.

> **EXPLORING THE WEB**
>
> Court TV recently offered an interactive seminar on the Ultimate Employee Handbook. Look at it on the web at:
> **http://www.courttv.com/seminars/handbook**
> for lots of examples of HRM policies.

### Feedback Says You Listened

Providing feedback to employees is critical. It could provide a concrete demonstration that management is listening. Nevertheless, 21 percent of the HR executives to the survey mentioned above said the results were not reported to employees. Further, when changes based on the survey results were made, only 64 percent said the changes were linked to the survey. If employees do not recognize that their opinions were part of the reason for the changes, they are less likely to buy into the process and accept change. The researchers conclude that organizations that do not link changes to employee opinion may not be getting the maximum value from the survey process. Top managers may think they are sending crucial messages about strategy, innovation, and product quality, but the employees may not be listening if the managers don't listen to their employees.

Johnson & Johnson incorporates a worldwide employee opinion survey as part of their "Signature of Quality Award" process. Exhibit 15.1 shows some of the questions asked employees from Japan to the United States to Germany. The J&J credo or statement of values includes four parts, with questions assessing how well J&J is doing on each part. Part I addresses external stakeholders: customers, suppliers, and distributors; Part II, employee treatment: compensation, security, opportunity for advancement; Part III, the community and environmental impact of J&J operations; and Part IV, stockholder concerns. The total questionnaire includes 244 items with the largest number in Part II. The J&J units compete for the corporatewide quality awards granted for achieving customer and employee satisfaction. The objective is to identify the best internal employee relations practices within the company for possible application worldwide.

J&J's corporate credo stating that, "Workers must have a sense of security" was so important to Daniel Tripodi, an R&D executive who was fired, that he took J&J to court for violating its mission statement. He argued that the credo lays out the company's responsibility to customers and employers and therefore is a binding contract. The jury sided with him and awarded him $434,000. But the judge set aside the verdict. He called the credo "aspirational rather than contractual."[5]

## EMPLOYEE INVOLVEMENT

To what extent will managers yield control to seek cooperative ways to solve workplace problems? And to what extent are employees interested in becoming involved in cooperative efforts? The highest degree of potential employee involvement in organizational decisions occurs when workers are also owners. Employees buying plants to save their jobs is not unusual. But research has found that most of such owner/employees view their ownership only as a financial investment and rarely exercise their full decision-making rights. U.S. tax law currently favors employee stock ownership plans (ESOPs) as a way to increase employee equity in a company. But even here, employee ownership does not typically alter the decision-making structure.

There is also some question whether concentrating an employee's major investment holdings in one company's stock is a good investment decision. A case in point is the unlucky IBM employee who poured retirement money and savings for children's tuition into IBM stock, which tumbled from nearly $140 a share to around $50 a share in a little over a year. (The stock has since recovered, but it has taken years to do so.) Some argue that diversity in stock holdings mitigates employee risk.

Some employers appear to have deliberately misused ESOPs to stave off hostile takeovers. Cone Mills of Greensboro, North Carolina, the largest U.S. denim manufacturer, fended off a raider in part with funds in its pension plan. Cone terminated its old pension plan, took out $69 million, and established a new ESOP that held "junior preferred" stock that had no voting rights but was valued at $100 a share. At the same time, 47 top managers and some outside investors bought 8.25 million shares of common stock with voting rights at $1 a share. In 1996, the managers' common stock was worth approximately $11 a share, but the employee-owned stock in the pension fund had not appreciated. Cone did pay dividends on the junior preferred stock, so that now each employee's stake is

## EXHIBIT 15.1 Johnson & Johnson Survey of Employee Opinions (excerpts)

**Part I of Our Credo**

**We believe our first responsibility is to the doctors, nurses and patients, to mothers and fathers and all others who use our products and services. In meeting their needs everything we do must be of high quality. We must constantly strive to reduce our costs in order to maintain reasonable prices. Customers' orders must be serviced promptly and accurately. Our suppliers and distributors must have an opportunity to make a fair profit.**

| How do you rate your COMPANY on . . . | Very Good | Good | Average | Poor | Very Poor | Not Applicable/ No Opinion |
|---|---|---|---|---|---|---|
| 2. Producing high quality products and services | 1 | 2 | 3 | 4 | 5 | 6 |
| 3. Constantly striving to reduce costs | 1 | 2 | 3 | 4 | 5 | 6 |
| 4. Maintaining reasonable prices | 1 | 2 | 3 | 4 | 5 | 6 |
| 5. Servicing customers' orders promptly and accurately | 1 | 2 | 3 | 4 | 5 | 6 |
| 6. Giving suppliers and distributors an opportunity to make a fair profit | 1 | 2 | 3 | 4 | 5 | 6 |

| My COMPANY . . . | Strongly Agree | Agree | Neither Agree nor Disagree | Disagree | Strongly Disagree |
|---|---|---|---|---|---|
| 7. Understands customer needs | 1 | 2 | 3 | 4 | 5 |
| 9. Provides good value to the consumer—quality at a reasonable price | 1 | 2 | 3 | 4 | 5 |
| 11. Is committed to customer satisfaction | 1 | 2 | 3 | 4 | 5 |
| **In my COMPANY . . .** | | | | | |
| 18. Management and employees agree on what constitutes good work | 1 | 2 | 3 | 4 | 5 |
| 19. I have enough information to do my job well | 1 | 2 | 3 | 4 | 5 |
| **My IMMEDIATE SUPERVISOR . . .** | | | | | |
| 20. Encourages me to do complete and accurate work | 1 | 2 | 3 | 4 | 5 |
| 21. Lets people know how they might achieve cost savings | 1 | 2 | 3 | 4 | 5 |
| 23. Gives me constructive criticism on how to improve the quality of my work | 1 | 2 | 3 | 4 | 5 |
| 24. Rewards employees who work in a cost-effective way | 1 | 2 | 3 | 4 | 5 |

**Part II of Our Credo**

**We are responsible to our employees, the men and women who work with us throughout the world. Everyone must be considered as an individual. We must respect their dignity and recognize their merit. They must have a sense of security in their jobs. Compensation must be fair and adequate, and working conditions clean, orderly and safe. We must be mindful of ways to help our employees fulfill their family responsibilities. Employees must feel free to make suggestions and complaints. There must be equal opportunity for employment, development, and advancement for those qualified. We must provide competent management, and their actions must be just and ethical.**

| How do you rate your COMPANY on . . . | Very Good | Good | Average | Poor | Very Poor |
|---|---|---|---|---|---|
| 29. Considering you as an individual | 1 | 2 | 3 | 4 | 5 |
| 30. Respecting your dignity | 1 | 2 | 3 | 4 | 5 |
| 31. Recognizing your merit | 1 | 2 | 3 | 4 | 5 |
| 32. Providing you with a sense of security in your job | 1 | 2 | 3 | 4 | 5 |
| 33. Providing fair and adequate compensation | 1 | 2 | 3 | 4 | 5 |
| 34. Maintaining clean, orderly and safe working conditions | 1 | 2 | 3 | 4 | 5 |

worth about $7,600. But each of the top 20 officers owns shares and options valued at more than $1 million. Nevertheless, the plan did foster employee involvement: Cone employees sued their employer.[6]

Encouraging employee involvement is an idea everyone can support. Involving people in the design of their work, and giving them the training and tools they need to perform effectively is a proven formula for boosting quality and productivity. The objective is to motivate people to be more creative and productive. Permit them to take pride in doing a good job.

But translating this ideal into practice steps on people's toes. An organization may be willing to provide necessary skills, but is it also willing to trust, to cede responsibility and authority to make decisions on behalf of the organization? Decision control translates into power, and most people do not like giving it up. Managers and supervisors may believe the most efficient way to accomplish a task is to make a decision and act on it, rather than increasing the number of people involved in the process. Employees may also be wary of a managerial interest in working together that does not square with past managerial behavior. So while employee involvement is an appealing notion, making it work is not always easy.

Despite a great deal of overlap, there are three main thrusts in employee involvement activities: quality-of-work-life programs, employee/management committees, and organization initiatives whose objective, at least in part, is to increase employee involvement.

## Quality of Work Life (QWL)

Quality of work life (QWL), or quality circles, stem from the recognition that the properly trained rank-and-file employee may be in the best position to identify unrecognized problems with product quality and/or how work is done. Shop-level worker committees are trained to use statistical and problem-solving analysis to improve quality and productivity in their particular work area. The focus is very much on the immediate work area; organization practices are of interest only in considering how they may interfere with product quality.

A program at General Motors Corporation is fairly typical. Participation is always voluntary, and the group avoids getting involved in issues covered in the union contract. Joint employee-management teams visited other facilities using QWL techniques, including some in Japan.

The initial thrusts of QWL typically involve training and quality control. Workers *and* suppliers enter training programs dealing with statistical quality control.

Reorganizing the inspection system is a critical component of quality control. Rather than inspection of the final product, a tally sheet stays with the product from start to finish, and all workers inspect their own work. As each step is completed, the worker records on the tally sheet if the job is completed correctly, or if there are problems. Thus, workers have more control over their work.[7]

But many QWL programs started in the 1970s have been abandoned. They have run into the following problems:

1. The change effort is isolated—either confined to one area of the plant or treated as an experiment.
2. The change is piecemeal—no change is made in management hierarchies and decision-making modes to support the new approach.

3. Worker involvement is limited to only a few issues that are not connected to how work is actually done or to critical business decisions.
4. First-line supervisors and middle managers are not involved in the change effort and so react negatively to employee participation.

Support for the changes must exist at all levels in the organization, or it will be ineffective. As you read in the previous chapter, the presence of a union may also be required to insist that the program be maintained.[8]

### Employee-Management Committees

Employees may also get involved in issues outside their immediate work area. Joint committees with greater authority and formalized structure are common in unionized plants, where they supplement collective bargaining; many nonunionized employers use joint committees, too, for a variety of purposes.[9] For example, many companies encourage employees to form groups based on ethnicity to provide mutual support and mentoring. The Black Caucus at Xerox includes both hourly and managerial employees of African American background. The group meets periodically to discuss such issues as salary equity and advancement. They then present their complaints to the company's chairman. Another example is 9 to 5: The Association for Working Women; it lobbies for women's concerns and runs public-relations campaigns and research to support its causes. Such groups assist employers meet their objectives for a culturally diverse workforce.

However, as we discussed in the previous chapter, committees must be careful that they do not interfere with employees' rights to self-organize. Many companies have backed away from supporting such committees rather than risk challenges by the NLRB.

### Organization Initiatives

Commonly, management must lead the way to greater cooperation by demonstrating a willingness to share control. Many human resource activities are initiated by management in the expectation that they may lead to increased employee involvement. Job redesign and gainsharing are just some of the many activities currently popular and discussed elsewhere in the text.[10]

## FAMILY/JOB CONFLICT

The increase in dual-career couples makes it likely that a sizable percent of students taking this course will experience family/job conflict. Conflict arises from simultaneous pressure to comply with competing demands.

1. Time devoted to one role makes it difficult to fulfill requirements in the other.
2. Stress from participation in one role makes it difficult to fulfill requirements in the other.
3. Specific behaviors required in one setting are completely different from behaviors in the other. For example, the aggressiveness required to close a sale may be incompatible with trying to get a toddler to go to sleep.

A number of options exist to ease this conflict: more flexible work scheduling, provided child care assistance, and making the work role requirements more flexible. The Family and Medical Leave Act provides some flexibility because the full 12 weeks of leave need not be taken at the same time. For example, an employee could take one day off a week at a 20 percent pay cut for a year.

## Work Schedule Adaptations

The number of hours of work a job requires, the arrangement of the hours, and freedom (or lack of it) in determining work schedules affect the nonwork part of a person's life: the time available for family, leisure and self-development.

A sizable portion of job dissatisfaction may be related to lack of control over hours of work, forced overtime, and lack of freedom to adjust hours to personal needs. Adaptations include flextime, permanent part-time positions, compressed work week, shift work, and telecommuting.

### Flexible hours (flextime)

Freedom to set one's own schedule can be invaluable for many individuals. Of course, many students will recognize that it merely means freedom to choose which 80 hours per week you will work—or study.

Probably the most popular version of flextime provides for all employees to be present for a specified period (core time), but the rest of the required hours may be completed at their discretion within a specified period.

### Part time

Voluntary part-time employment has been growing more than twice as fast as full-time employment. Twenty to 30 percent of the workforce were working part time in 1993, according to the Bureau of Labor Statistics, and women made up two-thirds of this group. Principal advantages to employers include flexibility in scheduling workers to meet peak demand periods and reduction in costs of benefits and overtime.

While part-time work has been hailed as beneficial for working parents, part-time workers earn only about 60 percent of the hourly wages of full-time workers. Very few receive benefits. It has been estimated that more than 30 percent of part-time workers would prefer to work full-time.[11]

There is some evidence that the increased use of part-time and temporary workers is part of a deliberate strategy to avoid a full-time workforce. The Bank of America, for example, admitted that in addition to cutting thousands of jobs, it turned 1,200 teller jobs into part-time positions, trimming health care costs and other benefits.[12] Soon only 19 percent of Bank of America employees will work full time; nearly 6 out of 10 will work fewer than 20 hours a week and receive no benefits. Ten years ago the bank had mostly full-time employees.

Whether the growing ranks of part-timers reflect worker preferences for flexibility or restructuring in the economy, better data are needed to determine whether protections and benefits customarily provided to full-time employees are also necessary for part-timers.[13] The combination of no health insurance and lower wages leaves part-timers in a vulnerable position. If involuntary part-time workers who cannot find full-time work are forced to use public services to get by (food stamps, medical assistance), then taxpayers are, in effect, subsidizing those employers who refuse to offer full-time employment.

**WHAT DO YOU THINK?**

A panel of HRM experts predicts that due to the financial and emotional costs of layoffs to employers and employees, the use of contingent workers will continue to increase. But critics of such arrangements label them a job rationing policy, inappropriate in our economy of abundance. If an employer uses contingent workers, what steps can it take to increase the equity and the efficiency of such an arrangement? How can the quality of work life for contingent workers be increased?

Job sharing Job sharing, a special type of part-time work, occurs when a single job is divided between two workers. Because it requires schedule compatibility between the two people sharing the job, as well as roughly equivalent or complementary skills, most job sharing is initiated by the employees.

Compressed workweek A compressed workweek is the scheduling of the normal hours of weekly work in less than five days. The typical compressed workweek follows a four-day schedule.

Research on the effects of compressed workweeks is uneven.[14] Some studies concluded it has positive effects on productivity, absenteeism, and other behaviors. Others conclude it does not. One pattern in the negative studies suggests that positive results occur shortly after the introduction of the compressed workweek; then they decline. Individual and job differences may explain many of the contradictions in the research findings. In general, older employees seem to find a compressed workweek undesirable, especially where the work is physically or mentally taxing. Younger workers tend to like the long weekends.

Telecommuting Working at home is not a recent innovation. What is new is its use by professional and managerial-level employees. Increasingly sophisticated and affordable communications technologies have eliminated many of the barriers to coordinating work activities among geographically dispersed employees. Amendments in 1990 to the Clean Air Act have given telecommuting a boost by requiring large employers in certain traffic-congested and polluted regions to reduce the number of single-occupant vehicles traveling to their worksites. To comply, employers are subsidizing vans, assisting rideshare arrangements, boosting parking fees, and reducing the number of days employees have to travel to work. Often it is the HR department's responsibility to develop compliance strategies.

A variety of studies report that employees who work at home experience less job-related stress as well as a greater sense of productivity and autonomy.[15] However, research on supervisors' attitudes toward work-at-home employees has uncovered strong resistance, stemming from concerns about loss of control and declines in employee productivity. "Invisible" workers are suspected of not working at all. From the perspective of employees, working at home has few negative effects on careers, according to a study at three companies.[16] Employees who worked at home received higher salaries than those who did not; however, this relationship may reflect the fact that those employees who were higher ranking and had a more valued status as employees were the ones able to make telecommuting arrangements. Mother Nature in the form of California's earthquakes and the East Coast's snowstorms could make many employers willing to look at the telecommuting possibilities provided by today's technology.

## Child Care Assistance

Eleven million children under the age of six have mothers in the labor force. One of the most frequently cited causes of work/family conflict is concern for adequate, affordable child care.

It is clear that the presence or absence of satisfactory child care affects work behavior.[17] The question is, What role shall an organization play? Corporations can provide options, ranging from care centers located at the work site, to coverage of expenses as part of flexible benefits, to referral services. The approach that an organization adopts depends on its employee relations philosophy as well as the needs of its employees. Child care probably is a more compelling issue in organizations that employ large numbers of young parents than in organizations with an aging workforce. Thus far, only about 11 percent of employers provide direct assistance, although 60 percent say they provide indirect assistance (flexible work schedules, part-time work, or information assistance). Because only a portion of employees require child care assistance, making it part of a flexible benefits package is an attractive option (see Chapter Thirteen). Assistance can be given to those employees who want it without the employer giving preferential treatment to certain groups of employees at the expense of others. For example, the 2,000-member Child Free Network is part of a backlash that says family-friendly workplaces really translate into child-friendly workplaces; consequently, benefits are inherently unequal to those who do not have children. Companies would do better, they assert, to recognize that workers have different lifestyles, and all workers have needs, either for insurance coverage for domestic partners, or for the same schedule flexibility to get cars repaired or the plumbing fixed that parents get for child care needs.

## PROTECTION

Every manager and employee wants a healthy and safe work environment; the issue confronting contemporary organizations is cost. What are the trade-offs between eliminating risks at the workplace and the costs involved?

Some work environments may be so bad that improvements are required by law. The Safety Appliance Act of 1893 reduced the death rate in the railroad industry discussed at the beginning of this chapter by 35 percent in less than three years. A current response to health and safety concerns is to compensate the victims with workers' compensation and insurance programs. This is necessary, but reactive. An alternative strategy focuses on prevention.

Prevention programs take many forms. They include redesigning jobs to diminish hazardous conditions, conducting safety training programs, even offering pay bonuses for good safety records. In an attempt to prevent accidents and improve overall safety records, Kerr-McGee Corporation considers applicants' accident records in selecting miners for work at its uranium and potash mines. However, the downside of this approach is the potential for blacklisting. Computerized databases can provide information on whether job applicants have filed previous workers' compensation claims for such elusive ailments as back strain or stress. If such claimants have difficulty finding jobs, this may intimidate others from filing workers' compensation claims, however just their complaints.

Other companies have involved employee teams on job redesign projects to ameliorate repetitive stress injuries and carpal tunnel syndrome.[18]

### Safety and Health Hazards

*Safety hazards* are those aspects of the work environment that have the potential for immediate and sometimes violent harm to an employee.

Loss of hearing or eyesight; cuts, sprains, bruises, broken bones; burns and electric shock are all potential results of safety hazards.

*Health hazards* are those aspects of the work environment that slowly and cumulatively (and often irreversibly) lead to deterioration of an employee's health.

Typical health hazards include physical and biological hazards, toxic and cancer-causing dusts and chemicals, and stressful working conditions. The causes of accidents and illness may lie in the job itself, the working conditions, or the employee.

Jobs Accidents and illnesses are not evenly distributed among jobs. Firefighters, miners, construction and transportation workers, roofing and sheet-metal workers, recreational vehicle manufacturers, lumber workers and woodworkers, and blue-collar and first-line supervisors in manufacturing and agriculture face serious health and safety dangers on the job. A few white-collar jobs are relatively dangerous: dentists and hospital operating room personnel, beauticians, and X-ray technicians.

Working conditions Poorly designed or inadequate repaired machines, lack of protective equipment, and the presence of dangerous chemicals or gases cause problems not only for an employee but also for all those nearby.

Employees Some employees seem to have more accidents than the average. The highest rate is for males under age 25, with a steady decline in following years. However, when older workers are injured, the costs per injury are higher. Females of all ages have substantially lower injury rates, due in large part to the differential occupational distribution of the sexes.[19]

In the mid-1980s, injury rates took a dramatic jump. Safety experts attribute the cause to workplace changes made in response to competitive pressures and the expanding economy. Smaller work crews, excessive overtime, and faster assembly lines all contribute. So do inexperienced workers. The Los Angeles district attorney's office claims that half of the workplace deaths they investigate involve non-English-speaking workers whose training was conducted in English.

Although statistics show that workplace fatality rates have halved since 1970, the number of workdays lost to occupational injury and illness has increased greatly.

### Lifestyle Factors

DuPont analyzed behavioral risk factors among employees and concluded excess illness and absenteeism due to certain employee behaviors were costing the company more than $70.8 million annually. The risk factors identified and the excess illness costs were smoking, $960; overweight, $401; excess alcohol, $389; elevated cholesterol, $370; high blood pressure, $343; inadequate seat-belt use, $272; and lack of exercise, $130. McDonnell Douglas found that over a five-year period, each worker with an alcohol or drug problem was absent 113 days more than the average employee (or 23 excess days a year) and filed $23,000 more in medical claims. The higher up in the organization the afflicted employee, the greater the costs.

The cost of behavioral risks provides an opportunity to control health care cost increases through health promotion, financial incentives for healthy lifestyles, and environmental changes that affect health behaviors. At least 6,000 companies now refuse to hire smokers; some dismiss smokers they discover on the payroll. However, several states have passed legislation protecting the employment rights of smokers, alleging that it may be appropriate to provide incentives to quit, but refusal to hire smokers constitutes lifestyle discrimination.

An application of utility analysis to assess the financial impact of safety intervention found that safety investments more than returned the costs of the interventions, though the returns may be long-term. The possibility of short-term safety expenses not being offset by immediate gains makes it more difficult to "sell" such safety interventions to decision makers.[20]

## Occupational Safety and Health Act

The Occupational Safety and Health Act (OSHA) is intended to remedy health and safety problems on the job by establishing safety standards. The standards affect any aspect of the workplace. OSHA does not try to inspect all industries equally, but it creates priorities based on known hazardous occupations. Similarly, all standards do not have equal emphasis. Those dealing with most hazardous conditions get highest priority.

> **WHAT DO YOU THINK?**
>
> A policy scholar makes the point that regulation often fails because it categorically treats safety as more important than convenience, or equality as more important than efficiency, and so misses the need to balance some of one for more of the other. Can you apply this argument to the various topics addressed in this chapter? How and who determines what the balance should be?

To increase employee awareness of hazards, OSHA established a communication standard in 1986. Often referred to as "right to know," the standard is intended to protect the safety of workers by keeping them informed of the dangerous substances with which they are working, the hazards and symptoms of exposure, and the proper steps to take if they have been exposed. Manufacturers, importers, and distributors of petroleum, stone, textiles, food, paper, and chemicals are covered by the standard.

Unions have played a major role in lobbying the government for stricter enforcement of OSHA and its regulations. This is consistent with their long history of concern for employee safety.

Hardly anyone has a kind word for OSHA. Employers say the rigidity and complexity of standards make compliance a nightmare. Unions say enforcement is spotty. And researchers say that evidence crediting OSHA with reducing accident and illness rates is hard to come by.[21]

Nevertheless, workplace safety continues to be a serious problem for several reasons. Technology is constantly introducing new chemicals whose potential hazards may not be fully appreciated for years. Additionally, OSHA focuses on design standards that dictate the physical characteristics of plant and equipment. The chemical leak at Bhopal, India, which killed over 2,000 people; the radiation leak at Chernobyl in the Ukraine; the Exxon oil spill at Valdez, Alaska; and the plant fire that killed 25 and injured 55 employees of Imperial Food Products in North Carolina all show that human error is frequently the culprit in large-scale disasters. People can circumvent almost any designed-in control system. At Imperial, emergency lights didn't work, an automatic fire alarm "didn't go off until everyone was dead," and, most appalling, exit doors had been deliberately locked.[22] The Imperial tragedy eerily resembles the 1911 Triangle Shirtwaist Factory fire in which 146 women and girls died when left without means of escape. But the Imperial fire did not occur in 1911. It occurred in 1991, more than 20 years after passage of OSHA.

### Applicant/Employee Screening

Many employers have begun screening people for factors that may affect health and safety on the job. Screening for drug or alcohol use, or both, is the most common example. Medical screening is extremely controversial, for a number of reasons. First, many believe it to be an invasion of privacy. Serious ethical issues arise if an employer has access to nonjob-related information about illnesses that carry a social stigma, such as sexually transmitted diseases or family histories of alcoholism or drug abuse.[23]

This objection can be overcome if medical information is kept in the hands of the medical staff, and the employer is given only relevant data. But that brings up the second objection: Is the quality of data adequate for use in selection decisions? Predictive screening for susceptibility to certain conditions has not been well developed scientifically. Studies have shown that neither drug testing at hire nor random drug testing had any affect on accident rates. However, a well-publicized and strictly enforced policy of testing for drugs and alcohol after every single accident did reduce accident rates.[24]

## Stress

This topic is receiving a lot of attention, at least in the popular press. It is a difficult area to study because what one person finds stressful another may find exhilarating. For example, there is no shortage of candidates (qualifications aside) to become astronauts, television talk show hosts, presidents, or prime ministers, occupations that surely involve stress.

One view of stress relates it to control: the lack of ability to make one's own decisions or use a range of skills. A recent medical study bypassed the popular picture of the executive under stress and found that workers in jobs that combine a high psychological demand with low decision control (mail workers, telephone operators) are approximately five times more likely to develop coronary heart disease than those who have greater control over their jobs.[25] Exhibit 15.2 locates jobs along the two dimensions of psychological demand and decision control.

If an objective of employee relations is to assist employees under stress, this study is important not only for its job design implications but also because it points out the importance of control as a factor related to stress. Helping employees to identify and alter areas in which they feel a lack of control should be a major objective of employee relations programs.

A Northwestern National Life Insurance Company survey of 1,300 employees conducted over two years at 37 diverse companies concluded that "companies that invest in (stress reduction) programs will earn a return in high morale and productivity, and lower sickness and turnover." Half the workers in the survey believed that on-the-job stress was cutting their productivity. However, these conclusions are employee responses to a survey, part of which is shown in Exhibit 15.3. As you can see, the survey items are extremely subjective. The survey reports that employees who believe their work is highly stressful are twice as likely to think about quitting their jobs as other workers. No measurements of actual turnover were taken, so we don't know if people who think their jobs are stressful actually quit them. Further, it is impossible to pin down whether the stress was the result of the job, the individual, or a poor match of individual to job.

EXHIBIT 15.2 Stress at Work

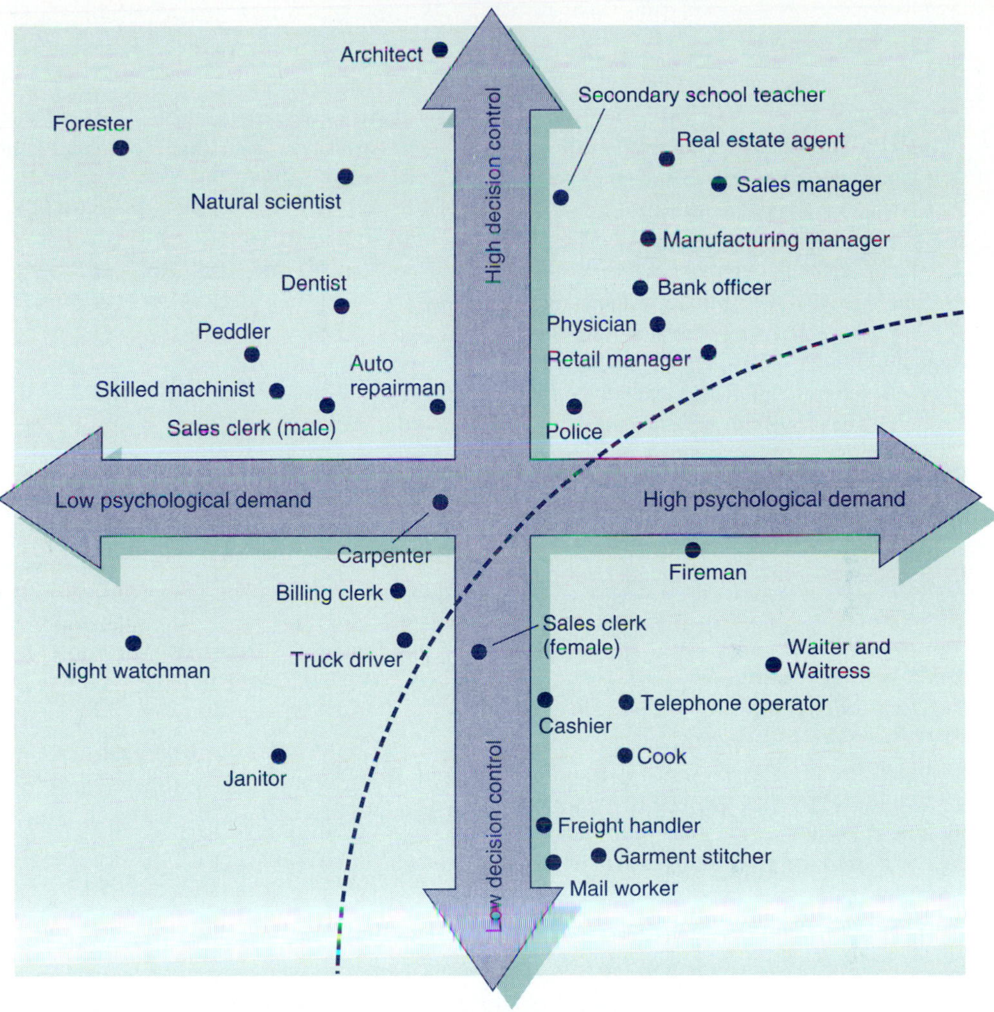


Source: Columbia University Department of Industrial Engineering and Operations Research.

The survey's 10 recommendations to relieve workplace stress are listed in Exhibit 15.4. They include a strong emphasis on multidirectional communication ("allow employees to talk freely with one another," "resolve conflict through open communications," "keep employees informed," and "give employees opportunities to air their concerns"); competitive benefits, clearly defined job expectations, and recognition and rewards for contributions. All of these recommendations fall within the purview of HRM. Thus, a well-run HR program may be the chicken soup and warm bath of the organization.

## EXHIBIT 15.3 The Workplace Stress Test

| | Response | | | | |
|---|---|---|---|---|---|
| **A. Employee Support and Training** | **Disagree strongly** | **Disagree somewhat** | **Neutral or don't know** | **Agree somewhat** | **Agree strongly** |
| 1. Management is supportive of employees' efforts. | ❑ 4 | ❑ 3 | ❑ 2 | ❑ 1 | ❑ 0 |
| 2. Management encourages work and personal support groups. | ❑ 4 | ❑ 3 | ❑ 2 | ❑ 1 | ❑ 0 |
| 3. Management and employees talk openly. | ❑ 4 | ❑ 3 | ❑ 2 | ❑ 1 | ❑ 0 |
| 4. Employees receive training when assigned new tasks. | ❑ 4 | ❑ 3 | ❑ 2 | ❑ 1 | ❑ 0 |
| 5. Employees are recognized and rewarded for their contributions. | ❑ 4 | ❑ 3 | ❑ 2 | ❑ 1 | ❑ 0 |
| 6. Work rules are published and are the same for everyone. | ❑ 4 | ❑ 3 | ❑ 2 | ❑ 1 | ❑ 0 |
| 7. Employees have current and understandable job descriptions. | ❑ 4 | ❑ 3 | ❑ 2 | ❑ 1 | ❑ 0 |
| 8. Management appreciates humor in the workplace. | ❑ 4 | ❑ 3 | ❑ 2 | ❑ 1 | ❑ 0 |
| 9. Employees and management are trained in how to resolve conflicts. | ❑ 4 | ❑ 3 | ❑ 2 | ❑ 1 | ❑ 0 |
| 10. Employees are free to talk with one another. | ❑ 4 | ❑ 3 | ❑ 2 | ❑ 1 | ❑ 0 |
| **B. Other Working Conditions** | **Disagree strongly** | **Disagree somewhat** | **Neutral or don't know** | **Agree somewhat** | **Agree strongly** |
| 11. Workloads vary greatly for individuals or between individuals. | ❑ 0 | ❑ 1 | ❑ 2 | ❑ 3 | ❑ 4 |
| 12. Employees have work spaces that are not crowded. | ❑ 4 | ❑ 3 | ❑ 2 | ❑ 1 | ❑ 0 |
| 13. Employees have access to technology they need. | ❑ 4 | ❑ 3 | ❑ 2 | ❑ 1 | ❑ 0 |
| 14. Few opportunities for advancement are available. | ❑ 0 | ❑ 1 | ❑ 2 | ❑ 3 | ❑ 4 |
| 15. Employees are given little control in how they do their work. | ❑ 0 | ❑ 1 | ❑ 2 | ❑ 3 | ❑ 4 |
| 16. Employees generally are physically isolated. | ❑ 0 | ❑ 1 | ❑ 2 | ❑ 3 | ❑ 4 |
| 17. Mandatory overtime is frequently required. | ❑ 0 | ❑ 1 | ❑ 2 | ❑ 3 | ❑ 4 |
| 18. Employees have little or no privacy. | ❑ 0 | ❑ 1 | ❑ 2 | ❑ 3 | ❑ 4 |
| 19. Performance of work units generally is below average. | ❑ 0 | ❑ 1 | ❑ 2 | ❑ 3 | ❑ 4 |
| 20. Personal conflicts on the job are common. | ❑ 0 | ❑ 1 | ❑ 2 | ❑ 3 | ❑ 4 |
| 21. Consequences of making a mistake on the job are severe. | ❑ 0 | ❑ 1 | ❑ 2 | ❑ 3 | ❑ 4 |

You can use these two key parts of the Workplace Stress Test, developed by Northwestern National Life Insurance Co., to assess your job's working conditions and how your workplace rates with a representative sampling of other workers who have taken this test:

| **Total points, support and training** | | **Total points, other working conditions** | |
|---|---|---|---|
| 0 to 14.1 points | Low stress | 0 to 17.8 points | Low stress |
| 14.2 to 19.6 points | Medium stress | 17.9 to 22.2 points | Medium stress |
| 19.7 to 40 points | High stress | 22.3 to 44 points | High stress |

For best results, experts suggest that several employees who work together take the tests to get an average score.

**EXHIBIT 15.4** Tips to Reduce Workplace Stress

Here are tips from the Northwestern National Life Insurance Co.'s report on workplace stress:

1. *Allow employees to talk freely with one another.* "Employees thrive in an atmosphere where they can consult with colleagues about work issues and defuse stress with humor."
2. *Reduce personal conflicts on the job.* Employers should resolve conflicts through "open communications, negotiations, and respect." Two basics: "Treat employees fairly." "Clearly define job expectations."
3. *Give employees adequate control in how they do their jobs.* "Workers take greater pride . . . are more productive and better able to deal with stress if they have some control and flexibility" in how they do their jobs.
4. *Ensure adequate staffing and expense budgets.* "Many organizations are facing the economic reality of smaller budgets," but "a new project may not be worth taking on if staffing and funding are inadequate."
5. *Talk openly with employees.* "Management should keep employees informed about bad news as well as good news," and should "give employees opportunities to air their concerns to management."
6. *Support employees' efforts.* By regularly asking employees how their work is going, listening to them, and addressing issues that are raised, "stress levels are significantly reduced."
7. *Provide competitive personal and vacation benefits.* "Workers who have time to relax and recharge after working hard are less likely to develop stress-related illnesses."
8. *Maintain current levels of employee benefits.* Cuts in pension, health insurance, vacation benefits and sick leaves invite employee stress. Employers must weigh dollar saving with the high costs of employee burnout.
9. *Reduce the amount of red tape for employees.* "Employers can lower burnout rates if they ensure that employees' time is not wasted on unnecessary paperwork and procedures."
10. *Recognize and reward employees.* "A pat on the back, a public word of praise, a raise or a bonus" for accomplishments and contributions can pay "big dividends in higher employee morale and productivity."

## Co-Worker Relations

What happens if the threat to health and safety, whether real or perceived, comes from co-workers: AIDS victims, alcohol or drug abusers, sexual harassers? Organizations must tread a narrow line here, so they do not trammel on the rights of one employee while protecting another. Court rulings generally provide guidance about how an employer may proceed.

### AIDS

AIDS has surpassed cancer as the disease people fear most. The fear is partly rational, because the disease is nearly always fatal and control has not been attained. But irrational fears exist, too, if people refuse to work with suspected AIDS victims. Legally, AIDS is considered a handicap; therefore, its victims are protected against job discrimination and cannot be fired or transferred, as long as they are able to perform their jobs.[26] This stance, however, does not allay

*Sexual harassment* is defined by federal guidelines as unwelcome sexual advances, requests for sexual favors, and other verbal or physical conduct of a sexual nature when such conduct creates a hostile or offensive work environment. If the conduct is (1) unwelcome and (2) occurs with sufficient frequency to create an abusive work environment (i.e., not an isolated incident), the employer is responsible for changing the environment by warning, reprimanding, and even firing the harasser.[28]

co-workers who are fearful of contracting the disease. Even though medical experts agree that the disease is not transmissible under normal workplace conditions, managers must take a strong role in educating the workforce to this fact. A vast amount of educational material concerning AIDS is available through public health services and government agencies, yet relatively few firms appear to utilize this material.[27]

### Sexual Harassment

Sexual harassment is a violation of Title VII of the Civil Rights Act.

Because an employer has the power to reprimand or fire an offender, an employer is legally liable for the sexual harassment acts of its employees, whether or not the employer knew they were occurring. However, liability is reduced if an employer has a clear, well-publicized policy forbidding harassment and follows up immediately on complaints.[29]

While a 1993 Supreme Court ruling (*Harris* v. *Forklift Systems, Inc.,* November 15, 1993) clarified the standard for judging sexual harassment as conduct that is sufficiently severe or pervasive to alter the conditions of the victim's employment, as judged by a reasonable person, little guidance exists thus far concerning what constitutes appropriate punishment versus insufficient response versus punitive actions. If a company reprimands but does not fire or transfer a harasser, it is unrealistic to assume that all parties will be able to act as if nothing happened. If the harasser is a highly productive employee not easily replaced, is it realistic to believe a company will fire the offender rather than transfer the victim? Another unresolved issue is the question of guilt. Wrongful accusations made out of malice can ruin careers and may be as hard to disprove as to prove. Particularly troublesome are harassment charges from salespeople working with the company's customers. Should a customer or the customer's employer be responsible for the customer's behavior? The area is rife with conflicting employee rights. A definition of sexual harassment, a policy statement, and a description of complaint resolution procedures should all be included in the employee handbook. Timely interviews of co-workers and managers, consideration of circumstances, keeping all parties informed, and providing them with an opportunity to respond seem to be wise precautions.

A nonprofit organization that helps women obtain and keep jobs in the coal mining industry offers advice to those who believe they are victims of harassment (see Exhibit 15.5). Some experts believe male-dominated workplaces are likely to be the most hostile to women. For example, in a 1990 Defense Department study, 64 percent of military women said they endured sexual harassment in the male-dominated armed services.[30]

A recent HR Net discussion on sexual harassment concluded with the following guidance on conducting investigations of allegations of sexual harassment.

1. Review company files about complainant and harasser.
2. Interview the complainant in a private setting of the complainant's choice to obtain the following information:
   *a.* Description of alleged harassment and employee actions in response.
   *b.* ID of alleged harasser or conditions thought to be offensive.
   *c.* Date/time/frequencies.

## EXHIBIT 15.5 If You Are Being Harassed

| | |
|---|---|
| **1. Don't quit your job.** | It won't solve anything, and you'll be out of a paycheck. Quitting may also work against you if you file an EEOC complaint, for the company will be under no pressure to negotiate. If the harassment intensifies because of your complaint, that only strengthens your case. |
| **2. Act quickly.** | The best defense to harassment is a strong offense. Confront the harasser. Say that the behavior is offensive to you and ask that it stop. |
| **3. Get support from your coworkers.** | Make sure the men and women who work with you are aware of the situation and your efforts to remedy it. Most men find sexual harassment as offensive as women do. Men also can be victims. |
| **4. Ridicule the harasser.** | Public exposure of sexual harassment can be the most effective way of stopping it. You may ask the harasser, "Does it make you feel like a big man to pick on a woman?" Or "Do you speak to your wife like that? Maybe I'll have to call her and ask." |
| **5. Use your union grievance procedures.** | Union members have additional protection under an antidiscrimination clause that is part of most contracts. Contact your union representative immediately and consider filing a grievance. |
| **6. Notify the company.** | Whether your harasser is a supervisor or a co-worker, tell the company. If you don't, your employer can claim ignorance and deny responsibility for the behavior. Put it in writing and keep a copy. |
| **7. Keep a diary.** | Indicate dates, times, and names of witnesses. Write exact quotes, if possible. The more evidence, the better. |
| **8. Find other victims.** | If you can build evidence that the harasser has abused others, or that harassment has been condoned by management, your case will be strengthened. |

Source: Adapted from Marat Moore and Connie White, *Sexual Harassment in the Mines* (Oak Ridge, TN: Coal Employment Project, no date).

*d.* Location/circumstances.
*e.* Names of possible witness(es).
*f.* Effect of conduct/conditions.
*g.* Names of others who are affected or subject to harassment.
*h.* Names of others the complainant has talked to in or out of work.
*i.* Find out if other employees voiced objections to harassments and what effect they had. Assure them that there will be no retaliation for reporting. Give no promises regarding course of action until all facts are obtained and assessed.
*j.* Require confidentiality. Assure complainants that only others with a "need to know" will be informed.

3. Interview other witnesses (Require confidentiality).
4. Interview others allegedly harassed (Require confidentiality).
5. Review evidence.
6. Interview alleged harasser.
7. Prepare report with recommendation for actions.
8. Take corrective action to resolve situation.
9. When matter is resolved, continue to monitor situation.
10. Follow up with parties to ensure that corrective actions were sufficient.

### Substance Abuse

Illegal drugs have become pervasive in American society. It is not surprising that they have also become an issue in the workplace. Yet, alcohol abuse is far more common in terms of impaired performance and absenteeism than drug abuse. The difference is that the mere possession of drugs is illegal, whether or not work behavior is affected.

Some employers advocate mandatory drug testing of all employees. More than one-third of all companies use drug testing, according to one survey.[31] One-fourth of responding companies require drug tests of all new employees. Current employees are tested only when drug use is suspected. Applicants who test positive for illegal drugs are rarely told that this is the reason for not being hired. However, current employees who test positive are given test results. Only 24 percent of them are fired; most are referred for treatment or counseling.

Testing may be justified for certain job classifications where the consequences of working while impaired are severe (e.g., bus drivers, pilots, or nuclear plant operators). For many jobs, proper supervision may make drug testing unnecessary. This does not imply the strict supervision and narrow employee discretion that was part of scientific management (see Chapter Three). It does imply managerial awareness of employee well-being. For example, Hewlett-Packard has a policy of Management by Wandering Around, shown in Exhibit 15.6. The policy requires managers to be aware of how employees are feeling about their jobs and of their personal well-being. The tone is positive. The emphasis is certainly not on substance abuse, yet it puts managers on notice that they share responsibility for the well-being of all H-P employees.

## EMPLOYEE ASSISTANCE

How does a manager respond when employees' problems impair their work behavior? It varies. One response is to search for ways to get rid of the troubled employee. Another is to assist employees through internal programs or outside professional assistance. Referral to outside sources of assistance is the most common response of organizations, but some type of in-house counseling, especially for alcoholism, is also common.[32] Such counseling may range from a brief chat with a supervisor who warns the troubled employee that failure to seek outside help will result in dismissal, to private appointments with professional counselors at the work site.

Employer assistance with personal problems is not new. In 1916, the Ford Motor Company's Legal Aid Department assisted employees "free of charge for all matters involving legal questions, insurance, investments, settlements of disputes, purchase of real estate, and filling out and securing naturalization papers."[33] Its medical department had its own modern operating room and six-bed ward, and its English School taught reading, writing, and speaking simple English to thousands of employees. The bulk of these assistance programs ended in the 1920s, however, as the result of pressures accompanying the phenomenal growth of the company, the complexity and cost of the programs, and the loss of influence of top managers who supported them.

## EXHIBIT 15.6 Hewlett-Packard: Management by Wandering Around and Open Door Policy

**Purpose**

Through the years a fundamental strength of the company has been the effectiveness of communication both upwards and downwards within the organization. Two key ingredients for making this happen are:

**I. Management by Wandering Around**

- To have a well-managed operation it is essential that the managers/supervisors be aware of what is happening in their areas—not just at their immediate level, but also at several levels below that.
- Our people are our most important resource and the managers have direct responsibility for their training, their performance, and their general well-being. To do this managers must get around to find out how their people feel about their jobs and what they feel will make their work more productive and more meaningful.

**II. Open Door Policy**

- Managers and supervisors are expected to promote a working environment, within which employees feel free and comfortable to either seek individual counsel, express general concerns, or offer ideas.
- All employees have the right, if in their opinion they feel such steps are necessary, to discuss their concerns with higher-level managers. Any effort to prevent an employee from seeking higher-level managers through intimidation or any other means is absolutely contrary to company policy and will be dealt with accordingly.
- Therefore, the intent of the open door policy is to encourage employees to seek the "appropriate" management level. Appropriate is defined as that level that can best act with the information.
- Utilizing the open door policy will not in any way impact any evaluation of the employee or subject him or her to any other adverse consequences.
- Employees also have responsibilities—particularly in keeping their discussions with upper-level managers objective and focused on significant concerns.

Today's assistance programs are structured in large part on the basis of research into alcoholism and effective ways to deal with employees who have this problem. Two components appear to be necessary for a successful program:

1. *Written policy.* While many of us help our friends if we become aware of a personal problem, most of us are unsure how to proceed. Our intentions may be honorable, but lack of expertise on how to proceed limits our usefulness. It is the same with organizations. Co-workers and managers are typically the first to be aware of a problem, and they are in a position to provide the necessary emotional support and motivation to confront the problem. A written policy guides them in how to proceed. Research has found managers' willingness to confront employees whose performance is impaired is highly related to a written policy outlining performance, discipline, and medical practices. Exhibit 15.7 is an excerpt from an employee assistance policy, which clearly spells out the supervisors' role. A written policy also demonstrates full managerial support for the policy and the options organizations pursue if performance does not improve.

## EXHIBIT 15.7 Excerpt from an Employee Assistance Policy (EAP)

**Policy**

The EAP operates within the following framework:

1. A wide range of problems may affect employees' job performance adversely. These include alcohol and drug addiction, marital and family difficulties, and emotional distress. The EAP will assist employees to resolve these problems and others for which employees may seek help.
2. Employees' current jobs and future advancement will not be jeopardized by using EAP services.
3. As with all health and personnel documents, EAP records will be maintained in a confidential manner.
4. When necessary, sick leave may be granted for treatment and rehabilitation on the same basis as it is granted for other health problems.
5. Employees will be responsible for complying with the EAP services' recommendations and treatment plans.
6. The EAP service will also be available to employees' families.

**Procedure**

1. Employees who need professional advice are encouraged to use the EAP counseling services, and those whose personal problems adversely affect their work are encouraged to seek help voluntarily from the EAP services.
2. Supervisors are responsible for confronting employees about their unsatisfactory performance and helping them to improve their work.
   *a.* Supervisors bring employees' unsatisfactory work to their attention and encourage them to solve the problem on their own or with the help of the EAP counseling services. Supervisors also point out to the employees that continued unsatisfactory performance will lead to formal discipline.
   *b.* If performance improves, no further action will be taken.
   *c.* If job performance continues to be unsatisfactory, regardless of whether or not employees have accepted help, regular disciplinary procedure will be followed, up to and including discharge.

At each step of the procedure, supervisors will encourage employees to seek help from the EAP counseling service.

2. *Program coordinator.* A coordinator ensures that procedures and policies are known and carried out throughout the workplace. A highly visible coordinator can advise managers, encourage them to confront the troubled employee, and can reassure employees about the confidentiality of the service.

## Approaches to Employee Assistance

There are two different approaches to intervention. Most assistance programs probably contain elements of both approaches.

### Constructive Confrontation

This strategy evolved as a technique for identifying employed alcoholics and for counteracting the typical responses of guilt, denial, rationalization, and manipulation. It focuses solely on job performance and documents to the employee clear instances of impaired performance. If a job performance is not impaired, there is no situation that warrants the organization's intervention. Confrontation is best combined with a progressive discipline strategy: Continued unacceptable performance will lead to progressively more severe discipline, culminating in dismissal.

That's the confrontation part of the strategy. The constructive part (1) expresses emotional support and group concern for the employee's welfare, (2) emphasizes that employment can be maintained if performance improves, and (3) suggests alternatives for the employee to regain satisfactory improvement. The support and the confrontation are offered in combination, and both focus heavily on job performance.

> WHAT DO YOU THINK?
>
> Although companies promise that the employee assistance program consultations are confidential, this confidentiality can be breached. If an employee sues the employer, EAP records may be turned over to the company's lawyer. Lawyers defend this practice by saying that they only get the information if the employee sues the company, and in such cases it becomes important evidence to determine if the employee had any problems that affected job performance and, if so, to demonstrate that the company tried to provide assistance with those problems. What do you think?

### Counseling

Improved job performance does not necessarily mean that the underlying problems have been resolved. Additionally, job performance may not be affected until the problem has become severe. Instead of focusing on job performance, a counseling approach focuses on the cause of the problem, either in the individual or the social relationships surrounding the individual. Professionally trained psychotherapists may be involved.

In spite of its tantalizing promise of tackling problems before they become severe, counseling appears to be most effective when it becomes clear that the problems have gone beyond employees' control. Before then, employees fear the stigma of being labeled mentally ill and so avoid contacting counselors.

Which approach, confrontation or counseling, has the better track record? Programs that maintain a balance between the two approaches are likely to have better outcomes than single-approach programs. Constructive confrontation motivates employees to change their behavior, and counseling provides one means of doing so.

Many organizations have established employee assistance or advisory programs. Programs range from 24-hour phone counseling and referral to classes on managing finances, stress, and health. Exhibit 15.8 shows the topics that come up most frequently at Claritas' Employee Advisory Resource (EAR). Personal problems account for about 60 percent of the calls; work-related problems account for 40 percent. A study of 6400 employees who used EAPs at 84 worksites found that 44 percent of the clients had problems of a psychological or emotional nature, followed by marital problems (28 percent) and other family problems (31 percent). Relatively few were diagnosed with alcohol or drug problems.[34]

## CONFLICT AND DISCIPLINE

Many of the policies and programs discussed in this chapter can go a long way to prevent discipline issues from arising. Prevention should be the objective of all organizations. However, when problems arise, having procedures in place to

**EXHIBIT 15.8** Types of Problems Brought to Employee Advisory Service

| **Personal Problems: 60%** | **Percentage of Calls** |
|---|---|
| Financial (bankruptcy, financial difficulties relating to inflationary costs, poor financial management) | 26% |
| Legal (most often family and tenant-landlord conflicts) | 21 |
| Chemical (10% alcohol, 3% drugs) | 13 |
| Mental health (mainly depression) | 9 |
| Familial (parent-child and parent-relative relationships) | 8 |
| Marital (difficulties with communication and problem resolution) | 8 |
| Personal (difficulties with identity, relationships, and sex) | 5 |
| Physical health | 5 |
| Miscellaneous (problems not characterized by one of the above groups) | 6 |
| **Problems at Work: 40%** | **Percentage of Calls** |
| Compensation and benefits (sick pay, health insurance coverage, vacation, overtime, sick leave, retirement) | 22% |
| Performance (disputes over the content of regular performance appraisals to specific disciplinary actions) | 19 |
| Transfers and promotions | 7 |
| Policies and procedures (requests for familiarization with specific written corporate policies) | 14 |
| Interpersonal relations (conflicts with supervisors or other employees) | 10 |
| Career counseling | 8 |
| Miscellaneous (including discrimination complaints, rehabilitation problems, complaints about working conditions, and other problems not characterized by another group) | 20 |

Source: David J. Reed, "One Approach to Employee Assistance," *Personnel Journal,* Aug. 1983, pp. 648–52.

deal with infractions can help safeguard the rights of all concerned. There are four elements to assure adherence to generally acceptable work rules of such a system.

1. *Establish rules.* The first element in a discipline system is the establishment of work and behavior rules. The rules can concern behavior that is directly or indirectly related to work productivity.
2. *Communicate the rules to all employees.* The employee handbook is an appropriate forum. Unless employees are aware of the rules, it is unfair to expect them to follow the rules. Closely related is a willingness to accept the rules and their enforceability. Employee participation in the formation of rules may help ensure that rules are fair and appropriate. For example, rules regarding hair length are relevant to job safety in some settings but irrelevant in most others. Though rules would ideally be kept to a minimum, they may need to be periodically revised to remain relevant.

3. *Assess behavior.* Performance evaluation typically assesses deficiencies in work behaviors at scheduled intervals; rule-breaking behavior is disclosed either as a result of observation or investigation (e.g., investigation of theft, falsifying records). Once again, the more constructive approach is to be aware of what's going on to forestall the need for discipline.
4. *Changing behavior.* Finally, the disciplinary process includes assistance in changing behavior and administering punishment. Counseling and confrontation to motivate change may be part of the program.

## Disciplinary Process

Discipline usually follows a progressive system because second or later infractions are dealt with more harshly than first offenses. The discipline policy in Exhibit 15.9 follows this approach. It progresses from a verbal reproach to a written warning, signed by the employee. A third offense within 12 months brings a final warning, with notification that additional problems will find the offender on the outside looking in.

A manager's first line of action is counseling; this is the most frequent method of disciplinary action. The supervisor determines if a violation took place, explains to the employee why the violation significantly affects productivity, and suggests that it should not happen again. This approach works for most violations.

If a second or more serious violation takes place, the supervisor again counsels the employee, this time noting that the incident will be entered in the employee's personnel file. If the violation was sufficiently serious, the employee may also be given a verbal or written warning of the consequences of a future recurrence.

If the incident concerns ineffective productivity, the employee may request a transfer or be asked to transfer to another job. The employee may have been placed in the wrong job, there may be a personality conflict between the employee and the supervisor, or more training might help. In some rare cases, demotions or downward transfers are used.

If counseling and warnings do not result in changed behavior, and if a transfer is not appropriate, the next step is normally a disciplinary layoff. If damage resulted from the deviant behavior, the deductions may be made from employee's pay over a period to pay for the damage. Most disciplinary action does not require this severe a step. The layoff is usually of short duration, perhaps a few days up to a week.

This next most severe form of punishment is getting an employee to quit. Getting the unsatisfactory employee to quit has many advantages over termination, for both employee and employer. Both save face. The employee finds another job and then quits, telling the peer group how much better things are at the new location. The employer is satisfied because an ineffective employee has left. However, this tactic may be unsavory from an ethical point of view. The employee may not be guilty.

While getting an employee to quit is not a forthright approach to discipline, many prefer it to the next step: firing the employee. To many inexperienced managers, discharge is the solution to any problem with a difficult employee. Often discharge is not possible, because of seniority rules, union rules, too few

## EXHIBIT 15.9 Progressive Discipline Policy

1. With the exception of offenses requiring more stringent action, employees will normally be counseled once verbally before receiving a written warning.
2. In the event of another performance problem or a violation of any employer policy or rule, a written warning should ordinarily be issued.
   *a.* The warning should be signed and dated by the employee. If the employee refuses to sign the warning, another supervisor should be immediately brought in and asked to sign and witness that the employee has seen, but refused to sign, the warning.
   *b.* The warning should inform the employee of the possible consequences, including final written warning, suspension and/or discharge, should additional violations or performance problems occur.
   *c.* A written warning need not pertain to the same or similar offense for which the verbal counseling was given.
3. If a third offense occurs within 12 months of the previous written warning, a final warning should be issued.
   *a.* The warning should be signed and dated by the employee. If the employee refuses to sign the warning, another supervisor should be immediately brought in and asked to sign and witness that the employee has seen, but refused to sign, the warning.
   *b.* The warning should inform the employee that termination may result if further violations or performance problems occur.
   *c.* A final written warning need not pertain to the same or similar offense for which any prior verbal or written warning was issued.
   *d.* In addition to the final written warning, the supervisor may also suspend the employee without pay or take other disciplinary action deemed appropriate.
4. If the employee violates any policy of the employer or fails to improve his or her level of performance, termination may result.

Reproduced with permission from *Employee Handbook and Personnel Policies Manual* by Richard J. Simmons. © 1983 Richard J. Simmons, Castle Publications, Ltd., P.O. Box 580, Van Nuys, California 91408.

replacements in the labor market, fear of wrongful discharge lawsuits, or a number of other reasons. Discharge is also costly, both directly and indirectly. Direct costs include a loss of all human resource investments already made in the person: recruiting, selection, and training. Severance pay may be added in exchange for a promise not to file a lawsuit. Indirect costs are the effect of the firing on other employees. These may not occur if it is a blatant case of deviant behavior or severe inability, but frequently the facts are not clear, and other employees may believe the action was arbitrary. If this is the case, productivity may drop, and valuable employees may leave, fearful of becoming victims of arbitrary action, too. Thus, discharge is a final resort—when all else fails or in very serious cases involving fraud or theft.

Documentation of actions and the behavior that precipitated them is required at every step of the way. This documentation may protect the employer from subsequent lawsuits accusing it of wrongful discharge, harassment, or violating employee rights.

## Conflict Resolution

Conflict must be handled in a way that protects employees' rights. In addition to discipline issues, conflict on the job may arise for a host of reasons: sexual harassment, equal opportunity complaints, disputes over promotions, pay, admission to training programs. Some organizations have designed procedures that provide a mechanism for employees and managers to voice their disagreements.

Employees who belong to a union collectively bargain some of these disputes and take others through a formal grievance procedure.

### Types of Systems

The type of system an organization uses may depend on the types of problems it deals with, and its compatibility with other organizational structures.

Procedures can vary on two dimensions:

1. *Degree of formality.* High formality means explicit statements concerning appealable issues, steps to follow, and roles and responsibilities of parties.
2. *Degree of independence from management.* Are workers forced to complain to their immediate superiors, or does the system use people further removed?

The most independent system would use an outside arbitrator, and it may even provide independent legal counsel to employees. At Wells Fargo Bank, the employee relations unit acts as an employee advocate within the organization. While many writers imply that the more formal and independent a process, the more accepted it will be, no research has so far addressed this issue.

The hierarchical system is the most formal, the least independent, and also the most common.

### Hierarchical Systems

Discipline is administered to most nonunion employees by the supervisor, who also evaluates the employee. When the employee is found to be ineffective, the supervisor decides what needs to be done. Hierarchical systems allow a supervisor, who might be arbitrary, wrong, or ineffective, to serve as cop, judge, and jury over the employee.

A person accused of a crime, such as speeding, in many of our courts can have counsel, the judge is not the arresting officer, and the penalty may be a $50 fine. In the employment situation, where the employee has none of these safeguards, the penalty for an infraction of work rules may be loss of job and salary. Even if the employee is convicted of speeding, appeal to a higher court is possible. What can employees do if they are unfairly treated by their supervisors?

Hewlett-Packard's open door policy encourages employees to express their concerns to managers and supervisors and to go to higher-level managers if they think it is necessary. But an inherent limitation of hierarchical systems is that the whole value system of the hierarchy is based on mutual support among supervisors to build a good management team. Therefore, while the system may offer *procedural* justice, in that employees are given the opportunity to be heard, *substantive* justice may be lacking if the system does not prevent arbitrary actions.[35]

### Peer Systems

In contract with hierarchical systems, where employees complain to superiors, peer systems rely on independent or related peers to assess the situation and recommend action. They can be implemented in several ways.

General Electric Company's conflict system for 1,800 nonunion production workers at a Columbia, Maryland, electric range plant uses a five-member panel, comprising the plant manager, a personnel officer, and three specially trained hourly employees. Thus, employees are in the majority.

An evaluation after five years' experience showed that, of 300 grievances filed, 100 went to the panel. The other 200 were resolved one-on-one with supervisors. This number was substantially higher than the complaints filed in the previous five years under an open door policy, where employees complained to management. Managers attribute the increase in complaints to greater employee confidence in fair treatment. They say the real value of the program is that it encourages better supervisor/employee interaction and makes supervisors more accountable.[36]

### Ombudsmen

Another approach to resolving conflicts is the use of an ombudsman, who will investigate complaints, hear all sides, and try to help the parties arrive at a solution they can all live with. The Intercom system at Chemical Bank of New York is an example. Bank employees receive special training and then serve three-year terms as Intercom representatives. Selected from all job levels and departments of the bank, Intercom representatives are trained to listen to employees and to talk with them about their job concerns. Management only becomes involved at the request of the employees.

## Judging the Judges

To be effective, conflict resolution systems must appear more attractive than quitting or suing. This standard leads to four criteria for evaluating such systems.

1. *Fairness of settlement.* Employees must perceive that an organization is both capable and willing to change a situation leading to the problem.
2. *Timeliness of settlement.* Reducing the period of uncertainty and the loss of benefits stemming from continuance of the dispute is one of the main advantages of complaining versus suing.
3. *Ease of utilization.* Time and effort required to file and follow through with an appeal must be minimal.
4. *Protection from recrimination.* Future raises and promotions must not be perceived to be threatened by filing a grievance or complaint.

> EXPLORING THE WEB
>
> The Employee Assistance Professionals Association has a web site at
> **http://www.jobweb.org/cohrma/eapa/eapa.htm**

A study of an open door complaint system found that the system had the potential to reduce turnover.[37] Researchers looked at the perceptions of both employees who have filed claims and those who have not. The sample of more than 4,000 employees at a Fortune 100 company indicated that a positive experience with the open door system increased perceptions of both distributive and procedural justice, which in turn influenced satisfaction levels and intent to remain with the organizations. And the effect went beyond those who used the system. A spillover effect occurs when filers talk about their experiences, positive or negative, with other employees.

Research is mixed concerning whether formalized hierarchical procedures deliver genuine organizational justice to employees. Supporters insist that formal procedures provide improved opportunities for employees to seek relief from unfair treatment when compared with informal open door policies with no institutionalized mechanisms. But skeptics say that the procedures are merely trying to look fair, without taking seriously the goal of actually being fair. In contrast with the mechanisms provided union members, nonunion employees usually must process grievances on their own and they must trust higher management to make a fair decision. Therefore, whether or not formal procedures provide employees with protection depends on the benchmark for comparison.[38]

Two researchers looked at a number of factors common within other justice systems which are presumed to help eliminate bias: (1) instructing decision makers to enforce the rule as it is written, whether or not they agree with the rule, (2) providing guidelines about what constitutes sufficient proof, and (3) limiting access to information on past work history.[39] While this study was performed in a laboratory setting instead of in an actual company, the researchers concluded that introducing these elements could strengthen nonunion grievance systems. Restricting the availability of work history information can gain the trust of employees by providing some protection from unwarranted disciplinary action; giving specific direction to enforce a rule as written and specifying a standard of proof helps reduce inconsistencies among decision makers. Thus, even though most conflict resolution systems in nonunion settings still give the lion's share of control to management, the structure of the system can enhance the degree to which its results are perceived as fair by employees.

## THE DARK SIDE OF THE NEW DEAL

Throughout this book, we have examined HR innovations that form the new employment relationship. They include shifts to greater role flexibility working for egalitarian employers; shifts from pay based on time and job to earnings based on profits and gainsharing; from adversarial to more cooperative, team-based relations, and so on. Others see a potentially dark side to these innovations.[40] They see not cooperation but cooptation; increased risk sharing and cost shifting to employees rather than success sharing; and diminished employment security rather than empowerment. Almost daily, the press describes another employer's decision to unilaterally restructure and redesign its employment relationship.

Depending on employment status, job and pay risk can range from limited to virtually all. For contract workers, the risks can be substantial. Unemployment insurance excludes contract workers by definition. Contract workers must provide their own health care, pensions, and training. They may or may not be able to accommodate family responsibilities, depending on the terms of the contract. But any accommodations are their responsibility; the employer is obligated to nothing outside the contract. Pay is risky because there are likely to be periods between contracts when no income is received.

The greatest risk to contingent workers is low employment stability. They can be laid off at the employer's discretion and are often excluded from collecting unemployment insurance. Their pay is likely to be predictable, however. As long as they are working, they receive the agreed-upon wage, which is typically lower than that for core employees. Pay does not vary with performance, however.

## Reciprocity in the Relationship

The magnitude of change in reciprocal obligations and shifting of risks from employers to employees demands thoughtful attention. As we observed in Chapter One, many of the current changes in the employment relationship are designed to better fit the particular circumstances of the employer. The impact on employees is ignored. Yet, those who believe that employees are going to remain passive in the face of perceived unfair treatment or violated implicit contract were asleep in their history classes. And those who don't know the history of changing employment relationships in the past century didn't learn from it. Unions, labor, and civil rights legalization all were reactions to perceived violation of implicit (and explicit) understandings.

Increasing the riskiness of pay for these who can least afford it, failing to create new jobs for a changing profile of the American workforce, underinvesting in education and training, and unilaterally shifting employees from core to other categories as a method to control labor costs have been called "a recipe for social and economic disaster."[41]

## Replacing the Contract with . . . What?

What to do about managing the changed employment relationship depends in some part on one's ideology. In addition to individuals and employers, these changes must involve a third key player, the government. Some call for corporations and the government to act in concert to synchronize technology and capital with a public policy that protects the interests of employees. Others praise the "creative destruction" that is inherent in market-based economies: assets, including human resources, are constantly being reconfigured to more productive uses.[42] AT&T is a case in point. For most of its life, it was a highly regulated monopoly with profits guaranteed and little incentive to control costs. Since its breakup and accompanying deregulation, the company has constantly been in the news for buying and/or spinning off units and laying off thousands and thousands of employees. In the meantime, the entire telecommunications industry has boomed, so that employment levels industrywide are at an unprecedented level at the same time that AT&T continues to reconfigure.

The ramifications of the changing employment contract, for employees and their dependents, and perhaps for society, too, have been virtually ignored. Perhaps, to ensure the efficient and equitable workings of a market-based economy, we need to help individuals mitigate the increased risks and costs they must bear. Additional HR innovations are going to be required. Some may include

- *Portable health and medical care* that employees carry with them when they change employers, are laid off, or move to contingent status.
- *Vouchers for education and training* that individuals can use to help ensure they will continuously learn valued skills.
- *Portable pensions and retiree programs* with some base level of coverage that would be owned by the employee.
- *Realistic employment relationship previews,* akin to realistic job previews that inform and alert employees to their changing obligations and returns to help them prepare for the increased risks.

- *Meaningful work* that provides opportunities for career development and learning.
- *Honest communication* regarding an individual's performance, prospects, and developmental needs as well as the company's prospects and future needs.

Without concern for social justice and fair treatment of employees, the sustained competitive advantage that all employers seek may well be impossible to achieve. HR managers need to understand the importance of the implicit social contract under which employees currently work as well as manage changes in this relationship.

## EVALUATING RESULTS

The effectiveness of employee relations lies in its efficiency and its equity outcomes for employees and employers.

### Efficiency

Efficiency measures of employee relations programs could include improved product quality (measured by reductions in reject rate), enhanced productivity (indicated by an increase in output per working hour), and reduced costs (measured in cost per unit produced). Obviously, these measures could change as a result of other factors besides employee relations, which makes evaluation difficult.

One empirical study correlated QWL programs at 18 General Motors plants with economic performance (labor costs, product quality), which could be characterized as efficiency, and industrial relations performance (grievance rates, absenteeism, attitudinal climate of union/management relationship), which could be characterized as equity. The authors were primarily interested in whether ongoing QWL programs could smooth collective bargaining relationships, as measured by the number of contract demands introduced in local, as opposed to national, bargaining. Despite having a common technology, employer, and union, the 18 plants experienced extreme variations in grievance rates, discipline rates, and other industrial relations and economic measures.

While the industrial relations performance measures were strongly related to economic performance, the authors were hesitant to conclude that QWL programs caused any of these improvements because of the incompleteness in data. The key test of QWL success, they say, is whether effective collaboration can be maintained at the workplace during periods of difficult negotiations at the bargaining table.[43]

#### Utility Measures of Efficiency

The utility approach to evaluation has been used to estimate the economic value of a job-based program. The economic value of a performance increase (or decrease) on a specific job is translated into an estimate of the program's value. The city of Phoenix, for example, used this approach to evaluate its alcoholism assistance program. Using public health estimates of the extent of alcoholism in the labor force (around 10 percent) and managers' estimates of the costs of impairment at various organization levels, the value of a program to reduce impairment was calculated.[44] The program for city employees in Phoenix claimed a higher degree of alcoholism rehabilitation than community treatment sources because of the added clout of threatened job loss. The estimated cost savings from the employee assistance program was more than $2 million a year.

A study of longitudinal data from 26 steel plants concluded that a single innovation in isolation has little effect on productivity. Consequently, trying to pin down the gains of an EAP or child-care service or flexible time is futile. Rather, what counts is the adoption of a coherent system of HR practices, including work teams, flexible job assignments, employment security, and training. Rather than a single program, it is the entire system of HR practice that can make a difference.

## Equity

Studies of effects of employee relations activities are difficult, because employee relations reflects an overall philosophy. It is difficult to disentangle its effects from anything else.

One way to examine effects is to consider employees' options absent strong employee relations. Valued employees who are disgruntled can easily leave an organization. Less-valued employees have fewer options to leave, but they can reduce their commitment and motivation, or even sabotage other employees' work efforts.

A second option for disgruntled employees is to unionize, thus pooling their efforts to change the workplace. A third option is to sue the employer. An increasing number of employees are taking this option, and it is costly. Wells Fargo Bank's cost estimates for lawsuits filed by employees who thought they were unfairly fired range up to $6 million. Avoiding even one lawsuit would pay for a considerable amount of employee relations activity.

Research to measure the results of cooperation programs views these programs as a variable affecting employee job satisfaction and motivation, or as an umbrella under which most organization development activities fit. The broadness of the definition makes it difficult to specify results. Also, most programs tend to be short-lived and have difficulty producing tangible, long-lasting results.

Nevertheless, the research does offer some guideline for success. To allow the more cooperative approaches to organization decision making to be successful, management must be willing to concede something of value to employees to obtain trust or credibility. The concession may be control over physical work conditions, or it may be job security. Additionally, there must be support for the new approach at multiple levels of the organization. The immediate supervisor may require training in how to make cooperative efforts a success.

With savings so difficult to document, you may ask why employers bother to offer counseling assistance, conflict resolution systems, or child care. But good intentions and a show of concern may be all the justification that is required. Some employers may be committed to such programs, just as they are committed to the wider communities in which they are located. Nevertheless, effective human resource management helps ensure that employee relations programs are well designed and managed.

## SUMMARY

There are a wide variety of activities in an organization aimed at enhancing the quality of the employment relationship. Some of the programs are formal, such as conflict resolution procedures or health and safety awareness programs. Other activities are more casual, such as organizing and funding an employee picnic. Encouraging a cooperative, rather than an adversarial, relationship is the goal. The underlying assumption is that this kind of atmosphere better allows employees to perform their jobs and unleash their creativity.

The effects of employee relations programs are difficult to assess. Most of their benefits take the form of cost avoidance—lawsuits that were not filed, turnover or absenteeism that did not occur, productivity that did not decline. Additionally, many of the programs contribute to a better atmosphere. They demonstrate that the employer is committed to cooperative relationships, respects the employees, views them as a source of profitable suggestions, and will make efforts to accommodate their preferences.

Because of the difficulty in justifying these programs on a cost basis, top management commitment to employee relations is essential. If this commitment falters (often through a change in management), it seems an easy choice to cut these programs to improve the bottom line. Therefore, human resource managers must link with employees to make sure that programs are working effectively and with top management to maintain their commitment.

## QUESTIONS

1. A Minnesota jury awarded $60,000 to a former bank teller who said she had suffered emotional damage because she had been pressed by her employer to take a polygraph, or lie-detector, test. The teller, who had passed the test but said she had nightmares afterward, had been questioned about missing funds. With the advantage of hindsight, what would you advise your employer, the Suburban National Bank of Eden Prairie, Minnesota, to do when it suspects internal theft?
2. A Texas insurance company fired its auditor for failing to complete a timely audit. The auditor claimed he could not complete the audit because his employer made claims that could not be verified and that the auditor believed were unrealistic. What would you do if you were the employer? The employee?
3. How might a successful assistance program for handling alcohol-impaired employees be structured?
4. Describe a progressive discipline system.
5. Is employee relations a good substitute for a union?
6. What other organization initiatives discussed in previous chapters could increase employee involvement?
7. How might a study of the cost effectiveness of a conflict resolution system be structured?
8. Do you think job stress should be a compensable factor on which pay systems are based?
9. What actions can individuals take to boost their economic security in the face of changes in employment relationships?

## YOUR TURN
### Saks Fifth Avenue

A former security guard for the fashionable Saks Fifth Avenue store in New York City is back in prison for sexual assault. This is his second conviction for a violent sex crime. While employed at Saks, he raped a 27-year-old assistant manager in her office. She did not report the first rape. Only after she was attacked again five days later and had an emotional breakdown did she go to the police.

Her attacker is now in jail, and the victim is suing the store for negligence. She says:

- Had the store done a better job of checking his background before hiring him, the store would have uncovered the previous conviction.
- He sexually harassed another woman at Saks before she herself was raped.
- The retailer negligently hired, retained, and supervised her attacker.

She further alleges that Saks intentionally failed to take action against the guard or warn or protect her from him. If the court allows this claim to stand, it will enable the woman to pursue the case in court rather than in the workers' compensation system.
Sak's position is to ask the judge to dismiss the woman's lawsuit. The store says:

- The filing of the lawsuit prevents the store from commenting on the hiring process.
- Because the incidents occurred at the store, the woman's only recourse is to pursue a worker's compensation claim.
- Allowing the lawsuit to go forward, in which the woman claims her injuries "didn't arise out of and in the course of employment . . . would render meaningless the entire workers' compensation system."

In response to the charge that Saks intentionally failed to take action, the store says that not only is there no support for the claim, but the woman waited too long to make it. The claim is merely a ploy to circumvent the legal requirement of filing her claim in the workers' compensation system where damages she could receive would be limited to lost wages and medical expenses.

Discuss the implications of a legal ruling in favor of the former employee.

Discuss the implications of a legal ruling in favor of the employer.

## NOTES AND REFERENCES

1. Reported by Charles Osgood, CBS radio network, March 9, 1996.
2. Thomas A. Kochan, Harry Katz, and Robert McKersie, *The Transformation of American Industrial Relations* (New York: Basic Books, 1986).
3. Charlene Marmer Solomon, "The Loyalty Factor," *Personnel Journal,* Sept. 1992, pp. 52–62.
4. William E. Wymer and Joseph A. Parente, "Employee Surveys: What Employers Are Doing and What Works," *Employment Relations Today,* Winter 1991/92, pp.-477–84.
5. *Business Week* February 20, 1995, p. 8.
6. Anne B. Fisher, "Employees Left Holding the Bag," *Fortune,* May 20, 1991, pp. 83–93.
7. Mike Parker and Jane Slaughter, *Choosing Sides: Unions and the Team Concept* (Detroit: Labor Notes/South End Press, 1988); Harry

Katz, *Shifting Gears: Changing Labor Relations in the U.S. Auto Industry* (Cambridge, MA: MIT Press, 1985).

8. Adrienne E. Eaton, "Factors Contributing to the Survival of Employee Participation Programs in Unionized Settings, *Industrial and Labor Relations Review* April 1994, pp. 371–89.
9. David F. Girard-di Carlo, Caren E. I. Naidoff, and Michael J. Hanlon, "Legal Traps in Employee Committees," *Labor Law Journal,* Oct. 1992, pp. 671–78; *Viewpoint: The Global Quest for Quality* (New York: Ernst & Young International, 1992).
10. Edward E. Lawler III, Susan Albers Mohrman, and Gerald E. Ledford, Jr., *Employee Involvement and Total Quality Management* (San Francisco: Jossey-Bass, 1992).
11. Jan Pierce, John Newstrom, Randall Dunham, and Alison Barber, *Alternative Work Schedules* (Boston: Allyn & Bacon, 1989); "The Changing Workplace: New Directions in Staffing and Scheduling," BNS Response Center, 9435 Key West Ave., Rockville, MD 20850, 1986; Diane S. Rothberg, "Part-Time Professionals: The Flexible Work Force," *Personnel Administrator,* Aug. 1986, pp. 27–39; Thomas J. Nardone, "Part-Time Workers: Who Are They?" *Monthly Labor Review,* Feb. 1986, pp. 13–19.
12. Joseph DeGiuseppe, Jr., "Flexible Work Arrangements: An Emerging Area of Law," *Benefits Law Journal,* Spring 1992, pp. 25–40.
13. Eileen Appelbaum, "Part-Time and Contingent Work: The Growing Dilemma for U.S. Workers" (address to Annual Meeting of National Committee on Pay Equity, Washington, DC, Dec. 6, 1991).
14. Janina C. Latack and Lawrence W. Foster, "Implementation of Compressed Work Schedules: Participation and Job Redesign as Critical Factors for Employee Acceptance," *Personnel Psychology* 38 (1985), pp. 75–92.
15. Robert Calem, "Working at Home, for Better or Worse," *New York Times,* Apr. 18, 1993, section C, p. 1.
16. Lotte Bailyn, *Breaking the Mold: Women, Men and Time in the New Corporate World* (New York: Free Press, 1993); Constance Perin, "The Moral Fabric of the Office: Panoptical Discourse and Schedule Flexibilities," *Research in the Sociology of Organizations,* vol. 8: Greenwich, CT: JAI Press, 1991), pp. 241–68; Pamela S. Tolbert and Tal Simons, "The Impact of Working at Home on Career Outcomes of Professional Employees," Working Paper 94-04, Cornell University Center for Advanced Human Resource Studies, Ithaca, NY, 1994.
17. S. L. Grover and K. J. Crooker, "Who Appreciates Family-Responsive Human Resource Policies: The Impact of Family-Friendly Policies on the Organizational Attachment of Parents and Non-Parents," *Personnel Psychology* 48 (1995), pp. 271–88.
18. Douglas R. May and Catherine E. Schwoerer, "Employee Health by Design: Using Employee Involvement Teams in Ergonomic Job Redesign," *Personnel Psychology* 47, 1 (1994), pp. 861–76.
19. Martin E. Personick and Ethel C. Jackson, "Injuries and Illnesses in the Workplace, 1990," *Monthly Labor Review,* Apr. 1992, pp. 37–38.

20. Amy K. Rajala, Jennifer L. DeNicolis, Ellyn G. Brecher, and Donald A. Hantula, "Investing in Occupational Safety: A Utility Analysis Perspective," presented at Eastern Academy of Management Meeting, 1995.
21. John W. Ruser and Robert S. Smith, "Reestimating OSHA's Effects: Have the Data Changed?" *Journal of Human Resources* 26, no. 2, pp. 212–35.
22. "North Carolina Fire Sparks National Outcry," *AFL-CIO News,* Sept. 16, 1991, pp. 1–12.
23. Kenneth Sovereign, *Personnel Law* (Englewood Cliffs, NJ: Prentice Hall, 1989).
24. Sandra E. Gleason and Karen Roberts, "The Impact of Union Membership on Perceptions of Procedural Justice of Injured Workers," *Proceedings of the Forty-Fourth Annual Meeting of the Industrial Relations Research Association,* 1992.
25. Columbia University, Department of Industrial Engineering and Operation Research, reported in the *New York Times,* Feb. 21, 1987.
26. *Privacy in the Workplace: When Employer-Employee Rights Collide* (New York: Alexander Hamilton Institute, 1987).
27. Information on the video "AIDS in the Workplace: Epidemic of Fear" can be obtained from the San Francisco AIDS Foundation, 333 Valencia St., San Francisco, CA 94103. John P, Kohl, Alan N. Miller, and Norval F. Phol, "Development of Personnel Policies to Deal with the Aids Crisis: A Study of the Practices and Procedures of Business Firms Today," *Labor Law Journal,* Feb. 1991, pp. 116–20.
28. David E. Terpstra and Douglas D. Baker, "Outcomes of Federal Court Decisions on Sexual Harassment," *Academy of Management Journal,* Mar. 1992, pp. 181–90.
29. Stephanie Riger, "Gender Dilemmas in Sexual Harassment Policies and Procedures," *American Psychologist,* May 1991, pp. 497–505.
30. E. LaFontaine and L. Tredeau, "The Frequency, Sources, and Correlates of Sexual Harassment among Women in Traditional Male Occupations," *Sex Roles* 15, (1986), pp. 433–42. The February 1993 issue of the *Journal of Vocational Behavior* is devoted entirely to sexual harassment in the workplace. The issue is edited by Howard E. A. Tinsley and Margaret S. Stockdale.
31. Eric Rolfe Greenberg, "Workplace Testing: Results of a New AMA Survey," *Personnel,* Apr. 1988, pp. 36–44.
32. *Employee Assistance Quarterly* 3 (1993), no. 3–4, is devoted entirely to the topic of evaluating employee assistance programs.
33. *Essays on American Industrialism: Selected Papers of Samuel M. Levin* (Detroit: Wayne State University, 1973).
34. Michael M. Harris and Michael L. Trusty, "Drug and Alcohol Programs in the Workplace: A Review of Recent Literature," *1997 International Review of Industrial and Organizational Psychology.* I. Robertson and C. Cooper, ed (New York: John Wiley, 1997).

35. Brian S. Klaas and Gregory G. Dell Omo, "The Determinants of Disciplinary Decisions: The Case of Employee Drug Use," *Personnel Psychology* 44, pp. 813–22; Michael M. Harris and Laura L. Heft, "Alcohol and Drug Use in the Workplace: Issues, Controversies, and Directions for Future Research," *Journal of Management* 18, no. 2 (1992), pp. 239–66.

36. Donna Blancero, "Nonunion Grievance Systems: Perceptions of Fairness." *Proceedings of the Forty-Fourth Annual Meeting of the Industrial Relations Research Association,* 1992, pp. 458–64; Jerald Greenberg, "A Taxonomy of Organizational Justice Theories," *Academy of Management Review,* Jan. 1987, pp. 9–22.

37. S. Antonio Ruiz-Quintanilla and Donna Blancero, "Open Door Policies: Measuring Impact Using Attitude Surveys," Working Paper 95-26, Cornell University Center for Advanced Human Resource Studies, Ithaca, NY, 1995.

38. P. Feuille and D. R. Chachere, "Looking Fair or Being Fair: Remedial Voice Procedures in Nonunion Workplaces," *Journal of Management* 21, no. 1 (1995), pp. 27–42.

39. Brian S. Klaas and D. C. Feldman, "The Impact of Appeal System Structure on Disciplinary Decisions," *Personnel Psychology* 47 (1994), pp. 91–108.

40. Steven C. Curral, "Labor-Management Trust: Its Dimensions and Correlates," *Proceedings of the Forty-Fourth Annual Meeting of the Industrial Relations Research Association,* 1992, pp. 465–74; Antonio LoFaro, "E. C. Social Policy and 1993: The Dark Side of European Integration?" *Comparative Labor Law Journal* 14, no. 1 (1992), pp. 1–32.

41. Robin Remick, "Reshaping Public and Private Policies to Reflect the Changing Nature of Work," working paper, Cornell University Center for Advanced Human Resource Studies, Ithaca, NY, 1993.

42. Roy J. Adams, "The Right to Participate," *Employee Responsibilities and Rights Journal* 5, no. 2 (1992), pp. 91–99; Joseph A. Schumpeter, *Capitalism, Socialism and Democracy,* 2nd ed. (New York: Harper, 1947).

43. Harry C. Katz, Thomas A. Kochan, and Kenneth R. Gobeille, "Industrial Relations Performance, Economic Performance, and QWL Programs: An Interplant Analysis," *Industrial and Labor Relations Review,* Oct. 1983, pp. 3–17.

44. Janice Beyer and Harrison Trice, "The Best/Worst Technique for Measuring Work Performance in Organizational Research," *Organizational Behavior and Statistics,* May 1984, pp. 1–21.

45. Casey Ichniowski, Kathryn Shaw, and Giovanna Prennushi, *The Effects of Human Resource Management Practices on Productivity* (Cambridge, MA.: National Bureau of Economic Research, 1995).

# The Evolving Human Resource Management Profession

*Nestling warm and sleepily in your company, like the asp in Cleopatra's bosom, is a department whose employees spend 80 percent of their time on routine administrative tasks. Nearly every function of this department can be performed more expertly for less by others. Chances are its leaders are unable to describe their contribution to value added except in trendy, unquantifiable, and wannabe terms—yet, like a serpent unaffected by its own venom, the department frequently dispenses to others advice on how to eliminate work that does not add value. It is also an organization where the average advertised salary for professional staffers increased 30 percent last year. I am describing, of course, your human resource department and have a modest proposal: Why not blow the sucker up?*

*—Thomas A. Stewart, "Taking on the Last Bureaucracy,"* Fortune, *Jan. 15, 1996.*

Suppose that one of your professors, not familiar with human resource management, showed you the article from *Fortune* and asked you to comment on it. Or, suppose that after you take a job in an organization, one of your managers brings you such an article, asking, "After all of your training in human resource management, can you tell me why we don't just abolish HR departments?" What would you say?

After reading the earlier chapters, you would probably guess that the authors of this book would say it's wrong to abolish HR departments. You have seen how important human resources are for accomplishing organizational goals. You have seen the quotes by leading top managers showing that they believe human resources are the key to achieving success, and that organizations ultimately stand or fall on the quality of the work and decisions made by their people. Finally, you have learned how managers can diagnose critical human resource issues, the key techniques that are used to build and improve the human capital of the organization, and the evidence that investing in people can and does have an impact on equity and efficiency. With such a wealth of knowledge and evidence, how can it be that columnists in leading business publications can still propose abolishing the HR department?

There are very good reasons why the traditional HR "department" may be an endangered species, particularly if it focuses on carrying out activities and administering processes. It goes back to our theme of "doing the right things" versus "doing things right." Increasingly, many of the administrative activities of human resources can be performed better by outside companies, line managers, or even the employees themselves. Doing payroll checks, changing employee personal data, or administering selection tests can be done "right" by internal HR professionals, but more frequently the "right thing" is to let outsiders do those things, and develop HR professionals within the company who can concentrate on doing the right things.

For example, Nucor Steel has become one of the best known steel "minimills," in part because the company claims to have no HR organization. Personnel manager James Coblin says that most plants have "no job description, no performance appraisals, and no human resource personnel and purchasing departments. The department manager does all the hiring, firing and purchasing." The secret? Coblin credits the company's incentive compensation plan, which typically pays production workers $9 an hour; in addition it pays 5 percent bonus for every ton of steel produced beyond the base quota. One crew has a quota of eight tons of steel and their machine has a capacity of 10 tons per hour, but the team has averaged 37 to 42 tons per hour. If employees are late, they lose that day's bonus. If they are absent or more than an hour late, they lose the bonus for the week. Not surprisingly, tardiness and absence are low.[1]

Of course, low tardiness and absence are only two indicators of HR effectiveness, and many leading companies would find it difficult to manage their workers solely on an incentive pay system. Still, the idea is appealing of having the plant manager responsible for staffing and giving employees maximum incentives and empowerment to do a good job. What's going on in HR anyway?

In this final chapter, we examine the changing HR profession, and the changing nature of the HR "function" within organizations. Recall Exhibit 5.3, where you saw how one element of an integrated HR plan includes deciding how to organize the human resource "department." This department traditionally contained a large number of HR professionals dedicated to the organization. Today, it increasingly includes line managers, employees, and outside service providers, so even calling it a "department" doesn't seem to fit; perhaps "function" is more appropriate. We'll discuss how organizations are working to organize and staff the function, so that it focuses on the doing the right things, including issues such as where HR professionals are located and to whom they report, the needed competencies for future HR professionals the way HR information is gathered and used, and how to track the success of the function. If you are interested in a career in the HR field, this chapter will help you understand the exciting and changing roles played by future HR professionals, as well as how to prepare for those roles.

## THE HR FUNCTION: FROM "ONE FOREMAN" TO "GLOBALLY HIGH-FLEX"

What form will the HR function take in the future? Historical perspective may be helpful, and instructive.[2]

### Industrial Model

As it turns out, Nucor Steel's approach is nothing new. The first HR practitioners were the foremen, who hired, fired, and supervised their workers. Over time, more specialized HR roles took shape. The 1920s saw "personnel departments" emerge as a result of labor shortages, the development of psychological testing, and increased attention to scientific studies of work, such as those by Frederick W. Taylor. Manufacturers of war material during World War I were required to have a personnel department. While the Great Depression of the 1930s decreased the attention paid to HR, the subsequent rise of unions and strike activity spawned more specialization—this time in the form of negotiators and labor relations specialists. World War II created production pressures, labor shortages, and the need for the military to select, train, and deploy huge numbers of people. Wartime restrictions on wage increases were the key motivation to develop "fringe" benefits, as yet another specialty emerged. During the 1950s, increasing unionism and strike activity led employers to search for ways to reduce unrest and codify the employment relationship. This led to the *industrial model* of human relations, with its focus on work rules, clear job ladders, seniority-based rewards, and administration of often complex contractual employment relationships. Performance appraisal systems, merit grids, and other specialized bureaucratic rules created a strong demand for HR specialists. At the same time, the Hawthorne experiments, a classic study of group behavior conducted in the 1920s and 1930s at the Hawthorne Works of the Western Electric Company in Chicago, showed that paying attention to employees could increase productivity and morale, so another set of processes was designed to enhance employment relations, such as job enlargement, employee communications, and so on.[3]

## Investment Model

The 1960s and 1970s saw a shift from the focus on labor relations to personnel management, and the emergence of the "personnel professional." Legislation was the key impetus to this development. As you have read, much of the equal employment opportunity legislation was passed in the 1960s, creating a need for professionals who could interpret the law and implement appropriate policies. There was also a shift in focus from traditional manufacturing organizations with largely unionized employees to fast-growing, technology-based companies relying on the knowledge of their workers who often were nonunion. In the 1960s and 1970s, the best examples were IBM and Eastman Kodak. Today, the list would include Microsoft, Intel and Disney. The *investment model* emerged, with a focus on giving employees discretion (compared with controlling them), enriching jobs, lifetime employment, and heavy investments in employee socialization and long-term compensation relationships. Morale became a key indicator of success, and the idea of HR as an integrated set of activities designed to help employees and the organization achieve its goals became accepted. The activities, discussed in earlier chapters, became well developed in the 1960s and 1970s; they usually were implemented by internal managers in human resource departments, who advised line managers, monitored practices for consistency and compliance, and even exercised financial responsibility for pay and benefits. Hordes of clerical employees processed the growing paperwork that came with this growing bureaucracy.

## Involvement Model

The 1980s and 1990s brought greater economic pressures and the realization that U.S. businesses and workers faced increasing and ongoing global competition—and opportunities. HR has not been immune to these pressures, as you have seen. One response has been the *involvement model,* with increasing employee involvement through enriched jobs, teams, high trust, and mutual goals, all of which are supported by careful selection, stable employment, a commitment to provide development opportunities, incentive pay, flexible benefits, and extensive communication. The era of the more self-reliant employee has emerged, in which employees take more of the responsibility and the risks in the employment relationship. Unlike the "child" employee, protected and instructed in return for loyalty and conformity, the "self-reliant" model is based on a more independent philosophy. The employee is free to build careers in new ways, to compete openly for opportunities, to share ideas, and to seek out opportunities for development. The employer makes few guarantees but provides pay structured to reward performance, many development opportunities, and a flexible approach to evaluating the worth of employees which does not depend on traditional hierarchies or reward structures. The role of HR in such organizations is evolving from the traditional advisor to top management and administrator of programs, to a much closer connection with the employees and the leaders of the business units. The involvement model relies on the idea that most employees still prefer to work for a single organization and that human resource management will still emanate from inside the organization. The increasing importance of people in the involvement model is an argument for more HR professionals within organizations.

## High-Flex Model

Even more radical models are emerging. Earlier chapters described how "reengineering" fundamentally examines how work is done. The same processes are being applied to HR. If work processes are moving toward flexible teams, why not reengineer activities such as selection, rewards, training, and communications, so that teams can do it themselves? If another organization can train your employees more cheaply or better, because it is dedicated to training, why not simply pay them to do it and abolish your internal training programs? If Touch-Tone telephones or personal computers can allow people to check their pension fund balances or update personal information, why is it necessary to have human resource administrators doing that? The result may be a *high-flex model* of the HR function, in which the organization is a loosely coupled set of alliances. Consider how the Rolling Stones or Phish put together a concert tour. They don't create the "Phish Corporation." Instead, they locate talented freelancers to handle travel, bookings, technical support, and all the other requirements. After the tour, these people move on to other projects. Can HR be operated in the same way? You have seen how activities such as benefits, selection, training, and pay system design can now be accomplished or enhanced by computers or outside consultants. Many organizations see this as the future.

Exhibit 16.1 depicts the ongoing transformation. Centralized and uniform HR is the tradition, with a large corporate staff to determine uniform policies for the organization. Those policies are then carried out and implemented by HR administrators assisting the business units. The creativity and authority rests at the corporate level. Decentralized and flexible HR may be evolving toward very small corporate staffs and made up mainly of a "SWAT" team of leaders with broad experience and knowledge about the business and its units. This leadership team chiefly provides broad guidance within which the business units determine policy. The "action" in the decentralized model rests with HR "account managers" and "vendors." The account managers serve as internal consultants to the business units, fashioning HR policies as needed to fit the business needs. Close alliances are formed with vendors who provide specialized knowledge and services (e.g., payroll, information systems, benefits administration). Notice the importance of the alliances in the decentralized model. Certain HR functions are indeed outsourced to the vendors, but these vendors become important contributors to organizational success. Outsourcing to the cheapest competitor just to cut costs is a recipe for disaster. Instead,

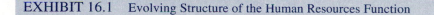

EXHIBIT 16.1 Evolving Structure of the Human Resources Function

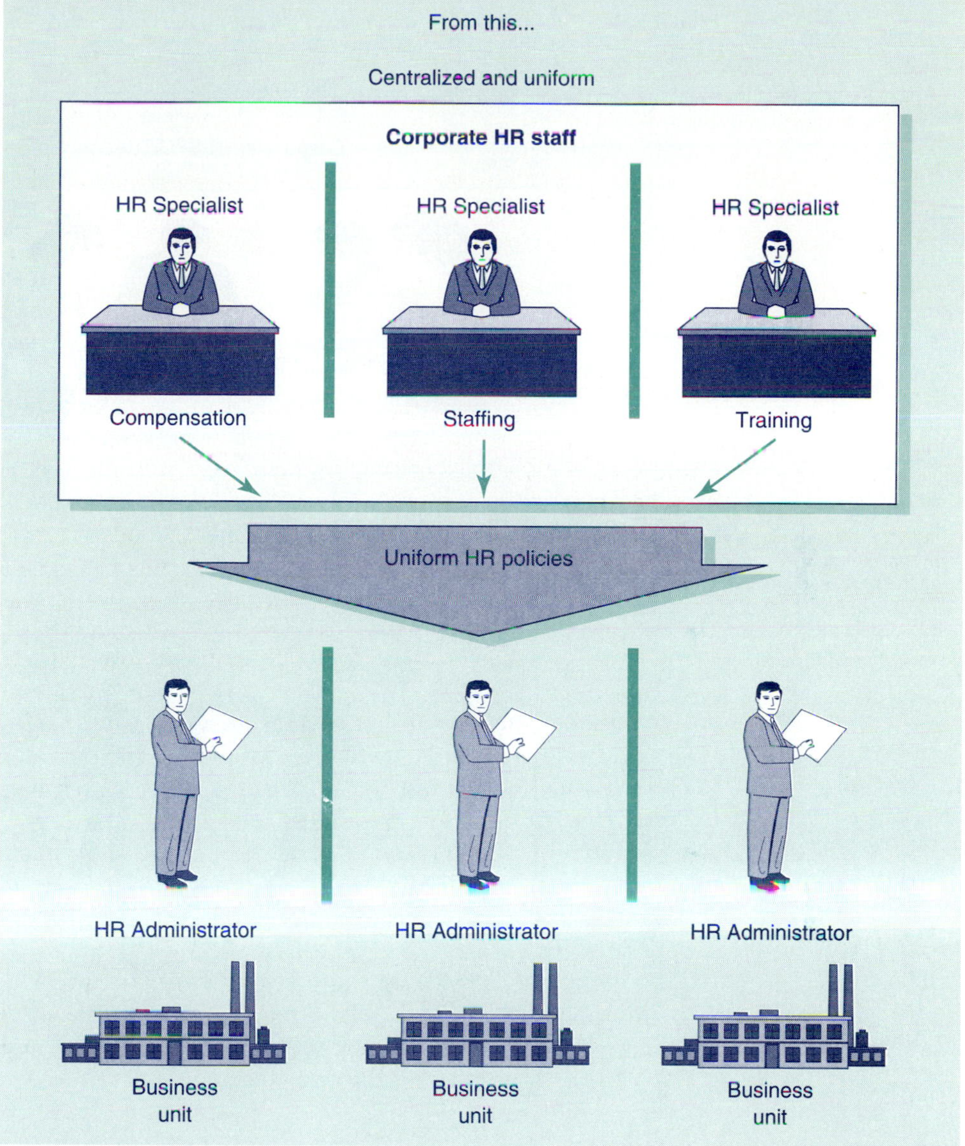


*Exhibit 16.1 continued on next page.*

carefully planned relationships with a few outside partners may become the norm. This approach has proven successful not only in maintaining the quality of service, but also in cutting costs.[4]

Has the HR function disappeared? No. Every organization must still identify, acquire, develop, reward, and nurture its human resources. The need for a diagnostic approach to HR doesn't disappear. However, as the decentralized model shows, organizations in the future may find that capability either inside or outside the organization, or even in the hands of managers and employees themselves. Therefore, it is important to understand the key capabilities on which HR will be built.

EXHIBIT 16.1 *Continued*

## THE BUILDING BLOCKS: HUMAN RESOURCE COMPETENCIES

We have dealt with the issue of competencies before. "Core competencies," such as understanding propulsion systems at Honda and computer chip technology at Intel, or how to make people feel like guests at Hyatt hotels or McDonald's restaurants, were defined as the key capabilities organizations need to compete effectively. We have seen how such competencies may imply certain skills and abilities among employees, and how HR can use those to better select, develop, reward, appraise, and communicate with employees. The same idea can be applied to those who carry out human resource activities, whether they are line managers or employees.

Human resource professionals need three general competencies:

- *Knowledge of the business,* which reflects understanding financial, strategic, technological, and organizational issues.
- *Delivery of HR practices,* which includes the ability to properly create and implement HR activities such as staffing, compensation, training, organizational design, labor relations, and communication.
- *Management of change,* which reflects the ability to make change happen (build relationships, manage data, lead, and influence), and to understand the needed changes (innovativeness and creativity).[5]

Considering the three competencies listed here, how should organization leaders ensure high-quality HR professionals? If you were hiring a vice president of HR, what questions would you ask candidates? If your college or university offers a degree in HR, does it reflect these competencies?

A survey of 1,400 leading companies asked those who work with HR professionals to rate their performance and to rate how much of each competency the professionals had. The competencies most related to performance perceptions were (in order) management of change, delivery of HR, and knowledge of the business. There was a small amount of evidence that organizations that had increased their HR competencies over a three-year period often had increased performance.[6]

Another way to look at HR competencies is to think about how they apply across different roles for HR professionals, and how careers might build competencies over time. Eastman Kodak surveyed its HR managers and employees who interact with them in order to identify competencies for the future and "clusters" of competencies that might define future HR roles. Exhibit 16.2 shows the results of Kodak's analysis. Notice how the two role titles, "Human Resource Competency Practitioner" and "Human Resource Initiative Leader," are very different from traditional titles emphasizing individual activities, such as "compensation manager," "benefits counselor," or "labor negotiator." Also notice how the competencies reflect results (problems solved) or general capabilities (vision) instead of specific HR tasks. Finally, notice how the two roles share some competencies but not others, perhaps suggesting that careers can be built by having people spend time in each role. If you have a job interview with Kodak, don't be surprised to find an HR competency practitioner conducting the interview or helping you if you decide to join the organization.

HR professionals must have information to carry out their roles and to support the new and changing business structures. You have read how every HR activity relies on information to diagnose gaps, choose appropriate strategies and activities, and evaluate results. You can't manage something in the dark, so information is indeed power in human resource management. Thousands of pieces of information might be used to help manage human resources, so HR professionals need a system to organize it and make it valuable.

## HUMAN RESOURCE INFORMATION SYSTEMS

Have you ever seen the computer kiosks outside Levi Strauss stores in shopping malls? Nationwide, these kiosks provide interactive multimedia presentations that show customers video clips of products, product information, and music in

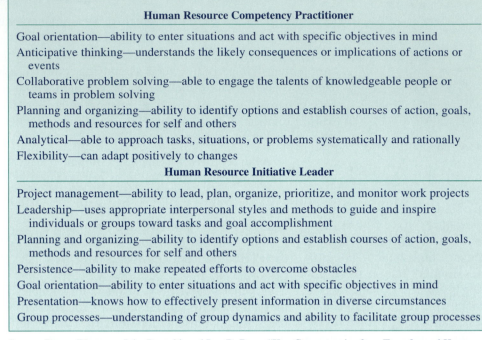

## EXHIBIT 16.2 Eastman Kodak's Human Resource Roles and Competencies

**Human Resource Competency Practitioner**

Goal orientation—ability to enter situations and act with specific objectives in mind

Anticipative thinking—understands the likely consequences or implications of actions or events

Collaborative problem solving—able to engage the talents of knowledgeable people or teams in problem solving

Planning and organizing—ability to identify options and establish courses of action, goals, methods and resources for self and others

Analytical—able to approach tasks, situations, or problems systematically and rationally

Flexibility—can adapt positively to changes

**Human Resource Initiative Leader**

Project management—ability to lead, plan, organize, prioritize, and monitor work projects

Leadership—uses appropriate interpersonal styles and methods to guide and inspire individuals or groups toward tasks and goal accomplishment

Planning and organizing—ability to identify options and establish courses of action, goals, methods and resources for self and others

Persistence—ability to make repeated efforts to overcome obstacles

Goal orientation—ability to enter situations and act with specific objectives in mind

Presentation—knows how to effectively present information in diverse circumstances

Group processes—understanding of group dynamics and ability to facilitate group processes

Source: Donna Blancero, John Boroski, and Lee D. Dyer, "Key Competencies for a Transformed Human Resource Organization at Eastman Kodak Company." *Human Resource Management,* forthcoming, 1996.

response to each customer's requests. Levi Strauss employees have OLIVER—On-Line Interactive Visual Employee Resource—an interactive computer network that allows all 2,500 employees to contact the central computer through their PCs to look at more than 500 screens of information on pay and benefits.[7] Major hotels, rental car agencies, and supermarkets use computer kiosks to provide information, to help customers fill out forms, or to provide a map directing them to the beer and pretzels. At companies such as Mobil, Harris Corporation, and Banc One, kiosks (often with touch-screen technology) allow employees to find out their outstanding balances on company-provided loans, calculate costs of a possible relocation, change their enrollment in the company savings plan, and get answers to questions about their benefits. Applicants can even apply for jobs with the company.[8] IBM has developed a multimedia selection test that presents applicants with video-action cases (such as seeing a co-worker deliberately hide a problem or mistake from a boss). Applicants then answer questions about what they would do by typing in their answers. The test does not yet feature a hall of fame showing the high scorers' initials.

The Internet presents astounding possibilities to reach employees and potential employees, as you have read in the chapters featuring on-line recruiting and other applications. Thus, while the majority of HR information systems are still only as sophisticated as the systems that generate a doctor's bill, their sophistication and scope are increasing rapidly. A CAT scanner or magnetic resonance imager (MRI) for HR is not yet on the horizon, but perhaps soon will be. However, the key to the value of information systems lies less in the technology and more on the principles on which these systems are built. Technology will continue to change, but the principles provide a constant guide.

## What Is a Human Resource Information System?

A *human resource information system* (HRIS) is a systematic procedure for collecting, storing, maintaining, retrieving, and validating data needed by an organization about its human resources, personnel activities, and organization unit characteristics.[9]

The HRIS need not be complex or even computerized. It can be as informal as the payroll records and time cards of a small boutique or restaurant, or as extensive and formal as the computerized human resource databases of major manufacturers, banks, and governments. HRISs can support planning with information for labor supply and demand forecasts; staffing with information on equal employment, separations, and applicant qualifications; and development with information on training program costs and trainee work performance. HRISs can also support compensation with information on pay increases, salary forecasts, and pay budgets; and labor/employee relations with information on contract negotiations and employee assistance needs. In every case, their purpose is to provide information that is either required by human resource stakeholders or supports human resource decisions.

## Information System Value: The Three C's

Exhibit 16.3 shows how HR information systems can add value along three dimensions—the "three C's." Each axis represents a different aspect of HR system value added. An HR information system or application can be located in the three-dimensional space, according to how it adds value.

### Communication

The first dimension, *communication,* shown on the vertical axis, has to do with how information gets into and out of the system. At the bottom are applications that use a local and single-medium approach, such as a spreadsheet operating on one person's PC. At the top are applications that go outside the organization and machine boundaries, using multiple media to communicate. This might include Internet-based recruiting through which applicants can submit résumés from anywhere in the world, or multimedia training on demand using CD-ROMS or on-line networks. Federal Express is famous for its on-line training network.

### Change

The second dimension is *change,* shown on the front-to-back axis. At the front are systems that contribute by cutting the costs of existing HR activities such as gathering information. Some information is gathered to satisfy an external stakeholder's requirement. Examples of this information include EEO forms describing minority and women representation, pay and benefit information related to unemployment compensation, wages and hours, or pensions. Other information is gathered because it is required to fulfill the employment relationship. Examples of this kind of information include payroll and employee benefit information needed to

EXHIBIT 16.3 Information System Value Dimensions

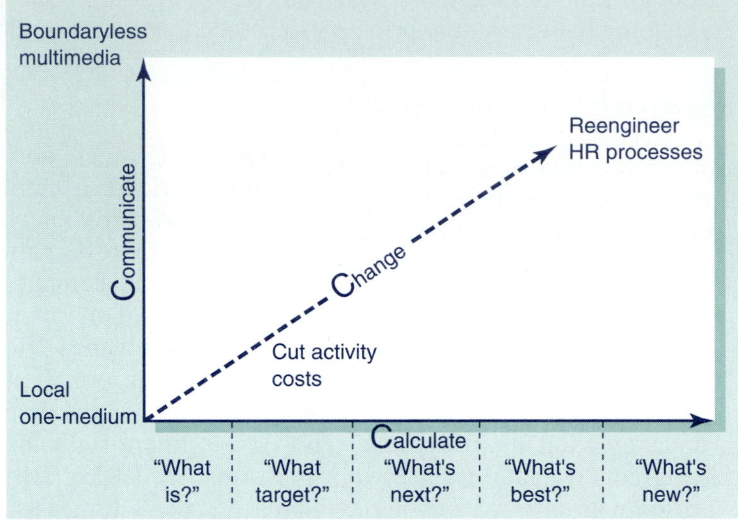


Source: John W. Boudreau. "HRIS: Exploiting its full potential," *HRMonthly The Australian Human Resources Magazine,* Summer 1995, pp. 8–13.

issue employee paychecks. Most HRISs begin with this required information; many of the computerized enhancements to information systems are designed to produce this information faster or at a lower cost. The benefits of the information are obvious—the organization would not be allowed to continue in business if it didn't use the information to produce the required reports or payments. Therefore, attention focuses on producing the information and completing the reports at the lowest cost. These kinds of applications are *administrative* because they emphasize doing administrative tasks faster, with less paper, or with fewer people. They are by far the most common HRIS applications because their value is relatively easy to calculate and the savings are tangible. Compaq Computer Company's experience is typical. Before computerizing their report distribution activities, Compaq's HR managers distributed 600 reports annually to 150 recipients. After computerizing, they distributed 7,200 reports annually to 600 recipients, saving an estimated $47,304 annually compared with the old manual reporting system. At Westin Hotels, computer integration saved more than $100,000 in processing fees and eliminated seven full-time staff positions.[10] However, saving money on traditional activities is not necessarily wise if those activities don't add value in the first place. It's important to use systems to do the right things, not just to do the old things better.

At the back of Exhibit 16.3 is the other end of the change dimension, "reengineering HR processes." You have seen examples of this type of reengineering in earlier chapters. Recall how the process of recruitment was fundamentally changed by allowing applicants to learn about companies and submit résumés over the Internet, changing the process from paper processing to remote communication. Think of how the training function is reengineered when technology allows employees to receive training wherever they are through networks, instead of in the traditional classroom. Finally, recall how companies such as Levi Strauss reengineered the way employees learn about benefits such as life insurance, pensions, and health care by allowing employees to log into computerized and graphical locations, where they can click on icons that link to constantly updated information. The process changed from a focus on human counselors answering routine questions in person to one in which employees answer the routine questions themselves, leaving HR professionals to concentrate on the tough questions that the system can't handle.

### Calculate

The final dimension, *calculate,* shown on the horizontal axis of Exhibit 16.3 has to do with how information is processed and how the user relates to it. At the left of this dimensions, the information system helps the user to know "what is," or the current state of things. Simple head-count summaries, reports of pay or training costs, or tallies of the numbers of employees in EEO categories all fit here. "What target?" is the next level, which adds a target or goal to show the gap between what is and what's expected. Now the user can focus on the key gaps and priorities. The third level, "what's next," adds forecasting to the system. Here an employee, manager, or HR professional can use the system to project possible future conditions. Examples would include computerized Markov analyses, as discussed in Chapter Five on planning, or forecasts of health care costs discussed in Chapter Thirteen on benefits. The fourth level, "what's best," reflects systems that not only forecast the future, but recommend a course of action. Typical examples might include expert systems that help line managers appraise performance and ensure compliance with the law, or systems that gather information about employees and use decision rules to recommend appropriate benefits. Finally, at the extreme right is "what's new." Here the system provides users with friendly ways to "move" through lots of information, so that they can explore relationships and perhaps discover new trends and patterns. A simple example might be a computerized statistics package that quickly identifies associations between different variables such as age, performance, pay, and gender. The user can ask the system to display these relationships in many different forms. A futuristic example occurs on *Star Trek, Deep Space Nine,* when Dax or Commander Sisco asks the computer to identify all ships leaving within the last 48 hours, then to identify any ships that carry Klingon registry, and to further identify any that have a Ferengi life form.

Generally, HR systems and applications evolve from the lower-left front to the upper-right back area of Exhibit 16.3. Few HR systems are as engaging as Zoop!, but things are improving beyond the old days of static paper reports or eye-straining spreadsheets.

## Designing the HRIS

No single best way to design and implement an HRIS has emerged. Exhibit 16.4 shows the process used by Chevron, TRW, and other corporations. It is widely agreed that the first and most important step is specifying the system requirements, especially the target users and the decisions the system is designed to support. These specifications include decisions about the type of data to collect, the amount of data to collect, how to collect the data, and when to collect it.

EXHIBIT 16.4 The HRIS Design Process at TRW

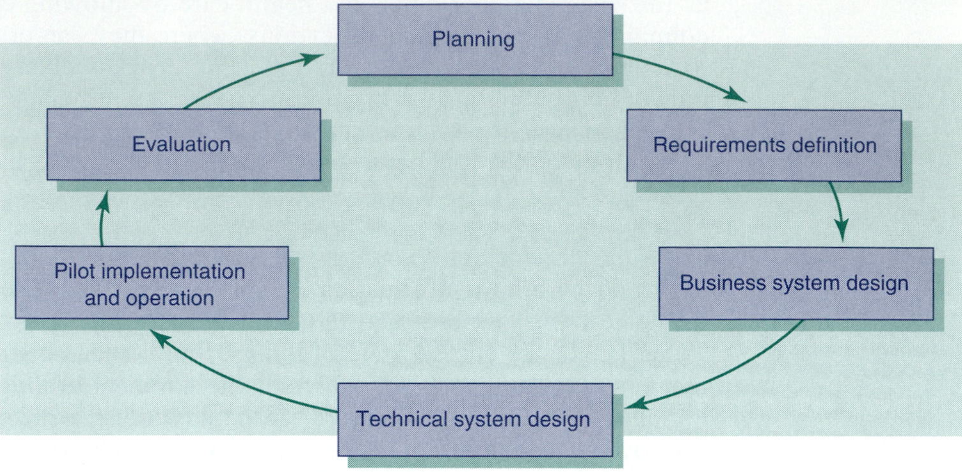


The next step is business system design. It involves answering questions about who will use the system, how they will access it, how it will be updated, and so on. Technical design includes software system development and programming. Then the system is tested at certain locations and evaluated. Once in operation, the system is evaluated, improvements are planned, and the process begins again.[11]

Many attempts to develop a HRIS start and stop at trying to determine the data requirements. Typically, a newly hired personnel specialist's first assignment is to visit all possible users and find out their data needs. An enormous wish list can result, containing so many items that the project is crushed by its own weight. Exhibit 16.5 lists typical data elements for a HRIS in alphabetical order. Even this list is not complete. In Australia for example, Coca-Cola Amatil suggested that its information system should include information on the type of automobile provided to executives. Apparently, executives have been known to roam the parking garages to discover whether any of their peers managed to negotiate extra features or more luxurious models. Automobile features had become an important reward and symbol of organization standing. Clearly, the principles of information value should be used to guide the choice of information to include in a HRIS. In addition to the choice of what information to include, the design of the HRIS must also account for organizational and user characteristics.

Increasingly, technology makes it possible to develop HRISs by simultaneously doing many of the processes in Exhibit 16.4. While one area of the HRIS may be in the planning stage, others may be in the pilot implementation stage. Object-oriented programming makes developing prototypes easier, so that users can see mock-ups before the actual systems go on-line, and users can be much more involved in the design process. The process is different for every organization. For example, Exhibit 16.6 shows how two high-technology companies, Hewlett-Packard and Apple Computer, reengineered their HR functions using technology. Notice how the Hewlett-Packard system focused on management

## EXHIBIT 16.5 Typical Data Elements in a Human Resource Information System

Address (work)
Address (home)
Birthdate
Birthplace
Child support deductions
Citizenship
Claim pending (description)
Claim pending (outcome)
Claim pending (court)
Claim pending (date)
Date on current job
Department
Dependent (sex)
Dependent (number of)
Dependent (relationship)
Dependent (birthdate)
Dependent (name)
Discipline (appeal date)
Discipline (type of charge)
Discipline (appeal outcome)
Discipline (date of charge)
Discipline (outcome)
Discipline (hearing date)
Division
Driver's license (number)
Driver's license (state)
Driver's license (exp. date)
Education in progress (date)
Education in progress (type)
Educational degree (date)
Educational degree (type)
Educational minor (minor)
Educational level attained
Educational field (major)
EEO-1 code
Emergency contact (phone)
Emergency contact (name)
Emergency contact (relation)
Emergency contact (address)
Employee weight
Employee number
Employee code
Employee status
Employee height
Employee date of death
Federal job code
Full-time/part-time code
Garnishments
Grievance (type)
Grievance (outcome)
Grievance (filing date)
Handicap status
Health plan coverage
Health plan (no. dependents)
Injury date
Injury type
Job location
Job position number
Job preference
Job title
Job location
Leave of absence start date
Leave of absence end date
Leave of absence type
Life insurance coverage
Marital status
Marriage date
Medical exam (date)
Medical exam (restrictions)
Medical exam (blood type)
Medical exam (outcome)
Miscellaneous deductions
Name
Organizational property
Pay status
Pension plan membership
Performance rating
Performance increase ($)
Performance increase (%)
Phone number (work)
Phone number (home)
Prior service (term, date)
Prior service (hire date)
Prior service (term, reason)
Professional license (type)
Professional license (date)
Race
Rehire code
Religious preference
Salary points
Salary compa ratio
Salary (previous)
Salary change date
Salary change reason
Salary change type
Salary
Salary range
Schools attended
Service date
Service branch
Service discharge type
Service ending rank
Service discharge date
Sex
Sick leave used
Sick leave available
Skill function (type)
Skill subfunction (type)
Skill (number of years)
Skill (proficiency level)
Skill (date last used)
Skill (location)
Skill (supervisory)
Social Security number
Spouse's employment
Spouse's date of death
Spouse's name
Spouse's birthdate
Spouse's sex
Spouse's Social Security number
Start date
Stock plan membership
Supervisor's name
Supervisor's work address
Supervisor's work phone
Supervisor's title
Termination date
Termination reason
Training Schools attended
Training schools (date)
Training schools (field)
Training schools completed
Transfer date
Transfer reason
Union code
Union deductions
United Way deductions
Vacation leave available
Vacation leave used
Veteran status

Source: Reprinted by permission of the publisher from "A Matter of Privacy: Managing Personnel Data in Company Computers," Donald Harris, *Personnel,* Feb. 1987, p. 37. 

**EXHIBIT 16.6** Reengineering HR Technology at Hewlett-Packard and Apple Computer

| | **Hewlett-Packard** | **Apple Computer** |
|---|---|---|
| Reengineered HR processes through information technology | PeopleBase Program is composed of the following components: Employment Management System, Telephone-Activated Benefits System, Management Compensation System, Paperless Wage Review, Training Management System. HR Information System, Personnel Document Management Systems, Optical File Imaging System, International Assignment, Worldwide Employee Data Base, etc. | Apple utilizes information technology to transform the delivery of routine but critical HR processes through desktop tools, phone (HR Helpline), and well-trained HR professionals. Desktop tools consist of four types: transactions (e.g., Merlin, MacFlex, Mac401(k)), information (e.g., AppleLink Extras, HotLinks Postings, Benefits Folders), dialogue (e.g., employee surveys, can we talk), and self-sufficiency tools (e.g., Job Finder, Directory DA, Apple U Catalog). |
| Objectives/benefits | Develop a single, integrated, and cross-functional information system that supports:<br>♦ People management<br>♦ Workforce management<br>♦ HR process improvement<br>♦ Relationships with external stakeholders | Reduced clerical/transaction expenses<br>♦ Increased knowledge-based, problem-solving activities<br>♦ More resources to leverage across organization<br>♦ Higher level of customer satisfaction<br>♦ Increased productivity through standardization |
| Costs involved | PeopleBase is a heavily funded project. But savings in Employment Management System alone provide the funding of the entire project. | Out-of-pocket costs are minimal as new information systems and processes are built upon existing Macintosh infrastructure and products. Staff time from Information System & Technology (IS&T) and HR professionals is required. |
| Implementation | Launched in 1990, the full PeopleBase program will be introduced in a phased, incremental approach over a ten year period. External vendors (e.g., PeopleSoft, Restrac) are involved. | Under the sponsorship of senior vice president of HR, IS&T took the lead in developing new information systems with participation and feedback from HR staff. |
| Key learnings | ♦ Ensure that information technology strategy is linked to clear HR strategy.<br>♦ Sustained sponsorship is critical, along with clear and agreed upon charters, roles, and responsibilities, particularly with respect to process/data ownership.<br>♦ Standardization in equipment, tools, and processes is vital.<br>♦ Seek "early victories" and immediate returns to build credibility and experience. | ♦ Clients are more receptive to embracing innovation when it is accessible, easy to use, and fulfills a primary need.<br>♦ Innovative technology solutions must fit into an overall HR strategy that supports client needs.<br>♦ Patience and courage to stick to the chosen strategy are essential.<br>♦ Any paradigm shift can be threatening because it requires a fundamental change in the way work is done.<br>♦ When there is a broad acceptance and use of technology within an organization, these types of solution can be implemented rapidly if they are good. |

Source: Arthur Yeung and Wayne Brockbank, "Reengineering HR Through Information Technology," Reprinted with permission from *Human Resource Planning* 18, no. 2 (1995), p. 29. Copyright 1995 by The Human Resource Planning Society.

tasks such as wage reviews, training management, and so forth while Apple focused on better delivery of routine services to employees. The objectives are different, but both systems reaped significant savings through more efficient activities, despite the high costs of the systems. Typically, fully developed HRIS systems can cost hundreds of thousands of dollars to develop. Also note the "key learnings" from each company. Clearly, the lessons reflect human issues such as support, credibility, minimizing threats, and early victories, but also they reflect the need to link HR technology to the larger organization and the value of standardization. It's easy to see why designing a HRIS frequently leads to fundamental reorganization for the HR function. Next, we consider the three main HRIS components: input, throughput and output.

## Input: Where Do You Get the Information?

The input function enters information into the HRIS. This includes the procedures such as who collects data, when, and how data are processed. In the past, data entry was often a laborious process requiring clerical staff to sit at a keypunch machine that punched patterns of holes in cards. Each card of 80 columns held only one line of information. Later, electronic links allowed data entry by typing in the information at a computer terminal and sending it electronically to other computers. Today, scanning technology allows computers to scan and store the actual image of the original document, including signatures and handwritten notes. Some scanners are like copy machines; instead of making a paper copy, they can read typed documents and feed the information directly to a computer as if it had been typed in. The quest to eliminate "administrivia," needless clerical tasks performed by humans, often centers on getting information into the system directly from employees and managers. Touch-tone telephone systems are common, much like the systems you access when you order from a catalog or make airline reservations. HR systems, like the system at IBM, use 800 numbers to allow employees to update their personal information. A study of 157 companies showed that the most common use of personal computer technology for human resources was to allow employees to log into a network to update their personal information. There's no reason why such input methods have to be dry and dull. Southwest Airlines, famous for its commitment to fun and informality in the workplace, got Second City, a Chicago comedy troupe, to record messages on its employee benefit phone link. Callers may talk to a psychic, impersonators of Elvis, Tonto, or the Lone Ranger, and those who press the wrong button three times get reprimanded by a phone "cop."[12]

## Data Maintenance and Processing

Once the data are in the system, how do you organize and maintain the system? Where are the data stored? Perhaps the most significant trend in HRIS is the emergence of the network—for years Sun Microsystems has been saying, "the Network's the Thing" in HR. Traditional human resource systems in the 1980s and early 1990s often stored data on a central mainframe computer; there it was accessible only to a few technicians, and it remained highly reliable and controlled. Or the systems were a hodgepodge of custom-designed systems on individual PCs, often scattered across business units and geographic locations, with considerable duplication and questionable reliability but with wide access. The dilemma was to keep the reliability of the centralized system while preserving the accessibility and customization of the more decentralized system. The answer is the "network," as shown in Exhibit 16.7. Notice how a central computer may still be used to integrate information from many company-level functions, such as finance, marketing, production, and human resources. However, this central computer then "serves" data to remote storage areas, which then process and integrate it with HR software, and finally present it to a variety of PCs, each within their own network. It doesn't matter to the PC user where the data came from. It all appears on his or her PC as if it were available locally. However, unlike data that reside on many PCs, updating the central server or the HR software involves only a few computers, not every single PC in the network. When employees at their PCs send data back to the servers, it can be checked at the local level and allowed into the central database only after verification. The users in the local area networks can customize their HR systems by placing the data into their own programs that they create or purchase from outside vendors.

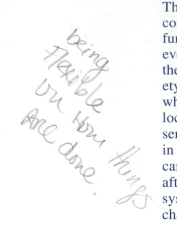

### The Internet and HR

Exhibit 16.7 shows that the Internet also can be a part of the network, offering immense possibilities but some trade-offs. The Internet was originally used primarily by research scientists in government and universities. It had been designed as a communication network for scientists and as a precaution against the loss of other communication networks during a national emergency. In the late 1980s, following the proliferation of personal computer and the development of commercial network providers such as America Online, virtually anyone with a personal computer connected by modem to a telephone line could obtain mail and join discussion groups on virtually any topic. As computers, software, and technology links grew in sophistication, the possibilities for remote communication have grown exponentially. Today, the Internet allows individuals seamless access to repositories of information at virtually very major university or company in the world, as well as the opportunity to send electronic messages to virtually anyone, including the president of the United States.

The *Internet* is a worldwide network of electronic information sources, which can be accessed using personal computers connected by telecommunications technology. Through this network, individuals may send mail, read reference material, share documents electronically, and send computer software directly from one computer to another.

The most exciting aspect of the Internet is the emergence of the World Wide Web. For HR professionals, the Internet offers extraordinary possibilities and the promise to change many HR activities fundamentally. Already, most major companies have Web sites through which potential customer and employees can learn about products and job openings, and can even submit electronic employment applications. Similar job-posting systems exist within many organizations. Commercial sites now exist to provide on-line recruitment, training, and expert advice to any individual who requests it. Major research centers, such as Cornell University's Center for Advanced Human Resource Studies and School of Industrial and Labor Relations, have sites that allow HR professionals to obtain the latest information from governments, academic institutions, and professional associations. Professional organizations, such as the Society for Human Resource Management and the Society for Industrial-Organizational Psychology also

EXHIBIT 16.7 The "Network" Is Key to Future HR Information Systems

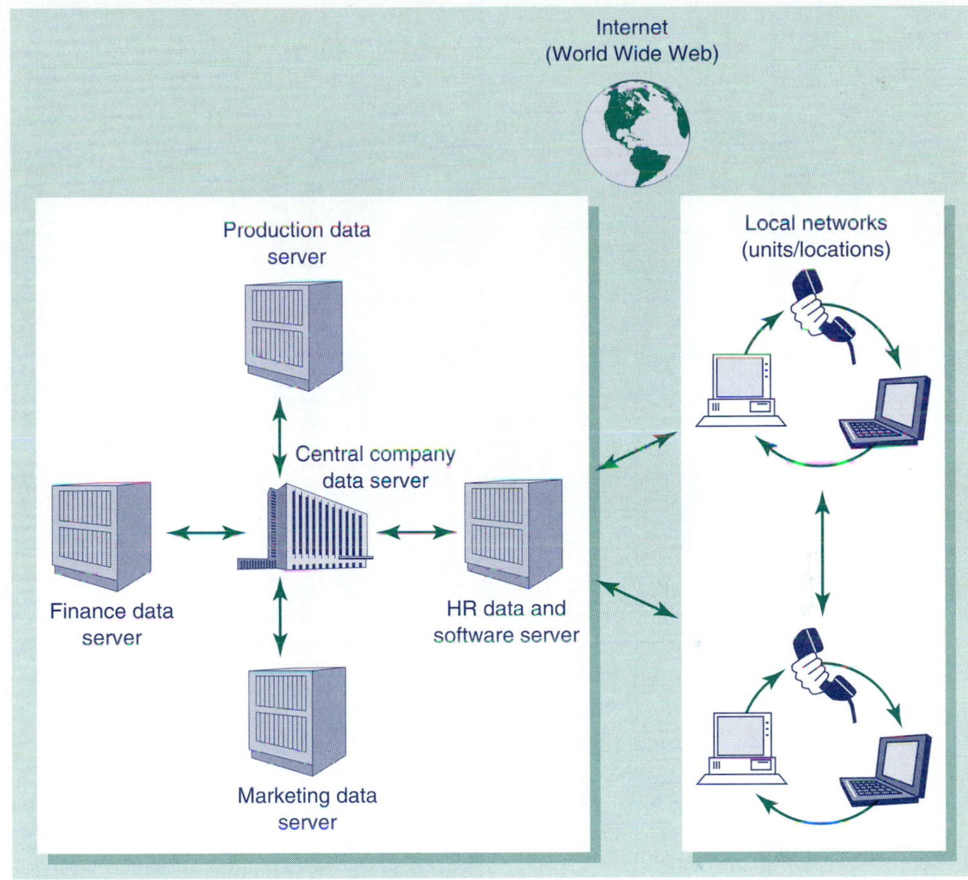


provide access. In the future, such access will make it less necessary to physically visit individuals or institutions having expertise, and much easier to obtain this expertise instantly and electronically. Throughout this book, you have seen examples of Web sites devoted to the different activities of HR.

EXPLORING THE WEB

Exhibit 16.8 shows the "home page" for the Society of Human Resource Management," which can link you to other useful resources. You can access it at:
**http://www.shrm.org/**

A variant of electronic mail (E-mail) is the electronic *discussion list,* or *interactive bulletin board,* which offers a single location to which individuals may "post" questions, comments, or ideas; these are then automatically distributed to everyone on the list through E-mail. The responses are distributed in the same way, so that any one can "listen" and participate in discussions. The largest and oldest of such lists, HRNET, was established through Cornell University under the auspices of the Academy of Management's Human Resource Division. HRNET has over 3,000 members worldwide. A single message posted to such lists commonly elicits 10 to 100 replies within

EXHIBIT 16.8 Home Page for the Society of Human Resource Management

Location: http://www.shrm.org/

# Welcome to SHRM® Online

**The Society for Human Resource Management's home on the World Wide Web.**

[ Join SHRM | News Update | Inside SHRM | HR Info Center |
| Reading Rack | Goods & Services | SHRM FAQ | HR Links ]

24 hours, often from all corners of the world, and it can bring together managers practicing the profession with researchers and content experts. Even internal E-Mail can improve relationships among employees.[13]

However, linking an organization's HR network to the Internet is not without risks. The proliferation of such sites makes it ever more difficult to determine the quality and relevance of the information. The Internet has been compared with the "world's largest library," but the information is hardly so well organized and cataloged. Instead, the Internet more closely resembles an infinitely large magazine and bookstore, where flashy graphics and compelling marketing is often enticing, but where the quality of the information must be judged carefully. As Exhibit 16.7 shows, once some of the employees link to the World Wide Web, that information can be quickly communicated to everyone on the network. Cookie recipes have been known to appear on professional discussion lists, but they may not be in good "taste" on a company network. Also, the Internet is addictive, so it's important not to "overdose."

WHAT DO YOU THINK?

The proliferation of the Internet poses a paradox for organizations. How can they encourage productive use of this powerful tool, while ensuring it does not become a time-waster, or worse, that inappropriate material exposes the company to copyright, privacy, or sexual harassment violations?

## Output: What You See Is What You Get

The most visible function of an HRIS is the output generated. To generate valuable output for users, the HRIS must process that output, make the necessary calculations, and format the presentation in a way that the user can understand. Noncomputerized systems do this by manually compiling statistics and typing reports. Highly computerized systems do this by using sophisticated programs to do thousands of calculations in minutes, produce color graphics, and simultaneously direct the results via cable modem and satellite to the PCs on the desks of executives worldwide.

Having information presented on a touch-screen is obviously much more pleasant and interesting than waiting several weeks for a typed report. However, no matter how compelling the technology, the *information* presented is still the heart of a system's value. Beautiful output that is incorrect or of the wrong type only makes it more likely that more people will rely on the information and make mistakes. Therefore, it is important to consider the users and how they employ the information system.

### Expert Systems

Earlier, we noted the emergence of the self-reliant employee model, in which many human resource activities that might previously have required an HR person can now be performed by employees or managers. HR professionals often make routine decisions. When these decisions have rules that can be captured by *expert systems* and programmed into a computer, other people can have the advantages of the expertise without the need to have an HR professional present for every routine decision. Mrs. Field's Cookies has developed expert systems that automate the preliminary interviews with job applicants and the testing procedures for evaluating training. Other expert-system applications include helping managers conduct legally proper performance appraisals, helping employees choose among flexible benefits, helping create employee handbooks, determining bonuses for executives, and authorizing leaves of absence.[14]

### "Events" versus "Activities"

One way to think differently about information output is to ask what makes the most sense to employees. Think about your own employment or that of your parents. When do they need to find and use HR information? How do they think about it? Suppose that someone has an accident at work. Does he or she say, "I need to access the databases on procedures, insurance, and medical benefits, so that I can gather the information to report and handle my accident?" Probably not, unless he or she is a system designer. Instead the person will want to have all the information needed for "accidents" at their fingertips. Similarly, people who relocate to a new location don't want to have to figure out that some information is in "records," other information in "travel," and still other information in "family services." They want it all to appear when they make a single inquiry about "relocation." "Events" such as relocation and accidents make the most sense to users while the HR "activity" databases are less friendly. To make information gathering easier, some companies are reorganizing the output function of their systems to provide a "map" based on events instead of activities.

## Avoiding "Disclosure"; Privacy and Security

In the movie *Disclosure,* Michael Douglas discovers that Demi Moore and other corporate rivals can read his E-mail and lock him out of key databases. Employees can connect to many different networks, use E-mail to communicate, and telecommute by carrying disks of information between the home and office. This creates immense dangers of privacy violations should information fall into the wrong hands. Who owns E-mail? The congressional hearings on Hillary Clinton's alleged involvement in the Whitewater events have shown that legal panels can subpoena E-mail messages as evidence.[15]

While the benefits of ready access to computerized HR information are often compelling, this technology creates new obligations and responsibilities for the HR professional. The data stored on computerized systems is often confidential and private and should be accessible only to approved individuals under controlled conditions. When HR data resided on mainframes and required special expertise to use, controlling access was somewhat easier. Cumbersome access procedures, for all their disadvantages, reduced the chance that unauthorized persons could see the data. Today, even a novice computer user may combine information in ways no one anticipated. For example, information on marital status, medical claim history, and age might be used to identify potential AIDS victims. Because HR professionals increasingly lead the development of HRISs, they are expected to shoulder the responsibility for achieving equity objectives by ensuring the privacy of personal information and access to that information only by those with a legitimate need to know.

William Safire, in a *New York Times* editorial, coined the phrase *data rape* to describe unauthorized eavesdropping and database manipulation that adversely affects individuals. A Louis Harris poll in 1990 showed that 79 percent of U.S. citizens believe that privacy ranks with life, liberty, and the pursuit of happiness as a fundamental right.[16]

### Tempting Technology

Corporate networks can just as easily become vehicles for supervisors to constantly peer over their subordinates' shoulders as they can mechanisms to empower employees by improving their access to necessary information. For instance, one draconian CEO devised a computerized blacklist,using Social Security numbers, to ensure that fired employees weren't sneaked back onto the payroll by soft-hearted co-workers. Technology must be tempered with strong organizational values.[17]

To enhance privacy, consultants recommend giving attention to:

1. *Management considerations,* such as who is authorized to use PCs, user training, inventories of equipment, and procedures for special events like power outages.
2. *Physical security,* such as access to PC areas, diskette handling, and secure housekeeping.
3. *Information security,* such as locking diskettes and hard drives, documenting PC applications, backup procedures, and network safety precautions.[18]

The Electronic Systems Sector of Harris Corporation uses a kiosk system called HEIDI containing information on employee retirement plans and company-provided loans. To prevent supervisors from unauthorized snooping, access to employee files is available only by using both the employee's social security number and PIN (personal identification number). Employees who wish an extra level of protection can establish an additional HEIDI PIN.[19]

Of course, even privacy can be taken to extremes. One Australian HR manager tells of a long and drawn-out meeting in which several of the organization's technical computer staff stubbornly insisted on very costly and restrictive security procedures as a prerequisite to approving a new HRIS. The HR professionals suggested that more modest security might be adequate. To illustrate their point, the HR professionals escorted the technical staff into a public hallway lined with unlocked filing cabinets containing the paper HR records the new system was designed to replace. Sometimes, even moderately secure PC systems can improve security over the status quo.

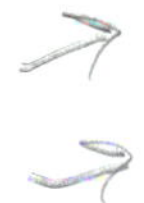

## Choosing the System

Obviously, choosing the information system, or even choosing one single application, requires weighing many factors. There is no one best set of factors to consider. Most experts recommend constructing a matrix, with the factors that are most important as rows, and the different system choices as columns. Each system receives a rating on each factor (perhaps from a low of 1 to a high of 100). Each factor receives a weight based on its importance relative to the other factors (perhaps by dividing 100 points among the factors). Then the rating on each factor is multiplied by the importance weight and the results added up for each option. The options with higher scores are considered further. Of course, the numbers from such a matrix are not perfect, but the exercise can be helpful in identifying the key considerations and in communicating the logic of a certain choice. Computerization can help.

> **EXPLORING THE WEB**
>
> The Human Resource Systems Professionals Society **(http://www.hrsp.org/)** offers a software product that compares a variety of different HR systems. Fittingly, it is called "HR Matrix."

## TRACKING VALUE-ADDED: A BALANCED SCORECARD

Once you build an HR organization that has the right structure, employs people with the right competencies, and uses the right information, how do you know if HR is really contributing value to the organization? As you've guessed by now, there is no single measure of value that captures the contribution of human resource management to the goals of efficiency and equity. A multifaceted approach to measurement is necessary. Many organizations apply the concept of a *balanced scorecard* to human resources.

Exhibit 16.9 shows how the four levels of the balanced scorecard are linked. Notice how human resources play a key role underlying each level of the scorecard. For the human resource function, the goal of measurement is to find a set of indicators that show the contribution of people to these goals, and the contribution of human resource management decisions to enhancing the value of people. We focus here on seven common approaches: Stakeholder opinions, human resource activities, audits, human resource budgets, activity/cost head-count ratios, human resource accounting, and return-on-investment in human resources.

*Balanced scorecard* measures the effectiveness of organizations using factors beyond the usual financial outcomes, including the perspectives of customers, internal processes, and learning/growth.[20] Applied to human resources, the approach means using multiple measures of performance and linking HR performance to the perspectives.

### Stakeholder Opinions/Perceptions

Former New York mayor Ed Koch was famous for asking his constituents, "How am I doing?" Similarly, the most obvious way to determine if the HR function is doing well is to ask the key stakeholders. Cliff Ehrlich, senior vice president, human resources for the Marriott Corporation bases decisions on what's fair to employees and actively markets the value of HR to employees.[21] Employees are only one of many groups of stakeholders whose opinions might make useful standards for HR planning. Other key stakeholders include the top personnel executives, managers of business operations, and external groups such as unions and governments. Canvassing stakeholder opinions has been called the *reputational* approach.[22] Research has sought constituent opinions on:

- Responsiveness (quick answers to questions, cooperation, objectivity, and neutrality).
- Proactivity and innovativeness (creative policies, measure of evaluations against goals, support line management).
- Overall effectiveness.

Reputational evaluations can be useful in identifying sources of dissatisfaction. They are also becoming more widespread as HR organizations try to embrace the notions of quality. Quality models emphasize meeting the needs of customers, and stakeholders are often seen as internal customers for HR. Of course, not all customers are created equal, and just as businesses should not waste effort trying to satisfy customers who don't expect or inspire creativity and new opportunities, neither should the HR function.[23]

EXHIBIT 16.9 The Four Levels of the Balanced Scorecard

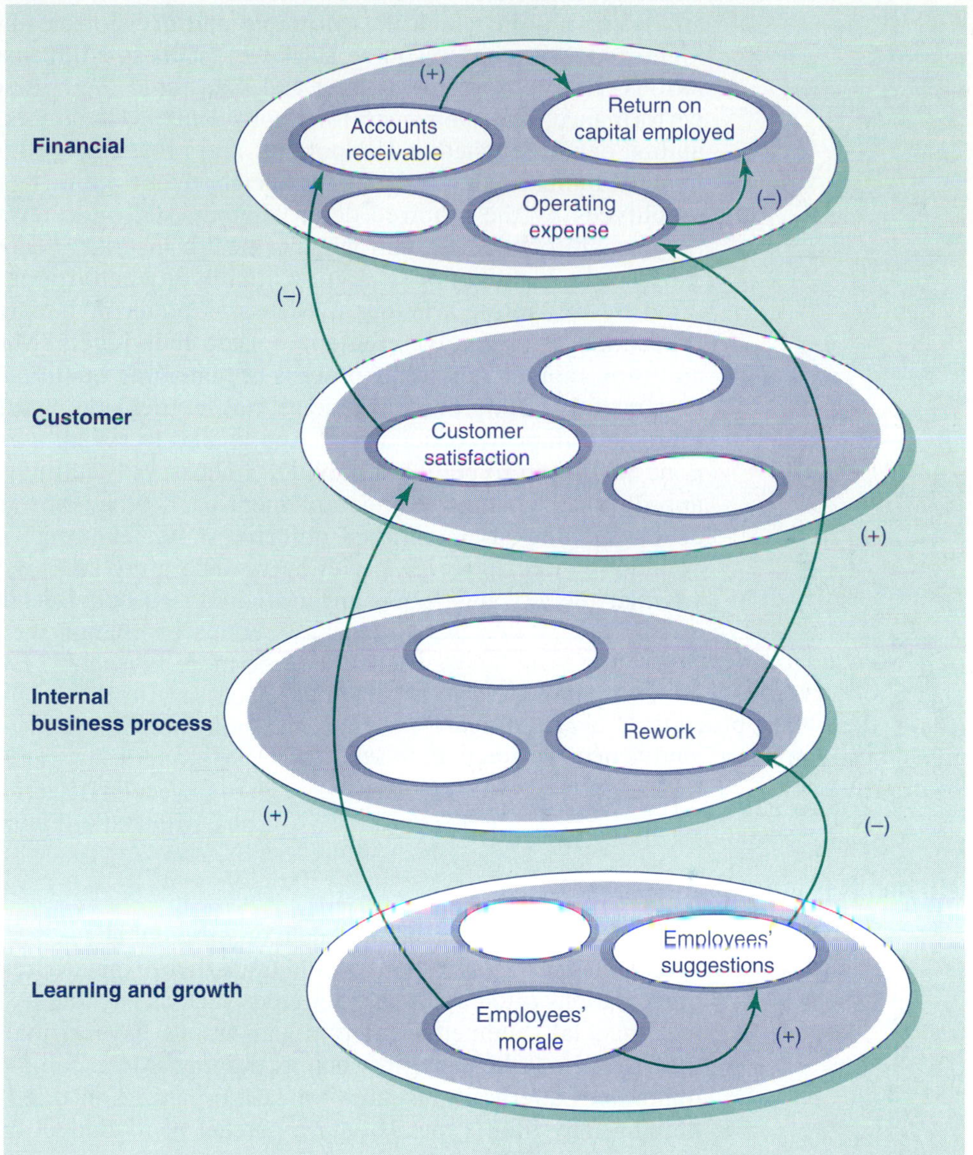


Source: Reprinted by permission of *Harvard Business Review*. Exhibit from "Using the Balanced Scorecard as a Strategic Management System" by Robert S. Kaplan and David P. Norton, January-February, 1995. 

## Auditing Human Resource Activities

Bruce R. Ellig, corporate vice president of personnel at Pfizer, Inc., described an HR review in which the corporate and division heads of human resources identified 18 human resource activities (such as compensation, community relations, EEO enforcement, etc.) and then rated their importance, their current performance, and their need for improvement. HR audits, like financial or tax audits, examine whether HR policies and practices are in place and being followed. Audits might track whether performance appraisals are completed on all employees by the required date, whether exit interviews with departing employees are conducted, and whether health insurance enrollments are properly processed when employees join. Virtually any activity or procedure can be audited by measuring whether it occurs as planned, is carried out according to procedures, and involves the appropriate individuals. Many HR functions see audits as another step in the process of managing quality. Audit information can be a useful starting point for identifying bottlenecks, wasted effort, and opportunities to improve efficiency.[23] Audits tend to reveal whether things are being done according to plan, but they don't necessarily tell whether the practices are appropriate, whether they complement each other, nor whether they relate to accomplishing organizational objectives. For example, if procedures call for conducting exit interviews with every separating employee, an audit can show whether the exit interviews are indeed carried out. But, do the interviews help reduce or change the separation pattern to be more favorable? Even though an audit is necessary to this analysis it doesn't tell the whole story.

A modern answer to the limits of audits is to observe HR activities *across* organizations, often called *benchmarking*.

**B***enchmarking* approaches send teams of observers to leading organizations to learn about their "best practices." Then, comparisons are made between "best" and "current" practice, to see how to improve.

## Human Resource Budgets

Budgets reflect dollar amounts spent on different HR activities. You might think it is obvious that organizations would track their expenditures for HR activities, but organizations often track only activities such as pay and benefits, that show up on the financial statements. Many organizations have virtually no idea how much they spend on HR activities such as training. More complete budgets can reveal important patterns in resource use. An organization that believes it emphasizes training may find it spends only 5 percent of its budget on training activities; it might spend $500 per employee on training compared with others in its industry who spend $2,000. Such information may cause the firm to reevaluate the true nature of its activities and try to bring them more in line with its stated goals. As one vice president of human resources says, "We don't have a miraculous and unlimited supply [of money]; it comes from them, the operating units."[25]

A survey by the Bureau of National Affairs showed that in 1995 the projected median expenditure on HR activities per employee was $823, compared with $792 in 1994.[26] This means that the HR budget for a company employing 10,000 employees would project a budget of $8,230,000 for HR activities—a significant investment. Moreover, HR expenditures were rising in real terms. The median increase in HR budgets between 1994 and 1995 was projected to be 4.3 percent, at a time when inflation was running about 3 percent. These numbers can provide guidance to HR professionals, but they never tell the whole story. As we have seen in prior chapters, the key questions is not how much is being spent, but what is the return on the investment. If only the costs of human resource activities are tracked, stakeholders will see HR only as spending money, not delivering valuable outcomes. It's much like parents who infrequently visit their children in college, so they tend to see only the bills, not the valuable social and educational experiences. Perhaps the next time your parents come to campus, you should bring them to your human resource management class.

## Activity, Cost, or Head-Count Ratios

A way to combine the audit and budgeting approaches is to construct ratios comparing activities, costs, and head-count levels. Typically, such ratios include the number of total employees divided by the number of HR staff employees, total training costs divided by total number of employees trained, total staffing costs divided by the total number of employees hired, total merit pay divided by the number of employees receiving merit bonuses, and average days to fill job vacancies.[27] For example, the Bureau of National Affairs survey for 1995 found that in companies with less than 250 employees, the average number of HR staff per 100 employees was 1.6, while in companies with over 2,500 workers, the average was 0.5 HR staff per 100 employees.[28] Since 1985, the Society for Human Resource Management (SHRM) and the Saratoga Institute have published the *HR Effectiveness Report,* which contains such ratios on over 600 companies in 20 industries.[29] A hypothetical excerpt from this type of report is shown in Exhibit 16.10. Notice how "your" company in this hypothetical report is below the average for its cost per hire. Still, company 1 managed to achieve an even lower cost than your company. Your company is above the average for its ratio of HR employees to total employees. Does this mean that some HR employees should be cut? Not necessarily. When an organization's ratio of HR staff to employees is higher than the industry average, it could indicate either excessive HR staff levels or that the organization has found unique ways to make that extra staff produce valuable contributions.

## Human Resource Accounting

Accountants have long recognized that HR activities generally appear on financial statements simply as costs of doing business, or unspecified overhead expenses that are arbitrarily allocated to business units. HR accounting (HRA) traces its roots to the 1970s, when accountants suggested the possibility of estimating the asset value of people according to how much it cost to obtain their services, or by projecting the dollar value of their expected economic activity in the organization.[30] While this idea is intriguing because it would value human resources similarly to financial and capital resources, it has not been widely applied and can be very complex to implement.[31] Many students who have taken accounting classes have first-hand knowledge of this complexity. HR activities do effect the organization's financial performance, but tracing these effects often requires working from the activity to the financial outcome, rather than measuring the total value of human assets. Nonetheless, HR provides valuable models for measuring the costs of acquiring, training, and separating employees, as we discussed in earlier chapters.

EXHIBIT 16.10 Hypothetical Benchmark Report on HR Ratios

| HR Ratio | Your Company | All Industry | Company 1 | Company 2 | Company 3 |
|---|---|---|---|---|---|
| HR employees per 100 employees | 1.9 | 1.6 | 1.2 | 1.5 | 1.7 |
| Total cost per hire | $2,010 | $2,540 | $1,855 | $2,600 | $2,222 |
| Percent employees receiving stock options | 10.00% | 8.00% | 2.50% | 12.30% | 11.22% |
| Average days to fill an open position | 12 | 15 | 10 | 13 | 20 |

## Return on Investment in Human Resources

Just as HR accountants recognize that it would be useful to measure the investment in human resources, some have suggested that the results of HR decisions be expressed as return on investment.[32] Typical return-on-investment (ROI) measures might include:

- Sales revenue divided by total employees.
- Sales revenue divided by total employee-related costs.
- Pretax earnings divided by total personnel expenses.
- After-tax earnings divided by total personnel expenses.
- Total asset value divided by the number of employees.
- Total yearly profit divided by the total pay and benefits of employees.

*Value-added* is the difference between the total sales revenue generated by an organization or unit, less the cost of the raw materials and purchased services it consumes to produce that sales revenue. Value-added can be used in return-on-investment ratios, such as value-added per employee or value-added per employee cost. One difficulty with calculating ROI for human resources is that the function doesn't directly generate revenue. However, some organizations are out to change that. IBM created Work Force Solutions to sell IBM's HR expertise both within and outside the company. Other leaders in HRM, such as Johnson & Johnson, AT&T, and DuPont, have marketed some of their individual HR programs as well.[33] Among the Fortune 100 companies, sales, assets, and equity rose by double-digit amounts between 1983 and 1993, while total employees fell by 12 percent during the same period. Thus, the overall productivity of employees appears to have risen sharply, as shown in Exhibit 16.11. Such overall measures can draw attention to the relationship between bottom-line measures and HR activities or employee staffing levels, but a complete set of indicators must look at the HR activities and their contribution to enhancing the human capital of the organization. A balanced scorecard means that measures of HR effectiveness reflect not only the broad financial outcomes, but also the individual activities that have been discussed in the previous chapters.

Exhibit 16.12 shows an example of performance factors that might comprise a balanced scorecard for HR, and possible measures for each factor.

## EXHIBIT 16.11 HR Productivity Increases among Fortune 100 Companies, 1983–1993

| | 1983 | 1993 | Percent Change |
|---|---|---|---|
| Sales | $1.2 trillion | $1.7 trillion | +42% |
| Assets | $914 billion | $2 trillion | +119 |
| Equity | $422 billion | $494 billion | +17 |
| Employees | 8.3 million | 7.3 million | −12 |
| Sales/employee | $144,578 | $232,877 | +62 |
| Assets/employee | $110,120 | $273,972 | +149 |
| Equity/employee | $ 50,843 | $ 67,671 | +33 |

Source: Adapted from Edward L. Gubman, "People Are More Valuable Than Ever," *Compensation and Benefits Review,* Jan.–Feb. 1995, p. 8.

## EXHIBIT 16.12 Balanced Scorecard

| Performance | | Measures |
|---|---|---|
| **Customers** | | |
| Value for money | | Pricing index |
| Competitive pricing | ⟷ | Customer ranking survey |
| Hassle free | | Customer attitudes |
| Reorder | | Market share |
| **Employees** | | |
| Labor cost | | Labor cost revenues |
| Quantity productivity | ⟷ | Zero defects |
| Satisfaction | | Employee surveys |
| **Internal Organization** | | |
| Restructuring | | Workforce flexibility |
| Teams | ⟷ | Employees on teams |
| Cycle time | | Project forecast ability |
| **Innovation and Learning** | | |
| Contacts on new products | | Percent of new product sales/revenues |
| Skill-based training | ⟷ | Training per employee |
| Work out | | Employee suggestions |
| **Financial** | | |
| Return on capital | | |
| Cash flow | ⟷ | Accounting and financial results |
| Project/unit profitability | | |
| Share price | | |

## EVALUATING THE HUMAN RESOURCE FUNCTION

### Efficiency

Like all organizational units, the HR function must contribute to efficiency goals. For the most part, this is accomplished by ensuring that the activities discussed earlier are integrated and evaluated for their payoff. You have seen many examples of how to calculate and track the costs and benefits of HR activities. In this chapter, we introduced the concept of an HR information system. This kind of system often can produce large returns on the investment, even though the investment is frequently very large. Exhibit 16.13 shows one sample calculation for moving from a mainframe-based information system to a system based on individual PCs using Windows software. While the new system costs $175,000 to implement, it saves through reduced operating costs and productivity improvements such as reduced advertising costs and more efficient production of benefit statements. Whether evaluating the HRIS or the HR function more generally, the balanced scorecard approach discussed here will produce the greatest value. HR contributions reflect multiple perspectives. The value of outsourcing, building HR competencies, and HR professionals as change agents can only be surmised by careful and multifaceted measurement.

### Equity

The increasingly prominent role played by HR professionals in organizations, and the increasing connections between HR information and organization members, creates great challenges to ensure equity, fairness, and privacy in the workplace. In previous chapters, you have seen how each of the HR activities contributes to equity goals. In this chapter, you see how important it is that HR professionals and the HR function have the structure and competencies needed to advocate for equity and ensure fairness and legal compliance. The nexus between information systems and fairness is always shifting. Even the ability to transmit photographs through computers can affect HR. Chevron recently agreed to pay $2.2 million to settle a lawsuit by four women who claimed they were sexually harassed through, among other activities, pornographic images sent through the company's E-mail system.[34] Clearly, the future equity challenges for HR professionals will be ever changing and ever more financially important.

## SUMMARY

We used to think of HR professionals as competent staff members, focused on compliance with rules and efficient administration of company policies. We used to think of HR careers as moving from specialties such as "recruiting manager" or "benefits analyst" through the ranks within a single company, and culminating with the job of "vice president of HR." Today, that career path is likely to have many more branches and many more options. The fundamental need to manage people well will continue to grow in importance, but the source of the competencies to do that may change. An HR professional's career may begin with a company, involve spending time as a consultant or private vendor, and perhaps end in the office of CEO. Some of the greatest organizational and information system challenges lie within the HR profession. We hope that the

EXHIBIT 16.13 Return-on-Investment for an HR Information System in an 800-Person Organization

| | 3-Years† |
|---|---|
| **Direct Costs** | |
| A = Operating cost of current mainframe system | $540,000 |
| B = Operating cost of new PC-based Windows system | 225,000 |
| C = One-time acquisition and implementation costs | 175,000 |
| **D = Savings from Productivity Improvements** | **3-Years** |
| Labor | 69,482 |
| Third-party administrators | 19,732 |
| Reduction in advertising | 13,790 |
| Producing annual benefits statement in-house | 11,424 |
| Cost avoidance (updating mainframe system) | 100,000 |
| Value of productivity gains | 77,438 |
| **Total dollars gained from productivity improvements** | **$291,866** |
| **Calculation of 3-Year Return on Investment** | |
| (A – B) – C + D = ROI | |
| ($540,000 – $225,000) = $315,000 | |
| $315,000 – $175,000 = $140,000 | |
| $140,000 + $291,866 = $431,866 | |

†Numbers account for a 4 percent inflation factor.

Sandra E. O'Connell, "Calculate the Return on Your Investment for Better Budgeting," *HR Magazine,* Oct. 1995, p. 40. Reprinted with the permission of *HR Magazine* published by the Society for Human Resource Management, Alexandria, VA.

reading of this book has given you a much better idea of the excitement, complexity, and impact that HR professionals experience in organizations. If you are interested in pursuing a career in human resources, you'll find information about accreditation in the appendix to this chapter.

## QUESTIONS

1. How has the job of the HR professional changed over time?
2. Discuss and contrast the industrial, investment, involvement, and high-flex models of the HR function.
3. Discuss the "competencies" that HR professionals need. Which competencies are likely to be enhanced by college classes? Which are developed through other activities? How does this suggest a definition of a "well-rounded" education?
4. Define human resource information systems. Discuss the purpose of an HRIS in an organization.
5. What are the "three C's" of HR information systems? Give an example of an application at each of the "corners" of Exhibit 16.3.
6. What is needed to develop a HRIS? How can HRIS designers decide what to include and what to leave out?
7. Discuss the HRIS components: input, throughput, and output. How has technology changed them over the years. What are two likely changes that will happen based on likely advances in technology, such as full-motion video, transmission of data through cable TV, and so forth?

8. What is the Internet? How has it changed the nature of HR information? What are its values? Its potential dangers?
9. What is a "balanced scorecard?" How is it used by organizations? How can it be used by human resource managers?
10. If a friend is contemplating a career in HR, what would you tell him or her about the likely career path? How many organizations will the person work for? How many jobs would the person hold? What is likely to be the HR professional's role and tasks over time?

## YOUR TURN: A Web Page for HR at a University

Now that you have read about all the HR activities and have an appreciation of the effects of technology on HR management, imagine that you are a highly paid design consultant. You have been asked by your college or university to design the layout of a "Web-page" that will be accessible by employees 24 hours a day. It needs to be user friendly and engaging. It needs to provide information in a form that the employees want, and it should be comprehensive, so that employees, managers, and HR professionals can use it. You can be as creative as you like, because the company is prepared to pay skilled technicians big bucks to implement your design.

The following questions may stimulate your thinking:

1. What "metaphor" will you use as the basis of your page? Will it be a simple menu with choices? Will it look like a desk, with clickable icons? Will it look like a life history or set of "events"? Discuss why you chose that metaphor in terms of value to the users.
2. What information will need to be available "behind" the page, so that it is useful? What "calculation" processes are necessary to make the page function?
3. Who will have access to what parts of the page, and how will you protect against breaches of privacy? How will you allay any fears of your users regarding the security of their information?
4. How would you judge the usefulness of the page? If a manager requests justification for the value of the page in one year, what measures would you track?

# APPENDIX Specialization in HRM

The human resource function has been moving toward greater education and professionalism. College training includes such courses as personnel management, human resource planning, equal employment opportunity, compensation administration, training, recruiting, staffing, labor law, and collective bargaining. Those who wish to become more specialized may join an association like the Society for Human Resource Management (SHRM), attend meetings, read professional journals listed in the notes and references in this book, or seek accreditation.

The Society for Human Resource Management has set up an accreditation institute to offer executives the opportunity to be accredited as specialists (in functional areas, such as employment, placement and planning, or training and development) or as generalists (multiple specialties). This institute is a nonprofit organization formed for the purpose of accrediting human resource professionals.

EXHIBIT 16.14 Specialties of the Personnel Administration and Industrial Relations Field as Defined by the Society for Human Resource Management

1. **Staffing:** Screening, interviewing, recruitment, testing, personnel records, job analysis, job description, staffing tables, promotion, transfer, and job enlargement.
2. **Personnel Maintenance:** Counseling, personnel appraisal inventories, turnover, health services and accident prevention, and employee benefits and services.
3. **Labor Relations:** Group relationships with organized or unorganized employees; negotiations, contract administration, grievances, arbitration, third-party involvement, and mutual aid pacts.
4. **Training/Development:** Job training, supervisor training, manager and executive development, preemployment and special-purpose training and retraining.
5. **Compensation:** Wage and salary surveys, incentive pay plans, profit sharing, stock ownership, financial and nonfinancial rewards, job enrichment, and wage and salary controls.
6. **Employment Communications:** House organ, employee handbook, rumor control, listening, attitude, morale and expectations surveys, and feedback analysis.
7. **Organization:** Structural design, planning and evaluation, innovation, utilization of formal and informal approaches to reducing conflict, and overcoming resistance to organizational change.
8. **Administrator:** Explanation and interpretation of options—authoritative, consultative, participative, self-management styles, and assistance in change.
9. **Personnel Policy and Planning:** Defining organization goals, policy guidelines and strategies; identifying, translating, and complying with public HR policy; forecasting HR needs, and selecting optional courses.
10. **Review, Audit, Research:** Program reporting and recording; evaluation of policies and programs; theory testing, innovation, experimentation, and cost/benefit studies.

Accreditation is based on mastery of a body of knowledge, as demonstrated by passing a comprehensive written examination and on varying amounts of full-time professional experience in the field as practitioners, consultants, educators, or researchers. Individuals must currently be serving in the role appropriate to the type of accreditation they seek. Accreditation can be changed or upgraded as roles change and experience accumulates. A generalist must pass an examination in five areas to demonstrate broad knowledge, whereas the specialist is expected to possess greater in-depth knowledge. Information and application materials are obtained from the Society for Human Resource Management, 606 North Washington Street, Alexandria, VA 22314. Exhibit 16.14 lists areas of specialization in HR management. To visit the Society for Human Resource Management on the World Wide Web, go to **http://www.shrm.org/.**

## NOTES AND REFERENCES

1. "Managing without HR," *HRM News,* Feb. 17, 1995, p. 3.
2. Material in this section is taken from Lee D. Dyer and Walton E. Burdick, "Personnel and Human Resource Management," in Jean McKelvey and Maurice Neufeld, eds., *A Half Century of Challenge and Change in Employment Relations* (Ithaca, NY: ILR Press, 1995).
3. R. Gillespie, *Manufacturing knowledge: A history of the Hawthorne experiments.* Cambridge, United Kingdom: Cambridge University Press, 1991.

4. "The Outing of Outsourcing," *The Economist,* Nov. 1995, pp. 57–58.
5. Dave Ulrich, Wayne Brockbank, Arthur K. Yeung, and Dale G. Lake, "Human Resource Competencies: An Empirical Assessment," *Human Resource Management,* Winter 1995, pp. 473–95.
6. Ibid.
7. Jennifer J. Laabs, "OLIVER: A Twist on Communication," *Personnel Journal,* Sept. 1991, pp. 79–82.
8. Jim Chandler, "Federal Express Corporation's Paperless Job Bidding System" *The Review,* Oct.–Nov. 1992, pp. 8–11; Sharon Wildman, "Employee Self-Service Kiosk: A Case Study at Harris Corporation," *The Review,* Oct.–Nov. 1992, pp. 20–22; Lars D. Perkins, "Replacing Paper Job Applications with an Employment Kiosk," *The Review,* Oct.–Nov. 1992, pp. 14–16.
9. This definition is adapted from A. J. Walker, *HRIS Development* (New York: Van Nostrand Reinhold, 1982).
10. Greg Bergin and Kathy Seesing, "CARD Deals with Report Distribution," *Personnel Journal,* Oct. 1991, pp. 109–13; Joyce E. Santora, "Data Base Integrates HR Functions," *Personnel Journal,* Jan. 1992, pp. 92–100.
11. For an excellent summary of a large-scale system development effort, see Jay F. Stright, Jr., "Creating Chevron's HRMS: An EPIC Tale," *Personnel Journal,* June 1990, pp. 72–81.
12. Emily Leinfuss, "HRIS: The Right Stuff," *Human Resource Executive,* Feb. 1995, pp. 22–23; "Virtual HR: Technology Drives a Trend," *HRM News,* May 8, 1995, p. 3; "Benefits: Turning Point for Outsourcing?" *HRM News,* Dec. 8, 1995, p. 3.
13. Eric Raimy, "'Net' working in Cyberspace," *Human Resource Executive,* Oct. 1995, pp. 53– 56; Mary R. Lind and Robert W. Zmud, "Improving Interorganizational Effectiveness through Voice Mail Facilitation of Peer-to-Peer Relationships," *Organization Science,* July–Aug. 1995, p. 445–61.
14. Paul S. Greenlaw and William R. Valonis, "Applications of Expert Systems in Human Resource Management," *Human Resource Planning,* no. 2, (1994), pp. 27–42.
15. "Whitewater Panel Seeks White House E-mail," Reuter News Service, Jan. 14, 1996.
16. William Safire, "Peeping Tom Lives," *New York Times,* Jan. 4, 1993, p. A15; Paige Amidon, "Widening Privacy Concerns," *ONLINE,* July 1992, p. 64.
17. Christian Duff, "Jack the Ripper," *The Wall Street Journal,* Jan. 11, 1993, p. A1; Michael Schrage, "When Technology Heightens Office Tensions," *The Wall Street Journal,* Oct. 5, 1992, p. A2; Glenn Rifkin, "Do Employees Have a Right to Electronic Privacy?" *New York Times,* Dec. 8, 1991.
18. Lynne E. Adams, "Securing Your HRIS in a Microcomputer Environment," *HR Magazine,* Feb. 1992, pp. 56–61; Donald Harris, "A Matter of Privacy: Managing Personal Data in Company Computers," *Personnel,* Feb. 1987, pp. 34–43.
19. Hal Glatzer, "Top Secret—Maybe," *Human Resource Executive,* Feb. 1993, pp. 26–28.
20. Robert S. Kaplan and David P. Norton, "Using the Balanced Scorecard as a Strategic Management System," *Harvard Business Review,* Jan.–Feb. 1995, pp. 75–84.
21. Martha Finney, "Profiles in Success: Fair Game," *Personnel Administrator,* Feb. 1989, pp. 44–48.
22. Anne S. Tsui, "Defining the Activities and Effectiveness of the Human Resource Department: A Multiple Constituency Approach," *Human Resource Management* 26, no. 1 (Spring 1987), pp. 35–69; Terry Connelly, E. J. Conlon, and S. J.

Deutsch, "A Multiple-Constituency Approach of Organizational Effectiveness," *Academy of Management Review* 5, no 2 (1980), pp. 211–18; Michael Keeley, "A Social Justice Approach to Evaluation," *Administrative Science Quarterly,* June 1978, pp. 272–92.

23. Michael Schrage, "Fire Your Customers!" *The Wall Street Journal,* Mar. 16, 1992, p. A14.
24. Bruce R. Ellig, "Improving Effectiveness through an HR Review," *Personnel,* June 1989, pp. 56–63; G. E. Biles, "Auditing HRM Practices," *Personnel Administrator,* Dec. 1986, pp. 89–93; G. E. Biles and Randall S. Schuler, *Audit Handbook of Human Resource Management Practices* (Alexandria, VA: American Society for Personnel Administration) 1986; Vicki S. Davis, "Self-Audits: First Step in TQM." *HR Magazine,* Sept. 1992, pp. 39–41; Carla C. Carter, "Seven Basic Quality Tools," *HR Magazine,* Jan. 1992, pp. 81–83.
25. Allan Halcrow, "The HR Budget Squeeze," *Personnel Journal,* June 1992, pp. 114–28.
26. "HR Budgets: How Are We Doing?" *HRFocus,* Oct. 1995, p. 13.
27. Jac Fitz-Enz, *How to Measure Human Resource Management,* 2nd ed. (New York: McGraw-Hill, 1995).
28. "HR Budgets: How Are We Doing," Ibid., p. 16.
29. Jonathan D. Weatherly, "Dare to Compare for Better Productivity," *HR Magazine,* Sept. 1992, pp. 42–46.
30. Eric G. Flamholtz, *Human Resource Accounting* (San Francisco: Jossey-Bass, 1985).
31. Vida Scarpello and Herman A. Theeke, "Human Resource Accounting: A Measured Critique," *Journal of Accounting Literature* 8 (1989), pp. 265–80.
32. Henry L. Dahl, Jr., "Human Resource Cost and Benefit Analysis: New Power for Human Resource Approaches," *Human Resource Planning* 11, no. 2 (1988), pp. 69–76.
33. "IBM to Sell HR/Benefits Know-How," *Human Resource Management News,* May 25, 1992, p. 4.
34. Associated Press, "Chevron Settles Women's Sexual Harassment Suit for $2.2 Million," *Los Angeles Times,* Feb. 22, 1995, p. D2.

# NAME INDEX

## C

## I



## J



## K

## N



## O



## P

## T

# SUBJECT INDEX

## D

## Q



## R



## S

**X**